Poetry Criticism

Guide to Gale Literary Criticism Series

For criticism on	Consult these Gale series
Authors now living or who died after December 31, 1999	*CONTEMPORARY LITERARY CRITICISM (CLC)*
Authors who died between 1900 and 1999	*TWENTIETH-CENTURY LITERARY CRITICISM (TCLC)*
Authors who died between 1800 and 1899	*NINETEENTH-CENTURY LITERATURE CRITICISM (NCLC)*
Authors who died between 1400 and 1799	*LITERATURE CRITICISM FROM 1400 TO 1800 (LC)* *SHAKESPEAREAN CRITICISM (SC)*
Authors who died before 1400	*CLASSICAL AND MEDIEVAL LITERATURE CRITICISM (CMLC)*
Authors of books for children and young adults	*CHILDREN'S LITERATURE REVIEW (CLR)*
Dramatists	*DRAMA CRITICISM (DC)*
Poets	*POETRY CRITICISM (PC)*
Short story writers	*SHORT STORY CRITICISM (SSC)*
Literary topics and movements	*HARLEM RENAISSANCE: A GALE CRITICAL COMPANION (HR)* *THE BEAT GENERATION: A GALE CRITICAL COMPANION (BG)* *FEMINISM IN LITERATURE: A GALE CRITICAL COMPANION (FL)* *GOTHIC LITERATURE: A GALE CRITICAL COMPANION (GL)*
Asian American writers of the last two hundred years	*ASIAN AMERICAN LITERATURE (AAL)*
Black writers of the past two hundred years	*BLACK LITERATURE CRITICISM (BLC-1)* *BLACK LITERATURE CRITICISM SUPPLEMENT (BLCS)* *BLACK LITERATURE CRITICISM: CLASSIC AND EMERGING AUTHORS SINCE 1950 (BLC-2)*
Hispanic writers of the late nineteenth and twentieth centuries	*HISPANIC LITERATURE CRITICISM (HLC)* *HISPANIC LITERATURE CRITICISM SUPPLEMENT (HLCS)*
Native North American writers and orators of the eighteenth, nineteenth, and twentieth centuries	*NATIVE NORTH AMERICAN LITERATURE (NNAL)*
Major authors from the Renaissance to the present	*WORLD LITERATURE CRITICISM, 1500 TO THE PRESENT (WLC)* *WORLD LITERATURE CRITICISM SUPPLEMENT (WLCS)*

ISSN 1052-4851

Poetry Criticism

Excerpts from Criticism of the Works of the Most Significant and Widely Studied Poets of World Literature

Volume 106

Michelle Lee
Project Editor

GALE
CENGAGE Learning™

Detroit • New York • San Francisco • New Haven, Conn • Waterville, Maine • London

GALE
CENGAGE Learning

Poetry Criticism, Vol. 106

Project Editor: Michelle Lee

Editorial: Dana Barnes, Sara Constantakis, Kathy D. Darrow, Kristen Dorsch, Dana Ferguson, Jeffrey W. Hunter, Michelle Kazensky, Jelena O. Krstović, Marie Toft, Lawrence J. Trudeau

Content Conversion: Katrina D. Coach, Gwen Tucker

Indexing Services: Factiva, Inc.

Rights and Acquisitions: Beth Beaufore, Barb McNeil, and Tracie Richardson

Composition and Electronic Capture: Gary Leach

Manufacturing: Rhonda Dover

Product Manager: Janet Witalec

For product information and technology assistance, contact us at **Gale Customer Support, 1-800-877-4253.**
For permission to use material from this text or product, submit all requests online at **www.cengage.com/permissions.**
Further permissions questions can be emailed to **permissionrequest@cengage.com**

While every effort has been made to ensure the reliability of the information presented in this publication, Gale, a part of Cengage Learning, does not guarantee the accuracy of the data contained herein. Gale accepts no payment for listing; and inclusion in the publication of any organization, agency, institution, publication, service, or individual does not imply endorsement of the editors or publisher. Errors brought to the attention of the publisher and verified to the satisfaction of the publisher will be corrected in future editions.

Gale
27500 Drake Rd.
Farmington Hills, MI, 48331-3535

LIBRARY OF CONGRESS CATALOG CARD NUMBER 81-640179

ISBN-13: 978-1-4144-4761-2
ISBN-10: 1-4144-4761-2

ISSN 1052-4851

Printed in the United States of America
1 2 3 4 5 6 7 14 13 12 11 10

Contents

Preface vii

Acknowledgments

Literary Criticism Series Advisory Board

v

Preface

*P*oetry Criticism (PC) presents significant criticism of the world's greatest poets and provides supplementary biographical and bibliographical material to guide the interested reader to a greater understanding of the genre and its creators. Although major poets and literary movements are covered in such Gale Literary Criticism series as *Contemporary Literary Criticism* (CLC), *Twentieth-Century Literary Criticism* (TCLC), *Nineteenth-Century Literature Criticism* (NCLC), *Literature Criticism from 1400 to 1800* (LC), and *Classical and Medieval Literature Criticism* (CMLC), PC offers more focused attention on poetry than is possible in the broader, survey-oriented entries on writers in these Gale series. Students, teachers, librarians, and researchers will find that the generous excerpts and supplementary material provided by PC supply them with the vital information needed to write a term paper on poetic technique, to examine a poet's most prominent themes, or to lead a poetry discussion group.

Scope of the Series

PC is designed to serve as an introduction to major poets of all eras and nationalities. Since these authors have inspired a great deal of relevant critical material, PC is necessarily selective, and the editors have chosen the most important published criticism to aid readers and students in their research. Each author entry presents a historical survey of the critical response to that author's work. The length of an entry is intended to reflect the amount of critical attention the author has received from critics writing in English and from foreign critics in translation. Every attempt has been made to identify and include the most significant essays on each author's work. In order to provide these important critical pieces, the editors sometimes reprint essays that have appeared elsewhere in Gale's Literary Criticism Series. Such duplication, however, never exceeds twenty percent of a PC volume.

Organization of the Book

Each PC entry consists of the following elements:

- The **Author Heading** cites the name under which the author most commonly wrote, followed by birth and death dates. Also located here are any name variations under which an author wrote, including transliterated forms for authors whose native languages use nonroman alphabets. If the author wrote consistently under a pseudonym, the pseudonym will be listed in the author heading and the author's actual name given in parenthesis on the first line of the biographical and critical introduction. Uncertain birth or death dates are indicated by question marks. Single-work entries are preceded by the title of the work and its date of publication.

- The **Introduction** contains background information that introduces the reader to the author and the critical debates surrounding his or her work.

- The list of **Principal Works** is ordered chronologically by date of first publication and lists the most important works by the author. The first section comprises poetry collections and book-length poems. The second section gives information on other major works by the author. For foreign authors, the editors have provided original foreign-language publication information and have selected what are considered the best and most complete English-language editions of their works.

- Reprinted **Criticism** is arranged chronologically in each entry to provide a useful perspective on changes in critical evaluation over time. All individual titles of poems and poetry collections by the author featured in the entry are printed in boldface type. The critic's name and the date of composition or publication of the critical work are given at the beginning of each piece of criticism. Unsigned criticism is preceded by the title of the source in which it appeared. Footnotes are reprinted at the end of each essay or excerpt. In the case of excerpted criticism, only those footnotes that pertain to the excerpted texts are included.

- Critical essays are prefaced by brief **Annotations** explicating each piece.

- A complete **Bibliographical Citation** of the original essay or book precedes each piece of criticism.

- An annotated bibliography of **Further Reading** appears at the end of each entry and suggests resources for additional study. In some cases, significant essays for which the editors could not obtain reprint rights are included here. Boxed material following the further reading list provides references to other biographical and critical sources on the author in series published by Gale.

Cumulative Indexes

A **Cumulative Author Index** lists all of the authors that appear in a wide variety of reference sources published by Gale, including *PC*. A complete list of these sources is found facing the first page of the Author Index. The index also includes birth and death dates and cross references between pseudonyms and actual names.

A **Cumulative Nationality Index** lists all authors featured in *PC* by nationality, followed by the number of the *PC* volume in which their entry appears.

A **Cumulative Title Index** lists in alphabetical order all individual poems, book-length poems, and collection titles contained in the *PC* series. Titles of poetry collections and separately published poems are printed in italics, while titles of individual poems are printed in roman type with quotation marks. Each title is followed by the author's last name and corresponding volume and page numbers where commentary on the work is located. English-language translations of original foreign-language titles are cross-referenced to the foreign titles so that all references to discussion of a work are combined in one listing.

Citing *Poetry Criticism*

When citing criticism reprinted in the Literary Criticism Series, students should provide complete bibliographic information so that the cited essay can be located in the original print or electronic source. Students who quote directly from reprinted criticism may use any accepted bibliographic format, such as University of Chicago Press style or Modern Language Association (MLA) style. Both the MLA and the University of Chicago formats are acceptable and recognized as being the current standards for citations. It is important, however, to choose one format for all citations; do not mix the two formats within a list of citations.

The examples below follow recommendations for preparing a bibliography set forth in *The Chicago Manual of Style,* 14th ed. (Chicago: The University of Chicago Press, 1993); the first example pertains to material drawn from periodicals, the second to material reprinted from books:

Linkin, Harriet Kramer. "The Language of Speakers in *Songs of Innocence and of Experience.*" *Romanticism Past and Present* 10, no. 2 (summer 1986): 5-24. Reprinted in *Poetry Criticism.* Vol. 63, edited by Michelle Lee, 79-88. Detroit: Thomson Gale, 2005.

Glen, Heather. "Blake's Criticism of Moral Thinking in *Songs of Innocence and of Experience.*" In *Interpreting Blake,* edited by Michael Phillips, 32-69. Cambridge: Cambridge University Press, 1978. Reprinted in *Poetry Criticism.* Vol. 63, edited by Michelle Lee, 34-51. Detroit: Thomson Gale, 2005.

Suggestions are Welcome

Readers who wish to suggest new features, topics, or authors to appear in future volumes, or who have other suggestions or comments are cordially invited to call, write, or fax the Associate Product Manager:

Product Manager, Literary Criticism Series
Gale
27500 Drake Road
Farmington Hills, MI 48331-3535
1-800-347-4253 (GALE)
Fax: 248-699-8054

Acknowledgments

The editors wish to thank the copyright holders of the criticism included in this volume and the permissions managers of many book and magazine publishing companies for assisting us in securing reproduction rights. Following is a list of the copyright holders who have granted us permission to reproduce material in this volume of *PC*. Every effort has been made to trace copyright, but if omissions have been made, please let us know.

COPYRIGHTED MATERIAL IN *PC*, VOLUME 106, WAS REPRODUCED FROM THE FOLLOWING PERIODICALS:

19th-Century Music, v. XVIII, autumn, 1994 for "The Echo, the Cry, the Death of Lovers" by Katherine Bergeron. Copyright © 1994 by The Regents of the University of California. Published by the University of California Press.—*Agenda*, v. 19, 1981-82 for "Keith Douglas" by Jon Silkin. Reproduced by permission of the Literary Estate of the author.—*Australian Journal of French Studies*, v. XXXVI, May-August, 1999 for "The Sound of Silence Points de suspension in Baudelaire's 'Les Fleurs du Mal'" by Russell Goulbourne. Copyright © 1999 by *Australian Journal of French Studies*. Reproduced by permission of the publisher and the author.—*Concerning Poetry*, v. 14, 1981. Copyright © 1981 Western Washington University. Reproduced by permission.—*Dalhousie French Studies*, v. 39/40, summer/fall, 1997. Copyright © 1997 Dalhousie University. Reproduced by permission.—*Diacritics*, v. 22, autumn-winter, 1992; v. 28, autumn, 1998. Copyright © 1992, 1998 by The Johns Hopkins University Press. Both reproduced by permission.—*Éire-Ireland*, v. XI, 1976; v. XVI, 1981; v. XVII, 1982. Copyright © 1976, 1981, 1982 by the Irish American Cultural Institute. All reproduced by permission of the publisher.—*English Studies*, v. 88, February, 2007 for "They Saw One They Knew: Baudelaire and the Ghosts of London Modernism" by Raphaël Ingelbien. Copyright © 2007 Taylor & Francis Group, LLC. Reproduced by permission of Taylor & Francis, Ltd., http//:www.tandf.co.uk/journals and the author.—*Explicator*, v. 45, winter, 1987; v. 49, winter, 1991. Copyright © 1987, 1991 by Helen Dwight Reid Educational Foundation. Both reproduced with permission of the Helen Dwight Reid Educational Foundation, published by Heldref Publications, 1319 18th Street, NW, Washington, DC 20036-1802.—*Hollins Critic*, v. 15, December, 1978. Copyright 1978 by Hollins College. Reproduced by permission.—*Irish University Review*, v. 19, spring, 1989. Copyright © 1989 *Irish University Review*. Reproduced by permission.—*Literary Review*, v. 22, winter, 1979 for "Global Regionalism: Interview with John Montague." Reproduced by permission of the author.—*Nineteenth-Century French Studies*, v. 20, fall-winter, 1991-92. Copyright © 1991 by *Nineteenth-Century French Studies*. Reproduced by permission.—*Pacific Coast Philology*, v. 37, 2002. Copyright © 2002 by Pacific Ancient and Modem Language Association. Reproduced by permission.—*Parnassus*, v. 8, fall/winter, 1979 for "Fretwork in Stone Tracery" by Paul Mariani; v. 9, spring/summer, 1981 for "A Sharp Enquiring Blade" by Reginald Gibbons; v. 26, 2001 for "Cows Have No Religion" by Gerald Mangan. Copyright © 1979, 1981, 2001 Poetry in Review Foundation, NY. All reproduced by permission of the publisher and the respective authors.—*PN Review*, v. 25, September-October, 1998 for "Shelf Lives: 1: Keith Douglas" by Peter Scupham. Copyright © 1998 *Poetry Nation Review*. All rights reserved. Reproduced by permission of the author.—*Poetry*, v. 171, February, 1998 for "Irish Voices" by Ben Howard. Reproduced by permission of the author.—*Romance Quarterly*, v. 45, summer, 1998. Copyright © 1998 by Helen Dwight Reid Educational Foundation. Reproduced with permission of the Helen Dwight Reid Educational Foundation, published by Heldref Publications, 1319 18th Street, NW, Washington, DC 20036-1802.—*Romanic Review*, v. 93, November, 2002. Copyright © 2002 by the Trustees of Columbia University in the City of New York. Reproduced by permission.—*Shenandoah*, v. 46, fall, 1996 for "A Second Tongue" by Eamonn Wall. Copyright © 1996 by *Shenandoah*. Reproduced by permission of the publisher and author.—*South Carolina Review*, v. 32, fall, 1999; v. 39, spring, 2007. Copyright © 1999, 2007 by Clemson University. Both reproduced by permission.—*South Central Bulletin*, v. 32, winter, 1972. Copyright © 1972 by The Johns Hopkins University Press. Reproduced by permission.—*Southern Review*, v. 34, winter, 1998 for "To Do Penance and Rejoice" by R. T. Smith. Reproduced by permission of the author.—*Symposium*, v. 62, spring, 2008. Copyright © 2008 by Helen Dwight Reid Educational Foundation. Reproduced with permission of the Helen Dwight Reid Educational Foundation, published by Heldref Publications, 1319 18th Street, NW, Washington, DC 20036-1802.

COPYRIGHTED MATERIAL IN *PC*, VOLUME 106, WAS REPRODUCED FROM THE FOLLOWING BOOKS:

Baudelaire, Charles. From *Flowers of Evil*. Translated by James McGowan. Oxford University Press, 1993. Translation copyright © James McGowan 1993. Reproduced by permission of Oxford University Press.—Blunden, Edmund. From the

Gale Literature Product Advisory Board

The members of the Gale Literature Product Advisory Board—reference librarians from public and academic library systems—represent a cross-section of our customer base and offer a variety of informed perspectives on both the presentation and content of our literature products. Advisory board members assess and define such quality issues as the relevance, currency, and usefulness of the author coverage, critical content, and literary topics included in our series; evaluate the layout, presentation, and general quality of our printed volumes; provide feedback on the criteria used for selecting authors and topics covered in our series; provide suggestions for potential enhancements to our series; identify any gaps in our coverage of authors or literary topics, recommending authors or topics for inclusion; analyze the appropriateness of our content and presentation for various user audiences, such as high school students, undergraduates, graduate students, librarians, and educators; and offer feedback on any proposed changes/enhancements to our series. We wish to thank the following advisors for their advice throughout the year.

Les Fleurs du Mal

Charles Baudelaire

French poetry collection, 1857.

For additional information on Baudelaire's life and career, see *PC*, Volume 1.

INTRODUCTION

Les Fleurs du Mal (1857; *The Flowers of Evil*) is the most famous work of French poet Charles Baudelaire, and his reputation as one of the most important lyric poets in literary history rests almost entirely on this one volume. Its shocking treatment of madness, perversity, and corruption, which attracted the attention of the French censors, made the work tremendously unpopular with both readers and critics. The work was, however, highly influential on the poetry of the twentieth century, and scholars today consider *Les Fleurs du Mal* the first true work of literary modernism.

BIOGRAPHICAL INFORMATION

Baudelaire was born April 9, 1821, into a well-to-do Parisian family. His father died when Baudelaire was a small child and his mother remarried a man the young boy despised. Baudelaire was, however, very close to his mother and remained so throughout his lifetime. Baudelaire was a rebellious young man, defying his stepfather by choosing a career in literature and leading a life of extravagance and profligacy, immediately spending every installment of his inheritance as he received it and then going into debt while waiting for the next installment to arrive. He was a regular customer of the taverns and brothels of Paris where he contracted both syphilis and gonorrhea and experimented with various drugs. He was, according to his own description, a "dandy," which he defined as one who follows "a cult of the self." It was while living in this dissipated manner that Baudelaire began writing critical essays as well as the poetry that would later appear in *Les Fleurs du Mal*.

TEXTUAL HISTORY

The first edition of the collection appeared in 1857 to a public shocked by its explicitly erotic content. The proofs were confiscated by the French censors, who excised six of the most offensive poems, which were later published in a Belgian edition as *Les épaves* (1866). Baudelaire, along with his publisher, was fined by the censors, and the ban remained in place until 1949 when it was officially reversed. In 1861, he published a second edition of *Les Fleurs du Mal*, excluding the censored poems and adding new ones; he was working on a third edition when he died on August 31, 1867.

MAJOR THEMES

Les Fleurs du Mal is comprised of six sections organized according to themes, entitled "Spleen et Idéal" ("Spleen and the Ideal"); "Tableaux Parisiens" ("Parisian Scenes"); "Le Vin" ("Wine"); "Fleurs du mal" ("Flowers of Evil"); "Révolte" ("Revolt"); and "La Mort" ("Death"). The work's preface is the poem "Au Lecteur," ("To the Reader"), which invites the reader into a world of ennui and corruption and suggests that by accepting the invitation, the reader will be implicated in that corruption along with the author. The poem ends with the oft-quoted lines "Hypocrite lecteur, mon semblable, mon frère" ("Hypocritical reader, my mirror image, my brother"). General themes that inform the book as a whole are sex and death, but individual poems cover such themes as loss of innocence, lesbianism, sadism, vampirism, and urban corruption. Many critics see the work as a conventional opposition between good and evil, or in more religious terms, between God and Satan, with man being simultaneously drawn to each of them. The poet's attitude towards women, as revealed in the love poems, suggest a similar conflict, with the poet/narrator appearing to both adore and despise women. The book ends with the poem "Le Voyage," an ambivalent conclusion that critics have alternately considered optimistic in that the poetic persona is prepared to strike out in a new direction after confronting the abyss, or pessimistic in that the inevitable conclusion is death.

CRITICAL RECEPTION

Les Fleurs du Mal was considered a failure among both readers and critics at the time of its publication. Although it had a small number of admirers, the work was generally received with shock and outrage by Baudelaire's contemporaries. T. S. Eliot praised it as the work that ushered in modernism, but Henry James was extremely negative in his review of the work, suggesting that Baudelaire had vastly overestimated himself in claiming to have confronted Evil. "You do yourself too much honor," was James's response to the poet, "This is not Evil; it is not the wrong, it is simply the nasty!" He contends that Baudelaire did not pick the flowers of evil, but rather "plucked the evil-smelling weeds . . . and he has often taken up mere cupfuls of mud and bog-water."

The censorship of six poems from the first edition of *Les Fleurs du Mal* continues to interest literary scholars, perhaps especially since the ban was not rescinded until 1949. E. S. Burt questions the decision to censor it in the first place, contending that lyric poetry's "subject matter and formalism remove it . . . from the experience of most readers" which would seem to make it "naturally exempt from state intervention, by virtue of a deliberate retreat from risky political subjects." Burt finds such censorship comforting though since, if the state is threatened in some way by the content of Baudelaire's poems, "it vindicates literary activity, which turns out not to be pointless after all, but instead invested with urgency and relevancy."

Edward K. Kaplan analyzes the poems of the "Fleurs du Mal" section of the volume, which deals primarily with sexuality and reveals the poet/narrator's complex attitude toward women, as he alternately sympathizes with women as victims and reviles them as "instruments of his destruction." This is further complicated by "ethical irony," which Kaplan describes as "a feigned promotion of crime and perversion meant to engage readers in dialogue"—a potential relationship between poet/narrator and reader that was introduced in the prefatory poem, "Au lecteur." Kaplan reports, however, that most contemporary readers "simply felt terrorized," missing Baudelaire's ironic stance and confusing the author with the poetic persona he assumed in the collection—a confusion that applied to the government's position as well. William Olmsted also discusses the complex and ironic misogyny of Baudelaire's poetry, in particular the poem "Une Charogne" ("A Carcass"), in which a woman is addressed as the poet/narrator's sun and then suddenly changes into a decaying animal who becomes "the object of his contempt and loathing." As Olmsted puts it, "clearly the poem not only deploys a novel style of misogynistic rhetoric but exposes in critical fashion the presence of misogyny in the very cultural and poetic traditions it deconstructs." Charles Minahen, in his discussion of "À celle qui est trop gaie," contends that the violence in the poem "is directed not just against the particular lady but also, at least implicitly, against the traditional conception of female beauty, extending back at least to the Renaissance." John Mc-

Cann, however, in his analysis of the same poem, maintains that while it is "technically brilliant," its representation of the woman has a negative edge because "the speaker finds her joy overpowering, he feels threatened by it." The woman is, according to McCann, "dismembered" by the metonymic references to her throughout the poem. Minahen, though, believes that Baudelaire was deliberately subverting the conventions of *le blazon de la femme*, a traditional form of homage to a woman wherein "the parts of the body were one by one extolled, but also, as we have seen, metonymically dismembered." McCann interprets it differently, concluding that in the poem "violence against women is inherent in the way they are thought about"; he believes that "unless we accept the villainy of the speaker along with the heroism, we will continue our complicity in the violence against *celle qui est trop gaie* which is violence against us all."

PRINCIPAL WORKS

Poetry

Salon de 1845 1845
Les fleurs du mal 1857; revised enlarged edition, 1861
Les paradis artificiels: Opium et haschisch (autobiography and poetry) 1860
Les épaves 1866
Petits poems en prose: Le spleen de Paris (prose poems) 1869

Other Major Works

La fanfarlo (novel) 1847
Histoires extraordinaires [translator; from the short stories of Edgar Allan Poe] (short stories) 1856
Nouvelles histoires extraordinaires [translator; from the short stories of Edgar Allan Poe] (short stories) 1857
Aventures d'Arthur Pym [translator; from the novel *The Narrative of Arthur Gordon Pym* by Edgar Allan Poe] (novel) 1858
Curiosités esthétiques (criticism) 1868
L'art romantique (criticism) 1869
Journaux intimes (diaries) 1887
Lettres: 1841-1866 (letters) 1905
Oeuvres completes de Charles Baudelaire. 19 vols. (poetry, criticism, essays, novel, letters, journals, autobiography, and translations) 1922-53
The Letters of Charles Baudelaire (letters) 1927
Baudelaire on Poe; Critical Papers (criticism) 1952
The Mirror of Art, Critical Studies (criticism) 1955
Baudelaire as a Literary Critic (criticism) 1964

Art in Paris, 1845-1862, Salons and Other Exhibitions Reviewed by Charles Baudelaire (criticism) 1965
Correspondance (letters) 1973
Selected Writings on Art and Artists (criticism) 1986

CRITICISM

Henry James (essay date winter 1876)

SOURCE: James, Henry. "Charles Baudelaire." *New England Review* 21, no. 1 (winter 2000): 194-98.

[*In the following negative review, originally published in 1876, James counts Baudelaire as a lesser genius than Edgar Allan Poe, Théophile Gautier, and possibly James himself. James asserts that Baudelaire overestimates the scope of his project in believing that he has confronted Evil or even great wrongs in* Les Fleurs du Mal.]

As a brief discussion was lately carried on (there had been an exchange of letters on the subject in an American journal,) touching the merits of the writer whose name we have prefixed to these lines, it may not be amiss to introduce him to some of those readers who must have observed the contest with littler more than a vague sense of the strangeness of its subject. Charles Baudelaire is not a novelty in literature; his principal work dates from 1857, and his career terminated a few years later. But his admirers have made a classic of him and elevated him to the rank of one of those subjects which are always in order. Even if we differ with them on this point, such attention as Baudelaire demands will not lead us very much astray. He is not, in quantity (whatever he may have been in quality), a formidable writer; having died young, he was not prolific, and the most noticeable of his original productions are contained in two small volumes.

His celebrity began with the publication of *Les Fleurs du Mal,* a collection of verses of which some had already appeared in periodicals. The "Revue des Deux Mondes" had taken the responsibility of introducing a few of them to the world—or rather, though it held them at the baptismal font of public opinion, it had declined to stand godfather. An accompanying note in the "Revue" disclaimed all editorial approval of their morality. This of course procured them a good many readers; and when, on its appearance, the volume we have mentioned was overhauled by the police a still greater number of persons desired to possess it. Yet in spite of the service rendered him by the censorship, Baudelaire has never become in any degree popular; the

lapse of twenty years has seen but five editions of *Les Fleurs du Mal.* The foremost feeling of the reader of the present day will be one of surprise, and even amusement, at Baudelaire's audacities having provoked this degree of scandal. The world has traveled fast since then, and the French censorship must have been, in the year 1857, in a very prudish mood. There is little in *Les Fleurs du Mal* to make the reader of either French or English prose and verse of the present day even open his eyes. We have passed through the fiery furnace and profited by experience. We are happier than Racine's heroine [*Phèdre,* in act III, scene 3], who had not

> Su se faire un front qui ne rougit jamais.
> [Known how to assume a countenance that never blushes]

Baudelaire's verses do not strike us as being dictated by a spirit of bravado—though we have heard that, in talk, it was his habit, to an even tiresome degree, to cultivate the quietly outrageous—to pile up monstrosities and blasphemies without winking and with the air of uttering proper commonplaces.

Les Fleurs du Mal is evidently a sincere book—so far as anything for a man of Baudelaire's temper and culture could be sincere. Sincerity seems to us to belong to a range of qualities with which Baudelaire and his friends were but scantily concerned. His great quality was an inordinate cultivation of the sense of the picturesque, and his care was for how things looked, and whether some kind of imaginative amusement was not to be got out of them, much more than for what they meant and whither they led and what was their use in human life at large. The later editions of *Les Fleurs du Mal* (with some of the interdicted pieces still omitted and others, we believe, restored) contain a long preface by Théophile Gautier, which throws a curious side light upon what the Spiritualist newspapers would call Baudelaire's "mentality." Of course Baudelaire is not to be held accountable for what Gautier says of him, but we cannot help judging a man in some degree by the company he keeps. To admire Gautier is certainly excellent taste, but to be admired by Gautier we cannot but regard as rather compromising. He gives a magnificently picturesque account of the author of *Les Fleurs du Mal,* in which, indeed, the question of pure exactitude is evidently so very subordinate that it seems grossly ill-natured for us to appeal to such a standard. While we are reading him, however, we find ourselves wishing that Baudelaire's analogy with the author himself were either greater or less. Gautier was perfectly sincere, because he dealt only with the picturesque and pretended to care only for appearances. But Baudelaire (who, to our mind, was an altogether inferior genius to Gautier) applied the same process of interpretation to things as regards which it was altogether inadequate; so that one is constantly tempted to suppose he cares more for his process—for making grotesquely-pictorial verse—than for the things themselves. On the whole, as we have said, this inference would be unfair. Baudelaire had a certain groping sense of the moral complexities of life, and if the best that he succeeds in doing is to drag them down into the very turbid element in which he himself plashes and flounders, and there present them to us much besmirched and bespattered, this was not a want of goodwill in him, but rather a dulness and permanent immaturity of vision. For American readers, furthermore, Baudelaire is compromised by his having made himself the apostle of our own Edgar Poe. He translated, very carefully, and exactly, all of Poe's prose writings, and, we believe, some of his very superficial verses. With all due respect to the very original genius of the author of the "Tales of Mystery," it seems to us that to take him with more than a certain degree of seriousness is to lack seriousness one's self. An enthusiasm for Poe is the mark of a decidedly primitive stage of reflection. Baudelaire thought him a profound philosopher, the neglect of whose golden utterances stamped his native land with infamy. Nevertheless, Poe was much the greater charlatan of the two, as well as the greater genius.

Les Fleurs du Mal was a very happy title for Baudelaire's verses, but it is not altogether a just one. Scattered flowers incontestably do bloom in the quaking swamps of evil, and the poet who does not mind encountering bad odors in his pursuit of sweet ones is quite at liberty to go in search of them. But Baudelaire has, as a general thing, not plucked the flowers—he has plucked the evil-smelling weeds (we take it that he did not use the word flowers in a purely ironical sense) and he has often taken up mere cupfuls of mud and bog-water. He had said to himself that it was a great shame that the realm of evil and unclean things should be fenced off from the domain of poetry; that it was full of subjects, of chances and effects; that it had its light and shade, its logic and its mystery; and that there was the making of some capital verses in it. So he leaped the barrier and was soon immersed in it up to his neck. Baudelaire's imagination was of a melancholy and sinister kind, and, to a considerable extent, this plunging into darkness and dirt was doubtless very spontaneous and disinterested. But he strikes us on the whole as passionless, and this, in view of the unquestionable pluck and acuteness of his fancy, is a great pity. He knew evil not by experience, not as something within himself, but by contemplation and curiosity, as something outside of himself, by which his own intellectual agility was not in the least discomposed, rather, indeed (as we say his fancy was of a dusky cast) agreeably flattered and stimulated. In the former case, Baudelaire, with his other gifts, might have been a great poet. But, as it is, evil for him begins outside and not inside, and consists primarily of a great deal of lurid landscape and unclean furniture. This is an almost ludicrously puerile view of the matter. Evil is represented as an affair of blood and carrion and physical sickness—there must be stinking corpses and starving prostitutes and empty laudanum bottles in order that the poet shall be effectively inspired.

A good way to embrace Baudelaire at a glance is to say that he was, in his treatment of evil, exactly what Hawthorne was not—Hawthorne, who felt the thing at its source, deep in the human consciousness. Baudelaire's infinitely slighter volume of genius apart, he was a sort of Hawthorne reversed. It is the absence of this metaphysical quality in his treatment of his favorite subjects (Poe was his metaphysician, and his devotion sustained him through a translation of "Eureka!") that exposes him to the class of accusations of which M. Edmond Schérer's accusation of feeding upon *pourriture* [putrescence] is an example; and, in fact, in his pages we never know with what we are dealing. We encounter an inextricable confusion of sad emotions and vile things, and we are at a loss to know whether the subject pretends to appeal to our conscience or—we were going to say—to our olfactories. "Le Mal?" we exclaim; "you do yourself too much honor. This is not Evil; it is not the wrong; it is simply the nasty!" Our impatience is of the same order as that which we should feel if a poet, pretending to pluck "the flowers of good," should come and present us, as specimens, a rhapsody on plumcake and *eau de Cologne*. Independently of the question of his subjects, the charm of Baudelaire's verse is often of a very high order. He belongs to the class of geniuses in whom we ourselves find but a limited pleasure—the laborious, deliberate, economical writers, those who fumble a long time in their pockets before they bring out their hand with a coin in the palm. But the coin, when Baudelaire at last produced it, was often of a high value. He had an extraordinary verbal instinct and an exquisite felicity of epithet. We cannot help wondering, however, at Gautier's extreme admiration for his endowment in this direction; it is the admiration of the writer who gushes for the writer who trickles. In one point Baudelaire is extremely remarkable—in his talent for suggesting associations. His epithets seem to have come out of old cupboards and pockets; they have had a kind of magical mustiness. Moreover, his natural sense of the superficial picturesqueness of the miserable and the unclean was extremely acute; there may be a difference of opinion as to the advantage of possessing such a sense; but whatever it is worth Baudelaire had it in a high degree. One of his poems—**"To a Red haired Beggar Girl"**—is a masterpiece in the way of graceful expression of this high relish of what is shameful.

> Pour moi, poëte, chétif,
> Ton jeune corps maladif,
> Plein de taches de rousseur,
> A sa douceur.
> [For me, a pitiful poet / Your sickly young body / Full
>   of freckles / Has its sweetness.]

Baudelaire repudiated with indignation the charge that he was what is called a realist, and he was doubtless right in doing so. He had too much fancy to adhere strictly to the real; he always embroiders and elaborates—endeavors to impart that touch of strangeness and mystery which is the very *raison d'étre* of poetry. Baudelaire was a poet, and for a poet to be a realist is of course nonsense. The idea that Baudelaire imported into his theme was, as a general thing, an intensification of its repulsiveness, but it was at any rate ingenious. When he makes an invocation [in **"The Two Good Sisters"**] to *"la Débauche aux bras immondes"* [Debauchery, with her filthy embrace] one may be sure he means more by it than is evident to the vulgar—he means, that is, an intense perversity. Occasionally he treats agreeable subjects, and his least sympathetic critics must make a point of admitting that his most successful poem is also his least morbid, and most touching; we allude to **"Les Petites Vieilles"** [**"The Little Old Women"**]—a really masterly production. But if it represents the author's maximum, it is a note that he is very rarely struck.

Baudelaire, of course, is a capital text for a discussion of the question as to the importance of the morality—or of the subject-matter in general—of a work of art; for he offers a rare combination of technical zeal and patience and of vicious sentiment. But even if we had space to enter upon such a discussion, we should spare our words; for argument on this point wears to our sense a really ridiculous aspect. To deny the relevancy of subject-matter and the importance of the moral quality of a work of art strikes us as, in two words, very childish. We do not know what the great moralists would say about the matter—they would probably treat it very good-humoredly; but that is not the question. There is very little doubt what the great artists would say. People of that temper feel that the whole thinking man is one, and that to count out the moral element in one's appreciation of an artistic total is exactly as sane as it would be (if the total were a poem) to eliminate all the words in three syllables, or to consider only such portions of it as had been written by candle-light. The crudity of sentiment of the advocates of "art for art" is often a striking example of the fact that a great deal of what is called culture may fail to dissipate a well-seated provincialism of spirit. They talk of morality as Miss [Maria] Edgeworth's infantine heroes and heroines talk of "physic"—they allude to its being put into and kept out of a work of art, put into and kept out of one's appreciation of the same, as if it were a colored fluid kept in a big-labeled bottle in some mysterious intellectual closet. It is in reality simply a part of the essential richness of inspiration—it has nothing to do with the artistic process and it has everything to do with the artistic effect. The more a work of art feels it at its source, the richer it is; the less it feels it, the poorer it is. People of a large taste prefer rich works to poor ones and they are not inclined to assent to the assumption that the process is the whole work. We are safe in believing that all this is comfortably clear to most of those who have, in any degree, been initiated into art by production. For them the subject is as much a part of their work as their hunger is a part of their dinner. Baudelaire was not so far from being of this way of thinking as some of his admirers would persuade us; yet we may say on the whole that he was the victim of a grotesque illusion. He tried to make fine verses on ignoble subjects, and in our opinion he signally failed. He gives, as a poet, a perpetual impression of discomfort and pain. He went in search of corruption, and the ill-conditioned jade proved a thankless muse. The thinking reader, feeling himself, as a critic, all one, as we have said, finds the beauty perverted by the ugliness. What the poet wished, doubtless, was to seem to be always in the poetic attitude; what the reader sees is a gentleman in a painful-looking posture, staring very hard at a mass of things from which, more intelligently, we avert our heads.

Note

Literal translations in brackets by the Editor, who wishes to thank John Bertolini for his assistance in locating the source of the quotation from Racine.

Dorothy M. Betz (essay date winter 1991)

SOURCE: Betz, Dorothy M. "Baudelaire's 'Bénédiction.'" *Explicator* 49, no. 2 (winter 1991): 92-4.

[In the following essay, Betz analyzes the figure of the angel in the "Bénédiction" of Les Fleurs du Mal.*]*

Even within the poem itself, the "Ange" of Baudelaire's **"Bénédiction"** plays an ambiguous role. In this opening poem of the autobiographical "Spleen et Idéal" section of *Les Fleurs du Mal,* the young poet, rejected by his mother, seems to find an alternate source of protection in the form of a guardian angel.

> Pourtant, sous la tutelle invisible d'un Ange,
> L'Enfant déshérité s'enivre de soleil,
> Et dans tout ce qu'il voit et dans tout ce qu'il mange
> Retrouve l'ambroisie et le nectar vermeil.
>
> Il joue avec le vent, cause avec le nuage,
> Et s'enivre en chantant du chemin de la croix;
> Et l'Esprit qui le suit dans son pèlerinage
> Pleure de le voir gai comme un oiseau des bois.[1]

The "tutelle invisible" (line 21) suggests that the angel has taken up the role that the mother has abandoned, that of caring for the child. But "tutelle," with its further implication of education, shows the angel to be guiding the child, whether toward a good or unfortunate end.

This ambivalence, together with the angel's tears, introduces ambiguity. Why should the angel cry upon seeing the child happy? Does this merely indicate that the angel foresees a corresponding unhappiness to come? Or does the angel share the animosity of other figures in the poem toward the child?

The ambiguity is strengthened by Baudelaire's repeated use of "s'enivre" (22 and 26). The concept of drunkenness for Baudelaire clearly transcends the physical phenomenon, as he states pointedly in his prose poem "Enivrez-vous": "Enivrez-vous sans cesse! De vin, de poésie ou de vertu, à votre guise" (p. 33). The exaltation inherent in this state does not necessarily contradict the religious element introduced by the "chemin de la croix" (line 26). But because drunkenness characterizes the poet while he is under the angel's guidance, its specific nature should help define the angel's influence.

The symbolic complexity of Baudelaire's images in *Les Fleurs du Mal* derives from a carefully structured process of redefinition, through which images gain additional nuance during their repetition in successive poems. Thus the recurring combination of the motifs of the angel and of drunkenness may serve to clarify Baudelaire's use of them here. Robert Cargo's concordance to *Les Fleurs du Mal* lists forty-six uses of *ange(s)* in the work.[2] Of these, only six occur in poems also referring to some form or "ivresse" or "enivrer." Of these six poems, three, **"Le Flacon," "Danse macabre,"** and **"La Mort des Pauvres,"** do not relate the angel directly to the poet. In the first, the flask contains a "poison préparé par les anges" (27), and the other two references are to the angel of death. The angel of death, however, cannot be discounted as not related to the poet. When the angel represents a woman ("Vous, mon ange et ma passion!" **"Une Charogne,"** [40]), or her seductive charms ("plus câlins que les Anges du mal," **"Les Bijoux,"** [21]), we recall that the woman has caused Baudelaire's spiritual death by distracting him from his ideal.

However, two additional poems linking the angel with drunkenness furnish analogies especially useful to the reading of **"Bénédiction"**—**"Un Voyage à Cythère"** and **"Le Voyage."** In the latter poem, with which Baudelaire ended *Les Fleurs du Mal* in the second edition, the poet concludes the voyage of his life, during which he has sought various forms of escape. He describes travelers, threatened by the figure of Circe, who echo the earlier experience of the child: "Pour n'être pas changés en bêtes, ils s'enivrent / D'espace et de lumière et de cieux embrasés" (13-14). Immediately afterward, the angel reappears, but this time as a clearly negative persona: "Comme un Ange cruel qui fouette des soleils" (28). Not only is this angel cruel and aggressive, but the references to the sun (or suns, reflecting the duration of the voyage) link this passage to the source of drunkenness in **"Bénédiction."**

The other poem to combine these motifs, **"Un Voyage à Cythère,"** provides a transition. The ship on which the poet travels evokes an angel no longer as passive as the spectator-angel of **"Bénédiction,"** but not yet as aggressive as the figure of **"Le Voyage":** "Le navire roulait sous un ciel sans nuages, / Comme un ange enivré d'un soleil radieux" (3-4). This time the angel, not the poet, becomes drunk. But the drunkenness, still produced by the sun, still represents a more generalized abandoning of mental faculties than that produced by alcohol. Both angel and poet in turn lose control to external influences. The angel, seen as analogous to the ship rolling in the waves, is externally directed, just as the travelers in **"Le Voyage"** flee dangers, represented by Circe, rather than determining their own course.

In the context of these other references, both the tears and the apparent ambiguity of the angel of **"Bénédiction"** make sense. The angel perceives the loss of control inherent in the young poet's drunkenness and foresees that it will leave the child at the mercy of others, most notably of the woman, also represented as an angel, to whose perfidy the other angels of the work may be linked. In a sense the angel may see his own role in the poet's destruction, for by the final poem, the angel himself, the "Ange cruel," will have joined with those who inflict suffering.

As the angel evolves toward a figure of cruelty, the angel as persona is more active. In **"Bénédiction,"** the action is that of the child, who becomes drunk, drinks, eats, plays, and chats. The angel's "tutelle invisible" remains passive. With action limited to "suit" and "pleure" (27 and 28), the angel reacts to the child but does not initiate an exchange with him. Further, Baudelaire also refers to the angel at this stage as "l'Esprit" (27), a term that he more frequently uses to describe himself. Soon after **"Bénédiction,"** he will describe "mon esprit" flying free in **"Elévation"** (5), suggesting a link between "ange," "esprit," and poet.

By **"Un Voyage à Cythère,"** however, it is the angel who is "enivré" (4), and in **"Le Voyage,"** the "ange cruel" becomes active with "qui fouette" (28). As a once-ethereal figure becomes active, the actions are perverse. The danger implicit in defining the angel's role parallels another suggestion of the poet's fall at the end of **"Bénédiction."** Just after describing his vision of the celestial crown "de pure lumière" (73), Baudelaire compares it with a more concrete object, "les yeux mortels" (75), the same eyes that will deceive him through the hypnotic gaze of a woman.

Thus the images of **"Bénédiction"** seem, on the surface, in harmony with the poem's title. But just as the title has an ironic dimension when the poet is cursed, figures such as the angel hide sinister meanings to be revealed in subsequent texts. Baudelaire's cluster of themes—the angel, drunkenness, and the sun—in **"Bénédiction"** typify his use of images—at first ambiguous, and growing through repetition into nuanced, composite symbols. The initial ambiguity serves to alert the reader to seek the true meaning in subsequent poems.

Notes

1. However, under the invisible guidance of an Angel,
   The disinherited Child becomes drunk on sunlight,
   And in all that he sees and all that he eats
   He finds ambrosia and scarlet nectar.

   He plays with the wind and chats with the cloud,
   And becomes drunk with singing the way of the cross;
   And the Spirit following him on his pilgrimage
   Cries upon seeing him gay as a bird in the woods.

                                          (lines 21-28)

   Charles Baudelaire. *Oeuvres complètes.* (Paris: Gallimard, 1975) 1; 7-8. All subsequent quotations from Baudelaire are from this edition. Translation is the author's.

2. Robert T. Cargo, ed., *A Concordance to Baudelaire's Les Fleurs du Mal* (Chapel Hill: U of North Carolina P, 1965) 15.

Karen A. Harrington (essay date fall-winter 1991-92)

SOURCE: Harrington, Karen A. "Fragmentation and Irony in *Les Fleurs du Mal.*" *Nineteenth-Century French Studies* 20, nos. 1 and 2 (fall-winter 1991-92): 177-86.

[*In the following essay, Harrington discusses the fragmentation of the self and the ironic uses to which Baudelaire put this fragmentation in* Les Fleurs du Mal.]

Fragmentation commands special significance in *Les Fleurs du Mal* and stresses an often contradictory split occurring at many levels such as the structural opposition between spleen and ideal. Thematic polarities of love and hate, time and space, good and evil, God and Satan abound in Baudelaire's work. Of greater importance, perhaps, is the position of the fragmented self that shapes the core or nucleus upon which other forms of fragmentation acquire meaning. It finds expression in various ways: the self identifies with others, thereby engaging in an interplay of its own absence and presence. The divided self also calls attention to the distancing of the poetic voice from the poem's movement, while at other times a self-conscious split alienates the self from its own identity.

Baudelaire touches upon this concept in *Les Paradis artificiels,* explaining how differentiation between object and subject is abolished as the self voluntarily renounces its own identity in favor of the object or "other."[1] His crucial quotation in *Mon Coeur Mis à Nu,* "de la vaporisation et de la centralisation du *Moi.* Tout est là," (1: 676) is also indicative of the role fragmentation plays. In such poems as **"La Chevelure,"** centralization or concentration of the self is accompanied by its dispersal, its capacity to permeate other objects, or to appropriate characteristics of "others." Dispersal precedes concentration as the self loses and subsequently regains its identity, but it is now infused with the richness of the experience of the other. In this respect, the loss or absence of the self creates a positive extension of the poetic act, a result of the harmonious transference between vaporization and centralization.

At other times, this interaction points to an impasse. In **"Obsession"** vaporization is hinted at with a potential diffusion of the self into ocean waves. However, vaporization and centralization remain polarized because the position of the poetic voice is too anchored in a self-reflective stance to allow such dispersal. In place of unification, fragmentation intensifies the separation between subject and object.

The paradoxically disruptive and harmonious nature of the divided self in Baudelaire's poetry can perhaps be best understood by exploring to what extent the relation between language and the self determines the ambivalence associated with fragmentation. In *De l Essence du rire* (2: 535) we find a paradigm that conveys how language alludes to divergent and often opposing expressions of fragmentation. Baudelaire refers to both smiling and joy as "le comique significatif" and argues that they are distinguished by their totality and sense of wholeness. To the contrary, laughter, or "le comique absolu," is associated with an irreconcilable split that denotes its ambiguous and irresolute nature.

"Le comique significatif" corresponds to a model in which the self's relation to the poem is framed by a clear and unequivocal notion of unity and closure. Fragmentation of this kind occurs with the partial or total abandonment of narrative control as the poetic persona assumes a chameleon-like stance to identify with "others." Jean Prévost terms this "le mimétisme de Baudelaire,"[2] a quality characteristic of many of the poet's love poems.

"Le Poison" illustrates this affinity, with the self consumed by the woman's presence. She serves as a guide to an illusory world, a means of transcending reality through the act of forgetting. Though dangerously linked to poison, her eyes are the embodiment of "oubli" and become the focal point through which the poetic self strives to revel in the much sought after oblivion. Other forms of possible transcendence (wine and opium) cannot compare to the woman's fascinating powers, which lure the poet to her:

Tout cela ne vaut pas le poison qui découle
   De tes yeux, de tes yeux verts,
Lacs où mon âme tremble et se voit à l'envers . . .
   Mes songes viennent en foule
Pour se désaltérer à ces gouffres amers.

Tout cela ne vaut pas le terrible prodige
   De ta salive qui mord,
Qui plonge dans l'oubli mon âme sans remords
   Et, charriant le vertige,
La roule défaillante aux rives de ia mort!

(1: 48)

Drawn to her green eyes and bitter saliva, he hopes to surpass the limits of time and space. But her association with a poisonous lake that quenches one's thirst points to her presence as not only enticing but also foreboding. The poet seeks and fears both the poison dwelling within the woman's eyes and the taste of her bitter saliva yet is cognizant of their imminent threat, projected in the "gouffres amers" and "rives de la mort."

This paradoxical influence marks the potential fulfillment of the poet's daydreams, but at the price of death. Though the woman epitomizes the oblivion that the poet is seeking, this ideal world is itself an illusion and, similar to wine and opium, she does not lead him beyond the ephemeral. Yet, chameleon fragmentation or mimetic association nonetheless offers a momentary escape, a temporary means of shutting out the world. Thus, loss of narrative control can be viewed as a desire to orchestrate and make sense of one's world.

When mimetic association is more closely related to sensory perceptions, as in **"Parfum exotique"** and **"L'Invitation au voyage,"** poetic reverie frequently suggests a more favorable outcome. Through a process of synesthetic transfer, the poetic voice relinquishes control to the sensory perceptions, thus showing the self's appropriation by others as a means of experiencing and yielding to the influence of the imagery.

"Parfum exotique" opens with the association between the olfactory sensory perception and the portrayal of a tropical setting, brought about by the woman's presence. As the sensory perceptions increasingly become the focus of the poem, narrative control weakens with the self relegated to the role of participant. In the last two stanzas the sensory perceptions transform the poet's vision into an imaginary setting:

Guidé par ton odeur vers de charmants climats,
Je vois un port rempli de voiles et de mâts
Encor tout fatigués par la vague marine,

Pendant que le parfum des verts tamariniers
Qui circule dans l'air et m'enfle la narine,
Se mêle dans mon âme au chant des mariniers.

(1: 25)

The woman's presence is soon consumed by her fragrance, transformed into the aroma of green tamarind trees. Circulating in the air, the olfactory sensory perception reveals its expansion as it becomes the subject of the poem. It also claims narrative control by exerting its far-reaching influence over and through the poetic self.

Sensory perceptions efface distinction between self and others, a position that Baudelaire justifies in *Les Paradis artificiels* by illustrating how the effects of various intoxicants lead the self to identify with the object of observation:

Il arrive quelquefois que la personnalité disparaît et que l'objectivité, qui est le propre des poètes panthéistes, se développe en vous si anormalement, que la contemplation des objets extérieurs vous fait oublier votre propre existence, et que vous vous confondez bientôt avec eux.

(1: 419)

In **"Parfum exotique"** the intoxicants are replaced by the woman's presence and the synesthetic associations it produces on the poet, through whom the expansive transformation occurs. The sensory perceptions link the real and the imaginary: the woman's fragrance is an indicator of the poet's real world, but its subsequent dispersal and consumption find expression in the realm of the imaginary ("Je vois un port rempli de voiles et de mâts / Encor tout fatigués par la vague marine"). Mimetic interaction in **"Parfum exotique"** thus prompts a timeless and inspiring movement that counteracts the cold-heartedness of reality.

While other poems show the mimetic stance as an intensification of harsh realities (**"Le Vampire"**), they all call attention to a self-contained world. There is a sense that, however pleasant or unpleasant the poem's outcome, it concludes on a decisive note and that the self's position, though fragmented, is not questioned. Mimetic association accordingly presents a straightforward view of the self in the world and corresponds to the autonomous vision associated with "le comique significatif."

By contrast, the laughter characteristic of "le comique absolu," symbolizes the duality of human nature, of man's fall from grace. In Baudelaire's estimation, "le comique absolu" is superior to "le comique significatif" yet is defined by its own negativity. Many of his poems show the fragmented self mirroring this negativity. Aware of its own duality, the self is unable to reconcile it, thus emphasizing an ambivalent and often self-deprecating position, which is essentially ironic. For Paul de Man the pervasive and obstructive influence of irony calls into play the paradoxical split of the self as both participant and detached observer of the poetic act.[3] The mimetic association of the aforementioned poems is replaced by ironic distancing, which differs from the former in terms of how language functions in the poem. The ironic stance highlights the self's failure to appropriate others to its own identity and magnifies the gulf between self and poem. Irony's relation to the divided self also denotes a separation owing primarily to an endless self-reflective questioning, symbolized by its lack of closure. These two perspectives are exposed either through the ironic severance of the self from the poem or through the status of the ironic self-consciousness and correspond roughly to Leo Bersani's distinction between the self as doomed artist and the prince-dandy figure.[4]

The ironic stance of the doomed artist implicates the self by relegating it to an alien world through various allegoric or metaphoric associations. Bersani alludes to this when discussing Lacanian theory and how the self moves from the Imaginary to the order of the Symbolic: "The self is still an appropriated self, but what is appropriated is language as the other, and not an ideal but alienated *image* of an individual self."[5] Thus appropriation is evidence of alienation in the form of language. Attaining its fullest potential through irony, language underscores distancing by means of dissimulation. As such, alienation of the fragmented self may be defined by its detachment from the object, thing, or person that it encounters.

Baudelaire's Spleen poems point to the technique of ironic distancing. In *"Pluviôse, irrité contre la ville entière"* the self's involvement in the various images depicted is diminished with its eventual separation from the poem's movement. Michael Riffaterre refers to the essence of this movement as a series of structural permutations through which the matrix of the "home" as "hearth" is subsequently transformed "into a code of the moral and physical discomfort a home is supposed to protect us against."[6] The poem thus operates on an interplay of words and their opposite in which "structural permutation . . . converts a mimesis of intimacy into a code negating intimacy and its attendant happiness."[7]

We can apply Riffaterre's insightful remarks to the fragmented self in the poem. The vision it portrays is progressively reduced to a single spot (a deck of cards), which engulfs the presence of the self. Here, fragmentation can be defined as the doubling of the poetic persona through an absent-present structure. Though responsible for the poem's articulation, narrative voice is enunciated only once ("Mon chat"). Its identity is never fully expressed and remains a floating or rather empty construct.

This problematic position occurs with the self stringing together the seemingly unrelated imagery as it is simultaneously being detached from the unfurling of the narrative. A disconcerting rift ensues between the language and the self, a division that transforms the house matrix into its negation while stressing the almost incidental and fortuitous role of the self.

As Riffaterre points out, the deck of cards and other objects as well reflect a scene of intimacy.[8] The reductive world of the Queen of Spades and Jack of Hearts almost assumes magnified proportions, depicting a true metonymic representation of the house system. The fact that the two cards converse grimly about their past loves creates the illusion of a coherent world. Yet, exclusion of the poetic voice from this self-contained universe gives rise to a gap in which language undermines the role of the self. It severs the poetic voice from the narrative, revealing a discord as the interplay of the self's absence and presence assists in refuting the house matrix. But ironic distancing not only joins forces with the house system, it also orients the reader's understanding of the poem's title, **"Spleen,"** laying bare the doomed poetic voice consumed by linguistic alienation.

Similar to Baudelaire's Spleen poem, **"La Béatrice"** paints the poet as doomed artist but at the same time, the ironic stance alludes to a "dédoublement" of the self with the poet adopting the pose of the prince or dandy. Ironic distancing emphasizes the self as a Hamlet-figure, a histrionic artist who is mercilessly berated by impish demons. Their attack aims at the heart of his artistic endeavors and becomes more poignant at the end when the beloved joins in the ridicule. Though overhearing their conversation, the narrator remains isolated from the demons since they do not suspect that he is listening. Even the poem's structure adds to the separation between subject and object: set apart by a direct quotation of the demons' conversation, the second stanza is disconnected from the first and last stanzas, which present the narrator's subjective perspective.

The reference to **"La Béatrice"** calls further attention to the poem's ironic and dual stance. Commenting upon the relation between self-consciousness and critical distancing, Claude Pichois stresses that "La Béatrice du poète n'est évidemment pas celle de Dante: elle est mêlée à la 'troupe obscène' des démons et parfois leur fait 'quelque sale caresse' . . . Le génie de Baudelaire est ici d'instaurer cette confrontation entre Shakespeare et Dante."[9] Questioning artistic enterprise, the irony of this confrontation pits a transformed Beatrice against Shakespeare's Hamlet-figure, which leads to the degradation of self. Yet the irony is twofold: owing to his self-awareness, the narrator also surpasses his ill-fated circumstances.

Another expression of the ironic stance, critical self-awareness also helps to frame the problematic nature between language and fragmentation. Approximating Leo Bersani's references to the prince or dandy in

Baudelaire's poetry, the ironic voice becomes a metaphor of the self as it appropriates others or objects, all contained within its own consciousness. Appropriation occurs as a result of the poem's irony, which is directed more at the narrator than at his rapport with others. Paul de Man notes that in Baudelaire's "comique absolu," "the ironic subject at once has to ironize its own predicament and observe in turn, with the detachment and disinterestedness that Baudelaire demands of this kind of spectator, the temptation to which it is about to succumb."[10] The dynamics of this critical position disclose irony as a self-reflective process that implicates the poetic persona: he becomes both the observer and victim of the poetic act who paradoxically knows and comprehends his situation but is unable to act upon such knowledge. Baudelaire refers to this as the "supreme" knowledge of the "Wise" ("le Sage"), a self-knowledge that is nonetheless concealed and frozen within the consciousness of the self. The ironic stance sets the stage for knowledge but prevents its materialization. It is, in other words, a reflection of negativity stemming from an entrapping discourse that mirrors an endless spiral.

Critical self-consciousness in **"La Béatrice"** supersedes the Hamlet-figure through a doubling of the self. In the first stanza the narrator sharpens the dagger of his mind against his heart. As Claude Pichois explains, "Le poignard de Baudelaire—sans doute l'ironie—n'est destiné qu'à le tuer lui-même."[11] The narrator knows that his awareness is self-incriminating and that he "is lost in that 'gouffre obscur,' one separated from God's grace. He must live on in the darkness of 'an unweeded garden / (grown) to seed'."[12] But the poem also hints at the narrator's "superiority," for he triggers irony's dagger. This critical play is more acutely brought to light with the portrayal of the demons as an imaginary construct of the poet's imagination, prompted by his reverie:

> Comme je me plaignais un jour à la nature,
> Et que de ma pensée, en vaguant au hasard,
> J'aiguisais lentement sur mon coeur le poignard,
> Je vis en plein midi descendre sur ma tête
> Un nuage funèbre et gros d'une tempête,
> Qui portait un troupeau de démons vicieux,
> Semblables à des nains cruels et curieux.

(1: 116)

An extension of the artistic self, the demons make disparaging remarks that question the poetic act. That the narrator is aware of their presence, however, not only reveals his deprecation but also his superiority in the knowledge of his victimization. Ironic self-consciousness thus transcends the narrator's position as artistic sham through the assimilation of the object (both the demons and the beloved) to the narrative self. As such, the role of "others" in this poem alludes to the narrator as the prince or dandy who is keenly cognizant of his preeminent status but unable to prevent his own denigration as the unfortunate Hamlet-character.

"L'Héautontimorouménos" similarly provides insight into the critical doubling of the narrative self. The ironic voice echoes Icarus' search for the impossible or the absolute as it seeks to establish the primacy of satanic order over divine rule. The opening stanzas show the poet inflicting pain upon the woman to satisfy and relieve his own suffering, thirst, and desires. This also reflects an effort to surpass conventional order and movement. However, it does not occur; instead, the poet's self-consciousness forces him to acknowledge his singularity as he becomes the vampire of his own heart. Treating the self-other relation in Baudelaire's work, Eric Gans writes, "'L'Héautontimorouménos' throws off the Other of the opening lines as a failed attempt at self-doubling which gives way to the intermediary figure of 'L'ironie,' whose doubleness the poet reflects. . . . The Self is finally revealed as its own double, and in so doing reacquires a new diabolic substantiality."[13] Irony's doubleness as the "vorace Ironie" tracking the self brings to light the destructive appropriation of the other. This awareness removes the critical self from the interplay of the empirical self-other rapport and forces it to acknowledge its own reflection as "la mégère," the shrew. With this recognition, the self becomes both perpetrator and victim, a position that is appropriated within the consciousness of the poetic voice.

In the last stanza this self-consciousness evokes a superiority in self-knowledge as it perceives the absolute ("le rire éternel"), thus bringing to mind the prince-dandy figure. But the poet's failure to smile also condemns him, revealing that he cannot participate in this knowledge. This is reminiscent of Melmoth's satanic laughter in *De l'Essence du rire*: it discerns its superiority but at its own expense, since it is always linked to a fall or self-destruction (2: 527).

That the ironic voice recognizes its split or fragmentation symbolizes its superiority. Though this realization ultimately occurs as a result of its fall, which the prince or dandy cannot halt, its prominent status brings it to an even higher, more self-conscious level. We are not far from the poem, **"L'Irrémédiable,"** which approaches the irony of ironies with the self revealed as the ultimate consciousness of desire. Both the imagery (others and objects) and the self are merged into one consciousness. Whereas the heart's "tête-à-tête" enjoys a unique role in this poem, it owes the recognition of its knowledge to its downfall. The fragmented consciousness in part one experiences several metaphoric descents, recognizing its imperfect or corrupt state but powerless to reverse its course:

—Emblèmes nets, tableau parfait
D'une fortune irrémédiable,
   Qui donne à penser que le Diable
Fait toujours bien tout ce qu il fait!

(1: 80)

Baudelaire places greater emphasis on the notion of awareness in part two. The self's preeminent status, though fragmented, is clearly delineated by various epithets:

Tête-à-tête sombre et limpide
Qu'un coeur devenu son miroir!
Puits de Vérité, clair et noir,
Où tremble une étoile livide,

Un phare ironique, infernal,
Flambeau des grâces sataniques,
Soulagement et gloire uniques, . . .

(1: 80)

These images prepare the last verse that points to a source of knowledge, "—La conscience dans le Mal!", ironically acquired at the price of a downfall. But irony probes deeper because this knowledge is locked within the self's own consciousness. All the images in the first part of the poem are ultimately appropriated by a heart that mirrors itself. Irony is further underscored as the narrative voice refers to this consciousness in indefinite terms ("Qu'*un* coeur devenu son miroir"). Accordingly, the heart or consciousness is isolated from the self with fragmentation assuming increasing significance. The self's superiority is discernible but since consciousness mirrors only itself, absolute knowledge remains enclosed in its own self-reflective form. Though **"L'Irrémédiable"** does not surpass the irony of this position, since this would be Baudelaire's description of pure poetry precluding the notion of a fall, it is nonetheless the exemplary testimony of a self-perpetuating and problematic stance in which the quest for knowledge or the absolute is deemed possible but impenetrable.

The irony framing Baudelaire's "comique absolu" inaugurates a critical process that, situated at the level of the narrative self, vigorously depicts a world constantly questioning itself. Though characterized by lack of closure, the ironic temper nevertheless verbalizes the ambiguities strewn in Baudelaire's poetry, ambiguities and paradoxes that could not otherwise be articulated. For it denotes a unique way of perceiving the world as it creates structures potentially rich and continuously varying in meaning while simultaneously challenging their effectiveness. The open-ended nature of irony and its relation to the fragmented self offer a viable perspective to new discoveries to be made about Baudelaire's poetry.

Notes

1. Charles Baudelaire, *Œuvres complètes,* 2 vols. (Paris: Gallimard, Bibliothèque de la Pléiade,

1975) 1: 419-420. Subsequent references will be in the body of the text.

2. Jean Prévost, *Baudelaire: Essai sur l'inspiration et la création poétiques* (Paris: Mercure de France, 1953) 89.

3. Paul de Man, *Blindness and Insight: Essays in the Rhetoric of Contemporary Criticism* (Minneapolis: University of Minnesota Press, 1971).

4. Leo Bersani, *Baudelaire and Freud* (Berkeley: University of California Press, 1977).

5. Bersani 116.

6. Michael Riffaterre, *The Semiotics of Poetry* (Bloomington: Indiana University Press, 1978) 67.

7. Riffaterre 68.

8. Riffaterre 69.

9. Claude Pichois, "Remarques sur Baudelaire et la conscience de soi," *Genèse de la conscience moderne: Etudes sur le développement de la conscience de soi dans les littératures du monde occidental,* ed. Robert Ellrodt (Paris: Presses Universitaires de France, 1983) 302-304.

10. de Man 217.

11. Claude Pichois, notes, *Œuvres complètes,* by Charles Baudelaire (Paris: Gallimard, Bibliothèque de la Pléiade, 1975) 1: 1067.

12. Rosette Lamont, "'The Hamlet-Myth' in Nineteenth-Century France," *Council on National Literatures/Quarterly World Report* 5.4 (1982): 15.

13. Eric Gans, "'Mon semblable, mon frère'," *Stanford French Review* 8.1 (1984): 81.

Elissa Marder (essay date autumn-winter 1992)

SOURCE: Marder, Elissa. "Flat Death: Snapshots of History." *Diacritics* 22, nos. 3 and 4 (autumn-winter 1992): 128-44.

[*In the following essay, Marder provides a detailed exigesis of "À une passante," primarily focusing on Walter Benjamin's analysis of the same poem.*]

Simply put, we might be tempted to call history that which has passed away—but any reflection on and of history encounters the trauma of how to be present not only to what has passed, but also to the activity of its passing. Both Baudelaire's **"À une passante"** and Roland Barthes's *Camera Lucida* are motivated by an impossible address to a female figure who has, as we say, "passed away." Baudelaire's sonnet **"À une passante"** is a lyric poem addressed to the figure of a woman who, having already "passed," cannot be present to receive the poem's address. *Camera Lucida,* Barthes's "note" on the ontology of photography, is centered and decentered by his attempt to speak about the death of his mother through a reflection on a photograph of her and on photography more generally. In both texts, the attempt to be present to a passing through the activity of mourning opens up the problem of how to represent history. The deaths that precede these two works are figured not by a passage, but rather by a ghostly, perpetually repeated and even mechanical "passing": the activity of passing is repeated to the point of immobility, and history is represented as "cliché." But before we look at these two works directly, we shall begin by looking at how Walter Benjamin sees the representation of history in "**À une passante.**" By examining the traces of a "hidden figure" in Benjamin's reading of "**À une passante,**" read through a series of relayed looks, we shall find that Benjamin uncovers a figure of history buried in this poem.

THE WIDOW

One should not read Walter Benjamin's writings on Baudelaire without being startled by his reading of the sonnet "**À une passante.**" His presentation of the poem occupies a pivotal position in the 1938 essay "The Paris of the Second Empire" as well as in the 1939 revision "Some Motifs in Baudelaire." In both essays, "**À une passante**" is the only poem from *Les fleurs du mal* that Benjamin quotes in its entirety. But although he reproduces the entire poem in both texts, his discussion of it concentrates primarily on a figure that the poem never directly names or represents. In order to understand what is at stake in his reading of this poem, as well as why it remains the cornerstone of all of his work on Baudelaire, we must begin by understanding that Benjamin's reading strategy is inextricable from the conclusions it enables him to reach. As Benjamin insists incessantly, "**À une passante**" must be read as a negative image, in relief, as it were, through the absence of its central figure—the crowd. In "Some Motifs in Baudelaire" he introduces the poem by claiming that "the masses had become so much a part of Baudelaire that it is rare to find a description of them in his works. His most important subjects are hardly ever encountered in descriptive form" [122]. To say that Benjamin reads the poem "as a negative image" is to claim that his specificity as both reader and thinker must be traced through this peculiar insistence on traces of absent figures. As the example of the crowd illustrates, Benjamin often bases his exegesis of Baudelaire by pointing out, with remarkable precision, the importance of specific details that Baudelaire leaves out of his poems.[1] Like the ancient prophets who attempted to read the future in the entrails of certain animals, Benjamin reads "modernity" in the traces of poetic history that Baudelaire leaves in his wake. In the "Motifs" essay he writes: "This crowd, of whose existence

Baudelaire is always aware, has not served as the model for any of his works, but is imprinted on his creativity as a hidden figure [*als verborgene Figur eingeprägt*]" [120]. By tracking the imprints of a "hidden figure" in Benjamin's reading of "**À une passante,**" we shall be able to read traces of a conception of the relationship among allegory, modernity and history that Benjamin might have made more explicit had he lived to complete the *Passagen-Werk* project.

Why, we might begin by asking, does Benjamin insist on reading this particular poem as a medium for his presentation of the motif of the crowd? As he himself points out, "In the sonnet '**À une passante**' the crowd is nowhere named in either word or phrase. And yet the whole happening hinges on it, just as the progress of a sailing-boat depends on the wind" ["Motifs" 124]. Through his analogy, Benjamin implies that the action depicted in the poem, like the progress of the ship to which he compares it, is primarily a medium for rendering visible an ineffable force that motivates it. Without a ship's sail, one can neither see the wind nor measure its velocity. For Benjamin, the action of the poem, like the sailboat's "progress," is read in its resistance to the force of the crowd through which the passing figure passes. Instead of focusing on the figure of the passing woman, he looks at the force (the mass of the crowd) through which her passage can be marked. By looking past her to the crowd, Benjamin turns our attention to what must have been passing around her and hence "present" to the eyes of the one who watches her. He goes on to discuss how the erotic encounter between the passing woman and the one who watches her is facilitated, rather than hindered, by the force of the crowd. It is the presence of the crowd itself that engenders this experience of modern love. In "Motifs" he writes: "The delight of the urban poet is love—not at first sight, but at last sight. It is a farewell forever which coincides in the poem with the moment of enchantment. Thus the sonnet supplies the figure of shock, even of catastrophe . . . like the kind of sexual shock that can beset a lonely man" [125]. Throughout his reading, Benjamin is consistently less concerned with the figure of the passing woman than with the impact that her passage produces on the one who watches her. For him, the force of the erotic encounter, as well as the poem it produces, can be read only in the aftershock of that encounter. His reading relies upon a dual structure of delayed action and relayed looks—Benjamin looks at the imprint of the wake of her passage reflected in the eyes of the one who watched her pass.

But it is curious that Benjamin appears to bypass the description of the passing woman almost altogether. While he does point out that she is in mourning (and we will return to this point in some detail later), he never refers to the poem's descriptions of her movement "Agile et noble, avec sa jambe de statue,"² or, even more surprisingly, to the fact that the final two tercets of the poem are, however impossibly, addressed to her. In his belated address to her (she is gone before he starts to speak), the poet calls out to the woman by calling her by the name of "fugitive beauté." Why does Benjamin choose not to comment on the obvious echoes between the invocation of a "fleeting beauty" in the poem and Baudelaire's definition of modernity as "fleeting beauty" in "The Painter of Modern Life"? Not only does Benjamin know the essay extremely well (he quotes from it constantly), but he uses that very essay as the foundation for his discussions of the flaneur, the crowd, and Poe's story "The Man of the Crowd" in both of his own essays on Baudelaire. We can only assume (and this assumption will be borne out by what follows) that Benjamin's silence concerning the figure of the "fleeting beauty" in the poem marks the site of a trace of a reading of Baudelaire's definition of modernity. By choosing to focus on this particular poem and by refusing to present it according to the paradigms that would be familiar to any reader of Baudelaire's discussion of modernity, Benjamin effectively *preempts* a reading that would claim that **"À une passante"** should be read as a poetic incarnation of Baudelaire's definition of modernity. The hidden figures embedded in Benjamin's reading of **"À une passante"** will allow us to read how, instead of relying on this poem in order to demonstrate Baudelaire's definition of modernity, Benjamin uses this poem precisely in order to challenge it.

In the 1938 essay "The Paris of the Second Empire in Baudelaire," Benjamin launches a direct attack on Baudelaire's definition of modernity in "The Painter of Modern Life." But the precise logic of this attack is so opaque that it provokes a critic as astute as Hans Robert Jauss to accuse Benjamin of a "violent" misreading of Baudelaire. Jauss begins his essay "Reflections on the Chapter 'Modernity' in Benjamin's Baudelaire Fragments" with the bold assertion that "It is paradoxical that Baudelaire's theory of modernity should have been misunderstood by the very critic whose work has done the most to propel us toward a new understanding of that poet" [176]. While it would be impossible to enter into the specifics of Jauss's argument without presenting a systematic analysis of the Baudelaire essay in relation to both Jauss and Benjamin, and while I believe that Jauss is wrong in his assessment that Benjamin "misunderstood" Baudelaire's theory of modernity, I point to Jauss's claim in order to stress the fact that Benjamin's argument is anything but self-evident. In the section entitled "Modernism" in "The Paris of the Second Empire," Benjamin quotes and glosses Baudelaire's definition of modernity:

> And in the final passage of his essay on Guys he says: "Everywhere he sought the transitory, fleeting beauty of our present life, the character of what the reader has

permitted us to call modernism." In summary form, his doctrine reads as follows: "A constant, unchangeable element . . . and a relative, limited element cooperates to produce beauty. . . . The latter element is supplied by the epoch, by fashion, by morality and the passions. Without this second element . . . the first would not be assimilable." One can hardly say that this is a profound analysis [*Man kann nicht sagen, dass das in die Tiefe geht*]. In Baudelaire's view of modernism, the theory of modern art is the weakest point. . . . None of the aesthetic reflections in Baudelaire's theory of art presented modernism in its interpenetration [*Durchdringung*] with classical antiquity, something that was done in certain poems of the *Fleurs du mal.*

[82]

It is rare, to say the least, to find Benjamin passing judgment on Baudelaire's thinking with a one-line verdict like "this is not a profound analysis." It is equally rare to find Benjamin abdicating the position of Baudelaire's ideal reader; when Baudelaire invokes the reader's permission to call the "transitory, fleeting beauty of our present life . . . modernism," Benjamin refuses to accord him that permission. In short, it would seem that Benjamin accuses Baudelaire-the-theorist of having a superficial appreciation of Baudelaire-the-poet's articulation of modernity. Benjamin's dissatisfaction would seem to lie in the way in which Baudelaire isolates the "constant, unchangeable element" from the "transitory, fleeting . . . element supplied by the epoch." For Benjamin, these two elements can never be understood as discrete entities—each element exists only in relation to the other—in the structure of what he calls here *Durchdringung*. By understanding *Durchdringung* as a forceful permeation, we understand that modernism exists for Benjamin only to the degree that it is thoroughly stamped with the marks of classical antiquity.

In the next paragraph, Benjamin explains that the more precise name for this penetrating process is allegory. He writes:

> Among these the poem **"Le Cygne"** [**"The Swan"**] is paramount. It is no accident that it is an allegory. The city which is in constant flux grows rigid. It becomes as brittle and as transparent as glass—that is, as far as its meaning is concerned—"The form of a city, alas, changes more quickly than a mortal's heart." . . . The stature of Paris is fragile; it is surrounded by symbols of fragility—living creatures (the negress and the swan) and historical figures (Andromache, "widow of Hector and wife of Helenus"). Their common feature is sadness about what was and lack of hope for what is to come. In the final analysis, this decrepitude [*Hinfälligkeit*] constitutes the closest connection between modernism and antiquity. Whenever Paris occurs in the *Fleurs du mal,* it bears the signs of this decrepitude.

[82-83]

In the 1935 "exposé," "Paris—Capital of the Nineteenth Century," in letters to Horkheimer, Scholem, and Adorno, and in numerous fragments of *Passagen-Werk,*

Benjamin reiterates that his interest in Baudelaire is first and foremost motivated by Baudelaire's distinctive use of classical allegory in his depiction of modernity. In the 1935 exposé, the chapter on Baudelaire bears the epigraph "Tout pour moi devient allegorie" ("Everything for me becomes allegory") from **"Le cygne,"** and in the first sentence of the exposé, Benjamin writes: "Baudelaire's genius, which drew its nourishment from melancholy, was an allegorical one" [170]. In a letter to Horkheimer dated 16 April 1938, he describes his project on Baudelaire:

> The work should have three parts. Their projected titles are: idea and image; antique and modern; the new and the always same. The first part will show the determining significance of allegory in the *Fleurs du mal*. . . . The second part develops the blinding over-exposure of the allegorical way of seeing [*der allegorischen Anschauung die Uberblendung*] as a formal element, by virtue of which the antique appears in the modern and the modern in the antique.

> [Briefe 751]

Moreover, it was precisely in relation to the question of allegory that Benjamin claimed that Baudelaire had been consistently misread. In *Passagen-Werk* he notes: "Baudelaire's allegorical way of looking at things was not understood by any of his contemporaries and, consequently, ultimately failed to be noticed altogether" ["J" 61.3; *GS* [*Gesammelte Schriften*] 1: 426]. Keeping these examples in mind, we can now understand that Benjamin's critique of Baudelaire's definition of modernity in "The Painter of Modern Life" is primarily concerned with the absence of an articulation of the role of allegory.

Benjamin's systematic invocation of the poem **"Le cygne"** as the privileged example of allegory in Baudelaire is *not* based, as one might expect, on the fact that the word *allegory* appears in the poem. For Benjamin, the allegorical quality of the poem resides in the poem's depiction of the city. As he remarks in his discussion of **"Le cygne,"** the city "becomes as brittle and as transparent as glass. . . . The stature of Paris is fragile; it is surrounded by symbols of fragility—living creatures (the negress and the swan) and historical figures (Andromache, 'widow of Hector and wife of Helenus')." The invisible but overpowering presence of the ruins of Troy in the poem shatters the newly built city of Paris at the level of its mythic foundation.[3] The image of the modern city is superimposed on the rubble of the ancient one—thus the modernity of the new city must be read through the figure of its past and future decrepitude. In a fragment from *Passagen-Werk*, Benjamin revises Baudelaire's definition of modernity by invoking the figure of "ruins" to collapse Baudelaire's distinction between a "constant, unchanging element" and a "fleeting, transitory" element. He writes: "The experience of allegory, which holds onto ruins, is,

actually, that of the eternally transitory" ["J" 67.4; *GS* 1: 439]. Benjamin reads Baudelaire's allegory to show that history is the site not of solid foundations but of ruins—it is no less fleeting than modernity. History is as fleeting as a bad dream that never fails to recur, and allegory is the form that the bad dream takes. In *Passagen-Werk* he writes: "Modernity has antiquity like one has a demon, which came over it in sleep" ["J" 82a.4; *GS* 1: 470].

While we have shown how Benjamin invokes **"Le cygne"** to prove that Baudelaire's poetic use of allegory challenges his own definition of modernity in "The Painter of Modern Life," how does Benjamin's discussion of allegory and modernity in **"Le cygne"** relate to our initial question concerning the "hidden figure" in Benjamin's reading of **"À une passante"** in "Motifs"? Moreover, given Benjamin's repeated claims (in the 1935 exposé, in *Passagen-Werk,* in the letters, and in the 1938 essay "The Paris of the Second Empire") that Baudelaire's use of allegory is the determining factor in his poetic depiction of modernity, why, in "Motifs," does Benjamin make no explicit reference either to allegory or to the poem that can be read as its insignia—**"Le cygne?"** The most obvious explanation for this omission is, of course, that the 1939 "Motifs" essay was conceived as a revision of only the "Flaneur" portion of the 1938 "Second Empire" essay: the passages we examined from the "Modernity" portion of the earlier essay were never intended to be part of the "Motifs" revision. There is, nonetheless, one tiny but significant trace of Benjamin's discussion of allegory, modernity, and history that emerges in his presentation of the "passante" poem in "Motifs." As I stated at the outset, **"À une passante"** is the only poem from *Les fleurs du mal* that Benjamin quotes in its entirety in both "Second Empire" and "Motifs." In both essays, Benjamin presents the poem in order to introduce a discussion of the hidden figure of the crowd. By adding one significant detail to his reading of the poem in "Motifs," Benjamin directs us to read **"À une passante"** through his reading of **"Le cygne."** In the opening lines of his analysis of **"À une passante"** in "Second Empire," he writes: "This sonnet presents the crowd not as the refuge of a criminal but as that of love which eludes the poet. One may say that it deals with the function of the crowd not in the life of the citizen, but in the life of the erotic person" [45]. But in "Motifs," he adds:

> In a *widow*'s veil, mysteriously and mutely borne along by the crowd, an unknown woman comes into the poet's field of vision. What the sonnet communicates is simply this: far from experiencing the crowd as an opposed, antagonistic element, this very crowd brings to the city dweller the figure that fascinates.

> [125; my emphasis]

Benjamin's invocation of the word *widow* is surprising because while the poem does refer to the fact that the passing woman is in mourning ("en grand deuil"), there is nothing in the poem to indicate that the mourning woman is a widow. In fact, one of the most compelling aspects of the poem lies in the fact that the passing woman mourns a death that is itself shrouded in mystery. Why does Benjamin, who is the very epitome of the meticulous reader and who had previously referred to the "passante" as "a female apparition in mourning" ["Second Empire" 46], now decide to give a name to the source of her mourning?

There are at least two ways of explaining why Benjamin might have wanted to force us to read the mourning woman as a widow. The more simple explanation would be to recall that Benjamin reads the erotic encounter depicted in the poem as an encounter characterized by loss. He argues that the poem speaks not of love at first sight but rather of "love at last sight." For Benjamin, "À une passante" is not merely a poem about love, but rather a poem about looking for love in all the wrong places (the street) and about losing it in the very moment it has been found. In *Passagen-Werk*, he repeatedly comments on the fact that Baudelaire modernizes the lyric by suffusing the love poem with images of sexual perversion.[4] By claiming that the mourning woman is a widow, he suggests that the erotic loss narrated in the poem was already figured in the widow's prior loss of her husband. The figure of the "lost husband" would thus stand as a synecdoche for the specifically *erotic* nature of the loss, as opposed to the loss of a noneroticized figure.

But another explanation for Benjamin's decision to cast the mourning woman in the role of a widow brings us back to our discussion of the relationship between antiquity and modernity in "Le cygne." Because while there is no explicit mention of a widow in "À une passante," in "Le cygne," the apostrophe to the widow, Andromache, constitutes the poetic source of the poem.[5] The entire poem emerges out of reflections cast in the stream of the widow's tears:

Andromaque, je pense à vous! Ce petit fleuve,
Pauvre et triste miroir où jadis resplendit
L'immense majesté de vos douleurs de veuve,
Ce Simoïs menteur qui par vos pleurs grandit,
A fécondé soudain ma mémoire fertile . . .

[85]

[Andromache, I think of you! This small river,
Sad and meager mirror where long ago,
The boundless majesty of your widow's grief glit-
  tered,
This lying Simoïs, which swelled with your tears,
Has quickened my memory . . .]

[my translation]

Read through the widow's veil, Benjamin encourages us to read "À une passante" as a palimpsest superimposed upon the ancient ruins of "Le cygne." The

bustling streets depicted in the first poem are haunted by the rubble of Troy invoked in the second one. Seen in this light, "À une passante" presents a vision of modernity that is permeated by the decay of history. In both poems, the city becomes visible only when it is seen through the veil of a mourning woman. Through the widow's veil, Benjamin invites us to read the stasis of modernity across the transitory flight of history.

In *Passagen-Werk*, Benjamin defines the figure of the crowd as an allegory of modernity and the figure of the city as an allegory of antiquity: "In Baudelaire, Paris stands as an emblem of antiquity, in contrast to his crowd, as emblem of the modern" ["J" 66a.2; *GS* 1: 437]. But, as our reading of Benjamin's reading of "À une passante" demonstrates, there is no simple historical progression *from* antiquity *to* modernity—they are frozen together in the form of a kind of static repetition. Instead of presenting history in terms of a fluid passage, Benjamin conceives of Baudelaire's depiction of history in architectural terms: history is seen as the rigid scaffold which binds allegorical antiquity to modernity. In one of the most opaque fragments of *Passagen-Werk*, Benjamin suggests that this construction of history can be understood only nondialectically:

The correspondence between antiquity and modernity is the only constructive conception of history in Baudelaire. Through its rigid armature, it excluded every dialectical one [*Die Korrespondenz zwischen Antike und Moderne ist die einzige konstruktive Geschichtkonzeption bei Baudelaire. Durch ihre starre Armatur schloss sie jede dialektische aus*].

["J" 59a.5; *GS* 1: 423]

If we recall Benjamin's discussion of the function of allegory in "Le cygne," we remember that, for Benjamin, history becomes visible when modernity is petrified by antiquity: "The city which is in constant flux grows rigid. It becomes as brittle and as transparent as glass." The very rigidity of this structure renders it both brittle and fragile. If history cannot be conceived of in dialectical terms here, it is because the petrification process cancels out the possibility of movement. Rather than appearing as the movement through which progress can be marked, this historical construction recalls the ossification of ruins. And it is no accident that the widow is the privileged witness to this model of history. The death that she mourns is, as Barthes will later say of the photograph, nondialectical; it is as irrevocable and static as the image of history that appears refracted through her veil.

THE WIDOW'S VEIL AND THE PHOTOGRAPHIC
CLICHÉ

In a letter dated 2 August 1935, written in response to the 1935 draft of the exposé for the Arcades Project, Theodor Adorno writes to Walter Benjamin: "I find the passage about the crowd as a veil wonderful." In that early text (which makes no mention of **"À une Passante"**), Benjamin had written: "The crowd was the veil from behind which the familiar city as phantasmagoria beckoned to the flaneur" [170]. Given his later reproach that Benjamin's "Second Empire" suffered from an excess of "immediate . . . materialism" compounded by the absence of a mediating theory,[6] it is not surprising that Adorno should have particularly appreciated the figure of the crowd as veil. In "Motifs," Benjamin introduces Baudelaire's view of the crowd through the figure of the veil. He writes: "The mass was the agitated veil; through it Baudelaire saw Paris" [123]. In attributing the figure of the veil to Baudelaire, instead of to the flaneur, Benjamin links this veiled vision to the experience of shock. At the end of "Motifs," he argues that while the flaneur is seduced and "bedazzled" by the "luster of the crowd," Baudelaire "was no flaneur"; he "singled out his having been jostled by the crowd as the decisive, unique experience. . . . This is the nature of something lived through [*Erlebnis*] to which Baudelaire has given the weight of an experience [*Erfahrung*]" [154]. Paradoxically, the figure of the veil illuminates rather than filters the shock of experience.

But the figure of the veil also serves as the medium through which Benjamin links the structure of repetition and relayed looks in **"À une passante"** to Baudelaire's place in literary history. In **"À une passante,"** the veil—the mark of death that separates the face of the woman from the look of the other—becomes the bearer of a relayed reflection of everything that passes around it. The mourner's veil functions like a mechanical mirror—or photographic apparatus—that turns our gaze away from the (perhaps nonexistent) face of the woman and back onto the amorphous crowd which is "present" all around her. It is by gazing at the veil that the "present" is represented. Through her veil, which is itself the mark of a prior passage, we can see that which could never otherwise be seen: the experience of the present.

Benjamin addresses the historical figure of Baudelaire in terms that recall those employed by the narrator of **"À une passante"** in his address to the figure of the passing woman. "Motifs" attempts to speak about the historical passing of lyric poetry by staging an encounter with Baudelaire, whom Benjamin calls the last lyric poet. In the final section of the essay, Benjamin enumerates the factors that contribute to Baudelaire's privileged position in relation to both lyric poetry and history. He writes:

> ***Les Fleurs du mal*** was the last lyric work that had a European repercussion; no later work penetrated beyond a more or less limited linguistic area . . . , it cannot be denied that some of his lyric motifs—and the present study has dealt with them—render the possibility of lyric poetry questionable. These . . . facts define

Baudelaire historically. They show that he imperturbably stuck to his cause and single-mindedly concentrated on his mission. He went so far as to proclaim his goal "the creation of a cliché."

[152]

Benjamin's essay both begins and ends with this reiteration, that Baudelaire was the "last lyric poet." But because Baudelaire is the last lyric poet, he is not merely historicized within the context of lyric poetry; he speaks of and to the problem of history in a different light. One might even say that Benjamin's essay is nothing other than an attempt to develop (like one develops a photograph) an image of history that he finds reflected in the relayed gaze of the figure of its last lyric poet.[7] Benjamin reads the passing of lyric poetry by looking through the veil of Baudelaire's experience of the city and the crowd. But to be the "last lyric poet" is precisely to be the first lyric poet after the last lyric poet: Baudelaire cannot simply be the "last lyric poet," because that position would imply the possibility that lyric poetry is still "present" in Baudelaire, a claim that Benjamin disputes when he writes that "some of his lyric motifs . . . render the possibility of lyric poetry questionable." Instead of being the last lyric poet, Baudelaire becomes lyric poetry's first simulacrum—its first stuttering ghost.

It is at this juncture that we can begin to understand why Benjamin ends his essay by insisting that Baudelaire proclaimed his goal to be the "creation of a cliché." But what does *cliché* literally mean, and where does it come from? The word that is translated in English as *cliché* appears as the word *poncif* in Baudelaire's original French text.[8] While the connotations of *poncif* are almost identical to those of the English word *cliché, poncif* has a very long history (*Le petit Robert* gives it the date 1551), whereas *cliché* (imported from French into English) relates directly to the technological advances (the printing press) and inventions (photography) of the nineteenth century.[9] But unlike the English word *stencil* (which is what a *poncif* is), *poncif* carries the connotation of a piece of work that lacks all originality. That Benjamin should have placed so great an emphasis on Baudelaire's characteristically perverse desire to "create a cliché" is a testimony to Benjamin's insight into Baudelaire's position in literary history.

The implications of Benjamin's claim that Baudelaire "went so far as to proclaim his goal 'the creation of a cliché'" are further complicated by a look at this passage in the German text. The German text reads: "Unbeirrbar war Baudelaire im Bewusstsein seiner *Aufgabe.* Das geht so weit, dass er als sein Ziel 'eine *Schablone* zu kreieren' bezeichnet hat" ["Motive," *GS* 1: 651]. There are two remarks to be made here. It is interesting that the word Benjamin uses to express mission is *Aufgabe: Aufgabe* immediately invokes the task of "Task of the Translator." And, more important for this analysis,

Benjamin uses the word *Schablone* as a translation of *poncif.* In a letter dated 2 August 1935, Adorno writes: "Incidentally, the idea of an early history of the feuilleton, about which so much is contained in your essay on Kraus, is most fascinating. . . . In this connection an old journalistic term occurs to me: (*Schablonstil*) [cliché style], whose origin ought to be investigated" [116].

Paradoxically, the history of the English word *cliché* may tell us more about Benjamin's understanding of history than the history of either *poncif* or *Schablone.* The English word has itself become a cliché—meaning that it has been reproduced and reiterated (keeping its French voice as it passes into English) to the point where the traces of its material history have been effaced. But embedded in the history of this word is a condensed history of the evolution of mechanical reproduction. The word *cliché* first emerges at the outset of the nineteenth century, and its meaning evolves throughout the nineteenth century and into the beginning of the twentieth century. *Le petit Robert* informs us that *cliché* first appeared around 1809 and was initially used in the context of typography.[10] In 1865 (eight years after the first publication of **Les fleurs du mal** and corresponding with the growth and emergence of photography) a new definition appeared: "negative image. See negative." The word *negative* presumably denotes a photographic negative—the inverted image through which we are able to make endless "positive" copies. Finally, in 1869 (according to the dubious chronology of the dictionary) we find that *cliché* finally assumed the definition through which we know it today: "Figurative and pejorative. An idea or expression that is used too often. A banality, a *lieu commun.*" What we find buried in the history of *cliché* is a certain passage from the mechanical reproduction of letters to that of photographs coupled with an emphasis upon an image that is cast in relief—what I have previously referred to as a "negative image." It is this model of cliché, in which we find the notion of mechanical reproduction linked to that of a negative image, that determines both Benjamin's reading of Baudelaire and his articulation of history. Like the frozen passage between modernity and antiquity that we found embedded in Benjamin's reading of "**À une passante**," *cliché* condenses the history of the development of mechanical reproduction and freezes the representation of that history into the rigid scaffold of a single imprinted word. Furthermore, the activity of that freezing process is precisely that of the photographic "click." As Benjamin writes in "Motifs": "Of the countless movements of switching, inserting, pressing, and the like, the "snapping" of the photographer has had the greatest consequences. A touch of the finger now sufficed to fix an event for an unlimited period of time. The camera gave the moment a posthumous shock, as it were" [132]. Benjamin claims not only that Baudelaire wanted to "create a cliché," but supports that claim by focusing his reading of

Baudelaire on images presented in *cliché*: he reads the *lieu commun,* or the common space (the street), that is presented in Baudelaire through its negative images. Only by reading "**À une passante**" as a negative image, one presented in relief, can Benjamin read the crowd as the primary (albeit negative) figure of the poem. In addition, it is only by reading Benjamin's reading of "**À une passante**" as a "cliché" that we understand how the modernity of "**À une passante**" is imprinted with the traces of the allegorical antiquity of "**Le cygne.**"

If we retain the memory of the notion of the "negative image" in the word *cliché,* we can begin to see how Benjamin reads history, through the figure of Baudelaire, as cliché. In the most complex and enigmatic lines of "Motifs," Benjamin attempts to describe how to read a change in the structure of experience. In an attempt to describe how history is represented in the passage from Bergson's supposedly ahistorical account of the structure of memory to Baudelaire's poetic "cliché" of history, Benjamin writes:

> It is, however, not at all Bergson's intention to attach any specific historical label to memory. On the contrary, he rejects any historical determination of memory. He thus manages to stay clear of that experience from which his own philosophy evolved or, rather, in reaction to which it arose. It was the inhospitable, blinding age of big-scale industrialism. In shutting out this experience the eye perceives an experience of a complementary nature in the form of its spontaneous after-image, as it were [*Dem Auge, das sich vor dieser Erfahrung schliesst, stellt sich eine Erfahrung komplementärer Art als deren gleichsam spontanes Nachbild ein*]. Bergson's philosophy represents an attempt to give details of this after-image and to fix it as a permanent record. His philosophy thus indirectly furnishes a clue to the experience which presented itself to Baudelaire's eyes in its undistorted version in the figure of his reader [*Sie gibt derart mittelbar einen Hinweis auf die Erfahrung, die Baudelaire unverstellt, in der Gestalt seines Lesers, vor Augen tritt*].
>
> [111; *GS* 2: 609]

Benjamin's reading of the view of history that can be developed in the passage between Bergson's philosophy and Baudelaire's reader mirrors the structure of a photographic apparatus and recalls his reading of the negative image of history in "**À une passante.**" Benjamin locates the imprint of history on Bergson's philosophy in the very gesture through which Bergson attempted to blot it out. It is "the blinding age" that forces Bergson to shut his eyes to the historical dimension of memory. But because he shuts his eyes in response to the blinding flash of history, his shut eyes perform the role of a photographic shutter: they retain the blotted image and allow it to be recorded (negatively) despite the fact that the recorded image was never seen directly. The trace of history that Bergson's philosophy records can be seen only when it is "developed" through the gaze of the figure of Baudelaire's reader. In order to read the trace of this photographic cliché of history, we shall return, once again, to **"À une passante."**

If we have not yet looked directly at **"À une passante,"** it is because it is not clear what one can see by looking directly at it. The central event in the poem occurs in the ellipsis of a blinding flash: "Un éclair . . . puis la nuit! [A flash . . . then night!]" But by following Benjamin's attempt to develop the negative image of history that is represented in it, we shall read this poem as Baudelaire's written photograph of history as cliché.

> La rue assourdissante autour de moi hurlait.
> Longue, mince, en grand deuil, douleur majestueuse,
> Une femme passa, d'une main fastueuse
> Soulevant, balançant le feston et l'ourlet.
>
> Agile et noble, avec sa jambe de statue.
> Moi, je buvais, crispé comme un extravagant,
> Dans son oeil, ciel livide où germe l'ouragon,
> La douceur qui fascine et le plaisir qui tue.
>
> Un éclair . . . puis la nuit!—Fugitive beauté
> Dont le regard m'a fait soudainement renaître,
> Ne te verrai-je plus que dans l'éternité?
>
> Ailleurs, bien loin d'ici! Trop tard! *Jamais* peut-être!
> Car j'ignore où tu fuis, tu ne sais où je vais,
> O toi que j'eusse aimée, ô toi qui le savais!
>
> [92-93]

> [The deafening street around me was screaming.
> Long, slim, in deep mourning, majestic grief,
> A woman passed, raising, with a delicate hand,
> The trim and hem of the flounces of her gown;
>
> Graceful and noble, with her statue's leg.
> And I drank, frozen like a madman,
> In her eye, livid sky where the storm breeds,
> The softness that fascinates and the pleasure that kills.
>
> A flash . . . then night!—O fleeting beauty
> Whose look made me suddenly be reborn
> Shall I not see you again but in eternity?
>
> Elsewhere, far from here! Too late! *Never,* perhaps!
> I know not where you flee, you don't know where I go,
> You, whom I would have loved, you who knew it was so.]
>
> [my translation]

The structure of the sonnet (which divides the poem into two quatrains followed by two tercets) also divides the action depicted in the poem. In the first half of the poem, the narrator makes a desperate attempt to represent the presence of the passing figure. The tercets in the second half of the poem reiterate the event represented in the quatrains—but they take the form of an impossible address relayed through a kind of photographic after-image. The pathos of the apostrophe resides in the fact that the poet's futile address to the woman coincides with and collapses into an equally futile attempt at recollecting the encounter. The fulguration or "lightning flash" that separates the two halves of the poem is, as Benjamin has indicated, precisely not the "coup de foudre" of love at first sight but rather like the flash of a camera, which explodes after the moment has vanished and through which the image of that moment is retained: "Un éclair . . . puis la nuit!" The lightning flash—the very mark of instantaneity—occurs long after the figure has presumably passed. What produces this flash? What is reiterated in it?

One of the greatest difficulties this poem presents depends on how we read the various grammatical tenses of the verb *passer* that appear in the poem. *Passer* is intransitive here and cannot have a simple present: how does one think the present tense of the verb that means to pass? The title of the poem, **"À une passante,"** transforms the present active participle of *passer* into a name (almost a proper name) that is given to the feminine figure.[11] In the designation "passante," the figure of the woman clings to the present tense of *passer* and vice versa. In the poem's title, the woman and the verb cannot be construed as separate entities: hence it would be an error to read "passante" synonymously with a phrase like "celle qui passe" or "she who passes." The present tense of the verb *adheres* to the figure of the woman in the same way that, as Barthes will later claim, the photographic referent *adheres* to the photograph.[12] It is only through their incarnation in the woman's body that *passer* can be represented in the present tense and that a moment of "passing" can appear as presence. The moment that the poem attempts to arrest can be read in the *décalage* between the time when the woman's body clings to the verb in the present active participle and the separation between the body of the woman and the action of the verb that occurs in the line "Une femme passa" ("a woman passed"). Before she is called a woman, this embodied feminine present is named *passante,* and *as passante* she is always perpetually passing. She is called *femme* ("woman") only in her absence, *after* she has already passed away. The poem attempts to arrest, photographically, the impossible temporal disjunction evoked by her passage.

So, let us ask naively, exactly *when,* in the poem, does the *passante* pass? The first line of the poem situates the narrator in the deafening presence of a noisy street. It would seem that it is the *passante*'s silence, in contrast to the noisy street, that first catches the narrator's attention. He does not notice her by chance— she stands out from the crowd. And it is *not* her beauty that draws the poet's attention to her: the poem does not refer to her beauty until after she has passed away.

It is the fact that she is "en grand deuil," dressed in mourning, that catches the poet's eye. But if he notices her because she is in mourning, in the very moment he looks *at* her, he has already looked past her—to the death that preceded her presence and marks her passage. This poem presents a vertiginous relay of deaths: the first death precedes the poem, the woman's veil is a figure of its passage, and then she, in turn, passes away. It is this relay of perpetual passings, layered upon one another, that the poem mourns repeatedly.

When does she pass? In the moment of her "arrival" she is hardly distinguishable from the description of the street itself. The figure for the street and for the woman converge in the adjectives through which she is introduced: "longue, mince." The figure for the woman detaches itself from the passing crowd only through the invocation of her mourning: "en grand deuil, douleur majestueuse." The third line presents us with the poem's central paradox: "Une femme passa, d'une main fastueuse / soulevant, balançant le feston et l'ourlet." *Une femme passa.* A woman passed. The verb tense that recounts her passage is the *passé simple,* the simple past. But in this poem this past tense is anything but simple. It is immediately followed and contested by the reemergence of two verbs in the present active participle: *soulevant* and *balançant.*

The continuous repetition of this passage, as an immobilized and even petrified "present," characterizes the remainder of the poem. The figure of the *passante* becomes literally petrified; she is a walking tombstone with "sa jambe de statue." It would seem to be this image of a petrified present that shocks and freezes the narrator: "Moi, je buvais, crispé comme un extravagant." It is only after this reciprocal petrification that the narrator looks directly in her eye: "Dans son oeil, ciel livide où germe l'ouragon / La douceur qui fascine et le plaisir qui tue." But the look that they presumably exchange is reconstructed only after the event—after she has already passed. And it is doubly impossible: not only is she gone before he gazes in her eye, but if she is "en grand deuil" she is veiled. Although she can see through her veil, her "eye" is precisely what cannot be seen through it. The veil becomes like a one-way mirror, a screen onto which the narrator projects a hallucination of the reciprocated gaze that can never take place but which he is eternally condemned to repeat. Furthermore, in the act of looking her "in the eye," he has the revelation (and this revelation is already figured by the notion that he "lifts her veil" to look her in the eye) that the eros "in her eye" is, like the veil it bypasses, imprinted by the mark of death. "In her eye," he reads the trace of a "pleasure that kills." The mark of a past death that was imprinted in the veil returns through the mark of a future death impaled "in the eye" of the hallucinated look.

Although it is bizarre enough that this hallucinated look takes place at all, it is even odder that the lightning flash which should logically precede or coincide with the look follows it, thereby transforming the flash into a posthumous shock of the event rather than as the sign of the event itself. The flash marks the aftermath of the encounter: it repeats the exchanged look in a cliché: "Un éclair . . . puis la nuit—fugitive beauté / Dont le regard m'a fait soudainement renaître, ne te verrai-je plus que dans l'éternité?" It would seem that the narrator is "reborn" in the flash of the mechanical reproduction of a look that is repeated without ever having actually occurred.

In the final tercet of the poem, the narrator's desperate attempt to conjure up the experience of this passage as "presence" terminates in cliché. The temporal disjunction that the poem has already set in motion returns in spatial terms: "Ailleurs, bien loin d'ici." Although in the previous stanza the word *éternité* invoked the cliched hope that there might be an "eternal" temporal and spatial utopia in which the poet could recover his lost object, in the final stanza all hope of restitution is abandoned. In apparent despair, the poet calls out to the lost woman by invoking more and more negative images of time and space: "Ailleurs, bien loin d'ici! Trop tard! *Jamais* peut-être! [Elsewhere, far from here, too late, *never* perhaps!]." As Benjamin remarks in "Second Empire," "The *never* marks the high point of the encounter, when the poet's passion seems to be frustrated but in reality bursts out of him like a flame. He burns in this flame, but no Phoenix arises from it" [45]. Although, as Benjamin indicates, there can be no future rebirth from the passion ignited by and in this *never,* we are reminded once again that the stuttering repetition of loss recounted in **"À une passante"** is itself a vertiginous replay of the losses depicted in **"Le cygne."** The emphasized word *jamais* in **"À une passante"** functions like a citation of the stuttering repetition of the word *jamais* in **"Le cygne."** In **"Le cygne"** Baudelaire writes: "A Quiconque a perdu ce qui ne se retrouve / Jamais, Jamais! [To whoever has lost that which is not re-found / Never, Never!]."

This depiction of an empty repetition of a death that can never be assimilated, transcended, or put to work is reminiscent of what Roland Barthes calls photographic death. Barthes's reflections on "his" photograph recall the crisis experienced by the narrator of **"À une passante."** Barthes writes:

> . . . the photograph—my photograph—is without culture: When it is painful, nothing in it can transform grief into mourning. And if dialectic is that thought which masters the corruptible and converts the negation of death into the power to work, then the photograph is undialectical: it is a denatured theater where death cannot "be contemplated" reflected and interiorized. . . .

[90]

Through its attempt to capture the movement from "passing" to "past" which is figured by repeated images of frozen movement, **"À une passante"** becomes a photograph in the Barthesian sense. This poem cannot get past the passing of its central figure: the symbolic pathos of the mourning figure collapses into a disarticulated repetition. The dead are neither buried nor put to rest; ghosts of history return in the form of stuttering clichés.[13] **"À une passante"** stages a strangely embodied, immobilized, and undialectical death where private mourning meets the banality, the *lieu commun,* of the public space. The passing woman never quite dies, but rather becomes a figure for death's immobile movement.

In the opening lines of *Camera Lucida,* Roland Barthes narrates an anecdote through which (and he later says so explicitly) we understand that he sees himself, historically, as the last witness to an amazement provoked by the sheer ontological fact of the photographic image. He writes:

> One day, quite some time ago, I happened upon a photograph of Napoleon's youngest brother, Jerome, taken in 1852. And I realized then, with an amazement I have not been able to lessen since: "I am looking at eyes that looked at the Emperor." Sometimes I would mention this amazement, but since no one seemed to share it, or even understand it (life consists of these little touches of solitude) I forgot about it. My interest in photography took a more cultural turn.

[3]

By recalling that, in "Motifs," Benjamin situates the shock of photography in the context of a study devoted to "the last lyric poet," we can begin to appreciate what might be at stake in Barthes's lonely amazement. By staring at the photographic, or clichéd, face of Napoleon's brother, Barthes implies that his amazement stems from the sense that he is staring history in the face. This impression (that he is looking directly at the face of history) could not have been produced, one understands, by a photograph of the emperor himself—even if such a photograph were indeed possible. If Barthes sees "history" in the photograph of the emperor's brother, it is because he reads that photograph as a negative image and thus perceives the absent face of the emperor that is depicted, in relief, through the relayed gaze of his brother. History, once again presented as cliché, can be seen here only by looking at a photographic representation of someone for whom the face of the emperor would be something other than merely a figure for history. It is through the suggestion of an absent "familiar look" (which recalls Benjamin's discussion of Baudelaire's use of the term *regards familiers*) at the emperor, that Barthes perceives the trace of history.

Toward the very end of *Camera Lucida,* Barthes gives another name to that relationship among history, death, and photography that we have been calling cliché. If, in

reading Baudelaire through Benjamin, we have seen how the look of history is sent back as cliché, in Barthes's text the operative word is *platitude.* It is through the use of the word *platitude* that Barthes explains, obliquely, why he insists upon staring at the ontological fact of photography rather than addressing the question of its history directly. Barthes explicitly chooses *not* to write a history of photography, but instead to look at how photography both produces and reproduces our contemporary conception of the image of History. History, as Barthes understands it here, is itself a product of the nineteenth century. He writes: "A paradox: the same century invented History and Photography" [93]. The history that Barthes sees in photography is a certain history of death. The word that he uses for the history of death read through the photograph is *platitude*: "With the photograph, we enter into *flat death.* One day, leaving one of my classes, someone said to me with disdain, 'You talk about death very flatly.'—As if the horror of Death were not precisely its platitude!" [92]. It is in relation to this vision of death as platitude that photography assumes its own, historical perspective. He writes:

> For photography must have some historical relation with what Edgar Morin calls the "crisis of death" beginning in the second half of the nineteenth century; for my part I should prefer that instead of constantly relocating the advent of photography in its social and economic context, we should also inquire as to the anthropological place of Death and the new image. . . . Contemporary with the withdrawal of rites, Photography may correspond to the intrusion, in our modern society, of an asymbolic Death, outside of religion, outside of ritual, a kind of dive into literal Death. Life/Death: the paradigm is reduced to a simple click, the one separating the initial pose from the final print.

[92]

The photograph is the veil of this asymbolic death. Its platitude lies in the fact that this asymbolic death can never be transcended, can never be put to work. It is nothing but a cliché, a stutter, a repetition, platitude.

* * *

Flat death: this inability to "go beyond" the passing of the past—the being caught in the relay of an infinite mechanical reproduction that we do not transcend—is the cliché that is contemporary history.

Notes

I would like to thank Tom Keenan for his generous "first reading" of this essay.

1. In *Passagen-Werk,* for example, he notes that "Just as in 'À une passante,' the crowd was neither named nor described, in 'Le jeu,' the instruments

of the gambling don't come up" ["J" 87a.6], and "In relation to the 'la rue assourdissante' and related formulations, one should not forget that the road surface at that time was, most frequently, cobblestones" ["J" 82a.8]. All references to *Passagen-Werk* come from *GS* [*Gesammelte Schriften*], vol. 1, and, except where indicated, all fragments have been translated by me with the help of Eric Marder.

2. The phrase "sa jambe de statue," read along with the phrase "fugitive beauté," clearly evokes a relationship between the "fleeting beauty" in "À une passante" and the allegorical figure of Beauty in the poem "La beauté": "Je suis belle, ô mortels, comme un rêve de pierre. . . ." For the purposes of this essay, however, I propose to demonstrate that Benjamin has a very precise stake in choosing not to acknowledge the relationship between these two poems.

3. I am glossing some of the issues that Susan Buck-Morss discusses in her chapter "Historical Nature: Ruin" in *The Dialectics of Seeing* [159-201]. Although I certainly agree with her statement that "In the Arcades project Benjamin himself practiced allegory against myth," I am not entirely convinced by her conclusion that "he was aware of its 'regressive tendency'" [201]. Or, to be more precise, I am not sure that Buck-Morss and I would agree about how to read the status of the "regression" to which she alludes. In any case, the passages she cites about the relationship between allegory and ruins, as well as her own discussion of the status of the ruins in "Le cygne," are both useful and illuminating. Among the important fragments that she translates in this chapter is one in which Benjamin writes: "If Baudelaire did not fall into the abyss of myth that constantly accompanied his path, it was thanks to the genius of allegory" ["J" 22.5; qtd. in Buck-Morss 182]. Fragments from *Passagen-Werk* taken from Buck-Morss are her translations.

4. As in the following fragment: "Baudelaire introduces the figure of sexual perversion, which looks for its objects in the street, into the lyric. But what is characteristic is that he does so in a line like 'crispé comme un extravagant' from one of his most successful love poems, 'À une passante'" ["J" 21a.4]. It might be useful to remember, however, that the enormous importance Benjamin accords to the figure of the lesbian in Baudelaire does not fall under the rubric of "sexual perversion," but rather the lesbian incarnates the figure of the "heroine of modernism" [90]. For Benjamin's discussion of the lesbian in Baudelaire, see "Second Empire" [90-94].

5. One might want to read the poetic "source" ("ce petit fleuve") depicted in "Le cygne" in relation to Samuel Weber's discussion of the "source" ("*Quellpunkt*") of poetry in his essay "Mediauras."

6. See the infamous letter dated 10 November 1938, reprinted in *Aesthetics and Politics* [New York: Verso, 1977] 126-33.

7. One fragment is particularly evocative: "The past has left images of itself in literary texts that are comparable to those which light imprints on a photosensitive plate. Only the future possesses developers active enough to bring these plates out perfectly" ["N" 15a.1; *GS* 5: 603; qtd. in Buck-Morss 250].

8. In "Fusées" Baudelaire writes: "créer un poncif, c'est le génie. Je dois créer un poncif" [662].

9. *Le petit Robert* defines *poncif* as a "Feuille de papier à dessin piqué . . . pour reproduire le contour du dessin [A piece of paper perforated with a design . . . for the purposes of reproducing the contours of the design]."

10. The original meaning of the word *cliché* related to the mechanical reproduction of letters on a page. *Le petit Robert* gives its definition as a "plaque portant en relief la reproduction d'une page de composition, d'une image, et permettant le tirage de nombreux exemplaires." To simplify matters, I have translated all further French definitions from *Le petit Robert* into English.

11. For a reading of the question of "feminine presence" in Baudelaire, in relation to "À une passante" and "La beauté," see Peggy Kamuf's "Baudelaire's Modern Woman."

12. In *Camera Lucida,* Barthes writes: "In short, the referent adheres. And this singular adherence makes it very difficult to focus on Photography" [6].

13. My thinking in this essay was initially motivated by an attempt to understand what the word history means in Paul de Man's writings. Although I cannot address this problem here, this essay is haunted, in particular, by the concluding lines of "Anthropomorphism and Trope in the Lyric" [see 262].

Works Cited

Adorno, Theodor. "Letters to Walter Benjamin." *Aesthetics and Politics*. London: Verso, 1980. 110-33.

Barthes, Roland. *Camera Lucida: Reflections on Photography.* Trans. Richard Howard. New York: Noonday, 1981.

Baudelaire, Charles. "À une passante." *OC* 1: 92-93.

———. "La beauté." *OC* 1: 21.

———. "Le cygne." *OC* 1: 85-87.

———. *Les fleurs du mal. OC* 1: 1-196. For the purposes of this essay, I have supplied my own, literal, English translations.

———. "Fusées." *OC* 1: 649-67.

———. *Oeuvres complètes*. 2 vols. Ed. Claude Pichois. Paris: Gallimard (Pléiade), 1975. [*OC*]

———. "The Painter of Modern Life." *The Painter of Modern Life and Other Essays*. Trans. and ed. Jonathan Mayne. London: Phaidon, 1964. 1-40.

Benjamin, Walter. *Briefe: Herausgegeben und mit Anmerkungen versehen von Gershom Scholem und Theodor W. Adorno*. Frankfurt: Suhrkamp, 1966. Vol 2.

———. *Charles Baudelaire: A Lyric Poet in the Era of High Capitalism*. Trans. Harry Zohn. London: Verso, 1983.

———. *Gesammelte Schriften*. Ed. Rolf Tiedemann and Hermann Schweppenhäuser. 7 vols. to date. Frankfurt am Main: Suhrkamp, 1972—. [*GS*]

———. "Paris—Capital of the Nineteenth Century." *Charles Baudelaire* 155-76.

———. "The Paris of the Second Empire." *Charles Baudelaire* 9-106.

———. *Das Passagen-Werk. GS,* vol. 5.

———. "Some Motifs in Baudelaire." *Charles Baudelaire* 109-54.

Buck-Morss, Susan. *The Dialectics of Seeing: Walter Benjamin and the Arcades Project*. Cambridge: MIT P, 1989.

de Man, Paul. "Anthropomorphism and Trope in the Lyric." *The Rhetoric of Romanticism*. New York: Columbia UP, 1984. 239-62.

Jauss, Hans Robert. "Reflections on the Chapter 'Modernity' in Benjamin's Baudelaire Fragments." *On Walter Benjamin: Critical Essays and Recollections*. Ed. Gary Smith. Cambridge: MIT P, 1991. 176-84.

Kamuf, Peggy. "Baudelaire's Modern Woman." *Qui parle* 4.2 (1991): 1-7.

Weber, Samuel. "Mediauras." *The Aura of Resistance*. Ed. David Ferris. Stanford: Stanford UP, [forthcoming].

Edward K. Kaplan (essay date 1993)

SOURCE: Kaplan, Edward K. "Baudelaire and the Vicissitudes of Venus: Ethical Irony in *Fleurs du Mal*." In *The Shaping of Text: Style, Imagery, and Structure in French Literature,* edited by Emanuel J. Mickel, Jr., pp. 113-30. Lewisburg, Pa.: Bucknell University Press, 1993.

[*In the following essay, Kaplan discusses the ethics—sexual ethics in particular—of* Fleurs du Mal.]

Respectful attention to literary context often helps resolve thorny theoretical issues. The "architecture" (or overall thematic structure) of *Les Fleurs du Mal* can be delineated, with some certainty, through analysis of certain sequences (or cycles), and Baudelaire's deliberate revisions of the first (1857) edition provide empirical confirmation. Here, quite briefly, are the changes. The second (1861) edition, which remained definitive, marks a radical shift from a poetics of transcendent Beauty to a poetics of compassion for imperfect, and afflicted, people. Most of the thirty-two added poems embrace the world as it exists.[1]

Baudelaire altered the first and final sections of *Les Fleurs du Mal* the most radically, and introduced a new one, *Tableaux parisiens*. He added poems to the "Beauty Cycle" (nos. 17-21) in the first section, *Spleen et Idéal*, which depict the poet-narrator's conversion from aesthetics to ethics; two of the new pieces, **"Le Masque"** and **"Hymne à la Beauté"** (nos. 20-21), explicitly repudiate idealized females who symbolize the untruth of art, its denial of human mortality. *Tableaux parisiens* reinforces this acceptance of imperfect life by countering the many attacks against idealized young women—understood in terms of "sadism"[2]—as it features the poet's artistic sympathy for older females, only some of them misshapen, "décrépites et charmantes." The mature Baudelaire favors a type of ethical inspiration revealed in **"Les petites vieilles":** "Je goûte à votre insu des plaisirs clandestins" (no. 91, v. 76.).[3]

Temporality as such assumes positive poetic value. The three poems Baudelaire added at the very end of the 1861 version of *La Mort*, the collection's concluding sequence, ratify its disenchanted realism. Transcendence of death is no longer preferred. **"La fin de la journée," "Le rêve d'un curieux,"** and especially **"Le Voyage"** (nos. 124-26) revise the idealist dreams of the preceding three sonnets—**"La mort des amants," "La mort des pauvres," "La mort des artistes"**—which had closed the original edition. Death becomes the "vieux capitaine" (no. 126, v. 137) of a grim but hopeful and courageous voyage.

The two penultimate sections—*Fleurs du Mal* and *Révolte*—form a unity that did *not* change drastically. They contain some of the earliest prepublications of *Les Fleurs du Mal* and anticipate the future collection's complex ethical thrust. Taken together, these notorious cycles defy conventional views of moral corruption.

The former appears to savor decadent sexual behaviors, whereas the latter attacks moralistic Christianity by claiming to repudiate Christ, the first "Christian" as it were, while promoting Cain, the first murderer, a proxy of proletarian rebellion. These were the poems most forthrightly condemned by the tribunal in 1857, earning the poet a perilous reputation he has never lost.

In both the 1857 and 1861 editions, *Fleurs du Mal* and *Révolte* preserved their structure despite censorship and subsequent displacement, retaining the same relation to each other and essentially the same contents. In 1857, *Fleurs du Mal* (containing twelve poems) was section 2, followed by *Révolte,* comprised of three poems considered blasphemous. But only three of the former section's offending pieces were excised by the authorities: **"Lesbos," "Femmes damnées. Delphine et Hippolyte"** (*A la pâle clarté . . .*), and **"Les Métamorphoses du vampire"** were suppressed, henceforth to be consigned as *Epaves* to the back of subsequent editions, where adolescents and amateurs of "curiosa" have conveniently relished them. Yet all the surviving poems maintain their undeniable poetic power. Questions of morality, inner psychological struggle, and literary meaning preserve the integrity of this apparently "perverse" section.

ETHICAL IRONY

Fleurs du Mal, section 4 of the 1861 edition, because of its title, and its content, provides a hermeneutical key to the entire collection. The male poet identifies with female love and sexuality, and establishes the poet-narrator's ambiguous ethics by providing a model of *ethical irony,* a feigned promotion of crime and perversion meant to engage readers in dialogue.[4] (At the time, the majority simply felt terrorized.) These disturbing poems render the pleasures of "vice" from the perspective of its practitioners, without moralistic complaining.

Baudelaire's masterpiece suffered—and succeeded—because we remain uncertain as to how far the poet as represented in the text leans on either side. He is not didactic, nor is he uncompromisingly rebellious. His lyricism of evil appeals directly to our ambivalence, and we can pleasantly contemplate private impulses we normally repress or at least guard unspoken. It was the author's misfortune that hostile critics ignored his warning, printed in 1857 as a preface to *Révolte,* that these outrageous poems represent "le pastiche des raisonnements de l'ignorance et de la fureur."[5] After his book was confiscated, Baudelaire wrote a memorandum to his lawyer that laments his misplaced trust: "Mon unique tort a été de compter sur l'intelligence universelle, et de ne pas faire une préface où j'aurais posé mes principes littéraires et dégagé la question importante de la Morale."[6] Readers still confused the author with the poet-narrator.

Fleurs du Mal is not objective in the manner of the *style indirect libre* of *Madame Bovary,* to use the most relevant historical parallel, nor is it resolutely perverse.[7] The poems' "immorality" has a Socratic function, to provoke complacent readers by probing our "hypocrisy," which can be analyzed, charitably, as unacknowledged inner conflicts. These poems juxtapose alluring images of vice with the poet's expressed horror at its causes, thus forcing readers to make moral (and hermeneutical) choices. What evidence of the poet's implicit literary "principles" can be adduced?

In the simplest terms, an overall structural symmetry, established before the collection took shape, provides precious clues. The definitive edition of **Les Fleurs du Mal** traces a path from the liminal poem, **"Au lecteur,"** through **"Voyage à Cythère,"** the cornerstone of section 4, *Fleurs du Mal,* ending with the poem added in 1861 as a finale, **"Le Voyage."** It is significant that, in their original prepublication in the *Revue des Deux Mondes* (1 June 1855), **"Un Voyage à Cythère"** directly follows **"Au lecteur."** Our analysis of ethical irony is justified by **"Au lecteur,"** which explains quite plainly that corruption is generated by Ennui, pathological apathy and depression ("Aux objets répugnants nous trouvons des appats"); the poet's snide celebration of "la ménagerie infâme de nos vices" (v. 14;32) challenges his readers' self-evasion. Yet its final lines establish an almost tender complicity between public and poet which the posturing of ethical irony disguises.

Fleurs du Mal, in both the 1857 and 1861 editions, expands the poet's complex dialogue with his "Hypocrite lecteur, mon semblable, mon frère." We can differentiate between his contradictory roles and attitudes. The 1861 version of *Fleurs du Mal* (which precedes *Révolte* and *La Mort*), provides the itinerary's pivotal moment. It consists of a cycle of nine poems (nos. 109-17) unified by examples of male and female sexuality, the search for authentic love with another person, and the limits of the body—of which death is the fundamental example. These poems' particular energy derives from the conflict between the passion for perfection and despair at being unable to reach it. Male and female characters alike endure the frustration of noble desires. All victims mirror the poet's vulnerability to social prejudices and to the fragility of his self-esteem.

Read as a single sequence, **Fleurs du Mal** interprets vice as a normal (though self-destructive) reaction against oppression, both spiritual and physical. Each poem explores variants of the insight that "evil" behavior often derives from desperation. So the word *mal* in the title of both the section and the collection should be interpreted in a nonjudgmental sense as *affliction* (or le *malheur,* to use Simone Weil's term). More precisely, **Fleurs du Mal** locates the poet's anger in his death anxiety, which he projects as horror of female otherness.[8] Idealized women usually appear in his poetry as victims of male hostility and lust. ***Fleurs du Mal*** will honor female scapegoats, shunned by polite society, as it relentlessly anatomizes the male imagination.

THE DESPAIR OF FINITUDE

The antepenultimate section is organized around the old theme of Love and Death; specifically, anxiety about the mortal body (male or female) may lead to vice, which is a form of distorted love (in Dante's terms). The poet of ***Fleurs du Mal*** is a self-aware man who strives both to love a woman and to write, and the poems mix fear, compassion, and moral polemic while lingering on the erotic charms of violence and female homosexuality. It is a psychological commonplace, but one worth recalling, that people (in this case, men) intimidated by women's independence fear for their own self-mastery. These poems combine the enchantments of "perversity" with an ethical challenge—expressed through irony—to those who condemn certain forms of loving.

Fleurs du Mal can be divided into four hermeneutic entities. The first two develop the dialectic of infinite desire frustrated by finitude: (1) **"La Destruction"** and **"Une martyre"** (nos. 109, 110) show that a man's violence is his primitive response to the impossibility of fulfilling his excessive emotional and sensual needs; (2) **"Femmes damnées"** (*Comme un bétail pensif . . .*, no. 111) (with **"Lesbos"** and **"Delphine et Hippolyte,"** censored from the first edition) present homosexuality as a woman's escape from society's hostility to *her* limitless quest for tenderness. The last two groupings portray male death anxiety through images of sexual intercourse: (3) **"Les Deux Bonnes Soeurs," "La Fontaine de sang," "Allégorie," "La Béatrice"** (nos. 112-15) depict frightened, vulnerable men who apprehend women as lethal. (4) The section closes with a long, metacritical poem, **"Un Voyage à Cythère"** (no, 116, followed by an emblematic clausula, **"L'Amour et le crâne"**), suggesting that a poet might overcome despair through literature.

The section is rigorously constructed and opens with a liminal sonnet which defines a table of contents, as does **"Au lecteur,"** which introduces both the 1855 *Revue des Deux Mondes* series and the 1857 and 1861 collections. **"La Destruction"** identifies the Devil, mortality itself, as responsible for humankind's inherent despair: "Je l'avale et le sens qui brûle mon poumon" (v. 3). (**"Au lecteur"** establishes these images: "la Mort dans nos poumons / Descend, fleuve invisible," v. 22-24). In **"La Destruction"** the poet's will, no longer passive, is powerful—though it remains ambivalent, uncontrollable, and infinite: "un désir éternel et coupable." The second quatrain applies our self-destructive

condition (i.e., mortality blamed on the Devil) to the aesthetic quest: "Parfois il prend, sachant mon grand amour de l'Art, / La forme de la plus séduisante des femmes."

This opening poem states quite clearly that misdirected or blocked religious impulses can provoke sadistic lust. Truth—not Beauty—is the poet's standard. Lust (or its metaphorical equivalent as existential self-assertion) is sophism, "de spécieux prétextes de cafard." (Baudelaire's expression "hypocrite lecteur" updates the traditional meaning of *cafard* as a religious bigot, used in the satires of Rabelais.) The poem's original title, "La Volupté" (also published in the *Revue des Deux Mondes* on 1 June 1855, perhaps emulating Sainte-Beuve's 1834 novel, *Volupté*) makes at least two levels of **"La Destruction"** explicit: (1) the joys of evil from the perspective of blindness or indifference; and (2) remorse for straying from the true path. The delights of illicit love are "des philtres infâmes," both magic and degrading.

"La Destruction" rather moralistically denounces the confusion of sensual love and art. The two tercets emphasize a traditional Christian judgment of a man addicted to this vicious inspiration. The woman as Devil alienates the man and undermines his drive toward goodness and even his desire to live. The poet unsuccessfully defends his yearning for spiritual companionship, the "regard de Dieu," and ends up "brisé de fatigue, au milieu / Des plaines de l'Ennui"; only apathy and "confusion" emerge from "l'appareil sanglant de la Destruction!" Because this moral outrage is so obvious, alert readers should not succumb to the ethical irony of the following poem.

The poet of **"Une martyre"** (no. 110) contemplates a female victim of male lust, preparing the ground for an analysis of violence against women. An apparently amoral perspective, however, introduces **"Une martyre,"** which describes enticingly a naked, decapitated female corpse. The poet's obscene complacency contradicts the title, which prepares us for an allegory of religious sacrifice. The ironic dissonance is reinforced by the subtitle, "Dessin d'un maître inconnu," identifying the poem as a *transposition d'art,* a literary reinterpretation of an already allegorical work. At the same time, the vivid description surpasses art as it plays the delicate notes of implied cruel joys. (This second poem of the section contains exactly sixty lines, as does **"Un Voyage à Cythère,"** the section's penultimate piece. That symmetry confirms ethical irony as an element of structure. It also establishes the figurative equivalence between the male and female victims.)

The poem reveals, gradually and quite concretely, the poet's complex sympathy with both man and woman, victim and assassin. This rhetorical process develops in four stages: (1) lines 1 to 28 describe the dead woman's seductive boudoir and her body; (2) lines 29 to 44 speculate on her "amour ténébreux"; (3) lines 45 to 52 evoke the man who killed her, and (4) the concluding lines 53 to 60 draw a surprising lesson: the poet lifts his cynical mask to condemn society's hypocrisy, declaring that the martyr will survive as a "forme immortelle."

The first nine stanzas (vv. 1-28) establish the ethical irony by maintaining a seductive atmosphere. A cinematographic sweep lingers over a sumptuous "chambre tiède où . . . l'air est dangereux et fatal," gradually to focus on "Un cadavre sans tête." Then the curious observer finds the head and examines its ambiguous gaze: "Un regard vague et blanc comme le crépuscule / S'échappe des yeux révulsés." Are they turned upward in terror or in the ecstasy of orgasm? These dead eyes, in either case, are segregated from her titillating body, as if the person were punished for her sexuality (or the thoughts her head contained):

> Sur le lit, le tronc nu sans scrupules étale
>   Dans le plus complet abandon
> La secrète splendeur et la beauté fatale
>   Dont la nature lui fit don.

> (v. 21-24)

An exquisite detail renders the victim's "coupable joie" all the more fascinating: "un bas rosâtre, orné de coins d'or." A marker of irony—the disjunctive "sans scrupules"—teases the voyeur's (i.e., the reader's) bourgeois prudery.

The next four stanzas (vv. 29-44) redirect the poet's attitude completely and prepare his compassionate intervention. The voyeur's ornate and lascivious description gives way to his (and our) empathy with the person. Suddenly he notices her "maigreur élégante" (v. 37) and, acknowledging her youth, he reflects on the "cadavre impur" who is—objectively—a teenager led astray and murdered. Description gives way to potential dialogue; the object *elle* becomes *tu*:

> Elle est bien jeune encor!—Son âme exaspérée
>   Et ses sens par l'ennui mordus
> S'étaient-ils entr' ouverts à la meute altérée
>   Des désirs errants et perdus?

> L'homme vindicatif que tu n'as pu, vivante,
>   Malgré tant d'amour, assouvir,
> Combla-t-il sur ta chair inerte et complaisante
>   L'immensité de son désir?

> (v. 41-48)

The poet questions the meaning of this scene and introduces moral judgments, though he does not "condemn" the crime. He suspects that her self-defeating "désirs errants et perdus" were imposed by pathological depression ("l'ennui"). Her man's vengeful

frustration, too, originates in infinite desire, a misdirected religious impulse. He goes so far as to suggest that the assassin's necrophilia (reconfirmed in the next stanza: "a-t-il sur tes dents froides / Collé les suprêmes adieux?") is the negative expression of a drive toward transcendence. The man's murderous lust degrades the young woman's pure intentions. Her pathetic dignity emerges when we realize that she could not satisfy her man "malgré tant d'amour."

Ethical irony enriches the expression "*cadavre impur!*" (v. 49). In reality, the prurient descriptions are meant to entrap "*la foule impure*" (v. 53), readers who will not own to their pornocratic aspirations. The repetition of *impur* condenses these contradictory perspectives and resolves them in the poem's conclusion, set off by its second dash. (The *cadavre*'s intentions seem to be morally pure.) At fault are guardians of public virtue who condemn private behavior without noticing the spiritual anguish at its inception.

The "sadistic" prologue had disguised the young woman's nostalgia for authentic love. Now freed from the irony, she emerges as a "martyre" in her anonymous death: "—Loin du monde railleur, loin de la foule impure, / Loin des magistrats curieux" (v. 53-54). (Baudelaire, by anticipation, appropriately impeaches the "magistrats curieux" who condemned *Les Fleurs du Mal* a scant fortnight after publication.) The poem ends by translating her sin into a sacrifice; the *cadavre impur* becomes redeemed as memory.

Yet the final ironies prevent us from sentimentalizing her too deftly. Her illicit lover becomes her husband through murder, and the bride receives a bitter recompense for her faith, a spurious immortality in the criminal's guilty conscience:

> Ton époux court le monde, et ta forme immortelle
>   Veille près de lui quand il dort;
> Autant que toi sans doute il te sera fidèle,
>   Et constant jusques à la mort.

> (v. 57-60)

The poet has thus transfigured her corpse into a poem, as he had at the end of **"Une Charogne"** (no. 29) when he assures his beloved, with an irony, this time, directed against mortality itself, "J'ai gardé la forme et l'essence divine / De mes amours décomposés" (v. 47-48). The corrupted female, victim of man's equally desperate "désir éternel et coupable," becomes vicious through despair. Baudelaire's poem restores her dignity—but without yielding to bourgeois indignation. The marriage of his "martyre" is consecrated—not by the Church—but by her murder and mutilation.

The next poem in the sequence, **"Femmes damnées"** (no. 111), recapitulates the poet's sympathy for the women represented in the two preceding pieces. His bold identification with women unjustly condemned is reinforced by this single poem about lesbian love that escaped the tribunal. The pleasures of sexual "deviation" in **"Femmes damnées"** challenges the hypocritical, and equally vicious, moral code that automatically dooms them. Its structure repeats the disequilibrium of **"Une martyre"**; it begins lyrically by nourishing our sympathy with these ostracized lovers, and ends, after the ambiguities are played out, by ratifying their spiritual aspirations.

The first part of **"Femmes damnées"** consists of five stanzas (vv. 1-24) that evoke various sorts of love between women, starting with the innocent need for companionship ("coeurs épris de longues confidences . . . l'amour des craintives enfances," v. 5, 7), through the questionable excitement of self-flagellation and hallucination ("Où saint Antoine a vu surgir comme des laves / Les seins nus et pourprés de ses tentations," v. 12). Two stanzas, in fact, seem to relish a pagan perversion of asceticism that diverts feelings of guilt ("O Bacchus, endormeur des remords anciens!" v. 16). (The section's true culmination, **"Voyage à Cythère,"** will recall and resolve this excruciating guilt.) Here, the poet's depiction of sadomasochistic joys ("L'écume du plaisir [mêlée] aux larmes des tourments," v. 20) challenges our moral tolerance to the limit—unless, of course, we view this fall from childhood intimacy to depravity as an amusing literary rebellion. Baudelaire would seem, in that instance, as in others (e.g., **"A celle qui est trop gaie," "Les Bijoux,"** and **"Les métamorphoses du vampire,"** also censored from the first edition), straightforwardly to advertise the naturalistic ethics of the Marquis de Sade.

"Femmes damnées" unveils its ethical irony only in the two final stanzas. The poet first expresses horror—pity for the suffering of lesbians and fear of their perversity—and then, somewhat sentimentally, he joins their search for perfected love. He first recapitulates the different female types in this poem and the preceding ones (including the two suppressed), in the penultimate stanza. The final stanza retranslates the entire sequence as the poet confesses his fraternal devotion:

> O vierges, ô démons, ô monstres, ô martyres,
> De la réalité grands esprits contempteurs,
> Chercheuses d'infini, dévotes et satyres,
> Tantôt pleines de cris, tantôt pleines de pleurs,
>
> Vous que dans votre enfer mon âme a poursuivies,
> Pauvres soeurs, je vous aime autant que je vous plains,
> Pour vos mornes douleurs, vos soifs inassouvis,
> Et les urnes d'amour dont vos grands coeurs sont
>   pleins!
>
> (v. 21-28)

The poet enters their *enfer* (recalling the double meaning of "femmes damnées") and deplores their anguish. He too repudiates a flat version of reality, and he shares the "mornes douleurs" of their "soifs inassouvis." Without a trace of irony he celebrates their spiritual passion, which physical love can either reinforce or subvert. The sincerity of his assent is reinforced, stylistically, by the final awkwardness (in line 28), which critics assailed without mercy. He loves the "femmes damnées," especially, for "les urnes d'amour dont [leurs] grands coeurs sont pleins!"[9]

This poem, which concludes with high affirmation and simple sincerity, subverts repressive norms in two areas. On a social level, it attacks wardens of the patriarchal family who would be loath to admit that evil does not inhere in this mode of loving. More profoundly, it repudiates conventional thinking that fears the thirst for the infinite, of which the pursuit of endless intimacy is but one poignant example. Baudelaire's irony upsets the self-satisfied who can endure existence only when they can restrict and control it, those who find it more convenient to scorn these female dissidents on principle than to defy life's limits.

FEMALE MESSENGERS OF MORTALITY

The next four poems (nos. 112-15) establish the poet as the central character of *Fleurs du Mal*. After having identified with female victims of desire—their own or a man's—he focuses on his own death anxiety. The reassuring women now metamorphose into instruments of his destruction, as anticipated in the liminal poem of that name (no. 109). The very obviousness of these "allegories," these self-translating poems, incites us to question the poet-narrator's stated delectation of death. The first two, **"Les Deux Bonnes Soeurs"** and **"La Fontaine de sang,"** develop a fundamental male fantasy, that sex drains the man: "Il me semble parfois que mon sang coule à flots / Ainsi qu'une fontaine aux rythmiques sanglots" (no. 113, 1-2). Even the poetic process (writing rhythmically) becomes a debilitating seminal ejaculation. The two longer pieces that follow, **"Allégorie"** and **"La Béatrice,"** further specify the woman's role as a projection of the male poet's need for nurturance and affection. His fear of death, however, makes all love impossible.

The two opening sonnets (nos. 112, 113) reassert the poet's irony. First and foremost, **"Les Deux Bonnes Soeurs"**—Death and Debauchery—are neither "bonnes" nor "aimables." Should we take more literally the narrator's characterization of himself as a "poète sinistre, ennemi des familles / Favori de l'enfer, courtisan mal renté" (v. 6-7)—malevolent but quick to complain that he is badly subsidized? He claims to surrender both to Love ("les myrtes infectes") and to Death ("tes noirs cyprès"). **"La Fontaine de sang"** continues this gloomy theme as it elaborates the nightmare of being drained of blood, the poet's death anxiety, "la terreur qui me mine" (v. 10). The narcotics he takes to escape only magnify his acute self-awareness: "Le vin rend l'oeil plus clair et l'oreille plus fine" and "L'amour n'est pour moi qu'un matelas d'aiguilles" (v. 11, 13). His expression of despair appears to be in earnest. Does the initial irony remain? Is woman only a relentless messenger of mortality?

These essentially misogynistic poems are more than exercises on an old theme. After all, everyone must die, and the intimacy of love and death came to Baudelaire with a distinguished history. An important clue to his barely voiced yearnings is condensed in the poet's pose as an *"ennemi des familles."* Does he claim to reject married life because of the bourgeois complacency it implies? Or is his "hatred" a Socratic mask? Two crucial lines allow us to unpack the pessimistic claim. **"Les deux bonnes soeurs"**—"Dont le flanc toujours vierge et drapé de guenilles / Sous l'éternel labeur n'a jamais enfanté" (v. 3-4)—are unreachable, not because they have refused sexual intercourse but because they are not mothers. This fleeting reference to childless women points to the poet's estrangement from *l'éternel labeur,* female fertility and nurturance.[10]

A veiled image of a childless woman unifies *Fleurs du Mal* and explains why the poet features the alienation of men and women from each other. He is the victim. Irremediably isolated, he can only share the tenderness of lesbians, including the sadomasochistic sisters. The male poet, too, is *eternally* sterile.

Negative images of women, in **"Allégorie"** (no. 114) and **"La Béatrice"** (no. 115), complete this cycle of four poems. The first one recalls the sonnet **"La Beauté"** (no. 17) in which a statuelike Muse, indifferent to the poet's passion, represents an abstract Ideal. The strong woman (or rather, the perfect body) of **"Allégorie"** is a "femme belle et de riche encolure, / Qui laisse dans son vin traîner sa chevelure" (no. 114, v. 1-2), a prostitute or courtesan whose coldness has two basic meanings: (1) she does not share the man's existential anxiety ("Elle rit à la Mort et nargue la Débauche," v. 5)—neutralizing **"Les Deux Bonnes Soeurs"**—which makes her inaccessible to his empathy; (2) she possesses no conscience ("Elle ignore l'Enfer comme le Purgatoire," v. 17), achieving an odd sort of innocence: "Elle regardera la face de la Mort, / Ainsi qu'un nouveau-né,—sans haine et sans remord" (v. 19-20, the final lines).

This logical impasse inserts us deeper into Baudelaire's text. How can a newborn consciously face death—as the image implies? The disjunction "ainsi qu'un nouveau-né" confronts us with a contradiction. The courtesan's absolute self-abandonment to sex ("Elle a dans le plaisir la foi mahométane," no. 114, v. 10) may suppress the drive toward Destruction that death anxiety can aggravate in both men and women; however, she

does so at the price of her sensitivity to others. The image of ultimate innocence (a newborn baby) as ultimate detachment from human finitude (or so-called Islamic fatalism) is ironic, because it requires moral indifference. Besides, would the poet, to alleviate his anguish, want to start anew, at birth? Perhaps he just wants his mother?

The poetic sequence as a whole reinforces an image of the poet as a victim of women. **"Les Deux Bonnes Soeurs"** and **"La Fontaine de sang"** assert that revolt is the only appropriate response to premature or arbitrary death: "Et la bière et l'alcôve en blasphèmes fécondes / [Nous offrent] De terribles plaisirs et d'affreuses douceurs" (no. 112, v. 9, 11). Debauchery, depicted as the magnificent but frigid courtesan of **"Allégorie"** (no. 114), represents another perilous denial of death anxiety. The sculptured female reminds the poet—whose trade consists in carving verbal allegories—of his isolation, vulnerability, and emotional sterility: "Tout glisse et tout s'émousse au granit de sa peau" (v. 4). She joins Love, Death, and lesbians on the list of *"vierges infécondes"* (v. 13). Sexually adept, they all shun motherhood and consequently deny the poet the sympathy he seeks from them.

"La Béatrice" (no. 115) completes this cycle of four as it applies images of female indifference to the poet's professional dilemma. The title continues the irony, because this mediator hardly inspires our postromantic Dante with a vision of cosmic and personal redemption. Jean Prévost's interpretation of the poem as a portrait of the author through the eyes of hostile critics is plausible.[11] Its significance is broader, however, when read within the sequence. **"La Béatrice"** mocks the poet's artistic self-consciousness, which makes his personal life unbearable: "—'Contemplons à loisir cette caricature / Et cette ombre d'Hamlet imitant sa posture.'" (The next poem, **"Un Voyage à Cythère,"** will redeem that *conscience malheureuse.*)

The three stanzas of **"La Béatrice"** systematically parody the idiom of romantic heroism. Lines 1 to 12 evoke a grim landscape ("Dans des terrains cendreux, calcinés, sans verdure"), similar to the wasteland of the prose fable, "Chacun sa Chimère" (no. 6). Another tone disturbs the solemn harmony, expressed by inflated, stereotyped images reminiscent of Musset or Chateaubriand's René: "Comme je me plaignais un jour à la nature. . . . J'aiguisais lentement sur mon coeur le poignard." The "démons vicieux" in the second stanza (vv. 13-22) question the poet's authenticity: "'Ce gueux, cet histrion en vacances, ce drôle / Parce qu'il sait jouer artistement son rôle.'"

These lines validate Baudelaire's repeated warnings that some of his offensive poems represent a "pastiche." At the same time, he could not expect his defensive critics to relish his polemics against self-deception. The government, unwilling to distinguish between narrator and author, would soon denounce *Les Fleurs du Mal* as subverting its moral (and literary) authority.

"Béatrice" reveals herself as the familiar courtesan in the third stanza (vv. 23-30): "La reine de mon coeur au regard nonpareil." The poet's elevated style makes all the more bitter the manner in which she humiliates his "orgueil aussi haut que les monts" by joining the "troupe obscène" of demons (or critics). Hyperboles reinforce the irony, but the images of betrayal decisively reinforce the implicit compassion of the preceding poems. The male artist is vulnerable, not only because his ideal cannot be captured but because the person who should incarnate his aspirations (a lover? his mother?) refuses even to understand his devotion. Finally, his defensive pride is crushed by the "sale caresse" (v. 30, the last words) that she lavishes ostentatiously on his enemies.

SEXUALITY: LOCUS OF HUMAN FINITUDE

"Un Voyage à Cythère" (no. 116), a cornerstone of Baudelaire's initial sequence (*Revue des Deux Mondes*, 1855), summarizes the section *Fleurs du Mal* and takes its place at a culminating moment in the masterwork of essentially the same name. *Fleurs du Mal* progresses from poems (nos. 110, 111) depicting "corrupt" women (with whom the poet touchingly identifies) to women who endanger him (nos. 114, 115). Acting out the man's internal conflicts, women can be either pure (and victimized) or menacing; the treacherous muse's *sale caresse* contradicts the teenaged martyr's "amour ténébreux" (no. 110, v. 2) and the lesbians' "soifs inassouvis" (no. 111, v. 27). All these women mirror the poet's struggles to reconcile infinite passion with its inevitable defeat ("—Son âme exaspérée / Et ses sens par l'ennui mordus," no. 110, v. 41-42). *Fleurs du Mal* fulfills the program of "Au lecteur," which had defined Ennui—pathological depression—as a two-edged remedy for existential pain.

"Un Voyage à Cythère" (no. 116) concludes *Fleurs du Mal* by interpreting sexuality philosophically, as the locus of a lover's confrontation with finitude. Baudelaire placed it at strategic intervals in both versions of the completed collection. Positioned in the 1861 edition at the end of the antepenultimate section (it was no. 88 in the first, when *Fleurs du Mal* was section 2), it recapitulates the struggle to differentiate self-destructive guilt from the plain facts of mortality. The title's ironic resonances would not be lost on contemporary readers: "*faire le voyage à Cythère* est une sorte d'euphémisme qui signifie se livrer aux plaisirs de l'amour" (the nineteenth-century Larousse, s.v. *Cythère*; the expression implies an erotic joke). More tragic than trivial, Baudelaire's grim voyage definitively translates his ethical irony.

In structural terms, "Un Voyage à Cythère" prepares the parallel with "Le Voyage" (no. 126), which Baudelaire added in 1861 as the final poem of *Les Fleurs du Mal*. Readers would in any case ponder "Un Voyage à Cythère" quite seriously, for it transposes a Watteau painting of that name and recalls Gérard de Nerval's prose piece, *Voyage à Cythère* (published in *L'Artiste*, 30 June, 11 August 1844), about the Ionian island, "l'antique Cythère," devoted to Venus. Baudelaire repudiates (however ambiguously) the ancient pagan cult whose disappearance Nerval laments. The ironic love journey recapitulates those of the entire section.

The prologue juxtaposes boundless aspirations and their eventual disillusion; the "ange enivré d'un soleil radieux" (v. 4) of the poet's free imagination faces "cette île triste et noire" (v. 5). It is another spiritual Odyssey that plays out the traditional Christian antagonism of body and soul: *coeur* appears in lines 1, 9, 15, 56, and 60, whereas *corps* appears in lines 23, 32, 52, and 60. Various birds (vv. 1, 17, 26, 29, and 51) mediate the conflict between the mobile spirit ("Mon coeur, comme un oiseau, voltigeait tout joyeux," v. 1) and carnivorous beasts that represent carnal sins ("Des corbeaux lancinants et des panthères noires / Qui jadis aimaient tant à triturer ma chair," v. 51-52). The island's history is an emblem of the traveler's past.

Ethical irony intensifies our emotional assent to "Un Voyage à Cythère." It arouses our prurient curiosity about the legendary island, "Eldorado banal de tous les vieux garçons" while denouncing its corruption. The idealized beginning of the excursion leads to the exclamation: "J'entrevoyais pourtant un objet singulier!" (v. 20). The poet teasingly does not name the "thing," and continues to play on the lost paradise; the preterition awakens erotic fantasies, before the shock:

> Ce n'était pas un temple aux ombres bocagères,
> Où la jeune prêtresse, amoureuse des fleurs,
> Allait, le corps brûlé de secrètes chaleurs,
> Entrebaillant sa robe aux brises passagères;
>
> Mais voilà qu'en rasant la côte d'assez près
> Pour troubler les oiseaux avec nos voiles blanches,
> Nous vîmes que c'était un gibet à trois branches,
> Du ciel se détachant en noir, comme un cyprès.

(vv. 21-28)

The narrative now becomes extremely bitter. The voyager contemplates a nauseating "punishment" for pagan delights as he details the work of the "féroces oiseaux," which eat the hanging corpse: "Chacun plantant, comme un outil, son bec *impur* / Dans tous les coins saignants de cette pourriture" (v. 31-32). The symbolism is quite literal: "ses bourreaux, gorgés de hideuses délices, / L'avaient à coups de bec absolument châtré" (v. 35-36). The poet seems to condemn the criminal's *impure* religion from a moralistic Christian perspective: "En expiation de tes *infâmes* cultes / Et des péchés qui t'ont interdit le tombeau" (v. 43-44). The opening poem, **"La Destruction,"** had anticipated this result of "des philtres *infâmes*" (no. 109, v. 8) of love worship (all emphases added).

Readers should not be fooled by the narrator's stated indignation. The expression "infâmes cultes" is ironic and cannot be taken moralistically. The poet favors the metaphysical aspirations of paganism, reinforcing his identification with the young female martyr and the persecuted lesbian lovers. The captivating young priestess makes the defiled man's "corps brûlé de secrètes chaleurs" all the more sympathetic. As he meditates on the male sacrifice, the poet becomes one with all victims of finitude:

> Ridicule pendu, tes douleurs sont les miennes!
> Je sentis, à l'aspect de tes membres flottants,
> Comme un vomissement, remonter vers mes dents
> Le long fleuve de fiel des douleurs anciennes;
>
> Devant toi, pauvre diable au souvenir si cher,
> J'ai senti tous les becs et toutes les mâchoires
> Des corbeaux lancinants et des panthères noires
> Qui jadis aimaient tant à triturer ma chair.
>
> (vv. 45-52)

The oxymoron *"ridicule pendu"* unveils the ethical irony, for there is nothing even remotely laughable about this mutilated corpse. The shocking adjective eliminates any bathos (such as "Pauvres soeurs, je vous aime autant que je vous plains," no. 111, v. 26), as does the poet's vomiting memories. The lesson is stark. Just as the "martyre" of poem number 110 had been decapitated for her loving, so the "enfant d'un ciel si beau" was robbed of his organs of generation. Acknowledging that the poem is, in part, a recollection (an experience of "jadis," or of Nerval's account), the poet revives his "douleurs *anciennes*." The witness becomes a brother ("mon semblable, mon frère") to this "pauvre diable au souvenir si cher."

This sixty-line poem completes the thematic symmetry of *Fleurs du Mal* because it completes the sixty-line **"Une martyre."** Male and female are equally sacrificed to "love," as the woman's decapitation anticipates the poet's "symbolic" castration. The rigorous structure of **"Un Voyage à Cythère"** confirms the section's overall logic: (1) lines 1 to 19 elaborate the contrast between the island's resplendent past and its grim present; (2) lines 20 to 44 particularize the lesson of love's decadence by describing, in gory detail, a rotted castrated corpse hanging from a gallows; and (3) finally, the poet (vv. 45-60) applies the image to his own sexual guilt. The conclusion revises the poet's anger or displaced aggression. Death now incites him to sublimate his despair though a literary symbolization.[12]

From Anguish to Redemption

The narrative of **"Un Voyage à Cythère"** has ended, but the two final stanzas lift the poet to a higher level of theoretical awareness. The poem's last eight lines translate the section's meaning as they recapitulate—and transcend—the despair of all the poet's proxies. The first concluding stanza—highlighted by a dash—returns to the poem's beginning and summarizes the thematic contrasts developed in the first fifty-two lines; then the poet introduces diacritical terminology usually reserved for analysis:

> —Le ciel était charmant, la mer était unie;
> Pour moi tout était noir et sanglant désormais,
> Hélas! et j'avais, comme en un suaire épais,
> Le coeur enseveli dans cette allégorie.
>
> Dans ton île, ô Vénus! je n'ai trouvé debout
> Qu'un gibet symbolique où pendait mon image. . . .
> —Ah! Seigneur! donnez-moi la force et le courage
> De contempler mon coeur et mon corps sans dégoût!
>
> (v. 53-60)

The final stanza imitates the emergence of poetry from anguish. Lines 57 and 58 summarize the adventure while the last two lines, after the ellipse, reject energetically the poet's self-condemnation. Death now reminds him of redemption within reach. The brusque leap between lines 58 and 59 conceals a complicated faith that allows the poet to survive and to hope. He faces his mortal body (and moral responsibility) through empathy with the corpse that becomes an *allegory* of his own experience. His assumption of guilt, as excruciating as it is, redeems his life.

Why does Baudelaire introduce the notions of "symbol" and "allegory"—so familiar to readers of Walter Benjamin and Paul de Man?[13] Our method of interpreting these poems as a sequence helps entangle this delicate, and often confusing theoretical problem. Context, here, provides an answer. The fact that the poet perceives the corpse as an *image* frees him from debilitating anxiety, despite his feeling that his heart is buried, *"comme en un suaire épais."* He confronts his earthly limits and then addresses God directly. His extraordinary prayer, in the poem's two final lines, without any irony, completes *Fleurs du Mal* and fulfills his poetic art.

A cognitive process seems to liberate the poet from suicidal despair when he perceives his encounter with lethal sex as symbolic. Of course Baudelaire's terminology is quite lax according to today's standards and is more expressive than rigorous; one cannot systematically distinguish between his use of the words "image" and "allegory." The terminology, as such, incites interpretation, however. Richard Stamelman has insightfully described Baudelaire's poetry as a positive construction of grief, "the shroud of allegory."

Whatever our theoretical preference, the ending of **"Un Voyage à Cythère"** definitely conveys meaning. What may be a cry of despair ("—Ah! Seigneur!") points to a higher design. The poet no longer submits to the irremediable conflict between his body and his spiritual strivings, but looks, with hope, toward their future integration. His past and present no longer inhibit productive desire.

The poet's prayer confirms the very force and courage for which he prays. He actively anticipates the harmony of his "body" and "heart," his inner and outer lives. Does he imply that a compassionate God listens and understands? We can only hypothesize his possible leap into faith. Although we cannot, in all honesty, interpret this allegory definitively, we finish the poem excited by its unresolved, open significance.

Literary Closure

The section *Fleurs du Mal* is now complete because the poet has formed his body-soul conflict into an aesthetic object. **"L'Amour et le crâne"** (no. 117) provides an emblematic clausula that corresponds to **"La Destruction,"** the opening piece (no. 109). Further proof of Baudelaire's policy of structural unity is the fact that he had changed the subtitle of **"L'Amour et le crâne"** from "D'après une vieille gravure" (see *Revue des Deux Mondes,* 1 June 1855, which it also closed) to "Vieux cul-de-lampe," a decorative piece at the end of a book chapter. The poem is a verbal icon that depicts Love as "Ce jeu féroce et ridicule" (v. 15), another "ridicule pendu" in the ultimate perspective of Death. With an ethical irony that is cruder, more obvious than in the preceding poems, the poet ratifies his truce with life's normal terrors. Readers, as well, have come to accept them, at least intellectually, as part of the reassuring construct of poetry. Allegories of mortality (nos. 109, 117) frame its meaning.

Could that be Baudelaire's point? Beautiful poems about mortality and affliction probe our anxiety and boundless thirsts, whereas our acts of interpretation can foster understanding and communion. The memory of John Porter Houston, a man of rigorous erudition and passionate scholarship, reminds us, with Baudelaire, that works of art can help us love the world and contemplate death with equanimity.

Notes

A preliminary version of this paper was presented at a Nineteenth-Century French Studies Conference, Vanderbilt University, October 1985. My thanks to Professors Laurence M. Porter and Katherine Perry for their helpful suggestions at earlier stages of revision.

1. See my articles "Baudelaire's Battle with Finitude: *La Mort,* Conclusion of *Les Fleurs du Mal,*" *French Forum* 4 (September 1973): 219-31; and

"Modern French Poetry and Sanctification: Charles Baudelaire and Yves Bonnefoy," *Dalhousie French Studies* 8 (Spring-Summer 1985): 103-25. Cf. D. J. Mossop, *Baudelaire's Tragic Hero: A Study of the Architecture of "Les Fleurs du Mal"* (London: Oxford University Press, 1961), based on a comparison of the two editions; also the elegant study of James Lawler, "The Order of 'Tableaux Parisiens,'" *Romanic Review* 56, no. 3 (May 1985), 287-306; John Porter Houston, "The Two Versions of *Les Fleurs du Mal* and Ideas of Form" in Fenoaltea, Doranne and David Lee Rubin, eds. *Ladder of High Designs: Structure and Interpretation of the French Lyric Sequence* (Charlottesville: University Press of Virginia, 1991), pp. 110-37.

2. See Georges Blin, *Le Sadisme de Baudelaire* (Paris: Corti, 1948), and Leo Bersani, *Baudelaire and Freud* (Berkeley: University of California Press, 1971).

3. My citations from *Les Fleurs du Mal* follow the text and numbering of the 1861 edition (see note 5 for complete reference). The prose fables published from 1861 on confirm the mature Baudelaire's focus on women (among others) who are particularly vulnerable to Time. In a previous study I have traced the poet's self-figuration as a bereaved mother, which I consider to be more basic than the failed clowns of "Le Vieux saltimbanque" or "Une Mort héroïque." See "Baudelaire's Portrait of the Poet as Widow: Three *Poëmes en prose* and 'Le Cygne,'" *Symposium* 34 (Fall 1980): 23-48. I applied this perspective in *Baudelaire's Prose Poems. The Esthetic, the Ethical, and the Religious in "The Parisian Prowler"* (Athens and London: The University of Georgia Press, 1990), 2-9; esp. chap. 4, "Poetry Versus Compassion. Conversion to the Ethical?" 56-75.

4. See the important study of Stephen Handwerk, *Irony and Ethics in Narrative. From Schlegel to Lacan* (New Haven and London: Yale University Press, 1985), and Wayne Booth, *A Rhetoric of Irony* (Chicago: The University of Chicago Press, 1974). Laurence M. Porter's rich chapter, "Baudelaire's Fictive Audiences," in *The Crisis of French Symbolism* (Ithaca and London: Cornell University Press, 1990), 113-90, provides a valuable, different perspective.

5. The 1857 note continues: "Fidèle à son douleureux programme, l'auteur des *Fleurs du Mal* a dû, en parfait comédien, façonner son esprit à tous les sophismes comme à toutes les corruptions," (Charles Baudelaire, *Oeuvres complètes,* vol. 1, ed. Claude Pichois [Paris: Gallimard, Editions de la Pléiade, 1975], 1075-76; hereafter abbreviated as *OC*). Baudelaire also emphasized the ethical problem in the first series he published under the

title *Les Fleurs du Mal* in the *Revue des Deux Mondes* (1 June 1855), with the epigraph from Agrippa d'Aubigné (*Les Tragiques*) later printed on the cover of the first edition, which ends: "Mais le vice n'a point pour mère la science, / Et la vertu n'est pas la fille de l'ignorance" (*OC* 1:807.) This series of eighteen poems includes four that were eventually published in the section *Fleurs du Mal* (see ibid., xxxviii, for the titles).

6. *OC* 1, 194. See also *Les Drames et les romans honnêtes* (1851): "Y a-t-il un art pernicieux? Oui. C'est celui qui dérange les conditions de la vie. Le vice est séduisant, il faut le peindre séduisant; mais il traîne avec lui des maladies et des douleurs morales singulières; il faut les décrire" (*OC* 2:41).

7. Referring to Eric Auerbach, *Mimesis* [Princeton University Press, 1953], 485, Hans Robert Jauss defines useful criteria for analyzing the reception, and misperception, of such morally provocative, and original, works: *Toward an Aesthetic of Reception* (Minneapolis: University of Minnesota Press, 1982), 42-44; and chap. 5.

8. See *Fusée* V: "Nous aimons les femmes à proportion qu'elles nous sont étrangères. Aimer les femmes intelligentes est un plaisir de pédéraste" (*OC* 1:653), among others. The prose poem, "Les yeux des pauvres" (no. 26), exclaims: "Vous êtes, je crois, le plus bel exemple d'imperméabilité féminine qu'on puisse voir." See the astute analysis of Ernest Becker, *The Denial of Death* (New York: The Free Press, 1973), esp. chap. 3, "The Recasting of Some Basic Psychoanalytic Ideas," 25-46, for the relationship between anxieties about sexuality and death.

9. Antoine Adam, ed. *Les Fleurs du Mal* (Paris: Editions Garnier, 1961), 413: "On notera l'incohérence de la métaphore: des coeurs pleins d'une urne d'amour."

10. Laurence Porter's psychoanalytical study of the presence of Baudelaire's mother in his poetry is quite relevant here; see sup. n. 4.

11. Jean Prévost, *Baudelaire. Essai sur l'imagination et la création poétiques* (Paris: Mercure de France, 1953), 126: "un romantisme tardif qui leur semblait désuet, une attitude mélancolique assez peu d'accord avec le dégoût avoué du plaisir, et enfin un ton outrancier."

12. I have analyzed "Un Voyage à Cythère" in "The Courage of Baudelaire and Rimbaud: The Anxiety of Faith," *The French Review* 52 (December 1978), 294-306, from which some of the following is taken. The most complete analysis remains that of Bernard Weinberg, *The Limits of Symbolism* (Chicago and London: The University of Chicago Press, 1966), 64-88.

13. To respect the relative simplicity of Baudelaire's poem, I will not rehearse the debates around Paul de Man's influential article, "The Rhetoric of Temporality." See Richard Stamelman's sensitive, judicious, and well-documented articles, "The Allegory of Loss and Exile in the Poetry of Yves Bonnefoy," *World Literature Today* (Summer 1979): 421-29; and "The Shroud of Allegory: Death, Mourning, and Melancholy in Baudelaire's Work," *Texas Studies in Literature and Language* 25 (Fall 1983): 390-409, revised and included in his important book, *Lost Beyond Telling: Representations of Death and Absence in Modern French Poetry* (Ithaca: Cornell University Press, 1990), an exemplary treatment, with remarkable depth and sensitivity, of these issues in the works of Baudelaire, Apollinaire, Jouve, Bonnefoy, Jaccottet, Jabès, and Barthes.

Katherine Bergeron (essay date autumn 1994)

SOURCE: Bergeron, Katherine. "The Echo, the Cry, the Death of Lovers." *19th-Century Music* 18, no. 2 (autumn 1994): 136-51.

[*In the following essay, Bergeron discusses Baudelaire's characterization of the poet as "a translator, a decipherer" in light of Walter Benjamin's seminal essay "The Task of the Translator," written as an introduction to a volume of Benjamin's translations of Baudelaire. Bergeron also discusses Debussy's 1889 compositions based on the work of Baudelaire as another aspect of translation.*]

Walter Benjamin once wrote that the task of the translator was to find an "echo," to discover an effect in the language of his translation that would resonate with the original.[1] The idea comes from an essay Benjamin completed in 1923 to introduce a volume of his own translations of Baudelaire. Since the present essay also concerns Baudelaire—in particular, what we might call different "translations" of Baudelaire—I should like to consider briefly Benjamin's metaphor, itself an "echo" of one of Baudelaire's most famous poems: "Unlike a work of literature," Benjamin writes, "translation does not find itself in the center of the language forest but on the outside facing the wooded ridge; it calls into the forest without entering, aiming at that single spot where the echo is able to give, in its own language, the reverberation of the work in the alien one."[2] The echo is the mark of a translator's success, because it signals distance, alienation from the original. Good translators must maintain this distance, keep the forest (now a wooded ridge) within view. If they let themselves be taken in by the alien language, they compromise the very position that allows them to speak as translators. They risk losing the echo of their own language, or— what amounts to the same thing—losing themselves.

But what is the meaning of such a risk? How is it possible to lose oneself in a work of art? It is significant that Benjamin's admonitions form the translator's preface to a book on Baudelaire, a poet whose critical writings point to translation as the inevitable task of the *poet* (from the well-known essay on Hugo: "What is a poet . . . but a translator, a decipherer?").[3] Yet the poet, at least as far as Baudelaire demonstrates, is more reckless than Benjamin would allow. Throughout **Les Fleurs du mal,** Baudelaire's ever-anxious attempts to render ineffable experience into language lead him to that dangerous region at the edge of the forest, to mark— and even to cross—a threshold between translation and oblivion, a scenario Baudelaire enacts in the very poem that was the inspiration for Benjamin's analogy: the sonnet entitled **"Correspondances."**

I begin, then, with this poem, to explore Baudelaire's idea of the poetic threshold, the limit of translation, a threshold marked even more explicitly, perhaps, in a second work from the same collection, **"La Mort des amants"** (The Death of Lovers). It was the latter poem, which opens the final chapter of **Les Fleurs du mal,** that Debussy set as the last in the cycle of songs he composed around 1889 on poems of Baudelaire—poems he "translated," so to speak, into music. I too shall save Debussy's translation for last (for very last, in fact), deferring my discussion of the song not only to raise issues that should serve to illuminate its analysis but also, I hope, to render it a true object of desire.

L'Écho et le tiret

"Correspondances" is, in effect, a poem about making poetry. Critics have tended to regard it as a didactic work, a sort of Baudelairean "aesthetic manifesto" harboring doctrines of symbolism, synesthesia, universal analogy, metaphorical unity.[4] By their very agenda, of course, such readings are limited; they avoid the poem, in a sense, in order to salvage laws and principles. Yet if the idea of correspondences—of making connections—is so important to Baudelaire's poetry, we might do better to contemplate the poem less as a manifesto than as a model: to look for such connection-making in the play of signs that motivates the poem's surface. It is useful to recall that the word *correspondances* refers to the connections, or transfers, made by a traveler in the course of a journey—a meaning that could hardly have been lost on Baudelaire in the golden age of *chemins de fer*. In Baudelaire's poetry, of course, such journeying becomes a function of the word, which, traveling along any number of possible paths, has the potential of reaching an even more remote terminus, far from its point of origin.[5] Hence it is not so much in specific statements or images that we should seek out this aesthetic as in a transit *between* images, a voyaging that, for Baudelaire, tends recklessly toward polysemous abandon or, to use Leo Bersani's expression, "mobile fantasy."

It all takes place in a forest. The poem's movement begins with the problem posed by the very first figure, "Nature" (capital *N*) in relation to that which surrounds it, "forests of symbols," or, to put it another way, with the dialectical tension between ineffable experience and language:

> La Nature est un temple où de vivants piliers
> Laissent parfois sortir de confuses paroles;
> L'homme y passe à travers des forêts de symboles
> Qui l'observent avec des regards familiers.
>
> (Nature is a temple where living pillars
> Sometimes issue forth confused words;
> Mankind traverses it through forests of symbols
> That watch him with knowing looks.)

Mankind's encounter with "Nature" is oblique, impeded by the dense "forests" through which he must pass, by which he is panoptically enclosed—language forests whose endless, material symbols "watch him with knowing looks." Speech thus not only mediates experience but emerges as a mode of surveillance, a field whose signs rigidly stand guard over meaning. Inside there is one kind of knowledge, which, while maintaining order over the world, also rules out a whole dimension of experience: Nature herself is lost, reduced to gibberish, a babbling temple of confusion.

The imaginary movement toward such lost experience appears, in the next quatrain, in the form of a sound: long echoes merging in an opaque, deep oneness.

> Comme de longs échos qui de loin se confondent
> Dans une ténébreuse et profonde unité,
> Vaste comme la nuit et comme la clarté,
> Les parfums, les couleurs et les sons se répondent.
>
> (Like long echos that mingle far away
> In an shadowy and deep unity,
> Vast as night as vast as light,
> The perfumes, colors and sounds answer each other.)

As a sound removed from its source, the echo suggests an escape from the strict surveillance of the forest; it is a condition of resonance, which (at some more distant point) effects the blending of those aspects of experience that are most particular, aspects that indeed *resist* description: sound, color, scent. Resonating in the spaces between the trees, so to speak, the echo circumvents obstacles that language imposes on subjective experience. It exploits, in its movement, everything that is *away* from the sign, promoting a kind of semiotic *Wanderlust*: signs move toward (and away from) each other in unthinkable ways.[6]

Such an image of "corresponding" suggests an analogy to what Jacques Lacan has called the "signifying chain," a linguistic structure that generates meaning through relations of contiguity—potentially endless series of signifiers, of differentiated linguistic elements. In promoting the making of meaning, such a chain has a remarkable creative potential of its own, for it empowers the subject who speaks to "make sense" in unexpected ways. As Lacan puts it:

> What the structure of the signifying chain discloses is the possibility I have, precisely in so far as I have [a] language in common with other subjects, to use [this language] in order to signify *something quite other* than what it says. This function of speech is [not a] "disguising of thought" . . . [but rather] an indication of the place of this subject in the search for the true.[7]

In other words, the subject, who is defined by language, searches for a "truth," a lost experience, that language has failed to capture—a search that is carried out by using words to signify something "other." The creation of a meaning that is potentially "other" thus begins to approximate, for the subject, a *truth* (call it "Nature") that is equally "other"—a truth that the subject believes to lie beyond the enclosing language forest. Such a creation is nothing less than the operation of metaphor, which, according to Lacan, "occurs at the precise point where sense emerges from nonsense."

In the poem **"Correspondances,"** the creative power of metaphor is displayed, somewhat conspicuously on Baudelaire's part, in the next formal division of the poem. The "proof" of resonance, of the echo, is carried out through an exemplary signifying chain, a poetic conjuring whose potential for sense-making appears as a creative *scent*-making: a mini-litany of perfumes whose endless attributes carry the poem away on cloud of incense, a dazzling (and unforeseen) peroration:

> Il est des parfums frais comme des chairs d'enfants,
> Doux comme les hautbois, verts comme les prairies,
> —Et d'autres, corrompus, riches et triomphants,
>
> Ayants l'expansion des choses infinies,
> Comme l'ambre, le musc, le benjoin, et l'encens,
> Qui chantent les transports de l'esprit et des sens.
>
> (There are perfumes fresh as infants' skin,
> Soft as oboes, green as fields,
> —And others, corrupt, rich and triumphant,
>
> Having the expansion of infinite things,
> Like amber, musk, benjamin, and incense,
> Which sing the ecstasies of the soul and the senses.)

Each scent opens a world of analogy that enfolds the next in the series. The freshness of a baby's skin evokes a smell as much as a touch: a softness that becomes the softness (and sweetness) of a sound: of a reed, which turns into grass, the color of a field. The power of the series lies precisely in this (metonymic) movement, in which each image gives rise to another link, a future displacement.[8] The apparently disconnected series of perfumes, like dream images, are thus joined along a chain that eventually *unites* sound, color, and scent—forming a new, reverberant whole in which new meaning is created ("sense emerging from nonsense") by metaphors that call back and forth like echoes from shadowy, distant places.

The very next moment in the poem, however, reveals the limits of such activity. It marks a boundary, an "end," a point of no return. I am speaking, of course, about the dash—what the French call a "tiret." The dash marks a transgression, interrupting the formal integrity of the first tercet, just as it interrupts the litany contained within it. It is not just a pause, but a threshold (in French, the verb *tirer sur* means "to border, or verge on"). It signals the extreme limit of the poem, that miniature forest, by symbolizing (like the minus sign) a negation, an inverted space where the very idea of the echo disappears; for it marks the place where the poem, even for only a moment, can no longer speak.

Such a limit point represents an absence within the poem, a loss of speech, that suggests at the same time a mysterious presence—the presence of that "other" meaning, or truth, sought by the poem's metaphorical movement. The dash materializes this truth, the unspeakable limit of correspondences, appearing on the poem's body like a stigma. A tiny opening, a slash in the poem's surface, it embodies the conceptual goal that Baudelaire describes as "the expansion of infinite things." It is as if meaning were like the inner surface of a bubble, which, brought to a point of bursting, continued to grow into unaccountable dimensions. Indeed, the "other things" (*d'autres*) that follow on the dash achieve their triumphant otherness precisely because of such an ontological shift. For they are no longer *like* anything at all. They simply sing. They chant, Baudelaire concludes, "the ecstasies of the mind and the senses."

LA MORT

Such an extravagant noise is, in a word, a *jouissance* marking the release from the symbolic order into ecstatic song, expressed in the musical space of what could be called, simply, a cry.[9] The cry defies the acoustical structure of the echo, so to speak, through a radical liberation of its terms; it suggests what the echo would be if it could break from its source, *stop* returning, a condition evoked by the Latin word that serves as a translation for the Greek *echo: vagere,* to wail. The cry is a release from language because it exists as sonorous material not yet subsumed *into* language, not hardened into a signifier. In it I find what existed before speech, and this discovery, in the end, has mortal consequences. For, as Lacan has argued, "When we wish to attain what was *before* the serial articulations of speech, and what is primordial to the birth of the symbols, we find it in death."[10] The liberation from the symbolic order is a discharge into oblivion.

Lacan thus reinterprets the Freudian notion of the death drive as a linguistic phenomenon, a movement toward an (ultimately) destructive truth outside the symbolic order that constitutes us as subjects. He defends the proposition by means of an analogy that illuminates, in an interesting way, the principal image of Baudelaire's poem:

> To say this mortal meaning [the object of our quest] reveals in speech a center exterior to language is more than a metaphor; it manifests a structure. This structure is different from the spatialization of the circumference or of the sphere in which some people like to schematize the limits of the living being and his milieu: it corresponds rather to the relational group that symbolic logic designates . . . as an annulus.[11]

This annulus, or ring, suggests a *correspondance* to the edge of Baudelaire's forest of symbols. To move beyond that border is thus to transgress the symbolic order—a step that, through the force of a pun (another kind of correspondence), constitutes *annulment*. Baudelaire's aesthetic achievement in the poem **"Correspondances"** is thus, one might say, to map out, like the mystic, a path toward poetic truth, a path that brings us to the limits of poetry, to a death that emerges in the poem, simply, as a blank.

We find Baudelaire tracing this same path—although across entirely different terrain—in the poem that opens the chapter on **"Death"** in *Les Fleurs du mal,* the sonnet entitled **"La Mort des amants."** I have lingered over Baudelaire's earlier poem in the hopes of demonstrating how this later work does, in fact, correspond to it, in an essential movement toward death that defines, to use Lawrence Kramer's term, a "structural rhythm" for both.[12]

> Nous aurons des lits pleins d'odeurs légères,
> Des divans profonds comme des tombeaux,
> Et d'étranges fleurs sur des étagères
> Ecloses pour nous sous des cieux plus beaux.
>
> Usant à l'envi leurs chaleurs dernières,
> Nos deux cœurs seront deux vastes flambeaux
> Qui réfléchiront leurs doubles lumières
> Dans nos deux esprits, ces miroirs jumeaux.
>
> Un soir, fait de rose et de bleu mystique
> Nous échangerons un éclair unique
> Comme un long sanglot tout chargé d'adieux.
>
> Et plus tard un Ange, entr'ouvrant les portes,
> Viendra ranimer, fidèle et joyeux,
> Les miroirs ternis et les flammes mortes.
>
> (We will have beds full of faint smells,
> Couches deep as tombs,
> And strange flowers on shelves
> Opening out for us beneath more lovely skies.
>
> Vying to consume their final heat,
> Our two hearts will be two vast torches

> That will reflect their double light
> In our two souls, these twin mirrors.
>
> One night all pink and mystic blue
> We will exchange a unique flash of light
> Like a long sob laden with goodbyes,
>
> And later an Angel, half-opening the doors,
> Will come, faithful and joyful, to revive
> The tarnished mirrors and the dead flames.)

Death appears in this poem, of course, as an inevitability, the poem's title articulating an *Ur*-metaphor in whose conceptual space the text will eventually unfold. There is no forest. It is the unspoken (even clichéd) equivalence between death and sexual communion that forms the resonant space of this text. The metaphor initiates, so to speak, an entire signifying chain, beginning with the title, that literally *motivates* the poem's subject—a subject that arrives in the form of a place marker, in the pronoun "nous." The movement of this "we" is represented, in fact, entirely in the future tense. It is a virtual movement, as if the death that begins the poem were its only true event, an event that, having just taken place (in the title), marks the subject in a state of postcoital languor in which the present, now past, can only be recuperated as a future: "We will have this death again."

This is, in other words, the space of a completely mobile fantasy. The fantasy death-drive outlines two stages within the sonnet. The first, which takes up the largest portion, is a magnificent act of conjuring, in which the "we" is expanded to a point of no return, through an evermore extravagant series of images marking out what that subject will have, and then be, and then do. The second stage occurs "later"; it marks a new temporal order, and with it (as we shall see) a new poetic order.

The first quatrain locates this fantasy subject en route to its pleasure. The "we" is implicated in a drive toward an ever-expanding object—which is, as it happens, a *direct* object of the verb to have: "We will have beds full of faint smells, couches deep as tombs." The expansion works like the expanding perfumes in **"Correspondances."** Beds turn into couches, while a sense of weightless atmosphere ("odeurs légères") modulates into the gravity and depth of the tomb. And then, another object: "strange flowers . . . beneath more lovely skies." The very attribute assigned to the flowers, that of "opening out," seems to comment on the activity of "corresponding" that constitutes this subject's fantasy (and even on the act of *making* poetry, as it puns on Baudelaire's entire collection of *fleurs du mal,* "sick flowers"). Such blossoming—a metaphor *for* the operation of metaphor—can be seen formally, too. As the following example attempts to show, the syntax of the first quatrain produces a form that itself "opens out" through cadences of ever-increasing duration and assonance:

Nous aurons . . .
1. des lits pleins d'o-deurs lé-gèr-es . . .
2. des di-vans pro-fonds com-me des
   tom-beaux . . .
Et . . .
3. d'é-tran-ges fleurs sur des é-ta-gè-res é-clo-ses
   pour nous sous des cieux plus beaux.

In the next quatrain, that metaphorical activity devolves on the subject itself. The "we" becomes "our two hearts," which, in "consuming their final heat," are also "two vast torches." And from the dual function of the torch—a source of both light and heat—ensues yet another series of doubles: a double light, two souls, twin mirrors. The "we," then, is caught up in a resonance *with itself,* a corresponding echo, so to speak, that redefines its plurality as a function not of two (the "you-and-I" of the lovers' discourse) but of one-and-its-double. Indeed, the final image, that of "twin mirrors," comprehends the ambiguous plural as a subject always already seized in (an infinite regress?) of its own reflection, a narcissistic desire for itself. The subjective journey toward the object of desire reaches its limit.

In **"Correspondances,"** the obstacles of language were circumvented through the operation of metaphor, an activity that served to propel meaning toward an imaginary "otherness" represented as the resonance of an echo. In **"La Mort des amants,"** the subject's unfolding fantasy tends toward the same goal, toward an "other" signified whose limit point is reached in the image of the mirror. The correspondence between the *two* poems, then, occurs as a function of the relationship between these limits—the relationship between Echo and Narcissus. For in both figures we see the structure of a duality: a continuity between poles, between a self and an "other" that is, in the end, a reflection of the self. Echo and Narcissus thus occupy the same register, but through a correspondence of two sensual dimensions: sound and image. Echo called out in love to Narcissus and got back the sound of her own voice; Narcissus, hearing the sound, looked out in love and saw his own reflection. The desire of the subject toward this "other" that it imagines always finds its limit at the same point, which Lacan, incidentally, identified as "the mirror stage."

To move beyond this point—to shatter the image in the mirror—is, as we have seen, deadly for the subject. Yet the move is also necessary to the Baudelairean aesthetic, an aesthetic that cannot be separated, as Leo Bersani has suggested, "from Baudelairean erotics, and in [which] jouissance is identical to the masochistic pleasure of self-shattering."[13] In **"La Mort des amants,"** this mortal conclusion, or "consummation," takes place in the very next division of the poem, in a single phrase of tiny, condensed narrative:

one night, all pink and mystic blue
we will exchange a unique flash of light
like a long sob laden with goodbyes.

The "exchange" marks the final, destructive act: the subject is consumed, "spent," in a dramatic movement toward the other-which-is-itself. In collapsing the distance that defines the double, the "we" literally *dis*integrates, loses its integrity as a subject. And Baudelaire imagines such a disintegration as a breaking-down: a "long sob," filled with the unutterable pathos of parting. It is, in other words, a moment of linguistic emptiness, a release from language that leaves the subject, once again, at a *loss*: a loss for words that is imagined as a nonverbal act, a loss of the sign.

After this long *adieu*, the "we" does, in fact, disappear from the surface of the poem—fading imperceptibly into the blank, the white space between the two tercets. The subject is, like the Barthesian lover, *engulfed.*[14] The last three lines establish a new temporality, as if this moment of loss for the amorous subject (the loss of his/her structure as a lover) altered the very structure of being-in-time. It is "later." But how much later? The tiny narrative of annihilation is followed by another story that upsets the flow of time: the screen fades out, then in; a phenomenological epilepsy.

We blink. There is a new agent, out-of-place, disrupting our sense of place: an "Angel." (Who are you?) This (capitalized) Angel is a figure—referring to an entire western discourse from at least the sixteenth century—for the sudden, the strange, the ungraspable. As Michel de Certeau has argued, one of the principal topoi of this discourse, that of the "angelic crossing" (*le passage angélique*), "take[s] the form of a speech that contests the order of things":

> The speech of angels restores eventfulness, a sense of the possible. In this sense it is "metaphorical": crossing to another genre, inventing another space, creating a possibility *on the inside* of that which facts pose as impossible. . . . The space of the dream gives thus to the angelic "metaphor" its fundamental figure: a word crosses the frontiers of beings or things, restores paradoxically a historicity within the limits of cosmic law, and, under the sign of suddenness and of the strange, opens a field of possibility.[15]

In Baudelaire's poem, the Angel represents the possibility of a redeemed speech, as it faithfully restores the very terms that had earlier compelled the subject in its fantasy. It makes speaking once again possible by reviving mirrors (now "tarnished") and flames (now "extinguished").[16] In other words, it restores the capacity for these terms to reflect or illuminate meaning, in effect by opening the possibility for them to mean something else. The angelic figure, "half-opening the doors," *is* an opening: it dis-locates the discursive space of the poem, introducing a narrative of the second order, another story.[17] Speaking, as it were, from *inside*—from the blank that had engulfed the we—it "invents another space" for the poem, as if to recuperate the white on the page (a "mere" formal convention) as another poetic frontier filled with new possibility, new meaning.[18]

Le chant

As a discursive figure, the Angel thus represents the possibility of an "other" dimension in this poem, much as the dash marked a space of "infinite things" in **"Correspondances."** A rupture of continuity (a tic in the narrative, a breach of form) opens up a new expressive realm—a transcendent "background," so to speak, which informs the shifting surface of correspondences, while it threatens the very integrity of such a surface. It suggests an unspeakable alternative to the poem, where things fall, flow, melt in a *jouissance* of nonspeaking. Such a structure is, in effect, essential to the Baudelairean aesthetic. The poem will always utter itself (indeed, struggle) *against* this imagined pleasure *hors du texte*; but it will never be able to express such pleasure directly—a dilemma that recalls, once again, the condition of the speaking subject as formulated by Lacan. In his words: "No one can in fact say *je jouis* ["I enjoy" or slang for "I come"] unless he or she is referring to past pleasure or pleasure to come, because as soon as he or she begins to speak, the subject ceases to enjoy in the true sense."[19] It's simply impossible to be transported beyond the "forests of symbols," to experience the ecstasy of leaving language behind, while you're still speaking.

But what about singing? Baudelaire was certainly attuned to the difference. It is something he asks us to imagine—to hear in our mind's ear—with the "singing" perfumes at the incantatory conclusion to **"Correspondances."** Even the restorative capacity he assigns to the Angel (whose unique speech act calls to mind the equally resonant image of the "angel choir") depends on a nonspeaking that suggests a form of singing: the "dead flames" rekindled ("ranimer") by a breath that could be, metaphorically speaking, a melody. It is perhaps not surprising, then, that we should also find Debussy, for whom melody was no mere metaphor, attuned to this special power of music—the power to transport a listener beyond language. Indeed, for him such a condition appears as a *donné,* an inevitable function of music in culture: "Ordinary people as well as the élite," he wrote in a short essay from 1902, "come to music to seek oblivion."[20] In Debussy's setting of **"La Mort des amants,"** which concludes his *Cinq poèmes de Baudelaire,* we can trace the means by which music, for both the ordinary listener and trained musicians, produces such oblivion.

In one sense, his song (like all song) fulfills the trajectory of the Baudelairean text. It invents an alternative "space" in which words are restored to a new life through a setting that makes them take on new, and—from Baudelaire's perspective, at least—wholly unexpected meanings. A song, we could say, realizes that promised frontier where all signs merge into a "shadowy and deep unity" largely through the presence of its melody, which, by its very nature, always makes speech "other." In turning speech into melody, a song disturbs the materiality of the spoken word. It eroticizes speech because, as individual words begin to lose their formal precision, they approach the condition of nonspeech; they become echoes of the prearticulate, more like sobs than signifiers.

Such a dis-integration of the material word, what Kramer refers to as the "topological distortion" of song,[21] effects a release from language and certainly accounts for the pleasure—as well as alienation—one might feel on hearing a familiar text set to music. In other words, pleasure is produced by translating the relations that order the surface of the poem into a set of purely *musical* relations. Singing "opens" the poem, allowing the boundaries of the word to be blissfully transcended, allowing speech to slip into new, unaccountable realms. It is precisely this unaccountability of the sung word that fosters the illusion of loss, the subject's temporary release from the spoken word and all its limitations. And such a release constitutes the "oblivion" that (according to Debussy) "ordinary" listeners always seek in music.

But what of Debussy's "elite" listeners? Can a song continue to function as a domain of blissful unaccountability for listeners who know music, so to speak, *as* a language, who are trained to read and interpret its signs? Trained musicians, the musical "elite," would seem to represent quite another audience, for whom the act of listening always involves a kind of discipline: a rigorous attention to all the musical signs in a given work, a comprehensive account of significant musical "events." A song, from this vantage point, becomes a site where a poem is not so much transcended, as heard and comprehended *through* a "substitute" language of music. Listening to music in this way would thus be linked, as Roland Barthes might say, to a "comfortable practice of reading,"[22] a reading that leads not to an experience of loss, but to its opposite: the set of collected musical "events" become markers, signposts, serving to show the listener precisely where she is, at every moment. In such a practice, music always maintains the poem in a certain relation to itself, a relation that, far from dissolving language, would seem to preserve it, by representing it.

A few examples from the first half of the song may serve to illustrate this sort of reading practice—instances of "local" correspondance (immediately gratifying) in which Debussy's music can be heard as a kind of literal translation of the poem, echoing the meaning of certain parts of the text. Consider, for instance, the curious whole-tone interruption, at the end of the first melodic period, that blossoms over a chromatic passing tone in the bass as if to "open out," like a strange flower, the tonal implications of the piece. Or the harmonic architecture of the next period, whose first and last measures reveal a foundation of two sonorities, having common tones and occupying a common register, that suggest the minimalist dramas of Satie, the endless cycling of two dominants caught in their own desire for each other—a drama that corresponds to the entrapment of the "we" in its mirror image.

Along the same lines, the sensuous color change at the beginning of the very next phrase, brought about by the revoicing of an already unresolved sonority, makes us "hear," with a kind of synesthetic pleasure, the poem's pink and mystic blue night. And this shading barely prepares us for the next correspondence—the poem's fatal climax—which Debussy marks by a sudden surging of the voice to claim a register it had not yet known, establishing at the same time (through the jarring effects of a most unexpected cadence) a tonal netherworld that seems to represent, in musical terms, the escape of the subject into its bliss.

Yet despite the pleasure they may afford me (or any other reader, for that matter), such observations remain merely topical—anecdotal, even—satisfying as they do my assumptions about the representation of poetic meaning within the *mélodie*. There is, however, another moment near the end of the song, a "non-event" that resists being drawn into this neat collection of text-and-music analogies: it is a peculiar moment whose difficulty raises (at least) two essential questions for our understanding of Debussy's setting—and perhaps for his entire musical practice in the face of shifting ideals in the 1880s. The first question has to do with what we might call the purely musical meaning of diatonicism in relation to chromaticism; the second, with the meaning of neither one—or, to put it another way, the escape from such a binary opposition.

So stated, the first concern is, of course, Parsifalian, a concern that has a moralistic ring, presupposing a "right" answer, a privileged term (such as that invoked, in Wagner's case, by means of having the "last word" in a five-hour opera). That *Parsifal* should figure somewhere in these works from the late 1880s is not surprising, since Debussy's involvement with the work at that time is well documented—an affair that Robin Holloway suggests Debussy never quite got over.[23] In this piece, the tribute to Wagner is unmistakable, if modest, occurring in the form of a pun at the climactic—and startling—cadence to E in the fourth phrase. The piano part, amidst a sinuous vocal melody that surely disguises what is happening, cites the grand cadence of the "Good Friday" music in act III, the cadence that

follows on Gurnemanz's lines: "All that blooms here and soon dies / Nature from which sin has been lifted / today wins her day of innocence."[24]

The pun brings to the moment of consummation—the climax of the poem—all of the spiritual and moral intensity of this moment in the opera, of Good Friday itself. The seriousness of the reference can be adduced, I think, by the way Debussy handles the original passage, whose mood, according to Pierre Louÿs, had long captivated him.[25] He treats the three parts of the contrapuntal complex (prominent descending seconds repeated at the octave, a chromatic inner voice, an extended pedal tone in the bass) with great reverence. In fact, he recomposes them slightly, making the inner voice ascend rather than descend, as if to prevent the quotation from seeming too obvious, or potentially comical.[26] The subtle insinuation of this musical idea into the song at this moment, then, radically revises the *Ur*-metaphor equating sex with death; through the lens of this corresponding image, the song suggests an alternative meaning where rapture is transposed into redemption, and "sin has been lifted."

Such a cleansing can be heard, in fact, in the very next phrase—with the piano interlude that rescues us from postcoital whimpering (the languorous *Poco ritardando* of the third period) and announces the recapitulation of the piece. After death, a resurrection. Here we find the same four measures that opened the song, now harmonically "transfigured" in a literal sense: figured *through* for the first time, with unambiguous voice leading supported by a fully functioning bass. This second passage seems to announce itself as the "truth" concealed by the song's opening measures. It supersedes that earlier passage, which, wearing its ambiguity with an attitude, had mixed triadic motives with chromatic counterpoint, clichéd diminished sevenths with an equally clichéd authentic cadence, and all of it articulated *without* the reassuring presence of a bass voice. The transfigured interlude, in other words, saves us from the omissions of the opening measures. Finally, we know how to hear the progression. And with that knowledge, the inevitable value of diatonicism for the whole song is made certain.

But how seriously are we to take this diatonic victory? It is worth noting, for example, that the song does *not* follow its operatic predecessor by closing at this redemptive moment. Indeed, it begins to seem that Debussy's punning was intended rather as a sleight of hand, a means to throw listeners gently off course—especially because what follows this moment constitutes much more than the peroration after the close: it's a mini-drama all its own, that leads to the "real" climax of the piece, an effect no one would have expected.

This brings me to the second question, and to my final point: the means by which the diatonic/chromatic dualism is ultimately transcended in the piece. Such transcendence, to be sure, is a function of the power-fully diatonic recapitulation just described. The reverberations of that tonal order continue well into the next phrase, which, in slipping away from C toward E♭, reproduces the same progression without variation for the next four measures. Over this an added vocal melody quotes the "death" motive from the *Tristan* prelude (at "entr'ouvrant les portes"),[27] as if to hint at yet another transfiguration of the musical text. The most harmonically venturesome (and aggressive) act of the entire piece then follows, in a chain of dominants whose meaning seems to emerge in a manner akin to the Lacanian "signifying chain": they lead continually toward another signified, and another, suggesting a process that need never end. In the meantime, under the pressure of all this movement, the vocal line is hard-pressed to keep itself together. For the first time in the setting, Debussy abandons his respectful "prosodic" declamation for something that is much more like an operatic melody—a line that dis-articulates the text as it soars higher and higher.

And then it happens. I reach the end of the dominant chain—and I don't know where I am. By the subtlest shift, a lowered semitone, the entire dominant frontier is shattered. I seem to have reached the other side, arriving on a sonority whose purpose, whose function, whose very name is (for the moment, at least) unspeakable. This arrival to nowhere marks the beginning of the end of the song. It is an arresting moment of musical emptiness: a poignant sound, leaking out on the humblest of parts of speech: the article *Les*. It is, as Poizat would say (speaking about the domain of opera), the moment when the libretto drops out of your hands, a moment, he says, "when singing deliberately presents itself as singing, as pure music free of all ties to speech; singing which literally destroys speech in pursuit of a purely musical melody, a melody that develops, little by little, until it verges on the cry."[28]

The top of the last phrase of **"La Mort des amants"** utters such a cry. Its poignancy lies in a pleasurable experience of disorientation: occurring as it does in that space between two tonal orientations, between two *edges* (diatonic and chromatic, normative and subversive), it marks a space of compromise.[29] To give the chord a name—to read it as if it belonged to the collection of diatonic sonorities that define the song's putative "key" of G♭ major (in this case, A♭ minor, or ii of G♭)—would be to deny the real pleasure of this compromise, of this edge between the established diatonic topos and the chromatic play that disturbs it. Indeed, Debussy himself, in this piece as elsewhere, seems to have been taking a kind of self-conscious pleasure in the new possibilities offered by such chromatic disturbance, a disturbance whose profound effect was to narrow the diatonic field, to eliminate harmonic functions beyond that of the tonic and the

dominant. In such a context, the A♭-minor sonority becomes exquisitely weightless—falling (or floating?) into a functionless abyss, a space emptied of syntactic value.

This momentary liberation from the musical symbol ultimately serves, like the Angel in Baudelaire's poem, to "open" a tiny passage—to invent a *new* space for the song that restores eventfulness to the music; confers new life on what follows; introduces, in fact, a delicious dysfunction into those stolidly "functional" functions, the two most nameable chords of the piece: D♭ and G♭. For in the long, sobbing descent that follows the "lost" chord, a descent whose melody echoes the dramatic vocal climax of the fourth phrase, these most predictable (one could even say "tarnished") of functions—the tonic and the dominant—seem transcended. The final cadence remains languorously suspended, reverberant, giving an odd impression of never actually touching ground. This feeling (this function?) is virtually impossible to name.

I have, in short, left my discipline behind. And this loss is bliss.

Notes

The ideas in this paper were developed in discussions among students at the University of California, Berkeley, in 1991-92. I would like to thank Ruth Charloff, Gregory Dubinsky, Michelle Dulak, Robert Fink, Mitchell Morris, David Pereira, Stephen Rumph, Leslie Sprout, and Steven Swayne for the intelligence and enthusiasm of their contributions to those discussions, and for many acts of friendship.

1. Walter Benjamin, "The Task of the Translator," in *Illuminations,* ed. Hannah Arendt, trans. Harry Zohn (New York, 1968), p. 76.

2. Ibid.

3. See Charles Baudelaire, *Œuvre complètes,* ed. Claude Pichois (Paris, 1975-76), II, 133.

4. The following claim offers an example of this traditional view: "'Correspondances' [is] Baudelaire's most important poem . . . , an anticipation of symbolism and surrealism . . . singled out . . . because it can be interpreted as Baudelaire's 'art poétique,' as the manifesto of a 'new' school of poetry" (Judd Hubert, "Symbolism, Correspondance and Memory," *Yale French Studies* 9 [1952], pp. 46-55). Paul de Man traces the view back to Marcel Raymond, *De Baudelaire au surréalisme* (Paris, 1940), by whose precedent "it [became] customary to take . . . 'Correspondances' as the fundamental statement of the symbolist aesthetic, a statement with which the majority of later experimentations and themes are merely a further

development" (see de Man's posthumously published essay, "The Double Aspect of Symbolism," *Yale French Studies* 74 [1988], 6, n. 9). Leo Bersani has also acknowledged this tradition, while offering a modification: "'Correspondances' does present itself as a doctrinaire poem (thus the countless critical efforts to extract the doctrine, to find its sources in nineteenth-century esthetics, philosophy, psychology), and the doctrine which the poem espouses and vaguely outlines has much less to do with symbolism in Nature than with metaphorical unity within Nature" (Bersani, *Baudelaire and Freud* [Berkeley and Los Angeles, 1977], pp. 32-34).

5. If Baudelaire had lived to know telephones, he surely would have appreciated the notion of "transfer" to which they also refer: i.e., the innumerable connections made possible, through a vast network of numbers and wires, by the hand of the switchboard operator.

6. This reading comes close to that of Bersani, who, in offering an alternative to the commonly held notion linking "correspondences" to a transcendental (or "vertical") symbolism, sees them as "horizontal" relations in which "objects are continuously moving toward and away from each other" (*The Culture of Redemption* [Cambridge, Mass., 1990], p. 75).

7. Jacques Lacan, "The Agency of the Letter in the Unconscious or Reason Since Freud," in his *Ecrits: A Selection,* trans. Alan Sheridan (New York, 1977), p. 155.

8. For Lacan, the power of metaphor is electric, a "creative spark" that "flashes between two signifiers, one of which has taken the place of the other in the signifying chain, the occulted one remaining present through its (metonymic) connection with the rest of the chain."

9. See Michel Poizat, "'The Blue Note' and 'The Objectified voice and the vocal object'," *Cambridge Opera Journal* 3 (1991), 195-211.

10. Lacan, "The Function and Field of Speech and Language in Psychoanalysis," in *Ecrits,* p. 105.

11. Ibid.

12. See Lawrence Kramer, *Music and Poetry: The Nineteenth Century and After* (Berkeley and Los Angeles, 1984).

13. Bersani, *The Culture of Redemption,* p. 72.

14. "The image of the other—to which I was glued, on which I lived—no longer exists . . . I am nowhere *gathered together*" ("'I am engulfed, I succumb . . .'," in Roland Barthes, *A Lover's Discourse: Fragments,* trans. Richard Howard [New York, 1978], p. 11).

15. Michel de Certeau, *Le Parler angélique: Figures pour une poétique de la langue,* Actes Semiotiques-Documents, vol. 54 (Paris, 1984), p. 9 (my trans.; emphasis added).

16. The two metaphors draw on an extensive literary heritage. Arthur Groos has discussed the Romantic tradition that, following ancient models, employed the extinguished torch as a common metaphor for death, a tradition that reaches its culmination, Groos argues, in the torches of the *Tristan* libretto—more or less contemporaneous with the *Fleurs du mal.* Isolde is compelled to extinguish her own (i.e., to commit suicide) "in order to realize her love in the transcendent realm of night" (Groos, "Wagner's 'Tristan und Isolde': In Defence of the Libretto," *Music & Letters* 60 [1988], 475-76). If not a Romantic topos, the image of the tarnished word was certainly familiar to a later (i.e., post-Baudelairean) generation of French symbolist poets. In a letter from 1893 to his friend Ernest Chausson, Claude Debussy reports the following conversation with the poet Henri de Régnier: "I had a visit from Henri de Régnier . . . obviously a man of delicate sensibilities. He was talking to me about certain words in the French language, saying that their gold had been tarnished from knocking about too much in the rude world, and I thought to myself it was much the same with certain chords" (*Debussy Letters,* ed. François Lesure and Roger Nichols, trans. Roger Nichols [London, 1987], pp. 51-52).

17. The image of the woman behind "half-opened doors" appears, interestingly, in J. K. Huysmans's *A Rebours* in a long reminiscence on legalized prostitution: "Through the half-opened [*entr'ouverte*] doors, and the windows only partially obscured by coloured panes or curtains, he could remember having caught glimpses of women walking up and down" (Huysmans, *Against the Grain* [New York, 1969], p. 161). Baudelaire's "Angel" might similarly be seen as such a prostitute, a figure that recurs in Baudelaire's critical writings to stand for the completely penetrated being, for one who is always "open" to otherness. Such a figure extends to the *flaneur,* to the lover, to God ("the most prostituted being"), and to the very idea of the artist, who is, for Baudelaire, always both absorbed and shattered by his "inspiration." As Bersani has noted, such a condition resembles in some respects the Freudian concept of primary narcissism: "The implicit equivalence in Freud between primary narcissism and the simultaneous constitution and shattering of ego boundaries is, in wholly different terms, anticipated in Baudelaire as the jouissance of a

self carried away (both ecstatically transported and removed from itself) by its own prostitution" (*The Culture of Redemption,* p. 73).

18. It may be instructive to compare this angelic function to that found in some of the late paintings of Turner (as it happens, one of Debussy's favorite painters). Jonathan Crary describes Turner's *Angel Standing in the Sun* (1846) as an attempt to represent "experience that transcends its possible representations." As Crary notes, "Turner's familiar vortex modulates into a pure spherical whirlpool of golden light: a radial conflation of eye and sun, of self and divinity, of subject and object. In the center of the . . . work is the figure of a winged angel raising a sword. . . . The recourse to the angel, an object with no referent in the world, is a sign of the inadequacy of conventional means for representing the hallucinatory abstraction of his intense optical experiences. The angel becomes a symbolic acknowledgment by Turner of his own perceptual anatomy" (Crary, *Techniques of the Observer: On Vision and Modernity in the Nineteenth Century* [Cambridge, Mass., 1990], pp. 142-43). Turner's angel is thus, like Baudelaire's Angel, a sign of the artist's relation to his own vision. The Angel's presence inside the painting (or poem) points to a dimension of experience beyond it, a dimension of nonrepresentability by which representation itself might be redeemed.

19. Quoted in Anika Lemaire, *Jacques Lacan,* trans. David Macey (London, 1977), p. 149.

20. Claude Debussy, "The Orientation of Music," in *Debussy on Music: The Critical Writings of the Great French Composer,* ed. and trans. Richard Langham Smith (Ithaca, N.Y., 1988), p. 85.

21. See Kramer, *Music and Poetry,* chap. 5.

22. Roland Barthes, *The Pleasure of the Text,* trans. Richard Miller (New York, 1975), p. 14.

23. Robin Holloway, *Debussy and Wagner* (London, 1979).

24. For this bit of musical wisdom, I owe thanks to Gregory Dubinsky. The translated passage is from Lucy Beckett, *Richard Wagner: Parsifal* (Cambridge, 1981), p. 54.

25. Louÿs's remarks are cited in Marcel Dietschy's biography of Debussy: "He loved to quote certain lines from *Parsifal,* nearly all of which have the same mood: a very gentle theme, unprepared, which lasts two bars and then fades out. For example: the theme of the Lake . . . the last page of the Good Friday Spell" (Dietschy, *A Portrait of Claude Debussy,* ed. and trans. William Ashbrook and Margaret G. Cobb [Oxford, 1990], p. 53).

26. The infamous *Tristan* quotation that appears ten years later in the "Golliwog's Cake-walk" of *The Children's Corner* (1908) has, of course, just such a mocking effect and belies the impatience with *Wagnerisme* that marked the later part of Debussy's artistic career.

27. Roger Parker pointed this out to me.

28. Poizat, "'The Blue Note'," p. 199.

29. See Barthes, *The Pleasure of the Text,* p. 6.

E. S. Burt (essay date December 1995)

SOURCE: Burt, E. S. "'An Immoderate Taste for Truth': Censoring History in Baudelaire's 'Les bijoux.'" *Diacritics* 27, no. 2 (summer 1997): 19-43.

[*In the following essay, first read at a December 1995 conference on censorship, Burt analyzes "Les bijoux," one of the poems censored by the French courts when* Les Fleurs du Mal *was first published in 1857.*]

In May 1949, a French Court of Appeals reversed an 1857 decision condemning six poems from *Les fleurs du mal* for obscenity, in a signal case of a public lifting of a ban against some lyric poems.[1] Among the several interesting features of this case not the least is the decision to proceed against the work in the first place. For lyric poetry does not appear an attractive target for censorship. Its subject matter and formalism remove it far enough from the experience of most readers that Gustave Flaubert, fresh from his troubles with the court over *Madame Bovary,* could express his surprise at the government's attack: "This is new," he wrote to Baudelaire, "this pursuit of a volume of verse." While Flaubert's comment was in point of fact inaccurate, he puts his finger on a problem worth considering.[2] Here we have a work that must seem naturally exempt from state intervention, by virtue of a deliberate retreat from risky political subjects, and it nonetheless did get censored by the state. Can anything be learned about "normal" state censorship from this exceptional case?

A key factor in the government's decision to pursue the book, according to the prosecutor Pinard, was that these poems would prove accessible to a large audience:[3] "An immoral book that had no chance of being read or understood would not be pursued" [1208], he states. In his argument, as in the judgment by the court that the condemned poems "lead necessarily to the exciting of the senses by a coarse realism offensive to modesty" [1182], the assumption is that the work is extraordinarily available, its pictures immediately referable to ordinary experience. In the six condemned poems, language is judged to be not a veil but a tool, and a sex tool at that. "Despite an effort of style" [1182], the poetic situation—in most of the poems that of the boudoir—is painted in a language insufficiently flowery.[4]

A further interesting feature in the case is that when it comes up again, under DeGaulle's Fourth Republic, the court summarily dismisses the 1857 judgment of coarse realism as just one possible interpretation, and a forced one at that. Instead, the 1949 court finds that the poems are self-referential, symbolic entities that do not represent ordinary experience:

> If some pictures, on account of their originality, were able to alarm some minds upon first publication and appeared to the first judges as offensive to morality, such an appraisal, attaching itself only to a realistic interpretation of the poems and neglecting their symbolic meaning, has proved to be of an arbitrary character, unratified by public opinion or by the judgment of the literary world.
>
> [St. John-Stevas 249]

The shocking representations of 1857, outraging morality, are now understood to deliver the Wordsworthian "shock of mild surprise" by which we recognize the original work of art. In 1949, the poems are precious artifacts; their language is not realistic but symbolical; its sensuous forms reveal an inner, spiritual meaning.

A crucial resemblance can be discerned between the actions taken by the two courts: both make their judgments in terms of a "reading pact," a set of "artificial rules" [1206] that are presumed to govern reading and to have currency in the context. *Les fleurs* gets policed in the name of this generic purity, with the prosecutor Pinard calling "the judge . . . a sentinel who must not let the border be crossed" [1206] and the 1949 decision confirming the opinion of the literary world that the supposed transgression against public morality was in point of fact a transformation in the rules regulating the narrow confines of lyric poetry.[5]

This concern that texts be framed by a reading pact aimed at constraining their interpretation is worth considering in any discussion of censorship that wants to move from the level of pragmatics to that of theory. It leads to queries about the possibility of getting rid of state censorship entirely and about the state's interest, as guardian and overseer of the archive, in the institutionalization and enforcement of such reading pacts. It raises the issue of an ambiguity in the role played by the literary establishment, which can be seen most often acting in collusion with the state on this matter of generic purity. That is partly a matter of empirical fact—in the case of *Les fleurs du mal* for instance, it was literary journalists who brought the whiff of scandal to the state's attention in 1857; in 1949 it was a Society of Learned Men who brought the suit to rehabilitate Baudelaire's memory, and critics who provided expert

testimony as to what Auerbach called the work's "aesthetic dignity." But it also touches on a region where censorship law flows over into copyright law, with the rights to profit from a work's reproduction and dissemination entailing, besides the responsibility to publish the names and coordinates of author, publisher, and printer, the implied requirement not to mislead readers as to the literary genre to which the work belongs. As for the works themselves, they can presumably collaborate with as easily as infringe upon the state's attempts to regulate linguistic indeterminacy. Where they help maintain the border between referential and self-referential language uses, they are presumably complicitous with the state, perfect mirrors of its ideology.

The point I'd like to pursue is somewhat different albeit related, and it entails a bit of introspection first. I suspect that part of the attraction of studying cases of state censorship for a critic like myself is that one can point to such cases as tangible proof that literature matters after all, that it sometimes does leave its ivory tower to touch the world. The state seems hit in a vital spot, as if some secret lay open in the work that its censorship laws want reburied. This is thrilling to critics, this notion that the state is somehow imperiled by the work. It vindicates literary activity, which turns out not to be pointless after all, but instead invested with urgency and relevancy.[6]

I cast this in the form of a confession, because I am somewhat suspicious of the drama of the scenario. It neatly pits a beleaguered text or author against the monolithic authority of the state threatened by and threatening to the literary work.[7] The reality of censorship is less reassuringly centralized; it is more diffuse, more disseminated, and less univocal in its functioning than such a model would suggest. Nor are works ever all black or white; their complicity with the state on matters of textual hygiene is at least partial. Partiality also afflicts the results of censorship, whose most repressive acts never can do more than partially or temporarily screen the offensive material.

Nevertheless, the scenario of the state vs. Baudelaire's poems helps focus the area of conflict on the threat posed by textual indeterminacy as it spills over to disturb the presumed unity and stability of the context. In the case of *Les fleurs,* poems the state allows once found to have a legible address and mode of meaning, the bone of contention turns out to have been a problematic relation between the literary work and experience, memory, and history.

The prosecutor provides the first hint that memory is at stake in complaining that the poems do not remove us from past, sensuous experience but instead *produce* and even *model* it. He says the poems have the effect of "giving back their senses to those who can no longer feel" [1208]. Into the reflective situation of reading considered as removed from the senses emerges a new experience of remembering, the sudden revival of deadened senses. This experience of memory as transgressive recollection has been analyzed by the eminent Baudelaire critic Walter Benjamin, in a discussion relevant enough to merit a brief summary.

Discussing Theodor Reik's distinction between memory and remembrance, Benjamin explains that remembrance (*Gedächtnis*) protects and preserves impressions whereas memory (*Erinnerung*) destroys and disintegrates them. Remembrance is a present act of retrieval that relies upon a forgetting of "what has not been experienced explicitly and consciously, what has not happened to the subject as an experience," says Benjamin [160]. It thus also conserves the past as past, subordinating it to the present act of consciousness. It confirms the view that whatever the present has lost in terms of immediacy or in proximity to natural experience is more than made up for by the progress in understanding. As for memory, it recalls uncollected and as yet unexperienced fragmentary impressions connected to the memory trace. Its act of recollection is at least doubly disintegrating. First, it calls into question the everyday experience of the subject by showing its conscious life to be an artificial construction, reliant on decisions and exclusions such as privileging vision (which is idealizing and totalizing) over the other senses. Second, it disrupts the temporal assumption of remembrance, which preserves the past as past with respect to its act. Memory is an experiencing *for the first time* of left-out impressions, for instance, the repressed sensations of the body as a tangle of parts and disconnected senses. Such a past has not taken place until it emerges, shattering the stability of the present, in the act of recollection. The knowledge provided by memory as *Erinnerung* can be termed negative knowledge, since in recalling what is left out by consciousness in remembering, one is faced with understanding the limits of the understanding. If, as Benjamin quotes Reik as saying, "becoming conscious and leaving behind a memory trace are processes incompatible with each other in one and the same system" [160], with memory consciousness gets engaged in the desperate and open-ended struggle of recalling traces it never can fully assimilate, but upon which its survival depends.

In question in Benjamin's Baudelaire is the notion that literature depicts a prior model, be that model to be found in nature, in other works, or in the author's transforming imagination. In such a view, the work of art preserves the image produced by the artist as a faithful remembrance of his act. It stands as a memorial to the mental activity of a conscious subject. But for Benjamin, Baudelaire's poems situate the work with respect to an experience that requires writing in order to

happen at all. The implication of Benjamin's argument is thus that Baudelaire's poems act against what Lawrence Douglas calls the "preserving of responsible memory."

Baudelaire's poems bring out a forgetfulness in the space of the public monument, which tries to place the past events remembered in a stable relation to the present of their interpretation. Such monuments, among which would be included those stockpiles of acquired knowledge called libraries, tell us that past events and past theories are over and done with; they shelter the present from a past so distant as to be unlikely to erupt into it as unassimilated shocks. Baudelaire's archive is rather to be conceived of as a cross between a heap of incomprehensible ruins and a fireworks factory set down in the midst of the bustling modern city. Memory and history are open-ended, future-oriented projects of recalling the conditions and limits of consciousness and of any history that would be modeled as a coming into consciousness. Small wonder that poems publicizing a faultline in the archive should be relegated to the Hell (*L'Enfer*) of the National Library, where nineteenth-century French law sent censored texts.

In a word, then, my hypothesis is that the question of how the text enters history lies at the heart of the censoring of *Les fleurs du mal*.[8] That is the problem I would like to discuss here, first nuancing the state's position on the text as public monument, and then pursuing, through the reading of a poem, the notion of a memory available in licentious writing that is incompatible with public, preserving memory. This disintegrating memory, I will contend, explains the uneasy relation of the state to the literary work: as disintegrating, its violence is perceived as a threat; as inventive, it is memory oriented toward the future, and has a productive energy to be exploited. Since poetry's ultimate task is that of giving the language, it is history carried in language that will provide the lens.

WRITING BETWEEN THE LINES: REMEMBERING LANGUAGE

Leo Strauss's "Persecution and the Art of Writing" provides a good starting point to complicate the state's position. Strauss's discussion of censorship is guided by a complex understanding of the relation of philosophical texts to history. The products of their time, philosophical texts preserve and pass on the opinion of that time. But they also engage in conflictual dialogue with opinion, and as such, transmit less a content than a critical method distinguished by a negative moment. Where state censorship has gotten in the way of the explicit expression of this dialogue between opinion and its critique, as it did in much of eighteenth-century Europe, for example, philosophical writers have had to have recourse to elaborate strategies of indirection, called by Strauss "writing between the lines," to transmit their philosophical method. To write between the lines is to write a text that, read as statement, is entirely orthodox but that, by the arrangement of the statements, devices of argument, and strategic asides, is revealed as criticizing the orthodoxy.

The recognition that the means of saying can intervene actively in signification allows Strauss first of all to formulate a critique of historicism as interpretative method. Historicism, he says, had as its principle that "no term of any consequence must be used in the interpretation of an author which cannot be literally translated into his language, and which was not used by him or was not in fairly common use in his time. The only presentations of an author's views which can be accepted as true are those ultimately borne out by his own explicit statements" [26-27]. By such methods, teaching texts like those of Plato, Averroes, Kant, or Rousseau were dumbed down into documents transmitting the most platitudinous orthodoxies. Against historicism, Strauss presents a theory of history as an ongoing process of interpretation of fundamental texts. Its method is that of active, self-critical dialogue over orthodox doctrine, a dialogue made available in works written in times of persecution by way of a disjunction between a statement and its mode of presentation; in short, as we would say nowadays, by way of a disjunction in an utterance between its force as a constative or statement and its performative affirmation or denial of the truth of whatever it states. Strauss can thus distinguish the true interpretation of a work from the merely correct, historicist one.[9] The true interpretation is neither the orthodox nor the heterodox opinion qua opinion; it is rather the interpretation that, having taken strategy into account, can teach a dialectical method to "the young men who love to think" [24].

What is most relevant in this account for our question is that the recollection that language actively affects meaning serves as a teaching moment, a privileged moment of progress and liberation from mere doxa. There is a crucial double effect on the concern of the liberal state with freedom of expression that can be extrapolated from Strauss's theory of history and of writing between the lines.[10] (1) If the "puppies of the race" [36] progress by recalling language, then a liberal state interested in the fostering of its puppies and the furtherance of progress has to tolerate to a certain degree the disruptiveness identified with Benjamin's disintegrating memory. Already we have to revise the simple opposition that pits the censoring state against the individual author, the public space of pious preservation of an heroic past against a private space where memory can be free to be disintegrative. Revealed here is a gray area of possible production and education where public and private interests overlap, where friendly disagreement of groups of reasonable citizens with one another

and with a state founded on reason can take place, and where agreements can be forged. The content of texts, statements qua statements, are in themselves revealed to be unthreatening. Once an opinion is of value only insofar as its truth is confirmed or belied by the force of its language, a state conceived along Straussian principles can easily liberalize its censorship of content. (2) Paradoxically, however, it would tend to tighten its control over the means of expression, hoping to limit the negative power of language to what can be assimilated as positive knowledge. Strauss notes the need to find such limits in his essay, in discussing the need for "criteria for distinguishing between legitimate and illegitimate reading between the lines" [32].

Censorship in such a state would hardly merit the name: its aim would be to shelter the means as inventive and educative, while limiting the potential for disruption. The aim is simply accomplished by the determination of those limits as those of knowledge. Any monological text whose structures confirm the liberal orthodoxy by saying what they mean would be allowable, as providing knowledge of a content. Any dialogical text whose presentation has a force discrepant with respect to the views it states would provide a lesson to the alert few on method. In either case, the relation of performative to constative enables education; but revelation of a potential, momentary discrepancy contributes the most by promising a dynamic, progressive education in which action and knowledge in the long run coincide. The axiomatic statement that "virtue is knowledge . . . and thoughtful men as such are trustworthy and not cruel" [25] would allow a Straussian state conceived along liberal principles to reduce the arena for positive censorship almost to nothing. The only texts offensive to public morality, and thus excisable, are those that provide for knowledge and action that do not confirm the axiom.[11]

The very few cases that could still fall under a positive censorship can be found in Strauss's own essay in the form of deafening silences on issues germane to his topic. One silence is on playful modes of writing between the lines—literature, especially poetry—where indirect expression is not a teaching method but an art.[12] Another silence is on obscenity, a language use that falls outside the interpretative scheme defining the work as the intentional act of a moral being.[13] Nor do any young women who love to think make an appearance in Strauss's essay; there is no thought of woman at all in his dreamed-of future; the only love moving "thoughtful men" [25] is for the male "puppies of the race" [36].

The reading of licentious writing, "profitable," in Baudelaire's words, "only to those minds possessed by an immoderate taste for truth" [**"La fanfarlo"** 555], leads in another direction. It demands that we take into account a dimension of language that may not ultimately confirm the harmonious convergence of knowledge and action. An *immoderate taste* for truth is the taste of someone who has not stopped with the revelation of the truth of method and of history as progress, but has developed an unhealthy appetite for revelation irrespective of whether it leads to positive knowledge. Obscene writing thrusts in our face a certain repetitive material, and a certain pleasure to be gotten from the material, that are rejected when writing is conceived in teleological terms. To recall obscenity is to threaten more than a prohibition on certain *topoi*. It threatens the very fundamental, convening assumption of the Straussian version of the liberal state that "virtue is knowledge." Its censorship, we may hypothesize, would constitute an attempt to keep the neglected material from returning to affect the public space of the liberal state, which is built, in short, by respectful, preserving remembrance and by the state's tolerant encouragement of a limited work of disruption by disintegrating memory.

Dirt for Dirt's Sake

Let me gather some support for my understanding of obscenity, and start filling in the gaps left in Strauss's discussion, by reference to a case settled in the American courts in 1933, the case of Joyce's *Ulysses,* where we see a liberal judge hard at work interpreting a literary work as productive of knowledge. Since it is a work of fiction that is in question, it is not logic and method but rather the language as used by its speakers that is the object, but the same axiom will turn out to be operative.

John M. Woolsey's ruling on the question of whether *Ulysses* could enter the United States became famous outside of legal circles because it was incorporated in several editions of the text as its foreword. In his discussion of the "dirty words" that pepper the text, Judge Woolsey explains what he takes to be Joyce's nonpornographic intent. It is the sincere and honest one proper to the artist of "show(ing) exactly how the minds of his characters operate" [ix].[14] For the judge, the artistic intent of bringing out "not only what is in the focus of each man's observation of the actual things about him, but also in a penumbral zone residua of past impressions" [ix] carries with it demands and responsibilities. Joyce, he says, would have "funked its necessary implications" [ix] had he not told fully what his characters think. Woolsey explains away the dirty words: Joyce's "attempt sincerely and honestly to realize his objective has required him incidentally to use certain words which are *generally considered* dirty words . . ." [ix-x].

For Woolsey, in this specific context—given the framing intent and the creative technique—words generally considered dirty are not really dirty. They are determined

otherwise, as the words that the author in all honesty must use. We might call them *honest dirt,* for they symbolize the sweat exuded from the brow of the inventing artist. In the specific context of *Ulysses* they have ceased to be filthy. The artist reconfigures the language, with the expletives as the clue.

What that means first of all is that the author does not really "use" the dirty words at all. He uses them, as Woolsey says, "incidentally." For a term to be judged obscene, it is clearly not enough that it refer to a sexual or excretory organ or function. Otherwise, any talking about such functions, never mind any talking about talking about such functions, would be forbidden, and obscenity trials themselves would become impossible.[15] The key to obscenity lies in the way language is being used. Like *tree* or *table*, dirty words are literal, referential terms properly designating entities in the physical world. If they nonetheless offend good linguistic hygiene, it is because when we use them we break the rule set forth in the work of empiricists like Locke or Condillac that dictates a one-to-one correspondence between the ideas we get from our senses or our reason and the terms designating them. In obscenity (as in certain theological discourses) the terms reserved to name a single referent—physical or metaphysical—proliferate, and a reserve of words piles up that can be substituted for or added to one another without loss or gain in meaning. Obscene terms guard one door to a secret place of play in language, where the substitution of names unregulated by meaning, unaccountable to knowledge, can go on and we can take pleasure in words for their own sake.[16] Language's public virtue as enabler of education is contested by the use of expletives (*explere*—to fill out), forceful verbal filler.

When Woolsey says Joyce does not use obscene terms except incidentally, I take it that he means the author does not himself commit the abuse. Rather, he collects and pins these obscene words into his text purposively, as *examples* of language abuse. Obscenities, Woolsey says, clutter the minds and speeches of Joyce's characters, but they are always in quotes so far as the author himself is concerned. He mentions them to fulfill an obligation he has to provide a full picture of the language. Adding quotes to a dirty word partially launders it by making it an example of a general possibility of language. It brings the prohibited material and the prohibition forward as objects of knowledge. Obscenity in quotes obtrudes the sheer physicality of language on us, but at a distance. By it the writer signals his debt and promise to represent the language in its entirety.

Quotation marks, literal or implied, are critical in Woolsey's discussion. They are laundry marks added by the artist that let him represent the whole body of language, without reserve.[17] The judge gives a glimpse of the stakes when he reminds us that the words that Joyce has reclaimed are "old Saxon words known to almost all men, and, I venture, to many women" [x]. Joyce accepts our English language as is, soiled by overuse and abuse, in parts reserved and shameless, with the aim of restoring its ideal Saxon integrity and purity. He takes terms eroded over time to the value of filler and makes them signify as examples of the transformation to which language is subject. By this move he arrests and even reverses the work of time. Language *shown* to be shopworn is language *revealed* to be subject to unacknowledged historical processes, and thus language brought into a certain conformity with the Straussian axiom: virtue is knowledge.

The point is worth tarrying over, for the judge is revealing an attitude toward the function of the work of art in purifying language by reversing the corrosion of time. In their account of the trial, Ernst and Schwartz insist that the explanation of "each four-letter word in historic terms" [94] was the turning point in the battle. Counsel for *Ulysses* gave etymological arguments that persuasively carried the terms back to a time before they had been set aside as obscene. These etymological arguments are in point of fact ahistorical, for they try to fix the term in an imagined pristine state, before any figurative extension, any reserve or repetition. Counsel states of the word *fuck,* for instance, that: "One etymological dictionary gives its derivation as from *facere*—to make—the farmer fucked the seed into the soil. This, your honor, has more integrity than a euphemism used every day in every modern novel to describe precisely the same event" [94].

Everything is revealing here, the definition, the example, the vague "this," the appeal to "your honor," the emphasis on the integrity of the past as opposed to modern prudishness, and so on. But most interesting is the example. Here we have the sort of man who might have newly minted the term to name his work, which is that of a farmer sowing his seed. This is an Adam before the fig leaf, who would have called things by their proper names, before figurative extensions, reserves, or euphemisms. *Fuck* was as innocent and honest a word as any in the English language. Counsel provides a glimpse of a nascent, agrarian people whose language was as fresh and virginal as the soil they planted. In contrast, the modern situation shows the same event of making, but everywhere repeated, in a banal, degraded version. The cause of corruption is overuse, unacknowledged quotation, and the veil of euphemism is interposed to hide it. Joyce partially reclaims the term by an acknowledged quotation that frames a mythic picture of a language once virginal but now prostituted, whose exemplary tale can serve as a warning about the rest of the language, still meaningful, still capable of being used with decency and respect.

The judge signals that he agrees with this recall to hygiene as a valuable service performed by the work of art. He does so partly by a slip, clumping the four-letter word *fuck* with the others, as criticized terms that are actually "old Saxon words." To say that *fuck,* derived from the Latin *facere,* is a Saxon word is, at the very least, to wipe out the Norman Conquest and the large-scale importation of Old French into the English language. It is to assume that there was a moment when the English language was entire, before contamination by suspect foreign influence, by transports this way and that. In the name of race, nation, people, some ideology of the proper, the judge goes along with what he takes to be the artist's function with respect to the language: the cordoning off of the ruined parts from the living language, together with the restoration of the ideal of a language as an intact whole.

Judge Woolsey also considers the same dirty words from the perspective of the world of the diegesis, in terms of the internal consistency of the characters depicted. Here, the quotation marks function somewhat differently. The obscene terms, he says, are "such words as would be naturally and habitually used . . . by the types of folk whose life, physical and mental, Joyce is seeking to describe . . . it must always be remembered that his locale was Celtic and his season Spring" [x]. From the perspective of the internal world of the novel, these dirty words are, so to speak, *natural dirt,* compost from which might spring flowers. So we are not surprised when Woolsey suggests that Joyce is truly inventive, opens up the unconscious of his characters by way of this dirt. Any other terms would have been euphemisms, the censored language of conscious thought, and would have kept locked the door to the world within the world of the novel which is that of the unconscious. Words from its unknown language, they point beyond the visible world of literal language and the spiritual world revealed by metaphor to a third world ordinarily repressed that obeys the logic of a logorrheic stream-of-consciousness. But that means that they are not really spoken by the characters, who are instead ventriloquized by them. As they erupt out of the mouths of the characters, they are the terms of an unfamiliar language pronounced by the characters, as one pronounces the words of a text written in a language one doesn't know. The obscene terms are the written language of the unconscious.

Placing the disruptive utterances in quotation marks helps contain the violence. A mouth of a single character or class of characters opens at a single moment to express the unconscious. Woolsey is very clear that this kind of talk is that of "persons of the lower middle class living in Dublin in 1904" [ix]. Joyce's quotation marks isolate as in a sick ward such utterances as are not spoken by conscious subjects from normal utterances of that character the rest of the time, the other characters, the world outside the fiction. Internal dikes in the elongated sentence that is the novel, they let us differentiate, say, between Molly Bloom's soliloquy and Judge Woolsey's prefacing opinion. Mentioning dirty words launders them doubly: first by preserving them as ruined terms recalling the originary state of the language in its integrity and propriety; second, by a partial censorship, a separating off of the disruptive talk from ordinary utterances.

Joyce's partial censoring provides a clue to a third kind of dirt, a dirt neither honest nor natural, potentially afflicting the whole of the language. Had Woolsey found it in *Ulysses,* he *would* have termed it obscene. He says of *Ulysses*: "although it contains . . . many words usually considered dirty, I have not found anything that I consider to be *dirt for dirt's sake*" [x]. This third kind of dirt the artist has caused to be rejected as unreclaimable excess. The phrase Woolsey uses—"dirt for dirt's sake"—tells us what is unreclaimable: it is dirt unendowed with a purpose; dirt as an index, just more of the dirt that it stands for. Dirty dirt puts the tautological and repetitive in the place of the teleological at the outset, and thus threatens Woolsey's myth of language as originarily an intact whole. Woolsey says that *Ulysses* expels such dirt. He knows that by the purging effect the work has on the reader: ". . . my considered opinion, after long reflection, is that whilst in many places the effect of 'Ulysses' on the reader undoubtedly is somewhat emetic, nowhere does it tend to be an aphrodisiac" [xii]. The dreck the work of art cannot purify it must cause to be expelled. *Ulysses* induces vomiting rather than pleasure. It makes its readers sick of sex.[18]

The case of *Ulysses* supports the contention that the censoring of obscenity operates according to a different logic than that of the censorship of philosophical texts. In the literary text, where knowledge of language use is at stake, the representation of obscenity can be seen as necessary. The judge, representative censor, lifts the quarantine on *Ulysses* because he finds it to be good for linguistic hygiene: it purifies and reclaims the language for use where it can by quoting, and purges dirt where it cannot.

Note the juridico-political situation of the literary text vis-à-vis the censor. Where message-oriented texts are concerned, the arena for legal censorship can be greatly restricted. Strauss's censor is bound by the law which demands proof of author's intent and of his vigilance over all his expressions. Structurally speaking, the censor is less intelligent than a writer even of average intelligence [26]. But where it is a matter of fictional texts whose aim is to represent the language, the protection of the law does not seem to apply. Implicit in Woolsey's argument is the view that artists have a duty to draw the line anew between those words and images that can be reassigned meaning and those that are unre-

claimable. Theirs is the Herculean task of mucking out the Augean stable of language made dirty by overuse and excessive euphemism. But that means that artists stand open to the accusation of obscenity precisely insofar as they try to keep their promise as artists. As for the censor's limits, it seems that the judgment of obscenity ought to stand on the success or failure of the work to reclaim the language as a whole. But since no one is or could be in a position to judge on such a matter, it relies instead on the intelligence and courage of the censoring judge. Judges are required to be informed about things that, for structural reasons, they cannot know. For instance, they have to know when an author is exemplifying language, mentioning a term in quotes, and when she is using it, speaking in her "own" voice.[19] They have to know when obscene talk is in quotes that clean up and contain the dirt, and when such quoting is just guilty pleasure taken in manipulating sensuous language, repetition without transformation.

As for the definition of obscenity, it is entirely problematic.[20] More than one author complains of the lack of any objective criteria to follow.[21] If the work is indeed engaged in the redefining of obscenity first by reclaiming "foul" language for meaning, and second, in causing to be regurgitated as excess what it cannot so reclaim, then it follows that the judge never could approach a new work armed with a prior definition, but would always have to rely on the work to provide a dividing line. To the extent that the work manages to assimilate "dirt," it defines it in terms of a purpose. To the extent that it cannot assimilate it to that purpose, to the extent that it expels it, it is mere tautology. By definition, *as* tautology, the obscene falls outside of definition. Indeed, Woolsey's own attempt at defining obscenity, which is one that enjoyed a certain currency in the writings of the mid-twentieth century on obscenity laws—"dirt for dirt's sake"—is really less a successful definition than a phrase coined to renounce definition. It gives up on determining a concept of dirt, gives in by just reiterating the term.[22] It indicates a symptomatic moment of breakdown, of unreclaimable excess in Woolsey's own writing. Because it fills in for a missing definition with a word that adds nothing, we can call it an expletive, a swearword in its own right: For dirt's sake, dirt![23]

These problems—the special risk and license of the artist, the special requirements of the censor, the necessary time lag in the law that makes it impossible for any author to know when she was breaking the law before having been called to account for it, the impossibility of defining obscenity—make the problem of censorship much murkier in the case of obscenity and the work of art than the rather optimistic one that Strauss presents for the philosophical text.[24]

Nonetheless, despite their differences, Strauss and Woolsey do agree on one thing, and that is the teleological nature of the understanding as mirrored in texts, with censorship legitimated as the act of reason overseeing transgressions against its rule. Woolsey's account can be said to complete Strauss's account, since it awards the work of art the function of reclaiming language to make it susceptible of bearing meaning. A question arises. Is this official view of the work of art as upholding the border between telos and tautos actually consonant with the nature of literary language?

ART FOR ART'S SAKE

To address this question, we require an example. What better place to look than the text of Baudelaire, the self-proclaimed theorist of "Art for Art's sake"? We may as well start with the slogan "l'art pour l'art," coined by Victor Cousin, imitated by Woolsey, and picked up by Baudelaire in defiance of Hugo's "l'art pour le progrès." Does Baudelaire mean by his slogan the opposite of what Hugo says, namely, that art does not serve an ideology outside itself but is responsible to its own truth, to no idea but that of autotelic beauty and formal perfection? Certainly, the preposition *pour* (for) can express purposiveness, and suggest a religion of art and a celebration of symbolic language. But a coined phrase comes with two sides. *Pour* can also state an equivalence between two different interchangeable things, as in "j'ai eu un pain pour cinq francs" (I got a loaf of bread for five francs) or even among similar exchangeable things, "oeil pour oeil, dent pour dent," an eye for an eye, a tooth for a tooth. The problem expressed by "l'art pour l'art" in such a reading would be to find two equivalents interchangeable with one another, one art for another art, say poetry for painting. Baudelaire often does call attention to this underside of the poetic economy, where the poet is engaged in sniffing out terms that are equivalent as terms—rhyme words, words of equal syllables, words with alliterative possibilities, or the like. With *l'art pour l'art,* then, Baudelaire may be pointing away from the teleological toward the tedious labor of the artisan with his material.

With this duality of the work in mind, let's look at one of the poems condemned by the 1857 court, **"Les bijoux"** (reproduced at the end of the essay). The poem was polemically rebaptized by the prosecutor "Naked woman, trying on poses before her fascinated lover," and its opening lines, as translated by J. McGowan, seem to support the point: "Knowing my heart, my dearest one was nude, / Her resonating jewellery all she wore, / Which rich array gave her the attitude / Of darling in the harem of a Moor." The artifices by which the woman attracts the lover, the epithet "la très chère" ironically suggesting that the dearest one is very dear indeed (the jewels she displays having been paid for by some rich lover), contribute so many details that might have served the prosecutor's contention that Baudelaire is attempting to "give senses back to those who no longer can feel." McGowan has pushed the poem in this direction by translating the impersonal "la très chere" (literally, "the very dear one") as the more intimate "*my* dearest one," and the rather sinister "les esclaves des mores" (literally, "the slaves of Moors") to whom she is likened, as the more innocuous "*darling* in the harem of a Moor." The poem is turned into a representation of an intimate moment between lover and expert courtesan, a moment that the poet—something of an exhibitionist as well as a voyeur—is letting us share.

This reading makes the poem blatantly contradict some of Baudelaire's strong statements of preference for draped women over the nude. In *Le peintre de la vie moderne,* for instance, he writes:

> [Woman] is a general harmony, not only in her bearing and the movement of her limbs, but also in the muslins, the gauzes, the vast and shimmering clouds of material with which she envelops herself, and which are, as it were, the attributes and pedestal of her divinity; in the metal and the mineral that snake about her arms and neck, that add their sparkle to the fire of her eyes, or that chatter softly at her ear. What poet would dare, in the depiction of the pleasure caused by the appearance of a beauty, to separate a woman from her costume? . . . the two, the woman and the dress [make for] an indivisible totality.
>
> [OC 2: 714]

The stark nudity of the woman in **"Les bijoux"** contrasts with this refusal to separate woman from her dress.[25]

With this in mind, looking back again at the first lines, another reading can be seen to emerge that would be more in keeping with the accent on the enveloping garb: "The very dear one was . . . a cloud, and knowing my heart, she had reserved only her sonorous jewels. . . ." *La nue,* from *nubes,* is a term for "cloud" that a working poet, one concerned with the formal requirements of the alexandrine or of a rhyme scheme, would do well to have in mind.[26] The poem, in this translation, would contain a daring metonymy representing the dearest one by her dress. It would be playing on something of a commonplace of mid-century parnassian poetry, the topos of the cloud-wrapped goddess descending from her mountain retreat, eagerly awaited by her priest-celebrant.[27]

We can thus give two readings to the female figure: one, the crude and fleshy nude, "la très chair" (*chair* means "flesh"), which links the poem to those addressed to the courtesan Jeanne Duval; the second, a veiled and enthroned idol, "la très chaire" (*chaire* means "throne, chair"), a figure close to that glimpsed in **"La beauté"** who "reign(s) in the azure" ("trône dans l'azur").[28] Whichever reading one starts from, it is shadowed by the other.

The problem is not which reading is the right one, since the poem can and does make sense of both. The problem is rather how the poet presents their relationship in the singular gift that is the poem. But that relation is puzzling. The poet quite deliberately does not provide us with the obvious itinerary, say, exploiting the protean shape of the cloud as a metaphor for desire, and then stripping away the cloud cover to reveal the nude.[29] In **"Les bijoux,"** where no natural landscape is provided—we are in a room illuminated by an uncertain fire, with occasional light refracting from the "clairvoyant" eyes, polished limbs and sonorous jewels—such an avenue is not available. It takes an act of the mind, an observation finer than that of the eye, to find in the fleshy nude a relation to a cloud-enveloped deity. The poet has to bypass visible nature and the analogies it makes available. He has to find an allegory.[30] If **"Les bijoux"** is an allegory, what is it an allegory of?

One thing it allegorizes is the poem itself, as engendered from the homonym. Take the seemingly insignificant detail of the sonorous jewels on which the poet fastens for the length of two stanzas. Whether we consider the poem as inspired by Goddess or Courtesan, the "sonorous jewels" point away from resemblances based on what we can see (and thus to the signified) to analogies prized for their sound alone. The jewels have the audibility of signifiers, and in celebrating them, the poet celebrates analogies based on sound. A nude courtesan can substitute for a cloud-wrapped goddess if one has only one's ears to rely on.

This is remarkable, and in a way scandalous. Here is a poem that takes a dirty postcard, the representation of a gentleman eyeing a nude courtesan, and the representation of an intoxicated priest awaiting a goddess, and treats them as indistinguishable. Not only that, writing a poem for poets, the poet is only interested in the double image as possibly owed to a homophony. Allegory, which gets its "didactic effectiveness," according to Paul de Man, by making "one forget the vices it sets out to represent" [*Allegories of Reading* 74], is the right term to use for a poem that sets aside so quickly the pleasures of sex and religion in favor of a discussion of poetic form. I take it that this is the sort of quotation of an obscene image that Woolsey might approve, since it lets us know that language's sensuous existence is being depicted, and not "dirt for dirt's sake." Read as an allegory, the central conflict of the first two stanzas is over whether the poet's attention to the signifier is degrading or elevating. On the outcome of this conflict will ride a second question, whether the homonym is indeed to be understood in terms of the sounded signifier at all.

On the one side in the conflict, we have the reading of *nue* as a nude courtesan who has kept on only the sonorous jewels. The poet-as-John no sooner catches sight of the nude than his attention is distracted to the jewels; the concupiscent eye intent on seizing its pleasure gives way to the ear. The ear, always open to the word of the other, is here the organ of conscience that starts to turn the voyeur poet away from pleasure, to contemplate such questions as the evanescence of things (stanza 5), the state of his soul (stanza 6), a new form of art (stanza 7), and even his own death (stanza 8). Beyond what words mean, the ear can receive chance words; chance words can awaken us to the consideration of language as speaking through what we say about itself. The poem provides an instance of a word received as if from on high at the beginning of the second stanza, where "son bruit vif et moqueur" stands out as significant. In context, in terms of the figure visualized, the phrase is easily translated as a description of an attribute of the courtesan's jewelry, "its lively and mocking noise." But given the invitation to listen to sound, and given the proximity of the term for "noise," *bruit,* we could well mistake the possessive adjective *son* (its) for its homonym *son* (sound). Reading the rest of the line in apposition, we get a sort of definition thrown off, "sound, lively and mocking noise." A statement made about the value of sound to the poet is interfered with by the sound of the words of the statement. The interruption reveals a meaning more "elevated," poetically speaking, than the mere pleasure taken in the sensuous signifier, since here the signifier can plausibly be said to have *produced* meaning, spinning off a theoretically sound definition of what sound is. It does not emerge from the poet, who receives it rather as a listener, but seems to come from the poem itself, as it were, "divinely inspired." The poet-as-John is shown distracted away from the sensuous pleasures associated first with eye and then with ear, toward an increasingly elevated mood of introspection. The possibility is that the play of the signifier, language in its independent action, recovers an earlier state of language when words shed light by their sound.

On the other side, the *nue* can be read as the cloud-veiled Goddess anticipated by her priest-celebrant. And here things take place very differently. Awaiting her imminent manifestation, the priest gets so impatient as to start hearing sounds of her approach in advance. In keeping with her veiled approach, she has "gardé" (kept back, in reserve) her sonorous jewels, and yet the poet starts to celebrate his furious love for sound. This is a rapid degradation: eagerly anticipating the arrival of the goddess, at the first chance he gets distracted and thinks only of his own senses. A movement of falling can be traced throughout the poem, down through the final stanzas where the priest compares his idol to other Goddesses, as a connoisseur in deities (stanza 7), until finally, letting the sanctuary light go out, the poem closes with a euphemistic veil partly drawn over the final sex act.[31]

There are instances of sound play in the first stanza to support this movement of degradation. The line describing the effect of her sonorous jewels, "Dont le riche attirail lui donnait l'air vainqueur" means "whose rich array gave her the conquering air." But it also adds, distractingly, a homophone, a word that sounds the same as *don* (gift), *dont* (whose). It sounds like the priest, talking about the air the jewels give her, is giving her another gift, *don(t) . . . don(nait)*. The gift is not as innocuous as it looks, or the priest is drunker than he first appears, for he says *don . . . don*. A *dondon* is an onomatopoeic term of some vulgarity meaning "fat lady," and it would be a wounding insult from a priest, officially charged with celebrating the cult of "the dear one." The excess carried by the chance words of the sounded signifiers get in the way, threatening the overall meaning of celebration. The poem can thus be seen as diverting our attention away from its meaning, which in this reading states that the play of the signifier is the source of a threat to meaning and leads to mental distraction (*fureur*).[32] Here, the play of language does not tend toward an ideal reconciliation of sound and meaning, force and signification, but instead has a disruptive, demonic origin. It leads toward the ventriloquizing of the very words in which the priest tries to celebrate his deity.

What, then, is the outcome of the conflict between the two readings? How does Baudelaire evaluate the play with the signifier, as a divinely inspired means for producing meaning or as a dangerous, degrading fall away from Art, into sensualism?

In one of its more remarkable moves, the poem discards the question as a false question that derives from the mistaken idea that poetic language is voiced, phenomenalized language and that poems are "meant to be read aloud."[33] There are several places where it is evident that the poem labors to reject sound patterns as a source of meaning or pleasure, and can consequently be construed as finding homophony to be a diversion away from the written homonym as figure for the poem. In the first line of the second stanza, the poet explains that he loves "this radiating world of metal and stones" "(w)hen it throws off in dancing its lively and mocking sound." The line summarizes the problem succinctly by way of the ambiguous term *jette,* which can mean "emit, throw out" (with the sensuous poet celebrating the jewels as emitting sound), and also "throw off, discard" (with the meditative poet celebrating the jewels as producing meaning in the shedding of sound). But the dilemma is dispensed with quickly once we understand that dancing is not the actual situation of the poem. The poet loves this world "(w)hen . . . dancing." But that "when" is hypothetical. It is not now. The *mundus mulierbus* does not now emit or discard any noise at all. The hypothesis, with all the razzle-dazzle effects of the signifier producing meaning, is a fiction by which he

points to the actual situation of the poem, which is one of stillness and deprivation—of voice, sensation, presence, sentiment, mobility, and so forth.[34]

The poem turns out after all to be a poem of mourning. It commemorates a spoken language stilled in the form of the homonym, an utterance redoubled as it strikes the ear. Our dulled ears cannot hear a difference between *nue* and *nue,* the result of an erosion of the sound value of the letter *b* of *nubes* and the *d* of *nudus.*[35] The erosion of the written word in the mouth is not important in itself. Sound is merely what obtrudes on our notice the central problematic of deprivation and redoubling associated with the writing system. Neither priestly nor laboring poet is responsible for this riddling redoubling. *Nue* is redoubled by *nue,* as a speech act by its quotation, or as an act of consciousness by a memory trace. The homonym provides evidence of language reiterated as it appears, of a language already a writing in the midst of what presents itself as lyric, expressive language. It requires us to consider the poem in terms of the *legibility* of its traces, and not of interpretation.

But that makes the collapse and withdrawal of the homonym foreseen by the poem significant. "I follow in vain the withdrawing God," Baudelaire says in **"Le coucher du soleil romantique,"** and that movement is quite literally what he has is seized here. In 1877, the *Littré* still sees *nue* as a cloud, a synonym for *nuage* and *nuée.* But by the end of the century, when Mallarmé writes, "She, dead *nue,* in the mirror . . ." he is already taking into account the fact that *nue* is dead as a common term for "cloud."[36] A new *âge* has dawned; *nuage,* already the usual term for Baudelaire, has entirely taken over in ordinary speech about the cloudscape. The recent *Trésor de la langue française* consecrates this change, saying the term *nue* is "archaic, poetic and literary" and subsists in only a few clichés in common parlance.

Clearly, from the perspective of the referent, it doesn't matter whether one calls a cloud a *nue* or a *nuage.* But what does matter is that in this poem, access to the allegory is available only if the figure remains legible as a metonym for the goddess figure. The homonym is the key to the riddle of writing as it reduplicates (for preserving remembrance) and deprives (as disintegrating memory) the speech act of its originary force. Its loss spells the possible end of the poem's legibility. The poem takes a snapshot of a little fissure in the archive, a fracture that by our period has so widened that we almost can't get access to the chief problem of the poem. It tries to capture in its snapshot the moment of collapse where the very memory of the departing *nue* is getting lost, and with it the memory of writing as redoubling the spoken language as it originates. Far from providing a reader's pact against which to measure the value of each of its enunciations, the poem concerns itself with its inability to transmit meaning without depriving itself of legibility. However we interpret the *nue,* we are forgetting that the poem, as given in the speech act, is preserved in a writing whose legibility is already in doubt.

This little fragment provides evidence that the act of re-configuring the language as a whole, healthy body entails a loss of its legibility. That it is a small piece is not comforting, since with it goes the poem's discussion of the idol of the time, the lesson on the play of the signifier as leading to madness, and so on, but also what the text has to say about a creeping sclerosis affecting the living language. In poems, it is possible to ask where the language is in its process of becoming, as André Chénier says, "an antique writing and no longer a language." In determining language as meaning, in terms of consciousness, we become estranged from our archive.

The poem is indeed concerned with the same question of history at work in the language as Woolsey's Joyce but to very different effect. In Woolsey's view, Joyce adds quotes to obscenity to give us back the language in its pristine state. In Baudelaire's poem, a fissure shows up in the act of giving the poem that shows language ruined at the outset. Obscene language reveals the truth that language never was an intact virgin. By it we learn of a language always already affected by deprivation, not a whole body but a catalogue of parts.[37]

The poem knows about this history at work rendering illegible its bicephalous figure. In an ensuing, crucial section of the poem (stanzas 5 and 6, the stanzas that came under direct fire in the 1857 trial), it sets its task in terms of it (with the verbs *Passaient* and *S'avançaient* establishing the meditation as concerned with the past and future of the language).[38] In this section, the examination of the double-sided figure and the development of the allegory proceeds in the relative calm provided by the knowledge that the poetic figure is stilled. She lies mute on her couch, and the term *couchée,* which means "prone," "abed," but which also can mean "consigned or inscribed in a text," again points to the textual allegory. Something disturbs the quiet, however, and when it does it provides a second glimpse of the poet, now working to slow down or speed up the work of history fracturing the archive. In the fifth and sixth stanzas, the poet differentiates between those parts of the figure that pass away before his serene surveying glance and those that advance, belly and breasts, to trouble his repose. In terms of the poetic allegory, these body parts are details that draw our attention to the structural parts of the poem, the organization of its stanzas and its syntax. The poem provides a striking instance of such structuring parts in the coordinating conjunction *et,* made visible by dint of its being repeated no fewer than nine times in eight lines, three times in positions of stress.

And plays two distinct grammatical functions in the fifth stanza. It adds together like things, body parts: ". . . arm and . . . leg and . . . thighs and . . . loins"; "belly and . . . breasts." But it also adds together things considered as different: thus, it adds the two verbs— "And . . . Passed . . . and . . . Advanced"—so as to present the widely different effects of the parts on the poet, *serene* in his mastery over the parade of some passing parts; *troubled* by the advancing belly and breasts. On being able to tell the difference between *et* as enumerating like things and *et* as enumerating different things reposes the understanding of a dramatic shift in the stance of the poet.

The poet is considering his task with respect to the corrosive work of usage on the parts of the language. Certain articulations he helps wear away further by repeating, polishing them to the point of near liquefaction: those parts are "polished as with oil." They are passing away, and the poet views with serenity the stream of conventional, polished parts, for he sees other parts still potentially able to make a difference. *Et* is exemplary of both movements. It makes no difference to interpretation and could almost be replaced by commas in the list of body parts. But in the list of verbs it makes a very big difference by making available *as different* the serene and the troubled poet. The poet knows himself to be engaged in a double process: he speeds up the polishing of *and* by repeating it, and he slows down that work by reactivating the differentiating function of the conjunction.

Things change in the sixth stanza, where follows an instance of *and* outside this pattern. For besides its grammatical role, *and* also has a role to play poetically, in the formal organization of the stanzas. It links the sixth stanza to the fifth, finishing out a pattern set in the fifth stanza by the opening words of the lines: "*Et* . . . Polis . . . Passaient . . . *Et* . . . S'avançaient . . . Pour . . . *Et.*"[39] Formal questions are not accidental in the sixth stanza, which is thematically concerned with the dominance of the figure for Poetry over the poet, with her ability to shake his tranquil assumption of mastery, and thus with his subservience to her in certain matters like those of stanza organization. If we ask what function this *and* serves in terms of meaning, moreover, we would have to say it is a negative or subtracting function. The poet indulges in what can only be called a pleonasm, a needless repetition, when he says that breast and belly advanced to trouble his soul's repose and to disturb it off its crystal rock (*pour troubler le repos où mon âme était mise / Et pour la déranger du rocher de cristal . . .*). *And* does not add like or different things; it adds the same thing, said again in different words. On account of poetry, the poet is in trouble, in trouble. Half of the stanza is an exercise in redundancy, with the poet as it were forced by the demands of formal unity to finish out the stanza despite his failing inspiration.

My point is not that Baudelaire is a bad poet who ekes out his stanza by repeating in other words thoughts he has said before. Clearly, the stanza is concerned with this issue, and Baudelaire is so good a poet, because, knowing that it is a possibility plaguing any poet, he acts out a loss of poetic inspiration before the poem is finished, to ask after its effect on poet and poem. The effect is dramatically negative with respect to the interpretation that makes the poet a serene surveyor of the scene of language, picking parts to polish off and parts with a differential value worth reactivating. This master is knocked off his perch by the poetic demand for formal order *irregardless* of meaning. The term *and* enacts the fall for us. It is an *and* deprived of its additive function altogether, having the value of a "minus" sign. Nothing is added by this pleonastic *and* except formal symmetry, unless one considers a verbal gesture dramatizing in advance the poet's fall into poetic senility a fresh addition.

It could be objected that *and* can sometimes be used emphatically, at the beginning of a sentence, to introduce something startlingly original.[40] Baudelaire's poem has an example of such an *and* in the last stanza, where is introduced a view of the room that appears unconnected to the earlier stanzas, with their concentration on the female figure. It is not farfetched to interpret stanza 6 in the same way. Throughout the poem, whenever the poet is talking about his own passion, his speech has inevitably turned out to be really about "the very dear one," and what is more likely than that he is again speaking of her when he states that her breasts and belly advance "pour *la* déranger" (to disturb *her*)?[41] But in that case what the poem says is something quite different: not, the poetic form overturns the poet by forcing him to repeat his utterances; rather, the poem advances against itself, pushing *poetry* off its pedestal. The stilled figure gets mobility. Poetry thrusts herself forward against the poet's tranquil ideal of "Art for art's sake" to posit the value of the work as that of "Art against art," as *antiwork*. The androgynous figure emerging in the seventh stanza represents the poem as self-divided in exactly this way.

Reading the stanza as disruptively self-toppling makes sense in the light of earlier patterns. Everything has had to be read twice—the naked figure / the veiled goddess; its lively and mocking noise / sound, lively and mocking noise, and so on. It is not surprising that the poem should repeat the pattern of doubling at the level of these lines. But what is disruptive is that it does what it says in a new way, inventively: it states, "And to disturb *her* off her rock," but it can state this only if the over-riding pattern of doubling is advanced to cover the ut-

terance. This is an unconventional performative. It neither confirms nor denies a truth presumed to be prior to it. Rather, it blindly posits a truth that becomes one only as a result of its act of positing. The poem ceases to have the immobility of an idol only when and if it thrusts forward the disruptive reading. It is impossible to determine the legitimacy of this reading, which is at once inevitable because it is in keeping with earlier formal patterns and radically unauthorized because it has emerged without the poet's say-so, in the very enunciation where his claim is that of a technician making concessions to sheer form. The poem makes use of the poet's attempt to resolve a purely formal problem as the occasion to impose its law. Like a Straussian interpreter, the poet is alerted to the fact that structure can produce meaning. But whereas Strauss's puppy cut his teeth on a work received from a thoughtful author whose structures are calculated to teach, this reader is the putative author of the poem. He discovers in his text a lesson still to be read about the nonconvergence of meaning and structure.

However we look at it, **"Les bijoux"** outrages the axiom that makes virtue converge with knowledge. It does so by bringing to the fore problems of reading and writing centered on the memory trace. On the one side, it commemorates a redoubled sign where can be read a disintegration affecting the archive and its legibility. It situates itself at the fracture line that disconnects the text's capacity to transmit knowledge from its capacity to be read, bearing the gloomy awareness that determining language for interpretation is forgetting "the writing on the wall," that is, the writing system and the accidents that affect its legibility. By censoring the poem in 1857, the court agreed with the prosecutor that it was its job to keep from view what the poem had to say about disintegrative memory and a destabilizing fault-line in the archive. In this light, the action of the 1949 court consisted less in a liberal, uncensoring move than in a confirmation that—with the loss of the homonym from the lexicon—the poem's shocking secret about a redoubling at the source of the poem had become a secret.

The advance of the poem against its own ideal of formal unity brings out another side of the predicament. By reproducing its pattern, the poem produced something new. It produced a certain reading, a certain future for itself, as antipoem or self-toppling symbol. Here the poem is still lively. If we need any proof of that, the court's deciding opinion in 1949 that Baudelaire's poems are to be interpreted symbolically can provide it. The attempt to regulate the means of expression by imposing a reading pact on the poem, the attempt to relegate the realistic interpretation of the poem to the dustbin of history as erroneous—both are attempts to recover the poem for "responsible memory" by a partial veiling of the destabilizing, wild performative that advances the poem against itself, and that certainly can be said to find more than one realistic referent in modern life. The free agency of human subjects with respect to linguistic structures, their ability to determine whether those structures are referential or symbolic, is in doubt in this poem. The rationale for the state's attempt to limit access to such a possibility is obvious enough: where freedom of expression is a fundamental right, there is a need for a convention assigning individuals like Baudelaire authorship over their speech acts, rather than, as in this case, assigning the poem the authorship of its reader Baudelaire.[42] But at the same time, there is a need to incorporate alternatives like the one glimpsed here, where the individual's freedom of expression turns out to be limited by a nonexpressive side to language. Otherwise, the rather threatening future given by this poem written in the age of revolution—the future of a repetitive toppling of old ideologies by new acts of blind positing—might well be ours. Our modern states, after all, have come into existence on the basis of blind performatives positing interpretations that were not true before their positing.[43] It is reasonable to suppose that their survival depends in part on their ability to mask or limit partially the public visibility of violent acts like the one by which they came into existence. But, following the evidence of the poem which showed the unconventional performative emerging in the midst of the poet's attempt to confine the independent force of language to a matter of form, the attempt to limit access too much could well provide the occasion for the realization of the threat. The move the poem makes that orients it toward the future, that makes it inventive and liberating with respect to the old ideology, is the one that calls into question the poet's agency. It asks for greater publicity for the dilemma making "freedom of expression" a statement of a text's ability to mean independent of its author, even more surely than a statement of a right guaranteed an individual.

The poem from *Les fleurs du mal* reveals a challenge to laws against obscene writing. Its censoring deprived us of a poem providing negative knowledge of a disintegrating memory at work in the archive, without managing to keep the ruin out. As for the obtrusive blind performative, an open secret in this text, to restrict access to it is to seek to foreclose on a source of invention as well as of threat. The challenge is to find ways to legislate that take into account pockets where the axiom that virtue is knowledge does not pertain, where freedom of an individual's expression is limited and extended by writing, and where the agency and autonomy of the reasonable, conscious subject are in question. The state has a vested interest in the pasts and futures given by the blind performative; it needs to extend more protection to those having developed "an immoderate taste for truth" and to obscene writing, as one place where those pasts and futures obtrude.

"Les Bijoux"

La très-chère était nue, et, connaissant mon cœur,
Elle n'avait gardé que ses bijoux sonores,
Dont le riche attirail lui donnait l'air vainqueur
Qu'ont dans leurs jours heureux les esclaves des Mores.
Quand il jette en dansant son bruit vif et moqueur,
Ce monde rayonnant de métal et de pierre
Me ravit en extase, et j'aime à la fureur
Les choses où le son se mêle à la lumière.
Elle était donc couchée et se laissait aimer,
Et du haut du divan elle souriait d'aise
A mon amour profond et doux comme la mer,
Qui vers elle montait comme vers sa falaise.
Les yeux fixés sur moi, comme un tigre dompté,
D'un air vague et rêveur elle essayait des poses,
Et la candeur unie à la lubricité
Donnait un charme neuf à ses métamorphoses;
Et son bras et sa jambe, et sa cuisse et ses reins,
Polis comme de l'huile, onduleux comme un cygne,
Passaient devant mes yeux clairvoyants et sereins;
Et son ventre et ses seins, ces grappes de ma vigne,
S'avançaient, plus câlins que les Anges du mal,
Pour troubler le repos où mon âme était mise,
Et pour la déranger du rocher de cristal
Où, calme et solitaire, elle s'était assise.
Je croyais voir unis par un nouveau dessin
Les hanches de l'Antiope au buste d'un imberbe,
Tant sa taille faisait ressortir son bassin.
Sur ce teint fauve et brun le fard était superbe!
—Et la lampe s'étant résignée à mourir,
Comme le foyer seul illuminait la chambre,
Chaque fois qu'il poussait un flamboyant soupir,
Il inondait de sang cette peau couleur d'ambre!

"The Jewels"

Knowing my heart, my dearest one was nude,
Her resonating jewellery all she wore,
Which rich array gave her the attitude
Of darling in the harem of a Moor.
When dancing, ringing out its mockeries,
This radiating world of gold and stones
Ravishes me to lovers' ecstasies
Over the interplay of lights and tones.
Allowing love, she lay seductively
And from the high divan smiled in her ease
At my love—ocean's deep felicity
Mounting to her as tides draw in the seas.
A tiger tamed, her eyes were fixed on mine,
With absent air she posed in novel ways,
Whose candour and lubricity combined
Made charming all her metamorphoses;
Her shoulders and her arms, her legs, her thighs,
Polished with oil, undulent like a swan,
Passed by my tranquil and clairvoyant eyes;
Then belly, breasts, those clusters on my vine,
Came on, tempting me more than devils could
To break the peace my soul claimed as its own,
And to disturb the crystal rock abode
Where distant, calm, it had assumed its throne.
Her waist contrasted with her haunches so
It seemed to me I saw, in new design,
A boy above, Antiope below.
The painting on her brown skin was sublime!

—And since the lamp resigned itself to die,
The hearth alone lit up the room within;
Each time it uttered forth a blazing sigh
It washed with tones of blood her amber skin.

From Charles Baudelaire, *The Flowers of Evil.* Trans.
James McGowan. Intro. Jonathan Culler. Oxford: Oxford
UP, 1993. 47-49.

Notes

This paper was presented by E. S. Burt at the December 1995 conference "Censorship and Silencing: Practices of Cultural Regulation," sponsored by The Getty Research Institute for the History of Art and the Humanities, The American Academy of Arts and Sciences, and the University of California Humanities Research Institute. A full-length version will be published in February 1998 in an anthology entitled *Censorship and Silencing: Practices of Cultural Regulation,* ed. Robert C. Post. Published with the permission of The Getty Research Institute for the History of Art and the Humanities, Santa Monica, CA.

1. The decision was made possible by a law passed in 1946 allowing a judgment on a book to be appealed after twenty years had passed.

2. The popular rhymster Béranger was successfully prosecuted in 1821, for instance. According to Jean Pommier, although Béranger was pursued for "outrage à la morale publique et religieuse," his aim was "political provocation" [7]. The first attacks in the press came from the Ultras, who noted the greater freedom of expression enjoyed by verse: ". . . here we must admire the marvellous privilege of rhyme: it is doubtless as powerful as the letters of inviolacy enjoyed by our Deputies, for an unprotected citizen who had said *in prose* what M. Béranger has said in verse would certainly have had a bone to pick with the King's Prosecutor." [qtd. in Pommier 9].

In his work *Obscenity and the Law,* which draws heavily on English cases, Norman St. John-Stevas remarks on violent attacks in the press against Keats, Byron, Shelley, Tennyson, and Swinburne. As a rule, these attacks did not lead to legal problems. St. John-Stevas cites only a pirated edition of *Queen Mab* prosecuted for blasphemy. Indeed, while deploring the attacks, St. John-Stevas nonetheless finds reason to take heart in the fact that to attack poetry is to acknowledge it as an important social force. "Critical excesses are indefensible," he writes, "but the assumption of the value and relevance of poetry to the life of the community which determined their approach was sound" [49].

3. Thus Pinard explains that the government does not lose its freedom to pursue a given work because it has not pursued others equally of-fensive. If the government is reserved in some cases, it is because, judging that the work will have "no chance of being read or understood, to bring it to justice would be to indicate it to the public and perhaps assure to it the day's success it would not have had without that" [qtd. in Baudelaire 1209]. References to the trial are to Claude Pichois's account, reproduced in the notes of the Pléiade edition of Baudelaire, *Oeuvres complètes,* vol. 1.

4. It is this paradoxical situation of poems whose style removes them from ordinary experience the better to make them represent modern experience that is the point of departure for Walter Benjamin's analysis in "On Some Motifs in Baudelaire."

5. The two charges brought against a total of eleven poems were "offense to public morality" and "offense to religious morality." Only the first charge was upheld in the condemnation of six poems.

6. There is a resemblance to be noted between the critic and Baudelaire's figure for the reader in "Au lecteur," the monstrous Ennui who dreams of dramatically violent deeds while yawning and smoking his dope.

7. This is somewhat the scene as Pinard paints it. He is acutely aware that he is cast in the role of persecutor by the world of letters, and boasts of his (anti)heroism in laboring for the good of the public nonetheless.

8. A recent writer in the *New York Times,* writing of billboards plastered with sexually explicit imagery, and of lone artists (Mapplethorpe, Alpern) targeted for censorship, supports my point that it is the medium and not that message that is the lightning rod here. Vicki Goldberg writes: "The sensationalistic images that flood the visual environment appear far more frequently and get immeasurably greater distribution in the popular culture than they ever do in art. Yet art bears the brunt of public attacks" [40]. The recent show of Merry Alpern's photos that is the occasion of the article bears the Baudelairian title "Dirty Windows." Speculating from the title and the single photograph that is shown in the *Times,* we can ask whether Alpern is not breaking the rule that an artwork view things through colored windows (roseate or not), whereas in ordinary commerce we are to see things through clear windows, that is, transparent language. What Alpern does in giving us *dirtied* windows is note the presence of "color" in the apparently transparent windows of real-life sexshop bathrooms. This is subversive, and makes the show a worthy successor to Baudelaire's "Mauvais vitrier."

9. This is the source of Gadamer's interest in Strauss [see *Truth and Method* 482-91]. See also Paul de

Man, "Dialogue and Dialogism," for a discussion of Strauss and Bakhtin.

10. We are extending Strauss's argument by suggesting its consequences for the liberal state.

11. All this is well known; discussion of silencing and hate speech—concentrated as it is on the discursive situation as on the exclusion of certain groups and speech acts from the scene of "friendly" dialogue—can only take place because it is acquired. If I rehearse it here, it is as the background necessary to raise two points. The first is that the Straussian liberal state gains an astonishing flexibility and durability as a result of its disregard of content. Once the state ceases to occupy itself with dictating what can be said, the positive content of its history, the details of a moral education, and so forth, it can occupy itself instead with what Judith Butler calls the "formation" of its subjects in "Vocabularies of the Censor." It produces, for instance, out of those who state their opinions freely and explicitly normal citizens, who say exactly what they mean (although what they mean is never more than mere opinion). As for those who make use of parody or irony to write between the lines, their heterodoxy may be suspect, but it is indulged on account of the inventive energy released in the unrepressing of the performative aspect. The liberal state goes out of the business of censoring messages; instead it feeds off the energy released by such unrepressions. The second point concerns the limits that Strauss effectively places on writing between the lines by determining it as educational. A writing that appears to state an opinion in order to criticize it is a writing whose use of parody, irony, strategy, and so forth, has been limited to what can be recuperated as critique, according to a teleology where the formation of subjects is the end. But it can be asked whether this limitation on the subversiveness of writing between the lines does not, as it were, leave out leaving out, censor its own censorship, and in doing so, lose sight of aspects of writing that do not lead to education, construed positively.

12. Strauss mentions Homer, but it is only to quote the cliché "even Homer nods from time to time" [26]. Milton is also mentioned, but in the *Areopagitica*. Literary works provide a stock of images to help out in Strauss's exposition, but do not figure as instances of texts persecuted.

13. Strauss is actively repressive of one aspect of language, figurative language. He remarks, for instance, that persecution teaches good writers to avoid flowery utterances when it is a matter of uttering the hidden doctrine ("he would silently drop all the *foolish excrescences* of the liberal creed"

[25]), and on the contrary to display a flowery style when it is a matter of uttering the orthodoxy being criticized ("The attack, the bulk of the work, would consist of *virulent expansions* of the most *virulent utterances* . . ." [25]).

14. Published as part of the prefatory material in the Modern Library edition of *Ulysses* from 1934 onward.

15. Morris Ernst and Alan Schwartz cite a case lost when the defense lawyer felt unable to "mention in court or print in his brief an Anglo-Saxon word used in the novel several times by one of the characters" [95]. His inability to mention the term showed the term to be censorable. At the other extreme, the defense attorney for Baudelaire spent most of his time reading long quotations from various literary sources, with the aim of defusing the effect made by the abbreviated textual "clippings" of Pinard. The length or brevity of quotations is a recognized ploy of argument.

16. That is true of expletives, for instance, where the names for the sexual organs or functions are not used as names, but as meaningless signifiers allowing the speaker to vent feeling in language freed from referential constraints. A "motherfucking verb paradigm" is an abusive use of terms properly used to describe an Oedipal situation carried over instead to express the speaker's frustration at having to learn a difficult Latin verb. It would be an error to think the verb paradigm is being accused of incestuous sexual practices. Obscene language shocks by virtue of an abusive transfer of a term valued as a name to express the pleasure or anger the speaker feels at language being so unanchored. It is as though by taking a name in vain one made naming in vain. It is obscene to persist in substitution where metaphor as an exchange of names between entities on the basis of an observable resemblance is no longer possible.

17. He says: "Each word of the book contributes like a bit of mosaic to the detail of the picture which Joyce is seeking to construct for his readers" [xii].

18. A somewhat similar view, reported in St. John-Stevas as that of Havelock Ellis, is the theory that obscene books are not aphrodisiacs but "safety valves protecting society from crime and outrage" [189].

19. They have also to judge the extent to which the work is successful at transforming custom. It was twenty years after Ulysses was published that Woolsey decided to let it into the United States. It took ninety, and a new law allowing cases of "offense against morality" to be reheard, for *Les*

fleurs du mal to be acquitted. The cases merely dramatize the time lag that is a necessary feature of obscenity cases, where one cannot know until after the publication whether an offense is felt, and until long afterward, whether custom has been effectively transformed. Writers on the subject of obscenity laws in America and in England consistently deplore the fact that the shock that the artist must deliver in order to be true to her art opens her to accusation by any reader, however untutored, who happens to pick up the work, and equally to the unjust verdicts of fearful or unknowing judges: "Any private person can start (a prosecution), any old lady who unluckily picks out of a twopenny library a book which shocks her" [Alan Herbert's introduction to St. John-Stevas xiii]. In Baudelaire's case, journalists raised the wind. Another writer, discussing the American situation in 1976, deplores the inability of most judges to discriminate between works allowable to artistic license and hard-core pornography [Lewis 247].

20. The American Supreme Court Justice Stewart once said, for instance, that "he knew hard-core pornography when he saw it but was unable to define it" [Lewis 247]. This is a recurrent theme. Ernst and Schwartz ironically entitle one chapter "The Word Obscenity 'Defies Misunderstanding',", and cite the dictionary to show that the terms lewd, lascivious, indecent, obscene are synonyms that do not help determine the concept, but repeat it.

21. Ernst and Schwartz state the problem:

    Not all law is as untidy as the Law of the Obscene. Lawyers and jurists have always had trouble defining in a courtroom words such as "negligence" or "reckless," or drawing a picture of "The Reasonable Man." But even "reckless," for example, has some objective definable outlines. "Reckless" driving can be described in terms of speedometer reading, condition of the road, density of population in the area and traffic on the road, infirmities of the driver, condition of the vehicle, and hundreds of factors on which factual testimony might be taken. Not so with censorship of the obscene. . . . when man has had fears of such concepts as blasphemy, impiety, or obscenity, law attempts avoidance rather than solution." [244-45]

22. Woolsey's *bon mot* gets cited and recited, on both sides of the Atlantic, as if it were a definition [see, for instance, St. John-Stevas xiv].

23. See Richard Sieburth's very interesting analysis in a Foucaultian vein, "Obscenity in Baudelaire and Swinburne."

24. It is a picture not without its irony, since the peculiar exposure of the work to accusation from the public offended is such as to make censorship laws protective of individual authors from discrepant readings.

25. This a consistent theme in Baudelaire. Women are always flashing clothing. We could cite "À une passante" [*OC* 1: 72] and "Avec ses vêtements ondoyants et nacrés" [*OC* 1: 29]. Even "À une mendiante rousse" [*OC* 1: 83] spends more time looking at the holes in the dress as signs of her poverty and beauty, than peering through them for a glimpse of skin. As for "Le serpent qui danse" [*OC* 1: 29], its very skin is a shimmering fabric, not just because of its light, but presumably because it can be discarded like a dress. For Baudelaire, nudes are clothed. In this he follows André Chénier: "C'est par ses vêtements qu'elle est nue à tes yeux" ("By her clothing she is nude / cloud to your eyes" [459]).

26. At the end of *Mon coeur mis à nu* Baudelaire cites a sonnet by Théophile de Viau that rhymes *nue* with *nue*. De Viau's homonym explains a state of error, in which a dreamer takes as an airy illusion what is actually a substantial shadow: "I dreamt . . . that Philis returned. . . . Wanted her phantom to make love again, / And that, like Ixion, I should embrace a cloud. // Her shadow slides into my bed all naked [*Je songeais . . . que Philis revenue. . . . Voulait que son fantôme encore fît l'amour, / Et que, comme Ixion, j'embrassasse une nue. // Son ombre dans mon lit se glisse toute nue*]" [*OC* 1: 708].

27. Leconte de Lisle, in a poem much appreciated by Baudelaire, "Le Manchy," roughly contemporaneous with *Les fleurs du mal*, starts out his description of the approaching Muse as follows: "Beneath a fresh cloud of clear muslin / Every Sunday morning / You came to the town in a rattan palanquin / Down the slopes of the hill. / The church bell rang out . . . [*Sous un nuage frais de claire mousseline / Tous les dimanches au matin, / Tu venais a la ville en manchy de rotin, / Par les rampes de la colline. / La cloche de l'église tintait . . .*]" [169]. The approach in a swirling cloud of muslin, with a poetic fanfare of exotic terms like *palanquin* (*manchy*) and *rattan* (*rotin*), the attention called to sound, makes "Le Manchy" a near cousin of Baudelaire's "Bijoux," with its sonorous jewelry, enveloped woman, and exotic Moorish detail.

La Fanfarlo contains a description of a deity in a "ravishing hovel, that owed at once to the place of ill-repute and the sanctuary." The "radiant and sacred splendor of her nudity" is rejected by the poet, who wants her back as Colombine "with her fantastic get-up and her clown's blouse" [*OC* 1: 576-77].

28. The poem, numbered XX in the first edition, occupied the transitional position between the cycle of idealized representations of Beauty and the Jeanne Duval cycle. The two poems that Baudelaire writes to replace "Les bijoux" both insist on the double face of Beauty. In "Le masque" [*OC* 1: 23], the statue turns out to be wearing a mask and is called a "bicephalous monster." As for the Beauty of "Hymne à la beauté" [*OC* 1: 24], a series of questions state her origin to be undecidably divine or satanic, her nature that of "Angel or Siren." Both poems help us read "Les bijoux" as concerned with a redoubled face, as the execrable pun *bi-joues* supports.

29. That is the itinerary followed in "Le voyage" [*OC* 1: 129], which starts out in a natural landscape and relies on a perceivable resemblance between the forms of cloud and woman.

30. It is against the argument that *Les fleurs du mal* is redeemed by way of an allegorical intention of this sort that the prosecutor Pinard directed his heaviest fire in the 1857 trial. Without naming allegory as such, he took it upon himself to refute the claim that the work contains a teaching by way of a counterexample. Certain argument would have it, states Pinard, that the "author wanted to depict evil and its deceitful caresses, for the sake of preserving against them" [1207]. Pinard is a more sophisticated reader than many modern day censors who assume that the representation of a vice automatically leads, by the seductive power of resemblance, to its imitation.

31. It is presumably this sort of rapid degradation that so shocks the prosecutor in this poem that he claims, against the argument that the poem provides a didactic allegory, that it makes grown (male) readers "pick up easily a taste for lascivious frivolities" [1208].

32. In the essay on Tassaert in the *Salon de 1846*, Baudelaire comments on the reverse tendency of obscene literature toward degrading the divine. "Genius sanctifies everything, and if these subjects were treated with all the care and self-collection necessary, they would not be soiled by that revolting obscenity that is rather a *flourish of trumpets* than a truth." In an aside, "revolting obscenity" is associated with the miserable drawings we find hanging above the "pots fêlés et les consoles branlantes" of a prostitute's room. The *double entendre* of *branlantes* ("shaky," but also the slang for "masturbating") provides another example of the way that the excessiveness of the signifier interferes with the meaning production [*OC* 2: 443].

Baudelaire identifies puns, tautology, expletives, whatever draws attention to the signifier as interfering with meaning production with the obscene.

33. Baudelaire's observation in *Mon coeur mis à nu* about the trial, as about the reading of *The Flowers of Evil*, is apposite: "Histoire des *Fleurs du mal*, humiliation par le malentendu, et mon procès" [*OC* 1: 682]. "Malentendu" means "misunderstanding," but it is the sort of misunderstanding to which the ear exposes one (*mal-entendre—mis-hear*).

34. Once again the *Salon de 1846* has a parallel. Baudelaire tells us that melancholy is the proper attitude in front of erotic drawings: "Has it happened to you, as it has to me, to fall into great melancholy after having spent long hours leafing through erotic engravings?" [*OC* 2: 443]. In other places, Baudelaire mimes noise-making the better to discuss the seduction that consists in giving voice to what has none. In *Fusées,* for instance, he says: "Do you hear these sighs . . . these wails, these cries, these death rattles?" [*OC* 1: 651] to draw attention to the lack of any such lively sound around, and to the figural means by which the poet can make the mute text appear as speaking.

35. Note that the poem spends a good deal of time collecting *b*'s and *d*'s, as if to draw attention to the crucial missing letters.

36. Mallarmé writes the line in the 1887 revision of the 1868 sonnet we know as "Sonnet en -yx" [68]. The 1868 version had no *nue.*

37. In "À une passante," the fascinating widow is afflicted with a statue's leg; here, the "dear one" displays a museumful of polished members.

38. The poem is written in the past tense and stands out from the poems in the Jeanne Duval cycle, which are mainly in the present tense, and from the poems of the cycle on beauty, which are also in the present tense. The commentators have not known what to make of the historical vision implied. F. W. Leakey speaks of the poem as "the recollection of a privileged moment of deep intimacy" [388] but gives no account of the rather terrifying "Passaient devant mes yeux clairvoyants et sereins . . . ," with its suggestion that the poet is watching a pageant of transitory forms passing before and vanishing.

39. Michael Riffaterre is certainly right when he reproaches Claude Lévi-Strauss and Roman Jakobson for noting too many formal patterns, many of them insignificant, in their classic analysis of "Les Chats." However, with a poet like Baudelaire, so insistent on the effects of the *labor* of

poetry on the poem, one has to take into account the possibility that he may have considered the potential interference of formal poetic patterns on the meaning of the poem.

40. The first chapter of the King James version of Genesis contains striking cases of the English *and* with this force: "And the Spirit of God moved upon the face of the waters. And God said, Let there be light: and there was light." Each phrase tries to translate the disruptiveness of God's creative positing.

41. The reading is all the more plausible because Baudelaire has a habit of using the vocative "my soul" as a term of ironic endearment, so that the problem would be that of a Galatea coming to life to disturb the poet's earlier tranquil assumption of the idol's immobility and his own agility [see "Une Charogne," *OC* 1: 31].

42. Pinard's recommendation of indulgence for Baudelaire, "who is a troubled and unbalanced nature" [1209], and condemnation for a work that tries to "paint everything, describe everything, say everything" [1209] confirms this point.

43. See Derrida's discussion in "Declarations of Independence," specifically of the wild performative bringing "the good people" into legal existence.

Works Cited

Baudelaire, Charles. *The Flowers of Evil.* Trans. James McGowan. Intro. Jonathan Culler. Oxford: Oxford UP, 1993.

———. *Oeuvres complètes.* Paris: Gallimard, 1976. [*OC*]

Benjamin, Walter. "On Some Motifs in Baudelaire." *Illuminations.* New York: Schocken, 1969.

Butler, Judith. "Vocabularies of the Censor." *Censorship and Silencing: Practices of Cultural Regulation.* Ed. Robert C. Post. Santa Monica: Getty Foundation and Oxford UP, 1998.

Chénier, André. *Oeuvres complètes.* Paris: Gallimard, 1958.

de Man, Paul. *Allegories of Reading.* New Haven: Yale UP, 1979.

———. "Dialogue and Dialogism." *The Resistance to Theory.* Minneapolis: U of Minnesota P, 1986. 106-14.

Derrida, Jacques. "Declarations of Independence." *New Political Science* 15 (summer 1986): 7-15.

Douglas, Lawrence. "Policing the Past: Holocaust Denial and the Law." *Censorship and Silencing: Practices of Cultural Regulation.* Ed. Robert C. Post. Santa Monica: Getty Foundation and Oxford UP, 1998.

Ernst, Morris, and Alan Schwartz. *Censorship: The Search for the Obscene.* New York: Macmillan, 1964.

Gadamer, Hans-Georg. *Truth and Method.* New York: Crossroad, 1975.

Goldberg, Vicki. "Testing the Limits In a Culture of Excess." *New York Times* 29 Oct. 1995, sec. 2: 40.

Joyce, James. *Ulysses.* New York: Random House, 1961.

Leakey, F. W. *Baudelaire: Collected Essays, 1953-1988.* Cambridge: Cambridge UP, 1990.

Leconte de Lisle, Charles. *Poèmes barbares.* Paris: Gallimard, 1985.

Lewis, Felice. *Literature, Obscenity, and Law.* Carbondale: Southern Illinois UP, 1976.

Mallarmé, Stéphane. *Oeuvres complètes.* Paris: Gallimard, 1945.

Pommier, Jean. *Autour de l'édition originale des "Fleurs du mal."* Geneva: Slatkine, 1968.

Riffaterre, Michael. "La description des structures poétiques: Deux approches du poème de Baudelaire." *"Les Chats" de Baudelaire: Une confrontation de méthodes.* Ed. Maurice Delcroix and Walter Geerts. Namur, Belg.: Presses Universitaires de Namur, 1980.

Sieburth, Richard. "Obscenity in Baudelaire and Swinburne." *Proceedings of the XXth International Congress of Comparative Literature.* Ed. Anna Balakian. New York: Garland, 1985-87. 464-71.

St. John-Stevas, Norman. *Obscenity and the Law.* London: Secker and Warburg, 1956.

Strauss, Leo. "Persecution and the Art of Writing." *Persecution and the Art of Writing.* Glencoe, IL: Free Press, 1952. 22-37.

Appendix

Stephen Walton (essay date summer/fall 1997)

SOURCE: Walton, Stephen. "Baudelaire and the Roots of 'Négritude.'" *Dalhousie French Studies* 39/40 (summer/fall 1997): 77-88.

[*In the following essay, Walton examines the twentieth-century influence of Baudelaire in political terms, focusing in particular on the work of Aimé Césaire and the concept of "negritude."*]

Vivrons-nous jamais, passerons-nous
jamais dans ce tableau qu'a peint mon
esprit, ce tableau qui te ressemble?

(Baudelaire, **"L'invitation au voyage"**)

J'attends le coup d'aile du grand albatros
séminal qui doit faire de moi un homme
nouveau.

(Césaire, "Aux écluses du vide")

In 1967, Henri Peyre marked the centenary of Baudelaire's death with a critical evaluation of his poetic
legacy. Entitling his article rather provocatively "Remarques sur le peu d'influence de Baudelaire," Peyre,
in addition to circumscribing the influence of the "father
of modernism," concludes by signaling certain "prosaic"
defects in Baudelaire's verses:

> La forme baudelairienne s'est en effet souvent efforcée
> de côtoyer ou de raser, la prose. Elle a, ce faisant, mul-
> tiplié des prosaïsmes qui répugnent aux oreilles de
> quelques-uns d'entre nous et brisent les ailes de nos
> élans imaginatifs. Mais peut-être y a-t-il un aventure
> courage [sic], de la part d'un poète, à ne pas s'envoler
> «au-dessus des étangs, au-dessus des vallées», à rester
> proche de la laideur quotidienne et de la boue pesante,
> à s'emparer de masses de prose et à tâcher de la sou-
> lever vers plus de poésie. Goethe n'avait pas toujours
> réussi; Lamartine, Hugo non plus; Sully-Prudhomme,
> Coppée, Walt Whitman, l'unanimiste Jules Romains
> moins encore. Mais la tentative doit être toujours
> reprise si la poésie doit continuer à parler aux hommes
> en un âge positif et démocratique.
>
> (436)

Peyre's remarks are surprising. Even a superficial
comparison between Whitman, Hugo or Romains and
the cynical dandy of modernism is difficult to accept,
but the implicit attribution of a democratic or positivist
impulse is clearly undermined in the draft prefaces to
Les fleurs du mal, in which Baudelaire mocks both:

> [. . .] aucun respect humain, aucune fausse pudeur, au-
> cune coalition, aucun suffrage universel ne me con-
> traindront à parler le patois incomparable de ce siècle,
> ni à confondre l'encre avec la vertu. [. . .] Malgré les
> secours que quelques cuistres célèbres ont apportés à la
> sottise naturelle de l'homme, je n'aurais jamais cru que
> notre patrie pût marcher avec une telle vélocité dans la
> voie du *progrès*. Ce monde a acquis une épaisseur de
> vulgarité qui donne au mépris de l'homme spirituel la
> violence d'une passion.
>
> (229-30)

The cynicism and poetic elitism expressed here are both
characteristic of Baudelaire's writing during the Second
Empire, but research since Peyre's article has also
documented an earlier period of republican sympathies
leading up to 1848.[1] During this early, lesser-known
phase, Baudelaire embraced the aspirations of the
revolutionaries of 1848, and traces of these radical
convictions persist in his later work, shading the recurrent Catholic strain of his ideas. It would, then, be erroneous to correct Peyre's characterization simply by
ignoring the democratic notions he evokes. Any accurate portrait of Baudelaire must render his many intellectual and artistic contradictions as well as his corrosive irony.[2]

If the nature and extent of Baudelaire's early political
thinking have been researched, however, another
important question remains, the response to which still
may cast the mature poet in a revolutionary (if not
engagé) light: to what extent does his *poetry* have an
enduring revolutionary import? Can his own artistic
goal of a "beau style" or the "frisson nouveau" that he
introduced to French poetry (in Hugo's words), can
these claim revolutionary import either within or beyond
literature?

The question lends itself to more than one response,
and considered together the responses can seem
contradictory. The State, which responded to **Les fleurs
du mal** by condemning six of the poems, clearly read it
as a subversive text, not for reasons of style, but of
content. Then, nearly a century later, in 1949, the State
rehabilitated the censored texts and effectively consecrated the whole collection by including it in school
curricula, thereby assuring its position in the literary
canon. The initial condemnation on the basis of "outrage
à la morale publique et aux bonnes mœurs"[3] does not,
however, suffice to qualify a work as revolutionary; for
some, moreover, the subsequent canonization of the
work is ironic testimony to its *diminished* revolutionary
import:

> Le résultat obvie de la commémoration [de Baude-
> laire], n'est-ce pas la vulgarisation de cette œuvre, la
> vaporisation de ses sortilèges agressifs, la distortion de
> sa structure? [. . .] Baudelaire n'est plus dangereux: il
> est domestiqué. Avec beaucoup d'habileté, le Père Tilli-
> ette constate [. . .] cette entrée dans le classicisme des
> classes [. . .].
>
> (Kopp and Pichois 182-83)[4]

If his official, institutional status offers one means of
gauging Baudelaire's impact, another means of approaching the question is to consider his influence on
his contemporaries and on subsequent generations of
poets. While Baudelaire's influence on the major poets
of the late nineteenth century is generally acknowledged,
Peyre asserts that "l'influence des **Fleurs du mal** sur la
poésie du *vingtième siècle* [my emphasis] est à peu près
inexistante" (426). Kopp and Pichois seem to agree
with Peyre on this point, contrasting Baudelaire's *"influence"* with his *"success."* In their view, the official
contemporary sanction is a foil to his enormous success
(i.e., readership) in this century, and his nineteenth-
century poetic influence contrasts with its ostensible
absence in the twentieth century.[5]

I propose to address the question of Baudelaire's influence by examining Aimé Césaire and the notion of
"négritude," for Césaire is one poet who affirms the
twentieth-century influence that Peyre and others deny.
Furthermore, if the example of Césaire undermines
certain aspects of Peyre's argument, it also confirms the

more interesting attribution of a revolutionary impulse to Baudelaire. For in his stated goal to "extraire la *beauté* du mal,"[6] the poet asserts the possibility of transforming the vulgar and the quotidian and elevating them to the status of poetry. While the poetic transformation of *spleen,* of *ennui,* of a rotting corpse, may not have any apparent political significance, the elevation of the abject is inherently subversive because it implicitly challenges the social forces that determine literary conventions. I propose to show that there is a clear filiation between this aspect of Baudelaire and the fundamental assertions of Césaire's work.

In an essay published in 1945 entitled "Poésie et connaissance," Aimé Césaire defines the essential characteristics of poetry, which he conceptualizes as a form of knowing, fundamentally different and more penetrating than the scientific mode of knowing.[7] In setting out his argument, which is strongly influenced by the Surrealists' tenets that he adopted in the 1930s, Césaire sketches a brief history of modern French poetry that begins with Baudelaire. "La France mourait de prose," he writes, when a dramatic change took place in literature, by which the Apollonian era of controlled, measured verse began to give way to the modern, Dionysian era:

> La nation la plus prose, en ses membres les plus éminents, par les voies les plus escarpées, [. . .] les seules que j'accepte de dire sacrées et royales—avec armes et bagages—passa à l'ennemi. Je veux dire à l'armée à tête de mort de la liberté et de l'imagination.
>
> La France prose passa à la poésie. Et tout changea.
> [. . .]
> La poésie devint une aventure. La plus belle des aventures . . . À son terme: voyance et connaissance.
> Donc Baudelaire . . .
>
> (1978b:159)

In characterizing its *littérateurs* and *littérature* as France's "membres les plus éminents, [s]es voies les plus escarpées, [. . .] sacrées et royales," Césaire celebrates the transfer of literary power from *prosateurs* to the poets of modernity. Although he is vague about what he means by "prose," the context suggests the kind of narrative description for which literary Realism claimed quasi-scientific objectivity.[8]

To illustrate Baudelaire's contribution to the literary and epistemological revolution, Césaire singles out three poems in *Les fleurs du mal* that speak of the poet's unique capacity for spiritual "pénétration de l'universe" (1978b:159). This is Césaire's way of denoting a form of knowing that, like automatic writing for the Surrealists, provides access to fundamental levels of existence closed to rationality and logic. The essential element in

his poetic epistemology is metaphor, and he traces modern metaphor to Baudelaire and to what literary history refers to as the symbolist notion of metaphor. He does not cite specific sources in this regard (his is a manifesto and not a scholarly article), but the following, slightly ironic pronouncement from the third draft preface to *Les fleurs du mal* seems to underly Césaire's understanding of metaphor:

> Que la phrase poëtique peut imiter (et par là elle touche à l'art musical et à la science mathématique) la ligne horizontale, la ligne droite ascendante [. . .]; qu'elle peut suivre la spirale, décrire la parabole, ou le zigzag figurant une série d'angles superposés;
>
> Que la poésie se rattache aux arts de la peinture, de la cuisine et du cosmétique par la possibilité d'exprimer toute sensation de suavité ou d'amertume, de béatitude ou d'horreur *par l'accouplement de tel substantif avec tel adjectif, analogue ou contraire* [. . .].
>
> (230-31; my emphasis)[9]

By facilitating the unlimited substitution of terms, and establishing relationships between otherwise antithetical categories and concepts, modern metaphor frees thought from the confines of rationality and opens truth to the imagination. Césaire even suggests that scientific truth, at its best, can only confirm the superior virtue of metaphor, or of the *image,* as it is referred to in the following passage:

> Parce que l'image étend démesurément le champ de la transcendance et le droit à la transcendance, la poésie est toujours sur le chemin de la vérité. Et parce que l'image sans cesse dépasse le perçu, parce que le dialectique de l'image transcende les antinomies, à tout prendre la science moderne n'est peut-être que la vérification pesante de quelques folles images lancées par des poètes [. . .].
>
> (1978b:167)

This understanding of metaphor owes much to the Surrealists; as we have seen, it also is grounded in Baudelaire.

Césaire develops his conception of poetic force based on metaphor in two distinct ways in "Poésie et connaissance," both of which are inspired and supported by Baudelaire. First, he claims for the true poet a privileged knowledge of nature, with which we are familiar from "Élévation" (159)[10]; second, he suggests that poets have the same power to tell the future that Baudelaire attributes to the Gypsies in "Bohémiens en voyage" (160). This power to tell the future is not prophetic in the normal sense of the word. Césaire conceives of poetry as a means for imaginative exploration of his psyche, of its weaknesses and its potential within his particular historical context. Since poetry in this sense enables the poet to define and discern himself, it is constitutive of his future.[11]

Finally, and most significantly, this poetic force is embodied in his work, in the proliferation of surrealistic metaphors *à la* Reverdy.[12]

In *Les fleurs du mal,* one of the salient signs of the poet's transformative power is the albatross. The seabird plays a comic role when it is forced by sailors to waddle awkwardly on deck, dragging its long wings; it is by virtue of those same wings, however, that it can soar far above the site of its humiliation and attain the ideal. In **"L'albatros,"** the emphasis is on the bird's alienation in the everyday world and the ridicule it provokes among the people, ignorant of and unmoved by its transcendent calling:

> Ce voyageur ailé, comme il est gauche et veule!
> Lui, naguère si beau, qu'il est comique et laid!
> L'un agace son bec avec un brûle-gueule,
> L'autre mime, en boitant, l'infirme qui volait!
>
> (36)

The albatross, symbolizing the poet, is misunderstood and ridiculed by society, but capable of transcendence by virtue of the same artistic wings that render him comical in the public's eyes.

In Césaire, one emblem of this same "albatrossness" is "négritude," which I will here characterize as Africans' literary affirmation of their people in response to and in defiance of a long history of colonialist social denigration.[13] The intertextual connection linking these two strands is made explicit by an allusion to Baudelaire's poem in Césaire's *Cahier d'un retour au pays natal.* The *Cahier* was first published in 1939, and it is the first poetic text in which Césaire's neologism "négritude" appears. Written in Europe near the end of his sojourn as *normalien,* the poem is an attempt to come to terms with the misery and wretchedness of his own people that confronted him during a return to Martinique in 1936. Near the middle of this long text the narrator describes a destitute *nègre* asleep on a bench in a tramway car, a man whose exaggerated features and pitiful condition all but caricature the stuff of racial stereotypes:

> La misère, on ne pouvait pas dire, s'était donné un mal fou pour l'achever.

> Elle avait creusé l'orbite, l'avait fardée d'un fard de poussière et de chassie mêlées.

> Elle avait tendu l'espace vide entre l'accrochement solide des mâchoires et les pommettes d'une vieille joue décatie. Elle avait planté dessus les petits pieux luisants d'une barbe de plusieurs jours. Elle avait affolé le cœur, voûté le dos.

> Et l'ensemble faisait parfaitement un nègre hideux, un nègre grognon, un nègre mélancolique, un nègre affalé, ses mains réunies en prière sur un bâton noueux. Un nègre enseveli dans une vieille veste élimée. Un nègre comique et laid et des femmes derrière lui ricanaient en le regardant.

> Il était COMIQUE ET LAID,
>
> COMIQUE ET LAID pour sûr.
>
> (1983:62)

"Comique et laid" is, of course, an allusion to the lines from **"L'albatros"** quoted above. Did the phrase occur only once, the allusion might go unnoticed, but Césaire takes it up twice more and places it in capitals. Marking the adjectives in this way produces a twofold effect: first, it seems to summarize the pathetic description of the *nègre* in an emphatic mode. Far more importantly, it invites and indeed demands that the reader recognize a parallel between this *nègre* and Baudelaire's albatross. This parallel serves as a catalyst which will ultimately transform the already overdetermined (one might even say "baroque") representation of *misère* in the passage. What appears to be the final, emphatic word on the tramway bum—his comic ugliness—is not to be read as the final word at all, for the flip side of the albatross's public humiliation is its capacity for flight and transcendence, and this potential will be actualized subsequently in the poem.[14]

In *Les fleurs du mal,* both humiliation and transcendence are a recurring theme. When they characterize the poet and his enterprise, they often attest to Baudelaire's elitist conviction that the poet and society stand in a relationship of fundamental otherness to each other.[15] This polarized relationship can have either a positive or a negative orientation. In many poems, Baudelaire's melancholy, his sense of persecution, his hatred of *ennui* and his anxiety in the face of death—his *spleen,* in short—are all unmitigated by any redemptive power. **"L'albatros"** offers such a negative example, since the sailors' negation of the bird's transcendence dramatizes the poet's exile and his alienation. Ultimately, however, the positive aspect of his imagination remains a defining trait of the poet. It is this trait which enables him to transform the sickly body of the *mendiante rousse* into an object of beauty, and the foulness of winter into spring:

> L'Émeute, tempêtant vainement à ma vitre,
> Ne fera pas lever mon front de mon pupitre;
> Car je serai plongé dans cette volupté
> D'évoquer le Printemps avec ma volonté.
>
> (**"Paysage"** 114)

In other instances, the imagination enables the poet to triumph over the people's scorn. In **"Bénédiction,"** for example, the religious lexicon underscores the poet's quasi-religious capacity to transform the mother's milk of hatred into goodness and light. It is this same potential for transformation that Césaire invokes in alluding to **"L'albatros."** The *Cahier* actualizes the same polarized relationship between bird and sailors, and its subsequent reversal, with colonial society and its attendant racist ideology playing the latter role, and the poet and his people playing the role of an ultimately triumphant albatross.[16]

The representation of the *nègre du tramway* is limited to a single page. He is represented only in a state of abject misery, no further mention of him being made in the poem, and he undergoes no transformation of the kind that I have been suggesting. He stands as an icon of the depravity and destitution of Martinican blacks, and his appearance is a culminating moment, for he epitomizes the *bassesse* of Fort-de-France—"cette ville plate-étalée" (1983:34)—evoked in the early lines of Césaire's text. As such, the tramway bum's *laideur comique* serves as a transition to the narrator's own identification with and confession of an ugliness that he has heretofore refused.[17] This ugliness is not only the ugliness of being black in a colonial society, the result of one's ideological and psychological position of "other" in the eyes of the white bourgeoisie; it is also the *moral* ugliness of his own complicity with that ideology. For, like the women on the tramway, he too snickers at the abjectness of the "tramway nigger," just as Baudelaire's sailors laugh at the albatross:

> [. . .] Un nègre comique et laid et des femmes derrière lui ricanaient en le regardant.
>
> Il était COMIQUE ET LAID,
> COMIQUE ET LAID pour sûr.
> J'arborai un grand sourire complice . . .
> Ma lâcheté retrouvée!
>
> (62)

The poet's *lâchete* consists not only in the amusement he shares with the women; it is implicit in the stereotypical terms of the representation, because the man's color and his wretchedness are correlative: the poet-onlooker's amusement is the natural manifestation of an alienated perspective, by which he looks on his own people with the "introjected" prejudice that he has acquired as a colonial subject. The poet's representation of the *nègre* tells as much about his own bad faith as it does about the one he describes.

From this point onward in the poem, the *mal* of blackness is understood to be both collective and personal: it comprehends both the poverty of his people and the poverty of his own spirit. Césaire devotes pages to an exploration of his complicity and its psychological and historical roots and ramifications, and it is this personal and social *autocritique* that initiates the Baudelairian transformation: liberated from the oppressive confines of institutionalized racism and his own complicity with it, the albatross can then soar to its splendid height. Colonial alienation is the soil from which the poet extracts the flower of "négritude," poetically transforming his "otherness" and ugliness by means of a collective affirmation of that otherness.[18]

The affirmation first begins with an acknowledgment and acceptance of his people's history and the depths of their suffering. The pathetic description of that history implicates both his own and his people's "lâcheté":

> Au bout du petit matin, flaques perdues, parfums errants, ouragans échoués, coques démâtées, vieilles plaies, os pourris, buées, volcans enchaînés, morts mal racinés, crier amer. J'accepte!
>
> [. . .]
>
> et le nègre chaque jour plus bas, plus lâche, plus stérile, moins profond, plus répandu au dehors, plus séparé de soi-même, plus rusé avec soi-même, moins immédiat avec soi-même,
>
> j'accepte, j'accepte tout cela.
>
> (76)

While this litany of colonial suffering hardly seems affirmative in nature, it does constitute an acceptance of history that was not yet evident in the representation of the *nègre du tramway*. Its significance is confirmed in the next lines, in which emerges, suddenly and without transition, the new affirmation:

> Et voici soudain que force et vie m'assaillent comme un taureau et l'onde de vie circonvient la papille du morne, et voilà toutes les veines et veinules qui s'affairent au sang neuf et l'énorme poumon des cyclones qui respire et le feu thésaurisé des volcans et le gigantesque pouls sismique qui bat maintenant la mesure d'un corps vivant en mon ferme embrasement.
>
> Et nous sommes debout maintenant, mon pays et moi, les cheveux dans le vent, ma main petite maintenant dans son poing énorme et la force n'est pas en nous, mais au-dessus de nous, dans une voix qui vrille la nuit et l'audience comme la pénétrance d'une guêpe apocalpytique.
>
> (76)

This climactic point is visionary in nature. The poet's exultation here is unmistakable, and is founded on the representation of a vibrant black community, united by its own symbols, its Antillean context, its history and a positive vision of its future. The poetic vision is of course not revolutionary in and of itself: the poet's work is a work of the imagination, and alone it does not transform the social, economic or political structures that have shaped and still shape the history of the African diaspora. We have seen already that poetry, for Césaire, is a means of individual self-exploration and self-transformation, a form of knowledge that is informed by the historical situation and attained through the imaginative power of metaphor.[19] As he states in "Poésie et connaissance":

> Quand arrive au zénith, le soleil de l'image, tout redevient possible . . . Les complexes de la malédiction se dissipent c'est le moment des émergences . . .
>
> Ce qui émerge c'est le fond individuel. [. . .]

[. . .] Nous sommes ici [. . .] au cœur même de
l'homme, au creux bouillonnant de son destin.

(1978b:167)

However, to say that Césaire's poetry serves first of all
a personal, individual function, is not to deny its efficacy as the initial movement in a broader, social and
historical transformation. In the *Cahier,* the poet speaks
of the efficacy of his poetic words, saying: "Je force le
membrane vitelline qui me sépare de moi-même; / Je
force les grandes eaux qui me ceinturent de sang" (56).
These lines evoke the active birthing of a new, disa-
lienated self, and at the same time they evoke the
transformation of a collective past, a forcing of the
ocean waters colored by the blood of Africans drowned
in the middle passage to the "New World." As Scharfman has suggested, the transformation begins with the
creation of the new signifier, "négritude," the new poetic
word that rises up to begin a new history, for the poet
and new generations of readers (Scharfman 61-62, 64).

In its broadest terms, then, this new signifier is part of
the Baudelairian legacy that is actualized by Césaire.
"Négritude" is in this sense fundamentally concerned
with a people's ability to refuse an ideologically-
imposed definition, and in so doing to renew and
transform its understanding of itself. It is not primarily
about essentialist formulations of biological or metaphysical characteristics that would distinguish blacks
from other races, but rather about the *value* that those
people can claim for themselves, and the human capacity to affirm that "il-est-beau-et-bon-et-légitime-d'être-
nègre" (1983:82). The seeds of that transformation lie
initially in the work of the poetic imagination, and it is
this assertion that Césaire found in Baudelaire. That it
takes a very different form in Césaire is not surprising,
since it is in the nature of a legacy to be transformed by
its heirs. In this instance, indeed, stasis would be impossible, since the legacy in question is itself the (poetic)
power to transform a given reality.

The question of Baudelaire's continuing influence thus
finds an answer in Césaire if the meaning of "influence"
is approached in a less obvious manner than Peyre allows. Kopp and Pichois at least seem to recognize the
fecundity of **Les fleurs du mal** in our own century as
well as Baudelaire's: "[. . .] les virtualités que contient
l'œuvre baudelairienne, sa charge (au sens électrique)
se révèlent parfois au contact d'une pensée poétique al-
lophyle" (182). So it is in the case of Césaire: the intertextual link between **"L'albatros"** and Césaire's *Cahier*
shows that the poetic current has continued to flow in
this century. Indeed, Césaire's work renews and
broadens our own understanding of the transformative
power of Baudelaire.

Notes

1. See the chronology outlined by Hambly, who
   shows that Baudelaire's radical republican sentiments, fervent prior to 1848, diminished significantly in the disillusion following 1848, and even
   more so after the fall of the Second Republic.

2. Cf. Burton: "The only enduring characteristic of
   the Baudelairean *homo duplex* is the consistency
   of his contradictions, the constancy of his dubieties
   and divisions" (356). Burton's thorough study
   presents an informed and engaging look at Baudelaire's political convictions and skillfully follows
   the twists and turns of the poet's political, artistic
   and religious thinking. He concludes that Baudelaire's *engagement* was the brief flower of a youthful commitment to radical ideas. Events after
   1848, and especially Napoléon III's *coup d'état,*
   caused Baudelaire to return to the Catholic
   bedrock of his worldview, and his republican sentiments were ultimately displaced by the cynical,
   elitist spirit of his later writing. Other useful
   analyses of Baudelaire's shifting sympathies can
   be found in Drost who considers the poem "As-
   sommons les pauvres," Baudelaire's response to
   Millet's work, and the role of Baudelaire's irony
   (see especially pp. 43-45). For a deconstructionist
   approach to socio-political and gender contradictions in one Baudelaire text, see G. Friedman.

3. "Jugement contre Baudelaire," in "Dossier des
   Fleurs du mal" (Baudelaire 242).

4. The entry of Baudelaire's poetry into the realm of
   "classic" literature does not, of course, signify its
   loss of æsthetic power. Indeed, when Austin
   discusses the prophetic power of this poetry, it is
   primarily to its æsthetic aspect, its capacity to
   move the reader, that he directs his attention: "The
   value of *Les fleurs du mal* as a whole lies not so
   much in the book's explicit subject-matter nor in
   its ideological superstructure, as in its implicit
   content and its underlying attitudes, and above all
   [. . .] in its art" (17-18).

5. This approach has some thorny aspects. Kopp and
   Pichois carefully distinguish between Baudelaire's
   "success," defined as the size and scope of his
   reading audience, and his "influence," defined as
   the impulse which a work transmits to other poets
   and a poetic tradition, as well as the extent to
   which it shapes academic literary scholarship
   (173-78). On this basis, they ultimately concur
   that Baudelaire's influence on poetry is limited to
   the nineteenth century: "La démonstration de M.
   Peyre serait-elle donc à reprendre? Nous ne le
   croyons pas. La difficulté naît de l'emploi du mot
   «influence». Ce que M. Peyre semble entendre par
   «influence» c'est, plus que la fécondation poétique, la réaction critique, l'hommage rendu à
   l'initiateur de la poésie moderne" (177). In my
   own view, however, their conclusion is unfounded
   or, at the very least, muddy. To suggest that Peyre

is speaking not of artistic fecundity but of the influence on *critics* is belied by the source: Peyre unambiguously states that the influence of *Les fleurs du mal* on twentieth-century *poetry* is non-existent.

6. "Projets de Préface" (Baudelaire 229).

7. For a critical discussion of Césaire's thesis, see Arnold 67.

8. It would be interesting to determine how much of Césaire's account owes its outlines to Marcel Raymond, since Raymond's classic text, *De Baudelaire au Surréalisme,* was published in 1933, at the same time Césaire was enrolled at the École Normale Supérieure. Arnold also notes this similarity in his analysis of "Poésie et connaissance" (65).

9. It is of course risky to attribute to Césaire an implicit reference to this or that statement of Baudelaire. This is especially true in this instance, since Césaire elsewhere takes pains to reject the notion of poetic *musicality* espoused by Valéry, claiming that "[l]a recherche de la musique est le crime contre la musique poétique qui ne peut être que le battement de la vague mentale contre le rocher du monde" (1978b:170). Even though he rejects the musical analogy, however, Césaire's claims for the virtue of the image and its performative aspect are otherwise analogous to Baudelaire's claims for the poetic line, and so I believe that the parallel is justified.

10. "Heureux celui qui [. . .] // comprend sans effort / Le langage des fleurs et des choses muettes!" (*Fleurs du mal* 32, vv. 15-20).

11. "[T]he most complex [of Césaire's] texts are often the working through of a particular solution to that poem's problems. [. . .] We read each text as an enactment of some conflict by or for the subject. The subject's self-imposed containment within the confines of poetic form has great metaphorical value. [. . .] Like Houdini, the subject experiments with its power to liberate itself from its own traps. The psychic function of such an exercise for a subject haunted by the memory of slavery should not be underestimated" (Scharfman 4-5).

12. "L'image est une création pure de l'esprit. / Elle ne peut naître d'une comparaison mais du rapprochement de deux réalités plus ou moins éloignées. / Plus les rapports des deux réalités rapprochées seront lointains et justes, plus l'image sera forte—plus elle aura de puissance émotive et de réalité poétique [. . .]" (Breton 31).

13. The basis of this definition of "négritude" is Césaire's *Cahier d'un retour au pays natal,* and the poet's proclamation that "il-est-beau-et-bon-et-légitime-d'être-nègre" (1983:82). This is close to Arnold's "minimal definition" of "négritude": "the right to be black and to affirm one's blackness" (62). By insisting here on the combined literary and historical contexts for the term, I hope to avoid the confusion which inevitably results when "négritude" is framed in terms of specific racial determinants. See also Arnold's discussion of this question and of the conceptual difficulties engendered by broader, Césairian formulations of "négritude" (61-63).

14. This same intertextual node linking the *Cahier* to "L'albatros" is the basis for Rosello's article. Rosello reads the first occurrence of "comique et laid" as a sign of the poet's alienation within the French language, since "the Baudelairian reference at first appears without any signs of quotation, [. . .] irrevocably absorbed by the word that the poet thinks he is speaking, but that in fact speaks him" (186). In her view, the two repetitions of the allusion reflect the narrator's coming to consciousness and his discovery of his own alienation within a poetic tradition that is not his own. While I am in complete agreement that the emphatic repetition is significant, I see two problems with this reading. First, it overlooks the fact that, in "L'albatros," "comique et laid" does not reflect the *poet*'s viewpoint of the bird (or of himself), but rather the *sailor*'s view, which the poet presents in order to undermine it. The original, ironic context of the allusion is an essential element, and it is carried intact into Césaire's text. Secondly, the relationship of the *Cahier* poet to Baudelaire is not problematic in the way that Rosello suggests. Baudelaire, "this canonized white poet, the origin of [the poet's] discourse" (188), does not represent the same "other" as the French-speaking slavemasters or even the instructors in colonial schools. Indeed, it seems more appropriate to say that Baudelaire exemplifies the very kind of opposition to dominant ideologies that Césaire espouses. That is why the literary timeline in "Poésie et connaissance" begins with Baudelaire. While Césaire's complicity with the snickering women *does* pose a moral problem for the narrator, and one the poem explores thoroughly, Rosello's characterization of his relationship to Baudelaire and modern French literature as a tragic and irreparable exile seems not to do justice to the poet. Furthermore, Césaire's own attitude toward the colonizer's language, while problematic, is not so fraught with anguish as she suggests. Language, in fact, is one forum where this "colonized" poet can exercise mastery, as he makes clear in an interview with Jacqueline Leiner: "Ah, moi, je ne suis pas prisonnier de la langue française! Seulement, j'essaie,

j'ai toujours voulu *infléchir* le français. Ainsi, si j'ai beacoup aimé Mallarmé, c'est parce qu'il m'a montré, parce que j'ai compris à travers lui, que la langue, au fond, est arbitraire" (Césaire 1978a:xiv). Ultimately the *Cahier* is a triumphant text in which the poet's own alienation is transformed; it is not a testament to despair.

15. Fairlie has pointed out that the notion of the creative artist spurned by the public is an important topos in the Romantic conception of the poet (36).

16. In Riffaterre's terminology, "L'albatros" could be seen as the "hypogram" of the entire *Cahier,* if we use the notion of a hypogram as defined in *Semiotics of Poetry*: "the production of the poetic sign is determined by *hypogrammatic derivation: a word or phrase is poeticized when it refers to [. . .] a preexistent word group* [e.g., "comique et laid"]. The hypogram is already a system of signs comprising at least a predication, and it may be as large as a text. The hypogram may be [. . .] actual, therefore observable in a previous text" (23). The word *albatros* is thus the hypogram that underlies the *Cahier* in the sense that the poem represents the oppression and abasement of the Martinican people (epitomized by the *nègre du tramway*), as well as the triumphant affirmation of "négritude." Oppression and transcendance are already contained in the alternate fates of Baudelaire's poetic bird. Moreover, the word *albatros* itself echos the word *atroce,* an epithet whose semes are actualized in the description of the *nègre du tramway.*

17. For a detailed analysis of the relationship between the poet's confession and critique of his own *lâcheté* and the subsequent transformation of blackness from a negative to a positive attribute, see Scharfman 55-57.

18. This does not mean, of course, that colonialism should be viewed as a salubrious influence in Césaire's experience. It is simply the given historical fact, which Césaire must and does transform in order to come to terms with his own alienation.

19. This notion of poetic self-discovery is central to Scharfman's analysis of Césaire's poetry: "[I]dentity is linked to the poetic praxis throughout the *Cahier.* In fact, it can be read as a dual apprenticeship in a common project, a coming-into-being-of-the-subject-as-writer, not unlike that of Proust's *À la recherche du temps perdu.* [. . .] The form, the scope, the themes, are of course different, but the project is similar" (30).

References

Arnold, A. James. *Modernism and Negritude: The Poetry and Poetics of Aimé Césaire.* Cambridge: Harvard University Press, 1981.

Austin, Lloyd. "Baudelaire: Poet or Prophet?" *Poetic Principles and Practice: Occasional Papers on Baudelaire, Mallarmé and Valéry.* Cambridge: Cambridge University Press, 1987. 1-18.

Baudelaire, Charles. *Les fleurs du mal.* Paris: Poésie/Gallimard, 1972.

Breton, André. "Manifeste du surréalisme" [1924]. *Manifestes du surréalisme.* Folio Essais. Paris: Gallimard, n.d. 12-60.

Burton, Richard D. E. *Baudelaire and the Second Republic: Writing and Revolution.* Oxford: Clarendon Press, 1991.

Césaire, Aimé. 1978a. "Entretien avec Aimé Césaire par Jacqueline Leiner." *Tropiques.* Paris: Jean-Michel Place. I:v-xxiv.

———. 1978b. "Poésie et connaissance." *Tropiques.* Paris: Jean-Michel Place. II (n° 12):157-70.

———. 1983. *Cahier d'un retour au pays natal. Aimé Césaire: The Collected Poetry.* Trans. Clayton Eshleman and Annette Smith. Berkeley: University of California Press. 32-85.

Drost, Wolfgang. "Baudelaire between Marx, Sade and Satan." *Baudelaire, Mallarmé, Valéry: New Essays in Honour of Lloyd Austin.* Eds. Malcolm Bowie *et al.* Cambridge: Cambridge University Press, 1982. 38-57.

Fairlie, Alison. *Baudelaire*: Les fleurs du mal. Studies in French Literature 6. Great Neck, NY: Barron's, 1960.

Friedman, Geraldine. "Baudelaire's Theory of Practice: Ideology and Difference in 'Les yeux des pauvres'." *PMLA* 104.3 (May 1989):317-28.

Hambly, Peter S. "Idéologie et poésie: notes sur Baudelaire et ses contemporains." *Australian Journal of French Studies* 16.2:198-213.

Kopp, Robert, and Claude Pichois. "La fortune de Baudelaire." *Les années Baudelaire.* Etudes baudelairiennes 1. Neuchâtel: Éditions de la Baconnière, 1969. 173-83.

Peyre, Henri. "Remarques sur le peu d'influence de Baudelaire." *Revue d'histoire littéraire de la France* 2 (avril-juin 1967):424-36.

Riffaterre, Michael. *Semiotics of Poetry.* Bloomington: Indiana University Press, 1984.

Rosello, Mireille. "One More Sea to Cross: Exile and Intertextuality in Aimé Césaire's *Cahier d'un retour au pays natal.*" *Yale French Studies* 83.2:176-95.

Scharfman, Ronnie Leah. Engagement *and the Language of the Subject in the Poetry of Aimé Césaire.* University of Florida Monographs, Humanities 59. Gainesville: University of Florida, 1980.

Songolo, Aliko. *Aimé Césaire: une poétique de la découverte.* Paris: L'Harmattan, 1985.

Nina Tucci (essay date 1997)

SOURCE: Tucci, Nina. "Baudelaire's 'La Vie antérieure.'" In *Understanding* Les Fleurs du Mal: *Critical Readings,* edited by William J. Thompson, pp. 16-34. Nashville, Tenn.: Vanderbilt University Press, 1997.

[In the following essay, Tucci examines the poem "La Vie antérieure" as a drug-induced vision, with reference to ideas present in the work of Aldous Huxley, C. G. Jung, and Gaston Bachelard.]

> J'ai longtemps habité sous de vastes portiques
> Que les soleils marins teignaient de mille feux,
> Et que leurs grands piliers, droits et majestueux,
> Rendaient pareils, le soir, aux grottes basaltiques.
>
> (4)
>
> Les houles, en roulant les images des cieux,
> Mêlaient d'une façon solennelle et mystique
> Les tout-puissants accords de leur riche musique
> Aux couleurs du couchant reflété par mes yeux.
>
> (8)
>
> C'est là que j'ai vécu dans les voluptés calmes,
> Au milieu de l'azur, des vagues, des splendeurs
> Et des esclaves nus, tout imprégnés d'odeurs,
>
> (11)
>
> Qui me rafraîchissaient le front avec des palmes,
> Et dont l'unique soin était d'approfondir
> Le secret douloureux qui me faisait languir.
>
> (14)

In general, critics agree that Baudelaire's **"La Vie antérieure"** is a drug-induced experience, a psychedelic vision, to use a more modern term (see, for example, Claude Pichois's commentary in the Pléiade edition of Baudelaire's complete works as well as other works listed in the bibliography). Indeed, a reassessment of the poem from this point of view is a timely task, for it creates a link to the modern drug culture, but more important, it continues to underscore the universal longing of the human psyche to transcend itself.

In the modern classic *The Doors of Perception,* the noted religious scholar Aldous Huxley states: "That humanity at large will ever be able to dispense with Artificial Paradises seems very unlikely. . . . [The] urge to escape, the longing to transcend . . . if only for a few minutes is, and always has been, one of the principal appetites of the soul" (62). Huxley's statement

is a commentary on his own chemically induced experience with the transcendent. He ingested mescaline to alter his ordinary state of consciousness in order to understand "from the inside" the vision of the seer, the medium, the mystic, the poet, and the artist (14). The drug temporarily suppressed the localized or subjective aspect of the self to allow what Huxley calls (and indeed what contemplatives, philosophers, mystics, and artists both Eastern and Western since time immemorial have called) the "Not-Self," the objective or nontransitory aspect of the human psyche, to emerge. The drug, he explains, rendered him indifferent to ordinary time and space, and his heightened sense of perception permitted him as Not-Self to participate in the Not-Self of all that surrounds him—in a word, the pure existence or eternal Being of all things ("this timely bliss of seeing"). Subject and object became one (35, 40). Speaking from beyond the boundary of ego, Huxley finds himself agreeing with Bergson's idea that each individual is potentially a "Mind-at-Large" (Not-Self). In other words, each person is "at each moment capable of remembering all that has ever happened to him and of perceiving everything that is happening everywhere in the universe" (22-23). "Mind-at-Large," continues Huxley, is necessarily filtered through the "reducing valve of the brain and the nervous system" to protect the ordinary mortal from being overwhelmed by an utter invasion of information (23). Yet a nostalgic intuition of this inherent potential for expanded awareness is ever present in the human psyche.

In recent history, the drug culture has claimed numerous adherents; however, only the artistic elite, contends Huxley, brings back reports from the transcendent country of the mind (see, for example, the winter 1993 issue of *Gnosis,* which examines psychedelics as harbingers of an awakening of human consciousness). The distinction between the poet (artist and so forth) and the untalented visionary resides not in the quality of the vision but rather in the inability of the latter to express and give form to the inner experience. Huxley concludes:

> From the records of religion and surviving monuments of poetry and the plastic arts, it is very plain that, in most places, men have attached more importance to the inscape than to objective existents, have felt that what they saw with their eyes shut possessed a spiritually higher significance than what they saw with their eyes open. . . . The outer world is what we wake up to every morning of our lives, is the place where . . . we must try to make our living. In the inner world there is neither work nor monotony. We visit it only in dreams and musings. . . . What wonder, then, if human beings in their search for the divine have generally preferred to look within!
>
> (46-47)

The accounts of poets, mystics, and artists attest to the universality of the spiritual experience and have created an ahistorical fraternity that transcends the barriers of time and space. Thus we can link, for example, Huxley's classic to Baudelaire's *Les Paradis artificiels.*

The poet's chronicle of his psychedelic experience is quasi-identical to that of Huxley. Baudelaire's unquenchable thirst for the infinite ("le goût de l'infini")— his desire to escape the human condition, if only for a few moments—drives him to create his own paradise through artificial means: "créer . . . l'Idéal Artificiel . . . par la pharamacie: [L'homme] . . . a . . . cherché . . . sous tous les climats et dans tous les temps, les moyens de fuir, ne fût-ce que pour quelques heures son habitacle de fange" (*OC* [*Œvres complètes*] I, 402-3). Though drugs temporarily obliterate the ego ("vous avez jeté votre personnalité aux quatre vents"), the experience will take on the hue of the temperament of the user: "[L'expérience] gardera toujours la tonalité particulière de l'individu" (*OC* I, 409). (This was only one of Huxley's unexpected insights during his experiment with mescaline: "But I had not reckoned . . . with the idiosyncrasies of my mental make-up, the facts of my temperament, training and habits" [*Perception* 15]).

Baudelaire describes the process as a progression from an incipient state of hyper well-being to one of inexorable ecstasy ("une extase implacable") to a state of absolute happiness ("C'est ce que les Orientaux appellent le kief; c'est le bonheur absolu"). The eyes have pierced the veil of profane reality, have opened onto infinity ("Les yeux visent l'infini") and there is a heightened acuity of all the senses: "C'est . . . à cette période de l'ivresse que se manifeste une finesse nouvelle, une acuité supérieure dans tous les sens. L'odorat, la vue, l'ouïe, le toucher participent également à ce propos" (*OC* I, 419). (Though not encompassing all the senses, Huxley reports an "enormous heightening . . . of the perception of color . . . under mescaline" [*Perception* 26]). In this radically altered state of consciousness, the Not-Self perceives and participates in the infinity of all things: "Les objets . . . se révèlent à nous sous des formes inconnues jusque-là. Puis ils se déforment, se transforment, et enfin ils entrent dans votre être, ou bien vous entrez en eux" (*OC* I, 392).

This cursory comparison of two strikingly similar accounts of chemically induced Artificial Paradises is an infinitesimal sampling of a substantial and controversial literature on the subject. It is important to mention that, although the alteration of consciousness remains constant, the experience varies from individual to individual (for additional bibliography, see the above-mentioned issue of *Gnosis*). For the modern individual whose horizons have been expanded experientially by drugs or meditation or psychologically by the study of the collective unconscious or objective psyche (Not-Self, Not-I, Mind-at-Large) as posited by the Swiss

psychologist C. G. Jung, the parcel of infinity encapsulated in **"La Vie antérieure"** can become a moment of shared participation. Enriched by an already substantial body of critical studies on the poem, we enter Baudelaire's visionary experience with the hope of gaining further insights into the infinite complexity of the poem. To this end, in addition to Huxley, I have also consulted the work of Gaston Bachelard and have drawn extensively on the psychological premises of C. G. Jung.

From the outset of **"La Vie antérieure,"** we are aware that a transformation has already occurred. The ego has receded to the wings and has assumed the role of witness. The drug has liberated the psychic forces, and we are immediately plunged into an "other" space that Huxley defined as the Not-Self, C. G. Jung as the collective or objective psyche, the matrix of all creativity (*Collected Works,* vol. 15, 97), and Gaston Bachelard as "l'immensité intime de la rêverie" (*La Poétique,* 168). The poet is already completely enveloped in the vision, and the reader as participant struggles to "see" and understand his personalized corner of infinity and at the same time to attach it to the primordial or archetypal image or images that have erupted from the depths of the unconscious.

A reading of the first quatrain tells us that the poet's unconscious is lodged in a familiar, serene, and well-structured space. Gaston Bachelard has noted that the inner house is our first piece of the universe, our private bit of the Cosmos: "Tout espace vraiment habité porte l'essence de la notion de maison" (24). The vast portals and the grand, majestic columns suggest that the imagination has sculpted a psychic structure that resembles a temple, an indication to our mind of the spiritual tenor of the vision. The affective tone of this first quatrain is one of leisure and passive well-being. But it is also a solemn participation in the autonomous unfolding of the idyllic scene and its subsequent transformation. Contemplating a splendid sunset from the protective grandeur of the portals (suggested by "sous"), the poet revels in the dance of sunlight on the surface of the sea that breaks into a prismatic orgy of color against the surface of the columns. In the evening, they are transmuted into columnar basaltic caves.

The use of the first person narration would seem to indicate that the essentially visual reverie of the first quatrain is anchored in a personal memory. Yet images such as the sea, the temple, the columns, and the caves, which have been individualized by the poet, belong to the immense repository of symbols of the collective psyche. The great images of mankind are both historical and prehistorical—that is, they belong to memory and to legend. Each image is rooted in an unfathomable oneiric source. On this oneiric source, the poet places the seal of his own personal past: "C'est sur ce fond onirique," says Bachelard, "que le passé personnel met des couleurs particulières" (*La Poétique*, 47). The accomplished state of extended perception is immediately rendered in the first line by the term "vastes." Bachelard, who has examined at length the use of the word in Baudelaire's poetry, helps us to understand its various shades of meaning (174-90). Drawing upon Baudelaire's essays on the use of drugs, he notes that the prerequisite for the visionary experience is an unbounded capacity for leisure: "Le mangeur d'opium, pour profiter de la rêverie calmante, doit avoir de 'vastes loisirs'" (114). Bachelard further postulates that the vowel "a" of the word ("l'immensité intérieure du mot") has the value of a mantra, or cosmic sound, that dissolves ego barriers and penetrates into the vastness of the human soul. The vibrating, ever-expanding vowel unites the double universe of the depths of the psyche and the Cosmos (181). In **"La Vie antérieure,"** the vast inner dwelling of the human psyche, symbolized by the temple with its grand, majestic columns and the basaltic caves, mirrors the immensity of the Cosmos, symbolized by the sea. From this inner abode, the poet, in a blissful state, contemplates his reflection in an intensely illuminated sea. As previously mentioned, it is a familiar, happy locus ("l'espace heureux"). It is also a locus that the poet possesses ("l'espace de possession") because of repeated periods of introversion ("J'ai longtemps habité"). Bachelard explains that "les lieux où l'on a *vécu la rêverie* se restituent d'eux-mêmes" (26). In addition, the image of the temple suggests that the poet has moved into a sacred space that will be further substantiated in the second quatrain by the phrase "solennelle et mystique."

Since time immemorial, man has constructed temples whose architecture images his concept of the sacred. When the image of the temple was interiorized, it became, psychologically speaking, one of the archetypes of man's spiritual inscape and the sacralization of the macrocosm. The temple is, however, also an image of the microcosm. In **"La Vie antérieure,"** the poet inhabits a temple that reflects his Occidental heritage, a symmetrical Hellenic structure, divided into upper and lower regions. Its classical proportions are reflected in the form and content of the first quatrain and, in terms of the division of light and dark, the entire poem. In the first two lines, the temple is bathed in light. The second half of the quatrain stands in direct opposition to the first yet is connected to it by the powerful columns extending from the light to be transmuted into basaltic caves in the obscure depths of its foundation.

This allusion to "grottes basaltiques" demands further attention. Basalt is a dark gray to black fine-grained volcanic rock and tends to assume a columnar structure (*Encyclopedia Americana*, III, 301). On the psychological level, this definition is significant, for the cave is also a prime symbol of the unconscious and as such is known to guard the secrets of humanity. From the erup-

tion of the treasure house of primordial images that is the human psyche, the poet has sculpted an edifice. He maintains a delicate balance between those secrets that have surfaced and become a part of his conscious substance and those that remain unknown. This balance will become increasingly clear as the poem unfolds, particularly in the relationship between the slaves and "Le secret douloureux." "La cave," says Bachelard, "est d'abord *l'être obscur* de la maison, l'être qui participe aux puissances souterrains" (35).

A complementary image of the cave is that of the womb. The return to the womb is the return to the origin of all things, to the innocence and purity of primal beginnings. It is an amniotic space of warmth and protection, but it is also a dark space of unrevealed phenomena. Therefore, the surface expanse of the sea, irradiated by the sun, symbol of consciousness and the masculine principle, masks its dark maternal aspect, which coincides with the unconscious or the cave (Jung, vol. 5, 219). The word "vaste" comes to mind once more, for it synthesizes the experience and unites the opposing forces of light and dark, or as Jung would say, the tension of the opposites. This juxtaposition of light and dark, it seems, would invalidate Michel Quesnel's assessment that "la grotte inaugure **'La Vie antérieure'**" (265). He has evidently overlooked the fact that the cave is the subterranean foundation of the temple. In addition, the dual symbols of the temple and the cave, upheld by the columns, illustrate the verticality of the inner house and represent the two poles of the psychic blueprint (Bachelard, *La Poétique*, 35). The contours of the poet's vision in this magnificently proportioned quatrain embrace the two "vast" categories of archetypal imagery, which are, to use Gilbert Durand's phraseology, "le régime diurne et le régime nocturne de l'image" (540, 543). The poet, however, has sensitized the objective immensity of these two values by creating, as we have seen, a temple to house and contain the vision. It is also significant that, despite the poet's awareness of the parallel forces of light and dark in this first quatrain, the dominant and overriding sensation is one of profound well-being. In the context of a drug-induced vision, it corresponds to the phase when the interior eye of the poet begins to apprehend the underlying aesthetic continuum in himself and in nature.

In the second quatrain, the static visual scene of the first four lines takes on an autonomous life of its own. The rounded ridges of the surf mirror the prismatic colors of the setting sun ("Les houles en roulant les images des cieux"). The collective, cadenced sound emanating from the slow, rhythmic swell and fall of the unbroken waves creates a solemn and mystical chant ("Mêlaient d'une façon solennelle et mystique / Les tout-puissants accords de leur riche musique"). The eyes of the poet become like magnets that synthesize and absorb this mighty union of heaven and earth unto himself, creating a triangle or, more pertinently, a sacred trinity ("Aux couleurs du couchant reflété par mes yeux"). It is far from the narcissistic experience of which Sartre accuses Baudelaire: "Il se regarde voir; il regarde pour se voir regarder" (25). The universe has entered the poet and has transported him beyond the boundaries of the individual self and the contradictions of relative existence. To our perceptions we may add Louis Morice's splendid appreciation of the poet's vision: "Et que fait Baudelaire dans ces deux quatrains sinon regarder et entendre le monde, comme le premier homme au matin de la création?" (45). For a precious, inestimable moment, Poet and Cosmos are one in a state of primordial innocence and purity. The form also renders the vision that has risen to consciousness and the poet's assimilation of it into his being. The rhyme scheme of the first quatrain, *abba,* is inverted in the second quatrain and becomes *baab,* suggesting that the poet has become the vessel for this sacred union. In *Les Paradis artificiels,* Baudelaire summarizes for us this final stage, which he compares to oriental "bliss consciousness": "Toute contradiction est devenue unité. L'homme est *passé* dieu" (*OC* I, 394).

It would not be an exaggeration to say that "vaste" also has a metaphysical value. Bachelard concurs: "Le mot vaste est, chez Baudelaire, un véritable argument métaphysique par lequel sont unis le vaste monde et les vastes pensées" (175). The sense of the immensity of the universe, which the poet cognizes in himself as a spiritual, aesthetic experience, converges and is recast in the second quatrain in the word "mystique." The mystical participation in which subject and object have become one is a mysterious poetic event that cannot be conveyed by rational language. "Mystique," which embraces the notion of "vaste," is an inexhaustible theme of our poem (and of poetry in general). The poem can be deciphered, and then only partially, through associative imagery. The poet, in an effort to express the inexpressible, couches the vision in symbolic language. In turn, the vision, when filtered through the individual psyche, takes on a humanized personal expression. As we saw, both Huxley and Baudelaire agreed that, despite the expansion of consciousness due to the influence of drugs, the core personality retained its identity. In this sense we can speak of the predilection of certain recurrent themes or images in an artist's work.

For the Baudelaire reader, **"La Vie antérieure"** is a prism that refracts a recognizable system of thought and impressions, for example: an insatiable thirst for the Absolute, the desire to escape the mundane, the ever-present tension between the forces of light and darkness, the fear of the void or the unknown (a theme that I will broach in our discussion of form at the end of our analysis), the theme of the inner voyage and the spiritual and sensual appreciation of this "other" space, the prevalence of sun and sea imagery, and above all, the

concept of synesthesia, a hallmark of Baudelaire's poetry that he defined in the celebrated poem **"Correspondances"** and enacted in the second quatrain of our poem. The convergence of the senses transports the poet beyond the individual frame and links him with his notion of ultimate Reality. An even more detailed description of the elements of the beatific scene of **"La Vie antérieure"** is found in "Le Poème du hachisch":

> Le hachisch s'étend alors sur toute la vie comme *un vernis magique*: il la colore en *solennité* et en *éclaire* toute la profondeur. Paysages dentelés, horizons fuyants . . . ou illuminés par les ardeurs concentrés des *soleils couchants,*—profondeur de l'espace, allégorie de la profondeur du temps. . . . *La musique,* autre langue chère aux esprits profonds, vous parle de vous-même et vous raconte le poème de votre vie; elle s'incorpore à vous, et vous vous fondez en elle. . . . Chaque note se transform[e] en mot, et le poème entier entr[e] dans votre cerveau comme un dictionnaire doué de vie. . . . *L'immensité bleue de la mer* s'étale comme une véritable enchanteresse.

> (*OC* I, 430-31; emphasis added)

The poet comes full circle and caps part of the event in the first two lines of the first tercet: "C'est là que j'ai vécu dans les voluptés calmes / Au milieu de l'azur, des vagues, des splendeurs." Syntax effects this partial, intertextual completion. The present perfect, "J'ai vécu" recalls its synonym "J'ai habité" in the first line and intensifies it with the introductory phrase "C'est là." It is as if the poet wishes to convince the reader of the veracity of this vast inner dimension for which he is the spokesman. In his prose writing, Baudelaire defines the poet as "une âme collective." Elsewhere, he asks: "qu'est-ce un poète (je prends le mot dans son acception la plus large), si ce n'est qu'un traducteur, un déchiffreur?" (*OC* II, 133, 139). Bachelard fleshes out Baudelaire's definition in terminology more reflective of our analysis: "Pour Baudelaire, le destin poétique de l'homme est d'être le miroir de l'immensité, ou plus exactement encore, l'immensité vient prendre conscience d'elle-même en l'homme. Pour Baudelaire, l'homme est un être vaste" (178-79).

"C'est là" also raises the specific question: Where is "là"? This "other" space is related to the title of the poem and has been the subject of some critical speculation. Paul Arnold sees in the title a clear allusion to the Pythagorean tenet of palingenesis. He equates the situation of **"La Vie antérieure"** with that in **"Le Mauvais moine,"** in which the poet, he feels, despite one or several previous existences, has failed to attain a state of purity: "Mon âme est un tombeau que, mauvais cénobite, / Depuis l'éternité je parcours et j'habite; / Rien n'embellit les murs de ce cloître odieux" (*OC* I, 16).

For him, the vision is a compensatory mental extravaganza that stands in direct opposition to "le secret douloureux" of the last line. Indeed, the painful secret invalidates the vision, says Arnold, because the poet has not succeeded in shedding karmic accretions accumulated over many lifetimes (126-28). The vision remains a haunting intuition of what was and the object of the poet's deepest longing. Louis Morice, on the other hand, rejects the notion of palingenesis. He proposes the Platonic theory of the Idea as a possible solution, admitting, nevertheless, that Plato also adhered to the doctrine of palingenesis. The Platonic Idea represents ultimate Reality. It is the archetype of absolute Being imperfectly expressed by man imprisoned in the human frame but in whom there remains the vague memory of the *Idea* of perfection. In the end, Morice decides that, despite misleading allusions to oriental and Hellenic notions of palingenesis and profound Platonic resonances, the title of the poem simply represents a privileged moment of "béatitude poétique." I would like to elaborate on these conclusions.

One of the metaphors that Baudelaire himself used to describe the unconscious was the palimpsest on which is transcribed the incommensurate collective memory of man. Images, ideas, and sentiments may drop below the level of consciousness, but they are never lost: "Rien ne se perd" (*OC* I, 507). The poems hidden in the artist's soul are not dead. They sleep: "L'oubli n'est donc que momentané . . . et généralement dans les excitations créées par *l'opium*, tout l'immense et compliqué palimpseste de la mémoire se déroule d'un seul coup, avec toutes ses couches superposées de sentiments défunts, mystérieusement embaumés dans ce que nous appelons l'oubli" (*OC* I, 506).

Baudelaire's discussion of the unconscious is strikingly akin to that of Jung, who defines it as an entity that tells the "story of mankind." When the brain "becomes creative, it creates out of this history" (Jung, vol. 10, 10). The point I wish to make is that the visionary mode of artistic creativity is irrational. Therefore, the Platonic theory of the Idea, the oriental and Pythagorean concepts of palingenesis, to which we might add the influence of Swedenborg, prevalent ideas in the nineteenth century, need not be dismissed. Rather, they should be regarded as tools of expression. Through the alchemy of the creative process, the imagination of the poet has dissolved them as philosophical systems and transformed aspects of them into a network of suggestions or usable metaphors, because, by their very nature, they speak of the immensity of the soul and its potential for perfectibility.

We must also consider the concept of time in the title. Time is a matter of perception. In ordinary reality, time is linear. Therefore, it would be appropriate to interpret "ante" of "antérieure"—which means "before" or "prior to"—as an allusion to a chronological past event. Barry Ulanov, in his work *Jung and the Outside World,* helps us frame the thought: "Here in the collective unconscious is where our roots go down into a shared history of soul to reach an inheritance that both *precedes* individual consciousness and is, at the same time, its nutriment" (x; emphasis added). "Anterior," however, also means "situated towards the front: before in place, as opposed to posterior" (*Webster's Third New International Dictionary,* s.v. "anterior"). We may remember Baudelaire's concept of the palimpsest, in which the psyche, in an altered state of consciousness, is capable of participating in the simultaneity of the human experience. In this state of extended awareness, the perception of time has changed. The ego, with its notions of sequence and logically connected events, has receded to the background, and Mind-at-Large (Not-Self), with its ability to perceive "All," has moved to center stage. Time is abolished, and the purview of the inner eye is all-encompassing. With one sweeping glance, the poet sees and experiences the sublime and the grotesque aspects of the human condition concurrently. In timelessness, both states cohabit and are eternally present. A more complete interpretation, then, must include both the chronological and nonchronological aspects of the title. In our poem, drugs yielded a panoramic view of a piece of man's psychic *history*— his eternal striving to create more light in the darkness. And the echoes of reincarnation discussed above can be reinterpreted to indicate not so much the problem of *a* previous existence or existences as *the collective unconscious life* that the poet shares with all mankind— "la vie antérieure"—and of which he, by virtue of his poetic gift, is a mediator. Indeed, the unconscious *reincarnates* each time the poet wrests from and expresses a part of this fertile Ground. The poem itself is the reincarnation, because it gives birth, or more accurately, rebirth to that which lives in the darkness of the womb, that matrix of all creativity. From this most profound level of human awareness, the poet says, "Quelque incohérente que soit une existence, l'unité humaine n'en est pas troublée. Tous les échos de la mémoire, si on pouvait les réveiller simultanément, formeraient un concert, *agréable* ou *douloureux,* mais logique et sans dissonances" (*OC* I, 506; emphasis added). This significant statement helps us create a harmonious transition from our discussion of the vision to the consideration of the slaves and the secret, for **"La Vie antérieure"** is both an agreeable and a painful concert.

In retrospect, we may note that the vision that comprises ten lines has disrupted the mechanics of the fixed form of the sonnet and has impinged upon two lines of the first tercet for its conclusion. The last line of the first tercet, when added to the last three lines, forms an equally divided quatrain. Just as the third line of the first quatrain connected the archetypal registers of light and dark, so also can lines 11 and 12 be considered pivotal. The exotically scented, nude slaves are affiliated with the world of light and the commingling of the senses of the second quatrain *and* the dark world of the secret.

In Baudelaire's poetic universe, the bouquet of a strong perfume has frequently served as a catalyst for transcending the finite (**"Parfum exotique," "La Chevelure," "Le Parfum"**). In **"La Vie antérieure,"** we can say that the poet is led by the scent of his own creative instincts, which seek expression and are symbolized by the slaves. There is more. The poet's choice of the word "front" is particularly auspicious, for it is linked to our interpretation of the term "antérieure" in the title. The notion of the poet as clairvoyant was widespread in the nineteenth century. The influx of oriental thought popularized the concept of the all-seeing third eye, located in the middle of the forehead (in oriental parlance, this corresponds to the sixth chakra). In "La Fonction du poète," Victor Hugo maintained that only the poet had the gift of vision: "Lui seul a le front éclairé" (*Œuvres poétiques* I, 1031). In "Le Poème du hachisch," Baudelaire makes the comment that "L'œil intérieur transforme tout" (*OC* I, 431).

I therefore disagree totally with Paul Arnold, who feels that "Le secret douloureux" of the final line annuls the vision. On the contrary, impending darkness, though muted by the splendor of the scene, permeates the poem. From the outset, we saw that darkness forms a part of the very structure of the poet's house ("grottes basaltiques"). That the event should occur at sunset is also psychologically telling, and critics have noted Baudelaire's predilection for sunsets. Marc Eigeldinger's interpretation is eminently appropriate for our poem: "Le soleil, à l'heure du couchant, ressuscite le passé, non seulement celui des souvenirs personnels, mais le passé immémorial et mythique de l'homme éternellement en quête de la lumière de l'âge d'or" ("La symbolique," 369). Eigeldinger adds that the setting sun in Baudelaire's poetry is often engulfed by the sea and is alchemically purified in its dark regenerative waters (368). Jung echoes the idea and completes it: "The sea devours the sun" in its maternal waters but brings it forth again. He who thirsts for the heights, adds the noted psychologist, must "descend into the dark depths," and this descent is an "indispensable precondition for climbing . . . higher" (Jung, vol. 5, 218; vol. 9i, 19). The tension between the upper and lower worlds is at the very core of Baudelaire's poetry and is an undeniable theme of our poem. Implicit in this habitually cultivated vision (note the use of the imperfect) is the cyclic movement of light to dark. These recurring encounters, which are meant to repel the darkness, are regulated by the slaves, the denizens of the inner abode.

The slaves acquire an even deeper meaning when viewed with a Jungian apperception. Jung maintains that the unconscious personifies itself to inform the individual ego (Jung, vol. 15, 81). In the structure of the poem, the slaves' function is complex. They officiate as custodians of the threshold that separates the light from the dark. If we accept them as vital inherent impulses of the psyche, as I suggested above, we can also say that they represent a deep intuition that points to things that are unknown and hidden and, by their nature, secret (Jung, vol. 15, 94). To ease the confrontation with the darkness, these incarnate elemental forces from the sea of the poet's unconscious draw refreshment for him from the corresponding sea of the Cosmos through the metrical strokes of palm leaves ("Qui me rafraîchissaient le front avec des palmes"). At the same time, this to-and-fro rhythm, which emulates the undulating movement of the waves, mesmerizes the poet and keeps the interior eye focused on the inner event. The slaves blur the boundaries of these contradictory worlds and turn the poet's attention from his experience of a spiritual union with the Cosmos to a consideration of the darkness, its psychic twin. This swing of the pendulum is necessary to authenticate the vision. "Every single virtue in this world," says the Jungian analyst Robert Johnson, "is made valid by its opposite. Light would mean nothing without dark. . . . one cannot exist without the other" (*Shadow,* 17, 82). The slaves' task, it seems, is to help the poet fold the dark into the light. These unclothed figures ("esclaves nus") lay bare the poet's inner truth, heretofore unknown, and allow it to filter up to ego consciousness gradually. Through this dialogue with the unconscious, or more precisely, through the mutual relationship between the poet and these inner "gods or daemons," as Jung sometimes calls them, the poet's Being becomes more conscious of itself and continues to expand its horizons. Jung gives a psychological explanation of the poetic experience: "However dark and unconscious this night world may be, it is not wholly unfamiliar. . . . The poet now and then catches sight of the figures that people the night world. . . . he feels the secret quickening of human fate . . . and has a presentiment of incomprehensible happenings in the pleroma" (Jung, vol. 15, 94-96). In **"La Vie antérieure,"** the concept of the psyche in a constant state of becoming is explained by the poet's ongoing quest to deepen his knowledge of "Le secret douloureux." And the process is contained in the well-chosen verb "approfondir."

The cryptic last line of the poem yielded an assortment of views. For René Galand, the secret pain is due to the fact that "Toutes les voluptés que peut offrir un lieu terrestre, si paradisiaque qu'il paraisse, ne peuvent satisfaire l'aspiration mystique à l'Absolu. Au lieu de l'apaiser, elles ne font que l'exacerber, que l'approfondir" (269). Carlo François seeks clues in the poet's account of his experience with hachisch: "Le rêveur du 'Poème du hachisch' confesse que l'euphorie des premiers moments du rêve est vouée à l'échec en vertu de l'existence préalable de son malheur" (199).

Hubert's evaluation is indecisive. He imputes the painful secret to existent causes in the actual life of the poet. The secret may be a permanent part of human nature, or it may even be linked to poetic creativity: "Ce secret douloureux marque un retour au présent, au secret qui fait souffrir le poète *maintenant* ou qui existe depuis toujours dans la nature humaine. . . . Il se pourrait que ce secret, existant semble-t-il, en dehors du temps, correspondît à la création poétique" (157).

In my opinion, we must probe the secret of **"La Vie antérieure"** from a double point of view: the objective, or impersonal, and the subjective, or personal. Objectively, the riddle of the secret is quite simple: the drug is the clue. Through its use, the vast, ever-present world of the human psyche that lies hidden behind the facade of ego emerges. It is secret because it cannot be perceived with ordinary vision. This secret world, which represents the psychic heritage of all mankind, is intuited and seen by the elite minority of which Huxley spoke in the statement that I quoted at the outset of this chapter. Within the context of the poem, the presence of this secret world was already implicit, as we saw, in my discussion of the word "antérieure" in the title and in the use of the word "front." Outside the framework of the poem, Baudelaire's own definition of the brain as a palimpsest whose many layers were simultaneously revealed to him under the influence of drugs further substantiates our premise. Yet the dissolution of profane vision does not make the poet immediately omniscient, for the inner world has its own inborn structure of secrets that remain dormant until ferreted out by the seer (June, vol. 15, 97).

Several of Baudelaire's poems reveal the various aspects of his anguish such as time, inimical to the poet (**"L'Horloge," "L'Ennemi"**); the isolation of the poet (**"L'Albatros"**); the chasm between the ideal and man's human estate (**"L'Élévation"**), and so on. Poetic creativity seems to be another central problem. To a degree, his pain is anchored in the conflict between simple human endurance and the imperatives of an ineluctable poetic calling. He expresses his concern in **"Le Guignon,"** which directly precedes **"La Vie antérieure"**:

> Pour soulever un poids si lourd,
> Sisyphe, il faudrait ton courage!
> Bien qu'on ait du cœur à l'ouvrage,
> L'Art est long et le Temps est court.

> (*OC* I, 17)

Though the unconscious is the cathedra of creativity, the poet accesses its treasures with much difficulty. Again in **"Le Guignon,"** he laments:

> Maint joyau dort enseveli
> Dans les ténèbres et l'oubli,
> Bien loin des pioches et des sondes;

> Mainte fleur épanche à regret
> Son parfum doux comme un *secret*
> Dans les solitudes profondes.

> (*OC* I, 17; emphasis added)

In a general comparison between man and the sea, the poet judges that neither will ever yield its secrets entirely:

> La mer est ton miroir; tu contemples ton âme

> Vous êtes tous les deux ténébreux et discrets:
> Homme, nul n'a sondé le fond de tes abîmes,
> O mer, nul ne connaît tes richesses intimes
> Tant vous êtes jaloux de garder vos *secrets*!

> (**"L'homme et la mer,"** *OC* I, 19; emphasis added)

In **"La Vie antérieure,"** the poet has prevailed on the unconscious and has wrenched one of its jewels from its clutches. Still, not only is the Source of the vision shrouded in a darkness that he can never fully penetrate, but its sparkle does not cast light on the myriad unborn secrets that remain unrevealed. As a collective man, says Jung, "the poet is everywhere hemmed round . . . by the Unconscious, the mysterious god within him; so that ideas flow to him—he knows not whence; he is driven to work and to create—he knows not to what end; and is mastered by an impulse for constant growth and development—he knows not whither" (Jung, vol. 15, 102). We may remember Jung's statement that to create more light, one must descend into the depths. Therefore, the continued deepening of the unfathomable secret of the depths of his own being, which coincides with the vision of light, both inherent facets of the psyche, is, to quote the poet once again, "logique et sans dissonances."

Reference to the mention of the "secret" in other poems in the proximity of **"La Vie antérieure"** emphasizes the poet's personal preoccupation with the unknown and also facilitates further speculation on "Le secret douloureux" as part of the paradox of the creative process. I will use the medieval concept of the mandorla to illustrate my point (I am indebted to Robert Johnson for this insight). The mandorla is the almond-shaped section that is created by two partly overlapping circles. It is, says Johnson, the home of all great poetry, the place where the poet has created a mystical synthesis of the opposites, the place where he has united the "beauty and the terror of existence," "l'horreur de la vie et l'extase de la vie," as Baudelaire himself put it (Johnson, *Shadow,* 98, 103; *OC* I, 703). Within the framework of the sonnet, the poet has created such a mandorla in which light and dark unite, for the vision that was once hidden has now surfaced to consciousness. On the affective level, the tension of the opposites is expressed by the bliss that is offset by the pain caused by that part of his psyche that he has not yet reclaimed ("Le secret douloureux").

The poet also demonstrates that the process by which the opposites are sustained must be constantly renewed. The inner secret world nourishes his creativity but only at the price of a continual sounding of the depths, and as we noted above, the process is rendered by the verb "approfondir." Another important verb to be taken into consideration is "languir." *Le Petit Robert* gives a definition that is germane to our analysis: "souffrir de quelque peine dont la continuité épuise" (972). From the outset, the poet informed us that he had been a longtime citizen of the inner world. As we saw, his inner temple was a protective fortress that permitted him to confront and to participate in the unfolding of the inner drama. Bachelard puts this idea into perspective: "Il faut participer au drame cosmique soutenu par la maison qui lutte. . . . Une telle maison . . . est un instrument à affronter le cosmos" (57-58). From this inner sanctuary, he allows the slaves to track the scent of his hidden resources. The creative struggle between the poet and his secret inner world has always been a painful one. In their wisdom, acquired through repeated encounters with the poet, the slaves cautiously gauge his journey, thus preventing the prodigious richness of the imaginative material from overtaxing and outstripping the poet's power to give expression and form to the event (Jung, vol. 15, 88). And herein lies the meaning of "languir." It is this gradual unveiling that saps his creative energy. He languishes after an ultimate ideal whose entirety he may never grasp, for the vast and complex secrets of the unconscious may never be reflected in the mirror of a single human consciousness. Nevertheless, the sonnet is a mandorla that absorbs unto itself a part of the two vast circles of light and dark that stretch beyond its boundaries into infinity. Light and dark are two aspects of the same coin. Paradoxically, the secret is a part of the light that has yet to be revealed. And the poem is a personalized miniature version of this most profound truth of the human condition, translated into language and form.

The enclosure of the vision into the specific form of the sonnet is significant. Given our hypothesis that the edenic scene of the poem is rooted in the undifferentiated formlessness of the unconscious, we could say that form is necessary to mold and give focus to the poet's discovery. The unconscious is the poet's cornucopia. As we saw in our discussion of the title, this silent, primordial domain, incapable of expressing itself, would remain forever hidden were it not glimpsed, formulated, and made concrete by the poet. He does not create the substance of his poetic vision but recreates it through form and gives it meaning (Jouve, *Baudelaire,* 78). Baudelaire is quite specific on the point, for in the *Salon de 1859* he states: Un poème ne se copie jamais: il veut être composé" (*OC* II, 661). Through *willed* composi-

tion of the reverie, the poet rediscovers and redeems the authentic state of primordial perfection. Form, then, regenerates and projects the spiritual longing of the human spirit onto the outside world (Jouve, *Baudelaire,* 78). This idea also links form to aesthetics, as Nicole Jouve spells it out: "Beauty [is] brought about by the 'Spirit' of man. . . . [It] only begins to *exist* once a landscape bears the sign of 'spiritual interference'" (76). In our poem, the drug-mandated reverie has displaced the intellect and has put the poet in contact with his absolute subjectivity. In this state, the poet as "seer" apprehends nature in its original, untainted, eternal beauty and gives it expression. Poetic reverie, it would seem, is the state of mind that reconciles absolute subjectivity with the absolute objectivity of nature. Baudelaire himself contended that Beauty exists not in and of itself "mais par moi, par ma grâce propre, par l'idée ou le sentiment que j'y attache" (*Curiosités esthétiques,* quoted by Jouve, *Baudelaire,* 78). In connection with this idea, Nicole Jouve appropriately comments, "The mind or the sensibility become for Baudelaire the repository of the beautiful because 'perception,' as well as a sense of values in man, remains relatively untouched by the fall" (78). In aesthetic contemplation, the poet transcends his local personality and, from this vantage point, externalizes his aesthetic intuition.

Form also assures the integrity of the vision and prevents the fragmentation of the psyche that gives it expression. The terse sonnet form is a particularly apt vehicle of expression for the poet's glimpse into the inexhaustible "superhuman world of contrasting light and darkness" (Jung, vol. 15, 90). Crystallizing the vision of light as well as the unfolding secret in artistic form serves to assuage the fears of the poet in his confrontation with the unknown. He confesses in **"Une Mort héroïque"** that "l'ivresse de l'Art est plus apte que toute autre à voiler les terreurs du gouffre" (*OC* I, 321).

Form is also inherently paradoxical. The poet has cognized and framed this "other" space, but he has not contained it. Peering into the gaping abyss reveals to him his own image and, by extension, man's human estate, "la tyrannie de la face humaine" (*OC* I, 483). He has not been able to sustain the moment of spiritual unity that is everywhere threatened by darkness. There is a dichotomy, then, between the power of art to recover primal innocence and to conceal the void and its inability to save him from the shadows of the human condition (Jouve, *Baudelaire,* 264). And of this Baudelaire was eminently aware: "La dualité de l'art est une conséquence fatale de la dualité de l'homme" (*OC* II, 685-86). In this sense, form is also inextricably linked to the secret. It is conceptualized in the fourteenth line of the poem, and it remains thus within the parameters of the traditional sonnet form. As a psychic reality, it wends its way past the grasp of poet and critic alike. The sonnet form has become a window that opens into a zone where only the elite few tread.

In succumbing to the temptation of trying to decode the personal topography of the poet's secret by alluding to poems that surround **"La Vie antérieure,"** we were just able to touch upon the great mystery that enshrouds the creative act. The fact remains that even this is not verbalized in the poem itself. The secret becomes a sort of vacuum, as Pizzorusso put it, that the reader must fill. To understand its transpersonal meaning, readers must allow it to mold them as it did the poet. They must descend into the depths of their own unconscious where all humans are united and from which space the poet has communicated his feelings and aspirations to humankind. Though the poet's lines seemingly express an aspect of his own personal myth—"un petit élément de mythologie spontané," as Bachelard phrases it—in essence, this is one of the myths of mankind. For **"La Vie antérieure,"** within the limited space of the sonnet, represents the archetypal quest for spiritual union. This "re-immersion in the state of *participation mystique*," says Jung, "is the secret of artistic creation and of the effect that art has upon us, for at that level of experience it is no longer the weal or woe of the individual that counts, but the life of the collective. . . . Great poetry derives its strength from the life of mankind" (Jung, vol. 15, 98, 105). A work of art can orient mankind toward the unfathomable depths of the secret but can never name it (Bachelard, *La Poétique,* 31).

References

Arnold, Paul. *Esotérisme de Baudelaire*. Paris: J. Vrin, 1972.

Bachelard, Gaston. *La Poétique de la rêverie*. Paris: Presses Universitaires de France, 1960.

———. *La Poétique de l'espace*. Paris: Presses Universitaires de France, 1989.

Baudelaire, Charles. *Œuvres complètes*. 2 vols. Edited by Claude Pichois. Bibliothèque de la Pléiade. Paris: Gallimard, 1975-76.

Durand, Gilbert. *Les structures anthropologiques de l'imaginaire*. Paris: Bordas, 1969.

Eigeldinger, Marc. "La symbolique solaire dans la poésie de Baudelaire." *Revue d'histoire littéraire de la France* 67:2 (April-June 1967): 357-74.

François, Carlo. "'La Vie antérieure' de Baudelaire." *Modern Language Notes* 73:3 (March 1958): 194-200.

Galand, René. *Baudelaire: Poétiques et poésie*. Paris: Nizet, 1969.

Gnosis 26 (Winter 1993).

Hubert, Judd David. *L'Esthétique des "Fleurs du mal": Essai sur l'ambiguïté poétique*. Geneva: Droz, 1953.

Hugo, Victor. "La Conscience." *La Légende des siècles*. Paris: Garnier-Flammarion, 1967.

———. *Œuvres poètiques de Victor Hugo*. 2 vols. Edited by Pierre Albouy. Bibliothèque de la Pléiade. Paris: Gallimard, 1964.

Huxley, Aldous. *The Doors of Perception*. New York: Harper and Row, 1970.

Johnson, Robert A. *Owning Your Own Shadow: Understanding the Dark Side of the Psyche*. San Francisco: Harper Collins, 1993.

Jouve, Nicole. *Baudelaire: A Fire to Conquer Darkness*. New York: St. Martin's, 1980.

Jung, C. G. *Collected Works*. Princeton: Princeton University Press, 1971.

Morice, Louis. "'La Vie antérieure.'" *Etudes littéraires* 1 (April 1968): 29-49.

Le Petit Robert. Paris: Société du Nouveau Littré, 1967.

Quesnel, Michel. *Baudelaire solaire et clandestin*. Paris: Presses Universitaires de France, 1987.

Sartre, Jean-Paul. *Baudelaire*. Paris: Gallimard, 1963.

Ulanov, Barry. *Jung and the Outside World*. Willmette, Ill.: Chiron Publications, 1992.

William Olmsted (essay date 1997)

SOURCE: Olmsted, William. "Immortal Rot: A Reading of 'Une Charogne.'" In *Understanding* Les Fleurs du Mal: *Critical Readings,* edited by William J. Thompson, pp. 60-71. Nashville, Tenn.: Vanderbilt University Press, 1997.

[*In the following essay, Olmsted analyzes the complex and ironic misogyny of "Une Charogne," touching on such ideas as the poem's relationship to the Christian conception of the body, Baudelaire's modernism, and his "anti-idealism."*]

> Rappelez-vous l'objet que nous vîmes, mon âme,
> Ce beau matin d'été si doux:
> Au détour d'un sentier une charogne infâme
> Sur un lit semé de cailloux,
>
> (4)
>
> Les jambes en l'air, comme une femme lubrique,
> Brûlante et suant les poisons,
> Ouvrait d'une façon nonchalante et cynique
> Son ventre plein d'exhalaisons.
>
> (8)

Le soleil rayonnait sur cette pourriture,
Comme afin de la cuire à point,
Et de rendre au centuple à la grande Nature
Tout ce qu'ensemble elle avait joint;

(12)

Et le ciel regardait la carcasse superbe
Comme une fleur s'épanouir.
La puanteur était si forte, que sur l'herbe
Vous crûtes vous évanouir.

(16)

Les mouches bourdonnaient sur ce ventre putride,
D'où sortaient de noirs bataillons
De larves, qui coulaient comme un épais liquide
Le long de ces vivants haillons.

(20)

Tout cela descendait, montait comme une vague,
Ou s'élançait en pétillant;
On eût dit que le corps, enflé d'un souffle vague,
Vivait en se multipliant.

(24)

Et ce monde rendait une étrange musique,
Comme l'eau courante et le vent,
Ou le grain qu'un vanneur d'un mouvement rhyth-
mique
Agite et tourne dans son van.

(28)

Les formes s'effaçaient et n'étaient plus qu'un rêve,
Une ébauche lente à venir,
Sur la toile oubliée, et que l'artiste achève
Seulement par le souvenir.

(32)

Derrière les rochers une chienne inquiète
Nous regardait d'un œil fâché,
Épiant le moment de reprendre au squelette
Le morceau qu'elle avait lâché.

(36)

—Et pourtant vous serez semblable à cette ordure,
A cette horrible infection,
Étoile de mes yeux, soleil de ma nature,
Vous, mon ange et ma passion!

(40)

Oui! telle vous serez, ô la reine des grâces,
Après les derniers sacrements,
Quand vous irez, sous l'herbe et les floraisons grasses,
Moisir parmi les ossements.

(44)

Alors, ô ma beauté! dites à la vermine
Qui vous mangera de baisers,
Que j'ai gardé la forme et l'essence divine
De mes amours décomposés!

(48)

More than sixty years ago, T. S. Eliot observed that Baudelaire's "stock of imagery" was less than adequate: "His prostitutes, mulattoes, Jewesses, serpents, cats, corpses, form a machinery which has not worn very well" (*Selected Essays,* 375-76). One might claim, however, that this "machinery" was not meant to last. In offering his list of the outmoded in Baudelaire's poetry, Eliot seized upon precisely those items that characterize *Les Fleurs du Mal* as "modern" in the sense Baudelaire gave it: "La modernité, c'est le transitoire, le fugitif, le contingent, la moitié de l'art, dont l'autre moitié est l'éternel et l'immuable" (*OC* [*Œuvres complètes*] II, 695). Nowhere in Baudelaire's poetry, perhaps, does the effort to seize the transitory—"dont les métamorphoses sont si fréquentes"—achieve greater force and irony than in **"Une Charogne."** The reader receives a detailed, dynamic depiction of an animal carcass undergoing decomposition. The descriptive stanzas by themselves constitute a tour de force in the poetry of nature, here seen in its most unpleasant yet energetic form of self-renewal. The carrion amounts to a little cosmos, its activities producing "une étrange musique / Comme l'eau courante et le vent." Yet the portrait of the corpse serves none of the rhetorical ends that a reader might customarily expect. The poem does not use its emblem of decomposition for the sake of a meditation on mortality or for the purpose of seduction ("gather ye rosebuds") or to celebrate the cycles of nature. If, in Michael Jenning's apt phrase, "the corpse is the ultimate allegorical object" (109), Baudelaire's speaker deliberately turns away from the opportunities for an allegorizing metacommentary in order to compare the rotting carcass to his beloved: "Et pourtant vous serez semblable à cette ordure." When the speaker describes in stanza 3 how

Le soleil rayonnait sur cette pourriture,
Comme afin de la cuire à point,
Et de rendre au centuple à la grande Nature
Tout ce qu'ensemble elle avait joint,

and goes on to instance this productive decomposition by depicting in stanza 5 how

Les mouches bourdonnaient sur ce ventre putride,
D'où sortaient de noirs bataillons
De larves, qui coulaient comme un épais liquide
Le long de ces vivants haillons,

the reader's nausea, indignation, and perplexity (or nervous laughter) signal the presence of what Hugo called the "frisson nouveau" made available by Baudelaire. This thrill or shock or jolt derives not merely from a new poetic diction (for example, the introduction of seemingly unpoetic terms like "exhalaisons" and deliberate clichés like "mon ange") but more from the reinterpretation of deeply rooted cultural expectations and beliefs.

The crux of the poem, the rhetorical move that transforms the title and the opening nine stanzas of description into lethal simile, occurs when the speaker reminds his companion

> —Et pourtant vous serez semblable à cette ordure,
> A cette horrible infection,
> Étoile de mes yeux, soleil de ma nature,
> Vous, mon ange et ma passion!

Star, sun, angel, passion: how utterly depleted of meaning these endearments seem, once the process of putrefaction has been transferred from the carrion to the beloved. And yet the repetition of the word "soleil" in stanzas 3 and 10 suggests that the comparison realigns not just objects (woman will be like decaying animal) but natural forces and relationships (the sun of his nature will become ordure). Whatever the "sunny" woman may once have meant to the poet, inevitably her effect on him will be like the cadaver's, a stimulus for disgust. The universe constructed in this poem displays a process character. Radical transformations and role reversals appear inevitable. These changes will affect nature, the poet and his beloved who was yesterday the poet's sun, tomorrow (and perhaps today) the object of his contempt and loathing.

But does he and will he loathe her? The repetition of terms of endearment in the last three stanzas raises the suspicion that more than irony is intended, that the prospect of her decay excites the speaker and adds a certain zest to his present passion. Leo Bersani includes **"Une Charogne"** within a Baudelairean project of sadistic sexuality that calls for the woman's immobilization, a deathlike frigidity that cooperates with fantasies of necrophilia (67-89). The poem undeniably fuses images of love and death in its final stanza:

> Alors, ô ma beauté! dites à la vermine
> Qui vous mangera de baisers,
> Que j'ai gardé la forme et l'essence divine
> De mes amours décomposés!

Yet a reading like Bersani's tends to reduce the poem to a symptom-laden fantasy. Instead of using diagnosis as a defense, we need to engage the issue of response. If we are to account for the poem's constructed character and the reader's role in that construction, we must refuse the temptation to take the moral high ground or otherwise pretend we are therapists immune to counter-transference. The poem's power depends on its capacity to create an intersubjectivity between the reader and the speaker as well as between the reader and the woman addressed. Operating simultaneously on linguistic and affective levels, this intersubjectivity encompasses and defines not only what Benveniste called the "réalité dialectique" of a poem's discursive poles of "locuteur" and "destinataire" (260) but also the reader who finds him/herself occupying now one and now the other of these poles. While Bersani's reading indicates what it would be like to entertain a fantasy such as the speaker's, we are left with no sense of what it would be like to be the object of such a fantasy, to find ourselves so conceived in the mind of one who calls us "mon ange" and "ma beauté."

Seen from the perspective of the addressee, **"Une Charogne"** performs several reversals. The theme of death is invoked not for purposes of seduction but to foretell the end of an affair, the decay of the rosebuds the speaker once had gathered. The theme of death is not invoked to celebrate the perpetuity of love-in-death or the lovers' joint metamorphosis and immortality. She will die and rot, but he will have created something immortal, which act would seem to be in the tradition, from Horace through Shakespeare, of the conceit of poetic immortalizing. Yet what has been immortalized is not the addressee as she is or at her best; paradoxically, her decomposed body becomes poetically "aere perennis." The poem's rhetorical structure of question-and-answer ("Rappelez-vous . . . telle vous serez") encourages the addressee to collude in the speaker's portrait of her. The stanzas describing the carrion, since they are framed by the command/invitation for her to recall, assume and reiterate the addressee's revulsion ("La puanteur était si forte, que sur l'herbe / Vous crûtes vous évanouir"); then the concluding stanzas solicit her self-disgust, the application of the images to herself. In this manner Baudelaire reverses the conventional trope of praise, the invitation of the beloved to admire herself in an idealized image. Finally, the imagery of corruption is not invoked for Christian moral considerations but for a peculiar kind of esthetic aim:

> Les formes s'effaçaient et n'étaient plus qu'un rêve,
> Une ébauche lente à venir,
> Sur la toile oubliée, et que l'artiste achève
> Seulement par le souvenir.

This stanza explicitly calls our attention to the way the poem plays off against the tradition of the artistic memento mori. The speaker finds himself intrigued by the unfinished, not yet realized, and sketchlike aspect of the carrion. The analogy between the artistic image and the loved one is arrested at the very point where memory has not yet been concretized in a stable image. To value the blurry sketch over the finished work, much as Baudelaire suggests in the *Salon de 1845* (*OC* II, 390), dematerializes and spiritualizes the artistic process. But in this instance we are concerned less with the ethereal artwork than with a decaying beast whose presently indistinct appearance is likened, by means of the sketch metaphor, to the beloved's future corpse. The speaker, in other words, asserts an aesthetic preference, what Baudelaire praised as "le goût de l'horrible" (*OC* I, 548-49), here manifested in his memory of the carrion and his projected image of the worm-eaten beloved. For the addressee, then, all the tropes that would identify her beauty with permanence are negated and replaced with the oxymoronic figure of perpetual rottenness.

How can putrefaction be immortalized? The question points toward the seemingly contradictory way that Baudelaire handles temporality. Given the poem's intense focus on the transformative aspect of decay, one might conclude that Baudelaire's representation of death agrees with the materialist conceptions of Bayle, Gassendi, and their Enlightenment followers. But the notion of cyclical processes in nature, whereby the corpse enters the food chain, is undercut by the notion of an indefinitely prolonged entombment for the beloved who, to make matters worse, may remain sentient ("ô ma beauté! dites à la vermine"). What ultimately distinguishes Baudelaire's rhetoric from materialist and Christian views of death is the emphasis on arrested development. Descartes and Bossuet alike would have agreed that the body's decomposition precedes its recomposition in some other form, but Baudelaire prefers to prolong indefinitely the time of decay, the moment of transition. What the speaker desires for his mistress is nothing less than a living death, a naturalized and de-Christianized version of eternal suffering.

Clearly the poem not only deploys a novel style of misogynistic rhetoric but exposes in critical fashion the presence of misogyny in the very cultural and poetic traditions it deconstructs. We need to correct, therefore, the view of Erich Auerbach that "corruption of the flesh means something very different in *Les Fleurs du Mal* and in the Christianity of the late Middle Ages" (219). On the contrary, it is the proximity of Baudelaire's decaying animal—"Les jambes en l'air, comme une femme lubrique"—to the images of medieval moralizing that gives **"Une Charogne"** its relative nihilism, its quite untraditional and un-Christian reduction of the corpse's moral significance. When Odilon of Cluny preached in the eleventh century on the body's frailty— "filth everywhere"—he did not neglect to conclude how intercourse with women was thus unthinkable: "We, who would be loath to touch vomit or dung even with our fingertip—how can we desire to clasp in our arms the bag of excrement itself?" (Ariès 110). For a theologian like Odilon, the loathsomeness of the medieval (feminine) body would not have been thinkable apart from the idealization of the resurrected body. But in Baudelaire's poem even a secular idealization of physical health or well-being has been removed. By

presenting misogyny so nakedly, **"Une Charogne"** challenges the metaphysical justifications for the privileging of the incorruptible poem (masculine) over the corruptible body (feminine).

Similarly, the poem challenges poetic conventions by inverting the Petrarchan sexual code, exchanging for the celestial the gritty and for the lovely the worm-eaten. A systematic violation of Petrarchan stereotypes (Tucker 892) was bound to offend contemporary readers. Indeed, Gustave Bourdin's review calling attention to the proliferation of vermine in *Les Fleurs du Mal* resulted in the book's prosecution for obscenity (Bandy and Pichois 13). And **"Une Charogne"** was probably on Sainte-Beuve's mind when he reproached Baudelaire for having "pétrarquisé sur l'horrible" (*OC* I, 890). No doubt Baudelaire's contemporaries would have agreed with a recent claim that the poem "strips poetry of its transcendent power" (McLees 22). But instead of congratulating Baudelaire for having created a new poetic genre (McLees 29), they tended to treat **"Une Charogne"** as an icon of Baudelaire's effeteness and buffoonery. Nadar's caricature of 1858 or 1859, showing the poet in a state of delectation and surprise over the presence of a fly-blown carcass, drew a somewhat injured response from Baudelaire, who claimed that he found it "pénible de passer pour le Prince des Charognes" (Bandy and Pichois frontispiece, 15; Pichois, *Album Baudelaire,* 162). After all, he objected to Nadar, "Tu n'as sans doute pas lu une foule de choses de moi, qui ne sont que musc et que roses" (*Correspondance* I, 573-74).

In this protest we can glimpse some ambiguities that pervade Baudelaire's poetry and his critical practice as well. A poem like **"Une Charogne"** stands against many instances of "musk and roses" and of love poems to women whose "chair spirituelle a le parfum des Anges" ("Que diras-tu ce soir") (*OC* I, 43). Likewise, the transformation of woman into carrion would appear to contravene those occasions when Baudelaire the critic abandons his misogyny to appreciate, as when speaking of the poet Marceline Desbordes-Valmore, "l'expression poétique de toutes les beautés naturelles de la femme" (*OC* II, 147). And if **"Une Charogne"** seems to parody the rhetoric of seduction and its trope of "tempus fugit," a poem like **"Chant d'automne"** employs this same trope without any undercutting whatsoever. Furthermore, the presence of the trope is presupposed by its very inversion in **"Une Charogne."** I emphasize these ambiguities to caution against reading the poem as purely the expression of aggression toward women.

Even the rhetorical extremism of **"Une Charogne"** and the sheer abundance of its images of decay suggest the presence of some obsession more powerful than misogyny. The poem itself is but one of many (most of them adjacent to each other in the 1861 edition) that link images of death and desire. Such images are, of course, omnipresent in Baudelaire's poetry. Here, however, I am referring to images not of death in general (**"La Mort des amants"** or **"La Mort des pauvres"**) nor of graves and the cemetery (**"La servante au grand cœur"**) but of the sexual and, as Baudelaire seems to indicate, *therefore decomposable* body. In **"Je t'adore à l'égal de la voûte nocturne,"** the speaker characterizes the relation between his erotic fervor and the beloved's coldness in these terms: "Je m'avance à l'attaque, et je grimpe aux assauts, / Comme après un cadavre un chœur de vermisseaux" (*OC* I, 27). In **"Le Vampire"** (*OC* I, 33) the speaker describes himself as bound to his lover "comme aux vermines la charogne" (now it appears that he is the corpse). And the following poem doubles the corpse image: "Une nuit que j'étais près d'une affreuse Juive, / Comme au long d'un cadavre un cadavre étendu" (*OC* I, 34). The body as corpse foregrounds the instability of flesh, its temporary and only semisolid quality. That this insubstantiality should not be limited to the female body becomes very apparent in a poem like **"Un Voyage à Cythère,"** where the speaker sees himself mirrored in the image of a hanged man being eaten by ravens:

> Les yeux étaient deux trous, et du ventre effondré
> Les intestins pesants lui coulaient sur les cuisses,
> Et ses bourreaux, gorgés de hideuses délices,
> L'avaient à coups de bec absolument châtré.

> (*OC* I, 118)

The body's vulnerability, its capacity for deformation and rot, and its liability to fragmentation are not restricted to women only, and Jacques Vier suggests the influence of Jansenist theology in the "décomposition généralisée" that links **"Une Charogne"** to **"Un Voyage à Cythère"** (48-49). But the decomposition of women in Baudelaire's poetry accompanies anger expressed by a male speaker, whereas the moldering of men accompanies expressions of despair, lassitude, and a self-hatred that the speaker would like to avoid. So concludes the speaker in **"Un Voyage à Cythère"**: "—Ah! Seigneur! donnez-moi la force et le courage / De contempler mon cœur et mon corps sans dégoût!"

Since the deity is invoked, we can hardly deny the speaker a Christian orientation; yet the sentiment expressed, the wish to be delivered from self-loathing, remains opposed to the Pascalian emphasis on the religious efficacity of self-hatred. **"Une Charogne"** similarly intersects but does not coincide with Christian attitudes toward the body. When Bourdaloue exhorts a "femme mondaine" to scrutinize a cadaver "pour réprimer cet amour infini de vous-même," the misogynistic and moralistic motives of his rhetoric greatly resemble those of the speaker in **"Une Charogne."** Like the seventeenth-century preacher, Baudelaire also mobilizes images of the cadaver for the sake of destroy-ing narcissism. Yet the context for this attack on self-love is not at all religious. Whatever may have been the historical origins for the hatred of the body as set forth in images of decomposition, a rhetoric that calls attention to the potential decay of the erotic body now aims to subvert contemporary attitudes and cultural values.

Baudelaire's remarks on what he called "L'école païenne" (1852) indicate what may have been the target of the subversions practiced in **"Une Charogne."** Attacking a resurgent taste for the classical and the mythological in literature, Baudelaire denounced the "malheureux néo-païens" for their affinities with the "sentimentalisme matérialiste" of Heine. Their "déplorable manie" for "les détritus anciens" could only result in sterility and pastiche, in a loss of reason and passion: "Est-ce Vénus Aphrodite ou Vénus Mercenaire qui soulagera les maux qu'elle vous aura causés? Toutes ces statues de marbre, seront-elles des femmes dévouées au jour de l'agonie, au jour de remords, au jour de l'impuissance?" (*OC* II, 47). At issue here is what Baudelaire perceives as the erotic idolatry of the neopagans, their elision of the potential evil caused by their Venuses, their blindness to women's capacity for solace, for devotion, suffering, and remorse. These strictures echo Baudelaire's slightly earlier criticism (in the 1851 review of Pierre Dupont) of the "philhellénisme" that succeeded the "individualité maladive" of the late romantics: "La puérile utopie de l'école de l'*art pour l'art,* en excluant la morale, et souvent même la passion, était nécessairement stérile" (*OC* II, 26). Baudelaire concludes his blast at the neopagans by imagining a poet whose obsession with "le beau, rien que le beau" leads him to rip his friends and vilify his wife. And since the "goût immodéré de la forme pousse à des désordres monstrueux et inconnus," Baudelaire concedes that he understands "les fureurs des iconoclastes et des musulmans contre les images" (*OC* II, 48-49). Is it not plausible to see in these objections to neopaganism the theoretical and critical confirmation of the poetic decomposition of the romantic image of the beloved in **"Une Charogne"**?

Although the poem may have been composed as early as 1843 (Pichois and Ziegler 185), its ironic attitude toward poetic idealization of the feminine recurs in a much later work, the prose poem **"Laquelle est la vraie?"** of 1863. The narrator recalls "une certaine Bénédicta, qui remplissait l'atmosphère d'idéal, et dont les yeux répandaient le désir de la grandeur, de la beauté, de la gloire et de tout ce qui fait croire à l'immortalité." But this miraculous woman soon dies, and the narrator buries her. As he gazes at her grave, her double appears, announcing herself as the true Bénédicta: "C'est moi, une fameuse canaille! Et pour la punition de ta folie et ton aveuglement, tu m'aimeras telle que je suis!" In shouting his refusal, he stamps his foot against the ground so violently that "ma jambe s'est enfoncée jusqu'au genou dans la sépulture récente, et que, comme un loup pris au piège, je reste attaché, pour toujours peut-être, à la fosse de l'idéale." The prose poem, rather more explicitly than **"Une Charogne,"** directs attention to what might be called the rhetoric of antiidealism. Here too there is a buried woman and a speaker/narrator who describes her as inspirational. And here too the romantic convention of love-in-death becomes subverted, although somewhat differently. Now it is the failure to immortalize his "decomposed love" that haunts the narrator and condemns him not only to a disillusioned love with "une fameuse canaille" but also to an immobilizing attachment to the grave of the ideal, a grave dug by himself. In sum, **"Laquelle est la vraie?"** contains a retrospective irony, Baudelaire's admission that he has in fact remained, both in reputation and temperament, "the Prince of the Corpses."

Although I have argued that Baudelaire's antiidealistic treatment of the body presupposes but undermines Christian attitudes, I do not mean to suggest that his stance lacks any spiritual dimension. Judging from remarks in his critical writings, it seems clear that he regarded the power of imagination to consist in the ability to decompose the world prior to creating it anew. This insistence on the imagination's capacity to radically reshape nature distinguishes Baudelaire's antiidealism from that of the realist painters and writers, who set out the facts of death and dying in a detached, undramatic fashion that emphasized the "sub-heroic banality" of the circumstances (Nochlin 68). Although **"Une Charogne"** reduces the dead person to the level of an animal, the process of putrefaction is dramatically and energetically rendered. There is no question of representing the dead woman as nonbeing, as a meaningless zero. On the contrary, the poem asserts the persistence of sensation and awareness after death, then compounds this paradox by drawing the analogy between her continued existence and the poem's own immortality. We can make sense of these puzzles if we recognize the extent to which Baudelaire separates form and matter, signifier and signified. As he put it in his journals, "Toute idée est, par elle-même, douée d'une vie immortelle, comme une personne. Toute forme créée, même par l'homme, est immortelle. Car la forme est indépendante de la matière, et ce ne sont pas les molécules qui constituent la forme" (*OC* I, 705). But the spiritualization of the formal in **"Une Charogne"** accompanies an ethical and not necessarily aesthetic devaluation of the material insofar as the material is subject to decay and evocative of disgust. Furthermore, this devaluation is not neutrally applied to all of creation but is focused rather on the beloved. Accordingly, we need to take a final look at the question of misogyny that **"Une Charogne"** raises.

Does the poem move in the direction of a cultural conservatism that would enforce the already low status of women by means of a rhetoric that subverts their romantic idealization and identifies them with decaying beasts? Can this be what Baudelaire meant when he claimed that woman is the being "pour qui, mais surtout *par qui* les artistes et les poètes composent leurs plus délicats bijoux" (*OC* II, 713)? Certainly it was by means of a woman, whether actual or imagined, that Baudelaire created **"Une Charogne"**; yet one would hardly describe the poem as a "delicate jewel." The response that we, as readers, must experience depends not simply on our repulsion at the spectacle of rotting animals and wormy women but equally, if not more powerfully, on our relation to the speaker and his "goût de l'horrible." This taste operates in the service of a final testament to a love that has or will be "decomposed." A love objectified in the body of a woman by metaphors that identify her with the natural world must, like the rest of nature, undergo change. Contrary to Nietzsche's notion of the eternal return, Baudelaire's poem instances a philosophy of the eternal departure. Love will decay, the body of the beloved will decay, and poetry cannot resist these processes. Insofar as we read this poem from the position of both speaker and addressee, we come to inhabit a world where the institution of love and its traditional poetic defenses have failed. Christian or pagan, metaphysical or material, the legitimations of a practice and a discourse that make the body of a woman depend on the soul of a man, on his instruction or adoration or poetry, are exposed by **"Une Charogne"** as rotten.

References

Ariès, Philippe. *The Hour of Our Death.* Translated by Helen Weaver. New York: Knopf, 1981.

Auerbach, Eric. "The Aesthetic Dignity of the 'Fleurs du mal.'" *Scenes from the Drama of European Literature.* New York: Meridian, 1959.

Bandy, W. T., and Pichois, Claude, eds. *Baudelaire devant ses contemporains.* Paris: Union Générale d'Editions (10/18), 1957.

Baudelaire, Charles. *Correspondance.* 2 vols. Bibliothèque de la Pléiade. Paris: Gallimard, 1973.

———. *Les fleurs du mal.* Edited by Antoine Adam. Classiques Garnier. Paris: Garnier, 1962.

———. *Œuvres complètes.* 2 vols. Edited by Claude Pichois. Bibliothèque de la Pléiade. Paris: Gallimard, 1975-76.

Bersani, Leo. *Baudelaire and Freud.* Berkeley: University of California Press, 1977.

Eliot, T. S. *Selected Essays.* New York: Harcourt, Brace, 1964.

Jennings, Michael W. *Dialectical Images: Walter Benjamin's Theory of Literary Criticism.* Ithaca: Cornell University Press, 1987.

McLees, Ainslie Armstrong. *Baudelaire's "Argot Plastique": Poetic Caricature and Modernism.* Athens: University of Georgia Press, 1989.

Nochlin, Linda. *Realism.* New York: Penguin Books, 1971.

Pichois, Claude. *Album Baudelaire.* Paris: Gallimard, 1974.

Pichois, Claude, and Ziegler, Jean. *Baudelaire.* Paris: Julliard, 1987.

———. *Baudelaire.* Translated by Graham Robb. London: Hamish Hamilton, 1989.

Tucker, Cynthia Grant. "'Pétrarchisant sur l'horrible': A Renaissance Tradition and Baudelaire's Grotesque." *French Review* 48:5 (April 1975): 887-96.

William Thompson (essay date 1997)

SOURCE: Thompson, William. "Order and chaos in 'A une passante.'" In *Understanding* Les Fleurs du Mal: *Critical Readings,* edited by William J. Thompson, pp. 145-59. Nashville, Tenn.: Vanderbilt University Press, 1997.

[*In the following essay, Thompson offers a line-by-line reading of "A une passante," focusing on the complicated interplay of order and chaos throughout the poem.*]

La rue assourdissante autour de moi hurlait.
Longue, mince, en grand deuil, douleur majestueuse,
Une femme passa, d'une main fastueuse
Soulevant, balançant le feston et l'ourlet;

(4)

Agile et noble, avec sa jambe de statue.
Moi, je buvais, crispé comme un extravagant,
Dans son œil, ciel livide où germe l'ouragan,
La douceur qui fascine et le plaisir qui tue.

(8)

Un éclair . . . puis la nuit!—Fugitive beauté
Dont le regard m'a fait soudainement renaître,
Ne te verrai-je plus que dans l'éternité?

(11)

Ailleurs, bien loin d'ici! trop tard! *jamais* peut-être!
Car j'ignore où tu fuis, tu ne sais où je vais,
O toi que j'eusse aimée, ô toi qui le savais!

(14)

In the midst of a bustling, noisy street scene, the poet crosses paths with a woman in mourning, who immediately captivates him. They apparently exchange a brief glance before being separated by the crowd and by their own paths in opposite directions. The poet regrets the brevity of this encounter and laments the impossibility of recapturing this moment in the anonymity of the large city. He even accuses the woman of having intentionally caused him great suffering. Reprising several familiar Baudelairean themes, **"A une passante"** is undeniably one of the great "Tableaux parisiens," an extraordinary poem of the city, a superb evocation of the anonymity of the modern urban setting and of the impossibility of pursuing a chance encounter or of halting the passage of time. Such occurrences are a regular feature of city life; strangers often exchange glances, knowing that little, if anything, will result of these encounters. But for the poet, apparently uncomfortable in these busy surroundings, one such meeting can have considerable consequences.

"A une passante" has been a particularly popular subject for Baudelaire scholars, who have brought to the interpretation of this poem a variety of perspectives, such as the erotic (Raser, Humphries), the biographical (Quesnel, reading the poem as an evocation of Baudelaire's mother), and the comparative (Heck, setting Baudelaire alongside Proust; LeBoulay, alongside Constantin Guys; Häufle, alongside Nerval; and Godfrey, alongside Lamartine); others have viewed the poem as street poetry (Chambers) and as an urban poem (Aynesworth; Benjamin, *Baudelaire: A Lyric Poet*). Indeed, one could devote an entire study to an overview of the critical exegeses of this poem (many of which appear in the bibliography).

The present analysis will focus on the fundamental opposition in **"A une passante"** between order and chaos, an opposition that makes difficult any exact interpretation of the poem. I will demonstrate how the tone of the poem shifts frequently and dramatically, from the chaos and seeming torment of both the street scene and later the poet's inner self, to the attempt on the poet's part to establish some sort of order, both in his own mind and in the syntax, vocabulary, and overall structure of the poem, as manifested in particular in the orderly depiction of the passerby and in his final comments on the impact of this woman on him.

For the purposes of this analysis, **"A une passante"** has been divided into six segments, each corresponding either to an atmosphere of disorder/chaos or to one of order/harmony in the development of the poem. That six possible divisions may be found in a poem of only fourteen lines demonstrates already an inherent instability in the structure of the poem (although I do not mean to argue that the poem must be segmented in this fashion). We will see that there is neither a gradual progression from one state to the other (chaos to order, order to chaos) nor a clear resolution of the consequences of this opposition. The poet never manages to escape completely the chaos introduced in the street scene described in the first line, since the most orderly element in the poem—the woman who appears in the street—will in turn cause his mental turmoil, another chaos. In this poem, chaos may lead to order, just as order leads to chaos. This uneasy opposition appears all the more remarkable if we attempt to hypothesize and reconstruct the process through which the poem has been composed: the poet undergoes this experience in the street, an event he will remember and later put on paper in the form of a sonnet. Yet even in this poetic creation, the chaos of the scene persists. In spite of the time that we assume elapses between the encounter and its commemoration on paper, the poet is not capable of recalling this experience and its impact in a uniformly clear and logical fashion. My analysis will proceed according to the following divisions:

l. 1: *disorder* of the street
ll. 2-5: *orderly* description of the woman
ll. 6-7: *disorder* of the poet's reaction to the woman
l. 8: *order* of his interpretation of this reaction
l. 9-12: *disorder* of his hopelessness
ll. 13-14: *order* of his final accusation and summary of the situation

The first line does much more than simply provide a physical setting for what is to transpire; it establishes the atmosphere of chaos that will reign over much of the remainder of the poem. The state of confusion is immediately evident in the opposition of the linearity suggested by the "rue" to the sense of disorder and confusion of "assourdissante" and "hurlait." The street is neither physically nor thematically a means of arriving at an end. On the contrary, the poet seems transfixed, incapable of movement or clear thought. The opposition between chaos and order is clear in the relationship of the poet to his surroundings. As Remacle notes, the street is described as "autour"—around—the poet (in itself a disorienting description), and the source of the noise, the grammatical subject of "hurlait," is the street itself. In addition, the two terms that qualify the street literally surround the poet in the first line: "*assourdissante* autour de moi *hurlait*." But the lack of detail about the precise sources of this noise (Benjamin notes that the crowd, if not mentioned, is implied) would seem to indicate that something—or someone—else will be the exclusive focus of the poet, who appears immobile, as if at the center of a whirlwind, the passive spectator of the action surrounding him. In fact, the title—**"A une passante"**—makes the mention of "la rue" virtually redundant, or at the very least predictable, as we can assume that the woman concerned is not an acquaintance and could only have been encountered in an anonymous public sphere.

The initial qualifier—"assourdissante"—is a key element in the poem. Not only does it establish the relationship between the poet and the street; it creates a

mood that will color the poet's depiction of the woman and, later, of his own mental state. One of his senses—his hearing—has been rendered ineffective from the beginning, and one might suggest that his ability to see (far more important in this poem) has been greatly impaired as well, as the constant, chaotic movement of the crowd impedes a clear or prolonged view of the individual passersby. The setting in which the poet finds himself overwhelms him in a potentially frightening and certainly incapacitating manner. In fact, the verb of the first line—"hurlait"—seems to evoke a bestial or monstrous imagery, reminiscent of the reference in **"Au Lecteur,"** the introductory poem of *Les Fleurs du Mal,* to "Les monstres glapissants, hurlants, grognants, rampants" (*OC* [*Œuvres complètes*] I, 6).

The effect of the setting on the poet is unpleasant, unlike that in another poem, **"Les Aveugles"** (the poem that immediately precedes **"A une passante"**), in which the poet says of the street: "tu chantes, ris et beugles." But the poet in **"Les Aveugles"** was also "hébété," overwhelmed by his environment, just as in **"A une passante"** the deafening street causes an initial disorder in the poet's thoughts. Ross Chambers, however, suggests that **"A une passante"** "is not out of control, like a howl; nor does it imitate a howl: its topic, indeed, is not lack of control but the subtle alliance of control . . . and disorder . . . in the one conjoined experience of beauty and death" ("Baudelaire's Street Poetry," 257). The importance of the initial line, then, is not to describe the street nor, for that matter, to establish an atmosphere of chaos but to set the (disordered) stage for, and to establish a contrast with, the subsequent description of the woman.

LINES 2-5

After the first, chaotic (albeit superbly constructed) introductory line, the focus shifts immediately to the exact, orderly description of the woman passing by. From the rapidity and chaos of the "rue assourdissante," we progress to the slow, relatively peaceful movement of the woman: "longue, mince, en grand deuil." She stands in stark contrast to the hustle and bustle of the surrounding street, as if part of an idealistic dream in the midst of the harsh reality of urban life. The movement from the general to the specific in the first stanza, from the crowd to the woman, also functions as a progression from disorder to order, from the chaotic goings-on in the street to the deliberate, careful (and quite specific) manipulation by the woman of her clothing in the fourth line ("Soulevant, balançant le feston et l'ourlet").

Ironically, the woman, before she is specifically mentioned, resembles the street. As both "rue" and "femme" are feminine, the two adjectives at the beginning of line 2 could very well be describing either (the street being the only noun in the poem thus far). If everything else around the poet is deafening confusion, the woman, like the physical street, is depicted as possessing a linear form ("longue"), and her progression (or the poet's focus on her progression) is distinct. But the woman and the street scene are far from identical, as Jean-Claude LeBoulay stresses: "Cette passante n'est pas un élément parmi d'autres de cette multitude, elle en est la négation" (25). While everything else around the poet provokes a confused aural response, the woman is described in clear, visual terms: tall, slender, and dressed in mourning.

Yet if the first hemistich of line 2 is marked by visual clarity, the second—"douleur majestueuse"—is ambiguous. At first glance, the majestic pain would appear to be that which the poet assumes the woman experiences in her mourning. If we allow for this interpretation, this line recalls the third line of another poem in the "Tableaux parisiens"—**"Le Cygne"**—in which the poet, speaking to Andromaque, refers to "L'immense majesté de vos douleurs de veuve." Yet if one reads to the end of **"A une passante"** and realizes in what state the seductive passerby will leave the poet, this "douleur" might well be the poet's own, an initial, violent "coup de foudre" when confronted with this apparition. At the moment when the poet attempts to understand the woman, to penetrate her exterior, we witness his lament. One might even suggest that, as the woman passes by him, the poet assumes the pain that he believes she feels. (It is worth noting the prominence and reverence accorded to "douleur" in Baudelaire's poetry; the word appears frequently and in *Les Fleurs du Mal* is capitalized on three occasions.) In whatever manner we interpret this word, "douleur" does certainly introduce, in the midst of a physical description of the woman, an element of unbearable emotion.

The first actual reference to the woman is strikingly straightforward—"Une femme passa"—especially in comparison with the "majestic" language that makes her stand out in the previous line and in comparison with the minuteness of the detail that will be devoted to her in the description that follows. The brevity of this initial reference undoubtedly parallels the brevity of the moment at which the poet catches sight of the woman (and subsequently loses sight of her). Yet following this key encounter, the poet seems capable of recalling every detail of this "tableau parisien." Indeed, the information in the latter half of line 3 (and later in line 4) is remarkably precise: from the woman in her entirety we pass immediately to the detail of one hand. Not only is a specific body part the focus of attention (which in itself is could hardly be considered unusual), but it is qualified in an extraordinary manner. What is the reader to make of "fastueuse"? Rich, sumptuous? Is this qualifier intended to reflect how the hand is perceived by the captivated poet, indicating his nearly obsessive (or

fetishistic) point of view? Or is this an indirect reference to the woman's social standing (Aguettant points out that these lines describe "détails de costume d'un goût bien bourgeois," 157)? From this might we imply that part of her attractiveness lies in her social standing? The subsequent lines would justify either interpretation, as they too focus on the details of the woman's clothing, yet from the perspective of an entranced male gaze. The precise vocabulary of this line is all the more striking in that it describes a woman who, chronologically speaking, is already a part of the past. She has, in fact, "passed by," the passé simple indicating that her action is complete and that she has already disappeared or is on the verge of doing so. In addition, as she disappears into the deafening, bustling activity of the street, any accurate description of her apparently becomes more problematic.

I have already stated that the description of the woman (in lines 2 through 5) is orderly, precise in opposition to the chaos of the street. This is particularly evident in the fourth line, where the two participles of the first hemistich—"soulevant, balançant"—suggest the rhythmic, flowing movement of the woman's skirts (in stark contrast to the general disorder of the street). That they are both composed of three syllables is hardly a coincidence, "balançant" in particular providing the line with both rhythmic and semantic equilibrium. This "balance" continues, in terms of the poetic structure, with the *3/3* syllabic division of the second hemistich (making the pattern for the entire line a perfectly orderly *3/3/3/3*).

The most specifically descriptive elements in the poem are, in fact, the references to the woman's outfit at the end of the first stanza: "le feston et l'ourlet," the lace border and the hem of her dress or skirt. (Again, as with her hand, the focus is on the details concerning the woman's extremities, those parts of her body that the poet can perceive when she makes any movement.) The orderly description of the woman, however, does not conclude at the end of the first quatrain, as one might expect. If lines 2 through 4 provide a physical description that one could probably perceive during a brief glance, the information in line 5 (which *is* the last line of the physical portrayal) is clearly more interpretive of the preceding lines and introduces a dramatic change in tone, moving beyond the objective (or quasi-objective) depiction by the poet and toward an obsessive preoccupation with the woman (this woman? any woman? all women?—yet another question left unanswered and perhaps unanswerable). Among the descriptive elements in this line, only "noble" would seem to coincide with what has preceded, falling within the same register as "majestueuse" and "fastueuse." It is the remaining elements that require further investigation, as they formulate a confusing depiction that troubles the apparent order that the woman has represented so far and stand as a transition point between the physical description of the woman (lines 2-4) and the reaction of the poet (lines 6-8).

"Agile," according to the *Petit Robert,* connotes "de la facilité et de la rapidité dans l'exécution de ses mouvements." Although, to be sure, the poet's exclusively visual encounter is brief, the description in line 2—"longue, mince, en grand deuil"—would appear to describe anything *but* quick, physically light movement. We have no indication of the woman's age, but perhaps Baudelaire means to suggest relative youth—although a widow, she might still be young, attractive, desirable. This qualifier also sets the woman in contrast to the poet who, for his part, will be described as "crispé," incapable of flowing movement. The brief, enticing, exhilarating glimpse of an ankle or foot, even one in mourning, is cause for an intense reaction. This woman—"agile et noble"—has perhaps both the physical attributes and the social position that the poet finds desirable.

Yet the description of the woman's leg, the ultimate point of focus in fact—"avec sa jambe de statue"—leaves another indelibly ambiguous impression. The poet captures only a brief view of this leg. But this leg—agile, if it too can be qualified by the preceding adjective—is also that of a statue: fixed and immobile. This ultimate orderly depiction renders the animate inanimate, the living immobile. The implications of this description are various: does the woman exemplify a perfect beauty, one that could be, or is worthy of being, immortalized in the form of a statue? If such is the case, is this a positive qualification, one that elevates the woman to the status of idealized being? Or is this description, in fact, the source of some degree of alienation between the woman and poet, a strange alienation indeed, considering that they do not know each other? Is the woman's beauty artificial, her leg (like the white leg of a statue) an unreal but stable presence in the hectic city scene in which this encounter takes place? At another level, one might see this immobile "jambe de statue" as an inevitable reflection of the brevity of the moment during which the poet catches a glimpse of the raised hem and what it dissimulates. Although the woman herself is "agile," this agility allows for only one excruciatingly brief view, so that what lies underneath appears motionless. Yet the brevity permits, ironically, a more ordered although less reliable description. It is relatively simple for the poet to describe what little he has seen. By focusing on one aspect or feature of one "isolated" individual, he escapes the chaos of the entire landscape. Perhaps there is an advantage to depicting what one sees in one brief moment, rather than over a prolonged period of time.

LINES 6-7

After the four lines devoted to description of the woman, the sixth line introduces a shift in focus from the seen to the seer, from the object to the subject of the gaze. The "moi" of the first line reappears, once again in a state of motionless disorder—"crispé comme un extravagant." "Crispé" itself may denote a variety of mental states causing tension, anguish, impatience, irritation, or pain, any of which we might offer to characterize the poet's state of mind in this case as he reacts to the woman. But more important, this adjective reflects the disorder in the poet's mind. His precise description of her physical appearance leads not to understanding but to upheaval on his part: "Significantly, the narration begins to break down at the moment when the man returns to himself and refers to his reaction . . . to the passante" (Aynesworth 330). We see that the chaos of the first line has not been eradicated or counteracted by the woman's brief presence but has been displaced into the mind of the poet, leading to his depiction of himself as "extravagant," meaning capable of bizarre actions or lacking in reason.

Although everything around him is "assourdissant," in line 6 we see that the poet is nonetheless capable of focus. Yet for the first time we also have some indication that the poet's glance (if not his fixation) is being reciprocated, that the woman is also looking either at him or in his general direction: "Je buvais . . . dans son œil." What is the nature of this reciprocated sighting (is it a glance, a gaze, a stare? does she actually look directly at him?), and is the poet capable of interpreting correctly the intent of the woman's gaze? Versluys suggests, "He is not so much drinking from the woman's eyes the meaning she possesses intrinsically as he is endowing her with his own meaning" (297). In other words, what the poet offers the reader is less an orderly and objective representation than a desperate attempt to understand her in the little time at his disposal before she fades from his memory. The preceding physical appearance (clear and orderly as it is) contrasts with the overall impact of the woman on the poet, especially the impact of her glance or gaze. Although the poet fully understands the implications of his situation, he is not spared the mental anguish that follows the woman's departure from his sight: "The woman . . . stands for two different ways in which human messages oppose disorder: as mediated, orderly communication (the beauty of her figure) and as unmediated communication (her glance). But in each of them, as we shall see, disorder inevitably lurks" (Chambers, "Storm," 159). She is both a cure for, and a cause of, the disorder in the poem and in the poet's mind.

This matter is complicated further by the depiction of her eye as a "ciel livide" (which itself is then qualified by "où germe l'ouragan"). The woman's gaze/glance appears to be dark and ominous albeit not immediately threatening. Similarly, in **"Horreur sympathique"** Baudelaire associates the "ciel livide" with potentially troubling thoughts:

> De ce ciel bizarre et livide,
> Tourmenté comme ton destin,
> Quels pensers dans ton âme vide
> Descendent? . . .

Even though these two individuals do not know each other, and undoubtedly never will, the potential for danger exists and succeeds in preoccupying the poet; perhaps any actual encounter with the woman would be disastrous. (For evidence, one need only examine Baudelaire's depictions of women and his relationships with these women in many of his other poems.)

What, in fact, would the "ouragan" describe: their potential relationship? the woman's volatile character? the poet's torment (the latter a likely candidate, considering the line that follows)? "Ouragan" is an appropriate choice of vocabulary, particularly in the context of our discussion of order and chaos; a hurricane might be considered a natural form of disorder, one that we might appose to the "civilized" disorder of the street scene (yet within which there is, ironically, some sense of order, in its circular motion centered on the "eye").

LINE 8

After the potentially threatening tone of the previous two lines, the eighth line unites the two aspects of physical and emotional relationships that permeate Baudelaire's oeuvre: on the one hand the idealized woman— gentle, captivating, enchanting—and on the other the (here) nearly violent, physical act. Grammatically, the line is the complement of "je buvais": "La douceur" and "le plaisir" both take on physical proportions; they are the "potent potables" that the poet would consume, thus intensifying his already heightened fascination with the woman. This line is also another wonderful syntactic construction: an orderly, lucid realization on the part of the poet of the effect of the woman on him, the sequence of two-syllable nouns and verbs—"douceur," "fascine," "plaisir"—reaching a climax with the shockingly violent, monosyllabic "tue," which concludes the quatrain. While "douceur" describes the woman herself in relatively flattering tones, "plaisir" describes the potential relationship between the poet and the woman, a physical one that would lead to death.

LINES 9-12

While the woman offers the poet both gentleness and pleasure, the poet's reaction to these qualities encompasses both hope and despair. After her departure, his frustration and tension, which have been building up

over the course of the description of the woman, reach a peak (a pseudosexual climax of sorts) in the ninth line, with the sudden flash followed by darkness, followed in turn by melancholic reflection. In discussing **"A une passante,"** Walter Benjamin states, "The delight of the urban poet is love—not at first sight, but at last sight" (45). The woman's presence in the poem is reflected in two ways: through the objective description that accompanies the initial sighting and in the emotional reaction after she has disappeared; the former is based on an event that lasted but a brief moment, the latter on a mental activity unrestricted even by the underlying reality.

The "éclair" is a most suitable image for conveying (once again) the brevity of the moment depicted. Yet this same word functions on a completely different level, introducing an opposition of light and dark, followed as it is by "la nuit" and referring back to the stormy vocabulary of "livide" and "ouragan." Obviously, this opposition does not occur exclusively at a spatiotemporal level. The night is not that which follows the setting of the sun but rather that void in the poet's soul as the passerby moves away from him, the glimmer of hope apparently extinguished, their brief encounter now history (and already obscured by the crowd and by the inevitably fading memory).

The poet's sudden realization of what has occurred, and his confused reaction to this event, are dramatically reflected in the punctuation of line 9. The ellipsis could signify the temporary blindness that occurs after a bolt of lightning has struck, the void in which he feels he has been left, or the ecstasy experienced by the poet as a reaction to the woman. Time, and the woman's progression away from him, continue, while the poet would wish both to stop, in what Remacle terms "la presque simultanéité de l'espoir et de la déception" (97). The exclamation point accentuates even further the poet's startled and consequently chaotic reaction to the woman's disappearance into the crowd. The diacritic mark preceding the second hemistich creates yet another break, a pause after the poet's exclamation, before he proceeds, in apostrophic style, to address this woman. I need hardly point out the obviously disjointed nature of this line, especially by comparison with the order of the preceding line. Its physical appearance on the page suffices to demonstrate the confusion felt by the poet at this moment as events happen all too quickly around him.

The lasting impression left in the poet's mind is that of a "Fugitive beauté," an expression that logically describes the woman in the context of the poem and one that allows again for several possible interpretations. There is undoubtedly a progression from the descriptive to the interpretive in this line, from a description emphasizing the brevity of this encounter

("Un éclair . . . puis la nuit!"), to a reflection on the part of the poet about what he has just experienced. Both suggest the frustration of the poet with the elusiveness of the woman. We might particularly note the use of vocabulary in the poem to indicate the (all too rapid) passage of time: "passa," "éclair," "fugitive," "soudainement," which might be opposed to the vocabulary of the negative question in the eleventh line: "Ne te verrai-je plus que dans *l'éternité?*" Yet "fugitive" may also signify flight, a conscious (or perhaps unconscious) effort to distance oneself. The lightning-quick exchange of glances between the poet and the woman inspires and impassions the poet, but the woman herself is out of reach, so that he is simultaneously frustrated.

Certainly there is an element of regret about the lack of fulfillment of the potential relationship, an interesting reworking of the common Baudelairean theme of the eventual demise of love or the beloved, as seen in **"L'Horloge":** "Le plaisir vaporeux fuira vers l'horizon." Ultimately, the woman is that which cannot be obtained, genuinely appreciated, or understood. The poet remains, describing something that has barely existed in his own personal world. It becomes apparent that the duration of the "regard" and of this "encounter" is irrelevant in relation to its impact on the object, the poet. As for the poet's rebirth, to which this line alludes, this may well be an attempt to extricate himself from the disorder and torment caused by his surroundings. Perhaps through some form of rebirth he will inherit the calm, orderly nature of the woman. (It is imperative as well to point out the maternal element introduced into the poem at this point, although I will not elaborate on this notion here.)

The poet's distress in line 11 stands in stark contrast to the all too brief hopefulness of the "rebirth" in the previous line (a rebirth that was, admittedly, "soudain"—thus only temporary—as the maternal figure disappears). The desperation takes the form of a question—"Ne te verrai-je plus que dans l'éternité?"—for which the poet already knows the answer all too well, as will be revealed in the final tercet. In poems such as **"Je te donne ces vers . . ."** and (albeit cruelly) **"Une Charogne,"** the poet states that long after her death (and decomposition), the woman will "live on," immortalized in the poet's memory and in the verses he composes. Yet in the case of **"A une passante,"** the poet clearly finds no solace in this memory. On the contrary, he despairs at having to content himself with one fleeting moment (one can scarcely even call it an "encounter"). Although he is inspired by the passerby's beauty, the poet would rather engage in an actual relationship with her. A desperate disorder results from his inability to "capture the moment," a disorder that the poet himself provokes (as opposed to that caused by the woman's immediate impact on him). The question in line 11 is hypothetical; the woman to whom it is ad-

dressed is long gone, and the poet is left questioning not only the nature of what has just transpired but his seemingly bleak future without her. Aynesworth suggests, "She is simply a fantasy by which the man maintains consciousness in the context of chaos and dereliction" (333). But I would counter that the poet is not merely daydreaming; the fantasy is more like a nightmare. Although one might posit that this woman is merely a model on which the poet will base his "fantasy," I believe that in this case the poet would prefer reality, however disappointing it may ultimately prove to be, to imagination.

The sense of hopelessness reaches a near-hysterical apex in the twelfth line (which resembles the ninth line in its disjointed construction). Again the poet laments how he and the woman have been forever separated, a fact that is stressed by the dual references to spatial ("Ailleurs, bien loin d'ici") and temporal ("trop tard! *jamais*") separation, with the second reference in each case suggesting a more extreme condition than the first; while "ailleurs" and "trop tard" evoke a missed opportunity, "bien loin d'ici" and "jamais" reflect the impossibility of recapturing the past or finding the woman. The restricted and precise nature of the setting for this poem (one instance on a city street) is now overwhelmed by an indeterminate future in an unknown, unattainable place. (Using a similar vocabulary, the ending of **"L'Horloge"** is even more despairing: "Meurs, vieux lâche! il est trop tard!") The negative "jamais" reveals the ironic impossibility of the title: how can the poem be addressed to the woman—"une passante"—who is no longer there and cannot be found? As Godfrey remarks, "In a dramatic demystification of the traditional lyric preoccupation with the theme of love, Baudelaire thus transforms the love sonnet—which in its very form recalls the ideals of Petrarchan love—into a "poème sur rien"" (41). The woman—"une passante"—is qualified in the title in terms of an ephemeral action that results in her disappearance. The only mitigating factor in this line is the final "peut-être"; in spite of his lament, the poet does seem to reserve some hope for a future encounter with the woman. Yet this hope seems empty; the obstacles to any future meetings are insurmountable, as will be clearly delineated in the final two lines.

Lines 13-14

After these lines of despair, the full realization of the futility of the situation leads the poet into a moment of striking clarity at the end of the poem. The poet liberates himself from the state of confusion caused by his surroundings and by the apparition (and disappearance) of the woman in order to formulate a cohesive, precisely structured summation about the encounter, an orderly structure that is particularly remarkable when opposed to the lamentation of line 12.

In the final two lines there are a total of eight pronouns ordered into four pairs: "j[e]" / "tu," "tu" / "je," "toi" / "je," "toi" / "le." In line 13 the two pairs form a perfect grammatical and semantic harmony (albeit one founded on ignorance!) as the "j'ignore" of the first hemistich matches the "tu ne sais" of the second, and as the "tu fuis" matches the "je vais." This line again suggests a mutual bond between the poet and the woman, an interest on the part of the poet perhaps reciprocated by the woman (however slightly), made even more personal by the poet's dramatic use of the familiar "tu."

Yet once again the emphasis is on the ephemeral nature of this event, the "fugitive" of line 10 recalled by the verb "fuis" (which is noticeably stronger than the "vais" used to convey the poet's own movement). Although the general state of confusion of the previous stanzas has dissipated, it has been replaced by two new states equally unacceptable to the poet: ignorance and nothingness; the ignorance of what has happened to the woman and what might have happened between them, and the nothingness that results from this ignorance, as the poet remains alone in the chaotic, anonymous bustle of this street, what Quesnel calls "l'impitoyable réalité" (100). And this ignorance and hopelessness, so clearly and logically presented in the penultimate line, lead to the final lament that closes the poem.

The last line is composed of two hemistiches with identical structures—apostrophic "ô toi," followed by relative clause—yet the implications of the two halves of this last line differ tremendously. In the first, the poet finally admits to the possibility of a romantic interest on his part, yet this can only be expressed in hypothetical terms through the use of the pluperfect subjunctive. The apostrophe makes the statement accusatory, blaming the woman for the power she does not know she possesses, for being the object of an unrequited "passion." The final hemistich, however, breaks from the pattern of the previous three by omitting the first person pronoun. Now only the woman is mentioned (in contradistinction to the "moi" of the very first line), the "passante" of the title being all that lingers in the mind of the poet, yet disembodied from the context in which she appeared. She is no longer merely a "passante," that activity having long ceased in any case but rather a (potentially) vindictive woman, conscious of her devastating impact on the poet.

It is evident from these final lines of **"A une passante"** that it is neither the physical depiction of the woman (lines 1 through 5) nor, for that matter, the poet's immediate reaction to this woman (line 6 through the first part of 9) that will ultimately dominate the structure of the poem and provide the greatest emotional and poetic impact. The key to a true comprehension of the poem (and the vacillation between order and chaos that has been the focus of this analysis) lies in the chaos-based

yet orderly summation by the poet (second part of line 9 to the end of the poem) and more specifically in the final accusatory address: "Seul l'anonymat permet le libre cours de l'imagination érotique inhérente à l'activité poétique qui, elle, est fondée sur le sentiment d'un manque, d'une absence, d'une nostalgie, de l'impossibilité de convergence de la réalité et du rêve" (Buvik 234). Only the disappearance of the woman before they can meet (and before the poet realizes that it is possible for them to meet) allows the poet to engage in the imaginative, poetic activity that subsequently results in the composition of the poem, and in the revelation of emotions that perhaps would not have existed in the case of an actual relationship. The real but chaotic event leads to an imaginary yet ordered summation.

Such an interpretation of the poem obviously emphasizes the tercets over the quatrains, a fact that the title of the poem itself would confirm as valid, since "à" implies an address rather than a mere depiction. What becomes clear after any reading of **"A une passante,"** although this fact is not evident in the lines that precede (which are, however, remarkable in themselves), is that the progress in the poem is assuredly in the direction not only of the final tercet but also of the final two lines: the ordered yet emotional conclusion by the poet regarding this encounter. The only order that the poet can construct in these final lines is sterile—based on the hopelessness of an unrealizable relationship. Far more beneficial to the poet's creative process is the frightening chaos that allows his imagination to run free in the first place. Is it possible, therefore, to determine which prevails in the poem—order or chaos? The answer is apparently neither. The only triumph is that of the passerby over the poet, in both orderly and chaotic fashion, which frustrates his desire to capture (or to recapture) this woman and this moment experienced in the midst of a deafening street.

References

Aguettant, Louis. *Baudelaire.* Paris: Editions du CERF, 1978.

Aynesworth, Donald. "A Face in the Crowd: A Baudelairian Vision of the Eternal Feminine." *Stanford French Review* 5:3 (Winter 1981): 327-39.

Baudelaire, Charles. *Correspondance.* 2 vols. Bibliothèque de la Pléiade. Paris: Gallimard, 1973.

———. *Les fleurs du mal.* Edited by Antoine Adam. Classiques Garnier. Paris: Garnier, 1962.

———. *Œuvres complètes.* 2 vols. Edited by Claude Pichois. Bibliothèque de la Pléiade. Paris: Gallimard, 1975-76.

Benjamin, Walter. *Charles Baudelaire: A Lyric Poet in the Era of High Capitalism.* Translated by Harry Zohn. London: New Left Books, 1973.

Buvik, Per. "Paris, lieu poétique, lieu érotique. Quelques remarques à propos de Walter Benjamin et de Baudelaire." *Revue Romane* 20.2 (1985): 231-242.

Chambers, Ross. "Baudelaire's Street Poetry." *Nineteenth-Century French Studies* 13:4 (Summer 1985): 244-59.

———. "The Storm in the Eye of the Poem." In *Textual Analysis: Some Readers Reading,* edited by Mary Ann Caws. New York: Modern Language Association, 1986.

Godfrey, Sima. "Foules Rush In: Lamartine, Baudelaire, and the Crowd." *Romance Notes* 24:1 (Fall 1983): 33-42.

Häufle, Heinrich. "Nervals und Baudelaires 'Schöne Unbekannte': 'Une allée du Luxembourg' und 'A une passante' im Vergleich." *Die neueren Sprachen* 88:6 (December 1989): 590-606.

Heck, Francis S. "Baudelaire and Proust: Chance Encounters of the Same Kind." *Nottingham French Studies* 23:2 (October 1984): 17-26.

Humphries, John Jefferson. "Poetical History or Historical Poetry: Baudelaire's Epouvantable Jeu of Love and Art." *Romance Quarterly* 30:3 (1983): 231-37.

LeBoulay, Jean-Claude. "Commentaire composé: Charles Baudelaire." *L'information littéraire* 41:3 (May-June 1989): 24-28.

Le Petit Robert. Paris: Société du Nouveau Littré, 1967.

Quesnel, Michel. *Baudelaire solaire et clandestin.* Paris: Presses Universitaires de France, 1987.

Raser, Timothy. "Language and the Erotic in Two Poems by Baudelaire." *Romantic Review* 79:3 (May 1988): 443-51.

Remacle, Madeleine. *Analyses de poèmes français.* Paris: Les Belles Lettres, 1975.

Edward K. Kaplan (essay date summer 1998)

SOURCE: Kaplan, Edward K. "Ecstasy and Insight: Baudelaire's Fruitful Tensions." *Romance Quarterly* 45, no. 3 (summer 1998): 133-42.

[*In the following essay, Kaplan focuses on the many tensions and oppositions of* Les Fleurs du Mal—*in particular the tension between the ethical and the aesthetic content of the work.*]

Baudelaire is acclaimed as the pre-Symbolist author of **"Correspondances"** (*FM* [*Les Fleurs du Mal*], no. 4), whose imagination joins light and dark, sound, savor, and touch to arouse "les transports de l'esprit et des sens."[1] Aromas are particularly evocative for the poet,

who shuts his eyes to evoke idealized worlds, such as the ones produced in **"La Chevelure"** (*FM,* no. 23): "Je plongerai ma tête amoureuse d'ivresse / Dans ce noir océan où l'autre est enfermé." The rhythmic refrains of **"Le Balcon"** (*FM,* no. 36) and especially **"Harmonie du soir"** (*FM,* no. 47) compose a communion of fantasy and memories, redeeming past pleasures from oblivion: "Ton souvenir en moi luit comme un ostensoir!" The refrain of **"L'invitation au voyage"** (*FM,* no. 53) summarizes these synesthetic utopias: "Là, tout n'est qu'ordre et beauté / Luxe, calme et volupté."

The affirmative ethical content of Baudelaire's works is also fundamental, nuancing the predominant view of him as an aesthete or "symbolist" as portrayed by Des Esseintes in Huysmans's *A rebours.* The poems Baudelaire added to the 1861 edition of *Les Fleurs du Mal* generate their energy from the struggle between "aesthetic" and "ethical" drives, that is, between the delights procured from inwardness and imagination versus the recognition of finite reality and compassion for other human beings.

This transition from a radical aesthetic position to ethical realism can be briefly summarized: Images of women in the first, 1857 edition glorify unreachable perfection; **"La Beauté"** (*FM,* no. 17), a widely taught favorite of anthologies, uses a statue to typify aesthetic idealism. Women in the second edition recall the poet to everyday life; added in 1861, **"Le Masque"** (*FM,* no. 20) initially displays Beauty's seductive qualities— "Cette femme, morceau vraiment miraculeux"—in order to emphasize his denounciation of the illusion: "O blasphème de l'art! ô surprise fatale!" At the end, the mortal beneath Art's mask provokes an almost hackneyed identification:

—Elle pleure, insensé, parce qu'elle a vécu!
Et parce qu'elle vit! Mais ce qu'elle déplore
Surtout, ce qui la fait frémir jusqu'aux genoux,
C'est que demain, hélas! il faudra vivre encore!
Demain, après-demain et toujours!—comme nous!

The poet-persona also changes character. **"La Beauté"** depicts him as solitary and "consumed" by the utopian quest. The poet of **"Le Masque,"** recalling the pathos of Hugo's preface to *Les Contemplations* ("Insensé qui crois que je ne suis pas toi"), establishes a solidarity with humankind.[2]

Baudelaire's literary innovations arise from a masterly *confluence* of profound visionary experience and critical analysis. Baudelaire the "philosopher" is inseparable from the imaginative voluptuary. In his 1861 essay on Wagner's operas, he summarizes his mature understanding of synesthesia by evoking and then examining the euphoria stimulated by the overture to *Lohengrin.* To explain the effect on his imagination he begins by quoting the first two stanzas of **"Correspondances"** ending with "Les parfums, les couleurs et les sons se répondent." Then, stating that his reverie was mediated by the composer's program notes and a book by Franz Liszt, he describes its climax as a combination of two normally distinct modes of consciousness: "Alors je conçus pleinement l'idée d'une âme se mouvant dans un lieu lumineux, d'une extase faite de volupté et de connaissance, et planant au-dessus et bien loin du monde naturel."[3] Soon after he defines his goal: "transformer ma volupté en connaissance." The complete poet is both dreamer and critic, both aesthetically hypersensitive and devoted to truth.

Baudelaire's prose poems—which I prefer to characterize as "fables of modern consciousness"—consistently perform this remarkable blending of opposites. Published in periodicals from 1855 to his death in 1867, fifty pieces were published together by Charles Asselineau and Théodore de Banville as *Le Spleen de Paris. Petits poèmes en prose* in the 1869 posthumous edition. This definitive order was based on a memorandum in Baudelaire's hand, written around 1865, which lists fifty pieces possessing an "architecture" or overall thematic progression.[4]

As a sort of preface, two prosaic fables, "L'Etranger" and "Le Désespoir de la vieille" (*SP* [*Le Spleen de Paris*], nos. 1-2), define the collection's polarity of ethical and aesthetic values. Conversations provide ethical possibilities whereas daydreaming encompasses the solipsistic pleasures of imagination. The alienated male of "L'Etranger" refuses to engage the narrator (or interviewer) who asks the fundamental ethical question, "Qui aimes-tu le mieux . . . ?" This outsider rejects all bourgeois values: family, friends, fatherland, money; he is committed only to "the goddess Beauty." At the end, the "extraordinaire étranger" deliberately spaces out on clouds: "—J'aime les nuages . . . les nuages qui passent . . . là-bas . . . là-bas . . . les merveilleux nuages!" Readers for decades have seen Baudelaire himself in this surrender to ever-changing desire.

The second panel of the diptych, "Le Désespoir de la vieille," also depicts a failed dialogue, but it ends with an ethical affirmation. Its heroine is "la petite vieille ratatinée" who attempts to coddle an infant with whom she shares, ironically, a certain beauty, "ce joli être, si fragile comme elle, la petite vieille, et, comme elle aussi, sans dents et sans cheveux." But the baby perceives her as ugly and shrieks with fear. At the end, she withdraws into "sa solitude éternelle" and weeps, accepting her failure to attract the baby as the inescapable condition of womankind: "—'Ah! pour nous, malheureuses vieilles femelles, l'âge est passé de plaire, même aux innocents.'" By contrast with the opening fable, here the narrator sympathizes with aged women whose ability to elicit tenderness fades with their youthful beauty.

ELUDING THE ETHICAL BAUDELAIRE

The appealing stereotype of the "aesthetic Baudelaire" has diverted attention from this stable ethical dimension—and its productive tensions with the aesthetic. Extrapolating from "L'Etranger," both Robert Kopp and Henri Lemaitre in their editions of *Le Spleen de Paris* cite Baudelaire's *Salon de 1859* to certify the author's putative preference for reverie as ultimate pleasure.[5] To validate the "stranger's" cloud fantasies, they truncate a lyrical passage from Baudelaire's analysis of Boudin's landscape paintings—ignoring, or implicitly denying, the fable's stated ethical probe.

Baudelaire's *complete* paragraph confirms the inseparability of the ethical and the aesthetic—as well as his ambivalence toward both. It describes how a painting arouses within him a synesthesia, then expanding into a lavish reverie that insulates him from the world; but then he thinks of other people:

> J'ai vu. A la fin tous ces nuages aux formes fantastiques et lumineuses, ces ténèbres chaotiques, ces immensités vertes et roses, suspendues et ajoutées les unes aux autres, ces fournaises béantes, ces firmaments de satin noir ou violent, fripé, roulé ou déchiré, ces horizons en deuil ou ruisselants de métal fondu, toutes ces profondeurs, toutes ces splendeurs, me montèrent au cerveau comme une boisson capiteuse ou comme l'éloquence de l'opium. Chose assez curieuse, il ne m'arriva pas une seule fois, devant ces magies liquides ou aériennes, de me plaindre de l'absence de l'homme.

Both Lemaitre and Kopp end their quotation here to claim that cloud reveries are the author's true commitment. But the passage continues by acknowledging, perhaps ironically, the public's vulgar pragmatism:

> Mais je me garde bien de tirer de la plénitude de ma jouissance un conseil pour qui que ce soit, non plus pour M. Boudin. Le conseil serait trop dangereux.

I could end my quotation here in order to promote Baudelaire's ethical concern, but he also applies irony toward his own resistance to reverie:

> Qu'il se rappelle que l'homme, comme dit Robespierre, qui avait soigneusement fait ses *humanités,* ne voit jamais l'homme sans plaisir; et, s'il veut gagner un peu de popularité, qu'il se garde bien de croire que le public soit arrivé à un égal enthousiasme pour la solitude.

Baudelaire censored his temptation to remain aloft.[6] If there is any lesson, it is ethical: meditation on richly colorful painting may release the mind through intense fantasy, but reason resists this inner plenitude and directs its focus back to earth.

Also to the point is Baudelaire's ambiguous attitude toward the ethical. His italicized reference to Robespierre's "humanities" undermines any didacticism. The theorist of the Terror hardly embodies civic virtue and it was unlikely that Robespierre himself "ne voit jamais l'homme sans plaisir."[7] More than a century before Emmanuel Lévinas defined the sanctity of "le visage de l'Autre," Baudelaire honestly confesses horror of "la tyrannie de la face humaine,"[8] which may also function as a defense against his agonized yearning for intimacy.

Multiple tensions thus emerge from the "jouissance" of imaginative autonomy described in this section of the paragraph. The combination of lyrical self-expression and critical self-awareness is the key.

THE GENESIS OF A GENRE

Roger Shattuck has located the possible inception of Baudelaire's prose poems in the opening paragraphs of "De la couleur," section 3 of **Salon de 1846**,[9] the poet's first significant published work. Generously naming other scholars who touched upon this idea (Ferran, Starkie, Leakey, Kelley), Shattuck interprets "Baudelaire's first attempt at the genre, partially set off as a separate whole, and reaffirming the early onset of his desire to develop a form of writing distinct from both formal verse and expository prose." He astutely demonstrates how a primitive prose poem arises from the author's dynamic synesthesia: "In the vibration of color [Baudelaire] sees a supreme *correspondance*, linking external reality and the mind." An analogous process characterizes "'Le *Confiteor* de l'artist' [*SP*, no. 3] which begins to throb between *immensité* and *petitesse*, between *les choses* and *moi*" (Shattuck 147). A similar "sense of wonder" inspires the imaginative whirling of the poem **"Harmonie du soir"** (*FM,* no. 47).

I would add one crucial element. The "vibratory organism" Shattuck plausibly identifies as a primal vehicle of Baudelaire's poetic liberation is also its downfall—since, at the same time, it opens a critical self-awareness. At the very center of **"Le *Confiteor* de l'artiste,"** the narrator's ecstasy collapses.[10] He then examines his sensations of transcendence objectively, like a phenomenologist, in order rationally to explain their origin:

> Toutefois, ces pensées, qu'elles sortent de moi ou s'élancent des choses, deviennent bientôt trop intenses. L'énergie dans la volupté crée un malaise et une souffrance positive. Mes nerfs trop tendus ne donnent plus que des vibrations criardes et douleureuses.

During the rapture, the dreamer had lost his ability to distinguish his mind from its productions. Now the narrator, who is both "philosopher" and "poet," experiences the pain of imagination's limits. He does not deny external reality. It is probable that the loss of his free will—Baudelaire's criterion for full humanity (see **"Au lecteur,"** *FM,* liminal poem)—explains his distress at the peak of his ego's ecstasy.

The fable ends by attempting to reconcile the fact of human finitude and the impossible but fated passion for the ideal: "L'étude du beau est un duel où l'artiste crie de frayeur avant d'être vaincu." Ecstasy cannot become a way of life. And yet the artist will not relinquish consciousness and free will. The modern seeker heroically, with sometimes tragic consequences, embraces the contradiction. Baudelaire's mature works honor, however ambivalently, finite exterior reality as a necessary counterpart of imaginative fullness.

Although Baudelaire's "prose poems" may have originated in such lyrical evocations of art, they make up an essentially ethical genre. Poetic prose, despite the author's stated "ambition" to realize "le miracle d'une prose poétique, musicale, sans rhythme et sans rime," even at that relatively early stage, was not his final destination. The diverse narratives labeled "prose poems" envisage a higher goal: "d'appliquer à la description de la vie moderne, ou plutôt d'*une* vie moderne et abstraite, le procédé qu'il [Aloysius Bertrand] avait appliqué à la peinture de la vie ancienne" ("A Arsène Houssaye," *OC* 146). They both perform and explore workings of the contemporary mentality—of the narrator, the author, and enlightened readers.

Their public gestation and birth justifies my (admittedly awkward) designation of "fables of modern consciousness." Extending Barbara Johnson's now classic deconstructive account, we can trace how Baudelaire's self-reflective fables far surpass the early stylistic experiments with prose and verse "doublets."[11] In 1855, two years before his poetic masterwork appeared, he contributed prose "versions" of two comparable poems to *Hommage à C. F. Denecourt,* with other contributions by Asselineau, Banville, Hugo, Nerval, and others. The prose pieces **"Le Crépuscule"** and **"La Solitude"** parallel **"Le Soir"** and **"Le Matin,"** poems later included in **Les Fleurs du Mal.**

The next stage emerged two years later, in 1857, four days after the poet's scandalous bouquet was confiscated by judicial order. On 27 August his first series conceived as a separate genre appeared in *Le Présent*. He had revised the two meditative narratives, **"Le Crépuscule"** and **"La Solitude"** (both from the 1855 anthology) and included them in a larger sequence, six pieces identified as *poèmes nocturnes*." The allegorical anecdotes **"Les Projets"** and **"L'Horloge"** were followed by **"La Chevelure"** and **"L'Invitation au voyage,"** rhythmical "prose poems" (as we usually understand the term). Yet self-reflective irony and analysis now became their hallmark—although the author did not yet anticipate the radical originality of the pieces that would follow.

The third stage introduces a more specifically "ethical" theme: the struggle between imagination and moral responsibility. In February 1861, the second edition of **Les Fleurs du Mal** went on sale. Matching his structural and philosophical revision of the poetry, Baudelaire had advanced his six "nocturnal poems" of 1857 and, on 1 November 1861, the *Revue Fantaisiste* published his series of nine *"poèmes en prose"*—so named for the first time—adding three very significant fables to the earlier sequence: **"Les Foules," "Les Veuves,"** and **"Le Vieux Saltimbanque"** (*SP,* nos. 12-14). This series of nine pieces in the *Revue Fantaisiste,* which ceased publication after the next issue, consolidates the birth of the Baudelairean fable of modern consciousness. Then, twenty-six pieces prepared for *La Presse,* August-September 1862, became the foundation of **Le Spleen de Paris.**

POETRY AND TRUTH

The originality of the fifty pieces that make up the collection consists, therefore, in a critical awareness generated within the lyrical process itself which liberates the narrator—and readers—from fantasy's enslaving naïveté. Two examples must suffice. The rhythmical meditation **"Un hémisphère dans une chevelure"** (*SP,* no. 17), first published in *Le Présent* in 24 August 1857, fulfills the author's ambition to perfect "une prose poétique"; but, more important, it subverts its own lyricism. It is one of *the only three* in the collection that are conventionally "poetic"; the others are **"L'Invitation au voyage"** and **"Le Crépuscule du soir"** (*SP,* nos. 18, 22).

Rythmical repetitions structure the seven brief paragraphs of **"Un hémisphère dans une chevelure"** as stanzas. The visionary narrator generates scenes of sensuality and repose from smelling a woman's head of hair: "Laisse-moi respirer longtemps, longtemps, l'odeur de tes cheveux, y plonger tout mon visage, comme un homme altéré dans l'eau d'une source." Self-reflection then arises in stanza three which explains how these images flow from an initial metaphor, tresses which generate fantasies: "Tes cheveux contiennent tout un rêve, plein de voilures et de mâtures; ils contiennent de grandes mers dont les moussons me portent vers de charmants climats."

This is the Baudelaire we love, the aesthete who savors subtle and intoxicating sensations of mind and feelings. The next three stanzas launch more images with parallel expressions: "Dans l'océan de ta chevelure . . . / Dans les caresses de ta chevelure . . . / Dans l'ardent foyer de ta chevelure. . . ." We are hooked: "sur les rivages duvetés de ta chevelure, je m'enivre des odeurs combinées du goudron, du musc et de l'huile de coco." And that is the point. The term *enivré* alerts us to the critical judgment that this utopia issues from fragile illusion.

The "prose poem" has deconstructed its own "poetic" world. The concluding stanza repeats and resolves the prelude, while the final refrain echoes the first paragraph, ending with a shocking literalism: "Laisse-moi mordre longtemps tes tresses lourdes et noires. Quand je mordille tes cheveux élastiques et rebelles, il me semble que je mange des souvenirs." The phrase "il me semble" undermines imagination's authority.

This skepticism internal to the prose poem raises fundamental ontological questions. Were his poetic productions memories, recollections of real experiences, or fictions of desire? Does reverie enhance memory or alienate the dreamer from the world by creating fantasies which then become memories, dreamed traces of desire? The prose **"L'Invitation au voyage"** (*SP,* no. 18), which directly follows, advances the self-analysis of this new, meta-linguistic genre.

A second subgenre combines rhythmical prose and symbolic self-interpretation. **"Le Crépuscule du soir"** (*SP,* no. 22) explores "Paris spleen" or urban depression, the turmoil lurking in our subconscious. The first version, published in the 1855 anthology, began with this paragraph: "La tombée de la nuit a toujours été pour moi le signal d'une fête intérieure et comme la délivrance d'une angoisse. Dans les bois comme dans les rues d'une grande ville, l'assombrissement du jour et le scintillement des étoiles ou des lanternes éclairent mon esprit." Baudelaire's first revision in the 1857 issue of *Le Présent* develops this insight both analytically and through images.

The final revision adds a new opening paragraph which generates the poetic process that follows. It depicts a detached observer who listens to the effects of "Le jour tombe. Un grand apaisement se fait dans les pauvres esprits fatigués du labeur de la journée; et leurs pensées prennent maintenant les couleurs tendres et indécises du crépuscule." Then, after devoting half the narrative to describing two of his crazy friends, the narrator returns to his own consciousness—at that very point where the primitive text had begun: "O nuit! ô rafraîchissantes ténèbres! vous êtes pour moi le signal d'une fête intérieure. . . ." The revised fable brings the dreamer's cosmic inspiration down to earth, a cityscape lit by the recently installed gas lamps.

The two final paragraphs maintain the excitement while contriving, self-analytically, the symbolism of nocturnal solitude. The first one consists of two sentences, one short, and a longer metaphoric amplification that ends with a gnomic formula. I transcribe the prose according to its syllables, assuming the suppression of several mute *e*'s:

> Crépuscule, comme vous êtes doux et tendre! (4, 6)
> Les lueurs roses qui traînent encore à l'horizon (4, 8)

comme l'agonie du jour (6)
sous l'oppression victorieuse de sa nuit, (10)
les feux des candélabres (6)
qui font des taches d'un rouge opaque (8)
sur les dernières gloires du couchant, (8)
les lourdes draperies qu'une main invisible attire (10)
des profondeurs de l'Orient, (8)
imitent tous les sentiments compliqués (10)
qui luttent dans le coeur de l'homme (8)
aux heures solennelles de la vie. (8) (emphases added)

The poem might end here, for its symmetry is quite impressive, and seductive. But the purpose of this verbal music is not simply to evoke and interpret urban reveries. The final paragraph adds metaphor to metaphor, leading us from a soothing meditation to an analytical supplement. Two comparisons lead to allegorical translations of the poetic process introduced by the verb *représenter*. Again I highlight the rhythmical units: "*On dirait* encore une de ces robes étranges de danseuses, / où une gaze transparente et sombre / laisse entrevoir les splendeurs amorties d'une jupe éclatante, / *comme* le noir présent transperce le déclicieux passé; / et les étoiles vacillantes d'or et d'argent, / dont elle est semée, / *représentent* ces feux de la fantaisie / qui ne s'allument bien / que sous le deuil profond de la Nuit" (emphases added). Insight penetrates the deceptively opaque fabric of consciousness.

Baudelaire's metaphors, anticipating Freud's pioneering paper, "Mourning and Melancholia" (1917), translate the insight that grief, which accepts loss, "the delicious past," can work through the unconscious ambivalences of depression, "the gloomy present." The urban poet allegorizes the dusk, unlike the madmen who are its victims. The personified "deuil profond de la Nuit" is another majestic widow who, in fable of that name (*SP*, no. 13), had inspired the lonely Parisian prowler. His bereavement generates poetry.[12]

HERMENEUTICAL KEYS

Baudelaire's so-called prose poems constitute a "critical poetry," in Barbara Johnson's words, which dramatizes within the process of inspiration a profound skepticism about its own productions. As we refine our taxonomic categories,[13] Baudelaire's fables, the second edition of **Les Fleurs du Mal,** and his critical writings constitute one hermeneutic entity.

Two fundamental insights connect the two literary masterpieces. First, the ontological paradox of the writer, as the ending of **"Les Fenêtres"** (*SP*, no. 35) defines it: "Qu'importe ce que peut être la réalité placée hors de moi, si elle m'a aidé à vivre, à sentir que je suis et *ce que* je suis?" Literature is inevitably solipsistic and, yet, can be more convincing than perceiving the outside world. Theoretical fables such as **"Laquelle est la vraie?"** **"Le Galant Tireur,"** and **"La Soupe et les**

Nuages"** (*SP*, nos. 38, 43, 44) confirm the skeptical realism of aesthetic fables such as "Un hémisphère dans une chevelure" and **"Invitation au voyage"** (*SP*, nos. 17-18), closer in time and in conception to the lyrical poems.

Baudelaire adds a metaphysical dimension. **"Mademoiselle Bistouri"** (*SP*, no. 47, the antepenultimate fable), summarizes previous conflicts between the aesthetic and the ethical and surpasses them. The narrator fails to communicate with a lovely, insane woman who refuses to share his rational version of reality. In despair, he cries out to God, implying that some explanation for her undeserved suffering exists: "O Créateur! peut-il exister des monstres aux yeux de Celui-là seul qui sait pourquoi ils existent, comment ils *se sont faits* et comment ils auraient pu *ne pas se faire*?" This authentic prayer acknowledges the possibility of ultimate meaning, a transcendent source of truth and justice beyond human ken, while challenging intellectual compromises.

Interpreters and teachers must refine binary categories and elaborate nuanced views of literature as *both* intoxication and cognition. Revising both his poetic monument and his poetics around 1860, Baudelaire relinquished the protective solitude of the unreal and made of literature's limits his generative theme. The ironic distance within even his hedonistic (or "voluptuous") fables confirms his power both to seduce us with beauty and to advocate an uncompromising commitment to truth.

Notes

1. All quotations taken from Baudelaire, *Oeuvres complètes,* ed. Marcel Ruff (Paris: Le Seuil, 1968), abbreviated as *OC*. The numbering of *Les Fleurs du Mal* (abbreviated as *FM*) follows the definitive second edition of 1861. *Le Spleen de Paris* is abbreviated as *SP*.

2. See the complementary piece, "Hymne à la Beauté" (*FM*, no. 21), which further revises "La Beauté" by promoting art's ameliorative function, "[rendre] L'univers moins hideux et les instants moins lourds." See E. Kaplan, *Baudelaire's Prose Poems. The Esthetic, the Ethical, and the Religious in "The Parisian Prowler"* (Athens & London: U of Georgia P, 1990): 4-9. The present paper applies several demonstrations from this book.

3. This and the next quotation from "Wagner et Tannhäuser à Paris," first published on 1 April 1861, *La Revue contemporaine, OC*, 513-14.

4. The memorandum retains the order of the twenty-six pieces published or printed for *La Presse* in 1862 and does not list the letter-preface to Houssaye or the verse "Epilogue" sometimes printed with *Le Spleen de Paris*. See Kaplan, *Baudelaire's*

Prose Poems, 9-12. "A Arsène Houssaye" was
first published as a preface to the 1862 *La Presse*
series. My translation of the prose poems, *The
Parisian Prowler* (U of Georgia P, 1989; 2nd ed.,
1996), places this "preface" in an appendix.

5. See *Petits poèmes en prose,* ed. Robert Kopp
(Paris: José Corti, 1969); *Petits poèmes en prose.
Le Spleen de Paris,* ed. Henri Lemaitre (Paris:
Garnier, 1962). See Kaplan, *Baudelaire's Prose
Poems,* 169-71; for my analysis of "L'Etranger,"
14-16. The following passage is from *Salon de
1859, OC,* 417.

6. Elsewhere in *Salon de 1859* he writes: "car la fantaisie est d'autant plus dangereuse qu'elle est plus
facile et plus ouverte [que la peinture du genre ou
la peinture romanesque]; dangereuse comme la
poésie en prose, comme le roman, elle ressemble
à l'amour qu'inspire une prostituée et qui tombe
bien vite dans la puérilité ou dans la bassesse;
dangereuse comme toute liberté absolue" (*OC*
407).

7. Robespierre's comment to the Comité du salut
public refers to an expedient for national celebrations not to his own compassion for other people.
See Cl. Pichois, ed., Baudelaire, *Oeuvres complètes,* vol. 1 (Paris: Gallimard, 1975), 1387-88,
n1. Baudelaire's 1860 essay *Un Mangeur d'opium,*
speaking of Thomas De Quincey's compassion for
his poverty-stricken female companion, alludes to
the historical context: "Pas d'autre séduction qu'un
visage humain, la pure humanité réduite à son
expression la plus pauvre. Mais, ainsi que l'a dit,
je crois, Robespierre, dans son style de glace ardente, recuit et congelé comme l'abstraction:
'L'homme ne voit jamais l'homme sans plaisir!'"
(*OC* 590).

8. "Enfin! la tyrannie de la face humaine a disparu,
et je ne souffrirai plus que par moimême," from
Le Spleen de Paris, "A une heure du matin," no.
10 (*OC* 152).

9. Roger Shattuck, *The Innocent Eye. On Modern
Literature and the Arts* (New York: Farrar, 1984);
the following quotations are from pp. 140, 142
respectively.

10. See Kaplan, *Baudelaire's Prose Poems,* 20-24.

11. See Barbara Johnson, *Défigurations du langage
poétique. La seconde révolution baudelairienne*
(Paris: Flammarion, 1979); Kaplan, *Baudelaire's
Prose Poems,* 81-83.

12. E. Kaplan, "Baudelaire's Portrait of the Poet as
Widow," *Symposium* 34.3 (1980): 233-48; Kaplan,
Baudelaire's Prose Poems, ch. 4, "Poetry versus
Compassion. Conversion to the Ethical?" Cf.

Richard Stamelman, *Lost Beyond Telling. On
Death and Absence in Modern French Poetry,
from Baudelaire to Yves Bonnefoy and Edmond
Jabès* (Cornell UP, 1990). Also E. Kaplan, ed. and
trans., Michelet, *Mother Death. The Journal of
Jules Michelet, 1815-1850,* selections with analytical commentary (U of Massachusetts P, 1984).

13. See Stamos Metzidakis, *Repetition and Semiotics.
Interpreting Prose Poems* (Birmingham, Ala.,
Summa Publications, 1986); Marie Maclean, *Narrative as Performance: The Baudelairean Experiment* (London & New York: Routledge, 1988):
"These texts include in perfect but minimal form
the *Märchen* or wonder-tale, the *Sage* or anecdote,
the fable, the allegory, the cautionary tale, the
tale-telling contest, the short story, the dialogue,
the novella, the narrated dream" (45).

Jonathan Culler (essay date autumn 1998)

SOURCE: Culler, Jonathan. "Baudelaire's Satanic
Verses." *Diacritics* 28, no. 3 (autumn 1998): 86-100.

[*In the following essay, Culler examines Baudelaire's
use of the figure of the Devil through* Les fleurs du
mal—*in the poems "Au lecteur," "La Destruction," and
L'irrémédiable" in particular—and questions the meaning of this usage for the characterization of Baudelaire
as the first Modern and for the understanding of
Modernity in general.*]

Paul Verlaine was perhaps the first to declare the
centrality of Baudelaire to what we may now call
modern French studies: Baudelaire's profound originality is to "représenter puissament et essentiellement
l'homme moderne" [599-600]. Whether Baudelaire
embodies or portrays modern man, **Les Fleurs du mal**
is seen as exemplary of modern experience, of the possibility of experiencing or dealing with what, taking
Paris as the exemplary modern city, we have come to
call the modern world. T. S. Eliot wrote, "Baudelaire is
indeed the greatest exemplar in modern poetry in any
language, for his verse and language is the nearest thing
to a complete renovation that we have experienced. But
his renovation of an attitude towards life is no less radical and no less important" [426]. And outside the field
of literature we find such affirmations as Harold Rosenberg's dating of "the tradition of the New" to Baudelaire, "who exactly one hundred years ago invited fugi-
tives from the too-narrow world of memory to come
aboard with him in search of the new" [11]. Baudelaire,
writes another critic, "did more than anyone else in the
nineteenth century to make the men and women of his
century aware of themselves as moderns. . . . If we
had to nominate a first modernist, Baudelaire would
surely be the man" [Berman 132-33].

There seems to be considerable agreement on this point, but, surprisingly, there is great difference of opinion about what it is that makes Baudelaire modern and worthy of special attention. Is it, as Albert Thibaudet and Walter Benjamin argue, that he was the first true poet of the city, the first to take the alienated experience of life in the modern city as the norm? Or is it, as Leo Bersani claims, that Baudelaire discovered and displayed the mobility of fantasy and of the desiring imagination? Or is it, as Paul de Man maintains, that Baudelaire invents modern self-consciousness about poetry itself, producing poems that allegorically expose the operations of the lyric?

There are many competing accounts of what is most particularly modern and important about Baudelaire, but the one thing on which contentious critics seem to agree is that there is a side of Baudelaire that is of no interest today, that belongs to a *bas romantisme* and is the very antithesis of Baudelaire's modernity, of Baudelaire the founder of modern poetry: this is the Baudelaire who invokes demons and the Devil. Most critics today pass over this in silence, but even those who explicitly address this Baudelaire seem to find him an embarrassment. Even the author of a book entitled *The Demonic Imagination: Style and Theme in French Romantic Poetry* begins his chapter on Baudelaire: "Baudelaire has, by now, ceased to interest us for the reasons which once appeared important: his diabolical Catholicism is a familiar, historical mode of sensibility which neither shocks nor has morbid appeal . . ." [Houston 85]. And Fredric Jameson distinguishes the modernist and the postmodernist Baudelaires—both worthy of our attention—from what he calls the "second-rate post-Romantic Baudelaire, the Baudelaire of diabolism and of cheap frisson, the poet of blasphemy and of a creaking and musty religious machinery that was no more interesting in the mid-nineteenth century than it is today" [427].

But Baudelaire called his collection **"Les Fleurs du mal"** and opens it with a poem that declares, "C'est le Diable qui tient le fils qui nous remuent [it's the Devil who holds the strings that move us]" [*OC* [*Oeuvres Complètes*] 1: 5; *FE* [*The Flowers of Evil.*] 5]. Can this be dismissed as an irrelevancy—something mistakenly appended to this quintessentially modern poetry? That critics of such different orientations should agree in shunting aside the Satanic Baudelaire suggests that there is something worth investigating here, something disquieting and embarrassing, which may not in fact be merely trivial—which may complicate the story of modernity that has come to depend on Baudelaire as its originator. Perhaps the Satanic Baudelaire would tell us things about modernity we don't want to know.

Certainly the idea of the Devil seems fundamentally at odds with accounts of modernity. Even Christianity itself seems to regard the Devil as outmoded mythol-ogy, irrelevant to a modern religion. The introduction to an issue of the Catholic review Communio devoted to "Satan, mystery of iniquity" declares, "we have trouble evoking him. Satan seems to us to belong to another age, part of the old terrorizing imagery of religions of fear" [2]. What could be less modern than Satan—a scrawny red man with horns, hooves, tail, and pitchfork?

Baudelaire, however, would have laughed at the idea of progress and enlightenment that lies behind all these comments—which present themselves as sophisticated while continuing to rely on notions of intellectual progress he would have regarded as simplistic and deluded. His prose poem **"Le joueur généreux"** reminds us, "n'oublier jamais, quand vous entendez vanter le progrès des lumières, que la plus belle des ruses du diable est de vous persuader qu'il n'existe pas!" [never forget, when you hear the progress of enlightenment praised, that the Devil's finest trick is to persuade you that he doesn't exist] [*OC* 1: 327, my translation]. Baudelaire reserves special scorn for George Sand, who had complained in the preface to one of her novels that modern Christians shouldn't be required to believe in the Devil, that a true Christian could not believe in Hell. This just shows, Baudelaire remarks, that the Devil does not scorn "imbeciles" but makes good use of them, to do his work for him. "Elle est possédée," he writes. She is possessed. "It's the Devil who has persuaded her to trust in her 'good heart' and 'good sense,'" in rejecting the idea of the Devil [*OC* 1: 686-87, my translation].

Satan appears in few poems of *Les Fleurs du mal,* but Baudelaire gives him a prominent place. Let me mention the most important moments before taking them up in more detail. The opening poem, **"Au lecteur,"** firmly declares, "C'est le Diable qui tient les fils qui nous remuent!" The first poem of the section of *Les Fleurs du mal* entitled "Fleurs du mal" also features Satan. **"La Destruction"** begins:

> Sans cesse à mes côtés s'agite le Démon;
> Il nage autour de moi comme un air impalpable.
>
> > [*OC* 1: 111]

> [The Fiend is at my side without a rest;
> He swirls around me like a subtle breeze.]
>
> > [*FE* 229]

And after *Les Fleurs du mal* had been condemned for offense to public morals, Baudelaire wrote an **"Épigraphe pour un livre condamné"** for the second edition of the collection—though in the end he did not include it. This poem claims that readers who haven't studied with Satan, that crafty dean, should throw away this book:

> Lecteur paisible et bucolique,
> Sobre et naif homme de bien,

Jette ce livre saturnien,
Orgiaque et mélancolique.

Si tu n'as fait ta rhétorique
Chez Satan, le rusé doyen,
Jette! tu n'y comprendrais rien
Ou tu me croirais hystérique.

[*OC* 1: 137]

[Reader, you of calm, bucolic,
Artless, sober bonhomie,
Get rid of this Saturnian book
Of orgies and despondency!

Just throw it out! unless you've learned
Your rhetoric in Satan's school
You will not understand a word,
You'll think I am hysterical.]

[*FE* 331]

But what does it mean for him to invoke the Devil in this way? Let me say straight away that it seems likely that Baudelaire himself did not have an answer to this question—"Se livrer à Satan, qu'est-ce que c'est? [What is it to give oneself to Satan?]," he asks in his Journaux intimes [*OC* 1: 663]. He would have been all too happy, one suspects, to sell himself to the Devil, if only he could discover what it entailed, for he spent his life vainly trying to sell himself to editors, publishers, even the Académie française. Indeed, one of the prose poems, **"Le Joueur généreux,"** represents just such a Satanic transaction, and at the end of the poem the sinner prays not for deliverance from the infernal pact but for the Devil to keep the bargain. "Mon Dieu! Seigneur, Mon Dieu! faites que le diable me tienne sa parole! [My Lord! God, my Lord! Make the Devil keep his word to me!]" [*OC* 1: 328].

But the fact that Baudelaire did not know what it would mean to give oneself to the Devil makes the question all the more important. What is the significance of the Devil in *Les Fleurs du mal*? Is it an unimportant bit of mythological machinery, or does the figure of the Devil, on the contrary, bring forward crucial problems and issues that we ignore by dismissing him? What threat does this figure pose that we need to set him aside? And if the threat is primarily to the idea of Baudelaire as the first modern or the quintessentially modern poet, why do we have such a stake in modernizing him? Let me emphasize that I am not just asking what it meant to write poems about the Devil in mid-nineteenth-century France—a question that certainly has no simple or single answer (Baudelaire says of his contemporaries, "it's harder for people of this century to believe in the Devil than to love him. Everyone feels him and no one believes in him" [*OC* 1: 182-83]). I am not just asking a historical question but am asking, rather, what sort of thinking can do justice to the force and distinctiveness of these poems today?

"Au lecteur" introduces the Devil. Here are the familiar opening stanzas.

La sottise, l'erreur, le péché, la lésine,
Occupent nos esprits et travaillent nos corps,
Et nous alimentons nos aimables remords,
Comme les mendiants nourissent leur vermine.

Nos péchés sont têtus, nos repentirs sont lâches;
Nous nous faisons payer grassement nos aveux,
Et nous rentrons gaiement dans le chemin bourbeux,
Croyant par de vils pleurs laver toutes nos taches.

Sur l'oreiller du mal c'est Satan Trismégiste
Qui berce longuement notre esprit enchanté,
Et le triste métal de notre volonté
Est tout vaporisé par ce savant chimiste.

C'est le Diable qui tient les fils qui nous remuent.

[*OC* 1: 5]

[Folly and error, stinginess and sin
Possess our spirits and fatigue our flesh.
And like a pet we feed our tame remorse
As beggars take to nourishing their lice.

Our sins are stubborn, our contrition lax;
We offer lavishly our vows of faith
And turn back gladly to the path of filth,
Thinking mean tears will wash away our stains.

On evil's pillow lies the alchemist
Satan Thrice-Great, who lulls our captive soul,
And all the richest metal of our will
Is vaporized by his hermetic arts.

Truly the Devil pulls on all our strings.]

[*FE* 5]

The movement of **"Au lecteur"** suggests that if, as the opening stanza has it, stupidity, error and sin occupy us and work us over, if we even nourish our remorse and proceed jauntily down the muddy road of sin, it is because our spirit is bewitched, because Satan has vaporized our will. We are his puppets. The opening line of the fourth stanza, "C'est le Diable qui tient les fils qui nous remuent!" comes with the force of an answer or explanation. The Devil pulls the strings; sometimes he makes us act, sometimes prevents us from having the will to act as we would.

The next two stanzas stress not this diabolical agency presumed to cause our weakness and wickedness but our resulting complaisance or connivance with vice: it seems that the Devil pulling the strings results in our finding repugnant objects attractive, passing through stinking darkness without horror, and furtively snatching pleasures from which we try to squeeze every drop of enjoyment.

C'est le Diable qui tient les fils qui nous remuent.
Aux objects répugnants nous trouvons des appas;

Chaque jour vers l'Enfer nous descendons d'un pas,
Sans horreur, à travers des ténèbres qui puent.

Ainsi qu'un débauché pauvre qui baise et mange
Le sein martyrisé d'une antique catin,
Nous volons au passage un plaisir clandestin
Que nous pressons bien fort, comme une vieille
    orange.

[Truly the Devil pulls on all our strings!
In most repugnant objects we find charms;
Each day we're one step further into Hell,
Content to move across the stinking pit.

As a poor libertine will suck and kiss
The sad tormented tit of some old whore,
We steal a furtive pleasure as we pass,
A shrivelled orange that we squeeze and press.]

But the seventh stanza reopens the question of who is responsible.

Si le viol, le poison, le poignard, l'incendie,
N'ont pas encore brodé de leur plaisants dessins
Le canevas banal de nos piteux destins,
C'est que notre âme, hélas, n'est pas assez hardie.

[If slaughter, or if arson, poison, rape
Have not as yet adorned our fine designs,
The banal canvas of our woeful fates,
It's only that our spirit lacks the nerve.]

If the banality or triviality of our lives has not been decorated by rape, murder, arson, etc., it is because our souls are not bold enough. There is a shift of agency in these first two lines, which makes rape and murder the agents that may or may not yet have put their designs on our fate. This shift seems to reinforce the notion that we are hapless creatures carrying out projects conceived elsewhere, but if, as the last line of this stanza sententiously declares, our lack of boldness is to blame, then what are we to think? Perhaps we are not the Devil's puppets after all—only mediocrities too timid for real sin (this is, I believe, the most common interpretation of the poem). Or is the timidity of our souls, rather, an example of what stanza three called Satan's vaporization of our will and thus an instance of his pulling the strings?

The last three stanzas shift the scene, in that strange way characteristic of Baudelaire: from an external scene where the speaker figures as a character to an allegorical space bounded by the speaker: it is as though Satan's pulling the strings of a hapless human puppet gave rise to this other space, which the poem calls "la ménagerie infâme de nos vices," where the beasts that are also demons clamor, groan, prance, or yawn.

Here is the rest of the poem:

Mais parmi les chacals, les panthères, les lices,
Les singes, les scorpions, les vautours, les serpents,

Les monstres glapissants, hurlants, grognants, ram-
    pants,
Dans la ménagerie infâme de nos vices,

Il en est un plus laid, plus méchant, plus immonde!
Quoiqu'il ne pousse ni grands gestes ni grands cris,
Il ferait volontiers de la terre un débris
Et dans un bâillement avalerait le monde;

C'est l'Ennui!—l'oeil chargé d'un pleur involontaire,
Il rêve d'échafauds en fumant son houka.
Tu le connais, lecteur, ce monstre délicat,
—Hypocrite lecteur,—mon semblable,—mon frère!

[But there with all the jackals, panthers, hounds,
The monkeys, scorpions, the vultures, snakes,
Those howling, yelping, grunting, crawling brutes,
The infamous menagerie of vice,

One creature only is most foul and false!
Though making no grand gestures, nor great cries,
He willingly would devastate the earth
And in one yawning swallow all the world;

He is Ennui—with tear-filled eye he dreams
Of scaffolds, as he puffs his water-pipe.
Reader, you know this dainty monster too;
—Hypocrite reader,—fellowman,—my twin!]

Though the Devil pulls the strings he is no longer on the scene when the poem turns to this zoo and to the ugliest, meanest, most disgusting of these monsters, *Ennui,* who dreams of executions and wouldn't mind swallowing the world in a yawn.

Is the presence of this monster in our world the work of the Devil or not? One can't be sure. The allegorical scene of yawning *Ennui* puffing his hookah like an oriental pasha seems far removed from that of Satan manipulating human puppets. Is it that, with the Devil pulling the strings and vaporizing our will, we are left vulnerable to this finicky monster? Is the very promotion of *ennui* to a fearsome monster of our inner life an example of the Devil's control?

This poem seems, in its development, to pose the problem of the Devil in a way that I would call forceful, were it not for the fact that critics succeed in ignoring it—no doubt because the poem ends not with the Devil but with *Ennui,* which becomes the focus of attention. But the poem announces, as though it were the explanation of the human predicament described in the first two stanzas, that the Devil holds the strings that move us. It then proceeds to offer further description of human complicity with vice in a scenario which reaches its climax with the worst monster, without telling us whether we know this fussy monster and lodge him in the menagerie of our vices *because* the Devil controls us or whether, on the contrary, as critics have sometimes suggested, it is the overpowering presence of *Ennui* that gives the Devil his power to seduce. What happens in the opening poem, I suggest, happens in the collection as a whole: the poems with an important framing function claim that the Devil is ubiquitous, but subsequent poems do not tell us whether the scenes or movements they narrate are examples of the Devil's work. Perhaps this is what is most worrying about the Devil—that we don't know what is his work and what is not.

The second framing poem I mentioned, **"La Destruction"**—the inaugural poem of the section entitled "Fleurs du mal"—begins with another assertion of the Devil's presence:

> Sans cesse à mes côtés s'agite le Démon;
> Il nage autour de moi comme un air impalpable.
> Je l'avale et le sens qui brûle mon poumon
> Et l'emplit d'un désir éternel et coupable.
>
> [*OC* 1: 111]

> [The Fiend is at my side without a rest;
> He swirls around me like a subtle breeze;
> I swallow him, and burning fills my breast,
> And calls me to desire's shameful needs.]
>
> [*FE* 229]

Impalpable but omnipresent, the Devil pulls the strings, seducing the speaker in the guise of a woman or proffering disgusting potions or drugs.

> Parfois il prend, sachant mon grand amour de l'Art,
> La forme de la plus séduisante des femmes,
> Et, sous de spécieux pretextes de cafard,
> Accoutume ma lèvre à des philtres infâmes.
>
> Il me conduit ainsi, loin du regard de Dieu
> Haletant et brisé de fatigue, au milieu
> Des plaines de l'Ennui, profondes et désertes.
>
> [Knowing my love of Art, he may select
> A woman's form—most perfect, most corrupt—
> And under sanctimonious pretext
> Bring to my lips the potion of her lust.
>
> Thus does he lead me, far from sight of God,
> Broken and gasping, out into the broad
> And wasted plains of Ennui, deep and still.]

Here the question left open in **"Au lecteur"** seems to receive a definite answer. If the speaker is in the plains of *Ennui*, it is because the Devil leads him there, in this way (*ainsi*): by always stirring at his side, by filling him with culpable desires, by taking the form of the most seductive of women and by accustoming him to infamous potions. Two peculiar things are worth noting here. First, the scenario hinted at in **"Au lecteur"** and affirmed in **"La Destruction"** differs from traditional tales of Satan, where the Devil doesn't lead you into *ennui* but out of it, by providing special powers, knowledge, or sensual opportunities (in exchange for your soul). In Baudelaire, though, *ennui* is not the

condition of or point of departure for the Devil's work but its result. This is singular and distinctive. Second, the poem ends with an allegorical event considerably more enigmatic than Ennui's dreaming of scaffolds in **"Au lecteur."** Here the Devil leads the speaker into the plains of Ennui:

> Il me conduit ainsi, loin du regard de Dieu,
> Haletant et brisé de fatigue, au milieu
> Des plaines de l'Ennui, profondes et désertes.
>
> Et jette dans mes yeux pleins de confusion
> Des vêtements souillés, des blessures ouvertes,
> Et l'appareil sanglant de la Destruction!
>
> [Then throws before my staring eyes some gowns
> And bloody garments stained by open wounds,
> And dripping engines of Destruction's will!]

The combination in these closing lines of the sonnet of strangely unresonant abstraction ("l'appareil sanglant de la destruction") and unlocated specificity ("vêtements souillés" and "blessures ouvertes") makes it difficult to grasp what the Devil might be throwing in his face, and this very difficulty seems to raise the possibility that any scenario elsewhere in Baudelaire's poems involving such things as wounds, destruction, blood, or soiled clothes can be seen as the Devil's work. One might imagine that since the Devil conducts me "*ainsi,*" in the guise of a woman, what the Devil as woman throws in the speaker's face is menstruation, as sign of the monstrousness of feminine sexuality. But this interpretation may fail to live up to the curious "appareil sanglant de la Destruction," which, unresonant though it may be, nevertheless has a *prima facie* importance since it provides or echoes the title of the poem. The difficulty of grasping what the Devil is about here, I'm tempted to conclude—here at the point where a poem of *Les Fleurs du mal* seems most explicitly to tell us what it is that the Devil does—heightens the question of the extent to which the Devil is at work in the adventures and obsessions of the speakers of these poems.

But there is one suggestion that needs to be pursued in the strange endings of the two poems cited so far. The puzzling "appareil sanglant de la destruction" recalls *Ennui*, who "rêve d'échafauds." In one case the Devil leads the speaker into the plains of *Ennui* and throws what might well be the guillotine before his eyes. In the other the Devil leaves us threatened by *Ennui*, who dreams of executions and would swallow the whole world in a yawn. Together the poems seem to carry the suggestion that the Devil is behind an *ennui* linked with revolutionary executions.

Associating Satan with the French Revolution was a right-wing commonplace. Baudelaire's *maître à penser,* Joseph de Maistre, had written, "The French Revolution has a Satanic character that distinguishes it from everything we have seen and perhaps from everything that we shall see" [55]. Baudelaire was certainly touched as well by the nineteenth-century tradition of revolutionary Satanism, which also identified Satan with those in revolt against authority. As Eugen Weber describes it,

> If, for the masters of the Restoration, freedom was diabolical, why shouldn't liberals take the devil's side? . . . If, for its enemies, the French Revolution was the work of Satan, the partisans of the Revolution ought to be grateful to him. If the enemies of the Revolution had God on their side, if the oppressors of the people . . . reigned by His grace, the liberal and the Romantic (often one and the same person) might very well wish to follow Satan into his exile and reject a heaven that was too reactionary and too bourgeois (depending on the current regime) to attract them.
>
> [11-12]

Baudelaire's **"Abel et Caïn,"** from the section of *Les Fleurs du mal* titled "Révolte," was written during his period of revolutionary enthusiasm in 1848 and concludes with the injunction (or possibly description in the present tense),

> Race de Caïn, au ciel monte,
> Et sur la terre jette Dieu.
>
> [*OC* 1: 123]

> [Race of Cain, assault the skies
> And drag him earthward—bring down God!]
>
> [*FE* 269]

But in general it is striking—given Baudelaire's interest in Satan—how little he participates in the reversals of romantic Satanism that make the Devil a hero, praised for his revolt against an oppressive despot. Baudelaire's only poem that places Satan in the title, **"Les Litanies de Satan,"** invokes him in liturgical accents, in the form of supplication and response, and substitutes Satan for Mary in the response or refrain, "O Satan, prends pitié de ma longue misère [Satan, take pity on my misery]" [*OC* 1: 123; *FE* 269]. This poem addresses Satan as one who, responsible for evil, may have pity for humans and even offer solace to human sufferers, but solace of a kind whose value is, to say the least, ambiguous. Satan, it is said, engenders hope (which may be a further illusion and source of torture); he teaches courage in adversity (a good thing, but which does not overcome adversity); he knows where metals and precious stones are hidden underground (which inspires greed and strife); he gives men gunpowder; he inspires perversions which bring solace (such as the "culte de la plaie et des guenilles [the love of rags, the cult of wounds and pain]"), and so on. This Satanic poem is remarkable, I think, for the modesty of its claims for the figure it addresses structurally as a kind of God: Satan is not a heroic rebel but a figure who offers minor consolations to social outcasts.

Though Baudelaire occasionally grants Satan the beauty and grandeur of a fallen archangel—as when he calls Milton's Satan the model of virile beauty [*OC* 1: 658] or speaks, in **"L'irrémédiable,"** of "la conscience dans le Mal" as a "flambeau des graces sataniques" and "soulagement et gloire uniques" ("torch of Satanical graces" and a "glory in consolation") he does not seek to reverse values and rehabilitate Satan. Indeed, a passage of romantic Satanism from Balzac's *Splendeurs et misères des courtisanes,* a passage sometimes thought to contain the germ of Baudelaire's title, ***Les Fleurs du mal,*** will help to measure Baudelaire's distance from the conceptions of his contemporaries. In *Splendeurs et misères,* Lucien de Rubempré says to Vautrin (Carlos Herrera):

> Il y a la postérité de Caïn et celle d'Abel, comme vous disiez quelquefois. Caïn, dans le grand drame de l'Humanité, c'est l'opposition. Vous descendez d'Adam par cette ligne en qui le diable a continué de souffler le feu dont la première étincelle avait été jetée sur Ève. Parmi les démons de cette filiation il s'en trouve, de temps en temps, de terribles, à organisations vastes, qui résument toutes les forces humaines, et qui ressemblent à ces fiévreux animaux du désert dont la vie exige les espaces immenses qu'ils y trouvent. Ces gens-là sont dangereux comme des lions le seraient en pleine Normandie: il leur faut une pâture, ils dévorent les hommes vulgaires et broutent les écus des niais. . . . Quand Dieu le veut, ces êtres mystérieux sont Moïse, Atilla, Charlemagne, Mahomet, ou Napoléon; mais, quand ils laissent rouiller au fond de l'océan d'une génération ces instruments gigantesques, ils ne sont plus que Pugatcheff, Robespierre, Louvel, et l'Abbé Carlos Herrera. Doués d'un immense pouvoir sur les âmes tendres, ils les attirent et les broient. . . . C'est la plante vénéneuse aux riches couleurs qui fascine les enfants dans les bois. C'est la poésie du mal.
>
> [473-74]

[There is Cain's posterity and that of Abel, as you sometimes said. In the great drama of humanity, Cain is the opposition. You descend from Adam by this line, into whom the devil has continued to breathe the fire whose first spark was given to Eve. Among the demons of this lineage, there have been, from time to time, those who were terrible indeed, whose vast structures encapsulate all human forces and who resemble those feverish animals of the desert whose life demands the immense spaces they find there. Such people are as dangerous in society as lions would be in the heart of Normandy: they need fodder; they devour ordinary men and graze on the coin of the unwary. . . . When God so wills, these mysterious beings are Moses, Atilla, Charlemagne, Mohammed, or Napoleon; but when they allow their gigantic capacities to rust at the bottom of the ocean of a generation, then they become Pugatcheff, Robespierre, Louvel, and Abbé Carlos Herrera. Endowed with immense power over tender souls, they attract them and crush them. . . . It's splendid. It's beautiful of its kind. It's the richly colored poisonous plant that fascinates children in the woods. It's the poetry of evil.]

[my translation]

In romantic Satanism we have Satanic characters—either Satan himself made a character in a substantial narrative (as in Hugo and Vigny) or other characters identified as Satanic surrogates, as in Byron or here in Balzac. Baudelaire, however, does not make Satan a character in a narrative—even in **"Les litanies de Satan"** he is an addressee with certain sympathies and achievements but not a figure in a story of reversal. Baudelaire, unlike many of his immediate precursors, does not participate in the rehabilitation of the Devil that structures such major efforts as Vigny's "Eloa," Lamartine's *La chute d'un ange* and, eventually, Hugo's *La fin de Satan*. The historian Ernest Renan wrote in 1855, two years before the publication of *Les Fleurs du mal*, "[o]f all the hitherto accursed beings whom the tolerance of our century has relieved of their curse, Satan is doubtless the one who has gained the most from the progress of enlightenment and of universal civilization" [231; my translation]. But Baudelaire was not an agent of the progress of enlightenment.

Unrehabilitated, the Devil takes his importance in *Les Fleurs du mal* from the way Baudelaire puts him into the poems that frame and present the book, such as **"Au lecteur,"** the opening poem of the book, **"La Destruction,"** the opening poem of the title section, and the epigraph projected for the second edition. Another poem where Satan is explicitly mentioned, **"L'irrémédiable,"** from the end of the section "Spleen et l'idéal," approaches the question of what the Devil controls in another way. (Note, incidentally, the appearance of *le diable* in the title **"L'irrémédiable."**) The first seven stanzas of the poem present a series of images of human oppression and entrapment—a being fallen into "un Styx bourbeux et plombé," a "malheureux" seeking vainly to flee "un lieu plein de reptiles," and so on—images that, the poem suggests, illustrate Satan's effectiveness:

> —Emblèmes nets, tableau parfait
> D'une fortune irrémédiable,
> Qui donne à penser que le Diable
> Fait toujours bien tout ce qu'il fait!
>
> [*OC* 1: 80]

> [Pure emblems, a perfect tableau
> Of an irremediable fortune,
> Which makes us think that the Devil
> Does well what he chooses to do!]
>
> [*FE* 161]

But the phrase "donne à penser" leaves open the possibility that we may be mistaken. These images make one *think* that the Devil always does his work well, but perhaps the Devil isn't really responsible for these disasters and entrapments after all—perhaps, for example, we are misled by the rhyme into seeing the Devil in any fate deemed *irrémédiable*. Since

"L'irrémédiable" immediately proceeds in the next stanza to speak of the

> Tête-à-tête sombre et limpide
> Qu'un coeur devenu son miroir!
>
> [It's a face-to-face sombre and clear
> When a heart gives its own image back!]

it is possible that the earlier images show not the Devil's efficacy and ubiquity but rather the heart's power of projection—displaying what is generated when, as in the production of the literary works from which these images or emblems are drawn, consciousness imaginatively reflects on itself. On the other hand, it could be that this somber self-reflection is another example of the Devil's work: he pulls the strings of self-reflexivity too, making hearts become their own mirrors, to disastrous effect. Perhaps no self-scrutiny would occur in an unfallen world or if the Devil hadn't led us into the plains of *Ennui*. Here, too, the appearance in the poem of the figure of the Devil seems to give rise to this problem: is he responsible? What is most diabolical about the Devil, I am tempted to conclude, is that we can never be sure when he is at work.

The foregrounding of Satan in the framing poems, and a few others, such as **"L'irrémédiable,"** poses the question of whether he is not responsible for what is described in the poems within the volume where he may make no obvious appearance. Are we observing the effects of Satanic control or his stimulation of perverse appetites, or is there some other explanation? For example, in **"Les sept vieillards,"** a poem from "Tableaux parisiens," the speaker encounters a sinister old man with an evil glitter in his eye, who staggers along,

> Comme s'il écrasait des morts sous ses savates,
> Hostile à l'univers plutôt qu'indifférent.
>
> [*OC* 1: 88]

> [As if his old shoes trampled on the dead
> In hatred, not indifference to life.]
>
> [*FE* 179]

This sinister figure seems to multiply himself—seven times:

> Son pareil le suivait: barbe, oeil, dos, bâton, loques,
> Nul trait ne distinguait, du même enfer venu,
> Ce jumeau centenaire, et ces spectres baroques
> Marchaient du même pas vers un but inconnu.
>
> [His double followed: beard, eye, back, stick, rags,
> No separate traits, and come from the same hell.
> This second ancient man, baroque, grotesque,
> Trod with the same step towards their unknown goal.]

The speaker suspects a plot:

A quel complot infâme etais-je donc en butte . . . ?

Is this a satanic plot? Or could it be mere chance that wickedly humiliates him by making him suspect a plot?

A quel complot infâme étais-je donc en butte,
Ou quel méchant hasard ainsi m'humiliait?
Car je comptais sept fois, de minute en minute,
Ce sinistre viellard qui se multipliait!

[To what conspiracy was I exposed?
What wicked chance humiliated me?
For one by one I counted seven times
Multiples of this sinister old man.]

This poem, like others, seems to prevent one from making a Satanic plot or Satanic influence an explanation on which one could rely.

The Devil, then, is the name of a problem. Sometimes—in Baudelaire's prose notes particularly—we may seem to be confronting a version of the traditional problem of the Devil's disguises. Writing of *Les liaisons dangereuses,* Baudelaire speaks of "Valmont Satan" and of Mme de Merteuil as "une Eve satanique." Apparently, Satan may take the form of or work through manifest villains, such as they, but these are eighteenth-century Satans, and in the nineteenth century, Baudelaire claims,

l'énergie du mal a baissé.—Et la niaiserie a pris la place de l'esprit. . . . En réalité, le satanisme a gagné. Satan s'est fait ingénu [manifesting himself, for instance, in George Sand]. Le mal se connaissant était moins affreux et plus près de la guérison que le mal s'ignorant. George Sand inférieure à de Sade. [the energy of evil has shrunk. And sappiness has replaced brilliance. . . . In fact, Satanism has won out. Satan has made himself the sweet innocent . . . Evil which knows itself was less horrible and nearer cure than evil ignorant of itself. George Sand inferior to Sade.]

[*OC* 2: 68, my translation]

In the eighteenth century, he continues, "on se damnait moins bêtement."

But if the Devil can manifest himself as easily in George Sand as in Melmoth or Madame de Merteuil, or Gilles de Rais, then he has become so ubiquitous as to be a different sort of figure—one which represents above all the possibility that anything or anyone, however innocent they may appear, can work for ill. As the supreme master of ruse and deceit, the Devil incarnates the ubiquity of deception, evil—or, to put it in other terms, the speculative possibility of dialectic, in which what looks beneficial at one level may prove at another to be horrible and oppressive. One can never tell where the Devil is at work. "Il nage autour de moi comme un air impalpable," says **"La Destruction,"** dissolved into the very air we breathe. Sometimes he takes the form of "la plus séduisante des femmes." So

there is always a question, it seems, whether a woman is a Satanic manifestation. "De Satan ou de Dieu, qu'importe?" or "Ange ou Démon, qu'importe?" exclaim Baudelaire's narrators in moments of great desperation (echoing Hugo's apostrophe to Napoleon: "Tu domines notre âge. Ange ou démon, qu'importe? [You dominate our age. Angel or demon, what matter?]") But the fact that this "qu'importe?" comes as the climax of agonized reflection shows that usually Baudelairian speakers care very much whether they are dealing with the Devil, though they can never know for sure. If what is most diabolical about the Devil is the difficulty of deciding whether he is at work in a particular scene or situation, then the figure of the Devil poses the general question of whether there is *meaning* to the scenarios in which we are caught up or misfortunes that befall us or whether they are simply accidents. Can we escape our sense that there are malignant forces that operate independently of human intentions or that the world often works against us? "Everyone *feels* the Devil and no one believes in him," wrote Baudelaire in a projected preface to **Les Fleurs du mal** [*OC* 1: 182-83].

But if the Devil is the name of a force that works on us against our will—if, as Baudelaire says in **"Au lecteur,"** "le riche metal de notre volonté / Est tout vaporisé par ce savant chimiste"—isn't he just a personification of aspects of the Unconscious or the Id, of forces that make us do what our conscious selves might reject? To make Baudelaire modern can't we just cross out *Devil* and write in *Unconscious* or, better, *Death Drive,* or *Repetition Compulsion*?

There is something to be said for this view, though one would have to work out the analogy and the substitution more precisely. Baudelaire, though, had anticipated such a possibility and in his prose poem **"Le mauvais vitrier"** he speaks of "cette humeur, hystérique selon les médecins, satanique selon ceux qui pensent un peu mieux que les médecins, qui nous pousse sans résistence vers une foule d'actions dangereuses ou inconvenantes" [that condition termed hysterical by doctors and Satanical by those who think rather more clearly than doctors, which pushes us unresisting towards a host of dangerous or unsuitable actions] [*OC* 1: 286]. The Satanical hypothesis is clearer thinking, one surmises, because it adduces not an individual disorder but impersonal structures and forces. When Gustave Flaubert objected to Baudelaire that he insisted too much on l'*Esprit du Mal,* Baudelaire replied,

de tout temps j'ai été obsedé par l'impossibilité de me rendre compte de certaines actions ou pensées soudaines de l'homme sans l'hypothèse de l'intervention d'une force méchante extérieure à lui.—Voilà un gros aveu dont tout le 19e siècle conjuré ne me fera pas rougir [I have always been obsessed by the impossibility of accounting for some of man's sudden actions or thoughts without the hypothesis of the intervention of an evil force outside him—Here's a scandalous avowal for which the whole nineteenth century ranged against me won't make me blush]

[*Correspondance* 2: 53, my translation].

Christian theology introduces the Devil to account for the presence of evil in the world. If God is not to be held responsible for evil, there must be another creature whose free choice in deviating from good introduced evil. The Devil, thus, is not a *symbol* of evil but an agent or personification whose ability to act is essential. Just as God is not a symbol of good but, if he is anything, an agent, a creator, or controller, so the Devil is the name for evil agency—evil as an active force, not evil as the absence of God, as modern theologians are wont to suggest. ***Les Fleurs du mal*** makes the Devil an actor, along with other unexpected agents, such as Prostitution, which lights up in the streets, Anguish, which plants its black flag in my skull, *Ennui,* who puffs on his hookah and dreams of the gallows. To dismiss Satan as *just* a "personification" of evil, though, and thus a fiction, requires remarkable confidence about what can and what cannot act, about what forces there are at work in the universe. Behind the wish to dismiss him as personification may lie the wishful presumption that only human individuals can act, that they control the world and that there are no other agents; but the world would be a very different place if this were true. Much of its character, its difficulty, its mystery, comes from the effects produced by actions of other sorts of agents, which our grammars may or may not personify: history, classes, capital, freedom, public opinion—forces not graspable at the level of the empirical actions of individuals but which seem to control the world and give events meaningful and often oppressive structures.

Baudelaire's poems, in which Anguish, Autumn, Beauty, Ennui, Hope, Hate, and others do their work, pose questions about the constituents and boundaries of persons, about the forces that act in the world, and about whether this level of allegorical action does not in fact best capture the realities of body, spirit, and history. This is, finally, a question about the sort of rhetoric best suited to explore our condition; Baudelaire's practice shows a commitment to hyperbolic scenarios involving diverse and unusual actors.

In his essay on Théodore de Banville, Baudelaire speaks of hyperbole and apostrophe as the forms of language not only most agreeable but also most necessary to lyric, and goes on to maintain that

l'art moderne a une tendance essentiellement démoniaque. Et il semble que cette part infernale de l'homme, que l'homme prend plaisir à s'expliquer à lui-même, augmente journellement, comme si le Diable s'amusait à la grossir par des procédés artificiels, à l'instar des engraisseurs, empâtant patiemment le genre humain dans ses basses-cours pour se préparer une nourriture plus succulente [modern art has an essentially demonic tendency. And it seems to me that this infernal part of man, which man takes pleasure in explicating to himself, grows larger daily, as if the Devil were amusing himself by fattening it through artificial means, inspired by forcefeeders, patiently stuffing humankind in his farmyards, to prepare more succulent food for himself].

[*OC* 2: 168, my translation]

This hyperbolic equation of the modern with the diabolical does not correspond at all with the critical reception of Baudelaire, which has left behind the gothic Baudelaire so splendidly encapsulated in this image of the Devil practicing a *gavage satanique,* like the producers of foie gras. Baudelaire here gives us, and claims as modern, an allegorical scenario with a highly original account of the forces behind a human activity that is increasingly swollen with evil. Such hyperbolic accounts may be well suited to a time when, as Baudelaire says, everyone feels the Devil but no one believes in him. Exploring and channeling this feeling without demanding belief, such allegories posit forces and meanings that might be at work in the infernal accumulations we characteristically feel but seem unable to control in what we persuade ourselves is the modern world. If one of the tasks of French Studies is to explicate the sense of a modern world and modern experience emanating from Paris, then Baudelaire's satanic verses should lie upon its path, requiring engagement and explanation.

Works Cited

Balzac, Honoré de. *Splendeurs et misères des courtisanes.* Ed. A. Adam. Paris: Gallimard, 1987.

Baudelaire, Charles. *Correspondance.* Ed. Claude Pichois et Jean Ziegler. 2 vols. Paris: Gallimard, 1973.

———. *The Flowers of Evil.* Trans. James McGowan. Oxford World Classics dual-language ed. Oxford: Oxford UP, 1993. [*FE*]

———. *Oeuvres complètes.* Ed. Claude Pichois. 2 vols. Paris: Gallimard, 1975. [*OC*]

Berman, Marshall. *All That Is Solid Melts into Air: The Experience of Modernity.* New York: Simon and Schuster, 1982.

Benjamin, Walter. *Charles Baudelaire: A Lyric Poet in the Era of High Capitalism.* London: Verso, 1973.

Bersani, Leo. *Baudelaire and Freud.* Berkeley: U of California P, 1977.

de Maistre, Joseph. *Considérations sur la France.* Vol. 1 of *Oeuvres complètes.* Lyon-Paris: Vitte et Perrussel, 1884.

de Man, Paul. "Anthropomorphism and Trope in the Lyric." *The Rhetoric of Romanticism.* New York: Columbia, 1983.

Eliot, T. S. "Baudelaire." *Selected Essays.* London: Faber, 1951: 419-30.

Houston, John Porter. *The Demonic Imagination: Style and Theme in French Romantic Poetry.* Baton Rouge: Lousiana State UP, 1969.

Jameson, Fredric. "Baudelaire as Modernist and Post-modernist: The Dissolution of the Referent and the Artificial 'Sublime.'" *Lyric Poetry: Beyond New Criticism.* Ed. Chaviva Hosek and Patricia Parker. Ithaca: Cornell UP, 1985.

Renan, Ernest. "La tentation du Christ." *L'Artiste* 27 May 1855: 47-50.

Rosenberg, Harold. *The Tradition of the New.* New York: Horizon, 1959.

Satan: Mystère d'iniquité. Communio 4.3 (1979).

Thibaudet, Albert. "Baudelaire," *Intérieurs.* Paris: Plon, 1924. 1-61.

Verlaine, Paul. "Charles Baudelaire." *Oeuvres en prose complètes.* Ed. J. Borel. Paris: Gallimard, 1972. 599-605.

Weber, Eugen. *Satan, Franc Maçon.* Paris: R. Juillard, 1964.

Russell Goulbourne (essay date May-August 1999)

SOURCE: Goulbourne, Russell. "The Sound of Silence . . . *Points de suspension* in Baudelaire's *Les Fleurs du Mal*." *Australian Journal of French Studies* 36, no. 2 (May-August 1999): 200-13.

[*In the following essay, Goulbourne discusses Baudelaire's usage of* points de suspension *or ellipses, noting that the poet paid "obsessive attention" to matters of punctuation.*]

Writing verse did not come easily to Baudelaire.[1] If the Romantic poets, seized by frenzied inspiration, suffered for their art, Baudelaire toiled for his: for him, the poet had to be a craftsman.[2] One aspect of Baudelaire's craftsmanship is the obsessive attention he paid to *mise en page,* the physical appearance of his poems on the page, the materiality of his text; checking proofs was a constant source of anxiety to him.[3] He had a particularly keen eye for punctuation; his attention to detail was far from conventional. When Gervais Charpentier published two of Baudelaire's prose poems, **"Les Tentations"** and **"La Belle Dorothée"**, in the *Revue nationale* in 1863, he received a sharp rebuke from the disgruntled poet:

J'y trouve d'extraordinaires changements introduits après mon *bon à tirer.* Cela, Monsieur, est la raison pour laquelle j'ai fui tant de journaux et de revues. Je vous avais dit: supprimez *tout un morceau,* si *une virgule* vous déplaît dans le morceau, mais ne supprimez pas la virgule; elle a sa raison d'être.[4]

Punctuation has its "raison d'être" in Baudelaire's poetry.

One aspect of the function of punctuation is suggested by Baudelaire's anxious letter to Poulet-Malassis, his publisher, when the 1861 edition of **Les Fleurs du Mal** was with Simon Raçon, the printer:

Sans doute le livre est d'un bon aspect général; mais jusque dans la dernière bonne feuille, j'ai trouvé de grosses négligences. Dans cette maison-là [Simon Raçon], c'est les correcteurs qui font défaut. Ainsi, ils ne comprennent pas la ponctuation, au point de vue de la logique; et bien d'autres choses.[5]

The reference to "la logique" points to what, since about the middle of the eighteenth century, has been the basic function of punctuation: to clarify the syntactic structure of a sentence.[6]

Baudelaire was also alive to the elocutionary function of punctuation, as he made clear to Poulet-Malassis when the 1857 edition of **Les Fleurs du Mal** was in proof: "*Quant à ma ponctuation, rappelez-vous qu'elle sert à noter non seulement le sens, mais* LA DECLAMATION".[7] Like dynamic markings on a musical score, punctuation is a key to performance: it indicates speech-derived pauses, it guides the respiration and intonation of the reader.[8] Baudelaire's awareness of the links between punctuation and rhythm is suggested by his comments on the line "Suivant un rythme doux, et paresseux, et lent" in **"Le Beau Navire"**. He noted on the proofs of the first edition: "Est-ce bien ainsi qu'il faut ponctuer? peut-être trouverez-vous que cette ponctuation rend bien la langueur du rythme".[9]

A third function of punctuation is to be suggestive, to imply, illuminate and embody the subjective meaning of a phrase. As Alison Fairlie observes: "No tiniest detail is irrelevant in [Baudelaire's] desire for total perfection of material presentation, where spacing, punctuation, capitals all have their suggestive functions".[10] The punctuation in a poem lends itself to interpretation. For Clive Scott, "punctuation in poetry is a matter of style rather than the observance of a code; the code may mark out certain parameters of use, but the specific value of the punctuation mark has constantly to be redefined, as it continually rebecomes an undeciphered hieroglyph".[11] It is the suggestive function of just one part of punctuation—suspension points—that I want to consider here, though I realize that this is just the tip of a (relatively unexplored) semiotic iceberg.[12]

Suspension points are particularly interesting since they can, by definition, fulfil only two of the functions of punctuation defined above, the elocutionary and the suggestive. They have no strict syntactic function, since they can appear anywhere in a sentence. Suspension points were first used in the seventeenth century, when Antoine Furetière saw them as an indication that "le sens est imparfait, qu'il y a quelque lacune, ou quelque chose à adjoûter".[13] In the late eighteenth century the grammarian Urbain Domergue defined them as "des morceaux de sentiment ou de force qu'on veut faire re- marquer". He also suggested that the length of the pause and the number of points could vary from two to four "selon le degré d'emphase que ces morceaux exigent".[14] In the nineteenth century Girault-Duvivier's *Grammaire des grammaires* indicated that suspension points "ne s'emploient que dans de grands mouvements de pas- sion, lorsque les sentiments qui oppressent l'âme ne pouvant se faire jour en même temps, on laisse échap- per des phrases interrompues et sans suite, qui peignent avec force le désordre intérieur".[15] Littré defined suspen- sion points as "un signe de ponctuation qui indique que le sens est suspendu";[16] for Larousse, they marked "une suppression, une interruption, une lacune".[17] And ac- cording to Grevisse's *Le Bon Usage* they can signal four things: incompletion, a non-grammatical pause, an unexpressed extension of thought, and an omission.[18] Nina Catach effectively summarizes all these views: "Ils [les points de suspension] rejoignent, d'une certaine façon, le non-dit, mais un non-dit explicite, expressif, car la ponctuation exprime toutes les sortes de si- lences".[19] Suspension points indicate incompletion and interruption, the breakdown of verbal language under the influence of strong passions; they are richly sugges- tive.

A recent study of Rimbaud's variants has shown that he consistently deleted suspension points in his definitive texts;[20] the opposite is true of *Les Fleurs du Mal*. Baudelaire never deletes suspension points; indeed, he frequently adds them specifically for the 1861 edition, which contains fifteen examples.[21] The ways in which he uses them deserve close attention.

Having identified the different potential functions of suspension points, I want to map some of the specific effects that Baudelaire creates with them. I will consider firstly their elocutionary function and then their power of suggestion. These categories are not watertight, but despite (or perhaps precisely because of) the overlaps between them, they offer a convenient framework for suggesting the different ways in which Baudelaire exploits suspension points as a mode of poetic significa- tion.

The primary effect of suspension points is elocutionary: they affect the way a poem is read; they constitute an audible pause as well as a visible space. Baudelaire

places five such pauses within lines. For some French prosodists, pauses cannot, or should not, occur within lines.[22] But suspension points, potentially like any punctuation within a line, will affect the rhythm. In the last line of **"Le Cygne"** suspension points give spatial and rhythmic emphasis to the poet's vision of an eternal future of exiled, suffering victims (ll. 49-52):

> Ainsi dans la forêt où mon esprit s'exile
> Un vieux Souvenir sonne à plein souffle du cor!
> Je pense aux matelots oubliés dans une île,
> Aux captifs, aux vaincus! . . . à bien d'autres encor!

The suspension points split the line visibly into its two hemistichs, interrupting the anaphora and foregrounding the dramatic climax of the enumeration.

A similarly dramatic effect is found in the deliberately shocking **"Le Reniement de Saint Pierre"**. The poet turns Christ's supposedly redemptive death into a symbol of man's failure to transform the present world, taking sides with St Peter and attacking Christ for submitting to the will of a tyrannical god. It is only in the final stanza that we understand the relevance of the title of the poem (ll. 29-32):

> —Certes, je sortirai, quant à moi, satisfait
> D'un monde où l'action n'est pas la sœur du rêve;
> Puissé-je user du glaive et périr par le glaive!
> Saint Pierre a renié Jésus . . . il a bien fait!

The last line is the key to the poem; the suspension points are central to its dramatic effect: they create suspense, and they highlight the shock of the poet's revolt against orthodoxy.

In **"Le Voyage"** Baudelaire twice uses suspension points within one hemistich. That their function here is primarily elocutionary is signalled by their use in direct speech, part of what Barthes saw as the "théâtralité puissante" of Baudelaire's verse.[23] The poem exposes the emptiness of illusions through the metaphor of the soul as a boat sailing for Utopia (ll. 33-36):

> Notre âme est un trois-mâts cherchant son Icarie;
> Une voix retentit sur le pont: «Ouvre l'œil!»
> Une voix de la hune, ardente et folle, crie:
> «Amour . . . gloire . . . bonheur!» Enfer! c'est un
> écueil!

The suspension points create a staccato rhythm; they separate, and draw attention to, the three abstract ideals. The ideals ring out, but they ring hollow: deflation fol- lows in the second hemistich as hopefulness is exposed as folly when the voice changes to that of the poet.

In **"A une passante"** the pause within the line is inextricably linked with what the poem is about: a fleet- ing encounter between the poet and a beautiful woman on a busy street in Paris. The first two quatrains of the sonnet narrate the encounter in the past; the first tercet injects a note of drama as the encounter is relived. The paratactic structure of the line is emphasized by the punctuation: "Un éclair . . . puis la nuit!—Fugitive beauté" (l. 9). The words suggest a rapid passing of time, from the flash of light of the woman's presence to the darkness of her absence: this passing of time is evoked both visually and audibly by the suspension points.[24] The pause may also have suggestive power. It may symbolize the poet's temporary blindness after the bolt of lightning, or the void in which he feels he has been left, or the ecstasy of the encounter: this is, in many senses, a climactic line. But "éclair" may also have negative connotations, echoing the earlier reference to the woman's eyes as a "ciel livide où germe l'ouragan" (l. 7). The pause is polysemic: as in so many of Baudelaire's poems, woman is both beautiful and deadly, the personification of "le plaisir qui tue" (l. 8).

This suggestive potential is the second characteristic of suspension points, which Baudelaire exploits by placing them ten times at line ends. One (not entirely frivolous) definition of verse poetry is "language printed in lines which stop short of the right-hand margin".[25] With suspension points Baudelaire visibly prolongs the line further towards the right-hand margin, disrupting the typographical terrain, emphasizing the pause, and frustrating any sense of completion or closure. This prolongation necessarily has suggestive power: language stops, silence starts, the unspoken and/or the unspeakable are foregrounded. Suspension points imply further layers of meaning by creating pregnant silences within the text: they are a vital part of that open-ended suggestiveness which Barthes referred to as "la pensivité des textes".[26]

"Harmonie du soir" offers a good example of this sort of suggestiveness. The suspension points occur at the end of the third line of the last quatrain: "Le soleil s'est noyé dans son sang qui se fige . . ." (l. 15). They create a pause on the last line of a paratactic pattern of repeated lines in this *pantoum*: the second and fourth lines of one stanza become the first and third of the next. When fourth lines become third lines, the effect is necessarily to lessen their impact; but the suspension points break this pattern and renew the emphasis on the line: the repetition of the image of the drowning sun at the end of the third stanza becomes unusually emphatic. The line is clearly significant, not least because it contains the only two metaphors in a poem otherwise dominated by similes. The metaphors of drowning and blood form a climax to the growing ambiguity in the text. The same lines take on different connotations in different contexts (ll. 9-16):

> Le violon frémit comme un cœur qu'on afflige,
> Un cœur tendre, qui hait le néant vaste et noir!
> Le ciel est triste et beau comme un grand reposoir;
> Le soleil s'est noyé dans son sang qui se fige.

> Un cœur tendre, qui hait le néant vaste et noir,
> Du passé lumineux recueille tout vestige!
> Le soleil s'est noyé dans son sang qui se fige . . .
> Ton souvenir en moi luit comme un ostensoir!

Line 12, after the reference to "ciel" in line 11, may suggest the harmony and natural beauty of the sunset, but the suspension points at the end of line 15 invite us to dwell on this passing moment of balance between day and night. The harmony is fragile: drowning and coagulated blood are both images of death, and the pause also conjures up the aftermath of the sunset, a descent into darkness. The suspension points set up conflicting currents of signification.[27]

That suspension points are a site of poetic ambivalence can be seen again in **"Le Poison"**. The poet establishes a contrast between the effects on him of wine and drugs and of his lover's eyes and saliva: the latter have greater transforming powers than the former. But the contrast is not entirely flattering. Wine and opium are described in ambivalent terms: they are both vivifying and deadly. This note of ambivalence is maintained in the description of the lover; as in **"A une passante"**, suspension points become a resource in this suggestion of hidden danger (ll. 11-15):

> Tout cela ne vaut pas le poison qui découle
> De tes yeux, de tes yeux verts,
> Lacs où mon âme tremble et se voit à l'envers . . .
> Mes songes viennent en foule
> Pour se désaltérer à ces gouffres amers.

The imagery suggests physical intimacy, strong visual contact between lover and poet: this may be part of what is left unsaid by the suspension points. The reference to the lover's green eyes leads into a second metaphor: her eyes are lakes in which the poet can see his reflection. The suspension points at the end of line 13 invite us to dwell on the implications of the image. The verb "trembler" both evokes the unstable nature of reflections in water and implies fear and anxiety: pleasure, like the surface of the water, is unstable. The adverbial expression "à l'envers" suggests both the reversal of reality in a reflection and a more painful distortion, the poet twisted by his lover into something distinct from his true self. The three points suspend these processes of meaning; they compel the reader to fill in the gaps.[28]

We need to fill in the gaps in **"Les Petites vieilles"** too. The final quatrain focuses on the paradoxical power of old women's eyes. In his love poems, Baudelaire exploits eyes as an erotic focus; but here they reflect suffering (ll. 33-36):

> —Ces yeux sont des puits faits d'un million de larmes,
> Des creusets qu'un métal refroidi pailleta . . .

Ces yeux mystérieux ont d'invincibles charmes
Pour celui que l'austère Infortune allaita!

By using suspension points Baudelaire invites the reader to pause on the ambiguous metaphor of eyes as "Des creusets qu'un métal refroidi pailleta . . ." (l. 34). The verb "pailleter" has connotations of beauty and adornment; linked with "métal", it recalls the images of light and radiance in stanza 5 as well as descriptions of jewellery in **"Un Fantôme"** (ll. 29-34) and **"Le Jeu"** (ll. 1-4). But here the verb is given an unusually violent force by being combined with the image of the crucible. The connotations of the crucible could be positive—the heat of passion—but heat is contrasted with cold metal, which suggests sharpness, pain and suffering; it may also recall the reference to tears in the previous line: tears become shards of metal.[29]

I suggested that in **"Le Poison"** part of the function of the suspension points may be to cloak sexual intimacy. Similarly intense emotions are evoked in **"Franciscæ meæ laudes"**. The five suspension points at the end of line 14 give an open-ended conclusion to a syntactic unit which runs across two stanzas (ll. 10-15):

> Quum vitiorum tempestas
> Turbabat omnes semitas,
> Apparuisti, Deitas,
>
> Velut stella salutaris
> In naufragiis amaris. . . . .
> Suspendam cor tuis aris!

The imagery is ecstatic: woman is a guiding light, an escape from the storms of vice. The five suspension points are unusual. As I indicated earlier, Urbain Domergue admitted in the late eighteenth century the possibility of using four suspension points to indicate a longer pause and to express heightened emotions. Compelling evidence of Baudelaire's sense of the importance and polysemy of suspension points is furnished by the fact that he both follows Domergue by using four points in **"Le Rêve d'un curieux"** and **"Causerie"**, and goes further than him by using five points in **"Franciscæ meæ laudes"**, **"Un Voyage à Cythère"** and **"Ciel brouillé"**. In **"Franciscæ meæ laudes"** the five suspension points effectively capture the poet's inconclusive crescendo of emotions; they also throw into relief the last line of the tercet, a blend of eroticism and solemnity.

Eroticism is foregrounded by the four suspension points in **"Causerie"**. We glimpse the poet in a moment of sexual intimacy with his lover, whom he repeatedly addresses directly, but his thoughts revolve around the impossibility of loving her because of the suffering it causes him. In the first tercet he is in introspective mood (ll. 9-11):

Mon cœur est un palais flétri par la cohue;
On s'y soûle, on s'y tue, on s'y prend aux cheveux!
—Un parfum nage autour de votre gorge nue!. . . .

The imagery mixes the military and the erotic, culminating in the reference to hair, an echo of **"La Chevelure"**. This sensual imagery prepares us for the typographical shock of the dash, which acts as a sort of dialogue marker, emphasizing the shift from the poet's introspection to his direct address to his lover, an address which is now more explicitly erotic. The four suspension points are combined with an exclamation mark: this is a moment of inexpressible wonder and sensuality for the poet; the reader is again left to fill in the blanks.[30] But the punctuation also invites us to dwell on the ambiguities of that eroticism: they reinforce, through a dramatic pause, the phonetic equivalence of "nue" and "tue" in the middle of the previous line: the woman is both sexually desirable and life-threatening.[31] They also make the transition to the final stanza all the more violent: the poet defiantly rejects all intimacy and launches into an attack on Beauty personified. Within the space of three lines, the poet shifts from introspection via eroticism to rejection; the shifts are highlighted and given suggestive power by Baudelaire's punctuation.

This articulation of shifts and transitions within the structural fabric of individual poems is a particular aspect of the suggestive power of suspension points that I want to explore more fully now. The transition can be between ignorance and insight. This is the case in **"Un Voyage à Cythère"**. The poet narrates his departure on a sea voyage to Cythera, the island of Venus; as he draws alongside, however, all he sees is a hanged man being ripped apart by wild animals: myth gives way to mortality. The poet identifies himself with the hanged man, executed for his sexual sins; the scene becomes an explicit allegory, symptomatic of the poet's self-disgust (ll. 57-60):

> Dans ton île, ô Vénus! je n'ai trouvé debout
> Qu'un gibet symbolique où pendait mon image. . . .
> .
> —Ah! Seigneur! donnez-moi la force et le courage
> De contempler mon cœur et mon corps sans dégoût!

The five suspension points emphatically signal the poet's dramatic moment of insight and self-awareness. They also split the quatrain into two halves, marking the shift, reinforced by the addition of a dash, from words of reproach to the pagan god to a plea to the Christian God, the capitalized "Seigneur".

Ignorance gives way to insight via suspension points in **"Le Rêve d'un curieux"**. The poet explores his ambiguous attitude to death: he both desires it and fears it. The two tercets revolve around the simile of the impatient child in the theatre waiting for the curtain to go up, which leads into the terror of realization: death disappoints. This movement from expectation to realization is articulated by suspension points (ll. 9-14):

J'étais comme l'enfant avide du spectacle,
Haïssant le rideau comme un obstacle. . . .
Enfin la vérité froide se révéla:

J'étais mort sans surprise, et la terrible aurore
M'enveloppait.—Eh quoi! n'est-ce donc que cela?
La toile était levée et j'attendais encore.

The four suspension points mark the climax of the poet's dream.[32] They keep the reader in suspense, wondering what will happen next: the whole significance of the poem hangs on this shift between lines 10 and 11. They also invite us to dwell on the everyday image of the child in a theatre, with the connotations of life as a game, death as a spectacle. They also foreground the last line of the tercet and the theme of disappointment.

This shift is also, in part, temporal, as it is in **"A une passante"** and in **"Le Vin de l'assassin"**; but in this last poem, the shift is backwards instead of forwards. The poetic persona, a murderer, delights in his freedom to get drunk now that he has killed his tiresome wife. His drunken happiness reminds him of his blissful past when first married (ll. 5-8):

Autant qu'un roi je suis heureux;
L'air est pur, le ciel admirable . . .
Nous avions un été semblable
Lorsque j'en devins amoureux!

To the drunken poet, all is well, the weather is fine. These sense impressions spark off a flight of memory, signalled by the suspension points: a hesitation in the poet's enunciation marks the temporal shift, underlined by the change to the past tense in line 7. The quatrain forms two halves, one in the present, the other in the past: drunkenness brings about the interruption of one time into another, suspension points articulate it.

Time is also evoked in **"Le Portrait"**, the fourth sonnet of **"Le Fantôme"**. This is a poem about the passing of time: the radiant image of the lover metaphorically dims with time into a pencil drawing: "[un dessein] que le Temps, injurieux vieillard, / Chaque jour frotte avec son aile rude . . ." (ll. 52-53).[33] The suspension points make the reader dwell on the image of Time's "aile rude", which recalls the bird imagery of **"L'Albatros"** and **"Elévation"**: whereas in the earlier poems wings are symbols of the poet's creative power, here the wing becomes an instrument of destruction. As in **"A une passante"**, the suspension points signal spatially and audibly the very passage of time which the line laments: the silence in the text itself evokes poetically the ravages of time. This is particularly striking as it disrupts the pattern established hitherto in the poem of the sense of each stanza running into the next: the pause pulls the reader up short, unlike the commas at the end of the previous two stanzas. The suspension points also articulate a structural divide in the poem, a dramatic

shift from lament to attack: the lover lives on in the poet's memory. The imagery of death in the first three stanzas provokes in the poet a dramatic challenge to Time itself, the "Noir assassin de la Vie et de l'Art" (l. 54). The suspension points bridge the gap between metaphor and apostrophe, between reflection and reaction.

This interruption of one discourse into another via suspension points is a key structural device in **"Ciel brouillé"**. The poem is a subtle evocation of a woman through the symbolism of the natural world: the woman's charms are as ambiguous as those of an autumn day. The woman's ambiguity makes describing her in words a difficult venture: suspension points highlight the inadequacy of language to describe external reality. The poet relies on analogy and simile until line 10; the breakdown is signalled by the five suspension points (ll. 9-12):

Tu ressembles parfois à ces beaux horizons
Qu'allument les soleils des brumeuses saisons. . . . .
Comme tu resplendis, paysage mouillé
Qu'enflamment les rayons tombant d'un ciel brouillé!

The deliberately extended pause interrupts the poet's enunciation, and it signals a shift from simile to metaphor: the pause is metalinguistic, a moment of poetic self-interrogation. As in **"Harmonie du soir"** the suspension points make us dwell on the pregnant image of a (setting?) sun. The poet continues with, not a simile, but a metaphorical identification of woman and landscape: the two are as one in the rest of the poem. The first two stanzas consist of one syntactic unit each; the third stanza disrupts this pattern with an unconventional number of suspension points: there is a significant change of direction after a dramatic pause. The distinctions between inner and outer, between human and physical, are blurred; comparison becomes impossible, the suspension points signal the poet's failure to maintain any sort of objective distance through language.

Suspension points are a sort of stop-look-and-listen sign in *Les Fleurs du Mal.* They affect timing and rhythm; they are a striking visual symbol of pause. They constitute a space, both visually and audibly, both literally and metaphorically, in which the reader is brought into play, invited to think, to use his/her imagination, to hear the unsaid, to read between the lines, or rather, to read between the points. They challenge the reader to listen to the sound of silence; in Valéry's words, "Entends ce bruit fin qui est continu, et qui est le silence. Ecoute ce qu'on entend lorsque rien ne se fait entendre".[34] They rely on suggestion and extension: they are polysemic. They play on, and serve to underscore, both what immediately precedes them and what immediately follows them. They are a perfect example of "le non-dit", of the absence of verbal language. They raise questions. They are the site of an unspoken drama.

Notes

1. All references to *Les Fleurs du Mal* will be to the text of 1861 in the edition by Georges Blin and Claude Pichois, Paris, Corti, 1968, which includes all the variants.

2. Baudelaire's observation that "Il n'y a pas de hasard dans l'art, non plus qu'en mécanique" is well known (*Œuvres complètes,* ed. C. Pichois, Paris, Gallimard, Bibliothèque de la Pléiade, 1975-1976, 2 vols, II, p. 432). For Yves Bonnefoy, Baudelaire's conception of poetry marks a turning point: "Un des moments décisifs de la modernité poétique ce fut quand Baudelaire, reprenant des indications de Poe, plaça l'idée de 'composition' au cœur de son écriture, là même où le Romantisme avait gardé vives celle du discours inspiré et une pratique de l'éloquence" ("La septième face du bruit", *Europe,* 760-761, 1992, pp. 5-19, see p. 5). For further discussion of Baudelaire's poetic craftsmanship see Graham Chesters, *Baudelaire and the Poetics of Craft,* Cambridge, Cambridge University Press, 1988, and Peter Broome, *Baudelaire's Poetic Patterns: The Secret Language of "Les Fleurs du Mal",* Amsterdam, Rodopi, 1999.

3. In his notes for a preface to *Les Fleurs du Mal,* Baudelaire explains that his poems are the products of unremitting effort and that they have behind them "les retouches et les variantes [. . .], les épreuves barbouillées" (*Les Fleurs du Mal,* pp. 369-370). See also his letter of 22 April 1860 to Poulet-Malassis, his publisher, about the art of careful proofreading: "Ce n'est que grâce à cet esprit minutieusement méthodique qu'on peut arriver à des résultats qui ne soient pas trop dégoûtants" (*Correspondance,* ed. C. Pichois, Paris, Gallimard, Bibliothèque de la Pléiade, 1973, 2 vols, II, p. 29; all further references to Baudelaire's correspondence will be to this edition).

4. *Correspondance,* II, p. 307 (letter of 20 June 1863; original emphasis).

5. Ibid., p. 127 (letter of 20 January 1861).

6. For a discussion of Baudelaire's use of, and interest in, punctuation see Henk Nuiten, *Les Variantes des "Fleurs du Mal" et des "Epaves" de Charles Baudelaire,* Amsterdam, APA-Holland University Press, 1979, pp. 80-101. Nuiten argues that Baudelaire's choice of punctuation indicates his desire for both clarity and suggestiveness in his syntax; he does not mention suspension points.

7. *Correspondance,* I, p. 384 (letter of 18 March 1857; original emphasis).

8. Roy Lewis highlights the elocutionary function of punctuation: "The texture of verse is made up not only of sound but also of the silences which serve to group syllables into rhythmic units. [. . .] Punctuation should therefore be carefully interpreted by the reader and expressed as sound" (*On Reading French Verse: A Study of Poetic Form,* Oxford, Clarendon Press, 1982, pp. 23, 240). For Paul Valéry's discussion of the affinities between punctuation and musical dynamic markings see his *Cahiers,* ed. J. Robinson, Paris, Gallimard, Bibliothèque de la Pléiade, 1973-1974, 2 vols, I, pp. 473-474. It is interesting to note that the tradition of reading aloud was still alive in the nineteenth century, as illustrated by the publication of treatises such as Louis Dubroca's *L'Art de lire à haute voix, suivi de l'application de ses principes à la lecture des ouvrages d'éloquence et de poésie,* Paris, chez l'auteur, 1824; 2nd edn, Paris, Johanneau, 1825.

9. *Les Fleurs du Mal,* p. 110.

10. Alison Fairlie, "'Mène-t-on la foule dans les ateliers?'—Some Remarks on Baudelaire's Variants", in E. M. Beaumont et al., eds, *Order and Adventure in Post-Romantic French Poetry: Essays presented to C. A. Hackett,* New York, Barnes and Noble, 1973, pp. 17-27, see p. 19. This article is reprinted in Alison Fairlie, *Imagination and Language: Collected Essays on Constant, Baudelaire, Nerval, and Flaubert,* ed. Malcolm Bowie, Cambridge, Cambridge University Press, 1981, pp. 228-249.

11. Clive Scott, *The Poetics of French Verse: Studies in Reading,* Oxford, Clarendon Press, 1998, p. 155. Scott's reference to punctuation as an aspect of a writer's style echoes one of Baudelaire's contemporaries, George Sand, who attacked printers for trying to impose syntactic regularity on authors: "La ponctuation a sa philosophie comme le style; je ne dis pas comme la langue; le style est la langue bien comprise, la ponctuation est le style bien compris. [. . .] On a dit 'le style, c'est l'homme'. La ponctuation est encore plus l'homme que le style" (quoted in Annette Lorenceau, "La Ponctuation au XIXe siècle: George Sand et les imprimeurs", *Langue Française,* 45, 1980, pp. 50-9, see p. 56). The dictum quoted by Sand is Buffon's: see his *Discours sur le style,* ed. C. E. Pickford, Hull, Department of French, University of Hull, 1978, p. xvii.

12. Critics are increasingly recognizing the importance of the study of punctuation in literary analysis. Such study has been greatly facilitated in recent years by two critics in particular: Malcolm Parkes, *Pause and Effect: An Introduction to the History of Punctuation in the West,* Aldershot, Scolar

Press, 1992, and Nina Catach, *La Ponctuation (histoire et système),* Paris, PUF, 1994. Nina Catach has also edited *Langue Française,* 45, 1980, which is devoted to punctuation in French literature. Jacques Drillon's *Traité de la ponctuation française,* Paris, Gallimard, 1991, gives a good account of the history and uses of punctuation in French; chapter 11 (pp. 404-426) deals with suspension points. Studies of punctuation in French poetry seem to have concentrated on Rimbaud and Valéry: see F. S. Eigeldinger, "Rimbaud et la transgression de 'la vieillerie poétique'. Ponctuation et rejets dans ses alexandrins", *Revue d'histoire littéraire de la France,* 83, 1983, pp. 45-64; G. M. Macklin, "Perspectives on the Role of Punctuation in Rimbaud's *Illuminations*", *Journal of European Studies,* 20, 1990, pp. 59-72; J.-M. Houpert, "Inutile le signe '? . . .'. Sémiotique de la ponctuation valéryenne", *Forschungen zu Paul Valéry / Recherches valéryennes,* 2, 1989, pp. 35-48; and G. Dessons, "La Ponctuation suspensive dans *Charmes* de Valéry", *Op. Cit.: Revue de littératures française et comparée,* 1, 1992, pp. 135-140. The ability of punctuation to affect meaning is illustrated, paradoxically, by poets like Mallarmé, Apollinaire, Eluard and Reverdy, who sometimes create suggestive ambiguity by not using any punctuation at all: see Clive Scott, *French Verse-Art: A Study,* Cambridge, Cambridge University Press, 1980, pp. 217-221, and R. A. York, "Mallarmé and Apollinaire: The Unpunctuated Text", *Visible Language,* 23, 1989, pp. 45-62.

13. Antoine Furetière, *Le Dictionnaire universel,* reprint of 1690 edition, Paris, SNL/Le Robert, 1978, 3 vols, III, s.v. "Point".

14. Urbain Domergue, *Grammaire françoise simplifiée, ou Traité d'orthographe,* Lyon, chez l'auteur, 1778, p. 188. By contrast, the *Encyclopédie* specifies only four points: "On dispose quelquefois quatre *points* horizontalement dans le corps de la ligne, pour indiquer la suppression, soit du reste d'un discours commencé, & qu'on n'acheve pas par pudeur, par modération, ou par quelqu'autre motif, soit d'une partie d'un texte que l'on cite, ou d'un discours que l'on rapporte" (article "Point", *Encyclopédie ou dictionnaire raisonné des sciences, des arts et des métiers,* Paris, Briasson et al., 1751-1765, 17 vols, XII, p. 870).

15. Charles-Pierre Girault-Duvivier, *Grammaire des grammaires, ou Analyse des meilleurs traités sur la langue française,* 5th edn, Paris, Cotelle, 1822, 2 vols, II, p. 1024.

16. Emile Littré, *Dictionnaire de la langue française,* Paris, Hachette, 1863, 2 vols, II, p. 1188.

17. Pierre Larousse, *Grand dictionnaire universel du XIXe siècle,* Paris, Larousse, 1866-1876, 15 vols, XII, p. 1257. Louis-Nicolas Bescherelle gives the same definition in his *Dictionnaire national,* Paris, Garnier, 1870, 2 vols, II, p. 923.

18. Maurice Grevisse, *Le Bon Usage,* 13th edn, Paris, Duculot, 1993, pp. 165-167.

19. Nina Catach, *La Ponctuation,* p. 63. Cf.: "Les points de suspension 'psychanalysent' le texte. Ils tiennent en suspens ce qui ne doit pas être dit explicitement" (Gaston Bachelard, *L'Eau et les rêves,* 2nd edn, Paris, Corti, 1947, p. 51).

20. F. S. Eigeldinger, art. cit., p. 49.

21. The fifteen examples occur in fourteen poems. Baudelaire used suspension points in the first published versions of five poems ("Le Portrait", "Le Cygne", "A une passante", "Le Rêve d'un curieux", "Le Voyage"). He introduced them into the 1857 edition of one poem ("Le Reniement de Saint Pierre"), and into the 1861 edition of eight poems ("Harmonie du soir", "Le Poison", "Ciel brouillé", "Causerie", "Franciscæ meæ laudes", "Les Petites Vieilles", "Le Vin de l'assassin", "Un Voyage à Cythère"). Of course, it is not simply the number of examples of suspension points that is interesting; their value is relative and can only be appreciated in context and in relation to other punctuation marks, together with which they constitute a system. The scope and focus of the present study rule out a systematic study of Baudelaire's punctuation as a whole. What I want to emphasize is the way in which suspension points act as one of Baudelaire's modes of poetic signification. In the course of this study I shall refer occasionally to dashes, or *tirets*. The *tiret* was imported into French syntax at the beginning of the nineteenth century. Used until then simply to signal dialogue, it came to be used, almost like the comma, singly to mark a new enunciation and in pairs to create a parenthesis; the Latin term for dash, *virgula plana,* suggests its links with the comma. For further discussion of the *tiret* see J. Drillon, op. cit., pp. 329-340, and G. Dessons, "Rythme et écriture: Le Tiret entre ponctuation et typographie", *Zeitschrift für französische Sprache und Literatur,* 21, 1993, pp. 122-134.

22. See, for example, Maurice Grammont, *Petit traité de versification française,* 17th edn, Paris, Colin, 1959, p. 20, and Jean Cohen, *Structure du langage poétique,* Paris, Flammarion, 1966, pp. 60-62.

23. Roland Barthes alludes to the theatricality of much of Baudelaire's writing in an essay originally published as a preface to Baudelaire's four

unfinished plays in the 1955 edition of his works: "Seulement, cette théâtralité puissante, elle n'est qu'à l'état de trace dans les projets de Baudelaire, alors qu'elle coule largement dans le reste de l'œuvre baudelairienne. Tout se passe comme si Baudelaire avait mis son théâtre partout, sauf précisément dans ses projets de théâtre" (*Essais critiques,* Paris, Seuil, 1964, p. 43). For a useful discussion of direct speech in *Les Fleurs du Mal* see Russell King, "Dialogue in Baudelaire's Poetic Universe", *L'Esprit Créateur,* 13, 1973, pp. 114-123.

24. The use of the dash, only added in 1861, is also significant: it marks a shift to the poet's apostrophe of Beauty personified, thus effectively isolating the first hemistich, which is itself divided by the suspension points.

25. Quoted in F. W. Leakey, *Sound and Sense in French Poetry: An Inaugural Lecture,* London, Bedford College, 1975, p. 27, n. 14.

26. Roland Barthes, *S/Z,* Paris, Seuil, 1970, p. 222.

27. Cf.: "The dots which follow 'se fige . . .' on its second appearance break down its former sharpness and make it more yielding [. . .]. It is, in the context, a highly expressive device. One could see the dots as representing the last faint disappearing remnants of light, a lingering but dying trail which makes all the more startling the switch to inner light which floods the following line. They might equally suggest the immeasurable, wordless distance which the mind has to traverse between outer and inner infinities, between visible horizons in space and mental horizons in time. But above all they dissolve the absolutism of 'se fige . . .', thaw its stern rigidity and give the mind release" (Peter Broome, op. cit, p. 179).

28. Cf.: "The dots which stretch beyond the actual rhythmic contour of the verse and may seem to have no syllabic or prosodic existence, contribute nevertheless their own rhythmic effect: that of a pause, a supernumerary or superfluous lull, during which the mind can feel the void, the inexpressible, the unfathomable, opening up before it—the hollow into which dreams can pour" (Peter Broome, op. cit., p. 215).

29. The image recalls earlier love poems: in "Le Serpent qui danse", the poet describes his lover's eyes as "deux bijoux froids où se mêle / L'or avec le fer" (ll. 15-16); and in "Le Chat", the poet longs to plunge into his lover's "beaux yeux, / Mêlés de métal et d'agate" (ll. 3-4). In these love poems, the metallic imagery suggests the paradoxical mixture of passion and coldness in the woman's eyes, the ambiguity of sexual desire; in "Les Petites vieilles" the connotations of coldness and pain dominate.

30. According to a nineteenth-century study of punctuation, the combination of exclamation mark and suspension points is used "dans les moments d'extase, d'un chagrin violent, ou d'une situation commandée par un tableau effrayant" (F. Raymond, *Traité raisonné de ponctuation,* in *Dictionnaire des termes appropriés aux arts et aux sciences* [. . .] *pouvant servir de supplément au Dictionnaire de l'Académie,* Paris, Masson, 1824, pp. i-xxxi, see p. xxvii).

31. This internal rhyme also serves to underline the shift in the first tercet from terminal *rime riche* to *rime pauvre,* a shift which parallels the poem's thematics of destruction and loss; the poem ends with a sense of resignation and acceptance, paralleled by a progression to *rime suffisante.* The ambiguities of beauty are reinforced phonetically by the links between "beau"/"Beauté" and "fléau", "lambeaux" and "bêtes".

32. The line ended with five points when the poem was first published in the *Revue contemporaine* on 15 May 1860.

33. The line ended with four points when the poem was first published in *L'Artiste* on 15 October 1860.

34. Paul Valéry, *Tel Quel,* in *Œuvres,* ed. J. Hytier, Paris, Gallimard, Bibliothèque de la Pléiade, 1957-1960, 2 vols, II, p. 656.

Peter Broome (essay date 1999)

SOURCE: Broome, Peter. "Introduction and *La Chevelure.*" In *Baudelaire's Poetic Patterns: The Secret Language of Les Fleurs du Mal,* pp. 7-39. Amsterdam: Rodopi, 1999.

[*In the following excerpts, Broome provides a general introduction to* Les Fleurs du Mal *and a detailed analysis of "La Chevelure," presenting the latter as a central example of Baudelaire's ability to represent the experiences of sensation in a transcendent light.*]

It would be almost superfluous, in the wake of so many searching critical studies, to attempt a survey of Baudelaire's enormous contribution to the realization of new directions in modern poetry, and to try to define the incomparable stimulus which he has given to a more problematical view of the possibilities of 'modernism'. What is clear is that *Les Fleurs du Mal* stands not at, but *as,* the busiest crossroads, multi-directional and endlessly complex, of the history of French poetry. Within its pages, Baudelaire has locked and interlocked all the repercussions of a major crisis of values, producing a poetry which is snared in contradictions, pulled this way and that by conflicting attractions and imperatives, animated, tormented and shaped by tensions running through the body of the verse.

To use the phrase the 'body of the verse' could hardly be more appropriate: not only in that Baudelaire is the most *physical* of poets, savouring the luxury of the senses to the full and venturing to the very brink of tolerance and beyond, but in that he turns the text itself into a pliable sensual medium which, beyond the hedonistic profusion of actual references to sight, scent, sound, taste and touch, moves and vibrates, resounds and reverberates, twists and wavers, fattens and thins as if of its own accord, manipulating and moulding, permeating and penetrating the intimate, perhaps unconscious, sensual instincts of the reader at the very instant of verbal contact and exposure. But to emphasize the indulgent physicality of **Les Fleurs du Mal** is not to suggest that this is a poetry which is only skin-deep. On the contrary, no poet has delved in greater depth into the extremism of the human passions: to uncover the obsessions, the treacherous undercurrents, the destructive deviations, the sophisticated compromises. No poet has refined more courageously the study of the psyche: partly through the fluctuating moods of drugs in a kind of *connaissance par les gouffres,* but essentially through the more versatile self-exploration of poetry, probing the ambiguities, confronting the censored and the half-confessed, bringing to light the hidden layers, the threatened frontiers and the points of conflict. And if the life of the senses is so acute, so overwhelming, in Baudelaire, this is not to the exclusion, but to the further enlargement, of more abstract dimensions, ontological issues and spiritual preoccupations. For the senses are a *translation.* They do not move without awakening and dislodging far-reaching implications. Their intensity, their very extravagance, their journeying to the edge, becomes the doorway of significance. They are meshed inseparably with what exceeds them: the great unfurling domain of analogies and equivalences, links and correspondences. The senses, then, for Baudelaire, are the touch-paper of the imagination: stimulating simile and metaphor in almost unprecedented abundance, creating a poetry which goes leaping far beyond, not only simple physicality, but the more insipid and self-contented *poésie du cœur* of the Romantics, so justifying his persuasive *caveat* that 'il ne faut pas confondre la sensibilité de l'imagination avec celle du cœur' (*OC [Œuvres Complètes]* II, p. 604).

And if the imagination is sensitized to an extraordinary degree and, with it, what one might call the intuitive visionary sense endowing all aspects of the material world with a 'double life', with the facility to unveil their own 'otherness', then so is the moral sense. The poetry of **Les Fleurs du Mal** is not an escapist poetry, despite symptomatic titles like **L'Invitation au voyage** (*OC* I, pp. 53-54) and **Any where out of the world** (*OC*

I, pp. 356-57). It is no more a poetry given to distraction and distant dreams than it is to sentimentality. It comes home to roost uncomfortably close to the festering breeding-ground of hypocrisies, guilty consciences and evasive feints. It injects into modern verse a new acuteness of moral urgency and perplexity, a probing awareness of the issues at stake in questions of truth and falsity, self-awareness and self-deception, love and hatred, commitment and alienation, creative and destructive impulses, responsibility and recklessness, discipline and *laisser aller,* self-betterment and whirling dissolution: to say nothing of liberty and enslavement.

It is a poetry also which opens up the most searching and perturbing spiritual dimensions, questioning from the very roots the tremors of faith and non-faith, the tormented relationships of spirit and matter, the intermittent glimpses of transcendence, the wayward possibilities for salvation or perdition. Nor are these simply *themes.* No-one, more than Baudelaire, has made of the poetic act, of the verbal mediation, of the transforming potentialities of art, a *sacred* or quasi-religious act: not just a prayer, a confession, an attempted exorcism, a sublimation, a yearning for the ideal (though it may be simultaneously all of these things), but a passage from intransitive to transitive and from one plane to another, a transmutation of one's own base matter, a self-purification and self-conquest through the mysterious alchemy of language, and a tentative communication between the inadequacies of the word as known to all poets and the unimaginable model to which it aspires which is the Word, reigning supreme like a mirage above the signs and symptoms of one's linguistic 'fall from grace' and suggesting a redemption. More than this, his poetry is one which enlists and puts to the test, if not on trial, all the opposites of one's deepest nature and of the human definition. It is a polarized poetry, racked between extremes (the divine and the satanical, ecstasy and horror, self-acceptance and self-refusal, the ethereal and the carnal, volatility and inertia, idolatry and universal indifference), which throws up the most restless and, one might say, the most ruthless self-awareness.

This is, then, a poetry of 'irresolutions': not of solved equations, secure values and safely closed doors, but of fractures, antitheses, clash and internecine warfare (registered as much in the form, style, tones and verbal textures as in the more patent emotional substance). It is a poetry shaped and deriving its rhythms from dualities of voice. Before the more systematic analyses of the twentieth century, Baudelaire has uncovered and explored the plurality of self: the voices at different levels, their ambivalent or ambiguous dialogues, their incompatibilities and compromises, those coming from undetermined sources and invisible horizons, their repressed shadows and refracted patterns, their ingenious proxies and *alter egos.* What this means, among other things, is that this is not an example of 'emotion recollected in tranquillity', however nostalgic or dreamy certain moods may be. It is the poem *as* struggle, the text *as* arena, the stanzas *as* debate. The drama, whichever of its many faces it may assume, is enacted 'live' in the pressure-chamber of the poem, which becomes the very crucible of self-confrontation, self-interrogation and the painful processes of potential self-transmutation. Hence the multifarious force of disturbance in Baudelaire's texts: stemming not simply from emotions which are disconcertingly two-faced and suspiciously ambivalent, from attitudes and implications which challenge moral stability, from probes into human psychology which hunt out demons, strip hypocrisy and show the subconscious as a sea of counter-currents, from a metaphysical or spiritual obstinacy which spirals between *ciel* and *gouffre* with howls of blindness and blasphemy, but, more importantly perhaps, from a verbal matter which is pulled between composition and decomposition, *forme* and *informe,* harmony and dissonance, to be characterized by its unpredictabilities, its sudden influxes of homeless energy, its *volte-faces,* its pockets of vertigo, its hollowing suction, its almost unmanageable changes of direction. It is Baudelaire's achievement to have grappled magnificently and, from the poetic point of view, triumphantly with a muse of Beauty who is not benign but embattled: whose resistant and perverse proximity has forced poetry away from the pallid, the tame, the platitudinous, and into new zones of vitality, energy and shock where language and expression have been obliged to invent new responses at the risk of their own *naufrage.*

* * *

So much is well known. What has not been so fully appreciated, however, is the extent to which Baudelaire has opened up for modern poetry, and immeasurably enlarged, the awareness of new dimensions of *active* form. It might be thought, glibly, that his 'modernism' lies essentially in his consciousness—the virulence of his passion, his revolutionary sensitivity to internal conflicts, the discomforting ambivalence of feelings, his incisive self-analysis and unearthing of multiple selves, the aggravated inner dialogues, the prickling confessions, the corrosive encounter with hypocrisy and its inventive disguises, the subversive challenge thrown out to simplistic notions of moral decency, the notes of blasphemy and wails of anguish which radically undermine facility of faith and sanguine reassurances of salvation—rather than in his poetic form which might be seen (with its predilection for the disciplines of the sonnet, its classic Alexandrines, its stout stanza-forms and fully fashioned rhyming patterns) to belong firmly to another century. This would be to overlook, however, what we have already stressed: that poetry, for Baudelaire, is a total commitment. It is a complete and uncompromising investment of the self—its intensities, its dilemmas, its perplexities and frustrations, its irreconcilables, its 'unacceptables'—in the living act of language. Thus form is not a mould, but an intimate correspondent; not an inheritance, but a willed invasion, an irruption / eruption of the moment. It fluctuates with each flicker of feeling. It advances and retreats, clenches and relents, with each wavelet of doubt or assertion, purpose or hesitation. It is the instantaneous and inseparable *translation* of every reverberation of the active self, never more problematical than in that moment of linguistic inflammation. So, if one sees 'modernism' as representing something more subversive, more fragmentary, more inquisitorial, split between selves and moving in a more complex play of mirrors, then this is not just a state of mind but a state of form and language—perhaps the essential realization of twentieth century criticism being that they are one and the same, virtually interchangeable, twin parts of that 'throw of the dice which will never abolish chance'[1]. Form, then, in the case of the poetry of Baudelaire, *is* its modernism. It is not simply a question of an increased responsiveness to the expressive potential of verse-form or the intuitive discovery of new possibilities for pattern, though the artist of **Les Fleurs du Mal** has enlarged the poetic medium in this respect, awakened it to its latent 'selves', almost beyond recognition. It is more that he has created a fabric, an inventive infinity of fabrics, in which self and style are consubstantial, in which the depth of the fluctuation or impulse within goes hand in hand with the visible reverberations, jolts, adjustments, contortions, unpredictabilities and palpitations of the expressive entity on the page, in which they mesh, multiply and define each other: in which every unfurling or blockage of syntax, every tentative affinity of rhyme, every irony or complicity of juxtaposition, every shimmering or occluded analogy, every variable pulse of rhythm, every gear-change or shift in tempo, every sensual ripple of sonority or deliberate clash of sound, every caressed syllable or lingering mute e̱, *are* the man, *are* the theme, *are* the battleground of spirit.

Much has been made of Baudelaire as a *lover.* Perhaps not enough has been made of Baudelaire as a *lover of form.* He admires in Poe

> des symptômes curieux de ce goût immodéré pour les belles formes, surtout pour les belles formes singulières
> *(OC* II, p. 335):

by which he means forms strangely moulded to the restless and eccentric imagination, creating their shapes in concordance with the (often discordant) play of initiatives and impulses. And he attributes Théophile Gautier's artistic distinction to 'ce goût inné de la forme et de la perfection dans la forme', adding

> Nul n'a mieux su que lui exprimer le bonheur que donne à l'imagination la vue d'un bel objet d'art, fût-il le plus désolé et le plus terrible qu'on puisse supposer
> *(OC* II, pp. 122-23):

a testimony to Baudelaire's own belief in the efficacy of form, regardless of the leanings of the subject-matter, creating a beauty in bleakness, tension and ugliness which is almost a redemption by form, a conversion into its second self. Of Poe, he also says: 'Sa poésie, profonde et plaintive, est néanmoins ouvragée . . .' (*OC* II, p. 274). And of an anonymous bard, no doubt referring, if only by reflection, to himself, he writes:

> Je connais un poète, d'une nature toujours orageuse et vibrante, qu'un vers de Malherbe, symétrique et carré de mélodie, jette dans de longues extases
>
> (*OC* II, p. 754).

Clearly, turbulence of poetic nature and a heaving, unruly inner inspiration are not incompatible with the delights of literary order, which, on the contrary, may be their necessary or ideal corollary; and æsthetic euphoria can be as powerful and overwhelming as, if not more complete than, its physical and emotional counterparts. Imagination, for Baudelaire, is not merely a free-wheeling adventurer. It is a structured sensitivity. It is meshed with *métier*. It discovers its own range through the disciplines and subtleties, the strategies and symmetries, of accomplishment of technique. Imagination demands its own versatile linguist, its travelling translator. So, he can state:

> Plus on possède d'imagination, mieux il faut posséder le métier pour accompagner celle-ci dans ses aventures et surmonter les difficultés qu'elle recherche avidement. Et mieux on possède son métier, moins il faut s'en prévaloir et le montrer, pour laisser l'imagination briller de tout son éclat
>
> (OC II, p. 612).

And speaking of Poe again he says admiringly:

> Non seulement il a dépensé des efforts considérables pour soumettre à sa volonté le démon fugitif des minutes heureuses, pour rappeler à son gré ces sensations exquises, ces appétitions spirituelles, ces états de santé poétique, si rares et si précieux qu'on pourrait vraiment les considérer comme des grâces extérieures à l'homme et comme des visitations; mais aussi il a soumis l'inspiration à la méthode, à l'analyse la plus sévère. Le choix des moyens! il y revient sans cesse, il insiste avec une éloquence savante sur l'appropriation du moyen à l'effet, sur l'usage de la rime, sur le perfectionnement du refrain, sur l'adaptation du rythme au sentiment
>
> (*OC* II, p. 331).

If, then, the poet of **Les Fleurs du Mal** can emphasize as the underlying intent of his collection the desire, the compulsion, to 'exercer mon goût passionné de l'obstacle' (*OC* I, p. 181), then that 'obstacle', setting its strictures and resistance against the imagination (the exercise of will, the application of technical means, the complex engineering of prosody), is not an imposition

but a partnership, not an impediment but a facilitator: an obstacle enabling the flood to break into an infinity of *passages* and to define itself multifariously as pattern. Technique, indeed, makes the imagination speak more articulately, refine and crystallize the most far-reaching of its intuitions, explore itself as a moving network of correspondences, expand and enhance its own complexity. 'Toutes les ruses du style' (*OC* II, p. 3) are put at the service of a *formal* imagination: such as that, perhaps, which prompts Baudelaire to promote the distinction between the 'imagination poétique' and the 'imagination de l'art' or 'imagination du dessin'; or, quoting Mrs Crowe, between mere *fancy* and

> 'the *constructive* imagination, which is a much higher function, and which, in as much as man is made in the likeness of God, bears a distant relation to that sublime power by which the Creator projects, creates and upholds his universe'
>
> (*OC* II, p. 624).

Might one therefore argue that the very *essence* of a text by Baudelaire may lie, not only in the manipulation of a chosen stanza-scheme or the broader symmetry of parallels and oppositions, but, within that framework, in the merest twist of a rhyme, in a curl of syntax, in the hesitation of a mute e̲ or the momentary giddiness of an *enjambement*? For few poets have stressed with such conviction, with such pressing personal commitment, the *virtues* of prosody. One of his earliest exercises in literary criticism laments the laxity and vagueness of form of M. de Senneville, saying:

> il ignore les rimes puissamment colorées, ces lanternes qui éclairent la route de l'idée; il ignore aussi les effets qu'on peut tirer d'un certain nombre de mots, diversement combinés
>
> (*OC* II, p. 11).

Gautier, by contrast, is seen as the perfect model of 'knowingness' in the apposite use of metre and finely focused rhyme:

> et il l'a parfaitement prouvé en introduisant systématiquement et continuellement la majesté de l'alexandrin dans le vers octosyllabique (*Émaux et Camées*). Là surtout apparaît tout le résultat qu'on peut obtenir par la fusion du double élément, peinture et musique, par la carrure de la mélodie, et par la pourpre régulière et symétrique d'une rime plus qu'exacte
>
> (*OC* II, p. 126).

Rhymes as lanterns, illuminating and furthering the progression of ideas; rhymes as part of a structured grandeur and solidity, as a regal colouring: to these he adds more sophisticated contributions, subtly attuned to twin or divergent strains of the human mind, as sensed, for instance, in the poetry of Leconte de Lisle whose rhymes répondent régulièrement à cet amour contradictoire et mystérieux de l'esprit humain pour la surprise et la symétrie

(*OC* II, p. 179);

or, in the case of Poe, the analytical awareness of the 'plaisir mathématique et musical que l'esprit tire de la rime' and the fact that, anticipating more disconcerting and ambivalent possibilities behind the customary chiming relationships,

il a aussi cherché à rajeunir, à redoubler le plaisir de la rime en y ajoutant cet élément inattendu, l'*étrangeté*, qui est comme le condiment indispensable de toute beauté

(*OC* II, p. 336).

Rhythm is no less alive, for Baudelaire, with renewable expressive potential: 'Rythme, parfum, lueur, ô mon unique reine!' (*OC* I, p. 25). Perhaps even more than rhyme, this is the soul of verse, its moving spirit, its animating force. He expresses his liking for a 'poésie profondément rythmée' (*OC* II, p. 131)—by which is meant one in which rhythm is not one of the range of cosmetics, but a power which transfuses, sets currents in motion, breeds highs and lows, surges and relapses, and wraps itself dynamically round the alternations and contrasts of thought and mood. In Banville, for example, he admires the facility with which 'la pensée se coule d'elle-même dans un rythme' (*OC* II, p. 162): the foretaste of a spontaneous fusion in which the self *becomes* the medium. And, as with the *étrangeté* of some of Poe's rhymes, he is open to the *dépaysement* and disturbance of texts, one might say,

dont les muscles ne vibrent pas suivant l'allure classique de son pays, dont la démarche n'est pas cadencée selon le rythme accoutumé . . .

(*OC* II, pp. 576-77):

open to the influence of 'new rhythms' which take tradition beyond its familiar boundaries. More than this, Baudelaire the rhythmic artist sees rhythm, not simply as an intimate correspondent, a kind of spiritual *alter ego*, but as an agent of transformation, working on and through the emotions in the course of the poetic act to turn them into a superior equivalent, intervening to effect an actual exorcism, transmuting pain, for instance, into an æsthetic serenity, phonetically and rhythmically induced, and absorbing and resolving what was a series of tensions:

C'est un des privilèges prodigieux de l'Art que l'horrible, artistement exprimé, devienne beauté, et que la *douleur* rythmée et cadencée remplisse l'esprit d'une *joie* calme

(*OC* II, p. 123).

Rhythm and rhyme, as exercised in verse, are part of the almost 'sacred' science of numbers. Hence Baudelaire's respect for Gautier in these terms:

Il y a dans le style de Théophile Gautier une justesse qui ravit, qui étonne, et qui fait songer à ces miracles produits dans le jeu par une profonde science mathématique

(*OC* II, p. 118).

In more general terms he adds, indicating how such mysterious permutations can conjure up and bring things to life on the page, give them relief, multiply their language, and turn sensations into a hub of analogical perceptions:

Il y a dans le mot, dans le *verbe*, quelque chose de *sacré* qui nous défend d'en faire un jeu de hasard. Manier savamment une langue, c'est pratiquer une espèce de sorcellerie évocatoire. C'est alors que la couleur parle, comme une voix profonde et vibrante; que les monuments se dressent et font saillie sur l'espace profond; que les animaux et les plantes, représentants du laid et du mal, articulent leur grimace non équivoque; que le parfum provoque la pensée et le souvenir correspondants . . .

(*OC* II, p. 118).

It is in this way that the word *jongleur* (*OC* II, p. 321), in its superior sense (that of ritual intermediary, transformer of appearances, magician or manipulator of occult signs, and not as mere juggler of words), can be applied to the poet as a supreme term of praise. In the pithy language of his *Journaux intimes,* Baudelaire homes in on the same hypnotic centre of thinking:

De la langue et de l'écriture, prises comme opérations magiques, sorcellerie évocatoire

(*OC* I, p. 658).

Rhythm and rhyme, then, not seen as casual or occasional literary devices, but as ministers of a demanding 'spiritual prosody':

Car il est évident que les rhétoriques et les prosodies ne sont pas des tyrannies inventées arbitrairement, mais une collection de règles réclamées par l'organisation même de l'être spirituel

(*OC* II, pp. 626-27),

he writes. The same point is made in numerous guises and with various shades of colouring. The author's *Projets de préfaces* for **Les Fleurs du Mal** emphasize

comment la poésie touche à la musique par une prosodie dont les racines plongent plus avant dans l'âme humaine que ne l'indique aucune théorie classique;

while the special 'porousness' of music as a language which can, with a minimum of resistance, espouse and express every movement of the inner being, enabling the transfusion between inner and outer worlds with an uncanny reflectiveness and a clinging precision, is doubly appreciated through the 'second state' of hashish-inspired perception:

> La musique [. . .] vous parle de vous-même et vous raconte le poème de votre vie; elle s'incorpore à vous, et vous vous fondez en elle. Elle parle votre passion, non pas d'une manière vague et indéfinie, comme elle fait dans vos soirées nonchalantes, un jour d'opéra, mais d'une manière circonstanciée, positive, chaque mouvement du rythme marquant un mouvement connu de votre âme, chaque note se transformant en mot, et le poème entier entrant dans votre cerveau comme un dictionnaire doué de vie
>
> *(OC* I, p. 431).

Such is this intuition of all notes (each sonority, each pulse of rhythm, each cadenced contour, each melodic thread or reverberation) contributing to a supreme harmonic entity—and a structure of the spirit—that the perfection of the text (its form, its proportions, its 'consonance') is almost, for Baudelaire, a moral re-integration, a redemption through harmony. It is in this way that he can write:

> Aussi, ce qui exaspère surtout l'homme de goût dans le spectacle du vice, c'est sa difformité, sa disproportion. Le vice porte atteinte au juste et au vrai, révolte l'intellect et la conscience; mais, comme outrage à l'harmonie, comme dissonance, il blessera plus particulièrement certains esprits poétiques; et je ne crois pas qu'il soit scandalisant de considérer toute infraction à la morale, au beau moral, comme une espèce de faute contre le rythme et la prosodie universels
>
> *(OC* II, p. 334).

If Baudelaire the poet is supremely sensitive (as a *duty*) to 'l'harmonie, le balancement des lignes, l'eurythmie dans les mouvements' *(OC* I, p. 432), and if, in venturing into the unversified form of the prose-poems of *Le Spleen de Paris,* he continues to seek through a new medium

> le miracle d'une prose poétique, musicale sans rythme et sans rime, assez souple et assez heurtée pour s'adapter aux mouvements lyriques de l'âme, aux ondulations de la rêverie, aux soubresauts de la conscience
>
> *(OC* I, pp. 275-76),

then rhythm and rhyme are not his only agents. The 'sorcellerie évocatoire', the 'spiritualization' of the word, enlist all the resources of style, form and expression: all the potentialities of *significant form.* It may be the shape of a phrase and its pattern of evolution, an intensification or a thinning out of syntax, a clausal concatenation or contraction, a thrust of development or a holding back, a crest or trough of intonational energy. It is in this sense that he can state so confidently, as if nothing is beyond the evocative (and therefore correspondent) flexibilities of form,

> que la phrase poétique peut imiter (et par là elle touche à l'art musical et à la science mathématique) la ligne horizontale, la ligne droite ascendante, la ligne droite descendante; qu'elle peut monter à pic vers le ciel, sans

essoufflement, ou descendre perpendiculairement vers l'enfer avec la vélocité de toute pesanteur; qu'elle peut suivre la spirale, décrire la parabole, ou le zigzag figurant une série d'angles superposés

> *(OC* I, p. 183).

Within such shapes and designs, no element of language is inactive. The poet, through the optic of the art critic, speaks of 'la science infinie des combinaisons de tons' *(OC* II, p. 753): a thought amplified when he writes, of the inexhaustible 'mix' of ingredients and interplay of savours available to his expressive art, that

> la poésie se rattache aux arts de la peinture, de la cuisine et du cosmétique par la possibilité d'exprimer toute sensation de suavité ou d'amertume, de béatitude ou d'horreur par l'accouplement de tel substantif avec tel adjectif, analogue ou contraire
>
> *(OC* I, p. 183).

Even grammar (the art of conjunctions and disjunctions, tenses and tempos, dominances and subordinations, action and description, movements and fine shadings, line and colour)—as the dynamics of hashish bring out to the 'visionary' with even greater impact and splendour—is a kind of resurrection, language leaving the limbo of its cocoon and taking flight, the abstraction of signs and functions turned into a host of living, creative energies on the page:

> La grammaire, l'aride grammaire elle-même, devient quelque chose comme une sorcellerie évocatoire; les mots ressuscitent revêtus de chair et d'os, le substantif, dans sa majesté substantielle, l'adjectif, vêtement transparent qui l'habille et le colore comme un glacis, et le verbe, ange du mouvement, qui donne le branle à la phrase
>
> *(OC* I, p. 431).

Similar notes elsewhere in Baudelaire's artistic jottings, such as

> La danse grammaticale
> La voix de l'adjectif me pénétra jusqu'à l'os
>
> *(OC* I, p. 594),

serve to convince one that one cannot approach his work with anything less than the assumption that each and every word, each and every part of speech, each intimation of movement (from whatever source) in the body of a text, is *necessary* and must *necessarily* form part of any appreciation. As he says in his earliest 'advice to young writers', 'Il faut donc que tous les coups portent, et que pas une touche ne soit inutile' *(OC* II, p. 17). The message is still there, visible in a pressing letter, at the time of the composition of the prose-poems, indicating that the presence and positioning of a mere comma can be crucial to the balance, emphasis and significance of a whole section, part of an inviolable interdependence, and that one cannot play fast and loose with it:

Je vous avais dit: supprimez tout un morceau, si une virgule vous déplaît dans le morceau, mais ne supprimez pas la virgule; elle a sa raison d'être

(*Corr.* II, p. 307).

A most interesting observation by Baudelaire the 'theatre critic' acts perhaps as a guide to any act of criticism of his own poetry. He writes:

Ce que j'ai toujours trouvé de plus beau dans un théâtre, dans mon enfance et encore maintenant, c'est *le lustre*—un bel objet lumineux, cristallin, compliqué, circulaire et symétrique [. . .]

Après tout, le lustre m'a toujours paru l'acteur principal, vu à travers le gros bout ou le petit bout de la lorgnette

(*OC* I, p. 682).

Should one approach **Les Fleurs du Mal** in the same way: imbued with the sense that it is the *lustre* which is the chief actor, that 'bel objet lumineux, cristallin, compliqué . . .' constituted by each and every individual text, almost regardless of its subject-matter, intricately fashioned, endlessly facetted, glimmering and inter-reflecting whichever way one looks at it, a unified centre of artistic activity surviving all opposites and available to an infinity of perspectives, somehow gathering to itself all elements of persons, places and plots and taking them into a superior realm which is both their sublimation and its own justification?

* * *

The approach represented by the present study respects above all the integrity of the individual poem. Each 'chapter' is a closely focused analysis of a single text from **Les Fleurs du Mal.** The aim in this way is to see all aspects of Baudelaire's poetic art working in concert towards a single end, under the influence of one surge or poetic moment of inspiration: rhymes, rhythms, cadences, sonorities, intonations, verbal textures, run-on effects, hiatuses, juxtapositions, structures of sentences, verse-forms, parallels and pairings, moulding the words, creating links, accentuating implications, shaping patterns and so on, as they conspire towards the same artistic unity. It is an approach which demands a certain 'comprehensiveness' of reading, in that the tiniest comma has its part to play, or the unobtrusive slippage of an *enjambement,* or the momentary slackness of an alleviated rhythm, or the intensified note of an exclamation, adjusting at each turn the space of the mind and imagination, modifying its trajectories, changing the tempos of the journey. For the flesh of the verse (the 'thickness' of its rhetoric, the mobility of its prosody, its verbal muscularity, the fitfulness of its textual moodiness, its expressive impulses and interventions) is inseparable from the aspirations and agitations of the 'âme intérieure'. The *âme is* the form, and vice versa. And if Baudelaire can say of Poe:

le style est serré, *concaténé*; la mauvaise volonté du lecteur ou sa paresse ne pourront pas passer à travers les mailles de ce réseau tressé par la logique

(*OC* II, p. 283),

then his own is all the more close-knit. It is a network which, if it is to be studied, traversed in all directions and brought together finally as a meaningful entity—as the full living expression of the poet at any given compositional moment—leaves little room for the convenience or casualness of mind of the reader more concerned for gobbets of theme or broader selective patterns skimmed from various points of the compass (a reader more given to the contents of the play than to the attractions of the *lustre*). Lamenting his inability to do justice, as translator, to Edgar Poe the poet, Baudelaire speaks of the impossibility of compensating for the 'voluptés absentes du rythme et de la rime' (*OC* II, p. 347). Perhaps it is just such a loss, as if one were slipping into a more distant language where certain correspondences are no longer possible, that one risks in any *critical* translation. But it is hoped that the technique of individual analysis, clinging through the most minute aspects of expression to the intimate movements and evolutionary stirrings of the single text, will best do justice to the *living* Baudelaire and to the very process of poetry, turning *volupté* into *connaissance* but without relinquishing the *volupté,* and enabling the reader to feel immersed in the whole of a text as it lives and breathes, finds patterns, and asserts itself finally as an indissociable unity.

But such a study would be soon expedited were it nothing but one amplified *explication de texte.* Nor, perhaps, would its interest be very far-reaching. For, of all poetic collections, **Les Fleurs du Mal** is bewilderingly varied, self-contradictory, multivocal and chameleon-like. No one poem, no matter how many lines of attack it can be made to reveal, could be thought to be representative. It is also a collection with an architecture: a structural entity, with groupings and evolutionary traces, mutually illuminating clusters, and parts which support and counterbalance each other. The present study is therefore a carefully chosen juxtaposition of fourteen poems: a kind of poetic 'constellation', made up of textual bodies of different shapes and sizes, with different degrees and tones of luminosity, in different phases of activity and emissions of energy. The texts are drawn from various quarters of the work as interreflective partners: to illustrate complementary and contrasting facets, disruptions and continuities, family-likenesses and disfigurements, coincidences and contradictions; but, above all, to give some idea, across the gaps and despite the inevitable *lacunes,* of the 'ténébreuse et profonde unité' (*OC* I, p. 11) of that cohesive universe which is **Les Fleurs du Mal,** to show in a new way and in new combinations that

tout, forme, mouvement, nombre, couleur, parfum
[. . .] est significatif, réciproque, converse, *correspon-dant*

(OC II, p. 133),

or that, both *within* the individual poem and *between* poems, all things are 'bien unies, conjointes, réciproquement adaptées [. . .] prudemment concaténées' (*OC* II, p. 803). So, by favouring the present approach, one is striving to keep in a delicate balance two overriding interests, always in harness: the unity of the single poem and the unity of the whole. While focusing on the *lustre,* one hopes never to lose sight of the whole play.

To have stretched the number of poems studied here would have been impossible or self-defeating, such is the detail of the analysis and the multiplication of comparative perspectives opened with the addition of each new text. Fourteen is, perhaps, an arbitrary limit. But it does have, obliquely, something of the authority of the author's own observations when he writes:

> Pourquoi le spectacle de la mer est-il si infiniment et si éternellement agréable?
>
> Parce que la mer offre à la fois l'idée de l'immensité et du mouvement. Six ou sept lieues représentent pour l'homme le rayon de l'infini. Voilà un infini diminutif. Qu'importe s'il suffit à suggérer l'idée de l'infini total? Douze ou quatorze lieues (sur le diamètre), douze ou quatorze de liquide en mouvement suffisent pour donner la plus haute idée de beauté qui soit offerte à l'homme sur son habitacle transitoire

(OC I, p. 696).

To choose the individual poem as the first 'frame' of study is to give the poetry (and all about it which is nebulous and uncontainable) a finite context: a limited contour designed to counter excessive dispersion or the vagueness of the undifferentiated, and within which to appreciate 'l'infini dans le fini' (*OC* II, p. 636), including all that conspires to make poetry 'tick'. Then to multiply that one example (say to twelve or fourteen) is to extend human attention—or in this case critical capaciousness—almost as far as it will go without its being overwhelmed and swallowed by sheer vastness: an 'infini diminutif' at another level, a structured and delimited sample, adequate and ideally proportioned enough to suggest the 'total' infinity of the collection as a whole and of Baudelaire's immeasurable genius. Adequate, too, one hopes, by its very restriction and the intensification which comes from it, and in its creation of a form conducive to innumerable other *dessins,* to give 'la plus haute idée de beauté qui soit offerte à l'homme' or something closely resembling it: the beauty of *Les Fleurs du Mal,* as one text and as a configuration of texts, almost without argument the greatest work of poetry in the history of French literature.

1. *La Chevelure*

Ô toison, moutonnant jusque sur l'encolure!
Ô boucles! Ô parfum chargé de nonchaloir!
Extase! Pour peupler ce soir l'alcôve obscure
Des souvenirs dormant dans cette chevelure,
Je la veux agiter dans l'air comme un mouchoir!

La langoureuse Asie et la brûlante Afrique,
Tout un monde lointain, absent, presque défunt,
Vit dans tes profondeurs, forêt aromatique!
Comme d'autres esprits voguent sur la musique,
Le mien, ô mon amour! nage sur ton parfum.

J'irai là-bas où l'arbre et l'homme, pleins de sève,
Se pâment longuement sous l'ardeur des climats;
Fortes tresses, soyez la houle qui m'enlève!
Tu contiens, mer d'ébène, un éblouissant rêve
De voiles, de rameurs, de flammes et de mâts:

Un port retentissant où mon âme peut boire
À grands flots le parfum, le son et la couleur;
Où les vaisseaux, glissant dans l'or et dans la moire,
Ouvrent leurs vastes bras pour embrasser la gloire
D'un ciel pur où frémit l'éternelle chaleur.

Je plongerai ma tête amoureuse d'ivresse
Dans ce noir océan où l'autre est enfermé;
Et mon esprit subtil que le roulis caresse
Saura vous retrouver, ô féconde paresse!
Infinis bercements du loisir embaumé!

Cheveux bleus, pavillon de ténèbres tendues,
Vous me rendez l'azur du ciel immense et rond;
Sur les bords duvetés de vos mèches tordues
Je m'enivre ardemment des senteurs confondues
De l'huile de coco, du musc et du goudron.

Longtemps! toujours! ma main dans ta crinière lourde
Sèmera le rubis, la perle et le saphir,
Afin qu'à mon désir tu ne sois jamais sourde!
N'es-tu pas l'oasis où je rêve, et la gourde
Où je hume à longs traits le vin du souvenir?

* * *

Sans avoir recours à l'opium, qui n'a connu ces admirables heures, véritables fêtes du cerveau, où les sens plus attentifs perçoivent des sensations plus retentissantes, où le ciel d'un azur plus transparent s'enfonce comme un abîme plus infini, où les sons tintent musicalement, où les couleurs parlent, où les parfums racontent des mondes d'idées!

(OC II, p. 596):

no poem, better than *La Chevelure,* could illustrate these thoughts, which hold the secret of Baudelaire's most euphoric poetic impetus, his addiction to heightened instants of perception when the senses communicate, between themselves and with deeper dimensions, sounding the infinite resonances of the ideal. The sonnet *Correspondances* is the exemplary summary of this æsthetic intuition: that objects of the phenomenal world speak a mysterious language, seem charged, on occasions, with immeasurable significance and testify to an immutable Reality beyond themselves; that, from the substance that they are, they release in rare moments an essence and a scent of transcendence. The poet in such transactions is 'un traducteur, un déchiffreur' (*OC* II, p. 133), entrusting himself to the intuitive mobility of imagination, that

> faculté quasi divine qui perçoit tout d'abord, en dehors des méthodes philosophiques, les rapports intimes et secrets des choses, les correspondances et les analogies
>
> (*OC* II, p. 329),

and admitted to a superior fusion of the senses, a 'métamorphose mystique de tous mes sens fondus en un' (*OC* I, p. 42), within which he is both translator and translated. Where **Correspondances,** however, might be seen more as a poetic manifesto, an imaginative but laconic statement of ideas, **La Chevelure** is the most sumptuous poetic performance, illustrating at its most dynamic and lavish that resurgence of the senses, that interlacing of analogy and ideal 'reference elsewhere', which transport perception into a realm where nothing is single or simply itself: a universe where 'les parfums, les couleurs et les sons se répondent' and nothing exists except 'ayant l'expansion des choses infinies' (*OC* I, p. 11). The text is an *invitation au voyage* with an extraordinary range of persuasions and caresses. It is a feast of the mind which temporarily dispels all lurking shadows or intimations of human poverty.

The opening is both impassioned sensual celebration and purifying litany. A love poem, yes. But one in which not woman, but one aspect of her absent person becomes the focus of the speaker's devotional mood and a stimulant for the flight of imagination. No other physical detail or episode from personal history is summoned or relevant. The hair is an immediate, abundant fund of analogy, transformed as soon as touched into 'toison', with its associative overlays, physical and mythical: on the one hand the fleecy profusion and the attractions of an animal freedom and vigour; on the other, the quest for the Golden Fleece and its links with the overtures and adventures of the sea. Sensual and spiritual converge. The words 'toison' and 'Extase', alpha and omega of the superlative first sequence, reach for each other through their subtle phonetic affinity. The *ouverture* could hardly be more emphatic or the text a more intense illustration of Paul Valéry's definition of lyricism as 'le développement d'une exclamation', as the expression of poetry

> qui suppose *la voix en action*—la voix directement issue de, ou provoquée par,—les choses que l'on voit ou que l'on sent comme *présentes*[2]:

the exclamatory fullness, the instant passage from emotional utterance (a single sound at the same time minimal and absolute) to sensual goal (a single word free from any subordinating context or function) by

which subject and object become as one, the repetition to excess which seems destined finally to burst and resolve itself in the consummate 'Extase!'. A concert of sensual appeals (dense texture for the touch, wisps of curl to catch the eye, perfume to induce a fragrant self-release) find their harmony in this one word which transcends and unifies. Few poets have been more sensitive than Baudelaire to the latent life of objects. **Le Flacon**—also a seven-stanza poem pursuing the analogy between the flight of scents and the flight of memory, both essences which float and linger when the substance has gone—depicts the magical metamorphosis of perfume thrusting improbably from its dark container to a rebirth of colour, movement and shimmering luminosity:

> Mille pensers dormaient, chrysalides funèbres,
> Frémissant doucement dans les lourdes ténèbres,
> Qui dégagent leur aile et prennent leur essor,
> Teintés d'azur, glacés de rose, lamés d'or
>
> (*OC* I, p. 48).

Here in **La Chevelure,** the hair itself is the dark metaphorical container with the power to envelop the physical one, the private universe of the 'alcôve obscure' with its fragrances of amorous intimacy. The tresses have an airy expansion. Shaken out like a handkerchief, a favour dropped for the attentive or devoted lover, to shed and disseminate their scented associations, they seem to give themselves in creative abandon. They wave before the mind's eye as a potential image of departure.

It is remarkable how many of Baudelaire's poems *realize* the idea of the sea, are drawn ultimately into its orbit as if compelled to acknowledge what was, initially, only implicit: 'Tu les conduis doucement vers la mer qui est l'Infini' (*OC* I, p. 303). In the first stanza the sea is a virtual presence not yet named, lapping the poem gently from a distance before exerting its full sway. It is, as the poet René Char says, 'la mer qui se fonde, qui s'invente'[3]. 'Moutonnant' and 'mouchoir', at the beginning and end of the stanza, blend in sound and connotation: the first evoking the rolling motions, the waviness, the foaming texture, the light-flecked tips of hair as it falls over a bold neckline; the second leaving one poised, as desires will themselves elsewhere, on the brink of a voyage. More persuasively, the opening tumbling rhythm mimes that of the sea: in the strong repetitive sequence, the revolving patterns, and the initiating surges of energy ('Ô toison . . . Ô boucles, Ô parfum . . .') which gradually subside as the intonation sinks and the violently propelled syllables make way for the smoother running sibilants ('. . . jusque sur l'encolure', '. . . chargé de nonchaloir', '. . . ce soir l'alcôve obscure', '. . . cette chevelure' and '. . . mouchoir') like a soft onomatopœic wash brushing over the ends of lines.

Suddenly, in this text of free-roaming transitions, vistas unfurl. 'Il y a des moments de l'existence', writes Baudelaire, 'où le temps et l'étendue sont plus profonds, et le sentiment de l'existence immensément augmenté' (*OC* I, p. 658). The poet, no less than Constantin Guys to whom the following words refer, is 'un homme épris d'espace' (*OC* II, p. 705). From the depths of the hair, from the confines of the darkened boudoir, vision expands: not only in space, through geographical perspectives which are more mythical distances and imaginative sensations than real places, but also in time, to be steeped in the influences of a *vie antérieure* irresistibly restored. In view of the preceding 'Je la veux agiter . . .', perhaps this is an instance of that '*enfance retrouvée* à volonté' (*OC* II, p. 690) which he sees in *Le Peintre de la vie moderne* as the sign of poetic genius: a genius for whose eye no aspect of life is dulled but all is seen afresh, whether at will or by mysterious instinct, in a mood which is 'animalement extatique'. The prosodic formation of 'Tout un monde lointain, absent, presque défunt, / Vit . . .' is especially influential. The graduation of adjectives ensures that the line, imitatively perfect, appears to dwindle to almost nothing—even their final vowels (-ain, -ent, -unt) become successively less resonant and more muffled—before the verb 'Vit . . .', acute, monosyllabic, initially vibrant, bursts free, prematurely accentuated, released to a new dimension of expressiveness, from the cavern of the nasals, setting in relief the paradox of a universe (one might say *the* universe) lost and rediscovered, absent and present, dead or progressively dying away yet intensely alive. (Even the rhymes of this stanza pick out the significant sound-contrasts of '. . . dé<u>funt</u> / <u>Vit</u>' and replay them in an unevenly matched contest between the sharp and the dull, the vivid and the subdued.) More importantly, this sentence typifies a pattern of rhythmic ebb and flow which will run dynamically through the entire poem: the dissipation and re-summoning of energy; the unexpected tide of stress (especially initial stress) which re-animates, gives new impetus or widens horizons ('<u>Fo</u>rtes tresses, soyez la houle . . .', '<u>Ou</u>vrent leurs vastes bras . . .'), so making the text itself an animated object which expands and contracts, rises and falls, swells and subsides. Opposites are juxtaposed, establishing polarity and alternation but invoking union and reconciliation: 'chargé de nonchaloir', 'La langoureuse Asie et la brûlante Afrique', 'défunt, Vit', 'mer d'ébène, un éblouissant rêve', 'l'alcôve obscur . . . ciel pur', 'Ouvrent leurs vastes bras . . . où l'autre est enfermé'. One senses simultaneously, in a single flow of inspiration, something laden yet levitational, dense yet virtually without substance; faint yet fierce, passive yet active, languid yet intense; dark yet dazzlingly light; enveloping yet revealing, enclosed yet infinitely extensive.

Imaginatively transfigured, the hair, first perfumed fleece, carrying the sensuality of the animal world, then becomes 'forêt aromatique', an exotic vegetal luxuriance, and finally 'mer d'ébène', a burgeoning, unfurling expanse of black sheen and rhythmic mobility. These unhurried transformations, and their secretive continuity (from perfumes to scented forest, and from forests to the glossed surface of ebony), evolve in widening circles. Writing of the effects of hashish, Baudelaire shows how the poetic mind, like an agile dancer, uses a single object or phrase (in this case 'la chevelure') 'comme d'un tremplin pour bondir dans des rêveries très lointaines' (*OC* I, p. 418), adding that 'les objets extérieurs prennent lentement, successivement, des apparences singulières' (*OC* I, p. 419). The suggestion of a mind overleaping itself in a series of maturing analogies echoes what the poet says in an essay on Banville on the implications of the word *lyre*, destined to translate, as he puts it, 'l'ardente vitalité spirituelle, l'homme hyperbolique' (*OC* II, p. 164). His thoughts here on hyperbole and apostrophe as features of the lyric state are richly applicable to **La Chevelure**:

> Tout d'abord constatons que l'hyperbole et l'apostrophe sont des formes de langage qui lui sont non seulement des plus agréables, mais aussi des plus nécessaires, puisque ces formes dérivent naturellement d'un état exagéré de la vitalité.

But more pertinently, the notion of '*hyperbolic* man', overstepping the real and 'projected beyond', is indissociably wedded to the leaps of metaphor by which the text and its central image mature: 'L'âme lyrique fait des enjambées vastes comme des synthèses' (*OC* II, p. 165). Even before the sea has emerged explicitly, a bond is already sealed here between the attractions of the aromatic forest and the liquid element on which, above all others, the poetic mind is borne aloft. The verbs 'voguent' and 'nage' are suggestively placed to gather stress as seventh syllables after the cæsura. Less powerful than the *rejet* 'Vit . . .', they inject nevertheless a wavelet of energy at the beginning of their own *hémistiches*, 'push out', as it were, from the cæsura, then to float freely to the end of their line with no need for further strokes or pulses of accentuation. One should also pick out in these lines the unmistakable signs of Baudelaire's phonetic genius, his exceptional sensitivity to the 'rapports intimes et secrets' of sounds themselves by which they, too, are resurrected to an ideal expressive life. In the phrases 'Vit dans tes profondeurs, forêt aromatique', not only are the letters of 'forêt' physically contained within '<u>te</u>s <u>profo</u>ndeurs' so that the depths of the hair seem to have engendered the analogy by a kind of necessity and corroborated a latent identity, but the key letters of the first *hémistiche* recur in perfect reverse order in the second ('<u>Vit</u> dans <u>te</u>s <u>pro</u>fondeurs, / <u>forê</u>t aroma<u>ti</u>que'), suggesting, if only in intermittent glimpses, an object contemplated and confirmed in its own mirror.

In his account of the sensations of hashish, more the vivid revealer of deep mental processes than their original creator, the poet writes:

> Il arrive quelquefois que la personnalité disparaît et que l'objectivité, qui est le propre des poètes panthéistes, se développe en vous si anormalement, que la contemplation des objets extérieurs vous fait oublier votre propre existence, et que vous vous confondez bientôt avec eux. Votre œil se fixe sur un arbre harmonieux courbé par le vent [. . .] Vous prêtez d'abord à l'arbre vos passions, votre désir ou votre mélancolie; ses gémissements et ses oscillations deviennent les vôtres, et bientôt vous êtes l'arbre

(OC I, pp. 419-20).

Here, in **La Chevelure,** in a line of the most gently cadenced and continuous iambic rhythm, where the words break into monosyllables and the lapping of liquid sounds conveys indolence and a supremely fluid union, 'l'arbre et l'homme' are infused with a single life-force and the same ecstatic swaying motion. The pantheistic osmosis does not exclude or eliminate, however, the continuing suggestion of sensual pleasure and amorous vertigo shared between lover and mistress. For just as the words 'forêt aromatique' keep a phonetic pairing with 'ô mon amour', so 'l'arbre' as a new poetic partner never loses its metaphorical bonding with 'forêt', with 'ébène' and therefore, by an indirect but unbreakable route, with the hair itself. In a far-reaching play of reverberations, the phrase '. . . pleins de sève, / Se pâment . . .' brushes the wavelength of the earlier '. . . chargé de nonchaloir' with its dual sense of fullness and airiness, of weight and pleasurable dizziness (or absence of mind); while 'Se pâment longuement sous l'ardeur des climats' keeps alive the complementary richness of 'La langoureuse Asie et la brûlante Afrique', with its dual strains of weakened abandonment and ardent desire.

The anagrammatic re-integration of the word 'forêt' into 'Fortes tresses' sustains hints of a link back to the imagery of vegetation while preparing the transition to a new element, 'houle' and 'mer'. So, certain sounds acquire an exceptionally extended span, one might say an 'after-life', within the text. More relevantly, the anagram exemplifies how language itself, caught in the field of force of a heightened imagination, promotes patterns in its own image and becomes its own rich analogical source. It is in such sonorous 'encounters', perhaps, that one responds to the intimation that 'Dieu a proféré le monde comme une complexe et indivisible totalité' (*OC* II, p. 784) and that, in the poetic word in its most sensitive states and in its ideal form, all is equally 'réciproque, converse, *correspondant*' (*OC* II, p. 133). For when the poet writes in his **Correspondances** that 'Les parfums, les couleurs et les sons se répondent', such echoing networks are not only taken to be abroad in the universe at large but are heard simultaneously in

the body of the sonnet itself. The line 'Fortes tresses, soyez la houle qui m'enlève!' is a most dynamic one. (Indeed no text illustrates more convincingly than this that beauty is energy for Baudelaire.) With its plunging initial stresses, its violently rolled alliterative consonants held apart only by the hollow of the mute e ('Fortes tresses, soyez . . .'), the tautness and elasticity of the imperative 'soyez' posted at the cæsura, and the propulsion of the aspirate h in 'la houle', it breaks the relaxed and fainting mood of the previous two lines in the most emphatic way, illustrating once more those powerful alternations which underpin even the poem's minor cadences. The rhythmic patterning of this three-line sequence is highly evocative. We have seen how a single line ('Ô boucles! Ô parfum chargé de nonchaloir!'), read horizontally, as it were, across the page, can have its own contour of turbulence and calm, surge and relapse. Here, as one reads vertically through the long body of the verse, the noisy energy of 'Fortes tresses, soyez la houle qui m'enlève!' is progressively broken down, like a double wave crashing itself out and dispersed, as it subsides, through the course of the three lines, from a two-part, then to a three-part ('Tu contiens, mer d'ébène, un éblouissant rêve') and finally to a four-part phrase ('De voiles, de rameurs, de flammes et de mâts'), softly articulated, verbless and gently repetitive. What Yves Bonnefoy calls the 'énergies invisibles'[4] of Baudelaire's poetry are no less at work here in the textures of the sounds themselves. Are the words 'Fortes tresses' meant to conjure up, by subliminal contact, the notion of a feminine 'forteresse', fragrantly impregnated but impregnable? And does 'soyez', conditioning the mind before one reaches the metaphorical vision of the sea's surface as 'moire', imprint the suggestion of silkiness ('soie') on to these radiant black tresses? By a different process, the opposites 'ébène' and 'éblouissant', thanks to their internal rhyme, are made to seem as if they owe their origins to one and the same source. 'Flammes', with its several possible meanings, reaches in many directions, so enjoying in yet another way that 'expansion des choses infinies': as nautical pennant it links hypothetically with 'pavillon'; as flame it guarantees the influence of 'brûlante' and 'ardeur' while helping to conjure up the spectacle of a 'sea of fire' ('rien . . . Ne me vaut le soleil rayonnant sur la mer', writes the poet of **Chant d'automne**); as a synonym for love, inherited from the lexicon of seventeenth century *précieux* verse, it finds its twin in the exclamatory 'ô mon amour'.

Words by Baudelaire on the complex æsthetic and spiritual attractions of seaports help to suggest why the fourth stanza is the centre and the climax of the poem:

> Un port est un séjour charmant pour une âme fatiguée des luttes de la vie. L'ampleur du ciel, l'architecture mobile des nuages, les colorations changeantes de la mer, le scintillement des phares, sont un prisme merveilleusement propre à amuser les yeux sans jamais

les lasser. Les formes élancées des navires, au gréement compliqué, auxquels la houle imprime des oscillations harmonieuses, servent à entretenir dans l'âme le goût du rythme et de la beauté

(*OC* I, p. 344).

Many such features loom large at the heart of *La Chevelure*: limitless sky, shimmering surface of the sea, tall-reaching ships. If there are no shifting clouds, there is instead a quivering heat-haze, and if the boats are not so much rocked as seen to slide smoothly through the water's silk, there are other 'oscillations harmonieuses' rippling through the structure and substance of the text itself. After the luxurious looping journey from 'l'alcôve obscure' through archetypal images of 'Asie' and 'Afrique' to a nameless 'là-bas' opening on to 'l'éternel' and 'l'infini', this stanza finally represents arrival. Placed in simple apposition to the previous stanza, an ever more remote extension of that tidal swell which began with 'Fortes tresses . . .' and slowly abated, it seems magically becalmed. The exclamatory tone, which recurrently willed the poem further and further on, now fades. No new *souffle* is required to direct it to its destination. The volitional presence of the poetic self is absorbed and erased. Lines from the text on hashish serve again to illuminate this poem of 'ivresse':

Ce n'est plus quelque chose de tourbillonnant et de tumultueux; c'est une béatitude calme et immobile, une résignation glorieuse

(*OC* I, p. 425).

This is also the stanza of unity. In that idealized 'métamorphose mystique de tous mes sens fondus en un', all sense impressions are drunk as a single spirit-like state. A spirituality (an 'âme') which has been dormant (for poet and reader alike) in a hidden layer of phonetic memory for some time ('Se pâment . . . rameurs . . . de mâts') now emerges as if from nowhere and seems all-pervasive. In a vision reminiscent of Rimbaud's lines:

Elle est retrouvée.
Quoi?—L'Éternité.
C'est la mer allée
Avec le soleil[5],

sea and sky, the two infinities, fuse in an immeasurable splendour. And just as the union of 'l'arbre et l'homme' never shook itself free from the penetrating influence of woman and from hints of a more erotic mingling of saps, so the final picture of masts and yard-arms opening wide to embrace the expanse of tropical sky retains enough of the physical vocabulary of love to suggest the warmth and tremor of a sexual acceptance and arrival. The speaker is drawn momentarily into an objectivity in which personality all but disappears: framed between two stanzas which begin with the assertive and self-summoning 'J'irai . . .' and 'Je plong-

erai . . .', the present one is comparatively selfless. It is also the only stanza of the poem which does not have recourse to the second personal address, to apostrophe or invocation: wishful calls to union between first and second person are, it seems, now rendered superfluous. For the first time, too, metaphorical reference to the hair ('toison . . . forêt . . . mer d'ébène' and subsequently 'noir océan . . . pavillon . . . crinière') is abolished. In a poetic purification allowing the emergence of what Coleridge called 'the translucence of the Eternal through and in the Temporal'[6], one has passed from the thickness of 'toison' to transparency, from sea to sky, from obscurity to light. 'L'éphémère ébloui vole vers toi [. . .] crépite, flambe', Baudelaire writes of the mysterious workings of Beauty in *Hymne à la Beauté* (*OC* I, p. 25). External nature as *incitamentum*, as 'un réveil pour les facultés sommeillantes' (*OC* II, p. 752), has fulfilled its role. The sensuous object, stroked by the imagination and by the far-reaching desires of awakening faculties, is here transcended. As the poet says of the potent *rêveur*:

il roule de déduction en déduction, et après une longue journée de rêverie, la cause première est tout à fait envolée, l'*incitamentum* a disparu

(*OC* II, p. 280).

La Chevelure is a superlative example of how a minimal starting-point can be exploited and expanded to create an infinite luxury, the proof of the rare poetic gift 'de savoir se parer avec un rien' (*OC* II, p. 310). It also illustrates how, for this author, a single sensual contact, deep in the past, can live on and on in seemingly immaterial but penetrating form:

J'en fus embaumé, pour l'avoir
Caressée une fois, rien qu'une,

he confesses in *Le Chat* (*OC* I, pp. 50-1). Since this fourth stanza is, more than any other, a visionary *tableau* set apart in a dimension of its own, it is interesting to test its qualities against those which the poet has most appreciated among certain visual artists. Of Fromentin's paintings he says:

Mais la lumière et la chaleur, qui jettent dans quelques cerveaux une espèce de folie tropicale, les agitent d'une fureur inapaisable et les poussent à des danses inconnues, ne versent dans son âme qu'une contemplation douce et reposée. C'est l'extase plutôt que le fanatisme. Il est présumable que je suis moi-même atteint quelque peu d'une nostalgie qui m'entraîne vers le soleil; car de ces toiles lumineuses s'élève pour moi une vapeur enivrante

(*OC* II, p. 650).

And of two canvases by Delacroix:

un tableau si prodigieusement lumineux, si aéré [. . .] Et toujours ces drapeaux miroitants, ondoyants, faisant se dérouler et claquer leurs plis lumineux dans l'atmosphère transparente

(*OC* II, p. 592).

Not only do light, warmth and contemplative tranquillity coincide at this climactic moment, but the poem as a whole is one, like the world of Delacroix, where undulating movements and luminous folds (of vision, syntax and rhythm) unfurl in a spacious transparent atmosphere.

From this point on, the poetic energies which urged imagination so irresistibly towards the exotic dream must, it seems, relapse. After the evocation of a splendid arrival, is it now the case that the journey must drift nostalgically away from its goal? No abrupt transition is apparent and it would be incorrect to speak of a structural hiatus or marked change of tone. Indeed the poem continues to open its doors of analogy and reinforce the themes which provide its groundswell. The hair is still a fathomless ocean, infinitely capacious, vaster than the real: it is a 'vault of heaven' more embracing than sky itself, a rounded universe, the symbol of eternal blue. Sea and sky are held within it as if within a mirror greater than themselves. It is a mythical 'pavillon': a canopy, a shaded haven, a lovers' retreat (like the enclosure of the 'alcôve' itself); or perhaps a dark nautical flag catching the light of the world as it streams in the wind (linking back simultaneously with 'Je la veux agiter dans l'air' and '. . . de flammes et de mâts'). And, though a multivalent symbol, it remains most potently an object of sensual delight. The hedonism of 'Je plongerai ma tête amoureuse d'ivresse', the gentle rhythmic inducements implicit in the verb 'caresse', the suggestions of downy softness combined with intermingled scents, ensure that it loses nothing of its complex physical appeal. The mood of creative indolence, established by the words 'parfum chargé de nonchaloir', floods back persuasively in the nearly synonymous 'féconde paresse' and 'loisir embaumé'. The 'oscillations harmonieuses' attributed to boats in the harbour's soft swell become the poet's own as he yields wishfully to 'roulis' (a rhyming continuation, on a lesser scale, of 'houle') and 'bercements' without end. The theme of intoxication, prefigured both in the liquid abundance and overflow of 'pleins de sève' and 'boire à grands flots' and in the headiness of 'Extase' and 'Se pâment', now acquires its most explicit expression. There is, moreover, in these few stanzas, a musical beauty almost unsurpassed elsewhere: the internal and reverse rhymes of 'Et mon esprit subtil que le roulis caresse' conspire to suggest a perfect reciprocity between external stimulus and inner satisfaction; the line 'Infinis bercements du loisir embaumé', freed from verbs and itself enjoying, at the end of the stanza, a suspended serenity conducive to notions of 'bercement' and 'loisir', has a sustained anapæstic rhythm which gives a lulling unhurried cadence and a sequence of sounds (i, b, m) repeated in the second *hémistiche* as if to suggest that 'Là, tout n'est qu'ordre et beauté, / Luxe, calme et volupté'; while the unusually rich internal rhyme of 'Sur les bords duvetés de vos mèches tordues'

causes this line to 'curl back' on itself in a way which rekindles one's response to the ardour of the opening apostrophe 'Ô toison! . . . Ô boucles!'.

And yet, after the transcendent vision of gold, silk and pure light, the poem slips almost imperceptibly towards loss. Perhaps the words 'Je plongerai', so forcibly positioned after the central stanza, are the discreet indicator of an impending downward movement. The emphasis veers more noticeably towards a paradise to be regained rather than a paradise possessed: 'Saura vous *re*trouver', 'Vous me *ren*dez'. A self-analytical note tinges the text. The phrases 'ma tête amoureuse d'ivresse' and 'mon esprit subtil que le roulis caresse' are the first to attach descriptive adjectives to the poet's mind, suggesting, after the irresistible outward movement of the first three stanzas, an attention tending now to contract back towards the self. The mood is more consciously self-indulgent. The poet, sophisticated sensualist savouring his own intoxication, says 'amoureuse d'ivresse' and not 'ivre d'amour'; and the self-enclosed reflexive form of 'Je m'enivre ardemment' leads suggestively to the threshold of the final stanza, with its growing awareness of separation and its pleading tone desperate to re-establish fullness of communication. One returns also to the physical particularity of the hair. As if one were now for the first time treading the shallows of the imagination, the word 'Cheveux' appears undisguised. Perfume, so far vague and indefinite, becomes more precisely identifiable as a blending of coconut oil, musk and tar; and after the excursion to an exotic dream-harbour, one reacts to the harshness and tang of 'goudron', tugging one's attention towards the more mundane realities of ports. Finally, the rhythmical agitation and excitement, so evident in the first three stanzas as they thrust and roll creatively towards a coveted 'là-bas', subside in Stanzas five and six where there are no more exclamations, no more surges of initial stress, and the accent falls regularly and more tamely, in classical fashion, at the cæsura. So, there emerges, in the structure of the whole, a forceful symmetrical contour: three stanzas of energetic upsure and 'movement towards', three stanzas of gradual distancing and relapse, and, at the centre, a luminous tableau which stands virtually motionless. The seven stanzas themselves are thus made to resemble a long wave which slowly rises, reaches its peak, and slowly falls.

A further structural motif crucial to the dynamics of the piece is the alternation between future and present, wishful projection and actuality. In an unusual poetic use of *pair* and *impair*, the first, third, fifth and seventh stanzas are all oriented by an act of volition or purposeful future idea ('Je la veux agiter . . .', 'J'irai . . .', 'Je plongerai . . .', 'Sèmera . . .'). The second, fourth and sixth, on the other hand, fall back exclusively into the present tense ('Vit..', 'Ouvrent . . .', 'Je m'enivre

. . .'), relinquishing the acquisitive energy and accepting a more passive satisfaction. So, a to-and-fro motion is established through the body of the verse between tension and relaxation, concentration of the resources of the self and their momentary suspension. There are many ways of interpreting this rhythmic duality. It is ideally attuned to a mood which hovers between the 'langoureuse' and the 'brûlante', at one moment 'chargé' and then as weightless as 'nonchaloir'. In a literary essay Baudelaire tells us that Leconte de Lisle was born

> dans une de ces îles volcaniques et parfumées, où l'âme humaine, mollement bercée par toutes les voluptés de l'atmosphère, désapprend chaque jour l'exercice de la pensée

> (*OC* II, p. 176).

Not only is there in **La Chevelure** a similar combination of the 'volcanique' and the 'parfumé', but one might see in its patterning a recurrent 'unlearning' of thought (or of wilful consciousness) followed by its partial recovery. In his famous essay on Wagner, the poet speaks of

> l'idée d'une âme se mouvant dans un milieu lumineux, d'une extase *faite de volupté et de connaissance,* et planant au-dessus et bien loin du monde naturel

> (*OC* II, p. 785).

The two qualities of 'connaissance' and 'volupté' are admirably fused in the single line 'Et mon esprit subtil que roulis caresse'; they intertwine more secretively still in the structure of the stanzas, which waver between greater and lesser self-awareness, between the firm formulation of intent and its disappearance. Reflecting on the title of Charles Asselineau's collection *La double vie* and on the resonances of the words *homo duplex,* Baudelaire summarizes one aspect of man's double nature in these terms: 'action et intention, rêve et réalité' (*OC* II, p. 87). One feels the hidden pulse of such a tension at work in the present text. Most telling of all, however, are these, the first words of *Mon Cœur mis à nu*: 'De la vaporisation et de la centralisation du *Moi.* Tout est là' (*OC* I, p. 676). They are all the more relevant to this poem of willed *ivresse* in that the author writes elsewhere, in words close enough to imply a similarity, even an interlinked affinity, between the two quotations: 'Il faut être toujours ivre. Tout est là: c'est l'unique question' (*OC* I, p. 337). In **La Chevelure** the self balances between active and passive, the condensed and the dissolved: at one moment forcibly superimposing itself, at another partially erased. The prose-poem **L'Invitation au voyage** speaks of 'mes pensers qui dorment ou qui roulent' (*OC* I, p. 303), a description finely applicable to a text in which the words 'dormant' and 'roulis' have such a prominent part to play. Not only do dormant memories take flight in unexpected profusion

and things fading to non-existence burst back to life with a vibrant intensity, but certain poetic sections roll like breakers, to be followed by a rhythmic lull or calm: in the first stanza the excited waves of 'Ô toison! . . . Ô boucles! Ô parfum . . . Extase!' then ease into a gentler continuous sequence, while in the third stanza the reverse pattern takes effect, with the soothing, unperturbed cadence of the first two lines overwhelmed by the violently propelled movement initiated by 'Fortes tresses, soyez la houle . . .'. The poet's own movements of 'centralisation' and 'vaporisation', finely traced into the structure, provide the perfect support for such rhythmical variations. Finally, in view of the poem's evolution towards a climactic objectivity transcending both the speaker himself and the physical reality of his inspiration, to be followed by a return to self-consciousness, separation and doubt, one might argue that another central drama of Baudelaire's work is being enacted in the texture: the inconclusive fluctuations of 'un *moi* insatiable du *non-moi*' (*OC* II, p. 692), intimately linked to a play of *fermeture* and *ouverture.*

The 'invisible energies' of Baudelaire's imagination produce a complex pattern of rhythms within rhythms. To quote René Char again as a revealing kindred spirit: 'mon onde au large est profonde, complexe, prestigieuse'. Contained within the slowly evolving rise and fall of the seven-stanza structure, individual lines heave and subside in a horizontal plane, sequences of lines summon up energy and gradually expend it in a vertical direction down through the body of the verse, while the alternating currents of a secret prosody ebb and flow from stanza to stanza. The poem itself celebrates the spell of 'ce noir océan où l'autre est enfermé'. It is an idea which recurs emphatically in the author's writing, fascinated as he is by objects containing or contained within their own mirror-image and by the intercommunications of analogy. Pricking the appetite of those anxious to know what love is like under the influence of hashish, he asks:

> Que peut être cette ivresse de l'amour, déjà si puissante à son état naturel, quand elle est enfermée dans l'autre ivresse, comme un soleil dans un soleil?

> (*OC* I, p. 432-33).

And in **Les Phares** he refers to the work of Rubens as a 'fleuve d'oubli [. . .] où la vie afflue et s'agite sans cesse, / Comme l'air dans le ciel et la mer dans la mer' (*OC* I, p. 13). In **La Chevelure** the ocean which embraces all others is that of rhythm: the 'ivresse de l'amour' is subordinate to vaster, more ingenious intoxicants. Could there be a more apt formula for the poem's interplay of rhythmic movements than 'la mer dans la mer': waves within waves, a global tidal cycle swept from within by a host of other, more variable and diminutive currents?

'Pourquoi le spectacle de la mer est-il si infiniment et si éternellement agréable?' asks Baudelaire: 'Parce que la mer offre à la fois l'idée de l'immensité et du mouvement' (*OC* I, p. 696). Any study of the verse-form of *La Chevelure* will conclude that the chosen stanza is ideally designed to suggest joint ideas of 'immensité' and 'mouvement'. Its fulsome Alexandrines spill beyond the more familiar four-line limit with an abundance, weightiness and lingering richness well suited to tresses that foam '*jusque sur* l'encolure', perfume which is '*chargé* de nonchaloir', ecstasy that is savoured '*longuement*', senses that are drunk '*à grands flots*', a flowing mane that is overwhelmingly '*lourde*', and draughts of memory which are inhaled '*à longs traits*'. This is not an expeditious verse-form. It conspires by nature to fulfil the words 'J'irai là-bas . . .', and responds intimately in its texture to the plea 'Longtemps! toujours!'. It gives time for the slow, sinuous unfurling of what the poet calls 'cette interminable imagination' (*OC* I, p. 420), evoking magnificently 'l'idée d'une évaporation lente, successive, éternelle' (ibid.)—the 'evaporation' here being that of material reality and the poet's own small-scale self-consciousness. The five-line stanza allows an exceptional intertwining of its two rhymes. It evades the finite quality of the matching four-line stanza where the rhymes, in 2+2 pairings, produce a sense of prosodic stability and an equation resolved. Could one not say of its imparisyllabic verse-structure what Verlaine says of the individual *vers impair*: that it is

> Plus vague et plus soluble dans l'air,
> Sans rien en lui qui pèse ou qui pose[8]?

One rhyming pattern is lighter and one has greater weight, one is more dispersed and the other more cohesive. Is there a hint here, even in the designs of rhyming, of a subtle 'vaporisation' and 'concentration'? Certainly the arrangement ensures an extended effect of 'roulis' and 'bercement'. The penultimate line of the stanza is, in this respect, influential: it postpones resolution, it prolongs the poem at a moment when the ear anticipates completion and symmetry, it plunges one deeper into the sway of the feminine rhymes (whose predominance can be used 'pour plus de moelleux'[9], according to Cassagne) before the balance is tipped back and the text restored to a more even keel with the locking of its masculine rhyme. *La Chevelure* has seven stanzas, as the corresponding prose-poem *Un Hémisphère dans une chevelure* has seven paragraphs. One is tempted to see in this a deliberate expressive choice. We have observed how the poem lends itself to a balanced structure of three stanzas on either side of a pivot: three of upsurge and movement towards, three of relapse and movement away, and at the centre a picture of suspended serenity. This in turn signals wider ternary reverberations in the text. The opening invocation ('Ô toison . . . Ô boucles! Ô parfum . . .') and various phrases throughout the text ('lointain, absent, presque défunt', 'le parfum, le son et la couleur', 'De l'huile de coco, du musc et du goudron', 'le rubis, la perle et le saphir') are compelling enough to establish a recurrent triple rhythm and mould the verse into wave-like patterns. In the rhyme-scheme itself there are three feminine rhymes which swell to fullness ('ayant l'expansion des choses infinies'), before being drawn back into the narrower compass of the masculine duality. Stanza arrangement, internal phrasing and movements of rhyme thus interlace their effects in a fascinating dimension of what could be called 'rhythms within rhythms'.

Writing of Poe, Baudelaire says:

> En effet, un poème ne mérite son titre qu'autant qu'il excite, qu'il enlève l'âme, et la valeur positive d'un poème est en raison de cette excitation, de cet *enlèvement* de l'âme. Mais, par nécessité psychologique, toutes les excitations sont fugitives et transitoires
>
> (*OC* II, p. 332).

That the excitement which animates *La Chevelure* is fugitive and transitory is intimated by the exclamation 'Longtemps! toujours!' which not only injects a new emotional urgency, but suggests the creeping encroachment of time and the need to perpetuate an experience progressively slipping from the poet's grasp. This is without doubt the most ambiguous of the stanzas. Perhaps it is natural that one should slip from the most earth-bound of words 'goudron' to an exclamation which, while fraught with intention, is already tinged with nostalgia. Relevant, too, that one should revert to the untamed animal quality of the hair (with 'crinière' harking back to 'toison' and 'encolure' and so closing a circle on the poetic voyage), hair which, though offered regal favours, stands as a defiant and primitive emblem of the sensual. In his *Éloge du maquillage* Baudelaire sees 'la parure' as an expression of the 'dégoût pour le réel', as a 'déformation sublime de la nature': proof on the part of those who seek to dress themselves in artificial finery of 'l'immatérialité de leur âme' (*OC* II, p. 716). That the poet's desires should here lavish precious tributes on these locks is the sign of the urge to transform the real and to ensure that, never again mere 'crinière', they will preserve those glints of light and artistic vitality which make them a 'fenêtre ouverte sur l'infini' (*OC* II, p. 717). The final stanza can thus be seen not only as a desire to repay favour with favour, each to his own, and to coax his magical mistress to remain forever so generous, a source of illumination; but also as the wishful conquest of artifice over nature. At no point in the poem, however, has the distance and division, even the incongruity, between artifice and nature been more apparent. Is it that the speaker, confronted with what Char calls 'ce seul être que l'absence s'efforce de placer à mi-longueur du factice et du surnaturel'[10], can only repay with self-conscious artistic adornment what took flight by natural association? In the finale of **Bénédiction** the symbolic Poet, describing the 'couronne mystique' to which he feels obscurely destined, writes:

> Mais les bijoux perdus de l'antique Palmyre,
> Les métaux inconnus, les perles de la mer,
> Par votre main montés, ne pourraient pas suffire
> À ce beau diadème éblouissant et clair;
>
> Car il ne sera fait que de pure lumière,
> Puisée au foyer saint des rayons primitifs,
> Et dont les yeux mortels, dans leur splendeur entière,
> Ne sont que des miroirs obscurcis et plaintifs!

> (*OC* I, p. 9)

There, the rarest 'bijoux' summoned from extremes of time and space cannot adequately reconstitute an original spiritual radiance beyond mortal capture. In **La Chevelure** the dreamer has re-awakened the 'rayons primitifs' of 'Tout un monde lointain, absent, presque défunt' and touched in imagination 'un *éblouissant* rêve' containing the glory of 'un ciel *pur*'. In comparison, his final offering of jewels and precious stones must appear a somewhat constrained and apologetic second-best. One sees the relevance of Yves Bonnefoy's words concerning Yeats: 'il opposait à l'oiseau réel éphémère l'automate d'or et de gemmes qui signifie le règne autonome de l'art'[11]. Is it that Baudelaire, sensing a finale and brushed by the conscious need to prolong, feels closing round him once again 'le règne autonome de l'art'?

The last stanza introduces a new function of the second personal address. Whereas it is the hair, through its metaphors, which has governed the *tu* form ('Vit dans tes profondeurs, forêt aromatique!', 'Tu contiens, mer d'ébène . . .'), the *toi* now invoked is woman herself. In an almost imperceptible change of focus, the enchantments of the single privileged object give way to a querying review of the function of woman in general. While providing a satisfying wider conclusion to the poem, this final transition may suggest an involuntary disengagement, an unconscious slipping away from the specific sensual and imaginative riches of the hair into which the mind has plunged and been enveloped. Baudelaire makes the following interesting distinction; he speaks of woman

> pour qui, mais surtout *par qui* les artistes et les poètes composent leurs plus délicats bijoux

> (*OC* II, p. 713).

La Chevelure is a love poem but one in which, as we have seen, the poet is essentially 'amoureux d'ivresse'. In this, woman is an intermediary, almost (and literally) a pre-text. The poem is not written for her but via her: she is not its goal, only its agent. Though described as oasis of dream and intoxicant vessel (images behind which lurk the not too distant shadows of desert wastes

and enslaving addiction), she is the means by which he departs for the horizons of his own imagination. In the prose-poem **L'Invitation au voyage** he writes,

> Chaque homme porte en lui sa dose d'opium naturel, incessamment sécrétée et renouvelée

> (*OC* I, p. 303).

She is the stimulus for the release of that inner opium: memory, metaphor, musicality and movement. The intoxication absorbed is the self-indulgent one of poetry itself. As he exclaims exclusively in **Hymne à la Beauté**: 'Rythme, parfum, lueur, ô mon unique reine!' (*OC* I, p. 25).

Just as the poem began with the animal sensuality of 'toison' and ended with that of 'crinière', so it began with the flight of 'souvenirs' and now returns ultimately to 'souvenir'. This places the perfect artistic clasp around the poem, as if the wishful journey must be consigned back whence it came. The lingering appeal of the word 'souvenir' left hanging in the air (that 'souvenir enivrant qui voltige' which is a crucial force in **Le Flacon,** and the last five letters of which form the perfect anagram of the first five of 'enivrant', fusing memory and drunkenness as one) provides a most appropriate finale. It carries with it, as it fades on its lengthened vowel, the last reverberations of 'saphir' and 'loisir', a word which in its turn leaves 'l'oasis', 'lointain' and 'nonchaloir' stirring like disappearing perfumes in one's own poetic memory. But what began in a mood of excited creativity slips towards one of plaintive nostalgia. Significantly, the poem was launched on a series of emphatic exclamations (affirmative apostrophes like the first words of each stanza of **Les Phares** which, according to Yves Bonnefoy, burst the containment of the self as 'un cri irréfréné d'adhésion'[12]). It ends, on the other hand, with a double question, unanswered, less confident, implying a presence lost. To quote Bonnefoy again:

> l'imagination trace là d'abord un grand signe de délivrance, mais bientôt [. . .] elle avoue sa secrète forclusion[13].

The contrasting grammatical forms, exclamation and question, thus leave the poem poised on the negotiations of other dualities: escape and enclosure, admission and exclusion, *plénitude* and *vide*.

Notes

Quotations from Baudelaire's work appearing in this study are identified by the following abbreviations:

OC I: *Œuvres complètes,* Vol. I, Bibliothèque de la Pléiade, Gallimard, 1975

OC II: *Œuvres complètes,* Vol. II, Bibliothèque de la Pléiade, Gallimard, 1976

Corr. I: *Correspondance,* Vol. I, Bibliothèque de la Pléiade, Gallimard, 1973

Corr. II: *Correspondance,* Vol. II, Bibliothèque de la Pléiade, Gallimard, 1973.

For all other quotations used, details are given in footnotes.

1. See Stéphane Mallarmé, *Œuvres complètes,* Bibliothèque de la Pléiade, Gallimard, 1965, pp. 453-77.

2. Paul Valéry, *Œuvres* II, Bibliothèque de la Pléiade, Gallimard, 1960, p. 549.

3. René Char, *Œuvres complètes,* Bibliothèque de la Pléiade, Gallimard, 1983, p. 343.

4. Yves Bonnefoy, *Le Nuage rouge,* Mercure de France, 1977, p. 12.

5. Arthur Rimbaud, *Œuvres,* ed. Bernard, Garnier, 1960, p. 160.

6. Samuel Taylor Coleridge, *The Statesman's Manual*: see J. Beer, *Coleridge the Visionary,* Chatto and Windus, 1970, p. 138.

7. Char, *Œuvres complètes,* p. 360.

8. Paul Verlaine, *Œuvres poétiques complètes,* Bibliothèque de la Pléiade, Gallimard, 1962, p. 326.

9. Albert Cassagne, *Versification et métrique de Charles Baudelaire,* Slatkine, 1972, p. 88.

10. Char, *Œuvres complètes,* p. 345.

11. Bonnefoy, *Un Rêve fait à Mantoue,* Mercure de France, 1967, p. 10.

12. Bonnefoy, *Le Nuage rouge,* p. 9.

13. Bonnefoy, ibid., p. 42.

Roland A. Champagne (essay date November 2002)

SOURCE: Champagne, Roland A. "The Devil's Advocate: Baudelaire's Cat as the Daîmon of Erotic Mysticism in *Les Fleurs du Mal.*" *Romanic Review* 93, no. 4 (November 2002): 427-44.

[*In the following essay, Champagne discusses the figure of the cat—in "Les Chats" as well as in other poems of* Les Fleurs du Mal—*as a representation of both sensuality and intellectual curiosity.*]

The cat is for Charles Baudelaire, the poet of *Les Fleurs du mal,* both a sign and a symbol. In Michael Riffaterre's analysis of the poem **"Les Chats,"** he isolates both meanings, the cat as the living sign of an erotic relationship (Riffaterre 226) and the cat as the symbol of the poet's "mystical communion with the universe" (Riffaterre 223). Between these erotic and mystical meanings lies the cat as *daîmon,* that Greek concept of otherness that sometimes was portrayed as an interpretive conscience, a mediator acting as a guardian according to Hesiod's *Works and Days* or sitting on one's shoulder visible only to those one encounters (Arendt 180). Baudelaire the poet has a special daîmonic vision insofar as the poet has insight into the daîmon described by Hesiod as unseen by the one being influenced (Jaeger 52). The poet likewise literally sees the cat with its need to "watch . . . [and] demand to be watched" (Riffaterre 227), thus leading the poet to be self-reflective as a consequence of this communication with the daîmon.

The word daîmon has also been confused historically with demon or devil and is thus linked with the evil that generates Baudelaire's vision for flowers or objects of beauty and delicacy. In a post-Lévinas world, we learn from Alain Finkielkraut that love is the basic model for ethical relationships "le Mal procède d'abord d'une volonté de punir l'Autre de son intrusion dans mon existence" (Finkielkraut 145). Hence, the poet looks for allies in this insight into the ethical consequences of Evil. The cat is such an ally to be reckoned with in the quasi-religious rituals that are Baudelaire's poems. While Georges Bataille speaks, out of inspiration from Baudelaire, about the need for a fundamental connection between religious ecstasy and eroticism (Bataille 1987 640), a contemporary of T. S. Eliot, Arthur Symons, comments that Baudelaire's poetry is "an eternal Mass served before a veiled altar" (Eliot 1932 62). Baudelaire's poems indeed create the ambience for Catholic ritual, the Mass, as a memento for Baudelaire from his father, Jean-François, who was a defrocked priest (Pichois and Ziegler 50). The role model for moving the sacred to the profane was thus already set for Charles. Jean-François, the ordained priest, became a teacher of Latin and Greek rhetoric. His son the poet was then sympathetic, almost symbiotically, with "un prêtre à qui on arracherait sa divinité" (*OC* I 338).

The poet conducts his poetic ritual before a "veiled altar," that is, one decorated as in a Black Mass. This ritual does not invoke a Romantic Satan, "a symbol of revolt and heroic energy" (Hyslop 80). Instead, the poet calls forth, as in his **"Les Litanies de Satan,"** what he would later call "le plus parfait type de Beauté virile" (Baudelaire 1949 22). This virility is in contradistinction with feminine wiles that threaten him because "la virilité de Baudelaire cherche à se confondre avec la féminité" (Bassim 12). Satan incarnates the poet's male sexuality, testosterone, driving the poet internally while eroticism leads the poet toward women who threaten him with emotional death and the chasm of self-destruction in his impotence (Antoine 97, n. 39) prior to being rejected by them. More than the Romantic myth, Baudelaire's Satan is the poet's salvation (Milner 10) as the artistic incarnation that the erotic drive leads to more. The poet has a larger mystical vision wherein his personal chasm is matched by an external abyss that promises escape in the company of others who are similarly rejected. This duality of chasms is developed by Pierre Guiraud as the opposition between a "gouffre marin" and a "gouffre terrestre" (Guiraud 1958 80 ff.) in Baudelaire's poetry. The unity of this opposition is also important to understand because the mystical vision of the poet seeks a refuge in the encompassing beauty of poetic art. And there is the rub because Baudelaire's misogyny tells us that this is a "beauté malade" (Anderson 27) and that we must search for the disorder of this sexual ideology in its apparent order.

Much has been said over time about the order or disorder of **Les Fleurs du mal.** While Claude Pichois argues that there is a pattern and a sequence to the collection (*OC* I 800), F. W. Leakey prefers to posit Baudelaire's fragmentary life and the lack of order for a poet in his thirties (Leakey 68). My reading prefers the pattern rather than a necessary sequence to the changing order of the three editions. As James Lawler remarks, however, "the secret architecture is a moral dialectic" (Lawler 37). The dialectical portion is clear as we consider what Baudelaire says about himself from early on in life: "Tout enfant, j'ai senti dans mon cœur deux sentiments contradictoires, l'horreur de la vie et l'extase de la vie" (*OC* I 703). The poet's sensibility reflects that same contradictory and unifying tension in the daîmonic relationship between the cat and himself. Meanwhile, the "moral" issues at stake have to do with Baudelaire's revision of the sacred as being a daîmonic capacity for understanding the self and its relationship to others.

Baudelaire's poetry worships what is revealed by the daîmon's look at the poet. As the daîmon /cat stares, the poet becomes self-aware. We recall that Sartre observes in the young Baudelaire the tendency to watch himself see (Sartre 1947 23). In this self-consciousness, the poet's religious ritual begins to disclose Baudelaire's hermeneutic in his temple of nature (**"Correspondances"**) with its horizontal and vertical connections. As Arthur Wenk reminds us, Baudelaire's temple is also "a place of worship, a place where truth is revealed" (Wenk 72). Part of the truth in this case is the identity of the cat, everywhere present during the ritual of worship, acting as an idol for the priest and a muse for the poet.[2] Théophile Gautier remarked in 1868 that the cat was "une espèce de signature" (Gautier 137), an obsessive presence in the very interior space of the poet. In one of the two poems entitled **"Le Chat,"** the poet describes this place of sacred, feline worship:

"Dans ma cervelle se promène, / Ainsi qu'en son appartement"[3] (50, ll. 1-2). The interior life of this poetic, secular temple divides humanity according to Baudelaire's later manichean reflection that "il y a dans l'homme, à toute heure, deux postulations simultanées, l'une vers Dieu, l'autre vers Satan" (*OC* II 682). Yet clearly the poet is more concerned with exploring the side named by Théophile Gautier as "un air passablement satanique" (Gautier 137).

This interior temple is revealed by the cat's gaze that becomes effectively the devil's advocate. The advocacy here is that of the poet's ritual that enables him to see the cat as daîmon with the accompanying conscience of the satanic side that drives male sexuality. This ritual will be discussed in its evolution from the erotic devotion by a mediator priest, secondly as the pious work of the poet transformed by his erotic vision, and third by the mystical communion attained once the poet transcends his erotic trance to enter the esthetic realm where he finds mystical communion. The feline presence enables the poet to use the words of his poems as a ritual of daîmonic self-reflection that is a kind of satanic Black Mass with three parts moving from devotion to eroticism to mysticism. Finally, in that mystical state, the poet finds the calmness to understand himself with the acceptance that the cat's stare compels him to find.

Some believe that there has been simply too much attention, "a kind of catmania" (Plottel 103) given to Baudelaire's cats, especially as reflected in the plethora of publications about the poem **"Les Chats"** (Delcroix and Geerts 1980). This, however, assumes that the problem of the feline presence has been adequately presented. Graham Robb responds pointedly: "y chercher le regard qui l'explique le mieux est une cure plus efficace, qui ne prend pas l'hypocondrie critique pour une maladie du texte" (Robb **"Les Chats"** 1010). Insofar as the feline mania exists in the poetry itself, then there is the problem of trying to address the nature of the sickness. Ross Chambers sees the issue as an ideological one with **"Les Chats"** representative of structuralism and its issues and that the shift toward concerns with Baudelaire's **"Les Cygne"** presenting a struggle with "modernist" concerns (Chambers "Du Temps"). To continue Chambers's argument, the figure of the cat, rather than the plural cats of a single poem, is emblematic of the relationships needed in a post-Lévinas environment where ethics develops the responsibility engendered by the face of the Other for the self and for renewing the communal bonds of society. The significance of the cat is now, in the ethical pursuit of engagement in the aftermath of postmodernism and the death of Lévinas, the living incarnation of the renewed ethical impact of the Baudelairean process from eroticism, to piety, and mysticism.

THE EROTIC DEVOTION OF A PRIEST

The cat's vertical resting position suggests folded praying hands in a position of devotion and the kneeling Catholic in the position of prayer. This feline presence (**"Le Chat"**: "ses prunelles pâles . . . me contemplent fixement" [51, ll. 38, 40]) as witness to the poet, by his side as he writes his poems, inspires him to think of the poem as a prayer. Of course, a prayer has many functions, beginning with the attitude of a request to a being that is in possession of more power than the one praying. The poet is the conduit of such a prayer, thus realizing the role of a prayerful mediator conducting a ritual of devotion. Baudelaire even uses the prayer to praise the cat next to him, whom he has internalized and with whom he is on intimate terms: "Que ta voix, chat mystérieux, / Chat séraphique, chat étrange, / En qui tout est, comme en un ange, / Aussi subtil qu'harmonieux" (51, ll. 21-24). This angelic devotion is only the beginning of the priestly function of the poet.

The poet uses prayer as a mediation of his own needs for blessing and expiation. The title **"Bénédiction"** for one of his poems suggests the blessing that sometimes accompanies prayers such as Grace prior to meals. Within this poem, however, Baudelaire refers to "mon expiation" (7, l. 8) as a result of his poetic prayer thus arguing for repentance usually requested as forgiveness from a powerful presence to whom one is confessing a prior wrong perhaps having to do with the poet's state of being *ennuyé*. The hypocrisy of his reader and himself ("Hypocrite lecteur,—mon semblable,—mon frère") is found in the lack of confrontation with *Ennui* through their "*mauvaise foi* by fleeing from it into habitual utilitarian routines" (Zalloua 7). While the poet is excusing himself and appealing to a superior presence, in this instance to free him from his *ennui* through forgiveness, the cat appears with its independence and coyness, much like Baudelaire's erstwhile female lovers. Jakobson and Lévi-Strauss assert that, in the two poems entitled **"Le Chat,"** ". . . the image of the cat is narrowly linked to that of the woman" (Jakobson and Lévi-Strauss "Les Chats" 145) either as an epithet ("mon beau chat" [35, l. 1]) or as a feline metaphor or simile ("Son regard, / Comme le tien" [35, l. 9-10]). When the poet mentions women, he often links them with his own virility, inspiring the remark by Michel Butor that "ces deux aspects: féminité, supervirilité, bien loin de s'exclure, se lient" (Butor 85).

The priestly function of the poet derives not only from poetry as ritual but also poetry as mediation between the erotic and the mystical. The physical sources of mysticism have been richly explored recently by two psychiatrists as they note that ritual and myth are the bases for the projection of the physical into the mystical (d'Aquili and Newberg 5). These projections from the physical are accomplished by mediators who perform rituals and myths for others in their communities. A priest is such a mediator as is the poet. The poet/lover identifies his erotic passion as a priestly one: "avec la dévotion / Du prêtre pour son idole" (59, l. 78). The priest's "idol" is similar to the lover's beloved.[4] In the introduction to all the variants of **Les Fleurs du mal,** **"Au Lecteur"** presents Satan as the one "qui tient les fils qui nous remuent" (5, l. 13). The poet respects this incarnation of Evil who tweaks our behavior. After all, Baudelaire's focus on evil, according to Bataille, is "un sentiment mûr (qui souvent le guidait dans la réflexion sur l'érotisme)" (Bataille 1957 67). And in one of the last poems added to the third edition, "Epigraphe pour un livre condamné," the poet calls this advocate of Evil "le rusé doyen" (137, l. 6), an expression of ironic respect. This follows upon the poet's prayer in **"Les Litanies de Satan"** using the intimate pronoun form in addressing Satan with the refrain: "prends pitié de ma longue misère" (123, l. 3-4). Perhaps this misery refers to Baudelaire's syphilis or simply to the frustration of erotic longing with Satan harassing him from the sidelines. In response, the poet must adapt his priestly role, in a rite of exorcism inspirational to Henri Michaux's poetry of rebellion in the twentieth century. This priestly role resembles that of the shamans of some cultures who use personal creativity to manipulate magic and reach ecstatic states as does the troubadour tradition of "les jongleurs sacrés" (29, l. 3). The poem **"Élévation,"** whose title suggests the central moment of the religious rite of the Mass when the priest shows those attending what has been transubstantiated into a mystical vision of God, is very much grounded in "une indicible et mâle volupté" (10, l. 8). The poet similarly recreates the charm and magical aura of a sacred place as the poet reminds his reader: "Lecteur, as-tu quelquefois respiré / Avec ivresse et lente gourmandise / Ce grain d'encens qui remplit une église. / Ou d'un sachet le musc invétéré? / Charme profond, magique, dont nous grise / Dans le présent le passé restauré! / Aussi l'amant sur un corps adoré / Du souvenir cueille la fleur exquise." (39, ll. 1-8). Within this aesthetic of poetry, eroticism and mysticism form the two extreme practices whose ritualized implementation not only purge the poet from the daîmonic—that is, as Aeschylus portrayed it, "a manifestation of a power from the beyond" (Vernant 37) on human character as the complement to the ethical, that is the innate, component of one's character-motivation on his behavior but also guide the poet to place himself in the company of exiled others through the art of his poetry.

The presence of the cat affects how the ritualized ceremony of the erotic and the mystical interact in Baudelaire's poetry. First of all, the cat is an erotic image and symbol and thus links the daîmonic with eroticism. To repeat, Riffaterre speaks of the "role of the cat in private erotic imagery" (Riffaterre 226). The erotic role of the cat is much more universal, however, and even becomes symbolic of the poet's obsession with his beloved. The poet at times even identifies with a cat, as in **"La Géante,"** when a cat is curled up at the feet of the giantess looking up admiringly as "un chat voluptueux" (22, l. 4). While the poem **"La Chevelure"** speaks of the appeal to the point of drunkenness of the beloved's pubic hair ("Je plongerai ma tête amoureuse d'ivresse / Dans ce noir océan où l'autre est enfermé" [26, ll. 21-22]), the cat is a moving, living representation (in **"Le Chat"**: "Je vois ma femme en esprit." [35, l. 9]) of the dangerous atmosphere of erotic attraction (also in **"Le Chat"**: "Et, des pieds jusques à la tête, / Un air subtil, un dangereux parfum / Nagent autour de son corps brun" [35, ll. 12-14]). Whether the "corps brun" refers to Jeanne Duval's dark complexion or not, the cat is often accepted by the poet as a sign of his beloved.

In the priestly devotion conducted by the poet, the poet/ priest also accomplishes the rite of sacrifice in his ritualized poetry. In Catholic liturgy, the Mass is considered to be a reenactment of the sacrifice of Christ. Baudelaire, however, is celebrating a Black Mass in which he is at once the celebrant and the victim. As with his **"L'Héautontimôrouménos,"** meaning in Greek the tormenter and his/her victim all in one person, Baudelaire sings his own Mass in order to question being a sour note in a well-orchestrated, divine symphony ("ne suis-je pas un faux accord / Dans la divine symphonie" [78, ll. 13-14]) in favor of his own music. His music is an incantation about what he calls "the horror of mystery": "Partout l'homme subit la terreur du mystère, / Et ne regarde en haut qu'avec un œil tremblant" (141, ll. 7-8). We must not forget that the thoughtful titles of Baudelaire's poems were often deliberate as he was proud of saying: "J'aime les titres mystérieux ou les titres pétards" (Mourot 89). The explosive potential of mystery is well-known in his translations of Edgar Allan Poe's explorations of the macabre. The "mystery" has to do with the darkness, traditionally relegated to a diabolical presence and contrasted with the revelation of the light. Baudelaire decides to celebrate this darkness and to explore it accompanied by his cat who not only sees in the darkness but is comfortable hunting and prowling for what lies in it, especially the Prince of Darkness, an alternate title for the diabolical other. The cat thus acts as the poet's assistant as we recall that the feline presence "Dans ma cervelle se promène" (50, l. 1) all the while talking to the poet ("sa voix s'apaise ou gronde" [50, l. 6]). It is the cat's meowing that has a magical, musical effect on the poet ("Cette voix, qui perle et qui filtre / Dans mon fonds le plus ténébreux, / Me remplit comme un vers nombreux / Et me réjouit comme un philtre." (50, 9-12). The feline music is crucial in providing the poet with a rhythm that many have called the hallmark of Baudelaire's poetry. His musical genius was cited by Gaston Bachelard, for example, in an analysis of the poem **"La Mort"** that

recalls how "Pour cetains rêveurs, l'eau est le mouvement nouveau qui nous invite au voyage jamais fait" (Bachelard *L'Eau* 103). Music becomes the carrier of the poet into his poetic vision.

Baudelaire's poetic vision is also a ritual surrounded by the aura of magic. This is the ethical model proposed by Lévinas whereby the Other can enchant through "une qualité différente de toutes les autres mais la qualité même de la différence" (Lévinas *Le Temps* 14). The poet is thus mesmerized by the "charmants yeux" (44, l. 9) of his beloved, recalling the staring eyes of his cat. The image of the beloved as a sorceress is very frequent (e.g., "sorcière aux yeux alléchants," [59, l. 4]; "ô molle enchanteresse", [51, l. 1]; "belle" and "adorable sorcière", [54, l. 2]; "obi" and "sorcière", [28, ll. 3, 4]), thus suggesting enchantment as a condition with which the poet is familiar as a beloved. Meanwhile, the cat's meowing and purring also gladden the poet as would a love potion ("un philtre," [50, l. 12]) governing "les cœurs ensorcelés" (49, l. 6). He uses the image of a magic potion in other poems ("népenthèse", [156, l. 22]; "divin élixir", [126, l. 3]), suggesting the priest's magic-like changing of wine into Christ's blood in the ceremony of the Mass, a Catholic ritual dedicated to celebrating the miracle of Transubstantiation, a metaphor for the process that takes Baudelaire from his materialistic eroticism to his abstract mysticism.

The poet's ritualistic performance, however, does not simply imitate a traditional daily Mass. In **"L'Imprévu,"** mention is made of "la joyeuse Messe noire" (171, l. 24) so that the Black Mass produces a certain elation in the poet, through its celebration of the Dead, of the dark past. Gretchen Schultz even goes so far as to say that there is "an often masochistic masculine poetic subject" (Schultz 137). This remark, however, overlooks the ritualistic process of self-negation and culpability that is involved in Catholic confession and that prepares the poet for the more elaborate celebration of the Black Mass. Henri Peyre does recognize the Catholic traditions influencing Baudelaire, and he finds that the poet seeks "martyrdom without name" (Peyre 34). Martyrdom, however, implies reward beyond death. The poet seems to seek pleasure in the bleak prospect of death rather than in its leading toward some sort of fulfillment or reward.

The title of one of Baudelaire's poems, **"De profondis clamavi,"** refers to the requiem Mass so that this ceremony is certainly within his ken. Another poem, **"Franciscae meae laudes,"** written entirely in Latin, the language of the Mass, is formally patterned, according to Claude Pichois (*OC* I 940), upon the litany called the *Dies Irae,* often sung at a Black Mass. Regarding the Black Mass itself, the celebrant mentions the ciborium (171, l.22), the vessel containing the transformed bread to be distributed at Communion, that ritual in the

Mass whereby the faithful ingest the sacred hosts as a group experience. This experience of Communion foreshadows the poet's mystical vision toward which his eroticism tends. First of all, the Communion is a physical act that must be appreciated for the changes that it enacts in the participants. The poet himself senses that a change is taking place within him such that the piety of his role as mediator/priest is changing.

THE MODIFIED SPIRIT OF THE PIOUS POET

The experience of revisiting his father, the defrocked priest whose priestly idol is removed ("Semblable à un prêtre à qui on arracherait sa divinité . . ." [*OC* I 338]), is a double-edged sword for Baudelaire. The cutting edge is the poet who learned piety before a creative power more awesome than his own and now wields the power of artistic creativity through his awe. The piety of Baudelaire the poet is not the humbling, contained reverence of a cowed and respectful idolater. Instead, his religiosity entails the fear and trembling, reminiscent of Kierkegaard's pre-conversion anxiety, at the prospect of the *gouffre*, that abyss both inside and outside the poet, as well as terrestrial and oceanic, that overflows from the inside like an ocean toward that other abyss of life itself. At times, the poet seems delighted at the prospect of a free-floating oceanic experience: "Et mon âme dansait, dansait, vieille gabarre / Sans mâts sur une mer monstrueuse et sans bords!" (88, ll. 51-2). The oceanic image is everywhere present in his poetry but especially in the poems **"Le Goût du néant"** and **"Le Gouffre."** The poet's *ennui* is frightful in its awe before that outer abyss represented by the external conditions of the weather and Time itself: "Et le Temps m'engloutit minute par minute, / Comme la neige immense un corps pris de roideur" (76, ll. 11-12). The *gouffre* is ubiquitous and unites internal and external threats: "En haut, en bas, partout, la profondeur, la grève, / Le silence, l'espace affreux et captivant / Sur le fond de mes nuits Dieu de son doigt savant / Dessine un cauchemar multiforme et sans trêve" (142, ll. 5-8). This God is malicious and threatens the poet who is guided by his cats walking the line between these abysses. Many of Baudelaire's contemporary readers—the hypocritical readers he calls his fraternal peers ("Hypocrite lecteur,—mon semblable,—mon frère" in **"Au Lecteur"** [6, l. 40])—could not adopt his stance as poet: "the cats that prowl through Baudelaire's work . . . aroused a furor on the part of the public, who attributed to them an almost diabolical significance" (Hyslop 36). In contradistinction, Lévinas reminds us that the fraternity, despite the qualification of hypocrisy, between Baudelaire and his reader, is felicitous as "l'heureuse rencontre d'âmes fraternelles qui se saluent et qui conversent" (Lévinas *Découvrant* 178). And so the poet's encounter with the diabolical begins an involvement of the reader in looking at Otherness together. Baudelaire, however, attributes his distinctive valuation to the concept of the

diabolical. As Sartre, influenced by Baudelaire, remarks: "The Devil is a symbol for Otherness" (Sartre *Notebook* 429)

Baudelaire, however, attributes his distinctive valuation to the concept of the diabolical. The otherness of the cat allows Baudelaire to find within himself both the oppression of his own phallocentric meaning (Hadlock 201) and the power of the imagination to transcend the threatening depths of *ennui* and self-destruction found in the images of the abyss. Jean Starobinski concludes that the poet and the cat bond as "le chat est le destinataire du chagrin que nul autre ne partage" (Starobinski 122). The poet finds comfort in this feline sharing because, according to his friend Théophile Gautier, "Baudelaire était lui-même un chat voluptueux, câlin, aux façons veloutées, à l'allure mystérieuse . . ." (Gautier 137). Baudelaire's personal identification with feline qualities allows him to use his poetic imagination to portray "la griffe effroyable de Dieu" (91, 1.84) and especially "les griffes de l'amour" (116, l. 3) thus intuiting, as he says in his "Fusées," that "la volupté unique et suprême de l'amour gît dans la certitude de faire le mal: et l'homme et la femme savent de naissance que dans le mal se trouve toute volupté" (Baudelaire *Journaux intimes* 11). The poet thus attains a moral vision with his imagination, one in which evil and physical desire are intimately linked in order to give him access to what he calls "the secret." His is a painful secret ("le secret douloureux" in **"La Vie Antérieure"** [18, l. 14]) whose access is controlled by the diabolical Other: "le Démon fait des trous secrets à ces abîmes" (71, l. 5). The result is the insight that the secret allows the poet to follow this diabolical Other in order to exit the abyss into the vastness of space that consoles him with the rocking motion of the lullaby of other choices. The poet often speaks about the ocean to represent this vastness as in **"Moesta et Errabunda"**: "La mer, la vaste mer, console nos labeurs! / Quel démon a doté la mer, rauque chanteuse / Qu'accompagne l'immense orgue des vents / De cette fonction sublime de berceuse? / La mer, la vaste mer console nos labeurs!" (63, ll. 6-10). Note the demonic endowment of the ocean, whose vastness is not containable for the poet.[5] Vastness—as expressed in variations of such words as *grand* (Mourot 205), *long,* and *vast*[6]—itself is one of the predominate motifs setting up the "metaphysical" (Bachelard *Poétique* 175) stakes for Baudelaire's spatial dimensions. To Bachelard's "metaphysical" I prefer "mystical," which is a word often used by Baudelaire to speak of the poet's vision ensuing from the pious ceremonies associated with eroticism. E. M. Cioran speaks appropriately about an anonymous Oriental insight into who a mystic is: "The mystic is a man who tells you about your mystery while you remain silent" (Cioran 7). And Baudelaire's inner vision has this effect over his reader who is overcome with awe at the grandeur of what is exposed.

The transition from the erotic to the mystical takes place in the poet's religious ceremony. Whereas the notion of magic has already been introduced to refer to the transformation taking place in the poet's soul, he also utilizes terms from alchemy to identify how these changes take place. In **"L'Alchimie de la douleur,"** for example, the poet proudly exclaims to his beloved that "pour toi je change l'or en fer et le paradis en enfer" (77, ll. 9-10). Curiously, he would reverse the alchemical process just as the presence of the beloved has changed his life. The poet often employs synesthesia, the process of using a single image to combine multiple sensations, to imitate the transformational process that transgresses the boundaries of apprehension, as in the poem **"Tout entière"** wherein "The perfume of the woman's breath creates musical harmony, and in the music of her voice a perfume can be sensed" (Dal Molin 88). In fact, all boundaries are broken for the poet as "Le souvenir de la Femme remet tout en question" (Bassim 111).

There is yet another factor in the transformational process, however. The diabolical presence is constantly hovering over the poet, especially when change takes place. Baudelaire himself reflected upon this presence in a letter to Flaubert: ". . . je me suis aperçu que de tout temps j'ai été obsédé par l'impossibilité de me rendre compte de certaines actions ou pensées soudaines de l'homme sans l'hypothèse de l'intervention d'une force méchante extérieure de lui" (Baudelaire 1973 II 53). In his obsession with open spaces like the ocean and the sea where his freedom can be openly expressed, the poet travels but cannot escape that even there, "Quel démon a doté la mer" (63, l. 7). Like the cat who accompanies the poet during the writing of the poems, the Devil is always attending: "Sans cesse à mes côtés s'agite le Démon" (111, l. 1). This last reflection, however, occurs in a poem entitled **"La Destruction,"** thus associating pejorative and diabolical influences. This pejorative influence can best be understood as a dialectical factor, similar to the principles of tantric philosophy—as differentiated from Christian theology with its positioning of evil as a privation of Good (and God), thus dependent upon the existence of Good for its definition—stipulating that "the yoga of non-duality of the profound and the manifest" (Hopkins 58). Tantrism exemplifies Baudelaire's interest in the exotic allure of Orientalism ("sa rêveuse allure orientale" [38, l. 11]) and its links between eroticism and mysticism. With the tantric focus away from the opposition of apparent dualities between appearance and truth, this insight qualifies Baudelaire's demon who is derivative of Christian theology. For example, the title of one of his poems **"Les Litanies de Satan,"** links the liturgical repetitive prayer to saints called a litany with Satan whom the poet calls "le Prince de l'exil" (124, l. 4). Of course, exile is well-known to the marginalized poet[7] who now has made a kind of patron saint and aristocrat

(as the Prince) out of his diabolical companion. The poet becomes a kind of tantric priest, that is a mediator who celebrates diabolical presence and thus accomplishes what Ross Chambers calls "a form of power that controls those mediations in the interests of what are called stability and order" (Chambers "Flâneur" 143). Effectively, the poet as priest celebrating a Black Mass is a mediator interested in creating his own "stability and order" independent of the relational opposition to God or Christ within Christian theology. Baudelaire's poet even acknowledges that there could be religion despite those "qui jamais n'ont connu leur Idole" (127, l. 9). The word "Idole" is Baudelaire's all-purpose term for a deity that represents any non-human intervention in human affairs. The poet's Black Mass is a celebration of his alternate religion that is so manifest in a poem like **"Les Litanies de Satan"** with its refrain asking for pity from Satan for the poet's woes, thus ascribing power to the recipient of the enchanting song/prayer. At times, the poet's feline prayer unites the attraction of women with the proximity of cats, as in the already mentioned example of **"La Géante":** "J'eusse aimé vivre auprès d'une jeune géante, / Comme aux pieds d'une reine un chat voluptueux" (22, ll. 3-4). This "chat voluptueux" exemplifies, for the poet, "la vocation de son érotisme" (Bonnefoy 26).

In the face of the poet's *ennui,* however, the cat calls forth a much more complex process in the diabolical ritual. The ritualized celebration of diabolical power as a cleansing process (the refrain of the request for pity as a methodical catharsis) is attended by the poet's cat. Michael Riffaterre provides insight into the direction of the poet's altered state as a result of the religious process: "the cat's image symbolizes the poet; the sublimation of the cat symbolizes love cleansed of feminine impurity and knowledge freed of its coldness; the poet is thus ready for a mystic communion with the universe" (Riffaterre 223). Hence, the third stage of the religious transformation of the poet is the mystical vision that taunts and pulls him away from the *ennui* that eroticism feeds if left to itself. This *ennui* is well-known to Lévinas who reminds us that "Dans l'amour—à moins de ne pas aimer l'amour—, il faut se résigner à ne pas être aimé" (Lévinas *Autrement* 153). Baudelaire already learned that ethical relationships should not be assumed to be symmetrical. Instead, there is the mystical pleasure derived thereby.

THE POET'S MYSTICAL COMMUNION

The devotional practices of the Black Mass lead the poet into curious acknowledgments about himself. For example, ". . . je cherche le vide, et le noir, et le nu!" (75, l. 11). These appear to be nebulous goals, but let us remember that the poet moves from eroticism through an altered piety toward mysticism. In an apparent echo of Bachelard, this pattern has been called "Baudelaire's metaphysics" by Graham Robb: "La métaphysique de Baudelaire le pousse donc à faire de l'érotisme . . . une des bases d'une esthétique" (Robb *La Poésie* 356). Thus the esthetic goals for the art of his poetry lay bare not only the direction of his traveling soul but also a scheme for a weltanschauung that transcends his situation and joins up with others, especially the "hypocritical reader" who partakes of the poet's vision. The poet often uses the word "mystical" in this way, as if the word for him meant a larger view of life that is inaccessible to most of us in our daily routines. Part of the nobility of cats ("les nobles attitudes" [66, l. 9]) is their suggestion of an intimation about a mystical vision ("leurs prunelles mystiques" [66, l. 14]). Their gaze reminds him of his own access to the *gouffre,* defined by Jean-Pierre Richard as "ce creux intérieur de la conscience" (Richard 95). This interior mystical abyss of the poet's consciousness, like the ambivalence of the French word *conscience,* is also the conscience searching for a communion among similar-minded souls. This is not the spontaneous self of the poet. Indeed, as Lévinas tells us, an ethical moment occurs when one "suspend son mouvement spontané d'exister" (Lévinas *Totalité* 34) in response to the call from the Other. Instead, a daîmonic reaction leads us to understand the poet along with Léon Somville: "Les chats (ou Baudelaire) choisissent la voie de quasi-rupture (la rupture totale aurait pris la forme d'une psychose); l'évasion dans le monde des idées, l'évasion mystique" (Somville 199). This is where the feline gaze, both toward and from the cat, leads the poet and his reader, toward the awareness of the void that is both internal and external to consciousness. The poet thus exemplifies the daîmonic influence of his cat as symbol with the critical, self-reflective gaze of conscience leading him to examine how the mystical enables him to project the personal into his vision of himself and others. He can speak intimately to an interior presence and chastise it for controlling him as an independent force, as in **"Recueillement"**: "Sois sage, ô ma Douleur, et tiens-toi plus tranquille. / Tu réclamais le Soir; . . ." (140, ll. 1-2). Through the meditation of the poet's self-reflective gaze, he thus acknowledges the complexity of his self-identity and his ability to be able to regulate its absorption by the exterior abyss of night, a metaphor for depression and perhaps even suicide, which Baudelaire is known to have attempted at least once (Pichois and Ziegler 211 ff.).

While Baudelaire's abysses are both internal and external, his mystical vision is rooted in his eroticism, and his eroticism has insights into his mysticism. Here is where Baudelaire participates in Blaise Pascal's insight into the two infinities (Pascal 115-122). While Pascal speaks of the infinities of minuteness (*petitesse*) and expansion (*grandeur*), Baudelaire's infinities are personal and communal. Baudelaire's chasms complement each other and create structural cohesion for his

postulate of the diabolical presence in the face of God. From his personal solitude in the ambience of his "diabolical" male sexuality, the absence of light, and the presence of darkness ("Ô rafraîchissantes ténèbres" [121, l. 14), the poet looks outward and finds "Un soir plein de rose et de bleu mystique" (126, l. 9). These colors suggest the richness of the community of others who people the world of the urban landscape. If they have already been "poor" in spirit or in life, they could inherit what he calls "le grenier mystique" (127, l. 12), a reward for their suffering. It does not matter, however, to the poet which abyss of suffering one inhabits because "De Satan ou de Dieu . . . Ange ou Sirène" (25, l. 25) there is a an ecstatic pleasure to be derived, as is mentioned by the pleasure of **"La Chevelure."** Ecstasy is not unlike the cat's sudden response to catnip, whose perfume drives it mad with pleasure. The poet's feline companion is likewise very sensitive to scents and becomes a model for the poet's sensitivity to the erotic and, ultimately, mystical associations with olfactory sensations. The cat's presence as a daîmonic inspiration is thus once again re-asserted to make the poet critically aware of himself by observing what is around him in the urban setting and creating poetry to set up a diabolical, alternate abyss peopled by marginalized beings such as himself and his cat. This poetry juxtaposes the dual systems of chasms because the poet is intent upon displacing a theocentric universe, as he wonders in his "Mon cœur mis à nu": ". . . la création ne serait-elle pas la chute de Dieu?" (*OC* I 688). Or at the very least, the poet's creativity substitutes an alternate place where the daîmonic activity of his self-reflection can enjoy expression without being marginalized as "evil" or a "paria" of the majority interest in society.

The creativity of the poet's daîmonic reflections can be especially appreciated in his predilection for the adjective "mystique." The poet's mystical vision provides alternatives to the darkness and the black entrapment of his internal *gouffre* in the insight about how things could be out there, in the alternate abyss among others. In **"La Mort des Amants,"** for example, the word "mystique" is associated with the sustained, yet brief (after all, this is "the death of lovers"), torches of light brought about in the darkness by the two hearts meeting each other: "nos deux cœurs seront deux vastes flambeaux, / Qui réfléchiront leurs doubles lumières / Dans nos deux esprits, ces miroirs jumeaux" (126, ll. 6-8).[8] Within this "mystical" colorful evening painted by the poet in rose and blue, the lovers will exchange "un éclair unique" (126, l. 10), that bright stroke of lightning so quickly occurring and then vanishing. The poet is indeed fond of this momentary "clarté mystique" that he derives from "les charmants yeux" (44, l. 9) of his beloved, but let us not forget his cats whose focused, unblinking eyes likewise beguile him with their suggestion of a transcendent vision ("leurs prunelles mystiques" [66, l. 14]) while reminding him of the subversive effect ("Un air subtil, un dangereux parfum" [35, l. 13]) that Jeanne Duval had over him ("Je vois ma femme en esprit" [35, l. 9]). This temporary flash of light contrasting with the darkness of the self enclosed in its inner abyss recalls the theological principle of *tsimtsum* (Ouaknin 1992), theorized by the twelfth-century Zohar, whereby God contracted divine, infinite light in order to make place for creation. This principle was revived by the Cathars in southeastern France where Baudelaire learned about them.[9] This space between light and dark, a kind of divine suspended animation, is where the poet inserts his mystical vision by continuously re-creating through his poetry and therein with his own contrasting inner and outward abysses providing his secularized version of divine creation. Indeed, the poet saw himself as being an exception to divine creation, a false note in the orchestrated creation. Instead, he proposes his own "accord mystique" (154, l. 65). In his alternate plan for the universe, Satan visits the poet to discuss the drastic change for the Prince of Darkness in this "métamorphose mystique" (42, l. 21). As we have discussed, this entails the veiled "Black Mass" dedicated to the devil, a ritual described by Théophile Gautier as "le bercement vague d'une incantation magique" (Gautier 145). This "rocking motion" lulls and thereby coopts the reader ("l'hypocrite lecteur") into accepting the poet's ecstatic alternative to divine creation. In **"Harmonie du soir,"** the poem that reverberates the poet's mystical vision, the perfume and color of the flower are transformed into a kind of incense: "Chaque fleur s'évapore ainsi qu'un encensoir" (47, l. 5). The even-metered verse rocks in imitation of the censer—secularized by the poet as an image for wafting the beloved's perfume in **"Chanson d'après-midi"** (59, ll. 13-15), for a secret evening memory in **"Hymne"** (162, ll. 11-12), and for the memory of a perfume in **"Un Fantôme"** (39, II, ll. 10-11)—used in Church rituals but appropriated by the poet as a metaphor for the poem itself. Richard has brilliantly discussed Baudelaire's poetry as "un brouillard qui se dissipe" (Richard 115) in the eyes of the informed reader. The dissipation does leave an image behind of what once was because the poet's power is that of his imagination creating analogies that Baudelaire identifies as part of his mystical ritual: "L'imagination . . . comprend l'analogic universelle qu'une religion mystique appela *la correspondance*" (Baudelaire 1973 I 336). As we remember, this is the same word Baudelaire used in its plural form as the title for the poem that is his *art poétique*. His reference to "a mystical religion" as his source prepares us for the secularizing rituals that re-appropriate the sacred in his poetry.

Baudelaire's mystical vision, especially in the analogy to the cat as sign and symbol of the daîmon, leads to a sense that ecstasy is possible when the self is aware of its own limitations and seeks to go beyond them. When Sartre noted that Baudelaire the man was the poet who could not contain the secret in his body in the present moment (Sartre 1947 164), we have the intimation that the poet has a mystical vision that transcends the present moment to create unifying beauty, the art of his poetry. Ecstasy is, after all, "a supreme expression of mystical knowledge . . . all senses melted into one flame" (Cioran 8). Hence, Baudelaire's synesthesia prepares the reader for this explosive inner vision linking the inner and the outer abysses. Returning to Riffaterre's analysis of **"Les Chats,"** we note his analogy of "apotheosis to infinity" (Riffaterre 194) of the cats as Baudelaire's style unites the cats to the cosmos: "substitution of parts of his body for the whole cat dissolves the beast into particles of matter, and the final identification associates these particles with desert sands and transmutes them into stars; the fusion of cats and cosmos has been accomplished" (Riffaterre 194). The integration of the feline into the cosmos is a crucial insight because the divine order is thus appropriated and partaken into the cat who accompanies the poet. By observing the cat, the poet sees that order is entailed by interaction. The pleasure of the exchange of interaction leads to respect for that bond and the intimation that therein lies the promise of accession to infinity. Similarly, regarding the form of many of the poems, the reader of Baudelaire's sonnets admires with Victor Brombert that the poet is "also celebrating the notion that constricting forms give a deeper sense of infinity" (Brombert 16). This melding of content and form regarding accession to infinity is a secularized alternative to a Christian afterlife. We thus return to Baudelaire's mediation at the "veiled altar" of his poetry. What are being hidden are the altar for the poet's table and the secularized mediation of the priest in the daîmon. On the poet's table is the cat who is both sign and symbol ("Dans ma cervelle se promène . . ." [50, l. 1]) for the poet of his own daîmonic ability to produce a mystical vision of a self-determined community of his readers. This is not the mystical vision of such saints as John of the Cross or Teresa of Avila with their sexualized renditions of their relationships to divinity. Instead, Baudelaire relies on the nobility of the cats ("leurs nobles attitudes" [66, l. 9]) to remind him that sensuality is balanced by intellectual curiosity ("amis de la science et de la volupté" [66, l. 5]) and that they inspire self-confidence in humans by actually seeking darkness and silence ("Ils cherchent le silence et l'horreur des ténèbres" [66, l. 6]). The feline example allows the poet to see beyond his personal, inner depression and to project his own "nobility" of a human association with others who are similarly isolated, that is, his readers. The cat thus also becomes symbolic of the daîmon, exemplifying what T. S. Eliot calls an "objective correlative" in order "to arouse a particular emotion in the reader . . . by a carefully elaborated poetical formula" (Galant 30). That emotion is the self-reflective, artistic vision of ecstasy. While for some mystics, "ecstasy replaces sexuality . . . [as] sexual orgasm pales beside the saints' ecstatic trance" (Cioran 19), for Baudelaire eroticism leads to ecstasy and is intimately linked with it. It is the "hypocrite lecteur," at once the Other and the fraternal equal, who offers to the poet the possibility for the renewal of this human association. The ritual of the poet's creativity is after all performed for his readers. Laurence Porter would have us consider "the idealized audience . . . [as] a single object of desire who seems to offer the hope of filling a void in the lyric self" (Porter 114). This "void" is projected in the other voice of daîmonic conscience that the poet so desperately needs as he glances at the cat gazing at him and becomes aware of his ritualized responsibility to respond to its alterity and its similarity to him.

Notes

1. *OC* will be used to indicate a reference to Baudelaire's *Œuvres Complètes* with the complete citation noted in the Works Consulted.

2. Jennifer Walkowiak has developed in discussion with me the cat not only as the poet's muse but also as his source of power and intelligence in the night similar to the owl (see Baudelaire's "Les Hiboux").

3. All citations of *Les Fleurs du mal* are from the first volume of the Pléiade edition in Works Consulted. To simplify the textual references while making them accessible, references to this work will be indicated parenthetically after the citation by page number first followed by l. or ll. indicating the specific verse or verses.

4. I thank Allen Pickett for developing this insight for me by discussing the similarities of the idol and the beloved for the priest as lover and the role of the cat as an objective correlative of that relationship for the poet/priest.

5. Amy G. Reiter-McIntosh, "L'Attirance du gouffre chez Baudelaire," 1981 Honors Thesis, University of Missouri-St. Louis, p. 20. She develops the crucial notion that the ocean is "insaisissable" in that it is always beyond the reach of the poet, thus spurring his need for the voyage in order to try to approach the "là-bas" of the expanding ocean.

6. Viprey (1997 324-5) speaks of a Greimas-inspired "zone isotropique" constituted by the words *mer* and *profond* such that the notion of *gouffre* is related to the frequency lists established by Giraud (1954) placing words with spatial dimensions as important relational *mots-thèmes* for *Les Fleurs du mal*.

7. In the trial against *Les Fleurs du mal* in 1857, Baudelaire was portrayed as "une nature inquiète et sans équilibre" ("Le Procès des *Fleurs du mal*" [Baudelaire 1975 1180]), thus a pariah to the French society whose moral fiber his poetry was threatening.

8. I especially thank Tracy Turnage for discussing this association of mysticism with the light shared by mutual lovers and, in the poem "Elévation," the notion that the spirit helps the poet to be buoyant in the sea of depression that threatens to engulf him.

9. Simone Weil researched the Cathar religion of the twelfth century, which was in large part destroyed by the Albigensian Crusade but whose remains were researched by contemporaries of Baudelaire—namely, Péladan and Huysmans—who provided him with information on their theology (O'Shea 254). Basically, the Cathars developed the principle of *tsimtsum* and "saw the created world as evil, believed in reincarnation, and held that the body was an obstacle to spiritual perfection" (Gray 155).

Works Consulted

Anderson, Jean. "Baudelaire Misogyne: Vers une lecture féministe des *Fleurs du mal*." *New Zealand Journal of French Studies*, 8.1 (1987): 16-28.

Antoine, Gérald. "Pour une nouvelle exploration 'stylistique' du *gouffre* baudelairien." *Le Français moderne*, 30. 2 (April 1962): 81-98.

Arendt, Hannah. *The Human Condition*. Chicago: University of Chicago Press, 1958.

Bachelard, Gaston. *L'Eau et les rêves*. Paris: Corti, 1942.

———. *La Poétique de l'espace*. Paris: Presses Universitaires de France, 1957.

Bassim, Tamara. *La Femme dans l'œuvre de Charles Baudelaire*. Neuchatel [Sw.]: Editions de la Baconnière, 1974.

Bataille, Georges. *La Littérature et le mal*. Paris: Gallimard, 1957.

———. *Œuvres complètes*, v. 10. Eds. Francis Marmande and Yves Thévenieau. Paris: Gallimard, 1987.

Baudclaire, Charles. *Journaux Intimes*. Eds. Jacques Crépit and Georges Blin. Paris: Corti, 1949.

———. *Correspondance*, v. I and II. Eds. Claude Pichois & Jean Ziegler. Paris: Gallimard, 1973.

———. *Œuvres complètes*, v. I and II. Ed. Claude Pichois. Paris: Gallimard, Bibliothéque de la Pléiade, 1975.

Bonnefoy, Yves. *Baudelaire: la tentation de l'oubli*. Paris: Bibliothèque Nationale de France, 2000.

Brombert, Victor. *The Romantic Prison: The French Tradition.* Princeton: Princeton University Press, 1978.

Butor, Michel. *Histoire extraordinaire: essai sur un rêve de Baudelaire.* Paris: Gallimard, 1961.

Chambers, Ross. "Du Temps des 'Chats' au temps du 'Cygne.'" *Œuvres & Critiques,* 9.2 (1984): 11-26.

———. "The *flâneur* as hero (on Baudelaire)." *Australian Journal of French Studies,* 28.2 (May 1991): 142-153.

Cioran, Emil M. *Tears and Saints.* Tr. from Romanian by Ilinca Zarifopol-Johnston. Chicago: University of Chicago Press, 1995.

d'Aquili, Eugene and Andrew B. Newberg. *The Mystical Mind: Probing the Biology of Religious Experience.* Minneapolis: Fortress, 1999.

Dal Molin, Eliane. "Toute Entière: A Mystifying Totality." *Understanding* Les Fleurs du mal. Ed. William J. Thompson. Nashville: Vanderbilt University Press, 1997, pp. 86-94.

Delcroix, Maurice and Walter Geerts, eds. *"Les Chats" de Baudelaire: une confrontation de méthodes.* Namur [Belgium]: Presses Universitaires de Namur, 1980.

Eliot, T. S. "Baudelaire in our Time." In his *Essays Ancient and Modern.* New York: Harcourt, Brace and Company, 1932, pp. 60-74.

Finkielkraut, Alain. *La Sagesse de l'amour.* Paris: Gallimard, 1984.

Galant, René. "T. S. Eliot and the Impact of Baudelaire." *Yale French Studies,* 6 (1950): 27-34.

Gautier, Théophile. "Notice." *Baudelaire par Gautier.* In eds. Claude-Marie Senninger and Lois Cassandra Hamrick. Paris: Klincksieck, 1986 reprint of 1868, pp. 113-167.

Giraud, Pierre. *Les Caractères statistiques du vocabulaire.* Paris: Presses Universitaires de France, 1954.

———. "Le Champ stylistique du gouffre de Baudelaire." *Orbis littérarum* (1958): 74-84.

Gray, Francine du Plessix. *Simone Weil.* New York: Penguin, 2001.

Hadlock, Philip G. "Sartre's Failure: Reading the Baudelairean Dilemma." *Neophilologus,* 85.2 (April 2001): 193-202.

Hopkins, Jeffrey. *The Tantric Distinction.* Boston: Wisdom, 1999.

Hyslop, Lois Boe. *Charles Baudelaire Revisited.* New York: Twayne, 1992.

Jaeger, Werner. *Paideia: The Ideals of Greek Culture.* Tr. Gilbert Highet. New York: Oxford University Press, 1973.

Jakobson, Roman and Claude Lévi-Strauss. "Charles Baudelaire's 'Les Chats.'" Tr. Fernande M. de George. *The Structuralists from Marx to Lévi-Strauss.* Eds. Richard and Fernande de George. New York: Anchor Books, 1962, pp. 124-146.

Lawler, James R. *Poetry and Moral Dialectic: Baudelaire's "Secret Architecture."* Madison [N.J.]: Fairleigh Dickinson University Press, 1997.

Leakey, F. W. *Baudelaire.* Cambridge [U.K.]: Cambridge University Press, 1990.

Lévinas, Emmanuel. *Totalité et infini.* The Hague: Martinus Nijhoff, 1971.

———. *En découvrant l'existence avec Husserl et Heidegger.* Paris: Vrin, 1974.

———. *Autrement qu'être ou au-delà de l'essence.* The Hague: Martinus Nijhoff, 1978.

———. *Le Temps et l'autre.* Montpellier [Fr.]: Fata Morgana, 1979.

Mauriac, François. "Charles Baudelaire, the Catholic." *Baudelaire.* Ed. Henri Peyre. Englewood Cliffs [N.J.]: Prentice-Hall, 1962, pp. 30-37.

Milner, Max. "Satan et le romantisme." *L'Information littéraire* (January 1961): 6-11.

Mourot, Jean. *Baudelaire,* Les Fleurs du mal. Nancy [Fr.]: Presses Universitaires de Nancy, 1989.

O'Shea, Stephen. *The Perfect Heresy: The Revolutionary Life and Death of the Medieval Cathars.* New York: Walker and Company, 2000.

Ouaknin, Marc-Alain. *Tsimtsoum: Introduction à la méditation hébraïque.* Paris: Albin Michel, 1992.

Pascal, Blaise. *Pensées.* Ed. Louis Lafuma. Paris: Seuil, 1962.

Pichois, Claude and Jean Ziegler. *Charles Baudelaire.* Paris: Fayard, 1987.

Porter, Laurence M. *The Crisis of French Symbolism.* Ithaca: Cornell University Press, 1990.

Plottel, Jeanine Parisier. "The Battle of Charles Baudelaire's 'Les Chats.'" *Romanic Review,* 74.1 (January 1983): 91-103.

Richard, Jean-Pierre. *Poésie et profondeur.* Paris: Seuil, 1955.

Riffaterre, Michael. "Describing Poetic Structures: Two Approaches to Baudelaire's 'Les Chats.'" *Structuralism.* Ed. Jacques Ehrmann. Garden City: Anchor Books, 1970, pp. 188-230.

Robb, Graham. "'Les Chats' de Baudelaire: Une Nouvelle Lecture." *Revue d'histoire littéraire de la France,* 85.6 (November-December 1985): 1002-1010.

————. *La Poésie de Baudelaire et la poésie française, 1838-1852.* Paris: Aubier, 1993.

Sartre, Jean-Paul. *Baudelaire.* Paris: Gallimard, 1947.

————. *Notebook for an Ethics.* Tr. David Pellauer. Chicago: University of Chicago Press, 1992.

Schultz, Gretchen M. "Baudelaire's Lesbian Connections." *Approaches to Teaching Baudelaire's* Flowers of Evil. Ed. Laurence M. Porter. New York: Modern Language Association, 2000, pp. 130-138.

Somville, Léon. "Le Poème 'Les Chats' de Baudelaire: Essai d'exégèse." *Études littéraires,* 5.2 (August 1972): 189-211.

Starobinski, Jean. "'Les Chats' de Charles Baudelaire." *Romanistische Zeitschrift für Literaturgeschichte,* 25.1-2 (2001): 105-122.

Vernant, Jean-Pierre and Pierre Vidal-Naquet. *Myth and Tragedy in Ancient Greece.* Tr. Janet Lloyd. New York: Zone Books 1988.

Viprey, Jean-Marie. *Dynamique du vocabulaire des* Fleurs du mal. Paris: Honoré Champion, 1997.

Wenk, Arthur B. *Claude Debussy and the Poets.* Berkeley: University of California Press, 1976.

Zalloua, Zahi. "Baudelaire and the Ethics of Demystification." *Tropos,* 26 (Spring 2000): 5-24.

Nicole Simek (essay date 2002)

SOURCE: Simek, Nicole. "Baudelaire and the Problematic of the Reader in *Les Fleurs du Mal*." *Pacific Coast Philology* 37 (2002): 43-57.

[*In the following essay, Simek argues that Baudelaire's poetry, in its relationship to the potential readers of* Les Fleurs du Mal, *presents a delicate tension between ethics, or morality, and aesthetics.*]

In his *Réflexions sur quelques-uns de mes contemporains* [*Reflections on Some of My Contemporaries*], Baudelaire praises Victor Hugo on many accounts, and identifies him as "un de ces esprits rares et providentiels qui opèrent, dans l'ordre littéraire, le salut de tous" [one of those rare and providential minds who effectuate, in the literary order, the salvation of all] (2: 131).[1] Unlike Hugo, however, in whose works politics and aesthetics become imbricated after 1830, Baudelaire seems here to separate this "literary order" from other spheres of influence, maintaining that Hugo brings about salvation in literature "comme d'autres dans l'ordre moral et d'autres dans l'ordre politique" [as some others do in the order of morality, and others in the order of politics] (2: 131). A few pages later Baudelaire nu-

ances this description, though, explaining that Hugo does have a moral impact on the reader, but that in his poetry "[il s'agit] d'une morale inspirée qui se glisse, invisible, dans la matière poétique [. . .]. La morale n'entre pas dans cet art à titre de but; elle s'y mêle et s'y confond comme dans la vie elle-même. Le poète est moraliste sans le vouloir, par abondance et plénitude de nature" [(it is a matter) of an inspired morality that slips invisibly into the poetic material (. . .). Morals do not enter this art as an intended objective; they mix with it and blend into it as in life itself. The poet is a moralist without wanting to be one, by abundance and plenitude of nature] (2: 137). The "poet" of this last line refers to Hugo himself, but the shift from the proper name to a general designation permits a conflation of Hugo and the different, ideal poet that Baudelaire intends to be. This fusion is striking in this passage because it seems to reflect Baudelaire's position at the junction between two opposing views of art: that supported by Hugo (that art should fulfill a social or moral function), and that of Gautier's *art pour l'art,* a "useless" art focused on form alone, destined for the small number of readers capable of appreciating it.

Here art is at once a salvation, but a limited one, moral, yet not determined by moral goals. Such a relationship is possible, Baudelaire explains elsewhere in his writings (and in his essay on Gautier in particular), through a notion of *correspondences.* Valorizing the poet who refuses to seek "le Vrai" and "le Bien" [the True and the Good] (which, he says, find their proper place in the distinct realms of science and morality, not poetry), and who devotes himself instead to "le Beau," the "but exclusif du Goût" [the Beautiful, the exclusive goal of Taste] (2: 112), Baudelaire emphasizes that poetry affects the realm of morality through its *correspondence* to it, by leading one to consider "la Terre et ses spectacles comme un aperçu, comme une *correspondance* du Ciel" [the Earth and her spectacles like a glimpse, or a *correspondence,* of Heaven] (2: 113-14).

If Baudelaire appears to reconcile Hugo's and Gautier's viewpoints in his theoretical criticism, his poetry displays unresolved tensions between the two, in particular concerning the potential reception of his work. While Gautier and the Parnassian poets who followed his lead emphasized their distance from the public, Baudelaire maintains a more ambivalent relationship with his readers,[2] questioning their capacity to receive poetry yet attempting to produce some sort of change within them. A closer examination of this relationship, taking *Les Fleurs du mal* [*Flowers of Evil*] as a foundation, and an exploration of how the collection is organized will help elucidate the stakes involved in Baudelaire's adoption of various positions with respect to his reading public(s), including his fellow writers. Beginning with Walter Benjamin's study of experience and the reception of the lyric in *Les Fleurs du mal,* I will then draw on Pierre Bourdieu's sociological analyses, in order to offer a critical assessment of Baudelaire's contribution to the development of lyric poetry and its audience in the second half of the nineteenth century.

Walter Benjamin begins his essay "On Some Motifs in Baudelaire" by noting that the "climate for lyric poetry" in France was becoming "increasingly inhospitable" in the mid-nineteenth century due to lyric poetry's lack of "rapport with the experience of its readers" (Benjamin 155-56). While examining Baudelaire's particular response to this crisis, Benjamin concentrates his study on the material conditions affecting reception, attributing the disjunction of lyric poetry and its readers to "a change in the structure of their experience" brought about by the industrialization of modern society. Drawing on the conceptions of trauma and memory set forth in Freud's *Beyond the Pleasure Principle,*[3] Benjamin argues that modern life is marked by shocks which, over time, lead to the buildup of automated responses or defense mechanisms against stimuli; the more effective these mechanisms are, "the less do [. . .] impressions enter experience [*Erfahrung*], tending to remain in the sphere of a certain hour in one's life [*Erlebnis*]" (163). Impressions can no longer be registered, or integrated into a meaningful whole grasped through memory. Instead, rapidly arriving stimuli are lived as momentary, passing sensations, briefly present to consciousness but never processed. The modern man in the crowd experiences [*erlebt*] life as does the assembly-line worker: as a series of unintegrated shocks. Benjamin goes on to explain the *Spleen et idéal* [*Spleen and Ideal*] cycle of *Les Fleurs du mal* in light of this absence or loss of experience which characterizes modern life: the *idéal* represents the aspiration to a reintegrated whole and "supplies the power of remembrance," which makes experience [*Erfahrung*] possible, whereas "the *spleen* musters the multitude of the seconds against it," recalling "the present state of collapse of that experience" (183-84).

Benjamin's interpretation helps elucidate this fundamental tension between *spleen et idéal* present throughout *Les Fleurs du mal* and particularly in the opening section of the *Fleurs du mal* collection, which bears the same title. The opening poems illustrate particularly well the aspiration of the lyric to the ideal and the hostile conditions surrounding its negative reception and "death" in modern times. Rather than suggesting a linear movement or chronological transition from one state to the other, however, Baudelaire maintains a tension between the two. Poems like **"Élévation," "Correspondances,"** or **"La Vie antérieure"** [**"Former Life"**], examples of this movement toward the ideal, are interspersed with portrayals of the decline of the lyric in poems such as **"L'Albatros"** [**"The Albatross"**], which depicts the poet's distance from a cruel

and uncomprehending public, or the two muse poems (**"La muse malade"** [**"The Sick Muse"**] and **"La muse vénale"** [**"The Muse for Hire"**]), in which poetic inspiration is compared first to a sickly woman pursued by nightmares of demons, then to a sorrowful "saltimbanque" forced to sell himself out—and thus to commodify his work—in a capitalist consumer society.

Each of these poems illustrates one of the two poles in the *spleen* and *idéal* opposition, while the tension between the two is maintained mainly through the juxtaposition of the poems with one another in the collection. **"Harmonie du soir"** [**"Evening Harmony"**], however, evokes at once both *le spleen* and *l'idéal,* further nuancing this opposition and bringing into question both lyric poetry's role in modernity in general and also Baudelaire's own particular poetic project. **"Harmonie du soir"** seems at first to celebrate the power of poetic language to represent experience, illustrating the correspondence of sights, sounds, and odors that Baudelaire had already described enthusiastically in his *Salon de 1846* [*Salon of 1846*]. In this piece of art criticism, Baudelaire explains the effects of changing light on color first through the metaphor of music. After describing the mutations of color values in a landscape over the course of a day, he concludes with the statement: "Cette grande symphonie du jour, qui est l'éternelle variation de la symphonie d'hier, cette succession de mélodies, où la variété sort toujours de l'infini, cet hymne compliqué s'appelle la couleur" [This great symphony of the day, which is the eternal variation of yesterday's symphony, this succession of melodies, where variety always springs from infinity, this complicated hymn is called color] (2: 423). On the following page, however, he expands on this reflection, suggesting that music not only provides a *metaphor* for color, but provokes a synesthetic *experience* in which correspondences between sight and other senses become fully manifest. It is Hoffmann, he writes, who best expressed this when he described music in these terms: "[L]orsque j'entends de la musique, [. . .] je trouve une analogie et une réunion intime entre les couleurs, les sons et les parfums. Il me semble que toutes ces choses sont engendrées par un même rayon de lumière, et qu'elles doivent se réunir dans un merveilleux concert" [(W)hen I hear music, (. . .) I find an analogy between, and an intimate uniting of, colors, sounds, and perfumes. It seems to me that all these things are engendered by one same ray of light, and that they must come together in a marvelous concert] (2: 425). Likewise poetry, through its music or its imagery, could then conceivably produce a synesthetic experience in its reader.

"Harmonie du soir" puts this hypothesis into practice, while paradoxically drawing an ambivalent conclusion. Besides evoking music in its title and content, the poem recalls a careful musical composition structurally as well. Arranged in four quatrains, the poem consists of ten alexandrines (of which six are repeated twice), makes extensive use of alliteration, and is rhythmically very regular (in only one line, 10 and repeated in 13, "Un cœur tendre, qui hait le néant vaste et noir" [a tender heart, which hates the huge black void] does the hemistich fall after the fourth rather than the sixth syllable). The repetitive rhyme scheme (abba baab abba baab) and the pattern by which the second and fourth lines of each stanza become the first and third lines of the next suggest that the poem could continue infinitely. Drawing on the past while constantly introducing new elements, never cyclically returning to its starting point, the poem creates a double movement of contraction and expansion, representing the "éternelle variation" of a theme described above. Ending after four stanzas, this infinite movement seems, on one side, to remain an unrealized potential. On another side, the poem also generates a different figuration of the infinite by suspending time at one moment, the "soir" [evening]. Baudelaire focuses on the *now*, employing present-tense verbs and vivid sensual descriptions (all five senses are solicited in the poem). The tension between the fixed and the mobile calls into question the poem's ability to freeze and transmit impressions, however. Nature is described as being or static: "le ciel *est* triste et beau" [the sky *is* sad and beautiful] (line 8, emphasis added); each "flower," though vibrant, is grounded by its "stem" (1-2). Nature is also described as becoming: "Chaque fleur s'*évapore*" [Each flower *exhales*] (line 2, emphasis added); and the death of the sun in the third stanza recalls the ephemerality of nature.

The reference to flowers compels the attentive reader to reflect on the *Fleurs du mal* as a poetic project intended to connect with a contemporary audience, as does the poem **"L'Ennemi" ["The Enemy"]**, for example, in which the narrator seems to comment on the collection even more directly when he poses the question: "Et qui sait si les fleurs nouvelles que je rêve / Trouveront dans ce sol lavé comme une grève / Le mystique aliment qui ferait leur vigeur?" [And who knows whether the new flowers I dream of / Will find in this soil washed like a shore / The mystic food which would create their strength?] (9-11). If the fertility of this "washed soil," or poetry's ability to survive in a world ravaged by violent storms, appears doubtful here, in **"Harmonie du soir"** Baudelaire examines more specifically poetry's capacity (or incapacity) to produce experience [*Erfahrung*] by fashioning memory out of impressions. Nature, described as a "temple" in **"Correspondances"** becomes a church in **"Harmonie du soir"**: flowers are likened to an "encensoir" [censer], the sky is a "reposoir" [altar], and the poet partakes in nature as in communion, incorporating as "souvenir" [memory] the sun, which, like the host, has been dipped in its own blood. The implications of this image remain uncertain, however. Interpreted as a critique of the lyric, the poem accentuates the absence of the sun in the verb "s'est noyé" [drowned], the only verb in the past tense in this poem, and the gap between this sun and the memory trace it leaves suggests that the poem is an instance of failed transubstantiation: the "souvenir" shines brilliantly, but is only an "ostensoir" [monstrance], a receptacle for the consecrated wafer, which fails to equal reality. ("Ostensoir," in the sixteenth century, meant "sundial," and here, like a sundial, it seems to capture only a shadow of the real.) The "melancoly" of the poem could then stem from the recognition of the disjunction between impressions and their poetic representation. Conversely, if the poem is read as celebrating the lyric, the "ostensoir" (whose Latin root means "to show") becomes an index to reality which suffices to preserve impressions as memory. According to this account, the melancholic tone of the poem could be attributed not to an inherent deficiency of lyric form as a possible vehicle for preserving experience, but to its limited ability to transmit experience to a wide, modern public. The sudden introduction of personal pronouns in the last line of the poem ("Ton souvenir en moi luit comme un ostensoir!" [Your memory shines in me like a monstrance!]), which breaks the potentially interminable pause created by the ellipses in the preceding line, draws attention to the particular or individual nature of this incorporation of memory. The poet himself seems to capture memory, yet the possible transmission of this capacity to his readers remains questionable.

While Benjamin's well-known analysis examines this distance between poet and reader through a reflection on the nature of experience, his formulation of the intensity of the melancholy or *spleen* provoked by this problematic relationship can be complemented and enriched through Bourdieu's reconstruction of the social space occupied by writers and artists under the Second Empire. The latter's studies point to what he terms a "structural subordination" by which these artists found themselves subjected to the increasingly powerful "industrialists and businessmen of colossal fortunes [. . .], uncultured *parvenus* ready to make both the power of money and a vision of the world profoundly hostile to intellectual things triumph within the whole society" (*Rules* 48). For this dominating class, supported by profits obtained from technical advancements in industries under its direction, as well as by the State, literature was at most a pleasure, but mainly a useless distraction from "serious" pursuits, an object of disinterest in which it was unwise to invest time and study (Bourdieu, *Rules* 49). Members of this upper bourgeoisie were not endowed through education (as, by contrast, the aristocracy had been) with what Bourdieu terms a *habitus* or disposition towards culture that would lead to viewing literary and artistic knowledge or skill as a valuable form of capital.⁴ Bourdieu cites two contemporary examples of the *doxa* characteristic of many industrialists of the period, André Siegfried, the son of a textiles entrepreneur, and André Motte, "one of the great patrons of the North" (48). The first, speaking of his father, notes:

> In [my father's] education, culture counted for nothing. To tell the truth, he never had intellectual culture and didn't worry about having any. He was educated, remarkably informed, knew everything he needed for acting on the spot, but the disinterested taste for things of the mind remained foreign to him.

(quoted in Bourdieu, *Rules* 48)

while the second writes:

> I repeat each day to my children that the title of *bachelier* [high school graduate] will never put a piece of bread into their mouths; that I sent them to school to allow them to taste the pleasures of intelligence, and to put them on their guard against all false doctrines, whether in literature, philosophy or history. But I add that it would be very dangerous for them to give themselves over to the pleasures of the mind.

(quoted in Bourdieu, *Rules* 48)

Through "the practice of having an official candidate in elections," Bourdieu continues, which functioned to confer political legitimacy on members of this "new" social group, strong ties were established between "the political world and the economic world," so that buying power and political consecration (through honors and pensions) and censure (aimed often at poetry, still too closely associated with the "major romantic battles") exerted a large, mutually reinforced hold over the literary field (*Rules* 49-50).

By raising the question of the poet's active response to this situation of domination by and disjunction from the public, a situation lived as a crisis, **"Harmonie du soir"** anticipates the "Tableaux parisiens" ["Parisian Scenes"] section (which Benjamin reads as a detailing of the conditions of modernity at the root of *spleen*) and also prepares a shift that occurs in "Tableaux parisiens," a shift toward a search for alternative lyric forms better adapted to the poet's (and poetry's) problematic position. This section, added to **Les Fleurs du mal** in 1861, opens with two poems, **"Paysage"** [**"Landscape"**] and **"Le Soleil"** [**"The Sun"**], which refer to "the poet at work," as Benjamin has noted (164). The tone of these two poems can be read at once as self-ironizing yet serious: the poet represents himself first as a Virgilian figure, composing "chastement mes églogues" [chastely composing my eclogues] (**"Paysage"** 1), and secondly as a fencer engaged in a sort of duel, "Flairant dans tous les coins les hasards de la rime, / Trébuchant sur les mots comme sur les pavés" [Sniffing out the hazards of rhyme in every corner / Tripping over words as over

pavement stones] (**"Le Soleil"** 6-7). Both poems emphasize the poet's elevation and solitude as well: in the first, the poet declares, "Je veux [. . .] / Coucher auprès du ciel, comme les astrologues" [I want (. . .) / to sleep close to the sky, like the astrologers] (1-2), while in the second, he enters into the fight alone—"Je vais m'exercer seul à ma fantasque escrime" [I go out to drill myself alone in my fantastic fencing match] (5). While these images can be taken as a parody of a romanticized view of the solitary writer-creator, through descriptive details the poems highlight the poet's urban situation as well, making clear that it is his present surroundings which provide the matter of his works.

Through his "Tableaux parisiens" section, then, Baudelaire illustrates and enacts his thesis, put forth as early as his 1846 essay "De l'héroïsme de la vie moderne" ["On the Heroism of Modern Life"], that poetry must recognize the particularity of modernity and the transitory nature of beauty. Baudelaire further develops this concept in **"Le Cygne"** [**"The Swan"**], pointedly addressing this poem to Victor Hugo, who, at the time (in 1859), was living in exile on the island of Guernsey. Three years earlier, Hugo had presented his *Contemplations* as a sort of memoir, a look back into the past, inviting readers to see mirrored in it the story of their own lives. In **"Le Cygne,"** Baudelaire problematizes this nostalgia, as well as the reader-poet relationship that works like *Les Contemplations* assume. As Benjamin puts it, this "image of the past, which Baudelaire regards as veiled by the tears of nostalgia," creates an impasse, "prevent[ing] our delight in the beautiful from ever being satisfied" (187). Baudelaire attempts to resolve this "crisis in perception," evoking sympathy for the potentially endless series of exiled figures who file through the narrator's mind in the poem, but criticizing a nostalgic yearning for that which is irrevocably lost ("ce qui ne se retrouve / Jamais, jamais!" [what can never / Be found again!] (45-46), insofar as this nostalgia can determine poetic expression. While Baudelaire seems to identify with the romantic poet in the "Spleen et idéal" section, comparing him favorably to an albatross, the "prince des nuées" ["prince of the clouds"] who finds himself "exilé sur le sol" ["exiled on the earth"] amidst an uncomprehending public, here his narrator adopts a critical, if not ironic, distance from this vision of the poet, and from Hugo in particular, represented in the swan. Though "sublime," the swan is also described as "ridiculous," and his desire to return to his past home, like that of Ovid's Icarus, to whom he is compared, appears condemned to frustration. The narrator, while drawing parallels between himself and the swan, is transfigured as a reader in this poem: a reader first of "le cygne," that is, of other poets and models of poetry, but also a reader of himself, and in particular of his "idéal" poems, suggested through the association of "le cygne" to its homonym "le signe" [the sign] and through coupling the latter with the forest image in the last stanza, which recalls the "forests of symbols" of the poem **"Correspondances."**

By positioning himself as a reader, Baudelaire might be read as extending a hand to the public, inviting his audience to identify with a narrator who has been put in their role. Although this gesture is not unusual in itself (Hugo makes a much more explicit claim to universality in *Les Contemplations,* where, in his preface, he declares "Homo sum" [2: 482]), it startles however through its contrast with **"Au Lecteur"** [**"To the Reader"**], the dedication to the *Fleurs du mal* collection, in which Baudelaire establishes an immediate but complex "text-reader relationship," as Ross Chambers writes (103). Throughout this dedication, Baudelaire emphasizes the unity of the poet and the reader by his repeated use of an inclusive "we" and the possessive "our," and the famous final line portrays the reader not only as resembling the writer ("mon semblable" [my likeness⁵]), but as his kin ("mon frère" [my brother]). However, verbal violence is performed on the reader through the process of defamiliarization to which he is paradoxically subjected when these lines of kinship are imposed accusingly from the very beginning of the poem. Vivid images and sensations assail the reader throughout. Satan is a chemist, vaporizing "le riche métal de notre volonté" [the rich metal of our will] (11), and a puppeteer pulling our strings, forcing us to descend into Hell "à travers des ténèbres qui puent" [through the darkness which smells rank] (16). No salvation seems possible in the first stanzas: the reader, likened to a "débauché pauvre" [lustful pauper] who devours "le sein martyrisé d'une antique catin" [the martyred breast of an aged whore] (18), takes pleasure in his sin, and, feeding his paradoxically "aimables remords" [polite remorse], runs gaily to the "chemin bourbeux" [muddy road] of evil (3, 7). The multiplication of plosive b's and p's in stanza 7 attack the reader through sound, as does the string of "monstres glapissants, hurlants, grognants" [monsters squealing, yelling, grunting] in stanza 8. In contrast, personified Ennui [Boredom], called a "monstre délicat" [delicate monster], menaces through *silence,* threatening to swallow up the world in a yawn. It is precisely because it is unremarkable that Ennui is "plus méchant" and "plus immonde" [more wicked and more foul] than these other creatures of the "ménagerie infâme de nos vices" [infamous menagerie of our vices (32-33): quietly, unnoticeably, Ennui overtakes the world more quickly than the rest. Yet by giving to Ennui corporeality—a yawning mouth and an "œil chargé d'un pleur involuntaire" [eye weeping an involuntary tear], the poet makes the invisible seen. "Monster" takes on its original etymological sense, and, so designated, it becomes a warning, reminding the reader not only of its danger ("delicate," it attracts insidiously), but also of its vulnerability ("delicate," it is also fragile). The poem's violent accusations attack

the "reader" in an attempt to force him into awareness of his apathy, much the way the narrator violently forces a beggar into action in Baudelaire's later prose poem "Assomons les pauvres!" ["Let's Beat Up the Poor!"].

Yet to what extent did Baudelaire believe in the efficacy of this procedure? Moreover, is the identity of his "lecteur" ever precisely defined? Drawing a parallel between the "reader" of the dedication to **Les Fleurs du mal** and the bourgeois "repu" [the "sated" bourgeois] addressed in *Salon de 1846,* it is doubtful that Baudelaire believed without question in the transformative capacity of his poetry, that is, it is unlikely that he hoped to be heard by a wide public or to produce any change within this audience. "C'est donc à vous, bourgeois," he concludes in his "Aux Bourgeois" ["To the Bourgeois"] introduction to the *Salon de 1846,* "que ce livre est naturellement dédié; car tout livre qui ne s'adresse pas à la majorité,—nombre et intelligence,—est un sot livre" [It is therefore to you, bourgeois, that this book is naturally dedicated; for any book which does not address itself to the majority,—multitude and intelligence,—is a foolish book] (2: 417), but the mocking tone of this piece, coupled with the unflattering portrait of the bourgeoisie's desire for self-satisfaction seems to reveal that Baudelaire views any attempt to address this class as a constraint, an undesired necessity, even a hopeless cause. The bourgeois' intractability persists as a theme in Baudelaire's later works as well: as Debarati Sanyal has noted, in the prose poem **"Une Mort héroïque"** [**"A Heroic Death"**], the "bewitched and credulous public" is portrayed not only as "mindless," but as a group of "unwitting accomplices to the perpetuation of absolute power, aesthetic or political (317-18). Under the Second Empire, this means that the public becomes complicit with a despotic and repressive regime, a fact, continues Sanyal, which provoked "rage" in Baudelaire (318).

What seems through an examination of **"Au lecteur"** and **"Le Cygne"** to represent an evolving attitude toward the public on the part of Baudelaire can then be reread as a vacillation between two targeted publics, a vacillation that stems from Baudelaire's particular position in the literary field at this specific moment in the field's history. Following Bourdieu's argument further, with the rise of capitalism in France and the development of a "veritable cultural industry" came the very possibility for the literary field to gain increasing autonomy from the dominant political and religious powers, met by writers with varying reactions toward their role as producers of symbolic goods in this new economy (113). Consequently, Bourdieu continues,

> By an apparent paradox, as the art market began to develop, writers and artists found themselves able to affirm the irreducibility of the work of art to the status

of a simple article of merchandise and, at the same time, the singularity of the intellectual and artistic condition.

(113-14)

Defining themselves in opposition to journalists and authors who produced works intended to sell to a large public, writers like Hugo,[6] Gautier, and Baudelaire contributed to the development of a field of restricted production within the literary field, that is, a field of literature destined for a small readership of other poets and novelists, their peers, whose works became increasingly distanced from those produced for the mass public as the literary field gained increasing autonomy; when Mallarmé was to propose his "Faune" ["Faun"] to the Théâtre Français in 1865, it would be well-received by de Banville and Coquelin, but rejected for the stage, as Mallarmé explains, with the recognition that "cela n'intéresserait que les poètes" [it would interest only poets] (207). These words attest to and exemplify this split in the reception of literature.

Dedicated to Hugo and, moreover, implicitly engaging Hugo in a dialogue over specific aesthetic concerns, Baudelaire's **"Le Cygne"** could then be interpreted as a work intended mainly for this restricted public of peers, whereas **"Au lecteur,"** addressed to a bourgeois reader similar to the one evoked in *Salon de 1846,* manifests Baudelaire's distaste for the mass public of complacent consumers. Furthermore, the addition of the "Tableaux parisiens" section to the *Fleurs du mal* after the trial and censure of several of its pieces (confirming the public's suspected incapacity to receive the work) reinforces this reading. However, returning to the two poems in question, it can be noted that if the harsh attack of **"Au lecteur"** contrasts with the softened attitude toward the reader Baudelaire adopts in **"Le Cygne,"** the difference is perhaps mainly one of degree: in both instances, what is at stake is the reader's perception, and in both cases Baudelaire employs the device of defamiliarization in an attempt to change this outlook.[7] If **"Au lecteur"** focuses on bringing about awareness of **"Ennui,"** in **"Le Cygne,"** the reader's perceptions of memory, history, and myth are all called into question. Baudelaire presents a modern Paris whose "forme [. . .] / Change plus vite, hélas! que le cœur d'un mortel" [form (. . .) / Changes more quickly, alas, than the heart of a man] (7-8), and whose mutating architecture, seen as disconnected pieces ("ce camp de baraques, / Ces tas de chapiteaux ébauchés et de fûts" [that camp of booths, / The piles of rough-hewn capitals and shafts] (9-10), has lost its sense, if, indeed, it ever had one. Unlike the Paris of Hugo's "A l'Arc de Triomphe" ["To the Arch of Triumph"], whose monuments become legible accounts of history once a poetic representation of their destruction has revealed their beauty (1: 936-48), Baudelaire's present-day Paris is severed from a historical past: rather than recollecting

the Empire to which it was designed to be a testament, the new Carrousel evokes mythical figures (the swan and Andromache). The "bric-à-brac confus" [crowded bric-à-brac] of the modern city is only comprehensible when it is allegorized in stanza 8, where "memories" become paradoxically more material ("plus lourds que des rocs" [heavier than rocks]) than the "blocks" of Paris' buildings, which have, conversely, become emblems. Memory here is not so much a process of retrieving past events as of creating associations, of reconfiguring the present. Both that which fertilizes and that which, "fertile," is labored, memory self-sufficiently cultivates itself.

Nostalgic memory, on the other hand, fails to sustain those who "tettent la Douleur comme une bonne louve" [suckle Grief as if she were a kind wolf] in stanza 12. Alluding to the legendary foundation of Rome in this line, Baudelaire suggests that the modern world is no longer nourished by myth and that modern poetry (referred to by the use of the word "flowers," which, here again, recalls the poetic project of the collection) cannot sustain itself if it remains fixated on a lost past. But the allegory which remains the only possible connection between literature and memory, or experience, is a personal allegory, underscored by the words "tout *pour moi* devient allégorie" in stanza 8 [everything becomes an allegory *for me*] (emphasis added) and by the possessive "my" which qualifies the "dear memories" of the following line. The poem attempts to initiate its readers into the process of perceiving allegorically, rather than presenting them with any resulting, universally valid vision that they should merely assimilate or consume.

In this sense, it would seem that **"Le Cygne"** both parallels and reworks the relationship established with the reader in **"Au lecteur."** If the new, persuasive tone of **"Le Cygne,"** as well as the call to a search for alternative lyric forms that characterizes the "Tableaux parisiens" section, implies a shift in audience, Baudelaire's placement of this section at the center of the *Fleurs du mal* (rather than publishing the poems as a separate volume, for example) reinforces its ties to the collection, re-inscribing the "new" text-reader relationship in an already established context. While Baudelaire seems to suspend his bitterness toward an uncomprehending public in **"Le Cygne,"** or rather, seems to disregard this public,[8] the similar strategy of "attack" employed here points to the fluidity of a field *in the process of formation.* The terms "mass" and "restricted" are convenient descriptors of trends of reception within the literary field, but should not mask the way in which a field is experienced by whoever participates in it, that is, as a *continuum* between constantly shifting positions and relations. Baudelaire's (softened) "attack" on other writers also recalls his position as a *still to be consecrated* poet,[9] struggling not only to impose a particular aesthetics, but, at the same time, to actually *forge* a receptive audience for this aesthetics, to create a certain type of reader not yet fully in existence. Baudelaire's 1868 **"Épigraphe pour un livre condamné" ["Epigraph for a Condemned Book"]**, which reworks the **"Au lecteur"** dedication to the 1857 edition, can be read precisely as recalling the uncertainty which Baudelaire faced in this attempt. Suggesting that his work can reach only certain readers—those who have studied their "rhétorique / Chez Satan, le rusé doyen" [rhetoric / With Satan, that wily dean] (5-6) and those who "suffer," who share with him, like the woman of **"A Une Passante" ["To a Passer-By"]**, a sense of the pain of modern life—the poem raises doubts about the positive reception of the text. From the hyperbolic accusations of **"Au lecteur,"** Baudelaire moves to threat (". . . Sinon, je te maudis!" [. . . Otherwise, I curse you!]), the force of which is problematized through the self-ironizing overtones of the poem. Contrary to **"A Celle qui est trop gaie" ["To Her Who is Too Gay"]**, one of the works condemned by the tribunal in 1857, where the poet's attack on the complacent reader becomes literally violent as he dreams of infusing his "venom" into the "joyful flesh" of a "too" happy woman, **"Épigraphe"** renounces depictions of such fantasy, emphasizing instead the poet's powerlessness before such a "peaceful" reader:

Lecteur paisible et bucolique,
Sobre et naïf homme de bien,
Jette ce livre saturnien,
Orgiaque et mélancholique.

Si tu n'as fait ta rhétorique
Chez Satan, le rusé doyen,
Jette! tu n'y comprendrais rien
Ou tu me croirais hystérique.

Mais si, sans se laisser charmer,
Ton œil sait plonger dans les gouffres,
Lis-moi, pour apprendre à m'aimer:

Âme curieuse qui souffres
Et vas cherchant ton paradis,
Plains-moi! . . . Sinon, je te maudis!

(124)

[Peaceful bucolic reader,
Sober naïve man of good will,
Throw away this saturnine
Orgiastic and melancholy book.

Unless you have studied your rhetoric
With Satan, that wily dean,
Throw it away! You would not understand it,
Or you would believe me hysterical.

But if, without allowing them to be spellbound,
Your eyes can see into abysses,
Read me, in order to learn to love me;

Curious soul who suffer
And are looking for your paradise,
Pity me! . . . Otherwise, I curse you!]

(113)

Despite this uncertainty, the poet does not renounce the possibility of communicating with the reader; the epigraph, however, might be directed more to a reader still to come, one yet to be formed (or persuaded) through Baudelaire's violent, performative rhetoric.

From a later perspective it is perhaps relatively easy to trace a general progression of the literary field toward autonomy during the 1800s, but what Baudelaire's work reminds us of particularly well is the continual redefinition of this field that was taking place throughout this period and the varying degrees of uncertainty (higher in Baudelaire's particular case, for example) of any writer's attaining a position of consecration, that is, of reaching the dominant reading public in the literary field or, moreover, of bringing such a receptive public *into existence.* If literature remained subject to external pressures (to censorship from the state in particular), it was no less subject to internal shifts, as writers like Baudelaire sought to define and impose their varying visions of the poet's role in literature and society. While the stances taken by Baudelaire at particular moments can be pinpointed in his literary criticism, his poetry, replete with ambiguities, irony, and continually shifting attitudes in relation to his public, reminds us of the contested boundaries of the literary field in the second half of the nineteenth century. It is precisely Baudelaire's figuration of an ambivalent attitude toward his audience, making his self-fashioning as a poet inextricably linked to the fashioning of his readers, which testifies to the seriousness with which he regarded questions of aesthetics, ethics, and literature's relation to the social.[10]

Notes

1. Charles Baudelaire, *Œuvres complètes.* Unless otherwise noted, all citations refer to this edition. Translations of Baudelaire's "Au lecteur," "Harmonie du soir," "L'Albatross," "Correspondances," "Le Cygne," "Épigraphe pour un livre condamné," and "De l'Héroïsme de la Vie moderne" are taken from Wallace Fowlie, *Flowers of Evil and Other Works/Les Fleurs du mal et Œuvres choisies.* All other translations are mine.

2. This, despite his overt dedication of the *Fleurs du mal* collection to Gautier:

Au poète impeccable
au parfait magicien ès lettres françaises
à mon très vénéré
maître et ami
Théophile Gautier

avec les sentiments
de la plus profonde humilité
je dédie
ces fleur maladives
C. B.
[To the impeccable poet
to the perfect magician of French literature
to my very dear and greatly venerated
master and friend
Théophile Gautier
with the expression of my most profound humility
I dedicate
these sickly flowers
C. B.]

(3, my translation)

3. See in particular chapter 5 of Michael G. Levine's *Writing Through Repression* for a discussion of Benjamin's reading and inflection of Freud.

4. *Habitus,* a key term in Bourdieu's thought, can be defined as "a system of acquired dispositions functioning on the practical level as categories of perception and assessment or as classificatory principles as well as being the organizing principles of [an agent's] action" (Bourdieu, *In Other Words* 13). Bourdieu develops this notion as a tool for understanding the practical sense or logic generating an individual's actions, interests, and tastes, a tool for conceptually overcoming the dichotomy between "a structuralism without subject [for example Althusserian Marxism] and the philosophy of the subject [for example Sartrean phenomenology]" (*In Other Words* 10). *Doxa* (in my next sentence) is a "practical belief" in the presuppositions of a given field; it is closely related to the notion of *habitus*: "Doxa is the relationship of immediate adherence that is established in practice between a *habitus* and the field to which it is attuned, the pre-verbal taking-for-granted of the world that flows from practical sense" (Bourdieu, *The Logic of Practice* 68). See chapters 3 ("Structures, *Habitus,* Practices") and 4 ("Belief and the Body") in *The Logic of Practice* for a more elaborate account of these terms.

5. My translation.

6. While I stress above the points of contention between Hugo and Baudelaire (Hugo's more openly didactic bent in matters of morality or politics, for instance), Hugo's commitment to the literariness of poetry (to the formal aspects of literature in general) places him, along with Baudelaire, in the emerging literary avant-garde, when contrasted with writers of "facile" literary forms (journalistic writing and serialized novels, for example) intended mainly to reap immediate economic profits. Although Hugo wishes to affect his public, he does not betray his poetic vision, refusing to adapt his poetry to suit the tastes of

this public. Hugo recognizes with frustration the difficulties encountered in his attempt to reach the reader in his preface to *Les Contemplations*: "On se plaint quelquefois des écrivains qui disent moi. Parleznous de nous, leur crie-t-on. Hélas! quand je vous parle de moi, je vous parle de vous. Comment ne le sentez-vous pas? Ah! insensé, qui crois que je ne suis pas toi!" [People sometimes complain about writers who say I. Tell us about us, people cry out to them. Alas! When I speak to you of myself, I speak to you of yourselves. How is it that you do not feel this? Ah! Senseless reader, who believe that I am not you!] (2: 482).

7. See Zahi Zalloua's "Baudelaire and the Ethics of Demystification" for an insightful discussion of Baudelaire's use of defamiliarization as an ethical tool.

8. It is this indifference towards the mass public, or an increasingly exclusive concern, in Bourdieu's terms, for the verdict of artistic peers that marks later writers.

9. Consecration, for Bourdieu, is the process of conferring legitimacy or authority on an individual or group through institutions (such as academies, universities, political institutions, honor societies and other social organizations).

10. I would like to thank Suzanne Nash for her helpful comments on earlier drafts of this paper.

Works Cited

Baudelaire, Charles. *Œuvres complètes.* Pléiade. Paris: Gallimard, 1975.

Benjamin, Walter. "On Some Motifs in Baudelaire." *Illuminations.* Trans. Harry Zohn. New York: Schocken Books, 1968. 155-200.

Bourdieu, Pierre. *In Other Words: Essays Towards a Reflexive Sociology.* Trans. Matthew Adamson. Cambridge: Polity Press, 1990.

———. *The Logic of Practice.* Trans. Richard Nice. Stanford: Stanford UP, 1990.

———. "The Market of Symbolic Goods."*The Field of Cultural Production.* New York: Columbia UP, 1993. 112-141.

———. *The Rules of Art: Genesis and Structure of the Literary Field.* Trans. Susan Emanuel. Cambridge: Polity Press, 1996.

Chambers, Ross. "Poetry in the Asiatic Mode: Baudelaire's 'Au Lecteur.'" *Yale French Studies* 74 (1988): 97-116.

Fowlie, Wallace. *Flowers of Evil and Other Works / Les Fleurs du mal et Œuvres choisies.* New York: Dover Publications, 1964.

Hugo, Victor. *Oeuvres poétiques.* 3 vols. Pléiade. Paris: Gallimard, 1964.

Levine, Michael G. *Writing Through Repression: Literature, Censorship, Psycho-analysis.* Baltimore: Johns Hopkins UP, 1994.

Mallarmé, Stéphane. *Poésies.* Paris: Gallimard, 1992.

Sanyal, Debarati. "Conspiratorial Poetics: Baudelaire's 'Une Mort héroïque.'" *Nineteenth-Century French Studies* 27.3-4 (1999): 305-22.

Zalloua, Zahi. "Baudelaire and the Ethics of Demystification." *Tropos* 26 (2000): 5-24.

John McCann (essay date 2004)

SOURCE: McCann, John. "Heroism or Villainy in *Les Fleurs du Mal.*" In *Heroism and Passion in Literature: Studies in Honour of Moya Longstaffe,* edited by Graham Gargett, pp. 145-56. Amsterdam: Rodopi, 2004.

[*In the following essay, McCann addresses the content of* Les Fleurs du Mal *in light of the poem's censorship and the question of Baudelaire's potential "heroism" in writing a work that so revolutionized contemporary aesthetics as to necessitate its censorship by the state.*]

À celle qui est trop gaie

Ta tête, ton geste, ton air
Sont beaux comme un beau paysage;
Le rire joue en ton visage
Comme un vent frais dans un ciel clair.

Le passant chagrin que tu frôles
Est ébloui par la santé
Qui jaillit comme une clarté
De tes bras et de tes épaules.

Les retentissantes couleurs
Dont tu parsèmes tes toilettes
Jettent dans l'esprit des poètes
L'image d'un ballet de fleurs.

Ces robes folles sont l'emblème
De ton esprit bariolé;
Folle dont je suis affolé,
Je te hais autant que je t'aime!

Quelquefois dans un beau jardin
Où je traînais mon atonie,
J'ai senti, comme une ironie,
Le soleil déchirer mon sein;

Et le printemps et la verdure
Ont tant humilié mon cœur,
Que j'ai puni sur une fleur
L'insolence de la Nature.

Ainsi je voudrais, une nuit,
Quand l'heure des voluptés sonne,

Vers les trésors de ta personne,
Comme un lâche, ramper sans bruit,

Pour châtier ta chair joyeuse,
Pour meurtrir ton sein pardonné
Et faire à ton flanc étonné
Une blessure large et creuse,

Et, vertigineuse douceur!
À travers ces lèvres nouvelles,
Plus éclatantes et plus belles,
T'infuser mon venin, ma sœur![1]

(For the woman who is too gay

Your head, your movements, your attitude
Are beautiful as a beautiful landscape;
Laughter plays across your face
Like a fresh breeze in a clear sky.

You lightly brush a passing sadness
And it is dazzled by the well-being
That gushes like a bright light
From your arms and shoulders.

The eye-catching colours
That spring from your clothing
Create in the minds of poets
The image of a ballet of flowers.

The mad disorder of these clothes
Is the emblem of your multicoloured spirit;
You are mad and I am mad for you,
I hate you as much as I love you!

Sometimes in a beautiful garden
Where I would drag along my listlessness,
I have felt the sun pierce
My breast like a bitter irony;

And the Spring and the greenness
Have so humiliated my heart,
That I have taken revenge on a flower
For the insolence of nature.

Thus, one night, I should love,
When the hour of voluptuousness chimes,
To creep like a coward up to the treasures
Of your person, without making a sound,

To punish your joyful flesh,
To damage your breast freed from sin,
And to inflict on your startled belly,
A large and deep wound,

And then feel the dizzying sweetness
As through these new lips,
More brilliant and more beautiful,
I inject my poison, oh my sister!)

Heroism, like villainy, may be defined as an indicator of the regard in which one is held. Heroes are perceived as being good people. However, it is usually a judgment arrived at by considering a selection of the actions of the person concerned. Thus, to be judged a hero, some actions are promoted at the expense of others, and the same is true of villains. It is as though a person's life has been broken down into constituent aspects and then reconstituted on the basis of some of them. The result is that good qualities are enhanced. Villains have their bad points stressed. Heroes and villains are made, not born. If a hero has some defects, these are construed as throwing into relief fundamental goodness. Similarly, the villain may have some admirable qualities but again these are perceived not to alter our basic judgment.

Although we may know that real people are more complex than this, we persist in wanting to divide humanity into heroes and villains, creating a special relationship with the former, as though some of the regard we ourselves bestow on them may be reflected back on us for being the only ones capable of truly appreciating them. In 1857 Baudelaire was tried and found guilty of offending public decency in *Les Fleurs du Mal* (*The Flowers of Evil*). This judgement is deemed perverse by many modern readers, who feel that it shows his contemporaries' foolish lack of understanding of Baudelaire's genius. The original trial may have found against him but nowadays it is the judges who are likely to be censured, as though readers today have some superior grasp of morality, one which aligns itself with Baudelaire who thereby becomes a heroic pioneer in such matters, as Sartre argues:

> Mais, ne l'oublions pas, c'est en faisant le Mal consciemment et *par sa conscience dans le Mal* que Baudelaire donne son adhésion au Bien.

> (But let us not forget that it is through doing Evil consciously and *conscientiously* that Baudelaire shows his support for Good.)[2]

It is not just that his contemporaries were wrong about him but also that what they deemed wrong was in fact right, and vice versa. That is why the breach of the rules has to be knowing rather than inadvertent. Baudelaire's supposed greater awareness overturns the moral basis on which a society rests. It is revolutionary. Sartre, by his argument, is legitimising Baudelaire's position but is, by association, deriving legitimacy from it, aided by the fact that, by the time of writing, most people would have little sympathy with the judgment handed down against *Les Fleurs du Mal.* Consequently, for Sartre, as for Sartre's Baudelaire, deliberately flouting the conventions of what constitutes goodness can further the cause of right. To do so in the face of public displeasure, to be dragged in front of the courts, is a tribute to the bravery of the hero. It confirms his heroism and provides an opportunity for later vindication and for subsequent generations to demonstrate their superior wisdom.

However, Graham Robb has remarked that

> Tout poète *maudit* exerce une puissante attraction: une fois traîné devant les tribunaux, il sera condamné à être défendu éternellement par des avocats littéraires. En

découvrant l'histoire du procès, le lecteur moderne peut se féliciter de ses vues éclairées, mais au risque de faire preuve d'une pudeur, tout aussi nuisible que l'autre. Depuis plus d'un siècle, *Les Fleurs du Mal* se purifient dans l'air supérieur de la critique académique.[3]

(Every *accursed* poet exercises a powerful attraction: once he has been dragged before the courts, he will be condemned to be forever defended by literary lawyers. On uncovering the history of the trial, the modern reader can congratulate himself on his enlightened views, but at the risk of demonstrating a censoriousness that is just as harmful as that of his predecessors. For more than a century the *Fleurs du Mal* have been purified in the superior air(s) of academic criticism.)

What Robb means can be illustrated by *À celle qui est trop gaie.* This was one of the poems which the trial judges found to be obscene, imposing a fine of 300 francs, later reduced to 50. As Pichois points out in his note on the trial, subsequent generations disagreed. A law passed in 1946 'déchargeait Baudelaire et ses éditeurs du délit d'outrage à la morale publique et aux bonnes mœurs' ('exculpated Baudelaire and his publishers of the crime of offending public decency and morality') (*OC* [*Œuvres complètes*], I, p. 1183). No doubt many would see this as the long overdue righting of a wrong and the victory of common sense and freedom of speech, the vindication of Baudelaire's heroic stance against the hypocritical pieties of his age.

However, before rejecting the official condemnation as being unenlightened, we should examine the text, for there are attitudes expressed in it that would not find approval in progressive circles nowadays and would indeed be deemed offensive:

> Ainsi je voudrais, une nuit,
> Quand l'heure des voluptés sonne,
> Vers les trésors de ta personne,
> Comme un lâche, ramper sans bruit,
>
> Pour châtier ta chair joyeuse,
> Pour meurtrir ton sein pardonné
> Et faire à ton flanc étonné
> Une blessure large et creuse,
>
> Et, vertigineuse douceur!
> À travers ces lèvres nouvelles,
> Plus éclatantes et plus belles,
> T'infuser mon venin, ma sœur!

> Thus, one night, I should love,
> When the hour of voluptuousness chimes,
> To creep like a coward up to the treasures
> Of your person, without making a sound,
>
> To punish your joyful flesh,
> To damage your breast freed from sin,
> And to inflict on your startled belly,
> A large and deep wound,
>
> And then feel the dizzying sweetness
> As through these new lips,

More brilliant and more beautiful,
I inject my poison, oh my sister!)

Sensitivities have changed. It is disturbing to find violence against women expressed in such a fashion. The domination of the woman by the protagonist is linked to her gender. The lips cut in her flesh recall not just the mouth but also the vagina and the *venin* carries suggestions of a venereal disease. Such an idea is denied by the *Note de l'éditeur* (*Publisher's Note*) that follows the poem:

Les juges ont cru découvrir un sens à la fois sanguinaire et obscène dans les deux dernières stances. La gravité du Recueil excluait de pareilles *plaisanteries.* Mais *venin* signifiant spleen ou mélancolie, était une idée trop simple pour les criminalistes.

Que leur interprétation syphilitique leur reste sur la conscience.

(*OC,* I, p. 157)

(The judges thought they had uncovered a meaning that was both bloody and obscene in the last two stanzas. The seriousness of the Collection ruled out such jokes. But *venin* (poison) meaning depression or melancholy was too simple an idea for the criminal experts.

Let their syphilitic interpretation be on their own consciences.)

This is a complex gloss on the poem. It stands on the edge of the main text, a paratext that creates a (false) intertext for, as Pichois points out:

Il y a lieu de remarquer que ni le substitut du procureur dans son réquisitoire, ni les juges dans le libellé du jugement n'ont proposé une «interprétation syphilitique»: celle-ci est du fait de Baudelaire! À qui fut seulement reprochée une atteinte à la morale publique.

(*OC,* I, p. 1133)

(It should be noted that neither the deputy public prosecutor in his closing speech nor the judges in their written judgment put forward a 'syphilitic interpretation': the latter is entirely due to Baudelaire! He was merely accused of outraging public morals.)

Baudelaire is seeking to control the reader's response. He is in fact guiding us towards a judgment on the judges by means of a testimony that is false—in Baudelaire's note they are not allowed to speak on their own behalf, but are represented by their prosecutor. In a further twist, by drawing attention to the obscene and violent meanings or, as Pichois claims, inventing or elaborating on them, Baudelaire is ensuring that they are very much in our minds. Thus at one level the note is being ironic, making fun of the legal profession's tendency to take things literally. On the other hand, ironic or not, it draws attention to the complex interaction of literal and metaphorical meanings.

What is so objectionable is not just the fact that the woman is imagined being attacked but the exultant language used to describe it in the last quatrain (quoted above). Up until that point, the attack could be described as the outcome of the speaker's sense of his own inadequacy, his *atonie,* when faced with a woman who has the power to lighten sorrow and inspire poets. The first quatrain shows a woman who is possessed of what the speaker lacks:

Ta tête, ton geste, ton air
Sont beaux comme un beau paysage;
Le rire joue en ton visage
Comme un vent frais dans un ciel clair.

(*OC,* I, p. 156)

(Your head, your movements, your attitude
Are beautiful as a beautiful landscape;
Laughter plays across your face
Like a fresh breeze in a clear sky.)

The images in the first line demonstrate a progression. *Ta tête* is physical appearance, *ton geste* is movement animated by her mind or spirit, while *ton air* is her spiritual essence. The woman is unconditionally beautiful in body and spirit, as the repetition of the adjective in the second line indicates. The image of the cool breeze in the clear sky is suggestive of a mixture of coolness and warmth that achieves a complementary wholeness and rightness. This rightness is apprehended by touch rather than sight and, although colour is an important element in the description of the woman, it is her ability to affect other senses that gives her portrait its strength. Thus the *retentissantes couleurs* of the third quatrain takes a visual image and gives it an aural dimension and indeed the adjective chosen makes it verge on the tactile.

Technically brilliant, the depiction of the woman is not entirely positive. The *trop* in the title casts a forward shadow. It evokes a sense of unease, stemming from a realisation that the speaker finds her joy overpowering: he feels threatened by it. Furthermore, although the woman is referred to as *tu* in the second and third quatrains and as *te* in the fourth (twice), the majority of references to her are metonymic, the part standing for the whole: *ta tête, ton geste, ton air, ton visage, tes bras, tes épaules, tes toilettes* and *ton esprit.* Thus, even in these quatrains, before the slashing of the later quatrains, the woman is, as it were, dismembered. Violence against women is inherent in the way they are thought about.

The only reference to the woman as a whole person, apart from the second person pronouns, is *folle* in the fourth stanza:

Ces robes folles sont l'emblême
De ton esprit bariolé;

Folle dont je suis affolé,
Je te hais autant que je t'aime!

(*OC,* I, p. 157)

(The mad disorder of these clothes is the emblem
Of your multicoloured spirit;
You are mad and I am mad for you,
I hate you as much as I love you!)

It originates in the description of her dress. What is applied initially to a non-essential attribute is appropriated to describe the person. This adjective-become-noun is her essence and all other qualities are subordinate. The word stands at the beginning of the third line, an object placed before its verb and acquiring extra emphasis. That verb is *je suis affolé* and here the echo (or extension) suggests that it is the woman's madness that has infected the speaker, a suggestion reinforced by the use of the passive. If at the end of the poem it is the woman who is the passive victim of the speaker's violence, here it is he who is supposed to be the victim.

She is not explicitly blamed, however. The inferences are subtly implied, crude control unnecessary. Baudelaire's power over words is described by Rivière:

> Sur les poèmes le poète ne cesse d'exercer son empire. Il les mène, lents et suivis. Il fléchit à son gré leur intention. Il les dirige par l'influence de son goût. Il aime appeler à son service les mots imprévus,—on pourrait presque dire saugrenus. Mais c'est pour réduire aussitôt leur étrangeté, pour faire couler sur elle une harmonie, pour modérer l'écart que par leur caprice il ouvrit. Comme ceux qui se sentent parfaitement maîtres de ce qu'ils veulent dire, il cherche d'abord les termes les plus éloignés; puis il les ramène, il les apaise, il leur infuse une propriété qu'on ne leur connaissait pas.
>
> Il est *poète,* c'est-à-dire qu'il façonne des vers comme un ouvrage audacieux, utile et bien calculé.[4]

(The poet ceaselessly exercises dominion over his poems. He painstakingly takes them in the direction he wishes. Their intention is submitted to his will. His taste directs them. He presses into service unusual words—one might almost call them crazy. But it is in order to reduce their strangeness, to pour a smooth harmony over them, to lessen the gap that through their wilfulness he opened. Like those who feel in complete command of what they wish to say, he first looks for the most outlandish expressions; then he reins them in, softens them and gives them a sense of propriety one did not know they had.

He is a *poet,* that is, he fashions verse like an audacious, functional and well thought-out artwork.)

An example of this is to be found in the ***Correspondances***:

> Il est des parfums frais comme des chairs d'enfants,
> Doux comme les hautbois, verts comme les prairies.

(*OC,* I, p. 11)

(There are perfumes that are fresh as children's flesh,
Sweet as oboes, green as prairies.)

Although they are not the rich, complex perfumes of decay that transport senses and spirit and which end the poem in triumph, these perfumes turn out to be just as fascinating since they testify to the power of Baudelaire's language to impose meaning. In the two lines quoted above, three adjectives are used to describe the *parfums*. These adjectives are in turn modified by the nouns or (in the first case) the noun-phrase that follows. The adjective *doux* stands out at the beginning of its line. On reflection, its application to oboes is problematical because the sound of the oboe is piercing. It can have a plangent quality, a bitter sweetness, but that is as close as we can get to justifying *doux* in semantic terms. It is possible to interpret it in phonetic terms since *hautbois* with its long vowel sounds and single pronounced consonant is itself soft. Even so, there is a slippage between the sense of the adjective as applied to *parfums* and to *hautbois*. *Doux* does not have a simple, stable meaning to which one can appeal. The meaning is not innate. The conventions of language (*mœurs*) are being attacked. Words are used as the poet wills, often wrenched far from what the public consensus is. In linguistic terms it is *une atteinte à la morale publique*. However, there is no linguistic authority or panel of judges to enforce a definitive judgment. Thus the adjective is foisted on the noun and the oboe is made to sound as Baudelaire wills. It has to accept the sound that is applied to it—like a perfume, an extraneous essence applied to oneself so that one's own scent (or sense) is changed.

The other two descriptions are no less problematical. The adjective *frais* joins *parfums* and *chairs d'enfants*. Yet, perfumes and the flesh of children are fresh in quite different ways. For example, the freshness of a child's flesh is warm while that of a perfume is cool. There is an antagonism between the elements as well as a sense in which they are apt partners, and the power of the image comes from this fact. Next to this, the application of *verts* to prairies is simple, bordering on the obvious—so obvious in fact that the application to *parfums* might pass unquestioned. But what exactly are *parfums verts*? The use of *frais* encourages us to interpret it in the sense of immature or unripe, but since unripe is, if anything, a negative description, fruits which are unripe are bitter in a positive sense. However, *prairies* are green in a different way. The adjective refers to colour when applied to them. Thus *verts* undergoes a metamorphosis of meaning as we read it. The two interpretations are not incompatible since freshness is connoted by the green colour of nature. The reader slips from one to the other, making sense of the whole description: *des parfums verts comme des prairies*. The process does not end there. Prairies extend for a great distance and give one the impression of going on for ever and, at the end of the first line of the tercet, when we find the complementary rhyme: *l'expansion des choses infinies,* the collocation casts backwards a sense of infinity, expanding the reach of these perfumes. This is in spite of the fact that it is not these perfumes but those that are *corrompus, riches et triomphants* that reach out towards infinity. Nonetheless, the rhyme and the comparison strongly suggest that this first set of perfumes also have (or have acquired) this attribute. They refuse to be limited, to be pinned down.

A similar semantic expansion is to be found with respect to the way *Folle* is manipulated in *À celle qui est trop gaie.* The first usage in *robes folles* is playful, suggesting freedom and lack of inhibition, a poetic disorder of the clothes that is attractive. When treated as a noun and applied to the woman as a whole rather than just her clothes, it diminishes her, treating her as someone who is incapable of reason. The verb-phrase that follows, *dont je suis affolé,* creates the impression that this madness has infected the speaker. The use of a verb gives the description a temporal dimension, implying that such a state is not his natural one nor, for that matter, necessarily permanent. A subtle distinction between the two madnesses is drawn, a distinction that is to the speaker's benefit.

This can happen because the speaker, as the word itself suggests, controls language and through it the image of the woman. She is what he says she is. His voice analyses her, dissecting her image and defining her as mad. She is deprived of a voice. This is underlined, ironically, by the description of the wound as *ces lèvres nouvelles.* The lips surround the mouth, the empty space from which the voice emerges. These marginalia, like Baudelaire's note, indicate in this instance a silencing of an alternative voice. The lips are displaced to the side of the body away from their natural place and away from their speaking function. Instead, their role as point of entry is given priority. Yet what they admit is Baudelaire's venom which dissolves the integrity of the other.

Thus the lips are displaced to the side but are these new lips the vagina or a gash in the side? Is it murder or rape or infection? In such circumstances meaning is uncertain. The adjective *éclatantes* may be applied to *lèvres* because of their bright red colour, a sign of beauty, or it might be applied because of the rawness of the wound. Similarly, *belles* could be applied because beautiful women traditionally have beautiful lips. However, if the adjective is referring to the image of the lips as wound, then its meaning is changed. Beauty is shown not to be an absolute. The beauty that excites the speaker and which he genuinely experiences is not a beauty that this reader can share in. In fact it is rather disgusting.

In this poem, there is something mean and spiteful. The speaker attacks the woman out of fear. Yet this fear does not originate specifically in the woman (or even in womankind). He feels under attack from the sun and punishes a flower on account of the *insolence de la Nature.* However, in claiming that the sun is cutting his chest open (the counterpart of his attack on the woman) and in attributing insolence to Nature, is not Baudelaire doing what he also does in respect of the judges—making it up by attributing malevolence to sources that cannot reply? Consequently, the conclusion, once we become aware of this strategy, is that Baudelaire's fears lie not in his apprehension of some real threat in the outside world, but rather are the projection of his own mind. If Baudelaire feels fear, it comes from within himself. If he attacks, it springs not from courage, the heroic virtue, but from fear.

It would then be tempting to see the poem as an exercise in crude sexism. The male speaker is thus a villain who attacks the woman, the weaker sex, because he is a coward and cowards attack only those who are weaker than themselves. (This could itself be seen as a piece of crude sexism, not least for its unquestioned assumption that women are the weaker sex.) *À celle qui est trop gaie* is more subtle than that. Baudelaire's inner fears are aroused by his confrontation with forces that might be deemed more powerful that he is: the sun, Nature and the judiciary. If therefore the woman arouses fear in him—and the verb is doubly appropriate in the context of this poem—then it is because he sees her as a threat on account of her greater strength. That strength is not physical—in that respect she is weaker and that is why the assault is described in physical terms. The power of the woman lies in her self-possession that allows her to be gay, in her ability to transform a mood of sadness into something beautiful and, not least, in her ability to plant images in the minds of poets.

This last is closer to the traditional poetic image of woman as source of inspiration of great artists. However, in this case the image goes further. It is not so much that the poets are reacting to the woman as that she is giving them an image. They have no choice in the matter. The individual poetic voice is stifled and all poets become mouthpieces (reduced, as she will be later, to *lèvres*). Thus the poets are forced to speak in the way that she deems appropriate. Baudelaire's attack on her, his attack on her voice, is his way of liberating his own. He is creating his own room to speak by silencing her—just as he is trying to establish his right to freedom of speech in the face of the judiciary.

Yet this freedom is still hemmed in by the image of the woman. If he speaks, it is still a speech dominated by her image. He cannot escape the ballet of flowers—which is why his reaction to the insolence of Nature is to attack a flower. The woman is his sister—the same as he is. If the images of horror and violence can be transmuted in his mind to *belles,* is that any different from the way she transmutes sadness into an image of light? Poetic power circulates between woman and speaker. Neither is completely in control.

The fact that the woman is perceived as having access to power and as being a threat may make the poem's analysis of the relationship between *bourreau* and *victime* more complex than implied by the sort of oversimplified view, given above, of the poem as a piece of sexism that denigrates women. For all that, the struggle is depicted as brutal and violent, a resort to physical violence that is less and less acceptable these days. As pointed out earlier, the response of fear to strength in another is not constructive engagement but to find the weakest aspect of the adversary (an adversary that is of one's own creation, as much a real adversary as the sound of an oboe is *doux*) and attack that. The question of how to respond to what is depicted still remains. Perhaps, like Borrell, one may dismiss content as being somehow beneath real artists:

> L'artiste n'est plus un miméticien; les miméticiens, ce sont les autres, les faux artistes, les «singes». S'il n'est pas miméticien, cela signifie qu'il n'a plus à représenter, le peuple ou l'idéal du beau. Travailleur de la singularité, il a pour tâche de pro-duire, de faire présent, de présenter, en amenant à la présence, ce qui est oublié, refoulé, rejeté ou «bizarre».[5]

> (The artist is not an imitator; imitators are different, false artists, mere monkeys. If he is not an imitator, that means that he is not constrained to reproduce—either people or the ideal of beauty. Working on the singular, his job is to pro-duce, to make present, to present, to bring into our presence, that which is forgotten, repressed, rejected or 'bizarre'.)

This appears reasonable. It argues against ideological impositions on the artist. However, when faced with a concrete example of the bizarre, we may hesitate. The moral dimension that has been eliminated from Borrell's argument returns. Would we accept a depiction of paedophilia or racial prejudice? Both involve issues of power, of domination by violence or the threat of it. The answer would have to be that it would depend on the stance of the author. A depiction seen to promote a positive image of paedophilia would get short shrift in many quarters. As would any promotion of racism. Similarly, the depiction of male violence against women in such a way that it is seen to be pleasurable or beautiful or part of a legitimate struggle against a perceived feminine threat is one that would arouse protests were it to be expressed in a newspaper or from the Bench.

Thus, to claim that Baudelaire has some special insight or knowledge that allows him to express violent thoughts towards women and thereby to demonstrate that he is, as Sartre puts it, showing 'son adhésion au

Bien', is an example of Robb's claim that Baudelaire's views are sanitised and falsified by critics determined to demonstrate that he (and they) are on the side of the angels. Compagnon, in his edition of *Les Fleurs du Mal,* argues that this is part of a wider trend:

> Chaque fois, un seul poème ou quelques-uns sont censés représenter «le vrai Baudelaire»; toute l'œuvre est perçue à partir de l'entrée qu'ils procurent. [. . .] Or nous isolons du recueil le poème que nous privilégions, comme s'il valait pour l'œuvre entière et qu'il lui conférait un sens absolu; Baudelaire est alors le poète *d'Une charogne,* ou celui *des Correspondances, du Vin des chiffonniers, des Chats, du Cygne,* des *Petites Vieilles* . . . Ces lectures ne sont jamais tout à fait fausses, mais pas non plus très fidèles. *Les Fleurs du Mal* sont tout cela à la fois: tous leurs poèmes et toutes les épithètes qu'on a appliquées à leur auteur.[6]

> (Each time, one or just a few poems are supposed to represent 'the true Baudelaire'; the entire work is approached from the viewpoint they provide. [. . .] We extract from the collection the poem to which we give a special status, as though it contained the whole truth about the entire body of work and we confer on it an absolute meaning; Baudelaire is then the poet of *A Rotting Carcass,* of *Correspondences,* of *The Rag-and-bone Man's Wine,* of *The Cats,* of *The Swan,* of *The Little Old Ladies* . . . These readings are never completely false, but they are not overly faithful either. The *Fleurs du Mal* are all of these at once: all their poems and all the epithets that have been applied to their author.)

Baudelaire, for Compagnon, is not a stable essence, an author of unique status about whom the truth may be recovered once and for all. He is an invention of each reader who builds up a picture based on a reading of one or of a selection of poems. The critical view is always a partial view—just as is this view based largely on *À celle qui est trop gaie.* The reader does to Baudelaire what he does to the woman in the first part of the poem. Both are treated as though the part were the whole. The woman is her clothing, her gestures and so on, while Baudelaire is seen as the poet of this or that poem. The result, as Compagnon points out, is a vision that is neither true nor false.

We can only ever have a partial judgement of a poet and that judgment reflects on us as much as on the subject of that judgement. Sartre's view of Baudelaire is one that reflects his own preoccupations. He recognises and identifies in Baudelaire that which resonates with his own needs and desires. In a like manner, Baudelaire identifies the features of the woman that most correspond to his inner needs and turmoil. He feels threatened and so identifies, in what for other people would be the most innocuous place, a source for that threat, a justification for it. The weakness is his. That he feels threatened by her is true. That she is a threat is more complex.

Truth is a process of investigation not a definitive judgment. Laws are not eternal or valid for all places. They are conventions—not convictions based on some Absolute. The only convictions possible are impermanent, like the one handed down by the judges—contested by the author, erased by the National Assembly and, as Robb points out, still debated. Dayan argues that this affected more poets than Baudelaire:

> Did Baudelaire, Rimbaud, Lautréamont, Mallarmé believe in God? The question is, in the end, irrelevant; because whatever they believed in, it does not speak with the authority of the Christian God. Whatever speaks, in their work, has no absolute authority; and wherever the ideal is, it does not speak.[7]

The notion of an absolute justice that can be used to regulate human activities is overthrown. The world is a place of contestation where voices struggle. Words are, as in *Correspondances, confuses paroles.* They lack clarity—not, however, because they are emptied of meaning but because, as we have seen in the extract from the poem, they are invested with a multitude of meanings. The word *confuses* suggests a fusing together of different elements, not unlike the process Rivière has pointed out above, resulting in complexity and richness. In this world no perfumes, no words can be simple.

Thus to seek understanding is futile, as **Les sept vieillards (The Seven Old Men)** shows:

> Exaspéré comme un ivrogne qui voit double,
> Je rentrai, je fermai ma porte, épouvanté,
> Malade et morfondu, l'esprit fiévreux et trouble,
> Blessé par le mystère et par l'absurdité!
>
> Vainement ma raison voulait prendre la barre;
> La tempête en jouant déroutait ses efforts,
> Et mon âme dansait, dansait, vielle gabarre
> Sans mâts, sur une mer monstrueuse et sans bords!
>
> *(OC,* I, p. 88)

> (Exasperated like a drunk seeing double,
> I went home and shut my door, in a state of shock,
> Ill and dejected, my spirits fevered and troubled,
> Wounded by the mystery and the absurdity!
>
> In vain my reason wanted to take the tiller;
> The tempest blasts undid its efforts,
> And my soul danced and danced like an old barge
> Without masts, on a limitless and monstrous sea.)

What is causing Baudelaire's distress is not the fact that he lives in a world that is emptied of significance but rather that he lives in one where there is order and pattern but whose design he cannot comprehend: there is too much of it. The soul is moving through a reality that is monstrous (non-human or resistant to the human) and limitless. This is reflected at a number of levels within the lines quoted above: for example, he is like a drunk who sees double and the adjective *exaspéré* is echoed at the end of the second verse of the last quatrain

by *épouvanté* in a way that creates a symmetry. The verb *dansait* is repeated like a dance step but its meaning is metaphorical rather than literal. Indeed the adverb *vainement* stands out because it connotes emptiness rather than plenitude. It reveals the futility of seeking to comprehend through the faculty of reason the richness of life. Like the sea, life is huge and without limits—*une mer monstrueuse et sans bords.* We are borne upon it but, as in a tempest, we cannot control the direction we take. Control is impossible. If we try to grasp the meaning of life, it runs through our fingers and we are left with nothing. Thus life is a *mystère,* suggestive of meaning, and an *absurdité,* beyond our comprehension. It is this tension that is captured in the poetry of Baudelaire.

Such a view is, of course, only a part of what Baudelaire's poetry—like a *vieille gabarre*—conveys. But, as Compagnon has argued, that is both true and false. There is always something modern in Baudelaire's poems—it is not just a *vieille gabarre.* Trying to pin Baudelaire's poem to one particular meaning is at once a heroic and barbaric action. It is an epic attempt to come to terms with the teeming multitude of mystery and meaning. At the same time it is an attack on the integrity of the poetry. The whole can never be inclusively comprehended and each selection is a cut in the body of the poetry. Compagnon, who has alerted us to the dangers, and inevitability, of selecting poems and generalising on that basis, himself selects two poems as the basis of what he recognises as *his* Baudelaire. His first choice is **À une passante (To a woman passing by)** 'parce qu'il n'en reste rien une fois qu'on arrive au bout' ('because nothing is left when you come to the end') (Compagnon, p. 390), a phrase that indicates that it is not just the woman who escapes the observer's grasp but that the poem too is evanescent. Meaning is a journey not a destination. His second poem is the second one named **Spleen (Despair)** 'parce que c'est le premier poème de Baudelaire que j'ai lu' ('because it is the first poem by Baudelaire that I read') (ibid.). This poem is contradictorily both second (twice over: the second **Spleen** and the second in Compagon's list) and first (because it was the first of Baudelaire's that he ever read). He continues:

> C'était pour une explication de texte au lycée et je n'ai pas cessé de vouloir retrouver le choc que j'ai ressenti alors, l'impression de la première fois.
>
> (It was for an exercise in practical criticism that I did at school and I have always wanted to reexperience the shock that I felt then, the first impression.)

It is an impossible search. The first and the second are now inextricably entangled. The exercise, the *explication de texte,* is an analysis of the text by means of a division into its several aspects before coming to a general conclusion that is supposed to let us now appreciate the totality. Interestingly, the *choc* that Compagnon felt on reading the poem suggests that, although he views the experience as pleasurable, it was nonetheless an upset. It threatened his previous mindset. Furthermore, it is an irruption into his life like that described in *À une passante.* His way of reading the poem involves breaking it down and subjecting it to his invasive scrutiny. Thus the *explication* may be seen as the equivalent of Baudelaire's slashing of the woman in order to appropriate her and neutralise the *choc* that she poses to him. It is a reminder that no analysis is neutral in that something of the investigator always gets in among the component parts, as he or she adds a new voice to the silent work—the *venin* is introduced into the body of the poem. A pure understanding is always denied us by the very investigative procedure that we undertake.

Consequently, no understanding is ever definitive. Something is always added by the investigator to the investigation. As we have seen, Sartre adds his own revolutionary concerns to his analysis. This is the dilemma of the critic who approaches a poem thinking, like Sartre, that his predecessors have not done full justice to the work. The problem is actually the reverse. Critics are prevented from having a full understanding of the poem because of what they inevitably add. Baudelaire's false accusation against the judges rings true precisely because of this. He claims that they read too much into his poems—they injected them with their own *venin.* That the *venin* turns out in fact to be his, added by him in his role as critic of their judgment, is only a further demonstration of the process.

Justice is impossible and distortion is inevitable. The result is that categories are upset and reassigned. This may be a cause for rejoicing, as Sartre claims. However, he seems to envisage not a process but rather an arrival at some ultimate settled state where justice prevails. This poem viciously attacks such a notion. It poisons the notion of justice. It provokes judgements that are never allowed to be final and it fascinates us like a venomous snake that hypnotises its prey. We the readers receive a shock, like the young Compagnon, and have our ways of thinking turned upside down. We are so fascinated by the beauty and power of the linguistic richness that we fail to see that the aggressor has gained our sympathy, through this assault on our senses and reason, and is accepted as the victim. He manages to be both but, unless we accept the villainy of the speaker along with the heroism, we will continue our complicity in the violence against *celle qui est trop gaie* which is violence against us all.

Notes

1. Charles Baudelaire, *Œuvres complètes,* ed. by Claude Pichois, 2 vols (Paris: Gallimard [Pléiade]. 1975: henceforth *OC*), I, pp. 156-57. All references are to this edition and are given in the text. All translations are mine.

2. Jean-Paul Sartre, *Baudelaire* (Paris, Gallimard, 1947; reprinted 1975), pp. 63-64.

3. Graham Robb, 'Érotisme et obscénité des *Fleurs du Mal*', *Europe,* 70 (1992), pp. 70-71.

4. Jacques Rivière, *Études* (Paris: Gallimard, 1948), pp. 15-16.

5. Joan Borrell, *L'Artiste-Roi: Essai sur les représentations,* Bibliothèque du Collège International de Philosophie (Paris: Aubier, 1990), pp. 158-59.

6. Charles Baudelaire, *Les Fleurs du Mal,* ed. by Antoine Compagnon (Paris: Seuil, 1993), p. 350.

7. Peter Dayan, 'The Romantic Renaissance', in *Poetry in France, Metamorphoses of a Muse,* ed. by K. Asply and P. France (Edinburgh: Edinburgh University Press, 1992), p. 144.

Keith Waldrop (essay date 2006)

SOURCE: Waldrop, Keith. "Translator's Introduction." In *The Flowers of Evil,* translated by Keith Waldrop, pp. xi-xxvii. Middletown, Conn.: Wesleyan University Press, 2006.

[*In the following essay, Waldrop outlines the poet's central themes and ideas, both in general and with respect to* Les Fleurs du Mal.]

The most famous characterization of Baudelaire's work is in a letter (actually a sort of blurb) from Victor Hugo: "You create a new thrill." Or "a new shiver." Or "shudder." The sentence is so well known that the original French is common even in English contexts: *un frisson nouveau.* The kind of thrill in question can be suggested to an American by noting that Baudelaire spent years translating the prose of Edgar Allan Poe, not—he insisted—because he was a translator, but because in Poe he found someone who resembled him.

He discovered Poe around 1847 or '48 (he was not the first translator) and by 1850 or '51 was enthralled. As for resemblances, we might note that Poe's gothic is strongly psychological, his horrors are mostly inner, *nervous,* horrors. He is, as his disciple aspires to be, not just a poet, not just this or that kind of writer, but a complete man of letters. Baudelaire sees Poe, as he sees himself: unknown abroad and, in his own country, unloved; a completely solitary figure; an emblem of bad luck. And by the time Baudelaire has thoroughly absorbed him, Poe is dead—still young, impoverished, rejected.

MOTHER AND MUSES

Baudelaire's father, François Baudelaire, took holy orders, worked as a teacher and in various administrative posts, lived through the Revolution, renounced his priesthood, married and had a son (our Baudelaire's elder half brother), and—two years after the death of his wife—retired in 1816 at the age of fifty-seven.

Three years later (at, you will already have counted, sixty) he married Caroline Dufay, aged twenty-six, the poet's mother-to-be. The marriage was in September 1819 and Charles was born in Paris the ninth of April 1821. The house he was born in, rue Hautefeuille, on the Left Bank, was torn down later in the century, when Boulevard Saint Germain was cut through. (The changing shape of the city is noted in Baudelaire's poem **"The Swan."**) Until recently there was a plaque on the house standing now at the intersection of Hautefeuille and the boulevard, claiming it as the birthplace of Charles Baudelaire. The plaque is no longer there. In the store that is there, speaking of changes, you can buy a computer.

Two months before Charles's sixth birthday, his father died. Long after, he seems to have tried to make much of his father's memory, not too successfully. François had been a Sunday painter and his son managed to retrieve one of his canvases. "Detestable," he pronounced his beloved father's art work. But he was furious, understandably, that no one could tell him exactly where, in the cemetery of Montparnasse, his father's ashes lay.

Caroline Dufay (the last name is a little uncertain, at least in spelling, but Baudelaire used it for his own on occasion) was born in London, but transplanted very early to France. Her father died before she was one year old, her mother a few years later. The orphaned Caroline was raised in a well-to-do lawyer's family (friends, as it happens, of François Baudelaire, who had, one may suppose, his eye on her already in her tender years).

Baudelaire, later (in 1861), writes his mother, "In my childhood there was a period of passionate love for you." There is no reason to doubt this act of memory (though it could be considered suspect, being in a letter begging for money) and it is likely that this period of passionate love was just after his father's death.

If so, it was brief. On the eighth of November 1828 his mother married a dashing fortyish army officer, Commandant—soon to be General, later Senator—Jacques Aupick. The bride was, in fact, already in advanced pregnancy. She gave birth, not quite a month later, to a stillborn daughter. Baudelaire never learned of his virtual half sister.

He got on well enough with his stepfather while in school, especially away in boarding school, but the relationship went sour around age eighteen. If there is anything unusual about such an enmity, it is that it did not come a bit earlier—and that it was so violent and sustained a hatred on the young man's part. When, in 1848, revolution broke out in Paris and Aupick was one of those in charge of government troops, Baudelaire—in a rare moment of activism—went onto the barricades shouting, "We've got to gun down General Aupick!" The general survived.

Aupick was not really the main problem. The great catastrophe of Baudelaire's life was his own doing. In 1842 (at his majority) he had come into an inheritance from his father: not a grand fortune but enough to live reasonably well. In the space of eighteen months, he went through almost half the capital. His mother then had him declared legally incompetent and a guardian was appointed to take care of his money and dole it out at intervals.

The doles were small and Baudelaire was a big spender. Black clothing for men was becoming fashionable in the mid-nineteenth century and Baudelaire took up the fashion, showing how a dandy could dress with severe good taste (if he could afford it). He liked good furniture, antiques. He liked high ceilings. He was also a bibliophile: he loved (it was not the least of his expenses) good books—and good bindings. He spent what he got in doles and what little he got for his writing—journalism, art criticism (the best of the age, by the way) the Poe translations, a few poems—and when it was all gone kept on spending. In letter after letter, he begs for money, mainly, but not exclusively, from his mother.

And she gave him money. But it could never be enough. His debts grew. He moved constantly; no matter where he went, presently the rent would be due and he claimed in one month to have moved six times. Eventually he fled his creditors across the border into Belgium.

There was another reason for his always unsettled location and shortage of money. He was keeping a woman and she turned out to be more, sometimes, than he was prepared for. Baudelaire, as we hear of so many nineteenth-century men, preferred prostitutes. They were easy to find; he had a notebook of names and addresses. But—again, like others—he fell for one of them. Maybe she was not really a prostitute; she was said to be a stand-in actress (which would not likely have provided a living wage). It was said she was six years his junior, that she came from the West Indies. None of this is certain and almost nothing is actually known about her. Baudelaire at different moments refers to her under several different last names, so she is often simply "Jeanne." Where she actually came from, where and how they met (in, or at least by, 1842), what she did after Baudelaire (she fades out for us when he leaves for Belgium), when she died—all such is missing. (The last recorded reference: Nadar, the famous photographer and balloonist, after Baudelaire's death, caught a glimpse of her on the street; Jeanne was on crutches.) *If* they met in 1842, he was twenty-one, and *if* she was six years younger, she was fifteen. The one "fact" about her is that she was a "woman of color"; Nadar called her Baudelaire's "black Venus." She impressed Banville by the way she held her head and he found her "at once divine and bestial." Courbet painted her next to Baudelaire in his enormous painting *The Artist's Studio,* then painted her out.

Oh yes, and she was "tall." And Baudelaire writes, in 1845, "Jeanne Lemer [he more often calls her Jeanne Duval] is the only woman I ever loved." This is in a suicide note. From time to time he refers to her as his wife, but they were certainly not legally married. Fifteen years later he describes her as "old and sick" (would she have been thirty?) and they are not living together (well, not at the moment), but Baudelaire, who cannot support himself, is still supporting her. Meanwhile another man is living with her (her "brother," having mysteriously appeared from "abroad") and she is supporting this alleged sibling, obviously, from the same dole. And Baudelaire complains bitterly about this in letters to his mother, and to others, but his many decisions to abandon Jeanne are as ineffectual as his threats of suicide.

Jeanne is one of the three most important women with whom specific poems of Baudelaire are connected, poems sometimes thought of as cycles. On the ninth of December 1852 (five years before the publication of *Flowers of Evil*; he was thirty-one) he began sending poems, anonymously, to a notorious figure known as Madame Sabatier, also known as La Présidente, the former title not very accurate and the latter purely honorary, a gift from Théophile Gautier. Madame Sabatier was born poor, but by a series of rich lovers lived well and gave dinners regularly at her house on the corner of Place Pigalle. Her guests included Gautier, Flaubert, Henri Monnier . . . a distinguished table.

Her wider fame was the result of one of her lovers' commissioning a statue of her. A sculptor, not yet famous—also a lover of La Présidente—Auguste Clésinger, agreed to carve it. Well, not exactly *carve*; he poured plaster over her to make a cast. She was to represent a bacchante in ecstasy and the ecstasy was, as it turned out, so clearly expressed that public exhibition became risky. (Did I mention that, under the plaster, she was naked?) The solution was to thicken the plot with a snake, and the statue, at the official Salon of 1847, was a sensation, entitled *Woman Bitten by a Serpent*. It is now, conspicuously, in the Musée d'Orsay.

It is not certain that Madame did not know who was sending the poems, but if she did, she kept it quiet. The first she received, by the way, was one of the poems that later got *Flowers of Evil* banned. (See, below, **"To Her, Too Merry."**) Her affair with Baudelaire, after the anonymity ended, was brief, but they remained friends.

The third muse was Marie Daubrun, a very successful boulevard actress who was known, from a spectacular role she had played on the stage, as the Gold-Haired Beauty (*la Belle aux cheveux d'or* sounds better). She was the mistress of Théodore de Banville, one of the poets of Baudelaire's generation who recognized Baudelaire's greatness (there were a few). She and Baudelaire had at least two brief bitter affairs, but she always went back to Banville, who helped edit the first posthumous edition of Baudelaire's writings.

The idea that Baudelaire wrote in cycles no doubt has some validity, but I have not tried to mark these out in my translation or notes; I believe his final arrangement to a large extent disperses them in the larger framework of the book. Those interested might consider those cycles critics most often isolate: the Jeanne cycle, from XXII to XXXIX, predominantly images of carnal love; the cycle of Mme. Sabatier, from XL to XLVIII, images of spiritual love; and the cycle of Marie Daubrun, from XLIX to LVII, perhaps meant to fuse the two kinds of love.

Readers might also turn with profit to the Penguin *Baudelaire: Selected Verse,* the French text with "plain prose" translations by the editor, Francis Scarfe, who attempts a rearrangement of the poems (not just those from *The Flowers of Evil*) into chronological groups.

The Book

From at least his early twenties, Baudelaire was writing poetry. He published some in magazines and by 1850 or '51 had a volume ready, a beautifully calligraphed manuscript bound in two volumes with gold stamping (seen by friends of his but now lost). After the catastrophe of the legal guardianship, he had become desperate to make money with his writing, and many letters to his mother inform her of the various ways he is going to make large earnings. He is going to edit a magazine, he is going to write a novel, a play . . . little comes of it. As a hack, he was a flop. Then in June 1857, *Les Fleurs du mal* is published.

Earlier the same year, a novel had appeared, by an author even more unknown than Baudelaire (who had, by this time, a certain underground reputation). Gustave Flaubert had brought out, finally, his first book—his masterpiece—*Madame Bovary,* and was immediately on trial for offending "public morality." Flaubert had a good lawyer, who answered the charge of obscenity with a four-hour tirade. *Madame Bovary* was vindicated (and assured, by the scandal, of large sales).

The Flowers of Evil, attacked on the same ground, was defended by a timid lawyer, himself probably rather shocked by the book. Even the title, after all, is outrageous (but had Baudelaire kept the title he first gave it, *The Lesbians,* it might not have been published at all). He thought the precedent of *Madame Bovary* would help his case but, on the contrary, the "morality" of the public had been alerted, and stiffened by its failure to destroy Flaubert's work. And the novelist, after all, was (when I say this he will, we can be certain, flip over twice in his grave) a solid bourgeois type, a *rentier* living quietly in the country. Baudelaire was an urban "bohemian," a "dandy," and (by extrapolating from certain poems) could easily be represented as a satanist and some sort of pervert.

Maybe—it's not beyond speculating—his stepfather the senator might (a word or two among the high-ups?) have counted for something in his favor, never mind their personal animosities. But the previous April, while the book was in production, General Aupick died.

The book, accused of (get this) "realism," was found injurious to "public morality"—*not,* by the way, to "public religion," a more serious charge. Six poems were cited as "obscene or immoral" and the author fined three hundred francs, the publisher fined also. The fine was later reduced, but the six poems were to be suppressed. Baudelaire had not, I think, expected this. It became one more proof of his birthright of bad luck.

Of his many complaints about the banning of *Flowers of Evil,* one (which he brings up often) is particularly important: he could never understand how the court could attack him for specific pieces—those six poems. What he had written was not a collection, but a book, a book that could only be judged *as a whole book.* He would not, now, try to republish the truncated—destroyed—book, but make it a new, different, book. The result, four years later, was the second *Flowers of Evil,* which omitted, necessarily, the six banned poems, but included thirty-two new ones (or thirty-five, depending how you count), and evidenced considerable rearrangement. This is the edition usually thought of as the definitive text. It is the book here translated—with the six banned poems added.

For the rest of his life the author made plans for another edition. He had not enough time. The next would be posthumous.

ORIGINAL SIN

The "natural" is an important category in Baudelaire's thought, and is always in some degree negative, a kind of original sin, very much in key with this favorite topic of Saint Paul, whose "natural man" is one for whom things of the spirit are "foolishness." Commerce,

for instance, Baudelaire condemns as *"natural, therefore vile."* Elsewhere he jots down, in reference to a writer of great importance to him, "We must always to go back to Sade, that is, to the *Natural Man,* to explain evil."

In "The Painter of Modern Life," he expounds this at length:

> It is this infallible nature that has created parricide and cannibalism and a thousand other abominations that modesty and manners forbid us to mention. [Except, he must silently have added, in poems.] It is philosophy (I speak of the good kind), and it is religion, that order us to feed our poor and infirm parents. Nature (which is nothing but the voice of our own interests) commands us to clobber them. Go through, analyse, everything natural—all actions and desires of the pure natural man. All you find will be atrocious. Anything beautiful and noble is the result of reason and calculation. Crime, a taste for which the human animal has drawn from his mother's womb, is natural in origin. Virtue, on the contrary, is *artificial,* supernatural, since it has been necessary, in all times and in all nations, for gods and prophets to teach animalistic humanity what man, alone, would never have managed to discover. Evil comes about without effort, *naturally,* by fatality; the good is always the product of an art.

So one is not surprised that his sense of beauty is less occupied with physical bodies than with the arts of makeup and adornment. His growing disdain for realism in the visual arts results in a predilection for caricature. And his most famous work, outside the poems and prose poems, is *Artificial Paradises,* a work he intended to bring out just after the second *Flowers of Evil,* but which (because his fiddling with the poems caused a delay) in fact appeared first. *Artificial Paradises* is a beautiful book in two parts, on hashish and on opium (though the part on opium is of less interest, being mainly a summary of De Quincey's *Confessions of an English Opium Eater.*)

Baudelaire had earlier attended sessions of *le Club des hachichins,* which met a few times in 1845 and '46; Gautier, Balzac, and Gérard de Nerval were also among its members. (The hashish, by the way, was not smoked, but put into some kind of cake or cookie, as later recommended by Alice B. Toklas.) Baudelaire does not promote the use of hashish or opium, because, he insists, wine is more effective. In spite of his interest in these substances, he is reported to have been rather abstemious or at least moderate, even with wine. But his notion of paradise is related to such "artificial" means—or sometimes to dreams. He drew an amusing caricature of himself under the influence of hashish.

By another train of thought (or trail of feeling) he comes to identify nature with woman: "Woman is *natural,* that is to say, abominable." This leads to extraordinary statements, such as one that attracted Eliot's attention:

Once someone asked, when I was present, what constituted the greatest pleasure in love. Someone replied, naturally: in receiving. Another: in giving. Someone said: the pleasure of pride! someone else: the ecstasy of humility! All these muckers making like the Imitation of Christ. Finally, an impudent utopian was found who insisted that the greatest pleasure of love was in forming new citizens for the fatherland.

Me, I said: what is uniquely, supremely voluptuous about love lies in the certainty of doing evil. And man and woman know from birth that in evil is to be found all voluptuousness.

Before writing off the poet as a simple misogynist (I stress here *simple*), let us consider some of Baudelaire's basic vocabulary.

Spleen and Ideal

For Baudelaire, the natural world, including ourselves, is the realm of *ennui*. A basic translation would be "boredom," but as "ennui" has been conveniently absorbed into English, I have kept the word wherever it is used in the poems. It enters very early, in the introductory verses **"To the Reader,"** where it denotes a force threatening to destroy the world, by engulfing it "in a yawn." It is the world as tedious and tasteless. The first, and longest, section of the book suggests two possible antidotes to ennui.

One is by embracing the Ideal, by a cult of beauty or by rejecting the physical world for the immaterial. The latter is sometimes regarded as Christian, but I see it more as Schopenhauerian. He means, it seems to me, not to change the world, but to stand apart from it and experience it in a kind of pure perception, to stand aside or apart (a bit above, let's say, and—like Joyce's artist—paring his nails) and experience it *in himself.* This is his role as *dandy,* a term he did not invent, but made in many ways his own. "The dandy," he jots in a notebook, "must aspire to sublimity without interruption; he must live and sleep before a mirror." The dandy is the "opposite of woman," unnatural, artificial.

But "Ideal" is balanced (or overbalanced) by "Spleen." I have left this word also in the original, as a kind of technical term. The French word is taken from English, but with a reduced spread of meanings. It is not used in French for the endocrine gland, nor for most of the current or obsolete senses you will find in the Oxford English Dictionary. The definition in the *Petit Larousse* corresponds exactly to Baudelaire's usage: "Ennui of all things; disgust with life."

Spleen, this ennui of all things, is the natural state. A life of ennui (Thoreau's "quiet desperation") may be accepted, consciously or unconsciously, controlled by religion or philosophy. It may be overcome by the Ideal. Or it may be allowed to follow its (natural) inclination for evil. An evil act, or thought (or poem) interrupts the natural tedium, signaling itself with a flash of horror that intensifies our awareness of existence. Baudelaire, from what we know of his life, could hardly be described as a great criminal; his horrors are literary representations. But though not actual events, they are real horrors; they throw a spotlight on real facets of human desire, which are of course dangerous, yet more dangerous if unlit. These are the flowers of Evil or, as in the final poem of the book, "an oasis of horror in a desert of ennui." No doubt this is what he meant when he insisted (as he sometimes, not always, did) that his book is a moral book.

He never made great claims for his own moral authority, but to his model Poe he allows a touch of the messianic: "I would like to say of him," he writes, "and of a particular class of men, what the catechism says of our Lord: 'He suffered much on our account.'"

After the book containing **"Spleen and Ideal,"** Baudelaire concentrated on putting together a volume of prose poems that he called (among other things) *Spleen de Paris,* as if dropping the Ideal. He wanted it to include a hundred poems, but only half that number are in the posthumous book.

An Attempt at Salvage

Baudelaire speaks often of bad luck (*guignon*), so much so that one is tempted to write it with capitals, Bad Luck. Applied to his life, it does not seem inappropriate. Beside the lack of critical acclaim, beside the humiliation of the guardianship, beside his debts (and a seeming ineptitude for any financial matter), he was ill much of his life, with a clutch of symptoms that are, at this distance, impossible to put in order. At some point he contracted syphilis. The letters to his mother are full, not only of growing debts, but of hair-raising medical details and constant talk of suicide. By the end of 1865, in Belgium, he mentions taking opium, digitalis, belladonna, and quinine. He cannot sleep but never feels quite awake. His right side becomes paralyzed and his language confused and diminished.

Baudelaire's publisher, Auguste Poulet-Malassis, had troubles of his own (including bankruptcy and a stint in debtors' prison) and made it to Brussels before Baudelaire. He had a reputation for publishing dirty books and he added to it by putting out a booklet—in Belgium—of twenty-three poems by Baudelaire, including the six poems banned in France. It was called *Épaves* ("wreckage," or better, maybe, something like "flotsam") and was published as Baudelaire was reaching the end. For this, Poulet-Malassis was condemned by a Belgian court to a fine of five hundred francs and a year in prison.

STRANGE SUNSET

Just before his final illness, which coincided with the collapse of his hope for a collected edition of his work (more bad luck), Baudelaire did begin to get words of appreciation from younger writers. While he was, of course, pleased by this, their poems sometimes puzzled him. Verlaine was one and, another, Mallarmé (who describes the effect of reading **The Flowers of Evil** as a "strange sunset"). Rimbaud was thirteen when Baudelaire died; a very few years later he would insist that Baudelaire was god.

His reputation has always been uneven. Valéry thought his importance (other than as the translator of Poe) was to have engendered three poets greater than himself, those mentioned in the last paragraph. Proust was enthusiastic, perhaps because of Baudelaire's evocations of involuntary memory (generally from perfumes rather than cookies; see, for instance, the second part of **"A Phantom,"** poem XXXVIII). The surrealists put Baudelaire under *Read* rather than under *Don't Read,* but paid more attention to Rimbaud and Nerval and Lautréaumont.

Swinburne was one of Baudelaire's earliest admirers and a fervent one, but Henry James was cool, denying that Baudelaire's flowers deserved to be called evil. He considered them merely "nasty" and essentially trivial, as if "a poet, pretending to pluck 'the flowers of good,' should come and present us, as specimens, a rhapsody on plumcake and *eau du Cologne*." James's sense of evil, no less profound than Baudelaire's, apparently required a less garish display.

Introducing an edition of **Les Fleurs du mal,** in 1955, Yves Bonnefoy begins, "Here is the principal book (*le maître-livre*) of our poetry." Pierre Jean Jouve's *Tombeau de Baudelaire,* the most beautiful book on the poet, almost stops one with its first (alexandrine) utterance (I don't think it necessary to translate): "O cher ô magnifique ô très saint Baudelaire." The rest of the book is excellent prose. I have the impression, but no statistics, that younger poets now writing in French pay more attention to Rimbaud and Mallarmé.

Eliot, whose more obvious links are with Gautier and Laforgue, after his conversion wrote a review of an English translation of the *Intimate Journals* (1930), in which he praises Baudelaire for maintaining a religious category, *evil,* rather than a merely social category such as *bad.* This strikes Eliot as making possible a return (by a negative route) to Christianity: hell is better than nothing. Whatever one thinks of this as a thesis, there are sentences in the essay that Baudelaire surely would have appreciated: "In all his humiliating traffic with other beings, he walked secure in this high vocation, that he was capable of a damnation denied to the politicians and newspaper editors of Paris."

DID BAUDELAIRE BELIEVE IN GOD?

I don't know. But he jotted down one of the more interesting theological claims I've come across. "God is the only being," he wrote, "who, in order to reign, need not even exist."

A BOOK'S AFTERLIFE

Baudelaire wrote prose poems and his essays often have the feel of poetry, but **Les Fleurs du mal** is a book of metrical rhymed verse, formally varied both in line and in stanza, but in its versification not at all innovative.

The translation into English of **Les Fleurs du mal** begins, alas, not with Swinburne, nor with Rossetti (would that one of them had taken it on!) but with Arthur Symons. Symons, in his essays, brought many French writers to the attention of Victoria's subjects, but his translations turned masterpieces into stale English verse. Since then, there have been versions in rhyme and meter, in blank verse, in free verse, in prose . . . I see no reason to reject any of these formal choices. The choice that is not available is "in the original meters," French and English meters being incommensurable.

My effort in this long line of attempts to make **Les Fleurs du mal** into **The Flowers of Evil** (it is not, as the shape on the page might suggest, a trot, but a literary translation) leans on the verset, a measured prose that allows the sentence to dominate, as in prose, checked by a sense of line that restricts it. The restriction is rhythmic, not metrical. The model, in English usage, is the biblical verse, especially that of the Psalms, as translated in early English versions, including the King James. If you glance at Baudelaire's original, you will see that his stanzas have become my versets. That Baudelaire never wrote in versets (his prose poems are prose) does not seem to me to be decisive; he never wrote free verse either and never, for that matter, in iambic pentameter. He did, at least on a few occasions, rewrite a verse poem in prose, and—possibly—make prose poems into verse. Part of **"Exotic Perfume"** (**Flowers** XXII), reappears in **Paris Spleen** XVII, and it is not certain whether that same prose poem was written before or after **"Hair"** (**Flowers** XXIII), its prototype or echo.

What I have tried to capture, in a different formal setting—translation, after all, is on some level collaboration—is the thought and feeling that Baudelaire put into the poems, coming as close as I can to his tone. He himself claimed that there are "two fundamental literary qualities: supernaturalism and irony." One recognizes from the former his antagonism to the "natural" and it comes to mind that the supernatural in a poem like Coleridge's *Ancient Mariner* was the aspect labeled "romantic." Baudelaire's supernatural is a literary artifice, like Coleridge's. It should cause no problem in reading him.

His irony has been less noticed. But here is his comment on the fashion I mentioned earlier—which he followed and, to some extent, led—for black attire:

> Note that black suit and coat have not only political beauty—as an expression of universal equality—but also poetic beauty: an expression of public spirit, an immense parade of political undertakers, love-stricken undertakers, bourgeois undertakers. We're all celebrating some burial or other.

In translating *Les Fleurs du mal,* there is a temptation to be deadly serious. After all, this is work by a genius of bad luck, for whom even beauty had to be painful, "a desire to live" necessarily connected with "a reflux of bitterness." But he is always pushing it a bit far at us. "I will not insist," he says,

> that Joy has no part in Beauty, but I do claim Joy as among its most vulgar ornaments; whereas Melancholy is, as it were, its steady companion—to the point that I can hardly conceive . . . any type of Beauty without *Unhappiness.* Supported (some would say obsessed) by these ideas, I would find it difficult, as you can see, not to conclude that the most perfect type of virile Beauty is *Satan*—as Milton represents him.

Joy a "vulgar ornament." Hmm. Some indeed might say . . . and it's certainly this side of him that has turned off some readers (good readers) like James, like Valéry. I have not tried to trim down this Lovecraftian side of Baudelaire, nor have I tried to foreground it. It's not that he wasn't serious—but not *only* serious. He is part of that long tradition of bugging the bourgeois (not exactly what my dictionary gives for *épater*). I'm aware that there are still those in America who regard Poe as gothic claptrap and think the French simply have peculiar taste (they also like Jerry Lewis).

Baudelaire may not be so much like Poe as he thinks he is, but Poe would surely have gone for a poem like **"Posthumous Remorse"** (XXXIII), a poem on the edge of humor and yet, yes, certainly serious. Baudelaire's sense of humor (one of the poems from **Paris Spleen** is in Breton's anthology of "black humor") does not cancel out seriousness. It has been said, rightly no doubt, that Satan is a mask for Baudelaire, but a mask, even a comic one, is not necessarily a sign of frivolity. He has been compared to Kafka's Josef K.—a character hard to put entirely under one term such as tragic or comic. I would add a kinship with Swift: the ending of **"A Voyage to Cythera"** (CXVI), has something of Gulliver's self-disgust (comic? . . . hmm, well . . .) after his stay among the Houyhnhnms.

Anyone who reads Baudelaire over a course of time will likely find passages that seem of particular significance in understanding the author. Here are two I have found, and put here, especially because they are not in **The Flowers of Evil. Artificial Paradises** is

dedicated (as is the important poem **"Heautontimoroumenos"** [LXXXIII]) to a woman identified only by the initials J. G. F. (The best critics seem inclined to think this is again Jeanne, perhaps *Jeanne glorieuse femme.* While I find this quite unbelievable, I have no name to suggest in its place.) The dedication begins:

> Common sense tells us that the things of this earth hardly exist, and that true reality is only in dreams. To digest natural (or artificial) happiness takes first of all the courage to swallow it down. And perhaps those worthy of happiness are precisely those for whom felicity, as mortals conceive it, has ever the effect of an emetic.

And a note, jotted in a journal:

> Life has but one true charm, the charm of Gambling. But if we can't care whether we win or lose?

BIG DEAL

In 1949, the French Supreme Court of Appeal reversed the decision of 1857 that had banned six poems in *Les Fleurs du mal* by Charles Baudelaire.

LAST THINGS

What Baudelaire died of, the thirty-first of August 1867 (he was forty-six), is impossible to say with any precision. Probably it's best to leave it that he died of complications.

A year before, he had been brought back to a hydrotherapy clinic in Paris. He lay paralyzed for months, unable to speak coherently. His mother visited him. The biographers insist that he loved his mother. I suspect that is true. I strongly suspect he also hated her. Friends played the piano for him, passages from Wagner's *Tannhäuser.* All he could say was *"Crénom!"* the single word, but over and again, which, had he been from Kansas, would surely have come out "God damn it! *GODAMMIT!"*

He was buried in the cemetery of Montparnasse, not with his father, whose gravesite is unknown, but with the person he had hated most in the world, his stepfather. Four years later, his mother joined them.

Raphaël Ingelbien (essay date February 2007)

SOURCE: Ingelbien, Raphaël. "They Saw One They Knew: Baudelaire and the Ghosts of London Modernism." *English Studies* 88, no. 1 (February 2007): 43-58.

[*In the following essay, Ingelbien discusses the influence of Baudelaire's novel poetic vision of urban modernity—most particularly in "Les Sept Vieillars" from the "Tableaux Parisiens" section of* Les Fleurs du Mal—*on T. S. Eliot's vision of London in* The Wasteland, *as well as on English modernism more generally.*]

In his *London: A Book of Aspects* (1909), Arthur Symons complained that few English poets had done for London what Baudelaire had done for Paris: to make the city "vital, a part of themselves, a form of creative literature".[1] Symons's remark partly comes as an implicit acknowledgement of failure: his own poems about the metropolis, collected as *London Nights* (1895), certainly suggest an influence, but they had apparently failed to put London firmly on the poetic map and to meet the challenge that Baudelaire's achievement represented in Symons's eyes. If anybody was bold enough to openly claim Baudelaire as a precursor in a poem about London, it was of course Eliot in *The Waste Land.*

Eliot's debt to Baudelaire went far beyond the development of a poetics of the city, and it was characterized by subtle misreadings to which Eliot criticism has long been alert. In his essays, Eliot repeatedly stressed Baudelaire's spiritual leanings, his awareness of sin, his classicism, and the formal orthodoxy of *Les Fleurs du Mal*.[2] Eliot was clearly determined to turn Baudelaire into an ally in his fight against Romanticism, and to propose a version of Baudelaire that would confound those who preferred Symons's decadent picture of the *poète maudit*—even if this meant that Baudelaire ended up as a rather improbable approximation of Dante. Eliot's insistence on Baudelaire's classical aspects, and his concomitant scorn for the "romantic detritus" that still littered some poems of *Les Fleurs du Mal* understandably prompted rejoinders: those who have tried to correct Eliot's misreading have thus generally emphasized Baudelaire's residual Romanticism.[3] Meanwhile, this debate has largely obscured the nature of the transformations that Baudelaire's urban poetics underwent in Eliot's work. The time may have come for a new look at Eliot and Baudelaire as specifically urban poets, and at the role Eliot's mediation played in shaping Baudelaire's influence on the modernist representation of London.

In such a comparison, I suggest that the terms in which Eliot's misreading of Baudelaire is most often discussed are largely unhelpful. Indeed, Eliot's enlistment of Baudelaire in a classical reaction against Romantic tendencies draws attention away from other questions surrounding the representation of urban experience, and of London in particular. Eliot's comment on Baudelaire as a poet who created a "means of expression for other men" through his elevation of urban imagery to "the first intensity—presenting it as it, yet making it represent something much more than itself",[4] has become a commonplace of Eliot criticism. But its vague and general tenor conceals some crucial shifts that occurred in Eliot's relation to Baudelaire even before his conversion to classicism and Anglo-Catholicism was made official. Ron Schuchard's most recent comments on Eliot's response to urban experience move nimbly between different locations, and stress the importance of "the city" as the scene where Eliot "would stage the drama of a spiritual consciousness under sensual assault": "the dark angel had descended on Eliot in the streets of Boston, Paris, and London". As Eliot's cities changed, however, so did the uses to which he put the urban poems of *Les Fleurs du Mal.* The move to London, in particular, signalled a major development—and not just because the personal nightmare of Eliot's early years in London meant that the city "would gradually become as 'Unreal' as Baudelaire's Paris".[5] It was not until Eliot dealt explicitly with London in "The Burial of the Dead" that he would flaunt his debt to Baudelaire, but it is also in that poem that Eliot's use of *Les Fleurs du Mal* became fraught with ironies.

Although *The Waste Land* takes the credit for turning London into the equivalent of Baudelaire's Paris (thus fulfilling Symons's wish with a vengeance), it is equally arguable that Eliot also domesticated Baudelaire's urban poetics and made them palatable for an English audience who would hail *The Waste Land* as a major text. Eliot actually reinscribed Baudelaire's vision of the city in two allegorical discourses that were familiar to some of the English readers of *The Waste Land,* but which have little to do with Eliot's later Anglo-Catholic and classical orthodoxies. For one thing, the conflation of Baudelairean intertexts and a Great War subtext in "The Burial of the Dead" partakes of a strategy that had already been developed by some English poets during the conflict. Then, most importantly—and most paradoxically—Eliot's vision of the "Unreal City" harks back to a Romantic tradition of London writing which the notes to *The Waste Land* try to suppress, but which unsettles the dichotomy between classicism and Romanticism that underpins Eliot's critical writings on Baudelaire.

These ironies can best be traced by contrasting Baudelaire's and Eliot's uses of urban spectrality. The first note that refers to Baudelaire in *The Waste Land* underscores the importance of two lines from *Les Fleurs du Mal*: "Fourmillante cité, cité pleine de rêves / Où le spectre en plein jour raccroche le passant" ("City of swarming, city full of dreams / Where ghosts in daylight tug the stroller's sleeve").[6] Later, Eliot would state that those two lines had a defining influence on his development. They "summed up" Baudelaire's "significance" for Eliot: "I knew what *that* meant, because I had lived it before I knew that I wanted to turn it into verse on my own account".[7] Eliot had apparently recognized himself as Baudelaire's "mon semblable, mon frère": the sudden insight into the phantasmagoric nature of the metropolis, according to Eliot, was an experience that he must have shared with the first major European poet of the city. The lines are taken from **"Les Sept Vieillards"** (**"The Seven Old Men"**), a poem which contains other images that appealed to Eliot as he started formulating his own poetic response to the modern city. The location of "Prufrock" remains indeterminate, and there has been speculation as to where its "yellow fog"[8] may have originated. Hugh Kenner argued for a persistent geographical indeterminacy: "[Eliot's] earlier poems immerse us in a city we cannot name. If we tend to suppose that Prufrock treads the streets of Boston, still his surname and his yellow fogs are from St Louis, and the Paris of Laforgue has left its impress".[9] But as Robert Crawford has noted, **"Les Sept Vieillards"**, where "un brouillard sale et jaune inondait tout l'espace" ("a dirty yellow steam filled all the space"—"fog" would be a better translation than "steam"), is a likely intertextual source.[10]

"Les Sept Vieillards" remains a defining moment in the development of Baudelaire's aesthetics. Even by the standards of what would become the revolutionary volume *Les Fleurs du Mal,* it stood out as a bold departure from the poems Baudelaire had written up to that point. Not only was Baudelaire taking unprecedented formal liberties with enjambements and caesuras, but this was the first poem of the "Tableaux Parisiens" in which the darker sides of Baudelaire's urban subject matter really took centre stage. In an admiring letter, Victor Hugo commented that, with this poem, Baudelaire had created "un frisson nouveau" ("a new thrill"), and Baudelaire himself wondered whether he had gone beyond the bounds of poetry.[11] The spectral nature of Baudelaire's vision has itself been related to a quintessentially modern experience of the city: as Christina Britzolakis argues, "in modernist texts, the metropolis becomes a theatre for the operations of dream, fantasy and memory", "the city as a poetic object . . . demands a discontinuous, fragmented and imagistic literary form which highlights the fleeting, ephemeral character of modern metropolitan existence". In Eliot's case, modernist "phantasmagoria" is evident in the adoption of the magic lantern as a metaphor for poetic vision in poems like "Prufrock" ("as if a magic lantern threw the nerves in patterns on a screen") or in the "flicker" of "sordid images" in "Preludes".[12] What happens to London in *The Waste Land,* however, suggests a significant transformation of those Baudelairean treatments of urban experience.

The "spectres" of Baudelaire's "fourmillante cité" are seven old cripples who follow each other down a street of Paris, all looking exactly similar and heading for some mysterious goal. It is not even certain whether they are ghosts or not. The speaker's response to their apparition is one of fascinated fear, queasiness and utter bafflement:

> Aurais-je, sans mourir, contemplé le huitième,
> Sosie inexorable, ironique et fatal,
> Dégoûtant Phénix, fils et père de lui-même?
> —Mais je tournais le dos au cortège infernal.
>
> Exaspéré comme un ivrogne qui voit double,
> Je rentrai, je fermai ma porte, épouvanté,
> Malade et morfondu, l'esprit fiévreux et trouble,
> Blessé par le mystère et par l'absurdité!
>
> (Could I still live and look upon the eighth
>   Relentless twin, fatal, disgusting freak,
>   Trick Phoenix, son and father of himself?
> —I turned my back on this parade from Hell.
>
>   Bedazzled, like a double-visioned drunk,
> I staggered home and shut the door, aghast,
>   Shaking and sick, the spirit feverous,
> Struck by this mystery, this absurdity!)[13]

These stanzas from the end of **"Les Sept Vieillards"** show the extent to which Eliot's reworking of the "fourmillante cité" into his own "Unreal City" deviates from his Baudelairean model:

>   Unreal City,
> Under the brown fog of a winter dawn,
> A crowd flowed over London bridge, so many,
> I had not thought death had undone so many.
> Sighs, short and infrequent, were exhaled,
> And each man fixed his eyes before his feet.
> Flowed up the hill and down King William Street,
> To where Saint Mary Woolnoth kept the hours
> With a dead sound on the final stroke of nine.
> There I saw one I knew, and stopped him, crying:
>   "Stetson!
> "You who were with me in the ships at Mylae!"[14]

It is widely accepted that the flowing crowd is "a cross between the inhabitants of Baudelaire's teeming and spectral city and those of Dante's hell",[15] and Eliot's appropriation of Baudelaire, in this common reading, once again emphasizes the spiritual and classical aspects of his urban poetics. Eliot's blend of Baudelaire and Dante thus seems to pave the way for the "recoil from the modernism of his earlier poems" into the Anglo-Catholic, classical orthodoxy of his later essays on Baudelaire, as well as the "Christianized reading of his own career".[16] But by taking this retrospective, teleological account for granted, critics neglect other readings that the mixed influences behind "The Burial of the Dead" made possible for Eliot's contemporaries. I suggest that if Eliot already retreated from Baudelaire's urban modernism in *The Waste Land,* the way in which he did so reminded some fellow modernists of earlier, mostly Romantic (and, to their eyes, more congenial) representations of London.

Robert Crawford has already shown how much Eliot's Dantean representation of London owed to late Victorian models he discovered before he became actively interested in either Dante or Baudelaire.[17] But poets like

James Thomson and John Davidson can in their turn be seen as part of a longer tradition of English urban writing whose literary and ideological associations Eliot should have been even keener to disown: indeed, much of it was unabashedly Romantic. Whether or not that tradition directly influenced the writing of the "Unreal City" passage is a moot point, but Eliot's fellow modernist readers did not fail to note its presence: if some famously condemned it, others (as is still too little recognized) seem to have regarded it as one of the poem's strengths. Ezra Pound had spotted this Romantic influence in the drafts of *The Waste Land* and made his disapproval clear through the damning note he wrote next to the line "Flowed up the hill and down King William Street": "Blake. Too often used". Such indictments from the quasi-editor of Eliot's poem were normally decisive—even when the resulting cuts actually took away from, rather than enhanced, the modernist aspects of the poem. Eliot thus bowed to a similar criticism from Pound when he left out a line from "The Fire Sermon" that was closer to Baudelaire's sense of spectrality than anything else in his drafts: "Phantasmal gnomes, burrowing in brick and stone and steel".[18] Yet the objectionable lines in "The Burial of the Dead", which evoke the "marks of weakness, marks of woe"[19] that Blake discerned in the faces of his fellow Londoners, did survive Pound's warning—a sign of their importance in Eliot's vision of the "Unreal City".

Pound's alertness to Romantic heresies could also have detected other worrying associations. Eliot's vision of London people "undone" by death even as they are walking the streets of the metropolis not only translates Dante's lines on the "doleful city" ("che morte tanta n'avesse disfatta") in *Inferno* (III.57), it also inadvertently echoes other treatments of London in English poetry. Years before Eliot used it, the rhyming pun on "London" and "undone" had already found its way in the work of writers whose approach to London was conditioned by a Romantic dislike of the metropolis. For A. E. Housman, London was also a scene of Blakean misery that caused the undoing of all who lived in it:

> But here in London streets I ken
> No such helpmates, only men;
> And these are not in plight to bear,
> If they would, another's care.
> They have enough as 'tis: I see
> In many an eye that measures me
> The mortal sickness of a mind
> Too unhappy to be kind.
> Undone with misery, all they can
> Is to hate their fellow man . . .[20]

The pun on "London" and "undone" has an even longer history. It was also used strategically by none other than Eliot's favourite Romantic bogeyman Shelley, who also developed a vision of the metropolis as a Dantean hell in the third part of *Peter Bell the Third*:

> Hell is a city much like London—
> A populous and a smoky city;
> There are all sorts of people undone,
> And there is little or no fun done;
> Small justice shown, and still less pity.[21]

Claude Rawson thus writes of Eliot's line: "'Undone' reverberates, fortuitously or otherwise, from Shelley's poem"—which, as he observes, also points forward to *The Waste Land* in its use of a mock-heroic tone.[22] Shelley's own debt to Dante, and his choice of a quasi-classical form in *Peter Bell the Third,* greatly complicate Eliot's contrast between Baudelaire's Dantean and classical leanings and the "romantic detritus" of *Les Fleurs du Mal.*[23] In purely spiritual terms, Baudelaire's poetry may well be marked by an opposition between the intuitions of Christianity on which Eliot insisted and the Satanism that fascinated Symons and other decadents. On the other hand, a focus on urban poetics reveals that Eliot has many more affinities with a long English tradition of urban writing than with his supposed French model.

The hostile view of London which is central to that English discourse has been diagnosed by historians as well as literary critics. It finds its most memorable expressions in (post)Romantic treatments of the city, but its pervasive influence in English culture means that it often transcends literary and ideological antagonisms.[24] A Baudelairean treatment of London might have challenged the assumptions of that peculiarly English tradition, but whether Eliot was equipped or willing to take urban poetics in radically new directions is highly debatable. In his own call for a new poetics of London, Symons had mentioned both Whitman and Baudelaire as possible models.[25] But Eliot's choice of a career in London, like Pound's, coincided with a reaction against a version of American culture that they identified with Whitman. Eliot may well have transplanted to London an alternative American discourse that was fundamentally anti-urban: an aversion to the city which is "a dominant attitude from Jefferson, through the writers of the American Renaissance, to Louis Sullivan and Frank Lloyd Wright", and which leaves Whitman relatively isolated in the nineteenth century.[26] Eliot was certainly keener to acknowledge Baudelaire's influence than Whitman's, but he may not have shared Baudelaire's vision of Paris any more than Whitman's vision of New York. Indeed, for all his gesturing towards Baudelaire, Eliot ended up reinforcing anti-urban assumptions that were ingrained in English literature. Even more ironically, the impact of *The Waste Land* would ensure that they lived on in English modernist writing that took its bearings from Eliot.

The idea of an "undoing" brought about by city life would have been largely alien to Baudelaire, who was an urban creature to his fingertips. The "undoing" that affects the London crowd presupposes a fall from a former state. If Housman's poem implies nostalgia for a pre-urban existence, Eliot's "undone" seem to be urban denizens who have sustained a more purely spiritual loss. But so have Shelley's: Eliot's Dantean allusion is tinged with spiritual critique, but the norm on which that critique is based is not fully worked out in "The Burial of the Dead". This means that Eliot's lines can be taken as perpetuating a home-grown and often Romantic denunciation of the British metropolis. In that view of London as a Dantean hell, specific sins are often recognizable. Shelley's critique of London life often singles out businessmen and speculators—one of whom interestingly "walks about a double ghost"[27]—and thus concentrates on the financial district of the City. Eliot's "Unreal City", with its significant capitals, provides a synecdochical bridge between the whole metropolis and the City defined by London Bridge, King William Street and St Mary Woolnoth. Whereas Baudelaire's ghosts marched to an unknown destination, Eliot's dead are definitely walking to the Royal Exchange and the Bank of England.

Eliot's London ghosts thus invite allegorical interpretations which Baudelaire's spectres actually resist. Baudelaire critics have been trying to tease out the symbolical meanings of the seven old cripples—these can be construed as repressed personal memories, hashish-induced hallucinations, the seven deadly sins, or as figures in a quasi-religious allegory.[28] To the *flâneur* of **"Les Sept Vieillards"**, however, they clearly remain a mystery: "le mystère et l'absurdité" dominate his mind both during and after the procession of the spectres. This procession is "infernal" because it horrifies and confuses, not because it can be interpreted in a specifically Christian sense—although English translators have not always resisted the Eliotic temptation to render Baudelaire's "cortège infernal" as "parade from Hell", with a tell-tale capital.[29] If Baudelaire was determined to "plunge into the depths of Heaven or of Hell", it was chiefly to "fathom the Unknown, and find the *new*".[30] Walter Benjamin argues that the procession of the cripples in **"Les Sept Vieillards"** is infernal precisely in this aesthetic sense, and that the poem reveals the paramount novelty of the "Tableaux Parisiens" to be "nothing else but [a] phantasmagoria of the 'always the same'", which he sees as the defining experience of life among the crowds of the modern metropolis. In Benjamin's reading, what is allegorical is not the ghosts themselves, but the mystery into which they temporarily plunge the speaker's feverish mind: the "anguish of the city dweller who is unable to break the magic circle of the type even though he cultivates the most eccentric peculiarities". The multiplication of the cripples thus testifies to the emergence of an urban poetry that cannot but acknowledge the loss of individuality, and is secretly fascinated by the aesthetic possibilities of that loss.[31]

Baudelaire's ghosts reveal the imbrication of the fantastic within the real in modern urban space, but they do not reduce the city to ghostliness. In the first poem of the "Tableaux Parisiens", Baudelaire explained that Paris's changing cityscapes became an allegory in his eyes ("tout pour moi devient allégorie"),[32] but the allegory is itself plural and shifting, fractured as it is by the ceaseless movement of *flânerie*. **"Les Sept Vieillards"** does not dismiss Paris as hell on earth. Instead, Baudelaire experiments with the aesthetic possibilities offered by his nightmarish vision; hell is part of the new poetic material afforded to the urban *flâneur,* but the city cannot be reduced to it. Eliot's vision of London as Hell, by contrast, flaunts its Baudelairean ancestry, but is only deceptively Baudelairean. Some critics have already pointed out how, in contrast to Baudelaire's Paris, "London [in *The Waste Land*] is never allowed to assume a life of its own, but remains [a] 'nightmare mirage'". But once again, this difference has been linked to Eliot's later Christian and classical misreading of Baudelaire: "the more one looks at Eliot's urban poetry in the context of another, expansive urban poet, the more one is convinced that it was indeed to another world that he had to turn from now on for inspiration".[33] This religious turn was announced in "What the Thunder Said", in which the city significantly "atrophies".[34] But "The Burial of the Dead" itself harks back to a Romantic tradition which the Anglican, classical Eliot is supposed to have disowned. If Eliot is not quite developing an equivalent of Baudelaire's urban poetry in *The Waste Land,* neither is he ridding Baudelairean poetics of Romantic trappings in his quest for an alternative City of God. Rather, "The Burial of the Dead" uses a Baudelairean allusion within a familiar English critique of London. As will be shown below, Eliot's perpetuation of this essentially Romantic critique facilitated the reception of *The Waste Land* among some of his English readers, including those who later felt alienated by his conversion to an Anglo-Catholic and classical orthodoxy.

Eliot's "Unreal City" passage also invited other recognitions. This is not to say that Eliot's lines are any less puzzling than the rest of *The Waste Land*, but the specific geography that they chart and the Romantic vision of London that they embody go some way towards explaining the popularity and the influence of the passage (as well as Pound's reservations). After his description of the "undone" crowd, Eliot's vision suddenly zeroes in on "Stetson!" The exclamations that follow can remind one of Baudelaire's own ejaculations when confronted with the spectres: "Ce sinistre vieillard qui se multipliait!", "Ces sept monstres hideux avaient l'air éternel!" ("Multiples of this sinister old man!", "These monsters smacked of all eternity!").[35] Yet Eliot's exclamations, confusing though they can be for the reader, proceed from the shock of sudden recognition ("I saw one I knew"), whereas the voice of **"Les Sept**

Vieillards" is baffled by an impenetrable mystery. The immediate recognition of "Stetson" provides an intriguing parallel to the way Eliot later described his response to the first lines of **"Les Sept Vieillards"**: "I knew what *that* meant, because I had lived it before I knew that I wanted to turn it into verse on my own account".[36] Baudelaire's haunted Paris of yellow fogs and incipient spectrality made their way subtly into the flickering world of *Prufrock and Other Observations*; but by the time Eliot declared his debt to Baudelaire in *The Waste Land,* he had apparently solved the enigma that the urban ghosts had represented in the "Tableaux Parisiens". "Stetson" may have remained a mystery for readers of *The Waste Land,*[37] but he clearly did not confront the speaker with the problems that had beset the hallucinating poet of **"Les Sept Vieillards"**. If the name of "Stetson" has puzzled to this day, the sentences that are addressed to him have been more amenable to interpretation: the references to "the ships at Mylae" and to buried corpses have become a privileged locus for the reading of *The Waste Land* as a Great War poem. Parallels between the Punic War and the conflict from which Europe had just emerged are an important key to the poem, ranging from Hugh Kenner's seminal essay "The Urban Apocalypse" to an editorial note in *The Norton Anthology.*[38] But the Great War subtext was part of the poem's reception from the beginning. As its buried corpses assumed the identity of war casualties, Eliot's "Unreal City" became associated with a perception of wartime horror and post-war gloom, or with the "unreality" of the post-war settlement that Keynes had denounced in *The Economic Consequences of the Peace.*[39] The allegory of London as Hell was complemented by another subtext that would give Eliot's urban ghosts recognizable identities. When some English readers were confronted with the apparition of Stetson among the flowing crowd of the dead, they too "knew what *that* meant": they had lived or read it before, and they would write it all over again.

Eliot was not the first poet who used Baudelairean themes to write about the War and its impact: Baudelaire's nightmarish images of carrion and skeletons recur in War poems published by Osbert Sitwell or Iris Tree in Edith Sitwell's *Wheels* between 1916 and 1919. As Patricia Clements tellingly observes, "that corpse, planted in the English garden in the 1860's, sprouts vigorously" in their poems, prefiguring Eliot's similar strategy in *The Waste Land.*[40] During and after the War, Eliot's relation to the Sitwells and their circle had been marked by a mixture of tactical collaboration, uneasy rivalry and private deprecation. In his letters, Eliot often seems to draw a firm line between English modernist insiders like the Sitwells and expatriates like himself, Lewis or Pound.[41] Although he is aware of a poetic kinship with the Sitwells, he is generally at pains to stress that this results from their imitation of him: "Heaven preserve me from being reviewed in the company of

Osbert. I may say that any poems of his which appear to have any affinity with mine were published *subsequent* to mine".[42] But whatever Sitwell immaturely borrowed from Eliot, the conflation of Baudelairean imagery and references to war in poems of *Wheels* could not possibly have been indebted to *The Waste Land.* Eliot, on the other hand, may well have been more inspired by *Wheels* than he cared to admit. In 1921, an invitation was apparently extended to Eliot: "*Would I think of contributing to Wheels? And so give the S[it-wells] a lift and the right to sneer at me?*"[43] Despite Eliot's hostile reaction, the "Unreal City" passage would certainly not have been out of place in that belittled organ of home-grown English modernism. Eliot's later portrayal of Baudelaire as an intensely moral poet was thus already foreshadowed by his and others' exploitation of the imagery of **Les Fleurs du Mal** as a source for sarcastic allegories of wartime horror. English poets were perhaps able to draw on an ethical dimension that was inherent in Baudelaire's wider "moral conception of his art".[44] What is remarkable in Eliot's case, however, is that this use of Baudelaire went hand in hand with a denunciation of the city that clearly runs against the grain of Baudelairean *flânerie.* When Eliot forged a link between a Romantic condemnation of London as Hell and the haunting presence of the Great War dead, he made a lasting contribution to the English modernist transformation of Baudelairean poetics, as Woolf's *Mrs Dalloway* best demonstrates.

Woolf's response to *The Waste Land* was extensive, as the many echoes of Eliot's poem in her fiction, and especially in *Mrs Dalloway,* suggest.[45] The "Unreal City" passage, and more particularly its association of Dantean spectrality with Great War traumas, would indeed echo throughout her portrayal of the shell-shocked visionary Septimus Warren-Smith. Septimus actually condenses various Eliotic aspects that have already been remarked on in Woolf criticism.[46] What needs stressing in this context is that Woolf's creation of Septimus brings out the latent Romanticism of Eliot's vision of London in "The Burial of the Dead", and also provides a foil to the quasi-Baudelairean *flânerie* found in other characters of *Mrs Dalloway.* The firmest intertextual link between those two key texts of English high modernism may thus be a Romantic approach to the metropolis that sets both Woolf and Eliot apart from a Baudelairean sense of the city, or from another model they both shared, i.e. the Joycean vision of Dublin in *Ulysses.*

Walking round Oxford Street and Regent's Park, Septimus hallucinates visions of his dead officer Evans. Like Stetson, the ghost who appears to Septimus has a specific identity that is immediately recognized; he actually makes explicit the Great War subtext that has long been felt to be a key to Eliot's "Unreal City". As if to underscore his Eliotic provenance, Septimus wants "to keep the dog far hence": "a Skye terrier snuffed his trousers and he started in an agony of fear. It was turning into a man!"; he also finds in Shakespeare an Eliot-like recoil from sex ("the business of copulation was filth to him before the end").[47] Septimus is also endowed with Messianic tendencies that strongly recall J. Alfred Prufrock's temptation to assume the role of a modern Lazarus "come back to tell you all": "I went under the sea. I have been dead, and yet am now alive". He knows "the meaning of the world" and feels the urge to impart it to the London crowd.[48] It is no coincidence that instead of resting when at home, he is often found reading Dante's *Inferno,* much to his worried wife's disapproval. Septimus's Dantean visionary powers make him see the London streets as a potential hell "about to burst into flames", an imminent conflagration where the Great War dead can appear to the living.[49] Yet Septimus is also a cross between the haunted, hallucinating urban wanderer of Eliot's early poems, and a more traditional Romantic type. As a young man freshly arrived in London, he went through certain "experiences" which once again remind one of "Prufrock" or the "Preludes": "the solitary ones, which people go through alone, in their bedrooms, in their offices, walking the fields and the streets of London". On the other hand, the changes that London brings about in Septimus make his plight symptomatic of a condition that was central to the Romantic critique of London. Septimus too is one of the "undone" of Romantic poems about the capital: "London had swallowed up millions of young men called Smith [. . .] there were experiences, again experiences, such as change a face in two years from a pink innocent oval to a face lean, contracted, hostile". Other traits identify Septimus with ill-fated Romantic figures: as a young man of literary tastes and aspirations, he half fell in love with a literature teacher, Miss Isabel Pole, who asked of him: "Was he not like Keats?".[50]

For Woolf, the visionary and Romantic elements in the Eliotic make-up of Septimus's character are not contradictory—they would only appear so to those who insist on reading *The Waste Land* in the light of Eliot's anti-Romantic pronouncements. My suggestion is that Woolf, at any rate, recognized the Romantic nature of the nightmarish vision of London presented in "The Burial of the Dead", and recycled it in *Mrs Dalloway.* Septimus's religious moments point not so much to Eliot's later conversion to High Anglicanism (which was received with considerable disappointment in Woolf's liberal circle), as to the "birth of a new religion" redolent of Romantic pantheism and hints of nature worship—elements that would have offended Eliot's later orthodox sensibilities:

> leaves were alive; trees were alive. And the leaves being connected by millions of fibres with his own body, there on the seat, fanned it up and down; when the

branch stretched he, too, made that statement. The sparrows fluttering, rising, and falling in jagged fountains were part of the pattern; the white and blue, barred with black branches. Sounds made harmonies with premeditation; the spaces between them were as significant as the sounds. A child cried. Rightly far away a horn sounded. All taken together meant the birth of a new religion—[51]

If Baudelaire is present here, however indirectly, it is not as the pioneering urban poet of the "Tableaux Parisiens", but rather as the author of the early **"Correspondances"**, that is a poet whose essentially Romantic interest in Unity of Being and Sweden-borgianism was often felt to be at odds with the radical modernity of *flânerie*:

> La nature est un temple où de vivants piliers
> Laissent parfois sortir de confuses paroles;
> L'homme y passe à travers des forêts de symboles
> Qui l'observent avec des regards familiers.
>
> Comme de longs échos qui de loin se confondent
> En une ténébreuse et profonde unité
> Vaste comme la nuit et comme la clarté
> Les parfums, les couleurs et les sons se répondent.
>
> (Nature is a temple, where the living
> Columns sometimes breathe confusing speech;
> Man walks within these groves of symbols, each
> Of which regards him as a kindred thing.
>
> As the long echoes, shadowy, profound,
> Heard from afar, blend in a unity,
> Vast as the night, as sunlight's clarity,
> So perfumes, colours, sounds may correspond.)[52]

This does not mean that the Baudelairean *flânerie* of the "Tableaux Parisiens" is absent from *Mrs Dalloway*—far from it. Recent Woolf criticism has made much of what it sees as her strategic adaptation of this Baudelairean motif for feminist purposes.[53] However, I suggest that in *Mrs Dalloway,* Woolf's main difference from Baudelairean models of *flânerie* does not lie in her feminization of a primarily masculine attitude, but rather in a critical distance towards *flânerie* that shows Woolf making common cause with Eliot (and, beyond him, a whole tradition of English urban writing) against Baudelaire.

The moments of *flânerie* in Woolf owe little to Eliot. Her vision of London was often very different from that of *The Waste Land*: countless passages in her letters and diaries attest to a deep love of the capital that Eliot could never have shared. *Mrs Dalloway* also voices that attachment. What Clarissa Dalloway loves about London is to be found "In people's eyes, in the swing, tramp, and trudge; in the bellow and the uproar; the carriages, motor cars, omnibuses, vans, sandwich men shuffling and swinging; brass bands; barrel organs . . .".[54] The paradoxical solitude of the urban crowd, which drew mournful comments from Eliot in "The

Burial of the Dead" ("Sighs, short and infrequent, were exhaled / And each man fixed his eyes before his feet") was "fascinating" to Woolf: "they all seemed separate, self-absorbed, on business of their own".[55] For her female characters in particular, London is a place of opportunity, and an alternative to domesticity. An elating sense of urban spectrality even emerges in some of her writings, like the significantly titled essay "Street Haunting",[56] which could fruitfully be compared to some of Baudelaire's prose poems about Paris.

But in *Mrs Dalloway,* Septimus experiences London very differently from Woolf's *flâneurs* and *flâneuses.* While Clarissa Dalloway, Peter Walsh and others can yield to the flow and the dispersal of the London streets, Septimus remains the anti-*flâneur* for whom the surface of London is deceptive. To him, starting motor-cars are pistols firing or shells exploding; every noise or sight conceals a hidden meaning; ghosts are not the metropolitan phantasmagoria of the "always the same" that Benjamin would diagnose, but reminders of the hell of the Great War. In this, he illustrates the transformation of Baudelairean urban poetics that took place in "The Burial of the Dead". Like Eliot, Woolf could also recoil from her beloved London. Septimus is the *doppelgänger* who voices her repulsion, and who exposes the fragility or even the vacuousness of the *flâneurs* and *flâneuses*'s response to the city. When Woolf read "The Burial of the Dead", Eliot's supposedly Baudelairean ghosts quickly revealed their significance: Woolf too, like Eliot (but unlike Baudelaire himself), seems to have known what they meant. They meant the very opposite of the *flâneuse*'s fascination with city life, of the temptations offered by metropolitan experience to modern (female) subjectivity, and of the ceaseless movements that Woolf's wandering style adopts as she follows her other characters. They implied, in short, a rejection of the modernity that Benjamin located at the heart of Baudelaire's experience of the city.

The London of English modernism may look as haunted as Baudelaire's Paris, but its ghosts are not fleeting visions in a city that swarms with experiences both real and fantastic. Rather, those ghosts open up a fantastic space that questions the ontological status of London through a Romantic critique of urban existence, or through the conjuring of a specific historical trauma which is the subtext of that ghostliness. Eliot's intervention was crucial in this adaptation of Baudelairean aesthetics to an English context, but it is easy to misunderstand the nature of the changes he effected. The transformation of the urban poetics of the "Tableaux Parisiens" that takes place in "The Burial of the Dead" is markedly different from the orthodox misreading later performed in Eliot's essays on Baudelaire.[57] Years after *The Waste Land,* Eliot would try to impose his version of a classical, Christian Baudelaire: a version which could not but alienate many of those who,

like Woolf, had hailed Eliot as radical voice of post-war fragmentation and disillusion. If the version of Baudelaire Eliot presented in "The Burial of the Dead" proved more recognizable and influential, it is largely because that version was more palatable to an English audience still imbued with a Romantic distrust of the metropolis, and for whom the aftermath of the Great War remained an inexorcizable trauma at the heart of London life.

Notes

Raphaël Ingelbien is affiliated with The University of Leuven, Belgium.

1. Symons, 89.

2. For some systematic treatments of Eliot's relation to Baudelaire, see Weinberg, Ward, Schuchard's "First-Rate Blasphemy", Clements and Coates. Eliot's two main essays on Baudelaire are "Baudelaire", reprinted in *Selected Essays* (1932), and "Baudelaire in Our Time", reprinted in *For Lancelot Andrewes* (1928).

3. Eliot, *Selected Essays,* 423. The first major reaction against Eliot's appropriation of Baudelaire was Victor Brombert's "T. S. Eliot and Romantic Heresy". Brombert insists that Baudelaire was "far more of a Romantic than Eliot is willing to grant" (14).

4. Eliot, *Selected Essays,* 426.

5. Schuchard, *Eliot's Dark Angel,* 13.

6. Baudelaire, *The Flowers of Evil,* 176-7. The translation is James McGowan's, which is preferred here for its semantic closeness to the original.

7. Eliot, *To Criticize the Critic,* 127.

8. Eliot, *Collected Poems,* 13.

9. Kenner, 27.

10. Crawford, 11. The translation is McGowan's.

11. Baudelaire, *Les Fleurs du Mal,* 309-10.

12. Britzolakis, 73, 78.

13. Baudelaire, *The Flowers of Evil,* 178-81.

14. Eliot, *Collected Poems,* 65.

15. Britzolakis, 76.

16. Ibid., 79.

17. Crawford, 39-55.

18. Eliot, *The Waste Land,* 9, 31. Pound's comment was "Palmer Cox's brownies" (31).

19. Wu, ed., 73.

20. Housman, 71-2.

21. Shelley, 306.

22. Rawson, 104-8.

23. Eliot's hostility to Shelley, most evident in *The Use of Poetry and the Use of Criticism* (33 in particular), is tempered elsewhere by a recognition of Dante's influence: Shelley was "the one English poet of the nineteenth century who could even have begun to follow those footsteps" (Eliot, *Selected Prose*, 227). Whether Eliot had *Peter Bell the Third* in mind is open to conjecture.

24. See for instance Stange and Wiener.

25. Symons, 89.

26. Stange, 480-1. Stange himself considers that poets like Symons eventually "cleared the way" and made "the twentieth-century city available to Joyce and Pound, Virginia Woolf and T. S. Eliot" (493). This sweeping conclusion represents a common view, but it overlooks what I think are important tensions and distinctions within the modernist writing of the city.

27. Shelley, 306.

28. See for instance the editorial note in *Les Fleurs du Mal*, 310, and also Chapman.

29. Baudelaire, *The Flowers of Evil*, 180-1.

30. Ibid., 293.

31. Benjamin, 22.

32. Baudelaire, *The Flowers of Evil*, 174-5.

33. Ward, 101, 104.

34. Versluys, 188.

35. Baudelaire, *The Flowers of Evil*, 178-9.

36. Eliot, *To Criticize the Critic*, 127.

37. Although the name has been interpreted in many ways, most commentators identify Stetson with soldiers or clerks and lawyers with City connections. See for instance Childs, "Stetson in *The Waste Land*".

38. Abrams et al., eds., 2372.

39. Eliot's reference to Baudelaire in his note may indeed conceal a borrowing from Keynes—see Harries, 144 and Paulin, 14-15.

40. Clements, 245.

41. Eliot's first recorded reference is to a poetry reading in late 1917, where he was invited together with "big wigs, OSWALD [*sic*] and EDITH Shitwell [*sic*]" (Eliot, *Letters*, 206). He later com-

plained that Osbert Sitwell enjoyed more critical attention in London than Ezra Pound (358). When Wyndham Lewis provided illustrations for the Sitwells, Eliot wrote to him that "it almost looked as if you were disparaging your own work in putting it alongside that of those people" (446).

42. Ibid., 378. Eliot's emphasis.

43. Ibid., 446.

44. Clements, 245-7.

45. See especially Childs, "Mrs Dalloway's Unexpected Guests", and Steinberg.

46. The most extensive treatment remains Steinberg's article. Steinberg is essentially concerned with possible parallels between Septimus and Eliot himself; in what follows, I will rather stress the intertextual relations between "The Burial of the Dead" and Woolf's novel.

47. Eliot, *Collected Poems*, 65; Woolf, *Mrs Dalloway*, 74, 97.

48. Eliot, *Collected Poems*, 16; Woolf, *Mrs Dalloway*, 75, 73-4.

49. Woolf, *Mrs Dalloway*, 96-7, 16.

50. Ibid., 92-3.

51. Ibid., 24.

52. Baudelaire, *The Flowers of Evil*, 18-19. On the tension between Romantic occultism and modern urban poetics in Baudelaire, see for instance Versluys, 145.

53. See especially Bowlby.

54. Woolf, *Mrs Dalloway*, 4.

55. Eliot, *Collected Poems*, 65; Woolf, *A Room of One's Own*, 86.

56. Woolf, *Collected Essays*, 155-66.

57. There is little space here to consider the Baudelairean aspects of the ghost that appeared much later in "Little Gidding". His features and demeanour are more stately and classical than those of the apparition in "The Burial of the Dead". But like Stetson, he also differs from Baudelaire's visions in his familiarity: "Both intimate and unidentifiable", he utters words that "sufficed / To compel the recognition they preceded". See Eliot, *Collected Poems*, 217.

References

Abrams, M. H. et al., eds. *The Norton Anthology of English Literature.* Vol. 1. New York: Norton, 2000.

Baudelaire, Charles. *Les Fleurs du Mal.* Edited by John E. Jackson. Paris: Livre de Poche, 1999.

———. *The Flowers of Evil.* Translated and edited by James McGowan. Oxford: Oxford University Press, 1993.

Benjamin, Walter. *The Arcades Project.* Translated and edited by Howard Eiland and Kevin McLaughlin. London: Harvard University Press, 1999.

Bowlby, Rachel. "Walking, Women, and Writing: Virginia Woolf as *flâneuse.*" In *New Feminist Discourses: Critical Essays on Theories and Texts,* edited by Isobel Armstrong. New York: Routledge, 1992.

Britzolakis, Christina. "Phantasmagoria: Walter Benjamin and the Poetics of Urban Modernism." In *Ghosts: Deconstruction, Psychoanalysis and History,* edited by Peter Buse and Andrew Stott. London: Macmillan, 1999.

Brombert, Victor. "T. S. Eliot and Romantic Heresy". *Yale French Studies* 13 (1954): 3-16.

Chapman, William Sharpe. *Unreal Cities: Urban Figuration in Wordsworth, Baudelaire, Whitman, Eliot, and Williams.* Baltimore, MD: Johns Hopkins University Press, 1990.

Childs, Donald J. "Mrs Dalloway's Unexpected Guests: Virginia Woolf, T. S. Eliot, and Matthew Arnold". *Modern Language Quarterly* 58, no. 1 (1997): 63-82.

———. "Stetson in *The Waste Land.*" *Essays in Criticism* 38 (1988): 131-48.

Clements, Patricia. *Baudelaire and the English Tradition.* Princeton, NJ: Princeton University Press, 1985.

Coates, Christopher. "Eliot's Baudelaire: 'Christ the Tiger' in the 'fourmillante cité'." *Yeats Eliot Review* 9, no. 4 (1988): 149-52.

Crawford, Robert. *The Savage and the City in the Poetry of T. S. Eliot.* Oxford: Clarendon, 1990.

Eliot, T. S. *Collected Poems 1909-62.* London: Faber, 1974.

———. *For Lancelot Andrewes.* London: Faber, 1928.

———. *The Letters of T. S. Eliot.* Vol. 1. Edited by Valerie Eliot. London: Faber, 1988.

———. *Selected Essays.* London: Faber, 1932.

———. *Selected Prose of T. S. Eliot.* Edited by Frank Kermode. New York: Farrar, Straus and Giroux, 1975.

———. *To Criticize the Critic and Other Writings.* Lincoln, NB: University of Nebraska Press, 1991.

———. *The Use of Poetry and the Use of Criticism.* London: Faber, 1946.

———. *The Waste Land. A Facsimile and Transcript of the Original Drafts, Including the Annotations of Ezra Pound.* Edited by Valerie Eliot. London: Faber, 1971.

Harries, Martin. *Scare Quotes from Shakespeare. Marx, Keynes and the Language of Reenchantment.* Stanford, CA: Stanford University Press, 2000.

Housman, A. E. *Collected Poems.* London, Harmondsworth: Penguin, 1956.

Kenner, Hugh. "The Urban Apocalypse." In *Eliot in His Time,* edited by A. Walton Litz. Princeton, NJ: Princeton University Press, 1972.

Paulin, Tom. "Many Cunning Passages." *Times Literary Supplement,* 29 November 2002, 14-15.

Rawson, Claude. *Satire and Sentiment 1660-1830.* Cambridge: Cambridge University Press, 1994.

Schuchard, Ron. *Eliot's Dark Angel.* Oxford: Oxford University Press, 1999.

———. "'First-Rate Blasphemy': Baudelaire and the Revised Christian Idiom of T. S. Eliot's Moral Criticism." *English Literary History* 42 (1975): 276-95.

Shelley, P. B. *Poems.* Vol. 1. Edited by A. H. Koszul. London: Dent, 1966.

Stange, Robert. "The Frightened Poets." In *The Victorian City: Images and Realities,* edited by H. J. Dyos and Michael Wolff. London: Routledge and Kegan Paul, 1973.

Steinberg, Erwin R. "*Mrs Dalloway* and T. S. Eliot's Personal Waste Land." *Journal of Modern Literature* 10 (1983): 3-25.

Symons, Arthur. *Poetry and Prose.* Edited by R. V. Holdsworth. Cheadle: Carcanet, 1974.

Versluys, Kristiaan. *The Poet in the City.* Tübingen: Gunter Narr Verlag, 1987.

Ward, Nicole. "'Fourmillante Cité': Baudelaire and 'The Waste Land'." In *The Waste Land in Different Voices,* edited by A. D. Moody. London: Arnold, 1974.

Weinberg, Kerry. *T. S. Eliot and Charles Baudelaire.* The Hague: Mouton, 1969.

Wiener, Martin J. *English Culture and the Decline of the Industrial Spirit 1850-1980.* 2nd ed. London, Harmondsworth: Penguin, 1985.

Woolf, Virginia. *Collected Essays.* Vol. 4. London, Harmondsworth: The Hogarth Press, 1967.

———. *Mrs Dalloway.* Edited by Elaine Showalter. London: Penguin, 1992.

———. *A Room of One's Own and Three Guineas.* Edited by Michèle Barrett. London: Penguin, 1993.

Wu, Duncan, ed. *Romanticism: An Anthology.* London: Blackwell, 2000.

Leslie Boldt-Irons (essay date 2007)

SOURCE: Boldt-Irons, Leslie. "In Search of the Archaic Mother: The Space of the Abject in Bataille's *My Mother* and Baudelaire's *Flowers of Evil*." In *Beauty and the Abject: Interdisciplinary Perspectives,* edited by Leslie Boldt-Irons, Corrado Federici, and Ernesto Virgulti, pp. 43-58. New York: Peter Lang, 2007.

[*In the following essay, Boldt-Irons compares the treatment of the mother figure in* Les Fleurs du Mal *and in Georges Bataille's* My Mother, *arguing that the former primarily employs the technique of metaphor, while the latter employs the technique of metonymy.*]

In an essay contained in *Desire in Language,* Kristeva declares: "[the] craftsmen of Western art reveal better than anyone else the artist's debt to the maternal body and/or motherhood's entry into symbolic existence— that is, translibinal jouissance, eroticism taken over by the language of art" (243). In *Tales of Love,* Kristeva raises the question of the power of the maternal body, and the confrontation or avoidance of it in Bataille's *My Mother* and Baudelaire's *Flowers of Evil.* This question is raised in the context of two issues: that of narcissism on the one hand, and the textual strategies of metaphor and metonymy on the other. Narcissism is seen, at best, to be an unstable refuge for a subject struggling with separation from an archaic relation to the mother; the refuge of narcissism is thus continually threatened by the "abject" at its borders. With respect to metaphor and metonymy, it becomes clear that the former is linked to the disguising of taboo, while the latter is associated with its displacement, or its circumvention. In what follows, I connect the use of metaphor and metonymy to Kristeva's discussion of the presence or absence of the maternal body in *Flowers of Evil* and *My Mother.* What interests me as well is the degree to which these tropes sustain or dismantle narcissism as a refuge, or as an avoidance strategy in the face of the maternal body. It is a question, then, of the way metaphor and metonymy are used in the poetic language of Baudelaire and Bataille to admit or avoid regression, in a fear-inspiring, but ultimately desire-filled movement towards that archaic, instinctual and maternal territory—a movement that Kristeva equates with a form of incest: "The point is to reach the threshold of repression by means of the identification with motherhood [. . .] to reach this threshold where maternal *jouissance,* alone impassible, is arrayed" (1980, 249).

It is principally Kristeva's *Revolution in Poetic Language* and her *Powers of Horror* that set the stage for understanding the way in which both narcissism and the

use of metaphor and metonymy may be linked to a confrontation with the maternal body in *Flowers of Evil* and *My Mother.* Based on notions contained in these two texts, notions such as the symbolic, the semiotic and the subject-in-process, the following questions may be asked: Do negativity and transgression permit *jouissance* to intrude fully upon the symbolic order in *Flowers of Evil* and *My Mother*? Can the texts of both Baudelaire and Bataille be said to challenge the symbolic order equally, and if so, to what extent are metaphor and metonymy linked in each case to this challenge? Does the passage of *jouissance* through textual transgression engage both Bataille and Baudelaire equally in a regression towards an archaic maternal territory?

To answer the questions raised above, one might consult Kristeva's *Powers of Horror,* a text in which she discusses narcissism, and the abject that threatens the stability of the narcissistic subject from its borders. In this text, Kristeva writes that the abject, neither subject nor object, is that which disrupts identity; it is the in-between, the composite, the ambiguous (4). It is that which is excluded or jettisoned from the speaking, proper (and therefore clean) subject. The jettisoned object (filth, excrement, the corpse, but also, more generally, "that which I cannot recognize as a thing" "draws me toward the place where meaning collapses" (2). That which "disrupts identity, system, order," that which "does not respect borders, positions, rules" causes abjection (4).

The abject, rendered accessible through *jouissance,* also challenges existing social and symbolic relations when the narcissistic subject is confronted with the "untouchable, impossible, absent body of the mother" (6). In *Powers of Horror,* Kristeva also writes that "[a]bjection preserves what existed in an archaism of pre-objectal relationship, in the immemorial violence with which a body becomes separated from another body in order to be" (10). However, literature brings about abjection when it "confronts us [. . .] within our personal archaeology, with our earliest attempts to release the hold of maternal entity even before ex-isting outside of her" (13). In *Tales of Love,* Kristeva suggests further that fear of the abject, brought about by severance from the maternal entity, causes the narcissistic withdrawal into a space where the subject meets the absence of object, or the self as object: "The object of Narcissus is psychic space; it is representation itself, fantasy" (116). "Narcissus is not located in the objectal or sexual dimension. He does not love youths of either sex; he loves neither men nor women. He loves Himself—active and passive, subject *and* object" (116). Narcissism may thus be seen as a strategy arising from fear of the abject brought about by severance from the mother.

Sublimation, for Kristeva, is a means of keeping the abject under control (1982, 11). For this reason, it is not surprising that the narcissist should resort to it in his writing. Sublimation allows one to name the "pre-nominal," the "pre-objectal" (1982, 11), which would appear to predate severance from the mother. Abjection, on the contrary, thwarts the capacity to "name" for, neither subject nor object, it is the ambiguous, the in-between, which disrupts order and identity. Sublimation, as a response to abjection, is identified by Kristeva in *Tales of Love* as a frequent strategy found in the poems of Baudelaire. For Kristeva, sublimation of the abject in Baudelaire's poems becomes a "process that neutralizes the body, passions, and everything that recalls, more or less closely, the family/cradle of desires" (1987, 325-26). Metaphor permits Baudelaire to attain an "*elevation* [. . .]" of meaning, through mingling significations, toward the *infinity* of connotation and the *void* of nonmeaning" (1987, 330). In this way, Baudelaire's metaphorical writing filters *jouissance* (which, according to Kristeva, his poetry tries to arrest nonetheless through recourse to the abject). The poem **"Elevation"** expresses this filtering of *jouissance*:

> Above the valleys, over rills, and meres,
> Above the mountains, woods, the oceans, clouds,
> Beyond the sun, past all ethereal bounds,
> Beyond the borders of the starry spheres,
>
> My agile spirit, how you take your flight!
> Like the strong swimmer swooning on the sea
> You gaily plow through the immensity
> With manly, inexpressible delight.
>
> Fly far above this morbid, vaporous place;
> Go cleanse yourself in higher, finer air,
> And drink up, like a pure, divine liqueur,
> Bright fire, out of clear and limpid space.

(17)

While Baudelaire's poetry often depicts an elevation away from abjection, Bataille's fiction in *My Mother* does not incorporate sublimation as a response to abjection. Rather, it is metonymical displacement as an avoidance strategy that one finds at work in the text. Pierre, the desiring son, initially circumvents taboo by loving his mother's lovers; however, the maternal body is ultimately confronted, not circumvented at the story's end. If the sublime in ***Flowers of Evil*** is tinged with the abject at its borders (an abject that metaphor is meant to alleviate) the abject in *My Mother*—though it may be temporarily circumvented through metonymic displacement—is ultimately joyed in, not sublimated.

An example of metonymic displacement first occurs in *My Mother* when Pierre discovers obscene photographs in his father's study:

> Lodged behind the books, in the glass-fronted book-cases my father kept locked but to which my mother had given me the keys, I came upon a heap of photographs. Most of them were very dusty. But in an

instant I saw that they were incredibly obscene [. . .]. I lost control and helplessly sent the remaining piles flying. But I had to pick them back up [. . .]. My father, my mother and this swamp of obscenity [. . .] out of despair, I decided to follow this horror through [. . .]. Interwoven joy and terror strangled me within [. . .]. The more those pictures terrified me, the more intense was my excitement at the sight of them [. . .]. I sensed that I was damned, I defiled myself before the filth in which my father—and perhaps my mother too—had wallowed.

(40, 41)

While he does not actually "see" his mother engaged in these indecent acts—indicating only that "perhaps" his mother had been a participant—Pierre has been led by her to a vision of bodies that may have had direct physical contact with her. Through displacement, Pierre is led to the experience of abjection in the face of the (imagined) maternal body—an imagining locked in a room to which his mother has provided the key. Metaphoric avoidance and metonymic displacement are, then, strategies that Baudelaire and Bataille use, respectively, to avoid or confront the abject, strategies that I will now examine more fully in the context of Kristeva's discussion of their work.

It is well known that Charles Baudelaire was extremely close to his mother. It has been suggested that

> [a]fter his father's death, [when Charles was only six, he] was drawn to his beloved mother in even closer intimacy. Her decision a year later to marry Captain Aupick, a brilliant career soldier, who was to become a general, an ambassador, and finally a senator, must have been a severe blow to the small child of seven who adored his mother and demanded all her love and affection for himself. Indeed, Baudelaire, who was inexhaustible on the subject of his disapproval of his mother's remarriage, is reported to have declared "When one has a son like me [. . .] one doesn't remarry."[1]

Baudelaire's correspondence is filled with letters in which intimacy with the mother is not only desired but prized over intimacy with other women, thus indicating the intensity of the bond between mother and son. The resistance to any real severance from the "maternal entity" could point to what Kristeva sees as Baudelaire's narcissistic withdrawal into a psychic space whose object is "representation itself, fantasy" (1987, 116). For Kristeva, it is metaphor that effects "an elevation toward the infinity of connotation and the void of non-meaning" (1987, 330).

Yet the abject is certainly present as a force in Baudelaire's poetry. One might say, with Kristeva, that the abject, used to arrest the erotic and *jouissance* in his poetry, provides an important and surprising counter-weight to sublimation (which, ironically, had been used as a strategy to avoid the abject). In **"The Carrion,"** the substitution of the carcass and its horrible infection for the lover's body means that the flowering of *jouissance* is checked by rot and swarming decomposition:

> And you in your turn, will be rotten as this:
> Horrible, filthy, undone,
> O sun of my nature and star of my eyes,
> My passion, my angel in one! [. . .]
> And then, o my beauty, explain to the worms
> Who cherish your body so fine,
> That I am the keeper for corpses of love
> Of the form and the essence divine.
>
> (61, 63)

In *Powers of Horror*, Kristeva writes that "devotees of the abject [. . .] do not cease looking [. . .] for the desirable and terrifying, nourishing and murderous, fascinating and abject inside the maternal body" (54), a body that is disguised by attributes that overdetermine its presence. Writers who incorporate the presence of a devouring woman into their writing, do so, writes Kristeva, "for want of having been able to introject [the mother] and joy in what manifests her, for want of being able to signify her" (1982, 54). Not having signified his mother directly by his writing, Baudelaire substitutes metaphors of aggressive, devouring, vampire-like figures, metaphors that are no doubt symptomatic, in Kristeva's eyes, of his failure to joy in what would manifest the maternal body in his writing. In **"The Metamorphoses of the Vampire,"** Baudelaire describes a woman who kneads her breast before giving it to those who would wish to bite it. The proffering of breast sedates the victim whose marrow is then sucked from his bones. When he wishes to return her kisses with kisses of his own, he awakes to find that the milk-giving breast has been transformed into a greasy leather flask that overflows with pus. From the perspective of Kristeva's theory, the substitution of leather flask for breast would be linked to the fact that *jouissance* (in this case, that in and of the maternal body, which is never given direct signification by Baudelaire) is typically arrested by abjection:

> Twisting and writhing like a snake on fiery sands
> Kneading her breast against her corset's metal bands,
> The woman, meanwhile, from her mouth of strawberry
> Let flow these fragrant words of musky mystery:
> —I have the moistest lip, and well I know the skill
> Within a bed's soft heart, to lose the moral will.
> [. . .]. When she had drained the marrow out of all
>   those bones,
> When I turned listlessly amid my languid moans,
> To give a kiss of love, no thing was with me but
> A greasy leather flask that overflowed with pus!
> Frozen with terror, then, I clenched both of my eyes;
> When I reopened them into the living light
> I saw I was beside no vampire mannequin
> That lived by having sucked the blood out of my skin,
> But bits of skeleton, some rattling remains
> That spoke out with the clacking of a weathervane,

> Or of a hanging shop sign, or an iron spike,
> Swung roughly by the wind on gusty winter nights.
>
> (253, 254)

Kristeva writes that Baudelaire's depiction of woman as "ferocious feral devouring beast" is particularly dangerous for one who "protect[s] [himself] from her through the mist of signs [he] call[s] beauty" (1987, 335). The vampire in his this poem exposes her flesh to the bone. "[S]tripped of her passion, devitalized, skeletonlike," [s]he has thus been made less dangerous than a mother who desires and abandons" (1987, 325).

The fact that Kristeva should base so much of her analysis of Baudelaire's writing on his use of metaphor (his is a text "wholly founded *on metaphor*" (1987, 318), requires that one examine more closely the function of metaphor in art and in dreams, since critical discussion of its nature and function has raised questions that are relevant to Kristeva's analysis.

Roman Jakobson's classic article on metonymy and metaphor "Two Aspects of Language and Two Types of Aphasic Disturbances" has been influential in the writings of linguists, aphasiologists, literary theorists, and semioticians. In this article, he describes what he calls the two poles or axes of language: the paradigmatic axis of metaphor, "which involves the association of substitutable entities," and the syntagmatic axis of metonymy, "which involves simultaneous or successive combinations" (115). Language operates along the two axes of selection (metaphor) and continuity (metonymy), whereby the metonymic axis of contiguity assumes that elements to be combined are *in praesentia,* that is "jointly present in an actual series" (19), while the metaphoric axis of selection suggests that items to be chosen are connected *in absentia,* that is, they are connected in the code of language but not in the message under consideration (119). While theorists like Paul Ricoeur point to the extreme simplicity of Jakobson's definition of metaphor, and its tendency to underestimate polysemy or lexical ambiguity,[2] I will nonetheless make use of several of the tenets of his classic article as a guideline for my discussion of metaphor and metonymy in the works of Baudelaire and Bataille.

Whether metaphor is considered to be the purveyor of truth, or to be its counterfeiter—and the nineteenth century provides us with a wide spectrum of views on this subject, from the Romantic poets to Nietzsche—there is a divergence regarding the source and the nature of its poetic charge. Jakobson, for example, provides the point of departure for this discussion when he writes that the process of selection upon which metaphor relies "implies the possibility of substituting one for the other, equivalent in one respect and different in another" (119). Once again, this relatively simple depiction is developed and refined by numerous theorists. Metaphors, seen to arise from the contradiction, clash or tension between a literal meaning and its context, are considered by some to actually *induce* similarity where none had previously existed.[3]

Ultimately, when they are viewed positively, metaphors are deemed capable of altering the "conceptual system in terms of which we experience and talk about our world."[4] Such a belief leads certain theorists to assert that, "any ontological description of the way things stand forth or reveal themselves to us as meaningful will itself be inextricably linked to metaphor."[5] This close association of metaphor with ontological description and, indeed, with speculative discourse, will be particularly relevant to my discussion of the collapse of metaphor in Bataille's fiction.

In the meantime, there is yet another view, which sets the creative power of metaphor against its disruptive force in the literary text. Jonathan Culler notes in this regard that "it is precisely literature's resistance to metaphor,"[6] that is, literature's resistance to the replacement operations that metaphor effects within a text, that will ensure the latter's power, a necessary counterbalance to that of metaphor. In a similar vein, Karsten Harries writes that, while poetry is metaphoric, it must struggle against metaphor if it is to preserve its unity (1978, 73). If indeed Kristeva is correct in her assertion that Baudelaire's poetry "is fully affirmed and exhausted within the metaphorical conveyance" (1987, 319), then one might ask whether his metaphoric language is properly disruptive, forcing his finished work to resist the aggression of metaphor in order to preserve its meaning. Kristeva writes that Baudelaire's corpus "has no other 'position' than to raise and shatter meaning" (1987, 319). This would suggest, then, that there is often little resistance to the metaphors in his text, a text in which metaphor is ultimately an agent of sublimation, moving meaning away from abjection and towards "the *infinity* of connotation and the *void* of non-meaning" (1987, 330). Kristeva writes that in Baudelaire's poetry the "Self" "vaporized" in generalized metaphoric form becomes the "ground not only of "lowly" passion, but of *jouissance* itself, which has been turned into beauty" (1987, 326).

Yet while metaphor is an agent of sublimation, of volatilization and deviation away from the abject, the abject is nonetheless frequently present, providing an aggressive resistance to sublimation, arresting *jouissance* (particularly when the source of *jouissance* is the maternal body, as Kristeva has observed). The theoretical positions on metaphor outlined above allow us to understand why it might be that the abject in Baudelaire's poetry appears so frequently to counter the opposite movement towards sublimation. To begin, the notion that metaphor should depend on a clash or tension for its poetic charge allows one to suggest, with

Kristeva, that the abject manages to arrest *jouissance* in Baudelaire's poetry through the clash and tension of metaphoric *substitution,* the abject providing, in this way, an important and surprising counterweight to sublimation as well as the very charge that recourse to sublimation was meant to circumvent. When Baudelaire writes, "[a]nd the sky cast an eye at this marvelous meat as over the flowers in bloom" (61), one notes that the evanescent beauty of this flower is rooted in the abject that checks its flight. Similarly, the substitution of the carcass and its horrible infection for the lover's body means that the flowering of *jouissance* is checked by rot and swarming decomposition:

> And you in your turn, will be rotten as this:
> Horrible, filthy, undone,
> O sun of my nature and star of my eyes,
> My passion, my angel in one! [. . .]
> And then, o my beauty, explain to the worms
> Who cherish your body so fine,
> That I am the keeper for corpses of love
> Of the form, and the essence divine.

> (61, 63)

Of course the substitution of pus-filled greasy leather flask for milk-laden breast, as seen earlier in **"Metamorphoses of the Vampire,"** constitutes another example of the metaphoric substitution of the abject for the sublime, thus arresting possible *jouissance* in the maternal body. One returns at this juncture to the views of Culler and Harries, who posit that literature must resist the replacement operations that metaphor effects in a text in order that the latter exert its own power and thereby preserve its unity. It would appear that two opposing impulses are at work in Baudelaire's text—the swerve away from abjection through sublimation and volatilization, as well as the metaphoric substitution of a monstrous abject for the absent maternal body, an abject that arrests *jouissance* and resists sublimation, forcing a return to a forbidden site that is replaced, disguised and overlaid by rot and decomposition. In both cases, the maternal body is occulted, having become an Other "present" only *in absentia.* In both cases as well, a metaphoric substitution is made, either through sublimation or through recourse to the abject. While the latter resists and arrests the movement towards sublimation, it would appear that Baudelaire's poetry is in each case relatively unable to resist the "replacement operations" mentioned by Culler and Harries in their descriptions of metaphor.

To what extent does Baudelaire's use of metaphor relate to his narcissism? One might say, with Kristeva, that Baudelaire's position is narcissistic to the extent that it is not directed to an object of desire, but aims, rather, at a lifting upwards towards an Other, rendered invisible through metaphoric substitution. Baudelaire's is a "paroxysm of identification, in which, without a stable object, the lover identifies with its contemplation; he passes into it, he is it—the artist, like the poet, is both 'cause and effect, subject and object, mesmerist and one entranced'" (1987, 333).

There are indeed many poems in *Flowers of Evil* that evoke this position of the narcissist, a position that is "predicated on the existence of the *ego* but not of an *external object*" (1987, 62). There are those in which he addresses his Muse, and those in which he addresses his death. In one of the poems, he even becomes his own executioner:

> I am the wound, and rapier!
> I am the cheek, I am the slap!
> I am the limbs, I am the rack,
> The prisoner, the torturer!
>
> **(Heautontimoroumenos,** 157)

Of this self-inflicted narcissistic suffering, Kristeva writes that it is a cover, an anaesthetization of painful emptiness: "In poetic art, the victim becomes a creator of his condition [. . .] the appearances put on are the bandages over unbeing, the anaesthesia against narcissistic pain" (1987, 337).

In Baudelaire's *Flowers of Evil,* then, metaphor permits the substitution of one signifier for another *in absentia,* a relationship by which the absent signifier is evoked by the one that has been selected to take its place: lover/vampire for mother; victim/torturer for self; vaporized, sublimated beauty/rotten filthy abject for maternal Other. Indeed as Karsten Harries writes: "Metaphors speak of what remains absent [. . .]. Thus metaphor implies lack" (1978, 82). Baudelaire compensates for this lack with a narcissistic plenitude achieved through desired union with a "non-object." The presence of the Other is absent, or rather evoked but also disguised by the metaphor that stands in its stead.

In the work of Georges Bataille, it is metonymy that is primarily at work. In *Tales of Love,* Kristeva does not, properly speaking, identify metonymy as the trope active in his writing. It is in fact metaphor that she mentions most frequently in this work. However, it is her reference to a writing "in-between-the-signs" (369) that leads me to discern metonymic practice.

To begin, Kristeva alludes to the presence of a clash or a tension in his writing, which the theorists mentioned earlier associate with metaphor. However, while metaphor normally arises from a "calculated category mistake" (Goodman, cited by Johnson, 1981, 32) that may actually induce a similarity where none had previously existed, any metaphor that might arise in Bataille's writing would result in a paradox, in a nonsynthetic combination that is more a juxtaposition than a substitution—in Kristeva's terms, an *antithetical* metaphor.

> When he writes, "Perfect darkness alone is similar to light," he confronts us with the unfolding of an antithetical metaphor that fuses two opposing semantic fields (darkness, light) and, through the tension caused by such nonsynthetic combination, produces a nonsense effect, a state of shock.
>
> (1987, 365)

The theoretical considerations raised earlier with respect to metaphor point to its more general function in language and thought, a function that links metaphor to the emergence of meaning: "any ontological description of the way things stand forth or reveal themselves to us as meaningful will itself be inextricably linked to metaphor," writes Mark Johnson (1981, 43). Kristeva notes as well that metaphor, according to the traditional view, "makes things visible" (1987, 366). However, she also asks: "How might one make visible that which is not visible because no code, convention, contract or identity holds it up?" (1987, 366). This is the challenge put forward in Bataille's work: to make visible that which has no code or identity to give it definition. Metaphor, which relies on the substitution of one signifier for another, does not in principle find a place in Bataille's work, since the occulted signified evoked by such a metaphor would, by its nature, resist any attempt to represent it.

And yet Kristeva maintains that literature must not draw back from the invisible, the inaccessible: "Figurative language, literature, then owe it to themselves to measure up to that invisible and also to its drive intensity" (1987, 366). According to Kristeva, Bataille's fiction takes on this challenge directly by reducing metaphor to an "ellipsis," to a scattering of multiple clues "along the narrative" (1987, 369). If metaphor traditionally speaks of "what remains absent," if it traditionally "implies lack" by substituting a presence, then Bataille's writing takes the metaphoric tendency to create a deferred meaning and exposes it to the impossible. Meaning is not deferred or sublimated by metaphoric substitution in his writing, but made jagged and incoherent through its collapse. "Since the metaphor is the sign of unbeing" writes Kristeva, "it reaches its peak and its completion in a deferment of meaning, at the very moment the narrative clarifies certain erotic stages of that unbeing" (1987, 369). If metaphor is considered by some the counterfeiter of presence and being, the lack or unbeing that in fact underpins it is exposed in Bataille's writing in a process that is at once metaphor's completion and its impossibility.

Kristeva expresses this notion in another way when she says that metaphor "with its retinue of idealization and mysteries" is out of place in Bataille's fiction (1987, 367). If in Baudelaire's writing metaphor is a vehicle for sublimation, for a movement away from the abject, in Bataille's narrative, a meditation on the sublime or on God is juxtaposed with the abject, with what is "obscene, aggressive, destructive, deadly, or simply painful" (1987, 367). Might one not speak in fact of a sort of reverse of sublimation, of an "abjectification" of the sublime? For Kristeva, Bataille's writing presents a sublime that *is* abject, an abject that *is* sublime. She writes that in his fiction the sublime is "this neither subject-nor-object entity I have called 'abjection'" (1987, 368). When it is revealed through its abject medium, the sublime becomes "degraded, breath-stopping, laughable" (1987, 367). In the following scene from *L'Abbé C.* for example, Robert the priest, his brother and the provocative Eponine find themselves in the bell-tower of his church. Eponine is nude beneath her coat; her nudity is suddenly revealed in a gust of wind, at the very moment that Robert is engaged in prayer:

> The priest knelt gently [. . .]. He bowed his head and extended his arms to form a cross [. . .]. After a few minutes he began to chant, slowly and lugubriously, as if he were calling to the dead: *Miserere mei Deus, Secundam magnam misericordiam tuam* [. . .]. It was a ravishingly melodious lament, but so ambiguous! Such a bizarre profession of horror before the delights of nudity! [. . .] that extraordinary beauty, in the night, was no longer anything more than a tribute to vice, the only object of that whole little scene [. . .]. The minute that she saw Robert, Eponine, visibly emerging from her dreamy stupor, broke into laughter so abruptly that she lost her balance: she turned around and, leaning over the balustrade, appeared to shake like a little child. She was laughing with her face in her hands and Robert, interrupted by a cackle she couldn't suppress, looked up, with his arms outstretched, only to behold her naked bottom: the wind had lifted up her coat which, when she was seized by laughter, she had been unable to keep closed.
>
> (43, 44, 45)

In this case, as in many others, the depiction of the sublime made abject leads to collapse, to the post-theological amorous "flash" (Kristeva 1987, 368), a "fading out of meaning at the same time as a conveyance of meaning" (1987, 366). Baudelaire's *Flowers of Evil,* writes Kristeva, is a text fully affirmed and exhausted within the metaphorical conveyance" (1987, 319). If metaphor in Bataille's writing has collapsed, if the sublime has been degraded in a vertiginous fall into the abject, then where or how does metonymy enter upon the scene of his writing? Metonymy is defined as a "figure of speech consisting of the name of one thing for that of another of which it is an attribute or with which it is associated." Jakobson stresses that contiguous elements of a sentence relate to one another metonymically; the syntagmatic axis of metonymy permits "simultaneous or successive combinations (*in praesentia*)" (1990, 115). The metonymic axis of contiguity assumes that elements to be combined are *in praesentia*, that is, "jointly present in an actual series" (1990, 119).

Earlier in this essay I gave the example of a metonymic displacement, thanks to which Pierre's viewing of the obscene photographs in his father's study brought him obliquely into contact with his mother's desiring body. Another more direct example of metonymic displacement occurs when Pierre, his mother and Rhea, her lover, leave for the theater and are thrown into amorous confusion in their brougham: "In the brougham we sat bunched close together. My mother's arm round Rhea's waist; Rhea nibbling her shoulder. Rhea, holding my hand, holding it as far up as her leg as she could get it. I shot a glance at my mother; she appeared radiant" (61). Pierre looks at his mother as she embraces her lover and as her lover arouses him with her touch. Desire may be said to be metonymically displaced to the extent that the mother and son express themselves contiguously, *in praesentia,* through and by means of another woman whom they share, before sharing each other.

There are perhaps two reasons why metonymic displacement is at work in this text. The first reason, as I have said earlier, is because metonymic displacement permits the circumvention of taboo. The second reason would be linked to the fact that incest, the sun and death cannot be stared at unblinkingly. As Kristeva writes, "they must be seen obliquely, through an erotic, meditative narrative—an amorous one" (1987, 370). Of course these two reasons may be likened to the two sides of a coin: one circumvents taboo because it signifies the impossible; the impossible brings about its circumvention because it is intolerable. As the following passage suggests, Pierre circumvents the possibility that he desires his mother sexually by claiming that neither one nor the other sought to give each other sexual fulfillment. What they sought, rather, was the very impossibility of desire: "Had we translated our trembling madness into the barren act of copulation, the cruel game we played with our eyes would have ceased [. . .] we'd have exchanged the purity of the unattainable for a mess of pottage [. . .]." (87-88). The text continues to give the impression that Pierre desired his mother's impossible desire, not her body, that his mother desired her anguish, loved the fruit of her womb—now empty—and not her son:

> Am I then to say of this love that it was incestuous? The insane sensuality we hovered in, was it not impersonal and similar to that so very violent sensuality which my mother had experienced when she wandered naked in the forest [. . .]. Was I even in love with my mother? I *worshipped* my mother, I did not love her. As for her, I was the forest child, creature of ungodly joy.
>
> (87, 89)

Yet these descriptions of an impossible desire do not allow us to discount the very contiguity of sexual exchange linking mother metonymically to son:

My mother on one side, I on the other, we leaned together over Rhea who drank between us. Up until this point our silence had only intensified our pleasure, revealed in the darkening of our faces. For several minutes, my mother and I used Rhea, doing to her, and just as deliberately, just as slyly, what a few moments before she had been doing to us. [. . .] once again my mother's gaze and mine met and they coupled.

(82)

What remains deliberately ambiguous in the text is the nature of the desire linking mother to son. Is this desire truly beyond mere incestuous longing (seen as the possible) or does incestuous longing (the impossible, the taboo) by its nature force its circumvention and metonymic displacement in the text? Does the mother's desire exceed the mere desire of a mother for her son? Or do both mother and son simply displace their desire to one that appears to be without and beyond object?

The answer to this question no doubt involves an impossible juxtaposition of both possibilities. Pierre's mother claims: "I am not sure whether I really have a taste for women [. . .]. I believe that all I love is love, and in love itself only the torment of loving" (73). When his mother leaves him, however, Pierre's emptiness and rage at being abandoned are expressed in moments of sexual paroxysm with Rhea: "I had made love with Rhea; or rather, more truthfully, I had spent my fury upon her. My mother had left me, I would have liked to cry, and those shudderings while we were embracing were the aching sobs that racked my heart" (83).

If metaphor has been reduced in Bataille's text to "multiple clues scattered along the narrative" (Kristeva 1987, 369), if its meaning, due to the collapse of its function, has been impossibly deferred, then metonymy, as the continued deferral of desire, is the trope that follows naturally upon the reduction of metaphor. What is of interest in this context is the comparison between sublimation in Baudelaire's poetry, which Kristeva sees as elevation away from the abject, the maternal body, and a displacement or deferral in Bataille's *My Mother* that paradoxically circumvents and confronts the maternal body and its desire. Perhaps it is the very nature of the abject, as a "'something' that I do not recognize as a thing" (Kristeva 1982, 2), that causes its representation in *My Mother* to surface in the spaces between the words, between the lines. After all, the abject (in Kristeva's words) "draws me towards the place where meaning collapses" (1982, 2). As that which disrupts identities, system and order, the abject brings me to "the edge of nonexistence and hallucination, of a reality that, if I acknowledge it, annihilates me" (1982, 2). If *My Mother* successfully utters the abject, it does so metonymically, contiguously, *in praesentia*, but in a way that causes presence to fade into absence. The sublime having been made abject,

metaphor collapses into metonymy, which in turn fades into an "in-between-the-signs" of an impossible utterance.

If one may speak of *re*placement operations in Baudelaire's poetry, one might say that *dis*placement operations in *My Mother* lead the reader around, but eventually to the confrontation of a *crisis*; a crisis in which meaning and presence fade, in which the abject disrupts order, in which the subject meets an archaic mother whose own desire has emerged and been given representation. In *My Mother*, the narrative strategy does not protect against death, against a *jouissance* found in the mother. Indeed, Bataille's fiction, unlike Baudelaire's poetry, attempts to signify the mother directly, "to introject her and joy in what manifests her" (Kristeva 1982, 54). In doing so—be it through the provisional strategy of metonymic displacement, and this because the maternal body cannot be stared at unblinkingly—Bataille's text brings the reader to a crisis, to a depiction of a subject-in-process.

In the final analysis it is not surprising that Baudelaire's metaphoric sublimation, though arrested by the abject, is less likely than Bataille's metonymic displacement—challenged in its turn by a confrontation with the abject—to bring the subject to a crisis, to its own process. Both writers refer, in Kristeva's words, to a "terrifying, abject referent" (1982, 38). For both, the relation to an archaic mother does not provide solace. In each case, the "narrative web is a thin film constantly threatened with bursting" (1982, 141) as the boundary between subject and object is shaken. Like all literature, theirs represents what Kristeva calls the "archeology" and "exhaustion" of abjection (1982, 210). The artist "even if he does not know it, is an undoer of narcissism and of all imaginary identity as well, sexual included" (1982, 208). In the hollowing out of this crisis in which identity becomes unraveled, both writers, in their different ways, reach for that "sublime point at which the abject collapses in a burst of beauty that overwhelms us—and that 'cancels our existence'" (1982, 210). Baudelaire reaches for that sublime point through the replacement operations of metaphor, the sublime replacing maternal abjection, the abject replacing *jouissance* with and in the mother. Bataille, on the other hand, reaches for the collapse of the sublime through the displacement operations of metonymy, thus circumventing maternal abjection before leading the subject to a crisis through *jouissance* with and in the mother, a *jouissance* marked by an "abjectification" of the sublime.

Notes

1. L. B. Hyslop and F. E. Hyslop, *Baudelaire: a Self-Portrait* (Westport: Greenwood P, 1957), p. 243.

2. P. Ricoeur, *The Rule of Metaphor*, trans. R. Czerny with K. McLaughlin and J. Costello (Toronto: U of Toronto P, 1977). In this text, Ricoeur views

Jakobson's descriptions of metaphor as suffering from an excessive or damaging emphasis on the noun or on naming, and this at the expense of a properly semantic treatment of metaphor that would proceed from a recognition of the sentence as the primary unit of meaning. In addition, the insistence on a "borrowed" word that "deviates" from normal usage ignores the fact that all words are defined to some extent by the frame of the sentence in which they are situated. In a sense, no single meaning can be said to "properly" belong to a word; nothing prevents a word from signifying more than one single thing. In Ricoeur's view, Jakobson's interpretation of metaphor does not pay sufficient attention to the potential polyvalence and semantic ambiguities of words.

3. Turbayne, for example, argues that metaphor "is a sort of 'sort-crossing' in which objects ordinarily falling under one category are seen as falling under some new category." Ed. M. Johnson, *Philosophical Perspectives on Metaphor* (Minneapolis: U of Minnesota P, 1981), p. 31. Goodman, in a similar vein, writes that metaphor is a "calculated category mistake," M. Johnson (1981, 32).

4. M. Johnson, (1981), p. 33.

5. M. Johnson, (1981), p. 43. Indeed, Paul de Man builds upon this notion when he suggests that: "Being and identity are the result of a *ressemblance* which is not in things but posited by an act of the mind which, as such, can only be verbal. And since, to be verbal in this context, means to allow substitutions based on illusory *ressemblance* [. . .] then mind, or subject, is the central metaphor, the metaphor of metaphors." "The Epistemology of Metaphor." *On Metaphor,* ed. S. Sacks (Chicago: The U of Chicago P, 1978), p. 23.

6. J. Culler, cited by K. Harries in "Metaphor and Transcendence," *On Metaphor,* ed. S. Sacks (Chicago: The U of Chicago P, 1978), p. 73.

7. Definition abridged from Webster's dictionary.

References

Bataille, Georges. *L'abbe C.* 1988. Trans. P. Facey. London: Marion Boyars.

———. *My Mother.* 1995. Trans. A. Wainhouse. London: Marion Boyars, 1995.

Baudelaire, Charles. *Flowers of Evil.* 1993. trans. J. McGowan Oxford: Oxford UP.

De Man, Paul. "The Epistemology of Metaphor," *On Metaphor.* Ed. S. Sacks. Chicago: The U of Chicago P., 1978.

Harries, Karsten. Metaphor and Transcendence. *On Metaphor,* ed. S. Sacks. Chicago: The U of Chicago P. 1978.

Hyslop, L. B. and Hyslop F. E. *Baudelaire: a Self-Portrait.* Westport: Greenwood P, 1957.

Jakobson, Roman. "Two Aspects of Language and Two Types of Aphasic Disturbances." *On Language.* Ed. L. Waugh and M. Monville-Burston. Cambridge: Harvard UP, 1990.

Johnson, Mark, ed. *Philosophical Perspectives on Metaphor.* Minneapolis: U of Minnesota P, 1981.

Kristeva, Julia. *Desire in Language: A Semiotic Approach to Literature and Art.* Trans. and ed. L. Roudiez. New York: Columbia UP, 1980.

———. *Powers of Horror: An Essay on Abjection.* Trans. L. Roudiez. New York: Columbia UP, 1982.

———. *Revolution in Poetic Language.* Trans. M. Waller. New York: Columbia UP, 1984.

———. *Tales of Love.* Trans. L. Roudiez. New York: Columbia UP, 1982.

Ricoeur, Paul. *The Rule of Metaphor.* Trans. R. Czerny with K. McLaughlin and J. Costello. Toronto: U of Toronto P, 1977.

Charles D. Minahen (essay date spring 2008)

SOURCE: Minahen, Charles D. "Irony and Violence in Baudelaire's 'À Celle Qui Est Trop Gaie.'" *Symposium* 62, no. 1 (spring 2008): 3-15.

[*In the following essay, Minahen analyzes the polar oppositions, ironic tension, and resultant descent into madness and fantasized violence on display in "À celle qui est trop gaie," one of six poems censored by the French courts as obscene and excluded from the 1857 edition of* Les Fleurs du Mal.]

Irony, like obscenity (as famously described by U.S. Supreme Court Justice Potter Stewart), is hard to define, but you know it when you see it. Philippe Hamon adds a cautionary note: "vouloir analyser ou réduire théoriquement cet objet [l'ironie], qui a fini par incarner le 'je ne sais quoi' le plus irréductible de toute œuvre particulière, voire de toute la littérature en général, c'est le détruire immanquablement" (3), which did not prevent him from undertaking a rigorous 159-page analysis of irony. Perhaps the elusive *je ne sais quoi* stems from the idea that "irony, like beauty, is in the eye of the beholder and is not a quality inherent in any remark, event, or situation," as D. C. Muecke avers (14). More than a convenient cliché, situating irony in a beholder reveals it to be primarily an intention that in fact involves at least two beholders: the producer and the receiver(s) of the ironic enunciation. The ambiguous *je ne sais quoi* is further heightened by the double nature of the enunciation, which contains a "contresens"[1] that must be perceived for the irony to take effect. In other words (to turn the previous dictum around): you see it (irony) when you know it (the *contresens*) is implied.

Charles Baudelaire's predication of his aesthetic on the well-known "deux postulations simultanées" toward God and Satan[2] (and implicitly other polar dualisms locked in a violent struggle for ascendancy in the poet's soul) makes his work particularly apt for the deployment of irony.[3] The qualification *simultanées* is particularly important here, because the sense and countersense are typically not presented as mutually exclusive. This simultaneity is everywhere apparent in the use of antithesis throughout his work, as exemplified by a poem such as **"Hymne à la beauté"** (Baudelaire 24-25), where it saturates every stanza. Its pithiest form is undoubtedly the oxymoron, which is also widely deployed, from the characterization of "Ennui" as a "monstre délicat" in the liminal **"Au lecteur"** (5-6), on through piece after piece, including, among other examples, "la superbe carcasse" of **"Une Charogne"** (31-32), "les soleils mouillés" of the exotic land that mirrors the lady's tearful eyes in **"L'Invitation au voyage"** (53-54), or the double oxymoron and chiasmus "Ô fangeuse grandeur! sublime ignominie!" that describes the "Femme impure" of the untitled poem XXV (27-28).

At face value, an oxymoron could be said to represent the romantic idea of irony expressed by Friedrich Schlegel as the "recognition of the fact that the world in its essence is paradoxical and that an ambivalent attitude alone can grasp its contradictory totality."[4] Concerning paradox, Anne-Marie Paillet-Guth notes, "[l]oin d'établir une hiérarchie entre deux sens dont l'un annulerait l'autre, le paradoxe postule une constante réversibilité de la signification" (qtd. in Mercier-Leca 97), an "unresolvable conflict"[5] and oscillation[6] between sense and countersense that is as unsettling as it is ambivalent. Oxymoronic irony thus involves a dialectical process of conflict between poles in which any intended or hoped-for synthesis ultimately fails. Resolution is not achieved; indecision and frustration prevail.

Yang (Yin)

In one of Baudelaire's most notorious poems, **"À celle qui est trop gaie"** (156-57), this type of irony is summed up in the antithesis of verse 16, "Je te hais autant que je t'aime!" where the contrary emotions are joined by *autant que,* denoting both simultaneity and equality. But the dynamic working out of the emotions through the poem would seem at first not simultaneous but sequential, with the first four and then the next five stanzas under the rubrics of, respectively, "love" and "hate," and with hate threatening to defeat and exclude love by having the last word. Like the opposing halves of the yin-yang symbol,[7] however, an element of antithesis is simultaneously present in the exposition of each term of the polar dualism, as can be seen first in the evocation of the lady. She epitomizes a classical ideal of beauty:

> Ta tête, ton geste, ton air
> Sont beaux comme un beau paysage;
> Le rire joue en ton visage
> Comme un vent frais dans un ciel clair.
>
> Le passant chagrin que tu frôles
> Est ébloui par la santé
> Qui jaillit comme une clarté
> De tes bras et de tes épaules.

(1-8)

The associations—beauty and clarity (both evoked twice), freshness, bedazzlement—bespeak her good looks and health. But the allusion to the passing chagrin that the latter dispels (the bit of yin within the yang) admits the theme of melancholy and presages the poem's second part. "La santé," moreover, "[q]ui jaillit comme une clarté," has a distinct erotic overtone, which not only unmasks the poet's sexual desire but also anticipates the imagined toxic insemination with which the poem concludes. (The association of *clarté* with ejaculation may prompt in the minds of some critics the Rimbaldian image of "l'hydrogène clarteux" possibly denoting spent sperm in the prose-poem "H.") Although the "retentissantes couleurs" of her dresses evoke musically "L'image d'un ballet de fleurs," they are "folles"[8] and "l'emblème / De ton esprit bariolé"—in other words, madly excessive and gaudy, like her too-gay spirit.[9] A subtle subversion of the lady's beauty that has inspired the poet's love is thus underway in the very portrayal of it. It is further compounded by the fact that, as John McCann points out, "the majority of references to her are metonymic, the part standing for the whole: *ta tête, ton geste, ton air, ton visage, tes bras, tes épaules, tes toilettes* and *ton esprit.* Thus, even in these quatrains, before the slashing of the later quatrains, the woman is, as it were, dismembered" (149). Not only is potential violence insinuated rhetorically into the text, also presaging the poem's outcome, but the emphasis on the physical, including body and dress, that overwhelms the belated reference to her *esprit* further exposes the poet's primarily sexual interest in her, because, as the object of desire, she is literally more object than subject. Reification of this sort is often a characteristic of the erotic imagination, as Verlaine's late erotica, which involves both female and male objects of desire, demonstrate (1387-1416).

There is, at this point, a triple allusion to madness, first in the adjective *folles* describing her dresses, then as a noun denoting the woman herself, and finally as an adjectival past participle that transfers significantly the attribute from the woman to the poet, who describes himself as "affolé." He is, in one sense, mad with desire but is also, in another sense, terror-stricken by this too-perfect woman, who makes him all too aware of his own melancholic inadequacies. There follows directly in the text the antithesis "Je te hais autant que je t'aime," signaling for the first time his conscious realization of the irony of his predicament, an irony that has been nascent in the latent connotations of sexual desire and violence that have subtly subverted the patent celebration of the lady's beauty and gaiety. This sudden, shocking irruption of hatred in extreme opposition to love creates an admixture so unstable, so intolerably ironic that, like jostled nitroglycerin, it explodes, triggering madness. In his discussion of irony, which focuses on the particular case of Baudelaire, Paul de Man claims that

> absolute irony is a consciousness of madness, itself the end of all consciousness; it is a consciousness of a non-consciousness, a reflection on madness from the inside of madness itself. But this reflection is made possible only by the double structure of ironic language: the ironist invents a form of himself that is "mad" but that does not know its own madness; he then proceeds to reflect on his madness thus objectified.
>
> (216)

Although Buvik asserts that de Man misreads Baudelaire's essay "De l'essence du rire" by associating madness with irony ("Le poète ne se prononce pas [. . .] sur l'ironie, mais sur le comique absolu [. . .]. Il ne dit pas non plus que l'ironie nous rapproche de la folie" [93]), de Man's point, if not that of Baudelaire in his essay, nonetheless sheds light on madness in the face of irony that precipitates a consciousness of madness, as verses 15 and 16 of the poem show. Here we encounter another dimension of irony that issues from the romantic and that Schlegel describes as "self-conscious" (Wellek 15). Hermann Wetzel terms it "[c]ette forme moderne, auto-ironique de l'ironie (qui prend sa source dans le romantisme)" and observes that "[d]ans le cas de l'auto-ironie, où l'auteur est son premier lecteur, cet auteur-lecteur, aussi bien que tout lecteur externe, peut être un destinataire à la fois complice et victime de sa propre ironie" (120). In verses 15 and 16 of the poem, the poet as the enunciating subject recognizes the madness of his ironic consciousness as subject of the enunciation in a cogent instance of auto-irony. What follows is a dizzying plunge into violence.

YIN (YANG)

The shift of focus from the lady to the poet in stanzas 5 and 6 of what I have deemed the second part of the poem under the rubric of "hate" represents her at first indirectly in the image of a "beau jardin" (the bit of yang within the yin) that mirrors the "beau paysage" with which she was identified in stanza 1. But it is now the poet overwhelmed by "atonie" who strolls glumly in the garden aware of his ironic predicament, expressed directly in the simile "comme une ironie" that reflects the contradictory role of the sun as the bright source that lights up the beautiful garden but also bathes with its sunny rays his profound melancholy, a contradiction that "tears him up," intensifying his *folie*. Coupled with the lush greenness of springtime, he feels humiliated and is angered by "L'insolence de la nature." In this ironic reversal of the pathetic fallacy, nature is independently evil and perverse, intentionally exacerbating his melancholy by cruelly contrasting with it.

> [C]ette esthétique [du mal] s'effectue à travers une *violence métatextuelle*. Le cliché traditionnel ne sert pas seulement d'objet d'ironie, ni ne se présente comme la norme contre laquelle se définissent le style ou le programme nouveaux—il devient la victime du texte, brisée et violée par la nouvelle écriture, dans l'espace textuel lui-même"
>
> (Shinabargar 126; emphasis in original).

The violence done to the cliché of the romantic view of nature is even more egregiously inflicted when the poet exacts punishment for nature's insolence on a flower by presumably crushing or killing it. The flower has been associated with the lady in "L'image d'un ballet de fleurs" of the third stanza. The punishing of the flower for being too beautiful in the sunny garden, as if to mock his own dark mood, thus foreshadows the violent punishing of the lady for being similarly too lovely and gay, as if in spite of his gloomy melancholy.

However, the violence is directed not just against the particular lady but also, at least implicitly, against the traditional conception of female beauty, extending back at least to the Renaissance. She was first presented in a manner that recalled *le blason de la femme* by means of which the parts of the body were one by one extolled, but also, as we have seen, metonymically dismembered. As a result of the poet's subversion of this traditional form of homage in conjunction with his evocation of the romantic adequation of woman's and nature's beauty, the punishing of the flower signifies a violence inflicted metatextually on the cliché of feminine beauty that has persisted through the ages. Candice Nicolas has recently shown how Rimbaud, while continuing this assault on conventional representation of the feminine, particularly that of the Parnassian ideal, moves beyond Baudelaire in his championing of a future liberated, independent, and self-actualized woman.[10]

But this is certainly not the way the lady is portrayed in the last three stanzas of **"À celle qui est trop gaie,"** which have attracted the greatest amount of critical attention. The initial "Ainsi" of verse 25 serves as a pivot that transfers the poet's desire to punish from the flower-scapegoat of the previous scene to the lady in her bedroom. The sexual assault is imagined as a sneak attack at night while she is asleep. The lack of any cooperation on her part is implied by the poet's description of himself as "un lâche," who is ready to take by force what he cannot obtain through seduction, and by his intention to creep up on her "sans bruit." The adjective *étonné* that describes her startled physical reaction to the actual infliction of a knife wound confirms that this is not a consensual sadomasochistic sex play, but a criminal assault that, as we will see, culminates in rape.

The episode unfolds in the mode of irony, which is in fact a double irony. The first of these is the irony carried over from the feeling of hatred the poet experienced as a result of the lady's too-beautiful beauty and too-gay gaiety. These attributes are represented by the images of "les trésors de ta personne" (27), "ta chair joyeuse," "ton sein pardonné" (pardoned for being too perfect?), and "lèvres" that are "éclatantes et [. . .] belles"—conventionally positive features whose value is negatively reversed by the poet's ironic perception of them. As negatives in his eyes, they deserve punishment—hence, his desire to "châtier ta chair joyeuse" (29) and "meurtrir ton sein pardonné" (30),[11] as well as to create "lèvres nouvelles, / Plus éclatantes et plus belles" (34-35) by opening "Une blessure large et creuse" (32) in her side and infusing her with poison (this last action is expressed in the poem's last line, to which I will return).

The second instance of irony, which might be termed irony of irony, is the sadistic pleasure he takes in mutilating and inflicting pain. Sadism (and masochism) are by definition ironic, as they are predicated on a reversal of the reality principle from a conception of pleasure and pain as mutually exclusive to one of interdependence. The expression in the poem of sadistic pleasure is the exclamation "vertigineuse douceur!" of verse 33. In his discussion of Baudelaire's essay on laughter, de Man observes that

> [i]rony possesses an inherent tendency to gain momentum and not to stop until it has run its full course; from the small and apparently innocuous exposure of a small self-deception it soon reaches the dimensions of the absolute. Often starting as litotes or understatement, it contains with itself the power to become hyperbole. Baudelaire refers to this unsettling power as *"vertige de l'hyperbole."*
>
> (215)

De Man's misreading of Baudelaire's notion of *le comique absolu* as absolute irony is curiously revealing about the way irony unfolds in the poet's poetry and particularly in this poem. From his self-deception that he loves the lady for her loveliness to the sudden realization that he actually hates her for the same

reason, a madness takes hold of him that shatters the precarious balance of oxymoronic love-hate and unleashes the ever-increasing power of irony expressed as violence, first in the innocuous act of punishing a flower, then in the hyperbolic violent sexual assault and wounding of the lady that culminates in the utterly mad experience of absolute irony as vertiginous pleasure. This reverses de Man's description of irony as "unrelieved *vertige,* dizziness to the point of madness" (215), because it is the poet's unrelenting and increasing madness in the face of intolerable irony that precipitates his vertigo.

ART IMITATING LIFE IMITATING ART

A substitution in the last line, and "Note de l'éditeur" tacked onto the poem, have caused much debate and have added a historical dimension to that debate that has affected the interpretation of the poem. Although it behooves critics to avoid confusing *vie* and *œuvre,* since the subject speaking in the poem is inevitably a construct not unlike a fictional character, the note, in particular, is a rare intrusion of the author into his work that invites recourse to biography and creates an ironic tension between text and context. The note appears in the Belgian publication of **"À celle qui est trop gaie"** as one of the "Pièces condamnées tirées des *Fleurs du mal*" in *Les Épaves.* Although Baudelaire gave his publisher, Auguste Poulet-Malassis, permission to publish the pieces, he took pains to hide his involvement with the instruction "et surtout que cela ait l'air d'être fait sans mon aveu" (Baudelaire 1120). Poulet-Malassis confirms that "'[l]es notes sont de lui [Baudelaire], bien qu'il les ait fait endosser par l'éditeur'" (813). The note appended to **"À celle qui est trop gaie"** takes a swipe at the judges who condemned the poem, specifying that the word *venin* of the last line signifies "spleen ou mélancolie" and mocking "leur interprétation syphilitique" (157).[12] Claude Pichois remarks that "ni le substitut du procureur dans son réquisitoire, ni les juges dans le libellé du jugement n'ont proposé une 'interprétation syphilitique': celle-ci est du fait de Baudelaire!" (Baudelaire 1133n3). McCann adds that "by drawing attention to the obscene and violent meanings or, as Pichois claims, inventing or elaborating on them, Baudelaire is ensuring that they are very much in our minds" (148).

It should be further noted that "T'infuser mon venin" is a variant in the published editions that originally read "T'infuser mon sang" in the original manuscript, which was enclosed in an anonymous letter sent to Madame Sabatier in 1852. The reference to blood in the version she first received could be read perhaps as a metaphor for the commingling of their love in an attempt at seduction à la John Donne, who offered just such a symbol in his poem "The Flea" (c. 1601); even the cut could be considered an exaggeration of the classical notion of love as a wounding. In 1857, Baudelaire gave Madame Sabatier a copy of **Les Fleurs du mal** as a gift that, according to Michel Butor, "lui aura ouvert les portes de la chambre de Mme Sabatier," but that "une fois cette victoire obtenue, il n'en a point profité" (65). In that copy, one of the original copies Baudelaire received before the trial, **"À celle qui est trop gaie"** appears with *sang* replaced by *venin,* which Steve Murphy, supporting Butor, identifies as "une représentation métaphorique du sperme vicié du poète syphilitique" (59), notwithstanding the denial of the editorial note added later. Baudelaire's syphilitic condition would explain why he did not, in Butor's view, take advantage of Madame Sabatier's intimate availability, because he would risk infecting her, and it is hard to believe he could inflict that kind of violence on a living person, as Butor observes: "Le lâche qui infuse son venin à une fille saine lui fait une irréparable offense, il la plonge dans un malheur définitif; c'est un impardonnable crime."[13] Would Baudelaire, the man, be capable of such an act?

Henri Troyat seems to think so, because in his account of events Baudelaire would not be able to refuse an offer he had for years so ardently sought, even if the woman now making it is a far cry, physically at least, from the erstwhile cherished ideal:

> Devant cette dame qui n'est plus une idole lointaine, ni l'élégante hôtesse des dîners de la rue Frochot, mais une opulente créature aux seins lourds, aux hanches larges, offerte à lui sans détour. Baudelaire se sent paralysé de la tête aux pieds. Elle est trop charnue, trop rieuse, trop provocante à son goût. Ne va-t-il pas flancher par manque d'appétit? Il voudrait fuir. Néanmoins, il s'execute.
>
> (234)

Gasarian, alleging that Butor mistook the facts, echoes Troyat's view: "Baudelaire a déjà donné son venin à la Présidente, comme en témoigne la lettre du 31 août, où il écrit: 'il y a quelques jours, tu étais une divinité, [. . .] Te voilà femme maintenant'" (42). To buttress the point, Gasarian refers to Pichois's note in his edition of Baudelaire's works that states: "Mme Sabatier, émue par la longue adoration de son poète, se donna à lui aux derniers jours d'août" (907). But this only asserts that Madame Sabatier offered herself to the poet, which letters written by her to him after their encounter confirm, letters brimming with amorous delight—"je suis la plus heureuse des femmes [. . .] jamais je n'ai mieux senti que je t'aime [. . .] je suis à toi de corps, d'esprit et de cœur" (Troyat 234). As for Baudelaire's reaction to Madame Sabatier's offer, we have only the letter of 31 August, cited by Gasarian as evidence that Baudelaire did infect her, even though the parts he quotes only indicate that the poet now regards her as a human being—a woman—as opposed to his previous conception of her as *une divinité,* to which he adds, "ce

qui est si commode, ce qui est si beau, si inviolable" (Moss 110). Attention might more convincingly have been drawn to this last word in which the *violence* of the poem resounds, indicating that perhaps the poet now (consciously or unconsciously) finds her violable, although no evidence of any such action taking place can be adduced.[14]

Gasarian's claim that Butor mistakenly overlooked this letter is mistaken, as Butor actually cites from it (65) to support his view that Baudelaire and Madame Sabatier did not consummate their relationship, as suggested by the remark "nous savons (moi surtout) qu'il y a des nœuds difficiles à délier" that implies reluctance on his part and disappointment on hers.[15] This excuse is preceded by another one: "[N]ous sommes tous les deux possédés de la peur d'affliger un honnête homme qui a le bonheur d'être toujours amoureux" (Moss 110). The *honnête homme* is obviously Alfred Mosselman, Madame Sabatier's "protecteur," and the reference to "knots difficult to untie" likely describes Baudelaire's entanglement with Jeanne Duval (Troyat 235). In fact, a reading of the entire letter seems to portray an awkwardly embarrassed and apologetic Baudelaire, suggesting that he may well have lost his nerve—or perhaps was unable to perform—when whatever intimacies occurred reached the culminating moment. Moss further draws attention to "un subit désenchantement" in the salutations of Baudelaire's letters to Madame: "De 'Chère Madame' le 18 août, Mme Sabatier devient 'Chère bien-aimée' le 31; après avoir été 'Très chère amie' [lettre du 24 août] un court espace de temps. Le 13 septembre, elle redevient abruptement 'Chère Madame'" (113). We will probably never know whether Baudelaire's distancing himself from Madame Sabatier after their amorous encounter represents guilt for having had intercourse with her that might have infected her or for his unwillingness (or inability) to achieve the intimate consummation she desired. My own inclination, after examining the evidence, is to conclude that life did not imitate art, in this case, and that the poet was ironically more daring and outrageous in the virtual phantasms of his poetry than in the actions he was actually willing to take. But if, in life, the self is constrained by mood, expectation, opinion, and other limitations of the real, in art, the poet, as fictive self in the text, is free to vent his spleen and to unleash his violent fury. In **"À celle qui est trop gaie,"** the substitution of *venin* in the last line, although shocking, actually brings the poem more logically to its conclusion as both *violence* and *viol,* the venom-sperm completing the implied image of the phallic serpent slithering toward the lady,[16] and the "lèvres nouvelles / Plus éclatantes et plus belles" now also evoking the vagina that is viciously raped and infected.

There is a coda to this story that occurred a few weeks after the disastrous encounter between Baudelaire and

Madame Sabatier that Butor has interpreted as a further example of the privileging of art over life:

> Puisqu'il n'a pu lui donner ce venin qu'elle désirait, il compensera ce manque amplement, en lui offrant cela même dont le "venin" n'est qu'une figure, n'est qu'une annonce, un venin incomparablement plus noir, plus purement noir [. . .] à savoir l'encre.
>
> A défaut de ce qui est finalement l'un des attributs du poète, elle aura cet autre attribut, l'emblème classique de l'écrivain, qu'est l'encrier.

(68)

Baudelaire has the inkwell sent without an accompanying note identifying the gift-giver, "une énorme sottise," he exclaims in a letter he sent to her the next day (25 September). Perhaps this oversight revealed a desire to return to the status of secret admirer that he enjoyed when he sent that first anonymous (and strange) token of affection, the poem **"À celle qui est trop gaie."** Psychologically, it may well have been the impossibility of satisfaction that had stoked the flames of desire that Madame's unexpected availability quickly doused. Pursuing Butor's metaphorical reading of the venom-ink, Gasarian associates the inkwell with the male and female sex organs, a correspondence that makes sense only in part. As a substitute for the vagina-womb, the inkwell is a receptacle that receives and contains the ink-venom-sperm, which is male, but not phallic. What is missing is the poetic pen, which, to extend Butor's interpretation, was also lacking in the actual amorous encounter (but is ironically present in the figurative penning of the poem). Gasarian's reading of the inkwell as androgynous and thus representative of the poet's own androgyny posits the inkwell as a "[s]ubstitut du phallus" that is not phallic (43). The episode does, in any case, illustrate Gasarian's and Butor's point that Baudelaire values the symbolic at the expense of the real.

It remains to explain the seemingly incongruous last word of the poem, *sœur*. In the context of "T'infuser mon sang" of the manuscript, it might have seemed strange but not altogether outrageous in a poem originally inserted in a billet-doux and intended to seduce, however perverse its violent hyperbole may now seem (Murphy points out that "Mme Sabatier n'était pas connue pour sa pudibonderie" [61]). But the substitution of *venin* adds a truly wicked criminal intention to poison and perhaps kill the lady. Pichois cites the Crépet-Blin edition's suggestion that the sense of the ending might be "'je t'infuserai mon venin *de façon à te rendre toute semblable à moi*'" (Baudelaire 1133n3; emphasis in original), which Gasarian echoes in his androgynous reading: "Baudelaire cherche à lui transfuser son venin, pour qu'elle devienne comme lui un être androgyne, une femme-frère, une sœur" (44). Georges Blin takes a Sartrean sadomasochistic view:

> "Comme Sartre l'a souligné, l'ivrogne sadique du drame projeté se conduit, lui aussi, en masochiste, et 'supplie,' et s'applique à se 'faire pardonner,' avant de commettre le meurtre. C'est la même ambivalence que répond encore l'apostrophe raffinée, *Ma Sœur*, sur laquelle se termine la pièce barbare *A Celle qui est trop gaie*" (38; emphasis in original). Blin further asserts that "Baudelaire recherche la femme pure pour la souiller" (38). Leo Bersani thinks

> [t]he word "sister" [. . .] is itself a sadistic simulacrum of the same word in **"L'Invitation au voyage."** In the latter poem, it was merely one element in the shifting patterns of the woman's identities. In **"A Celle qui est trop gaie,"** it is of course an ironic conclusion to the fantasy of violence, but it also expresses a finalization of the woman's identity as the poet's spiritual companion: like him, she is now filled with death.

(74)

Beyond the fleeting moments of an imagined sexual union, I do not see the poet attempting to identify with the lady, who remains ineluctably *other* in the poem, isolated by an essential gap (or *gouffre*, to use a more Baudelairean term) that no transfusion of blood or venom could ever adequately overcome. The use of the word *sœur* in **"L'Invitation au voyage"** is telling. It is employed as a nonthreatening, nonsexualized salutation meant to soothe the lady, who is in tears, perhaps after a lovers' quarrel. If it were sexually charged, it would harbor an incestuous intent, which would be doubled by the concomitant reference to her as a child: "Mon enfant, ma sœur" (53). The tenor of this most peaceful and ideal of Baudelaire's poems would seem to exclude any possibility of incestuous and pedophilic desire. In **"À celle qui est trop gaie,"** which originally employed *sang* in the last verse as part of an attempt at seduction as we have seen, the use of the comforting "ma sœur," I would argue, brings the poem to a reassuring conclusion, with the poet suddenly assuming the role of a teasing, tormenting brother, as if to say, "Did I shock you? I was only joking." By substituting *venin* in the published version, however, after five years of undoubtedly frustrating self-restraint, Baudelaire not only indulges in a sadistic phantasm of fulfilled desire but also does violence metatextually to the now irrelevant cliché of the seductive lyric or, as Shinabargar puts it, "le poète écrase le langage que la tradition lui offre" (128). At the same time, *venin*, sharing the last line with *sœur*, reestablishes the oxymoronic love-hate antithesis of verse 16, from which the violence of the intervening stanzas irrupted, returning the poet to the all-too-human condition of unresolved ironic ambivalence and reminding us that the poem is not life, but rather theater of the mind.

Notes

1. Term borrowed by Hamon from Balzac and Hugo. From the latter's *L'Homme qui rit,* he cites the description of a character's "déstinée ironique" as

a "'contresens entre ce qu'on semble et ce qu'on est' [. . .] ce qui serait une bonne définition de la phrase ironique, où ce qui 'semble' être dit n' 'est pas ce qui est dit'" (Hamon 21n1).

2. "Il y a dans tout homme, à toute heure, deux postulations simultanées, l'une vers Dieu, l'autre vers Satan. L'invocation à Dieu, ou spiritualité, est un désir de monter en grade; celle de Satan, ou animalité, est une joie de descendre" (*Mon cœur mis à nu* XI; Baudelaire 682-83).

3. According to Per Buvik, "l'ironie n'est rien d'autre que la dualité même à laquelle l'homme ne peut pas échapper [. . .]. Ainsi, l'ironie est pour Baudelaire bien plus qu'un procédé rhétorique, bien plus qu'une attitude que l'on peut choisir ou ne pas choisir; elle n'est pas, non plus, une réaction, ni au comportement d'une personne, ni à un incident: selon le poète, l'homme *est* par définition ironique" (92; emphasis in original).

4. René Wellek's summary of Schlegel's view based on his translation of the original German quoted in the notes (14).

5. Taken from Muecke's quotation in English of Friedrich Schlegel's Lyceums-Fragment 108 in his Chapter VII titled "Romantic Irony" (Muecke 195).

6. Linda Hutcheon suggests "that we stop thinking of irony only in binary *either/or terms* of the substitution of an 'ironic' for a 'literal' (and opposite) meaning, and see what might happen if we found a new way of talking about ironic meaning as, instead, *relational, inclusive,* and *differential* [. . .]. [I]t would involve an oscillating yet simultaneous perception of plural and different meanings" (66; emphasis in original). Similarly, Debarati Sanyal states that irony "keeps the poetic subjectivity in a constant oscillation or 'double postulation' between *spleen et idéal*" (57) in her study of irony and violence in Baudelaire (which does not examine "A celle qui est trop gaie").

7. My reference to this symbol is meant only to illustrate Baudelaire's dialectic and does not go beyond the very basic association of yin with black (dark) and yang with white (light), which reflects the poem's opposing dynamics of hate and love.

8. Armand Moss remarks that "Baudelaire aimait les robes d'une élégance raffinée, originale, un peu indécente, les robes 'folles' dont se vêtait Mme Sabatier [. . .] celles où, explique Gautier, 'se mêlent quelque chose de la comédienne et de la courtisane'" (47).

9. Gérard Gasarian, supporting Baudelaire's own contention, in *L'Exposition universelle* of 1855, that *"'le beau est toujours bizarre'"* (Gasarian

27n24; emphasis in original), remarks that "[s]elon Littré, le mot 'bariolé' s'applique à la peinture comme au style et désigne un assemblage de couleur 'qui ne s'accordent pas,' étant 'bizarrement assortie'" (38). With regard to the musical image, "le bariolage de l'esprit féminin semble tenir à la bizarrerie d'un faux accord, tel une 'note criarde'" (38); that is to say, the woman's too-loud beauty is as shrill and irritating to the poet as her excessive gaieté.

10. See, in particular, the section of her dissertation titled "Ironie et dérision chez Rimbaud: de Vénus à l'anus" (26-35).

11. This constitutes an ironic reversal of the notion, in "La Beauté," of poets as victims bruised at beauty's breast; here, the poet is the victimizer and beauty's breast the object of the bruising.

12. The full text of the note reads:

> Les juges ont cru découvrir un sens à la fois sanguinaire et obscène dans les deux dernières stances. La gravité du Recueil excluait de pareilles *plaisanteries*. Mais *venin* signifiant spleen ou mélancolie, était une idée trop simple pour les criminalistes.
>
> Que leur interprétation syphilitique leur reste sur la conscience
>
> (Note de l'éditeur). (Baudelaire 157; emphasis in original)

13. Butor, conflating Baudelaire with the subject speaking in the poem, adds, "et Baudelaire s'accuse lui-même de cette lâcheté" (67), a reference to the perpetrator's (not necessarily Baudelaire's) masochistic sense of guilt and humiliation that is part of the erotic phantasm in the text.

14. Another similarly curious choice of words in the letter is the assertion that there are people who would imprison those who fail to pay their debts, "mais les serments de l'amitié et de l'amour, personne n'en punit la violation" (Moss 109). On the one hand, Baudelaire seems to be admitting to nothing more serious than violating an oath of friendship or love, but again, the choice of "violation," like that of "inviolable," evokes the violent scenario of the poem, which the use of the verb *punir* further underscores.

15. If the reluctance was because of his fear of infecting her, he would not have been able to tell her, Butor explains, because "la liaison si étroite qui s'établit entre poésie et virilité lui interdit de communiquer ce mal à une femme, puisque ce serait lui faire partager seulement la malédiction sans qu'elle ait les moyens de la faire tourner en bénédiction" (64).

16. This is suggested by the verb *ramper* of line 28. Murphy offers further evidence in support of this reading:

L'image du serpent n'était qu'implicite et pour ainsi dire latente dans la version du manuscrit donnée à Mme Sabatier. Elle surgit plus explicitement lorsque *T'infuser mon sang* devient *T'infuser mon venin.* Il nous paraît fort difficile de ne pas voir dans cette image une référence fort précise, qui aurait été tout à fait évidente à l'époque. Baudelaire fait allusion à la très célèbre sculpture de Clésinger, *La Femme piquée par un serpent,* exposée en 1847. Nul n'ignorait l'identité de cette femme piquée: il s'agissait précisément de Mme Sabatier, qui était en 1847 la maîtresse de Clésinger.

(60; emphasis in original)

Mme. Sabatier not only posed for the piece but also allowed a cast to be molded on her body to assure an exact likeness (Troyat 199). Nicolae Babuts detects in the snake image a biblical link: "For his part, the poet crawls to the beloved, in a parodic, staged repetition of the primal scene in the garden, and mimics the serpent's temptation of the first woman" (74).

Works Cited

Babuts, Nicolae. *Baudelaire: At the Limits and Beyond.* Newark: U of Delaware P, 1997.

Baudelaire, Charles. *Œuvres complètes.* Ed. Claude Pichois. Vol. 1. Bibliotheque de la Pleiade 1. Paris: Gallimard, 1993. 2 vols.

Bersani, Leo. *Baudelaire and Freud.* Berkeley: U of California P, 1977.

Blin, Georges. *Le Sadisme de Baudelaire.* Paris: Corti, 1948.

Butor, Michel. *Histoire extraordinaire: Essai sur un rêve de Baudelaire.* Paris: Gallimard, 1961.

Buvik, Per. "La Notion baudelairienne de l'ironie." *Revue Romane* 31.1 (1996): 87-98.

de Man, Paul. "The Rhetoric of Temporality." *Blindness and Insight: Essays in the Rhetoric of Contemporary Criticism.* 2nd ed. Minneapolis: U of Minnesota P, 1983. 187-228.

Donne, John. *Donne.* New York: Dell, 1964.

Gasarian, Gérard. *De loin tendrement: Étude sur Baudelaire.* Paris: Champion, 1996.

Hamon, Philippe. *L'Ironie littéraire: Essai sur les formes de l'écriture oblique.* Paris: Hachette, 1996.

Hutcheon, Linda. *Irony's Edge: The Theory and Politics of Irony.* London: Routledge, 1994-95.

McCann, John. "Heroism or Villainy in *Les Fleurs du mal*: The Problem of *À celle qui est trop gaie.*" *Heroism and Passion in Literature: Studies in Honour of Moya Longstaffe.* Ed. Graham Gargett. Amsterdam: Rodopi, 2004. 145-56.

Mercier-Leca, Florence. *L'Ironie.* Paris: Hachette, 2003.

Moss, Armand. *Baudelaire et Madame Sabatier.* Paris: Nizet, 1975.

Muecke, D. C. *The Compass of Irony.* London: Metheun, 1969.

Murphy, Steve. "*Qui* est trop gaie?" *Bulletin Baudelairien* 26.2 (1991): 57-62.

Nicolas, Candice. "Cataclysmes poétiques: Du poète maudit aux poètes déchéants: Rimbaud, Cocteau, Vian." Diss. Ohio State U, 2006.

Sanyal, Debarati. *The Violence of Modernity: Baudelaire, Irony, and the Politics of Form.* Baltimore: Johns Hopkins UP, 2006.

Shinabargar, Scott. "L'Esthétique du mal: La Violence des œuvres de D'Abigné et de Baudelaire." *Papers on French Seventeenth Century Literature* 32.62 (2005): 125-42.

Troyat, Henri. *Baudelaire.* Paris: Flammarion, 1994.

Verlaine, Paul. *Œuvres poétiques complètes.* Ed. Jacques Borel. Paris: Bibliothèque de la Pléiade, 1989.

Wellek, René. *The Romantic Age.* New Haven: Yale UP, 1955. Vol. 2 of *A History of Modern Criticism (1750-1950).*

Wetzel, Hermann H. "'Les Points d'ironie' dans *Une Saison en enfer.*" *Dix études sur* Une Saison en enfer. Ed. André Guyaux. Neuchâtel: La Baconnière, 1994. 117-26.

FURTHER READING

Criticism

Baker, Jr., J. M. "Vacant Holidays: The Theological Remainder in Leopardi, Baudelaire, and Benjamin." *MLN* 121 (2006): 1190-219.
Explores the motif of the "vacant holiday," a time once devoted to ritual and ceremony that has lost its meaning within a culture.

Ladenson, Elisabeth. "The Imperial Superreader, or: Semiotics of Indecency." *Romantic Review* 93, nos. 1/2 (January-March 2002): 81-90.
Discusses literary obscenity trials, including that of Baudelaire.

Wing, Nathaniel. "Baudelaire's *Frisson Fraternel*: Horror and Enchantment in 'Les Tableaux Parisiens.'" *Neophilologus* 81 (1997): 21-33.

Presents an in-depth analysis of three poems from the "Tableaux Parisiens" section of *Les Fleurs du Mal,* arguing that these poems present a view of the relationship between the poet and his subject that is quite different than that of the remainder of the poems in the section.

Additional coverage of Baudelaire's life and career is contained in the following sources published by Gale: *Dictionary of Literary Biography,* **Vol. 217;** *Discovering Authors; Discovering Authors 3.0; Discovering Authors: British; Discovering Authors: Canadian Edition; Discovering Authors Modules: Most-studied Authors* **and** *Poets; European Writers,* **Vol. 7;** *Guide to French Literature 1789 to the Present; Literary Movements for Students,* **Vol. 2;** *Literature Resource Center; Nineteenth-Century Literature Criticism,* **Vols. 6, 29, 55, 155;** *Poetry Criticism,* **Vol. 1;** *Poetry for Students,* **Vol. 21;** *Reference Guide to World Literature,* **Eds. 2, 3;** *Short Story Criticism,* **Vol. 18;** *Twayne's World Authors;* **and** *World Literature Criticism,* **Ed. 1.**

Keith Douglas
1920-1944

English poet, short story writer, and essayist.

INTRODUCTION

Virtually unrecognized during his lifetime, Douglas has since been considered one of the finest poets of the Second World War. He is known for producing emotionally detached poetic representations of his combat experiences as a British tank commander in North Africa—writing as though he were a journalist reporting on the events rather than a soldier living them.

BIOGRAPHICAL INFORMATION

Born Keith Castellain Douglas on January 24, 1920, in Tunbridge Wells, the future poet was the son of Keith Sholto Douglas, a retired army officer, and Marie Josephine Castellain Douglas, the descendent of a French aristocrats. Although the family was middle class, they experienced financial troubles after the senior Douglas left the military following World War I. Douglas's parents separated when he was six years old and he spent the remainder of his childhood in boarding schools. From 1931 to 1938, Douglas attended Christ's Hospital, where he was recognized as gifted both academically and athletically; he was a promising poet and artist, as well as an accomplished sportsman in swimming, rugby, and riding. He was also known as a rebellious student and was nearly expelled in 1935, after which he seemed to take his education more seriously. Douglas began writing poetry while in school and published his first work at the age of sixteen. In 1938, his poem "Dejection" was accepted by *New Verse,* a prestigious literary magazine. He received a scholarship to attend Merton College, Oxford, where he studied under the poet Edmund Blunden; however, his education was cut short by the impending war in Europe. In 1939 Douglas volunteered in the military, began service in 1940 as a cavalryman, and later assumed command of a tank troop in North Africa. In early 1943 he was wounded by a land mine and spent several months recuperating, writing all the while. When he recovered, he rejoined his regiment which was assigned to participate in the invasion of Normandy in June of 1944. Douglas was killed on June 9, three days after the Normandy landing; he was 24 years old.

MAJOR WORKS

The amount of writing Douglas produced during his brief lifetime was understandably limited, but impressive nonetheless. His work attracted the attention of T. S. Eliot and he was featured in the 1942 anthology, *Eight Oxford Poets.* In 1943, *Selected Poems* was published, featuring the poetry of Douglas, J. C. Hall, and Norman Nicholson. The poetry of Douglas's early student days became known as a demonstration of his technical skill, while his time at Oxford seems to have been spent developing his personal style. His war poetry, however, exhibited a change in style and poetic voice. It became less emotional—even callous according to some critics—and detached from the horrific events he witnessed in combat.

The remainder of Douglas's poetry was published after his death. *Alamein to Zem Zem,* a volume containing both poetry and prose, appeared in 1946. *The Collected Poems of Keith Douglas* was published in 1951 and a volume of *Selected Poems* in 1964, followed by *The Complete Poems of Keith Douglas* in 1978. His single short story, along with his essays and correspondence, appeared in 1985 under the title *Keith Douglas: A Prose Miscellany.*

CRITICAL RECEPTION

Considered a war poet by many critics, Douglas was nearly forgotten after interest in war-related literature waned, according to Ted Hughes (see Further Reading), who introduced the 1964 volume, *Selected Poems.* Hughes contends, though, that in the 1960s it was "becoming clear that he offers more than just a few poems about war, and that every poem he wrote, whether about war or not, has some special value." Philip Gardner (see Further Reading) points out that even his reputation as a war poet was slow in coming since "of the poems of direct war experience, too few appeared during his lifetime to make a concerted impact and establish his stature as a war poet." Stephen Matterson reports that Douglas has long had a reputation as a war poet who offered "a fresh and challenging perspective on warfare." The critic maintains that what set Douglas apart from others writing in the genre is that "rather than concentrating on the terrible conditions, waste and death . . . he provides a view of warfare as it appeared to the professional, highly-trained soldier."

Peter Scupham comments on Douglas's apparently detached view of events surrounding him: "In ["How to Kill"] there is a sense of something being said from a great distance, as if a disembodied voice we can hardly bear is saying something alien and imperative."

Edmund Blunden, Douglas's tutor at Oxford, remarks on the pictorial quality of his former student's poetry, claiming that his work was that of a painter-poet and that even his manuscripts were "written freely and gracefully, as though he saw his abstractions as definitely as physical objects." Desmond Graham has studied the composition of "Bête Noire," a poem that Douglas attempted to write several times, and traces of which turned up in a number of his other works. Graham considers the beast, and Douglas's preoccupation with it, to be "a richly creative presence" that "dislodged Douglas from his early romanticism and taught him the themes of mortality and loss," and thereby "equipped him ideally to write of the experience of war." David Ormerod (see Further Reading) also focuses on the poet's inability to complete "Bête Noire," contending that "Douglas' basic psychological impasse is concerned with the nature of perception, and involves the issue of the speaking poet's identity and the putative reality of the external world." Ormerod explores Douglas's attempt to work through the impasse by employing imagery associated with visual perception—masks, lenses, mirrors, windows, and even gunsights—throughout his poetry.

Douglas's poetic diction and style have been studied by a number of critics. Hughes, for example, comments on the simplicity of Douglas's language, calling him a "renovator of language," whose "triumph lies in the way he renews the simplicity of ordinary talk, and he does this by infusing every word with a burning, exploratory freshness of mind." Scupham considers Douglas's style "colloquial yet disciplined," and Reginald Gibbons maintains that Douglas "possessed an innate skill with words and a gift for figurative language and compression." Commenting on the use of "spread-eagled" and "unusual" in the poem "The Marvel," Gibbons acknowledges that Douglas's employment of such words may "prompt the conjecture that his diction was at times arbitrary, yet one begins to see that a certain kind of oddity was precisely Douglas' gift."

PRINCIPAL WORKS

Poetry

Selected Poems [includes poems by J. C. Hall and Norman Nicholson] 1943
Alamein to Zem Zem (prose and poetry) 1946

The Collected Poems of Keith Douglas 1951
Selected Poems 1964
The Complete Poems of Keith Douglas 1978

Other Major Works

Keith Douglas: A Prose Miscellany (short story, letters, and essays) 1985

CRITICISM

Edmund Blunden (essay date 1966)

SOURCE: Blunden, Edmund. Introduction to *Keith Douglas: Collected Poems,* edited by John Waller, G. S. Fraser, and J. C. Hall, pp. 17-20. New York: Chilmark Press, 1966.

[*In the following introduction, Blunden, who was Douglas's Oxford mentor, discusses the pictorial quality of Douglas's poetry.*]

To my constant regret my impressions of Keith Douglas are almost confined to that sad and wild time when the second World War was imminent and when it was actual, though I did not see much of him once he had begun his special training and duly taken his commission. At least I had the good fortune of meeting, in their health and strength, two of the chief poets whom that War did not allow to live on and exert their imaginative and personal powers on the world which has moved along such mysterious ways since 1945. The other, Sidney Keyes, I knew but little. With Keith Douglas naturally, our background being the same ancient school and ancient College at Oxford, my meetings were many and on many concerns; that is, in 1938 and 1939 particularly, between his schooldays and his going to the wars.

His school, as his editors duly note, was Christ's Hospital, and I had only to be with him for ten minutes—he came to me while I was the tutor in English Literature at Merton College—in order to know his two predominant loyalties. One was to his mother, the other to the Bluecoat School. Keith had the advantage of being well befriended by one of his schoolmasters, the late D. S. Roberts, who wrote that 'with his death Christ's Hospital has lost one of her most gifted and vivid personalities.' It is typical of his feeling for his old school that in his war journal, *Alamein to Zem Zem,* Douglas returns, right in the crash of battle, to Christ's Hospital chapel and one of Frank Brangwyn's murals there for a comparison.

Keith was one of the most outspoken of people, as many accounts agree, but to his Tutor (capital T in those days) he was infallibly gentle and attentive. He took plenty of trouble over his weekly essay, even when his passion for horsemanship (and his friendship with the amusing Hamo Sassoon, another pupil of mine) preoccupied him. Handwriting—ever clear and flowing; but then, so was the expression. Brevity—but nothing impecunious about it. Substance—as matter-of-fact as he could make it! He did not care about novelty when he was finding his way.

Outside our tutorial sessions I remember one or two Oxford, typically Oxford schemes, in which he took pleasure and for which he worked as he could work once he accepted the cause. I proposed a miscellany of prose and verse to be entitled *Augury,* and Keith quickly joined his friend Alec Hardie in assembling it. It was eventually published by Messrs. Blackwell; and for the senior and junior members of the university who contributed to it, it had the purpose of recommending the humanities at a time when the inhumanities were gathering round.

Another engrossing scheme was a performance of Dryden's *Secular Mask*—on the ending of an old age and the beginning of a new. Now we realized, if we had not already done so, that Keith was deeply devoted to the stage; he assisted us in all the preparations for this operatic piece (a shame that there was no part for him to act), spending many hours unseen to us in attempting to supply papier-mâché masks. These were revealed and had merit, but unfortunately collapsed before they could be displayed to the audience. After the show Keith used all his art (and he was a painter always looking about for some opportunity, some untried nicety) on a decorated poem in honour of the cast and, if I may say it here, of the senior member who played Chronos with a beach-ball as the globe he was compelled to carry.

With Keith Douglas, indeed, poetry and painting were twin preoccupations. Another Mertonian, Douglas Grant, has ventured the opinion that Keith 'might have excelled eventually as the artist rather than as the poet.' It was to nature, especially to horses and their settings, that he first applied his art and his fresh bright colours. Later, he used the same painter's skill to depict the turmoil and 'nightmare ground' of the desert campaign.

Keith's character was, I believe, complex in the manner of many artists. Against his generosity and zest for life must be placed, if the portrait is to be (as he would have wished it to be) true to life, certain less endearing qualities—an impulsive and obstinate streak which was sometimes the despair of even his closest friends. His intellect was as I now feel on the verge of greatness. It is on this account that his poetry, and his poetry was not only the fruit of his war experiences, looks like

answering the demand of his distant school predecessor Coleridge: the best poets utter a philosophy. Keith Douglas was (in the words of one of his schoolmasters) 'one of the ablest of our History Grecians', and had formed his panorama of life and time out of his historical contemplations. His mythology was energetic, for he had not noticed that the classical world had been sent to Coventry. He was a young man who often did not notice such things.

Introducing Douglas's **Selected Poems** in 1964, Mr. Ted Hughes gave the opinion that 'he offers more than just a few poems about war, and that every poem he wrote, whether about war or not, has some special value. His poetry in general seems to be of some special value. It is still very much alive, and even providing life. And the longer it lives, the fresher it looks'. It is good to find a poet of a later generation writing thus of Keith twenty years after his death. For myself, I will shelter behind the ample solidity of Samuel Johnson when in his short life of the poet William Collins he brought back what he had written on Collins in earlier years. The critical notice that follows is dated winter 1944, and the reader will easily adjust it in minor points to the present time; like Dr. Johnson in the case of Collins, I think it is clearer than what I might write now, notwithstanding all the fuller 'materials'.

> As the poems of Keith Douglas are as yet uncollected (though there is a volume in preparation), it is not easy to express a full opinion on them; but one especial characteristic is clear—they were the work of a painter-poet, and highly pictorial. His thoughts and fancies were curious, his emotions were not everybody's, and he strove to present these in sharp designs of image and allusion. His observation of the arts, no matter what the period or the place, was extremely keen, and provided him when he wrote verse with these figures and their strong colours. As yet, his topics were principally personal, yet his mind's eye saw in them the recurrence of experience of wider range and longer date than his own. We must grieve that it happened with him as with some young writers of the generation before, writers whom he honoured; it was war which brought him towards the maturity of his poetry. Some of his latest pieces are, I think, his best; the complexity which overlaid much that he meant has gone, and he is governed by the great argument of the time—that becomes the rhythm and the feeling of his lyrics. But still the singular touch of his pictorial sense signs the poems.

> He hated decoration without anything behind it, but his verse is decorative, and, thinking of it, I think of figureheads and lamias, or of the masks which he devised so eagerly; yet it was his real aim in pleasing the imagination thus to impress truths of human affairs which he came at in his independent way. He did not wish to startle with novelty, but to fashion his work as best suited his kind of thinking, whether that was unanticipated or after all of an ancient kind. The very look of his manuscripts is interesting as a help to understanding his poetic mood; they are written freely

and gracefully, as though he saw his abstractions as definitely as physical objects. And this he maintained throughout his varied circumstances on active service.

Desmond Graham (essay date 1974)

SOURCE: Graham, Desmond. "England: December 1943-June 1944." In *Keith Douglas: 1920-1944*, pp. 229-53. New York: Oxford University Press, 1974.

[*In the following excerpt, Graham discusses the process by which Douglas wrote "Bête Noire," a poem he found extremely difficult to compose.*]

> For the heart is a coal, growing colder
> when jewelled cerulean seas change
> into grey rocks, grey water-fringe . . .
> cold is an opiate of the soldier.

('On a Return from Egypt')

I

The voyage to Britain on a ship well supplied with nurses and other female passengers was almost as pleasant as that from Durban to Port Said two and a half years earlier, though the officiousness of the officer in charge of troops on board brought some annoyance to the Sherwood Rangers and to Douglas in particular. As the Straits of Gibraltar were now clear, they were able to spend a week in Augusta harbour, Sicily, and still arrive off the Scottish coast on 9 December, only three weeks after leaving Egypt. After two frustrating days offshore, waiting for a berth, the regiment had the consolation of the most cursory customs inspection—no one declared anything and no questions were asked—and at once the Sherwood Rangers travelled south to a camp at Chippenham, arriving on 12 December. It was a curious homecoming, for many their first sight of Britain since 1940; but the pleasure of return was conditioned by the knowledge that they had come back to prepare for another campaign. For the present, however, at least three weeks leave was granted to all those who had served in the Middle East, and Douglas set off to see his mother at East Grinstead where she had kept house for the Babers since December 1942.

It was a more secure and pleasant situation than Mrs. Douglas had known for many years. Much of the time she had the house to herself as Colonel Baber and his wife Jocelyn were both engaged in war work in London, and when they were staying at East Grinstead she was accepted as a member of the family. Finding his mother well settled, and having pleased her with the more mature and relaxed manner he seemed to have gained from his service abroad, Douglas set off for a few days in Oxford.

There he found Joan Appleton busily arranging the dance for a charity pantomime and running a club for Allied servicemen and women, the Charter Club. At Joan's invitation he gave a talk to the club on his experience of the desert war. To his audience of servicemen, many of whom were also waiting for the invasion, Douglas spoke of the desert's landscapes and flowers, the variety of its scenes and noises and the moods of its day. Joan was pleased by the sensitivity of the talk but impressed above all by the fact that Douglas did not once mention the fighting. With such a subject and audience one might have expected soldierly panache and adventure; instead there was a thoughtful and pacific curiosity.

In the evenings he wandered round some of his old haunts in the city. He saw little of Joan, who worked till late each night, but he slept at her parents' house at Boars Hill. On departing for Christmas, Joan recalls, Douglas told her not to forget his birthday. She asked what he wanted. 'Cigarettes and Baudelaire' was his reply. (The copy of Baudelaire is in Mrs. Douglas's possession.)

Douglas and his mother had in fact been invited to spend the holiday in Cornwall with Jack Holman of C Squadron, who, learning during the voyage of the uncertainties of Douglas's family situation, had offered to put them up. The return of the Babers to East Grinstead, however, meant a postponement of the visit. If the prospect of staying in a household where his mother worked had aroused unhappy memories, they were dispelled by the Babers' welcome. By the end of the holiday Douglas was happy to accept the position of honorary son. Mrs. Baber's forthright manner, her fund of experience from the work she was doing with refugees, and her love of argument made her excellent company, and some months later Douglas was to comment affectionately in a letter to her, that she was someone he could have 'fallen heavily for' if they had been twenty at the same time.

With her husband he established an impressive understanding. A veteran of the Great War who had stayed on in the army, only to have his hopes of a military career frustrated by ill health, Colonel Baber now had to content himself with an army desk job. His values were traditional, but Douglas respected him for having known what fighting was like and having returned from it with a gentler and more conventional creed than his own. To Colonel Baber Douglas's cynicism was an echo of his own response to the experience of the trenches, and he felt confident that Douglas's evident honesty and manliness would lead him back to the values he now humorously disparaged. Douglas had once more been cast in the role of rebellious young man, but he assumed the part with a grace and sense of humour which delighted his mother.

The week in Cornwall after Christmas was equally successful, with Mrs. Douglas much enjoying the chance to talk to someone who had served with her son in the desert, and Jack Holman's mother making sure that they had a relaxed and leisurely time. But the return to Chippenham in particularly hard weather, early in January, to find there living conditions reminiscent of those at Lulworth Cove three years before, bitterly ended a good first month in England. A letter from Jean Turner, whom Douglas had not seen on his leave, gave him the chance to revert to an earlier tone:

> At the moment it's no good writing you a letter as I feel so savage about this filthy country and the way it is run that I couldn't say anything entertaining or amusing. I now live in a tin hut and a sea of mud (which freezes every few days) and no laundry arrangements or showers, with about half as much food as civilians are eating.

Since leaving the Middle East the Sherwood Rangers had assumed that their eventual destination would be the mainland of Europe; and at the beginning of February they had their first training in '"European" type of country', at a firing camp in Kirkudbright. Back in Chippenham, they learnt that they were indeed to open a second front, and when, in the middle of February, B and C Squadrons left Chippenham for training with amphibious tanks, it was evident that the regiment was to be in the leading wave of a sea-borne invasion. With the pace of training certain to quicken with the spring, leave was granted, and it was with this knowledge of the nature of his fate, and ignorance of its timing, that Douglas left Chippenham for eleven days in East Grinstead and Oxford.

In Oxford Douglas again stayed with the Appletons, visiting Tony Rudd's aunt, who was now in Oxford, and at the Appletons' meeting Joan's sister Betty, now married with a child. Betty recalls his seriously chiding her for marrying so soon when she could have had his pension: for he would not survive Europe.

The Charter Club had a spare room at the back, so while Joan served tea and sandwiches to Americans, Poles, Frenchmen, and Chinese, Douglas worked at his war narrative and prepared illustrations for it. For the rest of his leave he concentrated on arrangements for the publication of his work. The Babers lent him and his mother their London flat, from which Douglas paid daily visits to Tambimuttu at his *Poetry* (*London*) office in Manchester Square. (One evening Douglas and his mother walked through the blackout to call on John Hall in Notting Hill; he also took her to meet Tambimuttu. On another occasion Michael Meyer remembers waving to Douglas across the floor of the Café Royal.) During his leave he signed a contract for a volume of his poems to appear in the Editions Poetry London series, published by Nicholson and Watson.[1]

If the imprint carried less prestige than that of Faber and Faber, it none the less promised reasonably large distribution and more lavish production than was customary; Editions Poetry London despite wartime austerity published some of the most finely produced and expensively illustrated books of the time. Tambimuttu suggested that Douglas should do illustrations to go with the poems, and Douglas, pleased at the prospect of presenting his talents as both poet and artist, produced some two dozen line drawings. The war narrative he left for Tambimuttu's consideration.

During these eleven days Douglas had a first opportunity of participating in London's literary life. *Poetry* (*London*) and its editor provided a real point of focus for the younger poets of the period, and Tambimuttu spent much of his time with writers, not all of them unknown, in the pubs of Fitzrovia. He found Douglas as impressive as his poetry, and would have been glad to take him along to meet some of his literary circle. But Douglas had little taste for the fellowship of London pubs. Instead he talked to Tambimuttu in his office, trying to get as much business as possible done, for it was unlikely that he would be able to watch over the publication of his work. Moreover, while Douglas responded to the charm of the editor on whose efficiency his reputation was likely to depend for some time, the fact that an issue of the bi-monthly *Poetry* (*London*) had not appeared for twelve months gave cause for apprehension.

At Nicholson and Watsons, however, Douglas had found in Tambimuttu's assistant, Betty Jesse, a potential ally for his work and a companion more attractive to him than those of the Wheatsheaf and Soho. Intelligent, sophisticated, and although only a little older than he, in the midst of a crumbling marriage, Betty was well used to the attentions of young writers who hoped she would put in a good word for them with Tambimuttu. She had been impressed by the poems Douglas had sent back from Africa and curious to find out what their author was like. In the Manchester Square office she and Douglas talked often, and hearing of his love of riding, Betty, who rode each week in Hyde Park, arranged horses for them on the last day of his leave. Although when the day came Betty seemed not to enjoy her ride, Douglas invited her for the evening to the Piccadilly. An evening's dancing with a woman whose company he enjoyed was the perfect climax to a successful leave. Towards its end, however, as Douglas wrote to Betty on his return to Chippenham, he had 'rather bitched the evening up'.

When he was telling her about his mother, Betty had suddenly said: 'It must be nice to have a mother who wants you all the time.' Douglas could not believe that she would make such a 'Little Nell' remark without some reason; he could only guess that she wanted to tell him a story. He wanted to hear it, and knowing how an exchange of stories could turn an acquaintance into a friendship, he wanted to tell his own. What followed he described in his letter.

When I was very small I climbed up some scaffolding once, and a workman underneath told me to jump off and he would catch me. After he said it three times I jumped and he did catch me. On Thursday night I repeated this performance, only you stepped out from underneath and grinned like a cat while you watched me 'working it out', as though anyone has to work it out when he's dived onto his neck. Then you lectured me like a Mother Superior while I was down and couldn't kick. No wonder I spilt your beer.

Of course it doesn't matter but I think you decided I was a bit dotty; so that's the explanation. I could provide a plot for Dickens myself (possibly in collaboration with Freud, now that they're both in Limbo) so you see you kind of set me off. Never mind, skip it; I'll behave quite properly and cattily again next time. I don't know (nor care) if you've commented on my erratic behaviour to Tambi or your husband or anyone; but anyway this letter is for you and the nearest waste paper basket. The Bête Noire style will begin again in our next issue.

The 'Bête Noire style' took up a comment Betty had made without being particularly serious: chiding Douglas for his arrogant, cynical manner with her, she had called him her *bête noire*. She meant little by it, but her comment had struck home. Before the close of his letter Douglas wrote, 'Now (and all your fault), I have to think of and write a poem called Bête Noire!'; and on the back flap of the envelope he sketched the creature, a bulbous little demon with stringy legs and forked tail, 'on Squander Bug lines'. Douglas had written to Betty as soon as he got back to camp—'writing letters at once, like one does after getting back to school'—and using the same notepaper as his letter,[2] he embarked confidently on his poem.

> This is my particular monster, I know him;
> he walks about inside me: I'm his house
> and his landlord. He's my evacuee
> taking a respite from hell in me
> he decorates his room of course
> to remind him of home. He often talks of going
>
> Such a persuasive gentleman he is
> I believe him, I go out quite sure
> that I'll come back and find him gone
> but does he go? Not him. No, he's a one
> who likes his joke, he won't sit waiting for
> me to come home, but comes

Here Douglas broke off. He had embarked on what he described the next day as five hours of writing which left all his muscles tired, in which, 'sitting down to try and describe'[3] the beast he had 'sensations of physical combat'.

His first attempt at the poem having stopped short, Douglas presented the beast as 'a toad or a worm curled in the belly', but within three lines he had turned from the beast to himself. He is the thing

> . . . I can admit only once to
> anyone, never to those who have not their own.
>
> Never to those who are happy, whose easy language
> I speak well, though with a stranger's accent.

Douglas had come too quickly to an understanding for the poem to need to be continued.

Next he gave up form and rhythm, listing the beast's features in the hope of finding his poem later. It is 'a jailer', allowing him out on 'parole' then bringing him back. Inside his mind, it breaks into his conversation, using Douglas's own words. It can overthrow him 'in a moment', and can be overthrown, 'if I have help'. But again the poem moved from the beast to a statement of personal fact:

> I have been trying to get help for about eleven years
> If this is the game it's past half time and the beast's
>   winning

Douglas's own voice breaks through the procedure of his poem. A little less than eleven years earlier, he had written of the need for a companion, seeking her at Eastbourne Baths, trusting that if she were found she could put out the *'ignis fatuus'* of his discontent. His first letter to Kristin had proposed such a role for her; in his first year at Oxford his poems had celebrated Yingcheng's assumption of it, and in his second, Antoinette had been told of it; again, for a few months with Milena, he had been able to elude the devils outside him. Betty's words had given him an image for something which he had known about himself for a long time; but the attempt to write **'Bête Noire'** had become a struggle to master destructive feeling through poetic control.

Twice more he approached the poem, no longer trying to establish metaphors for the beast's behaviour, but to place it as a counter-current to a mood.

> The trumpet man to take it away
> blows a hot break in a beautiful way
> ought to snap my fingers and tap my toes
> but I sit at my table and nobody knows
> I've got a beast on my back.
>
> A medieval animal with a dog's face
> Notre Dame or Chartres is his proper place
> but here he is in the Piccadilly
> sneering at the hot musicians' skill. He
> is the beast on my back.
>
> Suppose we dance, suppose we run away
> into the street, or the underground
> he'd come with us. It's his day.
> Don't kiss me. Don't put your arm round
> and touch the beast on my back.

Setting the beast in the world where Betty had first conjured its presence, Douglas holds it in the safety of his syncopated rhythms for two stanzas. Then the poetic impulse, which had depended upon the detachment of his wit, is lost. Again he had started to care too much about the experience itself for it to remain poetically viable; and again the poem had stopped.

His fifth attempt returned to the unconcealed lyrical intimacy on which his second version had foundered. Now the creative activity of his fragment is devoted to an affirmation of the imaginative powers which the creature cannot destroy, but having encompassed a perfect gesture, he leaves the beast with all its power at the foot of the poem.

> If at times my eyes are lenses
> through which the brain explores
> constellations of feeling
> my ears yielding like swinging doors
> admit princes to the corridors
> into the mind, do not envy me.
> I have a beast on my back.

Douglas's efforts to locate the beast had drawn him back through almost an anthology of his earlier work, which started with **'The House'** and ended with that poem's corridors and princes. In his 'stranger's accent' he had echoed the 'separative glass cloak / of strangeness' which clothed the visitor to **'Syria'**, and the language of the girl from Monte Nero, which he found hard to speak in **'Forgotten the Red Leaves'**. The 'medieval animal with a dog's face' had first been seen in **'Soissons'**, to return as the **'Devils'** inside and outside his mind in 1942; and the exploring mind of the final attempt was that which had created **'The Hand'**. In another effort to find the poem he wanted Douglas had even revised the loneliness of his poem on **'Saturday Evening in Jerusalem'** to contain his new discovery, incorporating into his revised draft the line 'I have a beast on my back'.

When, a week or so later, Douglas wrote again to Betty, he admitted defeat: 'I'm sending up an excuse (to be used as a preface)' for not writing a poem called Bête Noire.' In his 'excuse', he gave **'Bête Noire'** as the name of the poem 'I can't write', offering two of his attempts and a couple of lines from a third, as quotations from his failures to write the poem. If his quest for the poem had been a failure, Douglas's 'excuse' none the less acknowledged a paradox within his defeat. The poem was also 'a protracted success I suppose':

> Because it is the poem I begin to write in a lot of other poems . . . if he [the beast] is not caught, at least I can see his tracks (anyone may see them), in some of the other poems.

The tracks are clear and the poems in which he had begun to write **'Bête Noire'** readily identifiable. Along with those echoed in his fragments, **'Menippus in Sussex'**, **'Triton'**, **'Russians'**, **'A Ballet'**, **'The Creator'**, and the first half of **'John Anderson'** are only the beginning of a list. The beast had ridiculed his early lyricism, introduced Time and Death and the skull of **'The Prisoner'**, and driven poem after poem towards an awareness of loss.

In providing these tensions, which established the dialectic on which virtually all Douglas's work was based, the beast could be seen in poetic terms as a richly creative presence. Having dislodged Douglas from his early romanticism and taught him the themes of mortality and loss, the beast had equipped him ideally to write of the experience of war. Douglas had gained access to the nihilism of the dead, the insensitivity of the killer and his calm damnation, because these were external manifestations of the creature he well knew. In the context of war, he had in fact already written his **'Bête Noire'** poem, in **'Landscape with Figures'**. There a demon had offered him the delights of war's destruction and the fascination of the dead, before revealing that Douglas himself was the centre of 'the dark strife / the arguments of hell with heaven'.

In his 'excuse' Douglas had written that he knew 'nothing about the beast' beyond the 'infinite patience and extent of his malignity'.

> My failure is that I know so little about him . . . he is so amorphous and powerful that he could be a deity—only he is implacable; no use sacrificing to him, he takes what he wants.

The battlefield had been similarly immune, but its very implacability had enabled Douglas to reveal that its world was 'not wholly terrible'.[5] Its defiance of his expectations released the participant from commitment to its horrors as the whole truth. Here, perhaps, in the knowledge that he could do nothing certain to placate his beast, was a similar release. Douglas had come to understand its creative effect on his poetry even if he could not write its poem, and in the assurance of his final comment, 'no use sacrificing to him, he takes what he wants', he placed the beast at a distance from which its personal hold on him could perhaps also be withstood.

2

At Chippenham in early March, the regiment was not particularly busy. Apart from training, Douglas had to attend to the personal problems of a hundred and nineteen men, but this still left him a fair amount of time if not freedom. When the invasion was to take place, he still did not know, so these weeks provided what looked like a good chance to complete arrangements for his work. For the war narrative he completed a series of illustrations:[6] wash drawings of tanks advancing across the desert, derelicts, a Cairo street scene, and a man in a burning tank, this last picture carrying words:

'a good many casualties in tanks are burnt to death', 'cannot get out of the turret', 'small arms ammunition explodes'. There were also line drawings showing dead men, dogs at a grave, men brewing up, and other desert scenes, among them a drawing titled 'Pietà', of a dead man lying in the midst of a group of comrades. In the manner of his school picture of soldiers at bayonet practice, Douglas had based its design on an early French painting of the School of Touraine, a postcard reproduction[7] of which he had on the wall of his hut.

Douglas awaited Tambimuttu's decision on the narrative's publication, with some impatience. Learning from Betty's first letter that there was not yet any decision, he had replied despondently:

> But I suppose you'll get someone to read it sometime: after all, I suppose they do read everything that's submitted sooner or later. Anyway it's sweet of you to try. If you finally come to the conclusion that it's no use trying, please send it back, and I'll scrap it.

On 10 March, he wrote in a different tone:

> About Tambi, is it any good my saying will he either make up his mind or send it back because someone else wants it? I am writing a letter to this effect and I'll put it in this one. If you think it's a good thing, give it him. If not, tear it up. Needless to say I don't want it back and no one else wants it, though I dare say I could persuade Faber's, who view me with a kindly eye (Uncle Eliot's) or Gollancz.

With the first of these letters, however, Douglas had been able to announce that the narrative had passed an important hurdle. His colonel, to whom he had submitted a copy of the book, had returned it with a 'masterpiece' of a letter: a response which Douglas found delightful enough to deserve paraphrase in his letter to Betty:

> I have read and enjoyed the MS. Now I am not quite sure what is expected of me. I assume I don't have anything to do with the security angle, which seems O.K.

> From the Regimental angle, it seems a pity to go for 'Sweeney Todd' to such a tune, if in the final form he is to be easily identifiable.

> Some of your remarks about Flash [Kellett] will raise a storm, but I suppose it's a free country and you can write what you like within the limits of the law.

Douglas considered that a person who could write like this was someone 'whose orders I don't mind obeying'. All the same, he hoped it 'shook him'.

On 13 March Betty was able to write that Tambimuttu had decided to publish, and on the 18th Douglas was given a contract,[8] promising advance royalties of £20 with a further £20 if the manuscript was delivered within a month. He had already received an advance of £10 for the volume of poems which now had not only a title, ***Bête Noire,*** but a drawing for its cover.[9] If Douglas had been unable to write the beast's poem he had drawn its picture. His final design showed a desert landscape with the square blocks of Arab houses on the horizon, in the foreground a rearing red horse. On its back was a rider, neither huntsman nor cavalryman, but a hunched, naked figure worthy of Bosch. On the man's back was a dog-faced devil, clinging so tightly to the rider that it seemed to grow into him.

Douglas had also heard that *Lilliput* were to pay six guineas for the publication of his story of the horse's dissection. He then submitted two other stories, 'Giuseppe' and 'The Little Red Mouth', but on the 27th they were returned as being too similar to the horse story.[10] ('Giuseppe', a story of war, remains unpublished. With unusual kindness, *Lilliput* had set a typist to type up a copy of one of his stories before returning it.) Douglas then tried them with *Horizon,* but although they found the stories 'well and vigorously written and certainly very interesting' they considered them 'not suitable for this magazine'.

At the same time as **'Bête Noire'** Douglas had written a poem describing the feelings of those who were **'Actors waiting in the wings of Europe'**. In **'Sandhurst'** he had similarly anticipated experience of battle, but now he could write at first hand. For those 'entering at the height of the din' it would be hard to hear their thoughts and hard to gauge 'how much our conduct owes to fear or fury': but it was the present period of waiting which preoccupied him.

> Everyone, I suppose, will use these minutes
> to look back, to hear music and recall
> what we were doing and saying that year
> during our last few months as people, near
> the sucking mouth of the day that swallowed us all
> into the stomach of a war . . .

Now they were no more people, but food for war, 'swirling in an uncomfortable digestive journey'. What they said and did had a 'slightly / fairytale quality', but there was an excitement in 'seeing our ghosts wandering'.

With the same equanimity Douglas made his farewell to **'Women of four countries'**. To reach this poem he moved through six successive drafts,[11] but as if to demonstrate that the intractability of **'Bête Noire'** had been a problem unique to that poem, this time he arrived at a perfected artefact. The poem was dedicated 'To Kristin Yingcheng Olga Milena'.

> Women of four countries
> the four phials full of essences
> of green England, legendary China,

cold Europe, Arabic Spain, a finer
four poisons for the subtle senses
than any in medieval inventories.

Here I give back perforce
the sweet wine to the grape
give the dark plant its juices
what every creature uses
by natural law will seep
back to the natural source.

These first days of March had proved remarkably creative; unfortunately, that month Douglas not only lost the colonel whom he had grown to respect ('[he] was too good for us and has gone,[12] militarily speaking, to a Better Place'), he and the regiment gained a colonel who felt they needed stiffening up. The regiment's historian recorded:

He was appalled by our Middle East habits,[13] and introduced us to early-rising, P.T. in the morning, and 'Inglese' clothes with boots and gaiters. It was trying for all, but by now we had learnt to suffer.

With Headquarters and A Squadron still at Chippenham and B and C Squadrons engaged elsewhere with their swimming tanks, it was difficult for Colonel J. D'A. Anderson to settle into command, and rumour did not help: Colonel Anderson was said to have been Brigade Major of a brigade which at the start of the war in France had gone into action with practice ammunition.[14]

Even before the rigours of Colonel Anderson's command began, life at Chippenham had severe limitations for Douglas. There was little social life. Occasionally he got into Cambridge, but even there he found 'not much wine, one very indifferent woman and no song'. There was a dance or two, once accompanied by five Chinamen: 'I didn't dance once with the Chinamen, though at a later dance I had one loopy foxtrot with a Chinese girl (national costume complete)'; and a party, with some 'incredibly stupid young students (can it be that I behaved like that only four years ago?).' Even another chance meeting with Joe Arsenault, in a Cambridge bookshop, led to nothing, for Arsenault was too busy training for the invasion to have free time. They did, however, agree to meet in Europe.[15]

In such a situation, Betty Jesse provided a natural focus for Douglas's necessitous imaginative scheming. He awaited her letters impatiently, and although when they came their main subject was the publication of his work, Betty's evening out with him had been curious enough to sustain some personal comment. Douglas had been 'delighted' to learn that his behaviour on their day together had been 'excellent in many ways';[16] and presumably Betty had suggested that he had been too sensitive, for in a postscript to his second letter he suggested that 'raw' was the word she wanted, 'only it doesn't sound so nice'.

You're a strange person if you don't want any sympathy—possibly you mean pity. Personally I can always do with any amount of sympathy, although I don't often get it, ask for it, or feel it for anyone else. (Sometimes I do all three.)

Such brusque confessions run through the few letters he wrote her from Chippenham, offering the same defensive intimacy as his earliest letters to Kristin and Olga: hoping to deepen a brief relationship while leaving his defences intact.

If I may say it without committing a breach of security (*my* security) it has seemed a long time between the letters, although I know you wrote as soon as you'd any reason to. I find it hard not to write to you sometimes, though I certainly shan't allow myself to do it too often: and I enjoy getting your letters more than most things (that's not saying much, au moment).

Drawing attention to his defences was of course a way of writing personally.

At the end of his second letter, however, Douglas explained the importance of this new acquaintance: 'My relationship with you has a lot of unknowns and I hope I never quite get the equation to come out, because it's fascinating and I need something to keep me from becoming mud.' Douglas had always needed such an interest, to give him a sense of purpose beyond his present, mundane preoccupations. It was not just a matter of providing material for his day-dreaming; he needed someone to whom he could communicate the substance of his daily life. The intimacy he desired could extend to seemingly simple things.

With his letter of 10 March he had enclosed 'a daffy letter' which was 'letting down my shield a bit'. The enclosure was a letter provoked by Bethell-Fox's return to the squadron at Chippenham.

Dear Betty,

Do you remember Johnny in the diary? . . . Well, he's come back—to see *me*. And he's pleased to see me, too: not just ordinary polite pleased, but like a puppy who's been left alone in a house. This amazes me, but it's nice, I suppose. Why should I write and tell, when I've already written you one letter which no-one has posted, and anyway, as you say, we don't know each other? The only thing to do is not to post it, or to pretend I'm not going to post it for a day or two (and then tear it up or post it). Really I feel quite happy and I didn't realise what a rare sensation this is. Nothing worries you, you say, so you wouldn't know what my state of mind has been like. Anyway I'm being terrifically unemotional with Johnny. . . .

Douglas then confessed that he did know why he was writing to Betty, drawing himself deeper into the feelings he desperately wished to express and equally wanted to hide.

I do know why I'm writing to you, as a matter of fact: because this evening is a little like the day I got your letter saying you'd got a horse and you were coming dancing. Gosh, this is drivel, isn't it. Betty I hope this isn't a mirage, this little golden age, even if it's only for a week or two. Please forgive this outburst, if I'm weak enough to send it you.

Douglas sent the letter because he felt that if Betty could understand it, 'it might do some good': if she could not, then he must be mistaken in her.

The part of Betty's letter about himself and the 'very small pieces, no more than a hint' about herself had reminded Douglas of his letters from Olga, 'who thinks she knows all about me, and herself, and life—presumably because the first two have made the same sort of mess of the third.' But Olga's letters, and now Betty's, were 'the most interesting' he received. As someone who had long professed a mistrust of introspection, a dialogue about himself, under cover of his correspondent's sophistication, fascinated him and answered a need. At Chippenham, waiting for the invasion, Douglas's emotions were once again acting out the conflict between too much and too little feeling. If he was afraid of becoming 'mud', his letter about his friend's return had really been a plea for help in the face of potentially overwhelming emotions. Trying to arrange a meeting with Betty, in March, he had suggested the source of such feelings:

> If I can manage that day, it'll be the last, I fear, because awful things happen after that, nameless and unnecessary, but not at first, perilous. Later on of course, I shall have to engage someone to pray hard: I don't suppose you'd be any better at that than I am.

By the end of March it was clear that they were shortly to leave Chippenham, already partly equipped and trained with the new Sherman Fireflies which they were to take into Europe. These, the 'most formidable tanks in the Allied armies' at that time,[17] were fitted with seventeen-pounder guns, powerful enough in their first test at Chippenham[18] to blow over a hut with their blast and produce a flash which made observation impossible and singed off the gunner's eyebrows.

On 2 April, Douglas managed a Sunday visit to Betty in London.

> Sunday was a wonderful day. These haywire occasions are what make people friends—and lovers, sometimes. In a sense everything couldn't have gone wronger, but in hundreds of other ways that was made up. If I never see you again, it's not a bad time to remember as the last day of a short and peculiar friendship, which has made me happier—and of course unhappier—than I have been for a long time. But, before you start bawling me out for being gloomy, I'll hasten to say I'm sure it's not the end, although the flap is definitely on, now.

Betty had at last told him of her 'cat's cradle of a life', and he was left feeling that his 'fair comprehension of what's happening' and a desire to help 'which quite shakes me up' were not enough. Trying to find a way of helping he turned to one of his own perennial problems, money, urging Betty to take seriously an offer of help from his salary once he was in action. It was a wild idea and Douglas recognized that it sounded pretentious 'when I'm notorious for being permanently broke and over borrowing', but just as at Oxford he had offered Jean part of his grant if it would facilitate her return to university, he desperately wanted to help others out of difficulties he knew so well. It was part of his long frustration at being dependent himself, a frustration which led to his passionate determination that someone should get his pension.

> Don't dismiss this idea at once, or be contemptuous of it or amused at it—and don't think it would make the least difference to either of us, as friends, or change our situation at all. It's simply that I'm mad about being free and about other people being free, and if you decide to take your courage in both hands, I would do anything in the world—short of completely sabotaging myself, which wouldn't help either of us—to help you.

Douglas was writing on Tuesday the 4th of April, two days before they left Chippenham. Their destination was to be an area prohibited to civilians, and in the first half of his letter Douglas had made a bid for a last meeting with Betty. It seemed unlikely that he would get leave, and at the end of the letter he suggested a plan for that contingency: 'If all else fails, come out of town one Sunday and meet me at the borders of the prohibited belt, and we'll really go for a walk.' There was a chance, however, that he would be able to escape for a day or two and he was determined not to miss it.

> I'm going to ask you in a letter—because so many things in conversation embarrass you—if you will stay a whole week-end with me, before the second (so-called) front opens—and if I get a week-end, which isn't likely. This isn't because I want, as your favourite phrase is, 'to climb into bed with you.' As you must know, of course, I am quite enough in love with you from a sex point of view, to want that. But what I do want is not to have to fight against the whole of London (or the clientèle of the Southern Railway) for every moment I spend with you. It would be marvellous to be in a room with you and shut the door on all the problems and perils of both of us. You will probably feel that actually sleeping together will only make you another complication, and I don't suppose you want to sleep with me, anyway. But I hope you can see that it needn't happen just because we shut ourselves up together. I'm afraid this is very pompous, but I always get pompous when I'm having a job to express myself (like an M.P.).

Douglas suggested the Grosvenor as a possible place, for although the idea of it revolted him, one could be anonymous there, and complete anonymity was 'almost as good as solitude'.

If Douglas did not know whether Betty would agree, at least he now had confidence enough to know that she would understand his request and not feel that it was 'an ordinary pass thinly wrapped up'. If she had nothing to say about it, he suggested that she could ignore it in her next letter and not be afraid of hurting his 'ridiculous' feelings. Having made clear his intentions, however, he now wanted to make clear these feelings.

> . . . as you see, references to being in love with you seem to creep into conversations and letters of mine from time to time. Actually, I know no more certainly what's happening to me than you know what *will* happen to you. But you can be quite sure whatever it is, it isn't another problem for you; I am not dependent on you, you have absolutely no responsibility for me or need to worry about hurting *me* as little as possible, etc. etc. You can skip me, unless I happen to open up a way of escape for you. If so use me as much as you like—you can be sure I'll use you just as much, if you do. What I asked at the beginning of this letter is something which means a hell of a lot to me, and so does everything else I have to do with you; I think about you a great deal, having an amorphous rather than complicated life otherwise. But it's all duty-free as far as you're concerned: I'm an extra piece of furniture, if you like you can use it, but you can leave it behind in any of a hundred cloak rooms. You'll be glad to hear from now on is just news, and you can read it when you like.

The news was unimportant: a trip to a tank range on the coast, a visit to a bad film, and a near-disastrous attempt to trick some fellow-officers out on a spree.

The next day Douglas received a letter from Betty which had crossed his in the post: 'Comparison of your letter . . . and mine . . . is rather amusing. I like yours better—probably if I'd been in a hurry mine would have been improved.' Having had tea in Cambridge that afternoon, with a Frenchman 'in a red velvet képi', at 'sparrowfart' the next morning, 6 April, the Chippenham squadrons moved south.

3

The regiment's living conditions within their 'prohibited area' at Sway were as comfortable as those of Chippenham had been uncomfortable. The weather became more benevolent, and surrounded by a New Forest spring, 'flowers and sunshine' attended them, 'however oily and mechanical'[19] their duties. Tanks had to be waterproofed and drivers instructed in the art of driving them ashore in five foot of water. Douglas, however, remained preoccupied with thoughts of a final meeting with Betty, impatiently awaiting her reply to his letter. On Monday, 10 April, he wrote to her:

> Dear Betty,
>
> I have been feeling very depressed waiting for your letter—which shows I am not so conceited—or at least that there are bounds to my conceit. Now it (in two

parts) has arrived, I feel very much encouraged and for some reason much less frightened of the future. I can understand your not wanting to sneak about in and out of hotels; I don't myself. In any case I don't think London will see me again for some time: I don't think they'll let us far out of here. But I am going to find out how near here you are allowed to come from London, and I'll try and slip across the border and join you on a Sunday or on a Saturday, staying overnight. So stand by for a telegram. . . . If we don't meet, DON'T consider it an 'unfinished story'; go on writing to me, and you know unless I'm killed or crippled I shall feel about you as I do now: so try not to be too impatient and rush off with someone else, my sweet.

Having explained that being crippled would not alter his feelings but could change his chance of expressing them, Douglas turned to the spring weather, which was 'going like a symphonic accompaniment to one of Sam Goldwyn's hits':

> just too sugary and sentimental for words, sun and olde worlde cottages and lovers everywhere—and I, like any other dope in the film audience, am taken in (I hope you'll come and hold my hand and watch the show with me). Will it happen? We must at least worry about it and get in a hell of a flap and then it *may*.

'So overcome' with spring, Douglas sent four men under a lance corporal to pick primroses to put in the rooms and huts: 'much raucous laughter from the remaining soldiery, and they (the four chosen) slunk away blushing.'

On the 17th the whole regiment gathered for the first time since February, to take part in a landing exercise in the Southampton area. None of them knew the date for the invasion, though Montgomery had announced the plans to a select group at St. Paul's School on 7 April. On the 28th Douglas was writing to Jocelyn Baber: 'We suspect the worst whenever anything arrives in an O.H.M.S. envelope—but of course it may be weeks.' Four days previously, however, he had managed his meeting with Betty.

Douglas and Bethell-Fox left the camp on Saturday night without leave.[20] Dining locally, they caught the overnight train to London, arriving at 4.20 a.m., and Douglas, having made his way to Nuffield House, first fell asleep on a sofa and then in the bath. The rest of the day until the midnight train was Betty's. After a busy journey back, Douglas and Bethell-Fox were in camp by 3.30 on Monday morning.

On the train from London they had first treated an American armed with a gin bottle to a lecture on the nature of poetry, with special reference to Gascoyne, Verlaine, and Louis Aragon. Then Douglas had informed a 'truculent civilian' that if his four-year-old daughter's drawings really were as good as Graham Sutherland's, he should try and retard the girl's growth, 'she was obviously at her best age and might grow like Daddy.' Their two-hour harangue ended by provoking the man to recite fourteen lines of *Richard II*, 'quite well'. Despite losing a belt, razor, shaving bag, flannel, and khaki sweater on his travels, Douglas had managed to keep safe the silk handkerchief which Betty had given him.

There was the customary two-mile run before a breakfast at which Douglas greeted the colonel as though he had never been away, and in the evening, a cocktail party at brigade headquarters. There Douglas met an aristocratic Land Girl who wrote short stories and poems, and after about four gins, he took her into the garden:

> After a bit I took her glasses off, to see if she looked better without them, but she didn't. I didn't want to be nasty so I said: 'You want to keep your face moving, then you'll be all right.' Thinking this over I didn't think it sounded so nice after all, so I tried to improve it by saying she had a nice dress anyway: but unfortunately about then I spilt a pint of gin down the front of her so I had to walk her round the garden to get her dry.

Still 'frightfully canned', Douglas was writing to Betty. Where previously he had apologized for the sentimentality brought on by such a state, however, he now welcomed the effect of his mood.

> I only hope being drunk will enable me to escape the various sorts of shyness that prevent me sounding sincere when I say nice things to you. But I want to say that I couldn't love you or anyone else more than I did at moments yesterday—not if I know you for years. You were so kind (in the sense that a girl is kind to her lover, not in the YMCA sense) and sweet (I am resuscitating old words that have been slaughtered but I am giving them back their virtue), and I blundered about and ended up annoying you with remarks about your face which were only prompted by a fear that you couldn't be as happy as you were making me. Dear Betty. Thank you for telling me your story: go on trusting me and perhaps I can do something to make you happier. . . . Never believe a single catty remark I make; you are a difficult person to address, and I am as shy as you.

Acknowledging that his next letter would 'no doubt be saner', Douglas urged Betty not to say 'Thank you for your incredibly sentimental letter': 'because now I've said it for you, and anyway I should come to London leave or no leave and spit in your eye.'

For two months Douglas's energies had mainly been given to his visits to Betty. He made no practical proposals: the fact that they were not ruled out by her was enough. What mattered was that during his time of waiting she had been there, and the continuance of their relationship would allow its imaginative development in his mind when the war once again took over. Against thoughts of death and negation, Douglas could pit thoughts of love and its positive feelings, acting out in his imagination a conflict which lay behind virtually all his poetry. Before leaving the Middle East, in '**I Experiment**', he had brought this conflict into the open: the poet's cycle of roles ended with a shell-burst, 'the apathetic buzz buzz / pirouetting to a crescendo BANG'.

> The finale if it should come is
> the moment my love and I meet
> our hands move out across a room of strangers
> certain they hold the rose of love

Drafting his valediction to **'Women of four countries'**,[21] he had seen their love 'as treasure for my grave / if I should die tomorrow'. Under the influence of the brigade cocktail party, Douglas had written:

> I don't need anything to fight for now, but at least
>   there is you to look at beyond
> the fighting, and I can get through any amount of
>   fighting, however little I care
> for it, if I can think about you and have your letters.

If the tone of his remarks was, as he suggested, sentimental, he was writing no less than the truth.

Early in May Douglas saw Betty again. Often he had said that he would like her to meet his mother, and Betty had responded that she had met too many people's mothers and had no desire for further boredom. Douglas insisted that his would prove different. Now he simply invited Betty to meet him at Christ's Hospital where he would show her his school. She arrived to find Douglas had also invited his mother and her annoyance was dispelled by the discovery that his previous assurance was right. Bethell-Fox was also there, Douglas having threatened not to visit his mother unless he came with him, and together they had tea on the Robertses' lawn,[22] David Roberts also meeting Mrs. Douglas for the first time. At tea Douglas met C. A. Humphrey of Lamb A, and as Edward Malins was back at the school, invalided home from the army in India, Douglas called on him. Malins found him 'a totally different person . . . prepared to discuss his poetry, his life, and his views in a civilized way, with none of his previous arrogance'.[23]

Douglas snatched one more unofficial visit to Betty on 22 May and took her for a day in the country. (On that visit, or another, he brought her his painting of Yingcheng to look after for him.) Having missed one train, the one in which they travelled was delayed. They arrived just in time to cross the line and catch the train back to London. Writing to Mrs. Baber a few days later, however, Douglas was able to announce a new confidence in his relationship with Betty: not only did Betty 'intrigue' him, luckily he 'intrigued' her. He had planned to see his mother after their walk in the country, but the timing of their journey had made the meeting impossible.

April and May had been filled with conferences, maintenance, training in co-operation with infantry and artillery, and exercises with landing craft which had culminated in a mock-invasion of Hayling Island on 30 April. What free time Douglas had was spent making his personal arrangements for departure. To his mother he wrote of sea boots, American drill slacks, the payment of royalties, bank accounts, and the checking of proofs. To Jocelyn Baber he wrote of the coming need for eau de cologne, razor blades, and baby powder, and defended his war narrative against her criticisms.[24] The book had passed a last fence with a note from Mrs. Kellett,[25] which thanked Douglas for allowing her to read it, and raised no objections; and now it was with the publisher, being checked for breaches of national security, the Official Secrets Act, military law, libel, and defamation. (Too late for Douglas to receive it before his departure, a full list of alterations[26] to be made on these counts was forwarded to him.) Undeterred by the problems of publication, Douglas wrote on 28 May to Jocelyn Baber: 'I hope a second book (and bags more loot) will emerge from these events. Well, fair stands the wind for————?'

Having been sealed into transit camps in the Romsey area on 1 June, the Sherwood Rangers departed for Southampton Docks the next day. The sun was shining, and whenever they stopped, civilians appeared with tea and buns, seeming fully aware of the import of events which security precautions had for months tried to conceal. On the 3rd, accompanied by their tanks, they were in their landing craft, moored ten deep along the quayside.

During his two busy months at Sway Douglas had found difficulty in thinking about their forthcoming action. Fixed 'in the stomach of a war',[27] his mind was 'too full of odd things'[28] most of the time. But his fellow-officers were not only disturbed by his unofficial visits to London, they were troubled by his indifference. On a trivial level, Christopherson noticed that during exercises Douglas's map board was covered with even more drawings than previously. On a more serious level, Semken saw no reason to doubt Douglas's candour when he stated that he was played out as a soldier. Douglas, sharing a room with Bethell-Fox and talking more personally with him than with anyone else in the regiment, explained his lack of interest by saying that he would not survive. He had left the same impression with Malins at Christ's Hospital.

On a final visit to Oxford from Chippenham, after a meal at the Taj Mahal restaurant, Douglas had given Joan Appleton his watch, saying that he would not need

it again, and he had asked her to get his poetry known, if he was not there to do it himself. He had said this simply, without sentiment: but the 'gloom' for which, in his letter to Betty, he had expected her to bawl him out had been talk of his lack of a future. Often he had spoken calmly to Betty of his conviction that he would not survive, and his very seriousness had led her to dismiss such talk as stupid.

The Sunday before the regiment's departure from Sway, their padre, Leslie Skinner, set up his altar beside Douglas's tank as the most convenient place in the squadron's line. Douglas, after directing his crew to tidy up the area and fold blankets to be used as kneelers, stayed to communion, and that evening, to Skinner's surprise, he joined the civilian congregation for evensong in the small village church, the only soldier there. After the service, Douglas came up to speak to the padre, and they walked in the New Forest, talking of Douglas's conviction that he would not return from Europe. 'He was not morbid about it,' Skinner recalls. 'He could talk of and even make plans for the days when the war was over, and having done so come back again to this feeling that it was unlikely he would survive. . . . We walked and talked together, only separating as dawn was breaking.'

At Chippenham, Douglas had embarked on a speculative poem[29] which first described his feelings on return from Egypt, then announced that 'Next month' was a window; after splitting its glass, the poet would find on the other side, 'woman or the ominous skull of time / stretch out lips or the bone of death to kiss'. There was another possibility.

> All this is the curtain. Who would say
> beyond are islands, clouds, rivers and people
> the eyes and limbs, real to the touch
> of the legendary people, whose bones are
> hollow like bird's bones, whose fluting voices
> from time immemorial have resembled the swallow
> the women with fine Lethean violet eyes . . .

By the close of his draft there were three possibilities:

> Tomorrow I set out across Europe to find
> these islands, this land beyond the mountains
> these are the things which may happen to me
> to find them suddenly at the end of years
> to continue to death like the Jew
> to trip suddenly and fall in the earth, disintegrating.

When Douglas was ready to make fair copies of this, the last poem he completed before his departure, his speculations had narrowed. The islands and land beyond the mountains had disappeared, leaving the ambiguities of metaphor to hold all the suggestions he desired to offer. After the disturbances which had run through his previous work and enforced its development, his poem presented a triumphant return to lyricism. But here, for the first time in his work, the affirmation of a poetic quest was wholly retrospective.

"On a Return From Egypt"

To stand here in the wings of Europe
disheartened, I have come away
from the sick land where in the sun lay
the gentle sloe-eyed murderers
of themselves, exquisites under a curse;
here to exercise my depleted fury.

For the heart is a coal, growing colder
when jewelled cerulean seas change
into grey rocks, grey water-fringe,
sea and sky altering like a cloth
till colours and sheen are gone both:
cold is an opiate of the soldier.

And all my endeavours are unlucky explorers
come back, abandoning the expedition;
the specimens, the lilies of ambition
still spring in their climate, still unpicked:
but time, time is all I lacked
to find them, as the great collectors before me.

The next month, then, is a window
and with a crash I'll split the glass.
Behind it stands one I must kiss,
person of love or death
a person or a wraith,
I fear what I shall find.

Notes

Regimental movements and activities: *SR*. KD with the regiment: recollections of JB-F, SDC, Holman, Semken, Skinner, and others as for chapter 5; letters to MJD, Baber, BJ, JT. On leave: recollections of MJD, BA, JA, Baber, BJ. Meetings with BJ: letters to BJ and her recollections. Dealings with publishers: MJT, 'Tenth Letter: In Memory of Keith Douglas', *Poetry* (*London*), no. x, n.d. [Dec. 1944]; contracts (BL 56356); letters to BJ; letters from BJ and MJT to KD and MJD (BL 56356); recollections of MJD, JB-F, BJ, MJT. Visit to Christ's Hospital: letters from Humphrey and Roberts to MJD (BL 56356); recollections of MJD, JB-F, Humphrey, BJ, Malins, Mrs. Roberts.

In the following notes, for the sake of brevity, I have referred to Keith Douglas as KD, and have also used initials for the following: Mrs. Marie J. Douglas (MJD); Joan and Betty Appleton (JA, BA); Major John Bethell-Fox (JB-F); Lt.-Col. S. D. Christopherson (SDC); J. C. Hall (JCH); Alec Hardie (AH); Betty Jesse (BJ); Norman L. Ilett (NLI); Margaret Stanley-Wrench (MS-W); M. J. Tambimuttu (MJT); Jean Turner (JT); John Waller (JW). KD's friends and correspondents are referred to here by the names under which they figure in the book (e.g. Antoinette, Kristin, Milena, Olga, Yingcheng). The full names of many others interviewed or quoted, cited here by their surnames only, are given in the list of ac-

knowledgements at p. xi. Other abbreviations and short forms used are given below.

1. undated, BL 56356.

2. BL 53773. The *'Bete Noire'* fragments are in *CP*, pp. 114-15 and 158-9; their order has been corrected here by collation of the MSS. with letters to BJ.

3. *CP*, p. 158.

4. ibid.

5. *Alamein*, p. 16.

6. BL 53775-6.

7. sent to BJ, saying it was from his wall (BL 56355).

8. referred to in BL 56356; a later, revised contract exists in BL 56356.

9. BL 53775-6.

10. letter from *Lilliput*, BL 56356; rejection letter from *Horizon* also in BL 56356.

11. BL 53773, ff. 126-8.

12. letter to BJ.

13. *SR*, p. 98.

14. ibid.

15. Arsenault arrived at Point 103 (see chapter 10) late on 9 June 1944.

16. letter to BJ.

17. H. C. B. Rogers, *Tanks in Battle* (Sphere Books ed., 1972), p. 199.

18. *SR*, p. 98.

19. letter to Baber.

20. details from letter to Baber.

21. BL 53773, f. 126b: the revised version is on p. 242.

22. letter from Roberts to MJD.

23. Malins to author.

24. TS. copy of part of his letter to Baber, BL 56355.

25. a copy of Douglas's reply is in BL 56355.

26. BL 53773.

27. 'Actors Waiting . . .'

28. letter to Baber.

29. 'On a Return from Egypt'; collation of MSS. (BL 53773, ff. 86-91) with letters to BJ suggests the date in *CP*, 'Egypt-England 1943-44', given on the MS. in the possession of JW, is merely descriptive, not referring to date of composition.

PRINCIPAL SOURCES CITED OR QUOTED

I BY KEITH DOUGLAS

PUBLISHED WORK

Collected Poems, ed. John Waller, G. S. Fraser and J. C. Hall, with an Introduction by Edmund Blunden (London: Faber and Faber, 1966). Cited as *CP*

All poems quoted or referred to are from this volume, and follow its text, unless otherwise noted.

Alamein to Zem Zem, ed. John Waller, G. S. Fraser and J. C. Hall, with an Introduction by Lawrence Durrell (London: Faber and Faber, 1966). Cited as *Alamein*

In periodicals: *The Outlook* (Christ's Hospital, Horsham), 1933-8; *The Cherwell* (Oxford), 1940-1; *Citadel* (Cairo), 1942-3; *Personal Landscape* (Cairo), 1944-5; *Poetry* (*London*), 1942-9

UNPUBLISHED MATERIAL

(i) Keith Douglas Papers, The British Library. Cited as BL

Add. MSS. 53773-6 and 56355-60, with some uncatalogued items, comprising virtually all the MSS. and papers in MJD's possession after her son's death: 53773, poems and a few prose pieces; 53774, MS. of *Alamein*; 53775-6, paintings and drawings; 56355, letters from KD, 1926-44; 56356, letters to KD and MJD, 1937-65; 56357, poems and stories supplementing 53773; 56358, school and Oxford notes and essays; 56359, school exercise books; 56360, diary recording reading 1937-9; uncatalogued, letters and postcards to Margaret Stanley-Wrench.

Except for material in private hands (as detailed below), or where otherwise indicated, all letters and unpublished writings cited or quoted are in this collection.

(ii) The Brotherton Collection, Brotherton Library, The University of Leeds

MSS. of nine poems sent to Mary Benson

(iii) In private hands

Two letters to MJD, two letters to Olga, the MS. of an unpublished story, miscellaneous documents, drawings and paintings, and KD's books, in the possession of MJD

Letters to Antoinette, Betty Jesse, Milena, Jean Turner, Yingcheng, and others in the possession of their recipients: Mrs. John Baber, Mrs. M. Gattegno, Mrs. Allan Guest, J. C. Hall, Alec Hardie, Mrs. A. G. Haysom, Mrs. M. Johnson, Mrs. J. F. O'Neill, Sir John Waller

MS. poems in the possession of Mrs. Guest, Alec Hardie, Mrs. Haysom, Mrs. O'Neill, Mrs. Phyllis Thayer, Sir John Waller, and author

Two school exercise books, the gift of H. R. Hornsby, titled by KD 'Poems 1934-6' and 'Poems 1936-7', in the possession of the author. Cited as *1934-6 1936-7*

Drawings and paintings in the possession of Lt.-Col. S. D. Christopherson, Mrs. Gattegno, Mrs. Douglas Grant, Mrs. Haysom, Mrs. David Roberts, and Mrs. Thayer

II OTHER SOURCES

PUBLISHED

The Christ's Hospital Book, published for a Committee of Old Blues (London: Hamish Hamilton, 1953)

T. M. Lindsay, *Sherwood Rangers* (London: Burrup Mathieson & Co., 1952). Cited as *SR*

B. H. Liddell Hart, *History of the Second World War* (London: Cassell, 1970)

Other published sources are cited in the notes below, or listed in the Select Bibliography at p. 259.

UNPUBLISHED

Service records of KD and his father, Captain K. S. Douglas, consulted at the Ministry of Defence

Personal war diary of Lt.-Col. S. D. Christopherson

Extracts from personal diaries of David Hicks and Roger Lancelyn Green

Extracts from letters of Margaret Stanley-Wrench to her mother

KD rarely dated his letters, which are cited throughout the notes by the names of their recipients. All works mentioned are by, and letters cited from, KD unless otherwise indicated.

Select Bibliography

A full bibliography of Douglas's work and relevant criticism is given in my thesis, 'A Critical Study of the Writings of Keith Douglas, 1920-1944', Leeds University, 1969. A full description of the MSS. in the British Library (Keith Douglas Papers) is in preparation, and will be published in a *Catalogue of the National Manuscripts Collection of Modern Writers 1963-1972,* by Jenny Stratford (Turret Books for the Arts Council of Great Britain, 1974). All works listed below published in London unless otherwise stated.

I BY KEITH DOUGLAS

BOOKS

Augury: An Oxford Miscellany of Verse and Prose, ed. K. C. Douglas and A. M. Hardie (Oxford: Basil Blackwell, 1940)

Selected Poems, Keith Douglas, J. C. Hall and Norman Nicholson, Modern Reading Library No. 3 (John Bale & Staples, 1943)

Alamein to Zem Zem [with poems and drawings], Editions Poetry London (Nicholson and Watson, 1946)

Collected Poems, ed. John Waller and G. S. Fraser, Editions Poetry London (Nicholson and Watson, 1951)

Selected Poems, ed. Ted Hughes (Faber and Faber, 1964)

Collected Poems [with drawings], ed. John Waller, G. S. Fraser and J. C. Hall (London: Faber and Faber; New York: Chilmark Press, 1966)

Alamein to Zem Zem [with drawings], ed. John Waller, G. S. Fraser and J. C. Hall (London: Faber and Faber; New York: Chilmark Press, 1966); reissued with corrections, Penguin Modern Classics (1969)

UNCOLLECTED POEMS IN PERIODICALS

The Outlook (Christ's Hospital, Horsham): 'Pan', Dec. 1934, p. 8; *'Ave Atque Vale'*, Dec. 1934, p. 13; *'Xaipe'*, April 1935, p. 5; 'Poem: The rabbits are out', July 1935, p. 14; 'The Alchymist', Dec. 1935, p. 4; 'Song of the Fisherman', Dec. 1935, p. 14; 'Countryside', April 1936, p. 4; 'Triton', March 1937, p. 12; 'For E. B.', July 1938, p. 11.

The Sussex County Magazine (Eastbourne): 'Pan in Sussex' ('Song: You asked me for a song to sing'), Jan. 1937, p. 38.

The Cherwell (Oxford): 'To a Lady on the Death of her First Love', 27 April 1940, p. 8.

UNCOLLECTED PROSE

'Death of a Horse' (story), *Lilliput,* July 1944, pp. 51-2

'Butterflies: *The Yellow Book'* (essay), *Citadel* (Cairo), March 1943, pp. 32-4

'The Little Red Mouth' (story), *Stand* (Newcastle upon Tyne), vol. XI, no. 2 (1970), pp. 9-11

'Poets in This War' (essay), *Times Literary Supplement,* 23 April 1971, p. 478

II ON KEITH DOUGLAS

R. N. Currey, 'Poets of the 1939-45 War', *Writers and their Work,* No. 127 (1960), pp. 26-9

G. S. Fraser, 'Keith Douglas: A Poet of the Second World War', Chatterton Lecture on an English Poet, in *Proceedings of the British Academy,* vol. XLII (1956), pp. 88-108

D. Grant, 'War and the Writer', *Penguin Parade,* 2nd series, no. 3 (1948), pp. 57-68

M. Hamburger, *The Truth of Poetry* (Penguin ed., 1969), pp. 193-8.

I. Hamilton, 'Poetry: The Forties, I', *London Magazine,* April 1964, pp. 83-9

G. Hill, '"I in Another Place": Homage to Keith Douglas', *Stand* (Newcastle upon Tyne), vol. VI, no. 4, n.d. [1964/5], pp. 6-13

T. Hughes, 'The Poetry of Keith Douglas', *The Listener,* 21 June 1962, pp. 1069-71

———, 'The Poetry of Keith Douglas', *Critical Quarterly,* Spring 1963, pp. 43-8

N. L. Ilett, 'Keith Douglas', in *The Christ's Hospital Book,* published for a Committee of Old Blues (1953), pp. 292-4

O. Manning, 'Poets in Exile', *Horizon,* Oct. 1944, p. 278

D. S. Roberts, 'Obituary: Captain K. C. Douglas', *The Blue* (Horsham), Nov.-Dec. 1944, pp. 22-3

A. Ross, 'The Poetry of Keith Douglas' (Personal Preference), *Times Literary Supplement,* 6 Aug. 1954, p. xxii

R. J. Sapsford, 'Edmund Blunden and Keith Douglas: Two Christ's Hospital Poets of the Two World Wars', *The Blue* (Horsham), Jan. 1966, pp. 62-8; correspondence, Sept. 1966, pp. 249-50; Jan. 1967, pp. 45-6

B. Spencer, 'Keith Douglas: an Obituary Note', *Personal Landscape* (Cairo), vol. II, no. 4 (1945), p. 20

M. J. Tambimuttu, 'Tenth Letter: In Memory of Keith Douglas', *Poetry* (*London*), n.d. [Dec. 1944], unnumbered pages (first article in issue)

C. Tomlinson, 'Poetry Today', in *Pelican Guide to English Literature,* vol. VII (1961), pp. 469-71.

J. Waller, 'Oxford Poetry and Disillusion, II', *Poetry Review,* May-June 1940, pp. 211-15

———, 'The Poetry of Keith Douglas', *Accent* (Urbana, Ill.), 8 (1948), pp. 226-35

Reginald Gibbons (essay date spring/summer 1981)

SOURCE: Gibbons, Reginald. "A Sharp Enquiring Blade." *Parnassus* 9, no. 1 (spring/summer 1981): 315-31.

[*In the following essay, Gibbons traces Douglas's development as a poet from his early school years to his service in the army, noting that he was preoccupied with the subjects of time and death almost from the beginning of his writing career.*]

With only minor exceptions, everything Keith Douglas wrote is contained in two volumes, one of poems, the other prose. He was twenty-four when he died a few days after the Allied invasion of Normandy in 1944, hit after a reconnaissance patrol as mortar fire burst over the tanks of his regiment, near a village called St. Pierre. The wound that killed him left no mark except the lifelessness in his limbs—and had he been able to see it, he would have found this worth pondering, for in his account of tank warfare in Africa it is the sight of dead men that most excites his curiosity and dread. In 1940, while still a student at Oxford, he had written a brief statement for a symposium on poetry, which began:

> Poetry is like a man, whom thinking you know all his movements and appearance you will presently come upon in such a posture that for a moment you can hardly believe it a position of the limbs you know. So thinking you have set bounds to the nature of poetry, you shall as soon discover something outside your bounds which they should evidently contain.

> *(Collected Poems, 123)*

That "something" was, on the battlefield, simply the death that invaded the bodies of men and removed them from the company of the living; and for Douglas to have implied, so early, an odd connection between disarranged, at first unrecognized limbs, and the surprise and strangeness of poetry, only reinforces the sense one has, reading his work, of his premonition of death.

The advantage, to a poem, of a special kind of surprise—the startling detail or connection that turns out to be the center of the whole poem (and which can be achieved through sound or rhythm, sometimes, as well as through imagery)—was something Keith Douglas keenly appreciated. He had a kind of genius for it, from an early age, that seemed both natural to him and at odds with his life and its limitations. As a soldier he was brave, impulsive, impatient, un-hierarchical and too independent, cool, and compassionate without being unsoldierly. He had been this way as a boy and a student, too: intemperate, brilliant, pugnacious, rebellious perhaps, driven to excel in whatever he tried. He was prodigiously talented as both poet and artist. A few poems from his fifteenth and sixteenth years hold up well enough to stand beside the better-known poems of the war years. And the very first poem that is preserved, written in 1934 (he was fourteen), established a stanzaic pattern that he continued to employ often, right through till the last poem he wrote: a six-line stanza usually rhymed ABCCBA (though Douglas varied the scheme, and often used slant rhymes of great subtlety and authority).

Of the more than one hundred poems in the new *Complete Poems* there are certainly twenty that are superb—and the special and difficult circumstances of Douglas' writing make that figure even more astounding. By his twenty-first year, when he was in the Army training for action, he wrote the poem most readers know him by, **"Time Eating"**:

> Ravenous Time has flowers for his food
> at Autumn—yet can cleverly make good

each petal: devours animals and men,
but for ten dead he can create ten.

> If you enquire how secretly you've come
> to mansize from the bigness of a stone
> it will appear it's his art made you rise
> so gradually to your proper size.

> But while he makes he eats: the very part
> where he began, even the elusive heart
> Time's ruminative tongue will wash
> and slow juice masticate all flesh.

> That volatile huge intestine holds
> material and abstract in its folds:
> thought and ambition melt, and even the world
> will alter, in that catholic belly curled.

> But Time, who ate my love, you cannot make
> such another. You who can remake
> the lizard's tail and the bright snakeskin
> cannot, cannot. That you gobbled in
> too quick: and though you brought me from a boy
> you can make no more of me, only destroy.

There cannot have been a poet's life in which death was more forcefully the mother of beauty, nor more literally.

It is a little uncomfortable to analyze and ponder the work of a child, and yet the reader's discomfort is dispelled by the precocity of the poet's talent. **"Distraction,"** from 1936, will serve as example:

> Now my mind's off again. No tears
> Of Catullus move me. Though I know in turn
> We too will praise these years
> Of watching clouds through windows, fluttering pages;
> Usefully sometimes, though the beckoning scents
> Rise always, wafted from summer grasses:
> Hearing the loud bees mumble at the glass,
> And sound of sunlight behind the scratching pens.

It seems to have the flavor of a schoolboy, classroom Rimbaud. And from this poem one can already glean, with hindsight, several aspects of Douglas' later work. His rhythmic talent was outside the conventions of meter; he was never able to write a poem that was metrically accomplished, but already at sixteen he had obviously been able to find in himself another kind of poetic rhythm, and it is not exactly free verse, for the ghost of the iambic foot continually whispers behind the lines. His rhyming was better when not full; and his characteristic rhythms are more abrupt than these, as we shall see. He was also a very careful poet, and did not scruple falsely at making changes in old work: the notes to the *Complete Poems* reveal that in 1943 or 1944 Douglas went back and cut some bad lines from the end of this little poem, discovering only later how to bring it to a close at a moment of potential, but not yet dissipated, energy.

As a schoolboy Douglas wrote five or six *good* poems. He served a lightning apprenticeship: in what is preserved, there is little youthful gushing or overwriting. He possessed an innate skill with words and a gift for figurative language and compression. In his years at Oxford he wrote ten poems in 1939, and twenty-one poems and four translations in 1940. This extraordinary productivity was to continue. The war was already gathering for its leap into bloodshed, and Douglas was quick to respond, as in the very serious, unblinking love poem, **"Invaders"** (1939):

> Intelligences like black birds
> come on their dire wings from Europe. Sorrows
> fall like the rooks' clatter on house and garden.
> And who will drive them back before we harden?
> You will find, after a few tomorrows
> like this, nothing will matter but the black birds.
>
> · · · · ·
>
> So keep a highlight in your handsome eye;
> still be fastidious, and I will write
> some well-intentioned words.

Douglas' morbidity, his obsession with death, grows more pronounced as he waits to be called up for service, and enters the Army. His one poem of this period that treats war, **"Russians,"** voices a bright, knowing irony that he discarded as soon as he put on uniform. But without needing war for a subject, Douglas could find decay and wounds around him (and notice how the Douglas stanza is abandoned after the first six lines as the poem edges away from his control):

> How cleverly the choreographer
> and costumier combine—
> the effects fine, and the young lady's line
> impeccable; with what grace her arabesque
> he caps with an entrechat, this stunningly dressed
> young person her partner.
>
> All the colours of spring
> they are dressed in:
> they whirl about,
> and the dance over, they gracefully leap out.
>
> But here they come again, I'm certain—or
> is this not the fair
> young sylph? I declare
> she has a dead face and a yellow eye
> and he has no limbs! How horribly spry
> he is on his stumps:
> he bleeds, but he jumps
> ten feet at a prance.
> I don't like this dance.
>
> ("A Ballet")

To quote this poem at all is to cite Douglas' worst work against him, but it is worth noting how, even here, there is a kind of painful grace, and a tone that suggests Douglas was not able to hold the poem back from the horrible fantastic vision toward which it drops at the end.

He does try—with the rhymes "fair" and "declare"; with the exclamation point and the words "horribly" and "prance"—but the poem drops into the grotesque nevertheless.

Almost as a farewell to academic life, Douglas translated two poems of Rimbaud, and in these, as well as in **"Soissons,"** **"Soissons 1940,"** and **"John Anderson,"** he shows far greater control and power. The Rimbaud poems are *"Le Dormeur du Val"* and *"Au Cabaret-Vert,"* and Douglas Englished them with great skill; his straightforward lines and magnifying eye exactly match Rimbaud's ease and love of the little detail, and both poems assume a place in Douglas' own work, bringing in both death in battle and the simple but overwhelming pleasure of a moment of vivacity and heartiness.

Then Douglas went into the Army, where he wrote four more poems in 1940—that makes twenty-five that year!—and thirteen in 1941, half of these while still in England, learning over again how to ride a horse, and then how to fight in the mechanized cavalry, the tank corps. He matured poetically while enduring conditions he considered miserable and suffering emotionally in several ways: overcoming another of his several broken engagements to marry, chafing under the control of his superior officers, and fuming at the entirely inappropriate class-distinctions that characterized personal relations, and even command, in the mechanized cavalry. In 1941 he wrote **"Time Eating,"** the first of his great poems, and followed it with **"The Marvel,"** of which these are the first four stanzas:

> A baron of the sea, the great tropic
> swordfish, spreadeagled on the thirsty deck
> where sailors killed him, in the bright Pacific
>
> yielded to the sharp enquiring blade
> the eye which guided him and found his prey
> in the dim country where he was lord;
>
> which is an instrument forged in semi-darkness
> yet taken from the corpse of this strong traveller
> becomes a powerful enlarging glass
>
> reflecting the unusual sun's heat.
> With it a sailor writes on the hot wood
> the name of a harlot in his last port.

Despoilment, death, oddness, and a lens that magnifies—these are a few of Douglas' hallmarks, each stamped sharply on this and on a number of poems to come. If the words "spreadeagled" and "unusual"—as Douglas employs them—prompt the conjecture that his diction was at times arbitrary, yet one begins to see that a certain kind of oddity was precisely Douglas' gift. Apart from the sinewy rhythms of the lines, and the deft slant rhymes, a careful reader would also want to praise the rareness with which Douglas presents such a rare event.

That sharp enquiring blade was what Douglas' own eye enacted, his curiosity stupendous, and his artist's attentiveness reminding one of the risks Goya took to sketch on battlefields at night, coming out from town with his servant to hold the lamp, and always in danger of capture by the French, and after that, imprisonment or death. The lens of the swordfish eye seems to have come back at Douglas several times, for it appears in various guises in other poems, as in the wrong-way telescope in the last poem Douglas wrote before being posted to join the Nottinghamshire Sherwood Rangers Yeomanry, **"Simplify Me When I'm Dead"**:

> Remember me when I am dead
> and simplify me when I'm dead.
>
> As the processes of earth
> strip off the colour and the skin
> take the brown hair and blue eye
>
> and leave me simpler than at birth,
> when hairless I came howling in
> as the moon came in the cold sky.
>
> Of my skeleton perhaps
> so stripped, a learned man will say
> "He was of such a type and intelligence," no more.
>
> Thus when in a year collapse
> particular memories, you may
> deduce, from the long pain I bore
>
> the opinions I held, who was my foe
> and what I left, even my appearance
> but incidents will be no guide.
>
> Time's wrong-way telescope will show
> a minute man ten years hence
> and by distance simplified.
>
> Through that lens see if I seem
> substance or nothing: of the world
> deserving mention or charitable oblivion
>
> not by momentary spleen
> or love into decision hurled,
> leisurely arrive at an opinion.
>
> Remember me when I am dead
> and simplify me when I'm dead.

It's worth noting how Douglas took his six-line stanza and opened it up for this poem, allowing him at the same time to achieve a lapidary concision and strength, conserve a six-line rhyme scheme (much gentler on the ear for being divided by threes and arranged ABC ABC), and further to emphasize syntactical reach across stanza breaks. In addition, the poem is arranged symmetrically in a way that is both ingenious and architecturally monumental, giving it the shape of an inscription on a funeral stele. The central six lines ("Thus when . . . no guide.") straddle, as a sentence, two sets of rhymes, but as the central sentence, these lines are bounded top and bottom by sentences that alternate in length, three lines, then six, then the opening and closing two line stanzas. Thus a pattern of reflection and interference is set up by the two simultaneous patterns: six-line rhyme scheme, and sentence-length. The poem's complexity serves its emotional complexity.

The Sherwood Rangers were a tank regiment in Palestine. Douglas did not join them in action till they had moved west and were advancing on El Alamein, about to engage Rommel's troops, who were standing in defensive positions. As it was, Douglas had to leave a staff position behind the lines, without proper authorization, in order to join the battle at all.

He escaped this impertinence without penalty, except to receive a curiously reticent and oblique dressing down by his general. He recounts this episode, and much else, in *Alamein to Zem Zem,* a memoir that covers the time from his joining his regiment to the aftermath of the last battle he saw in Africa. Douglas did not fit in well, despite his early love of weapons, drill, and the paraphernalia of the military. He was not one of the upperclass officers, born to command and to dress and speak as they did. One of the things that most fascinated and exasperated him was the transference, from a complacent civilian hierarchical society to a battle front, of rituals and habits that could not survive the war, and could even endanger combatants. In the memoir, we find such observations as these:

> The Colonel, beautifully dressed and with his habitual indolence of hand, returned my salute. . . . Edward [was] full of polite pleasure at finding me back, overwhelming me with enquiries about myself, and answering my descriptions with incredulous exclamations. "Really? *No.* Did you? How perfectly terrific, etc." exactly as if he were still at a garden party, where presumably he had learnt this kind of repartee. He cleverly seemed to ignore what was said to him, having, I suppose, evolved this protective barrage of small talk against effusive acquaintances at home. For Edward is what is called in our current idiom "a social type." Unfortunately this inability to pay attention hampers him in action, where he often sits in his tank with the earphones on and doesn't hear what is said to him at critical moments . . .

And when Douglas' colonel is observed waiting for the chaplain to conclude his prayer with the troops, so that he may address them militarily, Douglas' eye is sharp and judgmental:

> Out stepped Piccadilly Jim, occupying the last few moments, though with bowed head, in giving a last twirl to his moustache and regarding his suede boots. The laces of these boots were tied in reef knots, with exactly equal ends hanging symmetrically on each side of the foot, ending at the welt of the boot.

To such figures as these, Douglas returned in the poem **"Sportsmen,"** which we will look at below. As he wrote in the first paragraphs of his memoir, Douglas did not intend to provide a record of military engagements, even from a tank commander's limited point of view. Rather:

> When I could order my thoughts I looked for more significant things than appearances; I still looked—I cannot avoid it—for something decorative, poetic or dramatic.

He had wanted to fight; he felt it was an experience he "must have." Yet throughout, as one can see in both poems and prose, he kept a distance, while a part of him—the artist and the poet—eyed each scene somewhat formally, scanning for the telling, often horrible, small touch that pulled the chaotic and confused spectacle of battle or rest into a pattern. "What remains in my mind," he wrote, is "a flurry of violent impressions. . . . Against a backdrop of indeterminate landscapes, of moods and smells, dance the black and bright incidents."

In action and out of it, Douglas wrote nine poems in 1942. His first reaction was perplexity and confusion at

> the hungry omens of calamity
> mixed with good signs, and all received with levity,
> or indifference, by the amazed mind.

("Negative Information")

The soldier's and the poet's small superstitions made a powerful mixture, stirred up by the jocularity that attenuated the threat of death, the great distance between the battlefield and the heart of the war in Europe, the virtual absence of civilians in the desert, the mobility and disorder—all very disturbing, and all flooding in on a poet who was only too avid to taste them to the fullest. It was inevitable that in such circumstances Douglas not only had to exercise great discipline and care merely to preserve copies of poems, but also found only rarely the time and quiet he needed to satisfy himself that a poem was finished. His method became one of recurring again and again to a theme, or to a figure (such as the lens). Typical of the problems associated with editing him, and reading him, is the difficulty of establishing "final" versions of some of his poems. **"The Sea Bird,"** for example, was originally thought by Douglas' biographer and editor, Desmond Graham, to be the first of two poems that share a number of stanzas in common. The second, longer one, **"Adams,"** suddenly shifts from the bird to a man, and in the connection it forges between the two it establishes a kind of haunting that afflicts the living when dead creatures, or dead men, fill the mind. But by the time these *Complete Poems* were assembled, Graham had found evidence that the shorter, simpler poem was the later one, and that Douglas had therefore given up yoking the two ideas, and settled for the one. Yet on the other hand, when Geoffrey Hill reviewed Douglas' *Se-*

lected Poems of 1964 (edited by Ted Hughes), he was irritated that **"The Sea Bird"** appeared in that volume instead of **"Adams,"** for he considered the latter, whether it was the final poem or not, to be the better of the two, thus suggesting that Douglas' revision had weakened the earlier poem.

"The Sea Bird" and **"Adams"** voice Douglas' metaphysical pondering of the ease with which what is living is transformed into what is lifeless. He came at things more than once, as other pairs of poems with common lines show. Hill notes too this recurrence, and writes:

> It would seem that he possessed the kind of creative imagination that approached an idea again and again in terms of metaphor, changing position slightly, seeking the most precise hold.

And Hill cites not only poems, but passages from *Alamein to Zem Zem* that bear obvious resemblances to lines from poems. It was mostly death that called him back for a new look. It is interesting to note how many poems end with death. Douglas and his fellow soldiers were

> the kindly visitors who meant
> so well all winter but at last fell
> unaccountably to killing in the spring.

("These grasses, ancient enemies")

The pun on "unaccountably" puts an edge on the wistfulness of the lines. And a love poem ends:

> your eyes look down on ordinary streets
> if I talk to you I might be a bird
> with a message, a dead man, a photograph.

("The Knife")

Douglas had so little time to write that images and ideas spill from one poem into the next. Here the bird recalls **"The Sea Bird,"** and the dead men are everywhere, and the photograph will reappear in the poem **"Vergissmeinnicht,"** to which we will return later.

Death invades even the living; Douglas describes the night before an offensive:

> . . . The mind
> mobile as a fox goes round
> the sleepers waiting for their wounds.

("The Offensive 1")

Or, when troops are resting after battle, and swimming in the Mediterranean near a village filled with the debris of fighting:

> O see my feet like stones
> underwater. The logical little fish

converge and nip the flesh
imagining I am one of the dead.

("**Mersa**")

What is remarkable is not that Douglas so constantly thought about death; it is that, thinking about it, he did not consider pain, or what happens to the dead after they die, but rather the effect they have on the living, who react with puzzlement that the form of a man should have no life in it, should have been changed, as Simone Weil put it in her study of the *Iliad,* into *objects,* the objects of pure force. Douglas' descriptions of the dead in **Alamein to Zem Zem** are arresting and fully imagined passages: true passages, to another realm of thinking. The dead were for him the true meaning and result of the war, the poor individual bodies left to mummify in the dry heat next to their tanks or guns, or pulled apart by wild dogs. As Jorge Guillén wrote in a little poem called *"Este muerto,"* confirming, as it were, Douglas' own intuition:

> Heme aquí frente al muerto irresistible
> Que revela, tranquilo, su verdad.
>
> I stand before the irresistible dead man.
> At peace at last, he tells me his truth.

Or as Hughes put it in the introduction to the 1964 **Selected Poems,** "not truth is beauty only, but truth kills everybody. The truth of a man is the doomed man in him or his dead body."

And when Douglas regarded the dead, it was neither coldly nor pitifully, but with the eye of an artist that does not blink at the macabre and the horrible, preferring to an emotional response to a compositional one. We must understand his "something decorative, poetic or dramatic" in a high sense: here "decorative" means an ornament that fulfills the latent significance of what it adorns.

The ink drawings—of burnt-out jeeps and guns, dead soldiers, tea-time in the shadow of a tank, a dead horse—give only a hint of Douglas' talent. While behind the lines or in the hospital with wounds, Douglas spent as much time as he could writing and drawing. "I like to write in comfort or not at all," he said in a letter to England. "What I have written has been written in hospitals, con.[valescent] depots, Base depots, etc." But on the other hand, Douglas felt a powerful compunction against writing "about" anything he had not himself seen or touched or smelled or heard whistling past his head. In another letter, he wrote:

> Did you ever receive the poems I wrote in hospital? I am not likely to produce anything but virtual repetitions of these, until the war is cleared up now, because I doubt if I shall be confronted with any new horrors or any worse pain, short of being burnt up, which I am not likely to survive.

And his mother wrote to the editors of the 1966 **Collected Poems** that Douglas had a "sense that if he did not face and share in every experience that came his way neither would he write any more. So for him there was no other choice despite his fear. So he went."

His desire to be thus faithful to his own experience, or rather, not to make up anything, seems tied to his demand of himself and of other poets that "lyricism," by which he meant an introspective sort of poem, be replaced by "reportage and extro-spective (if the word exists) poetry." From the writing of **"The Marvel"** through almost all of the desert poems, Douglas found this attitude a necessary mode of poetic thinking, because

> . . . by a day's traveling you reach a new world
> the vegetation is of iron
> dead tanks, gun barrels split like celery
> the metal brambles have no flowers or berries
> and there are all sorts of manure, you can imagine
> the dead themselves, their boots, clothes and posses-
>   sions
> clinging to the ground, a man with no head
> has a packet of chocolate and a souvenir of Tripoli.

("**Cairo Jag**")

"You can imagine"—that is, you can *see,* it is *there,* very little remains to be imagined in the old sense, and therefore the poem has to respect that hard light, that brutal frankness, that commonplace catastrophe.

It may have been as a result of no great striving on his part, but merely because of having gone through battle, and having been wounded, that Douglas went all the way through this way of looking at things and emerged in a realm of compassion, in his last poems. The dramatic detail is still there, and he still writes honestly, the "something decorative" may still be shocking. But the ascetic, careful rhythms, the slant rhymes that are a gesture of control, not slackness, and the artist's composure: these unite in a sympathy that produces both sorrow and rage, and most important, hones skill till it brings wisdom—not just beauty—out of technique. In addition to love poems like "I listen to the desert wind" and "Jerusalem," he wrote of the demise of heroes, and the survival of civilians. Perhaps the best of the twenty-two poems he wrote in 1943 are the two best known, **"Sportsmen"** and **"Vergissmeinnicht."** In the latter, Douglas approaches the body of the soldier who appears as a mere target in the poem **"How to Kill."** And the tender surprise at death is mixed with wonder at the almost intrusive presence of love among the carnage, when the observer and his comrades, as always on the lookout for booty and souvenirs routinely inspect the dead man's pockets:

> Three weeks gone and the combatants gone
> returning over the nightmare ground

we found the place again, and found
the soldier sprawling in the sun.

The frowning barrel of his gun
overshadowing. As we came on
that day, he hit my tank with one
like the entry of a demon.

Look. Here in the gunpit spoil
the dishonoured picture of his girl
who has put: *Steffi. Vergissmeinnicht*
in a copybook gothic script.

We see him almost with content,
abased, and seeming to have paid
and mocked at by his own equipment
that's hard and good when he's decayed.

But she would weep to see today
how on his skin the swart flies move;
the dust upon the paper eye
and the burst stomach like a cave.

For here the lover and killer are mingled
who had one body and one heart.
And death who had the soldier singled
has done the lover mortal hurt.

We are drawn in as accomplices, fellow witnesses, with
that one word, "Look." And a little word Douglas used
several times, "swart," here finds its perfect place, as an
English sound for the German word. The dead man's
girlfriend's voice sounds like a bell among this ruin and
waste, yet she does not yet know what the soldiers see.
Nor, as Douglas discovers at the end, would she or
anyone understand how these two contradictory roles of
a man, soldier and lover, have impinged on each other
and merged in a lifeless husk.

In **"Sportsmen"** Douglas eulogized those archaic
surviving creatures of domestic, pre-war England whose
command of troops or manner of behavior could also
irritate him. Here Douglas avoids the rhymes that
punctuate **"Vergissmeinnicht."** He submerges the
iambic foot much further, allowing it only the first and
last lines with authority. In the revisions, as Desmond
Graham points out, Douglas changed "leg" to "foot" in
the last line of the second stanza, so as to give Peter a
chance to euphemize his horrible wound. The rhythms
go somewhat limp in the long lines of the third stanza,
but it is almost a way of setting up the terseness and
greater symbolic weight of the last stanza, in which the
cricket-field terminology, which the Sherwood Rangers
used as their radio code in battle, brings the title to bear
on these figures in their "famous attitudes of unconcern."
Douglas the observer here becomes Douglas the singer
of elegy, and if, as some would say, the horn of the
ending is meant to suggest, however quietly, Ron-
cevaux, it is not inappropriate to an attempt to give
these doomed, out-of-place, inept heroes a place to
stand.

The noble horse with courage in his eye,
clean in the bone, looks up at a shellburst:
away fly the images of the shires
but he puts the pipe back in his mouth.

Peter was unfortunately killed by an 88;
it took his leg off; he died in the ambulance.
When I saw him crawling, he said:
It's most unfair, they've shot my foot off.

How then can I live among this gentle
obsolescent breed of heroes, and not weep?
Unicorns, almost. For they are fading into two legends
in which their stupidity and chivalry are celebrated;
the fool and the hero will be immortals.

These plains were a cricket pitch
and in the hills the tremendous drop fences
brought down some of the runners, who
under these stones and earth lounge still
in famous attitudes of unconcern. Listen
against the bullet cries the simple horn.

Now too Douglas looks at the living, as they try to
recover their lives:

Now the daylight coming in from the fields
like a labourer, tired and sad,
is peering about among the wreckage, goes
past some corners as though with averted head
not looking at the pain this town holds,
seeing no one move behind the windows.
But already they are coming back; to search
like ants, poking in the debris, finding in it
a bed or a piano and carrying it out.
Who would not love them at this minute?

("**Enfidaville**")

In the last weeks of his life Douglas was at work, back
in England, on a sequence it seems unlikely he could
have finished, even given the time. For time itself, so
visible a demon in his world, had come to obsess him
thoroughly, perhaps beyond the point of poetic usefulness. As an instrument of decay and death, it made a
new impression on him, not as a possibility, nor even as
an inevitability, but almost as a necessity—the force
that gave his genius strength. And this realization was a
heavy one to bear. His morbidity, perhaps even the
artist's dispassionate eye (for the two seem related,
perhaps in every artist), made these lines almost stagger
under the emotional weight:

If at times my eyes are lenses
through which the brain explores
constellations of feeling
my ears yielding like swinging doors
admit princes to the corridors
into the mind, do not envy me.
I have a beast on my back.

("**Bête Noire**")

As Graham points out, for the first time in Douglas' short life a retrospective view filled Douglas' eyes; looking back, he saw failures he knew he would not have the time to retrieve and correct. Having survived the desert war, though with painful wounds, he hurriedly prepared a book of poems, he wrote *Alamein to Zem Zem,* he fell in love again—while waiting in England for new orders. He left poems, paintings, drawings, and papers, fortunately, in capable hands, however tardy. Before embarking for Normandy with his regiment, he wrote **"On a Return from Egypt,"** a poem which supplies his epitaph, though it is too harsh:

> And all my endeavors are unlucky explorers
> come back, abandoning the expedition;
> the specimens, the lilies of ambition
> still spring in their climate, still unpicked;
> but time, time is all I lacked
> to find them, as the great collectors before me.[1]

Note

1. I have wanted to introduce Douglas to new readers, so I have put bibliographical information here, as a footnote.

The reader will have gathered that there are several different editions of Douglas' work, each of which differs from its predecessor. The *Collected Poems* were first published in 1951; Ted Hughes edited *Selected Poems* for Faber and Faber in 1964; then the *Collected Poems* were re-edited and republished in 1966. Desmond Graham's new edition of the *Complete Poems* omits the drawings and woodcuts that illustrated the 1966 *Collected,* but follows the same chronological sequence of poems. The difference resides in the far greater number of notes to the poems, and greater certainty about the texts and their variations, though not always about what Douglas himself preferred. Some of the textual variants are substantial and important. The lack of illustrations is somewhat compensated for by those included in Graham's biography, *Keith Douglas* (Oxford Univ. Press, 1974), a very sympathetic account of Douglas' life, although the critical analyses—which amount to a considerable part of the book—do not always seem to get to the heart of the poems, perhaps because there is simply too much biographical information surrounding them, and the poems are not free to stand clear. The republication of *Alamein to Zem Zem,* like the publication of the *Complete Poems,* is an occasion to thank Oxford University Press; one's gratitude would increase if the paperback *Complete Poems* were available in this country. Desmond Graham, effectively Douglas' curator, has performed a great labor of love in editing these books.

Jon Silkin (essay date 1981-82)

SOURCE: Silkin, Jon. "Keith Douglas." *Agenda* 19, nos. 2-3 (1981-82): 49-58.

[*In the following essay, Silkin praises Douglas for his courage and his wit, offering illustrations of both from his poetry.*]

In 1971, six years after Alan Ross had published *The Poetry of War 1939-1945,* its editor, Ian Hamilton, told me that although I might consider Keith Douglas the best poet of the Second War, I was to go away and re-read Alun Lewis. I was, he said, wrong. Such certainty requires courage, but I reckon, after several re-readings, that not only had Keith Douglas needed to have greater courage than either myself or Ian Hamilton, but that he had greater talent as a *poet* than Alun Lewis. Lewis's prose fiction is another matter.

Douglas's courage, of which as his prose *Alamein to Zem Zem* indicates he had plenty—sufficient, that is,—no-one can have too much—is as inseparable from his talent as is his wit. The courage finds expression in the wit, and the wit is the point at which the meaning becomes poetry. It is the poetry's expressive thrust. That's my thesis. I define wit, not only in the current sense of verbal sharpness that may induce amusement—the product of a mind that, as Ted Hughes put it,[1] 'reposes at a point . . . by a feat of great strength'; I also define it in the eighteenth-century sense of imagination, metaphysical imagination, which Pope makes use of in his 'Elegy to the Memory of an Unfortunate Lady':

> Most souls, 'tis true, but peep out once an age,
> Dull sullen pris'ners in the body's cage:
> Dim lights of life, that burn a length of years
> Useless, unseen, as lamps in sepulchres.

The deliberately-made vehicle of 'sullen pris'ners' and 'cage' has as much or even more *life* than what it stands for—body/soul. In the sense that Pope was affected by the metaphysicals Douglas, I think, was more affected by Eliot, and his metaphysics, than by Auden. Auden, for the most part, he left to his contemporaries Keyes and Lewis. It is Douglas's tough but not grimacing animation to which some of us respond.

This animation is best expressed in his facing death's foreshortening of life through war. But there are additional "places" ('I in another place') where courage is in order—love, for instance: and in love—or so I read the poems written from what was the Palestine of the British Mandate (Tel-Aviv and Jerusalem)—the voice grows lonely, aware of its loneliness:

> But among these Jews I am the Jew
> outcast, wandering down the steep road
> into the hostile dark square:

and standing in the unlit corner here
know I am alone and cursed by God
like the boy lost on his first morning at school.

('**Saturday Evening in Jerusalem**')

They are not the lines of a man afraid, but neither do they have the sheeing "wit" of the gun-barrel, such as we find in his "desert" poems. Once more from Palestine:

your face, flower that draws down my lips
our hands meet like strangers in a city
among the glasses on the table-top
impervious to envy or pity
we two lost in the country of our eyes.

('**Jerusalem**')

I wonder if for Douglas it might, at times, have appeared more difficult to endure the continuing pain of love, in survival, than the prospect of extinction in war.

I don't think a guess of that nature is much use to a biographer, or of any use to a literary critic, except in that it helps to distinguish between the morose, almost for Douglas lugubrious, verses of love, and this more alert poetry of war.

The poems I name, some of which I'll consider, are those the reader of Douglas might expect: '**Adams**', '**The Knife**', '**Mersa**', '**Dead Men**', '**Cairo Jag**', '**Snakeskin and Stone**', '**Desert Flowers**', '**Enfidaville**', '**Aristocrats**', '**Vergissmeinnicht**', '**How to Kill**', and '**Behaviour of Fish in an Egyptian Tea Garden**'; enough poems, in my opinion, to ensure Douglas's reputation as a fine poet, if not the finest of the War. And what for me stands out, stands forth, is, as I have defined it, the wit. But it is the nature of the wit, and its type of recurrence, its thoughtful unselfprotecting energy which both interests me and compels my admiration.

In '**Enfidaville**', for instance

In the church fallen like dancers
lie the Virgin and St. Thérèse
on little pillows of dust.

'Like dancers' brings out, perhaps, gestures of the religious ecstatic—beatitude beamed from the uplifted face; 'fallen', however, 'like dancers' reminds us (as Owen reminded us in 'Le Christianisme'—'One Virgin still immaculate / Smiles on for war to flatter her')—reminds us that earthly manifestations of the sacred are as vulnerable in war as the profane. The wit continues its trajectory. The 'little pillows of dust' brings about the age-old conjunction of death with its likeness 'sleep'. We have of course tomb-stone clichés of this. But 'little' reminds us that this is illusion, and that

'dust' is indeed the aptest conjuration of death, in which we rest and into which we at length crumble. Who else is Douglas reminding if not, among others, himself?

In the last line of the first stanza the 'detonations' '*shivered* the hands of Christ' (my italics)—'shivered' makes effective its pun on both the sacred (= frightened) and temporal (= shattered) levels. The second stanza reverses an earlier emphasis. Where the saints were 'like dancers' (temporal comparison) the 'men and women' of the town are now said to have 'moved like candles' (sacred comparison). Damaged by bombardment, 'The white houses are bare/black cages', but they let in more than they keep in—except for darkness. As 'cage' may associate with caged prisoners, so it may remind us of the body's 'cage'—that is, mortality. In all these I see wit, and in the wit an unflinching courage such as Rosenberg expressed when he wrote

I am determined that this war, with all its powers for devastation, shall not master my poeting; that is, if I am lucky enough to come through all right. I will not leave a corner of my consciousness covered up, but saturate myself with the strange and extraordinary new conditions of this life, and it will all refine itself into poetry later on.

(Letter to Laurence Binyon, Autumn 1916)

From '**Desert Flowers**' we know Douglas admired Rosenberg, and we can guess why. At the close of '**Enfidaville**' Douglas, operating wit, clashes the sacred with the temporal by evoking in the eyes of the saints those of the living:

I seem again to meet
the blue eyes of the images in the church.

Or is it the other way round—a temporary piety induced by suffering and seen in the eyes of the returning townsfolk?

In '**Cairo Jag**' he clashes two modes of life, of existence, and produces some third thing—a judgement. The *Marcelle* of civilian Cairo—where the fortunate spend their leave—is provocative and, apart from her grace,—she 'dances . . . by levitation'—Douglas finds little to commend her to the poet-annalist. 'All this', the poem tells us, 'takes place in a stink of jasmin'. In reversing the expectation of the flower's lovely odour by means of the poem's giving us 'stink', instead, Douglas is able to focus his judgement—disgust. In the third and final stanza, a different reversal occurs. This is the desert, not its city; it is war, not a temporary release from it:

But by a day's travelling you reach a new world
the vegetation is of iron
dead tanks, gun barrels split like celery
the metal brambles have no flowers or berries
and there are all sorts of manure, you can imagine

the dead themselves, their boots, clothes and posses-
    sions
clinging to the ground, a man with no head
has a packet of chocolate and a souvenir of Tripoli.

The contrasting reference to Donne's sexual Elegy 19
'To His Mistress Going to Bed'—'O my America, my
new found land'—is nothing compared to the 'dead
tanks' and, more powerfully still, to 'gun barrels split
like celery'. The power of the wit here depends on Douglas's ability to have the visual exactitude of 'guns split
like celery' to neither outweigh nor be outweighed by
the poised contrast with life in Cairo; which, among
other dispensations, provides the relative luxury of—
celery. And 'you can imagine' puts into mind something
else, the sharp staccato voice of Sassoon, making his
prose protest of 1917:

> I am not protesting against the conduct of the War, but
> against the political errors and insincerities for which
> the fighting men are being sacrificed. On behalf of
> those who are suffering now I make this protest against
> the deception which is being practised on them; also I
> believe that I may help to destroy the callous compla-
> cency with which the majority of those at home regard
> the continuance of agonies which they do not share,
> and which they have not sufficient imagination to real-
> ize.
>
> (*The Complete Memoirs of George Sherston*, p. 496)

Douglas (and Sassoon) may as well remind us of the
last stanza of Owen's 'Insensibility'—'By choice they
made themselves immune / To pity'. It is to provoke
our sympathetic imagination that Douglas, with wit,
works in the double meaning of "you could perceive it
if you cared" *and* "I'm sure you'll really have no trouble
in imagining it". By how much this doubleness has
been worked for may be appreciated if the last two
lines of the stanza above are compared with the prose
entry in *Alamein to Zem Zem*:

> The bodies of some Italian infantrymen still lay in their
> weapon pits, surrounded by pitiable rubbish, picture
> postcards of Milan, Rome, Venice, snapshots of their
> families, chocolate wrappings, and hundreds of cheap
> cardboard cigarette packets. Amongst this litter, more
> suggestive of holiday-makers than soldiers, there were
> here and there bayonets. . . . The Italians lay about
> like trippers taken ill.
>
> (pp. 54-5)

The journal-entry has been sifted to make a point. One
is reminded of the "rain" passage[2] in Edward Thomas's
The Icknield Way, and by how much Thomas re-shaped
that in his poem 'Rain'.

A similar conjunction to that of **'Cairo Jag'** and its
contrasting "lifes" is enacted in the last three lines of
the first stanza of **'Dead Men'**:

Tonight the white dresses and the jasmin scent
in the streets. I in another place
see the white dresses glimmer like moths. Come

    to the west

—to the almost entrancing desert war, that is. The ending of the poem is, clearly, not witty, yet wit of a different kind is as visible as that in **'Cairo Jag'**. The 'wise
man' will settle for no less or more than love; the dog,
wise as a philosopher, settles for *his* bone. If we are
'prudent', we will be like lovers and dogs. Thus is our
temporal nature defined, humbled, and given a modest
chance of a slightly more assured survival.

Douglas was an omniverous learner: from Pope as much
as from Donne, or Eliot; from Owen as much as from
Rosenberg. Owen in his poem 'Beauty' (unfinished)
makes an extremely complex notation on the word—

> A shrapnel ball
> Just where the wet skin glistened when he swam.
> Like a full-opened sea-anemone.
> We both said 'What a beauty! What a beauty, lad!'
> I knew that in that flower he saw a hope
> Of living on, and seeing again the roses of his home.
> Beauty is that which pleases and delights
> 'Not bringing personal advantage'
>
>   —Kant.

When Owen speaks of the soldier's wound being 'a
beauty', he implies both a substantial wound (it was
subsequently lethal) but one that, in the context, was
desirable in that it served to transport him back to the
safety of blighty. In **'Vergissmeinnicht'** ("Forget me
not"—the lover's plea) Douglas says in stanza four:

> We see him almost with content,
> abased, and seeming to have paid
> and mocked at by his own equipment
> that's hard and good when he's decayed.

'Hard and good' works in contrast to the now 'decayed'
soldier (and lover); but what is 'good' for the soldier is
not so for the human being and lover. 'Good' has about
it all the wit of Owen's 'beauty' and, by bifurcating the
two persons, 'killer' from 'lover', Douglas prepares us
for the last stanza where the distinction becomes explicit
which was implicit in stanzas three and four:

> For here the lover and killer are mingled
> who had one body and one heart.
> And death who had the soldier singled
> has done the lover mortal hurt.

Is the half-rime intentional? At any rate, 'singled' is
another pun—the soldier in his death is separated from
his love; but 'singled' also suggests "singled out for the
full works". Instances of compression also occur in the
poem (wit is just one form of it); the sleek barrel of the
gun is 'frowning' with one supposes death. The 'paper
eye' is fragile, dry of its life; the 'burst stomach', cave-
like, is now empty.

I wish to refer to two more poems—**'Desert Flowers'** and **'How to Kill'**. In the former there is again the reprise of Owen who in 'A Terre' speaks of

> The dullest Tommy hugs that fancy now,
> "Pushing up daisies" is their creed you know.

In Douglas's poem we get

> but the body can fill
> the hungry flowers . . .

The spoken, colloquial force of Owen has perhaps been sacrificed, but the savage voracity of nature (and of war) is much intensified by 'hungry flowers'. And in the artificial, theatre imagery with which stanza three opens

> Each time the night discards

> draperies on the eyes and leaves the mind awake
> I look each side of the door of sleep
> for the little coin it will take
> to buy the secret I shall not keep.

—in this theatre imagery, we are reminded by how much the mind "constructs" its perceptions, bringing together the unpalatable true meanings that lie about waiting for the poet's wit, and courage perhaps, to make a union of them in a poem. Johnson of course formulates this in his essay on Cowley, when he writes of the metaphysical poets:

> Of wit, thus defined, they have more than enough. The most heterogeneous images are yoked by violence together . . .

Johnson's judgement was adverse.

The 'secret' (in the stanza above) that Douglas will not keep consists in such memories of the horror of war which the mind, with wit, sets out. The coin, paid to Charon to ferry the dead across the Acheron, ought to purchase secrecy, for secrets are supposed to perish with the dead. And the dead, by drinking the waters of Lethe, were supposed to be blessed with forgetfulness. Douglas cleverly reverses these superstitions; the coin will not buy any collusion from him:

> Lay the coin on my tongue and I will sing
> of what the others never set eyes on.

Wit has its explicit task. It will tell the truth,[3] it will 'sing'—if with the irony of that word—to sing, *cantare*—the unsuitability of war for such song is understood. This will again be touched on in Douglas's letter to his fellow-poet John Hall, quoted below.

In **'How to Kill'** we take the most delicate of Douglas's cruxes

> I cry
> NOW. Death, like a familiar, hears

> and look, has made a man of dust
> of a man of flesh. This sorcery
> I do. Being damned, I am amused
> to see the centre of love travel into vacancy.
> How easy it is to make a ghost.

In his affirming essay '"I in Another Place": Homage to Keith Douglas' (*Stand,* Vol 6, no 4, 1963) Geoffrey Hill nevertheless indicates that

> 'Douglas clearly relished many of the techniques and some of the machinery of war'

and then goes on to quote a passage concerning how proud 'we were . . . of our Crusaders' (tanks)—from ***Alamein to Zem Zem.*** He might as easily, though perhaps with more hurt, have quoted the stanza above. The wound, I suggest,—it is our wound—is located not only in the 'Being damned'; if that were all, the self-condemnation and the almost mawkish confessional of the 'killer' would find no restraint in its self-pity; though even this we ought to find it hard in *ourselves* to condemn who are presently living 'at peace'. It is of course the unassailably clear 'I am amused' that pains, and who but Douglas would have the "nerve" to say this? Owen wrote in a letter to his mother dated 4th (or 5th) October 1918 and headed 'Strictly private', 'I lost all my earthly faculties, and fought like an angel'. Private indeed. And Rosenberg momentarily preened himself, 'I must be looking smart, for I was offered a stripe which I declined' (letter to Sydney Schiff, December 1915). Grenfell, in 'Into Battle', saw himself as combining the roles of Roland and Nimrod. But 'amused'? Is this the reposing point of the civilized ego? What terminus is this, one wonders.

It is the ease with which he can kill, as well as the sudden transformation of the victim, that amuses Douglas. 'Being damned' one has, has one (?), "earned" the right to amusement, for what else remains to one in combat but the perception of such lethal efficiencies? I don't justify, supposing, that is, that Douglas needs to be justified; but I do suggest that the skin which separates amusement from horror is, like the eye, 'paper' thin. And as Douglas's victim is vulnerable to 'the mosquito death' so was Douglas, killed three days after his D-day landing, June 9th, 1944. Douglas didn't not know his vulnerability. He knew.

In a by-now famous letter to his fellow-poet, John Hall, Douglas in 1943 wrote from Palestine:

> I don't know if you have come across the word Bullshit—it is an army word and signifies humbug and unnecessary detail. It symbolizes what I think must be

got rid of—the mass of irrelevancies, of 'attitudes', 'approaches', propaganda, ivory towers, etc., that stands between us and our problems and what we have to do about them.

To write on the themes which have been concerning me lately in lyrical and abstract forms, would be immense bullshitting . . . I never tried to write about war . . . until I had experienced it. Now I will write of it, and perhaps one day cynic and lyric will meet and make me a balanced style. Certainly you will never see the long metrical similes and galleries of images again . . . To be sentimental or emotional now is dangerous to oneself and to others. To trust anyone or to admit any hope of a better world is criminally foolish, as foolish as it is to stop working for it. It sounds silly to say work without hope, but it can be done; it's only a form of insurance; it doesn't mean work hopelessly.

(The Complete Poems, pp. 123-4)

No *cantare,* no cantata. The way from that *cantare,* from the *morbido* of poetry, such soft unctious lyric utterance, is wit. It took not merely physical courage to fight, but imaginative courage to take the route Douglas describes in the letter(s) quoted above—a route (with the possible exception of Webster and his verse) new to the matter of war and violence; the route of wit and its spoken poetry. Douglas took this route. No bullshit.

Notes

1. *Keith Douglas: Selected Poems,* edited with an introduction by Ted Hughes; p. 11

2. *Out of Battle* by Jon Silkin; pp. 91-5

3. "Sing" is also convicts' talk for "squeal" or 'betray'

Brief Bibliography

The Complete Poems of Keith Douglas edited by Desmond Graham; OUP, 1979

Alamein to Zem Zem edited with an introduction by Desmond Graham; OUP, 1979.

Keith Douglas 1920-1944: A Biography by Desmond Graham; OUP, 1974

Stephen Matterson (essay date winter 1987)

SOURCE: Matterson, Stephen. "Douglas' 'Vergissmeinnicht.'" *Explicator* 45, no. 2 (winter 1987): 57-9.

[*In the following essay, Matterson examines Douglas's handling of the contradictory roles of soldier and lover in the poem "Vergissmeinnicht."*]

Keith Douglas has often been considered a war poet offering a fresh and challenging perspective on warfare. That is, rather than concentrating on the terrible condi-

tions, waste and death that the two world wars have involved, he provides a view of warfare as it appeared to the professional, highly-trained soldier. While he is not an apologist for war and aggression, his work reminds the reader that if wars have to be fought (as apparently they must), they have to involve the use of well-prepared, technically competent, dispassionate killers. Douglas himself was one of these, voluntarily enlisting for service as soon as World War II began and considering himself a professional soldier. However, in some poems Douglas examines the contradictions involved in the life of such a soldier, and particularly the idea that to be a killer at all, one must suppress or discard ("for the duration") a certain degree of human feeling, of kinship with others. His poem **"Vergissmeinnicht"** examines precisely this: the relationship between "soldier" and "lover."

In the opening stanzas, the tone is detached but not, apparently, euphemistic or evasive. While the soldier's death is not sentimentalized or mourned, neither is it rejoiced over. The men consider the body with a special kind of professional pride; a task was presented to them and they have performed it with economy and efficiency. But their detachment functions also as a defense, saving the men from deeper reflection on their actions. The separation of human and professional is necessary to the men since it exonerates them from human responsibility in the killing. The men are thus "content" with the dead soldier, knowing him as their own would-be killer. The detached tone is sustained during the first two stanzas of the poem, but it then begins to break down:

> Look. Here in the gunpit spoil
> the dishonoured picture of his girl
> who has put: *Steffi. Vergissmeinnicht*
> in a copybook Gothic script.

Douglas' use of "Look" with which to open this stanza is deft and significant. The word generates a variety of effects. First, it directly invites the reader's involvement in the poem, whereas the first two stanzas kept the reader distant and unacknowledged. Second, "Look" rehearses the discovery made by the soldiers, adding some sense of the dramatic to the poem. Third, the word suggests that the soldiers or the poem's narrator are to "look" more closely at the subject, to scrutinize and perhaps reappraise their views. During this stanza, the carefully maintained objectivity of the poem begins to weaken. The photograph of the dead man's lover obviously intrudes upon the enclosed world of the professional soldiers, reminding them of their kinship with him and of his life beyond the field of battle. Her message of **"Vergissmeinnicht"**—forget me not—is clearly ironic, since professional soldiers must forget their humanity in order to sustain their profession with equilibrium.

At this point in the poem, a central opposition becomes apparent, a conflict between the two different lives led by the soldiers. On the one hand, they are naturally humans, with friends, family, and other established human attachments. However, they are also killers who must suppress temporarily their knowledge of those attachments. In either sphere, they might be comfortable, but when both are brought together, as they are in this stanza, doubt and discomfort arise. The photograph and its message disturb the narrator and deprive him of the comfortably detached view he was earlier able to assume. Douglas subtly reinforces the conflict at several points; for example, the phrase "his girl" both echoes and contradicts "his gun" from the previous stanza.

However, this conflict does not work in the poem merely in a simple way. An explicit contrast emerges in the next two stanzas between different ways of viewing the corpse. The men seem to continue seeing it as before, with professional "content." But in imagining the lover's view of the body the narrator has been forced to concede the existence of an alternative perspective:

> But she would weep to see today
> how on his skin the swart flies move;
> the dust upon the paper eye
> and the burst stomach like a cave.

The tone of steady detachment is almost maintained, but the whole stanza differs radically from the earlier stanzas. For one thing, it is foregrounded by the imagined emotions of the lover, certainly in direct contrast to the necessarily unemotional soldiers. But further, the physical description itself achieves a power through its very detachment. The tone of the poem has altered as the narrator acknowledges an alternative view of the soldier. Again, an explicit contrast is made between this realistic view of the corpse and the established view of the soldiers. They saw it "sprawling in the sun," with all that phrase's connotations of pleasant inertia. Because of this later perspective, one might now begin to consider the soldier's view as somewhat evasive, euphemistic, and tendentious to the point of self-deception, whereas earlier this did not appear to be the case.

By this point in the poem, Douglas has firmly established its central conflict between the views of soldier and lover. The centrality of this conflict has been emphasized by a variety of factors and details, including, it should be noted, a conflict between masculine and feminine. The war is depicted as a specifically masculine activity, with the powerful phallic image of the "frowning barrel of his gun" linking male sexuality and aggression. On the other hand, the woman's photograph is located in the womb-like pit of the gun emplacement, where the soldier attempts to simulate a home.

However, although the poem is largely concerned with exploring the conflict between soldier and lover, it ends by radically asserting the irrelevance of this conflict. It contends that the conflict is an illusion deriving from the needs of both soldier and lover to deny the existence of the other at any given moment:

> For here the lover and killer are mingled
> who had one body and one heart.
> And death who had the soldier singled
> has done the lover mortal hurt.

The distinction between lover and soldier may be vital if wars are to be fought, but it is clearly a false and dangerous distinction. While humans may be both soldiers and lovers, and attempt to keep these identities distinct, one cannot kill the professional soldier without also destroying the lover. Thus the conflict which the poem has established and sustained is now exposed as a vicious and fatal illusion. Now, too, the aptness of the title becomes clear—and the reason why Douglas preferred it to the earlier title of **"The Lover."** For the soldier did indeed forget the lover; not only his real, living lover, but that part of himself which was lover. It is when humans lay aside or temporarily forget their humanity, the poem asserts, that killing and war can continue.

Peter Scupham (essay date September-October 1998)

SOURCE: Scupham, Peter. "Shelf Lives: I: Keith Douglas." *PN Review* 25, no. 1 (September-October 1998): 22-4.

[*In the following essay, Scupham praises Douglas's poetry for its "colloquial yet disciplined style."*]

> Remember me when I am dead
> and simplify me when I'm dead.

Keith Douglas's poems have been re-published by Oxford:[1] a reminder to these softer climes that once upon a time there was a mind-set in Western civilisation which set the plumed helmets nodding, saw maps all frontiers and railway lines, dressed its children as mimic sailors and celebrated physical courage as the primary masculine virtue: a mind-set now deep in hiding. Many of those middle-class children of the 1890s who read 'The Dumb Soldier' in R. L. Stevenson's *A Child's Garden of Verses*—

Under grass alone he lies,
Looking up with leaden eyes,
Scarlet coat and pointed gun,
To the stars and to the sun

—fought their garden wars and marched their armies through the pleasant land of counterpane, now lie in Tyne Cot at Passchendaele, or buried more deeply as names on the Menin Gate. And many of *their* children lie in iron graves under sea in names which still clench on power and loss—Hood, Repulse, Renown—or are dispersed in air and sand. In the late 1930s my parents saw no incongruity in giving me a boxed machine-gun section as an Easter present. The be-chickened chocolate egg which accompanied it seems in retrospect to be the one in Saki's tale, 'The Easter Egg', which the stolid four-year-old stooge carries as a present for the Prince—and which ticks life away, the carapace of an anarchist's bomb.

And Douglas? A product of that mind-set, he had long been consciously in training to be an actor on a martial stage, and, from the age of fourteen, a poet. The bent of his psyche was inevitably turned towards the codes and value-systems of war by his period and background. As he sees himself at the age of four, in 'An Untitled Autobiographical Story' written when he was about twelve: 'Most of the time he was down in the field, busy, with an absurdly purposeful look on his round face, about a tent made of an old sheet, and sign-posted with a board saying "sergeants' mess".' His dates place him squarely in the iron time, born in 1920; killed in 1944. He only knew his father, Captain Keith Sholto Douglas, M.C., for some eight years, before the hero-worshipped Captain deserted his family, unable to cope after his wife had been diagnosed with sleepy sickness, encephalitis lethargica, a train of events which led to her slow recovery and a nomadic life as a genteel companion and help. What is left of Douglas's life can be found in Desmond Graham's biography:[2] Prep School, Christ's Hospital, the OTC, Merton College Oxford, girls, Sandhurst, The Sherwood Rangers, horses, tanks, Palestine, girls, Egypt, The Western Desert, Normandy, death in action. The constants which link these experiences are a deep affinity with patterns of order and control so long as they could be imposed by himself upon experience, not by authority upon him, a love of action and accomplishment and some distaste for the company of fellow-writers, a search for love, and a growing fatalism which sees himself as *maudit*, the one who will not survive. John Barton's advice to his actors playing Shakespeare, 'Play it for the contradictions', holds good for Douglas, the literary sensitive shying energetically from too close an identification with that role. So the young man who enlisted in the cavalry three days after the declaration of war could also shout 'You shits! You shits! You shits!' at a cinema audience cheering a newsreel show-

ing a German plane crashing after a dogfight. And out of that quarrel over the contradictions comes the dispassionate power of poems which cannot be simplified, though for the dead man himself simplification comes with the territory.

Many factors go to make the colloquial yet disciplined style which is Douglas at his best. From early on he had, as Donne or Ivor Gurney have, the gift for arresting attention with an opening line. The following invitations all come from poems written by the time Douglas was seventeen, and allowing for a little period garlic there is a security about these opening gambits which doesn't build up to an awful let-down: 'Put by your stitching, spread the table . . .'; 'Now my mind's off again. No tears . . .'; 'Yesterday travellers in summer's country'; 'Over and over the street is repeated with sunlight'; 'This season like a child with airy points . . .' The structures which follow demonstrate that he had a silver ear for cadence and that Auden's question: 'How does this contraption work?' was, for Douglas, a conscious question from early on. In a school exercise book dated for his sixteenth birthday Douglas scans his poem 'Strange Gardener' by quantity rather than stress, and gives his imagery a running commentary. He explains his choice of 'swift' in a 'swift, sad face' by saying 'the swiftness of his face is in the lines of it, his high cheek-bones and the curved hang of his hair', and his comment 'The lapses in metre are put in purposely, in an attempt to make it less stereotyped and more interesting' shows how quickly he knew those silver ears needed boxing. Some seventeen poems date from his schooldays, the best of them being poems of disparities, telling of aches in time between was, will be, and the poised landscape of is, with its 'turkish shadows on the down, / the busybody engine in the distance'.

The inevitable climax was approached with a kind of brilliant indifference. At Oxford—his year there was a grace-year, as he had already enlisted but not been called up—Douglas, who was determined to 'bloody well make my mark on this war' must have seen himself in prospect as an image, the young officer casually posed by horse, tank or armoured car for perpetuity. He was fortunate to have as his tutor Edmund Blunden, a very different kind of animal, whose own elegiac poems for the war in which he had fought and been decorated have been found guilty of insufficient savage indignation in the face of Armageddon. Blunden paid Douglas final tribute with an affectionate, avuncular introduction to the Faber **Collected Poems** of 1966, dwelling as ever on the links between Douglas and himself as Old Blues from Christ's Hospital, poets in the line of Coleridge, Lamb and Leigh Hunt. The Oxford poems are possessed by Death and the Maiden, but the war was still in the background for Douglas, and his love affairs at the time were not particularly lucky for him or his poetry: self-conscious epiphanies and valedictions in a landscape of water, leaves and sunlight on stone do not conspire to bring out that sharply focused imagery which is Douglas's trademark. Some of those formally over-wrought, self-conscious Oxford poems, with their echoes of Donne or Crowe Ransom, would seem regressive—but for the fact that the poems Douglas wrote in his school-days frequently surpass them. Those 'stones of the city, her venerable towers; / dignified, clothed by erudition and time', that 'green foliage indefinite and flowery' have their own lulling trance-effect to juxtapose against the coming violence, but sing their repetitive song too strongly for Douglas to make it individual.

Then come Egypt, Palestine and the intense armoured combat in the Western Desert. Desmond Graham writes of Douglas's final experiences that he 'had gained access to the nihilism of the dead', presented as he was with a simplified landscape in which the shapes of destruction were revealed iconically: wrecked men, wrecked machinery, sand. The fighting itself had a quality absent from warfare in the European Theatre in that it was essentially abstracted from civilian involvement, a mobile war of fighting soldiers, and as such capable of being focused under Douglas's burning glass the more effectively. With a Jacobean intensity the young man who will die studies the shapes of death with the same distanced involvement which made Manet note the colours in his dying sister's face. An earlier essay in this mode is the short prose piece 'Death of a Horse'—companioning Orwell's 'Shooting an Elephant'—where an experience at the Army Equitation School at Weedon is clinically taken apart. A horse, broken-legged, is shot and cut up until 'the wreck of the horse lay in a flurry of colours, the stench cemented them into one chaos'. *Alamein to Zem Zem*[3], Douglas's prose account of the desert war, is full of such minutiae, and in the final poems we find 'the dead men, whom the wind / powders till they are like dolls', 'vehicles / squashed dead or still entire, stunned / like beetles', and in **'Cairo Jag'**

> you can imagine
> the dead themselves, their boots, clothes and posses-
>   sions
> clinging to the ground, a man with no head
> has a packet of chocolate and a souvenir of Tripoli.

Douglas's visual sense was always phenomenally acute—see the vivid, nervous drawings he made in the Western Desert which accompany the editions of *Alamein to Zem Zem,* one of the few books from the Second World War which can stand by Sassoon's *Memoirs of an Infantry Officer* or Remarque's *All Quiet on the Western Front.* The continuous unfolding excitement his best poems create in the reader lies in the meticulous, authoritative nature of an imagery which carries the conviction that *this was so,* and being so, it can bear the full weight of that charged ambivalence this theatrical but emotionally reticent poet can give it.

At his best Douglas, like Louis MacNeice, makes poems of complete assurance in which the poet's identity is silverily elusive, as in **'Negative Information'**:

> As lines, the unrelated symbols of
> nothing you know, discovered in the clouds,
> idly made on paper, or by the feet of crowds
> on sand, keep whatever meaning they have
>
> and you believe they write, for some
> intelligence, messages of a sort;
> these curious indentations on my thought
> with every week, almost with each hour come.

It is a truism that major experiences such as war do not create first-rank poets; they come to such experiences equipped: first words, then ammunition. The First World War poets, Owen, Rosenberg, Sassoon, Graves, Thomas, were all primary makers immersed in a war which, as chance would have it, keeps some part of them in its petrifying amber, and it is interesting that both Thomas and Douglas, temperamentally poets of dubiety and ambivalence, have poems entitled **'Words'** which home in on the resilient, autonomous fragility of language. Both see themselves as being said through rather than saying. Thomas wishes the words to choose him 'As the winds use / A crack in a wall / or a drain, / Their joy or their pain / To whistle through', and Douglas sees himself as the stealthy collector and disperser of words:

> The catch and the ways of catching are diverse.
> For instance this stooping man, the bones of whose
>   face
>   are
> like the hollow birds' bones, is a trap for words.
> And the pockmarked house bleached by the glare
> whose insides war has dried out like gourds
> attracts words.

The best of the other poets of the Second World War—Alun Lewis, Sidney Keyes—carry more of the air of being literary civilians in uniform (which, of course, they were) than Douglas, and their poems have a greater admixture of unshaken out romantic and vatic imagery, more also to say of pain, home, loss, and the suffering self; they lack the cold, eager panache Douglas seems to share at times with a Julian Grenfell. The apparent absence of those more user-friendly qualities was excoriated by Geoffrey Grigson in a review of Desmond Graham's biography, 'What is a War Poet?', republished in *Blessings, Kicks and Curses* (Allison & Busby, 1982), in which Grigson quite amazingly says, 'but I must express my own disappointed conviction that Keith Douglas's poems are almost uniformly bad. Desmond Graham—and it is not his fault—does not find a convincing stanza, a convincing line to quote, let alone a convincing poem', and adds that 'his poems transmit no warm, attractive individuality of feeling'. Ah, if only to be nice was to be accomplished. Feeling is there, admiration is there, though with a saving ironic ambivalence, as in **'Aristocrats'**:

> Here then
> under the stones and earth they dispose themselves,
> I think with their famous unconcern.
> It is not gunfire I hear, but a hunting horn.

Douglas is thinking of such men as his commanding officer, Colonel Kellett. Desmond Graham calls 'Flash' Kellett 'a natural focus for Douglas's dissatisfaction'. Their mutual antipathy was, to some degree, redeemed by Douglas's completely unauthorised flight, with his batman, from a Camouflage School posting to rejoin his fighting regiment for the battle of El Alamein. It is amusing that Colonel Kellett's antipathy was not to poets as such. I have a copy of 'Poems by Michael Rivière', then a young officer in the Sherwood Rangers, printed in Palestine in 1940—and dedicated to his horse, Black Blossom—to which Kellett contributed a foreword commending what he hoped would be 'the beginning of many talented and delightful contributions to poetry.' Prescience, for Michael Rivière, captured in Crete and held in Colditz, later wrote a handful of the best poems to come out of that war. He and Douglas never met.

The whole complex amalgam of disciplined preparation, both for war and poetry, the feeling arrogance, the lack of self-pity, the thinking stance, the artist's eye, all come together in such a poem as **'How to Kill'**:

> Now in my dial of glass appears
> the soldier who is going to die.
> He smiles, and moves about in ways
> his mother knows, habits of his.
> The wires touch his face: I cry
> NOW. Death, like a familiar, hears
>
> and look, has made a man of dust
> of a man of flesh. This sorcery
> I do. Being damned, I am amused
> to see the centre of love diffused
> and the waves of love travel into vacancy.
> How easy it is to make a ghost.

In such poems there is a sense of something being said from a great distance, as if a disembodied voice we can hardly bear is saying something alien and imperative. Such a froideur is miles away from our post-modernist hall of mirrors; actions are being performed, under great stress, of great importance. Someone has been simplified, someone, perhaps, remembered. In the current Reith Lectures, *War and Our World,* John Keegan quotes Johnson's dictum 'Every man thinks meanly of himself for not having been a soldier' and amends it to 'Every man would think better of himself for having been a soldier, could he bear the strain'. For Keegan,

the era of the big wars is over. Keith Douglas's poems remind us what some of that strain was and how it could not only be borne but transposed into something obdurate, extraordinary and beautiful.

Notes

1. Keith Douglas, *The Complete Poems.* Edited by Desmond Graham. Introduction by Ted Hughes (Oxford Poets, 1998).

2. *Keith Douglas 1920-1944*: A Biography by Desmond Graham (Oxford, 1974).

3. Keith Douglas: *Alamein to Zem Zem.* Edited & Introduced by Desmond Graham (Faber & Faber, 1992). Keith Douglas: *A Prose Miscellany.* Compiled & Introduced by Desmond Graham (Carcanet, 1985).

FURTHER READING

Criticism

Gardner, Philip. "Keith Douglas and the Western Desert." In *A Festschrift for Edgar Ronald Seary: Essays in English Language and Literature Presented by Colleagues and Former Students,* edited by A. A. Macdonald, P. A. O'Flaherty, and G. M. Story, pp. 182-200. St. John's, Newfoundland, Canada: Memorial University of Newfoundland, 1975.

   Explores the real-life events that served as source material for Douglas's war poetry.

Hughes, Ted. Introduction to *Selected Poems,* edited by Ted Hughes, pp. 11-14. New York: Chilmark Press, 1964.

   Praises Douglas as a "renovator of language," whose poetic diction is fresh and natural.

Ormerod, David. "Keith Douglas and The Name of the Poem I Can't Write." *Ariel* 9, no. 2 (April 1978): 3-22.

   Examines Douglas's use of images of mirrors, windows, lenses, and masks to deal with the issue of perception—a problem he wrestled with in repeatedly trying, and failing, to write the poem "Bête Noire."

Scammell, William. "The Early Poems." In *Keith Douglas: A Study,* pp. 62-95. London: Faber and Faber, 1988.

   Explores issues of unity and paradox in Douglas's

schoolboy and undergraduate poetry.

Sherry, Vincent. "Hectic Stasis: The War Poetry of Keith Douglas." *University of Toronto Quarterly* 58, no. 2 (winter 1988-1989): 295-304.

Studies Douglas's treatment of war and its relationship to immobility.

Additional coverage of Douglas's life and career is contained in the following sources published by Gale: *British Writers,* **Vol. 7;** *Contemporary Authors,* **Vol. 160;** *Dictionary of Literary Biography,* **Vol. 27;** *Encyclopedia of World Literature in the 20th Century,* **Ed. 3;** *Literature Resource Center;* *Modern British Literature,* **Ed. 2;** *Poets: American and British; Reference Guide to English Literature,* **Ed. 2; and** *Twentieth-Century Literary Criticism,* **Vol. 40.**

John Montague
1929-

American-born Irish poet, short story writer, translator, and critic.

INTRODUCTION

One of Ireland's most famous contemporary poets, Montague has published several volumes of poetry as well as a number of prose collections. He composes in a wide range of poetic forms and covers subject matter both personal and political, drawing on experiences from his own life, on the history and mythology of Ireland, and on the political turmoil in Northern Ireland.

BIOGRAPHICAL INFORMATION

Montague was born on February 28, 1929, in Brooklyn, New York, to James Terence and Molly Carney Montague. His parents, Catholics from County Tyrone, had left Ireland because of his father's political activities. Four years later, Montague and his two older brothers were sent back to Ireland, the older boys to live with their maternal grandmother, and Montague to live with his father's unmarried sisters on their farm in Garvaghey, County Tyrone, Ulster. When his mother returned to Ireland, she reclaimed Montague's brothers, but chose to leave him in the care of his aunts. His father, meanwhile, stayed in America until 1952. Montague was educated at the local schools, Garvaghey and Glencull Primary Schools, and at St. Patrick's College in County Armagh. In 1945 he won a scholarship to University College, Dublin, where he studied history and English, graduating with a first in both subjects in 1949. He earned a Master's degree in Anglo-Irish literature, also from University College, and was awarded a Fulbright fellowship to attend graduate school at Yale University in 1953. He spent one year at Yale before transferring to the University of Iowa where he earned a Master of Fine Arts degree (1955) while teaching part time at the Iowa Writers' Workshop. At Iowa Montague met a number of prominent writers and poets, including William Carlos Williams, who would become an important influence on his writing career. Montague also met Madeleine de Brauer, a Fulbright scholar from France; the couple married in 1956. They were divorced in 1972; the following year Montague married Evelyn Robson, with whom he had two daughters, Oonogh and Silylle. His second marriage also ended in divorce; Montague's third wife is the New York novelist Elizabeth Wassell.

Montague has traveled extensively throughout Europe and North America and has lived in Dublin, Paris, and Berkeley among a number of cities, working at a variety of jobs—as a film critic for a Dublin newspaper, as an executive with the Irish tourist board, and as the Paris correspondent for *The Irish Times*. In 1972 he accepted a teaching position at University College, Cork, and retained that post for many years while also teaching at several other institutions throughout Europe and North America, including the University of California at Berkeley, the University of Dublin, the State University of New York at Buffalo, the University of Vermont, and the Sorbonne.

Montague has been the recipient of numerous awards over the course of his writing career. These include a Fulbright fellowship (1953-54), the May Morton Memorial Award for Poetry (1960); an Arts Council of Northern Ireland grant (1970); the Irish American Cultural Institute Prize (1976); the Marten Toonder Award (1977); the Alice Hunt Bartlett Memorial Award (1979); a Guggenheim fellowship (1979); the Hughes Irish Fiction Award (1988); the Irish American Foundation Award (1995), and The Vincent Buckley Poetry Prize (2000). In 1998 Montague was named the first Ireland Professor of Poetry by the Arts Councils of Dublin and Belfast, Queen's University, Belfast, Trinity College, Dublin, and University College, Dublin.

MAJOR WORKS

Montague published his first poems in 1949, having won a poetry competition as a student at University College. His first collection, *Forms of Exile,* was published in pamphlet form in 1958 and features themes of exile and failure to belong in any given place—themes that would be an important element of his work throughout his career. Montague's first major collection, *Poisoned Lands and Other Poems* (1961), consists of twenty-nine poems, some of them from his first collection; it was substantially revised and reworked for its 1977 reissue. Like much of his later work, the poems of *Poisoned Lands* deal with his ambivalent feelings toward Ireland, nostalgia for the Ireland of the past, and concerns about a country and a world undergoing dramatic changes at an ever-accelerating pace. In 1967, Montague published *A Chosen Light,* which includes one of his most celebrated individual poems, "A Bright Day." This was followed by *Tides* in 1970, featuring "The Wild Dog Rose" and a translation of a ninth-century Irish ballad, "The Hag of Beare."

Montague's most ambitious effort is *The Rough Field* (1972), a lengthy historical epic of County Tyrone that is often compared to William Carlos Williams' *Paterson.* The volume represents more than ten years of work and consists of eleven cantos, five of which were published earlier. These include *Home Again* (1966), *The Bread God* (1968), *Hymn to the New Omagh Road* (1968), *Patriotic Suite* (1968), and *A New Siege* (1970). In 1975, Montague produced *A Slow Dance,* a volume that juxtaposes nightmare images with nostalgic reminiscences. This was followed by *The Great Cloak* (1978), which deals with the disintegration of his first marriage and his new union with his second wife. It is believed that the volume's poems were composed at least four years earlier than the publication date. In the 1980s Montague published *The Dead Kingdom* (1984) and *Mount Eagle* (1988). The appearance of *The Collected Poems* in 1995 led to renewed interest in his poetry by both readers and critics. Montague's most recent collections include *A Love Present* (1997), *Smashing the Piano* (1999), and *Drunken Sailor* (2005). He has also produced three collections of short stories, a novella, and two memoirs. The most recent, *The Pear Is Ripe: A Memoir,* was published in 2008.

CRITICAL RECEPTION

Montague's poetry covers two major themes: love and the political problems of Ireland. Some critics, such as Frank L. Kersnowski, contend that Montague's early political poetry has been ignored by critics, who seem to feel that he could produce only love poetry at that stage of his career. The critic, however, points out a number of politically inspired early poems, most notable among them *A New Siege* (1970). Conor Johnston (see Further Reading) compares the political poetry of Montague with that of Derek Mahon and Seamus Heaney, noting that Montague "is acutely conscious of the history from which the present troubles arise," and in his poetry "he mourns part of that history—the British expulsion from Ireland of the Catholic Irish blue-bloods, the natural leaders of the people." Johnson reports on other political issues that turn up in Montague's work, such as the oppression of Catholics based on the eighteenth-century Penal Laws, as well as the loss of the Gaelic language. Eamonn Wall claims that Montague "brings together national and personal voices" in *The Rough Field,* which he considers Montague's masterpiece. The poet "has not only produced a confes-

sional poetry of the highest order, but he is also the writer who has articulated best the tragedy, and the context, of the Troubles," according to Wall. Ben Howard reports that Montague is "a gifted lyric poet and a passionate cultural historian," who "has limned the convergences of history and self."

Like many Irish poets, such as Patrick Kavanagh and Seamus Heaney, Montague exhibits mixed feelings about Ireland. The circumstances of Montague's life—his birth in America, his childhood in County Tyrone, his education in Dublin, and his occasional residence in Paris as well as a variety of other European and North American cities—made him prone to what Michael Faherty (see Further Reading) calls the Robinson Crusoe complex; that is, the feeling of belonging and at the same time, not belonging, in any of those places, most especially in Ireland. A. K. Weatherhead considers him "the poet of exile, literal and metaphorical, recognizing the conflicting claims of the old country and the new—claims, that is, of Ireland and New York and of old and new Irelands." Elmer Kennedy-Andrews (see Further Reading), addressing the same set of personal circumstances in Montague's life, reports that the poet believed the best position for someone of his profession was to be a "global regionalist," eschewing both the narrow regionalism of some of his fellow Irishmen, as well as the "boundless globalism" of Ezra Pound. Thomas Dillon Redshaw examines this feature of Montague's writing, noting that "his biography's details make the wanderings of his life and the diverse accomplishments of his writing one personal, morally sensitive embassy from Ireland to the world, and from the world back to Ireland," perhaps best exemplified by the poems of *The Rough Field.*

Antoinette Quinn finds another factor that may account for Montague's sense that he belongs nowhere—that is, his relationship with his mother. After a difficult birth and disappointment that she'd given birth to a third son, Montague's mother refused to nurse him and turned him over to a wet nurse. When she returned to Ireland, she left him in the care of the spinster aunts while reclaiming his two older brothers. This virtual abandonment by his mother informs much of Montague's poetry according to Quinn, particularly in the poems of *The Dead Kingdom,* in which he represents her "as a Janus-headed Muse, poetically enabling and emotionally disabling simultaneously." Eamon Grennan also refers to the "wound of abandonment" which seems to find its way into a number of Montague's poems including "Like Dolmens Round My Childhood, the Old People," "A Flowering Absence," and "The Locket." Grennan notes that "a preoccupation with loss will mark many of Montague's later poems" such as "Hymn to the New Omagh Road," "Process," and "Gone."

Montague is known for producing work in a wide variety of poetic forms and styles. Interviewer Kevin T.

McEneaney comments that Montague's poems "have great variety: imagism, free verse, rhymes, internal rhymes, prose poems, litanies, mythopoetic poems, and even concrete poems." Montague responded that modern poets have inherited all those various forms and can employ them as they see fit and that poets "have a renewed sense of tradition as well as an armory of techniques to wrestle or woo raw experience." Weatherhead compares Montague's ambivalent attitude toward Ireland with a similarly ambivalent attitude toward traditional poetic forms, contending that the regular metrical patterns of the early poems gave way to increasingly flexible patterns of rhyme and meter later in his career. Douglas Sealy also points to the "diversity of poetic form and the subtle handling of rhythm" that characterizes Montague's work.

PRINCIPAL WORKS

Poetry

Forms of Exile 1958
Poisoned Lands and Other Poems 1961
Old Mythologies: A Poem 1965
Home Again 1966
Patriotic Suite 1966
A Chosen Light 1967
Tides 1970
The Wild Dog Rose 1970
The Rough Field 1972
A Slow Dance 1975
The Great Cloak 1978
Selected Poems 1982
The Dead Kingdom 1984
Mount Eagle 1988
Born in Brooklyn (poetry and prose) 1991
The Love Poems 1992
Time in Armagh 1993
The Collected Poems 1995
A Love Present 1997
Smashing the Piano 1999
Selected Poems 2001
Drunken Sailor 2005

Other Major Works

Death of a Chieftain and Other Stories (short stories) 1964
The Lost Notebook (novella) 1987
The Figure in the Cave (essays) 1989
An Occasion of Sin (short stories) 1992
A Love Story and Other Stories (short stories) 1997

Company: A Chosen Life (memoir) 2001
A Ball of Fire (collected prose) 2008
The Pear Is Ripe: A Memoir (memoir) 2008

CRITICISM

Frank L. Kersnowski (essay date winter 1972)

SOURCE: Kersnowski, Frank L. "The Poet and Politics: John Montague." *South Central Bulletin* 32, no. 4 (winter 1972): 224-27.

[*In the following essay, Kersnowski refutes the common assumption that Montague could only write love poetry, contending that his political poetry has been ignored by critics.*]

John Montague has been known to his contemporaries as a lyric poet concerned with love. A poem such as **"All Legendary Obstacles"** gives credence to the view:

> You had been travelling for days
> With an old lady, who marked
> A neat circle on the glass
> With her glove, to watch us
> Move into the wet darkness
> Kissing, still unable to speak.[1]

Implicit, and sometimes explicit, in this praise is the suggestion that Montague can only write one kind of poetry. And that one is distinctly non-political. Valentin Iremonger and M. L. Rosenthal, two of his most perceptive reviewers, realize that Montague has based his poetry on an understanding of humanity rather than on an understanding of literature.[2] To be only a lyric poet writing of love would limit him to being the student of a genre. Ignored, though, is Montague's long and continuing political poetry and the change in it as Ireland becomes what I must regard as a violently stagnant culture.

As is generally true of Irish poetry in the 1950's, Montague's early verse fought a father-son battle with the precedent of Yeats and Co. To free the self from the Anglo-Irish personage that strode across literature dressed in bowler and spats, often thought of as helmets and greaves, then became a dominating theme, even an obsession:

> Ancient Ireland, indeed! I was reared by her bedside,
> The rune and the chant, evil eye and averted head,
> Formorian fierceness of family and local feud.[3]

With the sound of Joyce to encourage them, Montague and many of his contemporaries continued to write of an Ireland peopled by human beings flawed by character and circumstance, graced by love and kindness. The impersonal love Yeats expressed for Anne in "A Prayer for my Daughter" belongs to another age.[4] All poets do not neglect the achievement. Probably all would like to write so well, and at times some do.

Freedom from the past came as Montague accepted the strength of his belief in the people of Ireland, citizens of a new age, and no longer titled on the plain of the past. Many poems in *A Chosen Light,* the second collection, speak of the new understanding that has come to the poets and to the "plain people of Ireland" as Myles naGopaleen called them.[5] **"Vigil"** recalls the bombing of the North in World War II:

> On the first Thursday of every month
> The sirens sound through Paris
> A warning exercise. It begins
> With the sobbing call of the Alert
> Which, against my will, seems
> A nostalgic, almost homely sound
> Recalling nights at Armagh school
> When, cramped in mud shelters,
> We heard planes prowling overhead,
> Saw, across Belfast, the night-sky
> Swollen with fire, like blood.
> That is the real border, the grit
> of different experience, of shared terror
> No swift neutral sympathy can allay
> Only the rising pulse of the All Clear
> Cleanses, permits the day.[6]

As the third and last part of **"Waiting," "Vigil"** stresses remembrance of destruction and relief that such danger has not gathered itself into form again. Nowhere does certain calm present itself, not even in Ireland stuck by its neutrality on the backshelf of Europe. Changes in the world have come and are to be seen even at a festival of traditional music:

> At the Flaedh Cheoil in Mullingar
> There were two sounds, the breaking
> Of glass, and the background pulse
> Of music. Young girls roamed
> The streets with eager faces,
> Pushing for men. Bottles in
> Hand, they rowed out a song:
> *Puritan Ireland's dead and gone,*
> *A myth of O'Connor and O'Faolain.*[7]

Though describing sexual and social attitudes among the young, the poem announces a revolution. It should be remembered that such festivals as these were created by Hyde's Gaelic League, an organization that provided the structure and impetus for the 1916 Uprising.

Probably no revolution is singularly political or cultural; for politics describes the ideal life that within a culture becomes modified, compromised by locale, time, and power. Montague's concern, almost without exception, has been the human, the cultural, the non-idealized part

of the revolution. From his enjoyment and love of all peoples, Montague has built poems that show the humanity of all men, even Irishmen. *Tides,* his most recent collection, is essentially lyrical on love. With some surprise a reader can discover that love poems have cultural-political values. The poem **"Omagh Hospital"** tells of a visit to an aunt's deathbed, an old woman from whom he gained understanding:

> Bring me home
> you whimper and
> I see a house
> shaken by traffic
> until a fault runs
> from roof to base.[8]

In the longer version called **"The Leaping Fire,"** Montague explains that this woman who thought of herself as a follower of St. Teresa actually combines the goddess of poetry and St. Brigid.[9]

Now, twenty years after Montague cast out Cathleen, he goes to the hag's hut, sits before her fire, and drinks his tea. I refer to **"The Wild Dog Rose"** and his translation of **"The Hag of Beare,"** poems celebrating ancient courtesies and pain. The emphasis remains on continuing pagan forms, even in a Christian country. The hag of Beare casts a more than Lawrentian eye on Christ as she remembers past lovers:

> Well might the Son of Mary
> Take their place under my roof-tree
> For if I lack other hospitality
> I never say 'No' to anybody—[10]

No longer shunning the past, Montague looks back at his own heritage and finds precedent for his praise of life, praise of extravagance and says in every poem, "Puritan Ireland's dead and gone!"

This "Puritan Ireland" might well seem an unfortunate pause in the development of distinctly Irish culture. To make Victoria responsible for the drinking and masturbating practices of the Irish is tempting. More likely, in the last half of the twentieth century the cycle of existence contemplates again problems and identities more basic and less complex than other people's sex lives and ideological hatreds. John Montague in the published parts of *The Rough Field* develops a contrast between these two ways of life by describing the cultural and political life of Ireland.

For the outsider to Irish culture, the part called *Hymn to the New Omagh Road* is most easily entered. The problem is the economic and ecological change caused by a super highway. The poem presents a balance sheet of loss and gain, then describes past beauty in the words of a local poet. Business, conservation, and dehumanization are all referents.[11] In New Orleans, San Antonio, and Arkansas, conservation is a political issue. Conservation is not limited to the counter-culture. The larger revolution, the one for which Montague speaks, contests the right of the few to use land and people opportunistically.

The specifically Ulster quality of this poem is revealed in Montague's reading. The sounds of a country poet, an Ulster businessman, and an European poet set boundaries which outline Ireland. The poem is not simply local, and Montague need not explain wider significances. In *The Bread God,* some explanation of historical problems helps. To describe his local parish, he quotes from a Jesuit uncle and Carleton. The innocuous joy of these, however, is interrupted by Protestant battle cries:

> Cromwell went to Ireland
>   TO STOP
> The Catholics murdering Protestants![12]

This is history reversed. But one must know the history, surely not too complex an effort on this level. The effect of Cromwell on the western world is part of our heritage. The bigotry and hatred the poem presents passes into the racial strife of America, perhaps into religious beliefs. Yet this poem is distinctly Irish, as is stressed in the ending, called **"An Ulster Prophecy"**:

> I saw the Pope carding tow on Friday
> A blind parson sewing a Patchwork quilt
> Three bishops cutting rushes with their croziers
> Roaring Meg firing Rosary beads for cannonballs
> Corks in boats afloat on the summit of the Sberrins
> A mill and a forge on the back of a cuckoo
> The fox sitting conceitedly at a window chewing
>   tobacco
> And a moorhen in flight
>   surveying
>   A United Ireland.[13]

These paradoxes, suggested by French Surrealist poetry, may well leave the uninitiated puzzled.[14] In spite of the efforts of her artists, Ireland today has not been found on the world's stage. Most people do not comprehend the violence in the North. Even the southern Irishman does not understand why people kill one another in the North. One wonders if people soliciting funds for the IRA on O'Connell Street understand.

The violence in Londonderry and Belfast as it becomes more intensified becomes more and more local. Its similarity to turmoil in the rest of the world becomes less. Ulster draws a ring of ascending violence around itself and becomes a community bound to its own violence and cut off from the understanding of the rest of the world by the violence. Stagnation by violence becomes a condition, if not a solution. What can an artist do with such as this if he will neither resign himself to immersion in the pool nor live completely apart from it, abandon his people, and out-exile Joyce?

Montague in *A New Siege* (1970) attempts an answer not only to that problem, but to a divided Ireland. The first stanza sets the particularity of Ulster's problem in a wider perspective:

> Lines of history
>   lines of power
> the long sweep
>   of the Bedside
> under the walls
>   up to Cretan
> the black muzzle
>   of Roaring Me
> staring dead on
>   the new Cathedral
> the jackal shapes
>   of James's army
> watching the city
>   stiffen in siege.

The particularity in the poem increases, as does Montague's attempt to force it into a wider perspective:

> Lines of protest
>   lines of change
> a drum beating
>   across Berkeley
> all that Spring
>   invoking the new
> Christ avatar
>   of the Americas
> running voices
>   streets of Berlin
> Paris, Chicago
>   seismic waves
> zigzagging through
>   a faulty world.[15]

Whether or not Montague has truly found mythic significance in Ulster's violence only history will be able to tell, as he admits. That the poem has importance in Ireland is obvious. Mr. Lynch began a speech urging peace by quoting from *A New Siege*: "Old moulds are broken in the North."

The sound of the break has been heard in rifle, grenade, and bomb. I await the sound of the new and must pessimistically wonder if Ireland in general, the North in particular, can escape the political lethargy that followed partition. Only a solution to Irish violence on categorically different grounds can, it seems to me, assure a country that will have a cultural existence which belongs to the present. The poets, especially, have brought to Ireland news of change, of new joy and pain; but the plain people of Ireland remain the world of 1950 American swing. Though perhaps caught up in the process of world-wide change, Ireland remains on the backshelf of Europe. And she has not heeded often enough her artists, the signalers of the processes of man. Violence sweeps over, as poets write avant-garde terms of radical solutions.

In particular, I must wonder if a friend of mine, John Montague, has tied his talent to a culture that cannot respect it; wonder if his poetry would not be furthered by his total rejection of Ireland, which he did not even do in the 1950's. The answer is an historical one. But it is possible to observe that Montague's poetry grows in technique as he increases his vulnerability. In *The Rough Field,* especially *A New Siege,* he risks much by believing contemporary Ireland is worth writing about. Only the sound of a new, peaceful order will prove him right.

Notes

1. *A Chosen Light* (London, 1967), p. 16. Research for this paper was made possible by grants from the National Foundation for the Arts and Humanities and the Research Committee of Trinity University.

2. "The Rune and The Chant," *The Irish Times* (Nov. 11, 1961), and "Poet of Brooklyn, Ulster and Paris," *The Nation* (May 17, 1971), p. 632.

3. *Poisoned Lands* (London, 1961), p. 19.

4. *The Collected Poems of W. B. Yeats* (New York, 1959), pp. 185-187.

5. *The Best of Myles* (London, 1958), pp. 79-111.

6. *A Chosen Light,* p. 52.

7. *Ibid.,* p. 60.

8. *Tides* (Dublin, 1970), pp. 51-52.

9. *Irish University Review,* I, 1 (Autumn, 1970), 62-66.

10. *Tides,* p. 22.

11. *Hymn to the New Omagh Road* (Dublin, 1968).

12. *The Bread God* (Dublin, 1968), p. viii.

13. *Ibid.,* p. xi.

14. Conversation with John Montague in Paris, France, on July 21, 1969.

15. *A New Siege* (Dublin, 1970).

Thomas Dillon Redshaw (essay date 1976)

SOURCE: Redshaw, Thomas Dillon. "Appréciation." *Éire-Ireland* 11, no. 4 (1976): 122-32.

[*In the following essay, Redshaw examines the international quality of Montague's teaching and writing, considering the details of his life as a "wandering scholar."*]

For nearly a decade the Irish American Cultural Institute has presented awards to Irish composers, painters, and writers—both in Irish and English—in recognition of their efforts to broaden and enliven modern Irish culture. The substantial sum of these monetary awards is, nevertheless, but a token "payment" of Irish America's debt to her ancestral heritage and is intended to serve as practical assistance to Irish artists at critical moments in their careers. The award for Irish writing has lately been presented to the Irish poet and translator Michael Hartnett, whose collection *A Farewell to English* (1975) and bilingual poem *Cúlú Íde* (1975) are experiments Hartnett might not otherwise have undertaken. Likewise, the novelist Breandán Ó hEithir received a similar bursary in recognition of the extraordinary popularity of his Irish-language novel *Lig Sinn I gCathú* (1975), whose appeal to a wide public has renewed hopes for a genuinely bilingual Ireland. This year the Irish American Cultural Institute has been pleased to recognize the character and achievements of the work of the Tyrone poet John Montague with a similar award presented at a reception in the National Gallery of Ireland on September 20, 1976. The President of the Institute, Dr. Eoin McKiernan, prefaced the presentation by observing that "Without the least diminution of his identity as an Irish writer, [John Montague] has functioned as an international relay station, a satellite orbiting Ireland, transmitting outward and inward poetic and humanistic forms, themes, and ideas for the mutual stimulation and enrichment of these cultures." While it is not surprising that figures from Irish artistic and cultural circles—such as the novelist Francis Stuart, or Thomas MacAnna of the Abbey Theatre—should have welcomed the Institute's recognition of John Montague, it is curious and welcome that both The Irish *Times* and The International Herald *Tribune* should have noted the award with generous *editorial* commentary. Such notice suggests, as all of Montague's writing also makes plain, that this Tyrone poet serves his readers as an ambassador of Ireland to the world, and of the world to Ireland.

The character of John Montague's lifework of the past twenty-five years—ranging from his journeyman prose for *The Bell* to his new lyrics in *A Slow Dance*—might be best displayed by setting back-to-back two lines from his most controversial poem, *The Rough Field* (1972). Montague prefaced this long poem with an epigraph from the Greek poet Seferis and also with a sentence "from the Afghan": "I had never known sorrow, / Now it is a field I have inherited, and I till it." Pose against this the first line of Montague's overture to one canto, **"The Bread God"**: *"I break again into the lean parish of my art. . . ."* Both are parallel, autobiographical statements. In the first, an Irish life is seen in worldly terms. In the latter, a worldly life is seen in terms of a single Irish townland, a single parish. Montague once closed a radio lecture on the place of Irish verse in the poetry of the world by observing that he seemed "to be advocating a deliberate programme of denationalization," and then countering that "all true experiments and exchanges only serve to illuminate the self, a rediscovery of the oldest laws of the psyche."

For twenty-five years Montague has never abandoned the pursuit of illuminating poetically the human compass of flaws and virtues, trivialities and greatnesses, in the particulars of a County Tyrone autobiography and in the universals of an international life encompassing the moral perplexities of European and American culture. In Ireland—whether working in Dublin or teaching in Cork—Montague has never forgotten his American birth and heritage. In America and Europe—whether reading in Toronto, New York, Paris, or teaching at Victoria, Berkeley, or Vincennes—Montague has never forgotten his Tyrone upbringing and heritage. His biography's details make the wanderings of his life and the diverse accomplishments of his writing one personal, morally sensitive embassy from Ireland to the world, and from the world back to Ireland.

Montague's *The Rough Field* dramatizes that illuminating "rediscovery of the oldest laws" in terms so particular, so parochial, that they become universal. His Ulster—the narrow triangle of Omagh, Clogher, and Ballygawley—he presents to the world, like William Faulkner, as a miniature proportion of it. For this "little postage stamp of native soil," to quote Faulkner, Montague has recreated himself, like Whitman and William Carlos Williams, as a representative man struggling with outward change and inner turmoil to give this small world the moral order, not of the best of all worlds, but of the unflinchingly accurate poem. Recreating himself in *The Rough Field,* Montague also creates a personal epic of change, a parochial epic displaying

> the rough field
>   of the universe
> growing, changing
>   a net of energies
> crossing patterns
>   weaving towards
> a new order
>   a new anarchy
> always different
>   always the same

Like the life it shapes, *The Rough Field* does not simply perform an embassy from modern Ireland to the waiting world. French, British, and American readers might learn much from it of Ireland—her history and geography, her political and social condition, her varied literary traditions—but so might Dubliners, Belfastmen, Galwegians, and Corkonians. *The Rough Field* is uniquely vivid because it also performs an embassy from the world, and from America in particular, to Ireland. The achievement of the poem's form is one no Irish poet but Patrick Kavanagh has hoped to attempt

before, while its successes many Irish poets will hope to build upon. Montague's ten cantos and epilogue surely adapt to an Irish setting the poetic means of the American epic devised by Whitman and refined in William Carlos Williams' *Paterson.* So, Montague has accomplished what Denis Devlin did not live to do. To all Irish poets coming after him he has freely given the choice of a modern American, rather than British or Continental, poetic.

The different virtues of *The Rough Field* may all be found in Montague's several collections: his allusive and moral humor in *Poisoned Lands* (1961); his fascination with intimate, clear images of passion in *All Legendary Obstacles* (1966) and *A Chosen Light* (1967); his celebration of the natural, psychic order of darkness and pain in *Tides* (1971); and his counterpointed celebrations of the mature patterns of human life in *A Slow Dance* (1976). The poems in these shapely collections perform their embassy with a diplomacy sometimes unusually subtle, sometimes frank, but always disciplined. The heart of that discipline—whether intellectual or emotional, formal or symbolic—many times creates well-considered prayer and sometimes, as in *A Slow Dance,* a litany for life renewed:

> Freshet of ease
>   flow for us
> Secret waterfall
>   pour for us
> Hidden cleft
>   speak to us
> Portal of delight
>   inflame us
> Hill of motherhood
>   wait for us
> Gate of birth
>   open for us

The prose of Montague's finely tuned, sly stories in *Death of a Chieftain* (1965) and of his uncollected essays contains a similar prayer for rebirth and performs a like embassy. Montague's first essay focused on Carleton and Goldsmith, for example, but his later criticism touches as frequently on American literature—Faulkner, Lowell and Berryman, the San Francisco poets—as on any other. In a poet's way, he has sought to bring America to Ireland. Likewise, Montague sought early on to bring Clarke, Kavanagh, and Kinsella to American readers when the achievements of post-war Irish verse were hardly known across the Atlantic. And the long-awaited American edition of Montague's *Faber Book of Irish Verse* (1974) will shortly bring to these same readers a comprehensive survey—from the Gaelic poets to Montague's younger contemporaries like Michael Hartnett and Richard Ryan—of the whole realm of Irish verse. This is not Montague's only generosity: as if to pay William Carlos Williams homage, Montague prefaces his *Faber Book* with a long essay entitled "In the Irish Grain."

Unlike other anthologies, Montague's *Faber Book* contains a wealth of skillful translations or "versions" from the Irish, a number by his own hand. Just as he has also translated from the French, so Montague has encouraged the translation of his Irish peers into French. Like his teaching, his translating is an obvious embassy, while Montague's patient editorial work has been a less noticed one. Now a contributing editor for the Toronto quarterly *Exile,* along with the Israeli poet Yehuda Amichai, Montague once served as an editor for *The Dolmen Miscellany* (1962) and for *Poetry Ireland* (1968). With some modesty, he also helped Patrick Kavanagh's **Collected Poems** into print. Not only has Montague recommended to Liam Miller's Dolmen Press the work of younger Irish poets, he has also encouraged other publishers to look into their work, sometimes with small thanks.

For long a wandering scholar—his studies taking him to Yale and the Universities of Iowa and California— Montague more lately has taken his peripatetic teaching to schools in North America—at Berkeley, Buffalo, and Victoria; in France—at the experimental Université de Vincennes; and in Ireland—at the University Colleges of Dublin and Cork. In France and America Montague has offered his students and colleagues not just an Irish understanding of Baudelaire or Whitman, for example, but a view into an Ireland—one hidden by time from Yeats and Joyce—epitomized in one his most quoted couplets: *"Puritan Ireland's dead and gone, / A myth of O'Connor and O'Faolain."* Lecturing in Ireland, Montague has given his students an international perspective on Irish letters. Kavanagh, Clarke, Kinsella, and Heaney he has presented on the large stage of the world in company with Ted Hughes, Robert Duncan, Francis Ponge, and Vasko Popa. In all of his writings this has been Montague's certain attitude towards Irish artists, like the painter Barrie Cooke or the late composer Seán Ó Riada, and their paintings and music figure as often in Montague's writings as those of Geerard David and Mozart.

As Montague's studies and teaching, his critical prose and fiction, and above all the range of his poetry from **Poisoned Lands** (1961) to **A Slow Dance** (1967) plainly demonstrate, his life and work have ever carried forward a two-fold mission as highly personal as it is principled. Of its motive Montague rarely has been reticent.

    (Dumb,
bloodied, the severed
head now chokes to
speak another tongue:—

    As in
a long suppressed dream,
some stuttering garb-
led ordeal of my own)

That motive Montague shares with all his readers. The inhibition, impulse, painful effort all are human, whatever the tongue to be learnt. From that humanity— from individual and private dreams and ordeals—has Montague finely drawn the sentences of his continuing, public embassy.

Works

John Montague, *Forms of Exile* (Dublin: The Dolmen Press, December 1958). Also 50 specially bound copies signed by the author.

————, *The Old People* (Dublin: The Dolmen Press, August 1960). Privately printed edition of 100 copies.

————, *Old Mythologies* (Dublin: The Dolmen Press, Christmas 1960;. Postcard-poem printed in an edition of 100 copies.

————, *Three Irish Poets: John Montague, Thomas Kinsella, Richard Murphy* (Dublin: The Dolmen Press, February 1961). Souvenir program printed in an edition of 250 copies.

————, *Poisoned Lands and Other Poems* (London: MacGibbon and Kee, 1961).

————, *Poisoned Lands and Other Poems* (Philadelphia: Dufour Editions, 1963).

————, *Death of a Chieftain and Other Stories* (London: MacGibbon and Kee, 1964).

————, *Cathedral Town* (Dublin: The Dolmen Press, Christmas 1964). Postcard-poem printed in an edition of 100 copies.

————, *All Legendary Obstacles,* Dolmen Editions II (Dublin: The Dolmen Press, February 1966). Signed edition of 350 copies.

————, *Patriotic Suite,* The New Dolmen Chapbooks (Dublin: The Dolmen Press, November 1966). Also 100 specially bound, signed copies in slip case.

————, *Home Again* (Belfast: Festival Publications, [Spring 1967]).

————, *Death of a Chieftain and Other Stories* (Chester Springs, Pa.: Dufour Editions, 1967).

————, *A Chosen Light* (London: MacGibbon and Kee, 1967).

————, *Hymn to the New Omagh Road* (Dublin: The Dolmen Press, May 1968). Privately printed, signed edition of 175 copies.

————and Seamus Heaney, *The Northern Muse* (Dublin: Claddagh Records, 1968). Lp recording.

————, *The Bread God: A Lecture,* Dolmen Editions VII (Dublin: The Dolmen Press, December 1968). Edition of 250 signed copies.

————, *A Chosen Light* (Chicago: The Swallow Press, 1969).

————, *A New Siege: An Historical Meditation,* Poet Card 1 (Dublin: The Dolmen Press, August 1970).

————, *Tides* (Dublin: The Dolmen Press, [September] 1970).

————and John Hewitt, *The Planter and the Gael: An Anthology of Poems* (Belfast: Arts Council of Northern Ireland, November 1970). Souvenir program.

————, *Tides* (Chicago: The Swallow Press, 1971).

————, *The Rough Field* (Dublin: The Dolmen Press, October [November] 1972). Paperback trade edition in large format.

————, *The Rough Field* (Dublin: The Dolmen Press, October 1972). Specially bound, colored, signed edition of 150 copies published in December, 1972.

————, *A Fair House: Versions of Irish Poetry* (Dublin: The Cuala Press, 1972 [July 1973]). Edition of translations limited to 350 copies.

————, *Tides* (Dublin: The Dolmen Press, 1970 [1973, 1974]). Second and third paperback trade editions.

————, *The Cave of Night* (Cork: Golden Stone, Spring 1974). Also special, signed edition of 50 copies.

————, *O'Riada's Farewell* (Cork: Golden Stone, Winter 1974). Also special, signed edition of 50 copies.

————, *The Rough Field* (Dublin: The Dolmen Press, 1974). Second, paperback trade edition re-set and newly paginated.

————, *A Slow Dance* (Dublin: The Dolmen Press, November 1975). Also specially bound, signed edition of 150 copies.

————, *A Slow Dance* (Winston-Salem, N. C.: Wake Forest University Press, November 1975).

Selected Anthologies

Six Irish Poets, ed. Robin Skelton (London: Oxford University Press, 1962).

New Poets of Ireland, ed. Donald Carroll (Denver, Co.: Alan Swallow, 1963).

The Mentor Book of Irish Poetry, ed. Devin A. Garrity (New York: The New American Library, 1965).

The New Modern Poetry: British and American Poetry since World War II, ed. M. L. Rosenthal (New York: Macmillan, 1967).

Twenty-three Modern British Poets, ed. John Matthias (Chicago: The Swallow Press, 1971).

The Sphere Book of Modern Irish Poetry, ed. Derek Mahon (London: Sphere Books, 1972).

Sampla: A Selection of New Writing . . . (Dublin: Irish Book Publishers' Association, 1972). Edition of 3,000 copies.

The Wearing of the Black: An Anthology of Contemporary Ulster Poetry, ed. Padraic Fiacc (Belfast: Blackstaff Press, 1974).

Editions

The Dolmen Miscellany of Irish Writing, eds. John Montague and Thomas Kinsella (Dublin: The Dolmen Press, 1962).

Patrick Kavanagh, *Collected Poems,* [eds. Martin Brian, John Montague] (London: MacGibbon and Kee, 1964). Later re-published from the Devin-Adair edition (1964) in paperback by W. W. Norton (1973).

A Tribute to Austin Clarke on His Seventieth Birthday . . . , eds. John Montague, Liam Miller, Dolmen Editions IV (Dublin: The Dolmen Press, May 1966).

Threshold ["Ulster Crisis Issue"], 23 (Summer, 1970).

The Faber Book of Irish Verse, ed. John Montague (London: Faber and Faber, 1974).

Selected Prose

John Montague, "The Tyranny of Memory: A Study of George Moore," *The Bell,* XVII, 5 (August, 1951), 12-24.

————, "Tribute to William Carleton," *The Bell,* XVIII, 1 (April, 1952), 13-24.

————, "A First Response," *Shenandoah,* 5, 2 (Spring, 1954), 28-31.

————, "Return to Europe," *Poetry,* 89, 3 (December, 1956), 180-83.

————, "The First Week in Lent: A Political Snapshot," *Threshold,* 1, 2 (Summer, 1957), 69-71.

————, "Letter from Dublin," *Poetry,* 90, 5 (August, 1975), 310-15.

————, "Contemporary Verse: A Short Chronicle," *Studies,* XLVII, 184 (Winter, 1958), 441-49.

————, "Rebellion," *Threshold,* 3, 2 (Summer, 1959), 6-16. Short story.

————, "Isolation and Cunning: Recent Irish Verse," *Poetry,* 94, 4 (July, 1959), 264-70.

————, "American Pegasus," *Studies,* XLVIII, 190 (Summer, 1959), 183-91.

———, "Tragic Picaresque: Oliver Goldsmith, The Biographical Aspect," *Studies,* XLIX, 193 (Spring, 1960), 45-53.

———, "Outward Bound," *Threshold,* 4, 2 (Autumn-Winter, 1960), 68-75.

———, "The Sentimental Prophecy: A Study of *The Deserted Village*," *The Dolmen Miscellany of Irish Writing* (Dublin: The Dolmen Press, September 1962), 62-79.

———, "The Rough Field," *The Spectator,* 210, 7035 (April 26, 1963), p. 531.

———, "Regionalism into Reconciliation: The Poetry of John Hewitt," *Poetry Ireland,* 3 (Spring, 1964), 113-18.

———, "The Painting of Barrie Cooke," *The Dubliner,* 3, 1 (Spring, 1964), 38-41.

———, "Under Ben Bulben," *Shenandoah,* 16, 4 (Summer, 1965), 21-24.

———, "Louis Le Brocquy: A Painter's Interior World," *Hibernia,* 30, 12 (December, 1966), p. 29.

———, "The Seamless Garment and the Muse," *Agenda,* 5-6, 4-1 (Autumn-Winter, 1967-68), 27-34.

———, "And an Irishman [On Thomas Kinsella]," *The New York Times Book Review,* August 18, 1968, p. 5.

———, "Tyrone: The Rough Field," *Conor Cruise O'Brien Introduces Ireland* (London: André Deutsch, 1969), pp. 203-5.

———, "A Primal Gaeltacht," *The Irish Times,* July 30, 1970, *An Ghaeltacht Inniu,* [p. 7].

———, "Tribute," in Seán Ó Riada, *Hercules Dux Ferrariae* (Dublin: Woodtown Publications, 1970). Edition of composer's score limited to 500 signed copies.

———, "Order in Donnybrook Fair," *The Times Literary Supplement,* 3655 (March 17, 1973), p. 313.

———, "D'une conversation du 4. IV. 72 avec Serge Faucherau," *Les Lettres Nouvelles,* 73 (Mars, 1973), 234-238.

———, "[Rhythm]," *Agenda,* 10-11, 4-1 (Spring, 1973), 41.

———, "The Impact of International Modern Poetry on Irish Writing," *Irish Poets in English,* ed. Seán Lucy (Cork: The Mercier Press, 1973), pp. 144-58.

———, "Primal Scream: The Later Le Brocquy," *The Arts in Ireland,* 2, 1 (Winter, 1973), 4-14.

———, "Despair and Delight," *Time Was Away: The World of Louis MacNeice,* eds. Terence Brown, Alec Reid (Dublin: The Dolmen Press, 1974), pp. 123-27.

———, "Wind and Wave: A Tribute to S. W. Hayter," *S. W. Hayter* (Dublin: The Neptune Gallery, July 1975), p. 6. Exhibition catalogue.

Selected Criticism

John Hewitt, "Poetry Review," *Threshold,* 3, 2 (Summer, 1959), 92-96.

Robin Skelton, "[Reviews *Poisoned Lands*]," *The Critical Quarterly,* 3, 4 (Winter, 1961), 375-77.

Philip Legler, "Four First Volumes," *Poetry,* 99, 3 (December, 1961), 184-87.

John Jordan, "Off the Barricade: A Note on Three Irish Poets," *The Dolmen Miscellany of Irish Writing* (Dublin: The Dolmen Press, September 1962), 107-116.

Mairtín Ó Direáin, "Borradh Fhiliocht an Bhéarla," *Inniu,* Nollaig 7, 1962, p. 3.

Thomas Kinsella, "Some Irish Poets," *Poetry,* 102, 5 (August, 1963), 324-29.

Maurice Kennedy, "Breakthrough," *The Irish Times,* September 24, 1964, p. 9.

Seamus McGonagle, "Britain's Deep South," *The Tribune,* October 30, 1964, p. 14.

Augustine Martin, "Report from Ireland," *The Chicago Review,* XVIII, 1 (August, 1965), 87-94.

Serge Faucherau, "Nouvelles de l'Irlande," *Critique,* 22 (November, 1965), 990.

Serge Faucherau, "Irelande: Vers un renaissance poétique?" *Les Lettres Nouvelles,* LV (Juillet-September, 1966), 128-36.

Seán McMahon, "The Black North," *Éire-Ireland,* I, 2 (Summer, 1966), 63-74.

Richard Kell, "Poetry 1966," *The Critical Survey,* 3, 1 (Winter, 1966), 57-60.

M. L. Rosenthal, *The New Poets: American and British Poetry since World War II* (New York: Oxford University Press, 1967), pp. 297-306.

Douglas Sealy, "Luminous Exactness," *The Irish Times,* August 19, 1967, p. 8.

Anon., "Seas of Disappointment," *The Times Literary Supplement,* 3428 (November 9, 1967), 1059.

Claude Esteban, "La Poésie irlandaise contemporaine," *Preuves,* 17, 202 (Décembre, 1967), 13-22.

Penelope Palmer, "Three Ways to a Centre," *Agenda,* 6, 2 (Spring, 1968), 81-90.

Serge Faucherau, "Tradition et révolution dans la poésie irlandaise," *Critique,* 276 (Mai, 1970), 438-56.

Anon., "[Review of *A Chosen Light*]," *Éire-Ireland*, V, 2 (Summer, 1970), 159-61.

Eavan Boland, "Love Story," *The Irish Times*, October 3, 1970, p. 8.

Derek Mahon, "Poetry in Northern Ireland," *Twentieth Century Studies*, 4 (November, 1970), 89-93.

Anon., "Donnish Comedy and Imagist Mythology," *The Times Literary Supplement*, 3587 (November 27, 1970), 1394.

James Simmons, "[Review of *Tides*]", *The Honest Ulsterman*, 26 (November-December, 1970), 29-30.

Vernon Young, "October Thoughts," *The Hudson Review*, XXIII, 4 (Winter, 1970-71), 733-46.

Anne Cluysenaar, "New Poetry," *Stand*, 12, 2 (Spring, 1971), 63-71.

M. L. Rosenthal, "Poet of Brooklyn, Ulster and Paris," *The Nation*, 212, 20 (May 17, 1971), pp. 632-33.

Michael Longley, "Poetry," *Causeway: The Arts in Ulster*, ed. Michael Longley (Belfast: The Arts Council of Northern Ireland and Gill and Macmillan, 1971), pp. 95-109.

Richard Lattimore, "Poetry Chronicle," *The Hudson Review*, XXIV, 3 (Autumn, 1971), 499-510.

James Brophy, "John Montague's Restive Sally-switch," *Modern Irish Literature: Essays in Honor of William York Tindall*, eds. R. J. Porter, J. D. Brophy (New York: Iona College Press and Twayne Publishers, 1972), pp. 153-69.

Thomas Dillon Redshaw, "Montague's *Aisling*," *The North Stone Review*, 3 (Summer-Fall, 1972), 119-23.

Benedict Kiely, "Poet in the O'Neill Country," *The Irish Times*, December 2, 1972, p. 13.

John MacInerney, "Montague's Irish Dimension," *Hibernia*, 36, 25 (December 15, 1972), p. 11.

Eavan Boland, "The Tribal Poet: John Montague," The Irish *Times*, March 20, 1973, p. 10.

Seamus Heaney, "Lost Ulsterman," *The Listener*, 89, 2300 (April 26, 1973), pp. 550-51.

Maurice Harmon, "New Voices in the Fifties," *Irish Poets in English*, ed. Seán Lucy (Cork: The Mercier Press, 1973), pp. 185-207.

Kevin Sullivan, "Poets in Crisis," *The Nation*, 216, 16 (June 25, 1973), pp. 821-22.

Derek Mahon, "[Review of *The Rough Field*]," *The Malahat Review*, 27 (July, 1973), 132-37.

Anne Cluysenaar, "New Poetry," *Stand*, 14, 3 (Summer, 1973), 70-73.

Maurice Harmon, "By Memory Inspired: Themes and Forces in Recent Irish Writing," *Éire-Ireland*, VIII, 2 (Summer, 1973), 3-19.

Hugh MacDiarmid, "John Montague's Ulster," *Agenda*, 11, 2-3 (Spring-Summer, 1973), 109-11.

D. E. S. Maxwell, "The Poetry of John Montague," *The Critical Quarterly*, 15, 2 (Summer, 1973), 180-85.

Seán Lucy, "Three Poets from Ulster," *Irish University Review*, 3, 2 (Autumn, 1973), 179-93.

Damian Grant, "Body Politic: The Function of a Metaphor in Three Irish Poets," *Poetry Nation*, 1 (Autumn, 1973), 112-25.

Douglas Dunn, "The Speckled Hill, the Plover's Shore: Northern Irish Poetry Today," *Encounter*, 20, 12 (December, 1973), 70-76.

Derek Mahon, "Mother Tongue," *The New Statesman*, 87, 2245 (March 29, 1974), pp. 451-52.

Denis Donoghue, "Icham of Irlaunde," *The Spectator*, 7606 (April 16, 1974), pp. 419-20.

Thomas Dillon Redshaw, "John Montague's *The Rough Field: Topos* and *Texne*," *Studies*, LXIII, 249 (Spring, 1974), 31-46.

Richard Ellmann, "Garden Party," *The New Review*, 1, 4 (July, 1974), 70-71.

F. S. L. Lyons, "Two Traditions in One," *The Times Literary Supplement*, 3776 (July 19, 1974), p. 763.

Thomas Dillon Redshaw, "*Rí*, as in Regional: Three Ulster Poets," *Éire-Ireland*, IX, 2 (Summer, 1974), 41-64.

John Jordan, "Contemporary Irish Verse," *The Arts in Ireland*, 2, 3 (Summer, 1974, 28-31.

Dillon Johnston, "'The Enabling Ritual': Irish Poetry in the Seventies," *Shenandoah*, XXV, 4 (Summer, 1974), 3-24.

Liam Ó Dochartaigh, "John Montague and 'Ceol na mBréag'," *Ulster Folklife*, 20 (1974), 85-88.

E. James Peterson, "Ulster—Ireland's Rough Field," *The Holy Cross Quarterly*, 6, 1-4 (1974), 60-67.

Frank Kersnowski, *John Montague*, The Irish Writers Series (Lewisburg, Pa.: Bucknell University Press, 1975).

David Black, "Montague's Rough Field," *Lines Review*, 52-53 (May, 1975), 76-83.

Seamus Deane, "Irish Poetry and Irish Nationalism," *Two Decades of Irish Writing: A Critical Survey*, ed. Douglas Dunn (Cheadle, Cheshire: Carcanet, 1975), pp. 4-22.

Edna Longley, "Searching the Darkness: Richard Murphy, Thomas Kinsella, John Montague and James Simmons," *Two Decades of Irish Writing: A Critical Survey,* ed. Douglas Dunn (Cheadle, Cheshire: Carcanet, 1975), pp. 118-53.

John Wilson Foster, "The Landscape of Planter and Gael in the Poetry of John Hewitt and John Montague," *The Canadian Journal of Irish Studies,* I, 2 (November, 1975), 17-33.

Terence Brown, *Northern Voices: Poets from Ulster* (Totowa, N.J.: Rowman and Littlefield, 1975), pp. 149-70.

Frank Kersnowski, *The Outsiders: Poets of Contemporary Ireland* (Fort Worth, Texas: The Texas Christian University Press, 1975), pp. 117-32.

Eileán ní Chuilleanáin, "Joyous Suite," *Hibernia,* 40, 6 (March 12, 1976), p. 18.

W. J. McCormack, "Rural Past, Urban Present," *The Times Literary Supplement,* 3862 (March 19, 1976), p. 324.

Terry Eagleton, "New Poetry," *Stand,* 17, 3 (Summer, 1974), 68-73.

M. L. Rosenthal, "[Reviews *A Slow Dance*]," *The New York Times Book Review,* September 19, 1976, pp. 6-7.

John Montague and *The Literary Review* (interview date 8 September 1977)

SOURCE: Montague, John, and *The Literary Review.* "Global Regionalism: Interview with John Montague." *The Literary Review* 22, no. 2 (winter 1979): 153-74.

[*In the following interview, conducted on September 8, 1977, Montague discusses his political poetry, Ulster history, and the concept of global regionalism, which he considers the proper perspective for a poet.*]

[*The Literary Review:*] *Born in New York, raised in Tyrone, educated in Ulster, in Dublin, and in America, you settled for a time in Paris before returning to Ireland to make a home in Cork. Do you consider yourself an Ulster, an Irish, or a Continental poet? Or are these terms of abstract allegiance meaningless?*

[John Montague:] I think circumstances have conspired to make all these influences come together in my work. I did not choose to be born in Brooklyn. It was because my father was on the run. Being raised in Ulster was, once again, outside my choice. There are two areas of a man's life—and by man, I mean man or woman—those that are chosen for you in your earlier years, and those you choose for yourself later on.

Secondly, being reared not only in Ulster, but on a farm. This meant I had moved from one of the most advanced areas of the twentieth century, New York, back to one of the more . . . shall we say, nineteenth century ways of life? An old-style farm where you had to go to the spring for water, where you had horses, and where our fire was fed with turf, which we had to win up on the high bog. These contrasts were unconsciously implanted in me.

Then I moved on to school, first in Armagh, then down to Dublin. In going to Dublin, I was again making a move, unconsciously, between two states: for Northern Ireland is still technically, officially part of the British Empire, excuse me, of the British Isles—when I was growing up it was part of the British Empire. Then there was the war. My infant psyche experienced in a not too remote way the 1939-1945 war because Ulster was part of it, and many American troops were trained there for D-Day. But when I came down south I moved to the Irish Free State, which, again, was a different world.[1]

Now my urge toward French. I cannot claim in any real way to be a Continental. I haven't spent that much time in Italy. I don't know that much German. So really it is French. I would imagine that I picked up in Dublin, from reading Joyce, and from Beckett, something which appears more frantically later—it is, for instance, very strong in the New Writer's Press group[2]—the idea that an Irishman would become himself if he went to Paris. In some way, he could see his divisions more clearly there. It was partly a leap toward a less smothered world, a leap out of the Republic. One doesn't see that the Ulster poets, apart from Derek Mahon, have much interest in going to the Continent. They head for London, where the publishers are. . . .

Now, why was France so attractive to me? I think when you have that triple pressure on you, three umbilical cords, although the New York one was more vestigial, then moving to another country makes you take a good look back. But I think my great interest in French poetry is connected with a classical training at school, and the haunting fact that I once got first place in Latin in the North of Ireland. I may have wished to continue this form of clarity, this edge.

But as for them being terms of allegiance: the three areas of the world in which I was placed are allegiances now, but they were just things that happened then. France would have been *chosen* as a kind of counteraction.

If one were to choose two poets who make up a watershed in twentieth century verse in English, one might well look to Robert Frost and Ezra Pound, the regionalist and the cosmopolitan, the traditionalist and the modernist. Which of those two poets, in your mind, provides the best example for the contemporary poet?

Well, I think you have outlined there two polarities which exist even in recent Irish writing. I remember a friendly, but slightly belligerent, argument with Seamus Heaney as to this, with his waving the bourbon bottle at me, and saying that Pound finally is not a very important writer and that Frost is much better. There was the author of a book on Pound in the room so Seamus may have wished to have some sport.

These questions are fundamentally unanswerable. Like all questions in poetry, it can only be answered by a poem. Frost, first of all, was not from the area in which he settled. He was from California. I detect, having been an unconscious farmer, that is to say, having worked to some small extent when I couldn't avoid it, having anyway actually worked on a farm, worked with corn, worked with bog, worked with cattle, I can recognize that Frost, in his attitude toward the farm, is not really a country poet. He is a pastoral poet. He may have inserted himself into that life, but the essential heart of Frost does not seem to me to belong to it as Patrick Kavanagh did, *inescapably*. So the work of Robert Frost seems to me to be a kind of pastoral metaphor, an adoption of allegiances—the opposite of what we were talking about in the first question. He chose to write that way in those places. He seemed to assert, certainly in his public persona, that life was far more simple on the farm. Nevertheless, the poems are haunted by madness, loss, absence of love, loneliness. I met him briefly when he came to Dublin. I remember seeing Patrick Kavanagh in the audience: the real farmer broken at the age of fifty, and the professional farmer, hale and hearty, doing his act on the stage. I found the contrast between the two men a very bitter one.

The case of Pound is a disappointing one. I was reading through the early poems which some enterprising professor has reprinted—poems Pound did not want to have reprinted. It shows from the beginning that he had an aesthetic, literary view of life. It is certainly excellent, especially for young poets, to have a desire to ransack a great many literatures, but the need to belong to some place, to come from some place, the need to have a family, the need to learn the elementary emotions of life, is just as important to the poet. There seems to me to be something lacking in either of the two poles of Frost and Pound. The plan, the program of Frost seems to me too simple. We cannot go back to the small farm and build up our fences against our neighbors. On the other hand, we cannot decide that there are no fences and that we can go from China to Japan and from Old English to medieval Provence and leave out some central area belonging particularly to yourself, the family and place that produced you as well.

Was Pound's rejection of formal and philosophical pieties of the Georgians a wrong turn for twentieth century poetry?

No, balls. That had to be cleared. It seemed desperately sad to find Philip Larkin dragging them back into his *Oxford Book of Twentieth Century Poetry.*

I think the ideal method for poetry (and this is where Larkin fails—I don't say he fails as a poet, but as an example) is, on the one hand continually to dig deeper in your own garden patch, in whatever garden patches you have been given or you have claimed, and on the other hand, to try to discover anything across the world which can become accessible to you.

Did you find much that was accessible to your work while you were at the Iowa Writer's Workshop?

I spent three years in America as a graduate student. I went there primarily to meet my father, who went home before I left. That's one of the curious ironies of my historical existence.

But I spent a year at Yale, where the New Criticism was in its . . . ah . . . ah . . . prickly flower. I actually worked a bit with Robert Penn Warren, whom I found to be a very impressive but rather silent man. Harold Bloom was a graduate student; Cleanth Brooks was around; Norman Pearson, Auden's friend, who was very kind to me. It didn't give me all I was looking for, so I headed off west, to the Iowa Writer's [Workshop].

Having been born in Brooklyn, I was rather fascinated by America. Unlike Mr. de Valera I did not feel obliged to change the place of my birth, because he was born there also, in Brooklyn, although he moved it later on over to Manhattan, for prestige. I was curious about the country.

So in the Midwest, in the Iowa Writer's [Workshop], I was very lucky: it was rather a rich class. There was Snodgrass, who was writing very well, rather unfocused, but much more elaborately skillful verse than I was used to in Ireland. I wasn't actually used to the idea of working on poems; in Ireland people gave birth to poems, often misbirths. And then there was Robert Bly, who would suddenly rise to denounce everything written in the class. Donald Justice had just left, but came back halfway through the year. Constance Urdang. A Japanese poet called Saturo Sato. There was Peter Everwine; there was Robert F. Dana and Bill Dickey. I am sorry if I have left anyone out, but certainly you will get the view that it was a very rich class. And Berryman taught us for a while, before being jailed.

As visitors, apart from the staff, we had Louis MacNeice, R. P. Blackmur (once again I was getting yet another member of the New Criticism), and William Carlos Williams, who I thought was the most interesting man I'd met in that year. It was after his stroke and he was a very moving figure to behold and hear: he hugged me, like a son.

Enthroned in the East you had Robert Lowell as the established younger poet and Richard Wilbur as the rising star; in the Midwest the workshop was just beginning to hatch its first prize crop of poets. Somewhere I began to get sick, however, of the well-made poem, so I hied off to Berkeley for a year. And lo and behold! there was a different kind of monster hatching there: Allen Ginsberg. I was at, I think, the second if not the first reading of *Howl.* And at the same reading I heard what I had not yet heard in America—a young man reading poems about physical work. That seemed to link up with where I'd come from, with Patrick Kavanagh. He was reading poems about logging, about working in fields. This, of course, was Gary Snyder. There I seemed to have completed the spectrum of my own generation of American poetry, with, obviously, a few missing names. I wish I had met Robert Duncan there, for example. Or Jack Spicer. But I had got some view of a very strong generation of American poets. And so I was home with my little cargo, satisfied, and prepared to face Ireland again.

Do you think that the work of Irish poets who have stayed in the British Isles is limited in vision or technique?

I can't prescribe for anyone else. I have described the conditions under which I was born and brought up, and which had given me allegiances to several different areas of the English-speaking world. I even have an uncle in Australia. This wide-flung family is the consequence of political dissidence in the state in which they had been brought up. It has given me an awareness which I can't prescribe for others who come from different families and backgrounds.

I do observe with interest that the best of the Irish writers from the South prior to independence, Yeats and Joyce, automatically went abroad, as Beckett did after independence.[3] Joyce and Beckett never came back, while Yeats shuttled back and forth in the most extraordinary way. I don't know how he got the energy—between London, Dublin, and the west of Ireland. He was as much at home in the Saville Club, or in the Cheshire Cheese, as in Sligo.[4]

Note that they are all from the South. The Ulster writers who have now come into their strength can now catch a straight plane from Belfast to London, where, of course, the publishers are. I would sound a warning: this is what the Irish writers of the nineteenth century did, people like Moore, Allingham, de Vere. Each one was related in a secondary way to a leading English poet. They became merely an outlying branch of English poetry, provincials.

So while one part of me—the pleasantly devious peasant part—says why shouldn't Ulstermen get all they can out of the British government *and* the government

of the Republic, the other part of me would ask if emotionally this is an honest attitude. I took out my Irish passport in 1948, although I was entitled to a British passport and an American one.

Isn't there a danger that writers living out of a suitcase where style is concerned. . . .

It has nothing to do with travel.

Well, to put it another way, isn't there a danger that Irish writers, whether living at home or on the road, who reject the Irish tradition and try to imitate the new work of Spanish, American, French, or Colombian poets, will lose a sense of critical standards? . . . that they will be unable to know a good from a bad poem either in English or Portuguese? Consider for instance the work of the New Writer's Press group: Brian Coffey, Augustus Young, and Michael Smith.

Well, I don't want to name names, but this is the opposite naiveté. The argument, on the one hand, that everything should be grounded in the soil, that you should stay home on the farm is falsely limited. None of them do, of course. You will find that the parochial poets are quite as liable to be flying to Toronto as anyone else. My argument with Seamus Heaney about Frost took place in Philadelphia, over Kentucky bourbon, with ice. The opposite and equally narrowing point of view, on the other hand, is the one that poetry takes place only elsewhere and that we should divest ourselves of this absurd Irishness. This was answered very simply by James Joyce, as quoted in the Ellman biography. Joyce met Arthur Power, a gentleman from Waterford, in Paris and asked him what he was reading. Arthur Power said that he was reading an eighteenth century French writer and wished to write in his style. Joyce said, No, you must write in your own tradition, in what is in your heart and blood. The difference between a George Moore and a James Joyce is that Moore was invaded by French examples; Joyce learnt from Flaubert, and he applied it most intensely to his own local word.

Some years ago you edited a collection of poems and essays as a tribute to Austin Clarke.[5] Did Clarke's aggressively critical stance on Irish life have any influence on your own view of either Irish society or the role of the poet?

I admired Austin. I thought him a sad and brave man. His obsession with the Church partly had to do with experiences in his own life which do not completely come through in the work, that is to say his inability to have a divorce in the Irish context and consequent personal problems.

I would have supported Austin as an example of the kind of poet, like Mac Diarmuid in Scotland, like David Jones for Wales, like Graves too, as an inheritor of a mass of tradition. I am interested in his effort to apply his knowledge of the Irish tradition, particularly the bardic area which was his interest, as a criticism of the contemporary Irish life of his time.

It wasn't really a book of essays, but a collection of brief tributes on his seventieth birthday because I wished to encourage him.

It is historically and psychologically true that the poet has a place in Irish society. Rejecting the idea of Irishness, Patrick Kavanagh still lived out the role of "The Poet" within the city of Dublin, an ancient Irish role. He was also unconsciously moved to be a satirist, more in the manner of Swift, the octyosyllabic, than Austin's more ingrown, mordant, and detailed way. But both their lives give evidence of the way a poet's position in this society has a deep historical basis.

You say you can accept Clarke as a poet-scholar of the Irish past. Somewhere I have it in my mind that you have written, "The racial aspect of a poet's heritage must always be unconscious." Didn't Clarke consciously attempt to acquire his racial past, not his family's past, but his national and racial past?

I think we are confusing several things here. The trouble with interviews is that they must always be *simpliste*.

Austin became a scholar of the Irish tradition of poetry. It was not the language in which he was reared, it was his national language but not his mother tongue, as Yeats phrases it. We discussed once how much Irish we had, and we both agreed that we didn't have that much. But he studied what had been done in Irish poetry as an example of something that could be done in the present time.

That's not quite the same thing as racial heritage, which would be historical pain. For example, what I have done in *The Rough Field,* what I have inherited through my family.

Austin went back to study medieval Irish poetry as a technical matter, especially to study a masterpiece like MacConglinne, and to take the persona of the straying cleric, since his name was Clarke, and to use that as a satirical poet-figure. Naturally, that material would have a more intense racial relationship to him than it would if he were studying medieval French.

Clarke never relaxed his effort to carry on what he called, after Thomas Macdonagh, "the Irish Mode." What do you think of that as a matter for a poet's consideration? Should a poet be deliberately Irish?

Ah, no! I think it is very obliging of Austin to have demonstrated this for us. We now have that example before us, an example, I would have to say, which is at

least a partial failure. I don't think a poet should restrict himself in this way, but historically, Austin probably had to. The same principle would apply as with George Moore: if you too deliberately make yourself over into a French writer, you will fail because the French will never accept it. So Austin trying to make himself into an Irish writer is excellent as a technical example for other Irish writers to follow. It is now unconscious with us. We use assonance and internal rhyme like billyoo. I use it, Seamus uses it, all the time. But Austin is not a Gaelic writer.

You would have to get the judgment on Austin from a Gaelic-speaker. He can never be an Irish writer as Sean O'Riordan was, as Martin O'Direan is, he cannot be an Irish writer in that immediate sense at all. But he can help us if Irish does die or fade away as a literature again. At least part of its power will have been transferred into English.

At what point in your own work did you decide to take on the national subject. Was it at the moment commemorated in **The Rough Field** *by the poem beginning "Home again . . ."?*

No, it was much earlier; indeed, it has been there from the beginning. I don't consciously know why I have a strong political side to my nature. I presume it is because of what happened to my family.

The first political poems really are in *Poisoned Lands,* in the sequence called **"The Sheltered Edge,"** which is about the miasma of the Republic after the war. It was a kind of "fen of stagnant waters," to quote Wordsworth. I think that an American-born Ulsterman, born in America because of exile, because of the political trouble of Ulster, who then moves from an Ulster at war to a Dublin at peace, is bound to be aware of these psychological differences in the air, and will attempt, in turn, to diagnose them. Perhaps I was thinking of the example of Auden, who was, of course, the diagnostician of England in the 1930's. His poetry was more or less forced down my neck when I came to UCD (University College Dublin).

The beginning of *The Rough Field* comes immediately after *Poisoned Lands.* It was written in 1962 and was published in an Ulster magazine *Threshold.* Those three sonnets at the beginning—where I catch the bus and come down from Belfast—appeared then. The poem slowly grew out of those sonnets.[6]

I don't know why, but people find it suspect that one should have a strong political side to one's nature. They seem to feel that this is the same kind of thing as voting for a party, which, of course, one does as a human being living in a particular area. But I mean politics in the widest sense—the spiritual atmosphere of a country, one's concern for its spiritual health—this, I think, is one of the strongest strains in contemporary poetry. You find MacDiarmuid now seeing as he ages a Scottish national party, and he may well see Scotland gaining its independence. When he began he was one of the few people who believed in this. Pablo Neruda incarnated the conscience of Chile for years. Octavio Paz's resignation after the Olympics massacre—I would associate this certainly with the position of the poet within the Irish language. He always had a position in relation to his prince, in relation to his polity. Yeats was certainly a political poet. To declare poetry to be a-political seems to me a failure of nerve. Once again I would make a distinction between the Yeats who goes down the streets of Dublin breaking the street lamps because Queen Victoria is due to arrive—that is a *political gesture*—and between the Yeats who wrote poems like "Easter 1916," and "Meditations in Time of Civil War," which are *political poems* in the highest sense.

In an essay on Ferguson, Yeats hinted that centrality and nationality were necessary to poetic greatness. In turning to your family in County Tyrone, and to Irish history as seen through their history, you moved to the center of the nation's problem. Would you agree with Yeats that a poet, to be great, must become the voice of his clan and nation?

Well, becoming the voice of a community is rather different from becoming a national voice. Indeed, the word "nation" in the latter part of this century—since Fascism—has become a colored word. Certainly, I think a poet should speak for his people, out of his people's pain. I could not describe myself as a national voice because Ireland is not yet a nation. It is a broken, incomplete nation. Part of the problem of *The Rough Field* is right here. It is clear from some scenes, such as the scene in the pub called **"The Last Sheaf,"** that the sense of community is a very faulty one.[7] These people only partially feel or know where they are.

But I do speak for a tribal consciousness in that poem.

*The recurrent lament of that poem,"**All my circling a failure to return,**" seems to confess that a poet's self-consciousness and the sophistication of his craft divide him from an idyllic harmony with his people. Can the modern poet really be more than an isolated special voice?*

No, I think this is one of the great strengths of Irish poetry. It may seem hard to believe, but if I had the strength right now, I could, if I am asked, paid for, packaged, and sealed, take a plane off to Vermont or Philadelphia to see Tom Kinsella. But on the other hand, I could drive up, as I hope to in the next fortnight, to see my brother in Ulster, and go to visit the people with whom I was in school and the older people around there.

Any separations between us are not so much the product of my over-education as of false cultures that have come into their lives. The local singing pubs, for instance, would often have country and western. The divisions would be inside them, not inside me. I would be able to go back and know when they were singing their own songs, but in so far as they had been submerged by the great American sub-culture, from Elvis Presley to Nashville, allied also to the big highroads now driven through all the rural areas, with the small farms being bought out in the North (there is almost a law now against staying on a small farm, you are bought out by the State), it is they who are being taken away from what they had, and it is I who am the possessor, and with the older people, the guardian, of what had been there. The family farm and parish are going; Garvaghey is now 205 Omagh Road.[8]

Although many poets have come to light in the North since the firing started, it is surprising how few of them, at least until recently, wrote directly about the Troubles. Do you sympathize with their reticence? Isn't there a danger of being tasteless and commercial in writing about the horrors of modern war, as in the many recent books about the Holocaust?

You mean the Auschwitz poems?

Yes.

Yes. I was rather displeased recently when I read an Irish critic referring to *The Rough Field* as an hysterical poem, and saying that myself and Kinsella were "serving up the horror of it hot." I was displeased because, as I explained earlier, *The Rough Field* was not in any sense an attempt to exploit the Troubles. The Troubles came after *The Rough Field* had been begun, in 1962, with a sense that something might happen. The same sense is in a short story called "The Cry," which is about someone being beaten up in the North, published in 1963. In 1968 came the outbreak in the North, the bursting of the boil; I call it a boil, but another writer, Eugene McCabe, has called it a cancer, a more violent image—with cancer there is a strong possibility of death . . . a body politic gone wrong.

So because of my family, the intense pain caused to not just one Ulster family, but on both sides: my father had been in the IRA and could not accept a job even if he had been offered one; on my mother's side it was much worse: both of her brothers were interned during the Black and Tan War.[9] Her side of the family was completely wrecked by what is called down in the South "The Troubles." They're great for euphemism: the last world war they called "The Emergency." So I inherited this double pain and began my investigation. I was aware that something might happen, or my unconscious was, or my artistic historical interests were directed in that way, whereas the younger Ulster writers, people like Seamus Heaney, Michael Longley—that would be one generation—and Jimmie Simmons, they just wanted to write poetry, they didn't want to have this awful corpse on the doorstep. So they approached it in a more hesitant fashion. I am sympathetic to their diffidence, although I think the bitterness of our province is inescapable. Ulster is something we have to come to terms with. Unless we come to terms with it, there will be a certain lack in us *as writers.*

Now as for "serving up the horror of it hot," my next book is a book of love poems. Having stated from my own point of view the problem in *The Rough Field,* all I added in the third sequence of *A Slow Dance* was to conjure up some images of violence as part of a world pattern of chaos.

When you explore Ulster history . . .

"In one small backward place . . ."[10]

When you explore Ulster history in one small backward place to discover the reason for its present troubles, you seem to imply that the modern Ulsterman is a victim of fate. Those that are blown up or shot become not the victims of the individual choice of the bomber or the sniper, but of an impersonal nexus of historical mistakes.

Not mistakes. . . . The destruction of the O'Neills and the plantation of Ulster were historical *acts.*[11] The systematic pogrom which kept Ulster Catholics in their places from the time of the plantation until now was no mistake. It was part of a deliberate program of . . . well, genocide is a very strong term . . . but certainly a program of victimization, subjection.

Does that sin against a people involve the entire nation in a tragic drama which can only be . . . what technical term should we use from dramaturgy?

Expiated?

Yes, a tragic drama which can only be expiated in blood, with due sacrifices?

O, these are fearsome questions. The historical foundation of Ulster is first of all in the Plantation, and it then was ratified in the Covenant, in our century. The implacable nature of the Ulster Protestant is not an isolated thing, it is allied, for instance, to the deep South. The same kind of Ulster Scots are there in both cases, as I found myself when I went down to Mississippi, Louisiana, and Georgia. It is a kind of rump Protestantism, a form of Calvinism that goes back to John Knox. It is a very powerful ethos—I don't mean theologically, but politically: Ian Paisley's degree is

from Bob Jones University in South Carolina, and Big Ian is straight Bible Belt.[12] We are faced with a group of people who possess power in the North, no, not really possess, they, the rump Protestants, were the puppets used by the Ulster landlords, who now have abdicated: the Chichesters, the Clarkes, the "new" O'Neills. Orangemen cannot historically but take a very poor view of Catholics. They would have had, let's say, the same view of Catholics as a Mississippi white, even Faulkner, would have had of blacks: they were slovenly, they were disloyal, they had too many children, like rabbits, and might outbreed their masters. This phenomenon therefore repeats itself in the American South because the Ulster Scots who were not satisfied with Ulster went on to America, and you know their history there. Of course they wanted freedom, but, unfortunately, in Ulster as well as in America, their freedom seemed to depend on the slavery of someone else. I read Faulkner with instinctive recognition, like a gifted neighbor, possessed by history.

But Ulster is also allied in a peculiar way to South Africa. "Oranje Boven" was the Orange war-cry, and the Dutch Reformed Church is also a form of Calvinism.

This form of rectitude found in the Ulster Protestant (one is upset at how one has to generalize) is an historical anachronism inside the present Irish context. Whether it will end or not depends on whether he can accept some sort of accommodation with his neighbors. But this he will not do, since he regards them as not of the elect. Therefore we have an impasse. An historical impasse is a very grievous thing.

The South has very little to do with it. Even the Declaration of 1916 *in Dublin* meant that the North, whether Protestant or Catholic, was being left to its own devices. The South only partially cares. It would like to see the problem solved, but it only partially understands. Now and again somebody speaks about "Our people in the North," meaning the Catholics, who promptly get hit on the head by somebody who says our people should include the Protestants, who then declare that they are not our people. You've got a Gordian knot, a misery-go-round.

I am not going to condemn, but I am certainly going to say that the central impediment is the refusal of the Ulster Protestant to share, to recognize his neighbors as his equal, to accept that we are all here on one island, Ireland not England.

How can you break that, ease that, without using violence? I do believe in solutions to conflicts in spite of that sequence in *The Slow Dance* which says that violence is inside man, that it begins in the farmyard, which is where I first saw it. That section is an attempt to understand the waves of violence. We now have a world situation in which there are small wars, internecine strife in small areas. The Protestant-Catholic struggle in Ulster is akin to Lebanon, South Africa, Israel, the clash of race *and* religion.

The Provisional IRA were born out of that historical situation, born out of the defencelessness of the Belfast and Derry Catholics, after the Civil Rights Movement had been attacked. Every civilized person in this island would prefer that the Civil Rights Movement had been successful. I would even go so far as to say that the march to Burntollet was a mistake, that it gave an excuse for violence on the Protestant side, that the Civil Rights Movement should have begun to take a low profile at that point because it had the support of the more civilized English.[13] A good many acts of government would have gone onto paper at least. But the Provisionals emerged in answer to this attack and violence began to spread. Since the Northern society would not change, the Provisionals adopted the guerilla technique of destroying the society. Their actions can be historically explained—not excused—explained, because violence begins from the top in a state. The violence which had been perpetrated in the system over three hundred and fifty years led to this campaign to destroy a state responsible for discrimination and partial genocide.

The IRA campaign now seems to have worn itself out. The Civil Rights Movement, in so far as it exists, has now hardened into the shape of the SDLP,[14] the vagueness of the Peace Movement. Things are slowly moving onto a political plane, although there is still a stalemate. You have a massive Army presence in the North, and an increasingly powerful police force. All moves of this sort are really outside the scope of a poet. They are political in the practical sense. The situation, politically, will also be changed by the impending redefinition of the British Isles. Will Scotland achieve independence, or at least nationality, because of the offshore oil? Will Wales achieve its own parliament, or will it be bought off by the big Ford plant? The game of restructuring the British Isles will involve Ulster, just as what's happening in the South will involve Ulster. You must also note the emergence of a small group of British Fascists, little Englanders. A highly intelligent Englishman recently said to me when I asked him what he meant by British, "All those that would like to be English but can never be." This, of course, hits the Ulsterman: he regards himself as British, but he can never be English.

So you can see the complexity of the game. As Conor Cruise O'Brien once said, "The pressures of a community are in inverse proportion to its size." Ulster, then, is a battleground of forces—Catholic and Protestant, English and Irish, smaller units and larger societies, rural and urban (because it was Belfast that tilted

the balance in the North)—there is *no* Protestant majority in the six counties of the North; there is in two counties, the large Belfast hinterland; there is not in the rural areas. My home areas of Tyrone and Fermanagh have consistently voted out, sometimes by narrow margins, despite the bleeding away of immigration. They should never have belonged to the North. Similarly for much of Derry. Similarly for South Armagh, where the Army gets blown up periodically, in what used to be a Gaeltacht, a center of Irish tradition, to which soldiers should never have come.

To move from the political criss-cross of motives to more imaginative solutions with which I amuse myself, I once said that Ireland lost its opportunity to be the first Cuba. If we had had a real revolution, we could have taken advantage of the fact that we are the offshore island of Europe. We could have offered Connemara as a rocket range to the Russians and our coast in the West as a harbor to the Russian fleet; we could have offered the same to the Americans. I don't see why we didn't play this international poker to amuse ourselves. We could have made ourselves rich long ago.

I often think of such visionary solutions to the North. For example, one of the more pathetic exiles from the North was MacGreedy from outside Portadown. He was the champion rose-grower of the world; he won the title in Paris. Now there's an example—breeding a rose in Ulster to win the world prize. Clearly a very great poet in his own line, both regional and global. But he had to exile himself because you can't grow roses anymore in the North of Ireland.

Now if they would all take to growing roses instead of planting bombs . . . you see? If they would all take to playing games which they shared. . . . For instance, I played Gaelic football when I was a boy; I didn't play Rugby football, but I would have liked to have had Protestants to charge against when I was playing my Gaelic games. There is an All-Ireland Rugby team, both Protestant and Catholic. They come down to Dublin and play at Landowne Road. If we had had an All-Ireland soccer team at the time when Georgie Best was here (he was from "gud Protestant stock," a Belfast minister's son, I think), and Johnny Giles from the South—in the 1960's there were half a dozen such brilliant players, Protestant and Catholic, North and South, playing soccer—if we had them all on one team, we might well have got the World Cup! That would have pleased to no end the Irish working class, because soccer is a working class game. That would have been far better than all the Catholics of Ireland going to hurling and Gaelic football, and all the Protestants going to cricket and Rugby.

That's at a semi-facetious level, but there should be mixed education. Absolutely! I will not have my daughter go to schools where she will not have to sit beside Protestants. In any case, since they read the Bible she might learn more about religion. Certainly, one of the blemishes of the North has been the Catholic hierarchy's stand against mixed education, and, until recently, against mixed marriages. I abhor such sectarianism.

So we go from rose-growing, to games, to mixed education, and I think finally, to miscegenation. I think that as much as possible Protestants and Catholics should make love together, any chance they get, providing that they find each other pleasant, of course.

I remember some time ago when I was speaking to a mass audience in O'Connell Street, I suggested a mass Gandhi march on the North, completely unarmed, to go across by every unapproved road and every lane. You couldn't do this now, but then, in 1969, the violence was just beginning. The whole damn South going up every lane singing songs. You could put the politicians in the front with the clergy behind, so that in case they began to shoot, we could get rid of the lot of them, with one good fusillade. Every man from the South could meet any man, Catholic or Protestant, from the North, shake hands, and say, "What's wrong?" or "What have you got against us?"

If I could weave a vast blanket, a blanket to cover the North of Ireland, I would take away all their arms except the arms God has given them and throw them all into this blanket and throw roses over them and let them fight and warm themselves with the arms God has given them.

Any final word?

Yes. I have kept a continuing interest in American poetry because I have had—who could not have?—an intense respect for that great generation of American poets at the beginning of the century. I don't need to number them; you know their names—Pound, Eliot, Stevens, Williams, Crane. They are probably the best generation of poets since the great Romantics. Then I was especially pleased to see such a strong generation in my own time, people ranging from Galway Kinnell to Gary Snyder.

That has been a continuing interest which is now less strong because there is a powerful poetry situation right here in Ireland. Irish poets are probably writing better now than at any time since the Revival, and then, of course, it really only was Yeats. So it seems to me a much more rich field, except, perhaps, for the absence of Yeats: rich and varied, from Kavanagh to Kinsella, Hartnett to Heaney. The linguistic pressures are fascinating; a largely Gaelic tradition expressing itself mainly through the language of the conqueror, many of whose

best poets, from Spenser to Hopkins, spent terms here. As a result, I read less American poetry, and with less hunger, than previously.

But, to return to the Pound-Frost polarity, with Heaney taking Frost, and with the adoption of Edward Thomas in England as an example—I've even heard a lecture comparing Yeats and Edward Thomas, if you don't mind—this polarity seems to me unacceptable. As well as the American poets, I have saluted several older figures in my own time: MacDiarmuid in Scotland, intensely Scots, but to an alarming extent involved in anything around the world he can get his hands on, from Armenian to Patagonian; David Jones for Wales, intensely interested in all kinds of things. If you read *The Anathemata,* it begins with a man saying Mass, and the Mass stone becomes the stones of all the ages as he sinks back through history. In each section he ransacks the cultures of the world; Wales becomes Greece, a hill in Wales becomes Troy. Or Robert Graves, who acknowledges an allegiance to Celtic myth. *The White Goddess* is a magnificent rag-bag, as splendid a rag-bag as *The Vision. The Vision* tries to cover all history, yet Yeats is an intensely local poet, and not only local, he is an intensely personal poet. In his Great Wheel, the mind is dizzy contemplating Alexandria, Babylon, Magi crossing the desert, astronomical and mathematical magic, Arabian lore—all this, and more! So I think the real position for a poet is to be a global-regionalist. He is born into allegiances to particular areas or places and people, which he loves, sometimes against his will. But then he also happens to belong to an increasingly accessible world. Outside my window there is a boat which goes to London. Over that hill is an airport with planes departing for Paris. You have just dropped in from Eliot's St. Louis, Robert Mezey is due next week from California, both of you bringing news of American friends, Wright, Kinnell, Dickey, etc. So the position is actually local *and* international. The irony of such arguments as the ones supporting the Edward Thomas or Frost point of view is that they usually take place against a modern background. such as Heaney and myself having this friendly but belligerent discussion over Pound and Frost while drinking bourbon in Philadelphia, where Tom Kinsella teaches *The Tain.*

—This interview was edited by Mr. Montague from a tape recorded in his home in Cork on Saturday, September 8, 1977.

Notes

1. The Irish Free State, under the leadership of Eamon de Valera, remained neutral throughout the Second World War.

2. The New Writers' Press, edited in Dublin by Michael Smith, publishes the poetry of Augustus Young, Trevor Joyce, Brian Coffey, Thomas MacGreevy, and Michael Hartnett.

3. The Treaty establishing the twenty-six Southern counties of Ireland as the Irish Free State was ratified in 1922.

4. Saville Club: an exclusive Dublin men's club, with membership primarily restricted to wealthy Protestants. Cheshire Cheese: a London pub, and a center of literary life in the 1890's.

5. John Montague and Liam Miller, ed., *A Tribute to Austin Clarke on his Seventieth Birthday, 9 May 1966,* Dublin: Dolmen, 1966.

6.
> To a gaunt farmhouse on this busy road,
> Bisecting slopes of plaintive moorland,
> Where I assume old ways of walk and work
> So easily, yet feel the sadness of return
> To what seems still, though changing.
> No Wordsworthian dream enchants me here
> With glint of glacial corry, totemic mountain,
> But merging low hills and gravel streams,
> Oozy blackness of bog-banks, pale upland grass;
> Rough Field in the Gaelic and rightly named
> As setting for a mode of life that passes on:
> Harsh landscape that haunts me.
> Well and stone, in the bleak moors of dream,
> With all my circling a failure to return.

—the third of the three sonnets at the beginning
of *The Rough Field.*

7.
> . . . Our light
> Is a grease fattened candle, but
> In our gloomy midnight cave
> No one minds, we have reached
> The singing stage. 'The Orange Flute',
> 'The Mountains of Pomeroy', the songs
> That survive in this sparse soil
> Are quavering out, until someone
> Remembers to call on Packy Farrel
> *To say a song.*

> With the almost
> Professional shyness of the folk-singer
> He keeps us waiting, until he rises,
> Head forced back, eyeballs blind.
> *An Bunnan Buidhe.* As the Gaelic
> Rises and recedes, swirling deep
> To fall back, all are silent,
> Tentacles of race seeking to sound
> That rough sadness. At the climax
> He grips the chair before him
> Until the knuckles whiten—
> Sits down abruptly as he rose.
> Man looks at man, the current
> Of community revived to a near-
> ly perfect round . . .

> Soon broken
> As talk expands in drunken detail.
> 'I said to him': 'He swore to me'.
>   . . . . .

It is the usual
Grotesque, half animal evening so
Common in Ireland, . . .

—from "Up For Sale," *The Rough Field,* pp. 44-45.

8. Garvaghey (*Garbh acaidh:* Gaelic for "a rough field") is the Ulster district in which Montague grew up, now an address on the new expressway running through Tyrone, the Omagh Road.

9. The Black and Tan War: conflict between English soldiers and Irish republicans in 1920 and 1921. The English soldiers wore a mixed dress of army khaki and police black, and so came to be called "Black and Tans."

10.
> . . . All around, my
> Neighbors sleep, but I am
> In possession of their past
> (The pattern history weaves
> From one small backward place)
> Marching through memory magnified . . .

—from "The Source," *The Rough Field,* p. 49.

11. Destruction of the O'Neills (the leading clan of Ulstermen) and colonization of their land by English Protestants was the standard policy of English regents since the Tudors, but it was firmly established by Cromwell in his Irish campaign of 1642. The plantation of Ulster formed the basis for the future division of Ireland in the Government of Ireland Act of 1920.

12. Ian Paisley: leader of the militant Free Presbyterian Church in Northern Ireland, and a fierce warrior against Popery.

13. On January 1, 1969, The People's Democracy (an offshoot of the Irish Civil Rights Association) led a protest march from Belfast to Derry, and were savagely attacked along the way by militant Protestants in Burntollet.

14. SDLP: The Social and Democratic Labour Party. The SDLP represents moderate Catholic opinion, and pursues social reform through parliamentary action.

Benedict Kiely (essay date December 1978)

SOURCE: Kiely, Benedict. "John Montague: Dancer in a Rough Field." *Hollins Critic* 15, no. 5 (December 1978): 1-14.

[*In the following essay, Kiely offers an overview of Montague's most important collections of poetry, noting the mixture of modern love and ancient mythology, of personal agony and national—even global—mourning that informs his best work.*]

I

If I were, as I am, beginning a re-reading of John Montague, or if I were advising others where to begin reading him, I would go, and send those others to the heart of his collection, *Tides,* which had the Poetry Book Society Recommendation in 1970. And to two works there, one of them a quite horrifying prose-poem entitled with a cold irony that is typical of Montague: **"The Huntsman's Apology."** As you will see, it is not likely to be used as an argument for the defense by the unspeakable who pursue the inedible, or by those genial knee-booted Kerrymen who know by the inner voice that little hunted hares really love the chase. This is it:

> "You think I am brutal and without pity but at least I execute cleanly because, like any true killer, I wish to spare the victim. There are worse deaths. I have seen the wounded bird trail her wing, and attract only the scavenger. 'Help me', he croaks as he hops near. One dart of her beak would settle him, for he is only a pale disciple of death, whom he follows at a distance. But when she needs sympathy and when he calls 'I am more unhappy than you' her womanly heart revives and she takes him tinder her broken wing. Her eyesight is poor and her senses dulled but she feels an echo of lost happiness as he stirs against her breast. She does not realize that he is quietly settling down to his favourite meal of dying flesh, happily enveloped in the smell of incipient putrefaction. The pain grows and spreads through her entire body until she cries aloud but it is too late to shake off his implanted beak. He grinds contentedly on and, as she falls aside, his bony head shoots up, like a scaldy out of a nest. His eye is alert, his veins coursing with another's blood, and for a brief moment as he steps across the plain without looking back, his tread is as firm as a conqueror's."

The second work is brief, called **"A Meeting,"** and is from the ninth-century Irish:

> "The son of the King of the Moy
> met a girl in green wood a mid-summer's day:
> she gave him black fruit from thorns
> and the full of his arms
> of strawberries where they lay."

The startling thing is that both are poems about varieties of love, or about love at different stages, of development or decay. They come at the heart of a book that holds other fine love-poems and in which the blurb, with perhaps an echo of the poet's voice, says with a great deal of justification that the directness and passion of Montague's love-poems have been admired, and his feeling for people and landscape, and claims that in this collection, *Tides,* all these are seen as a part of a larger struggle where life and death are interwoven like the rhythms of the sea. Love in green woods at midsummer has its black fruit from thorns and a plenteousness of strawberries. Love can also be a rasping and cankerous death.

He has a nightmare in which he lies "strapped in dream helplessness" and some hand unseen, unknown is cut-ting up the body of the beloved, till the rhythm of the blade rising, descending, "seems the final meaning of life." Released from the dreadful dream, he lies in a narrow room, "low-ceilinged as a coffin," while outside the Liffey knocks against the quay walls and the gulls curve and scream over the Four Courts: Gandon's great domed building, the flower of the 18th century, the heart in Ireland of unalterable law. There is much agony in these love-poems, a something not allowed—for when, in one of the most celebrated passages of raving about love, Shakespeare allows Berowne to take off for seventy or so lines, and a lover's eye will gaze an eagle blind, a lover's ear will hear the lowest sound, a lover's feeling is more soft and sensible than are the tender horns of cockled snails: but Berowne had not at that moment, and as Shakespeare well knew, arrived at consummation not to speak of satiation. Montague, lean and sharp and soft and sensible, as Berowne uses the word, sees his lovers absurdly balanced on the springs of a bed, shadows swooping, quarreling like winged bats, bodies turning like fish "in obedience to the pull and tug of your great tides." A wind-swept holiday resort on the shore of the North sea becomes a perfect setting for the monster of unhappiness, "an old horror movie come true," to crawl out of the moving deeps and threaten love. The hiss of seed into a mawlike womb is the whimper of death being born: and lovers whirl and turn in their bubble of blood and sperm before, from limitless space, the gravities of earth claim them. Back from the business of loving, resuming workaday habits with the putting-on of clothes, the lover finds himself, comically driving through late traffic, and changing gears with the same gesture that a while ago had eased the "snowbound heart and flesh" of the beloved. It is a bitter sort of comedy.

II

It is scarcely then by accident that he places in the middle of all these love-poems the best rendering, from the Irish of the ninth-century, of the love-dirge, or bitter memory of past loves and bitter consciousness of bodily decay, of the Cailleach Beara, the Hag or Old Woman of Beare: which is the southwestern peninsula between Bantry Bay and Kenmare Bay, the land of the O'Sullivans. The Cailleach, a formidable ancient, overburdened with all knowledge and weariness and sometimes, all wickedness, is a recurring figure in Celtic mythologies and shows her face, on occasions and on various bodies, in Montague's poetry.

A one-eyed hag, she—or the poet who interpreted her, as Montague does eleven centuries later—reckons that her right eye has been taken as a down-payment on her claim to heaven, a ray in the left eye has been spared to her that she may grope her way to heaven's gate. Her life has come to be a retreating sea with no tidal return. Gaunt with poverty she, who once wore fine petticoats, now hunts for rags to cover her body. The great and generous gentlemen who once made love to her have now ridden on into eternity, their places taken by skin-flints, well-matched with girls who now think less of love than of money: and she looks at her arms, now bony and thin, that once caressed with skill the limbs of princes. Yet she gives thanks to God that she has lived and loved and feasted royally and misspent her days, even though now, to offer up that gratitude, she prays by candlelight in a darkened oratory and drinks not meat nor wine with Kings, but sips whey in a nest of hags: a memory. Never more can she sail youth's sea, she hears the cry of the wave, "whipped by the wintry wind," and knows that today no one will visit her, neither nobleman nor slave: and the poem rises to that recurring consideration of life as ebb **** and flow, and it may be that it was that very image that attracted Montague so strongly to the ancient poem:

> "Flood tide
> And the ebb dwindling on the sand!
> What the flood rides ashore
> The ebb snatches from your hand
>
> "Flood tide
> And the sucking ebb to follow!
> Both I have come to know
> Pouring over my body. . . . . . .
>
> "Man being of all
> Creatures the most miserable—His
> flooding pride always seen
> But never his tidal turn.
>
> "Happy the island in mid-ocean
> Washed by the returning flood. . . ."

In this collection, one of the two most striking poems is certainly: **"Life Class."** It opens calmly, clinically, a cool detailed survey of the body there to be studied, the hinge of the ankle-bone defining the flat space of a foot, the calf's heavy curve sweeping down against the bony shin, the arm cascading from shoulder-knob to knuckle, shapes as natural, as inanimate almost, as sea-worn caves, as pools, boulders, tree-trunks. This is the artist in the neolithic cavern recording in wonderment the skeleton of the life he sees, an art that may have been as utilitarian as modern engineering. Until the awakening comes to the existence of secret areas: "hair sprouting crevices, odorous nooks and crannies of love awaiting the impress of desire." Thereafter, the frenzy of the desert father tormented by images and visions that drag man down "to hell's gaping vaginal mouth." Until the eye and the mind swing the other way and the phantom of delight (Wordsworth did not follow it neither into the desert nor to helps mouth—as far as we know, that is) becomes an ordinary housewife earning a few shillings extra, a spirit, good or evil, yet a woman too: and the very soul of the machine blossoms, "a late flower," into a tired smile over a chilled cramped body.

The other poem, **"The Wild Dog Rose,"** follows the woman into more terrible and more holy places. It confronts again the cailleach, the ancient enchanted hag who recurs in our mythologies and in Montague's poetry. The image of the cailleach in this poem is a figure who haunted his childhood, lived in a cottage, circled by trees and with a retinue of whining dogs, on a hill-slope in South Tyrone. A grown man, a young poet, he walks to see her and the outside appearance is as it was when she used to terrify his boyhood: the great hooked nose, the cheeks dewlapped with dirt, staring sunken eyes, mottled claws, a moving nest of shawls and rags. But she talks to him gently and sadly about her memories of youth, her own unimportant sorrows: she is kin to the Gailleach Beara and in her own coulisse in time, and the dogrose shines in the hedge: and there is no sense of horror until she tells him of the night when a drunken oaf staggered into her cottage and attempted to rape her. She prays to the Blessed Virgin for help and after a time she breaks his grip, he sleeps and snores on the floor, then awakes in shame and lurches away across the wet bogland:

> ". . . . . . . The wild Rose
> is the only rose without thorns,
> she says, holding a wet blossom
> for a second, in a hand knotted
> as the knob of her stick.
>
> "Whenever I see it, I remember
> the Holy Mother of God and
> all she suffered."

That image of the Cailleach reappears again when in his poem-sequence, *The Rough Field,* he stands squarely facing into the past and present of his own place and people, and meditates also on some of his own personal agonies. He has a regulated passion for retracing his steps, changing and rearranging.

There is much more in the collection, *Tides,* than I have here indicated: more than love and lust, and woman, young and old, and ancient mythologies. There are, for instance, wise words to and about Beckett, and about Joyce, and a moving farewell to places and parents, and a seagull's view of his own town which misses only history and religion: which Montague is not to miss when later he takes a more-than-seagull's view of Garvaghey (Garbh Achaidh), *The Rough Field,* where he comes from. The collection, too, is rich, as is his earlier poetry, with the preoccupations of a man who has known, and to the bone, the ways of three countries: Ireland, France and the USA.

III

He was born in New York in 1929 of Irish parents who had left Ireland in the confusion following the Troubles of the 1920's. From an early age, as he said to Mary

Leland in an interview article in *The Irish Times,* (Nov. 23, 1976), he was aware of the confusion of the time through the unhappiness of his parents and had also an "emerging sense of hi-location" out of which he was to make a theme. As a child he was shipped back to Ireland and grew up on a farm in South Tyrone, in Ulster, with his father's unmarried sisters, somewhat isolated from the rest of his family, a situation that has also left its mark on his work.

Something of this I myself was aware of from away back. In my final year in high school, in 1936, a young fellow called Montague, American-born, came into third year and right away became of a group who were attempting to found a school magazine. Several of us then thought that this young man was so bright in a literary way that he was destined, or doomed, to become a writer. As it happened he became a medical doctor, and it wasn't until the late 1940's that a young man, whose name I was already aware of in the magazines and elsewhere, came into my house in Clontarf, in Dublin city, with some other college people of the time and said, quietly and confidently, that he would be the writer of the Montagues and that I had, for a while, gone to school with his elder brother.

By his own words, written down two years ago for a revised edition of his first collection, *Poisoned Lands,* he was not at that time as confident as he seemed. In the early 1950's he was 'discovering with awe' that he might possibly 'be able to write something like the kind of modern poetry' he admired. But in the 'acrimony and insult' of the poetic world of Dublin at the time he found out that the atmosphere was against doing anything of the kind. To explain the subtleties, more social than literary, involved in all that would need an essay five times as long as this one. The easiest way to understanding would be to do as I have done: come to Dublin permanently, say at the age of twenty and in 1940, and live there ever since, seeing it, I hope, steadily and seeing it whole. Voltaire, you'll remember, suggested to somebody who was anxious to do something of the sort that one way to found an enduring religion would be to be crucified and to rise from the dead.

IV

In 1977 he reworked his first collection, *Poisoned Lands,* which had originally appeared in London in 1961. The nature of the revisions, additions and subtractions, from one edition to the other, has been thoroughly examined by the poet, Seamus Deane, in a review in *Hibernia* for June 10, 1977. Montague himself said: "It became not so much the case of an older writer wishing to correct his younger self as of trying to release that earlier self from chains of time and place." He pleasantly recorded that in the years between, Mr. T. S. Eliot had

said: "I have, indeed, found Mr. Montague's poems worthy of study." We are all allowed those little moments in the sun, eyes happily closed when, that is, we get the chance to enjoy them.

Sidney Keyes, the young English poet who went to his death in the battle of North Africa, was garrisoned for a while with the British Army in my native town of Omagh, Co. Tyrone, sixteen miles away from Montague's Rough Field—Garvaghey or Garbh Achaidh. A friend of mine (now living in Indiana but coming from that same garrison town) who knew Keyes well, says that he told her that he, an Englishman, was never happy in Ulster; he said the land brooded, waiting. A pity that the young American-Irish Montague and the doomed English soldier-poet never could have met: they could easily have walked within arm-reach of each other on Omagh street: and right in the middle of *Poisoned Lands,* and for reasons that have to do with the same long history of the offshore islands, Montague senses the brooding and waiting that had disturbed Keyes.

"At times," he writes, "on this island at the sheltered edge of Europe. . . . . green enclosure of monks and quiet poetry . . . . . . we are afraid as the hints pile up a disaster . . . . . . Our best longings," are, "helpless, as the clouds begin hanking for a more ominous day." So he considers and incantates in a time of peace: and a brutal farmer who hates country people strides across symbolically-poisoned lands with four good dogs dead in one night and "a rooster, scaly legs in air, beak in the dust." The poet remembers how, as a boy, he carried water twice a day from a spring-well, and he sets the scene and crystallises the experience in a poem as pure and lucid as the water, and hopes to stylise that experience "like the portrait of an Egyptian water-carrier," but is halted and entranced "by slight but memoried life": a phrase of great subtlety and significance. The Cailleach, the Sean Bhean Bocht (the Poor Old Woman) of myth and of patriotic balladry, appears to him "her eyes rheumy with racial memory." She could be Mother Ireland, she could be that lovely Cathleen who followed St. Kevin to his cave in Glendalough and was, by the chaste and irate saint, thrown into the deeper of the two lakes. The poet, at home on his own hills, climbs up through red cornfields at the end of summer to see on the summit the secret spirals on the pre-historic burial stone and to wonder "what hidden queen" lies there in dust: and turning the page from that moment he comes on one of those golden phrases that happen only to the most fortunate poets: "Like dolmens around my childhood, the old people." It is one of his most important and most memorable poems and later on he is to work it into the intricate pattern of *The Rough Field.* He remembers some old people Orange and Green, who lived around his early rural years. He concludes splendidly:

"Ancient Ireland, indeed! I was reared by her bedside,
The Rune and the chant, evil eye and averted head,
Fomorian fierceness of family and local fend,
Gaunt figures of fears and friendliness,
For years they trespassed on my dreams,
Until once, in a standing circle of stones,
I felt their shadows pass.

"Into that dark permanence of ancient forms."

In that poem and, generally, in **Poisoned Lands,** and in the following collection, **A Chosen Light,** he has hammered his thoughts, and his places. into unity, and, also, the past and present of his own country. The shape of his mind has been made clear and his style has a sinewy sort of seeming nonchalance on which he is steadily to work and rework giving "slight but memoried life" a deep, universal significance. He casts a careful eye even on an old-style country byte and sees the milking-machine at work, and the old ways changing. He follows Murphy, an Irish worker, to the factories of Manchester, and balances his lot there against the possibilities of stagnation and madness in an Irish midland village.

He walks among mythologies on the grassy mounds of the hill of Tara that was the residence of the High Kings of pre-Christian Ireland, and wonders was it a Gaelic acropolis or a smoky hovel, and sees wolf-hounds "lean as models," follow at the heels of heroes out of the sagas: a sardonic bringing-together of the images of two ages. In Bernini's baroque Rome he watches Irish pilgrims, "matrons, girdled in nun-like black," marching with head and book relentlessly towards their God. The strangest variety of objects and people become symbols before his clear and wondering eye: an aging Irish priest watching bathing beauties on an Australian coast and remembering his own youth: a crazy old priest on an Irish street seeing young girls lilting their light skirts, hearing them (or imagining he hears them) cry out at a listless man in sunshine, wearing black: the pantomimic figures of the rural mummers. St. Patrick, St. George, Satan, remembered from a winter in boyhood: a tortured Catalan Christ seen in a cultural centre in New Haven, Connecticut: tired travellers dwarfed by snowy mountains at a bus-stop in Nevada: thirty quids worth of silky hair, a neighbour's dog, "shameless manhood, golden fleece . . . . . with a visage as grave as Richelieu," that he walks in the Champ de Mars in Paris . . . This is a rich and varied world.

In a mountain-brook, as a boy, he fingers for trout and years later, in a Paris street, he can feel on his hands the taste of the terror the hunted has for the hunter. Remembering a girl who spent herself too easily, and for whom he had a sort of distant, undefined affection, he realises that in that countryside "even beauty cannot climb stairs." He walks with an Irish virgin in the Dublin mountains: and crosses the American continent to meet a love not so virginal: and an uncle, a folk-musician, leaves for the New World in an old disgrace, and the nephew watches the abandoned violin gather dust and decay, and remembers that uncle in a poem and knows that "succession passes through strangest hands."

By the end of his second collection, **A Chosen Light,** he has gathered together and arranged like ornaments his foreign experiences, he can cast a calm eye even if it is an eye of foreboding, on his own country: and the calmness and foreboding can burst into bawdy laughter when he walks out at a folk-music festival in Mullingar at which, to judge by reports at the time, fornication was rife:

"At the Fleadh Cheoil in Mullingar
There were two sounds, the breaking
of glass, and the background pulse
of music. Young girls roamed
the streets with eager faces,
Pushing for men. Bottles in
Hand, they rowed out for a song:
Puritan Ireland's dead and gone
A myth of O'Connor and O'Faolain."

V

Utter assurance comes to Montague with the composition and arrangement of **The Rough Field,** his most remarkable book and one of the most interesting statements made in this century about Ireland past and present.

From a rump parliament of old friends who spend a night discussing a crate of bottles in a mountain cabin, the poet staggers home through the sleeping countryside. He peers over a humped bridge listening in the dark to the:

"Unseen rattle of this mountain
Stream, whose lowland idlings
Define my townlands shape."

He remembers the day he climbed to find the stream's source, through the lifeless, lichened thorn of MacCrystal's Glen and on and up until he came to a "pool of ebony water fenced by rocks," and groped under the rocks in the pool for the monstrous legendary trout to find only the cold source of the stream's life, the spring beating like a heart. Wondering if that was the ancient trout of wisdom he was meant to catch he goes seven-league-booting it on through the darkness, remembering an old man who raged at him to keep cows away from a well that is now "boarded-up," like the old man himself, remembering how he and the old man's son had once at that place kicked honeycombs around the grass until their boots smelled sweet for days afterwards, remembering how "every crevice held a secret sweetness" in summers gone forever. Now in the night:

". . . . . all around, my
Neighbors sleep, but I am
in possession of their past
(The pattern history weaves
from one small backward place)
Marching through memory magnified:
Each grassblade bends with
Translucent beads of moisture
And the bird of total meaning
Stirs upon its hidden branch."

There, you could perhaps say, is the core of **The Rough Field.** It is a unity, a movement and sequence of poems as strong and steady as the mountain stream descending on the lowlands to define a world, taking with it the past and present of that one small backward place, but a place over-burdened with history: for it is part of the country of the great Hugh O'Neill who warred for nine years against Elizabeth the first of England. Montague glosses his text, indeed, with fragments of ancient history, with a clipping now and then from current news, even with a bigot's letter pushed through a letter-box and ranting against the Romish wafer.

The bookmaker, Liam Miller of the Dolmen Press, a supreme artist in the making of books, has ornamented this one with woodcuts from John Derricke's: "The Image of Irelande with a Discoverie of Woodkerne, 1581." The result is a book of full meaning and exceptional beauty, and Montague's steady advance towards his mastership in verse brings him to great achievement.

The place, as I've said, is Garvaghey, a rough field, on the road between Ballygawley and Omagh as you go north: I pass it myself on the way to my own early haunts. The father who stayed in New York, when the infant son was brought back to Ireland, revisits the family, and father and son walk Garvaghey together, not smiling, "in the shared complicity of a dream," for when "weary Odysseus returns, Telemachus must leave." But the memory of his father stays with him on those hills and in New York City. Family history and his own personal agony, and the history of the place over three and a half centuries, onward from the end of the great O'Neill to the calamities of the present, are all twisted together, strands in a strong rope. Beginning this book he goes west by bus from Victoria station in Belfast and the historical gloss tells us how that Lord Mountjoy who had inherited the land from Charles Blount, the victor for Elizabeth over O'Neill at the battle of Kinsale, arrived first on the same route by coach in Omagh all that time ago. Ending almost the book, he celebrates the city of Derry through which from the translantic liner, the poet himself came home to Garvaghey.

Nowhere in the book is the tight razor-edged discipline of his verse and his uncanny knack for gathering the ages together more on display than in the movement that deals with the present problems of Derry City, **"A**

Second Siege." Derry (Doire) the Oak-Grove of the Celtic St. Colmcille is there, and the Londonderry of the settlement by the London merchants of the 17th century, and of the first renowned siege in the wars between William of Orange and James Stuart, and the shattered Derry of the bombs and the battle in the Bogside in the last nine dreadful years:

"Once again it happens
Under a barrage of stones
and flaring petrol bombs
the blunt, squat shape of
an armoured car glides
into the narrow streets
of the Catholic quarter
leading a file of helmeted,
shielded riot police;
once again it happens,
like an old Troubles film,
run for the last time. . . . . . ."

An extra dimension is introduced from his experiences elsewhere and Irish troubles are seen as part of the world's experiences. He was in Berkeley, California, for the beginning of the campus tumults there, and bombs in the Bogside and napalm in Vietnam are all part of the human condition:

"Lines of protest
lines of change
a drum beating
across Berkeley
All that Spring
invoking the new
Christ avatar
of the Americas
Running voices
Streets of Berlin
Paris, Chicago
Seismic waves
Zigzagging through
a faulty world."

He means faulty as in earthquakes and he surveys a world that may, as because of the San Andreas fault, California may, fall apart any of these days. Although he can be agonized and terrified by memory it could still be that he is happiest with those old people who, like dolmens, surrounded his childhood: Jamie MacCrystal who sang to himself a broken song without tune: Maggie Owens who was "a well of gossip defiled": the Nialls who lived among blooming heather bells but were all blind; Billy Harbinson who married a Catholic servant girl and was forsaken by both creeds, but who still aggressively wore howler and sash when the great day came around. Dolmens may be immune to earthquakes.

He is so well aware that he was reared by the bedside of an ancient Ireland that another poet said "knew it all." He knows (as I've quoted) the rune and the chant, the head averted from the evil eye, the Fomorian fierceness of feud. Even when he wrote those words he never dreamed that they could become as bitterly true as they have become in north-east Ulster since 1969. Standing in his rough field on a Tyrone hillslope he surveys his world and finds it precarious. He travels south through the county of Cavan and sees the same changing patterns from Ulster to the Ukraine and wonders as he also does in the **"Hymn to the New Omagh Road"** on the balance sheet of change:

> "Harsh landscape that haunts me,
> Well and stone, in the bleak moors of dream
> with all my circling a failure to return
> to what is already going,
> > going. . . .
> > GONE.

VI

Since *The Rough Field* there have been two collections, *A Slow Dance* and *The Great Cloak*. Little space have I left myself to consider them, but you will find that they richly reward reading and re-reading, right through—so to speak, for the pace, arrangement and continuity are insistent, and they amply justify Robin Skelton's strong claim that Montague is: "clearly one of the most skilled and interesting poets alive, and one of the most original and disturbing." The poet, approaching fifty, has the confidence and assurance, and for very good reasons, that the young man thirty years ago pretended to have. The pared-down lines are rich in irony, humanity, the sense of transience and mortality in love, in men and women, in nations and civilizations: a keen, exact expression.

That slow dance is a dance of life and death, of calm observation alternating with strange fantasy:

> "Darkness, cave
> drip, earth womb
>
> We move slowly
> back to our origins
>
> the naked salute
> to the sun disc
>
> the obeisance
> to the antlered tree
>
> the lonely dance
> on the grass"

He sees a sawmill on the road to Geneva; sees life emerge, a calf licked clean by a cow, from the cave of an old limekiln in Ireland: life and death and despair in a wintry courtyard with (in a fine refrain) snow curling in on the cold wind: writes a song for the shade of John Millington Synge: studies a snail, whorled house and all, that playing children have left on the table full of

books at which he works: speaks for an old bitch of a dowager in a western castle: returns home to walk with neighbors under Knockmany hill: sees strange symbols, a Celtic Moloch, a modern high-rise hotel gutted by terrorist bombs, in the Cave of the Night: "Godoi, godoi, godoi! Our city burns and so did Troy." Sees his father returning from America through the customs at Cobh, and travels with him to a moment of recognition. Sees an old French colonel in his final retreat in a Normandy chateau. Writes a lament "so total" that it mourns no one but the great globe itself.

"The Great Cloak" is an intensely personal poem-sequence about the death of love, and abandonment and betrayal, about the birth and growth of a new love:

> "As my Province burns
> I sing of love,
> Hoping to give that fiery
> wheel a shove."

The only poem I can compare it with, and it is very much a unity and no haphazard collection, is George Meredith's, "Modern Love": yet if it can, at times. be tense with agony and regret, it does not end as Meredith does in a sort of half-resigned despair, but rises to hope and renewal and a new life being born. No mortal who has realized that life is not a straight line can fail to be moved by this poem: happier people should cross themselves and thank whatever gods there be for something like good fortune.

> "I'll tell you a sore truth, little understood.
> It's harder to leave, than to be left . . . . . ."
>
> "A feel of warmth in this place.
> In winter air, a scent of harvest.
> No form of prayer is needed,
> when by sudden grace attended.
> Naturally, we fall from grace.
>
> "Mere humans, we forget what light
> led us, lonely, to this place."

As I end this essay I see in *The Irish Times* a new Montague poem: writing, as Spenser and others did about Mutabilitie bat with, you might say, a touch of return divilmecarum:

> "Sing a song for
> things that are gone,
> minute and great,
> renowned or unknown.
>
> "The library of Alexandria,
> the swaying Howth tram,
> the Royal city of Hue,
> the pub of Phil Ryan.
>
> "Now, nearing fifty, I
> have seen substantial things
> hustled into oblivion . . . . . ."

Paul Mariani (essay date fall/winter 1979)

SOURCE: Mariani, Paul. "Fretwork in Stone Tracery." *Parnassus* 8, no. 1 (fall/winter 1979): 249-59.

[*In the following review of* A Slow Dance *and* The Great Cloak, *Mariani contends that although the two volumes were published three years apart, they both deal with the same subject matter—"old laments and modern loves and their different musics."*]

John Montague published these two sequences three years apart, though their subjects—old laments and modern loves and their different musics—cover the same five-year period in his life. But for the accidents of economics and publishing schedules, these two sequences might have been printed together in 1975. *A Slow Dance* is by far the stronger of the two books and I cannot read it without thinking of the old, pre-Nineteenth Century Irish tunes that belong to a primitive world with its convoluted melodic line, dirge-like and unearthly, like a keening. Only Seamus Heaney among Irish writers today can compare with Montague when it comes to evoking this old Irish music with its vigor, its subtle webbing, its rainsoaked landscape of gray rock and burren, hedgerow and hawthorn and bog. And if *A Slow Dance* is not Montague's most ambitious book—that honor belonging to his earlier sequence on the Irish troubles, *The Rough Field* (1971)—then it is still his strongest and most satisfying to date, touching a world aligned to Ireland's distant past: somber, unrelenting, pagan, aristocratic, like fine fretwork in stone tracery.

It is Yeats who stands behind this music, though Montague has managed to come close to the unadorned, stubborn ground of Ireland's being, without Yeats's Romantic overlay and without recourse to his vatic posturing and myopic rhetoric. At its best, Montague's language is more attuned than Yeats's to the rare phosphorescence of Ireland's ancient past. There is in Montague a clearing of the field, a greater knowledge of the past understood in its own uncompromising terms, with less guesswork, less anxiety over generating all-encompassing Irish myths. What we hear are the old instruments resurrected: the shrill and beat of tin whistle, fiddle, harp, *bodhrán,* and bones, as in the jagged rhythm of

> Darkness, cave
> drip, earth womb
>
> we move slowly
> back to our origins
>
> the naked salute
> to the sun disc
>
> the obeisance

to the antlered tree

> the lonely dance
> on the grass. . . .

Or here, in the poet's tribute to the modern Irish composer, Ó Riada:

> two natives warming themselves
> at the revived fire
> in a ceilinged room
> worthy of Carolan—
>
> clatter of harpsichord
> the music of leaping
> like a long candle flame
> to light ancestral faces
>
> pride of music
> pride of race.

Yeats claimed to be among the last Romantics, yet forty years later we have still not escaped his valedictory note. Nor is this any less true for Montague. The difference, however, between his Romanticism and Yeats's is that he has cut his Romantic stance closer to the bone, making it more of a tribal affair, grafting his own line onto Yeats's late wintry branch: that stark, disconsolate, percussive line we find in the last plays and poems. (One other poet comes to mind when I read *A Slow Dance* the H. D. of the *Trilogy* and *Helen in Egypt.* Montague is as much the druid priest as H. D. is the ancient priestess.)

Besides the melodic line there is in Montague the realist's lens, images heightened and isolated by the jagged contours of the lines themselves:

> His vestments
> stiff with the dried blood
> of the victim, old Tallcrook advances
>
> singing & swaying
> his staff, which shrivels & curls:
> a serpent ascending a cross.

Or consider this portrait of an old French colonel, retreating into the prison of the self, silent, sliding towards his own extinction:

> I heard the floorboards creak
> as, cloudhuge in his nightgown,
> he prowled the house, halting
> only when, gnawed by the worm
> of consciousness, disappointment
> at disappointment, he stood
> on the porch to inhale
> the hay and thistle scented
> air of a Normandy harvest;
> piss copiously in salutation
> towards a shining moon.

A Slow Dance reveals a great deal about how Montague takes hold of a subject and finds a style to work it with. He claims a field and marks it with his own

scratches the way animals stake out territorial preroga-
tives. He wrestles forms—a wide variety of them, both
closed and open—and makes them his own, even if it
means twisting their necks into submission. He has
used the sequence to ride over a 64-page format (a limit
defined as much by the printer as anyone). Of the four
sequences he published in the 1970s, only *The Rough
Field* spilled over to a crowded 88 pages.

And these *are* true sequences. *A Slow Dance,* for
example, begins with a seven-poem section celebrating
the old blood-hungry gods of Ireland. The section
salutes the old dolmens and stone circles that dot the
Irish and English countryside, dating back to a time
before Ireland's memories of England turned so
violently bitter. It is no surprise, then, that in this ancient
Ireland the venerable litany to the Blessed Mother
should give way to a litany for the Hillmother, the
female earthsource, renewer, delighter, beginning and
end:

> Moist fern
>   unfurl for us
> Springy moss
>   uphold us
> Branch of pleasure
>   lean on us . . .
> Hidden cleft
>   speak to us.

A contrapuntal melody, the male of it facing the female,
the slow, stately dance cleansing and healing, putting
one in touch with one's humble beginnings in the earth
and transforming the dancer into the greatrooted blos-
somer. "Totally absent," a prose piece runs, "you shuffle
up and down, the purse of your loins striking against
your thighs, sperm and urine oozing down your lower
body like a gum."

The poem's last section closes like a diptych. Lining up
with the opening sequence, this powerful, elemental lament is for Ó Riada, the Irish composer who worked so
successfully in the old Irish musical tradition and who
died in 1971. It is an antiphon calling across to the
slow dance at the beginning of the volume, Ó Riada's
impersonal, tormented music merging with Montague's
sad lines until we too hear that keening,

> Beyond the flourish
> of personality, peacock
> pride of music or language:
> a constant, piercing torment!

There are moments of earned privilege in Montague's
dirge when he summons the whole weight of the pres-
ences of Ireland's tradition to welcome their dead
brother into the ancient blackness that for Montague is
older than Homer, Virgil, or Carolan:

> The slant of rain on void eye sockets,
> The shrill of snipe over mountains

> Where a few stragglers nest in bracken—
> After Kinsale, after Limerick, after Aughrim,
> After another defeat, to be redeemed
> By the curlew sorrow of an aisling.

For the most part, Montague maintains an icy control
over his subjects; syntax chafes against line break and
the chiseled images pluck pizzicato against eye and ear.
But sometimes, ever the Irish republican, he slips over
into sentimentality, especially when he tries to deal with
human love. For if Ireland has its proud, aloof blind
bards strumming the golden hairs of ancient harps, their
visions blazing into the dark skull as words begin to
tumble into the thin air, she also has her tradition of
beerhall and pub, where patriotic ballads recall the old
tragedies and stir us in spite of ourselves. No less a
figure than Joyce himself was wary of this all-devouring,
sentimental popular music, with its come-hithers and
"Wild Colonial Boys." Only by turning the tradition on
its head and keeping a safe distance from those sirens
was he able to escape that sentimentality which
sometimes catches up Montague.

Looked at from the angle of cultural retrieval, however,
Montague and the other Irish poets have been more
fortunate than their American cousins. For if the English
conquerors cut out the Irish tongue in the Eighteenth
Century by proscribing Gaelic, the present-day Irish
have grown a new one in order that they might once
again sing the grave songs of their ancestors. Refined
over milennia rather than decades, the old melodies
have escaped the tyrannies of the musical bar and the
English lyric tradition. And while it is true that few
Irish would willingly surrender their facility with
English to return to a language for which there are
perhaps 20,000 native speakers (there are more speakers of Gaelic, for example, in western Massachusetts
than there are in all of Ireland), still, what the Irish
have done with their new tongue is extraordinary.

An old tongue and the old gods—half-effaced, moulder-
ing, melting back into the steaming earth from which
they once came—are elemental forces which Montague
knows remain very much with us, as in the ritual
bloodletting of Irishman against Irishman:

>   we exchange sad notes
> about the violence plaguing these parts;
> last week, a gun battle outside Aughnacloy,
>
> machine gun fire splintering the wet thorns,
> two men beaten up near dark Altamuskin,
> an attempt to blow up Omagh Courthouse.

In the Iron Triangle, young British tank crews, eyes red
with fatigue and fear, patrol gutted streets where anyone
may harbor a bomb, not a homemade amateur sort, but
a sophisticated model made by experts who have had

ten years of practice in which to perfect their craft. So the killing trickles on in the north—in Tyrone and along the Falls Road or outside Belfast—at the average of one death each day. Under the shadow of the old gods the poet's countrymen continue to do what they have been doing for centuries, as his free translation from the Eleventh Century Irish tells us. Still the Irish cry out and mutilate their bodies, and "from this worship of dolour" they named one blood-stained field the "Plain of Adoration."

In Montague's world the passage of time is an illusion, for the old terrors still dominate his landscapes. So in one poem he recalls a night spent in a Belfast high-rise hotel, where "jungleclad troops" ransacked the Falls area, running down the "huddled streets" in search of terrorists, until the "cave of night" bloomed "with fresh explosions." Ireland's landscape of nightmares is like Bosch's fevered vision, where a "woman breasted butterfly / copulates with a dying bat" and a "pomegranate bursts slowly / between her ladyship's legs," her eggs "fertilizing the abyss."

A man racked with nameless guilts and a stiff pride, so his poems tell us, Montague is at home, finally, with bog and farmyard, tides and rivers, seagull and wren and curlew, with phallic tumuli and stone outcroppings, death and the scent of death, the release afforded by strong whiskey and copulation . . . all bought at the cost of the knowledge of his own mortality. He has not escaped his Jansenist background, though we know from these poems he has tried. Out of his struggle for some sort of order and his willingness to surrender himself to some kind of primordial fate, he has created a slow dance, a somber music, set to a few dark chords to which he clings as to a birthright.

When he turns in **The Great Cloak** to sing of modern love, as though he had won through to it, what we hear is a frailer, more fragmented music. Here the sequence follows the chronology of personal history in a triad Montague calls **"Search," "Separation,"** and **"Anchor,"** the sections which divide the text into thirds. These poems, he tells us in his quarter-page plot,

> should not only be read separately. A married man seeks comfort elsewhere, as his marriage breaks down. But he discovers that libertinism does not relieve his solitude. So the first section of the book ends with a slight affair which turns serious, the second with the despairing voices of a disintegrating marriage, the third with a new and growing relationship to which he pledges himself.

Approaching the subject of modern love, Montague has tried to use the strategy of detachment. It is thus Stendhal whom he seats across the entrance to the **"Search"** section of the poem, in order to reinforce the particular tone he is after: urbane, slightly amused, even

somewhat disgusted and enervated by the rutting that goes on in (semi-) secret places. This man is hard on himself, harder than perhaps he need be. How studiously he avoids the personal, self-implicating eye in this first section. Both partners—or is there more than one woman enmeshed in Montague's curiously impersonal language and syntax?—remain unrealized shadow figures, tracks, where the bit actors—porters and provincial chambermaids and even flowers—seem to take up a more substantial space:

> *I shall miss you*
> creaks the mirror
> into which the scene
> shortly disappears:
> the vast bedroom
> a hall of air, the
> tracks of our bodies
> fading there, while
> giggling maids push
> a trolley of fresh
> linen down the corridor.

Flat, distant, even self-parodic, like *The Chess Game* in Eliot's *Waste Land* or the dreamlike world of *Last Year at Marienbad,* Montague's language struggles to cope with a world of tenuous love between a man and a woman. One thinks back to poems Montague has written about male camaraderie in which he remembers old friends from boyhood, all-night drinking sessions, a father finally applauding the poems of a son he does not quite understand. But in **"Search,"** man and woman are wisps, ghosts: a hand resting on a table, a clenched fist, long fingernails stroking the skin like a butterfly caressing pollen, hands clasped defensively on small breasts, a closed hand trembling inside a more powerful one like some frightened animal seeking shelter.

It is a pattern of liaisons which has been repeated a thousand times, where

> Slant afternoon light
>
> on the bed, the unlatched
> window, scattered sheets
> are part of a pattern
> hastening towards memory.

This pattern hastening towards memory defines the whole first part of **The Great Cloak,** culminating in the terrible realization that the poet has after all been "searching through" the woman's body

> for something missing
> in your separate self
> while profound night
> like a black swan
> goes pluming past.

And so, for all its sense of a confession, **"Search"** remains very much a private affair, to be dealt with in the refined tones of a dozen cosmopolitan writers from Chaucer to Proust: a French set piece, almost, in spite of its Belfast setting.

But if terror and pain are kept in a minor key in the opening section of the poem, anger and suffering make themselves felt everywhere in the poem's center, as the poet's marriage to his first wife falls violently apart. We hear the pain growing, from the plangent cry of the screech owl in the June night air to the flat unhooded words of accusation flailing out against accusation, coupled with the knowledge that, certain things said and done, there can be no way out except separation. "We shall never be," the refrain insists, "what we were, again."

The problem for Montague here is to be fair to his first partner, despite his anger and hurt. One way for the "gentle man" to do that is to "assume / the proffered blame." But no use. Even in his recounting the old angers force their way to the surface: "It takes / two to make or break / a marriage. / *Unhood the falcon.*" Montague has tried to let his wife speak for herself in such poems as **"She Walks Alone,"** and **"She Daydreams, By the Blue Pool." "She Dreams,"** the strongest of the interior monologues spoken by the wife, points to one of the reasons—presumably—for the dissolution of this relationship. "I came to a place," his wife dreams,

> to where the eggs lay in the grass.
> I watched them for a long time, warming them
> With my swollen eyes. One after another
> They chipped and scraggy heads appeared;
> The embryos of our unborn children.
>
> They turn towards me, croaking "Mother!"
> I gather them up into my apron
> But the shape of the house has fallen
> And you are asleep by the water's edge:
> A wind and wave picked skeleton.

Childlessness is personal tragedy too deep even for the poet's words, and the bone sticks in the singer's throat:

> Grief, an unashamed,
> unconstrained, teeth-baring
> lament, one creature
> in a fury of loss
>
> bearing witness to
> the passage of another. . . .
>
>   (**"Lament"**)

This passage would seem to key the inner music of the whole middle section, before it subsides into the final lyric afterthought, a revisitation to the old home on Herbert Street when these two were first married. To sing of old happiness is to recollect the old times: Georgian Dublin architecture, Nurse Mullen with their old black tomcat, the pony and donkey across the way.

We feel Montague's lacerated wounds as he once again evokes that lost gossamer playland world, and we understand his failing attempt to keep faith with his wife's injunction not to betray whatever truth it was that belonged to them both.

The final section, **"Anchor,"** like a kind of extended *Midsummer Night's Dream,* focuses on the dream of the girl who moved through the opening sequence and to whom the poet returns once more. Montague fleshes her out now, as she emerges out of the shadows to become first some mythic corngoddess and finally a woman named Evelyn. Days of wine and roses: a world of sweet-smelling hay and "warm Constable" scenes, where deer by night are disturbed by headlights to move "stiff-legged, in short, jagged / bursts" at the couple's approach. As lyric gives way to lyric, we come to know this other woman more intimately, learning her little secrets and then her big ones: the shared intimacies and sudden, unexpected grace notes, the lullaby sung a little off key as the woman's wounds are touched. Thus Ceres gives way to another human being. And the new love leads—as with the old—to new quarrels. It is the pattern of fallen human nature reenacted once again. A man and a woman, like a team of horses, race together in the same direction, "close," yet "separate"; bitter quarreling is followed by sweet reconciliation, where thigh melts "into thigh, / mouth into mouth, breast / turning against ribcage." Love's old sweet song again, but with this difference, that in the book's last few pages, this new wife swells out with the promise of new life, caught up in the pattern of mother and child.

So **"Protest"** enacts the ritual of birth, with the poet present to comfort his wife in her need (Montague concentrates on her trembling hands, symbol of her vulnerability and need for comfort), "while our daughter was hauled / and forced into this breathing world," "born, as we die, reluctantly." Una, his firstborn, will inform everything he writes from now on with her presence: "love's invisible ink, / heart's watermark."

In the book's last two poems, Montague manages to see his two wives embedded in the seashore landscape of his new home. In the first of these, **"The Point,"** he recalls the sound of the foghorn mourning like a cow who has lost her calf, a sound which brings home to us Montague's obsession with his first wife's barrenness. Once, the poem remembers, he had assisted at the futile attempt to save a calf whose neck had been broken during the violent transit into life. Now the memory of the cow's disconsolate crying after its lost calf echoes the disembodied cry of the foghorn off the coast of Cork; echoes too the cry of his first wife, and—finally—Montague's own deep cry, even as he insists—unconvincingly—that the sound of the foghorn is nothing more than "a friendly signal in distress." As the poem ends and he bids a final good-bye to his first wife, he chooses to see the fog lifting to reveal their past in the same way that he now sees the opposite shore reveal itself, "Bright in detail as a painting, / Alone, but equal to the morning" of their shared life together.

The last poem is in turn addressed to Evelyn, and it too takes place along the Cork seashore by their new home. But now Montague's central metaphor is not the foghorn but the lighthouse. His new marriage, he says, must be—as all marriages are—a sailing out into unchartered waters, though the comfort of a sheltering home lies behind their excursions outward. Father, mother, child mark a new beginning, ambiguous as the image of the shore's edge itself, where the edge between domestic harbor and the vast sweeps of the Atlantic keep shifting, though for the moment they are quiet.

I am uneasy with **The Great Cloak,** though probably no more so than Montague himself was. He has moved beyond the momentary stasis of that poem's quiet edge, and that newborn child is now nearly seven. For even beneath those delicious embraces in the summer hay reminiscent of Constable's world, I can feel in the lines themselves a hornet swarm, a muscular tension, the deep angers and unresolved conflicts which also constitute one of Montague's strengths as a poet. What he managed to do in **The Great Cloak** was to wrestle his demons into some sort of formal pattern: a snarl of lusts, of anger, pathos, pain. But this sequence is—I think—only an interlude, an interruption, from that harsher, darker music one hears in **A Slow Dance.** It is that music which will probably draw him back to itself.

> Start a slow
> dance, lifting
> a foot, planting
> a heel to celebrate
>
> greenness, rain
> spatter on skin,
> the humid pull
> of the earth.

Transmute that music how he will, it will surface again and again. It is his own double-edged gift.

A. K. Weatherhead (essay date 1981)

SOURCE: Weatherhead, A. K. "John Montague: Exiled from Order." *Concerning Poetry* 14, no. 2 (1981): 97-113.

[*In the following essay, Weatherhead finds connections between the poet's ambivalent feelings toward Ireland and a similar attitude toward the order associated with conventional patterns of rhyme and meter.*]

John Montague is agnostic about the validity of conventional poetic form: he questions it, but he needs it there to be questioned, rather as Thomas Hardy

needed the idea of God. He is divided in loyalty between formal patterns which are associated with the past and the values of an organic living present with its strong claims against conserved convention. He is the poet of exile, literal and metaphorical, recognizing the conflicting claims of the old country and the new—claims, that is, of Ireland and New York and of old and new Irelands. He responds to the losses and gains incurred in the renunciation of a tradition or, in his latest volume, in the alienation of one love and the adoption of another.

> I'll tell you a sore truth, little understood.
> It's harder to leave, than to be left:
> To stay, to leave, both sting wrong.[1]

His verse reflects his ambivalence not only in its substance but in its manner.

> When I was young, it was much simpler;
> I saw God standing on a local hill,
> His eyes were gentle and bright birds
> Sang in chorus to his voice. . . .[2]

The prodigal son in a poem so titled in the same volume, **Poisoned Lands,** returns once a year to a landscape and a village that is "Unchanged in age or shape since childhood. . . ." The figure in **"Murphy in Manchester,"** on the other hand, lives with "Half-stirred memories and regrets. . . ." The poet himself knows the condition of exile: born in Brooklyn whither his father had emigrated from Ireland, he subsequently returned to the ancient turf.

The conflict of this exile, in the poetry and no doubt in life, is that between the conditions that made it "right" for the poet's father

> to choose a Brooklyn slum
> rather than a half-life in this
> by-passed and dying place[3]

and, on the other hand, the appeal of home *because* it is home and ancient Ireland is the poisoned land which indirectly gives title to the early volume. At the same time, however, it may be

> The last flowering garden of prayer and pretence,
> Green enclosure of monks and quiet poetry,
> Where the rivers move, without haste, to a restless
>   sea,
> And the rain shifts like a woven veil
> Over headland and sleeping plain. . . .[4]

But such images present a land too idyllic to be real. In **"The Road's End,"** a return to Ireland offers the poet only a sense of loss, as seeing the present he recalls the past

> Like shards
> Of a lost culture, the slopes

Are strewn with cabins, emptied
In my lifetime.[5]

And the ordered life of traditional Ireland is also continually threatened from outside by waves, weather, and seasons.

The old peaceful terrain thus assailed is identified with a metaphysical space: in his statement in *Contemporary Poets of the English Language* the poet says:

. . . my effort to understand as much of the modern world as possible serves only to illuminate the destruction of that small area from which I initially came, and that theme in turn is only part of the larger one of continually threatened love.[6]

And throughout all the poetry love is associated with an enclosed place, though it is insecure there:

. . . we two have come
Into love as to a lighted room
Where all is gaiety and humbling grace.[7]

But

There is a secret room
of golden light where
everything—love, violence,
hatred is possible;
and, again love.[8]

In the lighted room there are, significantly, "redeeming patterns":

Hearts long bruised with indolence,
With harsh fatigue of unrelated fact, can trace
Redeeming patterns of experience.[9]

Outside such enclosures, pattern can only be hoped for, as in the poem **"Boats,"** in which, moving from the "arms of the harbour," a female image, we come to the open sea, upon the periodic rhythms of which "we balance and slide, / hoping for pattern."[10] The shielding of the place may be impaired: in **"Enclosure"** in *A Chosen Light*

Through the poplars we spy the broken
Shape of the chateau. . . .

But

Around the landscaped woods
The high stone wall no longer defines
But falters.[11]

Violence may encroach. Even childhood, that place that in memory is safe, is compromised by knowledge and, like the innocent farm in **"Fern Hill,"** tainted with violence and death. **"Return,"** in *A Chosen Light*, opens with an entry into the childhood world:

the pines
wait, dripping.

Crumbling black-
berries, seized from a rack
of rusty leaves, maroon tents
of mushroom, pillars uprooting
with a dusty snap. . . .

But

the cleats of your rubber boot crush
a yellow snail's shell to a smear
on the grass
(while the wind starts
the carrion smell of the dead fox
staked as warning).[12]

The need for an enclosed place intensifies through the volumes of this poet as the threats of violence from outside become more dangerous. The latest volume, **The Great Cloak,** is itself such a sanctuary: the epigraph begins, "As my Province burns / I sing of love . . ." the enclosed place has religious associations in this volume; in one poem, **"Blessing,"**[13] grace attends there; in another, **"Allegiance,"**[14] the poet in a dolmen circle drops to one knee; the great cloak in the poem so titled will encompass the woman, the lover, or the child,

to wrap the morsel tenderly
while beasts browse around them
naturally as in Bethlehem.[15]

Threats to the enclosed place come variously. They may come in pale light, and in a poem titled **"The Pale Light,"** appears the "putrid fleshed woman / Whose breath is ashes," who

Tears away all
I had so carefully built—
Position, marriage, fame . . .[16]

In another poem, **"North Sea,"** a stormy scene is

Perfect setting for
the almost forgotten monster
of unhappiness to clank ashore . . .[17]

But monsters of one kind or another may enter any scene for that matter: the old *Cailleach* who stands for Ireland in **"The Wild Dog Rose"**[18] is threatened with rape; lovers in **"The Cave of Night"**[19] are assailed by nightmares and physical terror; there is always fear:

At times in this island, dreaming all day
In the sunlight and rain of attained revolutions,
We are afraid, as the hints pile up, of disaster
Enlarged as a dinosaur, rising from the salt flats . . .[20]

The complex of ambivalent attitudes toward Ireland and the enclosed scene of love—the desire for home, the recognition of the father's need to emigrate, and the sense of vulnerability—these may be taken as an index of the poet's complex attitude toward traditional order and, in turn, toward the order of formal verse structure. The early poems are mostly in regular metrical form, tightened on occasion by rhyme. But the form is flexible: metre can give way to free verse; if there are rhymes, they are rarely in a single pattern. Later the form becomes even more flexible: the poet-exile leaves the ordered poem as he left the ordered and archaic world. By 1972 Montague expresses an attitude to form which is not consonant with his own earlier practices and for which there is a parallel, partly no doubt a cause, and certainly an apt metaphor in his sojourn in America where apparently along with the husks of the Prodigal he was fed some of the new poetic principles. In his contribution to an *Agenda* symposium on rhythm, he says,

> there is an inhibiting traditionalism in contemporary English poetry on this side [i.e., the British side] of the Atlantic which saps inventiveness. It is only a habit of the mind which makes us expect a poem to march as docile as a herd of sheep between the fence of white margins. And what about all that waste paper, not reserved for silences but left fallow at the poem's edge? No farmer would allow such poor ploughing.[21]

For the most part, Montague had not up to the time of this comment made functional use of his margins. In *Tides,* however, in the poem **"Life Class,"**[22] he shows some good husbandry in deriving effects from the space at the edges of the page as he moves the short-line text across and back into three different positions in order to indicate different attitudes to the subject, the nude woman posing for the class. In the first eight stanzas, which adhere to the left margin, the body of the model is considered structurally—the hinge of the ankle bone, the calf's heavy curve, and so on. The second part, of about the same length but centered on the page, surveys the subject lustfully; the third, eight stanzas, again, set against the right margin, considers her humanly, as "a mild housewife / earning pocket money. . . ." Then in two more shorter sections the poem moves back to the left margin, combining the attitudes that have been individually declared. **"The Cave of Night"** in *A Slow Dance* similarly shifts the margin as the topic or perspective shifts.

Between 1966 and 1972 Montague was producing—composing and assembling—the long work, *The Rough Field,* of which parts were published separately before the whole was brought out. In this work the poet has occasional recourse to the collage as a substitute for the logical ordering of a poem. In Part I the description of the poet's homecoming to Garvaghey is counterpointed by excerpts from the *Ulster Herald,* set in the margin, recalling the arrival of Lord Mountjoy at Omagh. Then opposite a description of the poet's grandfather, a marginal note quotes the announcement of the appoint-

ment by the Lord Chancellor of John Montague, among others, to the Commission of the peace for Tyrone County.

Some of the other parts of the poem have similar notes commenting directly or obliquely on the main stream of the verse. But it is noticeable that the collage technique is used most extensively in those parts which deal with formal disruption of one kind or another, whether the despoliation of nature for the making of a highway or the civil turbulence that attends denominational differences. Part III, **"The Bread God,"** subtitled "A Collage of Religious Misunderstandings," is concerned with such disorder. Here is a miscellany of passages of prose and verse: a letter to the prime minister deploring the entry of the United Kingdom into the Common Market, Carleton's description of Christmas in Tyrone, a letter from the poet's uncle a Jesuit priest, and passages such as the following, a communication the poet had received after being put on the mailing list of an extreme Protestant organization:

"The Bread God"

the DEVIL *has* CHRIST *where he wants* HIM

A HELPLESS INFANT IN ARMS: A DEAD CHRIST ON THE CROSS

ROME'S CENTRAL ACT OF WORSHIP IS THE EUCHARISTIC WAFER!

IDOLATRY: THE WORST IDOL UNDER HEAVEN NOSELESS, EYELESS, EARLESS, HELPLESS, SPEECHLESS.[23]

These prose passages alternate with brief poems which deal at a rather low pitch with Church occasions.

Part VII, **"Hymn to the New Omagh Road,"** also makes use of the collage technique. It opens with two lists, in prose, one titled, "Loss," the other "Gain," the titles being in Gothic type. They itemize the disadvantages and the advantages of the new road. Then there follows a passage called "Glencull Waterside," in which verse describing the construction of the road alternates with lines of a pretty poem of an earlier date, reprinted in reduced type:

> From the quarry behind the school
> the crustacean claws of the excavator
> rummage to withdraw a payload,
> a giant's bite . . .

Then, on the other hand:

> 'Tis pleasant for to take a stroll by Glencull Waterside
> On a lovely evening in spring (in nature's early pride);
> You pass by many a flowery bank and many a shady dell,
> Like walking through enchanted land where fairies used to dwell.[24]

"All that remains of the glen as it has been," writes a critic, "is the poetry written about it."[25] But the *kind* of poetry preserved suggests the poet's ambivalence toward the flowery past. This part of *The Rough Field* closes with **"Envoi: the Search for Beauty,"** a little poem in a William Carlos Williams vein which mentions a farmer who, being drunk, bought "a concrete swan / for thirty bob," to deposit "on his tiny landscaped lawn," an anecdote which contributes ironically to the complex theme of beauty in the collage.

As D. E. S. Maxwell has noticed, the unity of *The Rough Field* is not imposed from an exterior scheme but grows with its composition, organically.[26] One of the paragraphs toward the end of Part IX begins,

> the emerging order
> of the poem invaded
> by cries, protestations
> a people's pain. . . .[27]

And this suggests that unity, the pattern, has been discarded, in part at least, so that the poem may accommodate protest, as if the artificiality of poetic order must give way before real grief—a principle like that by which Dr. Johnson found genuine grief lacking in *Lycidas* which had leisure for fictions and trappings of a convention. We may note the parallelism here between Montague's strategy and the whole ambivalence of his attitude to Ireland: as by constraint he is exiled from the country and from the enclosed place of love and order, so he leaves the patterned poem for the collage, relinquishing an order to which, all the same, he repeatedly shows commitment.

In its substance, *The Rough Field* reflects the quandary of the returned exile, who wants the past for its orderliness—the world, as he puts it, "where action had been wrung / through painstaking years to ritual"—but who recognizes also that such a world, on account of its harshness, "only a sentimentalist would wish to see . . . again."

The exile has returned in this poem, however, in order to fulfill the need of self-determination. In its various parts, Montague encounters his grandfather, uncle, father, mother, and other figures out of his past who together constituted his ordered childhood. In other parts of the poem, particularly Part III, the "Collage of Religious Misunderstandings," he presents parts of the feuding, past and present, that caused exile.

The loss, though, is not just Ireland, but by extension the loss of childhood innocence. In Part VI, **"A Good Night,"** the poet remembers how once he climbed to the source of a mountain stream until he came upon "a pool of ebony water / Fenced by rocks. . . ." Here, at the source of the stream and the source of his own be-

ing, he tried and failed to catch the "Ancient trout of wisdom" that legend declared inhabited the pool. But now memory itself irradiates the present; and, so it seems, "the burden of the mystery" is lightened:

> Each grassblade bends with
> Translucent beads of moisture
> And the bird of total meaning
> Stirs upon its hidden branch.[28]

If there is less involved here than there is in Wordsworth, whose phrase seems apt enough, certainly there is more than a boyish excursion. (Indeed, is there *any* boyish excursion in literature which is *only* a boyish excursion?) Loss of innocence appears similarly, in Part V, **"The Fault,"** which in verse like Robert Lowell's describes the role of the poet's father in the Troubles, describes also a scar, a mark both the poet and his father bear, apparently in fact a coincidence but symbolically the inherited human flaw, original sin:

> The line on my left temple
> Opened by an old car accident.
> My father had the same scar
> In the same place, as if
> The same fault ran through
> Us both: anger, impatience,
> A stress born of violence.[29]

The poem proceeds from Part IX, the collage of violent occasions, to X, **"The Wild Dog Rose,"** which appeared first in *Tides* and describes how the poet goes to visit the *Cailleach,* the old woman or hag, symbolizing Ireland, who tells him the terrible story of an assault and attempted rape by a drunkard, the whole episode and the telling of it framed by images of the dog rose that "shines in the hedge," the only rose without a thorn. Finally the old woman gathers the rose, love superseding violence, though the flower is unmistakeably emaciated:

> Briefly
> the air is strong with the smell
> of that weak flower, offering
> its crumbled yellow cup
> and pale bleeding lips
> fading to white. . . .[30]

Finally the epilogue, **"Driving South,"** leaves the poet hankering after the old, yet knowing that it not only cannot return but is not even to be hankered after. The poem ends on a note of lost innocence with lines used in its beginning:

> Harsh landscape that haunts me,
> well and stone, in the bleak moors of dream
> with all my circling a failure to return. . . .[31]

But return he does, constantly. In *A Slow Dance,* 1975, his commitment to the homeland has become stronger. In the opening and title poem, he moves back to his origins and in a slow cleansing and healing dance he is reborn from the Irish earth. In this volume he repeatedly returns to Ireland's mythic past. And the historic Ireland, also, still has its romantic appeal and the present it claims. **"The Errigal Road"** parades local memories, irradiated by the imagination but due to be effaced by the Troubles, which have perhaps sharpened them in the first place. They are shared now with an "old Protestant neighbour"—"old neighbours / can still speak to each other around here." But love is threatened and so is the enclosed place of order: "Soon all our shared landscape will be effaced."[32] In **"Dowager,"** another thoroughly Irish anecdote, an old woman relates memories and reports the satisfactions of age. If she is not a symbol for Ireland as the Cailleach was in *Tides* she surely embodies it; she and her situation as described (notwithstanding reminiscences of William Carlos Williams) could exist nowhere else. Most of the lines are end-stopped and suggest the limitations of age; but the enjambment between the last two stanzas and the emblem on her Rolls Royce suggest the constantly springing life of the spirit in the old satisfied body:

> I ride through a damp tunnel of sweetness,
> The bonnet strewn with bridal hawthorn
>
> From which a silver lady leaps, always young.
> Alone, I hum with satisfaction in the sun,
> An old bitch, with a warm mouthful of game.[33]

After the earliest volumes Montague's poems are less lyrical. In *A Slow Dance,* they are more formal than some in *The Rough Field*; there are no unstructured items of protest that have resisted form. Often the poet is talking in verse which, though not by any means flat, does lack the intensity of the earlier lyrics. Sometimes the talk comes in the voice of Yeats, an element of the past of Ireland that Montague is not about to relinquish, which we hear with every use of the word pride. One poem in particular, **"Hell Fire Club,"** Part VI of **"O Riada's Farewell,"**[34] in which the poet holds a girl child in his arms during a night when demons are abroad, is reminiscent of "A Prayer for my Daughter" and is no doubt a conscious reference. Sometimes the verse reminds us of the conflict expressed earlier between "emerging order" and protest: the talking becomes uncertain as if the poet had failed to settle whether to present facts in their own bleak facticity or, with a little "leisure for fiction," to hold them to a more intense poetic pitch with figurative expression. Some passages of **"O Riada's Farewell,"** a personal testament, quite poignant though in places quite private, may momentarily recall Stephen Spender who faced a similar quandary.

> Instinct wrung and run
> awry all day, powers idled

> to self-defeat, the vacuum
> behind the catalyst's gift.
>
> . . . . .
>
> A playing with fire, leading
> you, finally, tempting you
> to a malevolence, the
> calling of death for another.[35]

The poems in this volume depend often on the juxtaposition of clear-cut images presented without intensity and deriving from each other no more than the slightest incremental meaning that this technique frequently offers. There are some short simple poems using this technique, such as **"Sawmill, Limekiln"**[36] and **"Homes."**[37] In other poems juxtaposition is more complex and used with more advantage. **"The Cave of Night"** in six separate sections combines Irish myth—the horrors of human sacrifice in the enclosure of a dolmen circle—with contemporary Irish history—lovers frightened in the night by bombs and nightmares. Proceeding on the similar principle of the juxtaposition of parts without editorial comment is **"Wheels Slowly Turning,"** a poem indebted to the memories of a medical orderly friend of the poet's, "who helped to clear many battlefields."[38] The poem has five six-line sections distinctly separated by asterisks, and then an *envoi*. The first of the five parts presents the image of an overturned army lorry with **"Wheels slowly turning."** In the following are images of corpses; these become "bridegrooms of death . . . 'knee-deep in knight's blood, / hip-deep in the blood of heroes.'" Then death appears as a woman, love making is war, and then as a Black Widow goddess. The lightly pitched *envoi* describes how the orderly lost a leg in a battle but lived to tell how its wooden replacement attracted women:

> "they beg
> to handle it", you say,
> and wake to find it dangling
> —a hunter's weapon—
> around their bedpost
> at peep of day.[39]

There are many mutually enriching relationships between the parts of the poem: the overturned lorry is like a beetle; death is a black widow; a destroyed battalion is a "crushed centipede." The knight's blood and the blood of heroes relate across the gap to the orderly's hunter's weapon; and death's love-making, of course, to that of the "toothsome ladies" in the *envoi*. An army veteran I knew, in the British days when it made sense to leave shoes outside a hotel room to be cleaned, would occasionally leave his wooden leg parked in one of them, sportively, jesting at scars who had certainly felt the wound. It is not in itself sinister that death, the sinister mistress, is so lightly traded off in this poem for an aphrodisiacal wooden leg, when the wheels have turned. But the transaction contributes to a sense that horrors have become such unsensational daily events as to be accommodated into our lives with no more than the insouciant raised eyebrow. In the poem following **"Wheels Slowly Turning"** is this vignette:

> Soldiers with lances and swords
> Probe the entrails of innocents.
> A burgomeister washes manicured
> Hands before the mourning citizens
> The snow on the gable is linen crisp. . . .[40]

But death, a regular preoccupation, is not always treated easily. The contemporary Ireland as pictured in a number of the poems, **"The Cave of Night,"** for one example, (and, of course, as pictured in the newspapers) is no longer an enclosure of love and order; and some kind of mental accommodation of death is no doubt an aching need. In **"O Riada's Farewell"** it is again personified,

> harsh black hair falling to her knees,
> a pale tearstained face.
>
> *How pretty you look,*
> *Miss Death!*[41]

With this volume the face of Montague's verse has become lined. It is concerned with death and, even more perhaps, with loneliness. The poet anticipates loneliness in **"The Errigal Road"** as the shared landscape is diminished; he feels the pathos of a friend dying alone and of a "heart locked in"; he knows the "secret shell / of loneliness" and the sense of loneliness when cars pass each other at night on the long country roads. But the volume closes with a vision of the loneliness on the earth itself; **"Lament,"** the last section of **"O Riada's Farewell,"** describes a voice "like an animal howling" lamenting

> . . . the globe itself
> turning in the endless halls
>
> of space, populated
> with passionless stars. . . .[42]

In these recent poems the place of order has become constricted and fearful. Meanwhile outside, everything, the great globe itself, swims in solitary vacancy.

The latest volume, **The Great Cloak,** confirms the ambivalence of this poet who is unwilling to relinquish what he has repudiated. It is, in itself, as suggested above, a deliberate withdrawal from the war-torn Province, where ignorant armies clash. The poet of "Dover Beach" called for human love as a haven in a torn world; Montague's haven, on the other hand, is apparently the poetry itself. The poems, which are to be read as a unified sequence, come in three parts, the first covering "libertinism"; the second, the disintegration of a marriage; the third, the growth of a new relationship. But in this last part, in **"The Point,"** the poet still turns back to his former wife as in earlier poems he turned back to the "bypassed" Ireland:

> Our two lives have separated now
> But I would send my voice to yours
> Cutting through the shrouding mist
> Like some friendly signal in distress.[43]

In the last poem of the volume, **"Edge,"** the poet has found a "sheltering home," an Edenic place with the uninsistent symbols of garden, lighthouse, vast lifting Atlantic tides, and harbour arms, where he and his new wife may rest. They are blessed. And yet the poem offers no sense of permanent security: the two people are there out of good luck, and fate relenting, and at last only on the edge:

> Hushed and calm,
> safe and secret,
> on the edge is best.[44]

Notes

1. "No Music," *The Great Cloak* (Dublin: The Dolmen Press, 1978), p. 34.

2. "Soliloquy on a Southern Strand," *Poisoned Lands* (London: MacGibbon and Kee, 1961), p. 26.

3. "Stele for a Northern Republican," *The Rough Field* (Dublin: Dolmen Press, 1972), p. 45.

4. "The Sheltered Edge," *Poisoned Lands*, p. 32.

5. *A Chosen Light* (Chicago: Swallow, 1969), p. 32.

6. (London: St. James Press, 1970), pp. 746-65.

7. "Pastorals," *Poisoned Lands*, p. 51.

8. "The Same Gesture," *Tides* (Dublin: Dolmen Press, 1970), p. 37.

9. "Pastorals," *Poisoned Lands*, p. 51.

10. *Tides*, p. 59.

11. P. 48.

12. P. 25.

13. P. 52.

14. P. 46.

15. P. 59.

16. P. 27.

17. P. 25.

18. *The Rough Field*, p. 82.

19. "The Cave of Night," *A Slow Dance* (Dublin: Dolmen Press, 1975), pp. 29-33.

20. "The Sheltered Edge," *Poisoned Lands*, p. 32.

21. *Agenda*, Vol. 10, No. 4-Vol. 11, No. 1 (Autumn-Winter, 1972), p. 41.

22. Pp. 39-42.

23. *The Rough Field,* p. 26.

24. Ibid., p. 62.

25. Frank Kersnowski, *John Montague* (Lewisburg: Bucknell University Press, 1975), p. 63.

26. "The Poetry of John Montague," *Critical Quarterly,* XV (Summer, 1973), 180-85.

27. *The Rough Field,* p. 77.

28. "The Source," *The Rough Field,* pp. 53-55.

29. Ibid., p. 45.

30. Ibid., p. 82.

31. Ibid., p. 85.

32. *A Slow Dance,* p. 27.

33. Ibid., p. 23.

34. Ibid., pp. 60-61.

35. Ibid., pp. 58-59.

36. Ibid., p. 15.

37. Ibid., p. 22.

38. "Acknowledgements," Ibid.

39. Ibid., pp. 40.

40. "Coldness," Ibid., p. 41.

41. Ibid., p. 59.

42. Ibid., p. 63.

43. P. 61.

44. P. 62.

Sidney B. Poger (essay date 1981)

SOURCE: Poger, Sidney B. "Crane and Montague: 'The Pattern History Weaves.'" *Éire-Ireland* 16, no. 4 (1981): 114-24.

[*In the following essay, Poger compares Hart Crane's* The Bridge *with Montague's* The Rough Field, *and finds that each poet wanted to produce an epic of his own time and place, but did not want to use traditional epic conventions to do so.*]

Since both John Montague in *The Rough Field* and Hart Crane in *The Bridge* faced some of the same problems, much may be discovered through a comparison of their poems. The initial problem each faced was how to find a particular sense of place that would embody the national consciousness at a particular time: for Crane, the America of the 1920s; for Montague, the Ireland of the 1960s. Although both poets are keenly aware of the past, each wants his poem to be modern. That is, neither wants to return to the traditional epic subjects of the founding of a nation or the wanderings of a hero. Each wants to combine the fixed counters of the epic, space and time. Although Ireland seems to have little in the way of space or geography, it has plenty of history. America has tremendous space, but a history inchoate, still malleable. Each wants something that embodies the present, not only as it contains the past, but as it implies the future. They also need some physical symbol to pull together the geography of the nation. For Crane, the proper symbol is Brooklyn Bridge, a marvel of modern technology which is heroic in conception and construction. The American experience, as Crane presents it, is filled with echoes of bridges, of spans, of joinings between old and new.[1] For Montague, the proper symbol is his family's heritage, Garvaghey, which in Irish means "rough field." The struggle between old and new, between the rough field and the wild flowers that bloom within it, resembles the contentious balance of forces within Brooklyn Bridge, forces that would either pull the bridge down or pull it apart.

Both poets try to write epics of their own time, but not of the kinds traditionally available to them. This has caused some confusion on the part of critics of the two poems. Timothy Kearney describes *The Rough Field* as a sequence "whose soul is lyrical but whose body is epic"; it is the epic part, he declares, which is weakest.[2] Critics have reacted in much the same way to *The Bridge*: they have, in one way or another, declared the incompatibility of lyric and epic in that poem since its publication.[3] What critics do not see is that both Crane and Montague combine epic and lyric into a form that has objectives of its own.

Crane did not wish to write a narrative epic. Vincent Quinn claims that Crane aroused certain expectations when he called his poem-in-progress an "epic." This led many critics to blame Crane for not living up to the expectations he himself had aroused. Quinn's own definition of an epic, as "coherent narration,"[4] at least justifies his feeling of its failure as an epic, even if his criterion is rigid. Montague's knowledge of American writing is well known. He is well acquainted, as was Hart Crane, with the older forms Walt Whitman had repudiated in putting together his own epic, *Song of Myself.* Whitman solved his problem by creating an epic personality that encompassed all of America, all of his own wide and voracious appetite for living and language. This personality contained country and self. What is Whitman as person is inseparable from what is Whitman as "kosmos." Crane and Montague do not adopt this single large figure but, instead, play down the role of the poetic persona. "In nearly every section of *The Bridge,* Crane presents a mask of the poet; that is, a poet-figure or 'ancient man,' who in some way reënacts the narrator's quest and serves as guide."[5] This figure differs in each part of the poem. Montague also buries his persona: the figure of the poet emerges only partially from the flow of the poem.

Both Crane and Montague tried to fashion their own forms. Samuel Hazo recognizes this when he notes that *The Bridge* centers on a quest, which makes Crane's poem proceed from an epic impulse rather than a lyric one.[6] He asks that the form be looked at for what is there, and be judged organically and not "by predetermined criteria."[7] When looking at these poems, we do find what I call, for want of a better term, the lyric-epic, which most resembles the poetic sequence. Sequences are often collections of lyrics that form a narrative, as does Crane's own sequence "Voyages," which tells the story of a love affair between Crane and a sailor. A sequence may also treat of a subject or place, like Seamus Heaney's "Glanmore Sonnets" in *Field Work,* or some biographical experience, like Robert Lowell's *Life Studies.* But a sequence is only loosely organized, not concerned with establishing a symbolic place. Nor does it have the breadth of the quest which marks the lyric-epic.

Even without the creation of an epic personality, the lyric-epic can contain autobiographical details. Parts of Crane's own life are buried in such poems as "Van Winkle," which celebrates memory. Crane recalls:

> . . . the whip stripped from the lilac tree
> One day in spring my father took to me,
> Or is it the Sabbatical, unconscious smile
> My mother almost brought me once from church
> And once only . . . ?

Memories in "The River" include Crane's memories of hobos, whom he saw behind his father's factory, combined with fabricated memories of hobos. This mixing of personal memories with fictitious ones gives authenticity to the imagined memories and resonance to the real ones. Montague also blends personal details with nonpersonal ones, although neither poet develops a consistent persona. Montague shows a more developed "I" in *The Rough Field* than there is in *The Bridge.* This "I" is seen primarily in the frame: the first section, **"Home Again,"** tells of returning to the place where the narrator grew up; the last, **"Driving South, An Epilogue,"** takes the narrator from the world of Garvaghey to the smoother world of the South.[8] While this frame may be based on a real-life journey, it functions—like the frame of *The Bridge*: "To Brooklyn Bridge" and "Atlantis"—as an entrance and exit to the poem that brings the reader back to his starting point, having grown through experiencing the poem.

Details of the narrator's background are not Montague's personal experiences but are, instead, family histories looked at for an objective purpose. They do not contribute to an expansive personality like Whitman's. Such an incident is the invocation of "my grandfather," which has some of the spirit of Whitman, but which conveys an attitude rather than a particular personality of either poet or ancestor.

> Let it be clear
> That I do not grudge my grandfather
> This long delayed pleasure!
> I like the idea of him
>
> Rising from the rotting boards of the coffin
> With his J.P.'s white beard
> And penalising drivers
> For traveling faster
> Than jaunting cars

While **"The Wild Dog Rose,"** the climactic poem of *The Rough Field,* details a personal incident, the narrator is the one to whom the incident is told, not the one to whom it happens. The story, about the rape of an old woman, has an effect on the narrator, which is the same effect experienced by the reader. It does not, however, contribute to the epic hero or to his personality. The effect is, instead, lyrical and Wordsworthian, as if the narrator were listening to someone living with nature who, after some terrible event, has been restored to equilibrium. An epic hero would not choose such suffering and cowering for the reward of "The smell / of that weak flower."

The use of women as multiple and shifting national symbols can be traced at least as far back as the beauteous Helen of ancient epic. One such symbol in William Carlos Williams's work, with which Montague is familiar, appears in *Paterson.* In that poem, all the women, beginning with the composite woman who represents the nine stages of a woman's life, as seen in the nine wives of an African chieftain described in Book 1, through the "woman in our town" of Book 5, who represents Williams's perfect audience, combine both Williams' muse and the spirit of Paterson, New Jersey. In the section of *The Bridge* Crane titled "Powhaten's Daughter," Pocahontas, his major symbol, represents the body of the continent. The exploration of America becomes the exploration of her body, most clearly in "The Dance." The speaker, Maquokeeta, sets out to know his land, exploring both land and woman in a ritual which ends in union:

> . . . winds across the llano grass resume
> Her hair's warm sibilance. Her breasts are fanned
> O stream by slope and vineyard—into bloom!
>
> And when the caribou slant down for salt
> Do arrows thirst and leap? Do antlers shine
> Alert, star-triggered in the listening vault
> Of dusk?—And are her perfect brows to thine?
>
> We danced, O Brave, we danced beyond their farms,
> In cobalt desert closures made our vows . . .

Now is the strong prayer folded in thine arms.
The serpent with the eagle in the boughs.

Pocahontas is later transformed, in "Three Songs," into a prostitute, a burlesque dancer, and the virgin Cathedral Mary, and then into three women: Isadora Duncan, Emily Dickinson, and the "wop washerwoman" of the tunnel section—each of whom represents some part of America.

Montague's composite woman is made up more of sufferer and firebrand than of sexual object. **"The Leaping Fire"** is dedicated to his grandmother, Brigid Montague, who tends the fire of life and inspiration. Her age has broken her down, but some beauty remains:

> & you, whose life
> was selflessness,
> now die slowly
>
> broken down by
> process to a pale
> exhausted beauty

Her death is announced by "a low, / constant crying / over the indifferent / roofs of Paris," which the poet hears. The section **"A New Siege,"** written "for Bernadette Devlin," tells of the recurring battles over Derry, fought now in the name of the newest avatar of Cathleen Ni Houlihan. The traditional poor old woman of Ireland, the *Sean Bhan Bhocht,* is left, in **"The Wild Dog Rose,"** with the still beauty of the rose, the only rose without thorns, which reminds her of "the Holy Mother of God and / all she suffered." This old woman's traditional guise pulls the poem together in an important way. Had Montague ended this lyric-epic with another of his poems about a *Cailleach* or old woman, **"The Hag of Beare,"** the effect would have been very different. The Hag of Beare mourns that "Alas, I cannot / Again sail youth's sea; / The days of my beauty / Are departed, and desire spent." She laments what has been lost and mourns the passing of the time when she could "never say 'No' to anybody," but the woman in **"The Wild Dog Rose"** has kept herself apart by never marrying "though a man came asking in her youth": "'You would be loath to leave your own' / she sighs, 'and go among strangers'—/ his parish ten miles off."

But, if the lyric quality of *The Bridge* and **The Rough Field** is, as Kearney called it, the soul of the poem,[9] it is the epic impulse, the embodiment of place and the sense of time, which gives the lyrics their coherence. Crane chose the Brooklyn Bridge for more than the fact that it physically connects Manhattan and Brooklyn. The Brooklyn Bridge was the most advanced structure of its time. It combined beauty of structure with respect for materials, connecting time and space. Montague chose Garvaghey, his birthplace, with a particular history which exists in letters, documents, and family story

and which, in its thickness, represents the various strands of the present. Montague's particular history reflects all of Irish history. This is why the place of his childhood, County Tyrone, is well suited for this poem, since it is on the border between Ulster and the Republic and connects them.

Crane begins at the Brooklyn Bridge that, in its particular details, gains an eminence having overtones of divinity: "And of the curveship lend a myth to God." He then portrays Columbus, not facing the New World and seeing its future, as Joel Barlow did in *The Columbiad,* but facing east in mid-ocean, on his way back to Spain. "Harbor Dawn" and "Van Winkle" are both located in New York, although "Van Winkle," by implication, spans the continent like a bridge: "Macadam . . . / Leaps from Far Rockaway to Golden Gate." "The River" connects the country from north to south, from the Dakotas to the Gulf of Mexico into which the river debouches. The serpent of time combines with the eagle of space in "The Dance" to reveal the heart of the continent through the union of Maquokeeta and Pocahontas. "Indiana" moves from west to east, repeating Columbus's movement. Having been as far west as she could go, the mother in that poem recounts to her son Larry how the family had gone west in 1859 to search for silver in Colorado but there found "God lavish . . . / But passing sly." She showed her son to the Indian woman riding west with her own baby on her back, making the connection between Indian woman and white. The first half of the poem ends back in Brooklyn, on the bridge, looking down at the harbor at the ghosts of the clipper ships. The country has been traversed from east to west and back again, the journey ending where it began. The poem is anchored in this bridge; no matter how far it may wander, the poem retains an intimate connection with the bridge, which embodies the complex pattern of history. The second half of *The Bridge* explores time rather than space. It recalls earlier literary figures—Whitman, Dickinson, Poe—who contribute to the present poem. Even though the first poem of the second half is called "Cape Hatteras," through its references to Whitman, it proves as involved with Whitman's Brooklyn as with the Wright brothers and the airplane, which is the poem's major symbol. The second half also recognizes a usable poetic past that justifies America's destiny. Toward the end of *The Bridge,* the poet descends symbolically into Hell as he enters the tunnel under the East River into Brooklyn, paralleling the bridge's connection but repeating it under the water. The concluding poem "Atlantis" once again soars into the heavens above the harbor, connecting Brooklyn and New York and making all the places in the poem one:

> O Choir, translating time
> Into what multitudinous Verb the suns

And synergy of waters ever fuse, recast
In myriad syllables,—Psalm of Cathay!

The fusion of time and space results in "One Song, one Bridge of Fire!" This is the pattern of history in all its complexity.

The Rough Field has no such clear pattern of movement in space. Indeed, except for the trip to Garvaghey in the first section of **"Home Again"** (via Lisburn, Lurgan, and Portadown) and the last section **"Driving South"** (passing through Cavan and Monaghan), only two sections are set outside Montague's home place of County Tyrone. More important than the journey through space is the recollection of time, the pattern history makes, which unites personal with historical time. Montague remembers his father, his uncle the fiddler whose music has passed into his own poetry, and the old people who gather like dolmens around his memory of childhood. **"The Leaping Fire"** celebrates his grandmother, all the older women who represent Ireland and who brought him up. At her death the cry of the banshee heard in Paris calls him back to Ireland. **"The Bread God"** mixes in the old religious divisions, historic and real, with letters from Thomas Montague, S. J., whose views are innocent but which complicate the divisions. Montague underlines the difficulty of seeing things whole in **"An Ulster Prophecy,"** which lists a series of impossible things culminating in "a curlew in flight / surveying / a United Ireland." **"A Severed Head"** tells of the loss of the past through the destruction of the O'Neills and the abandonment of the Irish language. One of Montague's finest small lyrics, **"A Grafted Tongue,"** is prepared for by the ironic comment—"We have the Irish again"—on the schoolroom Irish learned by the poet:

The last Gaelic speaker in the parish
When I stammered my school Irish
One Sunday after mass, crinkled
A rusty litany of praise;
Tá an Ghaedilg againn arís . . .

This older tongue is the present's abandoned heritage: "To grow / a second tongue, as / harsh a humiliation / as twice being born." The earlier loss of language was a change of identity forced by English-speakers who could see no need for the older language: as they pointed out, "You can't sell the cow in Irish." Now, the search to recover that language marks a search for the past, for the pattern that would give meaning to the present. That past took place, and is best understood, at both the personal and the historical level, in Garvaghey, the field made rough by the exploding shells of history but from whose soil the present springs.

Section V, **"The Fault,"** goes back to Montague's immediate past, to his father in Brooklyn, and to the line on the poet's forehead opened by a car accident. His father had "the same scar / In the same place." This scar represents a fault line running from one generation to the next, reinforcing historical patterns. Section VI recalls a meeting at a pub called The Last Sheaf, where, in the company of a pubkeeper who "began to diminish / His own stock," the men drink during and after hours. Much like the old sailor in "Cutty Sark" from *The Bridge,* the men stumble onward, having lost their relation to time through drink. The men argue among themselves in the same way as two boys once fought over a swallow's nest that belonged to neither, but which each felt it necessary to worship or destroy. "The seventh sense of drunkenness" leads the speaker back to the road that overlooks the dance hall housing "an industry built / on loneliness"—the loneliness of the present assuaged only "with vague dreams"—in a district dominated by the "elegant remains" of the gutted castle of St. John's, "which my father helped to burn." Montague's dance hall recalls that of Emily Dickinson and Isadora Duncan of *The Bridge,* where the Friends Meeting House has degenerated into the New Avalon Hotel. Both poems show a present lived in the shadow of the ruins of the past.

The **"Hymn to the New Omagh Road"** views what modern society does in order to grow: it cuts out the past for dubious advantages, trivialized in Montague's list of gains. The account sheet does not favor the new, except in an ironic manner:

Item: a man driving from Belfast to Londonderry can
     arrive a
     quarter of an hour earlier, a lorry load of goods
     ditto thus making Ulster more competitive in the
     international market.

And even these gains are won at great cost:

Item: The uprooting of wayside hedges
     with their accomplices, devil's bit and pee
     the bed,
     prim rose and dog rose, an unlawful
     assembly of thistles.

This gain in speed is characterized by "the living / passing at great speed, sometimes quick enough to come / straight in" to the graveyard. Such travel recalls the plane, in Crane's "Cape Hatteras," crashing in a bunched heap of metal. Neither of these machines seems to go anywhere, but, in trying to go faster, ends up smashed. Crane's hopes for technology remain unfulfilled. The bridge, as the sum of man's knowledge and power, promises new fusions of "harp and altar" but the promise is never fulfilled; it is only repeated in "Atlantis," which holds out yet more hope for a fusion of space and time, or of eagle and serpent, but without moving any further than the last line of the introductory poem. The descent through the Hell of the tunnel has been accomplished by the new technology; so is the ascent over the harbor of the bridge. Technology for

Crane holds out hope for the future at the same time that it is indifferent to the effects it has on the present. For Montague, the new Omagh Road is the only notice of the new technology. What he wants to see are the patterns of history, the patterns of life and the mold from which they have come. Crane wants the future to be one unity, the fusion of harp and altar. What he finds combined with this vision is a fear of the past, of the losing of time, the "stilly note / Of pain that Emily, that Isadora knew!"

"Patriotic Suite," dedicated to musician Seán Ó Riada, collects poems and songs describing the political conditions in the South of Ireland. Since Crane described his poem as symphonic in form,[10] he felt free to use the musical motifs of crowd sounds and traffic noises. For example, in "The Tunnel," the voices of the crowd on the subway, with their repetitions and syncopation, contribute to the musical structure.

> "what do you want: getting weak on the links?
> fandaddle daddy don't ask for change—IS THIS
> FOURTEENTH? it's half past six she said—if
> you don't like my gate why did you
> swing on it, why *didja*
> swing on it
> anyhow—"
> And somehow anyhow swing—

His suite begins with a recall of the note which, in Paris, told him of the death of his grandmother: "Again that note! A weaving / melancholy, like a bird crossing / moorland," which also recalls the "curlew in flight / surveying / a United Ireland" from the only height at which that country's political divisions become invisible. But what the poet sees now are the shrunken remains of the heroic ancient Ireland reduced to the middle-class Irish present:

> The mythic lyre shrunk to country size:
> The clatter of brogues on the flagstones,
> The colourless dram of poteen—
> Is that the world we were made for?

What remains now are "the gloomy images of a provincial catholicism." The ancient heroes had been invited down from the hills by the revolutionaries to show "nervous majesty" and "forgotten grace," but soon bored the people. Some returned to the hills, others remained in the town, trying to accommodate to the new language. Both groups are now dying out, "A tragedy anticipated in the next government report." The once tragic music is arranged carefully by the government to harmonize with its own scoring. Now the nation has been reduced to council houses and emptiness, where:

> Only a drift of smoke
> And the antlike activity of cars
> Indicate life; with the wild flap
> Of laundry in a thousand backyards.

And the faith has deserted Ireland, since the Republic's success in the growth of its economy leads all but the Vatican to welcome Ireland as a nation. With the Vatican's indifference, without the ancient spiritual ties, even Jansenism has fled Ireland, which has become a wholly modern nation without faith. Everything is summed up in a "Line simple as a song: / *Puritan Ireland's dead and gone, / A myth of O'Connor and Ó Faoláin.*" The call of the birds above the cliffs now sounds "above a self-drive car."

"A New Siege," subtitled "An Historical Meditation," looks at the history of the North of Ireland through a view of the succession of battles for control of Derry, from the siege of 1689 to the civil rights marches of 1969. The same battles are repeated *"like an old Troubles film"* run through again and again. Each attempt leads only to more destruction. The civil rights march—"tired marchers / nearing Burntollet / young arms linked / banners poled high"—leads only to the inevitable reaction—

> Lines of action
>   lines of reaction
> the white elephant
>   of Stormont, Carson's
> raised right claw
>   a Protestant parliament

—and this leads to the division that still keeps North from South. Ireland remains united only in the view of a high-flying bird and in the hearts of the people:

> Across the border
>   a dead man
> drives to school
>   past the fort
> at Greene Castle
>   a fury of love
> for North, South
>   eats his heart

Because Ireland remains divided, the speaker recalls his meeting with an old hag, a *Cailleach,* who represents Ireland united. She tells her history, "a story so terrible / that I try to push it away, / my bones melting." She relates how, one night, she was attacked by a drunk who, like her, was "crazed / with loneliness." She struggled till she broke his grip and he fell asleep, "to lurch back across / the wet bog" in the morning when the whining of the dogs woke him. Still, after the terror of the story, she tenaciously holds on to the dog rose.

> 'The wild rose
> is the only rose without thorns,'
> she says, holding a wet blossom
> for a second, in a hand knotted
> as the knob of her stick.
> 'Whenever I see it, I remember

the Holy Mother of God and
all she suffered.'

It is the suffering of Ireland, as well as the suffering of the old woman, which culminates in the "smell / of that weak flower," of the sweetness of the rose which has grown from that suffering.

Although the epilogue, **"Driving South,"** does not ask for the old order to be restored, "something mourns." The "changing rural pattern means clack / of tractor for horse"; this substitution of machine for man's hard, physical labor is happening all over the world, "from Ulster to the Ukraine," so: "Finally lost [is the] dream of man at home / in a rural setting!" This rural dream has been lost by both Catholic and Protestant, for, in earlier times, "the priest blessed / the green tipped corn, or Protestant / lugged pale turnip, swollen marrow / to robe the kirk for Thanksgiving." This epilogue celebrates "what is already going, / going, / GONE." What remains after the experience of the poem is the memory of the rough field, the struggle to live one's own life, the attack of the old drunkard, and the scent of the dog rose, "'the only rose without thorns.'" All these suspended together constitute one symbol for Montague, just as the Brooklyn Bridge holds all in suspension for Crane.

Both Crane and Montague made their symbols, not through the conventional epic form, but through a lyrical impulse to invest their symbols with epic proportions. To do this, they both used autobiographical details with a submerged personality; a composite female figure to represent the nation and what one derives from a relationship with it; and the counters of both space and time. Their poems are triumphs of a new form which weaves together all the strands of the old world and the new into the patterns of history.

Notes

1. The text of Crane's *The Bridge* cited throughout this essay is that found in *The Complete Poems and Selected Letters and Prose of Hart Crane* (Garden City, N.Y.: Doubleday, 1966). In *The Bridge,* Crane sees the ocean as a connecting span—"For here between two worlds, another, harsh, / This third of water, tests the word . . ."; the memory as a highway between past and present, east and west—"Macadam, gun-grey as the tunny's belt, / Leaps from Far Rockaway to Golden Gate . . ."; and the Mississippi as river holding together continent, like the tunnel under the East River—"Here by the River that is East—/ Here at the waters' edge the hands drop memory. . . ."

2. Timothy Kearney, "The Poetry of the North: A Post-Modernist Perspective," *The Crane Bag,* III, 2 (1979), p. 48.

3. R. W. B. Lewis calls the poem "the epic effort of an initially lyric poet" in *The Poetry of Hart Crane: A Critical Study* (Princeton: Princeton University Press, 1967), p. 225. L. S. Dembo, on the other side, calls it "a romantic epic given lyric implications" in *Hart Crane's Sanskrit Charge: A Study of "The Bridge,"* (Ithaca: Cornell University Press, 1960), p. 10. Yvor Winters utters the most damning judgment: "*The Bridge* is a loosely joined sequence of lyrics, and some of the individual pieces have only a tenuous connection with the principal themes." Those poems which follow the "Powhaten's Daughter" section "are thrown haphazardly together," he goes on in *In Defense of Reason* (Denver: University of Denver Press, 1947), pp. 591, 594.

4. Vincent Quinn, *Hart Crane* (New York: Twayne Publishers, 1963), p. 73.

5. Dembo, p. 30.

6. Samuel Hazo, *Hart Crane: An Introduction and Interpretation* (New York: Barnes and Noble, 1963), p. 68.

7. Hazo, p. 120.

8. The text of *The Rough Field* cited in this essay is that of the first edition: John Montague, *The Rough Field* (Dublin: The Dolmen Press, October 1972).

9. Kearney, p. 48.

10. "To Gorham Munson," "To Waldo Frank," *The Letters of Hart Crane,* ed. Brom Weber (New York: Hermitage House, 1952), pp. 125, 242.

Thomas Dillon Redshaw (essay date 1982)

SOURCE: Redshaw, Thomas Dillon. "That Surviving Sign: John Montague's *The Bread God* (1968)." *Éire-Ireland* 17, no. 2 (1982): 56-91.

[*In the following essay, Redshaw offers a thorough analysis of Montague's* The Bread God *(1968) and explores the influence of William Carlton, an eighteenth-century writer from County Tyrone, on the work.*]

Although *The Bread God* (December, 1968) appeared after the printing of *Hymn to the New Omagh Road* (May, 1968), John Montague set the latter as the seventh canto and the former as the third of *The Rough Field* (1972). Both cantos exploit the typographical largesse of Liam Miller's design to display Montague's early understanding of the sentiments of his persona. As a fictive character, Montague's autobiographical persona achieves dramatic presence in each canto through signs of thought and feeling commingled and sometimes at odds. *Hymn to the New Omagh Road* exploits parody and satire to delineate the influence of modernization upon Tyrone, while *The Bread God* employs memoir and elegy to celebrate familial ties to a place or *topos* offering "that surviving sign of grace," and of vocation. Each canto's formal display and span of allusion present signs, also, of the persona's inward *psychomachia,* set in relief by the contrast between a remembered world, *"a local pride,"* and the tangible, changing present. If *The Bread God* is rooted in memory, then part of its substance has been inherited from the Tyrone romancer William Carleton, whose memories of Tyrone Montague claimed as also his:

> For a youngster living on the edge of the Clogher Valley the stories of Wiliam Carleton were not fiction but fact; gradually one learnt the genealogy of the various houses, gathered a hint of the intricate law-cases and local feuds, saw Orange drummers practising before a tin-roofed lodge. . . . Clamping turf in an upland bog, one could see, across the cramped heathery hills, the mountain which had haunted all of Carleton's work, particularly his longing imitative verse, an image of thoughtless happy youth in green fields.[1]

Behind Montague's early appreciation of the 19th-century Irish novelist lies the same autobiographical focus that shapes Montague's later essays "The Rough Field" (1963) and "A Primal Gaeltacht" (1970). In this manner Carleton's own sensibility, despite its Victorian manners, models Montague's. But Montague's "Tribute to William Carleton" (1952) primarily displays Carleton's vision of Ireland languishing between the Penal Days and the Famine in implied comparison with Ireland just emerging from the austerity of the "Great Emergency."

William Carleton's fiction has its roots in the erratic circumstances of his early life. In his *Autobiography* he states that he was born on February 20, 1794, in Prillisk near the episcopal "city" of Clogher, and from there he made his way to Dublin, marriage, and Protestantism. Like Kavanagh's *The Green Fool,* Carleton's *Autobiography* shows that his memories informed the sectarian stories he wrote for Rev. Caesar Otway's *Christian Examiner* during the years 1827-31. Carleton gave these stories final form in the 1842 edition of his *Traits and Stories of the Irish Peasantry,* which went through eleven editions by 1876. After outlining his own biography in the 1854 edition of *Traits and Stories,* Carleton explains that ". . . in undertaking to describe the Irish peasantry as they are, I approached that difficult task with advantages of knowing them, which perhaps few other Irish writers ever possessed; *and this is the only merit which I claim.*"[2] Carleton's most remarkable novels—*Faradarougha the Miser* (1837), *The Black Prophet* (1846), and *The Emigrants of Ahadarra* (1847)—offer documentary portraits, in folk-Gothic and melodramatic frames, of a rural Ireland fall-

ing into the Famine. To describe Carleton's melodramas as documentaries might seem misleading, yet, in *Poor Scholar,* Benedict Kiely quotes Carleton's introduction to his *Tales of Ireland* (1834) thus:

> I found them [the people of Ireland] a class unknown in literature, unknown by their own landlords, and unknown in whose hands much of their destiny was placed. If I became the historian of their habits and manners, their feelings, their prejudices, their superstitions and their crimes, if I have attempted to delineate their moral, religious and physical state, it was because I saw no person willing to undertake a task which surely must be looked upon as an important one.[3]

The reasonableness of Carleton's essays masks the sensibility out of which sprang his fictions. In each story and novel Carleton mixes sincere industry with his social conscience, and in the mixing arises his Dickensian sense of vital contradiction. His fictions are arrested by juxtapositions that embrace the comic and the melodramatic, the parochial and the provincial, the Catholic heart and the Protestant mind *without* attempting to seek harmonious unities. Anachronisms satisfy his fiction. Kiely's *Poor Scholar* presents Carleton as a tragicomic hero caught between his extravagant sense of comedy, and his unflinching sense of actuality—his vision of the "black sky." Carleton's sensibility tended at every unexpected turn to seek puritan simplicities of natural fact and of human nature. This quality of heart and mind Montague focuses on in his tribute:

> A large part of Carleton's genius was, that although the urge was in him to go far afield, to win fame in cities by the power of the written word, he always remained a countryman at heart, irascible and emphatic, marked for life by that kind of broad ruthless simplicity which sees things in their lowest common terms and refuses to be deceived by the trappings; a reaction which to the townsman seems only one stage removed from mysticism.[4]

Montague remarks upon Carleton's sensibility rather equivocally: he refrains from enlarging the peasant's "brute sense of acceptance" into a *Gaeilgeoir* nobility, unlike F. R. Higgins, Daniel Corkery, or Liam O'Flaherty. Montague emphasizes Carleton's "ruthless simplicity" as one source of spiritual endurance in the face of changeless change, which Carleton met in the Famine. Such survival forms the first theme of the third canto of Montague's *The Rough Field,* whose title—*The Bread God*—takes a rather Augustan subtitle—"A lecture / with illustrations in verse / on the recent history of the church in the ancient parish of Errigal Kieran / already referred to in the Annals of the Four Masters as being a monastic centre twelve centuries ago"—and anachronistically links it with a tongue-in-cheek warning: "Listeners are warned that reception may be interfered with by pirate stations, but every effort will be made to provide undisturbed contemplation."[5] The joking contrast of the Radio Telefís Éireann announcer with the Church of Ireland antiquary masks the sobriety of Montague's intent. Montague orients *The Bread God*'s "lecture"—in six verses—and its "illustrations"—in six prose passages—towards "the recent history of the church" revealed by memory in the prose and complemented by present perception in the verse. The site in the landscape of Tyrone that Montague's *paruchia* of Errigal Kieran measures out about its parishioners extends the fact of spiritual survival back fifteen centuries beyond the vicissitudes of clerical rigidity, the Famine, and the Penal Days to the time of the native, Celtic church.

During the 5th century the missions of Palladius and Patrick established in Ireland a Celtic church whose individuality arose in the nature of its organization. The Celtic church was founded by roving *peregrini* who settled alone on hills and islands, by wells and fords. They built stone huts, or *clocháin,* and became hermit-priests. Montague's Errigal Kieran was once such a settlement. The *Annals of the Four Masters* records the death of a monastic scribe there in 810, when the site was known as *Aireagal Dachíaróg (Do-Chíaróg),* "The Residence of Saint Dachiarog."[6] Other hermit-priests built *clocháin* and soon a monastery grew up, which was governed by an abbot-bishop who asserted authority over the local population of regular clergy, anchorites, and wandering friars known as the Culdees or *Céile dé.* Even after the Synod Whitby (663), the Celtic church emphasized eremetic religious life. While Irish monasteries were famed for their learning from the Celtic Romanesque period to their disestablishment during the Tudor Plantations, the religious life they sustained stressed the simplicity and individuality of devotion.

A millenium later, the Catholic church in Ireland reverted to its original peregrinal, anchoritic state. During the Williamite Plantations (1691-1703), the Protestant Ascendancy of Ireland passed through the Dublin Parliament legislation securing their colonial status as land-holders against the claims of native Catholics and northern Dissenters. Phrased in a strictly sectarian manner, as in the "Anti-Popery Acts" of 1704, the Penal Laws made it nearly impossible for any Roman Catholic to acquire land or to hold what property still remained his. The Penal Laws also contained disabling statutes excluding both Catholics and Dissenters from political life. Ancillary legislation, in petty detail, instituted a *Kulturkampf* against the society of native, Catholic Ireland, thus stripping the church of its properties, its schools, and its regular episcopal clergy.[7] Only the most elementary features of the church survived: the priest and his congregation. The church went "underground," for both the priests and their congregations disappeared into the wild camouflage of the Irish landscape. Until Catholic Emancipation in 1829, the solitary priest was

an independent missionary in a land made alien by the power of legislation. For the greater part of a century, priests imitated the vagrant life of itinerant polymaths. They became hedge-priests going in disguise from one congregation to another to celebrate the Eucharist in unmarked "mass-houses," or in the open air, under the eyes of a colonial, Protestant militia. William Carleton was ministered to in just this way:

> Within my own memory, there was nothing in existence for the Catholics for the worship of God except the mere altar, covered with a little open roof to protect the priest from rain, which it was incapable of doing. The altar was about two feet in depth, and the open shed which covered it not more than three, . . . In my early life, three such 'altars' were the only substitutes for the chapels in my native parish, which is one of the largest in the diocese. There was always a little plot of green sward allowed to be annexed to the altar, on which the congregation could kneel; . . .[8]

Carleton bases his fictional description of illicit acts of Catholic worship on just such memories. In the melodrama *Willy Reilly and His Dear Cooleen Bawn* (1855), Carleton depicts a forbidden Mass celebrated by a courageous bishop and his acolyte, the hero Willy Reilly:

> The neighbourhood in which they resided was, as we have said, remote, and exclusively Catholic; and upon Sundays the bishop celebrated mass upon a little grassy platform—or rather a little cave, into which it led. This cave was small, barely large enough to contain a table, which served as a temporary altar, the poor shivering congregation kneeling on the platform outside. . . . Messengers had been sent among them . . . and the consequence was that they not only kept the secret, but flocked in considerable numbers to attend mass.[9]

This humble ceremony is suddenly arrested by the arrival of Captain Smellpriest, who shouts: "You idolatrous Papist, stop that mummery—or you shall have twelve bullets in your heart before half a minute's time." Before Carleton launches into this melodramatic moment, he evokes the spirit of the ceremony: "two or three hundred persons kneeling" had "that gladsome opportunity of approaching the forbidden altar of God, now doubly dear to them that it *was* forbidden."[10] Earlier, in *Traits and Stories* (1842), Carleton based "The Midnight Mass" on a Christmas Eve Mass attended by a whole parish, each resident proceeding to the outdoor service by the light of a "blazing flambeau of bog-fir":

> He who stood at midnight upon a little mount which rose behind the chapel, might see between five and six thousand torches, all blazing together, and forming a level mass of red dusky light, burning against the horizon. These torches were so close to each other that their light seemed to blend, as if they had constituted one wide surface of flame; and nothing could be more preternatural looking than the striking and devotional

countenance of those who were assembled at their midnight worship, when observed beneath this canopy of fire.[11]

Montague opens *The Bread God* with precisely this passage, an "illustration" that alludes, through the intensity of Carleton's description, to the rift between past and present from which the poem draws its initial impetus. Quoting Carleton, Montague begins by suggesting the intense pre-Famine reverence of those who lived near Errigal Kieran by accenting Carleton's own emphasis on, not the Mass itself, but the custom of the torchlit progress that the people themselves invented. Certainly the significance of the torches partially derives from biblical sources: the prophets Isaiah and Zechariah; in the New Testament, St. Paul makes messianic fire the test of enduring faith (I Cor. 3: 13). In the circumstances Carleton describes, and which Montague emphasizes, any hedge-priest must have perceived the condition of his parishioners in those terms. And, perhaps, these communicants understood their reverence in the same biblical terms, having chosen to bear the fires that test their devotion, thus illumining and proving its survival.

Represented by a candle, the torch figures in the church's rite of the consecration of the font,[12] but the "blazing flambeau of bog-fir" carried by Carleton's characters probably takes its significance from Irish folk ways. Before the Famine, the Irish countryman often extinguished his hearth-fire during times of pestilence, famine, or civil disturbance. He would then take an ember from the fire of his parish priest and kindle his own fire, as if to purify his hearth in troubled times. Patrick prevailed over the druids of Ireland at Tara by lighting the Paschal fire.[13] At *Samhain* and *Beltaine,* bonfires customarily were lit for prophetic or propitiatory purposes. The *Beltaine* or May Day bonfires provided ritual sport, as young men and women would jump through them to show their desire for early marriage. And, according to the mythical history of Ireland, the *Beltaine* fires commemorate the discovery of fire by the druid Mide.[14] Irish myth plays also upon the cosmic duality that finds in the individual hearth the general altar, in the home-body wife the guardian goddess, and in the humble turf fire the divine flame. So, fire stands for the luminous masculine principle and, as well, symbolizes spiritual transformation in all its illuminating power. And Carleton's description exactly focuses on this sense of surviving spiritual growth.

Montague juxtaposes his "illustration" from Carleton's *Traits and Stories* with the first poem in *The Bread God*'s "lecture." Like **"Process"** in *Hymn to the New Omagh Road* (*TRF* [*The Rough Field*] 53), **"Christmas Morning"** presents one sentence whose argument avoids poetic statement until the sentence reaches its close. So, at first, the "lecture" seems just to extend Carleton's description into a record of one particular Christmas. The fabric of the poem's images—held together by a long warp of assonance and consonance—seems intent on simply describing Montague's **"Christmas Morning"** so as to show how like past and present are: "Lights outline a hill / As silently the people, / Like shepherd and angel / On that first morning, . . ." (*TBG* [*The Bread God*] iv). The patient understatement of Montague's verse reinforces this effect. The shift of sonic patterns follows the sentence's gradual syntax— ". . . March from Altcloghfin, / Beltany, Fallaghearn, / Under rimed hawthorn, . . ."—as if to imitate the gradual arrival of "the people" at the "Gray country chapel."

"Christmas Morning" faintly echoes Carleton's description: the lights that "outline a hill" seem to be candles carried by the arriving congregation. Their quiet assembly suggests that certain pieties have survived, and so even "that first morning" seems to have returned. Yet, by presenting the "rimed hawthorn, / Glinting evergreen," these lines withhold the mystery of commemoration "the people" have come to celebrate, like the Magi. Precisely as the poem's "lecture" attends to each detail, so the poem's tone modulates and, as the parishioners approach, the poem discovers that they are not shepherds, the Magi, nor angels, but just local folk who gather "in the warmth / and cloud of their breath." The image's ambiguity offers a first hint of irony: although breath may be taken as spirit or *pneuma,* the assembly of Mass-goers also may seem to be patient cattle. But the poem's observations do not pause; they follow the congregation past the *crèche* into the

> . . . country chapel
> Where a gas-lamp hisses
> To light the crib
> Under the cross-beam's
> Damp curled message:
> *Gloria in excelsis.*

Montague's slant rhymes abandon consonance for the sibilance of "paths" and "ice," and his assonance concentrates on the steady hissing of the "gas-lamp." The spirit of the Christmas holiday seems gradually more half-hearted, gray and dreary, as if the congregation expected more than a "Damp curled message." Montague wields an equivocal precision in these last lines in order to evade both sentiment and criticism. Yet, his precision's slight ironies announce the "lecture": that the survival of piety does not ensure its achievement; that the rigors of survival pare away the warmth of emotion and leave but a skeleton of religious observation; and that, paradoxically, the survival of a faith so reduced to duty signifies its loss.

The survival of dutiful piety may signify less than it appears to do. *The Bread God*'s second "illustration" confirms the anticlimactic intimations of **"Christmas**

Morning" by striking through objectivity with personal witness, while also confounding the first "illustration": "Yes, I remember Carleton's description of Christmas in Tyrone, but things had changed at the end of the century" (*TBG* v). The voice is that of the poet's uncle, the Rev. Thomas Montague, S.J.; the "illustration" is an excerpt from a letter dated "Christmas, Melbourne, 1960." The quotation alludes to *The Bread God*'s dedicatory quatrain and, also, to Montague's early monologue **"Soliloquy on a Southern Strand"** (1958), in which Montague's spiritual hero declines into perplexity: "No martyrdom, no wonder, no real loss, / An old man ailing on the Australian coast: / Is it for that poor ending that I / Have carried all this way my cross?"[15] Montague's poem romanticizes this predicament, while the priest's letter describes from memory a lost condition of communal piety:

> . . . We had one mass at 10 o'clock on Sundays at which a handful went to communion. We went to confession and communion about every four months. The priests did not take much interest in the people and did not visit them except for sick calls.
>
> (*TBG* v)

By bringing familial testimony into *The Bread God,* Montague inches his "illustrations" towards chronological congruence with his poetic "lecture" so as to document the loss of spirituality in his native parish. At the century's turn, religious life in Tyrone had become more a matter of class than of devotion: ". . . I became a priest because we were the most respectable family in the parish but what I really wanted to do was to join the army: so you see how your uncle became a Jesuit!" This particular "illustration" also obtains a less documentary effect. Its familial background, its personal locutions, and its confidential intimacy present a living voice that disturbs the chilly objectivity of **"Christmas Morning."** The insertion of this voice also foreshadows the poet's insertion of his own persona into *The Bread God.* Such an infusion complicates and then resolves the whole canto's ironic stance towards the Christmas celebration that forms the simple topic of the "lecture."

Just as the poetic "lecture" of *The Bread God* continues despite the interrupting "illustrations," so the Christmas Mass begins despite the breathless arrival of the "late-comer": "Hesitant step of a late-comer: / Fingers dip at the font, fly / Up to the roof of the forehead / With a sigh" (*TBG* v). In **"Late-Comer"** the "lecture" again takes up its documentary stance to observe the wary arrival of a tardy parishioner who, at first, seems contrite and reverent. Yet, just as the epistolary "illustration" confirmed the critical intimations of **"Christmas Morning,"** so **"Late-Comer"** more concretely suggests the equivocality of rural piety.

> On St. Joseph's
> Outstretched arm, he hangs his cap

> Then spends a very pleasant mass
> Studying the wen-marked heads
> Of his neighbours, or gouging
> His name in the soft wood
> Of the choirloft, with the cross
> Of his rosary beads.

At this point Montague's management of detail brings to every observation a critical tone. This parishioner's "very pleasant mass" evidently means little more to him than social custom. His interest wanders away from the simple responses of the ceremony. St. Joseph is his hatrack; Mass is a social occasion; his crucifix is only a tool for his own minor immortality. By suspending the telling point of attention until last, Montague's "lecture" obtains its closure: ". . . with the cross / Of his rosary beads." By carving his "name in the soft wood / Of the choirloft," the "late-comer" seems to have forgotten the trials his ancestors underwent during the 18th and early 19th centuries to maintain the privilege of celebrating the Eucharist. Yet, his uncaring gesture—"gouging"— recalls the carving of "Penal Crosses" that once were popular, illicit signs of faith. In particular, his casual gesture negates the craft of such carving, which originated around the junction of Counties Donegal, Fermanagh, and Tyrone during the first years of the Penal Days.[16]

The Bread God's two units of "illustration" and "lecture" display a restraint that, thus far, apparently prepares for critical intimations no more harsh than those in **"Late-Comer." "Christmas Morning"** and **"Late-Comer"** record a 20th-century Mass-going, which concludes in **"After Mass"** (*TBG* vii). The Christmas Mass itself takes up two units of the "lecture": **"Late-Comer"** and **"The Crowds for Communion."** The third and fourth of *The Bread God*'s "illustrations" coincide, however, with the ceremony's chief acts: oblation, consecration, and communion. Remarkably—for here the canto's equanimity suffers brutal disturbance—the third "illustration" coincides with the climactic mystery of consecration and transubstantiation. Emotionally and intellectually, this forms the most important moment in the ceremony, for then the sacred idea of the agapic love-feast, or *deipnon,* ritually emerges out of the inevitable possibilities of the act and idea of sacrifice.[17]

In *The Bread God,* this sequence of sacred gestures and events—the heart of the Eucharistic ceremony—is withheld from the reader's direct view, as if the whole third "illustration" formed a verbal *iconostasia.* This highly ornamented, verbal screen between the reader and the sacral event interrupts suddenly, surreptitiously offered "*In a plain Envelope marked* IMPORTANT" (*TBG* vii).[18] The dramatic shock here derives from the voice of this "illustration": anonymous, alien, negative. Free of personal identity and responsibility, it revels in a traditionally ritualized hysteria that reflects what it wishes to hide and accentuates what it desires to destroy.

THE BREAD GOD
the DEVIL *has* CHRIST *where he wants* HIM
A HELPLESS INFANT IN ARMS: A DEAD CHRIST ON THE CROSS
ROME'S CENTRAL ACT OF WORSHIP IS THE EUCHARISTIC
WAFER:
IDOLATRY: THE WORST IDOL UNDER HEAVEN
NOSELESS, EYELESS, EARLESS, HELPLESS, SPEECHLESS.

(*TBG* vi)

The *"plain Envelope"* delivers slogans of a sort brushed on the walls of Sandy Row and Donegal Road in Belfast, or of Fountain and Irish streets in Derry. Culturally and sociologically more *"Important"* than icons of "King Billy," such sentiments display the mentality of the antagonist. Their intrusion into *The Bread God* makes them dramatically shocking, psychotic. Hysterical propaganda of an uncomfortably familiar sort, these words of a true believer attain, in anonymity, flawless intemperance. Their argument is an overtly Orange one founded less on anti-Catholic bigotry, and even less on Protestant concerns, than on dim issues distorted by three centuries of uncomprehending paranoia. The most static-ridden of these interferences from "pirate stations," this "illustration" introduces the two that, in the midst of *The Bread God,* take up the most harshly ironic stance towards the "lecture" of the poem.

The first propagandistic assertion attempts to reduce the Mass to a diabolical—*"the* DEVIL *has* CHRIST *where he wants* HIM"—celebration of death, which assertion inverts the significance of the Christmas Mass presented in *The Bread God*'s "lecture." It understands crucifixes, like the Penal Crosses, as displays of only a mortal image: "A DEAD CHRIST ON THE CROSS." The second assertion comprehends "ROME'S CENTRAL ACT OF WORSHIP" literally. So, the material symbols of the Eucharist, rather than the ceremony itself, are mistaken for the object of worship, as if the anonymous voice can understand only death and material things. Thus, this blinkered formula follows: "THE EUCHARISTIC / WAFER: / IDOLATRY: THE WORST IDOL UNDER HEAVEN." Such a formula constitutes nothing so sophisticated as Fundamentalism. Only inbred fear could conclude that such a ceremony renders Christ powerless as "THE BREAD GOD . . . NOSELESS, EYELESS, EARLESS, HELPLESS, SPEECHLESS." The literal incomprehension of these grotesque visions has, however, the ironic effect of heightening the significance of the Christmas Mass quietly described in *The Bread God*'s "lecture." Indeed, in the timing of the poem's fiction, this anonymous outburst coincides with the Christmas Mass's *elevatio.* The contorted tone of this "illustration" also suggests that this "illustration" may announce a symbol of other than Christian import whose significance may lie outside the poem's local ironies.

Montague's deployment of coincidence sustains the dramatic antiphony between "illustration" and "lecture"

in *The Bread God.* The "lecture" provides—in **"Christmas Morning," "Late-Comer,"** and then **"The Crowds for Communion"**—the continuing fiction of one Christmas Mass-going that the "illustrations" interrupt. Yet, through timing, irony, and *logopoeia,* the interruptions achieve dramatic harmony. So, while the poem's alternation of poetic "illustration" with "lecture" implies an interior drama of intimation countered by intimation, the responsive tensions do not find argumentative statement, as they do in **Hymn to the New Omagh Road**'s **"Balance Sheet"** (*TRF* 54-55). The cultivated reticence of *The Bread God*'s "lecture" forbids such declarations. The calm description in **"The Crowds for Communion"** hardly answers the hysteria of the first Orange "illustration." Pose the shrill of "*the* DEVIL *has* CHRIST *where he wants* HIM" against:

> The crowds for communion, heavy coat and black
> shawl,
> Surge in thick waves, cattle thronged in a fair,
> To the oblong of altar rails, and there
> Where red berried holly shines against gold. . . .

(*TBG* vi)

Imitating the approach of the congregation to the altar and communion, the period of **"The Crowds for Communion"** paces slowly through the poem's one octet. The sentence's texture reflects pauses of attention as well as the moving sounds of the congregation. The subdued tone of the holiday—bitterly flavored by the ironies of **"Christmas Morning"** and **"Late-Comer"**—apparently bespeaks the lifelessness that the "illustration" accusingly perceived in "ROME'S CENTRAL ACT OF WORSHIP." The appositive "cattle thronged in a fair" suggests a congregational apathy first hinted at in **"Christmas Morning."** Direct and bleak, the comparison briefly colors the poem: "the oblong of altar rails" resembles a cattle pen, but that intuition does not survive the sight of the altar. The octet's fourth line flows around images so bright they hark back to the medieval Irish lyric. Before the altar's glow of candle-lit ewer, paten, chalice and monstrance, the parishioners ". . . wait patient / And prayerful and crowded, for each moment / Of silence, eyes closed, mouth raised / For the advent of the flesh-graced Word."

While the first quatrain moved toward exclamatory images, the second gradually focuses on the individual communicant, rather than the whole congregation. What first appears to be bovine passivity becomes individual certitude. Human anticipation of atonement and salvation through the Host, evoked in "the advent of the flesh-graced Word," gives the scene's particulars a simple nobility. As the gestures—"eyes closed, mouth raised"—become distinct they deny *Thanatos* and contradict the threatening Orange "illustration." This one moment has changed little since the parishioners of Errigal Kieran worshipped in the *scathláin* of the Penal Days.

DEAR BROTHER!
ECUMENISM *is* THE NEW NAME *of the* WHORE OF BABYLON!
SHE *who* SHITS *on the* SEVEN HILLS

(*TBG* vii)

Just as the third "illustration" shocked the "lecture," so the fourth interferes with **"The Crowds for Communion"** and screens the moment of communion. The reticence of that "lecture" cannot resist the revivalist salutation, ironic as it is. This interruption distracts even as it offends, for the anonymous voice taunts the idolatry of "papishry" and the "pope-heads." If such words express thought at all, then the ideas they broadcast are all *idées reçues* passed on by a long history of religious disputation that began with the Lollard Wyclif. Thus, the chief device of the "illustration" constitutes an irrationally charged commonplace. William Tyndale's arguments in *The Obedience of a Christian Man* (1528) and *The Practise of Prelates* (1530) so frequently employed such conceits that they passed, via pamphlets and popular preaching, into the dissenting English vernacular.[19] Strangled and burnt for heresy, William Tyndale (1495-1536) adopted the conceit while translating his New Testament (1525) from Erasmus's Greek Testament. The conceit figures largely in the visions of The Revelation of St. John the Divine (Rev. 17: 5-6). Tutored in the vernacular Bible by centuries of vigorous preaching, the dissenting imagination kept the vision of the "Whore of Babylon" alive as, at least, an angry expletive. Certainly the notion gained currency in Ulster with the arrival of the Scots Presbyterians during the Cromwellian and Williamite Plantations, as Andrew Fairservice's description of Glasgow Minster in *Rob Roy,* Sir Walter Scott's Jacobite romance, suggests.[20]

The ritualized anger indulged in by the anonymous voice reduces the symbol to an absurdity, for, by "shitting" on the seven hills—or seven heads or kings—the "MOTHER OF HARLOTS" punishes those who "shall make war with the Lamb." Such a contradiction compounds that in the salutation—"DEAR BROTHER!"—and prepares for an exclamatory syllogism of inherited attitudes: "ONE CHURCH, ONE STATE / WITH THE POPE THE HEAD OF THE STATE: BY RE-UNION / ROME MEANS ABSORPTION / UNIFORMITY MEANS TYRANNY." The import of this "illustration" rests in the argument's confusion, one which characterizes the speaker's emotional fidelity to his own liberties. The speaker focuses so obsessively on presumed evils— "ONE CHURCH, ONE STATE"—that his sense of his own liberty seems insecure. In a dissenting manner, he opposes a harmony between church and state that he considers "papist," yet his Unionist allegiance to Great Britain upholds a state church. He finds a papist plot in the term "RE-UNION," which excites his fear of being dominated by a Roman Catholic state upon the reunification of Ireland. Such a speaker could not admit that, in the 1790s, Orange Lodges throughout Ireland

campaigned against Castlereagh's coercion of the Dublin Parliament into accepting the 1801 Act of Union.[21] More ironically, he would take pride in the fact that, because the Orange Order opposed Home Rule, Ulster Unionists achieved a degree of home rule eight years before the Irish Free State was established.

One element welds these contradictions into the Ulster Unionist stance. Since the Cromwellian Plantations, an aggressive ignorance of Roman Catholicism has always been exacerbated by historical and class anxieties in Ulster. This again and again appears in the dissenter's defense of the primacy of individual conscience. However, even before the "Penal Days," this defense had taken on an Orwellian flavor.[22] "UNIFORMITY MEANS TYRANNY" is an Orwellian expression, as is the whole syllogism. Such language preaches only to the converted. To look back a century, Carleton's experience of Unionist "UNIFORMITY" aptly describes the Orange "TYRANNY" such arguments ignore:

> Merciful God! In what a frightful condition was the country at that time. I speak now of the North of Ireland. It was then, indeed, the seat of Orange ascendancy and irresponsible power. To find a justice of the peace *not* an Orangeman would have been an impossibility. The grand jury room was little less than an Orange lodge. There was no law *against* an Orangeman, and no law *for* a Papist.[23]

And, as if to heap contradiction upon contradiction, Montague permits his propagandist to plead for the very pluralism his words attack: "*But* GOD DELIGHTS IN VARIETY / NO *two leaves are* EXACTLY *alike*!"

The Bread God's Christmas congregation cannot perceive, of course, the two Unionist "illustrations" that Montague offers the reader. Conversely, the second Orange "illustration" masks the congregation's moments of individual communion. Montague completes this dramatic irony in **"After Mass,"** whose tone and measure echo **"Christmas Morning."** However, more than Montague's management of tactical irony makes it difficult for these parishioners to sense, as the reader does, the atmosphere of insult and threat overshadowing their modest Mass-going. The manner of those who wait outside the chapel—"already assembled / Around the oak-tree, / Heavy brogues, thick coats" (*TBG* vii)— shows that they see nothing remarkable in the Christmas Mass, nor do they take much account of the atmosphere that clouds their lives. Typically, the men stand about "Staring at the women, / Sheltering cigarettes." Montague's objectivity expresses the atmosphere by making no attempt to lighten or penetrate it. The people observed by **"After Mass"** seem ruled by an awkward impassivity: they wait and "stare" and "shelter" only the glow of cigarettes in their cupped hands. No one holds an extinguished candle, let alone Carleton's "blazing flambeau of bog-fir." Their apathy seems but resignation complicated by distrust:

Once a politician came
Climbed on the graveyard wall
And they listened to all
His plans with the same docility;
Eyes quiet, under caps
Like sloped eaves.

(*TBG* v)

In Irish communities like Garvaghey, more than a topographical fate forces the "politician" to set out his "plans" from the "graveyard wall." His words fall "dead" at the feet of the "dead" in the land of the "dead." The "docility" of the congregation puts them beyond politics or "plans." After decades of contradiction and crisis, survival has resolved into a matter of remaining private, immovable. Like politicians, Christmases come year after year: continuities of life depend on familiar events announced, not in exclamations of *Gloria in excelsis,* but in mimeographed notices: "a football match; / Pearses v's Hibernians. . . ." The failure of politics echoes in the names of the football teams: Pádraic Pearse captaining the Easter Rising's insurrectionists against the Ancient Order of Hibernians led by the Home Rule nationalists like Joe Devlin, which "match" precedes "a Monster Carnival / In aid of Church Funds / Featuring Farrel's Band."[24]

The "docility" of the parishioners in **"After Mass"** finds explanation in the next "illustration," whose protestations document the Orange inheritance by incarnating a nightmare of sectarian vengeance as well as a political myth of numberless wrongs—of innocent blood spilt on Ulster soil: "LOYALISTS REMEMBER! / MILLIONS *have been* MURDERED *for refusing to* GROVEL / *Before Rome's Mass-Idol*: THE HOST" (*TBG* viii). The Unionist propagandist stridently alludes—"LOYALISTS REMEMBER!"—to the Irish Rising (1641-1650), which culminated in the Cromwellian Plantation of Ireland. The Orange version of the Rising's first phase inaccurately interprets "The War of the Three Kingdoms": "*King Charles I and his Frog Queen Henrietta* GLOAT *in their* / LETTERS / *that they have almost* EXTERMINATED THE PROTESTANTS OF / IRELAND / *The* PRIESTS *in every* PARISH *were told to record* HOW MANY / *killed!*"

This Orange myth originates in the rebellion of Rory O'More and Sir Phelim O'Neill against the Long Parliament in support of Charles I. Although More's coup failed, his and O'Neill's followers—displaced Gaelic Ulstermen—killed some ten thousand of the Ulster Scots Planters loyal to the Long Parliament.[25] After Charles I broke with Parliament, the Irish organized the "loyalist" Catholic Confederation of Kilkenny (1642). Ulster Planters and Irish Protestants quickly established the "convention that the Ulster Catholics had risen and slaughtered the Ulster Protestants to . . . a plan worse than that of St. Bartholomew."[26] Encrusted by centuries of myth-making, that conviction still twists history into

such contradictory exaggerations as: "*Under* ROGER MORE AND SIR PHELIM O'NEILL / *Instruments of Rome / 40,000 loyal protestants were* MASSACRED *like game-fowl* / IN ONE NIGHT." The timing of the insurrection is a patent fantasy; moreover, the Ulster Scots Planters were "loyal" only to Parliament and not the Stuart monarchy. After Oliver Cromwell took command of Parliamentary forces, the notion that the Irish Rising was designed by malign Papist intelligence seemed confirmed by Owen Roe O'Neill's victory at Benburb in Tyrone, thus: "'*Cromwell went to Ireland* / TO STOP / *The Catholics murdering Protestants!*'" Cromwell followed his occupation of Dublin in 1649 with the sack of Drogheda and Wexford. Some 3,500 Royalists were executed at Drogheda alone. Under the terms of the Cromwellian Settlement (1652) Parliament suppressed Protestant and Catholic Royalists by turning their lands throughout Ireland over to Cromwellian veterans. Those Irish who held to Gaelic, Old English, or Catholic ways were banished to Connachy by the 1653 Act of Satisfaction.[27] Thus, the history of Cromwell's campaigns provided the primal myth of Orangeism:

> . . . the plantation, the wilderness settled with bible and sword, the massacres of 1641, and the martyrdom of the settlers by the treacherous and barbarous uprising of the natives; the threat to 'freedom, religion and laws' caused by the accession of the popish James II, the glorious revolution which overthrew him, the sufferings, endurance, valour and triumph of the cause at Derry, Enniskillen, Aughrim and the Boyne.[28]

The third Orange "illustration," climactically tests the poetic "lecture." This middle movement of *The Bread God* balances "lecture" against "illustration" so as to make increasingly severe the tensions moving *The Bread God* forward: tensions between versed lines of attention and the prose of the "found" poem; between tones of ironic apathy and incensed fear; tensions between discordant allusions and contrary symbols. As the documentary thrall of both "lecture" and "illustration" increases by repetition, so the dramatic tension strains towards resolution.

Resolution comes in **"Penal Rock / Altamuskin,"** and in the form of wedded poetic and personal gestures of conscious identification and defiance. Formally, the fifth "lecture," a recognizable sonnet, compromises Spenserian and Shakesperian forms by weaving assonance and consonance into terminal slant rhyme without, however, closing its periods of expression up in quatrains before the couplet. Such a surprising assertion of a traditional, closed form draws attention to the poetic gesture. The formal gesture completes Montague's dramatic design by accenting the design's personality in recalling Montague's dedicatory quatrain to the whole of *The Bread God*:

> I break again into the lean parish of my art
> Where huddled candles flare before a shrine

And men with caps in hand kneel stiffly down
To see the many-fanged monstrance shine.

(*TBG* [iii])

Following the dedication—"for Thomas Montague, S.J."—this quatrain links the strict, closed verse form with personal, self-conscious expression that distinguishes **"Penal Rock / Altamuskin,"** from the rest of *The Bread God.* The quatrain frames a personal stance as well as a poetic one. "Lecture" and "illustration" thus break in with self-conscious observation, with their "art." The "lean parish" of Errigal Kieran contains camouflaged privacies—present and past, communal and individual, emotional and devotional—that abide in tradition and, so, shape the parish's spiritual topography. These intimacies live in the quatrain's vocabulary of nouns—"candles," "shrine," "caps," "monstrance"— and verbs—"flare," "kneel," "see," "shine"—that grow from a description of the actual. Yet, synonymy and repetition, analogy and variation weave the same vocabulary into the whole cloth of *The Bread God.* This vocabulary intensely marks off communal and individual privacies. By "breaking" out of intent or emotion "into the lean parish," Montague challenges the forbidden. Standing apart, his persona does not kneel before the Host, nor does he refuse to acknowledge it. Symbolic or real, the Eucharistic presence is by communal belief an actual one—at once glorious and threatening, terrible and forgiving. Both technically and thematically, Montague maintains a critically chosen stance between accepting worship and doubting rejection throughout *The Bread God* until it "breaks" into the resolving gesture of **"Penal Rock / Altamuskin."**

The formal gesture of **"Penal Rock / Altamuskin"** consists of its performance of the sonnet as a form, which achieves a more subtle effect than Montague's sudden, direct use of the "I" persona. Breaking the thrall of the intimidating "illustrations" and the passive "lecture," the sonnet's assertion of an individual personality closes the poem's address after both the persona and reader have consented "To learn the massrock's lesson. . . ." Such assent begins an invitation to Platonic learning: the persona breaks into his "lean parish"—down from the borrowed Austin on the road— into the realm of memory—from individual to familial to communal—that the isolated "Penal Rock" has stood for since the late 17th century. The sonnet's initial period—"To learn the massrock's lesson, leave your car, / Descend frost gripped steps to where / A humid moss overlaps the valley floor" (*TBG* viii)—leads into a landscape like that in **"The Lure"** in *Patriotic Suite* (*TRF* 60). The stressed assonances of these lines evoke stately simplicity. By taking up the consonants of the last rhymes, the sonnet's opening vowels predict the close of the quatrain in the start of the sonnet's second period:

Crisp as a pistol-shot, the winter air
Recalls poor Tagues, folding the nap of their freize
Under one knee, long suffering as beasts,
But parched for that surviving sign of grace,
The bog-Latin murmur of their priest.

The sights the mind "recalls" when startled out of contemporaneity arise first from familial and then communal memory as evanescent as the "lost cry / of the yellow bittern!" (*TRF* 60). The memory proves communal in an odd sense: "Teigue" or "Tague" once was the root of the poet's name, whose genealogical etymology foreshadows the sonnet's closing emphasis upon the presence of a persona in *The Bread God.*[29] The same etymology also links Montague's autobiographical persona back through two hundred "winters" to his people who, "long suffering as beasts," had endured the "freize" of poverty and persecution under the Penal Laws. As the sibilance of "freize" gathers the partial rhymes of the quatrain, so the pun on "freize" gathers the intuition of the stanza into an allusion to **"Emigrants"** in *Patriotic Suite* (1966) and also—by way of "long suffering as beasts"—back to the passive congregation in **"Christmas Morning"** and **"The Crowds for Communion."** Waiting in the cold and damp, the "poor Tagues" suffer in their wasted land—denied the reassurance of "that surviving sign of grace, / The bog-latin murmur of their priest." The nostalgia of the octet finds discipline in a critical note: the Latin is not pure or learned. It is "bog-latin" mumbled by a hedge-priest, the equivalent of the vagrant polymaths—like Carleton's Mat Kavanagh—of the 18th and early 19th centuries.

At the start of the sonnet's sestet, the attending mind begins to withdraw from the inherited image of congregations worshipping at this *scáthlán* in the open, wintry air:

A crude stone oratory, carved by a cousin
Commemorates the place. For two hundred years
People of our name have sheltered in this glen
But now all have left. A few flowers. . . .

Noticing the "massrock," the persona identifies it as "carved by a cousin." Engraved on that Tyrone stone appears the sign *crux* or *Christus,* rather than a name gouged in the soft wood / Of the choirloft, with a cross . . ." (*TRF* 23). In **"Penal Rock / Altamuskin"** the persona is no **"Late-comer,"** for a welcome identification with the place arises from familial history: "People of our name have sheltered in this glen." For two centuries the "Tagues," the MacTeagues and Montagues, found refuge there, "But now all have left."[30] Aware of the wintry isolation of the "massrock," the perceiving persona fails to realize that not "all have left," for the prodigal has returned. Even so, his eye picks out the symbol—"a few flowers"—of shared prodigality and reverence. The consonance of that rhyme draws the quatrain together in preparation for the closing gesture of the sonnet's couplet: "A few flowers / Wither on the altar, so I melt a ball of snow / From the hedge into their rusty tin before I go."

The simplicity of this gesture, and of the couplet, heightens the ambiguities of its significance. The "few flowers"—perhaps the frail blooms in *The Wild Dog Rose* (*TRF* 76-77)—were left to weather wind and sleet by some impulsive passer-by. Out of a like impulse, one restrained throughout *The Bread God,* the persona tries to rescue them. Figuratively anointing or baptizing, he waters them with snow melted by the shaping, transforming heat of his hands as if he momentarily were playing a priestly role in a rite as propitiatory and commemorative as the Eucharist documented by *The Bread God*'s "Lecture."

That intuition suggests an overly direct interpretation. The couplet's rhyme on "snow" and "go" proposes coincidence between the persona's presence and the negative season. Yet, the resonance of the gesture as a symbolic donation of life overwhelms those implications, especially since this one gesture takes a penultimate place in *The Bread God*'s "lecture." Melted from the "snow / From the hedge," as if from the mute essence of Daniel Corkery's "hidden Ireland," the water is intended to revive the altar flowers. Literally, it will not; figuratively it may, for the turn of season will melt all of Altamuskin's snow. Of course, the snow represents what *The Bread God* understands as powerful forces of negation: the Penal Days, Orangeism, contemporary apathy; thus the massrock's "few flowers" represent the positive *élan vital*: enduring simplicities of patient, parochial faith. So, by cross association, the persona makes a gesture of bloodless sacrifice in his private Mass when he gives his transforming energies to the "dead" snow and changes it into the "water of life." Yet, in their subtlety, the couplet's symbols do not distract emphasis from the couplet's most dramatic gesture. The witnessing persona of *The Bread God* breaks from his stubbornly impersonal stance to reassert his own character, as if the "massrock" at Altamuskin had identified him when he had personally recognized it.

Like other self-assertions through *The Rough Field,* and particularly in *A New Siege* (1970), the tone of such a gesture has been mistaken as self-serving. Shortsightedly, *The Honest Ulsterman* critics in particular have misread *The Rough Field*'s installments. Whenever and wherever expressed, such complaints usually betray a shallow understanding of *The Rough Field*—of its origins and history, its forms, and surfaces, and above all its informing symbolic drama.[31] The couplet closing *The Bread God*'s "Penal Rock / Altamuskin"—

> A few flowers
> Wither on the altar, so I melt a ball of snow
> From the hedge into their rusty tin before I go.

—does not casually or exploitatively stake out an exclusive claim to the Matter of Tyrone, let alone "The Ulster Goldmine." Rather, like **"Balance Sheet"** in *Hymn to the New Omagh Road,* or that canto's *"Envoi: The Search for Beauty"* (*TRF* 57), the couplet enacts a climactic gesture in *The Bread God*'s similar drama. Conflicting with the poem's documentary discipline, *The Bread God*'s understated ironies, its shifts in tonal direction, and its whole movement create a tension that, in **"Penal Rock / Altamuskin,"** at last discovers resolution in personal statement, assertion and gesture. Essentially *The Bread God* enacts an implicit *psychomachia* in which Montague's representative persona survives a struggle against what the documentary "lecture" and "illustrations" represent. As in *Hymn to the New Omagh Road,* the symbolic *agon* reënacts the "Hero Myth" in which consciousness, allegorized as the poem's Ego-Hero by Montague's manipulation of point of view, confronts a uroboric dragon of consuming unconsciousness. Thus, two sorts of unconsciousness—apathy and antagonism, documented in the "lecture" and "illustrations"—intensify the *psychomachia* of *The Bread God*'s persona.

Montague's design subjects the poem's implicitly autobiographical persona to the two-headed dragon of unconsciousness by alternating poetic units of "illustration" with units of "lecture," echoing the structural mode of **"Balance Sheet."** As in that section of *Hymn to the New Omagh Road* (*TRF* 54-55), **"Lecture"** and "illustration" discover dramatic relationships, in both vertical and lateral sequence throughout *The Bread God.* Of course, the tones struck in *The Bread God* differ in origin and effect: the whole poem's particular *logopoeia* does not pretend to the ironic comedy of *Hymn to the New Omagh Road.* Up to **"Penal Rock / Altamuskin,"** *The Bread God*'s "lecture" forms a documentary, lyric narrative that follows, despite interruptions, the plot of attending an ordinary Christmas Mass in rural Tyrone. Except for the dedicatory quatrain, Montague's persona keeps a critical distance from this particular Mass-going. Though the impulse to respond personally can be felt, rarely does the lyric narrative abandon its essential reserve. The congregation joins the Eucharistic celebration, but Montague's persona refuses that traditional comfort.

In *The Bread God*'s underlying symbolic drama, such participation would be a willful surrender of identity and selfhood to the congregation and, in turn, to the mystery in which both priest and congregation momentarily lose themselves. *The Bread God*'s persona withholds himself from the unifying round of incarnation and transformation enacted by the Mass. This persona's *non serviam* resists the conventional occasion for accepting the mystical unity and body of the church. That the poem's persona hesitates to offer up his own *prinicipium individuationis* does not indicate lack of familial or communal love, nor must it signify the persona's repudiation of pastoral authority. Montague's tones reflect his persona's prodigal alienation, yet their tenor in each "lecture" expresses a principled emotional inclination to put off the relief of participation in the unconsciousness of patient faith, conventional belief. Notably, Montague plots his "lecture" so that it cannot present, either out of modesty or anxiety, the climactic moment of the Mass. Yet, including the "illustrations," the whole of *The Bread God* parallels, in ritual sequence from oblation to communion, the symbolic events of the Latin Mass.

If "lecture" and "illustration" make a mural of the Mass, then both also picture the Janus-like, sectarian mentality of the Ulsterman—just as "LOSS" and "GAIN" record one phenomenon in **"Balance Sheet"** (*TRF* 54-55). Each face of Janus elicits a different response. The "lecture" tenders the persona the chance to rest in accepting belief, and he hesitates, withdraws, despite his sympathies. The "illustrations," thus, encounter little resistance from the "lecture" and compose themselves into a snapping, bellowing dragon-head of unconsciousness. A simpler and more obvious symbolism to follow, its presentation is neither the creation of narrative consciousness in the "lecture," nor an expression of *the Bread God*'s persona. The poem's point of view in the "lecture" reaches out to record experience, at least, while the climactic "illustrations" assault both the reader and the persona. The imagination comprehending the "illustrations" is dramatically rhetorical: each "illustration" is a quotation—from Carleton's *Traits and Stories,* from the letters of the poet's uncle, or from broadsides of Orange invective. While the "lecture" documents experience in a lyric narrative, the "illustrations" constitute "found poems."

Each "found" selection has the designed effect of adding to a curve of tones—from amazement and wonder to wry reflection to anxiety, bigoted paranoia—that counters the muted ironies of the "lecture." This curve also submerges the humane voices of William Carleton and the Rev. Thomas Montague in the hysterical anonymity of the Orange voice in the third, fourth, and fifth "illustrations." Unthinking, unfeeling, unconscious passions, thus, appear to devour identity, individuality. This assault shocks and repels both the reader and *the Bread God*'s persona. The unalloyed emotion of these "illustrations" helps them seem more intimidating then the solace offered by the "lecture." Yet, since they threaten, the persona resists them more instinctively than he does the repose in belief offered by the "lecture."

Until its resolution in **"Penal Rock / Altamuskin,"** *The Bread God*'s figurative *psychomachia* lets the

unconsciousness manifest in the "illustrations" push the persona toward escape into the Mass. But the Mass-going raises varied sensations of passive unconsciousness which, in the "lecture," repel him. Never insensitive to such conflicts of feeling, the persona—the particular consciousness that informs *The Bread God*—finds himself isolated twice over: as the prodigal stranger; as the valuing, discriminating participant in a spiritual life he has unavoidably inherited. At the same time, he must preserve his independence so as not to lose identity in either the calm or the hysterical unconsciousness of the true believer. His haunted *non serviam* seems, at heart, dramatically particular, rather than ideologically general. His stance proves as private as the gesture expressing it at the close of **"Penal Rock / Altamuskin."** Apart from the persona's renewed identification with the chosen symbol of the "mass-rock," that gesture consists of his impulsively watering the wilted bouquet on the altar. With this, Montague's persona takes on the role of priest by figuratively performing the *commixtio,* symbolizing resurrection, as would an ordained priest before offering the transubstantiated Host to the communicants. Thus, in Protestant way, Montague's persona becomes his own ministering priest, and so he confronts and comprehends both sorts of unconsciousness in one gesture. Having survived both, he asserts his powers, becomes the Ego-Hero, and momentarily resolves the *psychomachia* symbolically presented in *The Bread God.*

This hidden evolution of the persona's symbolic role during the dramatic conflict of "lecture" and "illustration" transforms the Mass itself into a ritual rooted more deeply in that hidden grammar of belief, recreated by mythologists like Robert Graves, than in the anchoritic culture of Celtic Christianity. Just as both priest and congregation mysteriously become both the sacrificers and the sacrificed during the Eucharist, so by a gesture the persona of *The Bread God* becomes his own priest, despite the risks. The privacy of this transformation, its wordlessness, finds protection in the "illustration" separating **"Penal Rock / Altamuskin"** from **"An Ulster Prophecy."** Another quotation from the Rev. Thomas Montague's letters, this acts like an *iconostasia* to the deliberate words of *The Bread God*'s "lecture," are the rather ordinary, hopeful words of an experienced priest of the Roman Catholic church:

> I sometimes wonder if anyone could have brought the two sides together. Your father, I know, was very bitter about having to leave but when I visited home before leaving for the Australian mission, I found our protestant neighbours friendly, and yet we had lost any position we had in the neighbourhood. Perhaps this new man will find a way to resolve the old hatreds. . . .
>
> (*TBG* ix)

Distanced, moderate, conciliatory—Rev. Montague's vision contains shades of optimistic commonsense and sympathetic pessimism. The Rev. Montague's reference to his brother—autobiographically, the poet's father—foreshadows the "bitter" sympathies of *The Fault* (1970), another canto of *The Rough Field* (*TRF* 37-42), in a way that contrasts with his hopeful allusion to "this new man"—to Captain Terence O'Neill, who became Stormont's prime minister in 1963. Such acceptance of an unresolved present and its traditional fixities disguises what cannot be conventionally expressed except in such gestures as *The Bread God*'s persona performs. The "illustration" assents to the present, and that resignation masks the climactic transformation of *The Bread God*'s feeling, forming sensibility.

This transformation signals its occurrence in diverse ways throughout **"An Ulster Prophecy."** What follow from the gesture enacted in **"Penal Rock / Altamuskin"** are visual, mental, add poetic symptoms of this transformation, whose monument is *The Bread God*'s final "lecture." Its typographical address to the reader and startling imagistic mode distinguish the lyric profile of its statement. And, like **"Penal Rock / Altamuskin,"** **"An Ulster Prophecy"** performs a comprehensive gesture, but this closes the symbolic drama *The Bread God*'s persona engages in. In these long eight lines Montague's persona, the Ego-Hero, makes known through "prophecy" that he has chanced those dangers of unconsciousness he had before evaded.

One obvious trait—an entirely visual one—distinguishes **"An Ulster Prophecy"** from the rest of *The Bread God*: the whole takes a different typeface—Hammer Uncial, not the Pilgrim and Pilgrim Italic faces used for the "lecture" and "illustrations"—which encourages the reader to overhear **"An Ulster Prophecy"** in new, more intense tones. But this effect is hardly singular: *The Bread God*'s title, subtitle, dedication and dedicatory quatrain receive the same neo-Gaelic characters. Such design invites responses leading to the heart of this last "lecture." Of these, the most alluring is to read the "prophecy" as an elaboration of the dedicatory quatrain, which highlights a peculiar contrast. The last two lines of the quatrain—"And men with caps in hand kneel stiffly down / To see the many-fanged monstrance shine" (*TBG* [iii])—point out how differently the lines of **"An Ulster Prophecy"** work: "Corks in boats afloat on the summit of the Sperrins / A mill and a forge on the back of a cuckoo / . . ." (*TBG* ix). Keeping in mind Montague's familiarity with French poetry, one might easily take these oneiric juxtapositions as borrowings from *Surréalisme*. However, the octet presents itself as a "prophecy," so its visions presuppose an intention, thus countering André Breton's original definition of *Surréalisme*.[32]

Essentially, the title defines this final "lecture"—**"An Ulster Prophecy"**—whose prime impact proceeds from the noun "prophecy." The article implies that this is but one catalogue of particular images that may arise from the conclusive *psychomachia* of *The Bread God*. Montague has founded the prophecy on experience peculiar to the Ulster that is *The Bread God*'s geographic and mental stage. The noun "prophecy" defines, first of all, the role of *The Bread God*'s persona just after the gestural resolution of his interior drama: he becomes an interpreter of the divine to men. Thus, after the Ego-Hero exclaims "I saw . . . ," the flow of images develops his role as priest. His catalogue of prophetic "conceits" contrasts with the moderation of Rev. Montague's prose in the last "illustration." This sort of extremity—"A mill and a forge on the back of a cuckoo /"—seems surrealistic. The images do not come, however, from purely human dreams, but, given the poem's title, work divinely. Though the images each line clasps together appear nonsensical, traumatic, they are not mystically parabolic. Unlike those set down by Saint John, the images in **"An Ulster Prophecy"** do not encourage allegorical gloss. Rather, Montague's conduct of *The Bread God* takes him back to the earliest visionary poetry in Irish.[33] **"An Ulster Prophecy,"** however, does not revive the *aisling*, which Montague alludes to in *Patriotic Suite* (*TRF* 59-66). Nor does **"An Ulster Prophecy"** revive the "ecstatic vision," or *baile*. Rather, in the context of *The Bread God*, the prophecy recalls the Latinate *visio*, or *fís*, which in medieval times was assumed to be oneiric, divine, and prophetically monitory.

According to visionary grammar, the Old Testament flourish of the formulaic "I saw . . ." creates a tonal colon. In the ensuring catalogue, the prophecy itself, syntax depends on present participials—"carding," "sewing," "cutting"—as if to itemize pictorially the future defined by *The Bread God* as perpetual, trivial activity. Each participial provides a link between visionary subject and object: "I saw the Pope carding tow on Friday / A blind parson sewing a Patchwork quilt / Three bishops cutting rushes with their croziers / . . ." (*TBG* ix). Alluding to the harvest of flax and the manufacture of linen, the participials suggest both severing and binding so equivocally that the subjects and objects so linked seem neither clearly figurative nor completely literal. They exist, rather, in a context of general allusiveness that can absorb cultural symbols and, yet, evade the emblematic. The linkage between the "Pope" and "tow," for instance, seems nonsensical, oneiric. By picturing, however, ecclesiastics of both Protestant and Roman Catholic churches engaged in Sisyphean "busywork," the opening three lines prophesy the benign triviality of organized Christianity. Yet, each ecclesiastic—from "Pope" to "blind parson"—in some small way reverses the role of some Northern churchmen by acting to bind together, not divide, Ulster. "Tow," or waste flax, must be "carded" in order to make twine; "cutting rushes" provides material for baskets and creels.[34] The "blind parson" binds up different parishes—green or orange—in a "Patchwork quilt" with what might be linen thread.

These trivializations of sectarian difference—by way of reversal of roles and inversion of stature—serve to exemplify the future of the tensions that the "lecture" and "illustration" of *The Bread God* document. Like parallel lines drawn to an abstract horizon—indeed, like the "lines" of *A New Siege* (**TRF** 67-71)—these converge in the reversal depicted in the octet's fourth line: "Roaring Meg firing Rosary beads for cannonballs. . . ." One of the cannon used by the Rev. George Walker's Protestant garrison to fend off General de Rosen's troops during the Siege of Londonderry (April 17-July 30, 1689), still commands the Catholic neighborhood of the Bogside from the old ramparts of Derry. "Roaring Meg" now symbolizes three centuries of *"une perpetuelle guerre fratricide."*[35] Denotatively, **"An Ulster Prophecy"** negatively inverts the significance of the cannon so that, by "firing Rosary beads," it seems to embody triumphant vengeance. "Rosary beads" as large as "cannonballs" seem ludicrous, but those of usual size would make fatal shot.

So, at this pivot of the prophecy, the vision remains highly ambiguous politically and morally. Final allegories drawn from hermetic visions, as from Revelation, do not brightly figure the prophecy, since it, like all of *The Bread God,* hardly denies the reality of time's continuing flow. However, the history understood by **"An Ulster Prophecy"** omits Yahweh's rescue of a chosen people. Old and New Testament prophecies seem inappropriate. Except as men acting in time, the role of religious ministers seems here to have passed away. And yet the divisions between men have not withered away precisely because history has not been cataclysmically suspended in the vision of **"An Ulster Prophecy."** The possibilities and impossibilities of right and wrong are still embraced in time so long as man lives to experience them. Consequently, the prophecy continues past "Roaring Meg firing Rosary beads for cannonballs" to: "Corks in boats afloat on the summit of the Sperrins / A mill and a forge on the back of a cuckoo /. . . ."

These lines lead away from the localized transformation of "Roaring Meg" to visions that give up formulaic inversion and reversal, along with the octet's domineering participial. The clarity of the images obscures the thematic base of their linkage: their allusive referents appear wholly absurd without, ironically, the sectarian dialectic of the prophecy's opening. The line of "Corks in boats afloat on the summit of the Sperrins /" tenuously recalls Noah's salvation; however, the allusion's particulars are disturbed by simultaneous allusion to both the Munster city of Cork and to Kirk's relief of the Siege of Londonderry. The figurative intelligence of the line suggests little more than an atmosphere, yet the

line's literal intelligence shares outright impossibility with the sixth—"A mill and a forge on the back of a cuckoo /"—which possibly pictures industrial Ulster in a Blakean manner. The barely tangible comparison between Cork and Derry, or the pastoral Republic and industrial Northern Ireland, suggests another future reversal of history. But, because a "cuckoo" cannot carry such machines, and because boats cannot "float" on top of mountains, both lines emphasize literal impossibility. This tellingly implies that history's continuance by way of predictable reversals, pictured in the prophecy's opening quatrain, itself is an impossibility.

If such a Bosch-like vista be inevitable, then the prophecy looks forward to more than a regional transformation. The character of this waste-land-to-come may be discovered in the vista itself: lines four through six fill the scene with mere objects; lines five and six present states of *stasis*; and line six introduces the perfidious "cuckoo" as if it were the prophecy's phoenix of the future. Man, in his human frame, seems to have been erased from this future. The transformation foreseen cannot be taken, though, as a millenial cataclysm, since man has apparently changed into "The fox sitting conceitedly at a window chewing tobacco / And a moorhen in flight / surveying / a United Ireland."

The flying moorhen and the conceited fox resolve **"An Ulster Prophecy"** into two opposed fables whose imagistic brevity allusion expands. While the triple fracture and elegaic tone of the last line obviously links the fable of the moorhen to *Patriotic Suite* (**TRF** 59-66), the fox's fable reaches outside Montague's *oeuvre* to Thomas Kinsella's *Nightwalker* (1967). In the latter third of *Nightwalker*'s first perambulation, Reynard appears in the role of the eternal trickster, betrayer, the spoiler:

> . . . how the Fox, long after
> Found a golden instrument one day,
> A great complex gold horn, left at his door;
> He examined it with little curiosity,
> Wanting no gold or music; observed the mouthpiece,
> Impossible to play with fox's lips,
> And gave it with dull humour to his old enemy
> The Weasel . . .[36]

Kinsella's Weasel entertains himself by destroying the "gold instrument," and the Fox nods his approval. Montague's Reynard likewise represents the triumphant ascent of "gombeen" mentality, which William Blake otherwise defined in "Proverbs of Hell": "The fox condemns the trap, not himself," and "The fox provides for himself, but God provides for the lion."[37]

Kinsella's *Nightwalker* (April, 1967) distinctly twins Montague's *Patriotic Suite* (November, 1966), whose first and last lyrics inform the last line of **"An Ulster Prophecy."** The close of **"1966 and All That"** in a broken line—"again that note // above the self-drive car"[38]—describes the plain of objects and automatons that the moorhen might see while "surveying // a United Ireland." Here, in *The Bread God,* both Spenser's "fatall destinie" and Engels's "real aims of a Revolution" come true in the prophecy's "United Ireland" ruled by a conceited Reynard. And, while "a moorhen in flight // surveying" alludes to "The Lure" (*PS* [*Patriotic Suite*] 7)—and to the "lost cry / of the yellow bittern!"—the specific allusion recalls, as well as *An Bunnán Buidhe,* Yeats's impatient melancholy in the fifth part of "Meditations in Time of Civil War."[39] Montague's "moorhen in flight" represents the alienated sensibility that finds no comfort in the fox-ruled fastness of an Ireland reduced to a wasted island. In this future, Montague's moorhen is as finally lost as Mac Giolla Ghunna's yellow bittern.

The particulars of **"An Ulster Prophecy"** have oneiric clarity but the paradoxical context of the prophecy renders them cryptic. The vision they make cannot fail to excite both wonder and despair; in this lies the prophecy's emotional "truth." Precise meanings served up here by interpretation matter less to *The Rough Field* as a whole than does the inward drama of *The Bread God.* Much like **"Penal Rock / Altamuskin,"** **"An Ulster Prophecy"** acts poetically as a compound gesture that distills evidence of the persona's *psychomachia,* whose resolution in **"Penal Rock / Altamuskin"** directly inspires the prophecy. The spiritual "plot" revealed in the sonnet's complex gesture showed that the Ego-Hero, by celebrating private Eucharist, accepted the role of priest and, so, had chosen to confront two sorts of powerful unconsciousness. The priest's role causes him to become his whole congregation by first accepting communion. The spiritual danger of this aspect of the rite, screened by the commonsensical last "illustration," supplies the crisis that lets the prophecy's symbolic images bloom. Writing to the Corinthians, St. Paul warms then not to date the spiritual dangers of the rite without having first prepared for it by strenuous self-examination:

> For as often as ye eat this bread, and drink this cup, ye do show the Lord's death till he come.
>
> Wherefore, whosoever shall eat this bread, and drink *this* cup of the Lord, unworthily, shall be guilty of the body and blood of the Lord.
>
> But let a man examine himself, and so let him eat of *that* bread, and drink of *that* cup.
>
> For he that eateth and drinketh unworthily, eateth and drinketh damnation to himself, not discerning the Lord's body.
>
> (I Cor. 11:26-29)

According to the Gravesian logic of John Allegro's *The Sacred Mushroom and the Cross,* the act of worship known to Christians as the Eucharist may be traced back to cognate, Near-Eastern cults. Their chief ceremony is the feast, or *deipnon,* of the communicants on the potent god, whose real presence abides in the Fly-Agaric mushroom, often called both "flesh" and "bread." Thus, the title of the whole poem—*The Bread God*—makes satiric and dramatic sense, and also syncretic sense. As worship, the feast was ritualized to protect the communicants and priests by forcing them to prepare for a spiritual trial, or *peirasmos,* since the god in his symbol—the *Amanita muscaria*—was sensed through neural poisons which cause an intense experience of paradox, an induced *psychomachia.* Having feasted, the communicant feels at once faint and strong, feverish and chilly, convulsed and paralyzed; hallucinations afflict him. So, the communicant dares to sense "death" as the immanence of total unconsciousness and "resurrection" as a struggle to regain consciousness and "life." Allegro characterizes the last stage of the ritual trial as a self-sacrificing act of atonement on the communicant's part,[40] which was understood to provide direct communion with the god. Consequently, Allegro's notion of the *peirasmos* inherent in the Mass illuminates even the dedicatory quatrain of *The Bread God*:

> I break again into the lean parish of my art
> Where huddled candles flare before a shrine
> And men with caps in hand kneel stiffly down
> To see the many-fanged monstrance shine.

The monstrance holding the "bread," or the Host, seems "many-fanged"—both glorious and terrible—because of the divinity it contains, which the persona ultimately chooses to encounter. In *The Bread God,* this episode of spiritual trial during the Ego-Hero's *psychomachia* occurs behind the screen of the last "illustration." The visionary incoherences of **"An Ulster Prophecy"** become, then, symptoms that the Ego-Hero, Montague's persona, has endured such a *peirasmos.* Also, they embody wisdoms the persona has salvaged from his "resurrection," but which continue to endanger, since they encourage *accidie.* Whatever the patterns of its paradoxes, allusions, or symbols, **"An Ulster Prophecy"** discourages reason by expressing the terrors of such knowledge gained by trial.

Despite its relevance to *The Bread God*'s covert drama, the octet's vision only partially succeeds precisely on account of its hallucinatory ambiguity. Its tantalizing failure to unify its own vision finds little compensation in its catalogue syntax, which permits—in lines five and six—an uncontrolled shift from the opening quatrain's pattern of reversal and inversion to the suggestive span of images in the closing vista. This flaw partly explains Montague's revision of *The Bread God*[41]—particularly **"An Ulster Prophecy"**—to give it its present form as the third section—set between *The Leaping Fire* and *A Severed Head*—of *The Rough Field* (October, 1972).[42] In this text *The Bread God* takes on a new subtitle: "A Collage of Religious Misunderstandings," while **"An Ulster Prophecy"** finds completion in three lines inserted between the original's lines five and six:

Corks in boats afloat on the summit of the Sperrins,
A severed head speaking with a grafted tongue,
A snail paring Royal Avenue with a hatchet,
British troops firing on the Shankill,
A mill and a forge on the back of a cuckoo, . . .

(*TRF* 26)

This addition extends the first quatrain's pattern of reversal so that the original octet's fourth line—"Roaring Meg firing Rosary beads for cannonballs"—discovers an echo in the revised eighth line: "British troops firing on the Shankill." By extending the original's pattern, the revision establishes imagistic continuity that makes more gradual the transition to the closing waste land vista. The three new lines also emphasize the probability of the impossible. Foreshadowing *A Severed Head* by alluding to its concern for language and by quoting part of its **"Old Rhyme"** (*TRF* 27), the images of the revision's first line express the rigors of prophecy while they accentuate the impossible. The next line defines the slow course of historical inevitability by looking forward to the destruction of Belfast's most "classy" shopping street. The revision's final line fulfills the pattern by echoing the original's fourth line: it confirms the probability of the impossible by describing what now is historical fact. British troops have already fired on the Shankill—the poorest of Belfast's Protestant, working-class neighborhoods—while trying to control the "Tartan" gangs and the Ulster Volunteer Force. **"An Ulster Prophecy"** has also become more severe, consistent and unified in other ways. The three new participials—"speaking," "paring," "firing,"—extend the prophecy's original syntactical pattern[43] Montague's revision consists, really, of expanding the original conception to turn it into a whole visionary catalogue:

I saw the Pope breaking stones on Friday,
A blind parson sewing a patchwork quilt,
Two bishops cutting rushes with their croziers,
Roaring Meg firing rosary beads for cannonballs,
Corks in boats afloat on the summit of the Sperrins,
A severed head speaking with a grafted tongue,
A snail paring Royal Avenue with a hatchet,
British troops firing on the Shankill,
A mill and a forge on the back of a cuckoo,
The fox sitting conceitedly at a window chewing
   tobacco,
And a curlew in flight
         surveying
              a United Ireland.

Notes

1. John Montague, "Tribute to William Carleton," *The Bell,* XVIII, i (April, 1952), 18.

2. William Carleton, *Traits and Stories of the Irish Peasantry,* 11th ed. (London: William Tegg, n.d.), i, xvii.

3. Benedict Kiely, *Poor Scholar: A Study of the Works and Days of William Carleton (1794-1869)* (Dublin: The Talbot Press, 1972), p. 37.

4. John Montague, "Tribute to William Carleton," 17-18.

5. John Montague, *The Bread God: A Lecture . . . ,* Dolmen Editions VII (Dublin: The Dolmen Press, December 1968), p. [i]. Hereafter cited parenthetically, thus: (*TBG* [i]). The preceding quotation, versed in black Hammer Uncial, stands as a subtitle, while below it appears the "warning" in red Pilgrim type. This typographical display does not appear in the final collation of *The Rough Field* (Dublin: The Dolmen Press, October [November] 1972), p. 21. Hereafter cited parenthetically, thus: (*TRF* 21).

6. *Annals of the Kingdom of Ireland, by he Four Masters, from the earliest period to the year 1616,* trans. John O'Donovan, 2nd ed. (Dublin: Hodges, Smith and Company, 1856), i, 416. See Nora K. Chadwick's "Celtic Christianity and Its Literature" in *The Celtic Realms* (London: Weidenfeld and Nicolson, 1967), pp. 174-85. The parish of Errigal Kerrogue, or Errigal Kieran, continued to be a center of religious activity through the Penal Days, as the Rev. Brendan MacEvoy shows in "The Parish of Errigal Kieran in the Nineteenth Century," *Seanchas Ardmhacha,* I, i (1954), 118-31.

7. Robert Kee, *The Green Flag: A History of Irish Nationalism* (London: Weidenfeld and Nicolson, 1972), pp. 19-20; J. C. Beckett, *The Making of Modern Ireland 1603-1923* (London: Faber and Faber, 1966), pp. 157-61.

8. William Carleton, *The Autobiography of . . . ,* introd. Patrick Kavanagh (London: MacGibbon and Kee, 1968), p. 43.

9. William Carleton, *Willy Reilly and His Dear Cooleen Bawn* (New York: George Routledge and Son, [1883]), p. 208. Carleton's accounts of the religious practices of the Catholic tenantry around Clogher are hardly as romanticized. Although the inhabitants of the parish of Errigal Kieran were tenants of Protestant Planter families—the Moutrays of Favor Royal and the Stewarts of Ballygawley House, for example—Catholic worship and education, in hedge schools, was less inhibited there than elsewhere in Ulster during the 18th century. Some 160 open-air Mass sites were used in the diocese of Clogher, of which the most popular were those sites around Glen-a-haltara—*Gleann na h-altora,* or "Altar Glen"—including

Altamuskin. Some Protestant families of lesser stature traditionally let Roman Catholic priests live on their lands, set up schools, and offer Mass at Mass-rocks, Mass-houses, and in Mass-glens. Traditional religious life did not go completely undisturbed, for the Verners of neighboring Armagh supported the "Killymen wreckers," a band of Orangemen, who sometimes raided Altamuskin. See Rev. Brendan MacEvoy, "The Parish of Errigal Kieran in the Nineteenth Century," *Seanchas Ardmhacha,* I, I (1954), 118-31.

10. *Willy Reilly,* p. 209.

11. *Traits and Stories,* p. 349.

12. Erich Neumann, *The Great Mother: An Analysis of the Archetype,* trans. Ralph Manheim, Bollingen Series, XLVII (Princeton: Princeton University Press, 1963), pp. 219, 310.

13. *The Tripartite Life of Patrick with Other Documents Relating to That Saint (Vita Tripartita),* ed. and trans. Whitley Stokes (London: H. M. Stationary Office [Eyre and Spottiswode]. 1887), I, 41-53.

14. E. Estyn Evans, *Irish Folk Ways* (London: Routledge and Kegan Paul, 1957), pp. 274-75; Alwyn and Brinley Rees, *Celtic Heritage: Ancient Tradition in Ireland and Wales* (New York: Grove Press, 1961), pp. 156-58, 162-63.

15. John Montague, *Forms of Exile* (Dublin: The Dolmen Press, December 1958 [May 1959]), pp. 16, 18.

16. A. T. Lucas, *Penal Crucifixes* (Dublin, 1958), which is an off-print from the *Co. Louth Archaeological Journal,* XIII, 2 (1954 [55]), 145-74.

17. C. G. Jung, "Transformation Symbolism in the Mass," *Psychology and Religion: West and East,* trans. R. F. C. Hull, Bollingen Series, XX (New York: Pantheon Books, 1958), pp. 204-205.

18. In his cover note to *The Rough Field,* Montague confirms the idea that his Orange "illustrations" are "found poems": "I managed to draft the opening and the close [of *The Rough Field*], but soon realized that I did not have the technique for so varied a task. At intervals during the decade I returned to it, when the signs seemed right. An extreme Protestant organization put me on its mailing list, for instance, and the only antidote I could find against such hatred was to absorb it into *The Bread God.*"

19. A. G. Dickens, *The English Reformation* (New York: Schocken Books, 1964), pp. 70-76; Philip Hughes, *The Reformation in England* (London: Hollis and Carter, 1950-54), I, 133-46.

20. Sir Walter Scott, *Rob Roy,* (Edinburgh: Adam and Charles Black, [1892?]), pp. 276-77.

21. Beckett, pp. 276-77.

22. The three Orange "illustrations" are Orwellian because their expressions are "designed to make lies sound truthful and murder respectable," in Orwell's words, "and to give an appearance of solidity to pure wind." See George Orwell, "Politics and the English Language," *Shooting an Elephant and Other Essays* (New York: Harcourt Brace and Company, 1950), pp. 85, 92, 77.

23. William Carleton, *The Autobiography of . . . ,* p. 37. See also Timothy Patrick Coogan, *Ireland Since the Rising* (London: Pall Mall Press, 1966), p. 288.

24. The revival of the Orange Order in opposition to Gladstone's Second Home Rule Bill (1886) was countered in industrialized Ulster by a Catholic, proletarian club: the Ancient Order of Hibernians. This organization became an essential element in Ulster politics when the Belfast M.P. "Wee Joe" Devlin (1871-1834) united the clubs under his presidency (1905-34). Devlin supported John Redmond's Nationalist Party in Westminster during the campaign for the Third Home Rule Bill. After the Anglo-Irish Treaty of 1921, Devlin was the only Ulster politician capable of disciplining the Ulster nationalist opposition to the Unionist Party. See Robert Kee's chapter "Volunteers in European War," *The Green Flag,* pp. 513-29, and Liam de Paor, *Divided Ulster* (Baltimore, Md.: Penguin Books, 1970), *passim.*

25. Edmund Curtis, *A History of Ireland,* 6th ed. (London: Methuen, 1965), pp. 243-47.

26. De Paor, p. 24.

27. Curtis, pp. 250, 252-53.

28. De Paor, p. 57.

29. *Tadhg* is an Irish noun that, by 1540, had come to mean "poet" and also was a Christian name. The *OED* notes that the Christian name, in its many Anglicized forms, came into English usage as a derogatory epithet during the late 17th century. While *Ó Tadhg* is a genuine Gaelic surname, *Mac Taidhge,* MacTeague, was never more than a patronymic: that patronymic evolved into the name Montague during the 17th century, when many Gaelic names were rendered in Norman form so as to identify those families as Old English. See Edward Mac Lysaght, *Irish Families: Their Names, Arms and Origins* (Dublin: Hodges Figgis, 1957), pp. 20, 26, 94; and also *More Irish Families* (Galway: O'Gorman, 1960), p. 186. Montague takes up the theme of his surname in "The Grafted Tongue" (*TRF* 34-35).

30. Owing to its removed location, Altamuskin—*Alt na Múscán,* meaning the "Cliff" or "Height" of the "Stench" or "Fungus"—continuously used of the open-air Mass sites. The Montague name is intimately connected with this site, for the vestments, altar table, and other liturgical necessities were kept nearby in the "inn" of a Brian Montague. During the first half of the 19th century some four men of the Montague name entered the priesthood and served in the parish, and one, a Rev. John Montague (d. 1848), became dean of Dungannon. See Rev. Brendan MacEvoy, "The Parish of Errigal Kieran in the Nineteenth Century," *Seanchas Ardmhacha,* I, 1 (1954), 118-31.

31. Michael Foley, "The Ulster Goldmine," *The Honest Ulsterman,* 28 (May—June, 1971), 2. *The Honest Ulsterman* critics, and other Irish readers, rather mistook the methods and aims of *The Rough Field* which I have attempted to more justly define in "John Montague's *The Rough Field: Topos and Texne,*" *Studies,* LXIII, 249 (Spring, 1974), 31-46; "*Rí* as in Regional: Three Ulster Poets," *Éire-Ireland,* IX, 2 (Summer, 1974), 41-64.

32. Breton's "The First Surrealist Manifest" (1924) offers pithy definitions of the imaginative mode he championed: "SURREALISM, n. Psychic automatism in its pure state, . . . the actual functioning of thought . . . in the absence of any control exercised by reason." See *Surrealists on Art,* ed. Lucy R. Lippard (Englewood Cliffs, N.J.: Prentice-Hall, 1970), p. 20. The surrealism of "An Ulster Prophecy" is far more Irish, and traditional, than one might expect. Much of Montague's poem adapts a "nonsense" rhyme for children recorded from oral tradition in Tyrone at the turn of the century. The Gaelic text and translation appear in John B. Arthurs, "A Tyrone Miscellany," *Ulster Folklife,* 3, 1 (1957), 44. Montague's use of this rhyme is the subject of Liam Ó Dochartaigh's "John Montague and 'Ceol na mBreág'," *Ulster Folklife,* 20 (1974), 85-88.

33. Accounts of the evolution of the *baile* genre into the *fís* may be found in Nora K. Chadwick's "Celtic Christianity and Its Literature," *The Celtic Realms,* pp. 196-204, and in St. John Seymour, "Studies in the Vision of Tundal," *Proceedings of the Royal Irish Academy (PRIA),* XXXVII, C (1924-27), 91-94, 99.

34. While many Irish households were furnished with containers and toys fashioned out of straw, flax, and rush, perhaps the most striking rushwork articles are the diamond or swastika "Briget's Crosses," whose forms have universal symbolic currency. See Evans, *Irish Folk Ways,* pp. 267-69.

35. Serge Fauchereau, "Tradition et révolution dans al poésie irlandaise," *Critique,* 276 (Mai, 1970), 453.

36. Thomas Kinsella, *Nightwalker,* The New Dolmen Chapbooks, 2 (Dublin: The Dolmen Press, April 1967), pp. 9-10.

37. William Blake, *The Poetry and Prose of . . .,* ed. David V. Erdman (Garden City, N.Y.: Doubleday, 1970), p. 36. Montague's personified fox appears to have evolved also from his description of Eamon de Valéra's last campaign in 1957. See John Montague, "The First Week in Lent—A Political Snapshot," *Threshhold,* 1, 2 (Summer, 1957), 69-71.

38. John Montague, *Patriotic Suite,* New Dolmen Chapbooks, [1] (Dublin: The Dolmen Press, November 1966), p. 14. Hereafter cited parenthetically, thus (*PS* 14).

39. W. B. Yeats, *The Collected Poems of . . .* (New York: Macmillan, 1956), p. 202.

40. John M. Allegro, *The Sacred Mushroom and the Cross* (Garden City, N.Y.: Doubleday, 1970), pp. 16-64, 176.

41. A Xerox copy of the 1968 edition of *The Bread God,* made from Montague's own copy in 1969, shows several holograph revision of "An Ulster Prophecy." The triplet that Montague eventually inserted between the original's lines five and six appears as a couplet. A version of this text was eventually published in *Open Poetry: Four Anthologies of Expanded Poems,* ed. Ronald Gross Richard Quasha (New York: Simon and Schuster, 1973), pp. 139-42. Montague worked a number of changes into the proofs for this printing, for aspects of "An Ulster Prophecy," in particular, differ both from the 1968 printing and from the text in *The Rough Field* (1972).

42. Montague began assembling *The Leaping Fire* after publication of *The Bread God* (December, 1968), for the canto appeared in the *Irish University Review,* I, 1 (Autumn, 1970), 62-66—concurrently with the publication of *Tides* (September, 1970). Portions of *A Severed Head* appeared from 1966 to 1971 before the whole canto was first printed in *The Journal of Irish Literature,* I, 3 (September, 1972), 24-34.

43. None of the revisions to *The Bread God* seems to reflect Montague's notice of public criticism. They wisely ignore Douglas Sealy's advice to "transmute" the documentary matter into verse. See Douglas Sealy, "Poetry and Documenta," *The Irish Times,* January 4, 1969, p. 10.

John Montague and Kevin T. McEneaney (interview date 1985)

SOURCE: Montague, John, and Kevin T. McEneaney. "John Montague." In *Writing Irish: Selected Interviews with Irish Writers from the* Irish Literary Supplement, edited by James P. Myers, Jr., pp. 27-35. Syracuse, New York: Syracuse University Press, 1999.

[In the following interview, originally published in 1985, Montague and McEneaney discuss Montague's critical reputation as well as his opinions on various poetic forms and his assessment of the work of a number of other poets.]

> I'm partly American, loving and loathing the place, but with the added irony that I see it from outside most of the time. And, of course, my central loyalty, or disloyalty, is to Ireland.
>
> —John Montague

John Montague was born on 28 February 1929 in Brooklyn, New York, but at the age of four his parents sent him to be raised by his aunts in Garvaghey, County Tyrone. As a poet, he has self-consciously tried to combine both Irish and American strains in his work: his approach to line and sound is influenced by William Carlos Williams while his subject matter has centered upon Ireland or his own biography. Montague attended both University College, Dublin, and Yale (where he studied under Robert Penn Warren). He experienced the now-legendary Dublin pub scene in the fifties and published his first book, *Forms of Exile* (Dublin: Dolmen Press) in 1958 with the Dolmen Press.

In *The Rough Field* (Dublin: Dolmen Press, 1972) Montague followed and surpassed Williams's historical epic, *Paterson,* giving a rural, Goldsmithian vision of Ireland and the Tyrone locale in which he grew up. Influenced by his stay in California during the heyday of the San Francisco poetry movement, he developed a historical vision that also contained resonant contemporary commentary. In addition to other volumes of poetry investigating romance and society Montague has also published short stories and a notable novella, *The Lost Notebook* (Cork: Mercier Press, 1987).

At the time of the interview I was both bookseller and apprentice poet, and Montague, a distinguished professor at University College, Cork, was working on his poetic sequence *The Dead Kingdom* (Mountrath, Ireland: Dolmen Press; Winston-Salem, N. C.: Wake Forest University Press, 1984),[1] a work melding family history and the Northern Troubles. While a graduate student, I had studied Elizabethan epyllion at Columbia University; we had some lively poetic and philosophic discussions when Montague stayed at my apartment in Manhattan Valley, overlooking Central Park. I recall being fascinated by Montague's probing sense of musical composition, in terms of how poems were arranged to form epyllion sequence. The upshot was a little interview with him (conducted in my basement bookshop off Fifth Avenue) for Bob Callahan's short-lived

Callahan's Irish Quarterly, but the publication folded before the piece could appear. I showed the interview to Robert Lowery and asked if he was interested in running it in *The Irish Literary Supplement.* Robert said, "Yes, but it's too short. Can you get him to expand it?" I wrote Montague, and he graciously agreed to redo it. [Kevin T. McEneaney]

[Kevin McEneaney] In your recent poem "Process" from **The Dead Kingdom** *you speak of everyone and the world "closed" in their dream of history, race, memory, and sense. Do you think that the present period is afflicted with a narcissistic* Zeitgeist? *Is the present an essentially confused period?*

[John Montague:] Of course. A global brain is growing, both in the crude sense of communications and the spiritual growth described by de Chardin.[2] But the other point of the gyre is a narrowing:[3] things have never been nastier, in Belfast or Beirut, Afghanistan or Central America. The old instincts of religion and race are fighting a rearguard action against centralization, which is both necessary and, if done for the wrong reasons, narcissistic. My solution would be both an intense attention to your home area and a sympathy for the endangered world—my old and doubtless boring cry of global regionalism.

The tradition of Irish poetry has been a second nature in your poetry—from early nature poetry, medieval heroic poetry, to W. B. Yeats. Yet you are completely a man of the modern world. How is such a synthesis or marriage possible?

Because of my American birth, I suppose. I mean, New York, even Depression Brooklyn, was the most modern city in the world, just as Ulster was nearly as backward as you could get, outside Donegal. That tension has kept me going. Though I am not proud of my Irish, I seem to have access to the literature. I'd love to put the Fenian cycle[4] together, but . . . A bilingual version of Michael Comyn's *Pursuit of Diarmuid and Grainne* was in Garvaghey and that was the book that set off Yeats *and* Clarke.[5] I loved it, especially Niamh of the Golden Hair; I'm still enchanted by her.

Most people who know the poem "All Legendary Obstacles" acclaim it as one of the great love poems of the century; yet it does not appear in American anthologies. Ironically, the poem is set in America, actually in California. Why do you think Americans have tended to neglect or ignore this poem?

There's a lot of typecasting around as if people couldn't face complexity of reaction. Of course, I'm partly American, loving and loathing the place, but with the added irony that I see it from outside most of the time. And, of course, my central loyalty, or disloyalty, is to Ireland. But I would like to gather my good American poems.

Sometimes I think the American poets and critics are more insular than they like to think though the "Roots" racket has a good side in that you need not be ashamed of being Irish-American, as John O'Hara[6] was. There was an awful lot of snobbery in American writers of Irish background, like F. Scott Fitzgerald. So I went to Yale as well as University College, Dublin. James Joyce seems a richer master than the few writers who survived New Haven! Still, I wish someone would put me in an American anthology for a change. I would think a real love poem is international—Cavafy[7] or Auden's "Lay Your Sleeping Head." The poem you speak of, though, has a specifically western landscape, and I don't remember that of many American love poems—so, yes, they should adopt it.

The Celtic revival of the late nineteenth century produced some great Celticists, two poets in particular—W. B. Yeats and Robert Graves. Some of your poems seem to be part of that revival. The little poem about Cernnunos, "The Split Lyre," is in that tradition but also in the tradition of Shelley's "Ode to the West Wind" and Francis Thompson's lesser poem "Ode to the Setting Sun".—Thompson's poem being Christian and Aristotelian, Shelley's being atheistic and Democritean; yours being pantheistic, or in terms of philosophy, Platonic. Like Plato, you have a way of integrating mythology into your aesthetics that is unobtrusive and instructive, integral and psychologically illuminating. Yet unlike Yeats's Vision or Graves's White Goddess, your poems don't need a coda or guide book. It seems that your poems are pretty much accessible to anyone. They have a simplicity although they retain an intellectual depth. How do you manage this?

God knows. I have great sympathy with the Celtic thing as a kind of nature religion, but I am prepared to argue for classical order if I feel it. I like Vivaldi's "La estro harmonico" *and* Bruckner's *Eighth*,[8] which I have just discovered—a marvelous monster! And good jazz sends me wild, controlled elation, *duende*.[9] I tried to do a double degree at college with philosophy as well as English, but I now agree with Beckett: *que c'est de la merde*.[10] Kant is a wonderful mental construct, but Pascal hurts.[11] *The Critique of Pure Reason* is like Bach's *Art of the Fugue*,[12] a wonderful exercise, the mathematics of our head. But Plato was a great writer who could dramatize our dilemma.

In the poem "Deities" you use both Greek and Irish mythology as if it were a part of a single continuum. This tradition is both international and classical as well as part of the native Irish poetic tradition: I am thinking of the profusion of Greek mythology in Middle Irish poetry and even in later folk songs such as "The Limerick Rake." Celtic mythology was certainly an Indo-European mythology and could not have been very far removed from Greek mythology. I think that Joyce

knew this. In the poem "Deities" the distinction between gods and heroes is blurred. This strikes me as very Celtic or early Greek, anarchically and pantheistically so.

Why not? The gods have fled from Greece, except maybe Delphi, and the tourists climb like ants over the sacred places. Some of Ireland still has presence as Mexico had when I visited it years ago. Greek is at the root of what we call "Western Civilization," and its pantheon has great psychological power. Many complexes are identified through Greek names—Oedipus, Electra, and even fair Psyche herself.[13] The Irish pantheon doesn't have the same currency, but if you use them together, you will see that Lugh and Apollo, for instance, are not that different.[14] Patrick Kavanagh loved Homer as if he were a local writer, and we were all taught that we were partly divine.

Your poems have great variety: imagism, free verse, rhymes, internal rhymes, prose poems, litanies (as in "For the Mother"), mythopoetic poems (as in "Mount Eagle" and "The Well Dreams"), and even concrete poems. You pointed out that "A Graveyard in Queens" is a concrete poem with the lines arranged on the page like rows of tombstones which the reader's eyes "walk" between. Do you think that the twentieth century is a collage of forms, an assembly in a kaleidoscopic time warp? Or do you think that the style of the century lies in imagistic concision and spoken voice?

The modern movement began with imagism—Pound, Eliot, Hulme—and it enlisted the verse of Lawrence and later Williams.[15] The spoken word, as opposed to the written word only, was an attempt to reinvigorate poetic language, rediscover natural rhythms. The French developed the prose form as well: early Ponge is marvelous, as was Baudelaire.[16] Now we have inherited all that and can do whatever we, or the poem, wants. We have a renewed sense of tradition as well as an armory of techniques to wrestle or woo raw experience.

The literary epic is a tricky thing. Most of them are failures—the Aeneid and Paradise Lost. Even Paterson[17] has, I think, its weak moments. The Rough Field is an epic that is personal, historical, and communal, and it is all of a piece. The choice of topic is important in such matters. Milton agonized over this problem for years. When Berryman and Merrill[18] came to the epic, they drifted into a solipsistic mode. What do you think are the pitfalls of the enterprise?

The long poem is a fascinating task. I say that, and yet I only drifted into my two efforts, and I wouldn't like to get a whopper on my line again for a while for the problems are ferocious. Biographically, it might be of some interest that as a student I made a special study of Milton although I haven't read him since. And I loved

Langland.[19] The supreme long poem of the West is *La Divina Comedia*,[20] and I have just begun to get a sense of, say, *Paradiso,* which is pure poetry, poetry of vision. But most people prefer the harsh facts of *Inferno* and don't understand that the greatest poetry redeems suffering, like Beethoven's *Ninth.* I find your list odd.

Well, it's pretty arbitrary. There's Allingham, Ariosto, and Ashbery.[21]

There is the classical epic, from the *Iliad* to the *Aeneid,* and then maybe the religious epic, Dante and Milton and du Bartas.[22] *The Faerie Queene* fails for me because of the ludicrous schema, but I haven't read Ariosto, so I can't judge the genre, romantic epic. Then there is the personal, Wordsworth's *Prelude* more than the labored *Excursion.*

The earlier version of the Prelude, *the 1805 version, is more spontaneous and flowing, more like a personal letter to Coleridge or the reader, less monumental symbolism. But Wordsworth hardly has the scope of somebody like Homer.*

The older epic summed up a civilization, but you still must have a pressure of community, the unexpressed feelings of an area seeking outlet. I hope that is obvious in both **The Rough Field** and **The Dead Kingdom.** But first one must be readable as I hope they also are. Give me Chaucer and Byron over Spenser every time; he was a great poet, but he had no momentum, no central thrust.

What of the modern effort?

The modern long poem is quite a problem. The canny Eliot settled for the very eighteenth-century shape of the Augustan essay poem. If *Paterson,* which I got published in England, doesn't work entirely, it is less indulgent than Olson's *Maximus* or Dorn's *Gunslinger,*[23] the lunatic notion of "open form." It is like the symphony: I can follow Beethoven through Brahms and Bruckner to Mahler,[24] but when Messiaen[25] adds bird calls, I say why not catcalls?

But there are some successful efforts.

There are poets like MacDiarmuid and David Jones,[26] who recall dying cultures, or the fabulous Neruda,[27] a volcano of good and bad. We are a bit less ambitious, I think. Kinnell's *Book of Nightmares* is less rhetorical than "The Bridge"[28] under which I was born. Whitman's influence may be releasing for South Americans but dangerous for us Irish. He wrote arias like Verdi and Victor Hugo, the warm blast of amplitude. Lord knows, I loved Berryman, but the *Dream Songs* needs to be dramatized, perhaps, to work. God has shrunk to a ouija board, which I presume is Merrill's point.

What do you think of Paul Muldoon's "Immran?"[29]

Good stuff. A bit smart-ass, but he joins a glimpse of the old with a *literary* version of American culture. You folks deserve it after flooding us with good and bad. "Immran" is very witty, mock-Gaelic, a new genre perhaps, and proof of how far we have come. I think he is wittier than his English contemporaries, but as with Pope, there is the question of how you let the emotions into a cool style. Miles Davis[30] could, but the Modern Jazz Quartet tinkled easy. Those who actually endure the North day-by-day—I almost said "die-by-die"—are bound to develop a macabre wit of survival, a sting.

Do you have anything to say about the young poets growing up in Cork? There's Tom McCarthy and Sean Dunne.[31] *Are there others?*

Theo Dorgan, Greg Delanty, Gerry Murphy, John Bourke—we could nearly put a team in the field. Tom is the most accomplished and may be the best poet of his generation, book-for-book, so far in the south. Tom won the Patrick Kavanagh award; and Greg has just done the same. No matter how they grow, they are a way-open group. All have a passion for poetry, which is very heartening. They love the stanza, and I like to think that bringing Graves and MacDiarmuid over in the '70s gave them an example.

Your poetry seems to have kept pace with life. Unlike many poets, you don't let art become an idol in your poetry. You keep to the bone and muscle, don't get lost in a wash of colors or begin placing a self-importance before your work. You are not distracted by flattery or fame. This is not easy. It is easier to succumb to these temptations.

All this is very flattering—will I succumb? I live in remote Cork, which is bad for my career, but good for my character. I partly believe in Keats's "negative capability"—to let things speak through you. I am continually an apprentice before life, but now nearing my mid-fifties, I feel I can, should, risk a few Yeatsian generalizations. My career has been slow, though steady, so I have only occasionally had to wrestle with the kind of public acclaim you describe, which is always partly an accident. If it were to come, it shouldn't distract me from the central thrust: to express what is essentially mine. I imagine that to be dishonest would be even more painful, but, to be certain, I listen to even the cat cries of the envious as remedies against self-deception. I think that Yeats handled fame by using it to keep others. He practically invented the Abbey and Synge. I would like to see more of that generosity around.

You said that this is the "age of the interview." Do you think that the interview is, at its best, an art form, a kind of Platonic or Erasmian[32] *dialogue? Or do you think that, at its worst, it is merely an aspect of society that relates to gossip?—I mean, that here is a part of society that has a jealous fear of artists and wants to cannibalize their every thought and act, to take from them the sources of their powers, and even to take away their very lives as was done to Orpheus?*

I resent interviews, and yet I give them. It can be justified, perhaps, if you have just published a book that people otherwise wouldn't read, or so seems the practice. I have given two long ones—to *The Literary Review,* another to *NER/BLQ*³³—and a handful of lesser ones, the last to *The Cork Examiner,* my local paper. They usually turn out well enough but are unnecessary in the sense that the information *should* be in the work, but if you are a poet, you can't be sure that they have read it. **The Rough Field,** of course, always crops up, notably in *The Crane Bag*'s³⁴ joint interview with John Hewitt. But my views on Irish, and indeed world history, are both so intimate and so detached that people must simplify them. Was my father a mad Republican dog? Does **"The Wild Dog Rose"** equal Mother Island? Perhaps ignorance is invincible, but one yields, with interest and shame, to yet another chance to explain, hoping, especially if it is to a friend, that it will not be a cheapening process. It is also connected with McLuhan's³⁵ vision of the global village. How many interviews did Joyce give? This is a media age, and we cannot escape it; we should try to use it. Any real poem is both simple and infinitely complicated, so perhaps it is fair to give a few simple signposts, as Joyce himself did.

Notes

1. Published in 1984 in Winston-Salem, N.C., and Mountrath, Ireland. Since the interview, Montague has published several important collections, including the following: *Mount Eagle* (Oldcastle, Ireland: Gallery Books, 1988; Newcastle-upon-Tyne, Eng.: Bloodaxe Books; Winston-Salem, N.C.: Wake Forest Univ. Press, 1989); *The Figure in the Cave and Other Essays* (Dublin: Lilliput Press, 1989); and *Collected Poems* (Liverpool: Gallery Books; Winston-Salem, N.C.: Wake Forest Univ. Press, 1995).

2. Teilhard de Chardin (1881-1955), French Jesuit, paleontologist, and philosopher, whose best-known work is *The Phenomenon of Man* (1953; English trans., London: Collins; New York: Harper and Row, 1959).

3. William Butler Yeats in *A Vision* and throughout his poetry employed the geometric figure of the cone or gyre, or two such interpenetrating gyres, to illustrate and describe phases of change.

4. The Fenian cycle, or *Fianaigheacht,* is one of the great medieval Irish compilations of heroic tales.

It centers on the deeds of Finn mac Cumaill (Finn McCool) and the Fiana, sometimes also known as the Red Branch Knights.

5. The Irish writer and critic Austin Clarke (1896-1974).

6. John O'Hara (1905-1970), American fiction writer and journalist.

7. Constantine Cavafy (1863-1933), Greek-Egyptian writer.

8. The Venetian composer Antonio Vivaldi (1678-1741) wrote his *L'estro harmonica* about 1711. Anton Bruckner (1824-1896), Austrian composer.

9. *Duende,* fiery spirit (Spanish).

10. That is, "that it's shit."

11. The German philosopher Immanuel Kant (1724-1804) published his *Critique of Pure Reason* in 1786. Blaise Pascal (1623-1662), French philosopher and mathematician important for his distrust of reason's ability to resolve metaphysical problems.

12. Johann Sebastian Bach (1685-1750), composer whose intellectual explorations of the fugue form climaxed in his *Art of the Fugue.*

13. In Greek mythology Oedipus killed his father and married his mother; Electra avenged her father's murder by killing her mother; and Psyche eventually destroyed herself in pursuing the boy-god with whom she had fallen in love.

14. Apollo and Lugh ("the Shining One") are, respectively, the classical and Celtic gods of the sun. (More often, however, Lugh corresponds to the classical Mercury/Hermes.)

15. Ezra Pound (1885-1972), American poet. T. E. Hulme (1883-1917), British poet; D. H. Lawrence (1885-1930), British writer. William Carlos Williams (1883-1963), American writer.

16. French writers Francis Ponge and Charles Baudelaire (1821-1867).

17. William Carlos Williams began publishing his long poem *Paterson* in 1946.

18. Possible references to American poets John Berryman's *Homage to Mistress Bradstreet* and James Merrill's "The Summer People."

19. William Langland (c. 1330-c. 1400), author of the long poem *The Vision of Piers the Plowman.*

20. Dante Alligheri began his *Divine Comedy* about 1300.

21. Each writer successfully authored at least one long poem: William Allingham (1824-1889), *Laurence Bloomfield in Ireland*; Ludovico Ariosto

(1474-1533; Italian), *Orlando Furioso*; John Ashbery (b. 1927), *Self-Portait in a Convex Mirror* (or, possibly, *Fragment*).

22. Gillaume de Salluste Du Bartas (1544-1590), French writer remembered chiefly for his *Divine Weeks and Works.*

23. Charles Olson (1910-1970), *American Maximus.* Edward Dorn, *Gunslinger* (1968).

24. For Bruckner see n. 8. Gustav Mahler (1860-1911), Austrian composer.

25. Olivier Eugéne Prosper Messiaen (1908-1992), French composer.

26. Hugh MacDiarmuid (1892-1978), sometimes considered the greatest Scottish poet since Burns, and David Jones (1895-1974), a strongly religious Welsh poet.

27. Pablo Neruda (1904-1973), Nobel prize-winning Chilean poet.

28. Galway Kinnell (b. 1927), American author of the *Book of Nightmares.* "The Bridge" is an allusion to Hart Crane's poem.

29. See interview with Irish poet Paul Muldoon.

30. Miles Davis (b. 1926), American jazz trumpeter.

31. Sean Dunne died in 1995.

32. Desiderius Erasmus (1466?-1536), Dutch humanist.

33. That is, the *New England Review and Bread Loaf Quarterly.*

34. See Timothy Kearney's interview with Montague and John Hewitt (1907-1987), in *The Crane Bag of Irish Studies, 1977-81* (Dublin: Crane Bag, 1983), 722-29 (this is the reprint of the original Crane Bag interview, 4 [1980]).

35. Marshall McLuhan (1911-1980), Canadian cultural historian and theorist on mass communications.

Works Cited

Bizot, Richard. "A Sense of Places: The Homing Instinct in the Poetry of John Montague." *Éire-Ireland* 30, no. 1 (1995): 167-76.

Dawe, Gerald. "Invocation of Powers: John Montague." In *The Chosen Ground*, edited by Neil Corcoran, 15-32. Bridgen, Wales: Poetry Wales; Chester Springs, Pa.: Dufour Editions, 1992.

Deane, Seamus. "John Montague: The Kingdom of the Dead." In *Celtic Revivals: Essays in Modern Irish Literature,* 146-55. Winston-Salem, N.C.: Wake Forest Univ. Press, 1985.

Frazier, Adrian. "Pilgrim Haunts: Montague's *The Dead Kingdom* and Heaney's *Station Island*." *Éire-Ireland* 20, no. 4 (1985): 134-43.

Garratt, Robert F. "Poetry at Mid-Century II: John Montague." In *Modern Irish Poetry: Tradition and Continuity from Yeats to Heaney,* 198-229. Berkeley and Los Angeles: Univ. of California Press, 1986.

Irish University Review 19, no. 1 (1989). Special John Montague issue.

Johnston, Dillon. "Devil and Montague." In *Irish Poetry after Joyce.* 2d ed., 167-203. Syracuse, N.Y.: Syracuse Univ. Press, 1997.

Kersnowski, Frank L. *John Montague.* Lewisburg, Pa.: Bucknell Univ. Press, 1975.

Martin, Augustine. "John Montague: Passionate Contemplative." In *Irish Writers and Their Creative Process.* edited by Jacqueline Genet and Wynne Hellegouarc'h, 37-51. Gerrards Cross, Eng.: Colin Smythe, 1996.

Montague, John. "The Sweet Way." In *Irish Writers and Their Creative Process.* edited by Jacqueline Genet and Wynne Hellegouarc'h, 30-36. Gerrards Cross, Eng.: Colin Smythe, 1996.

Poger, Sidney. "Crane and Montague: The Pattern History Weaves." *Éire-Ireland* 16, no. 4 (1981): 114-24.

Redshaw, Thomas Dillon. "John Montague." *Éire-Ireland* 11, no. 4 (1976): 122-33.

———. "*Ri,* as in Regional." *Éire-Ireland* 9, no. 2 (1974): 41-64.

Skelton, Robin. "John Montague and the Divided Inheritance." In *Celtic Contraries,* 225-46. Syracuse, N. Y.: Syracuse Univ. Press, 1990.

Douglas Sealy (essay date spring 1989)

SOURCE: Sealy, Douglas. "The Sound of a Wound: An Introduction to the Poetry of John Montague from 1958 to 1988." *Irish University Review* 19, no. 1 (spring 1989): 8-26.

[*In the following essay, Sealy discusses thirty years of Montague's poetry, covering each volume of poetry in chronological order beginning with* Forms of Exile *(1958) up to and including* Mount Eagle *(1988).*]

John Montague and I were born in the same year and his poetry has been part of my growing up. I have not felt able to make a detached survey from the height of a critical Olympus; I have chosen rather to approach each book in turn and tried to recreate something of what I thought at the time of each publication, without the benefit of hindsight. I have made a web of quotation and commentary and hope that certain matters that I have not had space to touch on, such as the diversity of poetic form and the subtle handling of rhythm, will be self-evident. I have not mentioned his translations from the Irish, collected in *A Fair House* (1972), nor discussed the revised second edition of **Poisoned Lands** (1977) nor his **Selected Poems** (1982). This last volume contains most of the poems I have quoted from. I would like to have quoted much more and written much more, I feel that what I have done is less than adequate; but I hope that it will arouse interest and stir memories and above all lead readers to the poems.

1

In 1958 the Dolmen Press issued a pamphlet of twenty poems at the rather high price of eight shillings and sixpence. I know it was high because I can remember not buying it for that reason, thus depriving myself of an early acquaintance with John Montague's **Forms of Exile.** Happily, thirteen of the poems were republished in a larger collection in 1961, in hardback, twelve shillings and sixpence, by MacGibbon and Kee, and whether I had more money at the time or not I could not resist the poem which the publishers had cunningly placed on the dustcover of **Poisoned Lands** instead of the usual list of other publications. The poem was called **"Old Mythologies"** and neatly eroded any lingering admiration I might have had for the heroes of myth and saga by turning them into the stars of fashion plates, totally unreal in their super-real detail. Now the warriors lie under meadows of grazing cattle, those "epicures of shamrock and the four-leaved clover", and the poem concludes:

> This valley cradles their archaic madness
> As once, on an impossibly epic morning,
> It upheld their savage stride:
> To bagpiped battle marching,
> Wolfhounds, lean as models,
> At their urgent heels.[1]

The word "models" gives the game away. Our image of that distant past, nurtured on centuries of romanticized and sanitized retellings, bears little relation to the swaggering, hard-drinking, foulmouthed headhunters that invaded Ireland around 400 BC.

This demystification had already begun in **Forms of Exile,** in particular in **"The Sean Bhean Vocht"**. The "poor old woman", who symbolizes Ireland, was presented as a garrulous crone, full of gossip and superstition and folk tale, who treasured a moth-eaten past and faced no happy future. She clung to a traditional framework that had outlived its usefulness, as did the pilgrims to Rome that the poet satirizes in **"Rome, Anno Santo"**:

> The olive-skinned impudent boys dive wildly past
> Thieving for pennies. In this splendid Italian sun

> Ranked facades proclaim a church's humanism:
> Bernini's baroque flares out in joyous ecstasy;
> But the Irish matrons, girded in nun-like black,
> Pilgrims from Georgian buildings above the Atlantic's wrack,
> March towards their Godhead, with bead and book, relentlessly.[2]

The almost pagan boys and the Jansenistic matrons make an effective contrast, the dead hand of the past confronted by resilience and optimism of youth, a contrast which is treated with more sympathy in **"Soliloquy on a Southern Strand"**, where an old priest in Australia recalls the simplicities of an Irish childhood and the assurance of a vocation. Faced by the apparently untroubled sensuality of the crowds of youthful holiday-makers the priest is visited by disabling doubts:

> No martyrdom, no wonder, no real loss,
> An old man ailing on the Australian coast:
> Is it for that poor ending that I
> Have carried all this way my cross?[3]

The confrontation between Christianity and paganism is expressed even more dramatically in **"Dirge of the Mad Priest";** but on the other hand the poet shows, in **"Footnote on Monasticism: Dingle Peninsula"**, a wry understanding of the appeal of anchoretic life and a handful of poems from his profane years in America are notable for their drabness. If one dispenses with old mythologies it may be necessary to find other mythologies to take their place, and if the American dream has turned sour and the beehive cell is far from draughtproof the poet must look elsewhere.

In a refashioning of the myth of Theseus and the Minotaur the poet sees himself as a mental explorer delving into strata of darkness, and tells how he:

> . . . came at last, with harsh surprise,
> To where in breathing darkness lay
> A lonely monster with almost human terror
> In its lilac eyes.[4]

The "almost human" must be the slightly more than animal, and what the poet discovered at the end of this poem, called **"The Quest"**, must have been no Minotaur but an embryonic version of himself, a primeval nucleus but not a mythology. More significant in the mythic context is the final verse of **"The Sean Bhean Vocht"** which I quote from the improved version of 1977:

> But in high summer as the hills burned with corn
> I strode through golden light
> To the secret spirals of the burial stone:
> The grass-choked well ran sluggish red—
> Not with blood but with ferrous rust—
> But beneath the whorls of the guardian stone
> What hidden queen lay dust?[5]

The poor old woman's traditional lore may have retained a vestigial link with ancient legends about the pre-Celtic megaliths, but the poet's choice of words in this verse implies that the tomb may have been the burial place of an Irish Demeter or Ceres or at least of her human representative. The poet is shaping a mythology for himself.

In **"Like Dolmens round my Childhood, the Old People"**, probably the best known poem in *Poisoned Lands* (1961), a similar theme comes to a different conclusion. After five vignettes of old and isolated people living on what might be called the borders of civilization—"Curate and doctor trudged to attend them"—the poet encompasses old people and megaliths in one synoptic vision:

> Ancient Ireland, indeed! I was reared by her bedside,
> The rune and the chant, evil eye and averted head,
> Fomorian fierceness of family and local feud.
> Gaunt figures of fear and friendliness,
> For years they trespassed on my dreams,
> Until once, in a standing circle of stones,
> I felt their shadows pass
>
> Into that dark permanence of ancient forms.[6]

It has been said that the medieval world lingered on in Ireland well into this century but here Montague has succeeded, against the odds, in identifying prehistoric myth and monument with the old people of his childhood; he has honoured them with one of those mysterious memorials that dot the Irish countryside, sometimes on a hilltop, sometimes in the corner of a field, and that never fail to stir the imagination. Their shadows no longer fall across his dreams but abide in his memory.

At times in *Poisoned Lands* he shows a sardonic humour, as in the title poem and in **"Wild Sports of the West"**, named after W. H. Maxwell's book about hunting, shooting and fishing in the West of Ireland, published in 1832: it is not a goose or a salmon that is the peasant's kill in the poem, however, but a bailiff, hated servant of the aristocratic landlord who, despite his red coat, rides safely home:

> . . . Evening brings the huntsman home,
> Blood of pheasants in a bag:
> Beside a turfrick the cackling peasant
> Cleanses his ancient weapon with a rag . . .[7]

The "transplanted bailiff" ends up happily patrolling God's "feudal paradise", an ironic suggestion that the relationship of church and state, landlord and tenant, is part of the eternal order!

Poisoned lands and murdered bailiffs are like fragments of a fairy tale compared with the newsreel of Auschwitz which Montague saw as a schoolboy on a "long dead Sunday in Armagh". In the poem entitled **"Auschwitz,**

mon Amour"**—this title was changed in the revised edition of *Poisoned Lands* (1977)—he tells how, faced by the human debris of the concentration camps, he had nothing to offer but "our parochial brand of innocence", the "Irish dimension" of his childhood was "to be always at the periphery of incident". This leads him to the reflection, omitted in the revised edition, that:

> It takes a decade and a half, it seems,
> Even to comprehend one's dreams:
> Continued operation on the body of the past
> Brings final meaning to its birth at last.[8]

He may not have been happy with the arbitrary "decade and a half" nor with the unwarranted assurance of the word "final", but "continued operation on the body of the past" seems as good a way as any of describing his way of working. He is possessed, some might say obsessed, by Irish history and landscape, by ancestors and family, and by mythology; and as we have seen in **"The Quest"** he painfully strips off "layer after layer of the darkness" to come nearer to truth or meaning.

In this next book, *A Chosen Light* (1967), the text is divided into sections, a method he was to make use of in his subsequent books. They function rather like chapters in a book of prose, outlining different but frequently overlapping themes, and offering breathing spaces to the reader. The first chapter here is devoted to love and contains the well-known **"All Legendary Obstacles"**, a description of lovers' reunion whose equal I have yet to find. There is nothing like it in the 164 pages of poems in *Poems about Love* (1968) by Robert Graves, a poet whose work, if it has not influenced Montague's, nevertheless often shares an attitude and a way with words. The lovers, separated by "the hissing drift of winter rain", for whom "water dripping from great flanged wheels" anticipates their reunion in the Californian railway station, are finally seen on the platform, as they "move into the wet darkness", by an old lady in a carriage, who has wiped away the condensation on a window pane in order to watch them. The rain has no logical connection with the love, and yet in some mysterious way, it is the love. It is for such rare moments of irrational insight that one reads poetry, not but that there are other reasons, and I would like to call attention to the bleak honesty of the dedicatory poem:

> My love, while we talked
> They removed the roof. Then
> They started on the walls,
> Panes of glass uprooting
> From timber, like teeth.
> But you spoke calmly on,
> Your example of courtesy
> Compelling me to reply.
> When we reached the last
> Syllable, nearly accepting
> Our positions, I saw that

The floorboards were gone:
It was clay we stood upon.[9]

The second chapter returns to the Irish or rather Ulster people and landscape and in the poem **"A Bright Day"** Montague reveals something of what poetry means to him as a poet: he sees it as:

. . . The only way of saying something
Luminously as possible.

. . . a slow exactness
Which recreates experience
By ritualizing its details—[10]

This luminous exactness is well displayed in the third chapter, mostly set in France, but ending with the poet's hurried journey home, with his wife, to see his dying father, who is described in **"The Cage"** as follows:

My father, the least happy
man I have known. His face
retained the pallor
of those who work underground:
the lost years in Brooklyn
listening to a subway
shudder the earth.[11]

His father haunts his imagination, as he does his later books, and it is a measure of the self-confidence attained by the poet that he now feels able to bring his immediate family into his work, although it is not until **The Dead Kingdom** (1984) that he can bring himself to disclose the troubled circumstances of his birth and upbringing.

The final chapter of **A Chosen Light** contains poems that are mostly, I consider, of a mythological slant, and among them is **"The Siege of Mullingar"**. I can remember that the poem's first appearance was in the autumn of 1963, in the second number of the magazine *Arena,* and though it had to compete for attention with poems by Austin Clarke and Patrick Kavanagh, its topical relevance and its expression of a shared hope that a new and more liberal age was about to dawn in Ireland made it immensely exciting:

At the Fleadh Cheoil in Mullingar
There were two sounds, the breaking
Of glass, and the background pulse
Of music. Young girls roamed
The streets with eager faces,
Pushing for men. Bottles in
Hand, they rowed out a song:
*Puritan Ireland's dead and gone,
A myth of O'Connor and O'Faolain.*[12]

A Chosen Light shows the poet in a mood of assurance and stability but in *Tides* (1970) all is restlessness and unease. This book is also in four sections, dealing more or less with mythology, old love, new love, Ireland and Ulster, and ends with a long coda of seven poems about the sea, related to colour engravings by S. W. Hayter; as usual the categories overlap. Images of age and decay and death preside over the collection and the poet is the plaything of wind and wave, but the tides must obey the moon and the poet's only hope of remaining sane, if that is not too strong a word, is to discern a pattern, to create a ritual. In **"Boats"** he invokes protective signs, mingling Christian and pagan beliefs, the Virgin Mary and the Mediterranean Poseidon, but there is no security on the sea and the rhythms of nature can be both friend and enemy:

. . . Horse-tailed kelp and dulse,
knotted wrack, the sway-
ing submarine forest of

the coastal waters recedes,
transparent passages of light
green expanding to the long

periodic rhythms of the open sea
upon which we balance and slide,
hoping for pattern.[13]

Is there a pattern, a refuge to be found in love? Many have thought so but love can be as subject to ebb and flow as the sea. Artemis, goddess of the hunt, protectress of femininity, is the presiding deity here, not Aphrodite. She is also, in another of her aspects, the moon-goddess and the lover cannot trust her. But that there are moments of radiance on love's path, who can doubt? The problem, as the poet sees it, is to ritualize these moments, so that they can be recalled, perhaps even recreated, as certain priests and shamans recreate the world daily, by the recital of the correct formulae or spells. It can be of help when reading Montague to see at least some of the poems as spells or invocations. The desirability of ritual is assumed in **"The Same Gesture"**:

There is a secret room
of golden light where
everything—love, violence,
hatred is possible:
and, again love.

Such intimacy of hand
and mind is achieved
under its healing light
that the shifting of
hands is a rite

like court music . . .[14]

Tides is also of interest in that it shows Montague experimenting with very short lines and continual enjambment to an even greater degree than before, and trying his hand at two prose poems, **"Coming Events"** and **"The Huntsman's Apology"**, which are more terrible in their icy cruelty than the story of attempted rape, narrated by a seventy year old spinster, in **"The**

Wild Dog Rose", and they lack even the modicum of comfort found by the old woman who gazes at the dog rose, not noticing its thorny stems.

>   . . . "The wild rose
> is the only rose without thorns"
> she says, holding a wet blossom
> for a second, in a hand knotted
> as the knob of her stick.
> "Wherever I see it, I remember
> the Holy Mother of God and
> all she suffered". . . .[15]

The publication of *The Rough Field 1961-1971* in 1972 showed that while Montague had been writing the books mentioned above he had also been planning and working on the ten sections and epilogue of *The Rough Field.* The book can be considered as one long poem in ten chapters or as a collection of ten sequences, some of which seemed perfectly satisfactory self-contained entities when they appeared previously as separate publications. In an afterword Montague wrote:

> I had a kind of vision, in the medieval sense, of my home area, the unhappiness of its historical destiny. And of all such remote areas where the presence of the past was compounded with a bleak economic future, whether in Ulster, Brittany or the Highlands. I managed to draft the opening and the close but soon realised that I did not have the technique for so varied a task. At intervals during the decade I returned to it when the signs seemed right . . . I never thought of the poem as tethered to any particular set of events. One explores an inheritance to free oneself and others . . . the violence of disrupting factions is more than a local phenomenon. But one must start from home—so the poem begins where I began myself, with a Catholic family in the townland of Garvaghey, in the county of Tyrone, in the province of Ulster.[16]

As Montague had continually been exploring his inheritance he was able to make fresh use of previously collected poems, one from *Poisoned Lands,* five from *A Chosen Light* and two from *Tides.* So in the first section about Garvaghey (from the Irish *Garbh-achadh* which means Rough Field) we meet again the old people like dolmens and from *A Chosen Light,* his uncle, the country fiddler who "left for the New World in an old disgrace" and abandoned his fiddle for the "discord of Brooklyn". Montague has altered his uncle's musical repertoire to make it more appropriate to the historical background of the new book, but it is a minor change as the poem is essentially about the inheritance and transmutation of artistic talent. The second section contains four elegiac poems in memory of his aunt Brigid Montague, one of which, **"Omagh Hospital"**, had appeared in *Tides.*

>   . . . & you, whose life
> was selflessness,
> now die slowly

> broken down by
> process to a pale
> exhausted beauty . . .

> *Bring me home*
> you whimper &
> I see a house

> shaken by traffic
> until a fault runs
> from roof to base . . .[17]

It is instinctively fitting that on the night of her death Montague, in Paris, should have heard "a low constant crying", as it were the banshee's traditional warning.

The third section is subtitled "A Collage of Religious Misunderstandings" and juxtaposes quotations from the startlingly offensive propaganda of an extreme Protestant organisation with poems about the quietly habitual religious observances of the Catholic countryman, at chapel or mass-rock. The conclusion is in the traditional form of a list of absurdities, the last of which is "a United Ireland"!

The fourth section is about loss: the loss of people, of the linguistic domain of Gaelic, of historical pride and of the very Irish sense of place:

>   . . . The whole landscape a manuscript
> We had lost the skill to read,
> A part of our past disinherited;
> But fumbled, like a blind man,
> Along the fingertips of instinct . . .[18]

From repression to revolution is a short step and in the fifth section we learn of the Republican activities of Montague's father, which led to flight to Brooklyn. For the poet this is not merely history; it is nightmare and resemblances between the poet and his father, both mental and physical, come to the fore in times of stress. Montague's bitterness about the conquest, or as it is now called the colonisation, of Ireland is an inheritance; "the vomit surge of race hatred", as he calls it in **"The Sound of a Wound"**, comes from his father. By curious coincidence both Montague and his father bore the marks of a car accident but in the context of the book they seem more an inheritance than a fortuitousness. The short poem **"The Fault"** reads:

> When I am angry, sick or tired
> A line on my forehead pulses,
> The line on my left temple
> Opened by an old car accident.
> My father had the same scar
> In the same place, as if
> The same fault ran through
> Us both: anger, impatience,
> A stress born of violence.[19]

And in **"The Cage"**, borrowed here from *A Chosen Light,* that mark is always beating on the father's "ghostly forehead".

The sixth section describes a drunken evening in Tyrone, full of old songs and childhood memories, and the attainment of "the seventh sense of drunkenness" in which:

> Each grassblade bends with
> Translucent beads of moisture
> And the bird of total meaning
> Stirs upon its hidden branch.[20]

The poet is stung into soberness by the sight of an unfinished dance hall, a gross symbol of the brief hunger of the young "for novelty, for flashing energy & change".

Change comes quickly in the seventh section, **"Hymn to the New Omagh Road"**, where the poet juxtaposes the conventional ballad lilt of "'Tis pleasant for to take a stroll by Glencull Waterside" with "the crustacean claws of the excavator" that are destroying the same waterside; and he draws up a balance sheet of profit and loss, a series of delicate observations of the natural world that is barely glimpsed, if at all, by the people who can now, thanks to the new road, drive past at high speed.

The eighth section **"Patriotic Suite"** presents the Irish Republic as it almost reluctantly forces itself into the modern world, eager to have its bite of the monetary cake, but loth to reject the mouldy shreds of the past. Economic greed is accompanied by cultural stagnation. **"The Siege of Mullingar"** reappears but it is only a minor local skirmish compared with **"A New Siege"** of section nine.

Events had overtaken the poem. In 1968 there was the first Civil Rights march, the near massacre of Burntollet, and in 1969 the arrival of British troops and the Battle of Bogside. The early part of the book now seems prophetic and to have been moving towards **"A New Siege"**, which gathers together the threads of history and family and patriotism, and links the new found pride and "flashing energy" of the Catholics of Derry with the student risings in the outside world:

> Paris, Chicago
>   seismic waves
> zigzagging through
>   a faulty world . . .[21]

The tenth and final section is the dying fall of **"The Wild Dog Rose"** and the epilogue bids goodbye to old rural poverty and degradation, through regretting the inevitable loss of a world where "action had been wrung through painstaking years to ritual". But the poet, in the verse which refers to the dedicatee of **"A New Siege"**, Bernadette Devlin, admits that everything is changing:

> the emerging order
>   of the poem invaded

> by cries, protestations
>   a people's pain
> the defiant face
>   of a young girl
> campaigning against
>   memory's mortmain . . .
> the rough field
>   of the universe
> growing, changing
>   a net of energies
> crossing patterns
>   weaving towards
> a new order
>   a new anarchy
> always different
>   always the same . . .[22]

The lines inscribed on the poet's forehead have become the lines of a geological fault that has altered the ground on which we stand, and in the poem the word "lines", repeated in many stanzas, bears a multiplicity of meanings. In a vignette we glimpse the young Montague, the first hint in his poetry that Derry had a private meaning for him:

> Lines of leaving
>   lines of returning
> the long estuary
>   of Lough Foyle, a
> ship motionless
>   in wet darkness
> mornfully hooting
>   as a tender creeps
> to carry passengers
>   back to Ireland
> a child of four
>   this sad sea city
> my landing place . . .[23]

2

It is not till the appearance of *A Slow Dance* (1975) that the reader realises that Montague's mother followed her husband to America, with her two eldest sons, and that the poet, the youngest son, was born in Brooklyn. But America was **"A Muddy Cup"** from which "she refused to drink" and she returned home four years later:

> a she cat,
> intent on safety,
> dragging her kittens
> to the womb-warm basket
> of home.[24]

This book is notable for its poems about nature viewed as a healing power. The sounds and sights of Ireland—fuchsias, whins, boglands, winds, snails, wrens, cattle, streams, squirrels embody a sense of beatitude and timelessness. But the grimmer aspects are not forgotten: the farm is built around the scream of the slaughtered pig and the earth goddess is also the queen of the land of the dead:

ease your
hand into the
rot smelling crotch

of a hollow
tree, and find
two pebbles of quartz

protected by
a spider's web:
her sunless breasts.[25]

The dance that in early times greeted the sun or revered the tree can also be the dance of death. And death figures largely in this book. In **"Ó Riada's Farewell"** we can sense a man driven to death by his own self-destructive impulses and in **"Courtyard in Winter"** with its masterly use of a chorus line—"Snow curls in on the cold wind"—a friend commits suicide:

What solace but endurance, kindness?
Against her choice, I still affirm
That nothing dies, that even from
Such bitter failure memory grows;
The snowflake's structure, fragile
But intricate as the rose when

Snow curls in on the cold wind.[26]

The troubles in the North get worse; "A burst of automatic fire solves the historical problem", as the poet ironically remarks, and happiness is briefly snatched from the jaws of destruction:

While jungleclad troops
ransack the Falls, race
through huddled streets . . .
you turn to me again
seeking refuge as the
cave of night blooms
with fresh explosions.[27]

That poem might well have found a place in Montague's next collection ***The Great Cloak*** (1978) for which the author has obligingly supplied a plot. "These poems should not be read separately. A married man seeks comfort elsewhere, as his marriage breaks down. But he discovers that libertinism does not relieve his solitude. So the first section of the book ends with a slight affair which turns serious, the second with the despairing voices of a disintegrating marriage, the third with a new and growing relationship to which he pledges himself."[28]

There are surprisingly few books of poems devoted entirely to love—*Berryman's Sonnets*, Neruda's *20 Poemas de Amor*, MacGilleain's *Dàin do Eimhir* come to mind among works of this century but I find ***The Great Cloak*** more akin to Meredith's *Modern Love* (1862), making due allowance for shifts in literary decorum. Meredith's XLVII

. . . Love that had robbed us of immortal things,
This little moment mercifully gave,

Where I have seen across the twilight wave
The swan sail with her young beneath her wings.[29]

is not so far from Montague's **"Song"**:

Let me share with you
a glimpse of richness:
two swans startled me
turning low over the Lee,
looking for a nestling place . . .[30]

and both authors show a grim appreciation of the dramatic possibilities inherent in the tragic situation of a broken marriage. I am particularly impressed by the poems spoken by the first wife, where Montague has gone outside himself to give expression to another's feelings, poems such as **"She Walks Alone"** in which a stranger begs her for a kiss:

. . . He looked so young, my heart went out to him.
I stopped in the shadows under the Cathedral.
We kissed, and the tears poured down my face.[31]

The poems cover a wide emotional range and the three main characters are portrayed with delicacy and sympathy. It is impossible for an outsider to judge to what extent fact had been fictionalised and the question is finally irrelevant; poems for reading are not lives to be judged. The words ring true: the anguish of the separation is totally convincing and the happiness of the new relationship is palpable in every poem of the third section, as for example in **"Waiting"**:

Another day of dancing summer,
Evelyn kneels on a rock, breasts
Swollen by approaching motherhood . . .
Seagulls aureoling her bowed head.
Translucent as Wicklow river gold;
Source of my present guilt and pride.[32]

Although the book contains the occasional Irish reference as in "Wicklow" above, it is a book without country, unlike all Montague's other books. Three translations from the French would not have been noticed as such if they had not been attributed; and the "Rue Daguerre" and "the white city of Evora" and "Herbert Street" belong not to France or Portugal or Ireland but to the world known to lovers. It is possible that the poems of ***The Great Cloak*** were written at more or less the same time as the poems of ***A Slow Dance***, but that the poet decided to make a separate volume of the love poems, releasing the dramatis personae from the burden of history and highlighting the intricacies of grief and passion at the purely personal level.

This particular strategy is abandoned in his next book ***The Dead Kingdom*** (1984). The epigraph, from Neruda, reads *"El reino muerto vive todavía"* (The dead kingdom still lives) and the book is peopled with the dead. It contains elements of myth, history, love and biography, much as his previous books do, but held together by the simple device of a journey across Ireland, from Cork to Tyrone, from South to North, from new home to old. It is the news of his mother's death that calls him home and on the journey memories of childhood rise, Ireland's troubled history surfaces, conjured by place-names, and back in Tyrone the poet makes his peace with the thronging ghosts of the ancestors. Though the book is composed, as usual, of separable lyrics, divided into sections, and bears some resemblance to *The Rough Field* it makes a more successful whole than the earlier work. I sometimes wonder if *The Rough Field* might not have been planned as a long narrative interspersed with lyrics—the forty-two lines of low-keyed description that open the first section would seem designed for that purpose—before the poet decided to leave it in a somewhat fragmentary state. I must add however that when it was presented publicly with various speakers, and music played by the Chieftains, it seemed no broken mosaic but a complete picture held together by strong bonds of emotion, a logic of the heart rather than the head. A similar logic prevails in *The Dead Kingdom,* assisted by an almost narrative thread.

Montague drives Northward through the midlands, passing towns where he had spent summer holidays as a child, noting the transient beauties of the rain-washed countryside, and letting his imagination dwell on the earlier inhabitants of deserted places—monks, vikings, lake-dwellers, Normans—and before entering "that lost finger of land from Swanlinbar to Blacklion" and crossing the Border, he finds a still centre in one of his favourite images, the well of pure water:

> . . . a tarnished coin is thrown in,
> sinking soundlessly to the bottom.
> Water's slow alchemy washes it clean:
> a queen of the realm, made virgin again.[33]

The well is more than a place to draw water or a place of pilgrimage, it has "its secret", its pulsations are "the hidden laughter of earth", it symbolises the untarnished source of healing.

The hostilities in the North are symbolized here by the mythical Black Pig, the wild boar with "flared nostrils, red in anger" but Montague cannot stop long with the ghosts of the past, he must go on to his mother's funeral and make his peace. He reprints **"The Muddy Cup"** from *A Slow Dance* but after the last stanza where the mother cat drags her kittens home he forces himself to add:

> (all but the runt
> the littlest one, whom
> she gave to be fostered
> in Garvaghey, seven miles away;
> her husband's old home.)[34]

This inexplicable abandonment of the four-year-old child by his mother is the wound whose sound has been present as the ground-bass of Montague's work. It can be heard in the voice of the lonely beast in the labyrinth of **"The Quest"**, in the cry of the banshee at the end of the four deeply felt poems dedicated to the aunt who fostered him, in the public humiliation of the child by his teacher:

> So this is our brightest infant?
> Where did he get that outlandish accent?
> What do you expect, with no parents,
> sent back from some American slum:
> none of you are to speak like him![35]

Though as a young man Montague often made his way over those seven miles to see his mother in her family home in Fintona, and though his father returned from America to live the last six years of his life in Tyrone, the consciousness of his abandonment can never have been dispelled even if in *The Dead Kingdom* he finally comes to terms with it. This book can be read as a sequel to *The Rough Field*—the first book is almost a public statement, the second a private commentary on the first. He attempts to make sense of his own past in relation to his country's past—for him the two are hardly separable—and *The Dead Kingdom* marks a pivotal point in the poet's career, so it is being considered separately elsewhere in this special issue.

The undercurrents of anguish, experienced or feared, that surface in the work indicate that had it not been for "the sweet oils of poetry" Montague might never have attained the serenity that can be glimpsed from time to time in *The Dead Kingdom* and becomes radiant in his latest book *Mount Eagle* (1988). Poetry gave him a medium in which his pain could be expressed and transmuted and thus prevented from eating him away from inside. The pain does not explain, or explain away, the poetry; the poetry is a gift that Montague has refined down the years and that has enabled him to speak not only for himself but for others. He is continually exploring ways of linking his private sensibility with his sense of what is happening to other people and of human inter reaction in "the rough field of the universe". Inevitably, in the shaping of raw material into poetry, words take on a life of their own and tempt the poet into byways of style and obsession, but in Montague's poetry he has managed to balance the insistence of what he wants to say against the pressure of the words he must use. His honesty, perhaps lucidity would be the better word, is admirable, as is his refusal to hide behind any grandiosity of rhetoric. His recourse to the world of myth is not an esoteric plumbing of the occult but an endeavour to restore an old instinctual human relationship with nature.

In his various books he has interwoven themes of age-old myth and present love, of personal life and national history, of natural process and of human failure, in continually changing patterns. The groups of poems that open and conclude *Mount Eagle* relate to the world of myth but them the other themes make fresh appearances. The sound of a wound, though mostly muted, is clearly to be heard in several poems, in particular in **"She Cries"**, where a desolating confession of human weakness finally conveys a message, not of despair, but of hope and of human endurance, and the creative power of the word is, against all odds, reaffirmed. I quote the beginning and ending of the poem:

> She puts her face against the wall
> and cries, crying for herself,
> crying for our children, crying
> for all of us . . .
>
> but most of all for her husband
> she cries, against the wall,
> the poet at his wooden desk,
> that toad with a jewel in his head,
> no longer privileged, but still
> trying to crash, without faltering,
> the sound barrier, the dying word.[36]

Notes

1. *Poisoned Lands and Other Poems* (London: MacGibbon & Kee, 1961), p. 36.

2. *Forms of Exile* (Dublin: The Dolmen Press, 1958), p. 9.

3. Ibid., p. 18.

4. Ibid., p. 15.

5. *Poisoned Lands* (Dublin: The Dolmen Press, 1977), p. 13.

6. *Poisoned Lands and Other Poems* (London: MacGibbon & Kee, 1961), p. 19.

7. Ibid., p. 29.

8. Ibid., p. 42.

9. *A Chosen Light* (London: MacGibbon & Kee, 1967), p. 9.

10. Ibid., p. 36.

11. Ibid., p. 54.

12. Ibid., p. 60.

13. *Tides* (Dublin: The Dolmen Press, 1970), p. 59.

14. Ibid., p. 37.

15. Ibid., p. 18.

16. *The Rough Field* (Dublin: The Dolmen Press, 1972), back cover.

17. *The Rough Field*, p. 20.

18. Ibid., p. 30.

19. Ibid., p. 39.

20. Ibid., p. 49.

21. Ibid., p. 70.

22. Ibid., p. 71.

23. Ibid., p. 69.

24. *A Slow Dance* (Dublin: The Dolmen Press, 1975), p. 46.

25. Ibid., p. 10.

26. Ibid., p. 19.

27. Ibid., p. 30.

28. *The Great Cloak* (Dublin: The Dolmen Press, 1978), p. 7.

29. *Poems*. Volume I (London: Constable & Co., 1913), p. 49.

30. *The Great Cloak* (Dublin: The Dolmen Press, 1978), p. 50.

31. Ibid., p. 28.

32. Ibid., p. 56.

33. *The Dead Kingdom* (Mountrath: The Dolmen Press, 1984), p. 39.

34. Ibid., p. 68.

35. Ibid., p. 91.

36. *Mount Eagle* (Loughcrew: The Gallery Press, 1988), p. 48.

Antoinette Quinn (essay date spring 1989)

SOURCE: Quinn, Antoinette. "'The Well-Beloved': Montague and the Muse." *Irish University Review* 19, no. 1 (spring 1989): 27-43.

[*In the following essay, Quinn discusses Montague's unhappy relationship with his mother and the way it informed the representations of women in his poetry.*]

> Raised by the fury of our need,
> supplicating, lusting, grovelling
> before the tall tree of Artemis,
> the transfiguring bow of Diana,
> the rooting vulva of Circe, or
> the slim shape of a nymph,
> luring, dancing, beckoning:
> all her wild disguises!

> **"The Well-Beloved"**

John Montague is a Muse-poet, obsessed by the eternal feminine, a votary of the Moon-goddess in her three phases, crescent, full or waning: laureate of woman as lover and wife, celebrant of the creative and destructive contraries of the maternal, and hag-ridden, too, fascinated by solitary crones who have abrogated the conventional female roles of lover, wife, mother.

In the most intimately confessional of his poetic sequences, *The Dead Kingdom,* he traces his imaginative cult of the female to its autobiographical origins in his own mother's repeated rejection of him as a child:

> All roads wind backwards to it.
> An unwanted child, a primal hurt.

Birth was for Montague only the first of several maternal expulsions. He portrays himself as virtually an orphan from the start, wet-nursed as an infant, banished from the parental home to be reared by his paternal aunts from the age of four, doubly abandoned to these foster-mothers when his natural mother later chose to care for his elder brothers but not for him, a denial so cuttingly cruel that he has not yet confronted it directly. The stanza dealing with it was omitted from *A Slow Dance*; in *The Dead Kingdom* it is included but bracketed, pain in parenthesis. Though he blames his childhood "stammer, impediment, stutter" on the public taunts of a schoolmistress one notices that this speech impediment first manifested itself in the year after his mother had finally deserted him. (The school-mistress acts *in loco parentis,* perhaps.) Writing was to become the aphasic's alternative mode of communication, and, therefore, a form of expression originating in deprivation and lovelessness. "Motherless", Montague reconceived himself as a poet, one "re-begot / Of absence, darkness, death; things which are not". Small wonder, then, that he should be imaginatively attracted towards female models of love, nurture, fosterage, plenitude, generosity, security; or that woman should also appear to him as a *femme fatale,* seductive but ultimately destructive; or that he should empathize with the loneliness, ostracism and otherness of the hag, finding in her an alter-ego, a mirror-image, so that when he peers into the well in *The Dead Kingdom* it is the Hag of the Mill whose face he sees reflected.

In *The Dead Kingdom* he attributes his mother's failure to nurse him, not to illness, but to a deliberate refusal, blaming it on the terrible travail his birth inflicted on her, on his "double blunder / coming out, both the wrong sex, / and the wrong way around", on the coincidence of his conception and the conclusion of his parents' conjugal relations. Through such editing of family history he manages to present himself as both culprit and victim and his mother as a Janus-headed Muse,[1] poetically enabling and emotionally disabling simultaneously:

fertile source of guilt and pain.

Montague's essay on his Northern Irish precursor, Louis MacNeice,[2] is in part an "Eclogue between the motherless" in which he traces MacNeice's nightmare vision to a "sense" and "scent" of guilt like that which had pervaded his own childhood, connecting maternal disapproval and deprivation with the pangs of childbirth:

> . . . The day I was born
> I suppose that that same hour was full of her screams. . . .

Like MacNeice's his sense of dispossession was further exacerbated by the fact that he was a pre-natal exile, "torn before birth from where (his) fathers dwelt", for Montague was born in Brooklyn, a child of the Northern Irish nationalist diaspora that followed on the Treaty of 1922. The offspring of a mother who had only recently emigrated from Ireland and suckled by other immigrant women, "new washed from the hold", he would have imbibed homesickness and alienation in the womb and at the breast and, consciously or unconsciously, passed his early years in an unsettled ambience. Aged four he suffered a reverse form of exile when he was transplanted from Brooklyn to Garvaghey, "transported" (again that implication of guilt and punishment) from bustling, modern, urban America to a "fading farm" at the back of beyond in rural Ireland, exchanging the familial home for a childless and unmanned household run by two spinsters. In *The Dead Kingdom* the Abbeylara household where he spent his childhood summers is clearly a surrogate home. What the schoolmistress taunted him with was his Brooklyn accent, an articulation of his foreignness and otherness. Soon, because of his status as star-pupil at the local school he was on the move again, separated geographically and culturally from his Garvaghey context as boarding-school in Armagh was succeeded by undergraduate and graduate studies at University College, Dublin, a Fulbright scholarship to Yale and further courses and teaching posts in a number of American universities. The adult Montague appears determined to play out his role of resident alien, basing himself in Paris for ten years and, even when domiciling himself in Ireland, choosing to live in Dublin and, later, Cork rather than in Northern Ireland. Now he is a nomad once again, commuting between France, Cork and New York. Significantly, both his marriages have been exogamous. The speed of modern air travel may have rendered the term "exile" melodramatic yet Montague's appears a belated and acute case of Irish literary deracination. Born a hyphenated Irish-American he is a perpetually displaced person, in permanent imaginative quest for a home.

As a virtual orphan Montague is continually seeking to compensate for the maternal bonding of which he was deprived in infancy. He is obsessed with fosterage and kinship, with genealogy, ancestry, tribe, inheritance, the sense of belonging, personal and local attachments. In his poetry he pores over old family photographs and letters, recounts recent and more remote family history, sees his verses as a perpetuation of his paternal family's musical gift, his uncle's fiddle-playing, his father's tenor singing. Critics who are perturbed by a lack of political objectivity in *The Rough Field,* expecting its collage-like structure to confer a multi-faceted complexity of perspective, underestimate the fact that Montague is primarily an autobiographical poet for whom provincial and local unrest and violence, whether historical or contemporary, are extensions of ancestral, familial and personal traumas. He is almost incapable of distinguishing between Clio and Mnemosyne. It is his own experience of deracination that has sensitized him to the plight of the dispossessed and culturally colonized. The child-immigrant mocked for his strange accent and his foreignness knows at first hand the problems of adapting to an alien culture. A longing to belong attracts him to the role of tribal and familial bard, articulate heir, the artist as Tague and Mon-tague. However, *The Rough Field,* for all its nationalist sympathies, is ultimately a regretful and resentful exploration of his own displacement, as much an outcry against technological change as against tribal disinheritance. Its opening poem, **"Home Again"**, is a doubly ironic comment on alienation and it concludes with his, by now notorious, admission of a dual estrangement:

> with all my circling a failure to return
> to what is already going
>
> going,
>
> GONE

Only a sentimentalist would wish to turn back the country calendar but Montague, one of whose favourite poems is *The Deserted Village,* is a pastoral poet manqué, an elegist pining for the stability of lost rural rituals. (Even the village pub is named "The Last Sheaf"; "The Last Straw", might have been more apt). *The Rough Field* is another narrative of the poet's expulsion from a "flayed womb".

Despite, or because of, his love-hate relationship with it, Garvaghey, his adoptive home, retains a powerful hold on his imagination:

> Harsh landscape that haunts me,
> well and stone, in the bleak moors of dream. . . .

"Well" and "stone" are recurrent images in his poetry from the first. "Well" or "source", his most obsessive trope, symbolizes his autobiographical fascination with his own origins and with the hiding places of his poetic power and also his abiding concern with creativity and the life-principle, with pulse and process, fluidity and fertility, tidal throb and threnody. "Stone" is expressive of his contrary attraction to stasis and permanence, to monumental art, ancient cultural artifacts and ancestral inscriptions, to Sheela-na-gigs, dolmens, passage-graves, "shards of a lost tradition", to poetry as a means of self-perpetuation and an enduring communication, to whatever survives and defies Mutability. This creative tension between flow and fixity is recognized and maintained in an early poem, **"The Water-Carrier"**, where realism triumphs over the impulse towards iconographic stylization, but, in what is perhaps Montague's best-known early poem, his eccentric old neighbours are imaginatively dignified by being translated into dolmens, "that dark permanence of ancient forms". As an elegant stylist in verse Montague's fatal Muse is the "Meduse", arresting the flow of process, simplifying and controlling through petrification, casting "in the mould of death".

One of his enabling Muses is the recurrent figure of the hag. Old, childless, unmarried, ugly and workworn she is, nevertheless, a foster-mother to the poet, an inspirational analogue to the spinster aunts who reared him. As a lonely, crazed and isolated woman she touches some profound chord in Montague's psyche and sometimes seems a female alter-ego. She may also appear as a manifestation of the mythological Irish hag who ensured the sovereignty of the prospective king if he drank a libation from her well and mated with her.[3] It is in this guise that she first enters Montague's poetry, introduced in his first collection, *Forms of Exile,* and in both versions of his second, *Poisoned Lands,* under the title, **"The Sean Bhean Bhoct"**,[4] a traditional poetic personification of Ireland. Here Montague is consciously assuming the role of Irish tribal bard, treating a legendary Irish theme in a contemporary Ulster accent. In her role of crone as chronicler this hag is a vital link between the recent and remote history of a region, bilingual, blending pagan and Christian beliefs, a living archive of local folklore and superstition. What she transmits to the young poet is the *dinnsheanchas* that once formed part of traditional Irish bardic training, a sense of the historical layers and legends which give character to an area, a local piety deeper than the topographical.[5] Though her listener evinces a young buck's contempt for her ugliness and repetitive, senile gibberings, he is spellbound by her narrative. In Irish mythology the "loathly lady" changed into a beautiful young queen when the initiation rites had been completed, symbolizing the renewed fertility of the land under its new ruler. Montague's hag is no "queen of the realm, made virgin again" yet, through her tales of well and queen, she, nevertheless, ensures the continuity of a cultural realm:

> So succession passes, through strangest hands.

The poem concludes with the prospective tribal bard striding over the fertile land to lay claim to his imaginative dominion, to conjure with the subterranean myths of the racial subconscious, to ponder the enduring inscriptions of neolithic poetic ancestors:

> But in high summer as the hills burned with corn
> I strode through golden light
> To the secret spirals of the burial stone:
> The grass-choked well ran sluggish red—
> Not with blood but ferrous rust—
> But beneath the whorls of the guardian stone
> What hidden queen lay dust?

"Well and stone" have a new custodian.

Two incarnations of the *cailleach* are juxtaposed in *Tides,* a local, near-contemporary land-hag in **"The Wild Dog Rose"**, a legendary ninth century, Southern Irish sea-hag, resuscitated through translation, in **"The Hag of Beare"**. The centrality of their presence in this volume and the interdependent formal relationship of the two poems are foregrounded in the folk tale epigraph:

> . . . Mariners know
> the glitter of the sea-hag,
> long-regarded, turns to a rose.

The *cailleach* encountered in **"The Wild Dog Rose"** is portrayed as a *genius loci,* the "final outcrop" of a bleak, barren landscape, her "untilled fields" seeming to symbolize both sexual and agricultural sterility, as in George Moore's stories. The hag as Muse is always at the outset a frightening figure, who impinges on the primitive childish imagination through her terrifying or repellent otherness, and the poet's confontation with her and her retinue of dogs here begins as the adult's laying of a childhood nightmare. He thinks he has her measure now, demythologizing her into "a human being / merely, hurt by event", befriending her, chatting her up, urbane auditor of her simple annals, "the small events of her life". As poet he diagnoses that her craziness is due to the lack of an audience:

> The only true madness is loneliness,
> the monotonous voice in the skull
> that never stops
> > > because never heard.

Yet the *cailleach* still retains her ancient capacity to disturb the complacent imagination. Her commonplace narrative suddenly veers into a 'tasteless' tale of violence and violation so shocking that the listening poet wants to shut it out. *Tides* is a volume which focusses on images of victimhood and opens with a nightmare image of woman as victim in **"Premonition"**. **"The Wild Dog Rose"** is crucial to this theme, its heroine a victim-narrator who succeeds in containing and controlling violence, managing her pain. Montague regards poetry as "a healing harmony", a therapeutic art, and the *cailleach* is here the consolatory Muse,

finding a symbolic antidote to near-defloration in a flower, turning to a dog-rose when canine protection has failed her. The *cailleach's* own Muse is female; Mary, as Blessed Virgin, is invoked during her attempted rape; Mary, as Holy Mother of God, is her customary foster-mother. In her maternal capacity Mary is represented as *Mater Dolorosa,* a mother who suffered the loss of her son. By associating this absent mother figure with the shining dog-rose the old woman transforms her into "a flowering presence", a "chosen light". In her solitariness and her sustaining bond with a caring maternal presence, her power to make her desert bloom, the *cailleach* of **'The Wild Dog Rose'** is an inspirational figure who touches Montague's imagination profoundly. No wonder he cannot "say goodbye" to her.

Certain of Montague's poems are multivalent, reintroduced in different sequences and gaining new resonances from their changed contexts. When **"The Wild Dog Rose"** reappears as the concluding poem (apart from the Epilogue) in *The Rough Field* its private symbolism acquires a public, historical and social dimension and it offers a final comment on the plantation and pillage of a province, on the loveless exploitation of the land by colonists and commercial developers, intent on quick returns of profit or pleasure. The *cailleach* assumes a mythological status, becoming a figure of the land of Ireland, the Sean Bhean Bhoct of Irish legend and poetry. The consolatory image of the rose now almost inevitably suggests the traditional symbolic depiction of Ireland as a rose, *Rosin Dubh*, "My Dark Rosaleen", "the little Black Rose", Yeats's "right rose tree". From her prominent position at the end of *The Rough Field* the *cailleach* of **"The Wild Dog Rose"** casts a retrospective significance on Maggie Owens and Mary Moore, those two, lonely old solitaries from **"Like Dolmens round my Childhood, the Old People"**, the concluding poem of the first movement. She is associated, too, through age, weatherbeaten spinsterhood, floral symbolism and Christian faith with the poet's old workworn foster-mother, the domestic Muse, Brigid Montague, memorialized in the second movement of the sequence. Brigid, as Montague has noted, was 'patroness of the hearth, the fire, the forge'[6] and here her metaphorical role is to fan the flames of the poet's inspiration. Like the *cailleach* she is exemplary of the artist as healer, gathering into her hands and taking responsibility for the pain of her family, thus anticipating the musician of the fourth movement, whose lament swells "to honour / a communal loss", assuage a "tribal pain". In the eighth movement, **"A Patriotic Suite"**, Yeats's beautiful Muse, Maud Gonne, hovers off-stage, but the only instance in Montague's poetry in which the Irish Muse is transformed into a young girl with the walk of a queen is the ninth movement, **"A New Siege"**, dedicated to Bernadette Devlin and saluting the defiance

of a young girl
campaigning against
memory's mortmain.

"The Wild Dog Rose" of *The Rough Field* draws on and is enriched by a cumulative female presence and symbolism in the poem while retaining its own angular and wayward integrity. An old countrywoman's mariolatry and a bedraggled flower seem weak and ineffectual responses to historical or contemporary violence and predatoriness. What Montague is portraying, perhaps, is not an exemplary ideological stance but the survival of the weakest.

The pairing of "The Wild Dog Rose" with "The Hag of Beare" in *Tides* again suggests the racial matrix of Montague's cult of the hag. On both occasions he communicates a solitary old woman's monologue, "bridging her time and truth to ours", but in the second poem he speaks with grafted tongue, as medium rather than narrator and commentator. His version of the lament of the *Cailleach Berri,* from the ninth century Irish, transcends the barriers of gender, age, history and language to achieve imaginative empathy with this celebrated hag. She lives and breathes as in no previous translation, resurrected in the present tense, not as the *puella senilis* of Irish myth, but as a tragic figure, a lonely, aged, post-sexual woman. The sea floods and ebbs throughout the poem, tidal images and rhythms recreating the diastole and systole of the human cycle: life at the full, beautiful and sensual and its inevitable decline into dearth and death. Montague has proclaimed that "Puritan Ireland" is now "dead and gone" but the Gaelic Ireland glimpsed in his versions of Irish poetry enjoys an almost uninterrupted sexual frolic. As a voluptuary's elegy, "The Hag of Beare" contrasts ironically with the repressed Gavaghey *cailleach's* tale of the assault on her long-preserved virginity. Unlike "The Wild Dog Rose", "The Hag of Beare" ends bleakly and negatively; its disconsolate speaker eludes Montague's healing vision and proffers no redemptive symbols of her own.

Mary Mulvey of "The Music Box" is the poet's most recent incarnation of the Irish hag as Muse, an "ageing guardian" of the well, preserving the purity of the source. She is the Muse as Terpsichore, introducing the farouche child poet to the formal elegance of music and choreography, starting him on his "slow dance". Discrepancy between inspiration and its source is deliberately emphasized, perhaps overemphasized, with Mary Mulvey portrayed as a hobbling, misshapen old woman in grotesque contrast to the gracefully twirling silver figurine she sets in motion on the music box. This Midlands crone is connected with an earlier Irish literary manifestation of Terpsichore, Sweeney's Hag of the Mill, who led the crazed, alienated poet-king a merry dance over his kingdom, challenging him to ever greater leaps, ever more daring expressions of freedom and delight in movement. Mary Mulvey's music box provides a more decorous and limiting model. The circling ripples of the Midland well mirror the wrinkled countenance of the mill hag, implicitly urging the poet to forego custom and ceremony, to journey recklessly, leap joyfully into unknown terrain, bestride his kingdom boldly. As

> The guardian of the well
> Source of lost knowledge

she directs the poet of *The Dead Kingdom* towards the ludic and lunatic, towards rhythms and energies that transcend the autobiographical: the pulsing wellhead of the universe, "the hidden laughter of earth",

> The whole world
> turning in wet
> and silence, a
> damp mill wheel.

To that recent incarnation of the hag, the aged Cassandra of "Cassandra's Answer",

> . . . Roots are obstructions
> as well as veins of growth.

A crucial poem in Montague's Irish female canon is "For the Hillmother", a Roman Catholic litany to the Blessed Virgin transposed into a pagan chant. This is not a hag poem but a prayer to the fecund, maternal earth, fertility goddess and poetic Muse. Apostrophized as *fons et origo* of all creativity, a cardinal principle of silence and sound, who expresses herself through the organic rhythms and lushness of vegetation and the cyclical alternations of darkness and colour; invoked as the secret source and generous dispenser of a plenitude that is at once chthonic and inspirational; the "Hillmother" is finally apotheosized as a primal embodiment of the relationship between pleasure and procreation, voluptuously vaginal, protuberantly pregnant, ultimately parturient:

> Hidden cleft
> speak to us
> Portal of delight
> inflame us
> Hill of motherhood
> wait for us
> Gate of birth
> open for us

This is Montague's hymn to the fine delight that mothers thought, his celebration of the erotic roll, rise and carol of creation. Reverting from mariolatry to a pagan worship almost as old as the hills, the suppliant poet penetrates beneath a grafted Roman Catholic culture to unearth the primitive Celtic Muse. In its attenuated lines, economical phrasing, the tentativeness of its intensity, Montague's catalogue of natural delights consciously recalls the spare, celebratory inventories of image in Gaelic nature poetry. The Muse-poet is here a supplicant, dependent on the female for the safe conception, gestation and deliverance of his offspring.

> . . . 'Can I find a love beyond the family
> And feed her to the bed my mother died in. . . .'.

Montague quotes these lines from "Eclogue between the motherless" in his essay on Louis MacNeice. His own love poetry, especially in **"The Great Cloak,"** betrays a similar anxiety to exorcise his guilty, painful relationship with his mother by establishing a permanent and fruitful partnership with another woman and setting up a home. Woman is cast in the roles of lover and wife in *The Great Cloak,* an autobiographical sequence whose 'plot' turns on the dissolution of his first marriage and the evolution and fruition of his second.

In the first phase, **"Search"**, in which the poet is an unhappily married Don Juan casually coupling to cure his loneliness, women are presented as an anonymous procession of sexual partners. Poetry is an expression of Montague's quest for permanence and he ponders the literary repercussions of these temporary trysts. What is so transitory may leave no impression on the consciousness and

> habitual sounds of loneliness
> resume the mind again.

Nude female bodies tend to be treated as blank pages by a libertine poet, preoccupied with inscription. In the paired poems, **"Snowfield"** and **"Tracks"**, he approaches passion's present tense from contrary perspectives.

The naked female body in **"Snowfield"** is "happily" regarded as a *tabula rasa,* having the potential to register the poet's print-marks:

> The paleness of your flesh.
>
> Long afterwards, I gaze happily
> At my warm tracks radiating
>
> Across that white expanse.

Stendhal's warning that the *chaleur* of coition is *passager* was quoted at the opening of the section but, through ambiguous use of the phrase, "long afterwards", and a pun on the spatial properties of radiance, Montague manages to prolong image into after-image, to perpetuate lust's after-glow and to expand the female nude into a metaphorically snowy expanse. Tracks are here a consequence of transitory encounter, marks that can only be made by melting and dissolving. What the poem records is an enduring impermanence.

Through ironic juxtaposition the tracks of **'Snowfield'** radiate into the succeeding poem which challenges its perpetuation of pleasure's imprint. **"Tracks"** inverts the proportions of **"Snowfield"**: at once more lengthy and more contained it is also more realist than its metaphorical predecessor, elaborating on the contextual while denying it imaginative extension. The metaphysical expanse of **"Snowfield"** contracts into the mockingly "vast" and humanly dwarfing enclosure of an hotel bedroom and then into a pyrotechnically exciting, orgasmic landscape bounded by "the walls of the skull". For all its eroticism **"Tracks"** focusses on the *tristesse* of tryst: present pleasure is pervaded by a knowledge of its future absence and irretrievability. Coleridge's ancestral voice echoes throughout the poem, prophesying both the destruction of the pleasure-dome and its resistance to poetic recreation. The melodiousness of the "hall of air" proves to be insubstantial dulcimer-music; the "tracks" are "fading" rather than "radiating"; the tauntingly valedictory mirror promises only an ephemeral mimesis; and giggling maids from Porlock hover in the corridors of the après-texte, bringing blank sheets to the writer's successors.

The Great Cloak is at its most contemporary in the first section, **"Search"**, where coupling takes place in hotel bedrooms and in afternoon light. Most of the poems in the other two sections, **"Separation"** and **"Anchor"**, are nocturnes set in dark, shadowy or moonlit interiors or alluding to night-time walks. This is a confessional poetry that does not aim at the density of reference or the contextual realism of a novel. Although the heroines of **"Separation"** and **"Anchor"** are named, as "Madeleine" and "Evelyn" respectively,[7] they are not fully realized dramatic characters and we learn almost nothing about their appearance, dress, gestures, habits, tastes, personal quirks and foibles, family background, careers. Such lack of reification is almost dictated by the decorum of the sequence, for this is no "well of gossip defiled". As an autobiographical poet Montague is committed to publicizing the secret and confidential files of other people's lives, trespassing on private ground. He attempts to preserve a respectful courtesy in his dealings, a gallantry which imparts a slightly old-fashioned air to the proceedings. One is not surprised to encounter him in medieval pose:

> Slowly, in moonlight
> I drop to one knee
> solemn as a knight
> obeying an ancient precept. . . .

Gentlemanliness demands gentleness. The problem of sustaining the chivalric mode while describing a disintegrating marriage is one of the themes of the second section:

> But the pose breaks.
> The sour facts remain.

It takes
two to make or break
  a marriage.
  Unhood the falcon!

We are spared the nitty gritty of marital rows in **"Separation"**, the bitter recriminations and flying crockery; instead the couple's estrangement from each other is usually obliquely conveyed, by isolating their voices into discrete lyrics or describing their divergent activities, as in that fine lyric, **"She Walks Alone"**, which subtly suggests the lacunae "Madeleine" experiences in her failing marriage. "Tearing" is a recurrent word, emphasizing the physicality of sundering and also, in **"Refrain"**, suggestive of weeping. A self-justifying note is occasionally sounded in these poems, especially in **"No Music"**, but there is a genuine attempt at dialogue, at allowing the "wife" to "thrash out / flat words of pain", write letters about her loneliness, reveal her psychic agonies through nightmare or daydream. She is always depicted as the more vulnerable partner, seeking comfort and reassurance, and it is only in the penultimate poem of the sequence that she is granted autonomy:

Alone, but equal to the morning.

Montague's ideal woman is maternal, flowring and fecund, the adult poet's compensation for the deprivation of a maternal presence in his childhood. Two poems in **"Separation"** focus on infertility. **"Childlessness"** is a cruel catalogue of negative definitions, representing the barren woman as abnormal and unnatural, a buried stone rather than a burgeoning plant. **"She Dreams"** is an horrific, surreal nightmare sequence in which the childless "Madeleine" is portrayed as subconsciously acknowledging the connection between her infertility and the dissolution of her marriage.

Montague insists that he is primarily a lyrical poet for whom music is a concord of sweet sounds and discord an alien mode:

To tear up old love by the roots,
To trample on past affections:
There is no music for so harsh a song.

Certainly the finest poem in **"Separation"** is also the tenderest, **"Herbert Street Revisited"**, dedicated to Madeleine and celebrating "old happiness". This poem is a triumph of evocation, recreating past contentment through precisely realized images, and also a reflexive masterpiece, enacting the release of imagery from the factual domain into the rhythmic control of the choreographic imagination. Its powerfully disturbing contrary is **"Wedge"**, deconstructing the idyllic context of the couple's Rue Daguerre home; but **"Separation"** chivalrously concludes with **"Herbert Street Revisited"**.

While "Madeleine" is undoubtedly at a disadvantage in having the narrative of her disintegrating marriage told by her divorced husband, she emerges as a more three dimensional character than her rival, "Evelyn". "Evelyn", who is never permitted to speak or think for herself, is idealized beyond recognition, aureoled, iconographed into "some / Generous natural image of the good", a "bowsprit Venus", a goddess but a wooden one, her humanity disappearing under her "mythic burden". In his attempt to universalize a personal passion Montague swathes her in a "great cloak" of mythological allusion; she is identified by turns with Eve, Mary, Ceres, Diana, Luna and the "angel of the house". By contrast with the barren "Madeleine" she is woman at her most fecund, a pregnant or maternal figure, associated with the frugiferous ninth-century Irish girl of **"A Meeting"**. Diana is both cover-girl and presiding Muse of *The Great Cloak*: a goddess revealed in several of her guises, as tamer of wild beasts, the moon in her fullness, ruler of the tides and patroness of childbirth. The female cycle is rendered in lunar imagery here and in *The Dead Kingdom.* Old Mrs. Montague's life wanes as "Evelyn" waxes pregnant with a daughter and the nascent "Lunula" exchanges familial spirits with her dying grandmother. It is peculiarly appropriate that Montague's wife should "bring forth" women "children only". Familial and literary continuity are inextricably related in **"Child"** (a contrary to **"Childlessness"**) where the poet's bond with his daughter, Una, is

love's invisible ink
heart's watermark.

For all his aesthetic delight in patterned process Montague cannot suppress a primal whimper that his daughter should enjoy the mothering he lacked.

The Muse-poet, as characterized by Robert Graves, has difficulty in reconciling the claims of heart and hearth; a domestic Muse is disallowed. Montague, on the contrary, seeks a nurturing, maternal Muse, a "capable", "bustling" woman, surrounded by children and household pets, "the wholesome / litter of love". The habitué of hotels in *The Great Cloak* is a reluctant nomad and a preoccupation with the image of home is evident in the **"Anchor"** section. However, it is surely not insignificant that in its concluding poem, **"Edge"**, Montague insistently employs positive imagery of anchorage, refuge, harbouring, shelter in describing his home and home life, deliberately ignoring the precariousness and marginalization implicit in his choice of location and locution:

on the edge is best.

Only an inherently deracinated imagination would opt for such a tenuous settlement.

In *The Dead Kingdom* the poet journeys back to the primal source of his fascination with the female, ostensibly to bury but really to resurrect and reproach his dead mother. The only rest he can wish her is *"a certain peace"*. Her death signifies her conclusive abandonment of him which he attempts to translate into a happy release, transforming bereavement into a begetting. Entrance to *The Dead Kingdom* is analogous to an act of sexual penetration since it is guarded by the figure of a Sheela-na-gig (*"motherfucka, thass your name"*). This Celtic "O" is, for Montague, an Irish sculpted version of the *femme fatale*, pointing to the vaginal as the life and death principle, source and sepulchre, enticing and creative but also negative, a vacuum. The tomb-like aspect of the vaginal is suggested through the placement of the Sheela-na-gig figure on the title page of *The Dead Kingdom,* connecting cunt and death. The sonnet, **"Sheela na Gig"**, from *Mount Eagle,* makes explicit what is implicit in this collocation of text and image:

> Cunt, or Cymric *cwm,* Chaucerian *quente,*
> the first home from which we are sent
> into banishment, to spend our whole life
> cruising . . .
> to return to that first darkness!

By an almost reverse representational strategy the next graphic image in *The Dead Kingdom,* that of the "Egyptian ship of the Dead" on the Nile, is starkly juxtaposed with the title, **"Upstream"**, an allusion to the salmon's journey to its breeding place in order to spawn. Again *Mount Eagle* is more forthright in its womb/home/tomb associations when, in **"Cassandra's Answer"**, the bombed-out ruin of "the old Carney home"[8] prompts the grim conclusion:

> you were born inside a skeleton.

It would appear that the ambivalent nature of the poet's relationship with his mother conditioned his choice of the female as a figure of death and destructiveness. So in *A Slow Dance* death is personified as a *belle dame,* "mistress of the bones":

> *How pretty you look,*
> *Miss Death!*

and woman is also the "Black widow goddess" who "believes in war". In *A Chosen Light* she is Coatlicue. At her most benign, woman in *The Dead Kingdom* is a personification of "Mutability":

> dark Lady of Process,
> our devouring Queen.

The "dead kingdom" is not dead, merely buried alive and about to be exhumed; Mnemosyne is the book's reigning muse. Oblivion is here "fuming oblivion", an anger subterraneously seething, a volcanic energy dormant but not extinct. Poetry is a "swaying rope-ladder" suspended over this potentially explosive psychic terrain, a risky balancing act between aggression and acceptance, or between self-pity and *lacrimae rerum.* The poet's mother, portrayed as a woman who regressed to the maternal home/tomb to avoid the pains of exile and a failing marriage, an escapist who refused life's "muddy cup", is never forgiven her parental neglect. His father, who drank himself into "brute oblivion" or sidestepped his problems with a sentimental song, if not fully exonerated, is let off lightly ("Surely my father loved me / teaching me to croon. . . ."). Their poet son, rather than shirk pain, tries "to manage" it. He is a self-consolatory autobiographer, perhaps, like Wordsworth, too anxious to ensure that "all" is "gratulant, if rightly understood". It was tempting to impose a happy ending on the painful story of the mother/son relationship in **"The Locket"**. An image of closure and disclosure, the locket reveals the mother's enduring, hidden affection for her son and offers a repressed response to the overt overtures of the Sheela-na-gig at the beginning of the sequence. As a consolatory image, however, it is too facile, appearing fictionally faked, even if factually true. The poet's "terrible thirst" for "love and knowledge" is too insatiable to be so easily slaked. Momentarily, he betrays a resemblance to his maudlinly musical father. *The Dead Kingdom* ends as it had begun (Montague considers circularity to be characteristic of the Irish aesthetic) with an image of his Cork house as "home", a brave attempt at a final severance of the imaginative umbilical cord. This concluding "hearth song of happiness" concedes the temporality and fragility of human bonds yet proclaims the poet's willingness to trust in traditional family values and salutes his discovery of

> A new love, a new
> litany of place names. . . .

What the actual rendering of his Cork context makes "manifest", however, is his repressed sense of bereavement, the funereal presence from the past that haunts his brave new world: "lambent" soon modulates into "lamenting", the "foghorn / at Roche's Point" holds a "hoarse vigil", "Mounts Brandon, / Sybil Head and Gabriel" are "shrouded". It would seem that a conscious censor is at work, intent on avoiding any destabilizing of *The Dead Kingdom*'s autotherapeutic scheme (Montague refused to conclude with a poem on the bombing of the Carney home, for instance), but that "fuming oblivion" is not always amenable to thematic control.

Because it is less schematic than *The Great Cloak* or *The Dead Kingdom, Mount Eagle* more readily accommodates disparate and discordant autobiographical material, celebration of "small daughter" and "lovely mother", bleak interrogation of the possibility of domestic contentment:

> When all the birds
> in the nest are there,
> is that the start
> of a new despair?

The problem now is how to make a presence flower! For the eagle of **"Mount Eagle"**

> Content was life in its easiest form. . . .
>   And
> a different destiny lay before him:
> to be the spirit of that mountain. . . .

One notices the aural similarity between the poet's name and the title poem of this recent collection, whose importance in Montague's canon was already indicated when it was made the concluding poem of *Selected Poems.* In his title role of **"Mount Eagle"** the poet projects himself as spiritually rooted in one perpetual place, yet as awesomely remote from human contact as the poet of "Kubla Khan". He is the aquilinely aloof loner whose attachment is local rather than personal. The role of *genius loci* here seems an expression of psychic petrifaction, a consummation devoutly to be resisted, not merely ambivalently entertained. Is his choice of a mountainy womb/home/tomb a supreme attempt to liberate himself from maternal dependency?

Readers must be grateful to Montague's mother for her "flowering absence" from his childhood. She is the poet's "fertile source", the "onlie begetter" of all his imaginings, the parent of his theme, his primary Muse. He has dedicated his poetic life to the courtship and creation of female figures and images that substitute for her, fashioning "out of absence's rib, a warm fiction": compensatory fosterers, nurturers, lovers. **"The Well-Beloved"**, as he acknowledges, may assume many guises. This poem's punning title alludes to woman's role as guardian of the "sacred well" and lover and, hearkening back to Hardy's novel, also reminds us that a man may pursue one ideal and image of the female to the exclusion of all others and that this ideal may be incarnated in a series of women. *The White Goddess* is, of course, one of Montague's sacred texts. **"The Well-Beloved"** was itself conceived as a poetic response to a retired manifestation of the White Goddess, Laura Riding, who had complained about Montague's uncritical championship of Robert Graves.[9] Apart from his resentment at the contemporary feminist's preference for equality of treatment over apotheosis, the bemused poet of **"The Well-Beloved"** is markedly ambivalent in his attitude to womanhood. He proclaims himself a worshipper of the female and pays tribute to her strange sorcery; yet he also affirms that the Muse is a male creation—the outcast filial poet's ultimate revenge on matriarchy. In Montague's creative schema, where

poetry is bred of an orgasmic relationship with the Muse, a woman poet is, psychologically, "an absurdity".[10]

Return Liadan and deal with this Cuirithir.

Notes

1. The ancient Janus-headed sculpture from Boa Island in County Fermanagh is represented on the cover of *The Dead Kingdom.*

2. *"Despair and Delight"* in *Time was Away,* ed. Terence Brown and Alec Reid (Dublin: The Dolmen Press, 1974), pp. 123-127.

3. Proinsias MacCana, "Women in Irish Mythology" and Muireann Ní Brolcháin, "Women in Early Irish Myth and Sagas" in *The Crane Bag,* 4 (1980), 520-532.

4. In *Forms of Exile* (1958) the title was "The Shean Bhean Vocht".

5. Based on Montague's own definition in *The Poetry Book Society Bulletin,* Spring, 1984.

6. "Jawseyes", *The Crane Bag,* 2 (1978), 159-160.

7. I use inverted commas to distinguish between Madeleine and Evelyn as the *dramatis personae* of Montague's poetic fictions and as actual persons.

8. Montague's mother's home in Fintona, Co. Tyrone.

9. *Encounter,* December 1986, pp. 79-80.

10. "In the Irish Grain", *The Faber Book of Irish Verse* (London: Faber and Faber, 1974), p. 22. This has been changed to "an anomaly" in a forthcoming edition of the essay.

Eamon Grennan (essay date spring 1989)

SOURCE: Grennan, Eamon. "'Of So, and So, and So': Re-Reading Some Details in Montague." *Irish University Review* 19, no. 1 (spring 1989): 110-28.

[*In the following essay, Grennan provides a detailed analysis of passages from two Montague poems, "Like Dolmens Round My Childhood, the Old People" and* 11 *rue Daguerre.*]

What I propose to do here is look closely at a few passages in Montague's poetry that I have always found compelling. I want to see, and try to explain if I can, why these particular passages appeal to me in the way they do.

The first piece is from what is probably the best, and best-known, poem in the 1961 volume, *Poisoned Lands*:

> Like dolmens round my childhood, the old people.
>
> Jamie MacCrystal sang to himself,
> A broken song without tune, without words;
> He tipped me a penny every pension day,
> Fed kindly crusts to winter birds.
> When he died, his cottage was robbed,
> Mattress and money box torn and searched.
> Only the corpse they didn't disturb.

First, I love the truncated, verbless grammar of the opening line, the way it turns the title—which it simply repeats—into a gesture of strong but not at all strident (the *sound* ensures that, all those soft consonants and open vowels seem nurturing, protective) affirmation. Lovely, too, the way the poet tucks his own childhood between the two impressive (parental?) entities—ancient monuments and "the old people" (the definite article in this phrase adds a dimension of grandeur to adjective and noun)—rhythmically isolating it (a spondee plus, after two iambs and before an iamb and trochee), but putting it protectively within a traditional line of descent. One of the triumphs of the stanza that follows is the way it shifts tonal gear and register out of the expansive rhetoric of the poem's opening line into the restrained indicative simplicity of description. Nothing could be more straightforward than Montague's manner here, showing how well he has learned the lessons of Kavanagh and of William Carlos Williams. Sentences lay themselves out without syntactical difficulty, each line at once a unit of rhythm and of sense, as natural as speech. The opening line of the poem—oddly structured, grammatically impacted, a passionate push for summary and fullness—reminds me of someone suddenly breaking into speech after long silence. The stanza, however, is the painstakingly simple speech of someone who wants to get things just right, precise, true to the facts. The language here is physical and factual: it resides among the surfaces of things and actions, entering no speculative depths, offering no overt commentary. The eye and the ear of the poet are alive to the facts of the matter; by presenting these facts unadorned he bears best witness to his subject. Almost without adjectives, the diction is plain, colloquial, to the point. The only two adjectives—"broken" and "kindly" (which is in truth an elastic adverb)—are chosen with exquisite justice and tact, since between them they seem to epitomise Jamie's nature and condition. Because of such tact, the picture Montague gives seems, for all its economy, complete. (This is equally true of the other stanza-portraits in the poem).

Part of its completeness comes from the way the stanza is divided in two. The first part describes the qualities of the man himself—his harmless kind habits, his solitude, his enduring heart. The second part—"When he died"—portrays the social environment which preys upon Jamie MacCrystal in death. Montague is equally alert to both of these realities, describing the cruelty in a dispassionate yet understanding and feeling way (the feeling is in the pathos of those details of mattress and money box). The passive impersonality of the verbs, the dispersed anonymity of "they", reveal his reluctance to set himself up in any way as judge. His rôle, rather, is that of witness, and he performs it flawlessly. So the private, personal, and social being of the dead man has been exhibited, as well as the environment in which he lived and died. The poet has found an adequate language, a language to acknowledge properly the real presence of this local character. The stanza composes an "historical" vignette, with the poet's own remembered self as an unobtrusive yet authenticating part of it.

Another source of my pleasure in this passage is observing the deftness and delicacy with which Montague coaxes the actual details towards emblematic status. For it seems to me that everything mentioned in connection with Jamie MacCrystal, all those personal details, may also be given a representative reading and interpretation. Read in this way, Jamie is the last relic of a civilization and way of life. Singing to himself "A broken song without tune, without words", he becomes an image of solitary craft, a whole tradition of music, song, even poetry dying away in his tuneless, wordless music. He reminds me of Wordsworth's "Solitary Reaper", although his predicament and what it represents are more pathetic. (Wordsworth may not understand the song he hears his reaper singing, but he knows the song itself has coherence—"For old, unhappy, far-off things / And battles long ago"—and suggests a live tradition). For Jamie's song is its own subject, is limited to his own hearing, is in every sense an end in itself. By putting the issue of song at the start an end in itself. By putting the issue of song at the start of his poem, Montague stresses the emblematic nature of the truth he wants to reveal: making his own music out of that cultural loss, he underscores his elegiac point and, perhaps, the deeper point of renewal. By taking upon himself the task of elegiac celebration, the poet both acknowledges the loss and establishes out of it a fresh beginning. And it's possible to detect some such double sense of "passing on" in the next detail, which also exists at factual and emblematic levels: "He tipped me a penny every pension day". In this quotidian image I can find at least a trace of ritual, a sort of laying on of hands, the old singer giving his gift to the boy who would become the poet. (A more self-conscious version of this appears in **"The Country Fiddler"**, from *A Chosen Light*). Obviously one doesn't want to overstress these possibilities, since the success of the poem lies, for me, in its beautifully balanced distance from any whiff of ideology, in the way these larger points remain latent. But Montague's sureness of touch here, the confidence with which he can summon up the real (the social, even sociological factuality of "pension day") and give it some extra air of the absolute, allows, without straining the text, for such extensions of meaning as I've mentioned. In this emblematic sense, then, the poem is not only an elegy for a culture but also a rite of poetic initiation. What's implicit and needs to be teased out at the start, however, becomes, as we'll see later, quite explicit in the last stanza.

The next line, "Fed kindly crusts to winter birds", has two possible metaphorical enlargements. First, those "winter birds" are an appropriate enhancement of the images of terminal song in the first two lines. As icons of hunger and need, they properly belong to this emotional landscape. As recipients of another kindness, another gesture of almost parental solicitude, they become kin to the boy. Second, they embody an active connection between the old man and the natural world, a relationship of an essentially benevolent kind. This sets up a category of description and understanding that continues through the portrait-stanzas following this one. All of "the old people", in fact, are bound closely to the natural world: Maggie Owens "was surrounded by animals"; on "the mountain lane" where the blind Nialls lived, "heather bells bloomed, clumps of foxglove"; Mary Moore's gatehouse is "crumbling" back to the state of nature, while "she tramped the fields"; and even Wild Billy Eagleson had "his flailing blackthorn". On the emblematic level these references suggest a vital continuity between the natural world and the civilisation these people represent. What Montague is instinctively insisting on here is the essential wholeness of that culture, a culture that inscribes an organic connection between man and nature, as well, indeed, as between dolmens and the old people. These old people are as native to their landscape as plants and animals (and dolmens), as integral to the natural world as Wordsworth's leech gatherer in "Resolution and Independence", who resembles "a huge stone" or "a sea-beast crawled forth", is "motionless as a cloud", an elemental particle of "the weary moors", and who is, like Montague's people, relic and reminder of another time, living into an age that has "dwindled long by slow decay".

The emblematic possibility of the next two lines (the account of the robbery) may be related to the idea of a fallen, a decayed age. The cruel treatment of the dead man suggests how an age of genuinely civilized benevolence can sink into one of savagery. And yet the mildness of Montague's language—the declarative sentence itself, with its initiating temporal adverb, "When", an image of inevitability—suggests the poet's own resignation before such unarguable proof of *process*. Given the deliberate (grammatical) absence of human agents, it might almost seem as if time itself, an inexorable and impersonal force, were responsible. What this manner manages to delineate is the sudden

violent extinction of certain values, values of community, their blatant absence from this post-mortem world.

I will make a small digression here, to point out that such a preoccupation with loss will mark many of Montague's later poems, notably **"Hymn to the New Omagh Road"** in *The Rough Field*—where human agency is more in evidence and the poem is making, satirically, an ideological point—and in two poems of a more truly philosophical bias in *The Dead Kingdom*— **"Process"** and **"Gone"**, both of them songs to "the goddess Mutability, / dark Lady of Process, / our devouring Queen". This engagement to loss is a strong consistent thread throughout the work (a dominant and plangent note, of course, in the poems about the breakdown of his first marriage that appear in *The Great Cloak*), making elegy one of Montague's most effective and affecting modes. In **"Like Dolmens Round My Childhood, the Old People"**, this "engagement to loss" receives early expression, significantly in a context that is both cultural and personal. What happens to Jamie MacCrystal, then, may be seen as an image of process writ large, the poet's own deep, unspoken sense of loss given violent embodiment. The pathetic felony is emblematic of a larger truth, a truth extending in different directions out of Montague's imagination. It suggests not only a world of cultural loss and decay, but also implies a world in which benign beginnings have unhappy outcomes. This latter sense of things, one could speculate (assisted by Montague's own later poems, poems in which he describes being abandoned as a child by his mother, and the absence of his father; In **"A Flowering Absense"** and **"A Locket"**, from *The Dead Kingdom,* for example, "All road wind backwards to it. / An unwanted child, a primal hurt"), is generated by an imagination trying to deal with the psyche's own appalled sense of being orphaned, in the grip of loss, at an irremediable loss. Some such interior motivation, deeper, more elusive and more mysterious than analytic expression can render, may account for this poem's existence in the first place, and for its occupying—as readers invariably feel it occupies, such an obviously cardinal spot in Montague's own genesis and evolution as a poet. He may simply be peopling his (cultural) past with parents. End of digression.

The final line of the stanza is also amenable to emblematic expansion. First of all, the simple fact reveals something of the true nature of the thieves, possessed by some residual moral feelings, is it? or by a delicate, if unlikely, scruple of taste, or merely by superstitious awe. In its own spare way, the line provides a quick sketch of a disintegrating community, the collapse of which is made seem all the more grievous and lamentable in this single quasi-religious observance, this hungover, morally hollow form. Linguistically, too, the line goes beyond its matter of fact. The word "disturb", after all, may betray an irony on the poet's part, an irony subtly levelled at the communal depravity. For does it have a simple physical meaning? or does it have the more emotionally animate sense of 'distract', 'call away the attention of?' (which, being obviously impossible in the case of a corpse makes the scrupulosity or residual civility seem ridiculously formulaic), or is it meant in the emotional sense of 'upset', an equally ridiculous proposition? Indeed the corpse—and this meaning may also be built into the line—is the only one not disturbed by the whole event, an event which in truth, at its most representative and emblematic levels, disturbs a whole fabric of existence, a total way of life. Such possible authorial irony is another indication of Montague's sense of the representative nature of his small event, and because of the ambivalent possibilities of meaning here, his own status as witness rather than judge remains essentially undisturbed. As with the picture of Jamie MacCrystal itself, the details of which can so easily grow into emblematic meanings, in the last line's potential for larger meanings, palpable delicacy of presentation is everything.

A last note on this line concerns it curious construction. "Only the corpse they didn't disturb": rhythmically satisfying, it is syntactically peculiar. Both the satisfaction and the peculiarity, however, reveal the poet's own implicit feeling of being a part of this broken community, a sense of belonging that he dramatizes by adopting such a distinctly colloquial locution. In his use of language—the recording instrument, the agent of memory, even the means of healing personal psychic wounds that, as it turned out, also impeded speech ("my tongue became a rusted hinge / until the sweet oils of poetry / eased it and light flooded in", he says later, in **"A Flowering Absence"**)—in his use of language the poet puts himself at one with his subject, endorsing its actuality, its emotional authenticity, and its emblematic significance.

The next passage (which I will not consider at such length) is also from **"Like Dolmens Round My Childhood, the Old People"**, from the end of the poem. And once again, through close engagement with some chosen details, I'd like to see what of Montague's special qualities as a poet can be revealed. Again my discussion is likely to wind out from the centre in a not necessarily logical way, in the hope of arriving at some revelation, however limited, of the nature and texture of Montague's imagination, at this early stage of his career:

> Ancient Ireland, indeed! I was reared by her bedside,
> The rune and the chant, evil eye and averted head,
> Formorian fierceness of family and local feud.
> Gaunt figures of fear and of friendliness,
> For years they trespassed on my dreams,
> Until once, in a standing circle of stones,

> I felt their shadows pass
> Into that dark permanence of ancient forms.

I suppose the first thing to say about these lines is that they reveal the source from which the rest of the poem actually flows. Because of the event described here (we do not know when it happened, only that it happened "once"—as in "once upon a time"?), the earlier stanzas take the form they do, have come into being at all. But that's not where I want to begin. I'll work up to that point, the point that makes such a powerful, enclosed, charmed circle of the poem.

What first compels my attention here is the vivid shift in tone brought about by that exclamatory opening. The last word in the preceding stanza is "death" and its final image is one of striking immobility, enlarging the pathetic figures of the old people who have died into emblematic "Silent keepers of a smokeless hearth / Suddenly cast in the mould of death". (The majestic calm and cultural implication of this image—tribal remnants struck dumb in front of the quenched fire of a whole way of life, a civilization—is proof of how Montague can shuttle between the actual and something beyond that, can perceive in the actual its ritual shadow, can find for the actual a language that can, without betraying its actuality, elevate its status to that of ritual, into what he calls in another early poem (**"Pastorals"**), "redeeming patterns of experience", intending that first word as noun and verb.) The unexpected scorn of "Ancient Ireland indeed!" shatters such a mood, thrusting the poem into a fresh direction, another idiom. It shows remarkable agility on the part of the poet, a confident streamlined fluency capable of emotional reversals and rapid shifts of attention. This lively, aggressive utterance punctures a conventional notion usually approached in attitudes of piety and homage. (In the later poem, **"The Siege of Mullingar"**—from *A Chosen Light*—he sees a whole generation, in the sixties, perform a similarly debunking act, this time on "Romantic Ireland"). By dismissing the conventional version, however, Montague clears the ground for a more personal version, as we'll see, of the same entity. In addition, the idiosyncratic individuality of his voice here acts as a bridge between the more or less objective narrative—descriptive mode of the earlier stanzas and the intensely subjective manner of this one.

Subjectivity is the norm here, the manner memorial. Everything is translated into the emotional vibration it had for the boy who became the remembering, recollecting poet. First he claims his own intimate relationship with "Ancient Ireland", having been "reared by her bedside". Maternal, grandmaternal, filial—however the relationship is named, the metaphor insists on its intensely familial nature, enabling the poet to provide for himself a (representative) cultural parent. In this context, the gender of "Ancient Ireland" seems especially revealing, since Montague might just as easily have written "*its* bedside" (as in Yeats's refrain about "Romantic Ireland": "It's with O'Leary in the grave"), but chose to write—deliberately or involuntarily—"her" instead.

In the next two lines, completing the first sentence, the potentially peaceful connotations of "bedside" are—in a condensed version of the pattern that shapes most of the poem—destroyed by a number of violent appositional phrases. This brief litany of "ancient" conditions suggests an ingrown, grimly enclosed, superstitious society, cruel by nature, violent in its habits. (It is, incidentally, a much more negative picture than that created by the particular portraits themselves, as if this generalisation, in a sense, *preceded* the more genially detailed memories of the individual people). The litany also implies a quick connection between private and public worlds, a rooted attachment to the past, cultural continuity, and a continuum of a palpable kind persisting between the worlds of matter and of spirit.

Meeting an accumulation of facts as powerfully, and for the most part negatively, evocative as these are, allied to the images of rearing, bedside, and motherhood which precede them, a reader might justifiably imagine a traumatic relationship between the child and his environment, both the general human environment—society, culture—and, by extension, the more immediate environment of the actual parents. Such a traumatic possibility is in fact endorsed by Montague in other poems, from the poem which precedes **"Like Dolmens"** in **Poisoned Lands, "The Sean Bhean Bhocht"** (1957)—"As a child I was frightened by her"—to the two poems from **The Dead Kingdom** (1984) that I have already mentioned—**"The Locket"** and **"A Flowering Absence"**. What's so important to me about **"Like Dolmens Round My Childhood, the Old People"** is the fact that in it Montague dramatizes, and therefore distances into understanding, the early wounds, both the wound of fear caused by the strange primeval otherness of "the old people", and the deeper wound of abandonment, being made a prey to such strangeness, being virtually orphaned, for which more primary wound the obsessive and frightened attachment to the old people is a form of emotional "displacement" (apt strategy for a psyche that must itself have felt—moving from Brooklyn to Northern Ireland, then from his mother to his father's relatives [see **"A Flowering Absence"**]—the acutest ache of a double displacement).

In the mysterious epiphany that ends the poem, the poet finds the true cure for these wounds, or at least the beginnings of such a cure. He also finds in it one of his own critical beginnings as a poet, since the moment of its occurrence—in "real" time—was, I suspect, one of the single most enabling moments in the life of Montague's imagination. It occupies the concluding five lines of the poem. What these lines dramatise is an exorcism and a birth. What's exorcized is incapacitating fear; what's born is poetic consciousness. the old people were "Gaunt figures of fear and friendliness", trespassing for years on the child's dreams. Larger than life, with an ambivalent emotional effect, they are a source of psychic uncertainty, embodying the child's fear of the unknown. In this case the unknown has, so to speak, a cultural body. The fear it causes is not unlike the ambivalent fears Stephen Dedalus has at different times of the peasantry and what they represent. Here is the very young Stephen's response to the peasants in Clane: "It would be lovely to sleep for one night in that cottage before the fire of smoking turf, in the dark lit by the fire, in the warm dark, breathing the smell of peasants, air and rain and turf and corduroy. But, O, the road there between the trees was dark! You would be lost in the dark. It made him afraid to think of how it was". Warm by the fire; lost in the dark: here are Montague's "figures of fear and of friendliness". In Stephen's later, more anguished brooding, it might be possible to find something of the dilemma of Montague's evolving imagination: after the satiric barb thrown at Synge-Mulrennan and the "old man" with "red eyes" who spoke Irish and was from the West of Ireland (Joyce's "Ancient Ireland indeed!"?), Stephen says in his diary, "I fear him. I fear his redrimmed horny eyes. It is with him I must struggle all through this night till day come, till he or I lie dead . . . No. I mean him no harm". Stephen leaves Ireland without really resolving this important issue for himself; Montague's resolution is this poem, for which he is prepared, initiated, by the experience described in the closing three lines.[1]

After the figures have "trespassed" on the most intimately private space of his dreams (becoming, I suppose, emanations of dread and of a desire for the human comfort of belonging), the poet is granted the gift of an exorcism that is authentic understanding, freeing him into a knowledge of *meanings*. In this silent and singular ("once") moment, located at a ritual centre, a standing circle that has to be womb and omphalos, he "felt their shadows pass". Verb and enjambment here both stress the motion that must accompany exorcism, a sense confirmed by the last line, with the shadows entering—a sort of image of possession—into the stones, and through them into the even more remote, but still vitally connected, "permanence of ancient forms". In this given instant of awareness, the old people become "the old people", at one with the icons of tradition and continuity, the dolmens, shadowy facts become permanent forms. And it is through this recognition that he comes to understand them also as emblems of a common loss, the sort of thing he gives expression to in the rest of the poem, these individuals glimpsed as exemplars of a traditional world that in their poor attenuated selves is at its last gasp. Seen in this way, the people may at least be dealt with as he actually deals with them in the poem, the manner, emotional texture, and assured vision of which derive from the moment dramatized at its conclusion. So the poem is a full circle, returning at the end to the first awareness of the condition stated in the opening line. By means of this epiphanal gift, Montague has managed to ritualize his sense of loss and exorcize many of the fears that surrounded it: the old people, transient and vulnerable, become a dark permanence, "ancient *forms*" that are themselves a consolation. Through this whole process his imagination, or at least a significant part of his poetic consciousness, is born. And this imagination, this poetic consciousness, is responsible for a great many of the poems that will come later. The moment is as important to Montague as the moment Wordsworth describes in Book One of *The Prelude,* the incident of the stolen boat. Montague's gaunt, trespassing figures could be related to the "huge peak, black and huge" which became for Wordsworth "huge and mighty forms" that were "a trouble to my dreams". Montague's last line, too, has something of a Wordsworthian amplitude, not unlike that "dim and undetermined sense / Of unknown modes of being" in the stolen boat passage.

The two passages I've just explored give something of the feel of Montague's imagination—its attachments, preoccupations, modes of procedure. They show, I'd say, the degree to which his sense of cultural vulnerability and loss—the sort of thing to be found in poems at every stage of his work—may grow out of some even deeper personal region of the spirit, a region where the issue of loss is a private matter co-extensive with the whole sentient personality itself. This is what gives these poems their rare emotional power, a power that does not necessarily inform poems where the issue of loss takes on—as it does in parts of *The Rough Field,* for example—a more explicitly ideological tinge, producing poems whose source is in the will rather than within that complex range of perceptions and receptions we call imagination. The passages also show one of Montague's most admirable traits—his ability to turn the keenly, lovingly observed actual detail into something larger, more representative, emblematic. Such an ability testifies, perhaps, to his awareness of inhabiting a border country between history and myth, but that must be the subject of another essay. In the present case I'd only point to the malleable vitality of his language, the way it enables him to occupy a number of contiguous zones of thought and feeling without any sense of strain. The passages might also reveal a poet who was, at least in his early phase, a responsive reader of Wordsworth. Finally, these lines and stanzas demonstrate the degree to which poetry is for Montague a necessary, deeply instinctive response to loss. Here, by imaginatively entering into the otherness of culture, he is essentially dealing with loss, offering (first to himself) some provisional restoration.

I want to expand this meditation (if art is "a warm brooding", as Montague, in a wonderfully maternal metaphor, says it is, then maybe that's what criticism should be too) by considering closely a few lines which may help me probe a little more the nature of what I most admire about the work of Montague's imagination. The lines are the last seven from *11 rue Daguerre,* which is Part I of the title poem from the 1967 collection, *A Chosen Light*:

> There is white light on the cobblestones
> And in the apartment house opposite—
> All four floors—silence.
>
> In that stillness—soft but luminously exact,
> A chosen light—I notice that
> The tips of the lately grafted cherry-tree
>
> Are a firm and lacquered black.

In the passages I quoted from **"Like Dolmens . . ."** it's possible to see the workings of imagination *in the world.* The way the poet focusses on the people he names and describes, the way their accidental natures become representative of meanings larger than themselves, mark the imagination's entrance into the world of history—of culture and society, of time. The role of the imagination is to seek out significance, finding a meaning for these transient inhabitants and the world for which they stand. The lines just quoted above, however, put one in touch, I believe, with the true lyrical centre of Montague's art, the imagination focussed on things for their own sake, the meaning utterly intrinsic to the object. It is a condition or point of consciousness where "the object of attention is the particularity of nature, and the imagination is disposed to reveal it in its plenitude, with the result that the objects contemplated take to themselves a certain radiance which marks the feeling they inspire".[2] In the passage from **"Like Dolmens . . ."** we see the source of imaginative action, the imagination's dedication to the world; in the lines from **"A Chosen Light"** it is the pure presence of imaginative being that confronts us. Let's take a closer look.

Tactful, unobtrusive, as silently watchful as the mood of the poem itself, these lines suggest a fine collaboration between eye and speech, the eye acknowledging what Terence Brown calls "the existential tingle of material objects",[3] while the speech refuses to do much more than name the phenomena—cobblestones, house, cherrytree, silence, light. A more or less neutral form of the verb "to be" is pervasive; the strongest verbal assertion resides in the speaker's own relaxed but ready attention, "I notice", an intransitive usage even less aggressive than the alternative "I see", since it takes no direct object. The wonderword in the passage is "chosen". Is it simply an adjective formed out of the past participle of the verb, as in "the chosen people?"

Or does it mean that Montague has himself 'chosen' it, an implicit gesture of mastery? It is not the answers to such questions that matter. What really matters is the poise of the word between such meanings, that brief enchantment of language the poet thought enough of to use as the title of his book. The language is all eyes and ears, making 'stillness' (absence of movement and sound) synaesthetically synonymous with 'light', "soft but luminously exact". And by means of such language, the poet at once inhabits and is absent from this moment.

What I love about this language is its calm reciprocity with the world of facts, of objects. The objective world seems splendidly available to a speech that is at once simple, deliberate, and polished. What Montague finds here is a language for and of pure awareness, a language emerging from the core of primary knowledge that must be one of the generative places of imagination. It's the space he inhabits in **"The Trout"** (also from *A Chosen Light*), describing the fish "where he lay, light as a leaf / In his fluid sensual dream", and the remembered self as "so preternaturally close / I could count every stipple". It's the lyrical centre of his art—an art of absolute attention to the living thing in the moment—as he describes it in **"A Bright Day"**, choosing "a slow exactness / Which recreates experience / By ritualizing its details" (in *A Chosen Light*). This language starts from things themselves and the mind's rapt attention to them, so "even the clock on the mantel / Moves its hands in a fierce delight / Of so, and so, and so" (**"A Bright Day"**). It is the perfect silence ("In that stillness . . . I notice") that houses the hart of Montague's imaginative being, close to what Yeats must have been thinking of when he described the (creative) mind as "a long-legged fly" that "moves upon silence". And in the poem **"Division"** (from *A Chosen Light*)Montague knows it as "my own best life"—not that "bitter, predatory thing", the head, but "the hypnotized field-mouse / Housed beneath its claws".

Thinking into such details as those in the lines I quoted from *11 rue Daguerre,* and trying to figure out what they tell me about the nature of Montague's imagination, two further things are of particular interest to me. The first of these is simply literary: I wonder what kind of literary kinships this small passage might suggest. The second is more personal: I wonder from what obsessive zone in Montague's own psyche comes this passionate attachment to the particular moment and the momentary particular. I wonder what it tells me, whether intending to or not, about the poet's deepest and least mediated apprehension of existence. I'll end this meditation on Montague by briefly considering each of these issues.

The first ghost conjured by these lines is Kavanagh's. Intense attention lodging in plain speech is one of the principal legacies Kavanagh left to Irish poets:

A boortree tried hard to
Let me see it grow,
Mere notice was enough,
She would take care of love.

("Ante-Natal Dream")

Montague has often acknowledged this aspect of the older poet. Indeed, it is to that he was most likely referring when he said (controversially) that Kavanagh had "liberated us into ignorance", since by "ignorance" I suspect he means a capacity for pure, uncontaminated awareness of the actual, the quotidian. Such an awareness is a decisive element in Kavanagh's own aesthetic, clearly seen in "The Hospital", where, after a litany of ordinary objects, he declares that "Naming these things is the love-act and its pledge; / For we must record love's mystery without claptrap".[4] In the poem, **"Waiting"** (from *A Chosen Light),* Montague echoes these sentiments when he says of his own literary habits, "This low-pitched style seeks exactness, / Daring only to name the event". The lines from *11 rue Daguerre* perform an intense excavation of a single moment of awareness, everything coming to a point in the tips of that cherry tree. In this exacting entrance into the moment—to acknowledge its presence, testify to its simple being—Montague seems to be obeying instinctively another of Kavanagh's poetic injunctions, the one that instructed poets to "Snatch out of time the passionate transitory" ("The Hospital"). Kavanagh's willingness to be still in the face of the objective world ("The only true teaching /. Subsists in watching / Things moving or just colour"—"Is") was tutor to Montague's central lyrical energy.

What might distinguish the younger poet from his master (one of his masters) is the way his sensibility, even where it is chiming with Kavanagh's, has a greater tendency to aestheticize (or, to use his own word, "ritualise") the moment and what inhabits it. Kavanagh's notice is just notice: "A year ago I fell in love with the functional ward / Of a chest hospital: square cubicles in a row / Plain concrete, wash basins—an art lover's woe" ("The Hospital"). (The rhyme, of course, is a force of "arrangement", but what it arranges is the poem—a sonnet—not the objects in the poem). Montague's descriptions, on the other hand, are more likely to be an "art lover's" delight. Cobblestones and white light, house and silence, black lacquer tips of the tree and a luminous exactitude—these elements seem to settle naturally into a framed, orderly picture. There's an inescapable and not unconscious refinement to the sensibility that thus arranges (very delicately) the world, rather than simply acknowledging it. Because of the nature of Montague's imaginative receptivity, the things of the world, as they enter his attention, somehow fall into place. This, I think, distinguishes his imagination from the more expansive tolerances of Kavanagh's, from Kavanagh's account of an actuality bristling with interior energies. Fascinating as it might be to explore the causes and consequences of such differences, however, they must remain the subject of another essay. It is enough to add here that, in a small example such as the one quoted, Montague's verse shows the influential presence of Kavanagh at its very centre.

A couple of minor influences might be noted here. The unhurried factual accumulation ("There is white light on the cobblestones . . ."), the utterly unjudged description, the definitive absence of commentary or evaluation—all these qualities evoke the tradition of Japanese haiku, poems which create a pellucid atmosphere of purified attention around an otherwise unremarkable and mundane moment. The "lacquered black" tips of the cherry tree (ubiquitous haiku subject) also suggest a certain Japanese effect, as if here Montague were trying to find something of the ritual precision of the haiku. Effects such as these, however, might also be under an influence closer to home—that of the Early Irish poets, whose poems of uncluttered radiance (moments of pure being uttered in a manner at once intense and simple) have always been deeply admired by Montague. He has called them "vernacular poems as delicate as haiku", would surely approve of Flann O'Brien's praise of their "steel-pen exactness"[5] (a quality particularly telling for him, given the "luminously exact" nature of his own "chosen light"), and has translated into English a number of their elegant and innocent celebrations of the natural world:

> The whistle
> of the bright
> yellow billed
>   little bird:
>
> Over the loch
> upon a golden
> whin, a blackbird
>   stirred.

("Belfast Lough")

Another possible influence on the lyrical habits responsible for such lines as those quoted from *11 rue Daguerre* is that of Synge. For what Montague is at here—which is fairly representative of his most intense and, for me, most satisfying lyrical mode—seems not unlike what Synge is at in the shining prose of *The Aran Islands*. A passage of Synge's like the following, for example, seems to blend facts, ritual, existential awareness of objects, and the poise between feeling and seeing, in more or less the same proportions as they are mixed in Montague:

> the walls [of a kitchen] have been toned by the turf smoke of a soft brown that blends with the grey earth-colour of the floor. Many sorts of fishing-tackle, and the nets and oilskins of the men, are hung upon the walls or among the open rafters; and right overhead,

> under the thatch, there is a whole cow-skin from which they make pampooties. Every article on these islands has an almost personal character, which gives this simple life, where all art is unknown, something of the artistic beauty of medieval life.[6]

Particularity such as this, edging into ritual, is certainly a determining element in the passage quoted from the rue Daguerre poem. It may be found in an even more obviously influential way in **"The Answer"** (*A Chosen Light*), where the poet stands in a country cottage, "tasting the neat silence / of the swept flags, the scoured delph / on the tall dresser where even something / tinny like a two-legged, horned alarm-clock / was isolated into meaning". Also in **"The Answer"**, the hint of a connection with Synge might be extended. For the politeness of the old woman's Irish, in Montague's poem, her "ritual greetings" and her general demeanour—all exemplifying "the only way, / the way of courtesy"—could call to mind a remark of Synge's on "the courtesy of the old woman of the house", and how he "could see with how much grace she motioned each visitor to a chair, or stool, according to his age, and said a few words to him".[7]

The pure affecting glitter of phenomenal presence; the recognition in an actual environment of ritual grace: these are the qualities Montague might have taken, consciously or unconsciously, from Synge. That he wrote a **"Song for Synge"** increases the likelihood of such speculations about influence having some truth to them. For in that poem, what he values in Synge is the way "Creation bright / each object shines and stirs", a lovely condensation of some of the qualities I'm suggesting he learned at least in part from Synge. Synge encourages in him an intensified state of awareness, that state in which things "shine", as well as a heightened sensitivity to the ritual possibility within objects, the "stir" in them that generates ritualizing patterns. (It may also have been Synge who helped bring this pure lyric sensibility to the borders of cultural, even ideological, awareness and expression—as happens in **"The Answer"**—since those are the borders on which Synge's own lyrical imagination is at home.)

What I would finally say about this whole more or less speculative issue of influences is that, in the conjunction of Kavanagh and Synge as lyric influences (an ironical conjunction, in that Kavanagh took many a critical swipe at Synge, accusing him, in a sense, of being "mock-Irish"), Montague manages to marry a natural "insider's" response to the world with the more sophisticated aesthetic habits of the enchanted "outsider". Under two such influences, Montague's lyric sense receives excellent training, tuned early to the real world and to his own responses to it.

The lines with which I began this discussion are a sign, as I said, of Montague's passionate attachment to the particularity of the moment and the momentary particular. I want to end by briefly considering this attachment.

The moment in question occurs at the close of *11 rue Daguerre*. What precedes it is an experience of process, the sight (in the garden) of "tendrils of green" that are "desperately frail / In their passage against / The dark, unredeemed parcels of earth". By juxtaposing the image of stillness against this image of "frail" but definitely kinetic energy, the poet draws the moment out of time, out of process, into a small island of being abstracted from the flow. Such an act seems native to Montague's imagination, a necessary reflex that becomes creative habit, a distinct presence and strategy in many of his best poems. In the very early **"Irish Street Scene, with Lovers"** (from *Poisoned Lands*), for example, "the world shrinks" to the compass of an umbrella, "its assembly of spokes like points of stars, / A globule of water slowly forming on each". Such minutely observed data contrasts with the normal street scene, stands up against passage the way "the guttering cry / of a robin . . . balances a moment". Or in that flawless poem, **"The Trout"** (*A Chosen Light*), the whole mesmerised, sensual action takes place inside a few moments epiphanally teased out of time, the poet "savouring my own absence". A similar strategy and habit may be found sprouting from a narrative of violence and horror, becoming an emblem of inexplicable consolation, as happens in **"The Wild Dog Rose"**:

> Briefly
> the air is strong with the smell
> of that weak flower, offering
> its crumbling yellow cup
> and pale bleeding lips
> fading to white . . .

A strategy and a habit like these compose epiphanal moments such as those visible in the small spots of time preserved in memory's amber in **"Salutation"** (from *The Rough Field*)—"The damp coats of the scholars / Stood breathing in the hall"—or can create the rapt, self-forgetting attentiveness that etches the image of the snail in **"Small Secrets"** (from a *A Slow Dance*), "rippling along / its liquid self- / creating path", or the even more richly evocative moment in **"Almost a Song"** (*A Slow Dance*): "At mealtimes / huge hobnails sparkled / a circle in the stiff grass / as we drank brown tea, bit / buttered planks of soda bread".

In spite of differences in content and context, what these examples have in common is a commitment—as total as it is exclusive—to the living moment. Implicitly they insist on the moment's own efficacy, asserting against the devouring, clouding energies of time and process its luminous intrinsic value. In each case—and they could be multiplied—the compound condition that's been revealed has on one side an awareness of inevitable loss, and on the other a countering or consol-

ing assertion of the value of the moment, with the poet's own habit of attention *enabling* that moment. It is possible, I believe, to see in all this a shaping base to Montague's imagination: a psyche conditioned by the sense of loss, seeking to temper that sense—and the sense of futility that may attend it—by its rapt attachment to the almost extra-temporal moment. Where culture may provide the poet with surrogate parents, this more primary and pre-cultural condition may provide him with no less than a feeling of meaningful existence. Such moments, that is, may convert "being" into "meaning".

Nowhere is this habit of imagination more active than in Montague's love poems, as if sexual love itself were a point of concentration for all these forces. (Given the central position of women—Woman?—in the history of his psyche—as this has been revealed through his own poems—it is hardly surprising that this should be the case). Most of Montague's best love poems, indeed, are either elegies, or celebrations of the moment—both of which impulses most likely grow from the one imaginative or psychic root, from the one complex way of receiving the world. This may be seen in his earliest love poem of original power—**"All Legendary Obstacles"** (from *A Chosen Light*)—where the terrible energies of process (time and space and weather) are finally overcome in one minutely observed moment of emotional relief, observed not by the poet himself but by "an old lady" who (like an eluded Fate) remains on the train that has brought his lover, and

> who marked
> A neat circle on the glass
> With her glove, to watch us
> Move into the wet darkness
> Kissing, still unable to speak.

The same breathless (and speechless) dissolution in the moment may be found in the more erotically charged **"Tracks"** (from *Tides*): "As I turn to kiss / your tight black / curls, full breasts, / heat flares from / your unmarked skin / & your eyes widen". But always these moments are threatened ("I shall miss you / creaks the mirror / into which the scene / will shortly disappear"— **"Tracks"**), since sexual love—"a greeting / in the night . . . a form of truth . . . an answer to death" (**"Love, A Greeting"**, in *Tides*)—is itself the prey of time and flux and circumstance. So affairs wear out, marriages collapse and shatter, proving the pattern of loss, provoking the poet to elegy. The best of his love elegies is the poem in *The Great Cloak* called **"Herbert Street Revisited"**, where celebration of the moment and elegiac acknowledgment of process, of loss, are—for one singular, emotionally flawless instant—the same thing. Beginning the poem outside the house in which he had spent part of his married life ("someone is leading our old lives!", he goes on to evoke some of the most vivid elements that constituted, and now reconstitute, that time and the texture of that stage of the marriage. (That the poem is *"for Madeleine"* provides, by happy accident, an initiating Proustian dedication to memory itself, a journey of the mind and heart "in search of lost time"). **"Herbert Street Revisited"** ends with a tender summoning of things past ("So put the leaves back on the tree, / put the tree back in the ground"), an unsentimental conjuring trick to outwit time and loss, a lovely moment of pure memorial magic, a triumph (*the* triumph) of pure lyricism:

> And let the pony and donkey come—
> look, someone has left the gate open—
> like hobbyhorses linked in
> the slow motion of a dream
>
> parading side by side, down
> the length of Herbert Street,
> rising and falling, lifting
> their hooves in the moonlight.

I seem to have wandered far from my starting point in **11 rue Daguerre.** But in truth not too far, for here again the poet—standing outside his "home" at night—loves himself in the contemplation of things, a lyrical contemplation enriched, this time, by its directly elegiac context. This time he is more explicit in affirmation, but what he's affirming is the same thing: the value of the object itself in its living moment—the only talisman we can know against the inexorable and inevitable reality of loss. In poems such as these—explicit and implicit acknowledgments of loss and affirmations of being— Montague reveals an important truth about the nature of his imagination and its creative sources and resources, a truth I have been circling about, warmly brooding, in these few pages. At his lyrical best (and to my mind, and to my pleasure, he is still at his best as a lyricist, though he himself might sometimes balk at any suggestion of confinement this might imply; the narrative instinct or need that composes *sequences* like **The Rough Field, The Great Cloak,** and **The Dead Kingdom** seems to me too willed a thing, seeking to establish order and pattern and understanding in a much more imposing—and overtly male—way than that in which he often *inadvertently finds* them in and through individual poems, poems that are lyrical reflexes to deep needs and habits of feeling and expression in the more involuntary and unrehearsed zones of his psyche; the sequences, that is, seem less than the sum of their parts)[8] at his lyrical best, as I say, he can embody a profound sense of loss *and* of affirmation *and* of celebration in a single poem, even in a few lines within a single poem. And in such lines, in such poems, he can summarize his sense of the world and show us "The only way of saying something / Luminously as possible" (**"A Bright Day"**). When this happens, and it often happens, he illuminates us all.

Notes

1. Oddly enough, Montague says he was going to use this Joycean passage as epigraph to his collection of short stories, *Death of a Chieftain.* See his "Work Your Progress", *Irish University Review,* 12 (Spring 1982), 49.

2. Denis Donoghue, "The Sovereign Ghost, part 1", *Sewanee Review,* LXXXIV, 1 (1976), 103.

3. Terence Brown, *Northern Voices* (Totowa, New Jersey: Rowman and Littlefield, 1975), p. 152.

4. Patrick Kavanagh, *Collected Poems* (London: MacGibbon & Kee, 1964), p. 153. The following quotation is also from this source; "Is", p. 154.

5. "In the Irish Grain", Introduction to *The Faber Book of Irish Verse* (London, 1974), p. 23. The O'Brien quotation may be found in Seamus Heaney's essay, "The God in the Trees", *Preoccupations* (London: Faber and Faber, 1980), p. 181.

6. John M. Synge, *Collected Works,* Volume 2, ed. Alan Price (Gerrards Cross: Colin Smythe, 1982), pp. 58-9.

7. Ibid.

8. Maybe his own *natural* tendency is revealed in a 1985 interview, where he said that his imaginative habit was "to let the lyric come as it will, let the spirit blow where it listeth, and now and then you can see some larger pattern". ("Elegiac Cheer", *The Literary Review,* 31, Fall 1987, p. 29). Some of the "larger patterns", however, seem less simply "seen", than deliberately made up.

Michael Faherty (essay date 1995)

SOURCE: Faherty, Michael. "The Strange Ones: John Montague, Ezra Pound and the Troubadour Tradition." In *Ezra Pound and the Troubadours,* pp. 123-41. Gardonne, France: éditions fédérop, 2000.

[*In the following essay, originally published in 1995, Faherty examines the influence of Ezra Pound on Montague's poetry, noting that both were interested in the poetic legacy of the medieval French troubadours.*]

As Antoinette Quinn has noted, the poet John Montague is

> *obsessed with fosterage and kinship, with genealogy, ancestry, tribe, inheritance, the sense of belonging, personal and local attachments. In his poetry he pores over old family photographs and letters, recounts recent and more remote family history . . . his uncle's fiddle-playing, his father's tenor singing*
>
> (29).

This obsession with family and belonging seems perfectly natural when one takes account of Montague's personal history. Born in Brooklyn in 1929, he was shipped back home to relatives in Ulster at the age of four; while his two older brothers went to live with his maternal grandmother, he was sent to live with his father's sisters in a nearby village where they ran a small farm and the local post office. When his mother returned to Ireland three years later, she set up home with her two older boys, but John was to remain with his aunts, only seeing his mother on her annual visits to Garvaghey and the occasional holiday, his father did not return until 1952, just before Montague himself left Ireland to study in the States. As if this was not enough to frustrate his desperate need to belong, one of the teachers at his primary school mocked his "outlandish" accent and warned the other pupils not to speak like him; while years later, when he left Ulster on a scholarship to study English and History at University College, Dublin, it was the turn of those south of the border to poke fun at his acquired "northern twang" (*FC,* [*The Figure in the Cave*] 9).

It is little wonder then that Montague's readers and critics have had difficulty placing him, not knowing whether he was properly Irish or American or, given his fondness for the culture and countryside of France, even French perhaps. Some have argued that his continuing fascination with his aunts' village in County Tyrone made him the rightful heir to Patrick Kavanagh's advocacy of parochialism in post-renaissance Irish poetry, while others suggested that his penchant for experimentalism and close association with poets like John Berryman, Robert Duncan and Gary Snyder placed him more comfortably within the post-war American tradition. And then there was still the nagging question of what to do with all those love poems: which tradition do they come from? Neither the Irish nor the American traditions have encouraged love poetry in recent years, and it seemed a rather odd way for a poet raised in rural Ulster—a place not known for its sense of comfort with either sex or the undraped body—to spend his time.

Perhaps sensing that the critics have had as much difficulty deciding exactly where he belongs as he himself has had, Montague has stated that he feels a "natural complicity in three cultures, American, Irish and French" (*FC,* 18). Despite the fact that he also occasionally describes himself as "the missing link of Ulster poetry" (*FC,* 8-9) or the poet who has taken over "where the last bard of the O'Neills left off" (*FC,* 55), Montague has long been an advocate of an international approach to Irish poetry, arguing that he sees no problem combining "local allegiances" with a "world consciousness", that one can be both "earthed in Ireland" and "at ease in the world" (*FC,* 18-19). This means, of course, that, for Montague, Pound is as much a literary

forefather as are Yeats and Joyce. Although Montague's hopes of meeting Pound were frustrated when he lost his letter of introduction to him at St Elizabeth's (*FC,* 15), he has consistently criticized contemporary Irish poets who continue to write as if Pound never existed, "as though the iambic line still registered the curve of modern speech" (*FC,* 218). Montague argues that it is not that Pound is "necessarily more important than Aodhagan O'Rathaille for an Irish poet . . . but the complexity and pain of the *Pisan Cantos* are certainly more relevant than another version of 'Preab san Ól'"(*FC,* 216). It is perhaps no wonder then that Montague's interest in the third tradition to which he inscribes himself, the French tradition, follows Pound's own interests there—in the poetry of the medieval troubadours. Like Pound, Montague's scholarship into the literature of France has been what Donald Davie would call a "pedestrian" one (210-17), from his first cross-country cycling trip in 1948, with a copy of Rimbaud in his pack, to his current semi-residence in the village of Mauriac in the Gironde, near the tower-study of Michel de Montaigne. In a recent essay written during one of his annual visits to Mauriac, Montague placed his work firmly within "a tradition of love poetry going back to the *amour courtois* which began here in the valley of the Dordogne" (*FC,* 15), adding that he feels "a natural affinity with the French attitude towards love which goes back to our poetic ancestors, the troubadours, and combines the ideal with the practical" (*FC,* 12). Although Montague acknowledges the debt his love poetry owes to the troubadour tradition in this essay, he fails to acknowledge the extent to which his understanding of this tradition may have been filtered through Pound's own reading of it or the extent to which his love poems differ from the usual conventions of courtly love.

Of course, Montague's understanding of courtly love does not all come from Pound; Robert Graves has played an acknowledged role here as well, as has, indeed, perhaps the greatest of Irish love poets, Yeats. It may be worth noting at this point that Pound and Yeats did not see a great deal of difference between the Celtic and Provençal traditions. As Stuart McDougal has pointed out, "Pound has always connected the pagan and mystic aspects of Provence with the Celts" (94-95), whether in "The Flame" where he states that what "Provence knew" in the time of the troubadours can also be found in "all the tales they ever writ of Oisín" (*CEP* [*Collected Early Poems*], 171) or in his conflation of the two traditions in "La Fraisne", where the speaker clearly owes half his character to Pound's interest in the troubadours and half to what he had gleaned from Yeats and the works of the Celtic Twilight. For both Pound and Yeats, however, the elements that most clearly linked the two traditions were the vestiges of pagan belief and worship that had somehow survived the best efforts of the monks in the West of Ireland and the popes in the South of France. While Yeats felt that he could detect a pre-Christian ember in the people and legends of places like Galway, Sligo and Donegal which might serve as an anecdote to the materialism and positivism of industrialized Europe, Pound thought that he had spotted a similar ember in the songs of the medieval troubadours. As Richard Sieburth has noted, Provence began to assume all the characteristics of "a secret Yeatsian land" for Pound (IX), a place that somehow maintained a pagan spirit in an otherwise distinctly un-pagan time. In his essay *Psychology and Troubadours,* Pound writes:

> . . . *Provençal song is never wholly disjunct from pagan rites of May Day. Provence was less disturbed than the rest of Europe by invasion from the North in the darker ages; if paganism survived anywhere it would have been, unofficially, in the Langue d'Oc*
>
> (*SR* [*The Spirit of Romance*], 90).

He even hoped that these vestiges of pagan culture might still be alive in the South of France and, like Yeats going from cottage to cottage with Lady Gregory in the West of Ireland, Pound walked from village to village in the summer of 1912, apparently hoping to find among the people of Provence what Yeats thought he had found among the peasants of Ireland. Although at first it seemed to Pound as if he would find no more than the odd fragment or ruin, he eventually wrote in his diary that a visit to a place like Arles

> *explains so much, so much why the great mass of Provençal canzons are what they are, why the whole thing "l'amour courtois" and the rest of it was just what it was and why there is no use trying to find subtle under- or over-currents*
>
> (*WT* [*A Walking Tour*], 65).

While Yeats was doing his best to revive a lost culture and vanishing tongue in Ireland, Pound had found a rhyme in the South of France, a place where Christianity had likewise not been completely successful in extinguishing the flame of paganism.

According to Robert Graves, one of the few contemporary poets besides Montague to dedicate so much of his career to the writing of love poetry and whose work has had not a small influence on the Irish poet, the role of the beloved in such a tradition is to embody the very "spark" that once existed in the world before it became the way it is today, while the role of the poet is to act as "keeper of the flame" in a world otherwise dead and benighted (109-12). Whether Graves borrowed this concept of the tradition from Pound is not clear but what is clear is that this is how Pound also envisioned the role of the beloved in the poetry of the troubadours. As Pound said, there are "half memories" buried in the praise of these medieval women that Christianity has not been able to erase: "fragments of the worship of

Flora and Venus as survived in the spring merrymakings" (*SR,* 39), "some non-Christian and inextinguishable source of beauty [that] persisted throughout the Middle Ages maintaining song in Provence . . . And this force was the strongest counter force to the cult of . . . asceticism" (*SP* [*Selected Prose*], 58). Like Graves and Pound, Montague believes that he can detect traces of a pre-Christian attitude towards the body and sexuality in a good deal of medieval art, whether in "the smile of the angels" in the cathedral at Chartres or the "sentiment that you find at the end of the *Divine Comedy*" (O'Driscoll, 69). Montague says that, despite whatever reputation the Irish people may have today for a general unease with such matters, this same attitude towards the sensual can be found in much of early Irish literature. Explaining why he began to experiment with love poetry in his early days as a poet in Dublin and responding to accusations that he is betraying his culture in such verse, Montague has said:

> *As for my transgressing the Irish inhibitions on the matter of sex, these were implanted in us by the Victorians. It was during the reign of that unlamented Queen that we learned to speak English, so (like some subject-races nowadays) we learned to be more polite than themselves. Whereas, if you turn to Irish literature, it's not explicit; it just takes an enormous pleasure in the fact of sex. It has a great deal of love in it and so do most great literatures. So I was just unconsciously bringing back what was already there in the Irish, going behind Queen Victoria . . . going behind the famine even, going back to the old Ireland and trying to find the true current of feeling which would illuminate this dismal scene*
>
> (O'Driscoll, 62-63).

Like Pound, Montague sees the practice of this sort of poetry as a "counter force" to the drabness of the modern world, opening a pathway between contemporary Ulster and the literature and spirit of the not-so-distant past.

Montague has said that the "the ultimate function of the poet is to praise. It may have taken somebody like Dante the long pilgrimage through the *Inferno* and the *Purgatorio* to get up to the praising point but nevertheless that is the end vision" (O'Driscoll, 68). Like Pound, Montague sees the act of praise as "ritual", as an essentially "religious" practice that transcends the everyday and, consequently, our usual perception of time and space. This is, perhaps, not surprising when one considers that Montague, like Joyce and his fictional double Stephen Dedalus before him, regards himself as a failed priest turned poet, who has instead become "a priest of the eternal imagination, transmuting the daily bread of experience into the radiant body of everliving life" (Joyce, 200). In fact, Montague has said that when he read Portrait for the first time at university, he felt that "it was like a case study of my own little psyche"

(*FC*, 7). For Montague, it is clear that to praise a woman in a poem in this manner is to leave the practical world and its petty concerns behind, that it is an escape of sorts to another time and place where the usual worries are temporarily put on hold. In a poem like **"The Well-Beloved"**, Montague acknowledges that such poems must seem extremely out-dated to some contemporary readers. He writes:

> To wake up and discover—
> a slairge *of chill water*—
> *that she was but a forthright woman*
> *on whom we had bestowed*
> (*because of the crook of an elbow,*
> *the swing of a breast or hip,*
> *a glance, half-understood)*
> *divinity or angelhood?*
>
> *Raised by the fury of our need,*
> *supplicating, lusting, grovelling*
> *before the tall tree of Artemis,*
> *the transfiguring bow of Diana,*
> *the rooting vulva of Circe, or*
> *the slim shape of a nymph,*
> *luring, dancing, beckoning:*
> *all her wild disguises!*
>
> *And now she does not shine,*
> *or ride, like the full moon,*
> *gleam or glisten like cascades*
> *of uncatchable, blinding water,*
> *disturb, like the owl's cry,*
> *predatory, hovering: marshlight,*
> *moonstone, or devil's daughter,*
>
> *but conducts herself like any*
> *Ordinary citizen, orderly or slattern,*
> *giving us a piece of her mind,*
> *pacifying or scolding children,*
> *or, more determinedly, driving*
> *or riding to her office, after*
> *depositing the children in a* crèche,
> *while she fulfills herself,*
> *competing with the best*
>
> (***ME***, [***Mount Eagle***] 46).

Montague admits in the poem that women no doubt feel the same way about men today, that

> *Of course, she is probably saying*
> *the same thing of us, as Oisín,*
> *our tall hero from Fairyland,*
> *descends or falls from the saddle*
> *to dwindle into an irritable husband,*
> *worn down by the quotidian,*
> *unwilling to transform the night*
> *with love's necessary shafts of light*
>
> (***ME***, 47).

Since the poem is reported to be Montague's response to an attack on him by Laura Riding for following too uncritically in Graves's footsteps, perhaps he has Graves's own caution in mind here that one cannot marry one's muse, or as Graves puts it, having had a rather disastrous marriage with Riding himself who had at one time served as his muse:

> *To marry the woman in whom the Muse is resident*
> *negates the poetic principle; if only because the*
> *outward view of marriage implies wifely subservience*
> *to a husband. Recognition of magic on the poetic level*
> *is irreconcilable with the routine of domesticity . . .*
> *For me, poetry implies a courtship of the Muse*
> *prolonged into a magical principle of living. There is*
> *no domestic poetry*
>
> (118).

Though a number of Montague's poems to his two French wives suggest that he does not see such an inevitable antagonism between marriage and the tradition of courtly love, it is clear that the domestic world and the romantic world cannot exist on the same plane, that one can be either in one world or in the other but not in both at the same time.

This may help account for Montague's obvious attraction to the *alba* in his love poetry. A number of his poems make use of the conventions of this sunrise song—which Pound himself was so fond of—to illustrate the intensity as well as the transitory nature of the romantic moment. In the standard *alba*, the tension is usually between the seemingly a-temporal pleasure of the moment and the threat of the rapidly approaching dawn, the re-introduction of the element of time which will shatter the moment and separate the lovers. But there is often a sense in these poems that the lovers have found a world apart that no longer has any connection with the external world of economics and politics. In some of Montague's poems, he describes this world apart from without, whether the couple that he observes with the eye of a painter walking down the road one "rainy quiet evening" in **"Irish Street Scene, With Lovers"** for whom the world is no larger than the width of an umbrella:

> *Dripping, they move through this marine light,*
>
> *Seeming to swim more than walk,*
> *Linked under the black arch of an umbrella,*
> *With its assembly of spokes like points of stars,*
> *A globule of water slowly forming on each.*
> *The world shrinks to the soaked, worn*
> *Shield of cloth they parade beneath*
>
> (***SP*** [***Selected Poems***], 9).

or his own reunion after a long separation at a station in California in **"All Legendary Obstacles"**, which is observed by an "old lady" from inside the train

> *who marked*
> *A neat circle on the glass*
> *With her glove, to watch us*
> *Move into the wet darkness*
> *Kissing, still unable to speak*
>
> (***SP***, 40).

the "neat circle on the glass" not unlike the circular fade-outs of the classic black-and-white movies on late-night television that Montague is said to be so addicted to. But far more often, as in the standard *alba*, this world apart is described from within. In **"Matins"**, it is a specific "balcony bed" at the top of the stairs, high above "a capital city", eventually shrinking in size to the beloved's "long hair tenting [her] head" (*ME,* 37), while in others it is the more oblique

> secret room
> of golden light where
> everything—love, violence,
> hatred is possible;
> and, again love
>
> (*SP,* 90).

In a couple of Montague's poems, this world apart assumes medieval characteristics, reminiscent of the love lyrics of the troubadours. In the poem just cited, **"The Same Gesture"**, he talks about "Such intimacy of hand / and mind" that "the shifting of hands is a rite / like court music" (*SP,* 90), just as in one of his most popular love poems **"Tracks"**, the "vast bedroom" that the lovers inhabit turns into a medieval scene:

> Behind our eyelids
> a landscape opens,
> a violet horizon
> pilgrims labour across,
> a sky of colours
> that change, explode
> a fantail of stars
> the mental lightning
> of sex illuminating
> the walls of the skull;
> a floating pleasure dome
>
> (*SP,* 160).

In some of the poems, this world apart becomes so intense and absorbing that the outside world seems to cease altogether, the threat of dawn that is so much a part of the *alba* convention simply disappears. For example, in one of his more comical love poems **"Uprooting"**, the couple become so oblivious to the world outside that their entire shelter is dismantled before they realize it:

> My love, while we talked
> They removed the roof. Then
> They started on the walls,
> Panes of glass uprooting
> From timber, like teeth.
> But you spoke calmly on,
> Your example of courtesy
> Compelling me to reply.
> When we reached the last
> Syllable, nearly accepting
> Our positions, I saw that
> The floorboards were gone:
> It was clay we stood upon
>
> (*SP,* 44).

However, even in this poem, particularly in the final line, it is clear that the romantic moment cannot be sustained, that try as they may to ignore it, the sun will eventually rise and they must part. Although in some of Montague's versions of the *alba* he retains the convention of the rising sun as the threat to the lovers' peace, in many of the poems it takes on a variety of considerably more modern guises, from the "city outside" and its

> twenty iron floors
>
> of hotel dropping
> to where the late sun
> strikes the shield of
> the lake, its chill towers
>
> (*SP,* 163).

to the modern world intruding on the medieval paradise of **"Tracks"**, embodied in the "giggling maids [who] push / a trolley of fresh / linen down the corridor" outside their room (*SP,* 161). As Montague suggests, these sensual moments in a world apart serve as a sort of charm for the lovers—and certainly, he would suggest, for the reader as well—as something that they can take with them and draw upon as "a talisman / of calm, to invoke against / unease, to invoke against harm" (*SP,* 163).

However, as both Pound and Montague have noted, one of the attractions of the poetry of courtly love is the glimpse it provides into the medieval world in which the troubadours lived. Pound's "love ethic", according to McDougal, insists that the woman described in the poem "characterizes the essentials of [the] medieval world" (88), and by getting to know her through the poet's physical description of her, one also gets to know quite a bit about the distant world she comes from. McDougal goes on to say that Pound began to realize that it was very difficult to translate this world and its spirit into the present time:

> *The spirit of Provence, as [Pound] interprets it, is "archaic" inasmuch as its values and sensibility do not function effectively in the modern world. Love has become debased . . . and we have lost the mystical reverence for Amor that permeated the medieval world*
>
> (138-39)

While Montague seems to have more faith than Pound in the ability of modern language and poetry to capture that spirit, it is interesting that whenever he attempts to dig beneath the surface of post-Victorian Ireland to see whether any embers are still glowing from those times, the women in his poems who embody that "spark" are not the beautiful, young women of his *alba* poems, but the *Cailleach* or "hag". Although Montague has stated that, in general, he goes along with what Graves has to say about the function of the muse in love poetry, for him the muse is "anything that excites you", including "wells, stones, old women and babies" (O'Driscoll, 63). In fact, stones and old women are often rhymed in his poetry as receptacles of ancient wisdom and culture, both of which may have frightened him as a child because of their reputed spells and powers, but which today he approaches with respectful amazement and awe. Such is the case with the old woman he listened to as a child from his "rough play-box" while she sat beneath the rafters, "Busy with her bowl of tea in a farmhouse chimney corner, / Wrapped in a cocoon of rags and shawls," prattling on about "The fairies of Ireland and the fairies of Scotland [who] / Fought on that hill all night" until "in the morning the well ran blood," or "Mrs McGurren [who] had the evil eye" and "prayed prayers on the black cow" upon which "It dropped there and died" (*SP*, 18). Montague remembers that while she "rocked and crooned" and "Her clothes stank like summer flax," her eyes were "rheumy with racial memory" and her rambling stories "Heavy with local history" (*SP*, 18-19). It is not until adulthood that he can appreciate all that has died with her, the culture that she embodied. In homage, he goes to visit her grave:

> . . . *in the high summer as the hills burned with corn*
> *I strode through golden light*
> *To the secret spirals of the burial stone:*
> *The grass-choked well ran sluggish red—*
> *Not with blood but ferrous rust—*
> *But beneath the whorls of the guardian stone*
> *What fairy queen lay dust?*
>
> (*SP*, 19)

An old woman that he meets by chance on the way to Gallarus on the Dingle Peninsula seems to him another of these embers of a lost culture, representing not only herself of course who guides him to the oratory but all the Irish women of the past who "when one entered a cottage / to ask directions . . ."

> *rose to greet you, not as a stranger*
> *but a visitor:*
> > *that was the old way,*
> *the way of courtesy*
>
> (*SP*, 12).

Everything in the woman's cottage begins to take on similar "luminous" meanings, from the way she keeps her flagstones swept to her "two-legged, horned alarm-clock". When he returns to the car with the directions he had sought and is asked by his partner what the woman has said, all he can do is

> . . . *point the way*
> *over the hill to where*
> > *obscured in sea*
> *mist, the small, grey stones of the oratory*
> *held into the Atlantic for a thousand years*
>
> (*SP*, 12).

Like the beloved in the tradition of courtly love, these figures have become sources of wisdom whose knowledge the lover can only hope to gain the faintest inkling of, his reach forever exceeding his grasp. In another poem, Montague writes of all the old men and women who seem to have populated his childhood, from Jamie MacCrystal who "sang to himself, / A broken song without tune, without words" and "Fed kindly crusts to winter birds" to Maggie Owens who "was surrounded by animals . . . Even in her bedroom [where] a she-goat cried" and who "was a well of gossip defiled, / Fanged chronicler of a whole countryside" (*SP*, 26). Whether, as a young boy, he found them friendly or frightening, Montague says they now surround his memories of childhood like "dolmens", with all the apparent significance of the stone circles one can find in the Sperrin Mountains of County Tyrone where these old people once lived.

As Quinn has noted, Montague has invented his very own "cult of the hag" in which each of these old women serves as "a vital link between the recent and remote history of a region, bilingual, blending pagan and Christian beliefs, a living archive of local folklore and superstition" (31). This nearly mariolatrous cult is nowhere more evident than in poems such as **"The Music Box"** and **"The Wild Dog Rose"**. The first poem is dedicated to Mary Mulvey, another smelly, hunched, old woman whom Montague and his boyhood friends used to terrorize, either by "clattering stones" on the roof of her cottage or by chanting "Maria Marunkey married a donkey" outside her half-door until she chased them away (*SP*, 186). The second poem is given over to an old spinster who apparently quarrelled with everyone in Montague's old neighborhood and whose countenance used to make him shake with

> . . . *ancient awe, the terror of a child*
> *before the great hooked nose, the cheeks*
> *dewlapped with dirt, the staring blue*
> *of the sunken eyes, the mottled claws*
> *clutching a stick . . .*
>
> (*SP*, 124).

Yet in both poems a metamorphosis takes place, the old woman assumes a beauty and significance in the poet's adulthood that she never could have had in his uncomprehending childhood. In his visit to the old woman in **"The Wild Dog Rose"**, Montague finds that they are able to "talk in ease at last, / like old friends, lovers almost, / sharing secrets", discovering one secret, however,

> > *so terrible*
> *that I try to push it away,*
> *my bones melting.*
>
> > *Late at night*
> *a drunk came beating at her door*

to break it in, the bolt snapping
from the soft wood, the thin mongrels
rushing to cut, but yelping as
he whirls with his farm boots
to crush their skulls.

> *In the darkness*
they wrestle, two creatures crazed
with loneliness, the smell of the
decaying cottage in his nostrils
like a drug, his body heavy on hers,
the tasteless trunk of a seventy-year-
old virgin, which he rummages while
she battles for life

> *bony fingers*
reaching desperately to push
against his bull neck. "I prayed
to the Blessed Virgin herself
for help and after a time
I broke his grip."

> *He rolls*
to the floor, snores asleep,
while she cowers until dawn
and the dogs' whimpering starts
him awake, to lurch back across
the wet bog

> (*SP*, 124-26).

While he makes no attempt in these poems to disguise either the ugliness of these women or their lives, whether the rape that Montague knew nothing about or the taunting that he took an active part in, he makes it clear that they are able to survive this ugliness with the aid of their individual talismans. While the old woman whose life Montague helped make a misery had her "magic music box" which, on the rare occasion, she would even treat her young tormentors to allowing them to enter her cottage and listen to its "light, regular sounds" and watch the "small figure on its rosewood top / twirling slowly" like a "tireless dancer" (*SP*, 187), the old woman who was raped by the drunk has her faith in the Virgin Mary and "the wild dog rose", the flower which constantly reminds her of "the Holy Mother of God and / all she suffered" (*SP*, 127). As a consequence, in his poetry Montague transforms the old women into their individual talismans, Mary Mulvey, who is eventually "too crippled to move", becomes that "tireless dancer" atop her music box, while the other old woman becomes the wild rose itself, its "Petals beaten wide by rain" and, for a moment, the air becomes

> *. . . strong with the smell*
of that weak flower, offering
its crumbling yellow cup
and pale bleeding lips
fading to white
> *at the rim*
of each bruised and heart-
shaped petal

> (*SP*, 127).

Just as the old women had their flowers and music boxes to draw upon for strength, Montague seems to be suggesting that these figures have assumed a similar function within the poetry, that they have become objects of veneration in their own right and can offer the sort of sustenance for the poet and reader that the beloved offered the troubadour and his audience in medieval times. As Peter Makin has argued, "courtly love was not 'religious' in the sense of being part of any Christian ethic; it was a religion in its psychology. The courtly lover did not think of his lady as the Church thought of her, but as the Church thought of God" (102).

For both Pound and Montague, the great attraction of the poetry of the troubadour tradition lies in its ability to act as a "counter force" to the drabness of everyday life, whether in the castles of Provence in the 12th century where Pound felt certain there was "unspeakable boredom" (*WT*, 93), or in London in the sad years following the First World War, or in the backwater of Dublin when Montague was learning to be a poet. The women praised in the poems embody an ember of a world that has all but ceased to exist and it is the poet's responsibility to see that it does not die out once and for all, perhaps never to be kindled again. In Montague's poem **"The Well-Beloved"**, he questions whether those who have criticized his obsession with love poetry will ever understand the emotional and psychological need for it, the tradition it represents. He writes:

> *Except that when the old desires stir*
> *—fish under weed-tangled waters—*
> *will she remember that we once were*
> *the strange ones who understood*
> *the powers that coursed so furiously*
> *through her witch blood, prepared*
> *to stand, bareheaded, open handed,*
> *to recognize, worship and obey:*

> *To defy custom, redeem the ordinary,*
> *with trembling heart and obeisant knee*
> *to kneel, prostrate ourselves again,*
> *if necessary, before the lady?*

> (*ME*, 47)

Works Cited

Donald Davie, *Studies in Ezra Pound,* Carcanet, Manchester, 1991.

Robert Graves, *Poetic Craft and Principle,* Cassell, London, 1967.

James Joyce, *A Portrait of the Artist as a Young Man,* 1916, Grafton, London, 1977.

Peter Makin, *Provence and Pound,* California UP, Berkeley, 1978.

Stuart McDougal, *Ezra Pound and the Troubadour Tradition,* Princeton UP, Princeton, 1972.

John Montague, *The Figure in the Cave and Other Essays,* ed. Antoinette Quinn, Lilliput, Dublin, 1989.

———, *Mount Eagle,* Bloodaxe, Newcastle upon Tyne, 1989.

———, *Selected Poems,* Oxford UP, Oxford, 1982.

Dennis O'Driscoll, "An Interview with John Montague", *Irish University Review,* 19. 1. (1989): 58-72.

Ezra Pound, *Collected Early Poems of Ezra Pound,* ed. Michael John King, Faber, London, 1977.

———, *Selected Prose, 1909-1965,* ed. William Cookson, Faber, London, 1973.

———, *The Spirit of Romance,* 1910, Peter Owen, London, 1970.

———, *A Walking Tour in Southern France: Ezra Pound among the Troubadours,* ed. Richard Sieburth, New Directions, New York, 1992.

Antoinette Quinn, "The Well-Beloved: Montague and the Muse", *Irish University Review,* 19. 1. (1989): 27-43.

Eamonn Wall (essay date fall 1996)

SOURCE: Wall, Eamonn. "A Second Tongue." *Shenandoah* 46, no. 3 (fall 1996): 113-18.

[*In the following review of Montague's* Collected Poems, *Wall contends that Montague, despite his many awards, is underrated both for his own poetry and for his influence on other poets.*]

This meticulously edited and beautifully produced volume is a fitting testament to the career and achievement of John Montague, a writer who occupies a central place in the narrative of Irish writing as it has unfolded during the contemporary period. He is a writer who, although he has been widely honored throughout his career, is perhaps underrated—both for his own work and for the influence he has exerted on a whole plethora of poets who have come after him. It would not be an exaggeration to suggest that contemporary Irish poetry begins with Montague and arrives at a type of culmination with Seamus Heaney being awarded the Nobel Prize. In the poetry of that island, Montague is the Irish Akhmatova to Heaney's Mandelstam: both are giants who speak on similar themes but see through different lenses. *Collected Poems* gathers most of the contents from Montague's principal collection—from *Forms of Exile* (1958), through *Time in Armagh* (1993)—and also some recent and older uncollected work. However, the book begins with and highlights the three extended poetic sequences—*The Rough Field* (1972), *The Great Cloak* (1978) and *The Dead Kingdom* (1984)—which frame Montague's career.

The Rough Field is a book of return. Montague arrives in the North of Ireland (where he grew up) during the 1960's to describe an area in crisis as a result of the resumption of the Troubles. Concerned with both the historical and political landscapes, with the personal arena of past and present and with the points at which these narratives intersect, *The Rough Field* is his masterpiece. In it, Montague brings together national and personal voices of the 1960's and synthesizes both into a long work as different from but as great as Patrick Kavanagh's articulation of the consciousness of the 1940's, *The Great Hunger.* The book is comprised of ten sections and an epilogue; in each, some aspect of the narrative is introduced and explored. The sections are glossed by quotations from Winston Churchill, Unionist pamphleteers and propagandists, Frederick Engles, Edmund Spencer and from the poet in other voices, which provide the work with both context, depth and added complexity. Missing from this edition are the illustrations from John Derrick's *A Discoverie of Woodkarne* (1581), which played an important role in earlier editions of *The Rough Field* and which suggested that Montague conceived the poem not just as a traditional literary text, but as postmodern collage, bringing to mind Larry Rivers' reinterpretation of American history in his collages. Despite these omissions, however, the text stands strong.

Montague begins in Belfast, an unattractive, uninspiring city to which he has journeyed in order to receive a poetry prize, and from there travels to Garvaghey, his home place:

> *Catching a bus at Victoria Station,*
> Symbol of Belfast in its iron bleakness,
> We ride through narrow huckster streets
> (Small lamps bright before the Sacred Heart,
> Bunting tagged for some religious feast)
> To where Cavehill and Divis, stern presences,
> Brood over a wilderness of cinemas and shops. . . .

At all times, Montague is conscious of the fact that others have traveled this road before, that each step he makes draws him deeper into history, but he is also aware that new travelers must come through to redefine an ancient landscape—physical and psychological—for an Ireland which is striving to belong to the modern world. Ancient Ireland, he tells us in **"Coole Park and Abbey Theatre 1951,"** has passed "into that dark permanence of ancient forms," as indeed has the poetry of Yeats, which treated of an Ireland which has ceased to be, if it ever existed in the first place:

> The visitor to Coole Park
> in search of a tradition
> finds
>   a tangled alley-way
> a hint of foundation wall
> (the kitchen floor)
>   high wire

to protect the famous beech-tree
from raw initials
                              and a lake
bereft of swans.

Montague, thinking of the tree outside Augusta Grego-ry's house (onto which many writers carved their initials) understands that a new poetry must be written to articulate a new consciousness and body politic. But despite an inexorable movement forward, Ireland remains tied to history, a mixed blessing, and to place, which is constantly celebrated. Loss—political, linguis-tic and personal—is a constant presence in Montague's work, and its political manifestation in *The Rough Field* echoes poems of more personal loss which appear in his work: loss of language due to a speech impediment, loss of parents when he was sent home to the North from Brooklyn as a child to be raised by his mother's family and the loss of love. What gives these poems power is Montague's mastery of the lyric, and his abil-ity to weave these themes and feelings together into a resonant mosaic. Irish life is complex in its interrela-tions and, of all living poets, Montague succeeds best in capturing this complexity at its deepest level.

The resumption of the Troubles brings history, religion and politics into the foreground again and stirs old animosities, "RELIGION POISONS US / NORTH AND SOUTH." Montague's attachment to Nationalism is defined by birth and culture; however, it is not just politics or religion which bind him, but the local places and small-scale occurrences from which both myths and, more important, personal narratives are created. Throughout *The Rough Field,* Montague highlights the tension which exists between the public and private worlds, between the thing as symbol and as object where even shoes, when placed into the Irish language, become part of a larger discourse:

The mythic lyre shrunk to country size:
The clatter of brogues on the flagstones,
The colourless dram of poteen—
Is that the world we were made for?

In common with many Irish writers, Montague is conscious of having lost his language; for him, English is a "grafted tongue" which he has had to learn to use. He strives to describe a world that has been lost (represented for him in *The Rough Field*'s fourth sec-tion by the Flight of the Earls as a consequence of the defeat at Kinsale in 1601) in a language which is not his mother tongue:

   To grow
a second tongue, as
harsh a humiliation
as twice to be born.

Montague's discourse on language echoes Joyce's in *Portrait* in the tundish/funnel scene between Stephen Dedalus and the English dean. Of course, the issue is a

central concern for all Irish writers, though many have managed to produce a dynamic and world-renowned literature from such a grafted tongue.

Montague spent a number of years in the 1950's and 1960's in the United States and France and found emerging in Ireland many of the movements for personal and political freedoms which he observed abroad. The Civil Rights Movement in the North of Ireland, influenced by Dr. King's efforts in the U.S., and the hijinks he notices at a traditional Irish music festival, show that a parallel drive towards sexual freedom is underway in Ireland, as he suggests in **"The Siege of Mullingar"**:

At the Fleadh Cheoil in Mullingar
There were two sounds, the breaking
Of glasses, and the background pulse
Of music. Young girls roamed
The streets with eager faces,
Shoving for men. Bottles in
Hand, they rowed out a song:
Puritan Ireland's dead and gone,
A myth of O'Connor and O'Faoláin.

The Fleadh Cheoil in Mullingar is an early, and an Irish, version of Woodstock.

Montague's presence in the United States has also influenced how he writes, and the influence of American poetry is particularly evident in the lyrics which comprise *The Great Cloak,* a collection which details love from birth through marriage and dissolution. Mon-tague is a confessional poet: he reveals more of his life in his work than any other poet of his generation. Yet, having said this, one cannot say his work is like Low-ell's or Sexton's because confession is just one aspect, one approach he has borrowed from American poetry. It's also evident that he has absorbed the work of Dun-can and Olson; however, in his shorter lyrics, in which he uses short lines and stanzas, his work resembles that of Robert Creeley and W. C. Williams. This mode of writing that Montague has introduced into Irish poetry has had a large influence on how poets younger than Montague have written their poems. The early poetry of Seamus Heaney, for example, owes much to Kavanagh for its themes and to Montague for its form. It is a mistake frequently made by critics to consider Mon-tague and Heaney, and sometimes all Northern Irish poets, to be of the same generation of Irish poets; whereas the former actually belongs to the school of Dolmen Press poets who began to publish in the 1950's, the latter emerged a decade later. Montague has been co-opted into Northern Irish poetry, but in fact, his work is more accurately compared to the poems of Thomas Kinsella and James Liddy.

The personal and political are interwoven impressively in the third sequence, *The Dead Kingdom.* The book is structured around the *dinnseanchas,* which in Irish literature is the lore of place, and is the account of a journey from Cork to the locale of Montague's early life in the Fermanagh-South Tyrone area, but it is also concerned with his mother's death and with the disappearance of a time she personified. Particularly moving are the poems which recall the years his mother and father spent in America. Both suffered the pain and disappointment which exile brought. Of his father's existence in Brooklyn, Montague notes:

> My long lost father
> trudging home through
> this strange, cold city,
> its whirling snows,
> unemployed and angry
> living off charity.

His mother's feelings of estrangement are equally harrowing:

> My mother
> my mother's memories
> of America;
> a muddy cup
> she refused to drink.

An underlying theme here is Montague's own recollection of the pain he suffered when his parents sent him home from America as a child to be raised by relatives. **The Dead Kingdom** is both an exploration of his parents' world and a peacemaking with it. Right at the end of **Collected Poems** is another strong sequence, **Border Sick Call,** an account of another journey—along the Fermanagh-Donegal border with his brother. Frequently, in volumes of collected poems, there is a tapering off towards the end; however, Montague's recent work is a welcome exception to this trend.

John Montague's poetry is notable for a number of reasons, not least for his ability to convey political and personal crises with deep feeling, clarity and elegance. He has not only produced a confessional poetry of the highest order, but he is also the writer who has articulated best the tragedy, and the context, of the Troubles. At the same time, Montague has never lost sight of the importance of craft in poetry and in the process has produced a body of work as beautiful as it is illuminating and moving. For sheer breadth of vision and writing skill, this book is perhaps the greatest volume of collected poems to emerge from an Irish poet since Yeats.

R. T. Smith (essay date winter 1998)

SOURCE: Smith, R. T. "To Do Penance and Rejoice." *Southern Review* 34, no. 1 (winter 1998): 180-95.

[*In the following essay, Smith discusses the publication of Montague's* Collected Poems, *hoping that it will spark interest among American readers who have failed to appreciate his work and his influence on the work of others.*]

The title of Thomas Cahill's best-selling *How the Irish Saved Civilization* makes an extravagant claim, but the book's argument is both cogent and persuasive. Cahill credits the written word's survival as something more than a utilitarian instrument to medieval scholar-monks who copied and illuminated manuscripts by hand; and it is tempting to attribute, in parallel fashion, the enduring love of highly charged language to poets whose words are vivid enough to provide their own illumination. A remarkable number of these poets are Irish, and one—who provides continuity from Yeats through Patrick Kavanagh and on to the younger voices, but whose influence has been little appreciated in America—is John Montague. With the publication of Montague's **Collected Poems,** this oversight should be mended, as American readers encounter his splendid and provocative blend of the personal with the political, the international with the local, and the formal with the spontaneous.

Cahill's book begins with the Roman Empire's fall from what Edward Gibbon called its "immoderate greatness"—the decline of style to manner and of substance to shadow. But civilization, Cahill maintains, survived in the hinterlands through the efforts of the unimperialized Irish, whose embrace of Christianity led to the painstaking labor of copywork in the scriptoria of a vast network of monasteries, from Hebridean Iona through Lindisfarne and Ghent to Bern and beyond. Montague writes of his appreciation for this era in **"A New Siege"**:

> Columba's Derry!
>   ledge of angels
> radiant oakwood
>   where the man-dove
> knelt to master
>   his fiery temper
> exile chastened
>   the bright candle
> of the Uí Néill
>   burns from Iona
> lightens Scotland
>   with beehive huts
> glittering manuscripts . . .

The codices wrought and preserved by these servants of words, including Columcille and Gall, range from the Gospels to lives of the church fathers and to pagan classics by Horace and Virgil.

As geographically and philosophically marginal in the grand scheme of the Roman Church as their beasts, vines, and other embellishments, the scribes still managed to shift the center of belief, less by launching a crusade to modify orthodoxy than by enclosing the standard Latin texts within their more private symbols. A similar industry characterizes many Irish poets today. Giving a local habitation and a name to the universal troubles and passions of the heart, they have spoken powerfully of preoccupations that assail all reflective people. In **"Patriotic Suite,"** written in the late '60s, Montague seems almost to have anticipated this current flowering, as he suggests, "Granted a saint, we might shepherd / Another Dark Ages home." Though he would never call himself a saint, Montague (b. 1929) has—as poet, critic, anthologist, and fiction writer—influenced and inspired a host of younger poets from Seamus Heaney to Paul Muldoon. His recurrent subjects include romantic love, exile and loss, sectarian divisiveness, the legacy of duress and reconciliation. His style, influenced as much by William Carlos Williams as by Irish ancestors, raises the particular to sharp focus through compression, "a slow exactness . . . ritualizing its details," while he sounds a fresh music by counterpointing the colloquial and the elevated.

Blessed early with the fine ear that drew him toward both *sean nós* storytellers and the traditional music revival, Montague has always been attracted to the pure lyric by the sheer physiology of utterance, but the course of his life has driven him, as Ben Howard writes in *The Pressed Melodeon,* "into the roles of activist, elegist, and interpreter of political upheaval." Montague was born in Brooklyn to Catholic parents who fled Ulster in the wake of the Treaty of 1922—thus branding him an outsider from the start. When he was sent at age four to the home of his maiden aunts in County Tyrone, Montague had not only to endure separation from his parents and brothers but to struggle against both his American accent and a speech impediment. Immersing himself in the natural world, where religious distinctions held no sway, he frequented the nearby bogs and shores but still could not wholly escape the clamor and anxieties of World War II, which were further complicated by the local sectarian struggle. As both a Catholic in Northern Ireland and a foster child, the youngster was caught in an ideological crossfire and in the perplexities of a fatherless household, where he had to half discover and half invent his identity. In his adult transatlantic existence—his education in Dublin and Iowa, his teaching at University College Cork and SUNY-Albany—Montague has always sought a peace and a melody that might heal these early rifts and displacements.

Any reader familiar with Montague's inclination to orchestrate lyrics and short narratives into larger dynamics will not be surprised that he chose not to arrange the **Collected Poems** according to simple chronology. In fact, that would be near-impossible for a writer who has carried poems over from one volume to another, always—in a way reminiscent of Robert Penn Warren—overlapping in search of an ideal context for dif-

ferent voices and impulses to speak to one another. The first of the three larger movements of this substantial book comprises Montague's three milestone sequences: **The Rough Field** (1972), **The Great Cloak** (1978), and **The Dead Kingdom** (1984). The second section consists of six collections published before, between, and after the sequences; and the final selection contains poems from the '90s.

Upon the initial publication of **The Rough Field,** which takes its title from a translation of the Montague family's native townland, *garbh acaidh* (Anglicized to "Garvaghey"), Seamus Heaney wrote, "An important poem, an utterance from the underworld of love and bitterness." Though critics have disputed whether or not the political and personal levels of this book clarify one another, it is a mysterious and compelling work, be it a sequence, a cycle, or a midden. Frank Kersnowski has described **The Rough Field** as a radio lecture punctuated with verse and violated by incursions from "pirate stations." Unfortunately, its full complexity is not captured in **Collected Poems,** for the language of the original 1972 version is wedded to its physical environment, including the seventeenth-century woodcuts by John Derricke that open each of the ten sections. This connection to the graphic arts is more intricate than that of Galway Kinnell's *The Book of Nightmares* or Francis Quarles's emblematic poems, and may follow consciously in the footsteps of manuscript illuminators. Fortunately, the quotations and snippets from letters, histories, ballads, and propaganda that cut across the poetry are retained in the new compilation, and the overall effect suggests a modernist symphony. In an interview, the poet once said of this method, "I place blocks of material against each other, in dissonance, as well as harmony." Dillon Johnston, Montague's editor at Wake Forest as well as an able critic of modern Irish poetry, describes the result of this stratagem as "destabilizing individual lyrics," but though Montague assembles a powerful and jarring mosaic from the historical, the legendary, and the private experience of both loss and recovery, most of these skillful poems do maintain their integrity as testaments.

Before **The Rough Field,** Montague was known primarily as a love lyricist, but the opening section dramatizes his return to Ulster after long absence, and he finds there not love's consolations but a larger version of his memories of division, decline, and separation. **"Like dolmens round my childhood . . . ,"** for instance, is a mysterious and beautiful poem that might be mistaken for unmitigated nostalgia were it not for the narrator's earlier claim that "Only a sentimentalist would wish / to see such degradation again." The ominous and vexing nature of the old people becomes clear when Montague describes their presence:

> Gaunt figures of fear and of friendliness,
> For years they trespassed on my dreams,

Until once, in a standing circle of stones,
I felt their shadows pass

Into that dark permanence of ancient forms.

Affiliated with the local flora and fauna, Montague's tutelary elders—from Jamie MacCrystal to Wild Billy Eagleson—all convey the kind of abiding resonance associated with ceremonial stones. The old women also carry particular significance in the sequence, for they appear as faces of Graves's White Goddess, who may find incarnation as muse, mother, lover, or crone.

Like the poet's psyche, the natural surrounds of Garvaghey are damaged (**"Balance Sheet"** records the loss of "all signs / of wild life"); but even more important to Montague, and more poignantly conveyed, are the symbolic implications of "progress." The lament **"A Lost Tradition"** claims "The whole landscape a manuscript / We had lost the skill to read." This interweaving of place, self, and language informs the most arresting sections of *The Rough Field.* Over and again Montague reminds the reader of the attempts to smother the Irish language and the difficulty for a Celt in making sense of the world through the medium of the oppressors' English. Though the volume abounds with references to torturous expression ("Suffering became a form of speech"), nowhere is the Irish-speaker's dilemma more painfully and memorably reported than in **"A Grafted Tongue,"** a poem worth quoting in full:

(Dumb,
bloodied, the severed
head now chokes to
speak another tongue—

As in
a long suppressed dream,
some stuttering garb-
led ordeal of my own)

An Irish
child weeps at school
repeating its English.
After each mistake

The master
gouges another mark
on the tally stick
hung about its neck

Like a bell
on a cow, a hobble
on a straying goat.
To slur and stumble

In shame
the altered syllables
of your own name;
to stray sadly home

And find
the turf-cured width
of your parent's hearth
growing slowly alien:

In cabin
and field, they still
speak the old tongue.
You may greet no one.

To grow
a second tongue, as
harsh a humiliation
as twice to be born.

Decades later
that child's grandchild's
speech stumbles over lost
syllables of an old order.

Tragically, that schoolmaster would likely have been Irish himself, and the severed head, reminiscent of piked heads of Irish nationalists, suggests the persistence of this violent division in the culture. The poem's hard consonants and sharp vowels, reinforced by the truncation of syntax across the lines and the crisp, angling-in rhymes, express anger but not rancor. The master, dominant as a priest or landlord, bells the shamed child like a cow—the animal that once measured Irish tribal wealth. "Altered" and "ordeal" underscore the religious and feudal elements of the predicament, but the "turf-cured" hearth may offer a gleam of hope. Montague's brother Seamus is a doctor, and poems from the early **"Sick Call"** to the one that ends *Collected Poems,* **"Border Sick Call,"** reiterate the ailing nature of the country without dismissing the possibility of remission.

Two other crucial features of Montague's lifework appear throughout *The Rough Field*: the necessary and hopeful survival of music, and the importance of names. "With an intricate / & mournful mastery"—**The Flight of the Earls"** recollects—"the thin bow glides & slides, / assuaging like a bardic poem / our tribal pain." The magical power that once resided in the harp has now passed on to the fiddle, which may have been relegated "to the rafters" by the poet's immediate family, but still enchants the nation as a whole, supplemented by choirs, drinking songs, keens, and even "Sony transistors" at the national music festival, the *Fleadh Cheoil.*

In old Irish, *taidgh,* from which the poet's family name is constructed, designated the son of a fool, a poet, or a philosopher, all identities Montague has gladly claimed. In contemporary slang, however, the word indicates a Catholic, and Montague is startled to see the syllable scrawled in an alleyway in **"A New Siege,"** dedicated to Bernadette Devlin and telescoping the 1689 Siege of Derry with the current raging of the Troubles: "Tague / my own name / hatred's synonym."

The national destruction is so deeply inscribed in Montague's experience that it is no wonder he has chosen to skew any narrative gesture that might suggest a rewarding homecoming. Yet the last poem before the epilogue recounts a scene of horrible violence survived and hints at a resulting beatitude. In **"The Wild Dog Rose,"** the narrator tells of going to visit an old neighbor whose appearance as *cailleach,* the crone of myth and bogey story, terrified him as a boy. Montague reexperiences "that ancient awe," but his fear passes, and he can view her as a fellow creature because she has openly shared her painful story. Late one night, "the bolt snapping / from the soft wood," a drunk battered his way into her cottage and attempted to rape "the tasteless trunk of a seventy-year-/ old virgin"; but she was able to thwart him, scuffling and praying to the Holy Virgin until he fell away and "snore[d] asleep." Awful as the experience and the story are, remembering brings the old woman to consider the wild dog roses, "the only rose without thorns," in her hedge. Seeing them, she meditates on the sufferings of the Virgin; and the poet, having discovered something about survival under duress, envisions

> its crumbling yellow cup
> and pale bleeding lips
> fading to white.
>
>   at the rim
> of each bruised and heart-
> shaped petal.

Despite the images of disappointment and the auctioneer's echo of "going / going / GONE" that concludes *The Rough Field,* one has the feeling that the music and the healing are imbedded in the struggle.

In *The Great Cloak,* Montague returns to an earlier splicing of images of woman, the sea, and the heavens, but he does not abandon his interest in juxtaposed texts and recurrences. From **"Caught,"** in which a "Conqueror turned plaintiff" steals "his pleasure in an idle dance," to the more caustic **"Don Juan's Farewell,"** the poet examines the nature of romantic passion and finds, if not satisfaction, at least inspiration in the range of love's delights and disappointments. Later in this book of searching disclosures about the beginning and demise of a marriage, the narrator comes home late and perceives his "stealthy prowler's tread" to be quietly scolded by his lover's repose, while in **"Separation"** he sees a pair of fish moving apart, one safe, the other feeling "the golden / marriage hook / tearing its throat."

Throughout this movement of the orchestrated poems, Montague finds the violence and the shining beauty of the hook inextricably linked, for the openness that soothes can also wound, perhaps *must* also wound. If the woman, the goddess, the muse is the source of self-discovery, intoxication, and guidance, she is also the impetus of frustration and self-recrimination. In poems as tactile and visual as Montague's, the enchantments of love never seem speculative, and even the laments for lost lovers are often erotic. Feminist readers have occasionally taken Montague to task for his seeming allegorizing of woman, but poems like **"A Dream of July,"** part of the **"Anchor"** sequence, subvert this criticism—in a strategy also favored by Heaney and Muldoon—by anticipating it:

> Like a young girl
> Dissatisfied with
> Her mythic burden
> Ceres, corn goddess,
> Mistress of summer,
> Steps sure-footed over
> The sweet smelling
> Bundles of grass.

He also struggles to give the wife, here called Madeleine, more voice than the Madeleine whose destruction is necessary to trigger Roderick Usher's art. **"She Writes,"** for instance, reveals the wife's injured but forgiving tone as she conveys the recent local news and does not hope for vengeance: "I wouldn't wish it upon anyone: / to live and dance in lonely fire." In these poems, where Montague speaks both directly and through masks of love's dilemma, the voice of the mythic Liadan echoes, "Joyless / what I have done; / to torment my darling one." Like his countryman Oscar Wilde, Montague knows that we will hurt the ones we love; he also knows that the self figures prominently among that number.

In moving from the historical to the personal, Montague may seem to retreat to safer, more conventional lyric territory, but the rich ambivalence of the poems in *The Great Cloak* undermines the credibility of simple witness even as it exposes the most intimate scenes between lovers. Shifting from frank confession to canny misdirection, Montague weaves a poetry whose theme lies somewhere between anacreontics and the wry sorrow of George Meredith's "Modern Love." His brittle symmetries may now appear the obvious way to make poems of love's decline, but in the '70s these strategies, which have evolved into a road, must have seemed at best a path. For example, in the first section of **"Tearing,"** the man who tries to sing his partner's pain "like a gentle man" concludes:

> But the pose breaks.
> The sour facts remain.
>   It takes two
> To make or break
>   a marriage.
> *Unhood the falcon!*

The rhyme, repetition, and alliteration in this tight construct suggest control and the certainties of reason, but the abrupt metaphor of the final line invades, disrupting the calm voice with a predatory image born of exasperation. The whole sequence of dissolution culminates with "'We shall never be // what we were, again.' / Old love's refrain," but the anger throughout is clearly the result of disappointment, not self-righteousness. *The Great Cloak* tells of a union gone wrong, with no clear culprit or victim, leaving the poet astonished and unable to exonerate himself completely. In this respect, the book is not appreciably different from *The Rough Field,* though here the contested ground lies within—for the poet, abandoned as a child, comes to each amatory encounter looking to suture an old rift, and he is aware of the possibility that his art depends more upon the exploration of that conflict than on its resolution. And yet Montague's central impulse is toward clemency, as in the collection's title poem, where he describes the traditional cloak of an Irish countrywoman as able to "swathe" her body, then "to encompass her lover," and finally to protect a child "tenderly / while beasts browse around them / naturally as in the peaceable kingdom."

The third sequence, *The Dead Kingdom,* extends the engagements of *The Rough Field* and follows in the path of Kavanagh's *The Great Hunger* while deeply personalizing Montague's depiction of an Ireland avoiding admission of its decline. The section begins with another return home, this time occasioned by the death of the poet's mother—whose loss, along with laments for the decaying landscape and a happier (if imagined) past, infuses this book. Divided into five distinct suites, the book carries an epigraph from Pablo Neruda: *El reino muerto vive todavia*; and in **"Abbeylara,"** Montague suggests that the dead but ubiquitous monarch may be disorder itself: "a small cleared realm / reverting to first chaos." The poems focus on the mother's death, the raucous and ineffectual return of the father after two decades, and the long-ago but unforgotten sorrows of the family's brief sojourn in America.

Stylistically, these poems reflect an acquaintance with broken two-beat lines often found in Williams or Robert Creeley, but they also rhyme, sometimes almost compulsively. The approximate Skeltonics in the extreme example of **"A Christmas Card"** supplement imagistic crispness in an effort to undermine the pathos. Unfortunately, the yearning for earlier times here does occasionally lead to an overweening sentiment. As he tries to "sing a song for / things that are gone," Montague fails to navigate successfully between memories of his mother "rigged out like a girlfriend" at the cinema and his larger task: "intent for a hint of evidence / seeking to manage the pain—/ how a mother gave away her son." The over-rhyming ("intent" / "hint" /"-dence") is an unusual miscalculation for a poet with such a fine ear.

One of the most valuable features of this collection, along with the *dinnseanchas* (place-wisdom) and scenes of sectarian conflict, is Montague's exploration of poetry as the only effective tool for understanding his past. **"A Muddy Cup"** shows the reader "a third son who / beats out this song / to celebrate the odours / that bubbled up / so rank & strong," and **"A Flowering Absence,"** perhaps the strongest poem from this stage of his career, ends with an embodiment of both desperate awkwardness and fluency:

> Stammer, impediment, stutter:
> she had found my lode of shame,
> and soon I could no longer utter
> those magical words I had begun
> to love, to dolphin delight in.
>
> And not for two stumbling decades
> would I manage to speak straight again.
> Grounded for the second time
> my tongue became a rusted hinge
> until the sweet oils of poetry
>
> eased it and grace flooded in.

Because this volume also concerns itself with the musicality of the absentee father, the boy's need to master his voice seems all the more urgent. In this place where "the iron circle of retaliation" proves inescapable, one must have a tune to wrap about the sorrow, and Montague feels the need of a "pressed melodeon" for revisiting "rushy meadows, / small hills and hidden villages." In a series shimmering with grief over the twice-lost mother, the sky over the Bog of Allen is "a great cloak torn into / tatters of light." This garment, reminiscent of the **"Great Cloak"** of the previous volume, no longer shelters anyone, and though the poet closes the sequence with a coda attempting to avoid the sorrow, it is a futile gesture; he cannot turn away, even in the presence of his new wife and child, from the damaging forces that have shaped him.

The middle section of *Collected Poems* begins with work from Montague's first two books, whose titles—*Forms of Exile* and *Poisoned Lands*—announce their central themes. Many of the poems originally in these books were reused in the collections already discussed, so these selections are sparse, yet the poems still suggest the range and pitch of the more intricate suites. One steady concern of Montague's, the merging of the real and the dreamed in poetic vision, appears immediately, as the adult artist recounts his return to a spring he hauled water from as a boy: "Some living source, half-imagined and half-real, // Pulses in the fictive water that I feel." These poems are full of hawthorns, doves, and "the trough of reality," but they are also further populated with mythic images and Yeatsian ghosts.

In **"The *Sean Bhean Bhocht,*"** a liberal translation and appropriation of the old Irish poem titled in English **"The Hag of Beare,"** Montague makes his earliest examination of the muse as crone, here concerning the witchery of a well guardian. The old woman is filthy and frightening, but she is also, like the dolmens of his childhood, a monumental figure to be puzzled out with wonderment. **"Old Mythologies"** presents the ancient warriors turning over in their graves, "Regretting their butchers' days," while "This valley cradles their archaic madness." The poem is full of elevated and savage sounds, but it pivots in the end on a surprising trope that reveals in the young Montague a penchant for extending, by means of a quirky surprise, what might otherwise have been a simpler poem. As they march to battle, the bold fighters have "Wolfhounds, lean as models, / At their urgent heels." The choice of "urgent" is risky enough, but when he reaches beyond the heroic diction of the poem to compare the hounds to fashion models, Montague brings past and present into uncomfortable but revealing juxtaposition. It is this delight and ingenuity, even in the midst of unearthing Ireland's bloody past, that justifies his spellbound attention in the next poem to a preacher's call "to do penance and rejoice."

A Chosen Light and *Tides,* the next two books excerpted in *Collected Poems,* were published before *The Rough Field,* and the poems focus on "lack of a language," the emotional intensity of lovers, the magnetism of old people with their stories, and that "slow exactness" of seeing and saying characterized in **"A Bright Day"** by the mantel clock's "fierce delight / of so, and so, and so." Sexual violence and literary history also appear, as well as rural scenes rendered with the general fluency now associated with Heaney. And **"Hill Field"** may serve to remind readers, with its "Starling, magpie, crow ride / A gunmetal sheen of gaping earth," that many of Heaney's characteristic virtues are refinements of an ore that the older poet has brought to the surface. Another poem, ***"11 rue Daguerre,"*** offers the kind of scene now often associated with Eavan Boland's work (both "Midnight Flowers" and "The Women" exhibit its influence). A sleepless householder goes to the door and breathes the garden:

> In that stillness—soft but luminously exact,
> A chosen light—I notice that
> The tips of the lately grafted cherry-tree
>
> Are a firm and lacquered black.

Itself "luminously exact," this poem from the '60s wears the influence of Pound gracefully without sacrificing any of Montague's own perspective.

A Slow Dance offers more image-rich, short-lined experiments in lyrical abbreviation, and the subjects again range from the mythical Sweeney, whose slow dance "celebrate[s] greenness," to place-wisdom, the famine, the diminishing family, and what Delmore

Schwartz called "the scrimmage of appetite." The book is reverberant with small carnage, whether from battlefield, woodland, or farmyard, and the language is frequently snaggled and staccato, sometimes reminiscent of Ted Hughes. This is not Montague's most distinctive book, but it continues on his course and offers a sobering "dance of pain" as the narrator visits his namesake uncle's grave in Queens:

> I submit again
> to stare soberly
>
> at my own name
> cut on a gravestone
>
> & hear the creak
> of a ghostly fiddle
>
> filter through
> American earth
>
> the slow pride
> of a lament.

Montague inscribes his name not only into the landscape but also, as a kind of anagram, into the title of his most recent full-length volume, *Mount Eagle,* included here with few omissions. It is a book populated with the poet's customary concerns and attitudes, but his artistic maturity has smoothed off many of the edges, and when he offers portraits of his seniors now, it is from a closer vantage. Instead of seeing them as looming and iconic, he now senses "their sweet assurance." The subjects of **"Postmistress," "A Real Irishman,"** and **"Respect"** are still full of rich contradictions, but now the speaker has joined the circle. Predictably, the volume contains some poems with political content, and though they are not the major chords here, two of them will stand strong with the earlier efforts. In **"Semiotics,"** the narrator is amazed to watch, after the murder of a member of "the Deaf Mute Club of Ireland," the memorial address by one of the victim's friends, "a fiery speech / in sign language" that carries great force in its silence, ending with "a flickering semaphore of fingers, / then an angry swirl of palms." The semiology the poet practices is more than sign language or "semaphore"; it is a questioning awareness of what it means to be speechless. Remembering the grafted tongue and the writer's speech impediment, the reader feels an unstated irony and primitive pain. **"Cassandra's Answer,"** less savage and graphic than Heaney's recent "Cassandra," also considers the role of seer and the pain of knowing. At the poem's close, visiting his childhood home reduced to rubble by a bomb, the poet summarizes the contemporary Irish situation grimly: "you were born inside a skeleton."

Despite these reminders of conflict and some graphic considerations of female anatomy, the overall tone of the recent book is much less agonized than earlier ones, due in great degree to the poems of love and longing. Many, such as the lovely and exuberant **"Matins"** with its "well-spring of sweetness," suggest a romantic devotion reminiscent of troubadour songs, and others express love for a child. Though he has touched on this subject before, Montague has never devoted so much of his imagination to fatherhood as in **"Sibyl's Morning"** or **"A Small Death."** The former displays a sprightliness he seems to have contracted from Sibyl, "a happy elf, / sister to the early train whistle," and the absence of strife is a relief as he dotes on his waking child, intoning, "O my human kettle!" The latter poem dramatizes a daughter's discovery of a dead bird amid the failing abundance of nature, "decay's autumnal weft." Any principles or allegiances beyond the instinct to protect innocence are absent in this moment when she asks, "Why not fly?" What the poet can offer is a ceremony, immediate and proximate, to begin both the healing and the journey into experience under the threatening weather. He not only offers symbols but, in a prose poem, accepts them, as he shares tea with the child while a plane crosses over: "Filtered through the apple blossom its sound is as distant and friendly as the hum of a honey-seeking bee." Of course, even in moments of peace, Montague cannot play the optimist entirely: the honey is sought rather than found.

The opening section of Part 3 of **Collected Poems** presents a baker's dozen of verses centering on childhood experiences from the perspective of the outsider running afoul of institutions, primarily the straitjacketing regulations of the Church. These short lyrics and prose poems do not much extend Montague's range, but they effectively refresh some characteristic themes. In **"Deo Gratias,"** the poet bribes a classmate to replace him as altar boy, thus helping him conceal "the halting, disagreeable manner" of his speech problem. As penalty for his manipulations, he is sentenced to chant at High Mass, but his tormentor has overlooked what has kept Montague aloft for the last half-century: "The brisk Dean had forgotten that to sing, / albeit tunelessly, is possible to the stammering."

"A Welcoming Party" reviews Montague's belief that he has existed "always at the periphery of incident." In a more comical mode than he usually allows himself, the poet recalls attempting to visit Bernadette Devlin back in his student days. When the guards of **"Outside Armagh Jail, 1971"** refuse him entrance, he "intone[s] the scop stresses of my Derry poem," only to hear a guard within snickering, "'Boys, that was great crack! The Fenians / must be losing. This time they sent a lunatic.'" Lunatic, fool, philosopher, poet, taidgh, Montague. From the vantage of age and experience the narrator can revel in his role as wise jester. Recalling that Derry poem from **The Rough Field,** **"A New Siege,"**

one can hardly imagine the British or unionist squaddie, despite that poem's scattering of Irish vocabulary and relentless dimeter, laughing to anyone's shame but his own at

> Lines of suffering
> > lines of defeat
> under the walls
> > ghetto terraces
> sharp pallor of
> > unemployed shades . . .

Although neither the earlier dispatch nor this rehearsal pretends to any objective, unmarred view, the stammering poet has learned to defend his position without violence of deed or word.

The concluding narrative poem, **"Border Sick Call,"** first published in 1995 in *The Southern Review,* recalls in its four hundred lines "a journey in winter" (as one epigraph signals) along marginal territory, and it might well represent the poet's most idealistic longstanding ambition, to transcend the disease of hatred and cross boundaries for the purpose of healing. Passing "a Customs Post that has twice / leaped into the air" from explosives, Montague accompanies his brother through the Dantesque precinct along the invisible border whose denizens are too tormented by hardship to concern themselves with taking sides. The pair travel—first by car, then tractor, finally on "Shanks' mare"—deeper into the severe beauty of the hibernal wilderness. Entering "the heart of whiteness," they suffer cold and exhaustion to bring comfort and treatment to the "shades who step out from the shadows." The narrator, well past the middle of his life, has lost his way, but in this disorientation he gains the opportunity to rediscover himself.

The great power of this poem, one of Montague's finest since **The Rough Field,** resides in the two-dimensional healing that occurs. After the brothers leave behind the fragmented borderland, a threshold where they observe *"the impossible as normal, / lunacy made local,"* they move among those desperate for medical care. In order to give or to receive the succor they need, the travelers must cross "the surface bright, hard, treacherous," hearing "boots / sink, rasp over crusted snow" until they reach "dumb desolation," where stunned silence may lead to understanding and acceptance.

This surreal anabasis shares some plot and thematic strangeness with Kafka's "The Country Doctor," but Montague lacks the earlier writer's fatalism, and when one host offers a phial of home-brew, saying, "Take that medicine with you for the road home," the poem's tone begins to brighten. They must still witness a rowboat "chained in ice" and other features reminiscent of the Inferno's innermost circles, but the two sojourners begin to approach restoration to a valuable wholeness. Acting as the spirit of benison, the brother comments that "the real border is not between / countries, but between life and death." By journey's end, back at their beginning, they find what Seamus Montague felt upon first hearing Beethoven—"In the face of suffering, unexpected affirmation."

The poem concludes with the rhetorical "But in what country have we been?" The reader knows it is less Byzantium or the Ulster/Republic border than the country of the conflicted heart, where even the most ancient and dangerous artifacts—"spiked with icicles, a leafless thorn, / where the gate scringes on its stone"— are rendered lovingly. What the brothers have found is the rough field smoothed and finally soothing, and despite the threat and anguish of the jagged images, the reader may half wish for the journey to continue, as the trajectory toward light carries an exhilaration that cannot fail to salve when it is chronicled so scrupulously.

Although Montague's career might almost serve as a synecdoche for the course of Irish poetry since Yeats, the organization of his **Collected Poems** discourages that approach, just as it hinders any attempt to trace his evolution as a poet: the deepening of his themes over time, his mounting linguistic dexterity. His arrangement of work here does, however, evoke his own early suggestion that significant achievement results when "a man's life-work can be seen as a pattern, with individual works existing not so much in themselves, but as a part of a total elaboration and an investigation of themes." Certainly the ingenious peregrinations in Montague's writing, from loss to revival across public and private parishes, qualify his work as a great achievement, and the weave of the various narratives into sequences recalls, once again, the spiraling vines and birds, cats and serpents, in the great codices of Kells and Durrow. Whether the revelations and meticulous craft of Montague and his fellow Irish poets will help preserve reverence for the skillfully written word is yet uncertain, but his efforts, reinforcing his belief that "a *scop* or *file* is a blend of historian and priest," will testify that no age is wholly dark when dedicated artists offer their labors to illumine the path, and no pain or anger falls beyond the range of penance and subsequent joy.

Ben Howard (essay date February 1998)

SOURCE: Howard, Ben. "Irish Voices." *Poetry* 171, no. 4 (February 1998): 279-82.

[*In the following review of* Collected Poems, *Howard praises the combination of personal experience and cultural history that Montague treats in his poetry.*]

For nearly four decades John Montague has probed the intricacies of history and the enigmas of selfhood. At once a gifted lyric poet and a passionate cultural historian, he has limned the convergences of history and self, taking his own difficult experience as prime example. Born in Brooklyn in 1929, eight years after the partitioning of Ireland and the creation of the Irish Free State, Montague was brought back as an infant to Ireland and reared by his aunts in rural County Tyrone. That primal dislocation has shaped his work, as has the experience of coming to maturity in an emerging nation-state, ghosted by its Gaelic past and uncertain of its present identity. In forms ranging from the brief lyric to the book-length sequence, Montague has lamented both his nation's losses and his own, shoring sacred Gaelic fragments against his secular ruins. By turns tender and brutally realistic, his poems have exposed their author's wounds and his culture's scars. Yet if Montague has remained acutely aware of fragmentation and defeat, of "change driving its / blunt wedge through / what seemed permanent," he has also envisioned unity and wholeness. And if his poems have sometimes been cries of anguish and bursts of anger, they have also been acts of healing and restoration.

Handsomely produced by Wake Forest University Press, Montague's **Collected Poems** gathers the work of ten previous collections. Departing from convention, Montague has chosen to place his major booklength sequences (**The Rough Field,** 1972; **The Great Cloak,** 1978; and **The Dead Kingdom,** 1984) at the beginning, followed by his earlier collections in chronological order. This bold format has the virtue of featuring the poet's most ambitious work, while also charting his artistic development. To follow the trail from Montague's first collection (**Forms of Exile,** 1958) to his most recent (**Time in Armagh,** 1993) is to witness an undistinguished formal style evolving into something far more supple and personal—a gentle, sensuous line that hovers somewhere between formal verse and "open" form. Less linear is the growth of Montague's vision, which from the beginning has embraced both the private and the public, the personal and the collective dimensions of experience. Montague's subjects range from sexual encounters to riots in Belfast to his harsh Catholic schooling in the County Armagh. But whether he is recalling his rural childhood or excoriating English oppression, celebrating the joys of love or chronicling the violent history of Ulster, Montague's habit of mind is to view the personal as bearing on the historical, and vice versa. And though he revels in local history and local color, he brings to his sometimes parochial subjects an internationalist's perspective, attuned to dissolution but yearning for centrality and continuity.

The themes of fragmentation and discontinuity are hardly new to Irish poetry. They have been prominent since the collapse of the Gaelic order in the early seventeenth century. But in Montague's poems the familiar themes take on renewed energy and personal urgency, embodied as they are in the multiple contexts of family, intimate relationships, and Irish cultural history. In **"The Country Fiddler,"** a personal reflection on the Irish diaspora, Montague becomes the "unexpected successor" of a fiddle-playing uncle, whose "rural art" was "stilled in the discord of Brooklyn." In **"Herbert Street Revisited"** the poet returns to the scenes of his first marriage, recalling the couple's neighbors, who "[tread] the pattern / of one time and place into history." And in **"A Grafted Tongue,"** set in the national schools of nineteenth-century Ireland, Montague portrays Irish school-children struggling to learn English—and to unlearn their mother tongue. Returning to their Irish-speaking homes, they find "the turf-cured width / of [their] parent's hearth / growing slowly alien." Like the poet brooding on his dispersed family and his broken marriage, the children endure the ache of separation.

Were Montague to dwell exclusively on exile, emigration, and the "shards of a lost tradition," he would tell, at best, a one-sided story. And the elegiac note, already prominent in his work, might well become a melancholy drone. But in the larger expanse of Montague's *oeuvre,* the elegiac strain, however prominent, is only one voice in a complex historical dialectic. Running counter to his lamentations is a voice which discerns lines of continuity and urges a reconciliation of past and present cultures. That voice speaks softly in **"Old Mythologies,"** an early poem, where a "whole dormitory" of Gaelic heroes, their "proud deeds done," stirs beneath the "soft spring grass." It can be heard again, thirty years later, in **"History Walk,"** a prose poem which recounts the poet's visit, as a schoolboy in Armagh, to the "magic mound of Emain Macha, the hillfort of the Red Branch knights" and haunt of Conor and Cuchulainn. Although compelled by the Northern Ireland school curriculum to study English and Modern History, Montague took the longer view, sensing the ancient resonances of a sacred site. In his imagination, "the lost city of Ard Macha [Armagh] coiled in upon itself, whorl upon whorl, a broken aconite."

Similar perceptions, developed on a larger scale, inform *The Rough Field,* Montague's booklength meditation on the province of Ulster, past and present. Taking its title from the place name Garvaghey, Montague's native townland in Co. Tyrone (Garvaghey, in Irish, is *garbh acaidh,* "a rough field"), this magisterial sequence juxtaposes lyric and narrative poems, interpolated documents, glosses, and marginalia to create a polyphonic, multi-layered composition. The effect is to underscore both the gap and the connection between early Irish civilisation and the modern British province:

> I assert
>   a civilisation died here;
>   it trembles

underfoot where I walk these
    small, sad hills:
it rears in my blood stream
    when I hear
a bleat of Saxon condescension,
    Westminster
to hell, it is less than these
    strangely carved
five-thousand-year resisting stones,
    that lonely cross.

Such affirmations of lineage and allegiance define the landscapes of Montague's poems, and while they are sometimes moving, their effect is not always salutary. At their most insistent, they are more polemical than historical. Analogously, Montague's struggle to uncover lines of continuity in his private life may strike the skeptical reader as selective and less than sufficient. A case in point is a poem entitled **"A Real Irishman,"** in which a Protestant named Billy Davidson, befriended by Montague as a child, offers his protection, decades later, in a Protestant pub: "Lay a hand on him and you deal with Billy Davidson." Affecting though it is, this anecdote stops short of examining its premises and assertions.

Yet if Montague's assertions of continuity, historical and personal, sometimes appear tendentious, his poems amply demonstrate another kind of consistency: that of a single, unfolding sensibility, reflected in a distinctive style. Among the virtues of that style are its deft concision, its sensuous immediacy, its prominent narrative element, and its subtle musicality:

> At the centre, I find her
> beneath black hemlock, red cedar,
> halted on a carpet, a compost
> of fallen leaves, rusty haws
> and snowberries, knobbly chestnuts:
> decay's autumnal weft.
>
> A SMALL DEATH

Describing his daughter, Montague plays conversational rhythms against a loose trimeter line, affirming the meter only in the closing line. Patterns of assonance, inner rhyme (*center/find, her/cedar*), alliteration, and parallel phrasing (*fallen leaves, rusty haws*) stylize and intensify colloquial speech. Clearly defined but softly enjambed, the lines feel both natural and formal.

By such quiet feats, as much as by his spacious historical visions, Montague has done much to shape the sensibility of postwar Irish poetry. And it is in such moments, frequent in his *Collected Poems,* that his work seems most destined to endure.

Thomas Dillon Redshaw (essay date fall 1999)

SOURCE: Redshaw, Thomas Dillon. "Abstracting Icons: The Graphic Ornamentation of John Montague's

The Rough Field (1972) and *The Dead Kingdom* (1984)." *South Carolina Review* 32, no. 1 (fall 1999): 100-17.

[*In the following essay, Redshaw discusses the cover art and graphic embellishments of various editions of two of Montague's works.*]

The solid rectangularity of John Montague's **Collected Poems** (1995) houses much of his work newly reorchestrated, as the publisher's afterword notes. The book opens with new settings of **The Rough Field** (1972), **The Great Cloak** (1978), and **The Dead Kingdom** (1984), all originally published by Liam Miller's Dolmen Press, which issued Montague's **Selected Poems** (1982). A very comprehensive selection, this earlier volume closes with a reorchestration of **A Slow Dance** (1975) with the three titles already mentioned, the title of **The Dead Kingdom** lacking a date.[1] The poems in Montague's **Selected** lack iconic decoration, though the first half opens with Louis le Brocquy's cover drawing for **A Chosen Light** (1967) and the second half opens with John Derricke's Elizabethan woodblock of the dancing bard and closes with the seal of the United Irishmen—both icons first employed by Liam Miller in his setting of Montague's **Patriotic Suite** (1966).[2] In contrast, the 376 pages of Montague's **Collected** offer the reader no sense of the poems' heritance of emblems, and by design, for the book expresses the design conventions favored by Peter Fallon and Dillon Johnston.[3] There, in those opening pages, **The Rough Field** and **The Dead Kingdom** appear as words, epigrams, lyrics, and strophes alone.

The Dead Kingdom appeared from The Dolmen Press after Liam Miller had moved the enterprise out of Dublin to Mountrath, near Portlaoise and but a few years before his death in the late spring of 1987. Montague's new sequence was published with what Miller counted as the fourth edition of Montague's **The Rough Field** (1972). The latter had earned Montague international prominence and the former earned him his third recommendation from London's Poetry Book Society. Both books were designed by Liam Miller; both were conceived as a pair; and both were issued as trade publications, almost as "pocket editions"—as near to mass-market books as collections of poems can come. Unfortunately, both were printed on inexpensive paper having a high acid content and, thus, both books display an alarming tendency to yellow rapidly. Both have the same dimensions (19.5 mm by 12.75). **The Rough Field** has a greeny-gold cover and bears John Derricke's figure of the harper under the title; **The Dead Kingdom** has a violet-grey cover and bears a high-contrast photograph of a fetish from Boa Island, County Fermanagh, on the cover.[4] Clearly, and with Montague's approval, Miller designed the books as a contrastive pair and that contrast of emblematic vocabularies may have its own significance.

Miller's fourth edition of **The Rough Field** merely repeats in smaller format the design of the original and gives it the least inspired cover of all the poem's editions, and it preserves the original's lexicon of decoration, of visual epigraphs, drawn from Small's 1883 facsimile edition of John Derricke's *The Image of Irelande with A Discourie of Woodkarne.* Derricke's "Notable Discouery" occupies a calendar of twelve wood-block plates, and these Liam Miller exploited so assiduously in the service of Montague's poetry that quotations of Derricke's propagandizing illustrations became, somewhat ironically, one of the hallmarks of the Dolmen style—the other being the brushwork of Louis le Brocquy associated with Thomas Kinsella's *The Tain* (1969).[5]

Of course, The Dolmen Press displayed the talents of many artists and typographers in Ireland during its thirty-five years, and Miller lists them fondly in his introduction to *Dolmen XXV* (1976). The study of architecture formed Miller's tastes, and Dolmen's vocabulary of design during its first decade owed much less to the precedent of the Yeats sisters and Cuala Press and more to the English example set by Eric Gill and René Hague in the 1930s.[6] Elizabeth Rivers's decorations as well as Michael Biggs's letter-cutting, for instance, all reflect the ethos of design advocated in the work of The Golden Cockerell Press and Hague and Gill in the 1920s and 1930s. In the 1960s, as The Dolmen Press came to be the representative Irish "art" publisher, Miller chose to celebrate the centenary of the birth of W. B. Yeats with the twelve fascicles of the *Yeats Centenary Papers* (1965-68) and the half-centenary of the Easter Rising with **Patriotic Suite** (November, 1966). This was the first of "The New Dolmen Chapbooks." Thomas Kinsella had presided over the twelve parts of the first *Dolmen Chapbook* (1954-60). Miller describes **Patriotic Suite** as having been published "With reproductions of old cuts," but it contains one new "cut"—the chapbook emblem graven in Gill's manner by Tate Adams.[7]

Patriotic Suite, in both its trade and collector's editions, offers the reader three "old cuts": the closing seal of the United Irishmen who were responsible for the Rising of '98, and two from plates illustrating the "state and condition of the Wild men in Ireland" rising against the Pale and at length submitting to Sir Henry Sidney in 1578. The cover cut for **Patriotic Suite** shows: "Here creepes out of *Sainct Filchers denne,* a pack of prowling mates, / Most hurtfull to the English pale. . . ."[8] The war-piper is followed by swordsmen and infantry bearing halberds. Miller left out the rest of Derricke's plate in which, to the right, pikemen burn a house on the edge of the Pale, and at the top other infantry drive cattle away—along with an unhappy tenant on horseback. The title page of **Patriotic Suite** bears an old cut from Derricke's third plate, displaying the feast of Mac

Sweynes, O'Neill's gallowglasses, after a cattle raid or *bodrag.* This version appears as the cover of the 1989 Bloodaxe and Wake Forest printings of *The Rough Field.* And from this third plate Miller selected the archetypal figure of the harper seated at the bottom right of the plate: "Both *Barde,* and Harper, is preparde, which by their cunning art, / Doe strike and cheare up all the gestes, with comfort at the hart" (Derricke 125). That figure of the harper decorates the cover of the 1984 edition of *The Rough Field,* while the figure of the "barde," really a *reacaire* or "reciter," heads the title page.

Derricke's figure of the "barde" occurs on the title pages of all editions of *The Rough Field* except those last issued in 1989 by Gallery Press and Bloodaxe Books. The latter's cover reproduces, however, the whole corner of the plate—bard, harper, and the two serving men baring their arses to the fire. The Gallery Press edition excerpts from Derricke's Plate V a trio of Sidney's soldiers bearing the severed heads of the rebel "woodkarne." The first edition's brown cover excerpts the scene from Plate II of the house-burning, as does the second, though the third departs from Derricke's visual diction by reproducing the seal of the United Irishmen on an orange field. Moreover, as Montague's readers know, all ten cantos of *The Rough Field* open with icons drawn from Derricke's plates—but not quite all. The decoration for Canto X, **"The Wild Dog Rose,"** derives from the verbiage sheltering John Derricke's initials ("ID") under the feet of "Donolle obreane, the messenger," in Plate VII, to whom Sir Henry is giving a letter of "peace" to deliver to The O'Neill.[9] But Miller's version leaves out the messenger, Sir Henry bending down from his steed, and the pikemen ranked on either side. Instead, he has drawn in the "wild dog rose," *rosa rugosa,* as if to echo the Tudor rose, and the peace that the "honour of that Queene" prefers. The image is Miller's, not Derricke's.

So, *The Rough Field*'s lexicon of visual decoration may, in the main, be traced back to Miller's selection of Derricke's imagery for the 1966 setting of *Patriotic Suite.* There is clear evidence, though, that Miller thought to provide *The Rough Field*'s cantos with an entirely different vocabulary of emblems. In 1972 the Irish Book Publishers' Association published *Sampla,* an anthology of sample typography and design by thirteen Irish book houses. Dolmen contributed *The Rough Field*'s first canto, **"Home Again,"** decorated with an ink drawing of "Dagda's Cauldron," a Bronze Age Celtic artifact recently unearthed in Monaghan.[10] It is likely that Miller executed the drawing himself, from archeological photographs, before June, 1971. A larger rendition of the cauldron appears on a "specimen" printing of the canto dated June, 1971. This suggests that, had his energies not been distracted by the business of publishing, Miller might have created a complete set of

drawings for the poem and, thus, a very different and differently evocative vocabulary of emblems.

But, after many meetings with Montague, Miller returned to the precedent of *Patriotic Suite.* Commemorating the fiftieth anniversary of the Easter Rising, Montague's sequence is dedicated to the composer Seán Ó Riada, who composed the film music for a trio of documentary films funded by Gael Linn: *Mise Éire* (1959), *Saoirse* (1960), and *An Tine Bheo* (1966). In the first film, for example, Ó Riada fatefully orchestrates variations on "Roisín Dubh" to go with documentary footage of the Rising edited by George Morrison. Thus, Miller set the cut of Derricke's "pyper" leading the kerne—a figure killed off in Plate IX—on the cover and at the head of *Patriotic Suite.* Montague's "suite" of poems steals some effects from American Modernism and others from Austin Clarke's curmudgeonly satire of the 1950s. Each movement in the suite satirizes the failure of the Easter Rising with atmospheric variations on the historical ironies created by raised expectations, as in **"Build-Up"**:

> Elegant port-wine brick, a colonial dream:
> *Now we own the cow, why keep the cream?*[11]

While Montague's poems here form little more than a narrative of scornful disappointments, the narrative of the Rising itself was one of immediate failure, and the narrative of Derricke's propagandizing plates is that of eventual "comming in of *Thirlaugh Leonaugh* the great *Oneale* of Ireland submitting himselfe to the right honorable Syr *Henry Sydney*" (Derrick 119).

In all editions of *The Rough Field* (1972-1989), *Patriotic Suite* opens with the same "old cut" from Derricke. Indeed, Miller raided Derricke's plates shamelessly, and in picking images from Derricke's pictorial narrative he let the topical force of Montague's lines, poems, and cantos determine the choice of icon in terms of direct correspondence. For instance, canto four, **"A Severed Head,"** opens not only with quotations from Sir John Davies and George Hill, but also with the image in Derricke's fifth plate of Sidney's men leading the troops back with two swordsmen holding Irish heads high like olives on toothpicks and a musketeer gripping a bleeding head by the glib. The same image appears on the cover of Peter Fallon's 1989 printing of *The Rough Field.* Here the images stolen from Derricke's Elizabethan narrative of a failed rising—of Irish submission and of English dominance—have been reordered according to cues raised by the distant and ultimately autobiographical effects of that rising in the raising of central persona of *The Rough Field.* And it is not entirely clear whether the modern autobiographical narrative of Mac an Teigue the poet succeeds in subverting the fragments Derricke's antique triumph of Sir Henry Sidney, the father of Sir Philip the poet.

Taking the 1984 "pocket edition" setting of *The Rough Field* together with that of *The Dead Kingdom* reveals, as noted before, a clear contrast. Taking the Exile Editions printing of *The Dead Kingdom* as an example, the cover image of the latter is a photograph of a "real" object that the tourist might witness at Boa Island. Like the cantos of *The Rough Field,* those of *The Dead Kingdom* come laden with epigraphs, but the proportions of sources is reversed: two-thirds of *The Rough Field*'s epigraphs come straight out of Irish history; two-thirds of *The Dead Kingdom*'s epigraphs come straight out of, for want of a better term, "world literature." Likewise, in *The Dead Kingdom,* the titular emblems heading each canto are photographic renditions of "real" objects, but those have "world" status, as the objects themselves depict mythic archetypes whose significances float free of the currents of history.

Like *The Rough Field,* the cantos of *The Dead Kingdom* document and enact another failure to return, a journey north to the purlieux of Fintona, the Sperrin hills, and County Tyrone—and to the burials of his aunt Winifred Montague and his mother Mary (or "Molly") Carney—foster mother and mother.[12] Montague orchestrates the phases of his return into five cantos. Each is tagged with epigraphs. The whole poem starts with a line from Pablo Neruda, and the cantos follow with epigraphs in prose and verse, with sources and without; from religion (*The Epic of Gilgamesh*); from world literature (Kafka, Beckett, Hesse); from Tyrone folksong and Cork pub-talk; and from poetry and pop song (Johns, Donne and Lennon). And the frame of allusion tends to shift from the archetypal to the typical, as if to incarnate the particular biography, the particular mourning of the poems with the universal, as if to assert the momentary inhabitation of the particular by the eternal. Likewise, from cover to last canto, *The Dead Kingdom*'s essentially photographic decorations have a similar framing effect on the suites of poems in the collection.

As noted before, *The Dead Kingdom*'s cover offers a high-contrast photograph of a sixth-century carving found on Boa Island—a head fetish related to the Horned God cult of northern Celtic culture of the La Tène period—a figure that identifies the poet and persona of the poems and echoes the autobiographical *tête coupée* motifs in *The Rough Field.* Answering or challenging that in a thoroughly Oedipal manner is the larger photographic image on the half-title page. The image seems both to represent and to cause overexposure. This, of course, is the legendary Sheelah-na-Gig (*Cíle na gCíoch*) beloved by aficionados of Gravesian muse-worship. The National Gallery has this piece in captivity in the Dawson Collection (725.2). It was taken from the Old Church in Cavan town. Myth critics offer parallel identifications of the figure: it is Babd or Baubo, the Personified Yoni, the Divine Hag, or the Heraldic

Woman. And here, in such precedential position, its meanings serve as premises for the agonies of mourning that the poems enact. Canto I, **"Upstream,"** offers a clearer, but smaller and less potent photographic emblem: a tomb model of a Nile boat meant to stand concretely for the transportation of the dead soul up the River of Life. This object, like the one following can be seen in the British Museum. For Canto II, **"This Neutral Realm,"** Miller's setting offers a starker and bigger emblem, but one from an actual Viking ship sunk in the River Scheldt and not a Nile model. The prow is four feet, nine inches tall in actuality, and the dragon finial aptly terminates in a depiction of fierce finality. Threat is the motive, as may be said of photographic emblem for Canto III, **"The Black Pig."** Montague's title there alludes to Irish mythology, but the object is Gaulish and was found at Neuvy-en-Sullias in Loiret. Though large (over two feet tall), this bronze is entirely typical of Celtic metal work, and the image is entirely conventional and figures in Continental Celtic lore.

The closing two cantos of *The Dead Kingdom* come prefaced by epigraphs explicitly framing the never-concluded family romance at the heart of Montague's mourning sequences. Canto V, **"A Flowering Absence,"** begins after John Lennon's lines: "Mother, you had me but I never had you / I wanted you but you didn't want me. . . ."[13] And the epigraph follows a selection from a newspaper illustration, perhaps from Walt Whitman's Brooklyn *Eagle*—a steel engraving depicting the Roeblings' Brooklyn Bridge on its opening day. It is a "real" image, a documentary image, but it also provides a symbol already defined by American popular culture and by Hart Crane. Despite its festivity, the symbol bridges past with present mourning, the sorrow of loss with the sorrow of abandonment, the unassuaged infantile trauma at the heart of the adult family romance. Preceding that comes **"The Silver Flask,"** Canto IV, and its epigraphic assertion of the same trauma:

> FIRST CUSTOMER: My mother? My mother was the real woman in my life. Every night I pray to her.

and:

> I never haid a mammy
> she soon gave me up
> I never haid a daddy
> he was always on the sup. . . .
>
> (*TDK* [*The Dead Kingdom*] 58)

These follow a photograph probably printed Victorian-style from a glass negative, for dimly in the upper left corner can be seen "Co. Tyrone" scratched in the negative by the photographer. This is a "real" image, a document. The man and woman posed stiffly against the *trompe-l'oeil* studio set are the parents. Though uncertain, the date can be no later than 1924 or 1925, when James Montague left Tyrone for Brooklyn owing to his Republican partisanship at the close of the Irish Civil War. Apparently mounted on a stiff card, the photograph seems something like a saint's card, something like a mass card. Though historically bound, the wedding photograph and the steel engraving have been posed to assume archetypal status that is both the equal of and the prior images and icons. The myths of history create the characteristic sacrifices of individuals.

A limited printing of *The Dead Kingdom*'s second canto, **"This Neutral Realm,"** from a small press in North Tonawanda, New York, reveals that other lexicons of design may be deployed as well in aid of Montague's themes.[14] Montague's published collections draw on two design traditions. Starting with the political ironies of *Patriotic Suite* (1966), Liam Miller exploited the resources of Derricke's sixteenth-century visual narrative depicting Sir Henry Sidney's triumphal command of Elizabethan Ireland from Dublin Castle. And Irish presses other than Dolmen followed suit, as may be seen in the example of the Arts Council of Northern Ireland's *Planter and Gael* souvenir program of 1970. In contrast, the Dolmen setting of *The Dead Kingdom* exploited photographs of objects assumed to have archetypal significance in the more fundamental narrative of human consciousness. Choosing these emblems to "lead" the stages of the persona's mourning journey seems an obviously encyclopedic tactic.

But the Bolt Court Press setting of **"This Neutral Realm,"** suggests that other, more abstract emblems may serve as well. Centered on the spine, the wrapper decoration squares the circle twice, giving four green fields outside the analogous and larger black fields of mourning. The dominant field of mourning or mortality is askew, not vertical, and it bounds a large circle containing a trinity of green circles—the primal family—each containing an ego conflicted but balanced. The Yin/Yang duality seems obvious, along with other archetypes redolent of Jung popularized in "New Age" spirituality—the whole circle, the mandala. The squared circle, the cross, the monstrance, the shackled sacred heart of North Republicanism appears again on the title page, but here the bounding, perhaps nationalist green square contains the square of mourning quartered, as if to represent the wafer of the Eucharist. By the time Montague's reader has read the canto's epigraphs on the flaps of the wrapper and has reached this page, it should be plain that this edition's designer, Joanne Dus-Zastrow, has given the Montague's canto a fresh lexicon of affecting emblems each composed of a primary color—green and red, the colors that dominate Stephen Dedalus's family romance—or of black and white and reduced, geometric shapes—square, circle, triangle, sections, and rules.

Once announced, the same abstracted elements may be combined and recombined not quite so suggestively as music and not so explicitly as illustration. Facing the poem **"Bog Royal,"** Dus-Zastrow poses a vertical square in thin black around an inner square in black, which contains the phallic image of domineering technology—one found throughout Europe—of the concrete cooling tower of a power plant, usually nuclear as at Sellafield alias Windscale. Here the allusion is to the Republic's peat-burning facility created by Bord na Móna and ESB. The border background of green squares suggests new-cut turves stacked in ricks according to the old custom. Both poem and emblem pose a Romantic irony by posing Ireland's willingness to burn both her Nature and her Fenian past to power what has lately become the feverish, high-employment economy of the "Celtic Tiger":

> Come back, Paddy Reilly
> to your changed world;
> pyramids of turf stored
> under glistening polythene:
> chalk white power stations,
> cleaned swathes of bog,
> a carpet sucked clean!

> (*TNR* [*This Neutral Realm*] 4)

Facing **"A Slight Fragrance,"** the next poem in **"This Neutral Realm,"** Dus-Zastrow poses the cover emblem against autobiographical memoir of a first summer romance "with one of the Caffrey's" during the austere years right after World War II, the wreckage of Europe around Ireland's "green" neutrality. Here is the promise of the family romance:

> I cycled
> with her to buy strawberries
> from the local big house,
> fairy-tale Tullynally;. . . .

> (*TNR* 7)

Memory provides the end of the idyll not only in the erotic and autumnal image of the bay hunter surprising them on the path, but also in the turning cycles or circles large and small: the image of the carbide-lamp reflector, of the whirling wheels of bicycles and traps, the roundness of turret and motte. As before, here the designer ends the text of the poem on the page with a small black square set askew. The next poem, **"Red Island,"** by contrast, gets no emblem of its own and is marked terminally by a small red square set askew. And here it may be that the poem's moments, not just its title, are squared in that period: the island and "sunstruck lake," the catch of perch and pike, the assault upon Sionnain, daughter of Lir, and the tragedy of Fionnuala.

What is plain, though, is that the bull emblem for **"Lake Dwelling: Crannóg"** also faces **"Red Island,"** as if **"Lake Dwelling"** were the story of **"Red Island"** continued, made consequential, as if loving and rowing, fishing and gutting, were reductions of hunting and slaughtering—the primal pursuits of the first family, the neolithic Irish tribe. The last stanza describes lying in wait for prey, alert for "the wary crackle of a hoof on grass." Literally, the bull emblem depicts the musk-ox of the poem. Alone, the emblem recalls the North, Ulster, the famous bulls of the *Táin-Bó-Cúailgne,* the ancient and very contemporary dependence of Ireland upon the wealth of cattle, the labor of herding and slaughtering, and the corrupting economics of their marketing as documented by Fintan O'Toole's analysis of the Beef Tribunal of the 1980s. And perhaps that is why the bull's nose the triangle hazard sign. But why might it be that a chalice rests on his forehead?

Turning to the next page reveals the heraldic intent of Zus-Dastrow's designs more clearly. These emblems have become several degrees more representative than before. As before, the next two poems are decorated by an elaborate emblem and punctuated by a red square skewed. **"Sword Land"** comes to one side of the emblem; **"This Neutral Realm"** faces it. While **"Sword Land"** dwells on the Viking and Norman depredations, it opens and closes with two versions of the sobriquet drawn from the Bardic poet Tadhgh Dall Ó hUiginn:

> Rehearse Tadhg Dall's phrase
> *Ferann cloidhimh, crioc Bhanba:*
> Mountjoy's name for this land—
> Ire land: Sword Land?

(TNR 10)

The question posed seems conclusively answered in Dus-Zastrow's emblem. The horns of the bull decorate the helm and hilt of the Viking sword. The blade of the sword and the nose guard of the helm are decorated with the red square skewed that closes the facing page. The whole is in a red rectangle a little less than twice the size of the usual large squarings. The vertical and horizontal lines in black seem also to suggest another, more Teutonic helmet. The sword intersects three crossed arcs in red suggesting a blooded fragment of Celtic ornament, a cradle, a chalice.

The canto's title poem faces this page, so it is worth noting that the colors are those of Nazi heraldry. **"This Neutral Realm,"** with its epigraph from the BBC broadcaster and Northern poet Louis MacNeice, articulates these themes directly.

> So we learnt to defend
> this neutral realm,
> each holiday summer,
> against all comers. . . .

(TNR 11)

The heraldic punctuation of this poem binds **"This Neutral Realm"** and **"Sword Land"** together around the Viking, Teutonic icon as if to insist upon the nearly

defenseless position of Ireland in Medieval times and modern. Here—culturally or biographically—militarism comes from the outside. The idyll of neutrality thus becomes native.

"The Music Box" concludes above one of Dus-Zastrow's more riddling emblems. The poem itself offers a placid recollection of one of Montague's more familiar tropes: the childhood encounter with the *cailleach.* The same Jungian type figures in Montague's early poem **"Like Dolmens Round My Childhood, The Old People"** (1958) and the very Marian last canto of *The Rough Field* (1972), **"The Wild Dog Rose."**[15] Here, by way of elegy, the poet remembers the crippled witch's music box, "a small figure on its rosewood top / swirling slowly, timeless dancer." The emblem shows the dancer as a trapezoid balanced on a red rectangle. This rests on a frieze of black squares placed inside a larger red square. Above the music box and dancer is a red oval and to the right of both appears to be a red protractor shape colored black inside. The two shapes together abstractly form the bend and mortal figure of the old woman. From another perspective, the red square lined with the black frieze becomes the table top and cloth over which she bends and the whitewashed, sooty walls of the cottage kitchen.

Directly after this imposing emblem comes another one leading and facing the three-part poem **"The Well Dreams."** Again, the colors are black and red. The elements of this emblem are new. A large square formed of wide black rules underscored by a thin and then a broad red rule. These do not intersect. Within the square Dus-Zastrow has arranged crescents of black whose interior points orbit and then intersect an off-center black circle. This is "the single eye / of the well" that "dreams on, / a silent cyclops" (*TNR* 15). In Ireland, a well may open down into the earth, or it may be a spring-fed pool in a cranny formed by stonework or by a path on the side of hill. Here, it seems, we are looking down into the earth of the page, as the perspective created by the falling, diminishing red triangles suggests. These are the poem's gross interruptions of coin and question. Montague's lines refrain from the usual concrete allusions to salmon or trout, to Fionn and his thumb, or even to so particular a saint as Gobnait, though the bushes around bear votive offerings.

The process of the poem recounts this: "And the well recomposes itself." That is why Dus-Zastrow closes the poem and the canto with a figure exceptional for its use of curves. This is not the divisive period of the skewed black or red square. The dominant is the suggestion of arcs completed as circles: the well opening, the dark of the water, the gleam of light off it, and then posed above it the body of the bird, the breast of the bird, its beak and cockade, the perfect circle of its seeing eye. The only square gives the green of Ireland watched over, guarded by—to recall Yeats—"those dying generations at their song." To the well, these seem "the same robin, / thrush, blackbird or wren" (*TNR* 16)—all potent totems in Irish folklore.

Three families of graphic ornament have accompanied the publication of John Montague's *The Rough Field* and *The Dead Kingdom,* and these have nuanced the visual reception of his poetry from 1967 through 1989. These are: the Antiquarian or Elizabethan, the Archival, and the Abstract. The first and most dominant family is ironically, the Elizabethan. Its antiquarian romance proved attractive to Liam Miller's eye not so much because his model of design was the work of Eric Gill and his heirs, nor because he espoused layered ironies latent in English representations of the quaint Irish from the age of Elizabeth on, nor even because these decorations bore a family resemblance to the typographic traditions represented by the Yeats sisters and their Cuala Press or by the Salkelds and their Gayfield Press editions. Rather, Miller saw in the crudeness of Derricke's imagery a counter to canons of ornament and design then dominant in England in the idiom of Eric Ravilious, John Luke, or Rowel Friers dating from the late 1940s. Dolmen printings of the 1950s and early 1960s present ornament in that tradition by, for example, Tate Adams, Michael Biggs, Mia Cranwell, and Elizabeth Rivers, among others. Miller's choice of the Elizabethan or the Antiquarian idiom based on borrowings from Derricke came to be a hallmark of "the Dolmen style." Likewise, it came to define Montague as a poet in a narrow, if interestingly ironic, manner. Unfortunately, of the three families of graphic ornament that Montague's printers have deployed on the page with his lines, poems, and cantos, the Elizabethan seems to dominate, and Montague's reader sometimes must strain through that dominance to see the poem and hear it aright.

Less frequently have Montague's poems been ornamented in the Archival mode, largely in limited, boxed editions coming from the Dolmen Press. The chief exemplar of this lexicon is *The Dead Kingdom* in the 1984 edition.[16] The decorations—scrapbook clippings, old photos—to this edition reinforce the reader's perception of Montague as an essentially autobiographical poet, and one who sees that story in both confessionally or genealogically specific and mythic terms. This perception has confirmed the impatience of some readers with Montague's familial sorrows, and that impatience can diminish the genuine stature of some of Montague's repeated themes—emigration and binationality, fosterage and abandonment. Such an impatience chances impoverishing the poems, many of which are more independent of their autobiographical anchorings than strophes from Allen Ginsberg, dream songs from John Berryman, or love letters from Ted Hughes.

It would be reassuring to resort to the metaphor of musical composition in order to set Joanne Dus-Zastrow's invention of an abstract lexicon of ornament for one canto of *The Dead Kingdom.* Certainly her novel manipulation of geometric figures into nearly representative emblems carries with it less pre-existing baggage and so does less to predetermine the reader's notion of the poet and the poem. Even so, her lexicon does suggest that *poesis* consists fundamentally of perceiving the basic shapes of things. the simple rudiments of human experience, and of recombining them for the reader and, thus, of asking the reader to listen to a stanza or a story as if it were an emblem composed of abstract elements, as if the burden of its gravity were more formal than thematic. Consequently, Montague's reader may be prompted to risk a reductive reading of a poem in hopes of arriving at an innovatory one. Even so, to have this poet's sequences and "orchestrations" liberated visually from the dominance of the Antiquarian or Archival—from the story of Ireland and the story of the poet—and nuanced anew by such designers as Dus-Zastrow would genuinely enrich both the critical and the common reader's understanding of John Montague's strophes and cantos.

Notes

1. Readers interested in the intricate transatlantic publishing history of Montague's writing may wish to consult the following descriptive checklists by Thomas Dillon Redshaw: "The Books of John Montague," in *Hill Field: Poems and Memoirs for John Montague* (Minneapolis: Coffee House Press; Oldcastle: The Gallery Press, 1989), pp. 95-108; or "Books by John Montague: A Descriptive Checklist, 1958-1988," *Irish University Review,* 19:1 (Spring, 1989), 139-58.

2. John Montague, *Selected Poems* (Dublin: The Dolmen Press; Winston-Salem, NC: Wake Forest UP, 1982), pp. 8, 99, 190. The limited, signed, and boxed Dolmen edition also bears an enlarged figure of the bard, printed on blue laid paper, on the front board of the binding.

3. Richard Eckersley, of the University of Nebraska Press, took the Dolmen *Selected* (1982) as the model for Montague's *Collected* (1995) and reset *The Rough Field* without the Derricke decorations. The musical analogy—"reorchestrations"— cited in the afterword of the *Collected* was supplied by Peter Fallon of The Gallery Press. E-letter, Dillon Johnston to author, October 3, 1996.

4. *The Dead Kingdom* was also issued in this format by Wake Forest University Press and by Exile Editions in Toronto, but Barry Callaghan also printed the book from the Dolmen plates in a larger, more rectangular format (22.5 mm by 14.5)

imitating that of the first Dolmen edition of *The Rough Field* (1972). The larger format made possible a clearer presentation of *The Dead Kingdom*'s emblems.

5. The last Dolmen mark—three brushstrokes giving the profile of a dolmen—was executed by the Irish artist Louis le Brocquy (1916), and le Brocquy created the other chief lexicon of Dolmen decoration with his brush drawings for Thomas Kinsella's often reprinted translation *The Tain,* published as Dolmen Edition IX in September, 1969. This boxed edition of 1,750 copies immediately became a rarity.

6. Montague's connection to the Gill-Hague artistic tradition is reflected in Douglas Sealy, "Three Snapshots," in *Hill Field: Poems and Memoirs for John Montague,* ed. Thomas Dillon Redshaw (Minneapolis: Coffee House Press; Oldcastle: The Gallery Press, 1989), pp. 90-92.

7. Liam Miller, *Dolmen XXV: An Illustrated Bibliography of The Dolmen Press 1951-1976* ([Dublin]: The Dolmen Press, 1976), p. 46.

8. John Derricke, *The Image of Ireland, with A Discouerie of Woodkarne* (1581), ed. John Small (Edinburgh: Adam and Charles Black, 1883), [p. 123]; hereafter cited parenthetically, thus: (Derrick 123).

9. Lucid summaries of these events may be found in: Edmund Curtis, *A History of Ireland* (1936; London: Methuen, 1965), pp. 167-220; G. A. Hayes-McCoy, "The Tudor Conquest (1534-1603)," in *The Course of Irish History,* ed. T. W. Moody, F. X. Martin (New York: Weybright and Talley, 1967), pp. 174-88.

10. John Montague, "*Home Again,* from *The Rough Field,*" in *Sampla: A Selection of New Writing under the Imprint of Nine Irish Publishers* (Dublin: Irish Book Publishers' Association / Cumann Leabhar-fhoilsitheoirí Éireann, 1972), pp. [11-18]. The canto appears set in Caslon of Dalmore laid paper with a short prose preface. The title, initial capital, and ending horizontal rule are printed in terra cotta. The cauldron drawing appears centered in black below the author's name and above the first line of Montague's preface.

11. John Montague, *Patriotic Suite* ([Dublin]: The Dolmen Press, 1966), p. 12. One of the New Dolmen Chapbooks, this pamphlet was also issued in a specially bound collectors' edition in slipcase. Both examples make extensive use of images excerpted from Derricke's plates, but the closing decoration is a woodcut by Tate Adams and the penultimate emblem is the seal of the United Irishmen struck from "the original woodblock" dating from the 1790s.

12. For more relevant biographical details, see the biographical notes appended to John Montague, *The Figure in the Cave and Other Essays,* ed. Antoinette Quinn (Dublin: Lilliput Press; Syracuse: Syracuse UP, 1989), 221-6.

13. John Montague, *The Dead Kingdom* (Mountrath: The Dolmen Press, 1984), p. 82. The same setting "Designed by Liam Miller," of the book was issued also by Blackstaff Press in England, Exile Editions in Canada, and Wake Forest UP in the United States.

14. The colophon gives the edition as one hundred numbered copies and twenty-six lettered copies, all signed by the author. See John Montague, *The Dead Kingdom*: Part II: *This Neutral Realm* (North Tonawanda NY: Bolt Court Press, December 1984), [p. 18]; hereafter cited parenthetically, thus: (*TNR* 18).

15. John Montague, *Poisoned Lands and Other Poems* (London: MacGibbon and Kee, 1961), pp. 18-19; John Montague, *The Rough Field* (Dublin: The Dolmen Press, 1972), pp. 75-77.

16. The boxed, limited edition of *The Dead Kingdom* was printed in a more rectangular format (213 mm by 130) and bound in gloomy marbled paper boards with a black calf spine and gold lettering. Limited to 125 signed copies, this printing of *The Dead Kingdom* succeeds in presenting the visual emblem more effectively than the trade edition simply because it has been printed on heavier, laid paper.

Works Cited

Curtis, Edmund. *A History of Ireland.* 1936; London: Methuen, 1965.

John Derricke. *The Image of Irelande, with a Discouerie of Woodkarne.* 1581; Edinburgh: Adam and Charles Black, 1883.

Hayes-McCoy, G. A. "The Tudor Conquest (1534-1603)," in *The Course of Irish History.* Ed. T. W. Moody, F. X. Martin. New York: Weybright and Talley, 1967.

Miller, Liam. *Dolmen XXV: An Illustrated Bibliography of The Dolmen Press 1951-1976.* Dolmen Editions XXV. [Dublin:] The Dolmen Press, 1976.

Montague, John. *A Chosen Light.* London: MacGibbon and Kee, 1967.

———. *Collected Poems.* Winston-Salem, NC: Wake Forest UP, 1995.

———. *The Dead Kingdom.* Mountrath: The Dolmen Press, 1984.

————. *The Dead Kingdom.* Toronto: Exile Editions, 1984.

————. *The Dead Kingdom.* Part II: *This Neutral Realm.* North Tonawanda, NY: Bolt Court Press, December 1984.

————. *The Figure in the Cave and Other Essays.* Ed. Antoinette Quinn. Dublin: The Lilliput Press; Syracuse: Syracuse UP, 1989.

————. *Home Again,* in *Sampla: A Selection of New Writing under the Imprint of Nine Irish Publishers.* Dublin: Irish Book Publishers' Association / Cumann Leabharfhoilsitheoirí Éireann, 1972.

————. and John Hewitt. *The Planter and the Gael.* Belfast: Arts Council of Northern Ireland, 1970.

————. *Patriotic Suite.* The New Dolmen Chapbooks. Dublin: The Dolmen Press, November 1966.

————. *Selected Poems.* Winstom-Salem, NC: Wake Forest UP, 1982.

————. *The Rough Field.* Dublin: The Dolmen Press, 1972.

————. *The Rough Field.* 4th ed. Winston-Salem, NC: Wake Forest UP, 1984.

————. *The Rough Field.* 5th ed. Notes by Thomas Dillon Redshaw. Winston-Salem: NC: Wake Forest UP, 1989.

Redshaw, Thomas Dillon. *Hill Field: Poems and Memoirs for John Montague.* Minneapolis: Coffee House Press; Loughcrew: The Gallery Press, 1989.

————. "Books by John Montague: A Descriptive Checklist, 1958-88." *Irish University Review,* 19: 1 (Spring, 1989), 139-58.

Gerald Mangan (review date 2001)

SOURCE: Mangan, Gerald. "Cows Have No Religion." *Parnassus* 26, no. 1 (2001): 247-62.

[*In the following review, Mangan discusses the poetry of Montague's 1995* Collected Poems *and the 2001 volume* Smashing the Piano, *contending that many of the poems are informed by Montague's "lifelong sense of dislocation."*]

John Montague concluded his **Collected Poems** with a long new sequence called **"Border Sick Call,"** which recounts a winter journey through the hills of the Donegal-Fermanagh border. It is undertaken in the company of his brother, a country doctor who is braving the white-out weather to visit his most isolated patients; and their destination is one of the wildest parishes of the region, a long way above the bomb-scarred customs-posts that demarcate the U.K. from the Irish Republic. The tortuous line of the border has grown indistinct by the time the travelers are forced to abandon their snow-blocked car, and it has effectively dissolved by the end of their uphill slog on foot. The political map proves to have little meaning for the inhabitants at this altitude, remote from urban amenities and conventions; and the border appears as no more than a figment in the eyes of one octogenarian hill-farmer, who reminisces at his fireside as the doctor tends his wife. He delivers one of the poem's most resonant remarks, as he recalls his pre-war career as a cattle-smuggler:

'I made a packet in the old days,
before this auld religious thing came in.
You could run a whole herd through
between night and morning, and no one
the wiser, bar the B-Specials . . .
Border be damned, it was a godsend.
Have you ever noticed, cows have no religion?'

"Border Sick Call" can be recommended as a useful introduction to the essential Montague. Its journey is one of the many return-visits to Ulster that have furnished a pretext for exploring his own 1930s childhood in rural Tyrone; but it takes us back much further, beyond history and autobiography, to a characteristic vision of nature that transcends the political definitions of the province. The travelers have climbed into the past by visiting this Sleepy Hollow, whose isolation has immunized it from the plague of sectarian strife; and it is soon clear that the poem's center of gravity lies in this wish-fulfilling image of a timeless Ireland, where the 1922 Partition Treaty has not yet divided the island into murderous factions. The farmer's story evokes the myth-shrouded, pre-Christian era of the Ulster cattle-raids ("the oldest of Irish traditions . . . / as old as the *Tain*"); and the poet's geological perspective reaches all the way back to the glaciers that formed the hills ("eskers of hardness / always within us, / a memory of coldness"). Even the snow serves as a unifying influence in this vision, by restoring the landscape to a condition of virginity:

When we stride again on the road,
there is a bright crop of stars,
the high, clear stars of winter,
the studded belt of Orion,
and a silent, frost-bright moon
upon snow crisp as linen
spread on death or bridal bed.

The image is best appreciated when we know how frequently Montague has imagined Ireland as the dismembered victim of a brutish imperialism. The border is an open wound, in the stark terms of this metaphor; and we must also remember that the violent consequences of Partition are closely associated with the emotional turmoils of his own early life. Revisiting the past has often been a deliberate act of recuperation, in more than one sense; and it is clearly no coincidence that his companion in this case should be his brother Seamus, a healer by profession, whose presence implies a measure of reconciliation with their common past. In a territory where the political wound is closed, his compassionate mission becomes doubly symbolic. ("'The real border,'" he says, after a tongue-loosening mouthful of poteen, "'is not between / countries, but between life and death. / That's where the doctor comes in.'") Echoes of Dante invite us to see him as a kind of Virgil, and the brothers' "purgatorial" journey as a soul-cleansing "pilgrimage," where the purity of the snow finally suggests the sacramental atmosphere of a procession to Lourdes. The wilderness has played this remedial role throughout Montague's work, in poems where nature mends the damaged spirit; but this nostalgic glimpse of redemption takes us deeper than ever into the heartland of his imagination. It's a wilderness with a clear view of paradise, whose fauna demonstrate the art of living in harmony.

* * *

In **"Border Sick Call"** we can also see an image of Montague's own career. He occupies an isolated and curiously ill-defined niche in the crowded pantheon of Irish poetry, and some of this must be due to his perception of himself as a born outsider, who has often chosen the least-trodden paths. In the earliest poems, from *Forms of Exile* (1958) to *Poisoned Lands* (1961), we can see him measuring himself for the mantle of Yeats, like most ambitious young Irish poets of that period. But his poetic lineage has been complicated by his birth in 1929 in New York, where he spent the first four years of his life with his Irish parents, and a formative period as a young post-graduate student in the U.S., which exposed him to the enduring influences of Lowell, Creeley, and the Beats. These American intonations were later to endow him with a certain maverick status in literary Belfast, a stuffy and predominantly Protestant milieu by his own account, which soon marked him out as a trouble-stirring spokesman for the unsung rural Catholic. Much of his subsequent career has been spent as a university lecturer in the more tolerant southern city of Cork, interspersed with long sojourns in France and the U.S.; but his exile from Northern Ireland has certainly not discouraged him from entering its fray, as poet and public figure. There is, indeed, some evidence that his physical distance from the conflict has induced him to internalize it, in ways which over-simplify the public issues.

Politics and autobiography have frequently converged in Irish literature, to dramatic effect. The political evolution of Yeats can be traced quite precisely through his friendships and infatuations; and he drew some inspiration from the tragic example of James Clarence Mangan, the early-Victorian *poète maudit,* who sublimated his personal frustrations in a Romantic patriotism of his own invention. Montague invokes this tradition in support of his own practice, when he identifies the "Troubles" of his country with the scars of his own past; but it is not quite so easy, in Montague's case, to establish exactly how or why this conflation occurs. It points to an intricate nexus of private traumas, originating in his fraught relationship with his separated parents, but it is woven so deeply into the texture of his imagination that he is inclined to take our complicity for granted, without benefit of elucidation. Before we stumble on the few poems that clarify the facts, we are allowed to imagine a whole house full of skeletons and unquiet ghosts, deriving from a dark family history of violence and bereavement. **"Like Dolmens Round My Childhood"** is a typically murky recollection of the forbidding presence of his elders:

> Ancient Ireland, indeed! I was reared by her bedside,
> The rune and the chant, evil eye and averted head,
> Fomorian fierceness of family and local feud.
> Gaunt figures of fear and of friendliness,
> For years they trespassed on my dreams . . .

There is a fine example of this obfuscation in his new collection *Smashing the Piano,* where a sequence called "Civil Wars" deals directly with some of the best-known chapters of recent Ulster history. After a requiem for the martyred I.R.A. hunger-striker Bobby Sands ("This is the sound of the bone / breaking through the skin / of a slowly wasting man . . ."), and a lament for the victims of the Omagh bomb ("We learn to live inside ruin / like a second home"), the sequence culminates in an affectionate elegy for his father, "Sunny Jim." It evokes his émigré years in Brooklyn during the Depression, as an "old nickel-pusher, / rough bar haunter," and it records his peaceful death in his native Tyrone, in the arms of the Church. But it neglects to explain his connection with the foregoing poems, except in one oblique allusion:

> Your faith I envy,
> Your fierce politics I decry.

We have to turn back some thirty years to trace the origins of this association, in a sequence called **"The Fault"**—a latter section of *The Rough Field* (1972), which brings the volume's sweeping historical narrative into his father's lifetime. **"Stele for a Northern Republican"** depicts him as a restless and hard-drinking farmworker ("the least happy man I have known"), who served as a part-time I.R.A. gunman during the Civil War, before his emigration to New York. The following poem, **"The Same Fault,"** which I quote in full, is one of several that explore the father-son affinities:

When I am angry, sick or tired
A line on my forehead pulses,
The line on my left temple
Opened by an old car accident.
My father had the same scar
In the same place, as if
The same fault ran through
Us both: anger, impatience,
A stress born of violence.

It's clear by the end of the sequence that the father's scar resulted from an equally banal accident, and not from any patriotic action. But the word "violence" is inevitably charged with a political meaning in the light of the preceding revelations about his freedom-fighting youth; and the final poem, **"Sound of a Wound,"** elaborates the paternal legacy on this doubtful premise, by means of a breathless conjunction of metaphors that invest the scar with a weight equivalent to Christian stigmata: "Scar tissue / can rend, the old hurt / tear open as / the torso of the fiddle / groans to / carry the tune / to carry / the pain of / a lost. . . . / pastoral rhythm . . ." In the context of a wrathful protest on behalf of the persecuted Gael, this devious abstraction has succeeded in making the scars synonymous with a righteous historical resentment:

> It rears in my blood stream
> when I hear
> a bleat of Saxon condescension . . .
> This bitterness
> I inherit from my father, the
> swarm of blood
> to the brain, the vomit surge
> of race hatred,
> the victim seeing the oppressor . . .

The origins of the "old hurt" can be glimpsed in many other family portraits, which allow us to re-assemble the story like the fragments of a torn snapshot. Among the most moving are two long sequences in *The Dead Kingdom* (1984), which recall his infancy in Brooklyn as the youngest son of an overextended family. Wrenched from the overcrowded parental home at the age of four, he is shipped back across the ocean ("transported to a previous century"), to the care of an aunt in Tyrone. His mother would leave his father some years later, to follow her children to Ireland ("Molly Bawn"); but the boy remains a foster child, brought up by her sister, and he is almost an adult before he renews his acquaintance with his father (**"At Last"**). By the time the family is reunited, for brief periods in the Fifties, the damage has long since been done. **"A Flowering Absence"** aches with an enduring sense of rejection and betrayal, by parents who had borne more children than they could afford to keep:

> Year by year, I track it down,
> intent for a hint of evidence,

seeking to manage the pain—
how a mother gave away her son.

. . . . .

All roads wind backwards to it.
An unwanted child, a primal hurt.

There are some indications that Montague's "bitterness" has been mollified by his explorations of its biographical sources. But he seems never to have regretted the virulence of the Anglophobic rage in *The Rough Field,* whose history of colonial injustice is so unashamedly partisan. He has in fact promoted the volume to a privileged position at the opening of the *Collected Poems,* in defiance of chronology; and this arrangement inadvertently draws attention to its qualities as a relic of its own time. Its indignation now seems redolent of the earliest campaigns for Catholic Civil Rights in the Sixties—a period whose radical innocence had not yet been stained by three decades of blood-letting, eye-for-eye vengeance, and vigilante-rule by paramilitary gangsters of all persuasions. The naïveté is well encapsulated in the penultimate section, **"A New Siege"**—a strident homage to the Republican folk-heroine Bernadette Devlin, on the occasion of a Bogside protest-march, which sometimes sounds as if Montague is contending for a post as the laureate of Provisional Sinn Fein. Among its anonymous voices is one calling for reconciliation ("RELIGION POISONS US / NORTH AND SOUTH"), but it is dominated by the poet's own finger-pointing accusations, which clearly identify his enemy: "a Protestant parliament / a Protestant people / major this and / captain that and / general nothing / the bland, pleasant / face of mediocrity . . ." His reference to the nationalist struggle as "the holy war to restore our country" is of a kind which diplomats on both sides would now call "unhelpful."

Montague has made his own high-minded pleas for mutual tolerance, and even an occasional gesture that looks like an act of contrition. In **"The Plain of Blood"** he concedes that "The evil sprang from / our own harsh hearts," and he recognizes elsewhere that "the punishment [has] slowly grown / more monstrous than the crime." But it is not much use to condemn hatred from one side of the barricades, if we are not prepared to denounce both sides equally from the middle. It is hard to find a poem that assumes the responsibility of repudiating his own antipathies, and **"Civil Wars"** testifies to an incurable ambivalence. Its response to the Omagh bomb is to wonder "Who can endorse such violent men . . . ?"—a hand-wringing rhetorical question that sounds a little faux-naïf on the heels of the tribute to Sands. ("This is the sound of his death; / but, turn the hour-glass, / also of his living on.") When Montague has not disavowed the ferocity of his own political verse, should we not be a little skeptical of the elegy that "decries" his father's "fierce politics"? His pride in his old insurrectionary role has not diminished, if we can judge from **"Outside Armagh Jail, 1971,"** from *Time in Armagh* (1993), which offers us a twenty-year-old memory of declaiming the pro-Devlin poem aloud to her prison-warders, at the gates where they have refused to admit him as a visitor. The point of the story is ostensibly self-mocking ("'The Fenians must be losing,'" he imagines a warder chuckling, "This time they sent a lunatic . . ."); but it merely exhibits an unrepentant self-satisfaction in the role of a quixotic champion of liberty, who is not afraid to risk ridicule at the hands of the Establishment's lackeys.

* * *

Montague has consciously shaped this role in the oldest tradition of the pre-Christian bard, whose primary function is to extol the virtues of his tribe. His liberal translations of early Gaelic poetry have heavily influenced his own voice in this vein, and they are often hard to distinguish from an extensive category of original poems, notably in *A Slow Dance* (1975), which weave a grandiloquent vision of Celtic autonomy at the height of a supposed Golden Age:

> a nomadic world of
> hunters and hunted;
> beaten moons of gold,
> a flash of lost silver . . .

Although the edges are hardened by a certain amount of decorative brutality ("bone biting axes, smoky / resinous torches"), it is otherwise very much a dream of a lost Eden, glowing with the sort of Burne-Jones colors that appealed to the adolescent Yeats. **"Bog Royal"** and **"Hero's Portion"** usher us into a world where the maidens are "slender-waisted," the deer-hunters "fleet-footed," and the poets rub shoulders with kings in the course of convivial, meaty feasts: "Timbers creak / in the banquet hall; / the harper's fingers / are ringed with blood / & the ornate battle sword / sheathed in its scabbard . . ." A sequence in the new collection, in praise of the Breton menhirs at Carnac ("warmed and hollowed / by tidal centuries"), is a strong reminder of the pagan-religious dimension of this vision in *The Great Cloak* (1978), where **"Allegiance"** contemplates prehistoric standing-stones in a mood of enraptured reverence:

> Slowly, in moonlight
> I drop to one knee,
> solemn as a knight
> obeying an ancient precept . . .

The poet in this incarnation has plainly assumed the offices of the high priest, who guards the runes and mediates with the gods. There is indeed a marked flavor of the hieratic in much of Montague's nature poetry, which routinely deifies the elements and casts him as a solitary interpreter of their mysterious signs. This Wordswor-

thian posture is conventional enough in its vanity, when he is responding to "the bird of total meaning" or "secret lonely messages / along the air, older than / humming telephone wires . . ." But it becomes a matter for regret when the most promising landscapes are ruined by Wordsworth's own worst failings, of egocentricity and overstatement. Montague has found it increasingly hard to contemplate a natural scene without insinuating his own superfluous presence into the picture, and those "lonely messages" are too often spelled out with a leaden hand, in florid generalities that require us to take the epiphanies on credit. **"Sea Changes"** informs us, largely out of the blue, that "There is no sea / except in the tangle / of our minds: / the wine dark / sea of history / on which we all turn / turn and thresh / and disappear . . ."

The more ambitious poems adopt the voices of animals and other features of the wild, caught between implacable nature and the cruel devices of man (**"Up So Doun"**); but these tend to develop the unmistakable accents of the poet at his most didactic and fatalistic. In **"Springs"** (1989), a salmon-study rashly dedicated to Ted Hughes, the particularity of the fish rapidly dissolves in a froth of ecological invective: "I mourn your passing / and would erase / from this cluttered earth / our foul disgrace: // Drain the poison / from the streams . . ." The falling-off can be measured by comparing this with **"The Trout,"** a similar poem from Montague's best collection, *A Chosen Light* (1967). In this much-anthologized account of river-guddling, Montague is more tactfully "savoring [his] own absence" as he homes in on his prey:

> Flat on the bank I parted
> Rushes to ease my hands
> In the water without a ripple
> And tilt them slowly downstream
> To where he lay, tendril-light,
> In his fluid sensual dream.

This genre includes most of Montague's best work, it must be said. The strong visual qualities of his imagination, which sometimes make him sound like a frustrated painter, are shown to the most striking effect in *A Chosen Light,* where small-framed and closely-focussed snapshots (**"Views," "Witness"**) dignify rural poverty with a perception of unassuming moments of grace. **"Hill Field"** concentrates with startling clarity on the labors of a tractor ("starling, magpie, crow ride / A gunmetal sheen of gaping earth"); and I cherish the overworked donkey in **"Time Out,"** who sits down in his tracks "sucking the sweet grass of stubbornness." There is one new poem, **"Between,"** that reminds us of his keen countryman's eye for the finer shades of meaning in the Irish landscape ("A wind flurry finecombing the growing grain . . ."). But this is over-painted, in a style of impasto reminiscent of the late-Victorian artist E. A. Hornel, whose paintings of druid ceremonies spring to mind particularly when the poem calls a bank of rhododendron "exalted as some pagan wedding-procession"; and it compares badly with **"Back Door,"** in *A Slow Dance,* a thumbnail watercolor that contains a finely-distilled essence of the West of Ireland:

> Oh, the wet melancholy
> of morning fields! We
> wake to a silence more
> heavy than twilight,
> where an old car finds
> its last life as a henhouse . . .

Some of the most intensely atmospheric landscapes prove, disappointingly, to be illustrations of the Celtic Eden (**"Crannog"**). But they all subscribe in varying degrees to a broader vision of nature, which is purely and even aggressively Lawrentian—a vision of "the human beast" driven by instinct, deservedly tormented by his self-imposed alienation from the wilderness reflected in his psyche. Montague professes an unshakable faith in instinct, in spite of the numerous poems which specify that it is "blind." **"Sweeney"** plunges head-first into the deepest and loamiest levels of Mother-Earth-worship, as if to out-Heaney Heaney: "to celebrate . . . / the humid pull / of the earth, // the whole world / turning in wet / and silence, a / damp mill-wheel . . ." The passion in this vision is unquestionably genuine, and it is a pity that so many poems exploit the full range of effects available to a writer who is not afraid of sounding like *Cold Comfort Farm.* Montague seems wholly unconscious of the Gidean paradoxes and absurdities that arise when an intellectual ritually exalts the instincts above the intellect; and the cup spills over most predictably when womanhood and sex enter the picture. His love-making-scenes are set with puzzling frequency in city hotel rooms, with the blinds drawn against the daylight; but the women tend to merge indistinguishably into a wild landscape, to the same extent that the landscape itself acquires a uniform femininity:

> With a body
> heavy as earth
> she begins to speak;
>
> her words
> are dew, bright,
> deadly to drink,
>
> her hair,
> the damp mare's
> nest of the grass . . .

Body parts, blood and other secretions proliferate abruptly around the period of *Tides* (1971), whose date probably indicates a deliberate attempt to expand Ireland's backward standards of permissiveness. ("Breasts, buttocks / the honey sac / of the cunt—// luring us to forget, / beget . . ."; "to drag man / down to hell's gaping / vaginal mouth.") Earlier love poems were constrained by the graceful influence of Robert Graves, whose reverence and vulnerability added an air of tender gallantry to the proceedings (**"All Legendary Obstacles"**). A new erotic sequence, **"Dark Rooms,"** includes a refreshing reminder of that younger Montague's rueful ironies ("Devious candour waits / outside the bedroom door.") But the effect is undermined by another new poem **"The Current,"** a strenuously honest memory of a first lesson in masturbation, as demonstrated by an older adolescent boy in a clump of riverside bushes. It labors a tenuous Heraclitean analogy between the ejaculated sperm and the "hidden, / overheard, swirl and pull" of the stream; and the heavy-handed anatomical descriptions suggest that he is loath to relinquish his once-controversial role as a spokesman for the imprisoned libido. When he hammers like this at a gate that is no longer manned by any censor, it is easy to recognize the poet whose futile declamations entertained the warders of Armagh Jail.

* * *

In Montague's vision of ancient Ireland, the tribal hierarchy reserves a privileged position for the music-maker. In **"The Flight of the Earls"** the violin is a shamanistic instrument of solace, "assuaging like a bardic poem / our tribal pain"; and he frankly aspires to this status in poems such as **"The Country Fiddler,"** a portrait of an uncle, which attributes his own verbal talents to a musical tradition in the family ("Succession passes through strangest hands . . ."). The self-image as a fiddler manqué invites us to consider the poetry as a performance attuned to a certain kind of sympathetic listener, eager to applaud a familiar repertoire; and it is obviously a key to understanding the extempore qualities of the verse. Montague often seems able to improvise at any length on a given theme—love, grief, exile, patriotism—on a jazz-like principle that allows for the recycling of formulae, favorite riffs, and whole phrases from previous performances. (There are no less than three poems that compare human life to a "rope-ladder" suspended over "oblivion.") The spontaneity can seem contrived, when it depends too routinely on Beat and Black Mountain devices—single-stress lines, sprinklings of ampersands, line-breaks after prepositions, and so on. But it does leave the impression of an impulsive writer, absorbed and compelled by his subject; and this is obviously not unsuitable to the Burns-like image of a blunt-speaking man-of-the-people, prepared to risk his neck in defense of freedom. The whimsical title poem of *Smashing the Piano* seems to be a celebration of avant-garde aesthetics on this wilful principle, sanctified once again by the instincts ("A jumble, jangle of eighty-eight keys . . . / John Cage serenading Stockhausen!"). It is reminiscent of a passage in **"Border Sick Call"** that announces his willingness to shatter some kind of sound barrier:

The poem is endless,
the poem is strong as our weakness,
strong in its weakness,
it will never cease until it has said
what cannot be said.

This is just blarney, of the most portentous variety. (If something really "cannot be said," not even poetry can say it. And if poetry could say it, why should it "cease" after saying it?) But it is hard to miss the Whitmanesque ambition of an all-saying yea-saying, and even the pea-soup fog of "strong in its weakness" can yield some light, if we consider Montague's own account of the sources of his writing in the pathology of his adolescence. **"Dumbshow"** and **"Poor Poll"** are the latest of several poems that recall a childhood handicapped by a paralyzing stammer: "Others giggle as / he fails, stumbles / pushes a consonant / slowly uphill . . ." The latter poem is a grateful memory of the moment when poetry-writing first fulfilled "his dream to stride / fluently through / fields of language"; and both poems send us back to the painful tangle of his family background in **"A Flowering Absence,"** where the original emotional impediment is identified. The stammer, which he suffered "for two stumbling decades, is blamed on the cruelty of his first Irish schoolmistress, who compounded his disorientation by mocking his "outlandish" hybrid accent ("'What do you expect, with no parents, / sent back from some American slum: / None of you are to speak like him!'") The poem ends with another image of the Muse as healer:

My tongue became a rusted hinge,
till the sweet oils of poetry
eased it, and grace flooded in.

These accounts invite us to see the writing as a long process of recovery from the years of enforced silence, "trying / to fishgasp something." They serve as a plausible excuse for loquacity, perhaps; and they also illuminate one of the more obscure mechanisms of his self-dramatization, as a victim of history. The muteness has obviously remained a sore point, but we have to reread *The Rough Field,* in the backglow of these later poems, to realize that the teacher's cruelty has been endowed with a large historical resonance. In **"A Grafted Tongue,"** one of the most rancorous sections, Montague identifies his own "stuttering, garb- / led ordeal" with the plight of his great-grandfather's Gaelic-speaking generation, forced by the British education system to suppress its native language: "To grow / a second tongue, as / harsh a humiliation / as twice to be born." The experiences seem hardly comparable, when his own punishment has been inflicted for the sin of not being sufficiently Irish. But it has stigmatized him as an outcast at an early age, and this has evidently been enough to convert the teacher into an instrument of the same colonial oppression that made his parents emigrate in the first place. Given his own subsequent embrace of

the Irish language, it has required only a minor adjustment of logic to perceive colonization as a source of his trauma, of which poetry is the cure.

* * *

This is more or less where we came in, at the point where the poet is toiling uphill in search of a miracle. Spread below him are the valleys of Ireland, a patchwork country that stands for the feminine principles of water, vegetation, and blood-knowledge. She is a victim of rape, by the arid intellect of the British Protestant, and we are persuaded by now that her predicament is the poet's own. The first step in the long healing process is to establish her innocence; and there is no task that raises Montague to quite the same heights of lyrical inspiration, when he resists the temptation to deliver a lecture. **"Windharp,"** from *A Slow Dance,* is so nearly perfect that it needs to be quoted in full:

The sounds of Ireland,
that restless whispering
you can never get away
from, seeping out of
low bushes and grass,
heatherbells and fern,
wrinkling bog pools,
scraping tree branches,
light hunting cloud,
sound hounding sight,
a hand ceaselessly
combing and stroking
the landscape, till
the valley gleams
like the pile upon
a mountain pony's coat.

Great poetry can be made of the struggle between the heart and the head; and in Montague this seems to correspond roughly to an unresolved conflict between the peasant and the professor—the headstrong ballad-singer versus the plodding lay preacher. Their tug-o'-war damages dozens of poems; but the professor allows the peasant to win most of the time, because he believes that the heart must have all the best reasons. Montague is not the sort of abstract thinker who makes a system of his world-view; and he often leaves us adrift in deep waters, when he casts the reader in the role of psychotherapist. But it's precisely the emotional grounding of the poetry that vouches for its authenticity, in the end; and it does invite more indulgence when we realize that its vanities and excesses arise from much the same source as its virtues. It's the lifelong sense of dislocation, as a casualty of an old injustice, that equips him to admire the resilience of the peasant in those bleak hill-regions, where we find the most lovingly unsentimental vision of his own immemorial Ireland. Even the lush green *paradiso* assumes a sharper meaning when we see it as a compensation for the missing family, a salving of the wound of separation, a salmon-like return to the source. On the last page of *Smashing the Piano,* when his plane comes to land in a country where he is still in love, I find myself relieved by the intensity of his serenity:

> I race homewards
> towards you, beside whom I now belong,
> *age iam, meorum finis amorum,*
> my late, but final anchoring.

David Gardiner (essay date 2001)

SOURCE: Gardiner, David. "'The Last Bard of The O'Neills.'" In *"Befitting Emblems of Adversity": A Modern Irish View of Edmund Spenser from W. B. Yeats to the Present,* pp. 121-68. Omaha, Neb.: Creighton University Press, 2001.

[*In the following essay, Gardiner discusses the influence of Edmund Spencer's literary legacy on Montague's poetry, contending that Montague embraced the work of Spencer as a way of opposing the Irish literary establishment associated with the poetry of William Butler Yeats.*]

> Historical sense and poetic sense should not, in the end, be contradictory, for if poetry is the little myth we make, history is the big myth we live, and in our living, constantly remake.
>
> —*Robert Penn Warren*

In 1966, the Republic of Ireland celebrated the fiftieth anniversary of the Easter Rising. At the same time, equally public commemorations of the hundredth anniversary of Yeats's birth were winding down. The National Gallery of Ireland had presented an extensive exhibit of paintings by W. B., Jack, and J. B. Yeats. The Abbey Theatre in Dublin and Lyric Theatre in Belfast both performed year-long festivals of Yeats's dramatic work. The Irish government also contributed to the reconstruction of Thoor Ballylee and, in late 1967, erected a statue to W. B. Yeats on St. Stephen's Green.[1] Like the Rising, Yeats had become a part of the official culture of the Republic of Ireland.

Concurrent with such public events, it is not surprising that many writers were also looking back over the preceding decades and giving voice to their views of the cultural and national direction of Ireland. One of the most significant of these writers was John Montague, who consciously took up Yeats's concerns with Spenser and the role of the national poet in Ireland. Employing lines from Spenser's poetry and prose in important moments of his own national self-presentations, Montague distinguished his work from Yeats's while claiming an equally national voice. As has been demonstrated in the previous chapters, Yeats's appropriation of Spenser

began in opposition to Dowden and the Dublin literary establishment. Similarly, Montague began his appropriation of Spenser through opposition; in this later instance, in opposition to Yeats and the literary establishment he had come to represent. Over the course of twenty five years, Montague would build upon his early occasions of opposition to Yeats and finally appropriate Spenser in a much more personal and enabling way than had Yeats. Whereas Yeats placed Spenser among a final collection of his noble friends in "Municipal Gallery Revisited," Montague ultimately places himself among Spenser's fictions and presents this approach as a means beyond the Yeatsian and Spenserian pasts. Engaging Spenser and Elizabethan Ireland over the course of his work, Montague sketched out an important and innovative poetic which significantly revised the idea of the renaissance poet and the Spenserian tradition and has influenced a number of succeeding Cork poets by whom Spenser seems finally to have been put to rest.

From his first publications, Montague was recognized as a significant voice of his generation. In 1958, Montague published his first collection of poetry, *Forms of Exile,* with Dolmen Press. Reviewing this publication, John Jordan called it and the establishment of Dolmen Press "one of the few important events in the history of Irish publishing since the inauguration of the Free State."[2] Montague's close affiliations with Austin Clarke and Patrick Kavanagh and his productive collaborations with the publisher Liam Miller and poet Thomas Kinsella placed him at the center of Irish writing as it emerged from Yeats's influence. Housed in the former residence of Yeats's Cuala Press, Liam Miller's Dolmen Press sought to break the hold of "tradition" in Irish poetry. The Dolmen agenda was presented in the 1962 *Dolmen Miscellany of Irish Writing,* which Montague edited.[3] In his introduction to the anthology, Montague claimed that it was the collective desire of these Dolmen authors "to avoid the forms of 'Irishism' (whether leprechaun or garrulous rebel) which have been so profoundly exploited in the past."[4] As Montague worked with Dolmen Press throughout the late sixties and early seventies, his poetic voice gained authority through his appropriation of Spenser and the renaissance model of the national poet which both Spenser and Yeats had constructed. Combining these poets' views, Montague envisioned a poet who had a right to speak on national matters and had the ability to change the direction of the people.

A decade before *The Dolmen Miscellany,* in the article which he contributed to Sean O'Faolain's symposium in *The Bell* and with which he announced his literary presence on the Irish scene, Montague reflected upon the "failure of talent" among contemporary Irish writers and stated:

> In purely literary terms it seems to be the aftermath of a conscious attempt to create a specifically Irish

literature—the tradition of the Revival exhausted, we find ourselves cut off from contemporary European literature, and with little or no audience in England, since our national preoccupations have left us miles behind in the race.[5]

Montague portrays the artistic failure of his generation as the result of the Irish Revival and its too "conscious attempt" to create a national literature. Ironically, Montague presents similar criticism of Yeats's Renaissance as Yeats had offered of Spenser's. In his interpretation, Yeats claimed that Spenser's efforts to create an English national literature forced the Elizabethan to conclude that "there was no right, no law, but that of Elizabeth, and all that opposed her opposed themselves to God, to civilisation, and to all inherited wisdom and courtesy, and should be put to death."[6] Montague drew similar conclusions about the diverse efforts of Yeats and the Revivalists. In his view of the Irish Renaissance, Montague concluded that similar "national preoccupations" with Irish-ness, as a race, have left the country behind in both economic and artistic "race." In answer to this failure of nerve and this isolation, Montague suggested that the young Irish writer "should be able to estimate his heritage without hastiness or bias, and having understood the present confusion and depression, move on to fresh and original work" (173).[7] For Montague, looking to the Spenserian past "without hastiness or bias" presented an opportunity to reclaim a source of poetic authority in the face of the "exhausted" inheritance of the Irish Revival. It provided a way around rebel, leprechaun, and most importantly, Yeats.

THE PASSAGE INTO SPENSER'S IRELAND

Like Yeats's, John Montague's first significant moment of national self-presentation was couched in Spenserian terms. In 1960, two years after the Dolmen publication of *Forms of Exile* (1958), Montague was awarded the prestigious May Morton Memorial Prize for poetry for his work, **"Like Dolmens Round My Childhood, The Old People."** Montague received his £50 award in the Assembly Hall of the Belfast Presbyterian Church and read the poem on the "Arts in Ulster" radio program on BBC (Northern Ireland). Montague was the first Northern Irish Catholic to read on the Northern Ireland Home Service since the partition, an anomaly emphasized by *The Belfast Telegraph* headline announcing: "Poetry Prize for Dubliner."[8] Reflecting upon this early poetic experience, Montague has stated:

[T]here was no tradition for someone of my background to work in . . . there had not been a poet of Ulster Catholic background since the Gaelic poets of the eighteenth century. . . . I describe myself as 'the missing link of Ulster poetry.'[9]

In this reflection upon his historical and literary place, Montague presents himself as someone outside the tradition, simultaneously recognizing his minority status in Northern Ireland and realizing that as a modern poet he might be free to create his own out of the elements he deems fit.[10] In Montague's efforts to invent a tradition, he consciously re-shaped the English literary tradition in light of his own situation in Ireland so as to present himself as a national poet. As an Ulster Catholic speaking within the Assembly Hall which had served originally as the Northern Irish Parliament, Montague was keenly aware of the cultural and political backgrounds with which he was contending.

In this first appropriation, Montague dignifies his Catholic rural heritage through means of Spenser. Within this new context, a Spenserian allusion serves to validate Montague's own poetic authority and the personal background which he is presenting. Yeats had undertaken a similar tactic in his first Dublin self-presentation, *The Island of the Statues* (1884). Yeats employed Spenserian names, allusions, and situations within his verse drama so as to portray himself as a poet poised to unite the English literary and the Irish political traditions into an Irish national art form. Though an early work, *The Island of the Statues* charted the later direction of Yeats's work. The forlorn lovers, mystic islands, and millennial prophecies which recurred throughout Yeats's work all appear within this early presentation. In **"Like Dolmens Round My Childhood, The Old People,"** Montague also assembles his most significant poet materials, casting the important figure, "Maggie Owens," in importantly Spenserian terms. **"Like Dolmens Round My Childhood"** presents the rural Ulster setting of his childhood and recalls an entire host of his elderly neighbors in detail. He writes about the figures of his Tyrone childhood: Jamie MacCrystal who "tipped me a penny every pension day"; Maggie Owens "surrounded by animals . . . Reputed a witch"; the Nialls "with Blind Pension and Wireless"; Mary Moore "Driving lean cattle from a miry stable"; and the Protestant Billy Eagleson, "Forsaken by both creeds" for marrying "a Catholic servant girl." The final stanza of the poem links these figures to Ireland's mythic history, concluding:

Ancient Ireland, indeed! I was reared by her bedside,
The rune and chant, evil eye and averted head,
Formorian fierceness of family and local feud.
Gaunt figures of fear and of friendliness,
For years they trespassed on my dreams,
Until once, in a standing circle of stones,
I felt their shadows pass

Into that dark permanence of ancient forms.[11]

These closing lines of the poem illustrate an important element upon which Montague would base the national voice he later assumed in *Patriotic Suite* (1966). This significant aspect of **"Like Dolmens Round My Childhood"** is the transformation of the personal into the mythic through, rather than in spite of, attention paid to the particular representation. Yeats's rural character, his peasant, was a type and pre-existed his depictions. Montague, having lived in the rural North, professed an equally mythic importance to the countryside but he moved inductively from particulars to that importance. The mythic importance that Montague granted to his rural upbringing is seen here as a resuscitation of the Gaelic past which preceded the Elizabethan conquest and which, according to **"Like Dolmens,"** outlived it as well.

Throughout his writing, Montague develops an historical sense—an awareness of what Oliver MacDonagh defines as "a dialogue between present apprehensions and knowledge of what has gone before."[12] In this important early moment, Montague enfolds his present apprehensions with his personal and communal past and links that inheritance with the mythic past of the island extending back to the first historical writing on Ireland, the twelfth-century *Leabhar Gabhála*, or "The Book of the Takings of Ireland." The "Formorian fierceness" about which Montague writes links the people of his neighborhood with the "Fomorii," the original, ancient inhabitants of the island who were defeated by the Tuatha De Danaan at the second battle of Magh Tuireach. They were "misshapen and violent people who are the evil gods of Irish myth. . . . They often appear with only a single hand, foot, or eye."[13] Stepping into this historical inheritance, Montague both personalizes and mythologizes it.[14] In **"Like Dolmens Round My Childhood,"** Montague's personal contemporaries occupy an equal place among the historico-mythic first inhabitants of Ireland. In his historical sense of the country, Montague's subjects join with the standing stones of Knockmany Hill as images of cultural inheritance as permanent and ancient as the myths which predate the English conquest as well as the properly "Irish" occupation of the island.

In his first public effort to find a place for his Ulster Catholic past within the difficult traditions of Northern Ireland, Montague reverses the flow of Spenser's fictions, subsuming the Elizabethan into the world of Irish myth, rather than the Irish world into the English view.[15] In the second stanza, Montague writes:

> Maggie Owens was surrounded by animals,
> A mongrel bitch and shivering pups,
> Even in her bedroom a she-goat cried,
> She was a well of gossip defiled,
> Fanged chronicler of a whole countryside;
> Reputed a witch, all I could find
> Was her lonely need to deride.

Through a Spenserian allusion, Montague grants dignity to Maggie Owens's character. Because his audiences in the North and the Republic would have been all too aware of Yeatsian images of the peasant, Montague avoids relying exclusively upon the "folk." The Spens-

erian allusion in the poem provides a new, although hardly precise, validation for an important member of Montague's past.

Returning to the lines from which Montague borrowed, a number of pertinent aspects about Montague's own project emerge. In Book Four of *The Faerie Queene,* Spenser presents the source his *Legend of Friendliness* as coming from,

> . . . that renowned Poet [who] . . .
> With warlike numbers and Heroicke sound,
> Dan *Chaucer,* well of English undefyled,
> On Fames eternall beadroll worthie to be fyled.
>
> (IV ii 32.6-9)

In the immediate context of *The Faerie Queene,* Spenser uses these lines to acknowledge his narrative debt to Chaucer since the episode from which these lines are taken is a continuation of Chaucer's "Squire's Tale." The lines function as more than simple citation in Spenser's epic. They also function as a homage to Chaucer's example. For Spenser, Chaucer was the national poet. Not only did Chaucer provide the characters for Spenser's story, he provided the authority for the narrative art which Spenser was nationalizing and updating in *The Faerie Queene*. Like Chaucer and Spenser, Montague sought to "compile" the materials of Irish history. In this first Spenserian borrowing, we see Montague's distinctly modern poetic working by accumulation and selection. Montague was concerned with memorializing what he perceived as heroic about his culture. In spite of "her lonely need to deride," Maggie Owens is granted a dignity in Montague's depiction because she shares in his cultural project. Surrounded by animals, Maggie stands initially as an ironic commentary on the renaissance inheritance. What further frees Montague's allusion from simple sarcasm is that Montague extends the comparison toward Spenser's rhetorically validating position by calling her a "chronicler."[16] Elizabeth's "chroniclers," such as the Dubliner Richard Stanihurst, sought through their efforts to commemorate the histories of the triumphs of England. These writers were the official, popular historians of the Elizabethan age. Richard Helgerson has stated: "Chronicle was the Ur-genre of national self-representation. More than any other discursive form, chronicle gave Tudor Englishmen a sense of national identity."[17] The most distinctive feature of Chronicle history is that it is "a story of kings. . . . To judge from books like these, England is its monarchs" (Helgerson 132). In **"Like Dolmens Round My Childhood,"** Montague's first national self-representation is the story of its old and defeated—its rural Ulster Catholic *and* Protestants. Like the Elizabethan chroniclers, Montague and Maggie Owens are the official custodians of Northern Irish culture. The images from Montague's rural past become "a standing circle of stones" with the same monumental importance as an English story of kings.

In his first Spenserian adaptation, Montague seems to be discovering the same "barbarous truth" of the countryside as had Yeats through Spenser. As has been discussed earlier in this study, Yeats's first published article alluded to Spenser to validate the poetry of Samuel Ferguson. Yeats wrote: "if I were asked to characterize, as shortly as may be, these poems, I should do so by applying to them the words of Spenser, 'barbarous truth'."[18] Spenser's "barbarous truth" emerged out of Una's encounter with "the salvage nation" of satyrs in the first book of *The Faerie Queene*. Una's truth was the essential, unwritten, and unspoken bond between the Reformed Church of England she represented and the unenlightened, illiterate masses symbolized by the satyrs.[19] Montague's appropriation takes significant liberties with its Yeatsian and Spenserian sources. Yeats saw the "barbarous truth" as the ancient materials of Ferguson's translations from the Irish heroic cycles. Throughout his career, Yeats envisioned this ancient heroic character residing in peasants like his proud, solitary "Fisherman" whom he imagined inhabiting "a grey place on a hill / In grey Connemara cloth."[20] Though Yeats admitted in "The Fisherman" that this ideal figure did not exist in his world, he never abandoned his belief that the particular people of the countryside ought to embody the type he imagined. Just as he would reverse the flow of Elizabethan logic, so Montague reverses the direction of Yeats's Irish Renaissance construction of the peasant. Working from the particulars of his own experience, Montague's depiction of Maggie Owens weaves a litany of folk-memory against the *inevitable* onslaught of modernization. Faced with the passing of a way of life, Montague does not seek to change the world in which these characters exist, but to memorialize them so that they might gain epic stature as elements of a newly formed communal memory. To draw attention to the "epic stature" of his provincial society in the North of Ireland, Montague has recourse to Spenser and, through him, the folk tradition of Chaucer to justify his own place as a poet. In this reference from *The Faerie Queene*, Maggie becomes the countryside's Chaucer and the "chronicler" of the region. Subsequently, Montague stands briefly as his society's Spenser, completing and circulating the national folk traditions of his country.[21]

"Like Dolmens Round My Childhood . . ." was included at an important point in Montague's long poem, *The Rough Field* (1972), and remains one of his most anthologized poems.[22] Significantly, the complex contemporary reception of the poem in 1960 demonstrates the difficulty Montague encountered as he used Spenser to grant validity to his contemporary efforts and his culture. The first and most obvious element is the problem of speaking of any sort of inclusiveness in Northern Ireland. Yeats's earliest use of Spenser occurred in a diverse, but like minded, group of Protestant Home Rulers at C. H. Oldham's Contemporary Club.

Montague's audience in the Belfast Assembly Hall and on the BBC would not have been so united. As he recorded in the original notes to *Poisoned Lands* (1961), Montague omitted the fifth stanza of the poem in his readings.

> Wild Billy Eagleson married a Catholic servant girl
> When all his loyal family passed on:
> We danced round him shouting "To hell with King Billy"
> And dodged from the arc of his flailing blackthorn.
> Forsaken by both creeds, he showed little concern
> Until the Orange drums banged past in the summer
> And bowler and sash aggressively shone.

Though BBC Northern Ireland may have been ready in 1960 to welcome a Catholic poet, it may not have been ready for such bald pronouncements on the long tradition of sectarian "creeds" division in the province. Though Montague seems to admire Billy Eagleson, the conflict which the character embodies was clearly too volatile at this point in time. Though his marriage crosses sectarian lines, Eagleson's "flailing blackthorn" might stand as an emblem for the ideology of sectarianism which would erupt at the end of the decade. Spenserian allusion in **"Like Dolmens Round My Childhood . . ."** could sophisticate and complicate the issue of the literary inheritance. Still, Eagleson's blackthorn seems to hang over the poet's head as a reminder that physical force is always more immediately threatening than literary interpretation.

The second element which originates in the reception of **"Like Dolmens Round My Childhood"** is the Yeatsian revision which Montague was undertaking. Before assuming a national platform in his later work, Montague had to contend with the much more immediate and significant example of Yeats. Though his use of Spenser at this point is original, Montague's self-presentation in **"Like Dolmens Round My Childhood"** remains distinctly Yeatsian. As has been demonstrated in regard to "The Municipal Gallery Re-visited," Yeats's last appropriation of Spenser sought to memorialize an artistic order that he saw passing in 1936. Montague uses Spenser for similar authoritative and elegiac purposes in **"Like Dolmens Round My Childhood."** Contrary to Yeats, Montague retained the rougher, fully human edges of the countryside. Though "defiled," Maggie Owens becomes the chronicle historian of the countryside. These distinctions were less evident to some than the Yeatsian appropriations in which Montague was also engaging. Reviewing *Poisoned Lands*, Donald Torchiana critiqued Montague and the writers of his generation who were presuming to a national poetic voice:

> . . . But when Montague slithers onto his Yeatsian Pegasus, he becomes like so many of his workshop comrades, downright offensive. . . . So it is that Montague's poem **"Like Dolmens Round My Childhood, The Old People"** becomes a travesty of Yeats's "The

Tower." Instead of a legendary appeal to the imaginative life of the locale that can set off and blend a poet's reveries, Montague's poem is merely [sic] a rag bag of grotesques, a gaggle of odd-balls and oddities, that are somehow deemed vatic and wise.[23]

What "offends" Torchiana is that Montague is treading on Yeatsian ground without any Yeatsian "reverie." Viewed in this way, any literary adaptation that is not celebration or commemoration will be viewed as "travesty." In Montague's next engagement with Spenser, he directly addressed the Yeatsian Pegasus through the use of Spenser. Building upon the validation the Spenserian allusion provided his community in **"Like Dolmens Round My Childhood,"** Montague looked to Spenser to provide authority for his poetic voice as he sought to speak on the destiny of the Republic of Ireland rather than the rural North.

PATRIOTIC SUITE (1966)

Issued to coincide with the events surrounding the fiftieth anniversary of the Easter Rising, *Patriotic Suite* (1966) provided Montague with the opportunity to assess his role as an Irish poet and to judge the cultural and political direction of the Republic of Ireland. As with the majority of the Dolmen publications, *Patriotic Suite* was issued as an elaborate chapbook. Although he had edited the *Dolmen Miscellany* (1962), from his first collection, *Forms of Exile* (1958), until *Patriotic Suite,* Montague had been publishing his work with the London printing house McGibbon & Kee. Consequently, *Patriotic Suite* marked Montague's return to both Dolmen and to Ireland.[24] Within the eleven poems that comprise this sequence, Montague interrogates the inheritance of Yeats's and Spenser's renaissance self-presentations. As we have seen, Spenser simultaneously condemned and memorialized the ability of the Irish poet to affect his countrymen. Yeats returned to Spenser to validate his own national efforts throughout his career. As Montague undertook a similarly national project in *Patriotic Suite* he assessed these related instances. The Renaissance pose of the poet enabled Montague to speak on contemporary issues in an authoritative way. Assuming the bardic power which Spenser reviled and revising the Irish peasant which Yeats extolled, Montague presented an entirely new element within modern Irish poetry. An equally important innovation within the sequence itself was Montague's adaptation of the more American influence of open form through which he could actually bring the words and images of Spenser and his contemporaries into his own texts.[25] For the first time, working by allusion and juxtaposition, Montague's *Patriotic Suite* places Spenserian Ireland in meaningful relation to contemporary Ireland. In doing so Montague attempts to cast poetic verdicts of equal authority upon the island and upon Yeats's part in the construction of the cultural myths of the Republic of Ireland.

In 1966, Romantic Ireland may have been dead and gone, but Yeats's unattractive Ireland of Falstaffian Irregulars and Paudeens still existed. The immediate context of Montague's publication underlines the interplay between Yeatsian and Spenserian elements. Because of the Yeats Centenary events of 1965 and the Rising Commemoration of the following year, Irish writers were acutely aware of the importance of Yeats within Irish culture. Not surprisingly, younger Irish writers such as Montague did not revel in the Yeats agenda. As a rather explicit commentary on the political direction of the Republic of Ireland, unknown Republican activists blew up Nelson's pillar on O'Connell street in 1966. In a sense, the bombing of Nelson's pillar might stand conversely for the literary undertaking of Montague's *Patriotic Suite.*[26] As that monument of Empire had become a defining characteristic of O'Connell street, so now the Yeatsian inheritance as revised and rehearsed through predictable commemoration rhetoric stood in the way of the Ireland which it had once created. It is this detrimental inheritance of the Irish Revival which Montague begins to critique and reconstruct in the sequence.[27]

Within *Patriotic Suite,* Montague assesses the Easter Rising, the Cultural Revival, the urbanization of Ireland, the burning of the Abbey Theater in 1951, and Ireland's entrance into the United Nations, before concluding with prose quotations from Friedrich Engels and Edmund Spenser. One of the most important aspects of the Dolmen Press printing of this chapbook is that it highlights the ways in which Montague's sequence is an extended exercise in literary influence which employs Elizabethan materials to throw off the tradition of Yeats's Revival. Liam Miller's contribution to Montague's reappropriation of renaissance materials cannot be overestimated since it was at his suggestion that *Patriotic Suite* was illustrated with woodcuts from John Derricke, Spenser's contemporary in Ireland.[28] Derricke's *Image of Irelande, with a Discovery of a Woodkarne* (1578) is a long verse epistle followed by a woodcut and doggerel verse portrayal of Sir Henry Sidney's three-year campaign against the O'Neills (1575-8). By mixing illustration with poetic explication, Derricke's text foregrounds the importance of controlling the interpretation of the situation in Ireland. Derricke's narrative of the Irish Woodkern proceeds from their "bodrags" (ritual cattle-raids) to the entertainment of the "Bard and Harper" before The MacSweeney. Derricke writes: "Both Barde and Harper is preparde, which by their cunning art, / Doe strike and cheare up all the gestes with comfort at the hart."[29] The progression seems to lead logically from the activities of the bard and harper to the "spoyling and destroying of her grace's loyall men." In his selection from Derricke, James P. Myers stated that the work "consummated the entire tradition" of Elizabethan colonial writings on Ireland.[30] Myers characterizes the work as "quaint and didactic

. . . the English perception at its most extreme" (38). Like Spenser's writings on Ireland, Derricke's work could be used quite against his intentions. Early in the nineteenth century, Sir Samuel Ferguson outlined the importance of this "specimen of this scurril school" of writing.[31] According to Ferguson, the importance of these Elizabethan tracts was that from them "we must now draw much of the material, for whatever history of the country we can be said to possess" (552). In the same year that Montague published his sequence, the highly-influential early modern historian D. B. Quinn drew heavily on Derricke's prints in *The Elizabethans and the Irish.*[32]

The cover of Montague's **Patriotic Suite** reproduces a section of a Derricke woodcut which depicts a piper leading a force of Irish kern. Originally subtitled "*Kern Pillaging Their Own People on a Bodrag,*" the full portrait shows light-armed Irish gallowglass marching behind a piper, then setting fire to an Irish nobleman's dwellings, before marching off with his cattle. From the Elizabethan English vantage point, this was, in the words of Derricke, "a pack of prowling mates" who crept "out of Saint Filcher's den" and "spare no more their country birth than those of th' English race" (40). By foregrounding this image of an Irish piper leading a band of armed Irish foot soldiers, the Dolmen design highlights the Spenserian emphasis on the interplay between Irish poetry and political action. The use of this illustration suggests that Montague will be leading a similar sortie. Underlining this visual suggestion, the first page furthers this implication by featuring an Irish harper who seems to stand for the work of both Montague and the press.

Building upon these first identifications, Montague's work enters into a dialogue with the Elizabethans which is very different than one would expect. By taking these illustrations out of their original negative contexts, the chapbook initially seems to be taking a simplistic, opposing stance to that offered by the Elizabethan testaments to Irish barbarity. Yet rather than assuming a contrary stance to the evidence of the pictures—assuming all negative English representations are positive Irish portrayals—Montague's work revises both this inheritance and the more recent inheritance of the Irish Renaissance. In *Patriotic Suite,* Montague parceled out Spenser's Elizabethan depictions of Ireland from Yeats's equally authoritative pronouncements. Yeats looked to Spenser to validate his own impressions of his national role as a poet and his ability to affect the polity. Against this Yeatsian and Spenserian background, Montague shapes his own more critical, but not entirely dismissive, view of the cultural and political direction of the Republic of Ireland. The first poem, **"The Lure,"** faces another reproduction of the cover print of the soldiers and piper and begins: "Again, that note! A weaving / melancholy."[33] Montague grants the patriotic suite of

the Republic the same sort of incantatory power of Irish poetry which Sir John Harington described in Elizabethan Ireland. Reporting to Queen Elizabeth about the maneuvers of Hugh O'Neill's army, he wrote that the Irish forces did not resemble any "soldierly exercise" so much as "a Morris dance trypping after their badge pypes."[34] Spenser and his contemporaries viewed Irish poets and poetry as the center of the resistance which English culture faced on the island. Consequently for the English, the "music" of Irish culture was a mixture of holiday and riot.[35] In his work, Yeats used this view to enable his search for a national audience susceptible to poetry. Montague, for his part, returned to Spenser's riotous bards and Yeats's poetic peasant so as to separate them from the official culture which had sprung up during the Yeats centenary and the Rising commemoration year. According to Montague's sequence, Ireland seemed to be following the morris dance of unjustifiably self-satisfied southern Irish Republicanism, rather than resuscitating what was truly worth commemorating in Irish culture. In the year *Patriotic Suite* was published, Montague contributed an introductory essay to the Dolmen tribute to Austin Clarke in which he referred drily to "our supposed commemoration year."[36] As Montague demonstrated, the national poetic vocabulary was sadly distant from its historic roots. Before he could continue the Spenserian appropriation of bardic power he had begun in **"Like Dolmens Round My Childhood,"** Montague first undertook a critique of the Irish Renaissance whose rhetoric had been adapted by de Valéra's Republic and which stood between Montague and the shaping cultural role he desired.[37] Adapting Montague's lines from **"The Lure,"** before capturing the "note" of Irish national poetry, he would have to face the "melancholy."

Montague's effort in **Patriotic Suite** is distinguished by the almost stifling presence of the Yeatsian national voice which echoes behind the poems. Robert F. Garratt has stated that "The demythologizing of the Yeatsian poetic tradition has become a regular and important act for almost every Irish poet who followed Yeats."[38] It was after all Yeats's "idea" of Ireland which had become ingrained in the English literary consciousness rather than the more revolutionary Easter Proclamation of 1916 which the "so-called commemoration year" was to be celebrating. Throughout the sequence, as Montague addresses the past in terms of the present, that past is equally Yeatsian and Elizabethan. Conflating the Irish and English Renaissances, Montague envisions them as equal, contending influences to move beyond. The English Renaissance had been a cultural commodity of considerable value during the early moments of the Irish literary Revival. The diligence with which Yeats, Dowden, and their circles had appropriated the English Renaissance for their different Irish cultural agendas nearly guaranteed that traces of the English Renaissance would be carried within Irish Renaissance literature and criticism. Montague's work confirms that for his generation the "Irish Renaissance" of the turn of the twentieth century appeared on an equal ground with the "English Renaissance" of the turn of the sixteenth century. Significantly, Montague's most effective demythologizing of Yeats is accomplished through his use of Spenser and the Elizabethans.

The confluence of these two periods may be read in the *Patriotic Suite* as the sequence moves towards conclusion through a pointed critique of the Irish Renaissance spear headed by Yeats. In the quatrain, **"Abbey Theatre 1951,"** Montague portrays the destruction of the original Abbey Theatre by fire on July 18, 1951:

> In this gutted building, a young man might stand,
> Watching a firehose play, like a soothing hand.
> It has earned little of his heart, beyond the abstract
> Duty and respect, accorded a public monument.

In Montague's poem, the emblem of Ireland's modern national literary movement burns down with no promise of rising from the ashes. As the Abbey Theater Company was returning to its original venue in 1966, Montague reminds his readership of the symbolic verdict of the fire.[39] In fact, in its echoes of the declamatory fifth section of Yeats's "Under Ben Bulben" where Yeats instructs Irish poets to "learn your trade," Montague seems to indicate that the only thing the writer of his generation has "learned" from Yeats is that his Irish Renaissance is a dead end. In an essay of this same year entitled, "Under Ben Bulben," Montague directly addressed this issue as he wrote,

> . . . though the level of achievement in recent Irish poetry has been high, it still seems largely a local matter, having more to do with the history of Irish poetry than with poetry in general. Which is almost what Yeats would have wanted, if we are to believe the extraordinary fifth section of "Under Ben Bulben," where he orders Irish poets to deliberately turn aside from contemporary literature. There are times when I wonder if that passage was not composed with malice aforethought. A friend told me once of interrupting two old men near Belmullet, in order to ask the way, and being shown a path which led onto a sea cliff: is that what Yeats meant by bequeathing us a catalogue of subjects that can now only be legitimately treated in parody?[40]

Montague casts this cold eye on the Yeatsian inheritance throughout *Patriotic Suite* as well. The burnt-out Abbey in Montague's poem comes to stand for the whole burnt-out Irish literary revival. To move beyond the merely negative assessments and the "inherited dissent" of his contemporaries, Montague plays the renaissance aspects of each poet off of the other and pares down the inheritance with which he is dealing so that he might discover what he might appropriate and present usefully as his own.

Though employing various traditional forms, the sequence is equally reliant upon the included prose passages and illustrations. Throughout the sequence, Derricke's Elizabethan woodcuts create an historical tone for the poems. **"Abbey Theatre, 1951"** is a poem which specifically plays off of the illustrations. In *A View of the Present State of Ireland* (c. 1596) and *Colin Clout Comes Home Again* (1595), Spenser recounts the "night alarms" which the Irish kern led against both the native Irish and the English settlers. From the Elizabethan Irish vantage point, the bodrag was an example of the ritualized violence which regulated early modern Irish civilization. Proinsias MacCana writes:

> So far as the poets were concerned, raiding and skirmishing among native chieftains was little more than a well-tried social lubricant that conferred certain benefits and carried few dangers for the [Gaelic] system. . . . Warfare and strife were indeed part of 'the natural order.'[41]

In his study of modern Irish literature, Seamus Deane has similarly deduced from this cultural background that "the idea of society and the assumption of stability have never been securely lodged in Irish experience. History is an inescapable category, violence a recurrent phenomenon."[42] As Montague's early, shifting perspectives illustrate, history is not "inescapable," but more appropriately "undiscovered" in how it relates to our personal circumstances. The first step of any "revival" or "renaissance" is to assess what precisely is being "re-born." Having been presented with nationally important images of Yeats and the Rising, Montague reassessed the full array of renaissance inheritances at his disposal. For Spenser's generation, it was the classical learning of ancient Greece and Rome which had come to roost in Troynovant on the banks of the Thames. As Joyce had demonstrated in regard to Irish literature, much more than classical learning and English literature seems to float down the Liffey. For Montague and poets of what was later to be called the "Northern Renaissance," both the English and the Irish Renaissance had to be reinterpreted.

In *Patriotic Suite,* Montague sets out on his own bodrag against the Irish cultural tradition. The burning of the Abbey Theatre seems an accurate metaphor for the changing of the guard from the peasant plays and Gaelic revivalists to the "new generation" of Irish writers which Montague and Kinsella championed in the first *Dolmen Miscellany.* Liam Miller's jacket note underlines Montague's innovative critique. Miller wrote: "The poets have been strangely silent during the 1916 commemoration. Is it because, as Lenin said, the Irish Revolution was premature, and bound to turn bourgeois?"[43] According to the judgement of Montague's poems upon the Irish Literary Revival, and this statement by Miller, the real revolution is taking place now—in the cultural realm. In **"Like Dolmens Round My Childhood,"** Montague presented rural Ireland with a level of objectivity that Yeats had eschewed. Maggie

Owens's animals and indignities are recounted as equal parts of her epic stature. Having revised the peasant, Montague turned towards revising the national poet.

The final pages of *Patriotic Suite* juxtapose a poem, **"1966 And All That,"** with a statement by Spenser regarding the "fatal destiny" of Ireland, the crest of the United Irishmen, and an untraced statement from Friedrich Engels: "The real aims of a Revolution, those which are not illusions, are always to be realised after that Revolution." It is the interplay of these images that reveals the direction of Montague's experimentation. The final poem calls attention to the discrepancies between national trends in Ireland and global modernization:

> The gloomy images of a provincial Catholicism
>
> (In a thousand schoolrooms
> children work quietly while
> Christ bleeds on the wall)
>
> wound in a native music
> curlew echoing tin whistle
> to eye-swimming melancholy
>
> Is that our offering?
>
> (14)

In a cultural analysis less ambitious than, but similar to, Yeats's "Among Schoolchildren," Montague places contemporary Ireland in relation to its cultural past and finds a marked, ironic discrepancy. In this instance, it is not Yeats's condemnation of the non-Quattrocento ways in which the children are learning, but rather the insistence on the old "Irish" ways, the "melancholy" and "provincial Catholicism" that provokes Montague's satiric dismay.

Following this topically entitled poem, the sequence concludes with the words of Spenser's *A View of the Present State of Ireland*: "They say it is the Fatal Destiny of that land that no purposes whatsoever which are meant for her good will prevail." Along with the quotation from Spenser, Montague juxtaposes the seal of Wolfe Tone's Society of the United Irishmen and the quotation from Frederick Engels. By placing an image of the Irish insurrectionary tradition with which he identifies[44] alongside Spenser's comment about the "fatal destiny" of Ireland, Montague was the first contemporary Irish poet to stand the contemporary political direction of the country in concrete relation to the occurrences (actual and written) of the past—specifically the Tudor Plantation in Ireland of which Spenser was significantly involved. In his work, Spenser had provided the clearest articulation of the English concern with Ireland's "fatall destiny" that his contemporaries Francis Walsingham, John Hooker, and Richard Stanihurst had posited.[45] Spenser's *View* attempted to prove

that attributing Irish intransigence to the English conquest as a matter of destiny was "a vayne conceipte of symple men," arguing that Irish social and cultural practices, rather than destiny, are at the root of Irish resistance.[46] In the late 1960s, as the island seemed to be obsessed with the various national vocabularies of the emerging Yeats industry, the Republic of Ireland and the Civil Rights movement in Northern Ireland, Montague and many others looked again to the "destiny" of Ireland. Like Spenser, Montague was also critical of attributing a "destiny" to Ireland.

Critiquing the cultural inheritance which Yeats had shaped and the Republic was currently commemorating, *Patriotic Suite* looks forward to Montague's next appropriation. No longer encumbered by the Yeatsian past, Montague returned to Spenserian Ireland in a more extensive way. Turning back to the English Renaissance example of Spenser which Yeats had so productively used, Montague discovered a pattern of self-representation which would sustain him throughout his prolonged attempt to find a national, artistic place for himself. By appropriating the Spenserian voice in *Patriotic Suite*, Montague discovered his first "right" to speak on the direction of the Republic, as opposed to simply his own Northern Irish community as he had in **"Like Dolmens Round My Childhood."** Montague revised the Elizabethans' negative images of the bards and assumed their authority at a time when, as Augustine Martin pointed out, the "acceptable stance" of the Irish writer shirked such responsibility as passe, Yeatsian or both.[47] Subsequent political events in Northern Ireland necessitated that Montague would no longer be able to separate his cultural roots in the North from the political direction of the Republic. In *The Rough Field* (1972), Montague would directly respond to the crisis in Northern Ireland by relying even more strongly upon the words and images of Edmund Spenser and his contemporaries.

THE ROUGH FIELD (1972)

In 1972, John Montague included *Patriotic Suite* as the eighth canto of his long poem, *The Rough Field*. In this inclusion, Montague added the poem, **"Siege at Mullingar, 1963,"** a poem which depicts the *Fleadh Cheoil*, the national music festival, held that year in Mullingar. This work juxtaposes this traditional Irish cultural event, the death that weekend of Pope John XXIII, and the wryly un-Irish and certainly un-Catholic goings-on of young women as they happily "roamed / The streets with eager faces, / Shoving for men."[48] The poem's thrice-repeated refrain—"Puritan Ireland's dead and gone / A myth of O'Connor and O'Faolain"—echos Yeats's "September 1913" and clearly indicates by its mention of the mid-century writers Frank O'Connor and Sean O'Faolain that Montague and his generation have put Romantic and Emergency Ireland behind them.

This **"Patriotic Suite"** no longer contends with Yeats, and looks more steadily toward a contemporary understanding of events in Ireland. An equally significant revision of the canto occurred in regard to Spenser's quotation regarding the "fatal destiny" of Ireland. Originally, Spenser's words concluded the sequence. In the canto as included in *The Rough Field,* Spenser's comment is placed as the first gloss at the opening to the entire movement. In these revisions, Montague presents **"Patriotic Suite"** as a canto which seeks to put to rest "dead and gone" epochs of Ireland. To do so, Montague focuses more closely upon the elements of Elizabethan Ireland which were not included in the 1966 publication of the sequence. While expanding his investigation of his literary and historical inheritance in this later work, Montague situates Spenser as a representative voice through which to begin his search. It is as if Elizabethan Ireland needs to be established as a myth of Spenser and his contemporaries before Montague can continue with his assessment of much more pressing contemporary events than the Rising commemoration and Yeats centenary had offered.

Between 1966 and 1972, the direction Irish politics and Irish society experienced a watershed far more significant than the cultural developments which were the center of focus for Montague in the earlier part of the 1960s. In his 1951 contribution to the young Irish writer symposium in *The Bell,* Montague seemed to lament that the contemporary Irish writer was not involved in some "national drama" like the war for Independence or the Civil War which had caused his father to emigrate from County Tyrone in 1925. With the Belfast and Derry riots of the late 1960s, the "drama" was to return in force. This re-emergence of armed struggle in Northern Ireland quickly curtailed the typically late-1960s mood of liberation to which Montague's work was contributing. In Northern Ireland, the establishment of the Dungannon Campaign for Social Justice (1964) and later organizations like the Northern Ireland Civil Rights Association (NICRA) and the People's Democracy (both founded in 1967) provided outlets for a generation desirous of change, and hoping to solve the old problems of partition and British rule by new means. These groups were based on the models of the Civil Rights movement in the United States and sought similar adjustments of economic and legislative powers for the Catholic minority of Northern Ireland. Like their later legislative inheritor the Social Democratic Labour Party, these groups were not narrowly defined "Republican" organizations centered exclusively in the Catholic minority of the province. Regardless of their intent, violent Loyalist resistance to these groups in Derry in 1968-1969 led to the current armed conflict frequently referred to euphemistically as the "Troubles."

The breakdown of the Northern Irish Civil Rights movement ushered in a period of increased introspection in Montague's poetry. During this period leading up to *The Rough Field,* Montague moved from aligning English Renaissance events with current events and towards identifying himself with the Irish bard of Elizabethan Ireland. Significantly, Montague was able to unite the commemorative project of **"Like Dolmens . . ."** with the prophetic role he critically assumed in *Patriotic Suite.* In the process of doing so, Montague constructed the voice and the form adequate for his most public poem, *The Rough Field,* which was published in response to the Northern Irish crisis which in many ways grew out of the legacy of the incomplete accomplishments of both Elizabethan conquest and the Easter Rising. Up until this point, Montague's use of Spenserian materials was a significant, but not an entirely shaping concern. In **"Like Dolmens . . . ,"** Spenser provided a way to connect Montague's Ulster countryside with an enabling literary and mythic tradition. In *Patriotic Suite,* Spenser granted a means to critique Yeats's Irish Renaissance and to enter into an historical consideration of what the Irish and English Renaissances provided the aspiring national poet. From this point forward, Montague united his personal tradition with the historical materials of the renaissances in a way that would allow him to conceptualize the events of Anglo-Irish history and subsequently to write out his own mature works from that coherence.

The Rough Field collects a number of Montague's earlier sequences and poetry in addition to *Patriotic Suite,* which was the earliest of the sequences to be published. Importantly, **"Like Dolmens Round My Childhood"** concludes the first canto, *Home Again,* and provides the context in which we are to enter into the vast historical meditation which will follow. In this revised context, the poem actually acts as a dolmen—a passage grave through which the spirit wanders into the afterlife. In Montague's work, as in Celtic mythology itself, the worlds of the dead and the living are not neatly separated. The spirits of the Spenserian past constantly impinge upon the rights of the living and vice versa. One of the most important revisions which occurs in *The Rough Field* is that Montague recalls both the spirits and the poetic responsibilities of the Elizabethans. Taking up the inheritance of the Gaelic O'Neill dynasty of early modern Ulster, Montague moves from being simply an historical poet to being a properly epic, or dynastic, poet in the Spenserian sense. Andrew Fichter defines the genre of the "dynastic epic":

> Their theme is the rise of *imperium,* the noble house, race, or nation to which the poet professes allegiance. . . . The "Poet historical" speaks of the past as if it were the future—a future to which he and his heroes are granted access only in extraordinary moments of prophetic vision during which the scroll of fate is unrolled and the divine plan is for an instant revealed.[49]

He continues, "[t]he strategy of the dynastic poet . . . is born of the desire, if not to order historical experience, to reveal whatever principle of order is thought to inform it" (2). The epic, or dynastic poem, originates in a "desire" to order, to cast form, upon the events of recent history in the perspective of the past. In this alone, *The Rough Field* may be said to be a profoundly "dynastic" poem. Montague's efforts with *The Rough Field* separate his adaptation of Spenser from Yeats's imitation. In Yeats's work, Spenser was brought back into the landscape of Irish literature, but not fully re-incorporated. When Yeats finally embraced the Spenserian pose in "The Municipal Gallery Re-visited," he did so to affirm the outside status Renaissance poets would, according to Yeats, always hold in Ireland. Spenser returns in Yeats's work, but as a figure transformed into a "beautiful lofty thing"—one aspect among many which Yeats memorialized. Though Yeats unquestionably championed the dynasty of the Big House, that dynasty practically by definition held no hopes of being resuscitated. In this later engagement with Spenser, Montague folds his own interpretations into formal as well as thematic instances. Spenser and Elizabethan Ireland are investigated as more than emblems. As has been seen in his experimentation in *Patriotic Suite,* Montague was willing to let Spenser speak out of his own work. In the attempt to write a modern Irish epic poem, Montague must follow Spenser's originating example. Yet, by allowing Spenser and his contemporaries historical voice with the open form of *The Rough Field,* Montague destabilizes the Elizabethan model and creates a very different national work than had either Spenser or Yeats. In his epic aspiration, Montague ambitiously attempts to let the whole of Elizabethan Ireland speak through *The Rough Field,* thereby addressing Spenser and the Elizabethan inheritance on their own terms.

A number of critics have drawn attention to the "epic" stature of *The Rough Field.* Most convincingly, Thomas Dillon Redshaw has outlined Montague's attempt in *The Rough Field* to undertake R. H. Pearce's "new epic."[50] In *The Continuity of American Poetry,* Pearce defined the "new epic" as

> . . . a poem of the breadth and scope of the epic, yet without its heroically plotted articulation; a poem, which working solely as a poem, would engage its reader's sensibilities in such a way as to reinvigorate and reform them and would then relate him anew to a world which, until it were poetically transubstantiated, could not give him this one thing he most wished for: humanity articulated by history.[51]

Like his previous uses of Spenser, Montague's inclusion of Elizabethan materials in *The Rough Field* serves to "reinvigorate" his reader's sensibility through an initial sense of novelty and then by contrast. Though not going so far as to attempt to reverse Pearce's

formula and articulate history by humanity, in its autobiographical origin, Montague's *The Rough Field* does seek to shift the balance more significantly toward the personal, human side.

Interestingly, criticism of Montague's "epic attempt" most frequently comes along nationalist lines. Placing *The Rough Field* in a pointedly national context, Seamus Deane observes:

> . . . in *The Rough Field,* he [Montague] is attempting the almost impossible task of inferring in a lyric sequence the existence of a whole civilization. . . . Although Ireland has, like most places, settled for a predominantly lyric tradition in its poetry, the anxiety on the part of many poets to incorporate the fragments of memory, history, and above all, the consciousness of having been subject to fragmentation, has led to a number of curious, sometimes brilliant, epic and narrative attempts. The epic bespeaks a culture which is whole; the lyric one which, while broken, is reconstituted in the fullness for the duration of the poem.[52]

As Deane points out, the epic speaks for a "whole" culture. According to this reasoning, the lyric tendency of Ireland grows out of tradition "broken" by empire. Montague's failure, according to Deane, is both his "lyric" tendency and the failure of his society to be whole. Regardless of the success or failure of his epic, Montague's achievement in *The Rough Field* has been generally recognized. Even Deane, underlining the aesthetic and politics implications of the poem, grants that

> after the publication of *The Rough Field* many of the facts of Irish poetry assumed shape and meaning; and the main fact is that the epic attempt in that poem marks the reuniting of the political and literary traditions which had previously been separated.[53]

Deane's guarded compliment of Montague's work points out the similarity of *The Rough Field* to many of the more Spenserian elements of the work of Yeats. Yeats painstakingly separated the political and literary traditions in his reading of Spenser. By returning to the dynastic epic, Montague returned to the genre in which political and literary realms had always coincided.

What most distinguishes Montague's work in *The Rough Field* is not his adaptation of *the* national Renaissance genre, but his modernization of it. He has combined the epic desire "to reveal whatever principle of order is thought to inform" historical experience with the open form's ability to include a vast array of experience, some historical and some not.[54] *The Rough Field* is an open poem which stakes its claims by turns in an epic, lyric, and elegiac voice. Ezra Pound re-defined the epic as simply "a poem including history."[55] In his epic, Montague attempts to fully incorporate Elizabethan history by re-animating it within his array of poems so as to investigate his relationship to his personal and national past.

As it was assembled, *The Rough Field* follows the psychological, religious, historical, and geographic searchings of the poem's central presence through the various layers of Northern Ireland. It begins with the poet's return from Dublin to his native Garvaghey and follows the sometimes present narrator through a number of conflicts into the center of the poem, **"A Good Night,"** and then back out the same route into the equally narrative conclusion, **"Epilogue: Driving South."** Retracing the route of Ireland's ancient epic the *Táin Bó Cúailnge*, Montague seeks to uncover the imaginative source of the contemporary personal and political conflict he was witnessing in Northern Ireland.[56] As it was finally published in 1972, *The Rough Field* is comprised of eleven cantos: **"Home Again"**; **"The Leaping Fire"**; **"The Bread God"**; **"A Severed Head"**; **"The Fault"**; **"A Good Night"**; **"Hymn to New Omagh Road"**; **"Patriotic Suite"**; **"A New Siege"**; **"The Wild Dog Rose"**; and **"Epilogue: Driving South."** Of these cantos, five—**"Home Again"** (1966), **"The Bread God"** (1968), **"Hymn to New Omagh Road"** (1968), **"Patriotic Suite"** (1968), and **"A New Siege"** (1970)—were printed in their entirety before being included along with Derricke's woodcuts in *The Rough Field*.[57] In some of the cantos, such as **"Home Again,"** Montague undertook extensive revision of his previous work. Significantly, in cantos where Elizabethan imagery figures most prominently, such as **"A New Siege"** and **"Patriotic Suite,"** fewer changes were made. In these "Elizabethan" cantos, Montague explicitly contrasted the current unrest with early modern Ireland.[58] The wholesale inclusion of these cantos seems to indicate that this juxtaposition was an original, satisfying imaginative answer for Montague as he sought to address poetically what was happening in Ireland.[59] Furthermore, where the Spenserian elements are most pronounced—as in the fourth canto, **"A Severed Head"**—Montague's work does more than align the crises of early modern and contemporary Northern Ireland. In this most historically engaged of the Elizabethan cantos within *The Rough Field,* Montague has, to a great extent, implicated himself in the progression of national, epic poets in Ireland from Spenser's time to his own and in this way outlines the risks and responsibilities involved.

In his "Preface" to *The Rough Field,* Montague claimed that he "sometimes saw the poem as taking over where the last bard of the O'Neills left off." A year earlier, he had stated this sentiment even more directly, writing: "I sometimes see myself as successor to the last bard of the O'Neills."[60] One of the last bards of these Ulster chieftains was Aodh MacAingill. MacAingill earned a place in the English literary tradition by being present at O'Neill's camp outside of Dundalk when Sir John Harington visited The O'Neill in 1599 after the Earl of Essex had abandoned his campaign in Ireland.[61] After O'Neill's defeat, MacAingill gained recognition on the

continent as the first professor of philosophy and theology at St. Anthony's College in Louvain and through his introduction of the works of Duns Scotus to the continent. Less known is that he is the author of a great deal of poetry, as most clerics in Gaelic Ireland were because they were frequently chosen from the ranks of the bardic families. MacAingill's most famous poem, *"Afhir fhéachas uait an chnáimh"* ["O thou who gazes on the skull"], depicts the head of Henry, the son of Hugh O'Neill, rising from out of the grave and condemning the state of Ireland since he died.[62] In *The Rough Field,* Montague journeys back to the geographic location of his own childhood and the center of the O'Neill country in County Tyrone to extend MacAingill's poem into a dialogue between Elizabethan and contemporary Ireland.

Following the example of the last bard of the O'Neills, in **"A Severed Head"** Montague presents his most concentrated effort to unite the politically empowered poet of Spenserian Ireland with his own autobiographical and historical situation. Montague wrote **"A Severed Head"** while assembling and composing the poetry of *The Rough Field* in early 1972. Quite literally taking over writing the work of the last bard of the O'Neills, this canto of the poem is the most Elizabethan of all Montague's work in both content and form. **"A Severed Head"** consists of six poems, the third of which is a series of poetic portraits recounting the history of the O'Neill dynasty of Tyrone. In this section, the fate of the O'Neill Earls of Tyrone comes to stand in for the fate of Montague's family and the whole of Ireland.

"A Severed Head" opens with an earlier poem, **"The Road's End."** Even though the title of this poem was omitted by Montague in its later inclusion in *The Rough Field,* as the first piece of the canto, the work suggests that the poem is journeying to the "end," or culmination, of Montague's historical considerations. The Elizabethan events retold in **"A Severed Head"** brought the early modern Anglo-Irish crisis to its climax in the North, resulting in the Flight of the Earls and the subsequent Plantation of Ulster with Scottish and English settlers in the seventeenth century. In the opening poem, Montague's casually recounts an afternoon driving cattle:

> May, and the air is light
> On eye, on hand. As I take
> The mountain road, my former step
> Doubles mine, driving cattle
> To the upland fields.

> (33)

Montague's speaker is driving cattle from their lowland winter pasturage to the "upland fields" in adherence to Irish pastoral ways dating back well before the Tudor conquest. Observing Irish pasturage practices in sixteenth-century Leinster and Munster, Spenser concluded in his *A View of the Present State of Ireland* that

> this keping of Cowes ys of yt self a verie Idle lyfe and a fytt nurserie for a theif: For which cause yee remember I disliked the Irish manner of keping of Bollies in sommer upon the mountaine and lyving after that salvage sorte.

Aside from providing cover for rebels, Spenser faults the *buaile* because it leads to isolated communities who are not "conversant in the view of the world."[63] Following in the ancient footsteps of Irish pastoral life, Montague's poetic voice aligns Elizabethan observation with contemporary experience before investigating the enduring conflict between the two. As testament to the development of Montague's poetic methods since the sometimes tendentious *Patriotic Suite,* the allusions within these opening lines are more subtle and ultimately more effective than in that earlier sequence. In this instance, Montague is uniting the topographical and the literary traditions in a complex and historical way. This journey in **"A Severed Head"** begins in May, the month following the April of both Geoffrey Chaucer's *Canterbury Tales* and T. S. Eliot's "Burial of the Dead." Situating his journey in the Irish and English literary tradition, Montague suggests an even deeper importance to this journey. Indicated by the echo of Dante's spiritual journey, Montague's interpretation builds upon the "former step" of Spenser's Elizabethan depictions. Just as Dante's "footfall rose above the last" as he tried to ascend out of the dark wood of error (*Inferno* I.31), Montague's narrator's confident footsteps are also about to encounter nearly insurmountable opposition. Dante confronted incontinence, violence, and fraud. Faced with a more personally affecting and consequently less explicit dilemma, Montague's narrator must simply turn back toward the dark wood of Elizabethan history to discover what he is up against.

Having begun the historical journey of **"A Severed Head,"** the narrator of *The Rough Field* observes, "No rock or ruin, dun or dolmen / But showed memory defying cruelty / Through an image-encrusted name" (35). Poetry covers this country according to Montague, providing an imaginative and a literary sediment of meaning. Significantly, *The Rough Field* itself originates in this read landscape. "Rough Field" itself is the literal translation of the Irish, *garbh achaidh*. Looking back at the folk tradition connected with the place-names of County Tyrone, the poem characterizes the landscape as "a manuscript / We had lost the skill to read, / A part of our past disinherited" (35). Shortly after the publication of *The Rough Field,* Montague stated that "a poet is someone who, through words, turns psychic defeats into victories."[64] Montague's project with *The Rough Field* is not simply to turn history on its head, but to re-enter the flow of history and

read it, as Walter Benjamin claimed, against the grain, analyzing each history encrusted image.[65]

In the first canto of *The Rough Field,* "Home Again," Montague underlined the importance of being able to recover the ability to read the historical manuscript of the North. In addressing the Elizabethan legacy of County Tyrone, Montague circles back to **"Home Again,"** the sonnet sequence which begins *The Rough Field.* In the second of the three opening sonnets, Montague turns from the octave through reference to the linguistic and political inheritance of Tyrone:

> . . . it was near the borders of Tyrone—
> End of a Pale, beginning of O'Neill—
> Before a stranger turned a friendly face,
> Yarning politics in Ulster monotone.
> Bathos as we bumped all that twilight road.
>
>   (10)

Although the Belfast-Omagh bus trip of the first sonnet already places the narrator well outside the Dublin Pale, the borders of Montague's imagined Pale are extended so as to surround the borders of Tyrone. Just as the Dublin Pale of Tudor Ireland was the sanctuary of English policy and custom on the island, so "Tyrone" now becomes the sanctuary of Catholic, Gaelic policy and custom as it had been until O'Neill's submission to Mountjoy. The O'Neill territory becomes the secret center, or Fifth Province, of the narrative quest of *The Rough Field.* It is the point around which biographical, historical, religious, political, and vocational concerns circle. Significantly, it is a point approachable only through Spenser's Ireland.

"A Severed Head" enters into the world of Tudor Ireland and the O'Neill dynasty by means of reading these "shards / Of a lost culture" (34). Montague's actual entrance into the past occurs abruptly via the Irish language. The active search into the historical materials of early modern Ireland is initiated by the speaker of the poem and his endeavor to speak "school Irish" to the "last Gaelic speaker in the parish." To his stammering attempt to speak the country's language, the Gaelic speaker responds, *"Tá an Ghaeilge againn arís . . ."* [We have the Irish again]. Immediately after this compliment, the narrative opens out into commentary that is neither the narrator's nor the old Gaelic speaker's:

> *Tír Eoghain:* Land of Owen,
> Province of the O'Naill;
> The ghostly tread of O'Hagan's
> Barefoot gallowglasses marching
> To merge forces in Dun Geanainn
>
> Push southward to Kinsale!
> Loudly the war-cry is swallowed
> In swirls of black rain and fog

As Ulster's pride, Elizabeth's foemen,
Founder in a Munster bog.

(35)

The Gaelic speaker's exclamation breaks the stanzas and leads to a consideration of who has "had" the land. The attempt to recover the language clears the path backwards to the historical content of the region. The family seat of the O'Neills at Dungannon, and the "ghostly tread" of their inaugurative family, the O'Hagans, bring back the memory of the defeat of O'Neill's army at Kinsale, at the opposite side of the island. Though linguistically O'Neill never "lost" County Tyrone,[66] Montague underscores the lost nature of the countryside he is "reading" as he concludes referring to the war-cry, or hubbub, of the Ulster O'Donnells, who accompanied Hugh O'Neill on the march to his defeat at Kinsale in 1603.

In the poems which follow, Montague immerses himself in Tudor Ireland to investigate the active and ongoing debt. A dead language, Montague indicates, may be a way backwards, but to come forward we must not only repossess that language but the past which has been described in the "foreign," English language which Montague speaks. In the poems which follow this entrance into Elizabethan Ireland, Montague imaginatively translates a number of English historical descriptions of Elizabethan Ireland back into Irish, in both language and perspective.[67] The O'Neill dynasty which Montague will repossess in the poems that follow was commemorated in the English literary imagination in the writings of St. Edmund Campion, Edmund Spenser, Sir John Harington, and William Camden. Returning to these depictions, Montague does not simply restylize the history so as to present complimentary portraits where critical ones existed. Instead, he highlights the complexities of the Elizabethan legacy in Ireland. Issues of cultural appropriation, English policy, and epic poetry are investigated in the O'Neill portraits.

The literary portraits of the third section of **"A Severed Head"** depict the O'Neill family from the first Earl of Tyrone, Con Bacach O'Neill (1484-1559), to his son Seán an Dimas (1530-67), to the diplomatic triumphs and defeats of Hugh O'Neill (1540-1616), the "Great O'Neill." The four poems which comprise the movement are written in short two- to four-foot lines of what Montague has called his "scopic" or "public meter."[68] Employing these bardic lines, Montague retells the history of the O'Neills as if he were providing counterpoint to how O'Neill's *seanachaí* would have recounted the ancient family's genealogy at public ceremonies. The O'Neill dynasty most significantly challenged Elizabeth's claims to Ireland and were directly responsible for Spenser's expulsion from Cork. By recalling these moments, Montague affirms their hold upon his imagination. Yet throughout this poetic movement, Montague

focuses upon the deconstructive potential of how England *reads* the Irish. In Montague's re-writing of this era, he reassembles these English fragments of policy and description into his own coherent, lost tradition of the earls of Tyrone.

The first poem, **"Con Bacach O'Neill, 1542,"** provides the date when "The O'Neill" became the first "Earl of Tyrone." In 1541, Henry VIII was declared King of Ireland by an act of Irish Parliament. One year later, in the effort to consolidate his authority in Ireland without wasting crown expenditures, Henry's Lord Lieutenant in Ireland, Anthony St. Leger, instituted the policy of "surrender and regrant." In that year, Con O'Neill "surrendered" his Gaelic title and privilege, "Uí Néill," and was "regranted" the English title, "O'Neill, Earl of Tyrone." Although this practice was to have marked effect on the leadership of Gaelic society, and particularly upon the O'Neills, the immediate effects of the policy were more ad hoc. D. B. Quinn summarizes:

> Some took titles. . . . Some promised to hold their lordships in feudal dependance from the Crown—which the Irish laws did not allow them to do, since the lord did not, as in feudal society, own the land. Others simply promised friendship and help in the king's wars.[69]

The inadequacy of the English policy of "surrender and regrant" may be illustrated by the immediate effects of Con O'Neill's example. Upon his assuming the title of the Earl of Tyrone, his illegitimate son, Matthew, was created the "baron of Dungannon" assuring, in the English tradition of primogeniture, his elevation to the Earldom upon his father's death. Much to the chagrin of English policy-makers, Irish society did not function along such clear lines. Instead, during the chieftain's lifetime, a *tánaiste,* or successor, would be chosen. This tánaiste was simply "the next strongest personality in the [extended family] group."[70] Since the leadership of the clan would be contested by force of arms if a tánaiste was not selected during the chieftain's lifetime, it was only logical to elect the family member who was in the best position to lead the clan. This could take into account both familial allegiances and military power. Not surprisingly, Matthew O'Neill, first baron of Dungannon, was killed by order of the more powerful and politically connected Seán O'Neill in 1558.

Montague's poem thematically enacts a similar act of surrender and regrant against the English depiction. **"Con Bacach O'Neill, 1542,"** works upon this irony of naming. A marginal gloss from Sir George Carew, a Provincial president in Elizabethan Ireland and an indefatigable officer in Ireland during Tyrone's Rebellion, underlines this interpretive gap: "O'Neill: A name more in price than to be called Caesar."[71] Preceding this entire sequence, Carew's comment, though sardonic, recognizes hereditary splendor of the O'Neill chieftain and his title. In Montague's first poem, Carew's recognition is undercut by the implication that an English title can be bought, at a considerable monetary and cultural price. The poem begins in medias res showing Conn "Heralded by trumpeters, / Prefaced by a bishop, / Sided by earls, Con" (35). As the description continues, more focus is granted to the financial expenditure of the title, than to Con's stature or the political or cultural cost of the event:

> Twenty angels for
> A fur lined gown,
> Ten white pounds
> To the College of Arms
> For a new eschuteon. . . .
> Forty shillings, by custom,
> Must go to the captain—
> His knee lifts rustily
> From English ground:
> *Arise, Earl of Tyrone.*
>
> (36)

Imaginatively returning to the event, Montague is quite literally cataloguing the naming of the earl of Tyrone. From the twenty gold coins to the captain's fee, the creation of the earl of Tyrone seems to be a bought privilege. The hypocrisy of paying an English guard, "by custom," is underlined by the fact that this literally occurs on "English ground," or metaphorically in an English field of reference.

A reading of the importance of that event for the "lost tradition" which Montague is investigating in this canto is available from the succession this event grants. At his death, Con was recorded to have

> left his curse to any of his posterity that would either learn English, sow wheat, or make any building in Ulster, saying that the language bred conversation and consequently their confusion, that wheat gave sustenance with like effect, and, in building, they should do as the crow doth, make her nest to be beaten out by the hawk.[72]

Con's curse is directed toward all English and modernizing innovations. Ironically, Hugh O'Neill was to have the greatest success against the English precisely by moving adeptly between the English and Irish worlds. In these poems, Montague is searching through his inheritance as recipient of this curse. He speaks English and is conversant with the historical and literary enemy. Though the first two poems of the canto do not recount the existence of wheat fields, they do focus upon the buildings dotting the countryside—"cottages" and "white-washed cells"—all in disarray but all against the dying wishes of Con.

The ambiguous cultural position of the first earl of Tyrone is accentuated by the next poem, which deals with his son and successor to the Gaelic title of "The O'Neill"—**"Seán an Dimas, 1562."** Upon Con's death, Shane, or "Seán the Proud," succeeded Con as "The O'Neill" on July 17, 1559 and immediately went into open rebellion against English. On the date given in the poem's title, Shane was summoned to Whitehall Castle where he arrived on January 6 to sue for pardon from Queen Elizabeth. Despite his father's formal surrender of "the name of O'Neeyle" and Gaelic custom, O'Neill appeared at Whitehall accompanied by a full retinue of advisors and gallowglass dressed "after the Irish fashion."[73] Edmund Campion recorded the English reactions to the O'Neill:

> the courtiers noting his haughtiness and barbarity devised his stile thus. Oneale the great, Cousin to St. Patricke, friend to the Queene of England, enemy to all the world besides.[74]

Despite his "barbarity," Shane was able to use his scant knowledge of English court politics to great effect. He was seen during his visit in the company of the Earl of Leicester and did, in fact, receive his pardon from the Queen. Not surprisingly, upon returning to Ireland, he resumed his warfare against the English and the other Irish clans in the area, eventually being killed by the Scottish gallowglass clan MacDonnell, among whom he had taken refuge from the O'Donnell Earls of Tyrconnell.

Montague's poem closely follows the popular description of Shane's visit to Whitehall:

> Swarthy and savage as
> The dream of a conquistador,
> Seán O'Niall, Shane
> The Proud struts before
> The first Elizabeth.
> Her fine-hosed courtiers
> Stare at his escort
> Of tall gallowglasses,
> Long hair curling
> Over saffron shirts
> With, on each shoulder—
> Under the tangle of
> The forbidden glib—
> The dark death-sheen
> Of the battle axe.
>
> (36)

The bardic poetry of the O'Neills traced their lineage back through the fifth century King Niall of the Nine Hostages to Noah's ark. Elizabeth, for her part, had only been Queen for four years at the time of Shane's visit and, despite the later efforts of her chroniclers, only had possession of the throne by right of two paltry generations of rule. Her designation in Montague's poem as "the first Elizabeth" underscores the potential irony of Montague's historical vision as it explores these Elizabethan elements. Placed against the backdrop of Elizabeth's chroniclers, apologists, and poets like

Spenser, Montague's investigation demonstrates the poetically constructed nature of the glories of the English Renaissance and the empire.

If history is happening again in Montague's poem, how that history recurs may be detected by tracing the element which unites each of the depictions. In these poems, Montague isolates the cultural practices of the O'Neills by use of the political descriptions presented by the Elizabethans. In the first portrait, a strangely silent and perhaps unknowing Con pays to become an Englishman. In the second portrait, Shane asserts his own claims of cultural autonomy in defiance of the English monarch. Emphasizing the cost of that defiance, the poem concludes on a foreboding note, drawing reference to the "forbidden glib" and "dark death-sheen / Of the battle axe." The Irish pole-axe which the gallowglass carry over their shoulder easily points towards the head which similar axes will "sever" from its body. The "glib," which Spenser describes as "a thicke curled bushe of haire hanginge downe over there eyes, and monstrouslie disguisinge them," had long been criticized by Elizabethan writers. Spenser is the most explicit on the sinister purpose of this cultural fashion:

> the Irish glibbes I sayed that besydes there salvage bruttishnes and loathlie fylthynes, which is not to be named, they are fytte maskes as a mantle is for a theif: For whensoever hee hath run him self into that perill of lawe that he will not bee knowen he eyther cutteth of his glibb quite by which he becometh nothinge lyke him self, or pulleth yt so lowe downe over his eyes, that it is verie hard to discerne his theivesh countenance. . . . Likewise theire goinge to battayle without Armour on theire bodies or heades, but trusting onelie to the thicknes of theire glibbs, the which they saye will sometymes beare of a good strooke.

(70; 74)

The threat of the "forbidden glib" for Spenser is the related threat of assimilation and resistance. As Spenser first explains, the hairstyle allows the rebels to hide their identity by either cutting off, or pulling down, their bangs. When not on the run and in open resistance, the rebels use their hair as armor. Far from simply having no redeeming quality, this Irish fashion demonstrated for Spenser that the kern could not be trusted in peace or war. Viewed from either cultural position, the Irish fashion threatens the possibility of a metaphoric loss of identity as well as the militant retention of that identity. The Irish cannot, according to Spenser's treatise, become good Englishmen.

Indicative of the complexity of his reassessment of the Spenserian inheritance, Montague does not simply turn these English condemnations into Irish affirmations. Instead he re-shapes these depictions toward highly personal ends. **"Like Dolmens Round My Childhood"**

and *Patriotic Suite* sought respectively to grant dignity and to align Montague's contemporary Irish subject matter through reference to Spenser. In this later more comprehensive effort, a more personal principle seems to be at work. This is evident in the last two poems, which address the legacy of Hugh O'Neill, Earl of Tyrone. **"Hugh, 1599"** recounts the visit of Sir John Harington to the O'Neill's camp outside of Dundalk on October 18, 1599. The poem is a loose adaptation of the words of Harington in his "Report of a Journey to the North of Ireland" which he presented to Queen Elizabeth upon his return to court after taking part in the second Earl of Essex's failed campaign in Ireland. Harington depicted the visit in largely cultural and literary terms so as to assure the queen of O'Neill's adherence to the "English ways" which his earldom supposedly necessitated.[75] Harington writes that while Sir William Warren and O'Neill spoke elsewhere, he

> took occasion the while to entertain his two sons, by posing them in their learning, and their Tutors, which were one Fryar Nangle, a Franciscan, and a younger scholer, whose name I know not; and finding the two children of good towardly spirit . . . in English cloths like a Noblemans sons; with velvet gerkins and gold lace; of a good and chearful aspect, freckle faced, not tall of stature, but strong, and well fet both of them their English tongue.

> I gave them, not without the advice of Sir William Warren, my English translation of Ariosto which I got at Dublin: which their Teachers took very thankfully, and soon afterwards shewed it the Earl, who call'd to see it openly, and would needs hear some part of it read; I turn'd, as it had been by chance, to the beginning of the 45th canto, and some other passages of the book, which he seemed to like so well, that he solemnly swore his boys should read all the book over to him.

(NA [Nugæ Antiquæ] 4)

Throughout Harington's "Report" there are significant problems of interpretation. Like Derricke's woodcuts, Harington's sketch was written out of the desire to illustrate how "Englished" O'Neill had become, but ended in being utilized to illustrate the Gaelic way of life. Much like Spenser's passages on the bards in his *View of the Present State of Ireland,* this voyeuristically detailed English condemnation of Elizabethan Ireland has the potential to become affirmation of an Irish way of life.

Montague utilizes this potential, but carefully revises his own self-presentation within the national tradition which he appears to be recovering. As he shapes Harington's prose into his own poetic account of the meeting, Montague writes:

> Around the table
> Of the Great O'Neill
> (Crushed bracken or
> A stone slab, under

A cloudless heaven)
Sir John Harington sees
The princely children
In velvet jerkin
And gold lace, after
The English fashion
With a bodyguard of
Beardless, half-naked
Boys, all listening
Meek as spaniels
While, with the aid
Of the shy poet tutor
He reads his translation
Of Ariosto's canto
On Fortune's Wheel
Whither "runs a
Restless round."

(36-7)

The changes which Montague makes to the passage from Harington are significant since they indicate how an English Renaissance epic, such as Harington's translation of *Orlando Furioso* might be perceived in Montague's version of Elizabethan Ireland. In Harington's account, the entire retinue is not present at the reading. Harington had described O'Neill's guard as "for the most part . . . beardless boys without shirts; who, in the frost, wade as familiarly through rivers as water-spaniels. With what charm such a Master makes them love him I know not" (*NA* 3). The other significant change in the passage is the emphasis now placed on the "shy poet tutor." In the original passage, Harington refers to an anonymous, not shy, "younger scholar." The "tutors" surrounding the O'Neills were part of their hereditary filidh and brehons, most of whom were now also priests. In this instance, the "younger scholar" was Aodh MacAingil. As the literal "last bard of the O'Neills," Mac Aingil's anonymity and shrewd ability to operate between cultures, like the half-present narrator of **"A Severed Head,"** holds out a direction for Montague to follow as he seeks to restore, as he wrote in the 1971 essay, the "lost intention of the O'Neills."[76] Montague stands as both Harington and Mac Aingil at this juncture. Like Harington, he is "translating" the work of epic poets. Like Mac Aingil, he recognizes that he is on the outside of a literary tradition that may certainly be bypassed, but which will all the same be present. The "shy" description of the poet-tutor signals the temerity with which Montague has entered into this complex inheritance since he first carefully presented **"Like Dolmens Round My Childhood."** Montague's development demonstrates a strikingly faithful adherence to the poetic he proposed as early as 1951, when he stated that it was the contemporary Irish writer's responsibility "to estimate his heritage without hastiness or bias" ("The Young Irish Writer and *The Bell*," 173). To recall and to reorganize the materials of early modern Ireland is daunting enough; to enter into them, Montague seems to suggest, may be overwhelming.

Like any prophetic vision, Montague's reflection on the O'Neill dynasty ends as abruptly as it begins. After depicting the surrender of Hugh O'Neill to Lord Mountjoy, **"A Severed Head"** returns to a more contemporary setting in the concluding poems. The poem immediately following the O'Neill vignettes is bordered by passages relating the Flight of the Earls, the fleeing of O'Neill and members of the remaining noble houses of Ulster in 1607. Montague's poem refers explicitly to the bardic poem "A nocht is uaigneach Éire," which recounts this event (*The Rough Field* 91). Depicting a country fiddler, Montague draws attention to how,

With an intricate
& mournful mastery
the thin bow glides & slides
assuaging like a bardic poem
our tribal pain . . .

(39)

It would seem that in spite of his long investigation into Spenser's Ireland, Montague has succumbed to **"The Lure"** of national eulogy which he critiqued so pointedly through his use of Spenser in *Patriotic Suite*. After all of these carefully appropriated historical portraits, Montague's poem invokes a traditional nationalist lament which surrounds the O'Neill's exile from Ireland. What distinguishes this later effort from the earlier critiques is the more purposeful autobiographical entrance at this point. The attempt of the poet's persona to take the part of the bard and sing out in the pain of the dying order occurs in the fifth poem. In the parallel stanzas of this poem, the poet recounts an autobiographical incident in which an Irish child "weeps at school / repeating its English." The poem itself emerges out of a dream:

(Dumb,
bloodied, the severed
head now chokes to
speak another tongue—
As in
a long suppressed dream,
some stuttering garb-
led ordeal of my own.)

(39)

The O'Neills' attempts to take on the English "garb" is now mirrored by the Irish child's "garb- / led ordeal of his own" enforced instruction in English. The "severed head" of the Great O'Neill which speaks out of MacAingill's bardic poem becomes the autobiographical figure of the poet as a child standing before two cultures from which he is alienated. Having journeyed through Spenser's Ireland, Montague's work returns to the present with an added, epic sense of authority.

The loss, or "tribal pain," of the English instruction, is not the loss of personal identity which Con predicted, although this is a continuing threat, but the loss of communal identity as seen in the child's separation from his parents:

> the turf cured width
> of your parent's hearth
> growing slowly alien:
>
> In cabin
> and field, they still
> speak the old tongue.
> You may greet no one.
>
> (39)

The poet's education in the "old tongue" began this historical meditation and might have united that child to the people of the countryside, the inheritors of the lands of the O'Neill retainers. In writing about the "history" of his province, Montague is seeking to educate his readers to another significance of those events. Ironically, "education" was the final solution to be imposed upon Gaelic culture. From the Elizabethan plans of Spenser to the compulsory English instruction of the National schools, "Education" and "Irishness" seemingly have been at logger-heads. In his *View,* Spenser presages this impasse. After the martial "reformation" of the Kingdom of Ireland, Spenser proposed that schoolmasters be sent out into the subdued provinces. These schoolmasters would instruct the Irish

> in grammar, and in the principles of scyences to whom they should be compelled to send their youthe to bee discyplined, whereby they will in shorte time growe upp to that Civill conversation, that both the children will loathe the former rudnesse in which they were bredd, and also there parence will even by thensample of there youge Children, perceave the fowleness of theire owne brutishe behavior compared to theirs, For learninge hath that wonderfull power of yt self that yt can soften and temper the most stearne and salvage nature.
>
> (205)

In the opening sonnets of *The Rough Field,* Montague claimed that "No Wordsworthian dream enchants me here" (11). A return to the rustic is not the aim of this poem because that would merely return the conflict back to the lost moment when the O'Neill dynasty died out. Throughout the poem, Montague privileges the rural setting over the urban, but he does not posit the return to a pre-lapsarian state which the Elizabethans, in spite of themselves, memorialized. As he is living in the wake of both Gaelic and Elizabethan Ireland, Montague chooses to retain both imagined communities in his text.

"A Severed Head" concludes with a poem which looks back upon the canto and states that this historical journey comprised "The longest journey / I have ever gone" (40). Throughout *The Rough Field,* as with any

contemplative investigation, the journey is more important than the arrival. Consequently, it is fitting that Montague does not bring to a close these historical meditations, and that the Elizabethan historical issues raised in this canto are left largely unresolved by the conclusion of the work. *The Rough Field* concludes where it began, with the narrator claiming: "With all my circling a failure to return, to what is already going // going // GONE" (83). In this work, Montague is charting the imaginative and historical landscape of his Spenserian inheritance. In the end, he seems to realize that a recollection of the noble history of Ulster was not a solution to the Troubles which prompted his historical investigations. In his brief autobiographical appearances in the Elizabethan sections of *The Rough Field,* Montague gestures a way through the current impasse which is as original as it is uncommented upon. Even in his "failure," the poet-protagonist illustrates certain generalizations about that history which may inform the present. In placing history in relation to the present, Montague does not finally "correct" or indict history, but highlights its direct personal relation to himself. Having made this connection, Montague returns to Spenser himself in his subsequent works and undertakes the next step—to rewrite the Tudor inheritance in Ireland in a startlingly personal way which would incorporate and transform Spenser and this history altogether. By investigating the Spenserian references in Montague's first publications after *The Rough Field* and in his final meditation addressing his autobiographical and historical inheritance, *The Dead Kingdom,* a pattern finally emerges in which Montague assesses and dismisses "memory's mortmain" (*The Rough Field* 75) in favor of even more personal and enabling poetic experimentations.

Notes

1. Liam Miller, "Introduction," *The Dolmen Press Yeats Centenary Papers MCMLXV,* (Dublin: Dolmen P, 1968) xiii-xvi. *The Dolmen . . . Centenary Papers* was the anthologized collection of twelve, monthly critical chapbooks by distinguished scholars such as Jon Stallworthy, Curtis Bradford, George Mills Harper, and Richard Ellmann. The other important publication of the Centenary was *In Excited Reverie: A Centenary Tribute to William Butler Yeats 1865-1939,* ed. A Norman Jeffares and K. G. W. Cross (New York: St. Martin's P, 1965).

2. "A Printing House That Fosters Poets," *Hibernia* (April 1959) 11.

3. This group consisted of writers who would become some of the most successful and critically acclaimed authors of the next three decades and included along with Kinsella and Montague, Aidin Higgins, John McGahern, Brian Moore, Richard

Murphy, and James Liddy. Originally conceived to be the first number of a new journal featuring the innovative work of contemporary Irish writers, a second number of the *Miscellany* never appeared.

4. *The Dolmen Miscellany of Irish Writing* (Dublin: Dolmen P, 1962) n.p.

5. "The Young Irish Writer and *The Bell* (1951)" *The Figure in the Cave and Other Essays,* ed. Antoinette Quinn (Dublin: Lilliput P, 1989) 170.

6. "Edmund Spenser," *Essays and Introductions* (New York: Macmillan, 1961) 361.

7. Echoing this sentiment, in 1966, the year that *Patriotic Suite* was published, Thomas Kinsella, Montague's co-editor of the *Dolmen Miscellany,* addressing the MLA on "The Irish Writer," put the matter in similar terms stating: "A writer who cares who he is and where he comes from looks about him and begins by examining his colleagues . . . I can learn nothing from them except I am isolated" ("The Irish Writer [1966]," *Davis, Mangan, Ferguson? Tradition and the Irish Writer* ed. Roger McHugh [Chester Springs: Dufour, 1970]: 57). Kinsella characterizes this isolation as a national *and* artistic condition related to the loss of the Irish language and lifestyle in Ireland which preceded the introduction of the English language: "I recognize simultaneously a great inheritance and a great loss. The inheritance is mine, but only at two enormous removes—across a century's silence, and through an exchange of worlds. The greatness of the loss is measured not only by the substance of Irish literature itself, but also by the intensity with which we know it was shared; it has an air of continuity and shared history which is precisely what is missing from Irish literature, in English or Irish, in the nineteenth century and today" (58-9). In his discussion of the role of the Irish writer who chooses to write in English, Kinsella motions towards the same sort of "culture-phase" which David Michael Jones had suggested in his "Preface to Anathemata." The "continuity and shared history" which is absent in contemporary Irish writing seems, for Kinsella, to be the defining characteristic of Irish literature before the coming of English. In the previous year, Augustine Martin had taken issue with the sort of "inherited dissent" which he detected in the work of Kinsella and others. Significantly, the only writer for whom Martin "made . . . exception" was John Montague ("Inherited Dissent: The Dilemma of the Irish Writer," *Studies* 54.213 [Spring 1965]: 21).

8. *The Belfast Telegraph* April 6, 1960: 22.

9. *The Figure in the Cave and Other Essays,* ed. Antoinette Quinn (Dublin: Lilliput P, 1989) 8-9. Hereafter cited parenthetically.

10. Seamus Deane has read this modernist characteristic as a particularly Irish trait, stating, "If tradition does not exist, it is necessary to invent it. This the Irish did. . . . Tradition is, in the end, an enabling idea rather than a fixed entity. Although knowledge of the past can affect it, it is the necessity of the present which activates it" ("An Example of Tradition," *The Crane Bag Book of Irish Studies,* 1971-1981 ed. Richard Kearney [Dublin: Blackwater P, 1982] 374).

11. *Poisoned Lands* (1961. Reprint, Dublin: Dolmen P, 1977): 15. The poem was first published in the Summer 1960 issue of *Threshold,* then republished by Montague four times without revision before its inclusion in *The Rough Field* (Redshaw, *The Northern Gate,* 612-22 passim).

12. *States of Mind: Two Centuries of Anglo-Irish Conflict, 1780-1980* (London: Pimlico, 1983) 127. T. S. Eliot defined the "historical sense" as "a perception, not only of the pastness of the past, but of its presence; the historical sense compels a man to write not merely with his own generation in his bones, but with a feeling that the whole of the literature of Europe from Homer and within it the whole literature of his own country has a simultaneous existence and composes a simultaneous order" (*The Selected Prose of T. S. Eliot,* ed. Frank Kermode [New York: Farrar, Straus & Giroux, 1975] 38).

13. Peter Beresford Ellis, *Dictionary of Irish Mythology* (New York: Oxford U P, 1987) 127.

14. In this poetic negotiation, Montague bridges between the distinctions R. G. Collingwood drew between "memory" and "history." Yeats's appropriations frequently reside in Collingwood's realm of memory where "the past is a mere spectacle . . . re-enacted." In "Like Dolmens Round My Childhood," Montague re-enacts the mythic history of Ireland in the present tense, entering into Collingwood's latter realm of history in which "history is re-enacted in present thought. . . . and my knowledge of myself is historical knowledge" (*The Idea of History,* ed. with an introduction by Jan Van Der Dussen [Oxford: Clarendon U P, 1993] 293).

15. The importance of Spenser for Montague's earliest self-presentations is evident as well in his earliest published poem. Two years earlier, he had published "The Sean Bhean Vocht" in *The Irish Times.* In this poem, the speaker encounters another old woman "[w]eaving a litany of legends against death" (*The Irish Times* 16 August 1958, "Books of the Week": 6). The poem concludes with the narrator wandering over Knockmany hill wondering "What faery queen lay dust" beneath its neolithic burial stones.

16. In a different, but closely related context, Thomas Dillon Redshaw reads Maggie Owens as one of Montague's many "heraldic women" in his work. See Thomas Dillon Redshaw, *The Northern Gate: A Study in the Poetry of John Montague,* Ph.D. diss., New York University, 1980: 64-79, 195-224 passim.

17. *Forms of Nationhood: The Elizabethan Writing of England* 132.

18. "The Poetry of Sir Samuel Ferguson" (Oct. 9, 1886), *Davis, Mangan, Ferguson? Tradition and the Irish Writer, Writings by W. B. Yeats and Thomas Kinsella,* ed. Roger McHugh (Chester Springs, PA: Dufour, 1970) 53. In the "Foreward," Prof. McHugh noted his gratitude to John Montague "who supplied the germ of this little book by suggesting that Yeats's article on Ferguson in the *Dublin University Review* should be reprinted" (11).

19. See Chapter Two, 41-3.

20. *W. B. Yeats: The Poems, Revised Edition,* ed. Richard J. Finneran (New York: Macmillan, 1983) 148.

21. At the time that Montague was beginning his career, the distinguished folklorist E. Estyn Evans, identified the same cultural transformation in the North of Ireland as did Montague: "These ancient diversities are being ironed out at an increasing rate, and the opportunity of seeing and, what is more important, placing on record these age-old crafts and rites will soon pass. The wonder is that so many have persisted through the political, economic and social upheavals of the last 150 years" (*Irish Folk Ways* [1957; London: Routledge & Kegan Paul, 1989] 2). In a note to a later English publication of his poems, Montague echoed this sentiment: "during my childhood, there were still pockets of Gaelic culture surviving in the remoter areas of the North of Ireland" (*Poisoned Lands, and Other Poems* London: McGibbon & Kee, 1961: 16).

22. Most recently, the poem has been included in *The Field Day Anthology of Irish Writing,* ed. Seamus Deane (Derry: Field Day Publications, 1991) Vol. 3: 1351, *The Penguin Book of Contemporary Irish Poetry,* ed. Peter Fallon and Derek Mahon (New York: Penguin, 1990): 38, and *Poets from the North of Ireland,* ed. Frank Ormsby, 2d ed. (Belfast: Blackstaff P, 1990) 97.

23. Cited by Redshaw, *The Northern Gate* 35.

24. Redshaw, *Northern Gate* 7.

25. In the 1950s, while studying at the University of Indiana, Yale, and the Iowa Writers' workshop, Montague was introduced by John Crowe Ransom and Robert Penn Warren to the work of Ezra Pound and William Carlos Williams. In his later experiences with John Berryman and lecturing at Berkeley during the 1960s, Montague became exposed to Berryman's work-in-progress, *The Dream Songs,* as well as Charles Olson's *The Maximus Poems* (1960). In *The Rough Field,* Montague adapted these poetic techniques so as to incorporate the disparate material of autobiography, history, and politics within his own work. See Thomas Dillon Redshaw, "John Montague's *The Rough Field: Topos and Texne*" (*Studies* 63.249 [Spring 1974] 31-46).

26. In a speech before the Irish Senate, Yeats had protested against contemporary motions to remove Nelson's pillar calling it a "very salutary" object "of meditation which may, perhaps, make us a little more tolerant" (*The Senate Speeches of W. B. Yeats* ed. Donald R. Pearce [Bloomington: Indiana UP, 1960]).

27. Contemporary commentaries on the sequence point out the scope of Montague's project in this respect. The Irish poet Basil Payne characterized *Patriotic Suite* as "poems which explore evocatively and/or provocatively the ideal of nationality" ("Rev. *A Chosen Light* (1967), *Patriotic Suite* [1966]," *Studies* 57.226 [Summer 1968]: 211). M. L. Rosenthal characterized the work as reflecting "lyrically and nostalgically on the idealism and the unrealized dream behind the Irish Revolution" (*The New Poets: American and British Poetry Since World War II* [New York: Oxford U P, 1967]: 267).

28. As early as the first Dolmen Press series of chapbooks published between 1954 and 1960, Liam Miller had demonstrated an interest in English Renaissance materials and more specifically Edmund Spenser. The seventh chapbook, *The Loves of Bregog and Mulla* (September 1956), reprinted an Irish topographical section of Spenser's *Mutabilitie Cantos.* For a discussion of Miller's part in the design of Montague's emerging project, *The Rough Field,* and other Dolmen projects see my "Reading the Renaissance: John Derricke's *Image of Irelande* (c. 1579) and the Dolmen Press (1966-72)." *Nua: Studies in Contemporary Irish Writing.* 1.2 (Fall 1998): 47-63.

29. *The Image of Irelande with a Discoverie of Woodkarne by John Derricke, 1581,* with the notes of Sir Walter Scott, edited with an introduction by John Small (Edinburgh: Adam and Charles Black, 1883).

30. "Introduction," *Elizabethan Ireland: A Selection of Writings by Elizabethan Writers on Ireland* (New York: Archon Books, 1983) 12.

31. "Curiosities of Irish Literature: No. 2—The Mere Irish," *The Dublin University Magazine* 9 (1837) 552.

32. *The Elizabethans and the Irish* (Ithaca: Syracuse U P, 1966).

33. *Patriotic Suite* (Dublin: Dolmen P, November 1966): 7. Hereafter cited parenthetically.

34. Harington's "Report" is contained in *Nugæ Antiquæ; Being a Miscellaneous Collection of Original Papers in Prose and Verse written during the Reigns of Henry VIII, Edward VI, Queen Mary, Elizabeth, and King James by Sir John Harington, Knt. And by others who lived in those times, Selected from authentic remains by the late Henry Harington, and newly arranged, with illustrative notes by Thomas Parks* [London: J. Wright, 1804] I: 43). Hereafter cited parenthetically, thus: *NA.* The morris dance was a traditional part of the may day festivities where men dressed as women (E. K. Chambers, *The Medieval Stage* 1903) i: 196.

35. See Stephen Greenblatt, "Murdering Peasants: Status, Genre, and the Representation of Rebellion," *Representing the Renaissance* ed. Stephen Greenblatt (Berkeley: U of California P, 1988) 1-30.

36. *A Tribute to Austin Clarke on His Seventieth Birthday* (Dublin: Dolmen P, 1966) 6.

37. De Valéra's use of the Revival images is best evident in his often quoted 1943 St. Patrick's Day Radio address, when he presented a hoped for vision of Ireland which "would be the home of a people who valued material wealth only as a basis of right living, of a people who were satisfied with frugal comfort and devoted their leisure to the things of the spirit; a land whose countryside would be bright with cosy homesteads, whose fields and villages would be joyous with sounds of industry, the romping of sturdy children, the contests of athletic youths, the laughter of comely maidens; whose firesides would be the forums of the wisdom of serene old age" (quoted in Terence Brown, *Ireland, A Social and Cultural History 1922 to the Present* [Ithaca: Cornell U P, 1981]: 113).

38. *Modern Irish Poetry: Tradition and Continuity from Yeats to Heaney* (Los Angeles: U of California P, 1989) 41.

39. From July 1951 until 1966 when the new Abbey Theater was rebuilt on the original site, the Abbey Theater company performed at the Queen's Theater on Pearse Street.

40. "Living Under Ben Bulben," *The Kilkenny Magazine* 14 (Spring-Summer, 1966) 46.

41. "Notes on the Early Irish Concept of Unity," *The Crane Bag Book of Irish Studies* 2. 1-2 (1978): 68-9.

42. *Celtic Revivals: Essays in Modern Irish Literature, 1880-1980* (London: Faber & Faber, 1985) 12.

43. Montague would later confirm this judgement in an interview where he stated: ". . . Ireland lost its opportunity to be the first Cuba. If we had had a *real revolution,* we could have taken advantage of the fact that we are the offshore island of Europe. We could have offered Connemara as a rocket range to the Russians and our coast in the West as a harbor to the Russian fleet; we could have offered the same to the Americans. I don't see why we didn't play international poker to amuse ourselves. We could have made ourselves rich long ago" (Adrian Frazier, "Global Regionalism: Interview with John Montague," *The Literary Review* 22, no. 2 [Winter 1979]: 171).

44. In an interview, Montague stated that he and his family "we're republicans . . . in terms of the eighteenth century and the United Irishmen." Earl Ingersoll and Ben Howard, "'Elegiac Cheer': A Conversation with John Montague," *Literary Review* 31 (Fall 1987) 24.

45. Sir Francis Walsingham reported to the Privy Council that it was "the cursed disteyne of that contrye being not ordayned to receyve any good of any determynacion agreed upon for the reformation thereof" (Cited by Nicholas Canny, *The Elizabethan Conquest of Ireland: A Pattern Established* [New York: Barnes & Noble, 1976] 157). John Hooker, in his contribution to Holinshed's *Chronicles,* wrote: "It is a fatall and inevitable destinie incident to that nation that they cannot brook anie English govenor; for be he never so just, upright, and carefull for their benefit, they care not for it" ("The Supplie of this Irish Chronicle Continued from the Death of King Henrie the Eighth, 1546, Untill this Present Year 1586," *Chronicles,* Vol. 6: 400). The most explicit of Spenser's contemporaries to address the destiny of Ireland was Richard Stanihurst, who in his contribution to Holinshed wrote: "whoso wisheth any goodness to the miserable country, and noble progenie, let him with all the veines of his heart beseech God" ("A Treatise Containing a Plain and Perfect Description of Ireland," *Chronicles,* Vol. 6:48).

46. *A View of the Present State of Ireland* ed. W. L. Renwick (1934; St. Clair Shores: Scholarly P, 1971) 3. See Chapter One, 47-50.

47. Elsewhere on the Celtic Fringe of Great Britain during Montague's early career, poets were undertaking similar cultural projects. The Welsh

poet, David Michael Jones defined such efforts as a recovery of the "bardic capacity" which might restore the non-British poet to the empowered role in English-speaking society which he had enjoyed until the modern period. In the preface to his open poem, *The Anathemata* (1951), Jones states that "There have been culture-phases when the maker and the society in which he lived shared an enclosed and common background, where the terms of reference were common to all." Against this belief, Jones admits: "We are, in our society today, very far removed from those culture-phases where the poet was explicitly and by profession the custodian, rememberer, embodier and voice of the mythus, etc., of some contained group of families, or of a tribe, nation, people cult" (117-8). In a later interview, Montague claimed that the bardic role "is denied . . . certainly in the British Tradition. Though when we think of the Gaelic Tradition, on the other hand, we do find that the poet's role is socially secure" ("Beyond the Planter and the Gael: Interview with John Hewitt and John Montague on Northern Poetry and The Troubles," *The Crane Bag Book of Irish Studies,* 727-8). Recently, Seamus Heaney has reflected upon the continued presence of the Irish poet in everyday society stating, poetry is "part of the . . . language, and it's part of the [cultural] possessions and the name of the poet is part of the cultural possessions of the tribe, still" (*Charlie Rose Show,* 19 April 1996, Transcript #1621 [Denver: Journal Graphics] 9.

48. *The Rough Field,* 5th edition, notes by Thomas Dillon Redshaw (Winston-Salem: Wake Forest U P, 1989) 68. All subsequent parenthetical citations will be from this edition.

49. *Poets Historical: Dynastic Epic in the Renaissance* (New Haven: Yale U P, 1982) 1.

50. *The Northern Gate* 282-3 and 552-8. See also Redshaw, "John Montague's *The Rough Field: Topos and Texne,*" *Studies* 63 (Summer 1974) 31-46 and "*Rí* as in Regional: Three Ulster Poets," *Éire-Ireland* 9.2 (Summer 1974) 54-5.

51. Roy Harvey Pearce, *The Continuity of American Poetry* (Princeton: Princeton U P, 1961) 163.

52. "Irish Poetry and Irish Nationalism," *Crane Bag Book of Irish Studies* 16-17.

53. "Irish Poetry and Irish Nationalism," 15. See also Edna Longley's "Searching the Darkness: Richard Murphy, Thomas Kinsella, John Montague, and James Simmons," *Two Decades of Irish Writing: A Survey* ed. Douglas Dunn [Chester Springs: Dufour, 1975] 145) for a similar recognition of Montague's achievement in *The Rough Field.*

54. Fichter *Poets Historical* 2.

55. *Literary Essays,* ed. T. S. Eliot [London: Faber & Faber, 1960] 86.

56. Montague's journey traces the length of the island as well as the path of the Ulster cycle. Like the *Táin,* Montague's journey North goes from Dublin to Tyrone. T. F. O'Rahilly "believed that the Ulster stories describe the historical circumstances of the invasion of Ulster by Uí Néill invaders from Leinster (not Connacht)" (Kinsella, xii).

57. *Home Again* (Belfast: Festival Publications, 1967). *The Bread God . . .* (Dublin: Dolmen P, 1968). *Hymn to the New Omagh Road* (Dublin: Dolmen P, 1968). *Patriotic Suite* (1966). *A New Siege: An Historical Meditation* (Dublin: Dolmen P, 1970).

58. For a discussion of the structural significance of the related, Jacobean elements of "A New Siege," see my "'Campaigning against memory's mortmain': Benjaminian Allegory in John Montague's *The Rough Field." Notes on Modern Irish Literature.* 8 (1996) 12-19.

59. Terence Brown has observed, "It was John Montague . . . who first gave eloquent expression to a sense of déjà vu in relation to Ireland's contemporary troubles, which has dominated much literary and artistic responses to the dreadful events of the last twenty years" (*Ireland's Literature: Selected Essays* [Mullingar: Lilliput P, 1988] 243).

60. "I Also Had Music" (1971), *The Figure in the Cave* 47-8.

61. For a detailed discussion of this encounter, see my "'These are not the thinges men live by now a days': Sir John Harington's visit to the O'Neill, 1599." *Cahiers Élisabéthains,* 55 (Spring 1999): 1-17.

62. Aodh De Blacam, *Gaelic Literature Surveyed* (Dublin: Talbot P, [1929]) 161.

63. *A View of the Present State of Ireland* 201. The "bollie," or *buaile,* was the summer encampment. D. B. Quinn writes: "One of [Gaelic Society's] . . . characteristic features was its transhumance, a movement of flocks and herds into summer pastures while the oats was growing" (*The Elizabethans and the Irish* 14).

64. *Faber Book of Irish Verse* 38.

65. "Theses on the Philosophy of History," *Illuminations* ed. Hannah Arendt (New York: Schocken Books, 1968) 253-64.

66. Tyrone is anglicized from the Irish, *Tir Eoghain,* "Land of Owen," a mythic ancestor of the O'Neills.

67. Terence Brown, in the only pointedly historical criticism of Montague's methods, claims that Montague, ". . . unambiguously responds to a vision of primitive martial splendor insolently parading as foppish sophistication" (*Northern Voice* 162). Though Brown's criticism does not take into account the complex undertones of the inclusion of O'Donnell's war-cry or the "last Gaelic speaker" within the poem, it does illustrate that unlike the earlier experiments with Spenserian, or early modern Irish materials, *The Rough Field* engages in topics which, at the time of its composition, were part of a larger, more serious, "debate" which fueled the Northern Irish crisis.

68. "The Impact of International Modern Poetry on Irish Writing," *Irish Poets in English: The Thomas Davis Lectures on Anglo-Irish Poetry,* ed. Seán Lucy (Cork: Mercier P, 1973) 157.

69. *The Elizabethans and the Irish* (Ithaca: Cornell U P, 1966) 3.

70. Quinn, 16.

71. Montague had access to this allusion through a number of contemporary biographies and most likely obtained it through Sean O'Faolain's popular, official work, *The Great O'Neill: A Biography of Hugh O'Neill Earl of Tyrone, 1550-1616* (1942; Cork: Mercier P, 1992).

72. This is recorded in the *Calendar of the Carew Manuscripts* ed. J. S. Brewer and William Bullen (PRO, 1867). C. L. Falkiner's *Illustrations of Irish History and Topography Mainly of the Seventeenth Century* (Longmans, Green & Co., 1904) and D. B. Quinn's *Elizabethans and the Irish.* These texts differ in that the latter two attribute the curse to Shane, while the *Carew Manuscripts* attribute it to Con.

73. For an account of the visit, see James Hogan, "Shane O'Neill comes to the Court of Elizabeth," *Feílscríbhinn Torna* ed. Séamus Pender (Cork 1947) 154-70.

74. "The Historie of Ireland," *Two Histories of Ireland,* ed. James Ware (Dublin, 1633) 189.

75. "'These are not the thinges men live by now a days': Sir John Harington's visit to the O'Neill, 1599." *Cahiers Élisabéthains* 55.

76. The phrase occurs in "I Also Had Music" (1971), *The Figure in the Cave* 47-8.

Maura Harrington (essay date spring 2007)

SOURCE: Harrington, Maura. "*Born in Brooklyn*'s Bifocal View of Time and Space: John Montague as a Hybridized Irish American." *South Carolina Review* 39, no. 2 (spring 2007): 18-29.

[*In the following essay, Harrington discusses Montague as an Irish-American writer, concentrating on the poetry and prose of his 1991 book* Born in Brooklyn.]

Charles Fanning's 1990 book *The Irish Voice in America: Irish-American Fiction from the 1760s to the 1980s* focuses only on Irish-American fiction because of the "complexity" of drama and the "simplicity" of poetry (40). Having few kind words for Irish-American poetry, Fanning asserts that

> The problem has been an endemic blight of programmatic melancholy or bravado that emerged from the experience and perception of forced exile. The stock-in-trade of Irish-American poetry has been the immigrant's lament for a lost, idealized homeland and the patriot's plea for Irish freedom from British oppression, Such materials make good songs but bad verse that exhibits simplistic strains of nostalgia or righteous indignation.
>
> (4)

Eamonn Wall takes Fanning up on this statement, and sets Montague forth as a poet who presents in his long work **The Dead Kingdom** "a substantial and unsentimental exploration of the complex nature of the diaspora and the beginning of mature, poetic reflection on the role of the immigrant Irish in the 'global' world" ("Grafted" 374). Wall is ebullient with praise for Montague, perhaps because the poet is filling the void that Fanning has pointed out. To Wall, Montague's **Collected Poems,** "For sheer breadth of vision and writing skill . . . is perhaps the greatest volume of collected poems to emerge from an Irish poet since Yeats" ("Second" 118). While Edna Longley believes that Montague is "a more complex poet" than his contemporaries Richard Murphy, Thomas Kinsella, and James Simmons (138-39), her praise of the writer is not unbridled. She criticizes **The Rough Field** because its depiction of history and landscape "disappoint hopes his poetry had previously encouraged" (144). Sections of this long, epic-like poem, according to Longley, "Fall for the inevitable temptation of barren historical collage" (144). Additionally, **The Rough Field** "seems too conscious of its synthesizing position in relation to events and to the sequence as a whole" (145). However, Longley believes that the poem "for all its flaws—*with all its flaws*—is perhaps the most characteristic and significant achievement of a generation," as it reflects the strengths and the weaknesses inherent in the poetry of its time (145-52). While Longley might consider consciousness of synthesis a weakness in Montague's work, it is precisely the act of synthesis necessitated by his awareness of hyphenated American hybridity that defines Montague's writings about the experience of being an Irish American.

At the 1976 presentation of an award from the Irish American Cultural Institute, then president Dr. Eoin McKiernan hailed John Montague as "'an international relay station, a satellite orbiting Ireland, and transmitting outward and inward poetic and humanistic forms, themes, and ideas for the mutual stimulation and enrichment of cultures'" (qtd. in Redshaw "Appréciation" 122). Daniel Tobin, in "'Lines of Leaving/Lines of Returning': John Montague's Double Vision," asserts that Montague's writing "anticipates the poetry of the New Irish in America and elsewhere. He therefore reveals himself as a poet not only of his time but, in crucial ways, a poet before his time" (164). Raised in County Tyrone, Montague nonetheless spent time in America from birth to age four and again during his graduate studies. Still, the reflections of the American experience in his poetry and prose have received surprisingly little critical attention, with critics choosing instead to focus on Montague's dealing with the Irish political landscape, as reflected in his varied lyrical and narrative poems. However, his poems, short stories, and essays anthologized in 1991 *Born in Brooklyn,* most previously published and some appearing in their print debut, contain a wealth of information on being an Irish American and bear further critical attention. As becomes clear through a reading of this collection, ethnic Americans, and in Montague's work, Irish Americans in particular, are in a unique position, able to simultaneously live in two cultures, providing them with the opportunity to understand American situations from the inside and from the outside. This multiplicity of points of view allows for an open-minded approach to both personal and national issues. Using the trope of the Irish American (often himself) as an anthropologist, both literally and figuratively digging up facts about his own past and synthesizing them to make meaning in his current situation, Montague demonstrates in the poetry, short fiction, and essays in *Born in Brooklyn* that "the complex fate of being an Irish American" (55) involves a responsibility to consider situations from multiple perspectives in order to avoid repeating, on both the personal and national level, mistakes from the past.

To Montague, it is important for a writer to have a sense of family and home, or at least to search for these two entities. Antoinette Quinn goes so far as to assert that "Montague's appears to be a belated and acute case of Irish literary deracination. Born a hyphenated Irish-American he is a perpetually displaced person, in permanent imaginative quest for a home" (29). Gerald Dawe believes that a "sense of dislocation . . . pervades Montague's poetry" (15) and that he must constantly search for his place. However, it seems that Montague has moved beyond a search for a home to an acceptance of the fact that he has multiple homes. Having moved to another country away from his immediate family at such a young age, Montague's sense of home is not lessened, but his search for a consanguinity between his home countries is heightened. Montague believes that a poet should both strive toward a familiarity with the work of other international poets, but that he should also "belong to some place, . . . come from some place" ("Global Regionalism" 155). Throughout and before his literary career, Montague has searched through the past, conducting an "investigation," since he believes that a failure "to come to terms" with Ulster's situation will cause "a certain lack in [him] as [a] writer" (166). Digging through the fields of his own mind, family artifacts, and the landscape of stories available to him, Montague set out on a lifelong trek to understand the components of himself that lie buried on either side of the Atlantic. Stipe Grgas believes that Montague's "ambiguous relationship with [the] Northern landscape" during his childhood "enabled him to negotiate an imaginative position between a suffocating localism and a liberating cosmopolitanism" (151); however, it seems that such an outlook of balance would be bred also by Montague's own transatlantic experiences. Montague locates the major influences on his life in America, Ireland, and France, leading to what Tobin refers to as "the exile's experience of displacement" (154). In *Born in Brooklyn*'s "The Evolving Logos," a tribute to Teilhard de Chardin, Montague betrays his search for connections among Ireland, America, and France, noting that although buried in New York, the French Jesuit is buried between two priests with Irish surnames (112). Clearly, this poet is searching for a way in which to connect the various geopolitical influences on his own life.

Montague expresses his acceptance of the Irishman's multiperspectivality, asserting that "the Irish writer is, at his best, a natural cosmopolitan" (*Book of Irish Verse* 38). He also believes that "An Irish poet [is] in a richly ambiguous position, with the pressure of an incompletely discovered past behind him, and the whole modern world around" (37). This is not the language of a threatened man, as some scholars seem to see him, but instead of an individual who sees opportunity for growth through his experiences in the world. Tobin concedes that Montague is a poet "whose birth fates him to be caught between the desire for a home lost before his birth and the recognition that the consciousness of being homeless may afford him a painful though privileged vantage point by which at once to survey the world and live within it" (154). However, Tobin considers "Montague's American inheritance . . . a profound psychic and social disruption" (151), rather than as, as Montague himself seems to indicate, an opportunity for further understanding his background, and therefore himself, and as a result, the world around him.

For Montague, the literary voice has both autobiographical and communal elements. Much of his writing is intensely personal, focusing on his own experiences and thoughts. Wall considers Montague to be "a confessional poet: he reveals more of his life in his work than any other poet of his generation" ("Second" 117). Montague himself believes that "a poet should speak for his people, out of his people's pain" ("Global Regionalism" 163). For Montague himself, this particular voice has yet to be fully uncovered, as "Ireland is not yet a nation. It is a broken, incomplete nation" (163). Robert F. Garratt considers even *The Rough Field,* a national poem, to be strongly colored by personal interpretations of history, "the distinct and autobiographical element which shapes the historical consciousness" rendering "the urge to discover the self [to] make possible the understanding of community" (94-95). The poet creates meaning by telling the story of history and by finding his own place within the story (102). Garratt points out that Montague is "aware of how personal a vision history can be" (101); Montague's writings are his way of sorting out the elements of his personal vision, selecting the aspects that are relevant and discarding useless preconceptions. As Thomas Dillon Redshaw notes, Montague's poetry has a reputation for being "essentially autobiographical," an impression which "can diminish the genuine stature of some of Montague's repeated themes—emigration and binationality, fosterage and abandonment" ("Abstracting Icons" 113). Through his exploration of personal experience, Montague gains the capacity to delve into universal issues. Montague's work thrives on a constant shifting between microcosm and macrocosm; in a Whitman-esque way, Montague reads himself as the world and the world as himself. Constantly striving to discover new evidence for who he is, Montague explains: "'my effort to understand as much of the modern world as possible serves only to illuminate the destruction of that small area from which I initially came, and that theme in turn is only part of the larger one of continually threatened love" (qtd. in Redshaw "*Topos* and *Texne*" 31).

Montague is willing to accept all parts of his experience, even the unsavory ones, that have helped to shape who he is. In **"A Muddy Cup,"** included in ***Born in Brooklyn,*** Montague recounts the negative experiences that his parents had in Brooklyn, focusing particularly on his mother's distaste for the whole adventure. Because even these experiences are part of the life story of Montague, as they led to his conception and surrounded his birth, Montague proclaims that he is

> a third son who
> beats out this song
> to celebrate the odours
> that bubbled up
> so rank & strong
>
> from that muddy cup.
>
>   (ll. 41-46)

Were he simply to discount the arguments, poverty, and urban setting that surrounded his young childhood exist-

ence, he would be missing, in the puzzle that is his adult self, significant elements that shaped him, and that, by extrapolation, shaped the American immigrant experience in the twentieth century. In ***Born in Brooklyn,*** Montague immediately follows this poem, which originally appeared in ***The Dead Kingdom,*** with **"Mother Cat,"** which debuted in *A Slow Dance.* Placing these two poems in the collection in this order allows Montague to capitalize on the image of mother as cat that ends the first poem and controls the second. Through this image connection between the two poems, Montague invites the reader to see **"Mother Cat"** not only as a confessional poem about the persona's feelings of having been neglected by his mother but also as a statement about the excessive competition to survive that all immigrants to America face upon arrival and about the need to be able to adapt. By arranging these two poems in this particular order, layers of meaning are added to each.

In ***Born in Brooklyn,*** Montague provides evidence that Fanning's assessment that Irish American poetry is characterized only by sentimentality and brashness falls short of the truth. Montague's portrayal of Irish American life, in poem, short story, and essay shows the many dimensions of such an existence. A longtime wish of Montague's was to "put all [his] American poems together, to suggest the complex fate of being an Irish-American" ("American-Irish" 35). He wants his writing to be seen neither merely as Irish nor merely as American: "Modern poetry used to be a common adventure, above national prejudice" (35). Or, as Montague wrote in 1972 "Having been born in America, and having spent many years there and in France, I see no reason to belong to any school, except that of good writing" ("Order in Donnybrook Fair" 313). Montague recounts how, by age four, he was "unwittingly the inheritor of three nationalities [American, Irish, and British]. . . . And yet [he has] kept a double vision, a part of [him] still profoundly moved by [his] American *patria,* [his] American heritage" ("American-Irish" 34). Because he has held on to all sorts of memories and has, in some cases, uncovered facts about himself, he has a realistic view of himself and therefore of his world. When asked, "Are you American, Irish, Irish-American? None of the above?" Montague responded "All of those" (Ingersoll and Howard 23). One is left to wonder whether Montague actually intended to say that he is also "None of the above." However, the way in which Montague labels himself or the various ways in which others might label him are not as important as the ways in which Montague pieces together the reality of who he is. He considers it important that "one slowly accepts all the parts of oneself so that they combine into a glorious whole" (24). Rather than fragmenting his work, his multiple allegiances and international background "provided him with a perspective and a voice with which he participates in" understanding the fluid boundaries of the modern world (Grgas 152).

Montague includes part of "The Figure in the Cave," a chapter of autobiography, as the first selection in **Born in Brooklyn.** With this work focusing on the relationship between his Irish and American backgrounds, Montague early sets out for the reader the idea of piecing together fragments in order to understand the whole person. Montague acknowledges that "losing a family and a country in one sweep must not have been easy, although for long I suppressed my earlier memories" (11). However, sweeping away this earliest part of his experience is not conducive to self-knowledge, and Montague notes that "though to understand, however, dimly, is to begin to forgive, a writer should not forget, and my American past keeps surfacing" (13). Knowledge is required for conflict resolution, and once attained, knowledge must be retained. Accepting of his fate of being multi-national, Montague thinks that such an existence "should seem natural enough in the late-twentieth century as man strives to reconcile local allegiances with the absolute necessity of developing a world consciousness to save us from the abyss. Earthed in Ireland, at ease in the world, weave the strands you're given" (14). This is not the voice of a rootless, exiled man, as some critics perceive Montague to be, but rather these are the words of an individual who has come to terms with his own history and is ready to share what he has learned. A poet should reject neither local influences nor international influences, and should instead be a "global-regionalist" ("Global Regionalism" 174). The key in Montague's experience as Irish and American, or as an Irish American, is balance. James D. Brophy notes that Montague's early poem **"The Water Carrier"** "is about equilibrium. . . . nothing is whole, . . . even water is of two kinds and must be balanced" (154-55). Similarly, the different aspects of one's nature must be tempered with one another. Not only is "creative anguish" born of multinationalism but also are "potential richness [and] comedy" (Montague "American-Irish" 32). He feels free to ponder, "Somewhere in New York my *alter ego,* my *doppelganger,* sits brooding over his destiny. . . . How would I have woven together my two worlds, the New World and the lost Ireland?" (32). By thinking along these lines, by carefully considering the inverse point of view, Montague gains a deeper understanding of his own situation, and invites other hyphenated Americans to do the same.

As he reveals throughout **Born in Brooklyn,** the poet's own quest for information began when he was very young. His earliest memories are, like James Joyce's Stephen Dedalus', impressionistic in nature. When he recounts memories of his very early childhood, Montague uses lists of sense impressions, rather than narra-

tives. His recollection of his uncle John is "as large-hatted, cheerful and kind, but [he] hear[s] no music in the background. Instead the sound of many voices, sometimes quarrelling, the clink of glasses. And then the sounds die away" (The Figure in the Cave" 10). In **"A Muddy Cup,"** Montague's recounting of the environs of his early childhood home in Brooklyn is thus:

> *(cops and robbers*
> *cigarstore Indians*
> *& coal black niggers,*
> *bathtub gin and*
> *Jewish neighbors).*

(ll. 51-55)

This is either a catalog of what the young Montague could reconstruct of his life in Brooklyn or a list of things that his mother emphasized to him about their life in New York. Either way, it shows not an understanding, but merely a recollection. Montague would later use memories like these as groundwork for his research on his own life. Not many years after he left Brooklyn, presumably when he was about ten years old, the action of the short story "The Letters" takes place. Again, his personal memories of New York are snapshots, with the narrative to be filled in. It is in this story that he shows his readers how he began to fill in the missing pieces from his life story. Feigning illness to stay home from church one Sunday morning, the young Montague will begin to excavate, this first excursion into the kitchen cabinet. In this work, Montague uses unexpected tense shifts to show that the experience of discovery that he had on that day many decades ago is still present to him. The first paragraph is in the present tense, but in the second and for the rest of Montague's adventure, he enters the past tense. His understanding of his parents' situation in New York is tied closely to material culture, as Montague claims "Finally I understood, standing there with the letters in my hand" (31). The items he has excavated have taught him what he needed to know. In the penultimate paragraph, after the boy awakes from his sobbing-induced sleep, the narration of the story returns to the present tense, indicating that there is a divide in the boy's understanding of himself between his innocence and newly-found knowledge. Unlike the rest of the story, which is narrated from the first-person point of view, the final sentences of the story are narrated from a third-person point of view, stating of the young Montague: "He will never be the same again and it is partly his own fault. Those who pry learn what they deserve" (31). Because of what he learned on that day about the circumstances surrounding his birth and early childhood, and because he has seen another person's view of these situations, Montague is able to view his own situation with some detachment.

Montague's methods of anthropological research into his own existence became increasingly varied. Rather than merely remembering tidbits of what he had seen in Brooklyn, the young Montague tried to unobtrusively interview those who knew his parents before they emigrated. However, his hopes were often not realized, as

> With the indifference of the hardworked, my aunts did not speak much of the past and failed to understand my secret pleas for information. My main hope lay then in what casual knowledge I could find. Patient as an archaeologist, I reconstituted the past from old books and photographs and the rambling conversation of the older men in the parish.
>
> ("Oklahoma Kid" 51-52)

When direct interviews failed, Montague continued his archaeological searches and even engaged in participant-observation. However, when he was a child, his understanding of the information he gleaned was incomplete, as he associated cowboy stories with his existence in New York, unaware that "Arizona was nearly a continent away from Bushwich [sic] Avenue, Brooklyn" (48). Also in his poems, Montague reveals that he continued his research into his past well into his adult life. In **"Stele for a Northern Republican,"** Montague discusses his adult understanding of his father's republican activities, about many of which he has learned since his father has returned to County Tyrone from Brooklyn. Still somewhat uncomfortable with some of the information he might unearth, Montague writes: "Hesitantly, I trace your part in / the holy war to restore our country" (ll.11-12). Montague then recounts, to the best of his ability, the secret battles that both of his parents fought for the cause of republicanism. Among the works in *Born in Brooklyn*, this poem marks a breakthrough, as it recounts the point at which the persona (who is, in fact, Montague) is able to critically examine the actions of even his own parents and to assess both the good and the damage that these actions have done, on not only a personal scale for Montague but on a national scale. His final assessment is that his parents and those of their generation who engaged in undercover military activities have done damage to the movement for a united Ireland because of the excessive violence and intolerance that they engendered, creating in the process "only a broken province" (ln. 53).

Montague's mission to learn about himself takes him again across the Atlantic, where, in New York, he attempts to research the circumstances surrounding his early life. He recounts his experience:

> I took the subway to the hospital
> in darkest Brooklyn, to call
> on the old nun who nursed you

> through the travail of my birth
> to come on another cold trail.
>
> (ll. 26-30)

Here, there are shades not only of research but also of detective work. Montague's birth is figured as a mystery, and he must travel into the darkness, through the subway, in which his father used to work, in order to uncover information about his origins. In trying to come into contact with his past, Montague is jarred into the present by his awareness of the rough neighborhood through which he must travel. Although he is considering the past and his mother's experience in giving birth to him, his mind immediately turns to the present and he notes the disparity between his own childhood and that of his daughter, between his mother and his wife as a mother. In his mind, Montague then travels back to his childhood, to his parent's dismissal of him to Ireland, sending him "to a previous century" (ln. 63). Travel across the ocean and across time, at least in his mind, are essential to Montague's ability to contextualize his findings and to gain the necessary perspective to make sense of what he learns. This transatlantic theme is further relied upon in **"The Locket,"** in which Montague recounts how he learns after his mother dies that she always, in life, wore a locket that contained a picture "of a child in Brooklyn" (ln. 42). Although by the time of his mother's death he has not been such a child for decades, it is significant that she always associated her son with his Brooklyn roots. And, ultimately, Montague is reminded of the impending end of his own life when, as an adult, he visits the grave of the paternal uncle after whom he was named:

> I submit again
> to stare soberly
>
> at my own name
> cut on a gravestone
>
> & hear the creak
> of a fiddle
>
> filter through
> American earth
>
> the slow pride
> of a lament.
>
> (ll. 93-102)

Not only does Montague see his own name on a gravestone but he also imagines his uncle's artwork, Irish fiddle music, coming through American earth; likewise, Montague's own poems, with both Irish and American dimensions, will outlive him and will serve to mediate between the two cultures for those who read them.

Fluidity of movement is at the heart of Montague's American poems. This movement is both transatlantic and transcontinental, both synchronic and diachronic.

While the movement is rarely meant as literal, it is nonetheless essential to the persona's synthesis of information gleaned from the traveled-to and traveled-from places. Seemingly paradoxically, the poem titled "The Cage" hinges on the relationship between the narrator and his father in America and then in Ireland. While the father's life in America was spent working in the subway and was marked by a dearth of opportunities for advancement, he returns to an open, untouched countryside in Ireland. Since the beginning of the poem is about the father's workday in New York, the line immediately following this discussion which reads "When he came back" (ln. 22) is expected to be about when he came back from work. Instead, it refers to the father's return to Garvaghey. Such a transition seems effortless, and the facility with which it appears that the father returns to Ireland suggests that the son frequently makes these trips in his imagination. The poem moves on to an injunction: "when / weary Odysseus returns / Telemachus should leave" (ll. 33-35), suggesting again an impending voyage for the son. Straightaway, the son is transported back to New York, where he imagines seeing his "ghostly" (ln. 42) father working in the subway once again. Immediately following this poem, which first appeared in **The Rough Field,** is "**A Christmas Card,**" which first was printed in **The Dead Kingdom.** In this poem, the narrator recounts his memories of his father at Christmastime in Brooklyn, and mutedly praises his father for working and living alone in Brooklyn for as long as he had to. However, at the end of the poem, there is ambiguity as to where the father goes when "the job was done; / and then [he] limped home" (ll. 35-36). While the home could be the Brooklyn boarding house, reading this poem in light of the previous poem, it is more likely that the home to which the poet refers is the father's birthplace. While it is physically impossible to limp from Brooklyn to Ireland, the use of such an image is an interesting one: it suggests a closeness between the two locales. Doubtlessly, in Montague's mind, such a closeness must exist. It is reaffirmed in "**Magic Carpet,**" the final selection in **Born in Brooklyn,** in which the narrator has achieved sufficient distance from terrestrial matters to see happiness and safety, and which can allow the rider to see from any perspective he desires, "from Cork to Upstate New York, / from Altcloghfin to Albany" (ll. 12-13).

In "Death of a Chieftain," Montague provides a prototype for many of the experiences of the Irish American as archaeologist. The story is of Bernard Corunna Coote, university-trained archaeologist and renegade Orangeman turned Bostonian, who decides to settle in San Antonio, Mexico, with the hopes of proving that Celts were the original inhabitants of the Americas. The short story contains some surprising links to Montague's own life. Aside from the penchant for archaeology, Montague, although a Catholic, did feel some alienation from his family for sending him into fosterage at such a young age. Montague considers himself to have Irish, American and French allegiances; Coote is an Irish American, and among his companions in San Antonio are a transplanted Frenchman and an American of English extraction, recalling County Tyrone's current alignment with Britain. Finding himself in the isolated, unusual atmosphere of San Antonio, Coote must learn the proper codes of behavior:

> After this rash beginning, Bernard Corunna Coote learned to offer his confidences with the same casualness as he played his cards. And though (unlike the latter) they lay without immediate comment, he knew that they were being picked up, one by one, gestures toward a portrait. Assembled, they made what Tarrou once smilingly called LE PETIT TESTAMENT DE BERNARD CORUNNA COOTE.
>
> (85-86)

Coote must adapt to his new environment. For his whole life, Coote had been made by his family to feel like "a sore disappointment. His whole career seemed a demonstration of the principle of cultural reversion, i.e., the invasion of the conqueror by the culture of the conquered" (86). Coote's *compadres* note that he is searching for something in a frenzied way, and they struggle to understand what he is doing: to them, his is "an alien discipline" (93). Hautmoc, the main proponent of the purity of the Indian race in Central America, tells Witchbourne that Coote "'is looking for something we both have lost'" (93). For Coote, proving his theory by finding sufficient evidence becomes an obsession, and his companions "felt that some incongruous struggle was going on, an almost physical rending, as though a blind man were trying to see, or a cripple to walk" (94). He searches for all kinds of evidence to prove his theory: he uses personality observations and physical characteristics, but continues to seek archaeological evidence that will indubitably link Celtic culture with that of the natives of the Americas. He is obsessed with his own brand of synthesis, through which he plans to link cultures around the world and to justify his own life's work to his family. Through a narrow-minded view of globalism, Coote hopes to combine multiple races under one banner, thereby obliterating the need for an individual home and self-identity. Tarrou, whose insulting Coote on the grounds of gender because of his insecurity in his own masculinity has caused Coote to go on this frenzied hunt for the origin of the civilization of the Western hemisphere, remarks of Coote's mission: "Who would have thought the irrelevant could have such deep roots?" (96), underestimating the importance that Coote placed on his own justification of his existence. When Coote discovers that the natives in his employ, led by Hautmoc, have constructed a stone formation that simulated an ancient Celtic burial site, Hautmoc says that he participated in this hoax "'because if the place you are searching for does not exist, then it should. Your dream and mine have much in common'"

(100). However, it is too late for Coote to find out if his dream is true and can be proven elsewhere: the pseudo-Celtic tomb is built, and it must serve its purpose. The search for purity and the single-minded pursuit of a goal cost Coote his life. In this story, we have an example of an archaeologist of the self gone awry: the challenge that faces the Irish American, as Montague suggests throughout **Born in Brooklyn,** is to piece together the parts of oneself, but not to search cease-lessly without accepting the factors of oneself that can-not be controlled. Coote could not find that his forefathers were the source of "the purest people in the world" (80), so he missed out on the opportunity for intercourse with the others who could have helped him to learn about himself.

For Montague, this challenge of being an Irish American has not only personal but also political implications. Noting the importance of politics in poetry, Montague stated:

> I do believe that there is some connection between poetry and politics. . . . Even the articulation of heal-ing is valuable. If you can get the private life right, or at least partly right, if you can achieve some intervals of peace inside marriage and love, then perhaps that would be some kind of paradigm of how people should behave towards each other.
>
> (Ingersoll and Howard 26)

Politics are endemic in poetry, in Montague's defini-tion: "I mean politics in the widest sense—the spiritual atmosphere of a country, one's concern for its spiritual health—this, I think, is one of the strongest strains in contemporary poetry. . . . To declare poetry to be a-political [sic] seems to me a failure of nerve" ("Global Regionalism" 163). Montague believes that "violence begins from the top in a state" (170), seeping from the government and infiltrating the people. When we combine Montague's ideas about the relationship between literature and politics with his presentation of the Irish American experience using the trope of anthropological research, the result is strong political poetry. In **"Visible Export,"** Montague identifies Eugene McCarthy as identifiably "an Irish politician" (ln. 3), one who would fit in well with his Irish contemporaries. However, punning on McCarthy's own House Committee on Un-American Activities, Mon-tague defines McCarthy himself as "un-American" (ln. 5). Short but powerful, this poem makes clear Mon-tague's position on the importance of a government's respect for its citizens. Having the privilege of both American and Irish vantage points, Montague can identify corruption and make connections between injustices perpetrated internationally, so that nations do not duplicate the mistakes of other nations. Likewise, it is clear that **"Vietnam"** is written by an individual who has been witness to long periods of conflict, and who

therefore has strong beliefs on how not to go about solving them. While taking the side of neither of the conflicting parties, Montague shows from a bird's eye view (quite literally, as the sky seems to be the place from which the persona narrates) the type of conflict that Vietnam appears to be: an old set of values repel-ling a comparatively new set of values. Having lived in Northern Ireland and having had the dubious benefit of looking at this war-torn area both from far away and from within, Montague believes that it is impossible to force a people away from something that it is intent on doing. In **"Sinnsear: Kindred,"** Montague makes no directly political statements; instead, he reflects on a set of events that profoundly impacted both Ireland and America. By drawing connections between John and Robert Kennedy and their ancestral past, comparing them with Cuchulain and observing a farmer who ploughs his fields as the Kennedys' "forebears might have done" (ln. 17), Montague suggests the continuity of the experience of Irish Americans with that of their homeland. Additionally, because in Montague's dream vision, the brothers are warned by "A far-off cottage window flash . . ., like Morse" (ln. 21) and are able to preserve the parts of their bodies that were in reality shot, Montague suggests that the dream of the Kennedys, and of the Irish in America, lives on.

For Montague, then, the Irish American experience involves seeking for the truth in the past, but not get-ting so caught up in it that no room is left for develop-ment in the future. As Eamonn Wall suggests, "Mon-tague is conscious of the fact that others have traveled this road before, that each step he makes draws him deeper into history. He is also aware, however, that new travelers must come through to redefine that ancient landscape—physical and psychological—for an Ireland beginning to strive to belong to the modern world" (366). Patricia Lynch believes that Montague's poetry requires him to "cut . . . living roots," but that this "violence" is tempered by the good that it will do the places mentioned in his poems to be discussed on an international stage (212). Likewise, Montague's digging through his own personal landscape, his family and national background, is tempered by the invitation he thereby extends to others to do the same and to create their own Irish, American, or Irish-American landscape. The "complex fate of being Irish-American," which Montague never explicitly defines, consists of deciding to what degree it is necessary to synthesize ancestral and personal elements. While learning about the past can help a person to understand his origins and the influences on his life, it is his own life that makes him who he is. Montague's experience as an Irish American is characterized by an anthropological interest in the influences on his own life. Montague invites only an open-minded curiosity, however. The challenge of being Irish American, as Montague presents it in his montage **Born in Brooklyn,** is to uncover and to understand one's own past—not to entrench ideas and preconceptions more deeply but to allow oneself an alternative vantage point, from which to accurately assess personal and political decisions and actions. Not all incongruities may be solved; some must be accepted. It is the acceptance of unresolved incongruities that Montague sets forth as the best part of the American experience, setting this also as the model for Ireland. Such acceptance, in order to be sincere, must come after an understanding of oneself and one's own past. Connections can be made with the experiences of others, but it is both unrealistic and unwise to expect others to conform entirely to one's own schema. Montague asks, perhaps facetiously, "I would try to keep the two things together in my head: to be forging forward and to be looking backwards. Is that possible?" (Ingersoll and Howard 31). Montague's answer to his own question is evident in his poems, short fiction, and essays: an emphatic "yes." In fact, in his creative work, Montague posits that one can look forward only by simultaneously looking backward, and that looking backward is fruitful only if it also inspires looking forward.

Works Cited

Brophy, James D. "John Montague's 'Restive Sally Switch.'" *Modern Irish Literature: Essays in Honor of William York Tindall*. Ed. Raymond J. Porter and James D. Brophy. New York: Iona College Press, 1972. 153-69.

Dawe, Gerald. "Invocation of Powers: John Montague." *The Chosen Ground: Essays on the Contemporary Poetry of Northern Ireland*. Ed. Neil Corcoran. Chester Springs, Pennsylvania: Dufour Editions, Inc., 1992.

Fanning, Charles. *The Irish Voice in America: Irish-American Fiction from the 1760s to the 1980s*. Lexington: The UP of Kentucky, 1990.

Garratt, Robert F. "John Montague and the Poetry of History." Murray 91-102.

"Global Regionalism: Interview with John Montague." *Literary Review* 22 (1979): 153-74.

Grgas, Stipe. "The Sense of Place in the Poetry of John Montague." *Studia Romanica et Anglica Zagrabiensia* 42 (1997): 145-53.

Ingersoll, Earl and Ben Howard. "'Elegiac Cheer': A Conversation with John Montague." *Literary Review* 31.1 (1987): 23-31.

Longley, Edna. "Searching the Darkness: The Poetry of Richard Murphy, Thomas Kinsella, John Montague and James Simmons." *Two Decades of Irish Writing: A Critical Survey*. Ed. Douglas Dunn. Chester Springs, Pennsylvania: Dufour Editions, Inc., 1975. 118-53.

Lynch, Patricia. "The Use of Place Names in the Poetry of John Montague and Seamus Heaney." *Poetry Now:*
Contemporary British and Irish Poetry in the Making. Ed. Holger Klein, Sabine Coelsch-Foisner, and Wolfgang Görtschacher. Tübingen, Germany: Stauffenburg, 1999. 201-14.

Montague, John. *Born in Brooklyn: John Montague's America*. Ed. David Lampe. Fredonia, New York: White Pine Press, 1991.

——. "Order in Donnybrook Fair." *Times Literary Supplement* 17 Mar. 1972: 313.

Montague, John, ed. *The Book of Irish Verse: An Anthology of Irish Poetry from the Sixth Century to the Present*. 2nd ed. New York: Macmillan Publishing Co., Inc., 1977.

Murray, Christopher, ed. *Irish University Review: John Montague Issue* 19.1 (Spring 1989).

Quinn, Antoinette. "'The Well-Beloved': Montague and the Muse." Murray 27-43.

Redshaw, Thomas Dillon. "Abstracted Icons: The Graphic Ornamentation of John Montague's *The Rough Field* (1972) and *The Dead Kingdom* (1984)." *South Carolina Review* 32.1 (Fall 1999): 100-15.

——. "Appréciation: John Montague." *Eire-Ireland* 11.4 (1976): 122-33.

——. "John Montague's *The Rough Field: Topos* and *Texne*." *Studies* 63 (1974): 31-46.

Redshaw, Thomas Dillon, ed. *Well Dreams: Essays on John Montague*. Omaha: Creighton UP, 2004.

Tobin, Daniel. "'Lines of Leaving/Lines of Returning': John Montague's Double Vision." Redshaw, ed. 147-66.

Wall, Eamonn. "'A Grafted Tongue': Montague's *Collected Poems* (1995)." Redshaw, ed. 363-75.

——. "A Second Tongue." *Shenandoah* 46.3 (Fall 1996): 113-18.

FURTHER READING

Criticism

Faherty, Michael. "Lost, Unhappy and at Home: The Robinson Crusoe Complex in Contemporary Irish Poetry." In *The Classical World and the Mediterranean*, edited by Giuseppe Serpillo and Donatella Badin, pp. 371-78. Cagliari, Italy: Università di Sassari/Tema, 1996.

    Examines the mixed emotions many Irish poets—including Seamus Heaney, Patrick Kavanagh, and Montague—feel for their homeland.

Johnston, Conor. "Poetry and Politics: Responses to the Northern Ireland Crisis in the Poetry of John Montague, Derek Mahon, and Seamus Heaney." *Poesis* 5, no. 4 (1984): 12-35.

Offers a comparison between Montague, Derek Mahon, and Seamus Heaney in the way each poet approaches the political crisis in Northern Ireland.

Kennedy-Andrews, Elmer. "John Montague: Global Regionalist." *Cambridge Quarterly* 35, no. 1 (2006): 31-48.

Discusses Montague's attempt to achieve a position of "global regionalism" in his writing—rejecting what he considered the extreme regionalism of some Irish poets as well as the "boundless globalism" of writers like Ezra Pound.

Additional coverage of Montague's life and career is contained in the following sources published by Gale: *Contemporary Authors,* **Vols. 9-12R;** *Contemporary Authors, New Revision Series,* **Vols. 9, 69, 121;** *Contemporary Literary Criticism,* **Vols. 13, 46;** *Contemporary Poets,* **Eds. 1, 2, 3, 4, 5, 6, 7;** *Dictionary of Literary Biography,* **Vol. 40;** *Encyclopedia of World Literature in the 20th Century,* **Ed. 3;** *Literature Resource Center; Major 20th-Century Writers,* **Ed. 1;** *Poetry for Students,* **Vol. 12;** *Reference Guide to English Literature,* **Ed. 2; and** *Twayne Companion to Contemporary Literature in English,* **Ed. 1:2.**

How to Use This Index

CDALBS = *Concise Dictionary of American Literary Biography Supplement*
CDBLB = *Concise Dictionary of British Literary Biography*
CMW = *St. James Guide to Crime & Mystery Writers*
CN = *Contemporary Novelists*
CP = *Contemporary Poets*
CPW = *Contemporary Popular Writers*
CSW = *Contemporary Southern Writers*
CWD = *Contemporary Women Dramatists*
CWP = *Contemporary Women Poets*
CWRI = *St. James Guide to Children's Writers*
CWW = *Contemporary World Writers*
DA = *DISCovering Authors*
DA3 = *DISCovering Authors 3.0*
DAB = *DISCovering Authors: British Edition*
DAC = *DISCovering Authors: Canadian Edition*
DAM = *DISCovering Authors: Modules*
    DRAM: *Dramatists Module;* **MST:** *Most-studied Authors Module;*
    MULT: *Multicultural Authors Module;* **NOV:** *Novelists Module;*
    POET: *Poets Module;* **POP:** *Popular Fiction and Genre Authors Module*
DFS = *Drama for Students*
DLB = *Dictionary of Literary Biography*
DLBD = *Dictionary of Literary Biography Documentary Series*
DLBY = *Dictionary of Literary Biography Yearbook*
DNFS = *Literature of Developing Nations for Students*
EFS = *Epics for Students*
EW = *European Writers*
EWL = *Encyclopedia of World Literature in the 20th Century*
EXPN = *Exploring Novels*
EXPP = *Exploring Poetry*
EXPS = *Exploring Short Stories*
FANT = *St. James Guide to Fantasy Writers*
FW = *Feminist Writers*
GFL = *Guide to French Literature,* Beginnings to 1789, 1798 to the Present
GLL = *Gay and Lesbian Literature*
HGG = *St. James Guide to Horror, Ghost & Gothic Writers*
HW = *Hispanic Writers*
IDFW = *International Dictionary of Films and Filmmakers: Writers and Production Artists*
IDTP = *International Dictionary of Theatre: Playwrights*
LAIT = *Literature and Its Times*
LAW = *Latin American Writers*
JRDA = *Junior DISCovering Authors*
MAICYA = *Major Authors and Illustrators for Children and Young Adults*
MAICYAS = *Major Authors and Illustrators for Children and Young Adults Supplement*
MAWW = *Modern American Women Writers*
MJW = *Modern Japanese Writers*
MTCW = *Major 20th-Century Writers*
NCFS = *Nonfiction Classics for Students*
NFS = *Novels for Students*
PAB = *Poets: American and British*
PFS = *Poetry for Students*
RGAL = *Reference Guide to American Literature*
RGEL = *Reference Guide to English Literature*
RGSF = *Reference Guide to Short Fiction*
RGWL = *Reference Guide to World Literature*
RHW = *Twentieth-Century Romance and Historical Writers*
SAAS = *Something about the Author Autobiography Series*
SATA = *Something about the Author*
SFW = *St. James Guide to Science Fiction Writers*
SSFS = *Short Stories for Students*
TCWW = *Twentieth-Century Western Writers*
WLIT = *World Literature and Its Times*
WP = *World Poets*
YABC = *Yesterday's Authors of Books for Children*
YAW = *St. James Guide to Young Adult Writers*

Literary Criticism Series
Cumulative Author Index

Amis, Kingsley 1922-1995 . **CLC 1, 2, 3, 5, 8, 13, 40, 44, 129**
See also AAYA 77; AITN 2; BPFB 1; BRWS 2; CA 9-12R; 150; CANR 8, 28, 54; CDBLB 1945-1960; CN 1, 2, 3, 4, 5, 6; CP 1, 2, 3, 4; DA; DA3; DAB; DAC; DAM MST, NOV; DLB 15, 27, 100, 139, 326, 352; DLBY 1996; EWL 3; HGG; INT CANR-8; MTCW 1, 2; MTFW 2005; RGEL 2; RGSF 2; SFW 4

Amis, Martin 1949- ... **CLC 4, 9, 38, 62, 101, 213; SSC 112**
See also BEST 90:3; BRWS 4; CA 65-68; CANR 8, 27, 54, 73, 95, 132, 166; CN 5, 6, 7; DA3; DLB 14, 194; EWL 3; INT CANR-27; MTCW 2; MTFW 2005

Amis, Martin Louis
See Amis, Martin

Ammianus Marcellinus c. 330-c. 395 .... **CMLC 60**
See also AW 2; DLB 211

Ammons, A.R. 1926-2001 .. **CLC 2, 3, 5, 8, 9, 25, 57, 108; PC 16**
See also AITN 1; AMWS 7; CA 9-12R; 193; CANR 6, 36, 51, 73, 107, 156; CP 1, 2, 3, 4, 5, 6, 7; CSW; DAM POET; DLB 5, 165, 342; EWL 3; MAL 5; MTCW 1, 2; PFS 19; RGAL 4; TCLE 1:1

Ammons, Archie Randolph
See Ammons, A.R.

Amo, Tauraatua i
See Adams, Henry

Amory, Thomas 1691(?)-1788 .... **LC 48**
See also DLB 39

Anand, Mulk Raj 1905-2004 ..... **CLC 23, 93, 237**
See also CA 65-68; 231; CANR 32, 64; CN 1, 2, 3, 4, 5, 6, 7; DAM NOV; DLB 323; EWL 3; MTCW 1, 2; MTFW 2005; RGSF 2

Anatol
See Schnitzler, Arthur

Anaximander c. 611B.C.-c. 546B.C. .... **CMLC 22**

Anaya, Rudolfo 1937- ...... **CLC 23, 148, 255; HLC 1**
See also AAYA 20; BYA 13; CA 45-48; CAAS 4; CANR 1, 32, 51, 124, 169; CLR 129; CN 4, 5, 6, 7; DAM MULT, NOV; DLB 82, 206, 278; HW 1; LAIT 4; LLW; MAL 5; MTCW 1, 2; MTFW 2005; NFS 12; RGAL 4; RGSF 2; TCWW 2; WLIT 1

Anaya, Rudolfo A.
See Anaya, Rudolfo

Anaya, Rudolpho Alfonso
See Anaya, Rudolfo

Andersen, Hans Christian 1805-1875 ...... **NCLC 7, 79, 214; SSC 6, 56; WLC 1**
See also AAYA 57; CLR 6, 113; DA; DA3; DAB; DAC; DAM MST, POP; EW 6; MAICYA 1, 2; RGSF 2; RGWL 2, 3; SATA 100; TWA; WCH; YABC 1

Anderson, C. Farley
See Mencken, H. L.; Nathan, George Jean

Anderson, Jessica (Margaret) Queale 1916- .... **CLC 37**
See also CA 9-12R; CANR 4, 62; CN 4, 5, 6, 7; DLB 325

Anderson, Jon (Victor) 1940- .... **CLC 9**
See also CA 25-28R; CANR 20; CP 1, 3, 4, 5; DAM POET

Anderson, Lindsay (Gordon) 1923-1994 .... **CLC 20**
See also CA 125; 128; 146; CANR 77

Anderson, Maxwell 1888-1959 .... **TCLC 2, 144**
See also CA 105; 152; DAM DRAM; DFS 16, 20; DLB 7, 228; MAL 5; MTCW 2; MTFW 2005; RGAL 4

Anderson, Poul 1926-2001 .... **CLC 15**
See also AAYA 5, 34; BPFB 1; BYA 6, 8, 9; CA 1-4R, 181; 199; CAAE 181; CAAS 2; CANR 2, 15, 34, 64, 110; CLR 58; DLB 8; FANT; INT CANR-15; MTCW 1, 2; MTFW 2005; SATA 90; SATA-Brief 39; SATA-Essay 106; SCFW 1, 2; SFW 4; SUFW 1, 2

Anderson, R. W.
See Anderson, Robert

Anderson, Robert 1917-2009 .... **CLC 23**
See also AITN 1; CA 21-24R; 283; CANR 32; CD 6; DAM DRAM; DLB 7; LAIT 5

Anderson, Robert W.
See Anderson, Robert

Anderson, Robert Woodruff
See Anderson, Robert

Anderson, Roberta Joan
See Mitchell, Joni

Anderson, Sherwood 1876-1941 ... **SSC 1, 46, 91; TCLC 1, 10, 24, 123; WLC 1**
See also AAYA 30; AMW; AMWC 2; BPFB 1; CA 104; 121; CANR 61; CDALB 1917-1929; DA; DA3; DAB; DAC; DAM MST, NOV; DLB 4, 9, 86; DLBD 1; EWL 3; EXPS; GLL 2; MAL 5; MTCW 1, 2; MTFW 2005; NFS 4; RGAL 4; RGSF 2; SSFS 4, 10, 11; TUS

Anderson, Wes 1969- .... **CLC 227**
See also CA 214

Andier, Pierre
See Desnos, Robert

Andouard
See Giraudoux, Jean

Andrade, Carlos Drummond de
See Drummond de Andrade, Carlos

Andrade, Mario de
See de Andrade, Mario

Andreae, Johann V(alentin) 1586-1654 .... **LC 32**
See also DLB 164

Andreas Capellanus fl. c. 1185- .... **CMLC 45**
See also DLB 208

Andreas-Salome, Lou 1861-1937 ... **TCLC 56**
See also CA 178; DLB 66

Andreev, Leonid
See Andreyev, Leonid

Andress, Lesley
See Sanders, Lawrence

Andrew, Joseph Maree
See Occomy, Marita (Odette) Bonner

Andrewes, Lancelot 1555-1626 .... **LC 5**
See also DLB 151, 172

Andrews, Cicily Fairfield
See West, Rebecca

Andrews, Elton V.
See Pohl, Frederik

Andrews, Peter
See Soderbergh, Steven

Andrews, Raymond 1934-1991 .... **BLC 2:1**
See also BW 2; CA 81-84; 136; CANR 15, 42

Andreyev, Leonid 1871-1919 ... **TCLC 3, 221**
See also CA 104; 185; DLB 295; EWL 3

Andreyev, Leonid Nikolaevich
See Andreyev, Leonid

Andrezel, Pierre
See Blixen, Karen

Andric, Ivo 1892-1975 .... **CLC 8; SSC 36; TCLC 135**
See also CA 81-84; 57-60; CANR 43, 60; CDWLB 4; DLB 147, 329; EW 11; EWL 3; MTCW 1; RGSF 2; RGWL 2, 3

Androvar
See Prado (Calvo), Pedro

Angela of Foligno 1248(?)-1309 .... **CMLC 76**

Angelique, Pierre
See Bataille, Georges

Angell, Judie
See Angell, Judie

Angell, Judie 1937- .... **CLC 30**
See also AAYA 11, 71; BYA 6; CA 77-80; CANR 49; CLR 33; JRDA; SATA 22, 78; WYA; YAW

Angell, Roger 1920- .... **CLC 26**
See also CA 57-60; CANR 13, 44, 70, 144; DLB 171, 185

Angelou, Maya 1928- ...... **BLC 1:1; CLC 12, 35, 64, 77, 155; PC 32; WLCS**
See also AAYA 7, 20; AMWS 4; BPFB 1; BW 2, 3; BYA 2; CA 65-68; CANR 19, 42, 65, 111, 133; CDALBS; CLR 53; CP 4, 5, 6, 7; CPW; CSW; CWP; DA; DA3; DAB; DAC; DAM MST, MULT, POET, POP; DLB 38; EWL 3; EXPN; EXPP; FL 1:5; LAIT 4; MAICYA 2; MAICYAS 1; MAL 5; MBL; MTCW 1, 2; MTFW 2005; NCFS 2; NFS 2; PFS 2, 3; RGAL 4; SATA 49, 136; TCLE 1:1; WYA; YAW

Angouleme, Marguerite d'
See de Navarre, Marguerite

Anna Comnena 1083-1153 .... **CMLC 25**

Annensky, Innokentii Fedorovich
See Annensky, Innokenty (Fyodorovich)

Annensky, Innokenty (Fyodorovich) 1856-1909 .... **TCLC 14**
See also CA 110; 155; DLB 295; EWL 3

Annunzio, Gabriele d'
See D'Annunzio, Gabriele

Anodos
See Coleridge, Mary E(lizabeth)

Anon, Charles Robert
See Pessoa, Fernando

Anouilh, Jean 1910-1987 ..... **CLC 1, 3, 8, 13, 40, 50; DC 8, 21; TCLC 195**
See also AAYA 67; CA 17-20R; 123; CANR 32; DAM DRAM; DFS 9, 10, 19; DLB 321; EW 13; EWL 3; GFL 1789 to the Present; MTCW 1, 2; MTFW 2005; RGWL 2, 3; TWA

Anouilh, Jean Marie Lucien Pierre
See Anouilh, Jean

Ansa, Tina McElroy 1949- .... **BLC 2:1**
See also BW 2; CA 142; CANR 143; CSW

Anselm of Canterbury 1033(?)-1109 .... **CMLC 67**
See also DLB 115

Anthony, Florence
See Ai

Anthony, John
See Ciardi, John (Anthony)

Anthony, Peter
See Shaffer, Anthony; Shaffer, Peter

Anthony, Piers 1934- .... **CLC 35**
See also AAYA 11, 48; BYA 7; CA 200; CAAE 200; CANR 28, 56, 73, 102, 133, 202; CLR 118; CPW; DAM POP; DLB 8; FANT; MAICYA 2; MAICYAS 1; MTCW 1, 2; MTFW 2005; SAAS 22; SATA 84, 129; SATA-Essay 129; SFW 4; SUFW 1, 2; YAW

Anthony, Susan B(rownell) 1820-1906 .... **TCLC 84**
See also CA 211; FW

Antiphon c. 480B.C.-c. 411B.C. .... **CMLC 55**

Antoine, Marc
See Proust, Marcel

Antoninus, Brother
See Everson, William

Antonioni, Michelangelo 1912-2007 .... **CLC 20, 144, 259**
See also CA 73-76; 262; CANR 45, 77

Ashbery, John Lawrence
See Ashbery, John
Ashbridge, Elizabeth 1713-1755 .... **LC 147**
See also DLB 200
Ashdown, Clifford
See Freeman, R(ichard) Austin
Ashe, Gordon
See Creasey, John
Ashton-Warner, Sylvia (Constance)
1908-1984 .... **CLC 19**
See also CA 69-72; 112; CANR 29; CN 1,
2, 3; MTCW 1, 2
Asimov, Isaac 1920-1992 ..... **CLC 1, 3, 9, 19,
26, 76, 92**
See also AAYA 13; BEST 90:2; BPFB 1;
BYA 4, 6, 7, 9; CA 1-4R; 137; CANR 2,
19, 36, 60, 125; CLR 12, 79; CMW 4;
CN 1, 2, 3, 4, 5; CPW; DA3; DAM POP;
DLB 8; DLBY 1992; INT CANR-19;
JRDA; LAIT 5; LMFS 2; MAICYA 1, 2;
MAL 5; MTCW 1, 2; MTFW 2005; NFS
29; RGAL 4; SATA 1, 26, 74; SCFW 1,
2; SFW 4; SSFS 17; TUS; YAW
Askew, Anne 1521(?)-1546 .... **LC 81**
See also DLB 136
Asser -c. 909 .... **CMLC 117**
Assis, Joaquim Maria Machado de
See Machado de Assis, Joaquim Maria
Astell, Mary 1666-1731 .... **LC 68**
See also DLB 252, 336; FW
Astley, Thea (Beatrice May)
1925-2004 .... **CLC 41**
See also CA 65-68; 229; CANR 11, 43, 78;
CN 1, 2, 3, 4, 5, 6, 7; DLB 289; EWL 3
Astley, William 1855-1911 .... **TCLC 45**
See also DLB 230; RGEL 2
Aston, James
See White, T(erence) H(anbury)
Asturias, Miguel Angel 1899-1974 .... **CLC 3,
8, 13; HLC 1; TCLC 184**
See also CA 25-28; 49-52; CANR 32; CAP
2; CDWLB 3; DA3; DAM MULT, NOV;
DLB 113, 290, 329; EWL 3; HW 1; LAW;
LMFS 2; MTCW 1, 2; RGWL 2, 3; WLIT
1
Atares, Carlos Saura
See Saura (Atares), Carlos
Athanasius c. 295-c. 373 .... **CMLC 48**
Atheling, William
See Pound, Ezra
Atheling, William, Jr.
See Blish, James
Atherton, Gertrude (Franklin Horn)
1857-1948 .... **TCLC 2**
See also CA 104; 155; DLB 9, 78, 186;
HGG; RGAL 4; SUFW 1; TCWW 1, 2
Atherton, Lucius
See Masters, Edgar Lee
Atkins, Jack
See Harris, Mark
Atkinson, Kate 1951- .... **CLC 99**
See also CA 166; CANR 101, 153, 198;
DLB 267
Attaway, William (Alexander)
1911-1986 .... **BLC 1:1; CLC 92**
See also BW 2, 3; CA 143; CANR 82;
DAM MULT; DLB 76; MAL 5
Atticus
See Fleming, Ian; Wilson, (Thomas) Woodrow
Atwood, Margaret 1939- . **CLC 2, 3, 4, 8, 13,
15, 25, 44, 84, 135, 232, 239, 246; PC 8;
SSC 2, 46; WLC 1**
See also AAYA 12, 47; AMWS 13; BEST
89:2; BPFB 1; CA 49-52; CANR 3, 24,
33, 59, 95, 133; CN 2, 3, 4, 5, 6, 7; CP 1,
2, 3, 4, 5, 6, 7; CPW; CWP; DA; DA3;
DAB; DAC; DAM MST, NOV, POET;
DLB 53, 251, 326; EWL 3; EXPN; FL

1:5; FW; GL 2; INT CANR-24; LAIT 5;
MTCW 1, 2; MTFW 2005; NFS 4, 12,
13, 14, 19; PFS 7; RGSF 2; SATA 50,
170; SSFS 3, 13; TCLE 1:1; TWA; WWE
1; YAW
Atwood, Margaret Eleanor
See Atwood, Margaret
Aubigny, Pierre d'
See Mencken, H. L.
Aubin, Penelope 1685-1731(?) .... **LC 9**
See also DLB 39
Auchincloss, Louis 1917-2010 ... **CLC 4, 6, 9,
18, 45; SSC 22**
See also AMWS 4; CA 1-4R; CANR 6, 29,
55, 87, 130, 168, 202; CN 1, 2, 3, 4, 5, 6,
7; DAM NOV; DLB 2, 244; DLBY 1980;
EWL 3; INT CANR-29; MAL 5; MTCW
1; RGAL 4
Auchincloss, Louis Stanton
See Auchincloss, Louis
Auden, W. H. 1907-1973 ... **CLC 1, 2, 3, 4, 6,
9, 11, 14, 43, 123; PC 1, 92; TCLC
223; WLC 1**
See also AAYA 18; AMWS 2; BRW 7;
BRWR 1; CA 9-12R; 45-48; CANR 5, 61,
105; CDBLB 1914-1945; CP 1, 2; DA;
DA3; DAB; DAC; DAM DRAM, MST,
POET; DLB 10, 20; EWL 3; EXPP; MAL
5; MTCW 1, 2; MTFW 2005; PAB; PFS
1, 3, 4, 10, 27; TUS; WP
Auden, Wystan Hugh
See Auden, W. H.
Audiberti, Jacques 1899-1965 .... **CLC 38**
See also CA 252; 25-28R; DAM DRAM;
DLB 321; EWL 3
Audubon, John James 1785-1851 . **NCLC 47**
See also AAYA 76; AMWS 16; ANW; DLB
248
Auel, Jean 1936- .... **CLC 31, 107**
See also AAYA 7, 51; BEST 90:4; BPFB 1;
CA 103; CANR 21, 64, 115; CPW; DA3;
DAM POP; INT CANR-21; NFS 11;
RHW; SATA 91
Auel, Jean M.
See Auel, Jean
Auel, Jean Marie
See Auel, Jean
Auerbach, Berthold 1812-1882 .... **NCLC 171**
See also DLB 133
Auerbach, Erich 1892-1957 .... **TCLC 43**
See also CA 118; 155; EWL 3
Augier, Emile 1820-1889 .... **NCLC 31**
See also DLB 192; GFL 1789 to the Present
August, John
See De Voto, Bernard (Augustine)
Augustine, St. 354-430 .... **CMLC 6, 95;
WLCS**
See also DA; DA3; DAB; DAC; DAM
MST; DLB 115; EW 1; RGWL 2, 3;
WLIT 8
Aunt Belinda
See Braddon, Mary Elizabeth
Aunt Weedy
See Alcott, Louisa May
Aurelius
See Bourne, Randolph S(illiman)
Aurelius, Marcus 121-180 .... **CMLC 45**
See also AW 2; RGWL 2, 3
Aurobindo, Sri
See Ghose, Aurabinda
Aurobindo Ghose
See Ghose, Aurabinda
Ausonius, Decimus Magnus c. 310-c.
394 .... **CMLC 88**
See also RGWL 2, 3

Austen, Jane 1775-1817 ...... **NCLC 1, 13, 19,
33, 51, 81, 95, 119, 150, 207, 210, 222;
WLC 1**
See also AAYA 19; BRW 4; BRWC 1;
BRWR 2; BYA 3; CDBLB 1789-1832;
DA; DA3; DAB; DAC; DAM MST, NOV;
DLB 116; EXPN; FL 1:2; GL 2; LAIT 2;
LATS 1:1; LMFS 1; NFS 1, 14, 18, 20,
21, 28, 29; TEA; WLIT 3; WYAS 1
Auster, Paul 1947- .... **CLC 47, 131, 227**
See also AMWS 12; CA 69-72; CANR 23,
52, 75, 129, 165; CMW 4; CN 5, 6, 7;
DA3; DLB 227; MAL 5; MTCW 2;
MTFW 2005; SUFW 2; TCLE 1:1
Austin, Frank
See Faust, Frederick
Austin, Mary Hunter 1868-1934 .... **SSC 104;
TCLC 25**
See also ANW; CA 109; 178; DLB 9, 78,
206, 221, 275; FW; TCWW 1, 2
Averroes 1126-1198 .... **CMLC 7, 104**
See also DLB 115
Avicenna 980-1037 .... **CMLC 16, 110**
See also DLB 115
Avison, Margaret 1918-2007 .... **CLC 2, 4, 97**
See also CA 17-20R; CANR 134; CP 1, 2,
3, 4, 5, 6, 7; DAC; DAM POET; DLB 53;
MTCW 1
Avison, Margaret Kirkland
See Avison, Margaret
Axton, David
See Koontz, Dean
Ayala, Francisco 1906-2009 .... **SSC 119**
See also CA 208; CWW 2; DLB 322; EWL
3; RGSF 2
Ayala, Francisco de Paula y Garcia Duarte
See Ayala, Francisco
Ayckbourn, Alan 1939- ...... **CLC 5, 8, 18, 33,
74; DC 13**
See also BRWS 5; CA 21-24R; CANR 31,
59, 118; CBD; CD 5, 6; DAB; DAM
DRAM; DFS 7; DLB 13, 245; EWL 3;
MTCW 1, 2; MTFW 2005
Aydy, Catherine
See Tennant, Emma
Ayme, Marcel (Andre) 1902-1967 ... **CLC 11;
SSC 41**
See also CA 89-92; CANR 67, 137; CLR
25; DLB 72; EW 12; EWL 3; GFL 1789
to the Present; RGSF 2; RGWL 2, 3;
SATA 91
Ayrton, Michael 1921-1975 .... **CLC 7**
See also CA 5-8R; 61-64; CANR 9, 21
Aytmatov, Chingiz
See Aitmatov, Chingiz
Azorin
See Martinez Ruiz, Jose
Azuela, Mariano 1873-1952 .. **HLC 1; TCLC
3, 145, 217**
See also CA 104; 131; CANR 81; DAM
MULT; EWL 3; HW 1, 2; LAW; MTCW
1, 2; MTFW 2005
Ba, Mariama 1929-1981 ...... **BLC 2:1; BLCS**
See also AFW; BW 2; CA 141; CANR 87;
DNFS 2; WLIT 2
Baastad, Babbis Friis
See Friis-Baastad, Babbis Ellinor
Bab
See Gilbert, W(illiam) S(chwenck)
Babbis, Eleanor
See Friis-Baastad, Babbis Ellinor
Babel, Isaac
See Babel, Isaak (Emmanuilovich)
Babel, Isaak (Emmanuilovich)
1894-1941(?) . **SSC 16, 78; TCLC 2, 13,
171**
See also CA 104; 155; CANR 113; DLB
272; EW 11; EWL 3; MTCW 2; MTFW
2005; RGSF 2; RGWL 2, 3; SSFS 10;
TWA

Babits, Mihaly 1883-1941 .... **TCLC 14**
  See also CA 114; CDWLB 4; DLB 215;
  EWL 3
Babur 1483-1530 .... **LC 18**
Babylas
  See Ghelderode, Michel de
Baca, Jimmy Santiago 1952- . **HLC 1; PC 41**
  See also CA 131; CANR 81, 90, 146; CP 6,
  7; DAM MULT; DLB 122; HW 1, 2;
  LLW; MAL 5
Baca, Jose Santiago
  See Baca, Jimmy Santiago
Bacchelli, Riccardo 1891-1985 .... **CLC 19**
  See also CA 29-32R; 117; DLB 264; EWL
  3
Bacchylides c. 520B.C.-c.
  452B.C. .... **CMLC 119**
Bach, Richard 1936- .... **CLC 14**
  See also AITN 1; BEST 89:2; BPFB 1; BYA
  5; CA 9-12R; CANR 18, 93, 151; CPW;
  DAM NOV, POP; FANT; MTCW 1;
  SATA 13
Bach, Richard David
  See Bach, Richard
Bache, Benjamin Franklin
  1769-1798 .... **LC 74**
  See also DLB 43
Bachelard, Gaston 1884-1962 ...... **TCLC 128**
  See also CA 97-100; 89-92; DLB 296; GFL
  1789 to the Present
Bachman, Richard
  See King, Stephen
Bachmann, Ingeborg 1926-1973 ..... **CLC 69;
  TCLC 192**
  See also CA 93-96; 45-48; CANR 69; DLB
  85; EWL 3; RGHL; RGWL 2, 3
Bacon, Francis 1561-1626 ..... **LC 18, 32, 131**
  See also BRW 1; CDBLB Before 1660;
  DLB 151, 236, 252; RGEL 2; TEA
Bacon, Roger 1214(?)-1294 ... **CMLC 14, 108**
  See also DLB 115
Bacovia, G.
  See Bacovia, George
Bacovia, George 1881-1957 .... **TCLC 24**
  See Bacovia, George
  See also CA 123; 189; CDWLB 4; DLB
  220; EWL 3
Badanes, Jerome 1937-1995 .... **CLC 59**
  See also CA 234
Bage, Robert 1728-1801 .... **NCLC 182**
  See also DLB 39; RGEL 2
Bagehot, Walter 1826-1877 .... **NCLC 10**
  See also DLB 55
Bagnold, Enid 1889-1981 .... **CLC 25**
  See also AAYA 75; BYA 2; CA 5-8R; 103;
  CANR 5, 40; CBD; CN 2; CWD; CWRI
  5; DAM DRAM; DLB 13, 160, 191, 245;
  FW; MAICYA 1, 2; RGEL 2; SATA 1, 25
Bagritsky, Eduard
  See Dzyubin, Eduard Georgievich
Bagritsky, Edvard
  See Dzyubin, Eduard Georgievich
Bagrjana, Elisaveta
  See Belcheva, Elisaveta Lyubomirova
Bagryana, Elisaveta
  See Belcheva, Elisaveta Lyubomirova
Bailey, Paul 1937- .... **CLC 45**
  See also CA 21-24R; CANR 16, 62, 124;
  CN 1, 2, 3, 4, 5, 6, 7; DLB 14, 271; GLL
  2
Baillie, Joanna 1762-1851 ...... **NCLC 71, 151**
  See also DLB 93, 344; GL 2; RGEL 2
Bainbridge, Beryl 1934- ...... **CLC 4, 5, 8, 10,
  14, 18, 22, 62, 130**
  See also BRWS 6; CA 21-24R; CANR 24,
  55, 75, 88, 128; CN 2, 3, 4, 5, 6, 7; DAM
  NOV; DLB 14, 231; EWL 3; MTCW 1,
  2; MTFW 2005

Baker, Carlos (Heard)
  1909-1987 .... **TCLC 119**
  See also CA 5-8R; 122; CANR 3, 63; DLB
  103
Baker, Elliott 1922-2007 .... **CLC 8**
  See also CA 45-48; 257; CANR 2, 63; CN
  1, 2, 3, 4, 5, 6, 7
Baker, Elliott Joseph
  See Baker, Elliott
Baker, Jean H.
  See Russell, George William
Baker, Nicholson 1957- .... **CLC 61, 165**
  See also AMWS 13; CA 135; CANR 63,
  120, 138, 190; CN 6; CPW; DA3; DAM
  POP; DLB 227; MTFW 2005
Baker, Ray Stannard 1870-1946 .... **TCLC 47**
  See also CA 118; DLB 345
Baker, Russell 1925- .... **CLC 31**
  See also BEST 89:4; CA 57-60; CANR 11,
  41, 59, 137; MTCW 1, 2; MTFW 2005
Baker, Russell Wayne
  See Baker, Russell
Bakhtin, M.
  See Bakhtin, Mikhail Mikhailovich
Bakhtin, M. M.
  See Bakhtin, Mikhail Mikhailovich
Bakhtin, Mikhail
  See Bakhtin, Mikhail Mikhailovich
Bakhtin, Mikhail Mikhailovich
  1895-1975 .... **CLC 83; TCLC 160**
  See also CA 128; 113; DLB 242; EWL 3
Bakshi, Ralph 1938(?)- .... **CLC 26**
  See also CA 112; 138; IDFW 3
Bakunin, Mikhail (Alexandrovich)
  1814-1876 .... **NCLC 25, 58**
  See also DLB 277
Bal, Mieke (Maria Gertrudis)
  1946- .... **CLC 252**
  See also CA 156; CANR 99
Baldwin, James 1924-1987 ...... **BLC 1:1, 2:1;
  CLC 1, 2, 3, 4, 5, 8, 13, 15, 17, 42, 50,
  67, 90, 127; DC 1; SSC 10, 33, 98, 134;
  TCLC 229; WLC 1**
  See also AAYA 4, 34; AFAW 1, 2; AMWR
  2; AMWS 1; BPFB 1; BW 1; CA 1-4R;
  124; CABS 1; CAD; CANR 3, 24;
  CDALB 1941-1968; CN 1, 2, 3, 4; CPW;
  DA; DA3; DAB; DAC; DAM MST,
  MULT, NOV, POP; DFS 11, 15; DLB 2,
  7, 33, 249, 278; DLBY 1987; EWL 3;
  EXPS; LAIT 5; MAL 5; MTCW 1, 2;
  MTFW 2005; NCFS 4; NFS 4; RGAL 4;
  RGSF 2; SATA 9; SATA-Obit 54; SSFS
  2, 18; TUS
Baldwin, William c. 1515-1563 .... **LC 113**
  See also DLB 132
Bale, John 1495-1563 .... **LC 62**
  See also DLB 132; RGEL 2; TEA
Ball, Hugo 1886-1927 .... **TCLC 104**
Ballard, James G.
  See Ballard, J.G.
Ballard, James Graham
  See Ballard, J.G.
Ballard, J.G. 1930-2009 ..... **CLC 3, 6, 14, 36,
  137; SSC 1, 53**
  See also AAYA 3, 52; BRWS 5; CA 5-8R;
  285; CANR 15, 39, 65, 107, 133, 198;
  CN 1, 2, 3, 4, 5, 6, 7; DA3; DAM NOV,
  POP; DLB 14, 207, 261, 319; EWL 3;
  HGG; MTCW 1, 2; MTFW 2005; NFS 8;
  RGEL 2; RGSF 2; SATA 93; SATA-Obit
  203; SCFW 1, 2; SFW 4
Ballard, Jim G.
  See Ballard, J.G.
Balmont, Konstantin (Dmitriyevich)
  1867-1943 .... **TCLC 11**
  See also CA 109; 155; DLB 295; EWL 3
Baltausis, Vincas 1847-1910
  See Mikszath, Kalman

Balzac, Guez de (?)-
  See Balzac, Jean-Louis Guez de
Balzac, Honore de 1799-1850 ... **NCLC 5, 35,
  53, 153; SSC 5, 59, 102; WLC 1**
  See also DA; DA3; DAB; DAC; DAM
  MST, NOV; DLB 119; EW 5; GFL 1789
  to the Present; LMFS 1; RGSF 2; RGWL
  2, 3; SSFS 10; SUFW; TWA
Balzac, Jean-Louis Guez de
  1597-1654 .... **LC 162**
  See also DLB 268; GFL Beginnings to 1789
Bambara, Toni Cade 1939-1995 ..... **BLC 1:1,
  2:1; CLC 19, 88; SSC 35, 107; TCLC
  116; WLCS**
  See also AAYA 5, 49; AFAW 2; AMWS 11;
  BW 2, 3; BYA 12, 14; CA 29-32R; 150;
  CANR 24, 49, 81; CDALBS; DA; DA3;
  DAC; DAM MST, MULT; DLB 38, 218;
  EXPS; MAL 5; MTCW 1, 2; MTFW
  2005; RGAL 4; RGSF 2; SATA 112; SSFS
  4, 7, 12, 21
Bamdad, A.
  See Shamlu, Ahmad
Bamdad, Alef
  See Shamlu, Ahmad
Banat, D. R.
  See Bradbury, Ray
Bancroft, Laura
  See Baum, L. Frank
Banim, John 1798-1842 .... **NCLC 13**
  See also DLB 116, 158, 159; RGEL 2
Banim, Michael 1796-1874 .... **NCLC 13**
  See also DLB 158, 159
Banjo, The
  See Paterson, A(ndrew) B(arton)
Banks, Iain 1954- .... **CLC 34**
  See also BRWS 11; CA 123; 128; CANR
  61, 106, 180; DLB 194, 261; EWL 3;
  HGG; INT CA-128; MTFW 2005; SFW 4
Banks, Iain M.
  See Banks, Iain
Banks, Iain Menzies
  See Banks, Iain
Banks, Lynne Reid
  See Reid Banks, Lynne
Banks, Russell 1940- . **CLC 37, 72, 187; SSC
  42**
  See also AAYA 45; AMWS 5; CA 65-68;
  CAAS 15; CANR 19, 52, 73, 118, 195;
  CN 4, 5, 6, 7; DLB 130, 278; EWL 3;
  MAL 5; MTCW 2; MTFW 2005; NFS 13
Banks, Russell Earl
  See Banks, Russell
Banks, Russell Earl
  See Banks, Russell
Banville, John 1945- .... **CLC 46, 118, 224**
  See also CA 117; 128; CANR 104, 150,
  176; CN 4, 5, 6, 7; DLB 14, 271, 326;
  INT CA-128
Banville, Theodore (Faullain) de
  1832-1891 .... **NCLC 9**
  See also DLB 217; GFL 1789 to the Present
Baraka, Amiri 1934- .. **BLC 1:1, 2:1; CLC 1,
  2, 3, 5, 10, 14, 33, 115, 213; DC 6; PC
  4; WLCS**
  See also AAYA 63; AFAW 1, 2; AMWS 2;
  BW 2, 3; CA 21-24R; CABS 3; CAD;
  CANR 27, 38, 61, 133, 172; CD 3, 5, 6;
  CDALB 1941-1968; CN 1, 2; CP 1, 2, 3,
  4, 5, 6, 7; CPW; DA; DA3; DAC; DAM
  MST, MULT, POET, POP; DFS 3, 11, 16;
  DLB 5, 7, 16, 38; DLBD 8; EWL 3, MAL
  5; MTCW 1, 2; MTFW 2005; PFS 9;
  RGAL 4; TCLE 1:1; TUS; WP
Baratynsky, Evgenii Abramovich
  1800-1844 .... **NCLC 103**
  See also DLB 205

Barbauld, Anna Laetitia
1743-1825 .... NCLC 50, 185
See also DLB 107, 109, 142, 158, 336;
RGEL 2

Barbellion, W. N. P.
See Cummings, Bruce F.

Barber, Benjamin R. 1939- .... CLC 141
See also CA 29-32R; CANR 12, 32, 64, 119

Barbera, Jack 1945- .... CLC 44
See also CA 110; CANR 45

Barbera, Jack Vincent
See Barbera, Jack

Barbey d'Aurevilly, Jules-Amedee
1808-1889 .... NCLC 1, 213; SSC 17
See also DLB 119; GFL 1789 to the Present

Barbour, John c. 1316-1395 .... CMLC 33
See also DLB 146

Barbusse, Henri 1873-1935 .... TCLC 5
See also CA 105; 154; DLB 65; EWL 3;
RGWL 2, 3

Barclay, Alexander c. 1475-1552 .... LC 109
See also DLB 132

Barclay, Bill
See Moorcock, Michael

Barclay, William Ewert
See Moorcock, Michael

Barea, Arturo 1897-1957 .... TCLC 14
See also CA 111; 201

Barfoot, Joan 1946- .... CLC 18
See also CA 105; CANR 141, 179

Barham, Richard Harris
1788-1845 .... NCLC 77
See also DLB 159

Baring, Maurice 1874-1945 .... TCLC 8
See also CA 105; 168; DLB 34; HGG

Baring-Gould, Sabine 1834-1924 ... TCLC 88
See also DLB 156, 190

Barker, Clive 1952- .... CLC 52, 205; SSC 53
See also AAYA 10, 54; BEST 90:3; BPFB
1; CA 121; 129; CANR 71, 111, 133, 187;
CPW; DA3; DAM POP; DLB 261; HGG;
INT CA-129; MTCW 1, 2; MTFW 2005;
SUFW 2

Barker, George Granville
1913-1991 .... CLC 8, 48; PC 77
See also CA 9-12R; 135; CANR 7, 38; CP
1, 2, 3, 4, 5; DAM POET; DLB 20; EWL
3; MTCW 1

Barker, Harley Granville
See Granville-Barker, Harley

Barker, Howard 1946- .... CLC 37
See also CA 102; CBD; CD 5, 6; DLB 13,
233

Barker, Jane 1652-1732 .... LC 42, 82; PC 91
See also DLB 39, 131

Barker, Pat 1943- .... CLC 32, 94, 146
See also BRWS 4; CA 117; 122; CANR 50,
101, 148, 195; CN 6, 7; DLB 271, 326;
INT CA-122

Barker, Patricia
See Barker, Pat

Barlach, Ernst (Heinrich)
1870-1938 .... TCLC 84
See also CA 178; DLB 56, 118; EWL 3

Barlow, Joel 1754-1812 .... NCLC 23, 223
See also AMWS 2; DLB 37; RGAL 4

Barnard, Mary (Ethel) 1909- .... CLC 48
See also CA 21-22; CAP 2; CP 1

Barnes, Djuna 1892-1982 .... CLC 3, 4, 8, 11,
29, 127; SSC 3; TCLC 212
See also AMWS 3; CA 9-12R; 107; CAD;
CANR 16, 55; CN 1, 2, 3; CWD; DLB 4,
9, 45; EWL 3; GLL 1; MAL 5; MTCW 1,
2; MTFW 2005; RGAL 4; TCLE 1:1;
TUS

Barnes, Jim 1933- .... NNAL
See also CA 108, 175, 272; CAAE 175,
272; CAAS 28; DLB 175

Barnes, Julian 1946- .... CLC 42, 141
See also BRWS 4; CA 102; CANR 19, 54,
115, 137, 195; CN 4, 5, 6, 7; DAB; DLB
194; DLBY 1993; EWL 3; MTCW 2;
MTFW 2005; SSFS 24

Barnes, Julian Patrick
See Barnes, Julian

Barnes, Peter 1931-2004 .... CLC 5, 56
See also CA 65-68; 230; CAAS 12; CANR
33, 34, 64, 113; CBD; CD 5, 6; DFS 6;
DLB 13, 233; MTCW 1

Barnes, William 1801-1886 .... NCLC 75
See also DLB 32

Baroja, Pio 1872-1956 .... HLC 1; SSC 112;
TCLC 8
See also CA 104; 247; EW 9

Baroja y Nessi, Pio
See Baroja, Pio

Baron, David
See Pinter, Harold

Baron Corvo
See Rolfe, Frederick (William Serafino
Austin Lewis Mary)

Barondess, Sue K. 1926-1977 .... CLC 3, 8
See also CA 1-4R; 69-72; CANR 1

Barondess, Sue Kaufman
See Barondess, Sue K.

Baron de Teive
See Pessoa, Fernando

Baroness Von S.
See Zangwill, Israel

Barres, (Auguste-)Maurice
1862-1923 .... TCLC 47
See also CA 164; DLB 123; GFL 1789 to
the Present

Barreto, Afonso Henrique de Lima
See Lima Barreto, Afonso Henrique de

Barrett, Andrea 1954- .... CLC 150
See also CA 156; CANR 92, 186; CN 7;
DLB 335; SSFS 24

Barrett, Michele
See Barrett, Michele

Barrett, Michele 1949- .... CLC 65
See also CA 280

Barrett, Roger Syd
See Barrett, Syd

Barrett, Syd 1946-2006 .... CLC 35

Barrett, William (Christopher)
1913-1992 .... CLC 27
See also CA 13-16R; 139; CANR 11, 67;
INT CANR-11

Barrett Browning, Elizabeth
1806-1861 ...... NCLC 1, 16, 61, 66, 170;
PC 6, 62; WLC 1
See also AAYA 63; BRW 4; CDBLB 1832-
1890; DA; DA3; DAB; DAC; DAM MST,
POET; DLB 32, 199; EXPP; FL 1:2; PAB;
PFS 2, 16, 23; TEA; WLIT 4; WP

Barrie, Baronet
See Barrie, J. M.

Barrie, J. M. 1860-1937 .... TCLC 2, 164
See also BRWS 3; BYA 4, 5; CA 104; 136;
CANR 77; CDBLB 1890-1914; CLR 16,
124; CWRI 5; DA3; DAB; DAM DRAM;
DFS 7; DLB 10, 141, 156, 352; EWL 3;
FANT; MAICYA 1, 2; MTCW 2; MTFW
2005; SATA 100; SUFW; WCH; WLIT 4;
YABC 1

Barrie, James Matthew
See Barrie, J. M.

Barrington, Michael
See Moorcock, Michael

Barrol, Grady
See Bograd, Larry

Barry, Mike
See Malzberg, Barry N(athaniel)

Barry, Philip 1896-1949 .... TCLC 11
See also CA 109; 199; DFS 9; DLB 7, 228;
MAL 5; RGAL 4

Barry, Sebastian 1955- .... CLC 282
See also CA 117; CANR 122, 193; CD 5,
6; DLB 245

Bart, Andre Schwarz
See Schwarz-Bart, Andre

Barth, John 1930- ... CLC 1, 2, 3, 5, 7, 9, 10,
14, 27, 51, 89, 214; SSC 10, 89
See also AITN 1, 2; AMW; BPFB 1; CA
1-4R; CABS 1; CANR 5, 23, 49, 64, 113;
CN 1, 2, 3, 4, 5, 6, 7; DAM NOV; DLB
2, 227; EWL 3; FANT; MAL 5; MTCW
1; RGAL 4; RGSF 2; RHW; SSFS 6; TUS

Barth, John Simmons
See Barth, John

Barthelme, Donald 1931-1989 ... CLC 1, 2, 3,
5, 6, 8, 13, 23, 46, 59, 115; SSC 2, 55
See also AMWS 4; BPFB 1; CA 21-24R;
129; CANR 20, 58, 188; CN 1, 2, 3, 4;
DA3; DAM NOV; DLB 2, 234; DLBY
1980, 1989; EWL 3; FANT; LMFS 2;
MAL 5; MTCW 1, 2; MTFW 2005;
RGAL 4; RGSF 2; SATA 7; SATA-Obit
62; SSFS 17

Barthelme, Frederick 1943- ...... CLC 36, 117
See also AMWS 11; CA 114; 122; CANR
77; CN 4, 5, 6, 7; CSW; DLB 244; DLBY
1985; EWL 3; INT CA-122

Barthes, Roland (Gerard)
1915-1980 .... CLC 24, 83; TCLC 135
See also CA 130; 97-100; CANR 66; DLB
296; EW 13; EWL 3; GFL 1789 to the
Present; MTCW 1, 2; TWA

Bartram, William 1739-1823 .... NCLC 145
See also ANW; DLB 37

Barzun, Jacques (Martin) 1907- ..... CLC 51,
145
See also CA 61-64; CANR 22, 95

Bashevis, Isaac
See Singer, Isaac Bashevis

Bashevis, Yitskhok
See Singer, Isaac Bashevis

Bashkirtseff, Marie 1859-1884 .... NCLC 27

Basho, Matsuo
See Matsuo Basho

Basil of Caesaria c. 330-379 .... CMLC 35

Basket, Raney
See Edgerton, Clyde

Bass, Kingsley B., Jr.
See Bullins, Ed

Bass, Rick 1958- . CLC 79, 143, 286; SSC 60
See also AMWS 16; ANW; CA 126; CANR
53, 93, 145, 183; CSW; DLB 212, 275

Bassani, Giorgio 1916-2000 .... CLC 9
See also CA 65-68; 190; CANR 33; CWW
2; DLB 128, 177, 299; EWL 3; MTCW 1;
RGHL; RGWL 2, 3

Bassine, Helen
See Yglesias, Helen

Bastian, Ann CLC 70

Bastos, Augusto Roa
See Roa Bastos, Augusto

Bataille, Georges 1897-1962 .... CLC 29;
TCLC 155
See also CA 101; 89-92; EWL 3

Bates, H(erbert) E(rnest)
1905-1974 .... CLC 46; SSC 10
See also CA 93-96; 45-48; CANR 34; CN
1; DA3; DAB; DAM POP; DLB 162, 191;
EWL 3; EXPS; MTCW 1, 2; RGSF 2;
SSFS 7

Bauchart
See Camus, Albert

Baudelaire, Charles 1821-1867 . NCLC 6, 29,
55, 155; PC 1, 106; SSC 18; WLC 1
See also DA; DA3; DAB; DAC; DAM
MST, POET; DLB 217; EW 7; GFL 1789
to the Present; LMFS 2; PFS 21; RGWL
2, 3; TWA

Bellamy, Edward 1850-1898 ..... NCLC 4, 86, 147
See also DLB 12; NFS 15; RGAL 4; SFW 4

Belli, Gioconda 1948- .... HLCS 1
See also CA 152; CANR 143; CWW 2; DLB 290; EWL 3; RGWL 3

Bellin, Edward J.
See Kuttner, Henry

Bello, Andres 1781-1865 .... NCLC 131
See also LAW

Belloc, Hilaire 1870-1953 ... PC 24; TCLC 7, 18
See also CA 106; 152; CLR 102; CWRI 5; DAM POET; DLB 19, 100, 141, 174; EWL 3; MTCW 2; MTFW 2005; SATA 112; WCH; YABC 1

Belloc, Joseph Hilaire Pierre Sebastien Rene Swanton
See Belloc, Hilaire

Belloc, Joseph Peter Rene Hilaire
See Belloc, Hilaire

Belloc, Joseph Pierre Hilaire
See Belloc, Hilaire

Belloc, M. A.
See Lowndes, Marie Adelaide (Belloc)

Belloc-Lowndes, Mrs.
See Lowndes, Marie Adelaide (Belloc)

Bellow, Saul 1915-2005 ...... CLC 1, 2, 3, 6, 8, 10, 13, 15, 25, 33, 34, 63, 79, 190, 200; SSC 14, 101; WLC 1
See also AITN 2; AMW; AMWC 2; AMWR 2; BEST 89:3; BPFB 1; CA 5-8R; 238; CABS 1; CANR 29, 53, 95, 132; CDALB 1941-1968; CN 1, 2, 3, 4, 5, 6, 7; DA; DA3; DAB; DAC; DAM MST, NOV, POP; DLB 2, 28, 299, 329; DLBD 3; DLBY 1982; EWL 3; MAL 5; MTCW 1, 2; MTFW 2005; NFS 4, 14, 26; RGAL 4; RGHL; RGSF 2; SSFS 12, 22; TUS

Belser, Reimond Karel Maria de 1929- .... CLC 14
See also CA 152

Bely, Andrey
See Bugayev, Boris Nikolayevich

Belyi, Andrei
See Bugayev, Boris Nikolayevich

Bembo, Pietro 1470-1547 .... LC 79
See also RGWL 2, 3

Benary, Margot
See Benary-Isbert, Margot

Benary-Isbert, Margot 1889-1979 .... CLC 12
See also CA 5-8R; 89-92; CANR 4, 72; CLR 12; MAICYA 1, 2; SATA 2; SATA-Obit 21

Benavente, Jacinto 1866-1954 .... DC 26; HLCS 1; TCLC 3
See also CA 106; 131; CANR 81; DAM DRAM, MULT; DLB 329; EWL 3; GLL 2; HW 1, 2; MTCW 1, 2

Benavente y Martinez, Jacinto
See Benavente, Jacinto

Benchley, Peter 1940-2006 .... CLC 4, 8
See also AAYA 14; AITN 2; BPFB 1; CA 17-20R; 248; CANR 12, 35, 66, 115; CPW; DAM NOV, POP; HGG; MTCW 1, 2; MTFW 2005; SATA 3, 89, 164

Benchley, Peter Bradford
See Benchley, Peter

Benchley, Robert (Charles) 1889-1945 .... TCLC 1, 55
See also CA 105; 153; DLB 11; MAL 5; RGAL 4

Benda, Julien 1867-1956 .... TCLC 60
See also CA 120; 154; GFL 1789 to the Present

Benedetti, Mario 1920-2009 .... SSC 135
See also CA 152; 286; DAM MULT; DLB 113; EWL 3; HW 1, 2; LAW

Benedetti, Mario Orlando Hardy Hamlet Brenno
See Benedetti, Mario

Benedetti Farrugia, Mario
See Benedetti, Mario

Benedetti Farrugia, Mario Orlando Hardy Hamlet Brenno
See Benedetti, Mario

Benedict, Ruth 1887-1948 .... TCLC 60
See also CA 158; CANR 146; DLB 246

Benedict, Ruth Fulton
See Benedict, Ruth

Benedikt, Michael 1935- .... CLC 4, 14
See also CA 13-16R; CANR 7; CP 1, 2, 3, 4, 5, 6, 7; DLB 5

Benet, Juan 1927-1993 .... CLC 28
See also CA 143; EWL 3

Benet, Stephen Vincent 1898-1943 ..... PC 64; SSC 10, 86; TCLC 7
See also AMWS 11; CA 104; 152; DA3; DAM POET; DLB 4, 48, 102, 249, 284; DLBY 1997; EWL 3; HGG; MAL 5; MTCW 2; MTFW 2005; RGAL 4; RGSF 2; SSFS 22; SUFW; WP; YABC 1

Benet, William Rose 1886-1950 ..... TCLC 28
See also CA 118; 152; DAM POET; DLB 45; RGAL 4

Benford, Gregory 1941- .... CLC 52
See also BPFB 1; CA 69-72, 175, 268; CAAE 175, 268; CAAS 27; CANR 12, 24, 49, 95, 134; CN 7; CSW; DLBY 1982; MTFW 2005; SCFW 2; SFW 4

Benford, Gregory Albert
See Benford, Gregory

Bengtsson, Frans (Gunnar) 1894-1954 .... TCLC 48
See also CA 170; EWL 3

Benjamin, David
See Slavitt, David R.

Benjamin, Lois
See Gould, Lois

Benjamin, Walter 1892-1940 .... TCLC 39
See also CA 164; CANR 181; DLB 242; EW 11; EWL 3

Ben Jelloun, Tahar 1944- .... CLC 180
See also CA 135, 162; CANR 100, 166; CWW 2; EWL 3; RGWL 3; WLIT 2

Benn, Gottfried 1886-1956 .. PC 35; TCLC 3
See also CA 106; 153; DLB 56; EWL 3; RGWL 2, 3

Bennett, Alan 1934- .... CLC 45, 77
See also BRWS 8; CA 103; CANR 35, 55, 106, 157, 197; CBD; CD 5, 6; DAB; DAM MST; DLB 310; MTCW 1, 2; MTFW 2005

Bennett, (Enoch) Arnold 1867-1931 .... TCLC 5, 20, 197
See also BRW 6; CA 106; 155; CDBLB 1890-1914; DLB 10, 34, 98, 135; EWL 3; MTCW 2

Bennett, Elizabeth
See Mitchell, Margaret

Bennett, George Harold 1930- .... CLC 5
See also BW 1; CA 97-100; CAAS 13; CANR 87; DLB 33

Bennett, Gwendolyn B. 1902-1981 .... HR 1:2
See also BW 1; CA 125; DLB 51; WP

Bennett, Hal
See Bennett, George Harold

Bennett, Jay 1912- .... CLC 35
See also AAYA 10, 73; CA 69-72; CANR 11, 42, 79; JRDA; SAAS 4; SATA 41, 87; SATA-Brief 27; WYA; YAW

Bennett, Louise 1919-2006 .... BLC 1:1; CLC 28
See also BW 2, 3; CA 151; 252; CDWLB 3; CP 1, 2, 3, 4, 5, 6, 7; DAM MULT; DLB 117; EWL 3

Bennett, Louise Simone
See Bennett, Louise

Bennett-Coverley, Louise
See Bennett, Louise

Benoit de Sainte-Maure fl. 12th cent. - .... CMLC 90

Benson, A. C. 1862-1925 .... TCLC 123
See also DLB 98

Benson, E(dward) F(rederic) 1867-1940 .... TCLC 27
See also CA 114; 157; DLB 135, 153; HGG; SUFW 1

Benson, Jackson J. 1930- .... CLC 34
See also CA 25-28R; DLB 111

Benson, Sally 1900-1972 .... CLC 17
See also CA 19-20; 37-40R; CAP 1; SATA 1, 35; SATA-Obit 27

Benson, Stella 1892-1933 .... TCLC 17
See also CA 117; 154, 155; DLB 36, 162; FANT; TEA

Bentham, Jeremy 1748-1832 .... NCLC 38
See also DLB 107, 158, 252

Bentley, E(dmund) C(lerihew) 1875-1956 .... TCLC 12
See also CA 108; 232; DLB 70; MSW

Bentley, Eric 1916- .... CLC 24
See also CA 5-8R; CAD; CANR 6, 67; CBD; CD 5, 6; INT CANR-6

Bentley, Eric Russell
See Bentley, Eric

ben Uzair, Salem
See Horne, Richard Henry Hengist

Beolco, Angelo 1496-1542 .... LC 139

Beranger, Pierre Jean de 1780-1857 .... NCLC 34

Berdyaev, Nicolas
See Berdyaev, Nikolai (Aleksandrovich)

Berdyaev, Nikolai (Aleksandrovich) 1874-1948 .... TCLC 67
See also CA 120; 157

Berdyayev, Nikolai (Aleksandrovich)
See Berdyaev, Nikolai (Aleksandrovich)

Berendt, John 1939- .... CLC 86
See also CA 146; CANR 75, 83, 151

Berendt, John Lawrence
See Berendt, John

Beresford, J(ohn) D(avys) 1873-1947 .... TCLC 81
See also CA 112; 155; DLB 162, 178, 197; SFW 4; SUFW 1

Bergelson, David (Rafailovich) 1884-1952 .... TCLC 81
See also CA 220; DLB 333; EWL 3

Bergelson, Dovid
See Bergelson, David (Rafailovich)

Berger, Colonel
See Malraux, Andre

Berger, John 1926- .... CLC 2, 19
See also BRWS 4; CA 81-84; CANR 51, 78, 117, 163, 200; CN 1, 2, 3, 4, 5, 6, 7; DLB 14, 207, 319, 326

Berger, John Peter
See Berger, John

Berger, Melvin H. 1927- .... CLC 12
See also CA 5-8R; CANR 4, 142; CLR 32; SAAS 2; SATA 5, 88, 158; SATA-Essay 124

Berger, Thomas 1924- .... CLC 3, 5, 8, 11, 18, 38, 259
See also BPFB 1; CA 1-4R; CANR 5, 28, 51, 128; CN 1, 2, 3, 4, 5, 6, 7; DAM NOV; DLB 2; DLBY 1980; EWL 3; FANT; INT CANR-28; MAL 5; MTCW 1, 2; MTFW 2005; RHW; TCLE 1:1; TCWW 1, 2

Bergman, Ernst Ingmar
See Bergman, Ingmar

Bissoondath, Neil Devindra
See Bissoondath, Neil
Bitov, Andrei (Georgievich) 1937- ... **CLC 57**
See also CA 142; DLB 302
Biyidi, Alexandre
See Beti, Mongo
Bjarme, Brynjolf
See Ibsen, Henrik
Bjoernson, Bjoernstjerne (Martinius)
1832-1910 .... **TCLC 7, 37**
See also CA 104
Black, Benjamin
See Banville, John
Black, Robert
See Holdstock, Robert
Blackburn, Paul 1926-1971 .... **CLC 9, 43**
See also BG 1:2; CA 81-84; 33-36R; CANR
34; CP 1; DLB 16; DLBY 1981
Black Elk 1863-1950 .... **NNAL; TCLC 33**
See also CA 144; DAM MULT; MTCW 2;
MTFW 2005; WP
Black Hawk 1767-1838 .... **NNAL**
Black Hobart
See Sanders, Ed
Blacklin, Malcolm
See Chambers, Aidan
Blackmore, R(ichard) D(oddridge)
1825-1900 .... **TCLC 27**
See also CA 120; DLB 18; RGEL 2
Blackmur, R(ichard) P(almer)
1904-1965 .... **CLC 2, 24**
See also AMWS 2; CA 11-12; 25-28R;
CANR 71; CAP 1; DLB 63; EWL 3;
MAL 5
Black Tarantula
See Acker, Kathy
Blackwood, Algernon 1869-1951 .... **SSC 107;
TCLC 5**
See also AAYA 78; CA 105; 150; CANR
169; DLB 153, 156, 178; HGG; SUFW 1
Blackwood, Algernon Henry
See Blackwood, Algernon
Blackwood, Caroline (Maureen)
1931-1996 .... **CLC 6, 9, 100**
See also BRWS 9; CA 85-88; 151; CANR
32, 61, 65; CN 3, 4, 5, 6; DLB 14, 207;
HGG; MTCW 1
Blade, Alexander
See Hamilton, Edmond; Silverberg, Robert
Blaga, Lucian 1895-1961 .... **CLC 75**
See also CA 157; DLB 220; EWL 3
Blair, Eric
See Orwell, George
Blair, Eric Arthur
See Orwell, George
Blair, Hugh 1718-1800 .... **NCLC 75**
Blais, Marie-Claire 1939- .... **CLC 2, 4, 6, 13,
22**
See also CA 21-24R; CAAS 4; CANR 38,
75, 93; CWW 2; DAC; DAM MST; DLB
53; EWL 3; FW; MTCW 1, 2; MTFW
2005; TWA
Blaise, Clark 1940- .... **CLC 29, 261**
See also AITN 2; CA 53-56, 231; CAAE
231; CAAS 3; CANR 5, 66, 106; CN 4,
5, 6, 7; DLB 53; RGSF 2
Blake, Fairley
See De Voto, Bernard (Augustine)
Blake, Nicholas
See Day Lewis, C.
Blake, Sterling
See Benford, Gregory
Blake, William 1757-1827 . **NCLC 13, 37, 57,
127, 173, 190, 201; PC 12, 63; WLC 1**
See also AAYA 47; BRW 3; BRWR 1; CD-
BLB 1789-1832; CLR 52; DA; DA3;
DAB; DAC; DAM MST, POET; DLB 93,

163; EXPP; LATS 1:1; LMFS 1; MAI-
CYA 1, 2; PAB; PFS 2, 12, 24; SATA 30;
TEA; WCH; WLIT 3; WP
Blanchot, Maurice 1907-2003 .... **CLC 135**
See also CA 117; 144; 213; CANR 138;
DLB 72, 296; EWL 3
Blasco Ibanez, Vicente 1867-1928 . **TCLC 12**
See also BPFB 1; CA 110; 131; CANR 81;
DA3; DAM NOV; DLB 322; EW 8; EWL
3; HW 1, 2; MTCW 1
Blatty, William Peter 1928- .... **CLC 2**
See also CA 5-8R; CANR 9, 124; DAM
POP; HGG
Bleeck, Oliver
See Thomas, Ross (Elmore)
Bleecker, Ann Eliza 1752-1783 .... **LC 161**
See also DLB 200
Blessing, Lee 1949- .... **CLC 54**
See also CA 236; CAD; CD 5, 6; DFS 23,
26
Blessing, Lee Knowlton
See Blessing, Lee
Blight, Rose
See Greer, Germaine
Blind, Mathilde 1841-1896 .... **NCLC 202**
See also DLB 199
Blish, James 1921-1975 .... **CLC 14**
See also BPFB 1; CA 1-4R; 57-60; CANR
3; CN 2; DLB 8; MTCW 1; SATA 66;
SCFW 1, 2; SFW 4
Blish, James Benjamin
See Blish, James
Bliss, Frederick
See Card, Orson Scott
Bliss, Gillian
See Paton Walsh, Jill
Bliss, Reginald
See Wells, H. G.
Blixen, Karen 1885-1962 ..... **CLC 10, 29, 95;
SSC 7, 75**
See also CA 25-28; CANR 22, 50; CAP 2;
DA3; DLB 214; EW 10; EWL 3; EXPS;
FW; GL 2; HGG; LAIT 3; LMFS 1;
MTCW 1; NCFS 2; NFS 9; RGSF 2;
RGWL 2, 3; SATA 44; SSFS 3, 6, 13;
WLIT 2
Blixen, Karen Christentze Dinesen
See Blixen, Karen
Bloch, Robert (Albert) 1917-1994 .... **CLC 33**
See also AAYA 29; CA 5-8R, 179; 146;
CAAE 179; CAAS 20; CANR 5, 78;
DA3; DLB 44; HGG; INT CANR-5;
MTCW 2; SATA 12; SATA-Obit 82; SFW
4; SUFW 1, 2
Blok, Alexander (Alexandrovich)
1880-1921 .... **PC 21; TCLC 5**
See also CA 104; 183; DLB 295; EW 9;
EWL 3; LMFS 2; RGWL 2, 3
Blom, Jan
See Breytenbach, Breyten
Bloom, Harold 1930- .... **CLC 24, 103, 221**
See also CA 13-16R; CANR 39, 75, 92,
133, 181; DLB 67; EWL 3; MTCW 2;
MTFW 2005; RGAL 4
Bloomfield, Aurelius
See Bourne, Randolph S(illiman)
Bloomfield, Robert 1766-1823 ..... **NCLC 145**
See also DLB 93
Blount, Roy, Jr. 1941- .... **CLC 38**
See also CA 53-56; CANR 10, 28, 61, 125,
176; CSW; INT CANR-28; MTCW 1, 2;
MTFW 2005
Blount, Roy Alton
See Blount, Roy, Jr.
Blowsnake, Sam 1875-(?) .... **NNAL**
Bloy, Leon 1846-1917 .... **TCLC 22**
See also CA 121; 183; DLB 123; GFL 1789
to the Present

Blue Cloud, Peter (Aroniawenrate)
1933- .... **NNAL**
See also CA 117; CANR 40; DAM MULT;
DLB 342
Bluggage, Oranthy
See Alcott, Louisa May
Blume, Judy 1938- .... **CLC 12, 30**
See also AAYA 3, 26; BYA 1, 8, 12; CA 29-
32R; CANR 13, 37, 66, 124, 186; CLR
15, 69; CPW; DA3; DAM NOV, POP;
DLB 52; JRDA; MAICYA 1, 2; MAIC-
YAS 1; MTCW 1, 2; MTFW 2005; NFS
24; SATA 2, 31, 79, 142, 195; WYA; YAW
Blume, Judy Sussman
See Blume, Judy
Blunden, Edmund (Charles)
1896-1974 .... **CLC 2, 56; PC 66**
See also BRW 6; BRWS 11; CA 17-18; 45-
48; CANR 54; CAP 2; CP 1, 2; DLB 20,
100, 155; MTCW 1; PAB
Bly, Robert 1926- ..... **CLC 1, 2, 5, 10, 15, 38,
128; PC 39**
See also AMWS 4; CA 5-8R; CANR 41,
73, 125; CP 1, 2, 3, 4, 5, 6, 7; DA3; DAM
POET; DLB 5, 342; EWL 3; MAL 5;
MTCW 1, 2; MTFW 2005; PFS 6, 17;
RGAL 4
Bly, Robert Elwood
See Bly, Robert
Boas, Franz 1858-1942 .... **TCLC 56**
See also CA 115; 181
Bobette
See Simenon, Georges
Boccaccio, Giovanni 1313-1375 ... **CMLC 13,
57; SSC 10, 87**
See also EW 2; RGSF 2; RGWL 2, 3; TWA;
WLIT 7
Bochco, Steven 1943- .... **CLC 35**
See also AAYA 11, 71; CA 124; 138
Bode, Sigmund
See O'Doherty, Brian
Bodel, Jean 1167(?)-1210 .... **CMLC 28**
Bodenheim, Maxwell 1892-1954 .... **TCLC 44**
See also CA 110; 187; DLB 9, 45; MAL 5;
RGAL 4
Bodenheimer, Maxwell
See Bodenheim, Maxwell
Bodker, Cecil
See Bodker, Cecil
Bodker, Cecil 1927- .... **CLC 21**
See also CA 73-76; CANR 13, 44, 111;
CLR 23; MAICYA 1, 2; SATA 14, 133
Boell, Heinrich 1917-1985 ..... **CLC 2, 3, 6, 9,
11, 15, 27, 32, 72; SSC 23; TCLC 185;
WLC 1**
See also BPFB 1; CA 21-24R; 116; CANR
24; CDWLB 2; DA; DA3; DAB; DAC;
DAM MST, NOV; DLB 69, 329; DLBY
1985; EW 13; EWL 3; MTCW 1, 2;
MTFW 2005; RGHL; RGSF 2; RGWL 2,
3; SSFS 20; TWA
Boell, Heinrich Theodor
See Boell, Heinrich
Boerne, Alfred
See Doeblin, Alfred
Boethius c. 480-c. 524 .... **CMLC 15**
See also DLB 115; RGWL 2, 3; WLIT 8
Boff, Leonardo (Genezio Darci)
1938- .... **CLC 70; HLC 1**
See also CA 150; DAM MULT; HW 2
Bogan, Louise 1897-1970 .... **CLC 4, 39, 46,
93; PC 12**
See also AMWS 3; CA 73-76; 25-28R;
CANR 33, 82; CP 1; DAM POET; DLB
45, 169; EWL 3; MAL 5; MBL; MTCW
1, 2; PFS 21; RGAL 4
Bogarde, Dirk
See Van Den Bogarde, Derek Jules Gaspard
Ulric Niven

Boyd, William 1952- .... **CLC 28, 53, 70**
See also CA 114; 120; CANR 51, 71, 131, 174; CN 4, 5, 6, 7; DLB 231

Boyesen, Hjalmar Hjorth
1848-1895 .... **NCLC 135**
See also DLB 12, 71; DLBD 13; RGAL 4

Boyle, Kay 1902-1992 .... **CLC 1, 5, 19, 58, 121; SSC 5, 102**
See also CA 13-16R; 140; CAAS 1; CANR 29, 61, 110; CN 1, 2, 3, 4, 5; CP 1, 2, 3, 4, 5; DLB 4, 9, 48, 86; DLBY 1993; EWL 3; MAL 5; MTCW 1, 2; MTFW 2005; RGAL 4; RGSF 2; SSFS 10, 13, 14

Boyle, Mark
See Kienzle, William X.

Boyle, Patrick 1905-1982 .... **CLC 19**
See also CA 127

Boyle, T. C.
See Boyle, T. Coraghessan

Boyle, T. Coraghessan 1948- ..... **CLC 36, 55, 90, 284; SSC 16, 127**
See also AAYA 47; AMWS 8; BEST 90:4; BPFB 1; CA 120; CANR 44, 76, 89, 132; CN 6, 7; CPW; DA3; DAM POP; DLB 218, 278; DLBY 1986; EWL 3; MAL 5; MTCW 2; MTFW 2005; SSFS 13, 19·

Boyle, Thomas Coraghessan
See Boyle, T. Coraghessan

Boz
See Dickens, Charles

Brackenridge, Hugh Henry
1748-1816 .... **NCLC 7**
See also DLB 11, 37; RGAL 4

Bradbury, Edward P.
See Moorcock, Michael

Bradbury, Malcolm (Stanley)
1932-2000 .... **CLC 32, 61**
See also CA 1-4R; CANR 1, 33, 91, 98, 137; CN 1, 2, 3, 4, 5, 6, 7; CP 1; DA3; DAM NOV; DLB 14, 207; EWL 3; MTCW 1, 2; MTFW 2005

Bradbury, Ray 1920- ... **CLC 1, 3, 10, 15, 42, 98, 235; SSC 29, 53; WLC 1**
See also AAYA 15; AITN 1, 2; AMWS 4; BPFB 1; BYA 4, 5, 11; CA 1-4R; CANR 2, 30, 75, 125, 186; CDALB 1968-1988; CN 1, 2, 3, 4, 5, 6, 7; CPW; DA; DA3; DAB; DAC; DAM MST, NOV, POP; DLB 2, 8; EXPN; EXPS; HGG; LAIT 3, 5; LATS 1:2; LMFS 2; MAL 5; MTCW 1, 2; MTFW 2005; NFS 1, 22, 29; RGAL 4; RGSF 2; SATA 11, 64, 123; SCFW 1, 2; SFW 4; SSFS 1, 20; SUFW 1, 2; TUS; YAW

Bradbury, Ray Douglas
See Bradbury, Ray

Braddon, Mary Elizabeth
1837-1915 .... **TCLC 111**
See also BRWS 8; CA 108; 179; CMW 4; DLB 18, 70, 156; HGG

Bradfield, Scott 1955- .... **SSC 65**
See also CA 147; CANR 90; HGG; SUFW 2

Bradfield, Scott Michael
See Bradfield, Scott

Bradford, Gamaliel 1863-1932 .... **TCLC 36**
See also CA 160; DLB 17

Bradford, William 1590-1657 .... **LC 64**
See also DLB 24, 30; RGAL 4

Bradley, David, Jr. 1950- ...... **BLC 1:1; CLC 23, 118**
See also BW 1, 3; CA 104; CANR 26, 81; CN 4, 5, 6, 7; DAM MULT; DLB 33

Bradley, David Henry, Jr.
See Bradley, David, Jr.

Bradley, John Ed 1958- .... **CLC 55**
See also CA 139; CANR 99; CN 6, 7; CSW

Bradley, John Edmund, Jr.
See Bradley, John Ed

Bradley, Marion Zimmer
1930-1999 .... **CLC 30**
See also AAYA 40; BPFB 1; CA 57-60; 185; CAAS 10; CANR 7, 31, 51, 75, 107; CPW; DA3; DAM POP; DLB 8; FANT; FW; GLL 1; MTCW 1, 2; MTFW 2005; SATA 90, 139; SATA-Obit 116; SFW 4; SUFW 2; YAW

Bradshaw, John 1933- .... **CLC 70**
See also CA 138; CANR 61

Bradstreet, Anne 1612(?)-1672 .... **LC 4, 30, 130; PC 10**
See also AMWS 1; CDALB 1640-1865; DA; DA3; DAC; DAM MST, POET; DLB 24; EXPP; FW; PFS 6; RGAL 4; TUS; WP

Brady, Joan 1939- .... **CLC 86**
See also CA 141

Bragg, Melvyn 1939- .... **CLC 10**
See also BEST 89:3; CA 57-60; CANR 10, 48, 89, 158; CN 1, 2, 3, 4, 5, 6, 7; DLB 14, 271; RHW

Brahe, Tycho 1546-1601 .... **LC 45**
See also DLB 300

Braine, John (Gerard) 1922-1986 . **CLC 1, 3, 41**
See also CA 1-4R; 120; CANR 1, 33; CD-BLB 1945-1960; CN 1, 2, 3, 4; DLB 15; DLBY 1986; EWL 3; MTCW 1

Braithwaite, William Stanley (Beaumont)
1878-1962 ...... **BLC 1:1; HR 1:2; PC 52**
See also BW 1; CA 125; DAM MULT; DLB 50, 54; MAL 5

Bramah, Ernest 1868-1942 .... **TCLC 72**
See also CA 156; CMW 4; DLB 70; FANT

Brammer, Billy Lee
See Brammer, William

Brammer, William 1929-1978 .... **CLC 31**
See also CA 235; 77-80

Brancati, Vitaliano 1907-1954 .... **TCLC 12**
See also CA 109; DLB 264; EWL 3

Brancato, Robin F(idler) 1936- .... **CLC 35**
See also AAYA 9, 68; BYA 6; CA 69-72; CANR 11, 45; CLR 32; JRDA; MAICYA 2; MAICYAS 1; SAAS 9; SATA 97; WYA; YAW

Brand, Dionne 1953- .... **CLC 192**
See also BW 2; CA 143; CANR 143; CWP; DLB 334

Brand, Max
See Faust, Frederick

Brand, Millen 1906-1980 .... **CLC 7**
See also CA 21-24R; 97-100; CANR 72

Branden, Barbara 1929- .... **CLC 44**
See also CA 148

Brandes, Georg (Morris Cohen)
1842-1927 .... **TCLC 10**
See also CA 105; 189; DLB 300

Brandys, Kazimierz 1916-2000 .... **CLC 62**
See also CA 239; EWL 3

Branley, Franklyn M(ansfield)
1915-2002 .... **CLC 21**
See also CA 33-36R; 207; CANR 14, 39; CLR 13; MAICYA 1, 2; SAAS 16; SATA 4, 68, 136

Brant, Beth (E.) 1941- .... **NNAL**
See also CA 144; FW

Brant, Sebastian 1457-1521 .... **LC 112**
See also DLB 179; RGWL 2, 3

Brathwaite, Edward Kamau
1930- ..... **BLC 2:1; BLCS; CLC 11; PC 56**
See also BRWS 12; BW 2, 3; CA 25-28R; CANR 11, 26, 47, 107; CDWLB 3; CP 1, 2, 3, 4, 5, 6, 7; DAM POET; DLB 125; EWL 3

Brathwaite, Kamau
See Brathwaite, Edward Kamau

Brautigan, Richard 1935-1984 .. **CLC 1, 3, 5, 9, 12, 34, 42; PC 94; TCLC 133**
See also BPFB 1; CA 53-56; 113; CANR 34; CN 1, 2, 3; CP 1, 2, 3, 4; DA3; DAM NOV; DLB 2, 5, 206; DLBY 1980, 1984; FANT; MAL 5; MTCW 1; RGAL 4; SATA 56

Brautigan, Richard Gary
See Brautigan, Richard

Brave Bird, Mary
See Crow Dog, Mary

Braverman, Kate 1950- .... **CLC 67**
See also CA 89-92; CANR 141; DLB 335

Brecht, Bertolt 1898-1956 .... **DC 3; TCLC 1, 6, 13, 35, 169; WLC 1**
See also CA 104; 133; CANR 62; CDWLB 2; DA; DA3; DAB; DAC; DAM DRAM, MST; DFS 4, 5, 9; DLB 56, 124; EW 11; EWL 3; IDTP; MTCW 1, 2; MTFW 2005; RGHL; RGWL 2, 3; TWA

Brecht, Eugen Berthold Friedrich
See Brecht, Bertolt

Brecht, Eugen Bertolt Friedrich
See Brecht, Bertolt

Bremer, Fredrika 1801-1865 .... **NCLC 11**
See also DLB 254

Brennan, Christopher John
1870-1932 .... **TCLC 17**
See also CA 117; 188; DLB 230; EWL 3

Brennan, Maeve 1917-1993 ... **CLC 5; TCLC 124**
See also CA 81-84; CANR 72, 100

Brenner, Jozef 1887-1919 .... **TCLC 13**
See also CA 111; 240

Brent, Linda
See Jacobs, Harriet A.

Brentano, Clemens (Maria)
1778-1842 .... **NCLC 1, 191; SSC 115**
See also DLB 90; RGWL 2, 3

Brent of Bin Bin
See Franklin, (Stella Maria Sarah) Miles (Lampe)

Brenton, Howard 1942- .... **CLC 31**
See also CA 69-72; CANR 33, 67; CBD; CD 5, 6; DLB 13; MTCW 1

Breslin, James
See Breslin, Jimmy

Breslin, Jimmy 1930- .... **CLC 4, 43**
See also CA 73-76; CANR 31, 75, 139, 187; DAM NOV; DLB 185; MTCW 2; MTFW 2005

Bresson, Robert 1901(?)-1999 .... **CLC 16**
See also CA 110; 187; CANR 49

Breton, Andre 1896-1966 .. **CLC 2, 9, 15, 54; PC 15**
See also CA 19-20; 25-28R; CANR 40, 60; CAP 2; DLB 65, 258; EW 11; EWL 3; GFL 1789 to the Present; LMFS 2; MTCW 1, 2; MTFW 2005; RGWL 2, 3; TWA; WP

Breton, Nicholas c. 1554-c. 1626 .... **LC 133**
See also DLB 136

Breytenbach, Breyten 1939(?)- .. **CLC 23, 37, 126**
See also CA 113; 129; CANR 61, 122, 202; CWW 2; DAM POET; DLB 225; EWL 3

Bridgers, Sue Ellen 1942- .... **CLC 26**
See also AAYA 8, 49; BYA 7, 8; CA 65-68; CANR 11, 36; CLR 18; DLB 52; JRDA; MAICYA 1, 2; SAAS 1; SATA 22, 90; SATA-Essay 109; WYA; YAW

Bridges, Robert (Seymour)
1844-1930 .... **PC 28; TCLC 1**
See also BRW 6; CA 104; 152; CDBLB 1890-1914; DAM POET; DLB 19, 98

Bridie, James
See Mavor, Osborne Henry

Brin, David 1950- .... **CLC 34**
See also AAYA 21; CA 102; CANR 24, 70, 125, 127; INT CANR-24; SATA 65; SCFW 2; SFW 4

Brink, Andre 1935- .... **CLC 18, 36, 106**
See also AFW; BRWS 6; CA 104; CANR 39, 62, 109, 133, 182; CN 4, 5, 6, 7; DLB 225; EWL 3; INT CA-103; LATS 1:2; MTCW 1, 2; MTFW 2005; WLIT 2

Brink, Andre Philippus
See Brink, Andre

Brinsmead, H. F.
See Brinsmead, H(esba) F(ay)

Brinsmead, H. F(ay)
See Brinsmead, H(esba) F(ay)

Brinsmead, H(esba) F(ay) 1922- ...... **CLC 21**
See also CA 21-24R; CANR 10; CLR 47; CWRI 5; MAICYA 1, 2; SAAS 5; SATA 18, 78

Brittain, Vera (Mary)
1893(?)-1970 .... **CLC 23; TCLC 228**
See also BRWS 10; CA 13-16; 25-28R; CANR 58; CAP 1; DLB 191; FW; MTCW 1, 2

Broch, Hermann 1886-1951 ... **TCLC 20, 204**
See also CA 117; 211; CDWLB 2; DLB 85, 124; EW 10; EWL 3; RGWL 2, 3

Brock, Rose
See Hansen, Joseph

Brod, Max 1884-1968 .... **TCLC 115**
See also CA 5-8R; 25-28R; CANR 7; DLB 81; EWL 3

Brodkey, Harold (Roy) 1930-1996 .. **CLC 56; TCLC 123**
See also CA 111; 151; CANR 71; CN 4, 5, 6; DLB 130

Brodskii, Iosif
See Brodsky, Joseph

Brodskii, Iosif Alexandrovich
See Brodsky, Joseph

Brodsky, Iosif Alexandrovich
See Brodsky, Joseph

Brodsky, Joseph 1940-1996 ..... **CLC 4, 6, 13, 36, 100; PC 9; TCLC 219**
See also AAYA 71; AITN 1; AMWS 8; CA 41-44R; 151; CANR 37, 106; CWW 2; DA3; DAM POET; DLB 285, 329; EWL 3; MTCW 1, 2; MTFW 2005; RGWL 2, 3

Brodsky, Michael 1948- .... **CLC 19**
See also CA 102; CANR 18, 41, 58, 147; DLB 244

Brodsky, Michael Mark
See Brodsky, Michael

Brodzki, Bella CLC 65

Brome, Richard 1590(?)-1652 .... **LC 61**
See also BRWS 10; DLB 58

Bromell, Henry 1947- .... **CLC 5**
See also CA 53-56; CANR 9, 115, 116

Bromfield, Louis (Brucker)
1896-1956 .... **TCLC 11**
See also CA 107; 155; DLB 4, 9, 86; RGAL 4; RHW

Broner, E(sther) M(asserman)
1930- .... **CLC 19**
See also CA 17-20R; CANR 8, 25, 72; CN 4, 5, 6; DLB 28

Bronk, William (M.) 1918-1999 .... **CLC 10**
See also CA 89-92; 177; CANR 23; CP 3, 4, 5, 6, 7; DLB 165

Bronstein, Lev Davidovich
See Trotsky, Leon

Bronte, Anne
See Bronte, Anne

Bronte, Anne 1820-1849 ..... **NCLC 4, 71, 102**
See also BRW 5; BRWR 1; DA3; DLB 21, 199, 340; NFS 26; TEA

Bronte, (Patrick) Branwell
1817-1848 .... **NCLC 109**
See also DLB 340

Bronte, Charlotte
See Bronte, Charlotte

Bronte, Charlotte 1816-1855 ...... **NCLC 3, 8, 33, 58, 105, 155, 217; WLC 1**
See also AAYA 17; BRW 5; BRWC 2; BRWR 1; BYA 2; CDBLB 1832-1890; DA; DA3; DAB; DAC; DAM MST, NOV; DLB 21, 159, 199, 340; EXPN; FL 1:2; GL 2; LAIT 2; NFS 4; TEA; WLIT 4

Bronte, Emily
See Bronte, Emily

Bronte, Emily 1818-1848 .... **NCLC 16, 35, 165; PC 8; WLC 1**
See also AAYA 17; BPFB 1; BRW 5; BRWC 1; BRWR 1; BYA 3; CDBLB 1832-1890; DA; DA3; DAB; DAC; DAM MST, NOV, POET; DLB 21, 32, 199, 340; EXPN; FL 1:2; GL 2; LAIT 1; TEA; WLIT 3

Bronte, Emily Jane
See Bronte, Emily

Brontes
See Bronte, Anne; Bronte, (Patrick) Branwell; Bronte, Charlotte; Bronte, Emily

Brooke, Frances 1724-1789 .... **LC 6, 48**
See also DLB 39, 99

Brooke, Henry 1703(?)-1783 .... **LC 1**
See also DLB 39

Brooke, Rupert 1887-1915 . **PC 24; TCLC 2, 7; WLC 1**
See also BRWS 3; CA 104; 132; CANR 61; CDBLB 1914-1945; DA; DAB; DAC; DAM MST, POET; DLB 19, 216; EXPP; GLL 2; MTCW 1, 2; MTFW 2005; PFS 7; TEA

Brooke, Rupert Chawner
See Brooke, Rupert

Brooke-Haven, P.
See Wodehouse, P. G.

Brooke-Rose, Christine 1923(?)- ..... **CLC 40, 184**
See also BRWS 4; CA 13-16R; CANR 58, 118, 183; CN 1, 2, 3, 4, 5, 6, 7; DLB 14, 231; EWL 3; SFW 4

Brookner, Anita 1928- . **CLC 32, 34, 51, 136, 237**
See also BRWS 4; CA 114; 120; CANR 37, 56, 87, 130; CN 4, 5, 6, 7; CPW; DA3; DAB; DAM POP; DLB 194, 326; DLBY 1987; EWL 3; MTCW 1, 2; MTFW 2005; NFS 23; TEA

Brooks, Cleanth 1906-1994 . **CLC 24, 86, 110**
See also AMWS 14; CA 17-20R; 145; CANR 33, 35; CSW; DLB 63; DLBY 1994; EWL 3; INT CANR-35; MAL 5; MTCW 1, 2; MTFW 2005

Brooks, George
See Baum, L. Frank

Brooks, Gwendolyn 1917-2000 .... **BLC 1:1, 2:1; CLC 1, 2, 4, 5, 15, 49, 125; PC 7; WLC 1**
See also AAYA 20; AFAW 1, 2; AITN 1; AMWS 3; BW 2, 3; CA 1-4R; 190; CANR 1, 27, 52, 75, 132; CDALB 1941-1968; CLR 27; CP 1, 2, 3, 4, 5, 6, 7; CWP; DA; DA3; DAC; DAM MST, MULT, POET; DLB 5, 76, 165; EWL 3; EXPP; FL 1:5; MAL 5; MBL; MTCW 1, 2; MTFW 2005; PFS 1, 2, 4, 6; RGAL 4; SATA 6; SATA-Obit 123; TUS; WP

Brooks, Gwendolyn Elizabeth
See Brooks, Gwendolyn

Brooks, Mel 1926-
See Kaminsky, Melvin
See also CA 65-68; CANR 16; DFS 21

Brooks, Peter 1938- .... **CLC 34**
See also CA 45-48; CANR 1, 107, 182

Brooks, Peter Preston
See Brooks, Peter

Brooks, Van Wyck 1886-1963 .... **CLC 29**
See also AMW; CA 1-4R; CANR 6; DLB 45, 63, 103; MAL 5; TUS

Brophy, Brigid 1929-1995 ...... **CLC 6, 11, 29, 105**
See also CA 5-8R; 149; CAAS 4; CANR 25, 53; CBD; CN 1, 2, 3, 4, 5, 6; CWD; DA3; DLB 14, 271; EWL 3; MTCW 1, 2

Brophy, Brigid Antonia
See Brophy, Brigid

Brosman, Catharine Savage 1934- ..... **CLC 9**
See also CA 61-64; CANR 21, 46, 149

Brossard, Nicole 1943- .... **CLC 115, 169; PC 80**
See also CA 122; CAAS 16; CANR 140; CCA 1; CWP; CWW 2; DLB 53; EWL 3; FW; GLL 2; RGWL 3

Brother Antoninus
See Everson, William

Brothers Grimm
See Grimm, Jacob Ludwig Karl; Grimm, Wilhelm Karl

The Brothers Quay
See Quay, Stephen; Quay, Timothy

Broughton, T(homas) Alan 1936- ..... **CLC 19**
See also CA 45-48; CANR 2, 23, 48, 111

Broumas, Olga 1949- .... **CLC 10, 73**
See also CA 85-88; CANR 20, 69, 110; CP 5, 6, 7; CWP; GLL 2

Broun, Heywood 1888-1939 .... **TCLC 104**
See also DLB 29, 171

Brown, Alan 1950- .... **CLC 99**
See also CA 156

Brown, Charles Brockden
1771-1810 .... **NCLC 22, 74, 122**
See also AMWS 1; CDALB 1640-1865; DLB 37, 59, 73; FW; GL 2; HGG; LMFS 1; RGAL 4; TUS

Brown, Christy 1932-1981 .... **CLC 63**
See also BYA 13; CA 105; 104; CANR 72; DLB 14

Brown, Claude 1937-2002 ..... **BLC 1:1; CLC 30**
See also AAYA 7; BW 1, 3; CA 73-76; 205; CANR 81; DAM MULT

Brown, Dan 1964- .... **CLC 209**
See also AAYA 55; CA 217; LNFS 1; MTFW 2005

Brown, Dee 1908-2002 .... **CLC 18, 47**
See also AAYA 30; CA 13-16R; 212; CAAS 6; CANR 11, 45, 60, 150; CPW; CSW; DA3; DAM POP; DLBY 1980; LAIT 2; MTCW 1, 2; MTFW 2005; NCFS 5; SATA 5, 110; SATA-Obit 141; TCWW 1, 2

Brown, Dee Alexander
See Brown, Dee

Brown, George
See Wertmueller, Lina

Brown, George Douglas
1869-1902 .... **TCLC 28**
See also CA 162; RGEL 2

Brown, George Mackay 1921-1996 ... **CLC 5, 48, 100**
See also BRWS 6; CA 21-24R; 151; CAAS 6; CANR 12, 37, 67; CN 1, 2, 3, 4, 5, 6; CP 1, 2, 3, 4, 5, 6; DLB 14, 27, 139, 271; MTCW 1; RGSF 2; SATA 35

Brown, James Willie
See Komunyakaa, Yusef

Brown, James Willie, Jr.
See Komunyakaa, Yusef

Brown, Larry 1951-2004 .... **CLC 73, 289**
See also CA 130; 134; 233; CANR 117, 145; CSW; DLB 234; INT CA-134

Brown, Moses
See Barrett, William (Christopher)

Burchill, Julie 1959- .... **CLC 238**
See also CA 135; CANR 115, 116
Burckhardt, Jacob (Christoph)
1818-1897 .... **NCLC 49**
See also EW 6
Burford, Eleanor
See Hibbert, Eleanor Alice Burford
Burgess, Anthony 1917-1993 . **CLC 1, 2, 4, 5, 8, 10, 13, 15, 22, 40, 62, 81, 94**
See also AAYA 25; AITN 1; BRWS 1; CA 1-4R; 143; CANR 2, 46; CDBLB 1960 to Present; CN 1, 2, 3, 4, 5; DA3; DAB; DAC; DAM NOV; DLB 14, 194, 261; DLBY 1998; EWL 3; MTCW 1, 2; MTFW 2005; NFS 15; RGEL 2; RHW; SFW 4; TEA; YAW
Buridan, John c. 1295-c. 1358 ...... **CMLC 97**
Burke, Edmund 1729(?)-1797 .... **LC 7, 36, 146; WLC 1**
See also BRW 3; DA; DA3; DAB; DAC; DAM MST; DLB 104, 252, 336; RGEL 2; TEA
Burke, Kenneth (Duva) 1897-1993 ... **CLC 2, 24**
See also AMW; CA 5-8R; 143; CANR 39, 74, 136; CN 1, 2; CP 1, 2, 3, 4, 5; DLB 45, 63; EWL 3; MAL 5; MTCW 1, 2; MTFW 2005; RGAL 4
Burke, Leda
See Garnett, David
Burke, Ralph
See Silverberg, Robert
Burke, Thomas 1886-1945 .... **TCLC 63**
See also CA 113; 155; CMW 4; DLB 197
Burney, Fanny 1752-1840 .... **NCLC 12, 54, 107**
See also BRWS 3; DLB 39; FL 1:2; NFS 16; RGEL 2; TEA
Burney, Frances
See Burney, Fanny
Burns, Robert 1759-1796 ... **LC 3, 29, 40; PC 6; WLC 1**
See also AAYA 51; BRW 3; CDBLB 1789-1832; DA; DA3; DAB; DAC; DAM MST, POET; DLB 109; EXPP; PAB; RGEL 2; TEA; WP
Burns, Tex
See L'Amour, Louis
Burnshaw, Stanley 1906-2005 ..... **CLC 3, 13, 44**
See also CA 9-12R; 243; CP 1, 2, 3, 4, 5, 6, 7; DLB 48; DLBY 1997
Burr, Anne 1937- .... **CLC 6**
See also CA 25-28R
Burroughs, Augusten 1965- .... **CLC 277**
See also AAYA 73; CA 214; CANR 168
Burroughs, Edgar Rice 1875-1950 . **TCLC 2, 32**
See also AAYA 11; BPFB 1; BYA 4, 9; CA 104; 132; CANR 131; DA3; DAM NOV; DLB 8; FANT; MTCW 1, 2; MTFW 2005; RGAL 4; SATA 41; SCFW 1, 2; SFW 4; TCWW 1, 2; TUS; YAW
Burroughs, William S. 1914-1997 . **CLC 1, 2, 5, 15, 22, 42, 75, 109; TCLC 121; WLC 1**
See also AAYA 60; AITN 2; AMWS 3; BG 1:2; BPFB 1; CA 9-12R; 160; CANR 20, 52, 104; CN 1, 2, 3, 4, 5, 6; CPW; DA; DA3; DAB; DAC; DAM MST, NOV, POP; DLB 2, 8, 16, 152, 237; DLBY 1981, 1997; EWL 3; GLL 1; HGG; LMFS 2; MAL 5; MTCW 1, 2; MTFW 2005; RGAL 4; SFW 4
Burroughs, William Seward
See Burroughs, William S.
Burton, Sir Richard F(rancis)
1821-1890 .... **NCLC 42**
See also DLB 55, 166, 184; SSFS 21

Burton, Robert 1577-1640 .... **LC 74**
See also DLB 151; RGEL 2
Buruma, Ian 1951- .... **CLC 163**
See also CA 128; CANR 65, 141, 195
Bury, Stephen
See Stephenson, Neal
Busch, Frederick 1941-2006 .. **CLC 7, 10, 18, 47, 166**
See also CA 33-36R; 248; CAAS 1; CANR 45, 73, 92, 157; CN 1, 2, 3, 4, 5, 6, 7; DLB 6, 218
Busch, Frederick Matthew
See Busch, Frederick
Bush, Barney (Furman) 1946- .... **NNAL**
See also CA 145
Bush, Ronald 1946- .... **CLC 34**
See also CA 136
Busia, Abena, P. A. 1953- .... **BLC 2:1**
Bustos, Francisco
See Borges, Jorge Luis
Bustos Domecq, Honorio
See Bioy Casares, Adolfo; Borges, Jorge Luis
Butler, Octavia 1947-2006 . **BLC 2:1; BLCS; CLC 38, 121, 230, 240**
See also AAYA 18, 48; AFAW 2; AMWS 13; BPFB 1; BW 2, 3; CA 73-76; 248; CANR 12, 24, 38, 73, 145, 240; CLR 65; CN 7; CPW; DA3; DAM MULT, POP; DLB 33; LATS 1:2; MTCW 1, 2; MTFW 2005; NFS 8, 21; SATA 84; SCFW 2; SFW 4; SSFS 6; TCLE 1:1; YAW
Butler, Octavia E.
See Butler, Octavia
Butler, Octavia Estelle
See Butler, Octavia
Butler, Robert Olen, Jr.
See Butler, Robert Olen
Butler, Robert Olen 1945- .... **CLC 81, 162; SSC 117**
See also AMWS 12; BPFB 1; CA 112; CANR 66, 138, 194; CN 7; CSW; DAM POP; DLB 173, 335; INT CA-112; MAL 5; MTCW 2; MTFW 2005; SSFS 11, 22
Butler, Samuel 1612-1680 .... **LC 16, 43, 173; PC 94**
See also DLB 101, 126; RGEL 2
Butler, Samuel 1835-1902 .... **TCLC 1, 33; WLC 1**
See also BRWS 2; CA 143; CDBLB 1890-1914; DA; DA3; DAB; DAC; DAM MST, NOV; DLB 18, 57, 174; RGEL 2; SFW 4; TEA
Butler, Walter C.
See Faust, Frederick
Butor, Michel (Marie Francois)
1926- .... **CLC 1, 3, 8, 11, 15, 161**
See also CA 9-12R; CANR 33, 66; CWW 2; DLB 83; EW 13; EWL 3; GFL 1789 to the Present; MTCW 1, 2; MTFW 2005
Butts, Mary 1890(?)-1937 ... **SSC 124; TCLC 77**
See also CA 148; DLB 240
Buxton, Ralph
See Silverstein, Alvin; Silverstein, Virginia B.
Buzo, Alex
See Buzo, Alexander (John)
Buzo, Alexander (John) 1944- .... **CLC 61**
See also CA 97-100; CANR 17, 39, 69; CD 5, 6; DLB 289
Buzzati, Dino 1906-1972 .... **CLC 36**
See also CA 160; 33-36R; DLB 177; RGWL 2, 3; SFW 4
Byars, Betsy 1928- .... **CLC 35**
See also AAYA 19; BYA 3; CA 33-36R, 183; CAAE 183; CANR 18, 36, 57, 102, 148; CLR 1, 16, 72; DLB 52; INT CANR-

18; JRDA; MAICYA 1, 2; MAICYAS 1; MTCW 1; SAAS 1; SATA 4, 46, 80, 163; SATA-Essay 108; WYA; YAW
Byars, Betsy Cromer
See Byars, Betsy
Byatt, A. S. 1936- .... **CLC 19, 65, 136, 223; SSC 91**
See also BPFB 1; BRWC 2; BRWS 4; CA 13-16R; CANR 13, 33, 50, 75, 96, 133; CN 1, 2, 3, 4, 5, 6; DA3; DAM NOV, POP; DLB 14, 194, 319, 326; EWL 3; MTCW 1, 2; MTFW 2005; RGSF 2; RHW; SSFS 26; TEA
Byatt, Antonia Susan Drabble
See Byatt, A. S.
Byrd, William II 1674-1744 .... **LC 112**
See also DLB 24, 140; RGAL 4
Byrne, David 1952- .... **CLC 26**
See also CA 127
Byrne, John Joseph
See Leonard, Hugh
Byrne, John Keyes
See Leonard, Hugh
Byron, George Gordon
See Lord Byron
Byron, George Gordon Noel
See Lord Byron
Byron, Robert 1905-1941 .... **TCLC 67**
See also CA 160; DLB 195
C. 3. 3.
See Wilde, Oscar
Caballero, Fernan 1796-1877 .... **NCLC 10**
Cabell, Branch
See Cabell, James Branch
Cabell, James Branch 1879-1958 .... **TCLC 6**
See also CA 105; 152; DLB 9, 78; FANT; MAL 5; MTCW 2; RGAL 4; SUFW 1
Cabeza de Vaca, Alvar Nunez
1490-1557(?) .... **LC 61**
Cable, George Washington
1844-1925 .... **SSC 4; TCLC 4**
See also CA 104; 155; DLB 12, 74; DLBD 13; RGAL 4; TUS
Cabral de Melo Neto, Joao
1920-1999 .... **CLC 76**
See also CA 151; CWW 2; DAM MULT; DLB 307; EWL 3; LAW; LAWS 1
Cabrera, Lydia 1900-1991 .... **TCLC 223**
See also CA 178; DLB 145; EWL 3; HW 1; LAWS 1
Cabrera Infante, G. 1929-2005 ... **CLC 5, 25, 45, 120; HLC 1; SSC 39**
See also CA 85-88; 236; CANR 29, 65, 110; CDWLB 3; CWW 2; DA3; DAM MULT; DLB 113; EWL 3; HW 1, 2; LAW; LAWS 1; MTCW 1, 2; MTFW 2005; RGSF 2; WLIT 1
Cabrera Infante, Guillermo
See Cabrera Infante, G.
Cade, Toni
See Bambara, Toni Cade
Cadmus and Harmonia
See Buchan, John
Caedmon fl. 658-680 .... **CMLC 7**
See also DLB 146
Caeiro, Alberto
See Pessoa, Fernando
Caesar, Julius
See Julius Caesar
Cage, John (Milton), (Jr.)
1912-1992 .... **CLC 41; PC 58**
See also CA 13-16R; 169; CANR 9, 78; DLB 193; INT CANR-9; TCLE 1:1
Cahan, Abraham 1860-1951 .... **TCLC 71**
See also CA 108; 154; DLB 9, 25, 28; MAL 5; RGAL 4
Cain, Christopher
See Fleming, Thomas

Cain, G.
See Cabrera Infante, G.
Cain, Guillermo
See Cabrera Infante, G.
Cain, James M(allahan) 1892-1977 .. **CLC 3, 11, 28**
See also AITN 1; BPFB 1; CA 17-20R; 73-76; CANR 8, 34, 61; CMW 4; CN 1, 2; DLB 226; EWL 3; MAL 5; MSW; MTCW 1; RGAL 4
Caine, Hall 1853-1931 .... **TCLC 97**
See also RHW
Caine, Mark
See Raphael, Frederic (Michael)
Calasso, Roberto 1941- .... **CLC 81**
See also CA 143; CANR 89
Calderon de la Barca, Pedro
1600-1681 . **DC 3; HLCS 1; LC 23, 136**
See also DFS 23; EW 2; RGWL 2, 3; TWA
Caldwell, Erskine 1903-1987 ... **CLC 1, 8, 14, 50, 60; SSC 19; TCLC 117**
See also AITN 1; AMW; BPFB 1; CA 1-4R; 121; CAAS 1; CANR 2, 33; CN 1, 2, 3, 4; DA3; DAM NOV; DLB 9, 86; EWL 3; MAL 5; MTCW 1, 2; MTFW 2005; RGAL 4; RGSF 2; TUS
Caldwell, (Janet Miriam) Taylor (Holland)
1900-1985 .... **CLC 2, 28, 39**
See also BPFB 1; CA 5-8R; 116; CANR 5; DA3; DAM NOV, POP; DLBD 17; MTCW 2; RHW
Calhoun, John Caldwell
1782-1850 .... **NCLC 15**
See also DLB 3, 248
Calisher, Hortense 1911-2009 .... **CLC 2, 4, 8, 38, 134; SSC 15**
See also CA 1-4R; 282; CANR 1, 22, 117; CN 1, 2, 3, 4, 5, 6, 7; DA3; DAM NOV; DLB 2, 218; INT CANR-22; MAL 5; MTCW 1, 2; MTFW 2005; RGAL 4; RGSF 2
Callaghan, Morley 1903-1990 ..... **CLC 3, 14, 41, 65; TCLC 145**
See also CA 9-12R; 132; CANR 33, 73; CN 1, 2, 3, 4; DAC; DAM MST; DLB 68; EWL 3; MTCW 1, 2; MTFW 2005; RGEL 2; RGSF 2; SSFS 19
Callaghan, Morley Edward
See Callaghan, Morley
Callimachus c. 305B.C.-c.
240B.C. .... **CMLC 18**
See also AW 1; DLB 176; RGWL 2, 3
Calvin, Jean
See Calvin, John
Calvin, John 1509-1564 .... **LC 37**
See also DLB 327; GFL Beginnings to 1789
Calvino, Italo 1923-1985 .... **CLC 5, 8, 11, 22, 33, 39, 73; SSC 3, 48; TCLC 183**
See also AAYA 58; CA 85-88; 116; CANR 23, 61, 132; DAM NOV; DLB 196; EW 13; EWL 3; MTCW 1, 2; MTFW 2005; RGHL; RGSF 2; RGWL 2, 3; SFW 4; SSFS 12; WLIT 7
Camara Laye
See Laye, Camara
Cambridge, A Gentleman of the University of
See Crowley, Edward Alexander
Camden, William 1551-1623 .... **LC 77**
See also DLB 172
Cameron, Carey 1952- .... **CLC 59**
See also CA 135
Cameron, Peter 1959- .... **CLC 44**
See also AMWS 12; CA 125; CANR 50, 117, 188; DLB 234; GLL 2
Camoens, Luis Vaz de 1524(?)-1580
See Camoes, Luis de

Camoes, Luis de 1524(?)-1580 . **HLCS 1; LC 62; PC 31**
See also DLB 287; EW 2; RGWL 2, 3
Camp, Madeleine L'Engle
See L'Engle, Madeleine
Campana, Dino 1885-1932 .... **TCLC 20**
See also CA 117; 246; DLB 114; EWL 3
Campanella, Tommaso 1568-1639 .... **LC 32**
See also RGWL 2, 3
Campbell, Bebe Moore 1950-2006 . **BLC 2:1; CLC 246**
See also AAYA 26; BW 2, 3; CA 139; 254; CANR 81, 134; DLB 227; MTCW 2; MTFW 2005
Campbell, John Ramsey
See Campbell, Ramsey
Campbell, John W(ood, Jr.)
1910-1971 .... **CLC 32**
See also CA 21-22; 29-32R; CANR 34; CAP 2; DLB 8; MTCW 1; SCFW 1, 2; SFW 4
Campbell, Joseph 1904-1987 .... **CLC 69; TCLC 140**
See also AAYA 3, 66; BEST 89:2; CA 1-4R; 124; CANR 3, 28, 61, 107; DA3; MTCW 1, 2
Campbell, Maria 1940- .... **CLC 85; NNAL**
See also CA 102; CANR 54; CCA 1; DAC
Campbell, Ramsey 1946- ... **CLC 42; SSC 19**
See also AAYA 51; CA 57-60, 228; CAAE 228; CANR 7, 102, 171; DLB 261; HGG; INT CANR-7; SUFW 1, 2
Campbell, (Ignatius) Roy (Dunnachie)
1901-1957 .... **TCLC 5**
See also AFW; CA 104; 155; DLB 20, 225; EWL 3; MTCW 2; RGEL 2
Campbell, Thomas 1777-1844 .... **NCLC 19**
See also DLB 93, 144; RGEL 2
Campbell, Wilfred
See Campbell, William
Campbell, William 1858(?)-1918 ..... **TCLC 9**
See also CA 106; DLB 92
Campbell, William Edward March
1893-1954 .... **TCLC 96**
See also CA 108; 216; DLB 9, 86, 316; MAL 5
Campion, Jane 1954- .... **CLC 95, 229**
See also AAYA 33; CA 138; CANR 87
Campion, Thomas 1567-1620 . **LC 78; PC 87**
See also CDBLB Before 1660; DAM POET; DLB 58, 172; RGEL 2
Camus, Albert 1913-1960 ...... **CLC 1, 2, 4, 9, 11, 14, 32, 63, 69, 124; DC 2; SSC 9, 76, 129; WLC 1**
See also AAYA 36; AFW; BPFB 1; CA 89-92; CANR 131; DA; DA3; DAB; DAC; DAM DRAM, MST, NOV; DLB 72, 321, 329; EW 13; EWL 3; EXPN; EXPS; GFL 1789 to the Present; LATS 1:2; LMFS 2; MTCW 1, 2; MTFW 2005; NFS 6, 16; RGHL; RGSF 2; RGWL 2, 3; SSFS 4; TWA
Canby, Vincent 1924-2000 .... **CLC 13**
See also CA 81-84; 191
Cancale
See Desnos, Robert
Canetti, Elias 1905-1994 .. **CLC 3, 14, 25, 75, 86; TCLC 157**
See also CA 21-24R; 146; CANR 23, 61, 79; CDWLB 2; CWW 2; DA3; DLB 85, 124, 329; EW 12; EWL 3; MTCW 1, 2; MTFW 2005; RGWL 2, 3; TWA
Canfield, Dorothea F.
See Fisher, Dorothy (Frances) Canfield
Canfield, Dorothea Frances
See Fisher, Dorothy (Frances) Canfield
Canfield, Dorothy
See Fisher, Dorothy (Frances) Canfield

Canin, Ethan 1960- .... **CLC 55; SSC 70**
See also CA 131; 135; CANR 193; DLB 335, 350; MAL 5
Cankar, Ivan 1876-1918 .... **TCLC 105**
See also CDWLB 4; DLB 147; EWL 3
Cannon, Curt
See Hunter, Evan
Cao, Lan 1961- .... **CLC 109**
See also CA 165
Cape, Judith
See Page, P.K.
Capek, Karel 1890-1938 .... **DC 1; SSC 36; TCLC 6, 37, 192; WLC 1**
See also CA 104; 140; CDWLB 4; DA; DA3; DAB; DAC; DAM DRAM, MST, NOV; DFS 7, 11; DLB 215; EW 10; EWL 3; MTCW 2; MTFW 2005; RGSF 2; RGWL 2, 3; SCFW 1, 2; SFW 4
Capella, Martianus fl. 4th cent. - .. **CMLC 84**
Capote, Truman 1924-1984 . **CLC 1, 3, 8, 13, 19, 34, 38, 58; SSC 2, 47, 93; TCLC 164; WLC 1**
See also AAYA 61; AMWS 3; BPFB 1; CA 5-8R; 113; CANR 18, 62, 201; CDALB 1941-1968; CN 1, 2, 3; CPW; DA; DA3; DAB; DAC; DAM MST, NOV, POP; DLB 2, 185, 227; DLBY 1980, 1984; EWL 3; EXPS; GLL 1; LAIT 3; MAL 5; MTCW 1, 2; MTFW 2005; NCFS 2; RGAL 4; RGSF 2; SATA 91; SSFS 2; TUS
Capra, Frank 1897-1991 .... **CLC 16**
See also AAYA 52; CA 61-64; 135
Caputo, Philip 1941- .... **CLC 32**
See also AAYA 60; CA 73-76; CANR 40, 135; YAW
Caragiale, Ion Luca 1852-1912 ...... **TCLC 76**
See also CA 157
Card, Orson Scott 1951- ...... **CLC 44, 47, 50, 279**
See also AAYA 11, 42; BPFB 1; BYA 5, 8; CA 102; CANR 27, 47, 73, 102, 106, 133, 184; CLR 116; CPW; DA3; DAM POP; FANT; INT CANR-27; MTCW 1, 2; MTFW 2005; NFS 5; SATA 83, 127; SCFW 2; SFW 4; SUFW 2; YAW
Cardenal, Ernesto 1925- .... **CLC 31, 161; HLC 1; PC 22**
See also CA 49-52; CANR 2, 32, 66, 138; CWW 2; DAM MULT, POET; DLB 290; EWL 3; HW 1, 2; LAWS 1; MTCW 1, 2; MTFW 2005; RGWL 2, 3
Cardinal, Marie 1929-2001 .... **CLC 189**
See also CA 177; CWW 2; DLB 83; FW
Cardozo, Benjamin N(athan)
1870-1938 .... **TCLC 65**
See also CA 117; 164
Carducci, Giosue (Alessandro Giuseppe)
1835-1907 .... **PC 46; TCLC 32**
See also CA 163; DLB 329; EW 7; RGWL 2, 3
Carew, Thomas 1595(?)-1640 ..... **LC 13, 159; PC 29**
See also BRW 2; DLB 126; PAB; RGEL 2
Carey, Ernestine Gilbreth
1908-2006 .... **CLC 17**
See also CA 5-8R; 254; CANR 71; SATA 2; SATA-Obit 177
Carey, Peter 1943- .... **CLC 40, 55, 96, 183; SSC 133**
See also BRWS 12; CA 123; 127; CANR 53, 76, 117, 157, 185; CN 4, 5, 6, 7; DLB 289, 326; EWL 3; INT CA-127; LNFS 1; MTCW 1, 2; MTFW 2005; RGSF 2; SATA 94
Carey, Peter Philip
See Carey, Peter
Carleton, William 1794-1869 ... **NCLC 3, 199**
See also DLB 159; RGEL 2; RGSF 2

Charby, Jay
See Ellison, Harlan
Chardin, Pierre Teilhard de
See Teilhard de Chardin, (Marie Joseph) Pierre
Chariton fl. 1st cent. (?)- .... **CMLC 49**
Charlemagne 742-814 .... **CMLC 37**
Charles I 1600-1649 .... **LC 13**
Charriere, Isabelle de 1740-1805 .. **NCLC 66**
See also DLB 313
Charron, Pierre 1541-1603 .... **LC 174**
See also GFL Beginnings to 1789
Chartier, Alain c. 1392-1430 .... **LC 94**
See also DLB 208
Chartier, Emile-Auguste
See Alain
Charyn, Jerome 1937- .... **CLC 5, 8, 18**
See also CA 5-8R; CAAS 1; CANR 7, 61, 101, 158, 199; CMW 4; CN 1, 2, 3, 4, 5, 6, 7; DLBY 1983; MTCW 1
Chase, Adam
See Marlowe, Stephen
Chase, Mary (Coyle) 1907-1981 .... **DC 1**
See also CA 77-80; 105; CAD; CWD; DFS 11; DLB 228; SATA 17; SATA-Obit 29
Chase, Mary Ellen 1887-1973 .... **CLC 2; TCLC 124**
See also CA 13-16; 41-44R; CAP 1; SATA 10
Chase, Nicholas
See Hyde, Anthony
Chase-Riboud, Barbara (Dewayne Tosi) 1939- .... **BLC 2:1**
See also BW 2; CA 113; CANR 76; DAM MULT; DLB 33; MTCW 2
Chateaubriand, Francois Rene de 1768-1848 .... **NCLC 3, 134**
See also DLB 119; EW 5; GFL 1789 to the Present; RGWL 2, 3; TWA
Chatelet, Gabrielle-Emilie Du
See du Chatelet, Emilie
Chatterje, Saratchandra -(?)
See Chatterji, Sarat Chandra
Chatterji, Bankim Chandra 1838-1894 .... **NCLC 19**
Chatterji, Sarat Chandra 1876-1936 .... **TCLC 13**
See also CA 109; 186; EWL 3
Chatterton, Thomas 1752-1770 ..... **LC 3, 54; PC 104**
See also DAM POET; DLB 109; RGEL 2
Chatwin, (Charles) Bruce 1940-1989 .... **CLC 28, 57, 59**
See also AAYA 4; BEST 90:1; BRWS 4; CA 85-88; 127; CPW; DAM POP; DLB 194, 204; EWL 3; MTFW 2005
Chaucer, Daniel
See Ford, Ford Madox
Chaucer, Geoffrey 1340(?)-1400 ... **LC 17, 56, 173; PC 19, 58; WLCS**
See also BRW 1; BRWC 1; BRWR 2; CD-BLB Before 1660; DA; DA3; DAB; DAC; DAM MST, POET; DLB 146; LAIT 1; PAB; PFS 14; RGEL 2; TEA; WLIT 3; WP
Chaudhuri, Nirad C(handra) 1897-1999 .... **TCLC 224**
See also CA 128; 183; DLB 323
Chavez, Denise 1948- .... **HLC 1**
See also CA 131; CANR 56, 81, 137; DAM MULT; DLB 122; FW; HW 1, 2; LLW; MAL 5; MTCW 2; MTFW 2005
Chaviaras, Strates 1935- .... **CLC 33**
See also CA 105
Chayefsky, Paddy 1923-1981 .... **CLC 23**
See also CA 9-12R; 104; CAD; CANR 18; DAM DRAM; DFS 26; DLB 23; DLBY 7, 44; RGAL 4

Chayefsky, Sidney
See Chayefsky, Paddy
Chedid, Andree 1920- .... **CLC 47**
See also CA 145; CANR 95; EWL 3
Cheever, John 1912-1982 ..... **CLC 3, 7, 8, 11, 15, 25, 64; SSC 1, 38, 57, 120; WLC 2**
See also AAYA 65; AMWS 1; BPFB 1; CA 5-8R; 106; CABS 1; CANR 5, 27, 76; CDALB 1941-1968; CN 1, 2, 3; CPW; DA; DA3; DAB; DAC; DAM MST, NOV, POP; DLB 2, 102, 227; DLBY 1980, 1982; EWL 3; EXPS; INT CANR-5; MAL 5; MTCW 1, 2; MTFW 2005; RGAL 4; RGSF 2; SSFS 2, 14; TUS
Cheever, Susan 1943- .... **CLC 18, 48**
See also CA 103; CANR 27, 51, 92, 157, 198; DLBY 1982; INT CANR-27
Chekhonte, Antosha
See Chekhov, Anton
Chekhov, Anton 1860-1904 ...... **DC 9; SSC 2, 28, 41, 51, 85, 102; TCLC 3, 10, 31, 55, 96, 163; WLC 2**
See also AAYA 68; BYA 14; CA 104; 124; DA; DA3; DAB; DAC; DAM DRAM, MST; DFS 1, 5, 10, 12, 26; DLB 277; EW 7; EWL 3; EXPS; LAIT 3; LATS 1:1; RGSF 2; RGWL 2, 3; SATA 90; SSFS 5, 13, 14, 26; TWA
Chekhov, Anton Pavlovich
See Chekhov, Anton
Cheney, Lynne V. 1941- .... **CLC 70**
See also CA 89-92; CANR 58, 117, 193; SATA 152
Cheney, Lynne Vincent
See Cheney, Lynne V.
Chenier, Andre-Marie de 1762-1794 . **LC 174**
See also EW 4; GFL Beginnings to 1789; TWA
Chernyshevsky, Nikolai Gavrilovich
See Chernyshevsky, Nikolay Gavrilovich
Chernyshevsky, Nikolay Gavrilovich 1828-1889 .... **NCLC 1**
See also DLB 238
Cherry, Carolyn Janice
See Cherryh, C.J.
Cherryh, C.J. 1942- .... **CLC 35**
See also AAYA 24; BPFB 1; CA 65-68; CANR 10, 147, 179; DLBY 1980; FANT; SATA 93, 172; SCFW 2; YAW
Chesler, Phyllis 1940- .... **CLC 247**
See also CA 49-52; CANR 4, 59, 140, 189; FW
Chesnutt, Charles W(addell) 1858-1932 .... **BLC 1; SSC 7, 54; TCLC 5, 39**
See also AFAW 1, 2; AMWS 14; BW 1, 3; CA 106; 125; CANR 76; DAM MULT; DLB 12, 50, 78; EWL 3; MAL 5; MTCW 1, 2; MTFW 2005; RGAL 4; RGSF 2; SSFS 11, 26
Chester, Alfred 1929(?)-1971 .... **CLC 49**
See also CA 196; 33-36R; DLB 130; MAL 5
Chesterton, G. K. 1874-1936 . **PC 28; SSC 1, 46; TCLC 1, 6, 64**
See also AAYA 57; BRW 6; CA 104; 132; CANR 73, 131; CDBLB 1914-1945; CMW 4; DAM NOV, POET; DLB 10, 19, 34, 70, 98, 149, 178; EWL 3; FANT; MSW; MTCW 1, 2; MTFW 2005; RGEL 2; RGSF 2; SATA 27; SUFW 1
Chesterton, Gilbert Keith
See Chesterton, G. K.
Chettle, Henry 1560-1607(?) .... **LC 112**
See also DLB 136; RGEL 2
Chiang, Pin-chin 1904-1986 .... **CLC 68**
See also CA 118; DLB 328; EWL 3; RGWL 3

Chiang Ping-chih
See Chiang, Pin-chin
Chief Joseph 1840-1904 .... **NNAL**
See also CA 152; DA3; DAM MULT
Chief Seattle 1786(?)-1866 .... **NNAL**
See also DA3; DAM MULT
Ch'ien, Chung-shu 1910-1998 .... **CLC 22**
See also CA 130; CANR 73; CWW 2; DLB 328; MTCW 1, 2
Chikamatsu Monzaemon 1653-1724 ... **LC 66**
See also RGWL 2, 3
Child, Francis James 1825-1896 . **NCLC 173**
See also DLB 1, 64, 235
Child, L. Maria
See Child, Lydia Maria
Child, Lydia Maria 1802-1880 .. **NCLC 6, 73**
See also DLB 1, 74, 243; RGAL 4; SATA 67
Child, Mrs.
See Child, Lydia Maria
Child, Philip 1898-1978 .... **CLC 19, 68**
See also CA 13-14; CAP 1; CP 1; DLB 68; RHW; SATA 47
Childers, (Robert) Erskine 1870-1922 .... **TCLC 65**
See also CA 113; 153; DLB 70
Childress, Alice 1920-1994 .... **BLC 1:1; CLC 12, 15, 86, 96; DC 4; TCLC 116**
See also AAYA 8; BW 2, 3; BYA 2; CA 45-48; 146; CAD; CANR 3, 27, 50, 74; CLR 14; CWD; DA3; DAM DRAM, MULT, NOV; DFS 2, 8, 14, 26; DLB 7, 38, 249; JRDA; LAIT 5; MAICYA 1, 2; MAIC-YAS 1; MAL 5; MTCW 1, 2; MTFW 2005; RGAL 4; SATA 7, 48, 81; TUS; WYA; YAW
Chin, Frank 1940- ..... **AAL; CLC 135; DC 7**
See also CA 33-36R; CAD; CANR 71; CD 5, 6; DAM MULT; DLB 206, 312; LAIT 5; RGAL 4
Chin, Frank Chew, Jr.
See Chin, Frank
Chin, Marilyn 1955- .... **PC 40**
See also CA 129; CANR 70, 113; CWP; DLB 312; PFS 28
Chin, Marilyn Mei Ling
See Chin, Marilyn
Chislett, (Margaret) Anne 1943- ...... **CLC 34**
See also CA 151
Chitty, Thomas Willes 1926- .... **CLC 6, 11**
See also CA 5-8R; CN 1, 2, 3, 4, 5, 6; EWL 3
Chivers, Thomas Holley 1809-1858 .... **NCLC 49**
See also DLB 3, 248; RGAL 4
Chlamyda, Jehudil
See Gorky, Maxim
Ch'o, Chou
See Shu-Jen, Chou
Choi, Susan 1969- .... **CLC 119**
See also CA 223; CANR 188
Chomette, Rene Lucien 1898-1981 .. **CLC 20**
See also CA 103
Chomsky, Avram Noam
See Chomsky, Noam
Chomsky, Noam 1928- .... **CLC 132**
See also CA 17-20R; CANR 28, 62, 110, 132, 179; DA3; DLB 246; MTCW 1, 2; MTFW 2005
Chona, Maria 1845(?)-1936 .... **NNAL**
See also CA 144
Chopin, Kate 1851-1904 .... **SSC 8, 68, 110; TCLC 127; WLCS**
See also AAYA 33; AMWR 2; BYA 11, 15; CA 104; 122; CDALB 1865-1917; DAB; DAC; DAM MST, NOV; DLB 12, 78; EXPN; EXPS; FL 1:3; FW; LAIT 3; MAL 5; MBL; NFS 3; RGAL 4; RGSF 2; SSFS 2, 13, 17, 26; TUS

Chopin, Katherine
See Chopin, Kate

Chretien de Troyes c. 12th cent. - . **CMLC 10**
See also DLB 208; EW 1; RGWL 2, 3; TWA

Christie
See Ichikawa, Kon

Christie, Agatha 1890-1976 . **CLC 1, 6, 8, 12, 39, 48, 110**
See also AAYA 9; AITN 1, 2; BPFB 1; BRWS 2; CA 17-20R; 61-64; CANR 10, 37, 108; CBD; CDBLB 1914-1945; CMW 4; CN 1, 2; CPW; CWD; DA3; DAB; DAC; DAM NOV; DFS 2; DLB 13, 77, 245; MSW; MTCW 1, 2; MTFW 2005; NFS 8, 30; RGEL 2; RHW; SATA 36; TEA; YAW

Christie, Agatha Mary Clarissa
See Christie, Agatha

Christie, Ann Philippa
See Pearce, Philippa

Christie, Philippa
See Pearce, Philippa

Christine de Pisan
See Christine de Pizan

Christine de Pizan 1365(?)-1431(?) ...... **LC 9, 130; PC 68**
See also DLB 208; FL 1:1; FW; RGWL 2, 3

Chuang-Tzu c. 369B.C.-c. 286B.C. .... **CMLC 57**

Chubb, Elmer
See Masters, Edgar Lee

Chulkov, Mikhail Dmitrievich 1743-1792 .... **LC 2**
See also DLB 150

Churchill, Caryl 1938- .... **CLC 31, 55, 157; DC 5**
See also BRWS 4; CA 102; CANR 22, 46, 108; CBD; CD 5, 6; CWD; DFS 25; DLB 13, 310; EWL 3; FW; MTCW 1; RGEL 2

Churchill, Charles 1731-1764 .... **LC 3**
See also DLB 109; RGEL 2

Churchill, Chick
See Churchill, Caryl

Churchill, Sir Winston 1874-1965 .... **TCLC 113**
See also BRW 6; CA 97-100; CDBLB 1890-1914; DA3; DLB 100, 329; DLBD 16; LAIT 4; MTCW 1, 2

Churchill, Sir Winston Leonard Spencer
See Churchill, Sir Winston

Chute, Carolyn 1947- .... **CLC 39**
See also CA 123; CANR 135; CN 7; DLB 350

Ciardi, John (Anthony) 1916-1986 . **CLC 10, 40, 44, 129; PC 69**
See also CA 5-8R; 118; CAAS 2; CANR 5, 33; CLR 19; CP 1, 2, 3, 4; CWRI 5; DAM POET; DLB 5; DLBY 1986; INT CANR-5; MAICYA 1, 2; MAL 5; MTCW 1, 2; MTFW 2005; RGAL 4; SAAS 26; SATA 1, 65; SATA-Obit 46

Cibber, Colley 1671-1757 .... **LC 66**
See also DLB 84; RGEL 2

Cicero, Marcus Tullius 106B.C.-43B.C. .... **CMLC 3, 81**
See also AW 1; CDWLB 1; DLB 211; RGWL 2, 3; WLIT 8

Cimino, Michael 1943- .... **CLC 16**
See also CA 105

Cioran, E(mil) M. 1911-1995 .... **CLC 64**
See also CA 25-28R; 149; CANR 91; DLB 220; EWL 3

Circus, Anthony
See Hoch, Edward D.

Cisneros, Sandra 1954- .... **CLC 69, 118, 193; HLC 1; PC 52; SSC 32, 72**
See also AAYA 9, 53; AMWS 7; CA 131; CANR 64, 118; CLR 123; CN 7; CWP; DA3; DAM MULT; DLB 122, 152; EWL 3; EXPN; FL 1:5; FW; HW 1, 2; LAIT 5; LATS 1:2; LLW; MAICYA 2; MAL 5; MTCW 2; MTFW 2005; NFS 2; PFS 19; RGAL 4; RGSF 2; SSFS 3, 13, 27; WLIT 1; YAW

Cixous, Helene 1937- .... **CLC 92, 253**
See also CA 126; CANR 55, 123; CWW 2; DLB 83, 242; EWL 3; FL 1:5; FW; GLL 2; MTCW 1, 2; MTFW 2005; TWA

Clair, Rene
See Chomette, Rene Lucien

Clampitt, Amy 1920-1994 .... **CLC 32; PC 19**
See also AMWS 9; CA 110; 146; CANR 29, 79; CP 4, 5; DLB 105; MAL 5; PFS 27

Clancy, Thomas L., Jr.
See Clancy, Tom

Clancy, Tom 1947- .... **CLC 45, 112**
See also AAYA 9, 51; BEST 89:1, 90:1; BPFB 1; BYA 10, 11; CA 125; 131; CANR 62, 105, 132; CMW 4; CPW; DA3; DAM NOV, POP; DLB 227; INT CA-131; MTCW 1, 2; MTFW 2005

Clare, John 1793-1864 .. **NCLC 9, 86; PC 23**
See also BRWS 11; DAB; DAM POET; DLB 55, 96; RGEL 2

Clarin
See Alas (y Urena), Leopoldo (Enrique Garcia)

Clark, Al C.
See Goines, Donald

Clark, Brian (Robert)
See Clark, (Robert) Brian

Clark, (Robert) Brian 1932- .... **CLC 29**
See also CA 41-44R; CANR 67; CBD; CD 5, 6

Clark, Curt
See Westlake, Donald E.

Clark, Eleanor 1913-1996 .... **CLC 5, 19**
See also CA 9-12R; 151; CANR 41; CN 1, 2, 3, 4, 5, 6; DLB 6

Clark, J. P.
See Clark-Bekederemo, J. P.

Clark, John Pepper
See Clark-Bekederemo, J. P.

Clark, Kenneth (Mackenzie) 1903-1983 .... **TCLC 147**
See also CA 93-96; 109; CANR 36; MTCW 1, 2; MTFW 2005

Clark, M. R.
See Clark, Mavis Thorpe

Clark, Mavis Thorpe 1909-1999 ...... **CLC 12**
See also CA 57-60; CANR 8, 37, 107; CLR 30; CWRI 5; MAICYA 1, 2; SAAS 5; SATA 8, 74

Clark, Walter Van Tilburg 1909-1971 .... **CLC 28**
See also CA 9-12R; 33-36R; CANR 63, 113; CN 1; DLB 9, 206; LAIT 2; MAL 5; RGAL 4; SATA 8; TCWW 1, 2

Clark-Bekederemo, J. P. 1935- ...... **BLC 1:1; CLC 38; DC 5**
See also AAYA 79; AFW; BW 1; CA 65-68; CANR 16, 72; CD 5, 6; CDWLB 3; CP 1, 2, 3, 4, 5, 6, 7; DAM DRAM, MULT; DFS 13; DLB 117; EWL 3; MTCW 2; MTFW 2005; RGEL 2

Clark-Bekederemo, John Pepper
See Clark-Bekederemo, J. P.

Clark Bekederemo, Johnson Pepper
See Clark-Bekederemo, J. P.

Clarke, Arthur
See Clarke, Arthur C.

Clarke, Arthur C. 1917-2008 .. **CLC 1, 4, 13, 18, 35, 136; SSC 3**
See also AAYA 4, 33; BPFB 1; BYA 13; CA 1-4R; 270; CANR 2, 28, 55, 74, 130, 196; CLR 119; CN 1, 2, 3, 4, 5, 6, 7; CPW; DA3; DAM POP; DLB 261; JRDA; LAIT 5; MAICYA 1, 2; MTCW 1, 2; MTFW 2005; SATA 13, 70, 115; SATA-Obit 191; SCFW 1, 2; SFW 4; SSFS 4, 18; TCLE 1:1; YAW

Clarke, Arthur Charles
See Clarke, Arthur C.

Clarke, Austin 1896-1974 .... **CLC 6, 9**
See also BRWS 15; CA 29-32; 49-52; CAP 2; CP 1, 2; DAM POET; DLB 10, 20; EWL 3; RGEL 2

Clarke, Austin C. 1934- .... **BLC 1:1; CLC 8, 53; SSC 45, 116**
See also BW 1; CA 25-28R; CAAS 16; CANR 14, 32, 68, 140; CN 1, 2, 3, 4, 5, 6, 7; DAC; DAM MULT; DLB 53, 125; DNFS 2; MTCW 2; MTFW 2005; RGSF 2

Clarke, Gillian 1937- .... **CLC 61**
See also CA 106; CP 3, 4, 5, 6, 7; CWP; DLB 40

Clarke, Marcus (Andrew Hislop) 1846-1881 .... **NCLC 19; SSC 94**
See also DLB 230; RGEL 2; RGSF 2

Clarke, Shirley 1925-1997 .... **CLC 16**
See also CA 189

Clash, The
See Headon, (Nicky) Topper; Jones, Mick; Simonon, Paul; Strummer, Joe

Claudel, Paul (Louis Charles Marie) 1868-1955 .... **TCLC 2, 10**
See also CA 104; 165; DLB 192, 258, 321; EW 8; EWL 3; GFL 1789 to the Present; RGWL 2, 3; TWA

Claudian 370(?)-404(?) .... **CMLC 46**
See also RGWL 2, 3

Claudius, Matthias 1740-1815 .... **NCLC 75**
See also DLB 97

Clavell, James 1925-1994 .... **CLC 6, 25, 87**
See also BPFB 1; CA 25-28R; 146; CANR 26, 48; CN 5; CPW; DA3; DAM NOV, POP; MTCW 1, 2; MTFW 2005; NFS 10; RHW

Clayman, Gregory CLC 65

Cleage, Pearl 1948- .... **DC 32**
See also BW 2; CA 41-44R; CANR 27, 148, 177; DFS 14, 16; DLB 228; NFS 17

Cleage, Pearl Michelle
See Cleage, Pearl

Cleaver, (Leroy) Eldridge 1935-1998 .... **BLC 1:1; CLC 30, 119**
See also BW 1, 3; CA 21-24R; 167; CANR 16, 75; DA3; DAM MULT; MTCW 2; YAW

Cleese, John (Marwood) 1939- .... **CLC 21**
See also CA 112; 116; CANR 35; MTCW 1

Cleishbotham, Jebediah
See Scott, Sir Walter

Cleland, John 1710-1789 .... **LC 2, 48**
See also DLB 39; RGEL 2

Clemens, Samuel
See Twain, Mark

Clemens, Samuel Langhorne
See Twain, Mark

Clement of Alexandria 150(?)-215(?) .... **CMLC 41**

Cleophil
See Congreve, William

Clerihew, E.
See Bentley, E(dmund) C(lerihew)

Clerk, N. W.
See Lewis, C. S.

Cleveland, John 1613-1658 .... **LC 106**
See also DLB 126; RGEL 2

Cliff, Jimmy
See Chambers, James
Cliff, Michelle 1946- .... **BLCS; CLC 120**
See also BW 2; CA 116; CANR 39, 72; CD-WLB 3; DLB 157; FW; GLL 2
Clifford, Lady Anne 1590-1676 .... **LC 76**
See also DLB 151
Clifton, Lucille 1936- ..... **BLC 1:1, 2:1; CLC 19, 66, 162, 283; PC 17**
See also AFAW 2; BW 2, 3; CA 49-52; CANR 2, 24, 42, 76, 97, 138; CLR 5; CP 2, 3, 4, 5, 6, 7; CSW; CWP; CWRI 5; DA3; DAM MULT, POET; DLB 5, 41; EXPP; MAICYA 1, 2; MTCW 1, 2; MTFW 2005; PFS 1, 14, 29; SATA 20, 69, 128; WP
Clifton, Thelma Lucille
See Clifton, Lucille
Clinton, Dirk
See Silverberg, Robert
Clough, Arthur Hugh 1819-1861 .. **NCLC 27, 163; PC 103**
See also BRW 5; DLB 32; RGEL 2
Clutha, Janet Paterson Frame
See Frame, Janet
Clyne, Terence
See Blatty, William Peter
Cobalt, Martin
See Mayne, William (James Carter)
Cobb, Irvin S(hrewsbury)
1876-1944 .... **TCLC 77**
See also CA 175; DLB 11, 25, 86
Cobbett, William 1763-1835 .... **NCLC 49**
See also DLB 43, 107, 158; RGEL 2
Coben, Harlan 1962- .... **CLC 269**
See also CA 164; CANR 162, 199
Coburn, D(onald) L(ee) 1938- .... **CLC 10**
See also CA 89-92; DFS 23
Cocteau, Jean 1889-1963 ... **CLC 1, 8, 15, 16, 43; DC 17; TCLC 119; WLC 2**
See also AAYA 74; CANR 40; CAP 2; DA; DA3; DAB; DAC; DAM DRAM, MST, NOV; DFS 24; DLB 65, 258, 321; EW 10; EWL 3; GFL 1789 to the Present; MTCW 1, 2; RGWL 2, 3; TWA
Cocteau, Jean Maurice Eugene Clement
See Cocteau, Jean
Codrescu, Andrei 1946- .... **CLC 46, 121**
See also CA 33-36R; CAAS 19; CANR 13, 34, 53, 76, 125; CN 7; DA3; DAM POET; MAL 5; MTCW 2; MTFW 2005
Coe, Max
See Bourne, Randolph S(illiman)
Coe, Tucker
See Westlake, Donald E.
Coelho, Paulo 1947- .... **CLC 258**
See also CA 152; CANR 80, 93, 155, 194; NFS 29
Coen, Ethan 1957- .... **CLC 108, 267**
See also AAYA 54; CA 126; CANR 85
Coen, Joel 1954- .... **CLC 108, 267**
See also AAYA 54; CA 126; CANR 119
The Coen Brothers
See Coen, Ethan; Coen, Joel
Coetzee, J. M. 1940- ..... **CLC 23, 33, 66, 117, 161, 162**
See also AAYA 37; AFW; BRWS 6; CA 77-80; CANR 41, 54, 74, 114, 133, 180; CN 4, 5, 6, 7; DAM NOV; DLB 225, 326, 329; EWL 3; LMFS 2; MTCW 1, 2; MTFW 2005; NFS 21; WLIT 2; WWE 1
Coetzee, John Maxwell
See Coetzee, J. M.
Coffey, Brian
See Koontz, Dean
Coffin, Robert P. Tristram
1892-1955 .... **TCLC 95**
See also CA 123; 169; DLB 45

Coffin, Robert Peter Tristram
See Coffin, Robert P. Tristram
Cohan, George M. 1878-1942 .... **TCLC 60**
See also CA 157; DLB 249; RGAL 4
Cohan, George Michael
See Cohan, George M.
Cohen, Arthur A(llen) 1928-1986 ...... **CLC 7, 31**
See also CA 1-4R; 120; CANR 1, 17, 42; DLB 28; RGHL
Cohen, Leonard 1934- .... **CLC 3, 38, 260**
See also CA 21-24R; CANR 14, 69; CN 1, 2, 3, 4, 5, 6; CP 1, 2, 3, 4, 5, 6, 7; DAC; DAM MST; DLB 53; EWL 3; MTCW 1
Cohen, Leonard Norman
See Cohen, Leonard
Cohen, Matt(hew) 1942-1999 .... **CLC 19**
See also CA 61-64; 187; CAAS 18; CANR 40; CN 1, 2, 3, 4, 5, 6; DAC; DLB 53
Cohen-Solal, Annie 1948- .... **CLC 50**
See also CA 239
Colegate, Isabel 1931- .... **CLC 36**
See also CA 17-20R; CANR 8, 22, 74; CN 4, 5, 6, 7; DLB 14, 231; INT CANR-22; MTCW 1
Coleman, Emmett
See Reed, Ishmael
Coleridge, Hartley 1796-1849 .... **NCLC 90**
See also DLB 96
Coleridge, M. E.
See Coleridge, Mary E(lizabeth)
Coleridge, Mary E(lizabeth)
1861-1907 .... **TCLC 73**
See also CA 116; 166; DLB 19, 98
Coleridge, Samuel Taylor
1772-1834 ..... **NCLC 9, 54, 99, 111, 177, 197; PC 11, 39, 67, 100; WLC 2**
See also AAYA 66; BRW 4; BRWR 2; BYA 4; CDBLB 1789-1832; DA; DA3; DAB; DAC; DAM MST, POET; DLB 93, 107; EXPP; LATS 1:1; LMFS 1; PAB; PFS 4, 5; RGEL 2; TEA; WLIT 3; WP
Coleridge, Sara 1802-1852 .... **NCLC 31**
See also DLB 199
Coles, Don 1928- .... **CLC 46**
See also CA 115; CANR 38; CP 5, 6, 7
Coles, Robert (Martin) 1929- .... **CLC 108**
See also CA 45-48; CANR 3, 32, 66, 70, 135; INT CANR-32; SATA 23
Colette 1873-1954 ... **SSC 10, 93; TCLC 1, 5, 16**
See also CA 104; 131; DA3; DAM NOV; DLB 65; EW 9; EWL 3; GFL 1789 to the Present; GLL 1; MTCW 1, 2; MTFW 2005; RGWL 2, 3; TWA
Colette, Sidonie-Gabrielle
See Colette
Collett, (Jacobine) Camilla (Wergeland)
1813-1895 .... **NCLC 22**
See also DLB 354
Collier, Christopher 1930- .... **CLC 30**
See also AAYA 13; BYA 2; CA 33-36R; CANR 13, 33, 102; CLR 126; JRDA; MAICYA 1, 2; SATA 16, 70; WYA; YAW 1
Collier, James Lincoln 1928- .... **CLC 30**
See also AAYA 13; BYA 2; CA 9-12R; CANR 4, 33, 60, 102; CLR 3, 126; DAM POP; JRDA; MAICYA 1, 2; SAAS 21; SATA 8, 70, 166; WYA; YAW 1
Collier, Jeremy 1650-1726 .... **LC 6, 157**
See also DLB 336
Collier, John 1901-1980 . **SSC 19; TCLC 127**
See also CA 65-68; 97-100; CANR 10; CN 1, 2; DLB 77, 255; FANT; SUFW 1
Collier, Mary 1690-1762 .... **LC 86**
See also DLB 95

Collingwood, R(obin) G(eorge)
1889(?)-1943 .... **TCLC 67**
See also CA 117; 155; DLB 262
Collins, Billy 1941- .... **PC 68**
See also AAYA 64; CA 151; CANR 92; CP 7; MTFW 2005; PFS 18
Collins, Hunt
See Hunter, Evan
Collins, Linda 1931- .... **CLC 44**
See also CA 125
Collins, Merle 1950- .... **BLC 2:1**
See also BW 3; CA 175; DLB 157
Collins, Tom
See Furphy, Joseph
Collins, Wilkie 1824-1889 ... **NCLC 1, 18, 93; SSC 93**
See also BRWS 6; CDBLB 1832-1890; CMW 4; DLB 18, 70, 159; GL 2; MSW; RGEL 2; RGSF 2; SUFW 1; WLIT 4
Collins, William 1721-1759 ...... **LC 4, 40; PC 72**
See also BRW 3; DAM POET; DLB 109; RGEL 2
Collins, William Wilkie
See Collins, Wilkie
Collodi, Carlo
See Lorenzini, Carlo
Colman, George
See Glassco, John
Colman, George, the Elder
1732-1794 .... **LC 98**
See also RGEL 2
Colonna, Vittoria 1492-1547 .... **LC 71**
See also RGWL 2, 3
Colt, Winchester Remington
See Hubbard, L. Ron
Colter, Cyrus J. 1910-2002 .... **CLC 58**
See also BW 1; CA 65-68; 205; CANR 10, 66; CN 2, 3, 4, 5, 6; DLB 33
Colton, James
See Hansen, Joseph
Colum, Padraic 1881-1972 .... **CLC 28**
See also BYA 4; CA 73-76; 33-36R; CANR 35; CLR 36; CP 1; CWRI 5; DLB 19; MAICYA 1, 2; MTCW 1; RGEL 2; SATA 15; WCH
Colvin, James
See Moorcock, Michael
Colwin, Laurie (E.) 1944-1992 .... **CLC 5, 13, 23, 84**
See also CA 89-92; 139; CANR 20, 46; DLB 218; DLBY 1980; MTCW 1
Comfort, Alex(ander) 1920-2000 .... **CLC 7**
See also CA 1-4R; 190; CANR 1, 45; CN 1, 2, 3, 4; CP 1, 2, 3, 4, 5, 6, 7; DAM POP; MTCW 2
Comfort, Montgomery
See Campbell, Ramsey
Compton-Burnett, I. 1892(?)-1969 .... **CLC 1, 3, 10, 15, 34; TCLC 180**
See also BRW 7; CA 1-4R; 25-28R; CANR 4; DAM NOV; DLB 36; EWL 3; MTCW 1, 2; RGEL 2
Compton-Burnett, Ivy
See Compton-Burnett, I.
Comstock, Anthony 1844-1915 ...... **TCLC 13**
See also CA 110; 169
Comte, Auguste 1798-1857 .... **NCLC 54**
Conan Doyle, Arthur
See Doyle, Sir Arthur Conan
Conde (Abellan), Carmen
1901-1996 .... **HLCS 1**
See also CA 177; CWW 2; DLB 108; EWL 3; HW 2
Conde, Maryse 1937- .... **BLC 2:1; BLCS; CLC 52, 92, 247**
See also BW 2, 3; CA 110; 190; CAAE 190; CANR 30, 53, 76, 171; CWW 2; DAM MULT; EWL 3; MTCW 2; MTFW 2005

Author Index

Dodgson, Charles Lutwidge
See Carroll, Lewis
Dodsley, Robert 1703-1764 .... **LC 97**
See also DLB 95; RGEL 2
Dodson, Owen (Vincent)
1914-1983 .... **BLC 1:1; CLC 79**
See also BW 1; CA 65-68; 110; CANR 24;
DAM MULT; DLB 76
Doeblin, Alfred 1878-1957 .... **TCLC 13**
See also CA 110; 141; CDWLB 2; DLB 66;
EWL 3; RGWL 2, 3
Doerr, Harriet 1910-2002 .... **CLC 34**
See also CA 117; 122; 213; CANR 47; INT
CA-122; LATS 1:2
Domecq, Honorio Bustos
See Bioy Casares, Adolfo; Borges, Jorge
Luis
Domini, Rey
See Lorde, Audre
Dominic, R. B.
See Hennissart, Martha
Dominique
See Proust, Marcel
Don, A
See Stephen, Sir Leslie
Donaldson, Stephen R. 1947- ... **CLC 46, 138**
See also AAYA 36; BPFB 1; CA 89-92;
CANR 13, 55, 99; CPW; DAM POP;
FANT; INT CANR-13; SATA 121; SFW
4; SUFW 1, 2
Donleavy, J(ames) P(atrick) 1926- .... **CLC 1,
4, 6, 10, 45**
See also AITN 2; BPFB 1; CA 9-12R;
CANR 24, 49, 62, 80, 124; CBD; CD 5,
6; CN 1, 2, 3, 4, 5, 6, 7; DLB 6, 173; INT
CANR-24; MAL 5; MTCW 1, 2; MTFW
2005; RGAL 4
Donnadieu, Marguerite
See Duras, Marguerite
Donne, John 1572-1631 ... **LC 10, 24, 91; PC
1, 43; WLC 2**
See also AAYA 67; BRW 1; BRWC 1;
BRWR 2; CDBLB Before 1660; DA;
DAB; DAC; DAM MST, POET; DLB
121, 151; EXPP; PAB; PFS 2, 11; RGEL
3; TEA; WLIT 3; WP
Donnell, David 1939(?)- .... **CLC 34**
See also CA 197
Donoghue, Denis 1928- .... **CLC 209**
See also CA 17-20R; CANR 16, 102
Donoghue, Emma 1969- .... **CLC 239**
See also CA 155; CANR 103, 152, 196;
DLB 267; GLL 2; SATA 101
Donoghue, P.S.
See Hunt, E. Howard
Donoso, Jose 1924-1996 ..... **CLC 4, 8, 11, 32,
99; HLC 1; SSC 34; TCLC 133**
See also CA 81-84; 155; CANR 32, 73; CD-
WLB 3; CWW 2; DAM MULT; DLB 113;
EWL 3; HW 1, 2; LAW; LAWS 1; MTCW
1, 2; MTFW 2005; RGSF 2; WLIT 1
Donoso Yanez, Jose
See Donoso, Jose
Donovan, John 1928-1992 .... **CLC 35**
See also AAYA 20; CA 97-100; 137; CLR
3; MAICYA 1, 2; SATA 72; SATA-Brief
29; YAW
Don Roberto
See Cunninghame Graham, Robert Bontine
Doolittle, Hilda 1886-1961 . **CLC 3, 8, 14, 31,
34, 73; PC 5; WLC 3**
See also AAYA 66; AMWS 1; CA 97-100;
CANR 35, 131; DA; DAC; DAM MST,
POET; DLB 4, 45; EWL 3; FL 1:5; FW;
GLL 1; LMFS 2; MAL 5; MBL; MTCW
1, 2; MTFW 2005; PFS 6, 28; RGAL 4
Doppo
See Kunikida Doppo

Doppo, Kunikida
See Kunikida Doppo
Dorfman, Ariel 1942- .... **CLC 48, 77, 189;
HLC 1**
See also CA 124; 130; CANR 67, 70, 135;
CWW 2; DAM MULT; DFS 4; EWL 3;
HW 1, 2; INT CA-130; WLIT 1
Dorn, Edward (Merton)
1929-1999 .... **CLC 10, 18**
See also CA 93-96; 187; CANR 42, 79; CP
1, 2, 3, 4, 5, 6, 7; DLB 5; INT CA-93-96;
WP
Dor-Ner, Zvi CLC 70
Dorris, Michael 1945-1997 .... **CLC 109;
NNAL**
See also AAYA 20; BEST 90:1; BYA 12;
CA 102; 157; CANR 19, 46, 75; CLR 58;
DA3; DAM MULT, NOV; DLB 175;
LAIT 5; MTCW 2; MTFW 2005; NFS 3;
RGAL 4; SATA 75; SATA-Obit 94;
TCWW 2; YAW
Dorris, Michael A.
See Dorris, Michael
Dorris, Michael Anthony
See Dorris, Michael
Dorsan, Luc
See Simenon, Georges
Dorsange, Jean
See Simenon, Georges
Dorset
See Sackville, Thomas
Dos Passos, John 1896-1970 ...... **CLC 1, 4, 8,
11, 15, 25, 34, 82; WLC 2**
See also AMW; BPFB 1; CA 1-4R; 29-32R;
CANR 3; CDALB 1929-1941; DA; DA3;
DAB; DAC; DAM MST, NOV; DLB 4,
9, 274, 316; DLBD 1, 15; DLBY 1996;
EWL 3; MAL 5; MTCW 1, 2; MTFW
2005; NFS 14; RGAL 4; TUS
Dos Passos, John Roderigo
See Dos Passos, John
Dossage, Jean
See Simenon, Georges
Dostoevsky, Fedor
See Dostoevsky, Fyodor
Dostoevsky, Fedor Mikhailovich
See Dostoevsky, Fyodor
Dostoevsky, Fyodor 1821-1881 ... **NCLC 2, 7,
21, 33, 43, 119, 167, 202; SSC 2, 33, 44,
134; WLC 2**
See also AAYA 40; DA; DA3; DAB; DAC;
DAM MST, NOV; DLB 238; EW 7;
EXPN; LATS 1:1; LMFS 1, 2; NFS 28;
RGSF 2; RGWL 2, 3; SSFS 8; TWA
Doty, Mark 1953(?)- .... **CLC 176; PC 53**
See also AMWS 11; CA 161, 183; CAAE
183; CANR 110, 173; CP 7; PFS 28
Doty, Mark A.
See Doty, Mark
Doty, Mark Alan
See Doty, Mark
Doty, M.R.
See Doty, Mark
Doughty, Charles M(ontagu)
1843-1926 .... **TCLC 27**
See also CA 115; 178; DLB 19, 57, 174
Douglas, Ellen 1921- .... **CLC 73**
See also CA 115; CANR 41, 83; CN 5, 6,
7; CSW; DLB 292
Douglas, Gavin 1475(?)-1522 .... **LC 20**
See also DLB 132; RGEL 2
Douglas, George
See Brown, George Douglas
Douglas, Keith (Castellain)
1920-1944 .... **PC 106; TCLC 40**
See also BRW 7; CA 160; DLB 27; EWL
3; PAB; RGEL 2
Douglas, Leonard
See Bradbury, Ray

Douglas, Michael
See Crichton, Michael
Douglas, (George) Norman
1868-1952 .... **TCLC 68**
See also BRW 6; CA 119; 157; DLB 34,
195; RGEL 2
Douglas, William
See Brown, George Douglas
Douglass, Frederick 1817(?)-1895 .. **BLC 1:1;
NCLC 7, 55, 141; WLC 2**
See also AAYA 48; AFAW 1, 2; AMWC 1;
AMWS 3; CDALB 1640-1865; DA; DA3;
DAC; DAM MST, MULT; DLB 1, 43, 50,
79, 243; FW; LAIT 2; NCFS 2; RGAL 4;
SATA 29
Dourado, (Waldomiro Freitas) Autran
1926- .... **CLC 23, 60**
See also CA 25-28R; 179; CANR 34, 81;
DLB 145, 307; HW 2
Dourado, Waldomiro Freitas Autran
See Dourado, (Waldomiro Freitas) Autran
Dove, Rita 1952- . **BLC 2:1; BLCS; CLC 50,
81; PC 6**
See also AAYA 46; AMWS 4; BW 2; CA
109; CAAS 19; CANR 27, 42, 68, 76, 97,
132; CDALBS; CP 5, 6, 7; CSW; CWP;
DA3; DAM MULT, POET; DLB 120;
EWL 3; EXPP; MAL 5; MTCW 2; MTFW
2005; PFS 1, 15; RGAL 4
Dove, Rita Frances
See Dove, Rita
Doveglion
See Villa, Jose Garcia
Dowell, Coleman 1925-1985 .... **CLC 60**
See also CA 25-28R; 117; CANR 10; DLB
130; GLL 2
Downing, Major Jack
See Smith, Seba
Dowson, Ernest (Christopher)
1867-1900 .... **TCLC 4**
See also CA 105; 150; DLB 19, 135; RGEL
2
Doyle, A. Conan
See Doyle, Sir Arthur Conan
Doyle, Sir Arthur Conan
1859-1930 ..... **SSC 12, 83, 95; TCLC 7;
WLC 2**
See also AAYA 14; BPFB 1; BRWS 2; BYA
4, 5, 11; CA 104; 122; CANR 131; CD-
BLB 1890-1914; CLR 106; CMW 4; DA;
DA3; DAB; DAC; DAM MST, NOV;
DLB 18, 70, 156, 178; EXPS; HGG;
LAIT 2; MSW; MTCW 1, 2; MTFW
2005; NFS 28; RGEL 2; RGSF 2; RHW;
SATA 24; SCFW 1, 2; SFW 4; SSFS 2;
TEA; WCH; WLIT 4; WYA; YAW
Doyle, Conan
See Doyle, Sir Arthur Conan
Doyle, John
See Graves, Robert
Doyle, Roddy 1958- .... **CLC 81, 178**
See also AAYA 14; BRWS 5; CA 143;
CANR 73, 128, 168, 200; CN 6, 7; DA3;
DLB 194, 326; MTCW 2; MTFW 2005
Doyle, Sir A. Conan
See Doyle, Sir Arthur Conan
Dr. A
See Asimov, Isaac; Silverstein, Alvin; Sil-
verstein, Virginia B.
Drabble, Margaret 1939- ...... **CLC 2, 3, 5, 8,
10, 22, 53, 129**
See also BRWS 4; CA 13-16R; CANR 18,
35, 63, 112, 131, 174; CDBLB 1960 to
Present; CN 1, 2, 3, 4, 5, 6, 7; CPW; DA3;
DAB; DAC; DAM MST, NOV, POP;
DLB 14, 155, 231; EWL 3; FW; MTCW
1, 2; MTFW 2005; RGEL 2; SATA 48;
TEA
Drakulic, Slavenka
See Drakulic, Slavenka

Drakulic, Slavenka 1949- .... **CLC 173**
　　See also CA 144; CANR 92, 198; DLB 353
Drakulic-Ilic, Slavenka
　　See Drakulic, Slavenka
Drakulic-Ilic, Slavenka
　　See Drakulic, Slavenka
Drapier, M. B.
　　See Swift, Jonathan
Drayham, James
　　See Mencken, H. L.
Drayton, Michael 1563-1631 . **LC 8, 161; PC 98**
　　See also DAM POET; DLB 121; RGEL 2
Dreadstone, Carl
　　See Campbell, Ramsey
Dreiser, Theodore 1871-1945 .... **SSC 30, 114; TCLC 10, 18, 35, 83; WLC 2**
　　See also AMW; AMWC 2; AMWR 2; BYA 15, 16; CA 106; 132; CDALB 1865-1917; DA; DA3; DAC; DAM MST, NOV; DLB 9, 12, 102, 137; DLBD 1; EWL 3; LAIT 2; LMFS 2; MAL 5; MTCW 1, 2; MTFW 2005; NFS 8, 17; RGAL 4; TUS
Dreiser, Theodore Herman Albert
　　See Dreiser, Theodore
Drexler, Rosalyn 1926- .... **CLC 2, 6**
　　See also CA 81-84; CAD; CANR 68, 124; CD 5, 6; CWD; MAL 5
Dreyer, Carl Theodor 1889-1968 ...... **CLC 16**
　　See also CA 116
Drieu la Rochelle, Pierre 1893-1945 .... **TCLC 21**
　　See also CA 117; 250; DLB 72; EWL 3; GFL 1789 to the Present
Drieu la Rochelle, Pierre-Eugene 1893-1945
　　See Drieu la Rochelle, Pierre
Drinkwater, John 1882-1937 .... **TCLC 57**
　　See also CA 109; 149; DLB 10, 19, 149; RGEL 2
Drop Shot
　　See Cable, George Washington
Droste-Hulshoff, Annette Freiin von 1797-1848 .... **NCLC 3, 133**
　　See also CDWLB 2; DLB 133; RGSF 2; RGWL 2, 3
Drummond, Walter
　　See Silverberg, Robert
Drummond, William Henry 1854-1907 .... **TCLC 25**
　　See also CA 160; DLB 92
Drummond de Andrade, Carlos 1902-1987 .... **CLC 18; TCLC 139**
　　See also CA 132; 123; DLB 307; EWL 3; LAW; RGWL 2, 3
Drummond of Hawthornden, William 1585-1649 .... **LC 83**
　　See also DLB 121, 213; RGEL 2
Drury, Allen (Stuart) 1918-1998 .... **CLC 37**
　　See also CA 57-60; 170; CANR 18, 52; CN 1, 2, 3, 4, 5, 6; INT CANR-18
Druse, Eleanor
　　See King, Stephen
Dryden, John 1631-1700 ..... **DC 3; LC 3, 21, 115; PC 25; WLC 2**
　　See also BRW 2; BRWR 3; CDBLB 1660-1789; DA; DAB; DAC; DAM DRAM, MST, POET; DLB 80, 101, 131; EXPP; IDTP; LMFS 1; RGEL 2; TEA; WLIT 3
du Aime, Albert
　　See Wharton, William
du Aime, Albert William
　　See Wharton, William
du Bellay, Joachim 1524-1560 .... **LC 92**
　　See also DLB 327; GFL Beginnings to 1789; RGWL 2, 3
Duberman, Martin 1930- .... **CLC 8**
　　See also CA 1-4R; CAD; CANR 2, 63, 137, 174; CD 5, 6

Dubie, Norman (Evans) 1945- .... **CLC 36**
　　See also CA 69-72; CANR 12, 115; CP 3, 4, 5, 6, 7; DLB 120; PFS 12
Du Bois, W. E. B. 1868-1963 .... **BLC 1:1; CLC 1, 2, 13, 64, 96; HR 1:2; TCLC 169; WLC 2**
　　See also AAYA 40; AFAW 1, 2; AMWC 1; AMWS 2; BW 1, 3; CA 85-88; CANR 34, 82, 132; CDALB 1865-1917; DA; DA3; DAC; DAM MST, MULT, NOV; DLB 47, 50, 91, 246, 284; EWL 3; EXPP; LAIT 2; LMFS 2; MAL 5; MTCW 1, 2; MTFW 2005; NCFS 1; PFS 13; RGAL 4; SATA 42
Du Bois, William Edward Burghardt
　　See Du Bois, W. E. B.
Dubus, Andre 1936-1999 ..... **CLC 13, 36, 97; SSC 15, 118**
　　See also AMWS 7; CA 21-24R; 177; CANR 17; CN 5, 6; CSW; DLB 130; INT CANR-17; RGAL 4; SSFS 10; TCLE 1:1
Duca Minimo
　　See D'Annunzio, Gabriele
Ducharme, Rejean 1941- .... **CLC 74**
　　See also CA 165; DLB 60
du Chatelet, Emilie 1706-1749 .... **LC 96**
　　See also DLB 313
Duchen, Claire CLC 65
Duck, Stephen 1705(?)-1756 .... **PC 89**
　　See also DLB 95; RGEL 2
Duclos, Charles Pinot- 1704-1772 .... **LC 1**
　　See also GFL Beginnings to 1789
Ducornet, Erica 1943- .... **CLC 232**
　　See also CA 37-40R; CANR 14, 34, 54, 82; SATA 7
Ducornet, Rikki
　　See Ducornet, Erica
Dudek, Louis 1918-2001 .... **CLC 11, 19**
　　See also CA 45-48; 215; CAAS 14; CANR 1; CP 1, 2, 3, 4, 5, 6, 7; DLB 88
Duerrematt, Friedrich
　　See Durrenmatt, Friedrich
Duffy, Bruce 1953(?)- .... **CLC 50**
　　See also CA 172
Duffy, Maureen 1933- .... **CLC 37**
　　See also CA 25-28R; CANR 33, 68; CBD; CN 1, 2, 3, 4, 5, 6, 7; CP 5, 6, 7; CWD; CWP; DFS 15; DLB 14, 310; FW; MTCW 1
Duffy, Maureen Patricia
　　See Duffy, Maureen
Du Fu
　　See Tu Fu
Dugan, Alan 1923-2003 .... **CLC 2, 6**
　　See also CA 81-84; 220; CANR 119; CP 1, 2, 3, 4, 5, 6, 7; DLB 5; MAL 5; PFS 10
du Gard, Roger Martin
　　See Martin du Gard, Roger
Duhamel, Georges 1884-1966 .... **CLC 8**
　　See also CA 81-84; 25-28R; CANR 35; DLB 65; EWL 3; GFL 1789 to the Present; MTCW 1
du Hault, Jean
　　See Grindel, Eugene
Dujardin, Edouard (Emile Louis) 1861-1949 .... **TCLC 13**
　　See also CA 109; DLB 123
Duke, Raoul
　　See Thompson, Hunter S.
Dulles, John Foster 1888-1959 .... **TCLC 72**
　　See also CA 115; 149
Dumas, Alexandre (pere) 1802-1870 .... **NCLC 11, 71; WLC 2**
　　See also AAYA 22; BYA 3; CLR 134; DA; DA3; DAB; DAC; DAM MST, NOV; DLB 119, 192; EW 6; GFL 1789 to the Present; LAIT 1, 2; NFS 14, 19; RGWL 2, 3; SATA 18; TWA; WCH

Dumas, Alexandre (fils) 1824-1895 ...... **DC 1; NCLC 9**
　　See also DLB 192; GFL 1789 to the Present; RGWL 2, 3
Dumas, Claudine
　　See Malzberg, Barry N(athaniel)
Dumas, Henry L. 1934-1968 . **BLC 2:1; CLC 6, 62; SSC 107**
　　See also BW 1; CA 85-88; DLB 41; RGAL 4
du Maurier, Daphne 1907-1989 .. **CLC 6, 11, 59; SSC 18, 129; TCLC 209**
　　See also AAYA 37; BPFB 1; BRWS 3; CA 5-8R; 128; CANR 6, 55; CMW 4; CN 1, 2, 3, 4; CPW; DA3; DAB; DAC; DAM MST, POP; DLB 191; GL 2; HGG; LAIT 3; MSW; MTCW 1, 2; NFS 12; RGEL 2; RGSF 2; RHW; SATA 27; SATA-Obit 60; SSFS 14, 16; TEA
Du Maurier, George 1834-1896 ..... **NCLC 86**
　　See also DLB 153, 178; RGEL 2
Dunbar, Alice
　　See Nelson, Alice Ruth Moore Dunbar
Dunbar, Alice Moore
　　See Nelson, Alice Ruth Moore Dunbar
Dunbar, Paul Laurence 1872-1906 .... **BLC 1:1; PC 5; SSC 8; TCLC 2, 12; WLC 2**
　　See also AAYA 75; AFAW 1, 2; AMWS 2; BW 1, 3; CA 104; 124; CANR 79; CDALB 1865-1917; DA; DA3; DAC; DAM MST, MULT, POET; DLB 50, 54, 78; EXPP; MAL 5; RGAL 4; SATA 34
Dunbar, William 1460(?)-1520(?) .... **LC 20; PC 67**
　　See also BRWS 8; DLB 132, 146; RGEL 2
Dunbar-Nelson, Alice
　　See Nelson, Alice Ruth Moore Dunbar
Dunbar-Nelson, Alice Moore
　　See Nelson, Alice Ruth Moore Dunbar
Duncan, Dora Angela
　　See Duncan, Isadora
Duncan, Isadora 1877(?)-1927 .... **TCLC 68**
　　See also CA 118; 149
Duncan, Lois 1934- .... **CLC 26**
　　See also AAYA 4, 34; BYA 6, 8; CA 1-4R; CANR 2, 23, 36, 111; CLR 29, 129; JRDA; MAICYA 1, 2; MAICYAS 1; MTFW 2005; SAAS 2; SATA 1, 36, 75, 133, 141; SATA-Essay 141; WYA; YAW
Duncan, Robert 1919-1988 ... **CLC 1, 2, 4, 7, 15, 41, 55; PC 2, 75**
　　See also BG 1:2; CA 9-12R; 124; CANR 28, 62; CP 1, 2, 3, 4; DAM POET; DLB 5, 16, 193; EWL 3; MAL 5; MTCW 1, 2; MTFW 2005; PFS 13; RGAL 4; WP
Duncan, Sara Jeannette 1861-1922 .... **TCLC 60**
　　See also CA 157; DLB 92
Dunlap, William 1766-1839 .... **NCLC 2**
　　See also DLB 30, 37, 59; RGAL 4
Dunn, Douglas (Eaglesham) 1942- .... **CLC 6, 40**
　　See also BRWS 10; CA 45-48; CANR 2, 33, 126; CP 1, 2, 3, 4, 5, 6, 7; DLB 40; MTCW 1
Dunn, Katherine 1945- .... **CLC 71**
　　See also CA 33-36R; CANR 72; HGG; MTCW 2; MTFW 2005
Dunn, Stephen 1939- .... **CLC 36, 206**
　　See also AMWS 11; CA 33-36R; CANR 12, 48, 53, 105; CP 3, 4, 5, 6, 7; DLB 105; PFS 21
Dunn, Stephen Elliott
　　See Dunn, Stephen
Dunne, Finley Peter 1867-1936 ...... **TCLC 28**
　　See also CA 108; 178; DLB 11, 23; RGAL 4

Ehrenburg, Ilya (Grigoryevich)
   1891-1967 .... **CLC 18, 34, 62**
   See also Erenburg, Ilya (Grigoryevich)
   See also CA 102; 25-28R; EWL 3
Ehrenburg, Ilyo (Grigoryevich)
   See Ehrenburg, Ilya (Grigoryevich)
Ehrenreich, Barbara 1941- ..... **CLC 110, 267**
   See also BEST 90:4; CA 73-76; CANR 16,
   37, 62, 117, 167; DLB 246; FW; LNFS 1;
   MTCW 1, 2; MTFW 2005
Ehrlich, Gretel 1946- .... **CLC 249**
   See also ANW; CA 140; CANR 74, 146;
   DLB 212, 275; TCWW 2
Eich, Gunter
   See Eich, Gunter
Eich, Gunter 1907-1972 .... **CLC 15**
   See also CA 111; 93-96; DLB 69, 124;
   EWL 3; RGWL 2, 3
Eichendorff, Joseph 1788-1857 .... **NCLC 8,**
   225
   See also DLB 90; RGWL 2, 3
Eigner, Larry
   See Eigner, Laurence (Joel)
Eigner, Laurence (Joel) 1927-1996 ..... **CLC 9**
   See also CA 9-12R; 151; CAAS 23; CANR
   6, 84; CP 1, 2, 3, 4, 5, 6, 7; DLB 5; WP
Eilhart von Oberge c. 1140-c.
   1195 .... **CMLC 67**
   See also DLB 148
Einhard c. 770-840 .... **CMLC 50**
   See also DLB 148
Einstein, Albert 1879-1955 .... **TCLC 65**
   See also CA 121; 133; MTCW 1, 2
Eiseley, Loren
   See Eiseley, Loren Corey
Eiseley, Loren Corey 1907-1977 .... **CLC 7**
   See also AAYA 5; ANW; CA 1-4R; 73-76;
   CANR 6; DLB 275; DLBD 17
Eisenstadt, Jill 1963- .... **CLC 50**
   See also CA 140
Eisenstein, Sergei (Mikhailovich)
   1898-1948 .... **TCLC 57**
   See also CA 114; 149
Eisner, Simon
   See Kornbluth, C(yril) M.
Eisner, Will 1917-2005 .... **CLC 237**
   See also AAYA 52; CA 108; 235; CANR
   114, 140, 179; MTFW 2005; SATA 31,
   165
Eisner, William Erwin
   See Eisner, Will
Ekeloef, Bengt Gunnar
   See Ekelof, Gunnar
Ekeloef, Gunnar
   See Ekelof, Gunnar
Ekelof, Gunnar 1907-1968 ... **CLC 27; PC 23**
   See also CA 123; 25-28R; DAM POET;
   DLB 259; EW 12; EWL 3
Ekelund, Vilhelm 1880-1949 .... **TCLC 75**
   See also CA 189; EWL 3
Ekman, Kerstin (Lillemor) 1933- ... **CLC 279**
   See also CA 154; CANR 124; DLB 257;
   EWL 3
Ekwensi, C. O. D.
   See Ekwensi, Cyprian
Ekwensi, Cyprian 1921-2007 .... **BLC 1:1;**
   CLC 4
   See also AFW; BW 2, 3; CA 29-32R;
   CANR 18, 42, 74, 125; CDWLB 3; CN 1,
   2, 3, 4, 5, 6; CWRI 5; DAM MULT; DLB
   117; EWL 3; MTCW 1, 2; RGEL 2; SATA
   66; WLIT 2
Ekwensi, Cyprian Odiatu Duaka
   See Ekwensi, Cyprian
Elaine
   See Leverson, Ada Esther
El Conde de Pepe
   See Mihura, Miguel

El Crummo
   See Crumb, R.
Elder, Lonne III 1931-1996 .. **BLC 1:1; DC 8**
   See also BW 1, 3; CA 81-84; 152; CAD;
   CANR 25; DAM MULT; DLB 7, 38, 44;
   MAL 5
Eleanor of Aquitaine 1122-1204 ... **CMLC 39**
Elia
   See Lamb, Charles
Eliade, Mircea 1907-1986 .... **CLC 19**
   See also CA 65-68; 119; CANR 30, 62; CD-
   WLB 4; DLB 220; EWL 3; MTCW 1;
   RGWL 3; SFW 4
Eliot, A. D.
   See Jewett, Sarah Orne
Eliot, Alice
   See Jewett, Sarah Orne
Eliot, Dan
   See Silverberg, Robert
Eliot, George 1819-1880 ...... **NCLC 4, 13, 23,**
   41, 49, 89, 118, 183, 199, 209; PC 20;
   SSC 72; WLC 2
   See also BRW 5; BRWC 1, 2; BRWR 2;
   CDBLB 1832-1890; CN 7; CPW; DA;
   DA3; DAB; DAC; DAM MST, NOV;
   DLB 21, 35, 55; FL 1:3; LATS 1:1; LMFS
   1; NFS 17, 20; RGEL 2; RGSF 2; SSFS
   8; TEA; WLIT 3
Eliot, John 1604-1690 .... **LC 5**
   See also DLB 24
Eliot, T. S. 1888-1965 .. **CLC 1, 2, 3, 6, 9, 10,**
   13, 15, 24, 34, 41, 55, 57, 113; DC 28;
   PC 5, 31, 90; TCLC 236; WLC 2
   See also AAYA 28; AMW; AMWC 1;
   AMWR 1; BRW 7; BRWR 2; CA 5-8R;
   25-28R; CANR 41; CBD; CDALB 1929-
   1941; DA; DA3; DAB; DAC; DAM
   DRAM, MST, POET; DFS 4, 13; DLB 7,
   10, 45, 63, 245, 329; DLBY 1988; EWL
   3; EXPP; LAIT 3; LATS 1:1; LMFS 2;
   MAL 5; MTCW 1, 2; MTFW 2005; NCFS
   5; PAB; PFS 1, 7, 20; RGAL 4; RGEL 2;
   TUS; WLIT 4; WP
Eliot, Thomas Stearns
   See Eliot, T. S.
Elisabeth of Schonau c.
   1129-1165 .... **CMLC 82**
Elizabeth 1866-1941 .... **TCLC 41**
Elizabeth I 1533-1603 .... **LC 118**
   See also DLB 136
Elkin, Stanley L. 1930-1995 ...... **CLC 4, 6, 9,**
   14, 27, 51, 91; SSC 12
   See also AMWS 6; BPFB 1; CA 9-12R;
   148; CANR 8, 46; CN 1, 2, 3, 4, 5, 6;
   CPW; DAM NOV, POP; DLB 2, 28, 218,
   278; DLBY 1980; EWL 3; INT CANR-8;
   MAL 5; MTCW 1, 2; MTFW 2005;
   RGAL 4; TCLE 1:1
Elledge, Scott **CLC 34**
Eller, Scott
   See Shepard, Jim
Elliott, Don
   See Silverberg, Robert
Elliott, Ebenezer 1781-1849 .... **PC 96**
   See also DLB 96, 190; RGEL 2
Elliott, George P(aul) 1918-1980 .... **CLC 2**
   See also CA 1-4R; 97-100; CANR 2; CN 1,
   2; CP 3; DLB 244; MAL 5
Elliott, Janice 1931-1995 .... **CLC 47**
   See also CA 13-16R; CANR 8, 29, 84; CN
   5, 6, 7; DLB 14; SATA 119
Elliott, Sumner Locke 1917-1991 ..... **CLC 38**
   See also CA 5-8R; 134; CANR 2, 21; DLB
   289
Elliott, William
   See Bradbury, Ray
Ellis, A. E. **CLC 7**
Ellis, Alice Thomas
   See Haycraft, Anna

Ellis, Bret Easton 1964- ..... **CLC 39, 71, 117,**
   229
   See also AAYA 2, 43; CA 118; 123; CANR
   51, 74, 126; CN 6, 7; CPW; DA3; DAM
   POP; DLB 292; HGG; INT CA-123;
   MTCW 2; MTFW 2005; NFS 11
Ellis, (Henry) Havelock
   1859-1939 .... **TCLC 14**
   See also CA 109; 169; DLB 190
Ellis, Landon
   See Ellison, Harlan
Ellis, Trey 1962- .... **CLC 55**
   See also CA 146; CANR 92; CN 7
Ellison, Harlan 1934- .... **CLC 1, 13, 42, 139;**
   SSC 14
   See also AAYA 29; BPFB 1; BYA 14; CA
   5-8R; CANR 5, 46, 115; CPW; DAM
   POP; DLB 8, 335; HGG; INT CANR-5;
   MTCW 1, 2; MTFW 2005; SCFW 2;
   SFW 4; SSFS 13, 14, 15, 21; SUFW 1, 2
Ellison, Ralph 1914-1994 .... **BLC 1:1, 2:2;**
   CLC 1, 3, 11, 54, 86, 114; SSC 26, 79;
   WLC 2
   See also AAYA 19; AFAW 1, 2; AMWC 2;
   AMWR 2; AMWS 2; BPFB 1; BW 1, 3;
   BYA 2; CA 9-12R; 145; CANR 24, 53;
   CDALB 1941-1968; CN 1, 2, 3, 4, 5;
   CSW; DA; DA3; DAB; DAC; DAM MST,
   MULT, NOV; DLB 2, 76, 227; DLBY
   1994; EWL 3; EXPN; LAIT 4; LATS 1:1;
   MAL 5; MTCW 1, 2; MTFW 2005; NCFS
   3; NFS 2, 21; RGAL 4; RGSF 2; SSFS 1,
   11; YAW
Ellison, Ralph Waldo
   See Ellison, Ralph
Ellmann, Lucy 1956- .... **CLC 61**
   See also CA 128; CANR 154
Ellmann, Lucy Elizabeth
   See Ellmann, Lucy
Ellmann, Richard (David)
   1918-1987 .... **CLC 50**
   See also BEST 89:2; CA 1-4R; 122; CANR
   2, 28, 61; DLB 103; DLBY 1987; MTCW
   1, 2; MTFW 2005
Ellroy, James 1948- .... **CLC 215**
   See also BEST 90:4; CA 138; CANR 74,
   133; CMW 4; CN 6, 7; DA3; DLB 226;
   MTCW 2; MTFW 2005
Elman, Richard (Martin)
   1934-1997 .... **CLC 19**
   See also CA 17-20R; 163; CAAS 3; CANR
   47; TCLE 1:1
Elron
   See Hubbard, L. Ron
El Saadawi, Nawal 1931- ...... **BLC 2:2; CLC**
   196, 284
   See also AFW; CA 118; CAAS 11; CANR
   44, 92; CWW 2; DLB 346; EWL 3; FW;
   WLIT 2
El-Shabazz, El-Hajj Malik
   See Malcolm X
Eluard, Paul
   See Grindel, Eugene
Eluard, Paul
   See Grindel, Eugene
Elyot, Thomas 1490(?)-1546 .... **LC 11, 139**
   See also DLB 136; RGEL 2
Elytis, Odysseus 1911-1996 .... **CLC 15, 49,**
   100; PC 21
   See also CA 102; 151; CANR 94; CWW 2;
   DAM POET; DLB 329; EW 13; EWL 3;
   MTCW 1, 2; RGWL 2, 3
Emecheta, Buchi 1944- ... **BLC 1:2; CLC 14,**
   48, 128, 214
   See also AAYA 67; AFW; BW 2, 3; CA 81-
   84; CANR 27, 81, 126; CDWLB 3; CN
   4, 5, 6, 7; CWRI 5; DA3; DAM MULT;
   DLB 117; EWL 3; FL 1:5; FW; MTCW
   1, 2; MTFW 2005; NFS 12, 14; SATA 66;
   WLIT 2

Flashman, Harry Paget
See Fraser, George MacDonald

Flaubert, Gustave 1821-1880 .... **NCLC 2, 10, 19, 62, 66, 135, 179, 185; SSC 11, 60; WLC 2**
See also DA; DA3; DAB; DAC; DAM MST, NOV; DLB 119, 301; EW 7; EXPS; GFL 1789 to the Present; LAIT 2; LMFS 1; NFS 14; RGSF 2; RGWL 2, 3; SSFS 6; TWA

Flavius Josephus
See Josephus, Flavius

Flecker, Herman Elroy
See Flecker, (Herman) James Elroy

Flecker, (Herman) James Elroy 1884-1915 .... **TCLC 43**
See also CA 109; 150; DLB 10, 19; RGEL 2

Fleming, Ian 1908-1964 ... **CLC 3, 30; TCLC 193**
See also AAYA 26; BPFB 1; BRWS 14; CA 5-8R; CANR 59; CDBLB 1945-1960; CMW 4; CPW; DA3; DAM POP; DLB 87, 201; MSW; MTCW 1, 2; MTFW 2005; RGEL 2; SATA 9; TEA; YAW

Fleming, Ian Lancaster
See Fleming, Ian

Fleming, Thomas 1927- .... **CLC 37**
See also CA 5-8R; CANR 10, 102, 155, 197; INT CANR-10; SATA 8

Fleming, Thomas James
See Fleming, Thomas

Fletcher, John 1579-1625 . **DC 6; LC 33, 151**
See also BRW 2; CDBLB Before 1660; DLB 58; RGEL 2; TEA

Fletcher, John Gould 1886-1950 .... **TCLC 35**
See also CA 107; 167; DLB 4, 45; LMFS 2; MAL 5; RGAL 4

Fleur, Paul
See Pohl, Frederik

Flieg, Helmut
See Heym, Stefan

Flooglebuckle, Al
See Spiegelman, Art

Flying Officer X
See Bates, H(erbert) E(rnest)

Fo, Dario 1926- .... **CLC 32, 109, 227; DC 10**
See also CA 116; 128; CANR 68, 114, 134, 164; CWW 2; DA3; DAM DRAM; DFS 23; DLB 330; DLBY 1997; EWL 3; MTCW 1, 2; MTFW 2005; WLIT 7

Foden, Giles 1967- .... **CLC 231**
See also CA 240; DLB 267; NFS 15

Fogarty, Jonathan Titulescu Esq.
See Farrell, James T(homas)

Follett, Ken 1949- .... **CLC 18**
See also AAYA 6, 50; BEST 89:4; BPFB 1; CA 81-84; CANR 13, 33, 54, 102, 156, 197; CMW 4; CPW; DA3; DAM NOV, POP; DLB 87; DLBY 1981; INT CANR-33; LNFS 3; MTCW 1

Follett, Kenneth Martin
See Follett, Ken

Fondane, Benjamin 1898-1944 ..... **TCLC 159**

Fontane, Theodor 1819-1898 . **NCLC 26, 163**
See also CDWLB 2; DLB 129; EW 6; RGWL 2, 3; TWA

Fonte, Moderata 1555-1592 .... **LC 118**

Fontenelle, Bernard Le Bovier de 1657-1757 .... **LC 140**
See also DLB 268, 313; GFL Beginnings to 1789

Fontenot, Chester .... **CLC 65**

Fonvizin, Denis Ivanovich 1744(?)-1792 .... **LC 81**
See also DLB 150; RGWL 2, 3

Foote, Albert Horton
See Foote, Horton

Foote, Horton 1916-2009 .... **CLC 51, 91**
See also AAYA 82; CA 73-76; 284; CAD; CANR 34, 51, 110; CD 5, 6; CSW; DA3; DAM DRAM; DFS 20; DLB 26, 266; EWL 3; INT CANR-34; MTFW 2005

Foote, Mary Hallock 1847-1938 .. **TCLC 108**
See also DLB 186, 188, 202, 221; TCWW 2

Foote, Samuel 1721-1777 .... **LC 106**
See also DLB 89; RGEL 2

Foote, Shelby 1916-2005 .... **CLC 75, 224**
See also AAYA 40; CA 5-8R; 240; CANR 3, 45, 74, 131; CN 1, 2, 3, 4, 5, 6, 7; CPW; CSW; DA3; DAM NOV, POP; DLB 2, 17; MAL 5; MTCW 2; MTFW 2005; RHW

Forbes, Cosmo
See Lewton, Val

Forbes, Esther 1891-1967 .... **CLC 12**
See also AAYA 17; BYA 2; CA 13-14; 25-28R; CAP 1; CLR 27, 147; DLB 22; JRDA; MAICYA 1, 2; RHW; SATA 2, 100; YAW

Forche, Carolyn 1950- .. **CLC 25, 83, 86; PC 10**
See also CA 109; 117; CANR 50, 74, 138; CP 4, 5, 6, 7; CWP; DA3; DAM POET; DLB 5, 193; INT CA-117; MAL 5; MTCW 2; MTFW 2005; PFS 18; RGAL 4

Forche, Carolyn Louise
See Forche, Carolyn

Ford, Elbur
See Hibbert, Eleanor Alice Burford

Ford, Ford Madox 1873-1939 ... **TCLC 1, 15, 39, 57, 172**
See also BRW 6; CA 104; 132; CANR 74; CDBLB 1914-1945; DA3; DAM NOV; DLB 34, 98, 162; EWL 3; MTCW 1, 2; NFS 28; RGEL 2; RHW; TEA

Ford, Henry 1863-1947 .... **TCLC 73**
See also CA 115; 148

Ford, Jack
See Ford, John

Ford, John 1586-1639 .... **DC 8; LC 68, 153**
See also BRW 2; CDBLB Before 1660; DA3; DAM DRAM; DFS 7; DLB 58; IDTP; RGEL 2

Ford, John 1895-1973 .... **CLC 16**
See also AAYA 75; CA 187; 45-48

Ford, Richard 1944- ... **CLC 46, 99, 205, 277**
See also AMWS 5; CA 69-72; CANR 11, 47, 86, 128, 164; CN 5, 6, 7; CSW; DLB 227; EWL 3; MAL 5; MTCW 2; MTFW 2005; NFS 25; RGAL 4; RGSF 2

Ford, Webster
See Masters, Edgar Lee

Foreman, Richard 1937- .... **CLC 50**
See also CA 65-68; CAD; CANR 32, 63, 143; CD 5, 6

Forester, C. S. 1899-1966 ..... **CLC 35; TCLC 152**
See also CA 73-76; 25-28R; CANR 83; DLB 191; RGEL 2; RHW; SATA 13

Forester, Cecil Scott
See Forester, C. S.

Forez
See Mauriac, Francois (Charles)

Forman, James
See Forman, James D.

Forman, James D. 1932- .... **CLC 21**
See also AAYA 17; CA 9-12R; CANR 4, 19, 42; JRDA; MAICYA 1, 2; SATA 8, 70; YAW

Forman, James Douglas
See Forman, James D.

Forman, Milos 1932- .... **CLC 164**
See also AAYA 63; CA 109

Fornes, Maria Irene 1930- .... **CLC 39, 61, 187; DC 10; HLCS 1**
See also CA 25-28R; CAD; CANR 28, 81; CD 5, 6; CWD; DFS 25; DLB 7, 341; HW 1, 2; INT CANR-28; LLW; MAL 5; MTCW 1; RGAL 4

Forrest, Leon (Richard) 1937-1997 .... **BLCS; CLC 4**
See also AFAW 2; BW 2; CA 89-92; 162; CAAS 7; CANR 25, 52, 87; CN 4, 5, 6; DLB 33

Forster, E. M. 1879-1970 .. **CLC 1, 2, 3, 4, 9, 10, 13, 15, 22, 45, 77; SSC 27, 96; TCLC 125; WLC 2**
See also AAYA 2, 37; BRW 6; BRWR 2; BYA 12; CA 13-14; 25-28R; CANR 45; CAP 1; CDBLB 1914-1945; DA; DA3; DAB; DAC; DAM MST, NOV; DLB 34, 98, 162, 178, 195; DLBD 10; EWL 3; EXPN; LAIT 3; LMFS 1; MTCW 1, 2; MTFW 2005; NCFS 1; NFS 3, 10, 11; RGEL 2; RGSF 2; SATA 57; SUFW 1; TEA; WLIT 4

Forster, Edward Morgan
See Forster, E. M.

Forster, John 1812-1876 .... **NCLC 11**
See also DLB 144, 184

Forster, Margaret 1938- .... **CLC 149**
See also CA 133; CANR 62, 115, 175; CN 4, 5, 6, 7; DLB 155, 271

Forsyth, Frederick 1938- .... **CLC 2, 5, 36**
See also BEST 89:4; CA 85-88; CANR 38, 62, 115, 137, 183; CMW 4; CN 3, 4, 5, 6, 7; CPW; DAM NOV, POP; DLB 87; MTCW 1, 2; MTFW 2005

Fort, Paul
See Stockton, Francis Richard

Forten, Charlotte
See Grimke, Charlotte L. Forten

Forten, Charlotte L. 1837-1914
See Grimke, Charlotte L. Forten

Fortinbras
See Grieg, (Johan) Nordahl (Brun)

Foscolo, Ugo 1778-1827 .... **NCLC 8, 97**
See also EW 5; WLIT 7

Fosse, Bob 1927-1987 .... **CLC 20**
See also AAYA 82; CA 110; 123

Fosse, Robert L.
See Fosse, Bob

Foster, Hannah Webster 1758-1840 .... **NCLC 99**
See also DLB 37, 200; RGAL 4

Foster, Stephen Collins 1826-1864 .... **NCLC 26**
See also RGAL 4

Foucault, Michel 1926-1984 . **CLC 31, 34, 69**
See also CA 105; 113; CANR 34; DLB 242; EW 13; EWL 3; GFL 1789 to the Present; GLL 1; LMFS 2; MTCW 1, 2; TWA

Fouque, Friedrich (Heinrich Karl) de la Motte 1777-1843 .... **NCLC 2**
See also DLB 90; RGWL 2, 3; SUFW 1

Fourier, Charles 1772-1837 .... **NCLC 51**

Fournier, Henri-Alban 1886-1914 ... **TCLC 6**
See also CA 104; 179; DLB 65; EWL 3; GFL 1789 to the Present; RGWL 2, 3

Fournier, Pierre 1916-1997 .... **CLC 11**
See also CA 89-92; CANR 16, 40; EWL 3; RGHL

Fowles, John 1926-2005 .... **CLC 1, 2, 3, 4, 6, 9, 10, 15, 33, 87, 287; SSC 33, 128**
See also BPFB 1; BRWS 1; CA 5-8R; 245; CANR 25, 71, 103; CDBLB 1960 to Present; CN 1, 2, 3, 4, 5, 6, 7; DA3; DAB; DAC; DAM MST; DLB 14, 139, 207; EWL 3; HGG; MTCW 1, 2; MTFW 2005; NFS 21; RGEL 2; RHW; SATA 22; SATA-Obit 171; TEA; WLIT 4

LMFS 2; MTCW 1, 2; MTFW 2005; NCFS 3; NFS 1, 5, 10; RGSF 2; RGWL 2, 3; SSFS 1, 6, 16, 21; TWA; WLIT 1

Garcia Marquez, Gabriel Jose
See Garcia Marquez, Gabriel

Garcilaso de la Vega, El Inca 1539-1616 .... **HLCS 1; LC 127**
See also DLB 318; LAW

Gard, Janice
See Latham, Jean Lee

Gard, Roger Martin du
See Martin du Gard, Roger

Gardam, Jane 1928- .... **CLC 43**
See also CA 49-52; CANR 2, 18, 33, 54, 106, 167; CLR 12; DLB 14, 161, 231; MAICYA 1, 2; MTCW 1; SAAS 9; SATA 39, 76, 130; SATA-Brief 28; YAW

Gardam, Jane Mary
See Gardam, Jane

Gardens, S. S.
See Snodgrass, W. D.

Gardner, Herb(ert George) 1934-2003 .... **CLC 44**
See also CA 149; 220; CAD; CANR 119; CD 5, 6; DFS 18, 20

Gardner, John, Jr. 1933-1982 ... **CLC 2, 3, 5, 7, 8, 10, 18, 28, 34; SSC 7; TCLC 195**
See also AAYA 45; AITN 1; AMWS 6; BPFB 2; CA 65-68; 107; CANR 33, 73; CDALBS; CN 2, 3; CPW; DA3; DAM NOV, POP; DLB 2; DLBY 1982; EWL 3; FANT; LATS 1:2; MAL 5; MTCW 1, 2; MTFW 2005; NFS 3; RGAL 4; RGSF 2; SATA 40; SATA-Obit 31; SSFS 8

Gardner, John 1926-2007 .... **CLC 30**
See also CA 103; 263; CANR 15, 69, 127, 183; CMW 4; CPW; DAM POP; MTCW 1

Gardner, John Champlin, Jr.
See Gardner, John, Jr.

Gardner, John Edmund
See Gardner, John

Gardner, Miriam
See Bradley, Marion Zimmer

Gardner, Noel
See Kuttner, Henry

Gardons, S.S.
See Snodgrass, W. D.

Garfield, Leon 1921-1996 .... **CLC 12**
See also AAYA 8, 69; BYA 1, 3; CA 17-20R; 152; CANR 38, 41, 78; CLR 21; DLB 161; JRDA; MAICYA 1, 2; MAIC-YAS 1; SATA 1, 32, 76; SATA-Obit 90; TEA; WYA; YAW

Garland, (Hannibal) Hamlin 1860-1940 .... **SSC 18, 117; TCLC 3**
See also CA 104; DLB 12, 71, 78, 186; MAL 5; RGAL 4; RGSF 2; TCWW 1, 2

Garneau, (Hector de) Saint-Denys 1912-1943 .... **TCLC 13**
See also CA 111; DLB 88

Garner, Alan 1934- .... **CLC 17**
See also AAYA 18; BYA 3, 5; CA 73-76, 178; CAAE 178; CANR 15, 64, 134; CLR 20, 130; CPW; DAB; DAM POP; DLB 161, 261; FANT; MAICYA 1, 2; MTCW 1, 2; MTFW 2005; SATA 18, 69; SATA-Essay 108; SUFW 1, 2; YAW

Garner, Helen 1942- .... **SSC 135**
See also CA 124; 127; CANR 71; CN 4, 5, 6, 7; DLB 325; GLL 2; RGSF 2

Garner, Hugh 1913-1979 .... **CLC 13**
See also CA 69-72; CANR 31; CCA 1; CN 1, 2; DLB 68

Garnett, David 1892-1981 .... **CLC 3**
See also CA 5-8R; 103; CANR 17, 79; CN 1, 2; DLB 34; FANT; MTCW 2; RGEL 2; SFW 4; SUFW 1

Garnier, Robert c. 1545-1590 .... **LC 119**
See also DLB 327; GFL Beginnings to 1789

Garrett, George 1929-2008 ... **CLC 3, 11, 51; SSC 30**
See also AMWS 7; BPFB 2; CA 1-4R, 202; 272; CAAE 202; CAAS 5; CANR 1, 42, 67, 109, 199; CN 1, 2, 3, 4, 5, 6, 7; CP 1, 2, 3, 4, 5, 6, 7; CSW; DLB 2, 5, 130, 152; DLBY 1983

Garrett, George P.
See Garrett, George

Garrett, George Palmer
See Garrett, George

Garrett, George Palmer, Jr.
See Garrett, George

Garrick, David 1717-1779 .... **LC 15, 156**
See also DAM DRAM; DLB 84, 213; RGEL 2

Garrigue, Jean 1914-1972 .... **CLC 2, 8**
See also CA 5-8R; 37-40R; CANR 20; CP 1; MAL 5

Garrison, Frederick
See Sinclair, Upton

Garrison, William Lloyd 1805-1879 .... **NCLC 149**
See also CDALB 1640-1865; DLB 1, 43, 235

Garro, Elena 1920(?)-1998 .. **HLCS 1; TCLC 153**
See also CA 131; 169; CWW 2; DLB 145; EWL 3; HW 1; LAWS 1; WLIT 1

Garth, Will
See Hamilton, Edmond; Kuttner, Henry

Garvey, Marcus (Moziah, Jr.) 1887-1940 ..... **BLC 1:2; HR 1:2; TCLC 41**
See also BW 1; CA 120; 124; CANR 79; DAM MULT; DLB 345

Gary, Romain
See Kacew, Romain

Gascar, Pierre
See Fournier, Pierre

Gascoigne, George 1539-1577 .... **LC 108**
See also DLB 136; RGEL 2

Gascoyne, David (Emery) 1916-2001 .... **CLC 45**
See also CA 65-68; 200; CANR 10, 28, 54; CP 1, 2, 3, 4, 5, 6, 7; DLB 20; MTCW 1; RGEL 2

Gaskell, Elizabeth 1810-1865 ... **NCLC 5, 70, 97, 137, 214; SSC 25, 97**
See also AAYA 80; BRW 5; BRWR 3; CD-BLB 1832-1890; DAB; DAM MST; DLB 21, 144, 159; RGEL 2; RGSF 2; TEA

Gass, William H. 1924- . **CLC 1, 2, 8, 11, 15, 39, 132; SSC 12**
See also AMWS 6; CA 17-20R; CANR 30, 71, 100; CN 1, 2, 3, 4, 5, 6, 7; DLB 2, 227; EWL 3; MAL 5; MTCW 1, 2; MTFW 2005; RGAL 4

Gassendi, Pierre 1592-1655 .... **LC 54**
See also GFL Beginnings to 1789

Gasset, Jose Ortega y
See Ortega y Gasset, Jose

Gates, Henry Louis, Jr. 1950- ... **BLCS; CLC 65**
See also BW 2, 3; CA 109; CANR 25, 53, 75, 125; CSW; DA3; DAM MULT; DLB 67; EWL 3; MAL 5; MTCW 2; MTFW 2005; RGAL 4

Gatos, Stephanie
See Katz, Steve

Gautier, Theophile 1811-1872 .. **NCLC 1, 59; PC 18; SSC 20**
See also DAM POET; DLB 119; EW 6; GFL 1789 to the Present; RGWL 2, 3; SUFW; TWA

Gautreaux, Tim 1947- .... **CLC 270; SSC 125**
See also CA 187; CSW; DLB 292

Gay, John 1685-1732 .... **LC 49, 176**
See also BRW 3; DAM DRAM; DLB 84, 95; RGEL 2; WLIT 3

Gay, Oliver
See Gogarty, Oliver St. John

Gay, Peter 1923- .... **CLC 158**
See also CA 13-16R; CANR 18, 41, 77, 147, 196; INT CANR-18; RGHL

Gay, Peter Jack
See Gay, Peter

Gaye, Marvin (Pentz, Jr.) 1939-1984 .... **CLC 26**
See also CA 195; 112

Gebler, Carlo 1954- .... **CLC 39**
See also CA 119; 133; CANR 96, 186; DLB 271

Gebler, Carlo Ernest
See Gebler, Carlo

Gee, Maggie 1948- .... **CLC 57**
See also CA 130; CANR 125; CN 4, 5, 6, 7; DLB 207; MTFW 2005

Gee, Maurice 1931- .... **CLC 29**
See also AAYA 42; CA 97-100; CANR 67, 123; CLR 56; CN 2, 3, 4, 5, 6, 7; CWRI 5; EWL 3; MAICYA 2; RGSF 2; SATA 46, 101

Gee, Maurice Gough
See Gee, Maurice

Geiogamah, Hanay 1945- .... **NNAL**
See also CA 153; DAM MULT; DLB 175

Gelbart, Larry 1928-2009 .... **CLC 21, 61**
See also CA 73-76; 290; CAD; CANR 45, 94; CD 5, 6

Gelbart, Larry Simon
See Gelbart, Larry

Gelber, Jack 1932-2003 ...... **CLC 1, 6, 14, 79**
See also CA 1-4R; 216; CAD; CANR 2; DLB 7, 228; MAL 5

Gellhorn, Martha (Ellis) 1908-1998 .... **CLC 14, 60**
See also CA 77-80; 164; CANR 44; CN 1, 2, 3, 4, 5, 6 7; DLBY 1982, 1998

Genet, Jean 1910-1986 .. **CLC 1, 2, 5, 10, 14, 44, 46; DC 25; TCLC 128**
See also CA 13-16R; CANR 18; DA3; DAM DRAM; DFS 10; DLB 72, 321; DLBY 1986; EW 13; EWL 3; GFL 1789 to the Present; GLL 1; LMFS 2; MTCW 1, 2; MTFW 2005; RGWL 2, 3; TWA

Genlis, Stephanie-Felicite Ducrest 1746-1830 .... **NCLC 166**
See also DLB 313

Gent, Peter 1942- .... **CLC 29**
See also AITN 1; CA 89-92; DLBY 1982

Gentile, Giovanni 1875-1944 .... **TCLC 96**
See also CA 119

Geoffrey of Monmouth c. 1100-1155 .... **CMLC 44**
See also DLB 146; TEA

George, Jean
See George, Jean Craighead

George, Jean C.
See George, Jean Craighead

George, Jean Craighead 1919- .... **CLC 35**
See also AAYA 8, 69; BYA 2, 4; CA 5-8R; CANR 25, 198; CLR 1, 80, 136; DLB 52; JRDA; MAICYA 1, 2; SATA 2, 68, 124, 170; WYA; YAW

George, Stefan (Anton) 1868-1933 . **TCLC 2, 14**
See also CA 104; 193; EW 8; EWL 3

Georges, Georges Martin
See Simenon, Georges

Gerald of Wales c. 1146-c. 1223 ... **CMLC 60**

Gerhardi, William Alexander
See Gerhardie, William Alexander

Gerhardie, William Alexander
1895-1977 .... **CLC 5**
See also CA 25-28R; 73-76; CANR 18; CN 1, 2; DLB 36; RGEL 2

Germain, Sylvie 1954- .... **CLC 283**
See also CA 191

Gerome
See France, Anatole

Gerson, Jean 1363-1429 .... **LC 77**
See also DLB 208

Gersonides 1288-1344 .... **CMLC 49**
See also DLB 115

Gerstler, Amy 1956- .... **CLC 70**
See also CA 146; CANR 99

Gertler, T. **CLC 34**
See also CA 116; 121

Gertrude of Helfta c. 1256-c. 1301 .... **CMLC 105**

Gertsen, Aleksandr Ivanovich
See Herzen, Aleksandr Ivanovich

Ghalib
See Ghalib, Asadullah Khan

Ghalib, Asadullah Khan
1797-1869 .... **NCLC 39, 78**
See also DAM POET; RGWL 2, 3

Ghelderode, Michel de 1898-1962 ..... **CLC 6, 11; DC 15; TCLC 187**
See also CA 85-88; CANR 40, 77; DAM DRAM; DLB 321; EW 11; EWL 3; TWA

Ghiselin, Brewster 1903-2001 .... **CLC 23**
See also CA 13-16R; CAAS 10; CANR 13; CP 1, 2, 3, 4, 5, 6, 7

Ghose, Aurabinda 1872-1950 .... **TCLC 63**
See also CA 163; EWL 3

Ghose, Aurobindo
See Ghose, Aurabinda

Ghose, Zulfikar 1935- .... **CLC 42, 200**
See also CA 65-68; CANR 67; CN 1, 2, 3, 4, 5, 6, 7; CP 1, 2, 3, 4, 5, 6, 7; DLB 323; EWL 3

Ghosh, Amitav 1956- .... **CLC 44, 153**
See also CA 147; CANR 80, 158; CN 6, 7; DLB 323; WWE 1

Giacosa, Giuseppe 1847-1906 .... **TCLC 7**
See also CA 104

Gibb, Lee
See Waterhouse, Keith

Gibbon, Edward 1737-1794 .... **LC 97**
See also BRW 3; DLB 104, 336; RGEL 2

Gibbon, Lewis Grassic
See Mitchell, James Leslie

Gibbons, Kaye 1960- .... **CLC 50, 88, 145**
See also AAYA 34; AMWS 10; CA 151; CANR 75, 127; CN 7; CSW; DA3; DAM POP; DLB 292; MTCW 2; MTFW 2005; NFS 3; RGAL 4; SATA 117

Gibran, Kahlil 1883-1931 ..... **PC 9; TCLC 1, 9, 205**
See also CA 104; 150; DA3; DAM POET, POP; DLB 346; EWL 3; MTCW 2; WLIT 6

Gibran, Khalil
See Gibran, Kahlil

Gibson, Mel 1956- .... **CLC 215**
See also AAYA 80

Gibson, William 1914-2008 .... **CLC 23**
See also CA 9-12R; 279; CAD; CANR 9, 42, 75, 125; CD 5, 6; DA; DAB; DAC; DAM DRAM, MST; DFS 2; DLB 7; LAIT 2; MAL 5; MTCW 2; MTFW 2005; SATA 66; SATA-Obit 199; YAW

Gibson, William 1948- .... **CLC 39, 63, 186, 192; SSC 52**
See also AAYA 12, 59; AMWS 16; BPFB 2; CA 126; 133; CANR 52, 90, 106, 172; CN 6, 7; CPW; DA3; DAM POP; DLB 251; MTCW 2; MTFW 2005; SCFW 2; SFW 4; SSFS 26

Gibson, William Ford
See Gibson, William

Gide, Andre 1869-1951 ..... **SSC 13; TCLC 5, 12, 36, 177; WLC 3**
See also CA 104; 124; DA; DA3; DAB; DAC; DAM MST, NOV; DLB 65, 321, 330; EW 8; EWL 3; GFL 1789 to the Present; MTCW 1, 2; MTFW 2005; NFS 21; RGSF 2; RGWL 2, 3; TWA

Gide, Andre Paul Guillaume
See Gide, Andre

Gifford, Barry 1946- .... **CLC 34**
See also CA 65-68; CANR 9, 30, 40, 90, 180

Gifford, Barry Colby
See Gifford, Barry

Gilbert, Frank
See De Voto, Bernard (Augustine)

Gilbert, W(illiam) S(chwenck)
1836-1911 .... **TCLC 3**
See also CA 104; 173; DAM DRAM, POET; DLB 344; RGEL 2; SATA 36

Gilbert of Poitiers c. 1085-1154 .... **CMLC 85**

Gilbreth, Frank B., Jr. 1911-2001 .... **CLC 17**
See also CA 9-12R; SATA 2

Gilbreth, Frank Bunker
See Gilbreth, Frank B., Jr.

Gilchrist, Ellen 1935- .... **CLC 34, 48, 143, 264; SSC 14, 63**
See also BPFB 2; CA 113; 116; CANR 41, 61, 104, 191; CN 4, 5, 6, 7; CPW; CSW; DAM POP; DLB 130; EWL 3; EXPS; MTCW 1, 2; MTFW 2005; RGAL 4; RGSF 2; SSFS 9

Gilchrist, Ellen Louise
See Gilchrist, Ellen

Gildas fl. 6th cent. - .... **CMLC 99**

Giles, Molly 1942- .... **CLC 39**
See also CA 126; CANR 98

Gill, Arthur Eric Rowton Peter Joseph
See Gill, Eric

Gill, Eric 1882-1940 .... **TCLC 85**
See Gill, Arthur Eric Rowton Peter Joseph
See also CA 120; DLB 98

Gill, Patrick
See Creasey, John

Gillette, Douglas **CLC 70**

Gilliam, Terry 1940- .... **CLC 21, 141**
See also AAYA 19, 59; CA 108; 113; CANR 35; INT CA-113

Gilliam, Terry Vance
See Gilliam, Terry

Gillian, Jerry
See Gilliam, Terry

Gilliatt, Penelope (Ann Douglass)
1932-1993 .... **CLC 2, 10, 13, 53**
See also AITN 2; CA 13-16R; 141; CANR 49; CN 1, 2, 3, 4, 5; DLB 14

Gilligan, Carol 1936- .... **CLC 208**
See also CA 142; CANR 121, 187; FW

Gilman, Charlotte Anna Perkins Stetson
See Gilman, Charlotte Perkins

Gilman, Charlotte Perkins
1860-1935 ...... **SSC 13, 62; TCLC 9, 37, 117, 201**
See also AAYA 75; AMWS 11; BYA 11; CA 106; 150; DLB 221; EXPS; FL 1:5; FW; HGG; LAIT 2; MBL; MTCW 2; MTFW 2005; RGAL 4; RGSF 2; SFW 4; SSFS 1, 18

Gilmore, Mary (Jean Cameron)
1865-1962 .... **PC 87**
See also CA 114; DLB 260; RGEL 2; SATA 49

Gilmour, David 1946- .... **CLC 35**

Gilpin, William 1724-1804 .... **NCLC 30**

Gilray, J. D.
See Mencken, H. L.

Gilroy, Frank D(aniel) 1925- .... **CLC 2**
See also CA 81-84; CAD; CANR 32, 64, 86; CD 5, 6; DFS 17; DLB 7

Gilstrap, John 1957(?)- .... **CLC 99**
See also AAYA 67; CA 160; CANR 101

Ginsberg, Allen 1926-1997 .... **CLC 1, 2, 3, 4, 6, 13, 36, 69, 109; PC 4, 47; TCLC 120; WLC 3**
See also AAYA 33; AITN 1; AMWC 1; AMWS 2; BG 1:2; CA 1-4R; 157; CANR 2, 41, 63, 95; CDALB 1941-1968; CP 1, 2, 3, 4, 5, 6; DA; DA3; DAB; DAC; DAM MST, POET; DLB 5, 16, 169, 237; EWL 3; GLL 1; LMFS 2; MAL 5; MTCW 1, 2; MTFW 2005; PAB; PFS 29; RGAL 4; TUS; WP

Ginzburg, Eugenia
See Ginzburg, Evgeniia

Ginzburg, Evgeniia 1904-1977 .... **CLC 59**
See also DLB 302

Ginzburg, Natalia 1916-1991 .... **CLC 5, 11, 54, 70; SSC 65; TCLC 156**
See also CA 85-88; 135; CANR 33; DFS 14; DLB 177; EW 13; EWL 3; MTCW 1, 2; MTFW 2005; RGHL; RGWL 2, 3

Gioia, (Michael) Dana 1950- .... **CLC 251**
See also AMWS 15; CA 130; CANR 70, 88; CP 6, 7; DLB 120, 282; PFS 24

Giono, Jean 1895-1970 .... **CLC 4, 11; TCLC 124**
See also CA 45-48; 29-32R; CANR 2, 35; DLB 72, 321; EWL 3; GFL 1789 to the Present; MTCW 1; RGWL 2, 3

Giovanni, Nikki 1943- ... **BLC 1:2; CLC 2, 4, 19, 64, 117; PC 19; WLCS**
See also AAYA 22; AITN 1; BW 2, 3; CA 29-32R; CAAS 6; CANR 18, 41, 60, 91, 130, 175; CDALBS; CLR 6, 73; CP 2, 3, 4, 5, 6, 7; CSW; CWP; CWRI 5; DA; DA3; DAB; DAC; DAM MST, MULT, POET; DLB 5, 41; EWL 3; EXPP; INT CANR-18; MAICYA 1, 2; MAL 5; MTCW 1, 2; MTFW 2005; PFS 17, 28; RGAL 4; SATA 24, 107; TUS; YAW

Giovanni, Yolanda Cornelia
See Giovanni, Nikki

Giovanni, Yolande Cornelia
See Giovanni, Nikki

Giovanni, Yolande Cornelia, Jr.
See Giovanni, Nikki

Giovene, Andrea 1904-1998 .... **CLC 7**
See also CA 85-88

Gippius, Zinaida 1869-1945 .... **TCLC 9**
See also CA 106; 212; DLB 295; EWL 3

Gippius, Zinaida Nikolaevna
See Gippius, Zinaida

Giraudoux, Jean 1882-1944 ... **DC 36; TCLC 2, 7**
See also CA 104; 196; DAM DRAM; DLB 65, 321; EW 9; EWL 3; GFL 1789 to the Present; RGWL 2, 3; TWA

Giraudoux, Jean-Hippolyte
See Giraudoux, Jean

Gironella, Jose Maria (Pous)
1917-2003 .... **CLC 11**
See also CA 101; 212; EWL 3; RGWL 2, 3

Gissing, George (Robert)
1857-1903 .... **SSC 37, 113; TCLC 3, 24, 47**
See also BRW 5; CA 105; 167; DLB 18, 135, 184; RGEL 2; TEA

Gitlin, Todd 1943- .... **CLC 201**
See also CA 29-32R; CANR 25, 50, 88, 179

Giurlani, Aldo
See Palazzeschi, Aldo

Gladkov, Fedor Vasil'evich
See Gladkov, Fyodor (Vasilyevich)

Gladkov, Fyodor (Vasilyevich)
1883-1958 .... **TCLC 27**
See also CA 170; DLB 272; EWL 3
Gladstone, William Ewart
1809-1898 .... **NCLC 213**
See also DLB 57, 184
Glancy, Diane 1941- .... **CLC 210; NNAL**
See also CA 136, 225; CAAE 225; CAAS
24; CANR 87, 162; DLB 175
Glanville, Brian (Lester) 1931- .... **CLC 6**
See also CA 5-8R; CAAS 9; CANR 3, 70;
CN 1, 2, 3, 4, 5, 6, 7; DLB 15, 139; SATA
42
Glasgow, Ellen 1873-1945 .... **SSC 34, 130;**
TCLC 2, 7
See also AMW; CA 104; 164; DLB 9, 12;
MAL 5; MBL; MTCW 2; MTFW 2005;
RGAL 4; RHW; SSFS 9; TUS
Glasgow, Ellen Anderson Gholson
See Glasgow, Ellen
Glaspell, Susan 1882(?)-1948 ..... **DC 10; SSC**
41, 132; TCLC 55, 175
See also AMWS 3; CA 110; 154; DFS 8,
18, 24; DLB 7, 9, 78, 228; MBL; RGAL
4; SSFS 3; TCWW 2; TUS; YABC 2
Glassco, John 1909-1981 .... **CLC 9**
See also CA 13-16R; 102; CANR 15; CN
1, 2; CP 1, 2, 3; DLB 68
Glasscock, Amnesia
See Steinbeck, John
Glasser, Ronald J. 1940(?)- .... **CLC 37**
See also CA 209
Glassman, Joyce
See Johnson, Joyce
Gleick, James (W.) 1954- .... **CLC 147**
See also CA 131; 137; CANR 97; INT CA-
137
Glendinning, Victoria 1937- .... **CLC 50**
See also CA 120; 127; CANR 59, 89, 166;
DLB 155
Glissant, Edouard (Mathieu)
1928- .... **CLC 10, 68**
See also CA 153; CANR 111; CWW 2;
DAM MULT; EWL 3; RGWL 3
Gloag, Julian 1930- .... **CLC 40**
See also AITN 1; CA 65-68; CANR 10, 70;
CN 1, 2, 3, 4, 5, 6
Glowacki, Aleksander
See Prus, Boleslaw
Gluck, Louise 1943- . **CLC 7, 22, 44, 81, 160,**
280; PC 16
See also AMWS 5; CA 33-36R; CANR 40,
69, 108, 133, 182; CP 1, 2, 3, 4, 5, 6, 7;
CWP; DA3; DAM POET; DLB 5; MAL
5; MTCW 2; MTFW 2005; PFS 5, 15;
RGAL 4; TCLE 1:1
Gluck, Louise Elisabeth
See Gluck, Louise
Glyn, Elinor 1864-1943 .... **TCLC 72**
See also DLB 153; RHW
Gobineau, Joseph-Arthur
1816-1882 .... **NCLC 17**
See also DLB 123; GFL 1789 to the Present
Godard, Jean-Luc 1930- .... **CLC 20**
See also CA 93-96
Godden, (Margaret) Rumer
1907-1998 .... **CLC 53**
See also AAYA 6; BPFB 2; BYA 2, 5; CA
5-8R; 172; CANR 4, 27, 36, 55, 80; CLR
20; CN 1, 2, 3, 4, 5, 6; CWRI 5; DLB
161; MAICYA 1, 2; RHW; SAAS 12;
SATA 3, 36; SATA-Obit 109; TEA
Godoy Alcayaga, Lucila
See Mistral, Gabriela
Godwin, Gail 1937- ...... **CLC 5, 8, 22, 31, 69,**
125
See also BPFB 2; CA 29-32R; CANR 15,
43, 69, 132; CN 3, 4, 5, 6, 7; CPW; CSW;
DA3; DAM POP; DLB 6, 234, 350; INT
CANR-15; MAL 5; MTCW 1, 2; MTFW
2005

Godwin, Gail Kathleen
See Godwin, Gail
Godwin, William 1756-1836 .. **NCLC 14, 130**
See also BRWS 15; CDBLB 1789-1832;
CMW 4; DLB 39, 104, 142, 158, 163,
262, 336; GL 2; HGG; RGEL 2
Goebbels, Josef
See Goebbels, (Paul) Joseph
Goebbels, (Paul) Joseph
1897-1945 .... **TCLC 68**
See also CA 115; 148
Goebbels, Joseph Paul
See Goebbels, (Paul) Joseph
Goethe, Johann Wolfgang von
1749-1832 . **DC 20; NCLC 4, 22, 34, 90,**
154; PC 5; SSC 38; WLC 3
See also CDWLB 2; DA; DA3; DAB;
DAC; DAM DRAM, MST, POET; DLB
94; EW 5; GL 2; LATS 1; LMFS 1:1;
RGWL 2, 3; TWA
Gogarty, Oliver St. John
1878-1957 .... **TCLC 15**
See also CA 109; 150; DLB 15, 19; RGEL
2
Gogol, Nikolai 1809-1852 .... **DC 1; NCLC 5,**
15, 31, 162; SSC 4, 29, 52; WLC 3
See also DA; DAB; DAC; DAM DRAM,
MST; DFS 12; DLB 198; EW 6; EXPS;
RGSF 2; RGWL 2, 3; SSFS 7; TWA
Gogol, Nikolai Vasilyevich
See Gogol, Nikolai
Goines, Donald 1937(?)-1974 .... **BLC 1:2;**
CLC 80
See also AITN 1; BW 1, 3; CA 124; 114;
CANR 82; CMW 4; DA3; DAM MULT,
POP; DLB 33
Gold, Herbert 1924- ... **CLC 4, 7, 14, 42, 152**
See also CA 9-12R; CANR 17, 45, 125,
194; CN 1, 2, 3, 4, 5, 6, 7; DLB 2; DLBY
1981; MAL 5
Goldbarth, Albert 1948- .... **CLC 5, 38**
See also AMWS 12; CA 53-56; CANR 6,
40; CP 3, 4, 5, 6, 7; DLB 120
Goldberg, Anatol 1910-1982 .... **CLC 34**
See also CA 131; 117
Goldemberg, Isaac 1945- .... **CLC 52**
See also CA 69-72; CAAS 12; CANR 11,
32; EWL 3; HW 1; WLIT 1
Golding, Arthur 1536-1606 .... **LC 101**
See also DLB 136
Golding, William 1911-1993 . **CLC 1, 2, 3, 8,**
10, 17, 27, 58, 81; WLC 3
See also AAYA 5, 44; BPFB 2; BRWR 1;
BRWS 1; BYA 2; CA 5-8R; 141; CANR
13, 33, 54; CD 5; CDBLB 1945-1960;
CLR 94, 130; CN 1, 2, 3, 4; DA; DA3;
DAB; DAC; DAM MST, NOV; DLB 15,
100, 255, 326, 330; EWL 3; EXPN; HGG;
LAIT 4; MTCW 1, 2; MTFW 2005; NFS
2; RGEL 2; RHW; SFW 4; TEA; WLIT
4; YAW
Golding, William Gerald
See Golding, William
Goldman, Emma 1869-1940 .... **TCLC 13**
See also CA 110; 150; DLB 221; FW;
RGAL 4; TUS
Goldman, Francisco 1954- .... **CLC 76**
See also CA 162; CANR 185
Goldman, William 1931- .... **CLC 1, 48**
See also BPFB 2; CA 9-12R; CANR 29,
69, 106; CN 1, 2, 3, 4, 5, 6, 7; DLB 44;
FANT; IDFW 3, 4
Goldman, William W.
See Goldman, William
Goldmann, Lucien 1913-1970 .... **CLC 24**
See also CA 25-28; CAP 2
Goldoni, Carlo 1707-1793 .... **LC 4, 152**
See also DAM DRAM; EW 4; RGWL 2, 3;
WLIT 7

Goldsberry, Steven 1949- .... **CLC 34**
See also CA 131
Goldsmith, Oliver 1730(?)-1774 .... **DC 8; LC**
2, 48, 122; PC 77; WLC 3
See also BRW 3; CDBLB 1660-1789; DA;
DAB; DAC; DAM DRAM, MST, NOV,
POET; DFS 1; DLB 39, 89, 104, 109, 142,
336; IDTP; RGEL 2; SATA 26; TEA;
WLIT 3
Goldsmith, Peter
See Priestley, J(ohn) B(oynton)
Goldstein, Rebecca 1950- .... **CLC 239**
See also CA 144; CANR 99, 165; TCLE
1:1
Goldstein, Rebecca Newberger
See Goldstein, Rebecca
Gombrowicz, Witold 1904-1969 .... **CLC 4, 7,**
11, 49
See also CA 19-20; 25-28R; CANR 105;
CAP 2; CDWLB 4; DAM DRAM; DLB
215; EW 12; EWL 3; RGWL 2, 3; TWA
Gomez de Avellaneda, Gertrudis
1814-1873 .... **NCLC 111**
See also LAW
Gomez de la Serna, Ramon
1888-1963 .... **CLC 9**
See also CA 153; 116; CANR 79; EWL 3;
HW 1, 2
Goncharov, Ivan Alexandrovich
1812-1891 .... **NCLC 1, 63**
See also DLB 238; EW 6; RGWL 2, 3
Goncourt, Edmond de 1822-1896 ... **NCLC 7**
See also DLB 123; EW 7; GFL 1789 to the
Present; RGWL 2, 3
Goncourt, Edmond Louis Antoine Huot de
See Goncourt, Edmond de
Goncourt, Jules Alfred Huot de
See Goncourt, Jules de
Goncourt, Jules de 1830-1870 .... **NCLC 7**
See Goncourt, Jules de
See also DLB 123; EW 7; GFL 1789 to the
Present; RGWL 2, 3
Gongora (y Argote), Luis de
1561-1627 .... **LC 72**
See also RGWL 2, 3
Gontier, Fernande 19(?)- .... **CLC 50**
Gonzalez Martinez, Enrique
See Gonzalez Martinez, Enrique
Gonzalez Martinez, Enrique
1871-1952 .... **TCLC 72**
See also CA 166; CANR 81; DLB 290;
EWL 3; HW 1, 2
Goodison, Lorna 1947- .... **BLC 2:2; PC 36**
See also CA 142; CANR 88, 189; CP 5, 6,
7; CWP; DLB 157; EWL 3; PFS 25
Goodman, Allegra 1967- .... **CLC 241**
See also CA 204; CANR 162; DLB 244,
350
Goodman, Paul 1911-1972 ..... **CLC 1, 2, 4, 7**
See also CA 19-20; 37-40R; CAD; CANR
34; CAP 2; CN 1; DLB 130, 246; MAL
5; MTCW 1; RGAL 4
Goodweather, Hartley
See King, Thomas
GoodWeather, Hartley
See King, Thomas
Googe, Barnabe 1540-1594 .... **LC 94**
See also DLB 132; RGEL 2
Gordimer, Nadine 1923- ...... **CLC 3, 5, 7, 10,**
18, 33, 51, 70, 123, 160, 161, 263; SSC
17, 80; WLCS
See also AAYA 39; AFW; BRWS 2; CA
5-8R; CANR 3, 28, 56, 88, 131, 195; CN
1, 2, 3, 4, 5, 6, 7; DA; DA3; DAB; DAC;
DAM MST, NOV; DLB 225, 326, 330;
EWL 3; EXPS; INT CANR-28; LATS 1:2;
MTCW 1, 2; MTFW 2005; NFS 4; RGEL
2; RGSF 2; SSFS 2, 14, 19; TWA; WLIT
2; YAW

Gordon, Adam Lindsay
1833-1870 .... NCLC 21
See also DLB 230

Gordon, Caroline 1895-1981 . CLC 6, 13, 29,
83; SSC 15
See also AMW; CA 11-12; 103; CANR 36;
CAP 1; CN 1, 2; DLB 4, 9, 102; DLBD
17; DLBY 1981; EWL 3; MAL 5; MTCW
1, 2; MTFW 2005; RGAL 4; RGSF 2

Gordon, Charles William
1860-1937 .... TCLC 31
See also CA 109; DLB 92; TCWW 1, 2

Gordon, Mary 1949- .. CLC 13, 22, 128, 216;
SSC 59
See also AMWS 4; BPFB 2; CA 102;
CANR 44, 92, 154, 179; CN 4, 5, 6, 7;
DLB 6; DLBY 1981; FW; INT CA-102;
MAL 5; MTCW 1

Gordon, Mary Catherine
See Gordon, Mary

Gordon, N. J.
See Bosman, Herman Charles

Gordon, Sol 1923- .... CLC 26
See also CA 53-56; CANR 4; SATA 11

Gordone, Charles 1925-1995 .... BLC 2:2;
CLC 1, 4; DC 8
See also BW 1, 3; CA 93-96, 180; 150;
CAAE 180; CAD; CANR 55; DAM
DRAM; DLB 7; INT CA-93-96; MTCW
1

Gore, Catherine 1800-1861 .... NCLC 65
See also DLB 116, 344; RGEL 2

Gorenko, Anna Andreevna
See Akhmatova, Anna

Gor'kii, Maksim
See Gorky, Maxim

Gorky, Maxim 1868-1936 ..... SSC 28; TCLC
8; WLC 3
See also CA 105; 141; CANR 83; DA;
DAB; DAC; DAM DRAM, MST, NOV;
DFS 9; DLB 295; EW 8; EWL 3; MTCW
2; MTFW 2005; RGSF 2; RGWL 2, 3;
TWA

Goryan, Sirak
See Saroyan, William

Gosse, Edmund (William)
1849-1928 .... TCLC 28
See also CA 117; DLB 57, 144, 184; RGEL
2

Gotlieb, Phyllis 1926-2009 .... CLC 18
See also CA 13-16R; CANR 7, 135; CN 7;
CP 1, 2, 3, 4; DLB 88, 251; SFW 4

Gotlieb, Phyllis Fay Bloom
See Gotlieb, Phyllis

Gottesman, S. D.
See Kornbluth, C(yril) M.; Pohl, Frederik

Gottfried von Strassburg fl. c.
1170-1215 .... CMLC 10, 96
See also CDWLB 2; DLB 138; EW 1;
RGWL 2, 3

Gotthelf, Jeremias 1797-1854 .... NCLC 117
See also DLB 133; RGWL 2, 3

Gottschalk, Laura Riding
See Jackson, Laura

Gould, Lois 1932(?)-2002 .... CLC 4, 10
See also CA 77-80; 208; CANR 29; MTCW
1

Gould, Stephen Jay 1941-2002 .... CLC 163
See also AAYA 26; BEST 90:2; CA 77-80;
205; CANR 10, 27, 56, 75, 125; CPW;
INT CANR-27; MTCW 1, 2; MTFW 2005

Gourmont, Remy(-Marie-Charles) de
1858-1915 .... TCLC 17
See also CA 109; 150; GFL 1789 to the
Present; MTCW 2

Gournay, Marie le Jars de
See de Gournay, Marie le Jars

Govier, Katherine 1948- .... CLC 51
See also CA 101; CANR 18, 40, 128; CCA
1

Gower, John c. 1330-1408 .... LC 76; PC 59
See also BRW 1; DLB 146; RGEL 2

Goyen, (Charles) William
1915-1983 .... CLC 5, 8, 14, 40
See also AITN 2; CA 5-8R; 110; CANR 6,
71; CN 1, 2, 3; DLB 2, 218; DLBY 1983;
EWL 3; INT CANR-6; MAL 5

Goytisolo, Juan 1931- .... CLC 5, 10, 23, 133;
HLC 1
See also CA 85-88; CANR 32, 61, 131, 182;
CWW 2; DAM MULT; DLB 322; EWL
3; GLL 2; HW 1, 2; MTCW 1, 2; MTFW
2005

Gozzano, Guido 1883-1916 .... PC 10
See also CA 154; DLB 114; EWL 3

Gozzi, (Conte) Carlo 1720-1806 .... NCLC 23

Grabbe, Christian Dietrich
1801-1836 .... NCLC 2
See also DLB 133; RGWL 2, 3

Grace, Patricia 1937- .... CLC 56
See also CA 176; CANR 118; CN 4, 5, 6,
7; EWL 3; RGSF 2

Grace, Patricia Frances
See Grace, Patricia

Gracian, Baltasar 1601-1658 .... LC 15, 160

Gracian y Morales, Baltasar
See Gracian, Baltasar

Gracq, Julien 1910-2007 ..... CLC 11, 48, 259
See also CA 122; 126; 267; CANR 141;
CWW 2; DLB 83; GFL 1789 to the
present

Grade, Chaim 1910-1982 .... CLC 10
See also CA 93-96; 107; DLB 333; EWL 3;
RGHL

Grade, Khayim
See Grade, Chaim

Graduate of Oxford, A
See Ruskin, John

Grafton, Garth
See Duncan, Sara Jeannette

Grafton, Sue 1940- .... CLC 163
See also AAYA 11, 49; BEST 90:3; CA 108;
CANR 31, 55, 111, 134, 195; CMW 4;
CPW; CSW; DA3; DAM POP; DLB 226;
FW; MSW; MTFW 2005

Graham, John
See Phillips, David Graham

Graham, Jorie 1950- .... CLC 48, 118; PC 59
See also AAYA 67; CA 111; CANR 63, 118;
CP 4, 5, 6, 7; CWP; DLB 120; EWL 3;
MTFW 2005; PFS 10, 17; TCLE 1:1

Graham, R. B. Cunninghame
See Cunninghame Graham, Robert Bontine

Graham, Robert
See Haldeman, Joe

Graham, Robert Bontine Cunninghame
See Cunninghame Graham, Robert Bontine

Graham, Tom
See Lewis, Sinclair

Graham, W(illiam) S(ydney)
1918-1986 .... CLC 29
See also BRWS 7; CA 73-76; 118; CP 1, 2,
3, 4; DLB 20; RGEL 2

Graham, Winston (Mawdsley)
1910-2003 .... CLC 23
See also CA 49-52; 218; CANR 2, 22, 45,
66; CMW 4; CN 1, 2, 3, 4, 5, 6, 7; DLB
77; RHW

Grahame, Kenneth 1859-1932 ...... TCLC 64,
136
See also BYA 5; CA 108; 136; CANR 80;
CLR 5, 135; CWRI 5; DA3; DAB; DLB
34, 141, 178; FANT; MAICYA 1, 2;
MTCW 2; NFS 20; RGEL 2; SATA 100;
TEA; WCH; YABC 1

Granger, Darius John
See Marlowe, Stephen

Granin, Daniil 1918- .... CLC 59
See also DLB 302

Granovsky, Timofei Nikolaevich
1813-1855 .... NCLC 75
See also DLB 198

Grant, Skeeter
See Spiegelman, Art

Granville-Barker, Harley
1877-1946 .... TCLC 2
See also CA 104; 204; DAM DRAM; DLB
10; RGEL 2

Granzotto, Gianni
See Granzotto, Giovanni Battista

Granzotto, Giovanni Battista
1914-1985 .... CLC 70
See also CA 166

Grasemann, Ruth Barbara
See Rendell, Ruth

Grass, Guenter
See Grass, Gunter

Grass, Gunter 1927- .. CLC 1, 2, 4, 6, 11, 15,
22, 32, 49, 88, 207; WLC 3
See also BPFB 2; CA 13-16R; CANR 20,
75, 93, 133, 174; CDWLB 2; CWW 2;
DA; DA3; DAB; DAC; DAM MST, NOV;
DLB 330; EW 13; EWL 3; MTCW 1, 2;
MTFW 2005; RGHL; RGWL 2, 3; TWA

Grass, Gunter Wilhelm
See Grass, Gunter

Gratton, Thomas
See Hulme, T(homas) E(rnest)

Grau, Shirley Ann 1929- .... CLC 4, 9, 146;
SSC 15
See also CA 89-92; CANR 22, 69; CN 1, 2,
3, 4, 5, 6, 7; CSW; DLB 2, 218; INT CA-
89-92; CANR-22; MTCW 1

Gravel, Fern
See Hall, James Norman

Graver, Elizabeth 1964- .... CLC 70
See also CA 135; CANR 71, 129

Graves, Richard Perceval
1895-1985 .... CLC 44
See also CA 65-68; CANR 9, 26, 51

Graves, Robert 1895-1985 ... CLC 1, 2, 6, 11,
39, 44, 45; PC 6
See also BPFB 2; BRW 7; BYA 4; CA 5-8R;
117; CANR 5, 36; CDBLB 1914-1945;
CN 1, 2, 3; CP 1, 2, 3, 4; DA3; DAB;
DAC; DAM MST, POET; DLB 20, 100,
191; DLBD 18; DLBY 1985; EWL 3;
LATS 1:1; MTCW 1, 2; MTFW 2005;
NCFS 2; NFS 21; RGEL 2; RHW; SATA
45; TEA

Graves, Robert von Ranke
See Graves, Robert

Graves, Valerie
See Bradley, Marion Zimmer

Gray, Alasdair 1934- .... CLC 41, 275
See also BRWS 9; CA 126; CANR 47, 69,
106, 140; CN 4, 5, 6, 7; DLB 194, 261,
319; HGG; INT CA-126; MTCW 1, 2;
MTFW 2005; RGSF 2; SUFW 2

Gray, Amlin 1946- .... CLC 29
See also CA 138

Gray, Francine du Plessix 1930- ..... CLC 22,
153
See also BEST 90:3; CA 61-64; CAAS 2;
CANR 11, 33, 75, 81, 197; DAM NOV;
INT CANR-11; MTCW 1, 2; MTFW 2005

Gray, John (Henry) 1866-1934 ...... TCLC 19
See also CA 119; 162; RGEL 2

Gray, John Lee
See Jakes, John

Gray, Simon 1936-2008 .... CLC 9, 14, 36
See also AITN 1; CA 21-24R; 275; CAAS
3; CANR 32, 69; CBD; CD 5, 6; CN 1, 2,
3; DLB 13; EWL 3; MTCW 1; RGEL 2

Gray, Simon James Holliday
See Gray, Simon
Gray, Spalding 1941-2004 .... **CLC 49, 112;
DC 7**
See also AAYA 62; CA 128; 225; CAD;
CANR 74, 138; CD 5, 6; CPW; DAM
POP; MTCW 2; MTFW 2005
Gray, Thomas 1716-1771 . **LC 4, 40, 178; PC
2, 80; WLC 3**
See also BRW 3; CDBLB 1660-1789; DA;
DA3; DAB; DAC; DAM MST; DLB 109;
EXPP; PAB; PFS 9; RGEL 2; TEA; WP
Grayson, David
See Baker, Ray Stannard
Grayson, Richard (A.) 1951- .... **CLC 38**
See also CA 85-88, 210; CAAE 210; CANR
14, 31, 57; DLB 234
Greeley, Andrew M. 1928- .... **CLC 28**
See also BPFB 2; CA 5-8R; CAAS 7;
CANR 7, 43, 69, 104, 136, 184; CMW 4;
CPW; DA3; DAM POP; MTCW 1, 2;
MTFW 2005
Green, Anna Katharine
1846-1935 .... **TCLC 63**
See also CA 112; 159; CMW 4; DLB 202,
221; MSW
Green, Brian
See Card, Orson Scott
Green, Hannah
See Greenberg, Joanne (Goldenberg)
Green, Hannah 1927(?)-1996 .... **CLC 3**
See also CA 73-76; CANR 59, 93; NFS 10
Green, Henry
See Yorke, Henry Vincent
Green, Julian
See Green, Julien
Green, Julien 1900-1998 .... **CLC 3, 11, 77**
See also CA 21-24R; 169; CANR 33, 87;
CWW 2; DLB 4, 72; EWL 3; GFL 1789
to the Present; MTCW 2; MTFW 2005
Green, Julien Hartridge
See Green, Julien
Green, Paul (Eliot) 1894-1981 .. **CLC 25; DC
37**
See also AITN 1; CA 5-8R; 103; CAD;
CANR 3; DAM DRAM; DLB 7, 9, 249;
DLBY 1981; MAL 5; RGAL 4
Greenaway, Peter 1942- .... **CLC 159**
See also CA 127
Greenberg, Ivan 1908-1973 .... **CLC 24**
See also CA 85-88; DLB 137; MAL 5
Greenberg, Joanne (Goldenberg)
1932- .... **CLC 7, 30**
See also AAYA 12, 67; CA 5-8R; CANR
14, 32, 69; CN 6, 7; DLB 335; NFS 23;
SATA 25; YAW
Greenberg, Richard 1959(?)- .... **CLC 57**
See also CA 138; CAD; CD 5, 6; DFS 24
Greenblatt, Stephen J(ay) 1943- ...... **CLC 70**
See also CA 49-52; CANR 115; LNFS 1
Greene, Bette 1934- .... **CLC 30**
See also AAYA 7, 69; BYA 3; CA 53-56;
CANR 4, 146; CLR 2, 140; CWRI 5;
JRDA; LAIT 4; MAICYA 1, 2; NFS 10;
SAAS 16; SATA 8, 102, 161; WYA; YAW
Greene, Gael **CLC 8**
See also CA 13-16R; CANR 10, 166
Greene, Graham 1904-1991 .. **CLC 1, 3, 6, 9,
14, 18, 27, 37, 70, 72, 125; SSC 29, 121;
WLC 3**
See also AAYA 61; AITN 2; BPFB 2;
BRWR 2; BRWS 7; BYA 3; CA 13-16R;
133; CANR 35, 61, 131; CBD; CDBLB
1945-1960; CMW 4; CN 1, 2, 3, 4; DA;
DA3; DAB; DAC; DAM MST, NOV;
DLB 13, 15, 77, 100, 162, 201, 204;
DLBY 1991; EWL 3; MSW; MTCW 1, 2;
MTFW 2005; NFS 16; RGEL 2; SATA
20; SSFS 14; TEA; WLIT 4

Greene, Graham Henry
See Greene, Graham
Greene, Robert 1558-1592 .... **LC 41**
See also BRWS 8; DLB 62, 167; IDTP;
RGEL 2; TEA
Greer, Germaine 1939- .... **CLC 131**
See also AITN 1; CA 81-84; CANR 33, 70,
115, 133, 190; FW; MTCW 1, 2; MTFW
2005
Greer, Richard
See Silverberg, Robert
Gregor, Arthur 1923- .... **CLC 9**
See also CA 25-28R; CAAS 10; CANR 11;
CP 1, 2, 3, 4, 5, 6, 7; SATA 36
Gregor, Lee
See Pohl, Frederik
Gregory, Lady Isabella Augusta (Persse)
1852-1932 .... **TCLC 1, 176**
See also BRW 6; CA 104; 184; DLB 10;
IDTP; RGEL 2
Gregory, J. Dennis
See Williams, John A(lfred)
Gregory of Nazianzus, St.
329-389 .... **CMLC 82**
Gregory of Nyssa c. 335-c. 394 ... **CMLC 118**
Gregory of Rimini 1300(?)-1358 . **CMLC 109**
See also DLB 115
Grekova, I.
See Ventsel, Elena Sergeevna
Grekova, Irina
See Ventsel, Elena Sergeevna
Grendon, Stephen
See Derleth, August (William)
Grenville, Kate 1950- .... **CLC 61**
See also CA 118; CANR 53, 93, 156; CN
7; DLB 325
Grenville, Pelham
See Wodehouse, P. G.
Greve, Felix Paul (Berthold Friedrich)
1879-1948 .... **TCLC 4**
See also CA 104; 141, 175; CANR 79;
DAC; DAM MST; DLB 92; RGEL 2;
TCWW 1, 2
Greville, Fulke 1554-1628 .... **LC 79**
See also BRWS 11; DLB 62, 172; RGEL 2
Grey, Lady Jane 1537-1554 .... **LC 93**
See also DLB 132
Grey, Zane 1872-1939 .... **TCLC 6**
See also BPFB 2; CA 104; 132; DA3; DAM
POP; DLB 9, 212; MTCW 1, 2; MTFW
2005; RGAL 4; TCWW 1, 2; TUS
Griboedov, Aleksandr Sergeevich
1795(?)-1829 .... **NCLC 129**
See also DLB 205; RGWL 2, 3
Grieg, (Johan) Nordahl (Brun)
1902-1943 .... **TCLC 10**
See also CA 107; 189; EWL 3
Grieve, C. M. 1892-1978 ... **CLC 2, 4, 11, 19,
63; PC 9**
See also BRWS 12; CA 5-8R; 85-88; CANR
33, 107; CDBLB 1945-1960; CP 1, 2;
DAM POET; DLB 20; EWL 3; MTCW 1;
RGEL 2
Grieve, Christopher Murray
See Grieve, C. M.
Griffin, Gerald 1803-1840 .... **NCLC 7**
See also DLB 159; RGEL 2
Griffin, John Howard 1920-1980 ..... **CLC 68**
See also AITN 1; CA 1-4R; 101; CANR 2
Griffin, Peter 1942- .... **CLC 39**
See also CA 136
Griffith, David Lewelyn Wark
See Griffith, D.W.
Griffith, D.W. 1875(?)-1948 .... **TCLC 68**
See also AAYA 78; CA 119; 150; CANR 80
Griffith, Lawrence
See Griffith, D.W.

Griffiths, Trevor 1935- .... **CLC 13, 52**
See also CA 97-100; CANR 45; CBD; CD
5, 6; DLB 13, 245
Griggs, Sutton (Elbert)
1872-1930 .... **TCLC 77**
See also CA 123; 186; DLB 50
Grigson, Geoffrey (Edward Harvey)
1905-1985 .... **CLC 7, 39**
See also CA 25-28R; 118; CANR 20, 33;
CP 1, 2, 3, 4; DLB 27; MTCW 1, 2
Grile, Dod
See Bierce, Ambrose
Grillparzer, Franz 1791-1872 .... **DC 14;
NCLC 1, 102; SSC 37**
See also CDWLB 2; DLB 133; EW 5;
RGWL 2, 3; TWA
Grimble, Reverend Charles James
See Eliot, T. S.
Grimke, Angelina Emily Weld
See Grimke, Angelina Weld
Grimke, Angelina Weld 1880-1958 ... **DC 38;
HR 1:2**
See also BW 1; CA 124; DAM POET; DLB
50, 54; FW
Grimke, Charlotte L. Forten
1837(?)-1914 .... **BLC 1:2; TCLC 16**
See also BW 1; CA 117; 124; DAM MULT,
POET; DLB 50, 239
Grimke, Charlotte Lottie Forten
See Grimke, Charlotte L. Forten
Grimm, Jacob Ludwig Karl
1785-1863 .... **NCLC 3, 77; SSC 36, 88**
See also CLR 112; DLB 90; MAICYA 1, 2;
RGSF 2; RGWL 2, 3; SATA 22; WCH
Grimm, Wilhelm Karl 1786-1859 .. **NCLC 3,
77; SSC 36**
See also CDWLB 2; CLR 112; DLB 90;
MAICYA 1, 2; RGSF 2; RGWL 2, 3;
SATA 22; WCH
Grimm and Grim
See Grimm, Jacob Ludwig Karl; Grimm,
Wilhelm Karl
Grimm Brothers
See Grimm, Jacob Ludwig Karl; Grimm,
Wilhelm Karl
**Grimmelshausen, Hans Jakob Christoffel
von**
See Grimmelshausen, Johann Jakob Christ-
offel von
**Grimmelshausen, Johann Jakob Christoffel
von** 1621-1676 .... **LC 6**
See also CDWLB 2; DLB 168; RGWL 2, 3
Grindel, Eugene 1895-1952 .... **PC 38; TCLC
7, 41**
See also CA 104; 193; EWL 3; GFL 1789
to the Present; LMFS 2; RGWL 2, 3
Grisham, John 1955- .... **CLC 84, 273**
See also AAYA 14, 47; BPFB 2; CA 138;
CANR 47, 69, 114, 133; CMW 4; CN 6,
7; CPW; CSW; DA3; DAM POP; LNFS
1; MSW; MTCW 2; MTFW 2005
Grosseteste, Robert 1175(?)-1253 . **CMLC 62**
See also DLB 115
Grossman, David 1954- .... **CLC 67, 231**
See also CA 138; CANR 114, 175; CWW
2; DLB 299; EWL 3; RGHL; WLIT 6
Grossman, Vasilii Semenovich
See Grossman, Vasily (Semenovich)
Grossman, Vasily (Semenovich)
1905-1964 .... **CLC 41**
See also CA 124; 130; DLB 272; MTCW 1;
RGHL
Grove, Frederick Philip
See Greve, Felix Paul (Berthold Friedrich)
Grubb
See Crumb, R.

Grumbach, Doris 1918- .... **CLC 13, 22, 64**
See also CA 5-8R; CAAS 2; CANR 9, 42, 70, 127; CN 6, 7; INT CANR-9; MTCW 2; MTFW 2005

Grundtvig, Nikolai Frederik Severin 1783-1872 .... **NCLC 1, 158**
See also DLB 300

Grunge
See Crumb, R.

Grunwald, Lisa 1959- .... **CLC 44**
See also CA 120; CANR 148

Gryphius, Andreas 1616-1664 .... **LC 89**
See also CDWLB 2; DLB 164; RGWL 2, 3

Guare, John 1938- .... **CLC 8, 14, 29, 67; DC 20**
See also CA 73-76; CAD; CANR 21, 69, 118; CD 5, 6; DAM DRAM; DFS 8, 13; DLB 7, 249; EWL 3; MAL 5; MTCW 1, 2; RGAL 4

Guarini, Battista 1538-1612 .... **LC 102**
See also DLB 339

Gubar, Susan 1944- .... **CLC 145**
See also CA 108; CANR 45, 70, 139, 179; FW; MTCW 1; RGAL 4

Gubar, Susan David
See Gubar, Susan

Gudjonsson, Halldor Kiljan 1902-1998 .... **CLC 25**
See also CA 103; 164; CWW 2; DLB 293, 331; EW 12; EWL 3; RGWL 2, 3

Guedes, Vincente
See Pessoa, Fernando

Guenter, Erich
See Eich, Gunter

Guest, Barbara 1920-2006 ... **CLC 34; PC 55**
See also BG 1:2; CA 25-28R; 248; CANR 11, 44, 84; CP 1, 2, 3, 4, 5, 6, 7; CWP; DLB 5, 193

Guest, Edgar A(lbert) 1881-1959 ... **TCLC 95**
See also CA 112; 168

Guest, Judith 1936- .... **CLC 8, 30**
See also AAYA 7, 66; CA 77-80; CANR 15, 75, 138; DA3; DAM NOV, POP; EXPN; INT CANR-15; LAIT 5; MTCW 1, 2; MTFW 2005; NFS 1

Guest, Judith Ann
See Guest, Judith

Guevara, Che
See Guevara (Serna), Ernesto

Guevara (Serna), Ernesto 1928-1967 .... **CLC 87; HLC 1**
See also CA 127; 111; CANR 56; DAM MULT; HW 1

Guicciardini, Francesco 1483-1540 ..... **LC 49**

Guido delle Colonne c. 1215-c. 1290 .... **CMLC 90**

Guild, Nicholas M. 1944- .... **CLC 33**
See also CA 93-96

Guillemin, Jacques
See Sartre, Jean-Paul

Guillen, Jorge 1893-1984 . **CLC 11; HLCS 1; PC 35; TCLC 233**
See also CA 89-92; 112; DAM MULT, POET; DLB 108; EWL 3; HW 1; RGWL 2, 3

Guillen, Nicolas 1902-1989 ... **BLC 1:2; CLC 48, 79; HLC 1; PC 23**
See also BW 2; CA 116; 125; 129; CANR 84; DAM MST, MULT, POET; DLB 283; EWL 3; HW 1; LAW; RGWL 2, 3; WP

Guillen, Nicolas Cristobal
See Guillen, Nicolas

Guillen y Alvarez, Jorge
See Guillen, Jorge

Guillevic, (Eugene) 1907-1997 .... **CLC 33**
See also CA 93-96; CWW 2

Guillois
See Desnos, Robert

Guillois, Valentin
See Desnos, Robert

Guimaraes Rosa, Joao 1908-1967 ... **CLC 23; HLCS 1**
See also CA 175; 89-92; DLB 113, 307; EWL 3; LAW; RGSF 2; RGWL 2, 3; WLIT 1

Guiney, Louise Imogen 1861-1920 .... **TCLC 41**
See also CA 160; DLB 54; RGAL 4

Guinizelli, Guido c. 1230-1276 ...... **CMLC 49**
See also WLIT 7

Guinizzelli, Guido
See Guinizelli, Guido

Guiraldes, Ricardo (Guillermo) 1886-1927 .... **TCLC 39**
See also CA 131; EWL 3; HW 1; LAW; MTCW 1

Guma, Alex La
See La Guma, Alex

Gumilev, Nikolai (Stepanovich) 1886-1921 .... **TCLC 60**
See also CA 165; DLB 295; EWL 3

Gumilyov, Nikolay Stepanovich
See Gumilev, Nikolai (Stepanovich)

Gump, P. Q.
See Card, Orson Scott

Gump, P.Q.
See Card, Orson Scott

Gunesekera, Romesh 1954- .... **CLC 91**
See also BRWS 10; CA 159; CANR 140, 172; CN 6, 7; DLB 267, 323

Gunn, Bill
See Gunn, William Harrison

Gunn, Thom 1929-2004 ..... **CLC 3, 6, 18, 32, 81; PC 26**
See also BRWR 3; BRWS 4; CA 17-20R; 227; CANR 9, 33, 116; CDBLB 1960 to Present; CP 1, 2, 3, 4, 5, 6, 7; DAM POET; DLB 27; INT CANR-33; MTCW 1; PFS 9; RGEL 2

Gunn, William Harrison 1934(?)-1989 .... **CLC 5**
See also AITN 1; BW 1, 3; CA 13-16R; 128; CANR 12, 25, 76; DLB 38

Gunn Allen, Paula
See Allen, Paula Gunn

Gunnars, Kristjana 1948- .... **CLC 69**
See also CA 113; CCA 1; CP 6, 7; CWP; DLB 60

Gunter, Erich
See Eich, Gunter

Gurdjieff, G(eorgei) I(vanovich) 1877(?)-1949 .... **TCLC 71**
See also CA 157

Gurganus, Allan 1947- .... **CLC 70**
See also BEST 90:1; CA 135; CANR 114; CN 6, 7; CPW; CSW; DAM POP; DLB 350; GLL 1

Gurney, A. R.
See Gurney, A(lbert) R(amsdell), Jr.

Gurney, A(lbert) R(amsdell), Jr. 1930- .... **CLC 32, 50, 54**
See also AMWS 5; CA 77-80; CAD; CANR 32, 64, 121; CD 5, 6; DAM DRAM; DLB 266; EWL 3

Gurney, Ivor (Bertie) 1890-1937 ... **TCLC 33**
See also BRW 6; CA 167; DLBY 2002; PAB; RGEL 2

Gurney, Peter
See Gurney, A(lbert) R(amsdell), Jr.

Guro, Elena (Genrikhovna) 1877-1913 .... **TCLC 56**
See also DLB 295

Gustafson, James M(oody) 1925- ... **CLC 100**
See also CA 25-28R; CANR 37

Gustafson, Ralph (Barker) 1909-1995 .... **CLC 36**
See also CA 21-24R; CANR 8, 45, 84; CP 1, 2, 3, 4, 5, 6; DLB 88; RGEL 2

Gut, Gom
See Simenon, Georges

Guterson, David 1956- .... **CLC 91**
See also CA 132; CANR 73, 126, 194; CN 7; DLB 292; MTCW 2; MTFW 2005; NFS 13

Guthrie, A(lfred) B(ertram), Jr. 1901-1991 .... **CLC 23**
See also CA 57-60; 134; CANR 24; CN 1, 2, 3; DLB 6, 212; MAL 5; SATA 62; SATA-Obit 67; TCWW 1, 2

Guthrie, Isobel
See Grieve, C. M.

Gutierrez Najera, Manuel 1859-1895 .... **HLCS 2; NCLC 133**
See also DLB 290; LAW

Guy, Rosa (Cuthbert) 1925- .... **CLC 26**
See also AAYA 4, 37; BW 2; CA 17-20R; CANR 14, 34, 83; CLR 13, 137; DLB 33; DNFS 1; JRDA; MAICYA 1, 2; SATA 14, 62, 122; YAW

Gwendolyn
See Bennett, (Enoch) Arnold

H. D.
See Doolittle, Hilda

H. de V.
See Buchan, John

Haavikko, Paavo Juhani 1931- .. **CLC 18, 34**
See also CA 106; CWW 2; EWL 3

Habbema, Koos
See Heijermans, Herman

Habermas, Juergen 1929- .... **CLC 104**
See also CA 109; CANR 85, 162; DLB 242

Habermas, Jurgen
See Habermas, Juergen

Hacker, Marilyn 1942- ...... **CLC 5, 9, 23, 72, 91; PC 47**
See also CA 77-80; CANR 68, 129; CP 3, 4, 5, 6, 7; CWP; DAM POET; DLB 120, 282; FW; GLL 2; MAL 5; PFS 19

Hadewijch of Antwerp fl. 1250- ... **CMLC 61**
See also RGWL 3

Hadrian 76-138 .... **CMLC 52**

Haeckel, Ernst Heinrich (Philipp August) 1834-1919 .... **TCLC 83**
See also CA 157

Hafiz c. 1326-1389(?) .... **CMLC 34**
See also RGWL 2, 3; WLIT 6

Hagedorn, Jessica T(arahata) 1949- .... **CLC 185**
See also CA 139; CANR 69; CWP; DLB 312; RGAL 4

Haggard, H(enry) Rider 1856-1925 .... **TCLC 11**
See also AAYA 81; BRWS 3; BYA 4, 5; CA 108; 148; CANR 112; DLB 70, 156, 174, 178; FANT; LMFS 1; MTCW 2; RGEL 2; RHW; SATA 16; SCFW 1, 2; SFW 4; SUFW 1; WLIT 4

Hagiosy, L.
See Larbaud, Valery (Nicolas)

Hagiwara, Sakutaro 1886-1942 .... **PC 18; TCLC 60**
See also CA 154; EWL 3; RGWL 3

Hagiwara Sakutaro
See Hagiwara, Sakutaro

Haig, Fenil
See Ford, Ford Madox

Haig-Brown, Roderick (Langmere) 1908-1976 .... **CLC 21**
See also CA 5-8R; 69-72; CANR 4, 38, 83; CLR 31; CWRI 5; DLB 88; MAICYA 1, 2; SATA 12; TCWW 2

Haight, Rip
See Carpenter, John

Hargrave, Leonie
See Disch, Thomas M.
Hariri, Al- al-Qasim ibn 'Ali Abu
Muhammad al-Basri
See al-Hariri, al-Qasim ibn 'Ali Abu Mu-
hammad al-Basri
Harjo, Joy 1951- ..... **CLC 83; NNAL; PC 27**
See also AMWS 12; CA 114; CANR 35,
67, 91, 129; CP 6, 7; CWP; DAM MULT;
DLB 120, 175, 342; EWL 3; MTCW 2;
MTFW 2005; PFS 15; RGAL 4
Harlan, Louis R. 1922-2010 .... **CLC 34**
See also CA 21-24R; CANR 25, 55, 80
Harlan, Louis Rudolph
See Harlan, Louis R.
Harling, Robert 1951(?)- .... **CLC 53**
See also CA 147
Harmon, William (Ruth) 1938- .... **CLC 38**
See also CA 33-36R; CANR 14, 32, 35;
SATA 65
Harper, F. E. W.
See Harper, Frances Ellen Watkins
Harper, Frances E. W.
See Harper, Frances Ellen Watkins
Harper, Frances E. Watkins
See Harper, Frances Ellen Watkins
Harper, Frances Ellen
See Harper, Frances Ellen Watkins
Harper, Frances Ellen Watkins
1825-1911 . **BLC 1:2; PC 21; TCLC 14,**
217
See also AFAW 1, 2; BW 1, 3; CA 111; 125;
CANR 79; DAM MULT, POET; DLB 50,
221; MBL; RGAL 4
Harper, Michael S(teven) 1938- ..... **BLC 2:2;**
CLC 7, 22
See also AFAW 2; BW 1; CA 33-36R, 224;
CAAE 224; CANR 24, 108; CP 2, 3, 4, 5,
6, 7; DLB 41; RGAL 4; TCLE 1:1
Harper, Mrs. F. E. W.
See Harper, Frances Ellen Watkins
Harpur, Charles 1813-1868 .... **NCLC 114**
See also DLB 230; RGEL 2
Harris, Christie
See Harris, Christie (Lucy) Irwin
Harris, Christie (Lucy) Irwin
1907-2002 .... **CLC 12**
See also CA 5-8R; CANR 6, 83; CLR 47;
DLB 88; JRDA; MAICYA 1, 2; SAAS 10;
SATA 6, 74; SATA-Essay 116
Harris, Frank 1856-1931 .... **TCLC 24**
See also CA 109; 150; CANR 80; DLB 156,
197; RGEL 2
Harris, George Washington
1814-1869 .... **NCLC 23, 165**
See also DLB 3, 11, 248; RGAL 4
Harris, Joel Chandler 1848-1908 ..... **SSC 19,**
103; TCLC 2
See also CA 104; 137; CANR 80; CLR 49,
128; DLB 11, 23, 42, 78, 91; LAIT 2;
MAICYA 1, 2; RGSF 2; SATA 100; WCH;
YABC 1
Harris, John (Wyndham Parkes Lucas)
Beynon 1903-1969 .... **CLC 19**
See also BRWS 13; CA 102; 89-92; CANR
84; DLB 255; SATA 118; SCFW 1, 2;
SFW 4
Harris, MacDonald
See Heiney, Donald (William)
Harris, Mark 1922-2007 .... **CLC 19**
See also CA 5-8R; 260; CAAS 3; CANR 2,
55, 83; CN 1, 2, 3, 4, 5, 6, 7; DLB 2;
DLBY 1980
Harris, Norman CLC 65
Harris, (Theodore) Wilson 1921- ... **BLC 2:2;**
CLC 25, 159
See also BRWS 5; BW 2, 3; CA 65-68;
CAAS 16; CANR 11, 27, 69, 114; CD-
WLB 3; CN 1, 2, 3, 4, 5, 6, 7; CP 1, 2, 3,
4, 5, 6, 7; DLB 117; EWL 3; MTCW 1;
RGEL 2

Harrison, Barbara Grizzuti
1934-2002 .... **CLC 144**
See also CA 77-80; 205; CANR 15, 48; INT
CANR-15
Harrison, Elizabeth (Allen) Cavanna
1909-2001 .... **CLC 12**
See also CA 9-12R; 200; CANR 6, 27, 85,
104, 121; JRDA; MAICYA 1; SAAS 4;
SATA 1, 30; YAW
Harrison, Harry 1925- .... **CLC 42**
See also CA 1-4R; CANR 5, 21, 84; DLB
8; SATA 4; SCFW 2; SFW 4
Harrison, Harry Max
See Harrison, Harry
Harrison, James
See Harrison, Jim
Harrison, James Thomas
See Harrison, Jim
Harrison, Jim 1937- .... **CLC 6, 14, 33, 66,**
143; SSC 19
See also AMWS 8; CA 13-16R; CANR 8,
51, 79, 142, 198; CN 5, 6; CP 1, 2, 3, 4,
5, 6; DLBY 1982; INT CANR-8; RGAL
4; TCWW 2; TUS
Harrison, Kathryn 1961- .... **CLC 70, 151**
See also CA 144; CANR 68, 122, 194
Harrison, Tony 1937- .... **CLC 43, 129**
See also BRWS 5; CA 65-68; CANR 44,
98; CBD; CD 5, 6; CP 2, 3, 4, 5, 6, 7;
DLB 40, 245; MTCW 1; RGEL 2
Harriss, Will(ard Irvin) 1922- .... **CLC 34**
See also CA 111
Hart, Ellis
See Ellison, Harlan
Hart, Josephine 1942(?)- .... **CLC 70**
See also CA 138; CANR 70, 149; CPW;
DAM POP
Hart, Moss 1904-1961 .... **CLC 66**
See also CA 109; 89-92; CANR 84; DAM
DRAM; DFS 1; DLB 7, 266; RGAL 4
Harte, Bret 1836(?)-1902 .. **SSC 8, 59; TCLC**
1, 25; WLC 3
See also AMWS 2; CA 104; 140; CANR
80; CDALB 1865-1917; DA; DA3; DAC;
DAM MST; DLB 12, 64, 74, 79, 186;
EXPS; LAIT 2; RGAL 4; RGSF 2; SATA
26; SSFS 3; TUS
Harte, Francis Brett
See Harte, Bret
Hartley, L(eslie) P(oles) 1895-1972 ... **CLC 2,**
22; SSC 125
See also BRWS 7; CA 45-48; 37-40R;
CANR 33; CN 1; DLB 15, 139; EWL 3;
HGG; MTCW 1, 2; MTFW 2005; RGEL
2; RGSF 2; SUFW 1
Hartman, Geoffrey H. 1929- .... **CLC 27**
See also CA 117; 125; CANR 79; DLB 67
Hartmann, Sadakichi 1869-1944 ... **TCLC 73**
See also CA 157; DLB 54
Hartmann von Aue c. 1170-c.
1210 .... **CMLC 15**
See also CDWLB 2; DLB 138; RGWL 2, 3
Hartog, Jan de
See de Hartog, Jan
Haruf, Kent 1943- .... **CLC 34**
See also AAYA 44; CA 149; CANR 91, 131
Harvey, Caroline
See Trollope, Joanna
Harvey, Gabriel 1550(?)-1631 .... **LC 88**
See also DLB 167, 213, 281
Harvey, Jack
See Rankin, Ian
Harwood, Ronald 1934- .... **CLC 32**
See also CA 1-4R; CANR 4, 55, 150; CBD;
CD 5, 6; DAM DRAM, MST; DLB 13
Hasegawa Tatsunosuke
See Futabatei, Shimei

Hasek, Jaroslav 1883-1923 ... **SSC 69; TCLC**
4
See also CA 104; 129; CDWLB 4; DLB
215; EW 9; EWL 3; MTCW 1, 2; RGSF
2; RGWL 2, 3
Hasek, Jaroslav Matej Frantisek
See Hasek, Jaroslav
Hass, Robert 1941- ...... **CLC 18, 39, 99, 287;**
PC 16
See also AMWS 6; CA 111; CANR 30, 50,
71, 187; CP 3, 4, 5, 6, 7; DLB 105, 206;
EWL 3; MAL 5; MTFW 2005; RGAL 4;
SATA 94; TCLE 1:1
Hassler, Jon 1933-2008 .... **CLC 263**
See also CA 73-76; 270; CANR 21, 80, 161;
CN 6, 7; INT CANR-21; SATA 19; SATA-
Obit 191
Hassler, Jon Francis
See Hassler, Jon
Hastings, Hudson
See Kuttner, Henry
Hastings, Selina CLC 44
See also CA 257
Hastings, Selina Shirley
See Hastings, Selina
Hastings, Victor
See Disch, Thomas M.
Hathorne, John 1641-1717 .... **LC 38**
Hatteras, Amelia
See Mencken, H. L.
Hatteras, Owen
See Mencken, H. L.; Nathan, George Jean
Hauff, Wilhelm 1802-1827 .... **NCLC 185**
See also DLB 90; SUFW 1
Hauptmann, Gerhart 1862-1946 .... **DC 34;**
SSC 37; TCLC 4
See also CA 104; 153; CDWLB 2; DAM
DRAM; DLB 66, 118, 330; EW 8; EWL
3; RGSF 2; RGWL 2, 3; TWA
Hauptmann, Gerhart Johann Robert
See Hauptmann, Gerhart
Havel, Vaclav 1936- ..... **CLC 25, 58, 65, 123;**
DC 6
See also CA 104; CANR 36, 63, 124, 175;
CDWLB 4; CWW 2; DA3; DAM DRAM;
DFS 10; DLB 232; EWL 3; LMFS 2;
MTCW 1, 2; MTFW 2005; RGWL 3
Haviaras, Stratis
See Chaviaras, Strates
Hawes, Stephen 1475(?)-1529(?) .... **LC 17**
See also DLB 132; RGEL 2
Hawkes, John 1925-1998 .. **CLC 1, 2, 3, 4, 7,**
9, 14, 15, 27, 49
See also BPFB 2; CA 1-4R; 167; CANR
47, 64; CN 1, 2, 3, 4, 5, 6; DLB 2, 7, 227;
DLBY 1980, 1998; EWL 3; MAL 5;
MTCW 1, 2; MTFW 2005; RGAL 4
Hawking, S. W.
See Hawking, Stephen W.
Hawking, Stephen W. 1942- ..... **CLC 63, 105**
See also AAYA 13; BEST 89:1; CA 126;
129; CANR 48, 115; CPW; DA3; MTCW
2; MTFW 2005
Hawking, Stephen William
See Hawking, Stephen W.
Hawkins, Anthony Hope
See Hope, Anthony
Hawthorne, Julian 1846-1934 .... **TCLC 25**
See also CA 165; HGG
Hawthorne, Nathaniel 1804-1864 ... **NCLC 2,**
10, 17, 23, 39, 79, 95, 158, 171, 191,
226; SSC 3, 29, 39, 89, 130; WLC 3
See also AAYA 18; AMW; AMWC 1;
AMWR 1; BPFB 2; BYA 3; CDALB
1640-1865; CLR 103; DA; DA3; DAB;
DAC; DAM MST, NOV; DLB 1, 74, 183,

223, 269; EXPN; EXPS; GL 2; HGG;
LAIT 1; NFS 1, 20; RGAL 4; RGSF 2;
SSFS 1, 7, 11, 15; SUFW 1; TUS; WCH;
YABC 2

Hawthorne, Sophia Peabody
1809-1871 .... NCLC 150
See also DLB 183, 239

Haxton, Josephine Ayres
See Douglas, Ellen

Hayaseca y Eizaguirre, Jorge
See Echegaray (y Eizaguirre), Jose (Maria
Waldo)

Hayashi, Fumiko 1904-1951 .... TCLC 27
See also CA 161; DLB 180; EWL 3

Hayashi Fumiko
See Hayashi, Fumiko

Haycraft, Anna 1932-2005 .... CLC 40
See also CA 122; 237; CANR 90, 141; CN
4, 5, 6; DLB 194; MTCW 2; MTFW 2005

Haycraft, Anna Margaret
See Haycraft, Anna

Hayden, Robert
See Hayden, Robert Earl

Hayden, Robert E.
See Hayden, Robert Earl

Hayden, Robert Earl 1913-1980 .... BLC 1:2;
CLC 5, 9, 14, 37; PC 6
See also AFAW 1, 2; AMWS 2; BW 1, 3;
CA 69-72; 97-100; CABS 2; CANR 24,
75, 82; CDALB 1941-1968; CP 1, 2, 3;
DA; DAC; DAM MST, MULT, POET;
DLB 5, 76; EWL 3; EXPP; MAL 5;
MTCW 1, 2; PFS 1, 31; RGAL 4; SATA
19; SATA-Obit 26; WP

Haydon, Benjamin Robert
1786-1846 .... NCLC 146
See also DLB 110

Hayek, F(riedrich) A(ugust von)
1899-1992 .... TCLC 109
See also CA 93-96; 137; CANR 20; MTCW
1, 2

Hayford, J(oseph) E(phraim) Casely
See Casely-Hayford, J(oseph) E(phraim)

Hayman, Ronald 1932- .... CLC 44
See also CA 25-28R; CANR 18, 50, 88; CD
5, 6; DLB 155

Hayne, Paul Hamilton 1830-1886 . NCLC 94
See also DLB 3, 64, 79, 248; RGAL 4

Hays, Mary 1760-1843 .... NCLC 114
See also DLB 142, 158; RGEL 2

Haywood, Eliza (Fowler)
1693(?)-1756 .... LC 1, 44, 177
See also BRWS 12; DLB 39; RGEL 2

Hazlitt, William 1778-1830 ...... NCLC 29, 82
See also BRW 4; DLB 110, 158; RGEL 2;
TEA

Hazzard, Shirley 1931- .... CLC 18, 218
See also CA 9-12R; CANR 4, 70, 127; CN
1, 2, 3, 4, 5, 6, 7; DLB 289; DLBY 1982;
MTCW 1

Head, Bessie 1937-1986 . BLC 1:2, 2:2; CLC
25, 67; SSC 52
See also AFW; BW 2, 3; CA 29-32R; 119;
CANR 25, 82; CDWLB 3; CN 1, 2, 3, 4;
DA3; DAM MULT; DLB 117, 225; EWL
3; EXPS; FL 1:6; FW; MTCW 1, 2;
MTFW 2005; RGSF 2; SSFS 5, 13; WLIT
2; WWE 1

Headley, Elizabeth
See Harrison, Elizabeth (Allen) Cavanna

Headon, (Nicky) Topper 1956(?)- ..... CLC 30

Heaney, Seamus 1939- . CLC 5, 7, 14, 25, 37,
74, 91, 171, 225; PC 18, 100; WLCS
See also AAYA 61; BRWR 1; BRWS 2; CA
85-88; CANR 25, 48, 75, 91, 128, 184;
CDBLB 1960 to Present; CP 1, 2, 3, 4, 5,
6, 7; DA3; DAB; DAM POET; DLB 40,

330; DLBY 1995; EWL 3; EXPP; MTCW
1, 2; MTFW 2005; PAB; PFS 2, 5, 8, 17,
30; RGEL 2; TEA; WLIT 4

Heaney, Seamus Justin
See Heaney, Seamus

Hearn, Lafcadio 1850-1904 .... TCLC 9
See also AAYA 79; CA 105; 166; DLB 12,
78, 189; HGG; MAL 5; RGAL 4

Hearn, Patricio Lafcadio Tessima Carlos
See Hearn, Lafcadio

Hearne, Samuel 1745-1792 .... LC 95
See also DLB 99

Hearne, Vicki 1946-2001 .... CLC 56
See also CA 139; 201

Hearon, Shelby 1931- .... CLC 63
See also AITN 2; AMWS 8; CA 25-28R;
CAAS 11; CANR 18, 48, 103, 146; CSW

Heat-Moon, William Least 1939- ..... CLC 29
See also AAYA 9, 66; ANW; CA 115; 119;
CANR 47, 89; CPW; INT CA-119

Hebbel, Friedrich 1813-1863 . DC 21; NCLC
43
See also CDWLB 2; DAM DRAM; DLB
129; EW 6; RGWL 2, 3

Hebert, Anne 1916-2000 . CLC 4, 13, 29, 246
See also CA 85-88; 187; CANR 69, 126;
CCA 1; CWP; CWW 2; DA3; DAC;
DAM MST, POET; DLB 68; EWL 3; GFL
1789 to the Present; MTCW 1, 2; MTFW
2005; PFS 20

Hecht, Anthony (Evan) 1923-2004 .... CLC 8,
13, 19; PC 70
See also AMWS 10; CA 9-12R; 232; CANR
6, 108; CP 1, 2, 3, 4, 5, 6, 7; DAM POET;
DLB 5, 169; EWL 3; PFS 6; WP

Hecht, Ben 1894-1964 ..... CLC 8; TCLC 101
See also CA 85-88; DFS 9; DLB 7, 9, 25,
26, 28, 86; FANT; IDFW 3, 4; RGAL 4

Hedayat, Sadeq 1903-1951 . SSC 131; TCLC
21
See also CA 120; EWL 3; RGSF 2

Hegel, Georg Wilhelm Friedrich
1770-1831 .... NCLC 46, 151
See also DLB 90; TWA

Heidegger, Martin 1889-1976 .... CLC 24
See also CA 81-84; 65-68; CANR 34; DLB
296; MTCW 1, 2; MTFW 2005

Heidenstam, (Carl Gustaf) Verner von
1859-1940 .... TCLC 5
See also CA 104; DLB 330

Heidi Louise
See Erdrich, Louise

Heifner, Jack 1946- .... CLC 11
See also CA 105; CANR 47

Heijermans, Herman 1864-1924 .... TCLC 24
See also CA 123; EWL 3

Heilbrun, Carolyn G. 1926-2003 ..... CLC 25,
173
See also BPFB 1; CA 45-48; 220; CANR 1,
28, 58, 94; CMW; CPW; DLB 306; FW;
MSW

Heilbrun, Carolyn Gold
See Heilbrun, Carolyn G.

Hein, Christoph 1944- .... CLC 154
See also CA 158; CANR 108; CDWLB 2;
CWW 2; DLB 124

Heine, Heinrich 1797-1856 .... NCLC 4, 54,
147; PC 25
See also CDWLB 2; DLB 90; EW 5; RGWL
2, 3; TWA

Heinemann, Larry 1944- .... CLC 50
See also CA 110; CAAS 21; CANR 31, 81,
156; DLBD 9; INT CANR-31

Heinemann, Larry Curtiss
See Heinemann, Larry

Heiney, Donald (William) 1921-1993 . CLC 9
See also CA 1-4R; 142; CANR 3, 58; FANT

Heinlein, Robert A. 1907-1988 .. CLC 1, 3, 8,
14, 26, 55; SSC 55
See also AAYA 17; BPFB 2; BYA 4, 13;
CA 1-4R; 125; CANR 1, 20, 53; CLR 75;
CN 1, 2, 3, 4; CPW; DA3; DAM POP;
DLB 8; EXPS; JRDA; LAIT 5; LMFS 2;
MAICYA 1, 2; MTCW 1, 2; MTFW 2005;
RGAL 4; SATA 9, 69; SATA-Obit 56;
SCFW 1, 2; SFW 4; SSFS 7; YAW

Held, Peter
See Vance, Jack

Heldris of Cornwall fl. 13th cent.
- .... CMLC 97

Helforth, John
See Doolittle, Hilda

Heliodorus fl. 3rd cent. - .... CMLC 52
See also WLIT 8

Hellenhofferu, Vojtech Kapristian z
See Hasek, Jaroslav

Heller, Joseph 1923-1999 . CLC 1, 3, 5, 8, 11,
36, 63; TCLC 131, 151; WLC 3
See also AAYA 24; AITN 1; AMWS 4;
BPFB 2; BYA 1; CA 5-8R; 187; CABS 1;
CANR 8, 42, 66, 126; CN 1, 2, 3, 4, 5, 6;
CPW; DA; DA3; DAB; DAC; DAM MST,
NOV, POP; DLB 2, 28, 227; DLBY 1980,
2002; EWL 3; EXPN; INT CANR-8;
LAIT 4; MAL 5; MTCW 1, 2; MTFW
2005; NFS 1; RGAL 4; TUS; YAW

Hellman, Lillian 1905-1984 . CLC 2, 4, 8, 14,
18, 34, 44, 52; DC 1; TCLC 119
See also AAYA 47; AITN 1, 2; AMWS 1;
CA 13-16R; 112; CAD; CANR 33; CWD;
DA3; DAM DRAM; DFS 1, 3, 14; DLB
7, 228; DLBY 1984; EWL 3; FL 1:6; FW;
LAIT 3; MAL 5; MBL; MTCW 1, 2;
MTFW 2005; RGAL 4; TUS

Hellman, Lillian Florence
See Hellman, Lillian

Helprin, Mark 1947- .... CLC 7, 10, 22, 32
See also CA 81-84; CANR 47, 64, 124;
CDALBS; CN 7; CPW; DA3; DAM NOV,
POP; DLB 335; DLBY 1985; FANT;
MAL 5; MTCW 1, 2; MTFW 2005; SSFS
25; SUFW 2

Helvetius, Claude-Adrien 1715-1771 .. LC 26
See also DLB 313

Helyar, Jane Penelope Josephine
1933- .... CLC 17
See also CA 21-24R; CANR 10, 26; CWRI
5; SAAS 2; SATA 5; SATA-Essay 138

Hemans, Felicia 1793-1835 ...... NCLC 29, 71
See also DLB 96; RGEL 2

Hemingway, Ernest 1899-1961 .. CLC 1, 3, 6,
8, 10, 13, 19, 30, 34, 39, 41, 44, 50, 61,
80; SSC 1, 25, 36, 40, 63, 117, 137;
TCLC 115, 203; WLC 3
See also AAYA 19; AMW; AMWC 1;
AMWR 1; BPFB 2; BYA 2, 3, 13, 15; CA
77-80; CANR 34; CDALB 1917-1929;
DA; DA3; DAB; DAC; DAM MST, NOV,
DLB 4, 9, 102, 210, 308, 316, 330; DLBD
1, 15, 16; DLBY 1981, 1987, 1996, 1998;
EWL 3; EXPN; EXPS; LAIT 3, 4; LATS
1:1; MAL 5; MTCW 1, 2; MTFW 2005;
NFS 1, 5, 6, 14; RGAL 4; RGSF 2; SSFS
17; TUS; WYA

Hemingway, Ernest Miller
See Hemingway, Ernest

Hempel, Amy 1951- .... CLC 39
See also CA 118; 137; CANR 70, 166;
DA3; DLB 218; EXPS; MTCW 2; MTFW
2005; SSFS 2

Henderson, F. C.
See Mencken, H. L.

Henderson, Mary
See Mavor, Osborne Henry

Henderson, Sylvia
See Ashton-Warner, Sylvia (Constance)

Henderson, Zenna (Chlarson)
1917-1983 .... **SSC 29**
See also CA 1-4R; 133; CANR 1, 84; DLB 8; SATA 5; SFW 4

Henkin, Joshua 1964- .... **CLC 119**
See also CA 161; CANR 186; DLB 350

Henley, Beth 1952- ... **CLC 23, 255; DC 6, 14**
See also AAYA 70; CA 107; CABS 3; CAD; CANR 32, 73, 140; CD 5, 6; CSW; CWD; DA3; DAM DRAM, MST; DFS 2, 21, 26; DLBY 1986; FW; MTCW 1, 2; MTFW 2005

Henley, Elizabeth Becker
See Henley, Beth

Henley, William Ernest 1849-1903 .. **TCLC 8**
See also CA 105; 234; DLB 19; RGEL 2

Hennissart, Martha 1929- .... **CLC 2**
See also BPFB 2; CA 85-88; CANR 64; CMW 4; DLB 306

Henry VIII 1491-1547 .... **LC 10**
See also DLB 132

Henry, O. 1862-1910 . **SSC 5, 49, 117; TCLC 1, 19; WLC 3**
See also AAYA 41; AMWS 2; CA 104; 131; CDALB 1865-1917; DA; DA3; DAB; DAC; DAM MST; DLB 12, 78, 79; EXPS; MAL 5; MTCW 1, 2; MTFW 2005; RGAL 4; RGSF 2; SSFS 2, 18, 27; TCWW 1, 2; TUS; YABC 2

Henry, Oliver
See Henry, O.

Henry, Patrick 1736-1799 .... **LC 25**
See also LAIT 1

Henryson, Robert 1430(?)-1506(?) ..... **LC 20, 110; PC 65**
See also BRWS 7; DLB 146; RGEL 2

Henschke, Alfred
See Klabund

Henson, Lance 1944- .... **NNAL**
See also CA 146; DLB 175

Hentoff, Nat(han Irving) 1925- .... **CLC 26**
See also AAYA 4, 42; BYA 6; CA 1-4R; CAAS 6; CANR 5, 25, 77, 114; CLR 1, 52; DLB 345; INT CANR-25; JRDA; MAICYA 1, 2; SATA 42, 69, 133; SATA-Brief 27; WYA; YAW

Heppenstall, (John) Rayner
1911-1981 .... **CLC 10**
See also CA 1-4R; 103; CANR 29; CN 1, 2; CP 1, 2, 3; EWL 3

Heraclitus c. 540B.C.-c. 450B.C. ... **CMLC 22**
See also DLB 176

Herbert, Edward 1583-1648 .... **LC 177**
See also DLB 121, 151, 252; RGEL 2

Herbert, Frank 1920-1986 ... **CLC 12, 23, 35, 44, 85**
See also AAYA 21; BPFB 2; BYA 4, 14; CA 53-56; 118; CANR 5, 43; CDALBS; CPW; DAM POP; DLB 8; INT CANR-5; LAIT 5; MTCW 1, 2; MTFW 2005; NFS 17; SATA 9, 37; SATA-Obit 47; SCFW 1, 2; SFW 4; YAW

Herbert, George 1593-1633 . **LC 24, 121; PC 4**
See also BRW 2; BRWR 2; CDBLB Before 1660; DAB; DAM POET; DLB 126; EXPP; PFS 25; RGEL 2; TEA; WP

Herbert, Zbigniew 1924-1998 ..... **CLC 9, 43; PC 50; TCLC 168**
See also CA 89-92; 169; CANR 36, 74, 177; CDWLB 4; CWW 2; DAM POET; DLB 232; EWL 3; MTCW 1; PFS 22

Herbert of Cherbury, Lord
See Herbert, Edward

Herbst, Josephine (Frey)
1897-1969 .... **CLC 34**
See also CA 5-8R; 25-28R; DLB 9

Herder, Johann Gottfried von
1744-1803 .... **NCLC 8, 186**
See also DLB 97; EW 4; TWA

Heredia, Jose Maria 1803-1839 ...... **HLCS 2; NCLC 209**
See also LAW

Hergesheimer, Joseph 1880-1954 ... **TCLC 11**
See also CA 109; 194; DLB 102, 9; RGAL 4

Herlihy, James Leo 1927-1993 .... **CLC 6**
See also CA 1-4R; 143; CAD; CANR 2; CN 1, 2, 3, 4, 5

Herman, William
See Bierce, Ambrose

Hermogenes fl. c. 175- .... **CMLC 6**

Hernandez, Jose 1834-1886 .... **NCLC 17**
See also LAW; RGWL 2, 3; WLIT 1

Herodotus c. 484B.C.-c. 420B.C. .. **CMLC 17**
See also AW 1; CDWLB 1; DLB 176; RGWL 2, 3; TWA; WLIT 8

Herr, Michael 1940(?)- .... **CLC 231**
See also CA 89-92; CANR 68, 142; DLB 185; MTCW 1

Herrick, Robert 1591-1674 .. **LC 13, 145; PC 9**
See also BRW 2; BRWC 2; DA; DAB; DAC; DAM MST, POP; DLB 126; EXPP; PFS 13, 29; RGAL 4; RGEL 2; TEA; WP

Herring, Guilles
See Somerville, Edith Oenone

Herriot, James 1916-1995
See Wight, James Alfred

Herris, Violet
See Hunt, Violet

Herrmann, Dorothy 1941- .... **CLC 44**
See also CA 107

Herrmann, Taffy
See Herrmann, Dorothy

Hersey, John 1914-1993 .. **CLC 1, 2, 7, 9, 40, 81, 97**
See also AAYA 29; BPFB 2; CA 17-20R; 140; CANR 33; CDALBS; CN 1, 2, 3, 4, 5; CPW; DAM POP; DLB 6, 185, 278, 299; MAL 5; MTCW 1, 2; MTFW 2005; RGHL; SATA 25; SATA-Obit 76; TUS

Hersey, John Richard
See Hersey, John

Hervent, Maurice
See Grindel, Eugene

Herzen, Aleksandr Ivanovich
1812-1870 .... **NCLC 10, 61**
See also DLB 277

Herzen, Alexander
See Herzen, Aleksandr Ivanovich

Herzl, Theodor 1860-1904 .... **TCLC 36**
See also CA 168

Herzog, Werner 1942- .... **CLC 16, 236**
See also CA 89-92

Hesiod fl. 8th cent. B.C.- .... **CMLC 5, 102**
See also AW 1; DLB 176; RGWL 2, 3; WLIT 8

Hesse, Hermann 1877-1962 ... **CLC 1, 2, 3, 6, 11, 17, 25, 69; SSC 9, 49; TCLC 148, 196; WLC 3**
See also AAYA 43; BPFB 2; CA 17-18; CAP 2; CDWLB 2; DA; DA3; DAB; DAC; DAM MST, NOV; DLB 66, 330; EW 9; EWL 3; EXPN; LAIT 1; MTCW 1, 2; MTFW 2005; NFS 6, 15, 24; RGWL 2, 3; SATA 50; TWA

Hewes, Cady
See De Voto, Bernard (Augustine)

Heyen, William 1940- .... **CLC 13, 18**
See also CA 33-36R; 220; CAAE 220; CAAS 9; CANR 98, 188; CP 3, 4, 5, 6, 7; DLB 5; RGHL

Heyerdahl, Thor 1914-2002 .... **CLC 26**
See also CA 5-8R; 207; CANR 5, 22, 66, 73; LAIT 4; MTCW 1, 2; MTFW 2005; SATA 2, 52

Heym, Georg (Theodor Franz Arthur)
1887-1912 .... **TCLC 9**
See also CA 106; 181

Heym, Stefan 1913-2001 .... **CLC 41**
See also CA 9-12R; 203; CANR 4; CWW 2; DLB 69; EWL 3

Heyse, Paul (Johann Ludwig von)
1830-1914 .... **TCLC 8**
See also CA 104; 209; DLB 129, 330

Heyward, (Edwin) DuBose
1885-1940 .... **HR 1:2; TCLC 59**
See also CA 108; 157; DLB 7, 9, 45, 249; MAL 5; SATA 21

Heywood, John 1497(?)-1580(?) .... **LC 65**
See also DLB 136; RGEL 2

Heywood, Thomas 1573(?)-1641 . **DC 29; LC 111**
See also DAM DRAM; DLB 62; LMFS 1; RGEL 2; TEA

Hiaasen, Carl 1953- .... **CLC 238**
See also CA 105; CANR 22, 45, 65, 113, 133, 168; CMW 4; CPW; CSW; DA3; DLB 292; LNFS 2, 3; MTCW 2; MTFW 2005

Hibbert, Eleanor Alice Burford
1906-1993 .... **CLC 7**
See also BEST 90:4; BPFB 2; CA 17-20R; 140; CANR 9, 28, 59; CMW 4; CPW; DAM POP; MTCW 2; MTFW 2005; RHW; SATA 2; SATA-Obit 74

Hichens, Robert (Smythe)
1864-1950 .... **TCLC 64**
See also CA 162; DLB 153; HGG; RHW; SUFW

Higgins, Aidan 1927- .... **SSC 68**
See also CA 9-12R; CANR 70, 115, 148; CN 1, 2, 3, 4, 5, 6, 7; DLB 14

Higgins, George V(incent)
1939-1999 .... **CLC 4, 7, 10, 18**
See also BPFB 2; CA 77-80; 186; CAAS 5; CANR 17, 51, 89, 96; CMW 4; CN 2, 3, 4, 5, 6; DLB 2; DLBY 1981, 1998; INT CANR-17; MSW; MTCW 1

Higginson, Thomas Wentworth
1823-1911 .... **TCLC 36**
See also CA 162; DLB 1, 64, 243

Higgonet, Margaret CLC 65

Highet, Helen
See MacInnes, Helen (Clark)

Highsmith, Mary Patricia
See Highsmith, Patricia

Highsmith, Patricia 1921-1995 ...... **CLC 2, 4, 14, 42, 102**
See also AAYA 48; BRWS 5; CA 1-4R; 147; CANR 1, 20, 48, 62, 108; CMW 4; CN 1, 2, 3, 4, 5; CPW; DA3; DAM NOV, POP; DLB 306; GLL 1; MSW; MTCW 1, 2; MTFW 2005; NFS 27; SSFS 25

Highwater, Jamake (Mamake)
1942(?)-2001 .... **CLC 12**
See also AAYA 7, 69; BPFB 2; BYA 4; CA 65-68; 199; CAAS 7; CANR 10, 34, 84; CLR 17; CWRI 5; DLB 52; DLBY 1985; JRDA; MAICYA 1, 2; SATA 32, 69; SATA-Brief 30

Highway, Tomson 1951- ..... **CLC 92; DC 33; NNAL**
See also CA 151; CANR 75; CCA 1; CD 5, 6; CN 7; DAC; DAM MULT; DFS 2; DLB 334; MTCW 2

Hijuelos, Oscar 1951- .... **CLC 65; HLC 1**
See also AAYA 25; AMWS 8; BEST 90:1; CA 123; CANR 50, 75, 125; CPW; DA3; DAM MULT, POP; DLB 145; HW 1, 2; LLW; MAL 5; MTCW 2; MTFW 2005; NFS 17; RGAL 4; WLIT 1

Holland, Marcus
  See Caldwell, (Janet Miriam) Taylor (Holland)
Hollander, John 1929- .... **CLC 2, 5, 8, 14**
  See also CA 1-4R; CANR 1, 52, 136; CP 1, 2, 3, 4, 5, 6, 7; DLB 5; MAL 5; SATA 13
Hollander, Paul
  See Silverberg, Robert
Holleran, Andrew
  See Garber, Eric
Holley, Marietta 1836(?)-1926 .... **TCLC 99**
  See also CA 118; DLB 11; FL 1:3
Hollinghurst, Alan 1954- .... **CLC 55, 91**
  See also BRWS 10; CA 114; CN 5, 6, 7; DLB 207, 326; GLL 1
Hollis, Jim
  See Summers, Hollis (Spurgeon, Jr.)
Holly, Buddy 1936-1959 .... **TCLC 65**
  See also CA 213
Holmes, Gordon
  See Shiel, M. P.
Holmes, John
  See Souster, (Holmes) Raymond
Holmes, John Clellon 1926-1988 ...... **CLC 56**
  See also BG 1:2; CA 9-12R; 125; CANR 4; CN 1, 2, 3, 4; DLB 16, 237
Holmes, Oliver Wendell, Jr.
  1841-1935 .... **TCLC 77**
  See also CA 114; 186
Holmes, Oliver Wendell
  1809-1894 .... **NCLC 14, 81; PC 71**
  See also AMWS 1; CDALB 1640-1865; DLB 1, 189, 235; EXPP; PFS 24; RGAL 4; SATA 34
Holmes, Raymond
  See Souster, (Holmes) Raymond
Holt, Samuel
  See Westlake, Donald E.
Holt, Victoria
  See Hibbert, Eleanor Alice Burford
Holub, Miroslav 1923-1998 .... **CLC 4**
  See also CA 21-24R; 169; CANR 10; CD-WLB 4; CWW 2; DLB 232; EWL 3; RGWL 3
Holz, Detlev
  See Benjamin, Walter
Homer c. 8th cent. B.C.- .... **CMLC 1, 16, 61; PC 23; WLCS**
  See also AW 1; CDWLB 1; DA; DA3; DAB; DAC; DAM MST, POET; DLB 176; EFS 1; LAIT 1; LMFS 1; RGWL 2, 3; TWA; WLIT 8; WP
Hong, Maxine Ting Ting
  See Kingston, Maxine Hong
Hongo, Garrett Kaoru 1951- .... **PC 23**
  See also CA 133; CAAS 22; CP 5, 6, 7; DLB 120, 312; EWL 3; EXPP; PFS 25; RGAL 4
Honig, Edwin 1919- .... **CLC 33**
  See also CA 5-8R; CAAS 8; CANR 4, 45, 144; CP 1, 2, 3, 4, 5, 6, 7; DLB 5
Hood, Hugh (John Blagdon) 1928- . **CLC 15, 28, 273; SSC 42**
  See also CA 49-52; CAAS 17; CANR 1, 33, 87; CN 1, 2, 3, 4, 5, 6, 7; DLB 53; RGSF 2
Hood, Thomas 1799-1845 . **NCLC 16; PC 93**
  See also BRW 4; DLB 96; RGEL 2
Hooker, (Peter) Jeremy 1941- .... **CLC 43**
  See also CA 77-80; CANR 22; CP 2, 3, 4, 5, 6, 7; DLB 40
Hooker, Richard 1554-1600 .... **LC 95**
  See also BRW 1; DLB 132; RGEL 2
Hooker, Thomas 1586-1647 .... **LC 137**
  See also DLB 24
hooks, bell 1952(?)- .... **BLCS; CLC 94**
  See also BW 2; CA 143; CANR 87, 126; DLB 246; MTCW 2; MTFW 2005; SATA 115, 170

Hooper, Johnson Jones
  1815-1862 .... **NCLC 177**
  See also DLB 3, 11, 248; RGAL 4
Hope, A(lec) D(erwent) 1907-2000 .... **CLC 3, 51; PC 56**
  See also BRWS 7; CA 21-24R; 188; CANR 33, 74; CP 1, 2, 3, 4, 5; DLB 289; EWL 3; MTCW 1, 2; MTFW 2005; PFS 8; RGEL 2
Hope, Anthony 1863-1933 .... **TCLC 83**
  See also CA 157; DLB 153, 156; RGEL 2; RHW
Hope, Brian
  See Creasey, John
Hope, Christopher 1944- .... **CLC 52**
  See also AFW; CA 106; CANR 47, 101, 177; CN 4, 5, 6, 7; DLB 225; SATA 62
Hope, Christopher David Tully
  See Hope, Christopher
Hopkins, Gerard Manley
  1844-1889 .... **NCLC 17, 189; PC 15; WLC 3**
  See also BRW 5; BRWR 2; CDBLB 1890-1914; DA; DA3; DAB; DAC; DAM MST, POET; DLB 35, 57; EXPP; PAB; PFS 26; RGEL 2; TEA; WP
Hopkins, John (Richard) 1931-1998 .. **CLC 4**
  See also CA 85-88; 169; CBD; CD 5, 6
Hopkins, Pauline Elizabeth
  1859-1930 .... **BLC 1:2; TCLC 28**
  See also AFAW 2; BW 2, 3; CA 141; CANR 82; DAM MULT; DLB 50
Hopkinson, Francis 1737-1791 .... **LC 25**
  See also DLB 31; RGAL 4
Hopley, George
  See Hopley-Woolrich, Cornell George
Hopley-Woolrich, Cornell George
  1903-1968 .... **CLC 77**
  See also CA 13-14; CANR 58, 156; CAP 1; CMW 4; DLB 226; MSW; MTCW 2
Horace 65B.C.-8B.C. .... **CMLC 39; PC 46**
  See also AW 2; CDWLB 1; DLB 211; RGWL 2, 3; WLIT 8
Horatio
  See Proust, Marcel
Horgan, Paul (George Vincent O'Shaughnessy) 1903-1995 .. **CLC 9, 53**
  See also BPFB 2; CA 13-16R; 147; CANR 9, 35; CN 1, 2, 3, 4, 5; DAM NOV; DLB 102, 212; DLBY 1985; INT CANR-9; MTCW 1, 2; MTFW 2005; SATA 13; SATA-Obit 84; TCWW 1, 2
Horkheimer, Max 1895-1973 .... **TCLC 132**
  See also CA 216; 41-44R; DLB 296
Horn, Peter
  See Kuttner, Henry
Hornby, Nicholas Peter John
  See Hornby, Nick
Hornby, Nick 1957(?)- .... **CLC 243**
  See also AAYA 74; BRWS 15; CA 151; CANR 104, 151, 191; CN 7; DLB 207, 352
Horne, Frank 1899-1974 .... **HR 1:2**
  See also BW 1; CA 125; 53-56; DLB 51; WP
Horne, Richard Henry Hengist
  1802(?)-1884 .... **NCLC 127**
  See also DLB 32; SATA 29
Hornem, Horace Esq.
  See Lord Byron
Horne Tooke, John 1736-1812 ..... **NCLC 195**
Horney, Karen (Clementine Theodore Danielsen) 1885-1952 .... **TCLC 71**
  See also CA 114; 165; DLB 246; FW
Hornung, E(rnest) W(illiam)
  1866-1921 .... **TCLC 59**
  See also CA 108; 160; CMW 4; DLB 70

Horovitz, Israel 1939- .... **CLC 56**
  See also CA 33-36R; CAD; CANR 46, 59; CD 5, 6; DAM DRAM; DLB 7, 341; MAL 5
Horton, George Moses
  1797(?)-1883(?) .... **NCLC 87**
  See also DLB 50
Horvath, odon von 1901-1938
  See von Horvath, Odon
  See also EWL 3
Horvath, Oedoen von -1938
  See von Horvath, Odon
Horwitz, Julius 1920-1986 .... **CLC 14**
  See also CA 9-12R; 119; CANR 12
Horwitz, Ronald
  See Harwood, Ronald
Hospital, Janette Turner 1942- .... **CLC 42, 145**
  See also CA 108; CANR 48, 166, 200; CN 5, 6, 7; DLB 325; DLBY 2002; RGSF 2
Hosseini, Khaled 1965- .... **CLC 254**
  See also CA 225; LNFS 1, 3; SATA 156
Hostos, E. M. de
  See Hostos (y Bonilla), Eugenio Maria de
Hostos, Eugenio M. de
  See Hostos (y Bonilla), Eugenio Maria de
Hostos, Eugenio Maria
  See Hostos (y Bonilla), Eugenio Maria de
Hostos (y Bonilla), Eugenio Maria de
  1839-1903 .... **TCLC 24**
  See also CA 123; 131; HW 1
Houdini
  See Lovecraft, H. P.
Houellebecq, Michel 1958- .... **CLC 179**
  See also CA 185; CANR 140; MTFW 2005
Hougan, Carolyn 1943-2007 .... **CLC 34**
  See also CA 139; 257
Household, Geoffrey (Edward West)
  1900-1988 .... **CLC 11**
  See also CA 77-80; 126; CANR 58; CMW 4; CN 1, 2, 3, 4; DLB 87; SATA 14; SATA-Obit 59
Housman, A. E. 1859-1936 . **PC 2, 43; TCLC 1, 10; WLCS**
  See also AAYA 66; BRW 6; CA 104; 125; DA; DA3; DAB; DAC; DAM MST, POET; DLB 19, 284; EWL 3; EXPP; MTCW 1, 2; MTFW 2005; PAB; PFS 4, 7; RGEL 2; TEA; WP
Housman, Alfred Edward
  See Housman, A. E.
Housman, Laurence 1865-1959 .... **TCLC 7**
  See also CA 106; 155; DLB 10; FANT; RGEL 2; SATA 25
Houston, Jeanne Wakatsuki 1934- .... **AAL**
  See also AAYA 49; CA 103, 232; CAAE 232; CAAS 16; CANR 29, 123, 167; LAIT 4; SATA 78, 168; SATA-Essay 168
Hove, Chenjerai 1956- .... **BLC 2:2**
  See also CP 7
Howard, Elizabeth Jane 1923- ..... **CLC 7, 29**
  See also BRWS 11; CA 5-8R; CANR 8, 62, 146; CN 1, 2, 3, 4, 5, 6, 7
Howard, Maureen 1930- .... **CLC 5, 14, 46, 151**
  See also CA 53-56; CANR 31, 75, 140; CN 4, 5, 6, 7; DLBY 1983; INT CANR-31; MTCW 1, 2; MTFW 2005
Howard, Richard 1929- .... **CLC 7, 10, 47**
  See also AITN 1; CA 85-88; CANR 25, 80, 154; CP 1, 2, 3, 4, 5, 6, 7; DLB 5; INT CANR-25; MAL 5
Howard, Robert E 1906-1936 .... **TCLC 8**
  See also AAYA 80; BPFB 2; BYA 5; CA 105; 157; CANR 155; FANT; SUFW 1; TCWW 1, 2
Howard, Robert Ervin
  See Howard, Robert E

Izumi Shikibu c. 973-c. 1034 .... **CMLC 33**
J. R. S.
　　See Gogarty, Oliver St. John
Jabran, Kahlil
　　See Gibran, Kahlil
Jabran, Khalil
　　See Gibran, Kahlil
Jaccottet, Philippe 1925- .... **PC 98**
　　See also CA 116; 129; CWW 2; GFL 1789
　　to the Present
Jackson, Daniel
　　See Wingrove, David
Jackson, Helen Hunt 1830-1885 .... **NCLC 90**
　　See also DLB 42, 47, 186, 189; RGAL 4
Jackson, Jesse 1908-1983 .... **CLC 12**
　　See also BW 1; CA 25-28R; 109; CANR
　　27; CLR 28; CWRI 5; MAICYA 1, 2;
　　SATA 2, 29; SATA-Obit 48
Jackson, Laura 1901-1991 . **CLC 3, 7; PC 44**
　　See also CA 65-68; 135; CANR 28, 89; CP
　　1, 2, 3, 4, 5; DLB 48; RGAL 4
Jackson, Laura Riding
　　See Jackson, Laura
Jackson, Sam
　　See Trumbo, Dalton
Jackson, Sara
　　See Wingrove, David
Jackson, Shirley 1919-1965 . **CLC 11, 60, 87;**
　　SSC 9, 39; TCLC 187; WLC 3
　　See also AAYA 9; AMWS 9; BPFB 2; CA
　　1-4R; 25-28R; CANR 4, 52; CDALB
　　1941-1968; DA; DA3; DAC; DAM MST;
　　DLB 6, 234; EXPS; HGG; LAIT 4; MAL
　　5; MTCW 2; MTFW 2005; RGAL 4;
　　RGSF 2; SATA 2; SSFS 1, 27; SUFW 1,
　　2
Jacob, (Cyprien-)Max 1876-1944 .... **TCLC 6**
　　See also CA 104; 193; DLB 258; EWL 3;
　　GFL 1789 to the Present; GLL 2; RGWL
　　2, 3
Jacobs, Harriet A. 1813(?)-1897 ... **NCLC 67,**
　　162
　　See also AFAW 1, 2; DLB 239; FL 1:3; FW;
　　LAIT 2; RGAL 4
Jacobs, Harriet Ann
　　See Jacobs, Harriet A.
Jacobs, Jim 1942- .... **CLC 12**
　　See also CA 97-100; INT CA-97-100
Jacobs, W(illiam) W(ymark)
　　1863-1943 .... **SSC 73; TCLC 22**
　　See also CA 121; 167; DLB 135; EXPS;
　　HGG; RGEL 2; RGSF 2; SSFS 2; SUFW
　　1
Jacobsen, Jens Peter 1847-1885 .... **NCLC 34**
Jacobsen, Josephine (Winder)
　　1908-2003 .... **CLC 48, 102; PC 62**
　　See also CA 33-36R; 218; CAAS 18; CANR
　　23, 48; CCA 1; CP 2, 3, 4, 5, 6, 7; DLB
　　244; PFS 23; TCLE 1:1
Jacobson, Dan 1929- ...... **CLC 4, 14; SSC 91**
　　See also AFW; CA 1-4R; CANR 2, 25, 66,
　　170; CN 1, 2, 3, 4, 5, 6, 7; DLB 14, 207,
　　225, 319; EWL 3; MTCW 1; RGSF 2
Jacopone da Todi 1236-1306 .... **CMLC 95**
Jacqueline
　　See Carpentier, Alejo
Jacques de Vitry c. 1160-1240 ...... **CMLC 63**
　　See also DLB 208
Jagger, Michael Philip
　　See Jagger, Mick
Jagger, Mick 1943- .... **CLC 17**
　　See also CA 239
Jahiz, al- c. 780-c. 869 .... **CMLC 25**
　　See also DLB 311
Jakes, John 1932- .... **CLC 29**
　　See also AAYA 32; BEST 89:4; BPFB 2;
　　CA 57-60, 214; CAAE 214; CANR 10,
　　43, 66, 111, 142, 171; CPW; CSW; DA3;

DAM NOV, POP; DLB 278; DLBY 1983;
FANT; INT CANR-10; MTCW 1, 2;
MTFW 2005; RHW; SATA 62; SFW 4;
TCWW 1, 2
Jakes, John William
　　See Jakes, John
James I 1394-1437 .... **LC 20**
　　See also RGEL 2
James, Alice 1848-1892 .... **NCLC 206**
　　See also DLB 221
James, Andrew
　　See Kirkup, James
James, C(yril) L(ionel) R(obert)
　　1901-1989 .... **BLCS; CLC 33**
　　See also BW 2; CA 117; 125; 128; CANR
　　62; CN 1, 2, 3, 4; DLB 125; MTCW 1
James, Daniel (Lewis) 1911-1988 ..... **CLC 33**
　　See also CA 174; 125; DLB 122
James, Dynely
　　See Mayne, William (James Carter)
James, Henry Sr. 1811-1882 .... **NCLC 53**
James, Henry 1843-1916 .... **SSC 8, 32, 47,**
　　108; TCLC 2, 11, 24, 40, 47, 64, 171;
　　WLC 3
　　See also AMW; AMWC 1; AMWR 1; BPFB
　　2; BRW 6; CA 104; 132; CDALB 1865-
　　1917; DA; DA3; DAB; DAC; DAM MST,
　　NOV; DLB 12, 71, 74, 189; DLBD 13;
　　EWL 3; EXPS; GL 2; HGG; LAIT 2;
　　MAL 5; MTCW 1, 2; MTFW 2005; NFS
　　12, 16, 19; RGAL 4; RGEL 2; RGSF 2;
　　SSFS 9; SUFW 1; TUS
James, M. R.
　　See James, Montague
James, Mary
　　See Meaker, Marijane
James, Montague 1862-1936 ...... **SSC 16, 93;**
　　TCLC 6
　　See also CA 104; 203; DLB 156, 201;
　　HGG; RGEL 2; RGSF 2; SUFW 1
James, Montague Rhodes
　　See James, Montague
James, P.D. 1920- .... **CLC 18, 46, 122, 226**
　　See also BEST 90:2; BPFB 2; BRWS 4;
　　CA 21-24R; CANR 17, 43, 65, 112, 201;
　　CDBLB 1960 to Present; CMW 4; CN 4,
　　5, 6, 7; CPW; DA3; DAM POP; DLB 87,
　　276; DLBD 17; MSW; MTCW 1, 2;
　　MTFW 2005; TEA
James, Philip
　　See Moorcock, Michael
James, Samuel
　　See Stephens, James
James, Seumas
　　See Stephens, James
James, Stephen
　　See Stephens, James
James, T. F.
　　See Fleming, Thomas
James, William 1842-1910 .... **TCLC 15, 32**
　　See also AMW; CA 109; 193; DLB 270,
　　284; MAL 5; NCFS 5; RGAL 4
Jameson, Anna 1794-1860 .... **NCLC 43**
　　See also DLB 99, 166
Jameson, Fredric 1934- .... **CLC 142**
　　See also CA 196; CANR 169; DLB 67;
　　LMFS 2
Jameson, Fredric R.
　　See Jameson, Fredric
James VI of Scotland 1566-1625 .... **LC 109**
　　See also DLB 151, 172
Jami, Nur al-Din 'Abd al-Rahman
　　1414-1492 .... **LC 9**
Jammes, Francis 1868-1938 .... **TCLC 75**
　　See also CA 198; EWL 3; GFL 1789 to the
　　Present
Jandl, Ernst 1925-2000 .... **CLC 34**
　　See also CA 200; EWL 3

Janowitz, Tama 1957- .... **CLC 43, 145**
　　See also CA 106; CANR 52, 89, 129; CN
　　5, 6, 7; CPW; DAM POP; DLB 292;
　　MTFW 2005
Jansson, Tove (Marika) 1914-2001 ... **SSC 96**
　　See also CA 17-20R; 196; CANR 38, 118;
　　CLR 2, 125; CWW 2; DLB 257; EWL 3;
　　MAICYA 1, 2; RGSF 2; SATA 3, 41
Japrisot, Sebastien 1931-
　　See Rossi, Jean-Baptiste
Jarrell, Randall 1914-1965 .... **CLC 1, 2, 6, 9,**
　　13, 49; PC 41; TCLC 177
　　See also AMW; BYA 5; CA 5-8R; 25-28R;
　　CABS 2; CANR 6, 34; CDALB 1941-
　　1968; CLR 6, 111; CWRI 5; DAM POET;
　　DLB 48, 52; EWL 3; EXPP; MAICYA 1,
　　2; MAL 5; MTCW 1, 2; PAB; PFS 2, 31;
　　RGAL 4; SATA 7
Jarry, Alfred 1873-1907 .... **SSC 20; TCLC 2,**
　　14, 147
　　See also CA 104; 153; DA3; DAM DRAM;
　　DFS 8; DLB 192, 258; EW 9; EWL 3;
　　GFL 1789 to the Present; RGWL 2, 3;
　　TWA
Jarvis, E.K.
　　See Ellison, Harlan; Silverberg, Robert
Jawien, Andrzej
　　See John Paul II, Pope
Jaynes, Roderick
　　See Coen, Ethan
Jeake, Samuel, Jr.
　　See Aiken, Conrad
Jean-Louis
　　See Kerouac, Jack
Jean Paul 1763-1825 .... **NCLC 7**
Jefferies, (John) Richard
　　1848-1887 .... **NCLC 47**
　　See also BRWS 15; DLB 98, 141; RGEL 2;
　　SATA 16; SFW 4
Jeffers, John Robinson
　　See Jeffers, Robinson
Jeffers, Robinson 1887-1962 .... **CLC 2, 3, 11,**
　　15, 54; PC 17; WLC 3
　　See also AMWS 2; CA 85-88; CANR 35;
　　CDALB 1917-1929; DA; DAC; DAM
　　MST, POET; DLB 45, 212, 342; EWL 3;
　　MAL 5; MTCW 1, 2; MTFW 2005; PAB;
　　PFS 3, 4; RGAL 4
Jefferson, Janet
　　See Mencken, H. L.
Jefferson, Thomas 1743-1826 . **NCLC 11, 103**
　　See also AAYA 54; ANW; CDALB 1640-
　　1865; DA3; DLB 31, 183; LAIT 1; RGAL
　　4
Jeffrey, Francis 1773-1850 .... **NCLC 33**
　　See also DLB 107
Jelakowitch, Ivan
　　See Heijermans, Herman
Jelinek, Elfriede 1946- .... **CLC 169**
　　See also AAYA 68; CA 154; CANR 169;
　　DLB 85, 330; FW
Jellicoe, (Patricia) Ann 1927- .... **CLC 27**
　　See also CA 85-88; CBD; CD 5, 6; CWD;
　　CWRI 5; DLB 13, 233; FW
Jelloun, Tahar ben
　　See Ben Jelloun, Tahar
Jemyma
　　See Holley, Marietta
Jen, Gish 1955- .... **AAL; CLC 70, 198, 260**
　　See also AMWC 2; CA 135; CANR 89,
　　130; CN 7; DLB 312; NFS 30
Jen, Lillian
　　See Jen, Gish
Jenkins, (John) Robin 1912- .... **CLC 52**
　　See also CA 1-4R; CANR 1, 135; CN 1, 2,
　　3, 4, 5, 6, 7; DLB 14, 271

EWL 3; FL 1:6; FW; INT CANR-13; LAIT 5; MAL 5; MBL; MTCW 1, 2; MTFW 2005; NFS 6; RGAL 4; SATA 53; SSFS 3; TCWW 2

Kingston, Maxine Ting Ting Hong
See Kingston, Maxine Hong

Kinnell, Galway 1927- ..... **CLC 1, 2, 3, 5, 13, 29, 129; PC 26**
See also AMWS 3; CA 9-12R; CANR 10, 34, 66, 116, 138, 175; CP 1, 2, 3, 4, 5, 6, 7; DLB 5, 342; DLBY 1987; EWL 3; INT CANR-34; MAL 5; MTCW 1, 2; MTFW 2005; PAB; PFS 9, 26; RGAL 4; TCLE 1:1; WP

Kinsella, Thomas 1928- .... **CLC 4, 19, 138, 274; PC 69**
See also BRWS 5; CA 17-20R; CANR 15, 122; CP 1, 2, 3, 4, 5, 6, 7; DLB 27; EWL 3; MTCW 1, 2; MTFW 2005; RGEL 2; TEA

Kinsella, W.P. 1935- .... **CLC 27, 43, 166**
See also AAYA 7, 60; BPFB 2; CA 97-100, 222; CAAE 222; CAAS 7; CANR 21, 35, 66, 75, 129; CN 4, 5, 6, 7; CPW; DAC; DAM NOV, POP; FANT; INT CANR-21; LAIT 5; MTCW 1, 2; MTFW 2005; NFS 15; RGSF 2

Kinsey, Alfred C(harles)
1894-1956 .... **TCLC 91**
See also CA 115; 170; MTCW 2

Kipling, Joseph Rudyard
See Kipling, Rudyard

Kipling, Rudyard 1865-1936 . **PC 3, 91; SSC 5, 54, 110; TCLC 8, 17, 167; WLC 3**
See also AAYA 32; BRW 6; BRWC 1, 2; BRWR 3; BYA 4; CA 105; 120; CANR 33; CDBLB 1890-1914; CLR 39, 65; CWRI 5; DA; DA3; DAB; DAC; DAM MST, POET; DLB 19, 34, 141, 156, 330; EWL 3; EXPS; FANT; LAIT 3; LMFS 1; MAICYA 1, 2; MTCW 1, 2; MTFW 2005; NFS 21; PFS 22; RGEL 2; RGSF 2; SATA 100; SFW 4; SSFS 8, 21, 22; SUFW 1; TEA; WCH; WLIT 4; YABC 2

Kircher, Athanasius 1602-1680 .... **LC 121**
See also DLB 164

Kirk, Russell (Amos) 1918-1994 .. **TCLC 119**
See also AITN 1; CA 1-4R; 145; CAAS 9; CANR 1, 20, 60; HGG; INT CANR-20; MTCW 1, 2

Kirkham, Dinah
See Card, Orson Scott

Kirkland, Caroline M. 1801-1864 . **NCLC 85**
See also DLB 3, 73, 74, 250, 254; DLBD 13

Kirkup, James 1918-2009 .... **CLC 1**
See also CA 1-4R; CAAS 4; CANR 2; CP 1, 2, 3, 4, 5, 6, 7; DLB 27; SATA 12

Kirkwood, James 1930(?)-1989 .... **CLC 9**
See also AITN 2; CA 1-4R; 128; CANR 6, 40; GLL 2

Kirsch, Sarah 1935- .... **CLC 176**
See also CA 178; CWW 2; DLB 75; EWL 3

Kirshner, Sidney
See Kingsley, Sidney

Kis, Danilo 1935-1989 .... **CLC 57**
See also CA 109; 118; 129; CANR 61; CD-WLB 4; DLB 181; EWL 3; MTCW 1; RGSF 2; RGWL 2, 3

Kissinger, Henry A(lfred) 1923- ..... **CLC 137**
See also CA 1-4R; CANR 2, 33, 66, 109; MTCW 1

Kittel, Frederick August
See Wilson, August

Kivi, Aleksis 1834-1872 .... **NCLC 30**

Kizer, Carolyn 1925- ..... **CLC 15, 39, 80; PC 66**
See also CA 65-68; CAAS 5; CANR 24, 70, 134; CP 1, 2, 3, 4, 5, 6, 7; CWP; DAM

POET; DLB 5, 169; EWL 3; MAL 5; MTCW 2; MTFW 2005; PFS 18; TCLE 1:1

Klabund 1890-1928 .... **TCLC 44**
See also CA 162; DLB 66

Klappert, Peter 1942- .... **CLC 57**
See also CA 33-36R; CSW; DLB 5

Klausner, Amos
See Oz, Amos

Klein, A. M. 1909-1972 .... **CLC 19**
See also CA 101; 37-40R; CP 1; DAB; DAC; DAM MST; DLB 68; EWL 3; RGEL 2; RGHL

Klein, Abraham Moses
See Klein, A. M.

Klein, Joe
See Klein, Joseph

Klein, Joseph 1946- .... **CLC 154**
See also CA 85-88; CANR 55, 164

Klein, Norma 1938-1989 .... **CLC 30**
See also AAYA 2, 35; BPFB 2; BYA 6, 7, 8; CA 41-44R; 128; CANR 15, 37; CLR 2, 19; INT CANR-15; JRDA; MAICYA 1, 2; SAAS 1; SATA 7, 57; WYA; YAW

Klein, T.E.D. 1947- .... **CLC 34**
See also CA 119; CANR 44, 75, 167; HGG

Klein, Theodore Eibon Donald
See Klein, T.E.D.

Kleist, Heinrich von 1777-1811 .... **DC 29; NCLC 2, 37, 222; SSC 22**
See also CDWLB 2; DAM DRAM; DLB 90; EW 5; RGSF 2; RGWL 2, 3

Klima, Ivan 1931- .... **CLC 56, 172**
See also CA 25-28R; CANR 17, 50, 91; CDWLB 4; CWW 2; DAM NOV; DLB 232; EWL 3; RGWL 3

Klimentev, Andrei Platonovich
See Klimentov, Andrei Platonovich

Klimentov, Andrei Platonovich
1899-1951 .... **SSC 42; TCLC 14**
See also CA 108; 232; DLB 272; EWL 3

Klinger, Friedrich Maximilian von
1752-1831 .... **NCLC 1**
See also DLB 94

Klingsor the Magician
See Hartmann, Sadakichi

Klopstock, Friedrich Gottlieb
1724-1803 .... **NCLC 11, 225**
See also DLB 97; EW 4; RGWL 2, 3

Kluge, Alexander 1932- .... **SSC 61**
See also CA 81-84; CANR 163; DLB 75

Knapp, Caroline 1959-2002 .... **CLC 99**
See also CA 154; 207

Knebel, Fletcher 1911-1993 .... **CLC 14**
See also AITN 1; CA 1-4R; 140; CAAS 3; CANR 1, 36; CN 1, 2, 3, 4, 5; SATA 36; SATA-Obit 75

Knickerbocker, Diedrich
See Irving, Washington

Knight, Etheridge 1931-1991 .... **BLC 1:2; CLC 40; PC 14**
See also BW 1, 3; CA 21-24R; 133; CANR 23, 82; CP 1, 2, 3, 4, 5; DAM POET; DLB 41; MTCW 2; MTFW 2005; RGAL 4; TCLE 1:1

Knight, Sarah Kemble 1666-1727 .... **LC 7**
See also DLB 24, 200

Knister, Raymond 1899-1932 .... **TCLC 56**
See also CA 186; DLB 68; RGEL 2

Knowles, John 1926-2001 ... **CLC 1, 4, 10, 26**
See also AAYA 10, 72; AMWS 12; BPFB 2; BYA 3; CA 17-20R; 203; CANR 40, 74, 76, 132; CDALB 1968-1988; CLR 98; CN 1, 2, 3, 4, 5, 6, 7; DA; DAC; DAM MST, NOV; DLB 6; EXPN; MTCW 1, 2; MTFW 2005; NFS 2; RGAL 4; SATA 8, 89; SATA-Obit 134; YAW

Knox, Calvin M.
See Silverberg, Robert

Knox, John c. 1505-1572 .... **LC 37**
See also DLB 132

Knye, Cassandra
See Disch, Thomas M.

Koch, C(hristopher) J(ohn) 1932- .... **CLC 42**
See also CA 127; CANR 84; CN 3, 4, 5, 6, 7; DLB 289

Koch, Christopher
See Koch, C(hristopher) J(ohn)

Koch, Kenneth 1925-2002 .... **CLC 5, 8, 44; PC 80**
See also AMWS 15; CA 1-4R; 207; CAD; CANR 6, 36, 57, 97, 131; CD 5, 6; CP 1, 2, 3, 4, 5, 6, 7; DAM POET; DLB 5; INT CANR-36; MAL 5; MTCW 2; MTFW 2005; PFS 20; SATA 65; WP

Kochanowski, Jan 1530-1584 .... **LC 10**
See also RGWL 2, 3

Kock, Charles Paul de 1794-1871 . **NCLC 16**

Koda Rohan
See Koda Shigeyuki

Koda Rohan
See Koda Shigeyuki

Koda Shigeyuki 1867-1947 .... **TCLC 22**
See also CA 121; 183; DLB 180

Koestler, Arthur 1905-1983 ... **CLC 1, 3, 6, 8, 15, 33**
See also BRWS 1; CA 1-4R; 109; CANR 1, 33; CDBLB 1945-1960; CN 1, 2, 3; DLBY 1983; EWL 3; MTCW 1, 2; MTFW 2005; NFS 19; RGEL 2

Kogawa, Joy 1935- .... **CLC 78, 129, 262, 268**
See also AAYA 47; CA 101; CANR 19, 62, 126; CN 6, 7; CP 1; CWP; DAC; DAM MST, MULT; DLB 334; FW; MTCW 2; MTFW 2005; NFS 3; SATA 99

Kogawa, Joy Nozomi
See Kogawa, Joy

Kohout, Pavel 1928- .... **CLC 13**
See also CA 45-48; CANR 3

Koizumi, Yakumo
See Hearn, Lafcadio

Kolmar, Gertrud 1894-1943 .... **TCLC 40**
See also CA 167; EWL 3; RGHL

Komunyakaa, Yusef 1947- . **BLC 2:2; BLCS; CLC 86, 94, 207; PC 51**
See also AFAW 2; AMWS 13; CA 147; CANR 83, 164; CP 6, 7; CSW; DLB 120; EWL 3; PFS 5, 20, 30; RGAL 4

Konigsberg, Alan Stewart
See Allen, Woody

Konrad, George
See Konrad, Gyorgy

Konrad, George
See Konrad, Gyorgy

Konrad, Gyorgy 1933- .... **CLC 4, 10, 73**
See also CA 85-88; CANR 97, 171; CD-WLB 4; CWW 2; DLB 232; EWL 3

Konwicki, Tadeusz 1926- .... **CLC 8, 28, 54, 117**
See also CA 101; CAAS 9; CANR 39, 59; CWW 2; DLB 232; EWL 3; IDFW 3; MTCW 1

Koontz, Dean 1945- .... **CLC 78, 206**
See also AAYA 9, 31; BEST 89:3, 90:2; CA 108; CANR 19, 36, 52, 95, 138, 176; CMW 4; CPW; DA3; DAM NOV, POP; DLB 292; HGG; MTCW 1; MTFW 2005; SATA 92, 165; SFW 4; SUFW 2; YAW

Koontz, Dean R.
See Koontz, Dean

Koontz, Dean Ray
See Koontz, Dean

Kopernik, Mikolaj
See Copernicus, Nicolaus

Kopit, Arthur (Lee) 1937- ..... **CLC 1, 18, 33; DC 37**
See also AITN 1; CA 81-84; CABS 3; CAD; CD 5, 6; DAM DRAM; DFS 7, 14, 24; DLB 7; MAL 5; MTCW 1; RGAL 4

Kopitar, Jernej (Bartholomaus) 1780-1844 .... **NCLC 117**

Kops, Bernard 1926- .... **CLC 4**
See also CA 5-8R; CANR 84, 159; CBD; CN 1, 2, 3, 4, 5, 6, 7; CP 1, 2, 3, 4, 5, 6, 7; DLB 13; RGHL

Kornbluth, C(yril) M. 1923-1958 .... **TCLC 8**
See also CA 105; 160; DLB 8; SCFW 1, 2; SFW 4

Korolenko, V.G.
See Korolenko, Vladimir G.

Korolenko, Vladimir
See Korolenko, Vladimir G.

Korolenko, Vladimir G. 1853-1921 .... **TCLC 22**
See also CA 121; DLB 277

Korolenko, Vladimir Galaktionovich
See Korolenko, Vladimir G.

Korzybski, Alfred (Habdank Skarbek) 1879-1950 .... **TCLC 61**
See also CA 123; 160

Kosinski, Jerzy 1933-1991 ..... **CLC 1, 2, 3, 6, 10, 15, 53, 70**
See also AMWS 7; BPFB 2; CA 17-20R; 134; CANR 9, 46; CN 1, 2, 3, 4; DA3; DAM NOV; DLB 2, 299; DLBY 1982; EWL 3; HGG; MAL 5; MTCW 1, 2; MTFW 2005; NFS 12; RGAL 4; RGHL; TUS

Kostelanetz, Richard (Cory) 1940- .. **CLC 28**
See also CA 13-16R; CAAS 8; CANR 38, 77; CN 4, 5, 6; CP 2, 3, 4, 5, 6, 7

Kostrowitzki, Wilhelm Apollinaris de 1880-1918
See Apollinaire, Guillaume

Kotlowitz, Robert 1924- .... **CLC 4**
See also CA 33-36R; CANR 36

Kotzebue, August (Friedrich Ferdinand) von 1761-1819 .... **NCLC 25**
See also DLB 94

Kotzwinkle, William 1938- ..... **CLC 5, 14, 35**
See also BPFB 2; CA 45-48; CANR 3, 44, 84, 129; CLR 6; CN 7; DLB 173; FANT; MAICYA 1, 2; SATA 24, 70, 146; SFW 4; SUFW 2; YAW

Kowna, Stancy
See Szymborska, Wislawa

Kozol, Jonathan 1936- .... **CLC 17**
See also AAYA 46; CA 61-64; CANR 16, 45, 96, 178; MTFW 2005

Kozoll, Michael 1940(?)- .... **CLC 35**

Krakauer, Jon 1954- .... **CLC 248**
See also AAYA 24; AMWS 18; BYA 9; CA 153; CANR 131; MTFW 2005; SATA 108

Kramer, Kathryn 19(?)- .... **CLC 34**

Kramer, Larry 1935- .... **CLC 42; DC 8**
See also CA 124; 126; CANR 60, 132; DAM POP; DLB 249; GLL 1

Krasicki, Ignacy 1735-1801 .... **NCLC 8**

Krasinski, Zygmunt 1812-1859 .... **NCLC 4**
See also RGWL 2, 3

Kraus, Karl 1874-1936 .... **TCLC 5**
See also CA 104; 216; DLB 118; EWL 3

Kraynay, Anton
See Gippius, Zinaida

Kreve (Mickevicius), Vincas 1882-1954 .... **TCLC 27**
See also CA 170; DLB 220; EWL 3

Kristeva, Julia 1941- .... **CLC 77, 140**
See also CA 154; CANR 99, 173; DLB 242; EWL 3; FW; LMFS 2

Kristofferson, Kris 1936- .... **CLC 26**
See also CA 104

Krizanc, John 1956- .... **CLC 57**
See also CA 187

Krleza, Miroslav 1893-1981 .... **CLC 8, 114**
See also CA 97-100; 105; CANR 50; CD-WLB 4; DLB 147; EW 11; RGWL 2, 3

Kroetsch, Robert (Paul) 1927- .... **CLC 5, 23, 57, 132, 286**
See also CA 17-20R; CANR 8, 38; CCA 1; CN 2, 3, 4, 5, 6, 7; CP 6, 7; DAC; DAM POET; DLB 53; MTCW 1

Kroetz, Franz
See Kroetz, Franz Xaver

Kroetz, Franz Xaver 1946- .... **CLC 41**
See also CA 130; CANR 142; CWW 2; EWL 3

Kroker, Arthur (W.) 1945- .... **CLC 77**
See also CA 161

Kroniuk, Lisa
See Berton, Pierre (Francis de Marigny)

Kropotkin, Peter 1842-1921 .... **TCLC 36**
See also CA 119; 219; DLB 277

Kropotkin, Peter Alekseieevich
See Kropotkin, Peter

Kropotkin, Petr Alekseevich
See Kropotkin, Peter

Krotkov, Yuri 1917-1981 .... **CLC 19**
See also CA 102

Krumb
See Crumb, R.

Krumgold, Joseph (Quincy) 1908-1980 .... **CLC 12**
See also BYA 1, 2; CA 9-12R; 101; CANR 7; MAICYA 1, 2; SATA 1, 48; SATA-Obit 23; YAW

Krumwitz
See Crumb, R.

Krutch, Joseph Wood 1893-1970 ..... **CLC 24**
See also ANW; CA 1-4R; 25-28R; CANR 4; DLB 63, 206, 275

Krutzch, Gus
See Eliot, T. S.

Krylov, Ivan Andreevich 1768(?)-1844 .... **NCLC 1**
See also DLB 150

Kubin, Alfred (Leopold Isidor) 1877-1959 .... **TCLC 23**
See also CA 112; 149; CANR 104; DLB 81

Kubrick, Stanley 1928-1999 .... **CLC 16; TCLC 112**
See also AAYA 30; CA 81-84; 177; CANR 33; DLB 26

Kueng, Hans
See Kung, Hans

Kumin, Maxine 1925- .... **CLC 5, 13, 28, 164; PC 15**
See also AITN 2; AMWS 4; ANW; CA 1-4R; 271; CAAE 271; CAAS 8; CANR 1, 21, 69, 115, 140; CP 2, 3, 4, 5, 6, 7; CWP; DA3; DAM POET; DLB 5; EWL 3; EXPP; MTCW 1, 2; MTFW 2005; PAB; PFS 18; SATA 12

Kumin, Maxine Winokur
See Kumin, Maxine

Kundera, Milan 1929- . **CLC 4, 9, 19, 32, 68, 115, 135, 234; SSC 24**
See also AAYA 2, 62; BPFB 2; CA 85-88; CANR 19, 52, 74, 144; CDWLB 4; CWW 2; DA3; DAM NOV; DLB 232; EW 13; EWL 3; MTCW 1, 2; MTFW 2005; NFS 18, 27; RGSF 2; RGWL 3; SSFS 10

Kunene, Mazisi 1930-2006 .... **CLC 85**
See also BW 1, 3; CA 125; 252; CANR 81; CP 1, 6, 7; DLB 117

Kunene, Mazisi Raymond
See Kunene, Mazisi

Kunene, Mazisi Raymond Fakazi Mngoni
See Kunene, Mazisi

Kung, Hans
See Kung, Hans

Kung, Hans 1928- .... **CLC 130**
See also CA 53-56; CANR 66, 134; MTCW 1, 2; MTFW 2005

Kunikida, Tetsuo
See Kunikida Doppo

Kunikida Doppo 1869(?)-1908 .... **TCLC 99**
See also DLB 180; EWL 3

Kunikida Tetsuo
See Kunikida Doppo

Kunitz, Stanley 1905-2006 ..... **CLC 6, 11, 14, 148; PC 19**
See also AMWS 3; CA 41-44R; 250; CANR 26, 57, 98; CP 1, 2, 3, 4, 5, 6, 7; DA3; DLB 48; INT CANR-26; MAL 5; MTCW 1, 2; MTFW 2005; PFS 11; RGAL 4

Kunitz, Stanley Jasspon
See Kunitz, Stanley

Kunze, Reiner 1933- .... **CLC 10**
See also CA 93-96; CWW 2; DLB 75; EWL 3

Kuprin, Aleksander Ivanovich 1870-1938 .... **TCLC 5**
See also CA 104; 182; DLB 295; EWL 3

Kuprin, Aleksandr Ivanovich
See Kuprin, Aleksander Ivanovich

Kuprin, Alexandr Ivanovich
See Kuprin, Aleksander Ivanovich

Kureishi, Hanif 1954- ...... **CLC 64, 135, 284; DC 26**
See also BRWS 11; CA 139; CANR 113, 197; CBD; CD 5, 6; CN 6, 7; DLB 194, 245, 352; GLL 2; IDFW 4; WLIT 4; WWE 1

Kurosawa, Akira 1910-1998 ..... **CLC 16, 119**
See also AAYA 11, 64; CA 101; 170; CANR 46; DAM MULT

Kushner, Tony 1956- ... **CLC 81, 203; DC 10**
See also AAYA 61; AMWS 9; CA 144; CAD; CANR 74, 130; CD 5, 6; DA3; DAM DRAM; DFS 5; DLB 228; EWL 3; GLL 1; LAIT 5; MAL 5; MTCW 2; MTFW 2005; RGAL 4; RGHL; SATA 160

Kuttner, Henry 1915-1958 .... **TCLC 10**
See also CA 107; 157; DLB 8; FANT; SCFW 1, 2; SFW 4

Kutty, Madhavi
See Das, Kamala

Kuzma, Greg 1944- .... **CLC 7**
See also CA 33-36R; CANR 70

Kuzmin, Mikhail (Alekseevich) 1872(?)-1936 .... **TCLC 40**
See also CA 170; DLB 295; EWL 3

Kyd, Thomas 1558-1594 .. **DC 3; LC 22, 125**
See also BRW 1; DAM DRAM; DFS 21; DLB 62; IDTP; LMFS 1; RGEL 2; TEA; WLIT 3

Kyprianos, Iossif
See Samarakis, Antonis

L. S.
See Stephen, Sir Leslie

Labe, Louise 1521-1566 .... **LC 120**
See also DLB 327

Labrunie, Gerard
See Nerval, Gerard de

La Bruyere, Jean de 1645-1696 .. **LC 17, 168**
See also DLB 268; EW 3; GFL Beginnings to 1789

LaBute, Neil 1963- .... **CLC 225**
See also CA 240

Lacan, Jacques (Marie Emile) 1901-1981 .... **CLC 75**
See also CA 121; 104; DLB 296; EWL 3; TWA

Laclos, Pierre-Ambroise Francois 1741-1803 .... **NCLC 4, 87**
See also DLB 313; EW 4; GFL Beginnings to 1789; RGWL 2, 3

La Colere, Francois
See Aragon, Louis

Macaulay, (Emilie) Rose
1881(?)-1958 .... **TCLC 7, 44**
See also CA 104; DLB 36; EWL 3; RGEL
2; RHW

Macaulay, Thomas Babington
1800-1859 .... **NCLC 42**
See also BRW 4; CDBLB 1832-1890; DLB
32, 55; RGEL 2

MacBeth, George (Mann)
1932-1992 .... **CLC 2, 5, 9**
See also CA 25-28R; CANR 61, 66;
CP 1, 2, 3, 4, 5; DLB 40; MTCW 1; PFS
8; SATA 4; SATA-Obit 70

MacCaig, Norman (Alexander)
1910-1996 .... **CLC 36**
See also BRWS 6; CA 9-12R; CANR 3, 34;
CP 1, 2, 3, 4, 5, 6; DAB; DAM POET;
DLB 27; EWL 3; RGEL 2

MacCarthy, Sir (Charles Otto) Desmond
1877-1952 .... **TCLC 36**
See also CA 167

MacDiarmid, Hugh
See Grieve, C. M.

MacDonald, Anson
See Heinlein, Robert A.

Macdonald, Cynthia 1928- .... **CLC 13, 19**
See also CA 49-52; CANR 4, 44, 146; DLB
105

MacDonald, George 1824-1905 .... **TCLC 9,
113, 207**
See also AAYA 57; BYA 5; CA 106; 137;
CANR 80; CLR 67; DLB 18, 163, 178;
FANT; MAICYA 1, 2; RGEL 2; SATA 33,
100; SFW 4; SUFW; WCH

Macdonald, John
See Millar, Kenneth

MacDonald, John D. 1916-1986 .. **CLC 3, 27,
44**
See also BPFB 2; CA 1-4R; 121; CANR 1,
19, 60; CMW 4; CPW; DAM NOV, POP;
DLB 8, 306; DLBY 1986; MSW; MTCW
1, 2; MTFW 2005; SFW 4

Macdonald, John Ross
See Millar, Kenneth

Macdonald, Ross
See Millar, Kenneth

MacDonald Fraser, George
See Fraser, George MacDonald

MacDougal, John
See Blish, James

MacDowell, John
See Parks, Tim(othy Harold)

MacEwen, Gwendolyn (Margaret)
1941-1987 .... **CLC 13, 55**
See also CA 9-12R; 124; CANR 7, 22; CP
1, 2, 3, 4; DLB 53, 251; SATA 50; SATA-
Obit 55

MacGreevy, Thomas 1893-1967 .... **PC 82**
See also CA 262

Macha, Karel Hynek 1810-1846 .... **NCLC 46**

Machado (y Ruiz), Antonio
1875-1939 .... **TCLC 3**
See also CA 104; 174; DLB 108; EW 9;
EWL 3; HW 2; PFS 23; RGWL 2, 3

Machado de Assis, Joaquim Maria
1839-1908 . **BLC 1:2; HLCS 2; SSC 24,
118; TCLC 10**
See also CA 107; 153; CANR 91; DLB 307;
LAW; RGSF 2; RGWL 2, 3; TWA; WLIT
1

Machaut, Guillaume de c.
1300-1377 .... **CMLC 64**
See also DLB 208

Machen, Arthur SSC 20; TCLC 4
See Jones, Arthur Llewellyn
See also CA 179; DLB 156, 178; RGEL 2

Machen, Arthur Llewelyn Jones
See Jones, Arthur Llewellyn

Machiavelli, Niccolo 1469-1527 ... **DC 16; LC
8, 36, 140; WLCS**
See also AAYA 58; DA; DAB; DAC; DAM
MST; EW 2; LAIT 1; LMFS 1; NFS 9;
RGWL 2, 3; TWA; WLIT 7

MacInnes, Colin 1914-1976 .... **CLC 4, 23**
See also CA 69-72; 65-68; CANR 21; CN
1, 2; DLB 14; MTCW 1, 2; RGEL 2;
RHW

MacInnes, Helen (Clark)
1907-1985 .... **CLC 27, 39**
See also BPFB 2; CA 1-4R; 117; CANR 1,
28, 58; CMW 4; CN 1, 2; CPW; DAM
POP; DLB 87; MSW; MTCW 1, 2;
MTFW 2005; SATA 22; SATA-Obit 44

Mackay, Mary 1855-1924 .... **TCLC 51**
See also CA 118; 177; DLB 34, 156; FANT;
RGEL 2; RHW; SUFW 1

Mackay, Shena 1944- .... **CLC 195**
See also CA 104; CANR 88, 139; DLB 231,
319; MTFW 2005

Mackenzie, Compton (Edward Montague)
1883-1972 .... **CLC 18; TCLC 116**
See also CA 21-22; 37-40R; CAP 2; CN 1;
DLB 34, 100; RGEL 2

Mackenzie, Henry 1745-1831 .... **NCLC 41**
See also DLB 39; RGEL 2

Mackey, Nathaniel 1947- .... **BLC 2:3; PC 49**
See also CA 153; CANR 114; CP 6, 7; DLB
169

Mackey, Nathaniel Ernest
See Mackey, Nathaniel

MacKinnon, Catharine
See MacKinnon, Catharine A.

MacKinnon, Catharine A. 1946- .... **CLC 181**
See also CA 128; 132; CANR 73, 140, 189;
FW; MTCW 2; MTFW 2005

Mackintosh, Elizabeth
1896(?)-1952 .... **TCLC 14**
See also CA 110; CMW 4; DLB 10, 77;
MSW

Macklin, Charles 1699-1797 .... **LC 132**
See also DLB 89; RGEL 2

MacLaren, James
See Grieve, C. M.

MacLaverty, Bernard 1942- ..... **CLC 31, 243**
See also CA 116; 118; CANR 43, 88, 168;
CN 5, 6, 7; DLB 267; INT CA-118; RGSF
2

MacLean, Alistair 1922(?)-1987 .. **CLC 3, 13,
50, 63**
See also CA 57-60; 121; CANR 28, 61;
CMW 4; CP 2, 3, 4, 5, 6, 7; CPW; DAM
POP; DLB 276; MTCW 1; SATA 23;
SATA-Obit 50; TCWW 2

MacLean, Alistair Stuart
See MacLean, Alistair

Maclean, Norman (Fitzroy)
1902-1990 .... **CLC 78; SSC 13, 136**
See also AMWS 14; CA 102; 132; CANR
49; CPW; DAM POP; DLB 206; TCWW
2

MacLeish, Archibald 1892-1982 ... **CLC 3, 8,
14, 68; PC 47**
See also AMW; CA 9-12R; 106; CAD;
CANR 33, 63; CDALBS; CP 1, 2; DAM
POET; DFS 15; DLB 4, 7, 45; DLBY
1982; EWL 3; EXPP; MAL 5; MTCW 1,
2; MTFW 2005; PAB; PFS 5; RGAL 4;
TUS

MacLennan, (John) Hugh
1907-1990 .... **CLC 2, 14, 92**
See also CA 5-8R; 142; CANR 33; CN 1,
2, 3, 4; DAC; DAM MST; DLB 68; EWL
3; MTCW 1, 2; MTFW 2005; RGEL 2;
TWA

MacLeod, Alistair 1936- .. **CLC 56, 165; SSC
90**
See also CA 123; CCA 1; DAC; DAM
MST; DLB 60; MTCW 2; MTFW 2005;
RGSF 2; TCLE 1:2

Macleod, Fiona
See Sharp, William

MacNeice, (Frederick) Louis
1907-1963 .... **CLC 1, 4, 10, 53; PC 61**
See also BRW 7; CA 85-88; CANR 61;
DAB; DAM POET; DLB 10, 20; EWL 3;
MTCW 1, 2; MTFW 2005; RGEL 2

MacNeill, Dand
See Fraser, George MacDonald

Macpherson, James 1736-1796 .... **CMLC 28;
LC 29; PC 97**
See also BRWS 8; DLB 109, 336; RGEL 2

Macpherson, (Jean) Jay 1931- .... **CLC 14**
See also CA 5-8R; CANR 90; CP 1, 2, 3, 4,
6, 7; CWP; DLB 53

Macrobius fl. 430- .... **CMLC 48**

MacShane, Frank 1927-1999 .... **CLC 39**
See also CA 9-12R; 186; CANR 3, 33; DLB
111

Macumber, Mari
See Sandoz, Mari(e Susette)

Madach, Imre 1823-1864 .... **NCLC 19**

Madden, (Jerry) David 1933- .... **CLC 5, 15**
See also CA 1-4R; CAAS 3; CANR 4, 45;
CN 3, 4, 5, 6, 7; CSW; DLB 6; MTCW 1

Maddern, Al(an)
See Ellison, Harlan

Madhubuti, Haki R. 1942- .... **BLC 1:2; CLC
2; PC 5**
See also BW 2, 3; CA 73-76; CANR 24,
51, 73, 139; CP 2, 3, 4, 5, 6, 7; CSW;
DAM MULT, POET; DLB 5, 41; DLBD
8; EWL 3; MAL 5; MTCW 2; MTFW
2005; RGAL 4

Madison, James 1751-1836 .... **NCLC 126**
See also DLB 37

Maepenn, Hugh
See Kuttner, Henry

Maepenn, K. H.
See Kuttner, Henry

Maeterlinck, Maurice 1862-1949 .... **DC 32;
TCLC 3**
See also CA 104; 136; CANR 80; DAM
DRAM; DLB 192, 331; EW 8; EWL 3;
GFL 1789 to the Present; LMFS 2; RGWL
2, 3; SATA 66; TWA

Maginn, William 1794-1842 .... **NCLC 8**
See also DLB 110, 159

Mahapatra, Jayanta 1928- .... **CLC 33**
See also CA 73-76; CAAS 9; CANR 15,
33, 66, 87; CP 4, 5, 6, 7; DAM MULT;
DLB 323

Mahfouz, Nagib
See Mahfouz, Naguib

Mahfouz, Naguib 1911(?)-2006 . **CLC 52, 55,
153; SSC 66**
See also AAYA 49; AFW; BEST 89:2; CA
128; 253; CANR 55, 101; DA3; DAM
NOV; DLB 346; DLBY 1988; MTCW 1,
2; MTFW 2005; RGSF 2; RGWL 2, 3;
SSFS 9; WLIT 2

Mahfouz, Naguib Abdel Aziz Al-Sabilgi
See Mahfouz, Naguib

Mahfouz, Najib
See Mahfouz, Naguib

Mahfuz, Najib
See Mahfouz, Naguib

Mahon, Derek 1941- .... **CLC 27; PC 60**
See also BRWS 6; CA 113; 128; CANR 88;
CP 1, 2, 3, 4, 5, 6, 7; DLB 40; EWL 3

Maiakovskii, Vladimir
See Mayakovski, Vladimir

Marx, Karl Heinrich
See Marx, Karl
Masaoka, Shiki -1902
See Masaoka, Tsunenori
Masaoka, Tsunenori 1867-1902 ..... **TCLC 18**
See also CA 117; 191; EWL 3; RGWL 3;
TWA
Masaoka Shiki
See Masaoka, Tsunenori
Masefield, John (Edward)
1878-1967 .... **CLC 11, 47; PC 78**
See also CA 19-20; 25-28R; CANR 33;
CAP 2; CDBLB 1890-1914; DAM POET;
DLB 10, 19, 153, 160; EWL 3; EXPP;
FANT; MTCW 1, 2; PFS 5; RGEL 2;
SATA 19
Maso, Carole 1955(?)- .... **CLC 44**
See also CA 170; CANR 148; CN 7; GLL
2; RGAL 4
Mason, Bobbie Ann 1940- ... **CLC 28, 43, 82,**
154; SSC 4, 101
See also AAYA 5, 42; AMWS 8; BPFB 2;
CA 53-56; CANR 11, 31, 58, 83, 125,
169; CDALBS; CN 5, 6, 7; CSW; DA3;
DLB 173; DLBY 1987; EWL 3; EXPS;
INT CANR-31; MAL 5; MTCW 1, 2;
MTFW 2005; NFS 4; RGAL 4; RGSF 2;
SSFS 3, 8, 20; TCLE 1:2; YAW
Mason, Ernst
See Pohl, Frederik
Mason, Hunni B.
See Sternheim, (William Adolf) Carl
Mason, Lee W.
See Malzberg, Barry N(athaniel)
Mason, Nick 1945- .... **CLC 35**
Mason, Tally
See Derleth, August (William)
Mass, Anna CLC 59
Mass, William
See Gibson, William
Massinger, Philip 1583-1640 .... **LC 70**
See also BRWS 11; DLB 58; RGEL 2
Master Lao
See Lao Tzu
Masters, Edgar Lee 1868-1950 ...... **PC 1, 36;**
TCLC 2, 25; WLCS
See also AMWS 1; CA 104; 133; CDALB
1865-1917; DA; DAC; DAM MST,
POET; DLB 54; EWL 3; EXPP; MAL 5;
MTCW 1, 2; MTFW 2005; RGAL 4;
TUS; WP
Masters, Hilary 1928- .... **CLC 48**
See also CA 25-28R; 217; CAAE 217;
CANR 13, 47, 97, 171; CN 6, 7; DLB
244
Masters, Hilary Thomas
See Masters, Hilary
Mastrosimone, William 1947- .... **CLC 36**
See also CA 186; CAD; CD 5, 6
Mathe, Albert
See Camus, Albert
Mather, Cotton 1663-1728 .... **LC 38**
See also AMWS 2; CDALB 1640-1865;
DLB 24, 30, 140; RGAL 4; TUS
Mather, Increase 1639-1723 .... **LC 38, 161**
See also DLB 24
Mathers, Marshall
See Eminem
Mathers, Marshall Bruce
See Eminem
Matheson, Richard 1926- .... **CLC 37, 267**
See also AAYA 31; CA 97-100; CANR 88,
99; DLB 8, 44; HGG; INT CA-97-100;
SCFW 1, 2; SFW 4; SUFW 2
Matheson, Richard Burton
See Matheson, Richard
Mathews, Harry 1930- .... **CLC 6, 52**
See also CA 21-24R; CAAS 6; CANR 18,
40, 98, 160; CN 5, 6, 7

Mathews, John Joseph 1894-1979 .. **CLC 84;**
NNAL
See also CA 19-20; 142; CANR 45; CAP 2;
DAM MULT; DLB 175; TCWW 1, 2
Mathias, Roland 1915-2007 .... **CLC 45**
See also CA 97-100; 263; CANR 19, 41;
CP 1, 2, 3, 4, 5, 6, 7; DLB 27
Mathias, Roland Glyn
See Mathias, Roland
Matsuo Bashō 1644(?)-1694 ...... **LC 62; PC 3**
See also DAM POET; PFS 2, 7, 18; RGWL
2, 3; WP
Mattheson, Rodney
See Creasey, John
Matthew, James
See Barrie, J. M.
Matthew of Vendome c. 1130-c.
1200 .... **CMLC 99**
See also DLB 208
Matthews, (James) Brander
1852-1929 .... **TCLC 95**
See also CA 181; DLB 71, 78; DLBD 13
Matthews, Greg 1949- .... **CLC 45**
See also CA 135
Matthews, William (Procter III)
1942-1997 .... **CLC 40**
See also AMWS 9; CA 29-32R; 162; CAAS
18; CANR 12, 57; CP 2, 3, 4, 5, 6; DLB
5
Matthias, John (Edward) 1941- .... **CLC 9**
See also CA 33-36R; CANR 56; CP 4, 5, 6,
7
Matthiessen, F(rancis) O(tto)
1902-1950 .... **TCLC 100**
See also CA 185; DLB 63; MAL 5
Matthiessen, Peter 1927- ... **CLC 5, 7, 11, 32,**
64, 245
See also AAYA 6, 40; AMWS 5; ANW;
BEST 90:4; BPFB 2; CA 9-12R; CANR
21, 50, 73, 100, 138; CN 1, 2, 3, 4, 5, 6,
7; DA3; DAM NOV; DLB 6, 173, 275;
MAL 5; MTCW 1, 2; MTFW 2005; SATA
27
Maturin, Charles Robert
1780(?)-1824 .... **NCLC 6, 169**
See also BRWS 8; DLB 178; GL 3; HGG;
LMFS 1; RGEL 2; SUFW
Matute (Ausejo), Ana Maria 1925- .. **CLC 11**
See also CA 89-92; CANR 129; CWW 2;
DLB 322; EWL 3; MTCW 1; RGSF 2
Maugham, W. S.
See Maugham, W. Somerset
Maugham, W. Somerset 1874-1965 ... **CLC 1,**
11, 15, 67, 93; SSC 8, 94; TCLC 208;
WLC 4
See also AAYA 55; BPFB 2; BRW 6; CA
5-8R; 25-28R; CANR 40, 127; CDBLB
1914-1945; CMW 4; DA; DA3; DAB;
DAC; DAM DRAM, MST, NOV; DFS
22; DLB 10, 36, 77, 100, 162, 195; EWL
3; LAIT 3; MTCW 1, 2; MTFW 2005;
NFS 23; RGEL 2; RGSF 2; SATA 54;
SSFS 17
Maugham, William S.
See Maugham, W. Somerset
Maugham, William Somerset
See Maugham, W. Somerset
Maupassant, Guy de 1850-1893 ..... **NCLC 1,**
42, 83; SSC 1, 64, 132; WLC 4
See also BYA 14; DA; DA3; DAB; DAC;
DAM MST; DLB 123; EW 7; EXPS; GFL
1789 to the Present; LAIT 2; LMFS 1;
RGSF 2; RGWL 2, 3; SSFS 4, 21; SUFW;
TWA
Maupassant, Henri Rene Albert Guy de
See Maupassant, Guy de

Maupin, Armistead 1944- .... **CLC 95**
See also CA 125; 130; CANR 58, 101, 183;
CPW; DA3; DAM POP; DLB 278; GLL
1; INT CA-130; MTCW 2; MTFW 2005
Maupin, Armistead Jones, Jr.
See Maupin, Armistead
Maurhut, Richard
See Traven, B.
Mauriac, Claude 1914-1996 .... **CLC 9**
See also CA 89-92; 152; CWW 2; DLB 83;
EWL 3; GFL 1789 to the Present
Mauriac, Francois (Charles)
1885-1970 .... **CLC 4, 9, 56; SSC 24**
See also CA 25-28; CAP 2; DLB 65, 331;
EW 10; EWL 3; GFL 1789 to the Present;
MTCW 1, 2; MTFW 2005; RGWL 2, 3;
TWA
Mavor, Osborne Henry 1888-1951 .. **TCLC 3**
See also CA 104; DLB 10; EWL 3
Maxwell, Glyn 1962- .... **CLC 238**
See also CA 154; CANR 88, 183; CP 6, 7;
PFS 23
Maxwell, William (Keepers, Jr.)
1908-2000 .... **CLC 19**
See also AMWS 8; CA 93-96; 189; CANR
54, 95; CN 1, 2, 3, 4, 5, 6, 7; DLB 218,
278; DLBY 1980; INT CA-93-96; MAL
5; SATA-Obit 128
May, Elaine 1932- .... **CLC 16**
See also CA 124; 142; CAD; CWD; DLB
44
Mayakovski, Vladimir 1893-1930 ... **TCLC 4,**
18
See also CA 104; 158; EW 11; EWL 3;
IDTP; MTCW 2; MTFW 2005; RGWL 2,
3; SFW 4; TWA; WP
Mayakovski, Vladimir Vladimirovich
See Mayakovski, Vladimir
Mayakovsky, Vladimir
See Mayakovski, Vladimir
Mayhew, Henry 1812-1887 .... **NCLC 31**
See also DLB 18, 55, 190
Mayle, Peter 1939(?)- .... **CLC 89**
See also CA 139; CANR 64, 109, 168
Maynard, Joyce 1953- .... **CLC 23**
See also CA 111; 129; CANR 64, 169
Mayne, William (James Carter)
1928- .... **CLC 12**
See also AAYA 20; CA 9-12R; CANR 37,
80, 100; CLR 25, 123; FANT; JRDA;
MAICYA 1, 2; MAICYAS 1; SAAS 11;
SATA 6, 68, 122; SUFW 2; YAW
Mayo, Jim
See L'Amour, Louis
Maysles, Albert 1926- .... **CLC 16**
See also CA 29-32R
Maysles, David 1932-1987 .... **CLC 16**
See also CA 191
Mazer, Norma Fox 1931-2009 .... **CLC 26**
See also AAYA 5, 36; BYA 1, 8; CA 69-72;
292; CANR 12, 32, 66, 129, 189; CLR
23; JRDA; MAICYA 1, 2; SAAS 1; SATA
24, 67, 105, 168, 198; WYA; YAW
Mazzini, Guiseppe 1805-1872 .... **NCLC 34**
McAlmon, Robert (Menzies)
1895-1956 .... **TCLC 97**
See also CA 107; 168; DLB 4, 45; DLBD
15; GLL 1
McAuley, James Phillip 1917-1976 .. **CLC 45**
See also CA 97-100; CP 1, 2; DLB 260;
RGEL 2
McBain, Ed
See Hunter, Evan
McBrien, William 1930- .... **CLC 44**
See also CA 107; CANR 90
McBrien, William Augustine
See McBrien, William

McNally, Terrence 1939- ... **CLC 4, 7, 41, 91, 252; DC 27**
See also AAYA 62; AMWS 13; CA 45-48; CAD; CANR 2, 56, 116; CD 5, 6; DA3; DAM DRAM; DFS 16, 19; DLB 7, 249; EWL 3; GLL 1; MTCW 2; MTFW 2005

McNally, Thomas Michael
See McNally, T.M.

McNally, T.M. 1961- .... **CLC 82**
See also CA 246

McNamer, Deirdre 1950- .... **CLC 70**
See also CA 188; CANR 163, 200

McNeal, Tom CLC 119
See also CA 252; CANR 185; SATA 194

McNeile, Herman Cyril 1888-1937 .... **TCLC 44**
See also CA 184; CMW 4; DLB 77

McNickle, D'Arcy 1904-1977 .... **CLC 89; NNAL**
See also CA 9-12R; 85-88; CANR 5, 45; DAM MULT; DLB 175, 212; RGAL 4; SATA-Obit 22; TCWW 1, 2

McNickle, William D'Arcy
See McNickle, D'Arcy

McPhee, John 1931- .... **CLC 36**
See also AAYA 61; AMWS 3; ANW; BEST 90:1; CA 65-68; CANR 20, 46, 64, 69, 121, 165; CPW; DLB 185, 275; MTCW 1, 2; MTFW 2005; TUS

McPhee, John Angus
See McPhee, John

McPherson, James Alan, Jr.
See McPherson, James Alan

McPherson, James Alan 1943- . **BLCS; CLC 19, 77; SSC 95**
See also BW 1, 3; CA 25-28R, 273; CAAE 273; CAAS 17; CANR 24, 74, 140; CN 3, 4, 5, 6; CSW; DLB 38, 244; EWL 3; MTCW 1, 2; MTFW 2005; RGAL 4; RGSF 2; SSFS 23

McPherson, William (Alexander) 1933- .... **CLC 34**
See also CA 69-72; CANR 28; INT CANR-28

McTaggart, J. McT. Ellis
See McTaggart, John McTaggart Ellis

McTaggart, John McTaggart Ellis 1866-1925 .... **TCLC 105**
See also CA 120; DLB 262

Mda, Zakes 1948- .... **BLC 2:3; CLC 262**
See also BRWS 15; CA 205; CANR 151, 185; CD 5, 6; DLB 225

Mda, Zanemvula
See Mda, Zakes

Mda, Zanemvula Kizito Gatyeni
See Mda, Zakes

Mead, George Herbert 1863-1931 . **TCLC 89**
See also CA 212; DLB 270

Mead, Margaret 1901-1978 .... **CLC 37**
See also AITN 1; CA 1-4R; 81-84; CANR 4; DA3; FW; MTCW 1, 2; SATA-Obit 20

Meaker, M. J.
See Meaker, Marijane

Meaker, Marijane 1927- .... **CLC 12, 35**
See also AAYA 2, 23, 82; BYA 1, 7, 8; CA 107; CANR 37, 63, 145, 180; CLR 29; GLL 2; INT CA-107; JRDA; MAICYA 1, 2; MAICYAS 1; MTCW 1; SAAS 1; SATA 20, 61, 99, 160; SATA-Essay 111; WYA; YAW

Meaker, Marijane Agnes
See Meaker, Marijane

Mechthild von Magdeburg c. 1207-c. 1282 .... **CMLC 91**
See also DLB 138

Medoff, Mark (Howard) 1940- .... **CLC 6, 23**
See also AITN 1; CA 53-56; CAD; CANR 5; CD 5, 6; DAM DRAM; DFS 4; DLB 7; INT CANR-5

Medvedev, P. N.
See Bakhtin, Mikhail Mikhailovich

Meged, Aharon
See Megged, Aharon

Meged, Aron
See Megged, Aharon

Megged, Aharon 1920- .... **CLC 9**
See also CA 49-52; CAAS 13; CANR 1, 140; EWL 3; RGHL

Mehta, Deepa 1950- .... **CLC 208**

Mehta, Gita 1943- .... **CLC 179**
See also CA 225; CN 7; DNFS 2

Mehta, Ved 1934- .... **CLC 37**
See also CA 1-4R, 212; CAAE 212; CANR 2, 23, 69; DLB 323; MTCW 1; MTFW 2005

Melanchthon, Philipp 1497-1560 .... **LC 90**
See also DLB 179

Melanter
See Blackmore, R(ichard) D(oddridge)

Meleager c. 140B.C.-c. 70B.C. ...... **CMLC 53**

Melies, Georges 1861-1938 .... **TCLC 81**

Melikow, Loris
See Hofmannsthal, Hugo von

Melmoth, Sebastian
See Wilde, Oscar

Melo Neto, Joao Cabral de
See Cabral de Melo Neto, Joao

Meltzer, Milton 1915-2009 .... **CLC 26**
See also AAYA 8, 45; BYA 2, 6; CA 13-16R; 290; CANR 38, 92, 107, 192; CLR 13; DLB 61; JRDA; MAICYA 1, 2; SAAS 1; SATA 1, 50, 80, 128, 201; SATA-Essay 124; WYA; YAW

Melville, Herman 1819-1891 ..... **NCLC 3, 12, 29, 45, 49, 91, 93, 123, 157, 181, 193, 221; PC 82; SSC 1, 17, 46, 95; WLC 4**
See also AAYA 25; AMW; AMWR 1; CDALB 1640-1865; DA; DA3; DAB; DAC; DAM MST, NOV; DLB 3, 74, 250, 254, 349; EXPN; EXPS; GL 3; LAIT 1, 2; NFS 7, 9; RGAL 4; RGSF 2; SATA 59; SSFS 3; TUS

Members, Mark
See Powell, Anthony

Membreno, Alejandro CLC 59

Menand, Louis 1952- .... **CLC 208**
See also CA 200

Menander c. 342B.C.-c. 293B.C. .... **CMLC 9, 51, 101; DC 3**
See also AW 1; CDWLB 1; DAM DRAM; DLB 176; LMFS 1; RGWL 2, 3

Menchu, Rigoberta 1959- .. **CLC 160; HLCS 2**
See also CA 175; CANR 135; DNFS 1; WLIT 1

Mencken, H. L. 1880-1956 .... **TCLC 13, 18**
See also AMW; CA 105; 125; CDALB 1917-1929; DLB 11, 29, 63, 137, 222; EWL 3; MAL 5; MTCW 1, 2; MTFW 2005; NCFS 4; RGAL 4; TUS

Mencken, Henry Louis
See Mencken, H. L.

Mendelsohn, Jane 1965- .... **CLC 99**
See also CA 154; CANR 94

Mendelssohn, Moses 1729-1786 .... **LC 142**
See also DLB 97

Mendoza, Inigo Lopez de
See Santillana, Inigo Lopez de Mendoza, Marques de

Menton, Francisco de
See Chin, Frank

Mercer, David 1928-1980 .... **CLC 5**
See also CA 9-12R; 102; CANR 23; CBD; DAM DRAM; DLB 13, 310; MTCW 1; RGEL 2

Merchant, Paul
See Ellison, Harlan

Meredith, George 1828-1909 .. **PC 60; TCLC 17, 43**
See also CA 117; 153; CANR 80; CDBLB 1832-1890; DAM POET; DLB 18, 35, 57, 159; RGEL 2; TEA

Meredith, William 1919-2007 ...... **CLC 4, 13, 22, 55; PC 28**
See also CA 9-12R; 260; CAAS 14; CANR 6, 40, 129; CP 1, 2, 3, 4, 5, 6, 7; DAM POET; DLB 5; MAL 5

Meredith, William Morris
See Meredith, William

Merezhkovsky, Dmitrii Sergeevich
See Merezhkovsky, Dmitry Sergeyevich

Merezhkovsky, Dmitry Sergeevich
See Merezhkovsky, Dmitry Sergeyevich

Merezhkovsky, Dmitry Sergeyevich 1865-1941 .... **TCLC 29**
See also CA 169; DLB 295; EWL 3

Merezhkovsky, Zinaida
See Gippius, Zinaida

Merimee, Prosper 1803-1870 . **DC 33; NCLC 6, 65; SSC 7, 77**
See also DLB 119, 192; EW 6; EXPS; GFL 1789 to the Present; RGSF 2; RGWL 2, 3; SSFS 8; SUFW

Merkin, Daphne 1954- .... **CLC 44**
See also CA 123

Merleau-Ponty, Maurice 1908-1961 .... **TCLC 156**
See also CA 114; 89-92; DLB 296; GFL 1789 to the Present

Merlin, Arthur
See Blish, James

Mernissi, Fatima 1940- .... **CLC 171**
See also CA 152; DLB 346; FW

Merrill, James 1926-1995 ...... **CLC 2, 3, 6, 8, 13, 18, 34, 91; PC 28; TCLC 173**
See also AMWS 3; CA 13-16R; 147; CANR 10, 49, 63, 108; CP 1, 2, 3, 4; DA3; DAM POET; DLB 5, 165; DLBY 1985; EWL 3; INT CANR-10; MAL 5; MTCW 1, 2; MTFW 2005; PAB; PFS 23; RGAL 4

Merrill, James Ingram
See Merrill, James

Merriman, Alex
See Silverberg, Robert

Merriman, Brian 1747-1805 .... **NCLC 70**

Merritt, E. B.
See Waddington, Miriam

Merton, Thomas 1915-1968 ..... **CLC 1, 3, 11, 34, 83; PC 10**
See also AAYA 61; AMWS 8; CA 5-8R; 25-28R; CANR 22, 53, 111, 131; DA3; DLB 48; DLBY 1981; MAL 5; MTCW 1, 2; MTFW 2005

Merton, Thomas James
See Merton, Thomas

Merwin, William Stanley
See Merwin, W.S.

Merwin, W.S. 1927- ..... **CLC 1, 2, 3, 5, 8, 13, 18, 45, 88; PC 45**
See also AMWS 3; CA 13-16R; CANR 15, 51, 112, 140; CP 1, 2, 3, 4, 5, 6, 7; DA3; DAM POET; DLB 5, 169, 342; EWL 3; INT CANR-15; MAL 5; MTCW 1, 2; MTFW 2005; PAB; PFS 5, 15; RGAL 4

Metastasio, Pietro 1698-1782 .... **LC 115**
See also RGWL 2, 3

Metcalf, John 1938- .... **CLC 37; SSC 43**
See also CA 113; CN 4, 5, 6, 7; DLB 60; RGSF 2; TWA

Metcalf, Suzanne
See Baum, L. Frank

Mew, Charlotte (Mary) 1870-1928 .. **TCLC 8**
See also CA 105; 189; DLB 19, 135; RGEL 2

Myers, L(eopold) H(amilton)
1881-1944 .... **TCLC 59**
See also CA 157; DLB 15; EWL 3; RGEL
2

Myers, Walter Dean 1937- ...... **BLC 1:3, 2:3;
CLC 35**
See also AAYA 4, 23; BW 2; BYA 6, 8, 11;
CA 33-36R; CANR 20, 42, 67, 108, 184;
CLR 4, 16, 35, 110; DAM MULT, NOV;
DLB 33; INT CANR-20; JRDA; LAIT 5;
LNFS 1; MAICYA 1, 2; MAICYAS 1;
MTCW 2; MTFW 2005; NFS 30; SAAS
2; SATA 41, 71, 109, 157, 193; SATA-
Brief 27; WYA; YAW

Myers, Walter M.
See Myers, Walter Dean

Myles, Symon
See Follett, Ken

Nabokov, Vladimir 1899-1977 ... **CLC 1, 2, 3,
6, 8, 11, 15, 23, 44, 46, 64; SSC 11, 86;
TCLC 108, 189; WLC 4**
See also AAYA 45; AMW; AMWC 1;
AMWR 1; BPFB 2; CA 5-8R; 69-72;
CANR 20, 102; CDALB 1941-1968; CN
1, 2; CP 2; DA; DA3; DAB; DAC; DAM
MST, NOV; DLB 2, 244, 278, 317; DLBD
3; DLBY 1980, 1991; EWL 3; EXPS;
LATS 1:2; MAL 5; MTCW 1, 2; MTFW
2005; NCFS 4; NFS 9; RGAL 4; RGSF
2; SSFS 6, 15; TUS

Nabokov, Vladimir Vladimirovich
See Nabokov, Vladimir

Naevius c. 265B.C.-201B.C. .... **CMLC 37**
See also DLB 211

Nagai, Kafu 1879-1959 .... **TCLC 51**
See also CA 117; 276; DLB 180; EWL 3;
MJW

Nagai, Sokichi
See Nagai, Kafu

Nagai Kafu
See Nagai, Kafu

na gCopaleen, Myles
See O Nuallain, Brian

na Gopaleen, Myles
See O Nuallain, Brian

Nagy, Laszlo 1925-1978 .... **CLC 7**
See also CA 129; 112

Naidu, Sarojini 1879-1949 .... **TCLC 80**
See also EWL 3; RGEL 2

Naipaul, Shiva 1945-1985 .... **CLC 32, 39;
TCLC 153**
See also CA 110; 112; 116; CANR 33; CN
2, 3; DA3; DAM NOV; DLB 157; DLBY
1985; EWL 3; MTCW 1, 2; MTFW 2005

Naipaul, Shivadhar Srinivasa
See Naipaul, Shiva

Naipaul, V. S. 1932- . **CLC 4, 7, 9, 13, 18, 37,
105, 199; SSC 38, 121**
See also BPFB 2; BRWS 1; CA 1-4R;
CANR 1, 33, 51, 91, 126, 191; CDBLB
1960 to Present; CDWLB 3; CN 1, 2, 3,
4, 5, 6, 7; DA3; DAB; DAC; DAM MST,
NOV; DLB 125, 204, 207, 326, 331;
DLBY 1985, 2001; EWL 3; LATS 1:2;
MTCW 1, 2; MTFW 2005; RGEL 2;
RGSF 2; TWA; WLIT 4; WWE 1

Naipaul, Vidiahar Surajprasad
See Naipaul, V. S.

Nair, Kamala
See Das, Kamala

Nakos, Lilika 1903-1989 .... **CLC 29**
See also CA 217

Nalapat, Kamala
See Das, Kamala

Napoleon
See Yamamoto, Hisaye

Narayan, R. K. 1906-2001 ..... **CLC 7, 28, 47,
121, 211; SSC 25**
See also BPFB 2; CA 81-84; 196; CANR
33, 61, 112; CN 1, 2, 3, 4, 5, 6, 7; DA3;
DAM NOV; DLB 323; DNFS 1; EWL 3;
MTCW 1, 2; MTFW 2005; RGEL 2;
RGSF 2; SATA 62; SSFS 5; WWE 1

Narayan, Rasipuram Krishnaswami
See Narayan, R. K.

Nash, Frediric Ogden
See Nash, Ogden

Nash, Ogden 1902-1971 ...... **CLC 23; PC 21;
TCLC 109**
See also CA 13-14; 29-32R; CANR 34, 61,
185; CAP 1; CP 1; DAM POET; DLB 11;
MAICYA 1, 2; MAL 5; MTCW 1, 2; PFS
31; RGAL 4; SATA 2, 46; WP

Nashe, Thomas 1567-1601(?) . **LC 41, 89; PC
82**
See also DLB 167; RGEL 2

Nathan, Daniel
See Dannay, Frederic

Nathan, George Jean 1882-1958 .... **TCLC 18**
See also CA 114; 169; DLB 137; MAL 5

Natsume, Kinnosuke
See Natsume, Soseki

Natsume, Soseki 1867-1916 .... **TCLC 2, 10**
See also CA 104; 195; DLB 180; EWL 3;
MJW; RGWL 2, 3; TWA

Natsume Soseki
See Natsume, Soseki

Natti, Lee 1919- .... **CLC 17**
See also CA 5-8R; CANR 2; CWRI 5;
SAAS 3; SATA 1, 67

Natti, Mary Lee
See Natti, Lee

Navarre, Marguerite de
See de Navarre, Marguerite

Naylor, Gloria 1950- . **BLC 1:3; CLC 28, 52,
156, 261; WLCS**
See also AAYA 6, 39; AFAW 1, 2; AMWS
8; BW 2, 3; CA 107; CANR 27, 51, 74,
130; CN 4, 5, 6, 7; CPW; DA; DA3;
DAC; DAM MST, MULT, NOV, POP;
DLB 173; EWL 3; FW; MAL 5; MTCW
1, 2; MTFW 2005; NFS 4, 7; RGAL 4;
TCLE 1:2; TUS

Ndebele, Njabulo (Simakahle)
1948- .... **SSC 135**
See also CA 184; DLB 157, 225; EWL 3

Neal, John 1793-1876 .... **NCLC 161**
See also DLB 1, 59, 243; FW; RGAL 4

Neff, Debra **CLC 59**

Neihardt, John Gneisenau
1881-1973 .... **CLC 32**
See also CA 13-14; CANR 65; CAP 1; DLB
9, 54, 256; LAIT 2; TCWW 1, 2

Nekrasov, Nikolai Alekseevich
1821-1878 .... **NCLC 11**
See also DLB 277

Nelligan, Emile 1879-1941 .... **TCLC 14**
See also CA 114; 204; DLB 92; EWL 3

Nelson, Alice Ruth Moore Dunbar
1875-1935 .... **HR 1:2; SSC 132**
See also BW 1, 3; CA 122; 124; CANR 82;
DLB 50; FW; MTCW 1

Nelson, Willie 1933- .... **CLC 17**
See also CA 107; CANR 114, 178

Nemerov, Howard 1920-1991 .... **CLC 2, 6, 9,
36; PC 24; TCLC 124**
See also AMW; CA 1-4R; 134; CABS 2;
CANR 1, 27, 53; CN 1, 2, 3; CP 1, 2, 3,
4, 5; DAM POET; DLB 5, 6; DLBY 1983;
EWL 3; INT CANR-27; MAL 5; MTCW
1, 2; MTFW 2005; PFS 10, 14; RGAL 4

Nemerov, Howard Stanley
See Nemerov, Howard

Nepos, Cornelius c. 99B.C.-c.
24B.C. .... **CMLC 89**
See also DLB 211

Neruda, Pablo 1904-1973 .. **CLC 1, 2, 5, 7, 9,
28, 62; HLC 2; PC 4, 64; WLC 4**
See also CA 19-20; 45-48; CANR 131; CAP
2; DA; DA3; DAB; DAC; DAM MST,
MULT, POET; DLB 283, 331; DNFS 2;
EWL 3; HW 1; LAW; MTCW 1, 2;
MTFW 2005; PFS 11, 28; RGWL 2, 3;
TWA; WLIT 1; WP

Nerval, Gerard de 1808-1855 ... **NCLC 1, 67;
PC 13; SSC 18**
See also DLB 217; EW 6; GFL 1789 to the
Present; RGSF 2; RGWL 2, 3

Nervo, (Jose) Amado (Ruiz de)
1870-1919 .... **HLCS 2; TCLC 11**
See also CA 109; 131; DLB 290; EWL 3;
HW 1; LAW

Nesbit, Malcolm
See Chester, Alfred

Nessi, Pio Baroja y
See Baroja, Pio

Nestroy, Johann 1801-1862 .... **NCLC 42**
See also DLB 133; RGWL 2, 3

Netterville, Luke
See O'Grady, Standish (James)

Neufeld, John (Arthur) 1938- .... **CLC 17**
See also AAYA 11; CA 25-28R; CANR 11,
37, 56; CLR 52; MAICYA 1, 2; SAAS 3;
SATA 6, 81, 131; SATA-Essay 131; YAW

Neumann, Alfred 1895-1952 .... **TCLC 100**
See also CA 183; DLB 56

Neumann, Ferenc
See Molnar, Ferenc

Neville, Emily Cheney 1919- .... **CLC 12**
See also BYA 2; CA 5-8R; CANR 3, 37,
85; JRDA; MAICYA 1, 2; SAAS 2; SATA
1; YAW

Newbound, Bernard Slade 1930- .... **CLC 11,
46**
See also CA 81-84; CAAS 9; CANR 49;
CCA 1; CD 5, 6; DAM DRAM; DLB 53

Newby, P(ercy) H(oward)
1918-1997 .... **CLC 2, 13**
See also CA 5-8R; 161; CANR 32, 67; CN
1, 2, 3, 4, 5, 6; DAM NOV; DLB 15, 326;
MTCW 1; RGEL 2

Newcastle
See Cavendish, Margaret

Newlove, Donald 1928- .... **CLC 6**
See also CA 29-32R; CANR 25

Newlove, John (Herbert) 1938- .... **CLC 14**
See also CA 21-24R; CANR 9, 25; CP 1, 2,
3, 4, 5, 6, 7

Newman, Charles 1938-2006 .... **CLC 2, 8**
See also CA 21-24R; 249; CANR 84; CN
3, 4, 5, 6

Newman, Charles Hamilton
See Newman, Charles

Newman, Edwin (Harold) 1919- ...... **CLC 14**
See also AITN 1; CA 69-72; CANR 5

Newman, John Henry 1801-1890 . **NCLC 38,
99**
See also BRWS 7; DLB 18, 32, 55; RGEL
2

Newton, (Sir) Isaac 1642-1727 ...... **LC 35, 53**
See also DLB 252

Newton, Suzanne 1936- .... **CLC 35**
See also BYA 7; CA 41-44R; CANR 14;
JRDA; SATA 5, 77

New York Dept. of Ed. **CLC 70**

Nexo, Martin Andersen
1869-1954 .... **TCLC 43**
See also CA 202; DLB 214; EWL 3

Nezval, Vitezslav 1900-1958 .... **TCLC 44**
See also CA 123; CDWLB 4; DLB 215;
EWL 3

DLBY 1981; EWL 3; EXPS; FL 1:6; FW; GL 3; HGG; INT CANR-25; LAIT 4; MAL 5; MBL; MTCW 1, 2; MTFW 2005; NFS 8, 24; RGAL 4; RGSF 2; SATA 159; SSFS 1, 8, 17; SUFW 2; TUS

O'Brian, E.G.
See Clarke, Arthur C.

O'Brian, Patrick 1914-2000 .... **CLC 152**
See also AAYA 55; BRWS 12; CA 144; 187; CANR 74, 201; CPW; MTCW 2; MTFW 2005; RHW

O'Brien, Darcy 1939-1998 .... **CLC 11**
See also CA 21-24R; 167; CANR 8, 59

O'Brien, Edna 1932- ..... **CLC 3, 5, 8, 13, 36, 65, 116, 237; SSC 10, 77**
See also BRWS 5; CA 1-4R; CANR 6, 41, 65, 102, 169; CDBLB 1960 to Present; CN 1, 2, 3, 4, 5, 6, 7; DA3; DAM NOV; DLB 14, 231, 319; EWL 3; FW; MTCW 1, 2; MTFW 2005; RGSF 2; WLIT 4

O'Brien, E.G.
See Clarke, Arthur C.

O'Brien, Fitz-James 1828-1862 ..... **NCLC 21**
See also DLB 74; RGAL 4; SUFW

O'Brien, Flann
See O Nuallain, Brian

O'Brien, Richard 1942- .... **CLC 17**
See also CA 124

O'Brien, Tim 1946- .... **CLC 7, 19, 40, 103, 211; SSC 74, 123**
See also AAYA 16; AMWS 5; CA 85-88; CANR 40, 58, 133; CDALBS; CN 5, 6, 7; CPW; DA3; DAM POP; DLB 152; DLBD 9; DLBY 1980; LATS 1:2; MAL 5; MTCW 2; MTFW 2005; RGAL 4; SSFS 5, 15; TCLE 1:2

O'Brien, William Timothy
See O'Brien, Tim

Obstfelder, Sigbjorn 1866-1900 ..... **TCLC 23**
See also CA 123; DLB 354

O'Casey, Brenda
See Haycraft, Anna

O'Casey, Sean 1880-1964 .... **CLC 1, 5, 9, 11, 15, 88; DC 12; WLCS**
See also BRW 7; CA 89-92; CANR 62; CBD; CDBLB 1914-1945; DA3; DAB; DAC; DAM DRAM, MST; DFS 19; DLB 10; EWL 3; MTCW 1, 2; MTFW 2005; RGEL 2; TEA; WLIT 4

O'Cathasaigh, Sean
See O'Casey, Sean

Occom, Samson 1723-1792 .... **LC 60; NNAL**
See also DLB 175

Occomy, Marita (Odette) Bonner
1899(?)-1971 ..... **HR 1:2; PC 72; TCLC 179**
See also BW 2; CA 142; DFS 13; DLB 51, 228

Ochs, Phil(ip David) 1940-1976 .... **CLC 17**
See also CA 185; 65-68

O'Connor, Edwin (Greene)
1918-1968 .... **CLC 14**
See also CA 93-96; 25-28R; MAL 5

O'Connor, Flannery 1925-1964 ..... **CLC 1, 2, 3, 6, 10, 13, 15, 21, 66, 104; SSC 1, 23, 61, 82, 111; TCLC 132; WLC 4**
See also AAYA 7; AMW; AMWR 2; BPFB 3; BYA 16; CA 1-4R; CANR 3, 41; CDALB 1941-1968; DA; DA3; DAB; DAC; DAM MST, NOV; DLB 2, 152; DLBD 12; DLBY 1980; EWL 3; EXPS; LAIT 5; MAL 5; MBL; MTCW 1, 2; MTFW 2005; NFS 3, 21; RGAL 4; RGSF 2; SSFS 2, 7, 10, 19; TUS

O'Connor, Frank 1903-1966
See O'Donovan, Michael Francis

O'Connor, Mary Flannery
See O'Connor, Flannery

O'Dell, Scott 1898-1989 .... **CLC 30**
See also AAYA 3, 44; BPFB 3; BYA 1, 2, 3, 5; CA 61-64; 129; CANR 12, 30, 112; CLR 1, 16, 126; DLB 52; JRDA; MAICYA 1, 2; SATA 12, 60, 134; WYA; YAW

Odets, Clifford 1906-1963 ..... **CLC 2, 28, 98; DC 6**
See also AMWS 2; CA 85-88; CAD; CANR 62; DAM DRAM; DFS 3, 17, 20; DLB 7, 26, 341; EWL 3; MAL 5; MTCW 1, 2; MTFW 2005; RGAL 4; TUS

O'Doherty, Brian 1928- .... **CLC 76**
See also CA 105; CANR 108

O'Donnell, K. M.
See Malzberg, Barry N(athaniel)

O'Donnell, Lawrence
See Kuttner, Henry

O'Donovan, Michael Francis
1903-1966 .... **CLC 14, 23; SSC 5, 109**
See also BRWS 14; CA 93-96; CANR 84; DLB 162; EWL 3; RGSF 2; SSFS 5

Oe, Kenzaburo 1935- .. **CLC 10, 36, 86, 187; SSC 20**
See also CA 97-100; CANR 36, 50, 74, 126; CWW 2; DA3; DAM NOV; DLB 182, 331; DLBY 1994; EWL 3; LATS 1:2; MJW; MTCW 1, 2; MTFW 2005; RGSF 2; RGWL 2, 3

Oe Kenzaburo
See Oe, Kenzaburo

O'Faolain, Julia 1932- .... **CLC 6, 19, 47, 108**
See also CA 81-84; CAAS 2; CANR 12, 61; CN 2, 3, 4, 5, 6, 7; DLB 14, 231, 319; FW; MTCW 1; RHW

O'Faolain, Sean 1900-1991 ...... **CLC 1, 7, 14, 32, 70; SSC 13; TCLC 143**
See also CA 61-64; 134; CANR 12, 66; CN 1, 2, 3, 4; DLB 15, 162; MTCW 1, 2; MTFW 2005; RGEL 2; RGSF 2

O'Flaherty, Liam 1896-1984 .... **CLC 5, 34; SSC 6, 116**
See also CA 101; 113; CANR 35; CN 1, 2, 3; DLB 36, 162; DLBY 1984; MTCW 1, 2; MTFW 2005; RGEL 2; RGSF 2; SSFS 5, 20

Ogai
See Mori Ogai

Ogilvy, Gavin
See Barrie, J. M.

O'Grady, Standish (James)
1846-1928 .... **TCLC 5**
See also CA 104; 157

O'Grady, Timothy 1951- .... **CLC 59**
See also CA 138

O'Hara, Frank 1926-1966 .... **CLC 2, 5, 13, 78; PC 45**
See also CA 9-12R; 25-28R; CANR 33; DA3; DAM POET; DLB 5, 16, 193; EWL 3; MAL 5; MTCW 1, 2; MTFW 2005; PFS 8, 12; RGAL 4; WP

O'Hara, John 1905-1970 . **CLC 1, 2, 3, 6, 11, 42; SSC 15**
See also AMW; BPFB 3; CA 5-8R; 25-28R; CANR 31, 60; CDALB 1929-1941; DAM NOV; DLB 9, 86, 324; DLBD 2; EWL 3; MAL 5; MTCW 1, 2; MTFW 2005; NFS 11; RGAL 4; RGSF 2

O'Hara, John Henry
See O'Hara, John

O'Hehir, Diana 1929- .... **CLC 41**
See also CA 245; CANR 177

O'Hehir, Diana F.
See O'Hehir, Diana

Ohiyesa
See Eastman, Charles A(lexander)

Okada, John 1923-1971 .... **AAL**
See also BYA 14; CA 212; DLB 312; NFS 25

O'Kelly, Seamus 1881(?)-1918 .... **SSC 136**

Okigbo, Christopher 1930-1967 ..... **BLC 1:3; CLC 25, 84; PC 7; TCLC 171**
See also AFW; BW 1, 3; CA 77-80; CANR 74; CDWLB 3; DAM MULT, POET; DLB 125; EWL 3; MTCW 1, 2; MTFW 2005; RGEL 2

Okigbo, Christopher Ifenayichukwu
See Okigbo, Christopher

Okri, Ben 1959- .... **BLC 2:3; CLC 87, 223; SSC 127**
See also AFW; BRWS 5; BW 2, 3; CA 130; 138; CANR 65, 128; CN 5, 6, 7; DLB 157, 231, 319, 326; EWL 3; INT CA-138; MTCW 2; MTFW 2005; RGSF 2; SSFS 20; WLIT 2; WWE 1

Old Boy
See Hughes, Thomas

Olds, Sharon 1942- .. **CLC 32, 39, 85; PC 22**
See also AMWS 10; CA 101; CANR 18, 41, 66, 98, 135; CP 5, 6, 7; CPW; CWP; DAM POET; DLB 120; MAL 5; MTCW 2; MTFW 2005; PFS 17

Oldstyle, Jonathan
See Irving, Washington

Olesha, Iurii
See Olesha, Yuri (Karlovich)

Olesha, Iurii Karlovich
See Olesha, Yuri (Karlovich)

Olesha, Yuri (Karlovich) 1899-1960 . **CLC 8; SSC 69; TCLC 136**
See also CA 85-88; DLB 272; EW 11; EWL 3; RGWL 2, 3

Olesha, Yury Karlovich
See Olesha, Yuri (Karlovich)

Oliphant, Mrs.
See Oliphant, Margaret (Oliphant Wilson)

Oliphant, Laurence 1829(?)-1888 .. **NCLC 47**
See also DLB 18, 166

Oliphant, Margaret (Oliphant Wilson)
1828-1897 ... **NCLC 11, 61, 221; SSC 25**
See also BRWS 10; DLB 18, 159, 190; HGG; RGEL 2; RGSF 2; SUFW

Oliver, Mary 1935- ... **CLC 19, 34, 98; PC 75**
See also AMWS 7; CA 21-24R; CANR 9, 43, 84, 92, 138; CP 4, 5, 6, 7; CWP; DLB 5, 193, 342; EWL 3; MTFW 2005; PFS 15, 31

Olivi, Peter 1248-1298 .... **CMLC 114**

Olivier, Laurence (Kerr) 1907-1989 . **CLC 20**
See also CA 111; 150; 129

O.L.S.
See Russell, George William

Olsen, Tillie 1912-2007 .... **CLC 4, 13, 114; SSC 11, 103**
See also AAYA 51; AMWS 13; BYA 11; CA 1-4R; 256; CANR 1, 43, 74, 132; CDALBS; CN 2, 3, 4, 5, 6, 7; DA; DA3; DAB; DAC; DAM MST; DLB 28, 206; DLBY 1980; EWL 3; EXPS; FW; MAL 5; MTCW 1, 2; MTFW 2005; RGAL 4; RGSF 2; SSFS 1; TCLE 1:2; TCWW 2; TUS

Olson, Charles 1910-1970 . **CLC 1, 2, 5, 6, 9, 11, 29; PC 19**
See also AMWS 2; CA 13-16; 25-28R; CABS 2; CANR 35, 61; CAP 1; CP 1; DAM POET; DLB 5, 16, 193; EWL 3; MAL 5; MTCW 1, 2; RGAL 4; WP

Olson, Charles John
See Olson, Charles

Olson, Merle Theodore
See Olson, Toby

Olson, Toby 1937- .... **CLC 28**
See also CA 65-68; CAAS 11; CANR 9, 31, 84, 175; CP 3, 4, 5, 6, 7

Olyesha, Yuri
See Olesha, Yuri (Karlovich)

Reed, Ishmael 1938- . **BLC 1:3; CLC 2, 3, 5, 6, 13, 32, 60, 174; PC 68**
See also AFAW 1, 2; AMWS 10; BPFB 3; BW 2, 3; CA 21-24R; CANR 25, 48, 74, 128, 195; CN 1, 2, 3, 4, 5, 6, 7; CP 1, 2, 3, 4, 5, 6, 7; CSW; DA3; DAM MULT; DLB 2, 5, 33, 169, 227; DLBD 8; EWL 3; LMFS 2; MAL 5; MSW; MTCW 1, 2; MTFW 2005; PFS 6; RGAL 4; TCWW 2

Reed, Ishmael Scott
See Reed, Ishmael

Reed, John (Silas) 1887-1920 .... **TCLC 9**
See also CA 106; 195; MAL 5; TUS

Reed, Lou
See Firbank, Louis

Reese, Lizette Woodworth
1856-1935 .... **PC 29; TCLC 181**
See also CA 180; DLB 54

Reeve, Clara 1729-1807 .... **NCLC 19**
See also DLB 39; RGEL 2

Reich, Wilhelm 1897-1957 .... **TCLC 57**
See also CA 199

Reid, Christopher 1949- .... **CLC 33**
See also CA 140; CANR 89; CP 4, 5, 6, 7; DLB 40; EWL 3

Reid, Christopher John
See Reid, Christopher

Reid, Desmond
See Moorcock, Michael

Reid Banks, Lynne 1929- .... **CLC 23**
See also AAYA 6; BYA 7; CA 1-4R; CANR 6, 22, 38, 87; CLR 24, 86; CN 4, 5, 6; JRDA; MAICYA 1, 2; SATA 22, 75, 111, 165; YAW

Reilly, William K.
See Creasey, John

Reiner, Max
See Caldwell, (Janet Miriam) Taylor (Holland)

Reis, Ricardo
See Pessoa, Fernando

Reizenstein, Elmer Leopold
See Rice, Elmer (Leopold)

Remark, Erich Paul
See Remarque, Erich Maria

Remarque, Erich Maria 1898-1970 . **CLC 21**
See also AAYA 27; BPFB 3; CA 77-80; 29-32R; CDWLB 2; DA; DA3; DAB; DAC; DAM MST, NOV; DLB 56; EWL 3; EXPN; LAIT 3; MTCW 1, 2; MTFW 2005; NFS 4; RGHL; RGWL 2, 3

Remington, Frederic S(ackrider)
1861-1909 .... **TCLC 89**
See also CA 108; 169; DLB 12, 186, 188; SATA 41; TCWW 2

Remizov, A.
See Remizov, Aleksei (Mikhailovich)

Remizov, A. M.
See Remizov, Aleksei (Mikhailovich)

Remizov, Aleksei (Mikhailovich)
1877-1957 .... **TCLC 27**
See also CA 125; 133; DLB 295; EWL 3

Remizov, Alexey Mikhaylovich
See Remizov, Aleksei (Mikhailovich)

Renan, Joseph Ernest 1823-1892 . **NCLC 26, 145**
See also GFL 1789 to the Present

Renard, Jules(-Pierre) 1864-1910 .. **TCLC 17**
See also CA 117; 202; GFL 1789 to the Present

Renart, Jean fl. 13th cent. - .... **CMLC 83**

Renault, Mary 1905-1983 .... **CLC 3, 11, 17**
See also BPFB 3; BYA 2; CA 81-84; 111; CANR 74; CN 1, 2, 3; DA3; DLBY 1983; EWL 3; GLL 1; LAIT 1; MTCW 2; MTFW 2005; RGEL 2; RHW; SATA 23; SATA-Obit 36; TEA

Rendell, Ruth
See Rendell, Ruth

Rendell, Ruth 1930- .... **CLC 28, 48, 50**
See also BEST 90:4; BPFB 3; BRWS 9; CA 109; CANR 32, 52, 74, 127, 162, 190; CN 5, 6, 7; CPW; DAM POP; DLB 87, 276; INT CANR-32; MSW; MTCW 1, 2; MTFW 2005

Rendell, Ruth Barbara
See Rendell, Ruth

Renoir, Jean 1894-1979 .... **CLC 20**
See also CA 129; 85-88

Rensie, Willis
See Eisner, Will

Resnais, Alain 1922- .... **CLC 16**

Revard, Carter 1931- .... **NNAL**
See also CA 144; CANR 81, 153; PFS 5

Reverdy, Pierre 1889-1960 .... **CLC 53**
See also CA 97-100; 89-92; DLB 258; EWL 3; GFL 1789 to the Present

Reverend Mandju
See Su, Chien

Rexroth, Kenneth 1905-1982 .... **CLC 1, 2, 6, 11, 22, 49, 112; PC 20, 95**
See also BG 1:3; CA 5-8R; 107; CANR 14, 34, 63; CDALB 1941-1968; CP 1, 2, 3; DAM POET; DLB 16, 48, 165, 212; DLBY 1982; EWL 3; INT CANR-14; MAL 5; MTCW 1, 2; MTFW 2005; RGAL 4

Reyes, Alfonso 1889-1959 .... **HLCS 2; TCLC 33**
See also CA 131; EWL 3; HW 1; LAW

Reyes y Basoalto, Ricardo Eliecer Neftali
See Neruda, Pablo

Reymont, Wladyslaw (Stanislaw)
1868(?)-1925 .... **TCLC 5**
See also CA 104; DLB 332; EWL 3

Reynolds, John Hamilton
1794-1852 .... **NCLC 146**
See also DLB 96

Reynolds, Jonathan 1942- .... **CLC 6, 38**
See also CA 65-68; CANR 28, 176

Reynolds, Joshua 1723-1792 .... **LC 15**
See also DLB 104

Reynolds, Michael S(hane)
1937-2000 .... **CLC 44**
See also CA 65-68; 189; CANR 9, 89, 97

Reza, Yasmina 1959- .... **DC 34**
See also AAYA 69; CA 171; CANR 145; DFS 19; DLB 321

Reznikoff, Charles 1894-1976 .... **CLC 9**
See also AMWS 14; CA 33-36; 61-64; CAP 2; CP 1, 2; DLB 28, 45; RGHL; WP

Rezzori, Gregor von
See Rezzori d'Arezzo, Gregor von

Rezzori d'Arezzo, Gregor von
1914-1998 .... **CLC 25**
See also CA 122; 136; 167

Rhine, Richard
See Silverstein, Alvin; Silverstein, Virginia B.

Rhodes, Eugene Manlove
1869-1934 .... **TCLC 53**
See also CA 198; DLB 256; TCWW 1, 2

R'hoone, Lord
See Balzac, Honore de

Rhys, Jean 1890-1979 .... **CLC 2, 4, 6, 14, 19, 51, 124; SSC 21, 76**
See also BRWS 2; CA 25-28R; 85-88; CANR 35, 62; CDBLB 1945-1960; CDWLB 3; CN 1, 2; DA3; DAM NOV; DLB 36, 117, 162; DNFS 2; EWL 3; LATS 1:1; MTCW 1, 2; MTFW 2005; NFS 19; RGEL 2; RGSF 2; RHW; TEA; WWE 1

Ribeiro, Darcy 1922-1997 .... **CLC 34**
See also CA 33-36R; 156; EWL 3

Ribeiro, Joao Ubaldo (Osorio Pimentel)
1941- .... **CLC 10, 67**
See also CA 81-84; CWW 2; EWL 3

Ribman, Ronald (Burt) 1932- .... **CLC 7**
See also CA 21-24R; CAD; CANR 46, 80; CD 5, 6

Ricci, Nino 1959- .... **CLC 70**
See also CA 137; CANR 130; CCA 1

Ricci, Nino Pio
See Ricci, Nino

Rice, Anne 1941- .... **CLC 41, 128**
See also AAYA 9, 53; AMWS 7; BEST 89:2; BPFB 3; CA 65-68; CANR 12, 36, 53, 74, 100, 133, 190; CN 6, 7; CPW; CSW; DA3; DAM POP; DLB 292; GL 3; GLL 2; HGG; MTCW 2; MTFW 2005; SUFW 2; YAW

Rice, Elmer (Leopold) 1892-1967 ...... **CLC 7, 49; TCLC 221**
See also CA 21-22; 25-28R; CAP 2; DAM DRAM; DFS 12; DLB 4, 7; EWL 3; IDTP; MAL 5; MTCW 1, 2; RGAL 4

Rice, Tim 1944- .... **CLC 21**
See also CA 103; CANR 46; DFS 7

Rice, Timothy Miles Bindon
See Rice, Tim

Rich, Adrienne 1929- ..... **CLC 3, 6, 7, 11, 18, 36, 73, 76, 125; PC 5**
See also AAYA 69; AMWR 2; AMWS 1; CA 9-12R; CANR 20, 53, 74, 128, 199; CDALBS; CP 1, 2, 3, 4, 5, 6, 7; CSW; CWP; DA3; DAM POET; DLB 5, 67; EWL 3; EXPP; FL 1:6; FW; MAL 5; MBL; MTCW 1, 2; MTFW 2005; PAB; PFS 15, 29; RGAL 4; RGHL; WP

Rich, Adrienne Cecile
See Rich, Adrienne

Rich, Barbara
See Graves, Robert

Rich, Robert
See Trumbo, Dalton

Richard, Keith
See Richards, Keith

Richards, David Adams 1950- .... **CLC 59**
See also CA 93-96; CANR 60, 110, 156; CN 7; DAC; DLB 53; TCLE 1:2

Richards, I(vor) A(rmstrong)
1893-1979 .... **CLC 14, 24**
See also BRWS 2; CA 41-44R; 89-92; CANR 34, 74; CP 1, 2; DLB 27; EWL 3; MTCW 2; RGEL 2

Richards, Keith 1943- .... **CLC 17**
See also CA 107; CANR 77

Richardson, Anne
See Roiphe, Anne

Richardson, Dorothy Miller
1873-1957 .... **TCLC 3, 203**
See also BRWS 13; CA 104; 192; DLB 36; EWL 3; FW; RGEL 2

Richardson, Ethel Florence Lindesay
1870-1946 .... **TCLC 4**
See also CA 105; 190; DLB 197, 230; EWL 3; RGEL 2; RGSF 2; RHW

Richardson, Henrietta
See Richardson, Ethel Florence Lindesay

Richardson, Henry Handel
See Richardson, Ethel Florence Lindesay

Richardson, John 1796-1852 .... **NCLC 55**
See also CCA 1; DAC; DLB 99

Richardson, Samuel 1689-1761 ...... **LC 1, 44, 138; WLC 5**
See also BRW 3; CDBLB 1660-1789; DA; DAB; DAC; DAM MST, NOV; DLB 39; RGEL 2; TEA; WLIT 3

Richardson, Willis 1889-1977 .... **HR 1:3**
See also BW 1; CA 124; DLB 51; SATA 60

Richardson Robertson, Ethel Florence Lindesay
See Richardson, Ethel Florence Lindesay

Richler, Mordecai 1931-2001 .... **CLC 3, 5, 9, 13, 18, 46, 70, 185, 271**
See also AITN 1; CA 65-68; 201; CANR 31, 62, 111; CCA 1; CLR 17; CN 1, 2, 3, 4, 5, 7; CWRI 5; DAC; DAM MST, NOV; DLB 53; EWL 3; MAICYA 1, 2; MTCW 1, 2; MTFW 2005; RGEL 2; RGHL; SATA 44, 98; SATA-Brief 27; TWA

Richter, Conrad (Michael)
1890-1968 .... **CLC 30**
See also AAYA 21; AMWS 18; BYA 2; CA 5-8R; 25-28R; CANR 23; DLB 9, 212; LAIT 1; MAL 5; MTCW 1, 2; MTFW 2005; RGAL 4; SATA 3; TCWW 1, 2; TUS; YAW

Ricostranza, Tom
See Ellis, Trey

Riddell, Charlotte 1832-1906 .... **TCLC 40**
See also CA 165; DLB 156; HGG; SUFW

Riddell, Mrs. J. H.
See Riddell, Charlotte

Ridge, John Rollin 1827-1867 ...... **NCLC 82; NNAL**
See also CA 144; DAM MULT; DLB 175

Ridgeway, Jason
See Marlowe, Stephen

Ridgway, Keith 1965- .... **CLC 119**
See also CA 172; CANR 144

Riding, Laura
See Jackson, Laura

Riefenstahl, Berta Helene Amalia
1902-2003 .... **CLC 16, 190**
See also CA 108; 220

Riefenstahl, Leni
See Riefenstahl, Berta Helene Amalia

Riffe, Ernest
See Bergman, Ingmar

Riffe, Ernest Ingmar
See Bergman, Ingmar

Riggs, (Rolla) Lynn
1899-1954 .... **NNAL; TCLC 56**
See also CA 144; DAM MULT; DLB 175

Riis, Jacob A(ugust) 1849-1914 ..... **TCLC 80**
See also CA 113; 168; DLB 23

Rikki
See Ducornet, Erica

Riley, James Whitcomb 1849-1916 .... **PC 48; TCLC 51**
See also CA 118; 137; DAM POET; MAI-CYA 1, 2; RGAL 4; SATA 17

Riley, Tex
See Creasey, John

Rilke, Rainer Maria 1875-1926 .... **PC 2; TCLC 1, 6, 19, 195**
See also CA 104; 132; CANR 62, 99; CD-WLB 2; DA3; DAM POET; DLB 81; EW 9; EWL 3; MTCW 1, 2; MTFW 2005; PFS 19, 27; RGWL 2, 3; TWA; WP

Rimbaud, Arthur 1854-1891 ..... **NCLC 4, 35, 82; PC 3, 57; WLC 5**
See also DA; DA3; DAB; DAC; DAM MST, POET; DLB 217; EW 7; GFL 1789 to the Present; LMFS 2; PFS 28; RGWL 2, 3; TWA; WP

Rimbaud, Jean Nicholas Arthur
See Rimbaud, Arthur

Rinehart, Mary Roberts
1876-1958 .... **TCLC 52**
See also BPFB 3; CA 108; 166; RGAL 4; RHW

Ringmaster, The
See Mencken, H. L.

Ringwood, Gwen(dolyn Margaret) Pharis
1910-1984 .... **CLC 48**
See also CA 148; 112; DLB 88

Rio, Michel 1945(?)- .... **CLC 43**
See also CA 201

Rios, Alberto 1952- .... **PC 57**
See also AAYA 66; AMWS 4; CA 113; CANR 34, 79, 137; CP 6, 7; DLB 122; HW 2; MTFW 2005; PFS 11

Rios, Alberto Alvaro
See Rios, Alberto

Ritsos, Giannes
See Ritsos, Yannis

Ritsos, Yannis 1909-1990 .... **CLC 6, 13, 31**
See also CA 77-80; 133; CANR 39, 61; EW 12; EWL 3; MTCW 1; RGWL 2, 3

Ritter, Erika 1948(?)- .... **CLC 52**
See also CD 5, 6; CWD

Rivera, Jose Eustasio 1889-1928 ... **TCLC 35**
See also CA 162; EWL 3; HW 1, 2; LAW

Rivera, Tomas 1935-1984 .... **HLCS 2**
See also CA 49-52; CANR 32; DLB 82; HW 1; LLW; RGAL 4; SSFS 15; TCWW 2; WLIT 1

Rivers, Conrad Kent 1933-1968 .... **CLC 1**
See also BW 1; CA 85-88; DLB 41

Rivers, Elfrida
See Bradley, Marion Zimmer

Riverside, John
See Heinlein, Robert A.

Rizal, Jose 1861-1896 .... **NCLC 27**
See also DLB 348

Roa Bastos, Augusto 1917-2005 ...... **CLC 45; HLC 2**
See also CA 131; 238; CWW 2; DAM MULT; DLB 113; EWL 3; HW 1; LAW; RGSF 2; WLIT 1

Roa Bastos, Augusto Jose Antonio
See Roa Bastos, Augusto

Robbe-Grillet, Alain 1922-2008 ..... **CLC 1, 2, 4, 6, 8, 10, 14, 43, 128, 287**
See also BPFB 3; CA 9-12R; 269; CANR 33, 65, 115; CWW 2; DLB 83; EW 13; EWL 3; GFL 1789 to the Present; IDFW 3, 4; MTCW 1, 2; MTFW 2005; RGWL 2, 3; SSFS 15

Robbins, Harold 1916-1997 .... **CLC 5**
See also BPFB 3; CA 73-76; 162; CANR 26, 54, 112, 156; DA3; DAM NOV; MTCW 1, 2

Robbins, Thomas Eugene 1936- . **CLC 9, 32, 64**
See also AAYA 32; AMWS 10; BEST 90:3; BPFB 3; CA 81-84; CANR 29, 59, 95, 139; CN 3, 4, 5, 6, 7; CPW; CSW; DA3; DAM NOV, POP; DLBY 1980; MTCW 1, 2; MTFW 2005

Robbins, Tom
See Robbins, Thomas Eugene

Robbins, Trina 1938- .... **CLC 21**
See also AAYA 61; CA 128; CANR 152

Robert de Boron fl. 12th cent. - .... **CMLC 94**

Roberts, Charles G(eorge) D(ouglas)
1860-1943 .... **SSC 91; TCLC 8**
See also CA 105; 188; CLR 33; CWRI 5; DLB 92; RGEL 2; RGSF 2; SATA 88; SATA-Brief 29

Roberts, Elizabeth Madox
1886-1941 .... **TCLC 68**
See also CA 111; 166; CLR 100; CWRI 5; DLB 9, 54, 102; RGAL 4; RHW; SATA 33; SATA-Brief 27; TCWW 2; WCH

Roberts, Kate 1891-1985 .... **CLC 15**
See also CA 107; 116; DLB 319

Roberts, Keith (John Kingston)
1935-2000 .... **CLC 14**
See also BRWS 10; CA 25-28R; CANR 46; DLB 261; SFW 4

Roberts, Kenneth (Lewis)
1885-1957 .... **TCLC 23**
See also CA 109; 199; DLB 9; MAL 5; RGAL 4; RHW

Roberts, Michele 1949- .... **CLC 48, 178**
See also BRWS 15; CA 115; CANR 58, 120, 164, 200; CN 6, 7; DLB 231; FW

Roberts, Michele Brigitte
See Roberts, Michele

Robertson, Ellis
See Ellison, Harlan; Silverberg, Robert

Robertson, Thomas William
1829-1871 .... **NCLC 35**
See also DAM DRAM; DLB 344; RGEL 2

Robertson, Tom
See Robertson, Thomas William

Robeson, Kenneth
See Dent, Lester

Robinson, Edwin Arlington
1869-1935 .... **PC 1, 35; TCLC 5, 101**
See also AAYA 72; AMW; CA 104; 133; CDALB 1865-1917; DA; DAC; DAM MST, POET; DLB 54; EWL 3; EXPP; MAL 5; MTCW 1, 2; MTFW 2005; PAB; PFS 4; RGAL 4; WP

Robinson, Henry Crabb
1775-1867 .... **NCLC 15**
See also DLB 107

Robinson, Jill 1936- .... **CLC 10**
See also CA 102; CANR 120; INT CA-102

Robinson, Kim Stanley 1952- ... **CLC 34, 248**
See also AAYA 26; CA 126; CANR 113, 139, 173; CN 6, 7; MTFW 2005; SATA 109; SCFW 2; SFW 4

Robinson, Lloyd
See Silverberg, Robert

Robinson, Marilynne 1943- ..... **CLC 25, 180, 276**
See also AAYA 69; CA 116; CANR 80, 140, 192; CN 4, 5, 6, 7; DLB 206, 350; MTFW 2005; NFS 24

Robinson, Mary 1758-1800 .... **NCLC 142**
See also BRWS 13; DLB 158; FW

Robinson, Smokey
See Robinson, William, Jr.

Robinson, William, Jr. 1940- .... **CLC 21**
See also CA 116

Robison, Mary 1949- .... **CLC 42, 98**
See also CA 113; 116; CANR 87; CN 4, 5, 6, 7; DLB 130; INT CA-116; RGSF 2

Roches, Catherine des 1542-1587 ...... **LC 117**
See also DLB 327

Rochester
See Wilmot, John

Rod, Edouard 1857-1910 .... **TCLC 52**

Roddenberry, Eugene Wesley
1921-1991 .... **CLC 17**
See also AAYA 5; CA 110; 135; CANR 37; SATA 45; SATA-Obit 69

Roddenberry, Gene
See Roddenberry, Eugene Wesley

Rodgers, Mary 1931- .... **CLC 12**
See also BYA 5; CA 49-52; CANR 8, 55, 90; CLR 20; CWRI 5; INT CANR-8; JRDA; MAICYA 1, 2; SATA 8, 130

Rodgers, W(illiam) R(obert)
1909-1969 .... **CLC 7**
See also CA 85-88; DLB 20; RGEL 2

Rodman, Eric
See Silverberg, Robert

Rodman, Howard 1920(?)-1985 .... **CLC 65**
See also CA 118

Rodman, Maia
See Wojciechowska, Maia (Teresa)

Rodo, Jose Enrique 1871(?)-1917 .... **HLCS 2**
See also CA 178; EWL 3; HW 2; LAW

Rodolph, Utto
See Ouologuem, Yambo

Rodriguez, Claudio 1934-1999 .... **CLC 10**
See also CA 188; DLB 134

Rowley, William 1585(?)-1626 ... **LC 100, 123**
See also DFS 22; DLB 58; RGEL 2

Rowling, J. K. 1965- .... **CLC 137, 217**
See also AAYA 34, 82; BYA 11, 13, 14; CA 173; CANR 128, 157; CLR 66, 80, 112; LNFS 1, 2, 3; MAICYA 2; MTFW 2005; SATA 109, 174; SUFW 2

Rowling, Joanne Kathleen
See Rowling, J. K.

Rowson, Susanna Haswell
1762(?)-1824 .... **NCLC 5, 69, 182**
See also AMWS 15; DLB 37, 200; RGAL 4

Roy, Arundhati 1960(?)- .... **CLC 109, 210**
See also CA 163; CANR 90, 126; CN 7; DLB 323, 326; DLBY 1997; EWL 3; LATS 1:2; MTFW 2005; NFS 22; WWE 1

Roy, Gabrielle 1909-1983 .... **CLC 10, 14**
See also CA 53-56; 110; CANR 5, 61; CCA 1; DAB; DAC; DAM MST; DLB 68; EWL 3; MTCW 1; RGWL 2, 3; SATA 104; TCLE 1:2

Royko, Mike 1932-1997 .... **CLC 109**
See also CA 89-92; 157; CANR 26, 111; CPW

Rozanov, Vasilii Vasil'evich
See Rozanov, Vassili

Rozanov, Vasily Vasilyevich
See Rozanov, Vassili

Rozanov, Vassili 1856-1919 .... **TCLC 104**
See also DLB 295; EWL 3

Rozewicz, Tadeusz 1921- ...... **CLC 9, 23, 139**
See also CA 108; CANR 36, 66; CWW 2; DA3; DAM POET; DLB 232; EWL 3; MTCW 1, 2; MTFW 2005; RGHL; RGWL 3

Ruark, Gibbons 1941- .... **CLC 3**
See also CA 33-36R; CAAS 23; CANR 14, 31, 57; DLB 120

Rubens, Bernice (Ruth) 1923-2004 . **CLC 19, 31**
See also CA 25-28R; 232; CANR 33, 65, 128; CN 1, 2, 3, 4, 5, 6, 7; DLB 14, 207, 326; MTCW 1

Rubin, Harold
See Robbins, Harold

Rudkin, (James) David 1936- .... **CLC 14**
See also CA 89-92; CBD; CD 5, 6; DLB 13

Rudnik, Raphael 1933- .... **CLC 7**
See also CA 29-32R

Ruffian, M.
See Hasek, Jaroslav

Rufinus c. 345-410 .... **CMLC 111**

Ruiz, Jose Martinez
See Martinez Ruiz, Jose

Ruiz, Juan c. 1283-c. 1350 .... **CMLC 66**

Rukeyser, Muriel 1913-1980 . **CLC 6, 10, 15, 27; PC 12**
See also AMWS 6; CA 5-8R; 93-96; CANR 26, 60; CP 1, 2, 3; DA3; DAM POET; DLB 48; EWL 3; FW; GLL 1; MAL 5; MTCW 1, 2; PFS 10, 29; RGAL 4; SATA-Obit 22

Rule, Jane 1931-2007 .... **CLC 27, 265**
See also CA 25-28R; 266; CAAS 18; CANR 12, 87; CN 4, 5, 6, 7; DLB 60; FW

Rule, Jane Vance
See Rule, Jane

Rulfo, Juan 1918-1986 .. **CLC 8, 80; HLC 2; SSC 25**
See also CA 85-88; 118; CANR 26; CD-WLB 3; DAM MULT; DLB 113; EWL 3; HW 1, 2; LAW; MTCW 1, 2; RGSF 2; RGWL 2, 3; WLIT 1

Rumi
See Rumi, Jalal al-Din

Rumi, Jalal al-Din 1207-1273 ...... **CMLC 20; PC 45**
See also AAYA 64; RGWL 2, 3; WLIT 6; WP

Runeberg, Johan 1804-1877 .... **NCLC 41**

Runyon, (Alfred) Damon
1884(?)-1946 .... **TCLC 10**
See also CA 107; 165; DLB 11, 86, 171; MAL 5; MTCW; RGAL 4

Rush, Norman 1933- .... **CLC 44**
See also CA 121; 126; CANR 130; INT CA-126

Rushdie, Ahmed Salman
See Rushdie, Salman

Rushdie, Salman 1947- .... **CLC 23, 31, 55, 100, 191, 272; SSC 83; WLCS**
See also AAYA 65; BEST 89:3; BPFB 3; BRWS 4; CA 108; 111; CANR 33, 56, 108, 133, 192; CLR 125; CN 4, 5, 6, 7; CPW 1; DA3; DAB; DAC; DAM MST, NOV, POP; DLB 194, 323, 326; EWL 3; FANT; INT CA-111; LATS 1:2; LMFS 2; MTCW 1, 2; MTFW 2005; NFS 22, 23; RGEL 2; RGSF 2; TEA; WLIT 4

Rushforth, Peter 1945-2005 .... **CLC 19**
See also CA 101; 243

Rushforth, Peter Scott
See Rushforth, Peter

Ruskin, John 1819-1900 .... **TCLC 63**
See also BRW 5; BYA 5; CA 114; 129; CD-BLB 1832-1890; DLB 55, 163, 190; RGEL 2; SATA 24; TEA; WCH

Russ, Joanna 1937- .... **CLC 15**
See also BPFB 3; CA 25-28; CANR 11, 31, 65; CN 4, 5, 6, 7; DLB 8; FW; GLL 1; MTCW 1; SCFW 1, 2; SFW 4

Russ, Richard Patrick
See O'Brian, Patrick

Russell, George William
1867-1935 .... **TCLC 3, 10**
See also BRWS 8; CA 104; 153; CDBLB 1890-1914; DAM POET; DLB 19; EWL 3; RGEL 2

Russell, Jeffrey Burton 1934- .... **CLC 70**
See also CA 25-28R; CANR 11, 28, 52, 179

Russell, (Henry) Ken(neth Alfred)
1927- .... **CLC 16**
See also CA 105

Russell, William Martin 1947- .... **CLC 60**
See also CA 164; CANR 107; CBD; CD 5, 6; DLB 233

Russell, Willy
See Russell, William Martin

Russo, Richard 1949- .... **CLC 181**
See also AMWS 12; CA 127; 133; CANR 87, 114, 194; NFS 25

Rutebeuf fl. c. 1249-1277 .... **CMLC 104**
See also DLB 208

Rutherford, Mark
See White, William Hale

Ruysbroeck, Jan van 1293-1381 ... **CMLC 85**

Ruyslinck, Ward
See Belser, Reimond Karel Maria de

Ryan, Cornelius (John) 1920-1974 ..... **CLC 7**
See also CA 69-72; 53-56; CANR 38

Ryan, Michael 1946- .... **CLC 65**
See also CA 49-52; CANR 109; DLBY 1982

Ryan, Tim
See Dent, Lester

Rybakov, Anatoli (Naumovich)
1911-1998 .... **CLC 23, 53**
See also CA 126; 135; 172; DLB 302; RGHL; SATA 79; SATA-Obit 108

Rybakov, Anatolii (Naumovich)
See Rybakov, Anatoli (Naumovich)

Ryder, Jonathan
See Ludlum, Robert

Ryga, George 1932-1987 .... **CLC 14**
See also CA 101; 124; CANR 43, 90; CCA 1; DAC; DAM MST; DLB 60

Rymer, Thomas 1643(?)-1713 .... **LC 132**
See also DLB 101, 336

S. H.
See Hartmann, Sadakichi

S. L. C.
See Twain, Mark

S. S.
See Sassoon, Siegfried

Sa'adawi, al- Nawal
See El Saadawi, Nawal

Saadawi, Nawal El
See El Saadawi, Nawal

Saadiah Gaon 882-942 .... **CMLC 97**

Saba, Umberto 1883-1957 .... **TCLC 33**
See also CA 144; CANR 79; DLB 114; EWL 3; RGWL 2, 3

Sabatini, Rafael 1875-1950 .... **TCLC 47**
See also BPFB 3; CA 162; RHW

Sabato, Ernesto 1911- ... **CLC 10, 23; HLC 2**
See also CA 97-100; CANR 32, 65; CD-WLB 3; CWW 2; DAM MULT; DLB 145; EWL 3; HW 1, 2; LAW; MTCW 1, 2; MTFW 2005

Sa-Carneiro, Mario de 1890-1916 . **TCLC 83**
See also DLB 287; EWL 3

Sacastru, Martin
See Bioy Casares, Adolfo

Sacher-Masoch, Leopold von
1836(?)-1895 .... **NCLC 31**

Sachs, Hans 1494-1576 .... **LC 95**
See also CDWLB 2; DLB 179; RGWL 2, 3

Sachs, Marilyn 1927- .... **CLC 35**
See also AAYA 2; BYA 6; CA 17-20R; CANR 13, 47, 150; CLR 2; JRDA; MAICYA 1, 2; SAAS 2; SATA 3, 68, 164; SATA-Essay 110; WYA; YAW

Sachs, Marilyn Stickle
See Sachs, Marilyn

Sachs, Nelly 1891-1970 .. **CLC 14, 98; PC 78**
See also CA 17-18; 25-28R; CANR 87; CAP 2; DLB 332; EWL 3; MTCW 2; MTFW 2005; PFS 20; RGHL; RGWL 2, 3

Sackler, Howard (Oliver)
1929-1982 .... **CLC 14**
See also CA 61-64; 108; CAD; CANR 30; DFS 15; DLB 7

Sacks, Oliver 1933- .... **CLC 67, 202**
See also CA 53-56; CANR 28, 50, 76, 146, 187; CPW; DA3; INT CANR-28; MTCW 1, 2; MTFW 2005

Sacks, Oliver Wolf
See Sacks, Oliver

Sackville, Thomas 1536-1608 .... **LC 98**
See also DAM DRAM; DLB 62, 132; RGEL 2

Sadakichi
See Hartmann, Sadakichi

Sa'dawi, Nawal al-
See El Saadawi, Nawal

Sade, Donatien Alphonse Francois
1740-1814 .... **NCLC 3, 47**
See also DLB 314; EW 4; GFL Beginnings to 1789; RGWL 2, 3

Sade, Marquis de
See Sade, Donatien Alphonse Francois

Sadoff, Ira 1945- .... **CLC 9**
See also CA 53-56; CANR 5, 21, 109; DLB 120

Saetone
See Camus, Albert

Safire, William 1929-2009 .... **CLC 10**
See also CA 17-20R; 290; CANR 31, 54, 91, 148

Sargeson, Frank 1903-1982 ..... **CLC 31; SSC 99**
See also CA 25-28R; 106; CANR 38, 79; CN 1, 2, 3; EWL 3; GLL 2; RGEL 2; RGSF 2; SSFS 20

Sarmiento, Domingo Faustino 1811-1888 .... **HLCS 2; NCLC 123**
See also LAW; WLIT 1

Sarmiento, Felix Ruben Garcia
See Dario, Ruben

Saro-Wiwa, Ken(ule Beeson) 1941-1995 .... **CLC 114; TCLC 200**
See also BW 2; CA 142; 150; CANR 60; DLB 157

Saroyan, William 1908-1981 ... **CLC 1, 8, 10, 29, 34, 56; DC 28; SSC 21; TCLC 137; WLC 5**
See also AAYA 66; CA 5-8R; 103; CAD; CANR 30; CDALBS; CN 1, 2; DA; DA3; DAB; DAC; DAM DRAM, MST, NOV; DFS 17; DLB 7, 9, 86; DLBY 1981; EWL 3; LAIT 4; MAL 5; MTCW 1, 2; MTFW 2005; RGAL 4; RGSF 2; SATA 23; SATA-Obit 24; SSFS 14; TUS

Sarraute, Nathalie 1900-1999 .... **CLC 1, 2, 4, 8, 10, 31, 80; TCLC 145**
See also BPFB 3; CA 9-12R; 187; CANR 23, 66, 134; CWW 2; DLB 83, 321; EW 12; EWL 3; GFL 1789 to the Present; MTCW 1, 2; MTFW 2005; RGWL 2, 3

Sarton, May 1912-1995 ... **CLC 4, 14, 49, 91; PC 39; TCLC 120**
See also AMWS 8; CA 1-4R; 149; CANR 1, 34, 55, 116; CN 1, 2, 3, 4, 5, 6; CP 1, 2, 3, 4, 5, 6; DAM POET; DLB 48; DLBY 1981; EWL 3; FW; INT CANR-34; MAL 5; MTCW 1, 2; MTFW 2005; RGAL 4; SATA 36; SATA-Obit 86; TUS

Sartre, Jean-Paul 1905-1980 . **CLC 1, 4, 7, 9, 13, 18, 24, 44, 50, 52; DC 3; SSC 32; WLC 5**
See also AAYA 62; CA 9-12R; 97-100; CANR 21; DA; DA3; DAB; DAC; DAM DRAM, MST, NOV; DFS 5, 26; DLB 72, 296, 321, 332; EW 12; EWL 3; GFL 1789 to the Present; LMFS 2; MTCW 1, 2; MTFW 2005; NFS 21; RGHL; RGSF 2; RGWL 2, 3; SSFS 9; TWA

Sassoon, Siegfried 1886-1967 .. **CLC 36, 130; PC 12**
See also BRW 6; CA 104; 25-28R; CANR 36; DAB; DAM MST, NOV, POET; DLB 20, 191; DLBD 18; EWL 3; MTCW 1, 2; MTFW 2005; PAB; PFS 28; RGEL 2; TEA

Sassoon, Siegfried Lorraine
See Sassoon, Siegfried

Satterfield, Charles
See Pohl, Frederik

Satyremont
See Peret, Benjamin

Saul, John III
See Saul, John

Saul, John 1942- .... **CLC 46**
See also AAYA 10, 62; BEST 90:4; CA 81-84; CANR 16, 40, 81, 176; CPW; DAM NOV, POP; HGG; SATA 98

Saul, John W.
See Saul, John

Saul, John W. III
See Saul, John

Saul, John Woodruff III
See Saul, John

Saunders, Caleb
See Heinlein, Robert A.

Saura (Atares), Carlos 1932-1998 .... **CLC 20**
See also CA 114; 131; CANR 79; HW 1

Sauser, Frederic Louis
See Sauser-Hall, Frederic

Sauser-Hall, Frederic 1887-1961 ..... **CLC 18, 106**
See also CA 102; 93-96; CANR 36, 62; DLB 258; EWL 3; GFL 1789 to the Present; MTCW 1; WP

Saussure, Ferdinand de 1857-1913 .... **TCLC 49**
See also DLB 242

Savage, Catharine
See Brosman, Catharine Savage

Savage, Richard 1697(?)-1743 .... **LC 96**
See also DLB 95; RGEL 2

Savage, Thomas 1915-2003 .... **CLC 40**
See also CA 126; 132; 218; CAAS 15; CN 6, 7; INT CA-132; SATA-Obit 147; TCWW 2

Savan, Glenn 1953-2003 .... **CLC 50**
See also CA 225

Savonarola, Girolamo 1452-1498 ...... **LC 152**
See also LMFS 1

Sax, Robert
See Johnson, Robert

Saxo Grammaticus c. 1150-c. 1222 .... **CMLC 58**

Saxton, Robert
See Johnson, Robert

Sayers, Dorothy L(eigh) 1893-1957 . **SSC 71; TCLC 2, 15**
See also BPFB 3; BRWS 3; CA 104; 119; CANR 60; CDBLB 1914-1945; CMW 4; DAM POP; DLB 10, 36, 77, 100; MSW; MTCW 1, 2; MTFW 2005; RGEL 2; SSFS 12; TEA

Sayers, Valerie 1952- .... **CLC 50, 122**
See also CA 134; CANR 61; CSW

Sayles, John (Thomas) 1950- .... **CLC 7, 10, 14, 198**
See also CA 57-60; CANR 41, 84; DLB 44

Scamander, Newt
See Rowling, J. K.

Scammell, Michael 1935- .... **CLC 34**
See also CA 156

Scannel, John Vernon
See Scannell, Vernon

Scannell, Vernon 1922-2007 .... **CLC 49**
See also CA 5-8R; 266; CANR 8, 24, 57, 143; CN 1, 2; CP 1, 2, 3, 4, 5, 6, 7; CWRI 5; DLB 27; SATA 59; SATA-Obit 188

Scarlett, Susan
See Streatfeild, Noel

Scarron 1847-1910
See Mikszath, Kalman

Scarron, Paul 1610-1660 .... **LC 116**
See also GFL Beginnings to 1789; RGWL 2, 3

Schaeffer, Susan Fromberg 1941- ..... **CLC 6, 11, 22**
See also CA 49-52; CANR 18, 65, 160; CN 4, 5, 6, 7; DLB 28, 299; MTCW 1, 2; MTFW 2005; SATA 22

Schama, Simon 1945- .... **CLC 150**
See also BEST 89:4; CA 105; CANR 39, 91, 168

Schama, Simon Michael
See Schama, Simon

Schary, Jill
See Robinson, Jill

Schell, Jonathan 1943- .... **CLC 35**
See also CA 73-76; CANR 12, 117, 187

Schelling, Friedrich Wilhelm Joseph von 1775-1854 .... **NCLC 30**
See also DLB 90

Scherer, Jean-Marie Maurice
See Rohmer, Eric

Schevill, James (Erwin) 1920- .... **CLC 7**
See also CA 5-8R; CAAS 12; CAD; CD 5, 6; CP 1, 2, 3, 4, 5

Schiller, Friedrich von 1759-1805 ...... **DC 12; NCLC 39, 69, 166**
See also CDWLB 2; DAM DRAM; DLB 94; EW 5; RGWL 2, 3; TWA

Schisgal, Murray (Joseph) 1926- .... **CLC 6**
See also CA 21-24R; CAD; CANR 48, 86; CD 5, 6; MAL 5

Schlee, Ann 1934- .... **CLC 35**
See also CA 101; CANR 29, 88; SATA 44; SATA-Brief 36

Schlegel, August Wilhelm von 1767-1845 .... **NCLC 15, 142**
See also DLB 94; RGWL 2, 3

Schlegel, Friedrich 1772-1829 .... **NCLC 45, 226**
See also DLB 90; EW 5; RGWL 2, 3; TWA

Schlegel, Johann Elias (von) 1719(?)-1749 .... **LC 5**

Schleiermacher, Friedrich 1768-1834 .... **NCLC 107**
See also DLB 90

Schlesinger, Arthur M., Jr. 1917-2007 .... **CLC 84**
See Schlesinger, Arthur Meier
See also AITN 1; CA 1-4R; 257; CANR 1, 28, 58, 105, 187; DLB 17; INT CANR-28; MTCW 1, 2; SATA 61; SATA-Obit 181

Schlink, Bernhard 1944- .... **CLC 174**
See also CA 163; CANR 116, 175; RGHL

Schmidt, Arno (Otto) 1914-1979 ...... **CLC 56**
See also CA 128; 109; DLB 69; EWL 3

Schmitz, Aron Hector 1861-1928 ..... **SSC 25; TCLC 2, 35**
See also CA 104; 122; DLB 264; EW 8; EWL 3; MTCW 1; RGWL 2, 3; WLIT 7

Schnackenberg, Gjertrud 1953- ..... **CLC 40; PC 45**
See also AMWS 15; CA 116; CANR 100; CP 5, 6, 7; CWP; DLB 120, 282; PFS 13, 25

Schnackenberg, Gjertrud Cecelia
See Schnackenberg, Gjertrud

Schneider, Leonard Alfred 1925-1966 .... **CLC 21**
See also CA 89-92

Schnitzler, Arthur 1862-1931 ..... **DC 17; SSC 15, 61; TCLC 4**
See also CA 104; CDWLB 2; DLB 81, 118; EW 8; EWL 3; RGSF 2; RGWL 2, 3

Schoenberg, Arnold Franz Walter 1874-1951 .... **TCLC 75**
See also CA 109; 188

Schonberg, Arnold
See Schoenberg, Arnold Franz Walter

Schopenhauer, Arthur 1788-1860 . **NCLC 51, 157**
See also DLB 90; EW 5

Schor, Sandra (M.) 1932(?)-1990 ..... **CLC 65**
See also CA 132

Schorer, Mark 1908-1977 .... **CLC 9**
See also CA 5-8R; 73-76; CANR 7; CN 1, 2; DLB 103

Schrader, Paul (Joseph) 1946- . **CLC 26, 212**
See also CA 37-40R; CANR 41; DLB 44

Schreber, Daniel 1842-1911 .... **TCLC 123**

Schreiner, Olive 1855-1920 ...... **TCLC 9, 235**
See also AFW; BRWS 2; CA 105; 154; DLB 18, 156, 190, 225; EWL 3; FW; RGEL 2; TWA; WLIT 2; WWE 1

Schreiner, Olive Emilie Albertina
See Schreiner, Olive

Schulberg, Budd 1914-2009 .... **CLC 7, 48**
See also AMWS 18; BPFB 3; CA 25-28R; 289; CANR 19, 87, 178; CN 1, 2, 3, 4, 5, 6, 7; DLB 6, 26, 28; DLBY 1981, 2001; MAL 5

Schulberg, Budd Wilson
See Schulberg, Budd

Schulberg, Seymour Wilson
See Schulberg, Budd
Schulman, Arnold
See Trumbo, Dalton
Schulz, Bruno 1892-1942 .. SSC 13; TCLC 5, 51
See also CA 115; 123; CANR 86; CDWLB 4; DLB 215; EWL 3; MTCW 2; MTFW 2005; RGSF 2; RGWL 2, 3
Schulz, Charles M. 1922-2000 .... CLC 12
See also AAYA 39; CA 9-12R; 187; CANR 6, 132; INT CANR-6; MTFW 2005; SATA 10; SATA-Obit 118
Schulz, Charles Monroe
See Schulz, Charles M.
Schumacher, E(rnst) F(riedrich) 1911-1977 .... CLC 80
See also CA 81-84; 73-76; CANR 34, 85
Schumann, Robert 1810-1856 ...... NCLC 143
Schuyler, George Samuel 1895-1977 . HR 1:3
See also BW 2; CA 81-84; 73-76; CANR 42; DLB 29, 51
Schuyler, James Marcus 1923-1991 .. CLC 5, 23; PC 88
See also CA 101; 134; CP 1, 2, 3, 4, 5; DAM POET; DLB 5, 169; EWL 3; INT CA-101; MAL 5; WP
Schwartz, Delmore (David) 1913-1966 . CLC 2, 4, 10, 45, 87; PC 8; SSC 105
See also AMWS 2; CA 17-18; 25-28R; CANR 35; CAP 2; DLB 28, 48; EWL 3; MAL 5; MTCW 1, 2; MTFW 2005; PAB; RGAL 4; TUS
Schwartz, Ernst
See Ozu, Yasujiro
Schwartz, John Burnham 1965- .... CLC 59
See also CA 132; CANR 116, 188
Schwartz, Lynne Sharon 1939- .... CLC 31
See also CA 103; CANR 44, 89, 160; DLB 218; MTCW 2; MTFW 2005
Schwartz, Muriel A.
See Eliot, T. S.
Schwarz-Bart, Andre 1928-2006 .... CLC 2, 4
See also CA 89-92; 253; CANR 109; DLB 299; RGHL
Schwarz-Bart, Simone 1938- . BLCS; CLC 7
See also BW 2; CA 97-100; CANR 117; EWL 3
Schwerner, Armand 1927-1999 .... PC 42
See also CA 9-12R; 179; CANR 50, 85; CP 2, 3, 4, 5, 6; DLB 165
Schwitters, Kurt (Hermann Edward Karl Julius) 1887-1948 .... TCLC 95
See also CA 158
Schwob, Marcel (Mayer Andre) 1867-1905 .... TCLC 20
See also CA 117; 168; DLB 123; GFL 1789 to the Present
Sciascia, Leonardo 1921-1989 .. CLC 8, 9, 41
See also CA 85-88; 130; CANR 35; DLB 177; EWL 3; MTCW 1; RGWL 2, 3
Scoppettone, Sandra 1936- .... CLC 26
See also AAYA 11, 65; BYA 8; CA 5-8R; CANR 41, 73, 157; GLL 1; MAICYA 2; MAICYAS 1; SATA 9, 92; WYA; YAW
Scorsese, Martin 1942- .... CLC 20, 89, 207
See also AAYA 38; CA 110; 114; CANR 46, 85
Scotland, Jay
See Jakes, John
Scott, Duncan Campbell 1862-1947 .... TCLC 6
See also CA 104; 153; DAC; DLB 92; RGEL 2
Scott, Evelyn 1893-1963 .... CLC 43
See also CA 104; 112; CANR 64; DLB 9, 48; RHW

Scott, F(rancis) R(eginald) 1899-1985 .... CLC 22
See also CA 101; 114; CANR 87; CP 1, 2, 3, 4; DLB 88; INT CA-101; RGEL 2
Scott, Frank
See Scott, F(rancis) R(eginald)
Scott, Joan CLC 65
Scott, Joanna 1960- .... CLC 50
See also AMWS 17; CA 126; CANR 53, 92, 168
Scott, Joanna Jeanne
See Scott, Joanna
Scott, Paul (Mark) 1920-1978 ...... CLC 9, 60
See also BRWS 1; CA 81-84; 77-80; CANR 33; CN 1, 2; DLB 14, 207, 326; EWL 3; MTCW 1; RGEL 2; RHW; WWE 1
Scott, Ridley 1937- .... CLC 183
See also AAYA 13, 43
Scott, Sarah 1723-1795 .... LC 44
See also DLB 39
Scott, Sir Walter 1771-1832 .... NCLC 15, 69, 110, 209; PC 13; SSC 32; WLC 5
See also AAYA 22; BRW 4; BYA 2; CD-BLB 1789-1832; DA; DAB; DAC; DAM MST, NOV, POET; DLB 93, 107, 116, 144, 159; GL 3; HGG; LAIT 1; RGEL 2; RGSF 2; SSFS 10; SUFW 1; TEA; WLIT 3; YABC 2
Scribe, Augustin Eugene
See Scribe, (Augustin) Eugene
Scribe, (Augustin) Eugene 1791-1861 . DC 5; NCLC 16
See also DAM DRAM; DLB 192; GFL 1789 to the Present; RGWL 2, 3
Scrum, R.
See Crumb, R.
Scudery, Georges de 1601-1667 .... LC 75
See also GFL Beginnings to 1789
Scudery, Madeleine de 1607-1701 .. LC 2, 58
See also DLB 268; GFL Beginnings to 1789
Scum
See Crumb, R.
Scumbag, Little Bobby
See Crumb, R.
Seabrook, John
See Hubbard, L. Ron
Seacole, Mary Jane Grant 1805-1881 .... NCLC 147
See also DLB 166
Sealy, I(rwin) Allan 1951- .... CLC 55
See also CA 136; CN 6, 7
Search, Alexander
See Pessoa, Fernando
Seare, Nicholas
See Whitaker, Rod
Sebald, W(infried) G(eorg) 1944-2001 .... CLC 194
See also BRWS 8; CA 159; 202; CANR 98; MTFW 2005; RGHL
Sebastian, Lee
See Silverberg, Robert
Sebastian Owl
See Thompson, Hunter S.
Sebestyen, Igen
See Sebestyen, Ouida
Sebestyen, Ouida 1924- .... CLC 30
See also AAYA 8; BYA 7; CA 107; CANR 40, 114; CLR 17; JRDA; MAICYA 1, 2; SAAS 10; SATA 39, 140; WYA; YAW
Sebold, Alice 1963- .... CLC 193
See also AAYA 56; CA 203; CANR 181; LNFS 1; MTFW 2005
Second Duke of Buckingham
See Villiers, George
Secundus, H. Scriblerus
See Fielding, Henry
Sedges, John
See Buck, Pearl S.

Sedgwick, Catharine Maria 1789-1867 .... NCLC 19, 98
See also DLB 1, 74, 183, 239, 243, 254; FL 1:3; RGAL 4
Sedley, Sir Charles 1639-1701 .... LC 168
See also BRW 2; DLB 131; RGEL 2
Sedulius Scottus 9th cent. -c. 874 .. CMLC 86
Seebohm, Victoria
See Glendinning, Victoria
Seelye, John (Douglas) 1931- .... CLC 7
See also CA 97-100; CANR 70; INT CA-97-100; TCWW 1, 2
Seferiades, Giorgos Stylianou
See Seferis, George
Seferis, George 1900-1971 .... CLC 5, 11; TCLC 213
See also CA 5-8R; 33-36R; CANR 5, 36; DLB 332; EW 12; EWL 3; MTCW 1; RGWL 2, 3
Segal, Erich 1937-2010 .... CLC 3, 10
See also BEST 89:1; BPFB 3; CA 25-28R; CANR 20, 36, 65, 113; CPW; DAM POP; DLBY 1986; INT CANR-20; MTCW 1
Segal, Erich Wolf
See Segal, Erich
Seger, Bob 1945- .... CLC 35
Seghers
See Radvanyi, Netty
Seghers, Anna
See Radvanyi, Netty
Seidel, Frederick 1936- .... CLC 18
See also CA 13-16R; CANR 8, 99, 180; CP 1, 2, 3, 4, 5, 6, 7; DLBY 1984
Seidel, Frederick Lewis
See Seidel, Frederick
Seifert, Jaroslav 1901-1986 . CLC 34, 44, 93; PC 47
See also CA 127; CDWLB 4; DLB 215, 332; EWL 3; MTCW 1, 2
Sei Shonagon c. 966-1017(?) ..... CMLC 6, 89
Sejour, Victor 1817-1874 .... DC 10
See also DLB 50
Sejour Marcou et Ferrand, Juan Victor
See Sejour, Victor
Selby, Hubert, Jr. 1928-2004 ..... CLC 1, 2, 4, 8; SSC 20
See also CA 13-16R; 226; CANR 33, 85; CN 1, 2, 3, 4, 5, 6, 7; DLB 2, 227; MAL 5
Self, Will 1961- .... CLC 282
See also BRWS 5; CA 143; CANR 83, 126, 171, 201; CN 6, 7; DLB 207
Self, William
See Self, Will
Self, William Woodward
See Self, Will
Selzer, Richard 1928- .... CLC 74
See also CA 65-68; CANR 14, 106
Sembene, Ousmane
See Ousmane, Sembene
Senancour, Etienne Pivert de 1770-1846 .... NCLC 16
See also DLB 119; GFL 1789 to the Present
Sender, Ramon (Jose) 1902-1982 ...... CLC 8; HLC 2; TCLC 136
See also CA 5-8R; 105; CANR 8; DAM MULT; DLB 322; EWL 3; HW 1; MTCW 1; RGWL 2, 3
Seneca, Lucius Annaeus c. 4B.C.-c. 65 .... CMLC 6, 107; DC 5
See also AW 2; CDWLB 1; DAM DRAM; DLB 211; RGWL 2, 3; TWA; WLIT 8
Seneca the Younger
See Seneca, Lucius Annaeus

Author Index

Senghor, Leopold Sedar
1906-2001 .. **BLC 1:3; CLC 54, 130; PC 25**
See also AFW; BW 2; CA 116; 125; 203; CANR 47, 74, 134; CWW 2; DAM MULT; POET; DNFS 2; EWL 3; GFL 1789 to the Present; MTCW 1, 2; MTFW 2005; TWA

Senior, Olive (Marjorie) 1941- .... **SSC 78**
See also BW 3; CA 154; CANR 86, 126; CN 6; CP 6, 7; CWP; DLB 157; EWL 3; RGSF 2

Senna, Danzy 1970- .... **CLC 119**
See also CA 169; CANR 130, 184

Sepheriades, Georgios
See Seferis, George

Serling, (Edward) Rod(man)
1924-1975 .... **CLC 30**
See also AAYA 14; AITN 1; CA 162; 57-60; DLB 26; SFW 4

Serna, Ramon Gomez de la
See Gomez de la Serna, Ramon

Serpieres
See Guillevic, (Eugene)

Service, Robert
See Service, Robert W.

Service, Robert W. 1874(?)-1958 .... **PC 70; TCLC 15; WLC 5**
See also BYA 4; CA 115; 140; CANR 84; DA; DAB; DAC; DAM MST, POET; DLB 92; PFS 10; RGEL 2; SATA 20

Service, Robert William
See Service, Robert W.

Servius c. 370-c. 431 .... **CMLC 120**

Seth, Vikram 1952- .... **CLC 43, 90, 277**
See also BRWS 10; CA 121; 127; CANR 50, 74, 131; CN 6, 7; CP 5, 6, 7; DA3; DAM MULT; DLB 120, 271, 282, 323; EWL 3; INT CA-127; MTCW 2; MTFW 2005; WWE 1

Setien, Miguel Delibes
See Delibes Setien, Miguel

Seton, Cynthia Propper 1926-1982 .. **CLC 27**
See also CA 5-8R; 108; CANR 7

Seton, Ernest (Evan) Thompson
1860-1946 .... **TCLC 31**
See also ANW; BYA 3; CA 109; 204; CLR 59; DLB 92; DLBD 13; JRDA; SATA 18

Seton-Thompson, Ernest
See Seton, Ernest (Evan) Thompson

Settle, Mary Lee 1918-2005 .... **CLC 19, 61, 273**
See also BPFB 3; CA 89-92; 243; CAAS 1; CANR 44, 87, 126, 182; CN 6, 7; CSW; DLB 6; INT CA-89-92

Seuphor, Michel
See Arp, Jean

Sevigne, Marie (de Rabutin-Chantal)
1626-1696 .... **LC 11, 144**
See also DLB 268; GFL Beginnings to 1789; TWA

Sevigne, Marie de Rabutin Chantal
See Sevigne, Marie (de Rabutin-Chantal)

Sewall, Samuel 1652-1730 .... **LC 38**
See also DLB 24; RGAL 4

Sexton, Anne 1928-1974 .. **CLC 2, 4, 6, 8, 10, 15, 53, 123; PC 2, 79; WLC 5**
See also AMWS 2; CA 1-4R; 53-56; CABS 2; CANR 3, 36; CDALB 1941-1968; CP 1, 2; DA; DA3; DAB; DAC; DAM MST, POET; DLB 5, 169; EWL 3; EXPP; FL 1:6; FW; MAL 5; MBL; MTCW 1, 2; MTFW 2005; PAB; PFS 4, 14, 30; RGAL 4; RGHL; SATA 10; TUS

Sexton, Anne Harvey
See Sexton, Anne

Shaara, Jeff 1952- .... **CLC 119**
See also AAYA 70; CA 163; CANR 109, 172; CN 7; MTFW 2005

Shaara, Michael 1929-1988 .... **CLC 15**
See also AAYA 71; AITN 1; BPFB 3; CA 102; 125; CANR 52, 85; DAM POP; DLBY 1983; MTFW 2005; NFS 26

Shackleton, C.C.
See Aldiss, Brian W.

Shacochis, Bob
See Shacochis, Robert G.

Shacochis, Robert G. 1951- .... **CLC 39**
See also CA 119; 124; CANR 100; INT CA-124

Shadwell, Thomas 1641(?)-1692 .... **LC 114**
See also DLB 80; IDTP; RGEL 2

Shaffer, Anthony 1926-2001 .... **CLC 19**
See also CA 110; 116; 200; CBD; CD 5, 6; DAM DRAM; DFS 13; DLB 13

Shaffer, Anthony Joshua
See Shaffer, Anthony

Shaffer, Peter 1926- ... **CLC 5, 14, 18, 37, 60; DC 7**
See also BRWS 1; CA 25-28R; CANR 25, 47, 74, 118; CBD; CD 5, 6; CDBLB 1960 to Present; DA3; DAB; DAM DRAM, MST; DFS 5, 13; DLB 13, 233; EWL 3; MTCW 1, 2; MTFW 2005; RGEL 2; TEA

Shakespeare, William 1564-1616 . **PC 84, 89, 98, 101; WLC 5**
See also AAYA 35; BRW 1; BRWR 3; CD-BLB Before 1660; DA; DA3; DAB; DAC; DAM DRAM, MST, POET; DFS 20, 21; DLB 62, 172, 263; EXPP; LAIT 1; LATS 1:1; LMFS 1; PAB; PFS 1, 2, 3, 4, 5, 8, 9; RGEL 2; TEA; WLIT 3; WP; WS; WYA

Shakey, Bernard
See Young, Neil

Shalamov, Varlam (Tikhonovich)
1907-1982 .... **CLC 18**
See also CA 129; 105; DLB 302; RGSF 2

Shamloo, Ahmad
See Shamlu, Ahmad

Shamlou, Ahmad
See Shamlu, Ahmad

Shamlu, Ahmad 1925-2000 .... **CLC 10**
See also CA 216; CWW 2

Shammas, Anton 1951- .... **CLC 55**
See also CA 199; DLB 346

Shandling, Arline
See Berriault, Gina

Shange, Ntozake 1948- .. **BLC 1:3, 2:3; CLC 8, 25, 38, 74, 126; DC 3**
See also AAYA 9, 66; AFAW 1, 2; BW 2; CA 85-88; CABS 3; CAD; CANR 27, 48, 74, 131; CD 5, 6; CP 5, 6, 7; CWD; CWP; DA3; DAM DRAM, MULT; DFS 2, 11; DLB 38, 249; FW; LAIT 4, 5; MAL 5; MTCW 1, 2; MTFW 2005; NFS 11; RGAL 4; SATA 157; YAW

Shanley, John Patrick 1950- .... **CLC 75**
See also AAYA 74; AMWS 14; CA 128; 133; CAD; CANR 83, 154; CD 5, 6; DFS 23

Shapcott, Thomas W(illiam) 1935- .. **CLC 38**
See also CA 69-72; CANR 49, 83, 103; CP 1, 2, 3, 4, 5, 6, 7; DLB 289

Shapiro, Jane 1942- .... **CLC 76**
See also CA 196

Shapiro, Karl 1913-2000 ... **CLC 4, 8, 15, 53; PC 25**
See also AMWS 2; CA 1-4R; 188; CAAS 6; CANR 1, 36, 66; CP 1, 2, 3, 4, 5, 6; DLB 48; EWL 3; EXPP; MAL 5; MTCW 1, 2; MTFW 2005; PFS 3; RGAL 4

Sharp, William 1855-1905 .... **TCLC 39**
See also CA 160; DLB 156; RGEL 2; SUFW

Sharpe, Thomas Ridley 1928- .... **CLC 36**
See also CA 114; 122; CANR 85; CN 4, 5, 6, 7; DLB 14, 231; INT CA-122

Sharpe, Tom
See Sharpe, Thomas Ridley

Shatrov, Mikhail CLC 59

Shaw, Bernard
See Shaw, George Bernard

Shaw, G. Bernard
See Shaw, George Bernard

Shaw, George Bernard 1856-1950 ..... **DC 23; TCLC 3, 9, 21, 45, 205; WLC 5**
See also AAYA 61; BRW 6; BRWC 1; BRWR 2; CA 104; 128; CDBLB 1914-1945; DA; DA3; DAB; DAC; DAM DRAM, MST; DFS 1, 3, 6, 11, 19, 22; DLB 10, 57, 190, 332; EWL 3; LAIT 3; LATS 1:1; MTCW 1, 2; MTFW 2005; RGEL 2; TEA; WLIT 4

Shaw, Henry Wheeler 1818-1885 .. **NCLC 15**
See also DLB 11; RGAL 4

Shaw, Irwin 1913-1984 .... **CLC 7, 23, 34**
See also AITN 1; BPFB 3; CA 13-16R; 112; CANR 21; CDALB 1941-1968; CN 1, 2, 3; CPW; DAM DRAM, POP; DLB 6, 102; DLBY 1984; MAL 5; MTCW 1, 21; MTFW 2005

Shaw, Robert (Archibald)
1927-1978 .... **CLC 5**
See also AITN 1; CA 1-4R; 81-84; CANR 4; CN 1, 2; DLB 13, 14

Shaw, T. E.
See Lawrence, T. E.

Shawn, Wallace 1943- .... **CLC 41**
See also CA 112; CAD; CD 5, 6; DLB 266

Shaykh, al- Hanan
See al-Shaykh, Hanan

Shchedrin, N.
See Saltykov, Mikhail Evgrafovich

Shea, Lisa 1953- .... **CLC 86**
See also CA 147

Sheed, Wilfrid 1930- .... **CLC 2, 4, 10, 53**
See also CA 65-68; CANR 30, 66, 181; CN 1, 2, 3, 4, 5, 6, 7; DLB 6; MAL 5; MTCW 1, 2; MTFW 2005

Sheed, Wilfrid John Joseph
See Sheed, Wilfrid

Sheehy, Gail 1937- .... **CLC 171**
See also CA 49-52; CANR 1, 33, 55, 92; CPW; MTCW 1

Sheldon, Alice Hastings Bradley
1915(?)-1987 .... **CLC 48, 50**
See also CA 108; 122; CANR 34; DLB 8; INT CA-108; MTCW 1; SCFW 1, 2; SFW 4

Sheldon, John
See Bloch, Robert (Albert)

Sheldon, Raccoona
See Sheldon, Alice Hastings Bradley

Shelley, Mary
See Shelley, Mary Wollstonecraft

Shelley, Mary Wollstonecraft
1797-1851 .... **NCLC 14, 59, 103, 170; SSC 92; WLC 5**
See also AAYA 20; BPFB 3; BRW 3; BRWC 2; BRWR 3; BRWS 3; BYA 5; CDBLB 1789-1832; CLR 133; DA; DA3; DAB; DAC; DAM MST, NOV; DLB 110, 116, 159, 178; EXPN; FL 1:3; GL 3; HGG; LAIT 1; LMFS 1, 2; NFS 1; RGEL 2; SATA 29; SCFW 1, 2; SFW 4; TEA; WLIT 3

Shelley, Percy Bysshe 1792-1822 .. **NCLC 18, 93, 143, 175; PC 14, 67; WLC 5**
See also AAYA 61; BRW 4; BRWR 1; CD-BLB 1789-1832; DA; DA3; DAB; DAC; DAM MST, POET; DLB 96, 110, 158; EXPP; LMFS 1; PAB; PFS 2, 27; RGEL 2; TEA; WLIT 3; WP

Shepard, James R.
See Shepard, Jim

Silverstein, Virginia B. 1937- .... **CLC 17**
See also CA 49-52; CANR 2; CLR 25; JRDA; MAICYA 1, 2; SATA 8, 69, 124

Silverstein, Virginia Barbara Opshelor
See Silverstein, Virginia B.

Sim, Georges
See Simenon, Georges

Simak, Clifford D(onald) 1904-1988 . **CLC 1, 55**
See also CA 1-4R; 125; CANR 1, 35; DLB 8; MTCW 1; SATA-Obit 56; SCFW 1, 2; SFW 4

Simenon, Georges 1903-1989 .... **CLC 1, 2, 3, 8, 18, 47**
See also BPFB 3; CA 85-88; 129; CANR 35; CMW 4; DA3; DAM POP; DLB 72; DLBY 1989; EW 12; EWL 3; GFL 1789 to the Present; MSW; MTCW 1, 2; MTFW 2005; RGWL 2, 3

Simenon, Georges Jacques Christian
See Simenon, Georges

Simic, Charles 1938- .... **CLC 6, 9, 22, 49, 68, 130, 256; PC 69**
See also AAYA 78; AMWS 8; CA 29-32R; CAAS 4; CANR 12, 33, 52, 61, 96, 140; CP 2, 3, 4, 5, 6, 7; DA3; DAM POET; DLB 105; MAL 5; MTCW 2; MTFW 2005; PFS 7; RGAL 4; WP

Simmel, Georg 1858-1918 .... **TCLC 64**
See also CA 157; DLB 296

Simmons, Charles (Paul) 1924- .... **CLC 57**
See also CA 89-92; INT CA-89-92

Simmons, Dan 1948- .... **CLC 44**
See also AAYA 16, 54; CA 138; CANR 53, 81, 126, 174; CPW; DAM POP; HGG; SUFW 2

Simmons, James (Stewart Alexander) 1933- .... **CLC 43**
See also CA 105; CAAS 21; CP 1, 2, 3, 4, 5, 6, 7; DLB 40

Simmons, Richard
See Simmons, Dan

Simms, William Gilmore 1806-1870 .... **NCLC 3**
See also DLB 3, 30, 59, 73, 248, 254; RGAL 4

Simon, Carly 1945- .... **CLC 26**
See also CA 105

Simon, Claude 1913-2005 ... **CLC 4, 9, 15, 39**
See also CA 89-92; 241; CANR 33, 117; CWW 2; DAM NOV; DLB 83, 332; EW 13; EWL 3; GFL 1789 to the Present; MTCW 1

Simon, Claude Eugene Henri
See Simon, Claude

Simon, Claude Henri Eugene
See Simon, Claude

Simon, Marvin Neil
See Simon, Neil

Simon, Myles
See Follett, Ken

Simon, Neil 1927- .... **CLC 6, 11, 31, 39, 70, 233; DC 14**
See also AAYA 32; AITN 1; AMWS 4; CA 21-24R; CAD; CANR 26, 54, 87, 126; CD 5, 6; DA3; DAM DRAM; DFS 2, 6, 12, 18,, 24; DLB 7, 266; LAIT 4; MAL 5; MTCW 1, 2; MTFW 2005; RGAL 4; TUS

Simon, Paul 1941(?)- .... **CLC 17**
See also CA 116; 153; CANR 152

Simon, Paul Frederick
See Simon, Paul

Simonon, Paul 1956(?)- .... **CLC 30**

Simonson, Rick CLC 70

Simpson, Harriette
See Arnow, Harriette (Louisa) Simpson

Simpson, Louis 1923- ... **CLC 4, 7, 9, 32, 149**
See also AMWS 9; CA 1-4R; CAAS 4; CANR 1, 61, 140; CP 1, 2, 3, 4, 5, 6, 7; DAM POET; DLB 5; MAL 5; MTCW 1, 2; MTFW 2005; PFS 7, 11, 14; RGAL 4

Simpson, Mona 1957- .... **CLC 44, 146**
See also CA 122; 135; CANR 68, 103; CN 6, 7; EWL 3

Simpson, Mona Elizabeth
See Simpson, Mona

Simpson, N(orman) F(rederick) 1919- .... **CLC 29**
See also CA 13-16R; CBD; DLB 13; RGEL 2

Sinclair, Andrew (Annandale) 1935- . **CLC 2, 14**
See also CA 9-12R; CAAS 5; CANR 14, 38, 91; CN 1, 2, 3, 4, 5, 6, 7; DLB 14; FANT; MTCW 1

Sinclair, Emil
See Hesse, Hermann

Sinclair, Iain 1943- .... **CLC 76**
See also BRWS 14; CA 132; CANR 81, 157; CP 5, 6, 7; HGG

Sinclair, Iain MacGregor
See Sinclair, Iain

Sinclair, Irene
See Griffith, D.W.

Sinclair, Julian
See Sinclair, May

Sinclair, Mary Amelia St. Clair (?)-
See Sinclair, May

Sinclair, May 1865-1946 .... **TCLC 3, 11**
See also CA 104; 166; DLB 36, 135; EWL 3; HGG; RGEL 2; RHW; SUFW

Sinclair, Roy
See Griffith, D.W.

Sinclair, Upton 1878-1968 ...... **CLC 1, 11, 15, 63; TCLC 160; WLC 5**
See also AAYA 63; AMWS 5; BPFB 3; BYA 2; CA 5-8R; 25-28R; CANR 7; CDALB 1929-1941; DA; DA3; DAB; DAC; DAM MST, NOV; DLB 9; EWL 3; INT CANR-7; LAIT 3; MAL 5; MTCW 1, 2; MTFW 2005; NFS 6; RGAL 4; SATA 9; TUS; YAW

Sinclair, Upton Beall
See Sinclair, Upton

Singe, (Edmund) J(ohn) M(illington) 1871-1909 .... **WLC**

Singer, Isaac
See Singer, Isaac Bashevis

Singer, Isaac Bashevis 1904-1991 .. **CLC 1, 3, 6, 9, 11, 15, 23, 38, 69, 111; SSC 3, 53, 80; WLC 5**
See also AAYA 32; AITN 1, 2; AMW; AMWR 2; BPFB 3; BYA 1, 4; CA 1-4R; 134; CANR 1, 39, 106; CDALB 1941-1968; CLR 1; CN 1, 2, 3, 4; CWRI 5; DA; DA3; DAB; DAC; DAM MST, NOV; DLB 6, 28, 52, 278, 332, 333; DLBY 1991; EWL 3; EXPS; HGG; JRDA; LAIT 3; MAICYA 1, 2; MAL 5; MTCW 1, 2; MTFW 2005; RGAL 4; RGHL; RGSF 2; SATA 3, 27; SATA-Obit 68; SSFS 2, 12, 16, 27; TUS; TWA

Singer, Israel Joshua 1893-1944 .... **TCLC 33**
See also CA 169; DLB 333; EWL 3

Singh, Khushwant 1915- .... **CLC 11**
See also CA 9-12R; CAAS 9; CANR 6, 84; CN 1, 2, 3, 4, 5, 6, 7; DLB 323; EWL 3; RGEL 2

Singleton, Ann
See Benedict, Ruth

Singleton, John 1968(?)- .... **CLC 156**
See also AAYA 50; BW 2, 3; CA 138; CANR 67, 82; DAM MULT

Siniavskii, Andrei
See Sinyavsky, Andrei (Donatevich)

Sinibaldi, Fosco
See Kacew, Romain

Sinjohn, John
See Galsworthy, John

Sinyavsky, Andrei (Donatevich) 1925-1997 .... **CLC 8**
See also CA 85-88; 159; CWW 2; EWL 3; RGSF 2

Sinyavsky, Andrey Donatovich
See Sinyavsky, Andrei (Donatevich)

Sirin, V.
See Nabokov, Vladimir

Sissman, L(ouis) E(dward) 1928-1976 .... **CLC 9, 18**
See also CA 21-24R; 65-68; CANR 13; CP 2; DLB 5

Sisson, C(harles) H(ubert) 1914-2003 .... **CLC 8**
See also BRWS 11; CA 1-4R; 220; CAAS 3; CANR 3, 48, 84; CP 1, 2, 3, 4, 5, 6, 7; DLB 27

Sitting Bull 1831(?)-1890 .... **NNAL**
See also DA3; DAM MULT

Sitwell, Dame Edith 1887-1964 ..... **CLC 2, 9, 67; PC 3**
See also BRW 7; CA 9-12R; CANR 35; CDBLB 1945-1960; DAM POET; DLB 20; EWL 3; MTCW 1, 2; MTFW 2005; RGEL 2; TEA

Siwaarmill, H. P.
See Sharp, William

Sjoewall, Maj 1935- .... **CLC 7**
See also BPFB 3; CA 65-68; CANR 73; CMW 4; MSW

Sjowall, Maj
See Sjoewall, Maj

Skelton, John 1460(?)-1529 ..... **LC 71; PC 25**
See also BRW 1; DLB 136; RGEL 2

Skelton, Robin 1925-1997 .... **CLC 13**
See also AITN 2; CA 5-8R; 160; CAAS 5; CANR 28, 89; CCA 1; CP 1, 2, 3, 4, 5, 6; DLB 27, 53

Skolimowski, Jerzy 1938- .... **CLC 20**
See also CA 128

Skram, Amalie (Bertha) 1846-1905 .... **TCLC 25**
See also CA 165; DLB 354

Skvorecky, Josef 1924- . **CLC 15, 39, 69, 152**
See also CA 61-64; CAAS 1; CANR 10, 34, 63, 108; CDWLB 4; CWW 2; DA3; DAC; DAM NOV; DLB 232; EWL 3; MTCW 1, 2; MTFW 2005

Skvorecky, Josef Vaclav
See Skvorecky, Josef

Slade, Bernard 1930-
See Newbound, Bernard Slade

Slaughter, Carolyn 1946- .... **CLC 56**
See also CA 85-88; CANR 85, 169; CN 5, 6, 7

Slaughter, Frank G(ill) 1908-2001 ... **CLC 29**
See also AITN 2; CA 5-8R; 197; CANR 5, 85; INT CANR-5; RHW

Slavitt, David R. 1935- .... **CLC 5, 14**
See also CA 21-24R; CAAS 3; CANR 41, 83, 166; CN 1, 2; CP 1, 2, 3, 4, 5, 6, 7; DLB 5, 6

Slavitt, David Rytman
See Slavitt, David R.

Slesinger, Tess 1905-1945 .... **TCLC 10**
See also CA 107; 199; DLB 102

Slessor, Kenneth 1901-1971 .... **CLC 14**
See also CA 102; 89-92; DLB 260; RGEL 2

Slowacki, Juliusz 1809-1849 .... **NCLC 15**
See also RGWL 3

Smart, Christopher 1722-1771 .... **LC 3, 134; PC 13**
See also DAM POET; DLB 109; RGEL 2

Smart, Elizabeth 1913-1986 .... **CLC 54; TCLC 231**
See also CA 81-84; 118; CN 4; DLB 88

Smiley, Jane 1949- ...... **CLC 53, 76, 144, 236**
See also AAYA 66; AMWS 6; BPFB 3; CA 104; CANR 30, 50, 74, 96, 158, 196; CN 6, 7; CPW 1; DA3; DAM POP; DLB 227, 234; EWL 3; INT CANR-30; MAL 5; MTFW 2005; SSFS 19

Smiley, Jane Graves
See Smiley, Jane

Smith, A(rthur) J(ames) M(arshall) 1902-1980 .... **CLC 15**
See also CA 1-4R; 102; CANR 4; CP 1, 2, 3; DAC; DLB 88; RGEL 2

Smith, Adam 1723(?)-1790 .... **LC 36**
See also DLB 104, 252, 336; RGEL 2

Smith, Alexander 1829-1867 .... **NCLC 59**
See also DLB 32, 55

Smith, Alexander McCall 1948- ..... **CLC 268**
See also CA 215; CANR 154, 196; SATA 73, 179

Smith, Anna Deavere 1950- ...... **CLC 86, 241**
See also CA 133; CANR 103; CD 5, 6; DFS 2, 22; DLB 341

Smith, Betty (Wehner) 1904-1972 .... **CLC 19**
See also AAYA 72; BPFB 3; BYA 3; CA 5-8R; 33-36R; DLBY 1982; LAIT 3; RGAL 4; SATA 6

Smith, Charlotte (Turner) 1749-1806 .... **NCLC 23, 115; PC 104**
See also DLB 39, 109; RGEL 2; TEA

Smith, Clark Ashton 1893-1961 .... **CLC 43**
See also AAYA 76; CA 143; CANR 81; FANT; HGG; MTCW 2; SCFW 1, 2; SFW 4; SUFW

Smith, Dave
See Smith, David (Jeddie)

Smith, David (Jeddie) 1942- .... **CLC 22, 42**
See also CA 49-52; CAAS 7; CANR 1, 59, 120; CP 3, 4, 5, 6, 7; CSW; DAM POET; DLB 5

Smith, Iain Crichton 1928-1998 .... **CLC 64**
See also BRWS 9; CA 21-24R; 171; CN 1, 2, 3, 4, 5, 6; CP 1, 2, 3, 4, 5, 6; DLB 40, 139, 319, 352; RGSF 2

Smith, John 1580(?)-1631 .... **LC 9**
See also DLB 24, 30; TUS

Smith, Johnston
See Crane, Stephen

Smith, Joseph, Jr. 1805-1844 .... **NCLC 53**

Smith, Kevin 1970- .... **CLC 223**
See also AAYA 37; CA 166; CANR 131, 201

Smith, Lee 1944- .... **CLC 25, 73, 258**
See also CA 114; 119; CANR 46, 118, 173; CN 7; CSW; DLB 143; DLBY 1983; EWL 3; INT CA-119; RGAL 4

Smith, Martin
See Smith, Martin Cruz

Smith, Martin Cruz 1942- .. **CLC 25; NNAL**
See also BEST 89:4; BPFB 3; CA 85-88; CANR 6, 23, 43, 65, 119, 184; CMW 4; CPW; DAM MULT, POP; HGG; INT CANR-23; MTCW 2; MTFW 2005; RGAL 4

Smith, Patti 1946- .... **CLC 12**
See also CA 93-96; CANR 63, 168

Smith, Pauline (Urmson) 1882-1959 .... **TCLC 25**
See also DLB 225; EWL 3

Smith, R. Alexander McCall
See Smith, Alexander McCall

Smith, Rosamond
See Oates, Joyce Carol

Smith, Seba 1792-1868 .... **NCLC 187**
See also DLB 1, 11, 243

Smith, Sheila Kaye
See Kaye-Smith, Sheila

Smith, Stevie 1902-1971 .... **CLC 3, 8, 25, 44; PC 12**
See also BRWR 3; BRWS 2; CA 17-18; 29-32R; CANR 35; CAP 2; CP 1; DAM POET; DLB 20; EWL 3; MTCW 1, 2; PAB; PFS 3; RGEL 2; TEA

Smith, Wilbur 1933- .... **CLC 33**
See also CA 13-16R; CANR 7, 46, 66, 134, 180; CPW; MTCW 1, 2; MTFW 2005

Smith, Wilbur Addison
See Smith, Wilbur

Smith, William Jay 1918- .... **CLC 6**
See also AMWS 13; CA 5-8R; CANR 44, 106; CP 1, 2, 3, 4, 5, 6, 7; CSW; CWRI 5; DLB 5; MAICYA 1, 2; SAAS 22; SATA 2, 68, 154; SATA-Essay 154; TCLE 1:2

Smith, Woodrow Wilson
See Kuttner, Henry

Smith, Zadie 1975- .... **CLC 158**
See also AAYA 50; CA 193; DLB 347; MTFW 2005

Smolenskin, Peretz 1842-1885 .... **NCLC 30**

Smollett, Tobias (George) 1721-1771 ... **LC 2, 46**
See also BRW 3; CDBLB 1660-1789; DLB 39, 104; RGEL 2; TEA

Snodgrass, Quentin Curtius
See Twain, Mark

Snodgrass, Thomas Jefferson
See Twain, Mark

Snodgrass, W. D. 1926-2009 .... **CLC 2, 6, 10, 18, 68; PC 74**
See also AMWS 6; CA 1-4R; 282; CANR 6, 36, 65, 85, 185; CP 1, 2, 3, 4, 5, 6, 7; DAM POET; DLB 5; MAL 5; MTCW 1, 2; MTFW 2005; PFS 29; RGAL 4; TCLE 1:2

Snodgrass, W. de Witt
See Snodgrass, W. D.

Snodgrass, William de Witt
See Snodgrass, W. D.

Snodgrass, William De Witt
See Snodgrass, W. D.

Snorri Sturluson 1179-1241 .... **CMLC 56**
See also RGWL 2, 3

Snow, C(harles) P(ercy) 1905-1980 ... **CLC 1, 4, 6, 9, 13, 19**
See also BRW 7; CA 5-8R; 101; CANR 28; CDBLB 1945-1960; CN 1, 2; DAM NOV; DLB 15, 77; DLBD 17; EWL 3; MTCW 1, 2; MTFW 2005; RGEL 2; TEA

Snow, Frances Compton
See Adams, Henry

Snyder, Gary 1930- . **CLC 1, 2, 5, 9, 32, 120; PC 21**
See also AAYA 72; AMWS 8; ANW; BG 1:3; CA 17-20R; CANR 30, 60, 125; CP 1, 2, 3, 4, 5, 6, 7; DA3; DAM POET; DLB 5, 16, 165, 212, 237, 275, 342; EWL 3; MAL 5; MTCW 2; MTFW 2005; PFS 9, 19; RGAL 4; WP

Snyder, Gary Sherman
See Snyder, Gary

Snyder, Zilpha Keatley 1927- .... **CLC 17**
See also AAYA 15; BYA 1; CA 9-12R; 252; CAAE 252; CANR 38, 202; CLR 31, 121; JRDA; MAICYA 1, 2; SAAS 2; SATA 1, 28, 75, 110, 163; SATA-Essay 112, 163; YAW

Soares, Bernardo
See Pessoa, Fernando

Sobh, A.
See Shamlu, Ahmad

Sobh, Alef
See Shamlu, Ahmad

Sobol, Joshua 1939- .... **CLC 60**
See also CA 200; CWW 2; RGHL

Sobol, Yehoshua 1939-
See Sobol, Joshua

Socrates 470B.C.-399B.C. .... **CMLC 27**

Soderberg, Hjalmar 1869-1941 ...... **TCLC 39**
See also DLB 259; EWL 3; RGSF 2

Soderbergh, Steven 1963- .... **CLC 154**
See also AAYA 43; CA 243

Soderbergh, Steven Andrew
See Soderbergh, Steven

Sodergran, Edith 1892-1923 .... **TCLC 31**
See also CA 202; DLB 259; EW 11; EWL 3; RGWL 2, 3

Sodergran, Edith Irene
See Sodergran, Edith

Softly, Edgar
See Lovecraft, H. P.

Softly, Edward
See Lovecraft, H. P.

Sokolov, Alexander V. 1943- .... **CLC 59**
See also CA 73-76; CWW 2; DLB 285; EWL 3; RGWL 2, 3

Sokolov, Alexander Vsevolodovich
See Sokolov, Alexander V.

Sokolov, Raymond 1941- .... **CLC 7**
See also CA 85-88

Sokolov, Sasha
See Sokolov, Alexander V.

Solo, Jay
See Ellison, Harlan

Sologub, Fedor
See Teternikov, Fyodor Kuzmich

Sologub, Feodor
See Teternikov, Fyodor Kuzmich

Sologub, Fyodor
See Teternikov, Fyodor Kuzmich

Solomons, Ikey Esquir
See Thackeray, William Makepeace

Solomos, Dionysios 1798-1857 .... **NCLC 15**

Solwoska, Mara
See French, Marilyn

Solzhenitsyn, Aleksandr 1918-2008 ... **CLC 1, 2, 4, 7, 9, 10, 18, 26, 34, 78, 134, 235; SSC 32, 105; WLC 3**
See also AAYA 49; AITN 1; BPFB 3; CA 69-72; CANR 40, 65, 116; CWW 2; DA; DA3; DAB; DAC; DAM MST, NOV; DLB 302, 332; EW 13; EWL 3; EXPS; LAIT 4; MTCW 1, 2; MTFW 2005; NFS 6; RGSF 2; RGWL 2, 3; SSFS 9; TWA

Solzhenitsyn, Aleksandr I.
See Solzhenitsyn, Aleksandr

Solzhenitsyn, Aleksandr Isayevich
See Solzhenitsyn, Aleksandr

Somers, Jane
See Lessing, Doris

Somerville, Edith Oenone 1858-1949 .... **SSC 56; TCLC 51**
See also CA 196; DLB 135; RGEL 2; RGSF 2

Somerville & Ross
See Martin, Violet Florence; Somerville, Edith Oenone

Sommer, Scott 1951- .... **CLC 25**
See also CA 106

Sommers, Christina Hoff 1950- ...... **CLC 197**
See also CA 153; CANR 95

Sondheim, Stephen 1930- .. **CLC 30, 39, 147; DC 22**
See also AAYA 11, 66; CA 103; CANR 47, 67, 125; DAM DRAM; DFS 25; LAIT 4

Sondheim, Stephen Joshua
See Sondheim, Stephen

Sone, Monica 1919- .... **AAL**
See also DLB 312

Song, Cathy 1955- .... **AAL; PC 21**
See also CA 154; CANR 118; CWP; DLB
169, 312; EXPP; FW; PFS 5
Sontag, Susan 1933-2004 ... **CLC 1, 2, 10, 13,**
31, 105, 195, 277
See also AMWS 3; CA 17-20R; 234; CANR
25, 51, 74, 97, 184; CN 1, 2, 3, 4, 5, 6, 7;
CPW; DA3; DAM POP; DLB 2, 67; EWL
3; MAL 5; MBL; MTCW 1, 2; MTFW
2005; RGAL 4; RHW; SSFS 10
Sophocles 496(?)B.C.-406(?)B.C. .... **CMLC 2,**
47, 51, 86; DC 1; WLCS
See also AW 1; CDWLB 1; DA; DA3;
DAB; DAC; DAM DRAM, MST; DFS 1,
4, 8, 24; DLB 176; LAIT 1; LATS 1:1;
LMFS 1; RGWL 2, 3; TWA; WLIT 8
Sordello 1189-1269 .... **CMLC 15**
Sorel, Georges 1847-1922 .... **TCLC 91**
See also CA 118; 188
Sorel, Julia
See Drexler, Rosalyn
Sorokin, Vladimir **CLC 59**
See also CA 258; DLB 285
Sorokin, Vladimir Georgievich
See Sorokin, Vladimir
Sorrentino, Gilbert 1929-2006 .... **CLC 3, 7,**
14, 22, 40, 247
See also CA 77-80; 250; CANR 14, 33, 115,
157; CN 3, 4, 5, 6, 7; CP 1, 2, 3, 4, 5, 6,
7; DLB 5, 173; DLBY 1980; INT
CANR-14
Soseki
See Natsume, Soseki
Soto, Gary 1952- ... **CLC 32, 80; HLC 2; PC**
28
See also AAYA 10, 37; BYA 11; CA 119;
125; CANR 50, 74, 107, 157; CLR 38;
CP 4, 5, 6, 7; DAM MULT; DFS 26; DLB
82; EWL 3; EXPP; HW 1, 2; INT CA-
125; JRDA; LLW; MAICYA 2; MAIC-
YAS 1; MAL 5; MTCW 2; MTFW 2005;
PFS 7, 30; RGAL 4; SATA 80, 120, 174;
WYA; YAW
Soupault, Philippe 1897-1990 .... **CLC 68**
See also CA 116; 147; 131; EWL 3; GFL
1789 to the Present; LMFS 2
Souster, (Holmes) Raymond 1921- .... **CLC 5,**
14
See also CA 13-16R; CAAS 14; CANR 13,
29, 53; CP 1, 2, 3, 4, 5, 6, 7; DA3; DAC;
DAM POET; DLB 88; RGEL 2; SATA 63
Southern, Terry 1924(?)-1995 .... **CLC 7**
See also AMWS 11; BPFB 3; CA 1-4R;
150; CANR 1, 55, 107; CN 1, 2, 3, 4, 5,
6; DLB 2; IDFW 3, 4
Southerne, Thomas 1660-1746 .... **LC 99**
See also DLB 80; RGEL 2
Southey, Robert 1774-1843 .... **NCLC 8, 97**
See also BRW 4; DLB 93, 107, 142; RGEL
2; SATA 54
Southwell, Robert 1561(?)-1595 .... **LC 108**
See also DLB 167; RGEL 2; TEA
Southworth, Emma Dorothy Eliza Nevitte
1819-1899 .... **NCLC 26**
See also DLB 239
Souza, Ernest
See Scott, Evelyn
Soyinka, Wole 1934- .. **BLC 1:3, 2:3; CLC 3,**
5, 14, 36, 44, 179; DC 2; WLC 5
See also AFW; BW 2, 3; CA 13-16R;
CANR 27, 39, 82, 136; CD 5, 6; CDWLB
3; CN 6, 7; CP 1, 2, 3, 4, 5, 6 ,7; DA;
DA3; DAB; DAC; DAM DRAM, MST,
MULT; DFS 10, 26; DLB 125, 332; EWL
3; MTCW 1, 2; MTFW 2005; PFS 27;
RGEL 2; TWA; WLIT 2; WWE 1
Spackman, W(illiam) M(ode)
1905-1990 .... **CLC 46**
See also CA 81-84; 132

Spacks, Barry (Bernard) 1931- .... **CLC 14**
See also CA 154; CANR 33, 109; CP 3, 4,
5, 6, 7; DLB 105
Spanidou, Irini 1946- .... **CLC 44**
See also CA 185; CANR 179
Spark, Muriel 1918-2006 .... **CLC 2, 3, 5, 8,**
13, 18, 40, 94, 242; PC 72; SSC 10, 115
See also BRWS 1; CA 5-8R; 251; CANR
12, 36, 76, 89, 131; CDBLB 1945-1960;
CN 1, 2, 3, 4, 5, 6, 7; CP 1, 2, 3, 4, 5, 6,
7; DA3; DAB; DAC; DAM MST, NOV;
DLB 15, 139; EWL 3; FW; INT CANR-
12; LAIT 4; MTCW 1, 2; MTFW 2005;
NFS 22; RGEL 2; TEA; WLIT 4; YAW
Spark, Muriel Sarah
See Spark, Muriel
Spaulding, Douglas
See Bradbury, Ray
Spaulding, Leonard
See Bradbury, Ray
Speght, Rachel 1597-c. 1630 .... **LC 97**
See also DLB 126
Spence, J. A. D.
See Eliot, T. S.
Spencer, Anne 1882-1975 ...... **HR 1:3; PC 77**
See also BW 2; CA 161; DLB 51, 54
Spencer, Elizabeth 1921- .... **CLC 22; SSC 57**
See also CA 13-16R; CANR 32, 65, 87; CN
1, 2, 3, 4, 5, 6, 7; CSW; DLB 6, 218;
EWL 3; MTCW 1; RGAL 4; SATA 14
Spencer, Leonard G.
See Silverberg, Robert
Spencer, Scott 1945- .... **CLC 30**
See also CA 113; CANR 51, 148, 190;
DLBY 1986
Spender, Stephen 1909-1995 ..... **CLC 1, 2, 5,**
10, 41, 91; PC 71
See also BRWS 2; CA 9-12R; 149; CANR
31, 54; CDBLB 1945-1960; CP 1, 2, 3, 4,
5, 6; DA3; DAM POET; DLB 20; EWL
3; MTCW 1, 2; MTFW 2005; PAB; PFS
23; RGEL 2; TEA
Spender, Stephen Harold
See Spender, Stephen
Spengler, Oswald (Arnold Gottfried)
1880-1936 .... **TCLC 25**
See also CA 118; 189
Spenser, Edmund 1552(?)-1599 ...... **LC 5, 39,**
117; PC 8, 42; WLC 5
See also AAYA 60; BRW 1; CDBLB Before
1660; DA; DA3; DAB; DAC; DAM MST,
POET; DLB 167; EFS 2; EXPP; PAB;
RGEL 2; TEA; WLIT 3; WP
Spicer, Jack 1925-1965 .... **CLC 8, 18, 72**
See also BG 1:3; CA 85-88; DAM POET;
DLB 5, 16, 193; GLL 1; WP
Spiegelman, Art 1948- .... **CLC 76, 178**
See also AAYA 10, 46; CA 125; CANR 41,
55, 74, 124; DLB 299; MTCW 2; MTFW
2005; RGHL; SATA 109, 158; YAW
Spielberg, Peter 1929- .... **CLC 6**
See also CA 5-8R; CANR 4, 48; DLBY
1981
Spielberg, Steven 1947- .... **CLC 20, 188**
See also AAYA 8, 24; CA 77-80; CANR
32; SATA 32
Spillane, Frank Morrison
See Spillane, Mickey
Spillane, Mickey 1918-2006 .. **CLC 3, 13, 241**
See also BPFB 3; CA 25-28R; 252; CANR
28, 63, 125; CMW 4; DA3; DLB 226;
MSW; MTCW 1, 2; MTFW 2005; SATA
66; SATA-Obit 176
Spinoza, Benedictus de 1632-1677 . **LC 9, 58,**
177
Spinrad, Norman (Richard) 1940- ... **CLC 46**
See also BPFB 3; CA 37-40R, 233; CAAE
233; CAAS 19; CANR 20, 91; DLB 8;
INT CANR-20; SFW 4

Spitteler, Carl 1845-1924 .... **TCLC 12**
See also CA 109; DLB 129, 332; EWL 3
Spitteler, Karl Friedrich Georg
See Spitteler, Carl
Spivack, Kathleen (Romola Drucker)
1938- .... **CLC 6**
See also CA 49-52
Spivak, Gayatri Chakravorty
1942- .... **CLC 233**
See also CA 110; 154; CANR 91; FW;
LMFS 2
Spofford, Harriet (Elizabeth) Prescott
1835-1921 .... **SSC 87**
See also CA 201; DLB 74, 221
Spoto, Donald 1941- .... **CLC 39**
See also CA 65-68; CANR 11, 57, 93, 173
Springsteen, Bruce 1949- .... **CLC 17**
See also CA 111
Springsteen, Bruce F.
See Springsteen, Bruce
Spurling, Hilary 1940- .... **CLC 34**
See also CA 104; CANR 25, 52, 94, 157
Spurling, Susan Hilary
See Spurling, Hilary
Spyker, John Howland
See Elman, Richard (Martin)
Squared, A.
See Abbott, Edwin A.
Squires, (James) Radcliffe
1917-1993 .... **CLC 51**
See also CA 1-4R; 140; CANR 6, 21; CP 1,
2, 3, 4, 5
Srivastav, Dhanpat Ray
See Srivastava, Dhanpat Rai
Srivastav, Dheanpatrai
See Srivastava, Dhanpat Rai
Srivastava, Dhanpat Rai
1880(?)-1936 .... **TCLC 21**
See also CA 118; 197; EWL 3
Ssu-ma Ch'ien c. 145B.C.-c.
86B.C. .... **CMLC 96**
Ssu-ma T'an (?)-c. 110B.C. .... **CMLC 96**
Stacy, Donald
See Pohl, Frederik
Stael
See Stael-Holstein, Anne Louise Germaine
Necker
Stael, Germaine de
See Stael-Holstein, Anne Louise Germaine
Necker
Stael-Holstein, Anne Louise Germaine
Necker 1766-1817 .... **NCLC 3, 91**
See also DLB 119, 192; EW 5; FL 1:3; FW;
GFL 1789 to the Present; RGWL 2, 3;
TWA
Stafford, Jean 1915-1979 .. **CLC 4, 7, 19, 68;**
SSC 26, 86
See also CA 1-4R; 85-88; CANR 3, 65; CN
1, 2; DLB 2, 173; MAL 5; MTCW 1, 2;
MTFW 2005; RGAL 4; RGSF 2; SATA-
Obit 22; SSFS 21; TCWW 1, 2; TUS
Stafford, William 1914-1993 ... **CLC 4, 7, 29;**
PC 71
See also AMWS 11; CA 5-8R; 142; CAAS
3; CANR 5, 22; CP 1, 2, 3, 4, 5; DAM
POET; DLB 5, 206; EXPP; INT CANR-
22; MAL 5; PFS 2, 8, 16; RGAL 4; WP
Stafford, William Edgar
See Stafford, William
Stagnelius, Eric Johan 1793-1823 . **NCLC 61**
Staines, Trevor
See Brunner, John (Kilian Houston)
Stairs, Gordon
See Austin, Mary Hunter
Stalin, Joseph 1879-1953 .... **TCLC 92**
Stampa, Gaspara c. 1524-1554 .. **LC 114; PC**
43
See also RGWL 2, 3; WLIT 7

Stitt, Milan 1941-2009 .... **CLC 29**
  See also CA 69-72; 284
Stitt, Milan William
  See Stitt, Milan
Stockton, Francis Richard
  1834-1902 .... **TCLC 47**
  See also AAYA 68; BYA 4, 13; CA 108;
  137; DLB 42, 74; DLBD 13; EXPS; MAI-
  CYA 1, 2; SATA 44; SATA-Brief 32; SFW
  4; SSFS 3; SUFW; WCH
Stockton, Frank R.
  See Stockton, Francis Richard
Stoddard, Charles
  See Kuttner, Henry
Stoker, Abraham
  See Stoker, Bram
Stoker, Bram 1847-1912 ... **SSC 62; TCLC 8,**
  144; WLC 6
  See also AAYA 23; BPFB 3; BRWS 3; BYA
  5; CA 105; 150; CDBLB 1890-1914; DA;
  DA3; DAB; DAC; DAM MST, NOV;
  DLB 304; GL 3; HGG; LATS 1:1; MTFW
  2005; NFS 18; RGEL 2; SATA 29; SUFW;
  TEA; WLIT 4
Stolz, Mary 1920-2006 .... **CLC 12**
  See also AAYA 8, 73; AITN 1; CA 5-8R;
  255; CANR 13, 41, 112; JRDA; MAICYA
  1, 2; SAAS 3; SATA 10, 71, 133; SATA-
  Obit 180; YAW
Stolz, Mary Slattery
  See Stolz, Mary
Stone, Irving 1903-1989 .... **CLC 7**
  See also AITN 1; BPFB 3; CA 1-4R; 129;
  CAAS 3; CANR 1, 23; CN 1, 2, 3, 4;
  CPW; DA3; DAM POP; INT CANR-23;
  MTCW 1, 2; MTFW 2005; RHW; SATA
  3; SATA-Obit 64
Stone, Oliver 1946- .... **CLC 73**
  See also AAYA 15, 64; CA 110; CANR 55,
  125
Stone, Oliver William
  See Stone, Oliver
Stone, Robert 1937- .... **CLC 5, 23, 42, 175**
  See also AMWS 5; BPFB 3; CA 85-88;
  CANR 23, 66, 95, 173; CN 4, 5, 6, 7;
  DLB 152; EWL 3; INT CANR-23; MAL
  5; MTCW 1; MTFW 2005
Stone, Robert Anthony
  See Stone, Robert
Stone, Ruth 1915- .... **PC 53**
  See also CA 45-48; CANR 2, 91; CP 5, 6,
  7; CSW; DLB 105; PFS 19
Stone, Zachary
  See Follett, Ken
Stoppard, Tom 1937- ... **CLC 1, 3, 4, 5, 8, 15,**
  29, 34, 63, 91; DC 6, 30; WLC 6
  See also AAYA 63; BRWC 1; BRWR 2;
  BRWS 1; CA 81-84; CANR 39, 67, 125;
  CBD; CD 5, 6; CDBLB 1960 to Present;
  DA; DA3; DAB; DAC; DAM DRAM,
  MST; DFS 2, 5, 8, 11, 13, 16; DLB 13,
  233; DLBY 1985; EWL 3; LATS 1:2;
  LNFS 3; MTCW 1, 2; MTFW 2005;
  RGEL 2; TEA; WLIT 4
Storey, David (Malcolm) 1933- . **CLC 2, 4, 5,**
  8
  See also BRWS 1; CA 81-84; CANR 36;
  CBD; CD 5, 6; CN 1, 2, 3, 4, 5, 6; DAM
  DRAM; DLB 13, 14, 207, 245, 326; EWL
  3; MTCW 1; RGEL 2
Storm, Hyemeyohsts 1935- ... **CLC 3; NNAL**
  See also CA 81-84; CANR 45; DAM MULT
Storm, (Hans) Theodor (Woldsen)
  1817-1888 ... **NCLC 1, 195; SSC 27, 106**
  See also CDWLB 2; DLB 129; EW; RGSF
  2; RGWL 2, 3
Storni, Alfonsina 1892-1938 . **HLC 2; PC 33;**
  TCLC 5
  See also CA 104; 131; DAM MULT; DLB
  283; HW 1; LAW

Stoughton, William 1631-1701 .... **LC 38**
  See also DLB 24
Stout, Rex (Todhunter) 1886-1975 ..... **CLC 3**
  See also AAYA 79; AITN 2; BPFB 3; CA
  61-64; CANR 71; CMW 4; CN 2; DLB
  306; MSW; RGAL 4
Stow, (Julian) Randolph 1935- ... **CLC 23, 48**
  See also CA 13-16R; CANR 33; CN 1, 2,
  3, 4, 5, 6, 7; CP 1, 2, 3, 4; DLB 260;
  MTCW 1; RGEL 2
Stowe, Harriet Beecher 1811-1896 . **NCLC 3,**
  50, 133, 195; WLC 6
  See also AAYA 53; AMWS 1; CDALB
  1865-1917; CLR 131; DA; DA3; DAB;
  DAC; DAM MST, NOV; DLB 1, 12, 42,
  74, 189, 239, 243; EXPN; FL 1:3; JRDA;
  LAIT 2; MAICYA 1, 2; NFS 6; RGAL 4;
  TUS; YABC 1
Stowe, Harriet Elizabeth Beecher
  See Stowe, Harriet Beecher
Strabo c. 64B.C.-c. 25 .... **CMLC 37**
  See also DLB 176
Strachey, (Giles) Lytton
  1880-1932 .... **TCLC 12**
  See also BRWS 2; CA 110; 178; DLB 149;
  DLBD 10; EWL 3; MTCW 2; NCFS 4
Stramm, August 1874-1915 .... **PC 50**
  See also CA 195; EWL 3
Strand, Mark 1934- .. **CLC 6, 18, 41, 71; PC**
  63
  See also AMWS 4; CA 21-24R; CANR 40,
  65, 100; CP 1, 2, 3, 4, 5, 6, 7; DAM
  POET; DLB 5; EWL 3; MAL 5; PAB;
  PFS 9, 18; RGAL 4; SATA 41; TCLE 1:2
Stratton-Porter, Gene 1863-1924 ... **TCLC 21**
  See also ANW; BPFB 3; CA 112; 137; CLR
  87; CWRI 5; DLB 221; DLBD 14; MAI-
  CYA 1, 2; RHW; SATA 15
Stratton-Porter, Geneva Grace
  See Stratton-Porter, Gene
Straub, Peter 1943- .... **CLC 28, 107**
  See also AAYA 82; BEST 89:1; BPFB 3;
  CA 85-88; CANR 28, 65, 109; CPW;
  DAM POP; DLBY 1984; HGG; MTCW
  1, 2; MTFW 2005; SUFW 2
Straub, Peter Francis
  See Straub, Peter
Strauss, Botho 1944- .... **CLC 22**
  See also CA 157; CWW 2; DLB 124
Strauss, Leo 1899-1973 .... **TCLC 141**
  See also CA 101; 45-48; CANR 122
Streatfeild, Mary Noel
  See Streatfeild, Noel
Streatfeild, Noel 1897(?)-1986 .... **CLC 21**
  See also CA 81-84; 120; CANR 31; CLR
  17, 83; CWRI 5; DLB 160; MAICYA 1,
  2; SATA 20; SATA-Obit 48
Stribling, T(homas) S(igismund)
  1881-1965 .... **CLC 23**
  See also CA 189; 107; CMW 4; DLB 9;
  RGAL 4
Strindberg, August 1849-1912 .... **DC 18;**
  TCLC 1, 8, 21, 47, 231; WLC 6
  See also CA 104; 135; DA; DA3; DAB;
  DAC; DAM DRAM, MST; DFS 4, 9;
  DLB 259; EW 7; EWL 3; IDTP; LMFS
  2; MTCW 2; MTFW 2005; RGWL 2, 3;
  TWA
Strindberg, Johan August
  See Strindberg, August
Stringer, Arthur 1874-1950 .... **TCLC 37**
  See also CA 161; DLB 92
Stringer, David
  See Roberts, Keith (John Kingston)
Stroheim, Erich von 1885-1957 ..... **TCLC 71**
Strugatskii, Arkadii 1925-1991 .... **CLC 27**
  See also CA 106; 135; DLB 302; SFW 4
Strugatskii, Arkadii Natanovich
  See Strugatskii, Arkadii

Strugatskii, Boris 1933- .... **CLC 27**
  See also CA 106; DLB 302; SFW 4
Strugatskii, Boris Natanovich
  See Strugatskii, Boris
Strugatsky, Arkadii Natanovich
  See Strugatskii, Arkadii
Strugatsky, Boris
  See Strugatskii, Boris
Strugatsky, Boris Natanovich
  See Strugatskii, Boris
Strummer, Joe 1952-2002 .... **CLC 30**
Strunk, William, Jr. 1869-1946 .... **TCLC 92**
  See also CA 118; 164; NCFS 5
Stryk, Lucien 1924- .... **PC 27**
  See also CA 13-16R; CANR 10, 28, 55,
  110; CP 1, 2, 3, 4, 5, 6, 7
Stuart, Don A.
  See Campbell, John W(ood, Jr.)
Stuart, Ian
  See MacLean, Alistair
Stuart, Jesse (Hilton) 1906-1984 ... **CLC 1, 8,**
  11, 14, 34; SSC 31
  See also CA 5-8R; 112; CANR 31; CN 1,
  2, 3; DLB 9, 48, 102; DLBY 1984; SATA
  2; SATA-Obit 36
Stubblefield, Sally
  See Trumbo, Dalton
Sturgeon, Theodore (Hamilton)
  1918-1985 .... **CLC 22, 39**
  See also AAYA 51; BPFB 3; BYA 9, 10;
  CA 81-84; 116; CANR 32, 103; DLB 8;
  DLBY 1985; HGG; MTCW 1, 2; MTFW
  2005; SCFW; SFW 4; SUFW
Sturges, Preston 1898-1959 .... **TCLC 48**
  See also CA 114; 149; DLB 26
Styron, William 1925-2006 .. **CLC 1, 3, 5, 11,**
  15, 60, 232, 244; SSC 25
  See also AMW; AMWC 2; BEST 90:4;
  BPFB 3; CA 5-8R; 255; CANR 6, 33, 74,
  126, 191; CDALB 1968-1988; CN 1, 2,
  3, 4, 5, 6, 7; CPW; CSW; DA3; DAM
  NOV, POP; DLB 2, 143, 299; DLBY
  1980; EWL 3; INT CANR-6; LAIT 2;
  MAL 5; MTCW 1, 2; MTFW 2005; NCFS
  1; NFS 22; RGAL 4; RGHL; RHW; TUS
Styron, William C.
  See Styron, William
Styron, William Clark
  See Styron, William
Su, Chien 1884-1918 .... **TCLC 24**
  See also CA 123; EWL 3
Suarez Lynch, B.
  See Bioy Casares, Adolfo; Borges, Jorge
  Luis
Suassuna, Ariano Vilar 1927- .... **HLCS 1**
  See also CA 178; DLB 307; HW 2; LAW
Suckert, Kurt Erich
  See Malaparte, Curzio
Suckling, Sir John 1609-1642 . **LC 75; PC 30**
  See also BRW 2; DAM POET; DLB 58,
  126; EXPP; PAB; RGEL 2
Suckow, Ruth 1892-1960 .... **SSC 18**
  See also CA 193; 113; DLB 9, 102; RGAL
  4; TCWW 2
Sudermann, Hermann 1857-1928 .. **TCLC 15**
  See also CA 107; 201; DLB 118
Sue, Eugene 1804-1857 .... **NCLC 1**
  See also DLB 119
Sueskind, Patrick
  See Suskind, Patrick
Suetonius c. 70-c. 130 .... **CMLC 60**
  See also AW 2; DLB 211; RGWL 2, 3;
  WLIT 8
Su Hsuan-ying
  See Su, Chien
Su Hsuean-ying
  See Su, Chien

Tan, Amy 1952- ..... **AAL; CLC 59, 120, 151, 257**
   See also AAYA 9, 48; AMWS 10; BEST 89:3; BPFB 3; CA 136; CANR 54, 105, 132; CDALBS; CN 6, 7; CPW 1; DA3; DAM MULT, NOV, POP; DLB 173, 312; EXPN; FL 1:6; FW; LAIT 3, 5; MAL 5; MTCW 2; MTFW 2005; NFS 1, 13, 16; RGAL 4; SATA 75; SSFS 9; YAW

Tan, Amy Ruth
   See Tan, Amy

Tandem, Carl Felix
   See Spitteler, Carl

Tandem, Felix
   See Spitteler, Carl

Tania B.
   See Blixen, Karen

Tanizaki, Jun'ichiro 1886-1965 ... **CLC 8, 14, 28; SSC 21**
   See also CA 93-96; 25-28R; DLB 180; EWL 3; MJW; MTCW 2; MTFW 2005; RGSF 2; RGWL 2

Tanizaki Jun'ichiro
   See Tanizaki, Jun'ichiro

Tannen, Deborah 1945- .... **CLC 206**
   See also CA 118; CANR 95

Tannen, Deborah Frances
   See Tannen, Deborah

Tanner, William
   See Amis, Kingsley

Tante, Dilly
   See Kunitz, Stanley

Tao Lao
   See Storni, Alfonsina

Tapahonso, Luci 1953- .... **NNAL; PC 65**
   See also CA 145; CANR 72, 127; DLB 175

Tarantino, Quentin 1963- .... **CLC 125, 230**
   See also AAYA 58; CA 171; CANR 125

Tarantino, Quentin Jerome
   See Tarantino, Quentin

Tarassoff, Lev
   See Troyat, Henri

Tarbell, Ida 1857-1944 .... **TCLC 40**
   See also CA 122; 181; DLB 47

Tarbell, Ida Minerva
   See Tarbell, Ida

Tarchetti, Ugo 1839(?)-1869 .... **SSC 119**

Tardieu d'Esclavelles, Louise-Florence-Petronille
   See Epinay, Louise d'

Tarkington, (Newton) Booth 1869-1946 .... **TCLC 9**
   See also BPFB 3; BYA 3; CA 110; 143; CWRI 5; DLB 9, 102; MAL 5; MTCW 2; RGAL 4; SATA 17

Tarkovskii, Andrei Arsen'evich
   See Tarkovsky, Andrei (Arsenyevich)

Tarkovsky, Andrei (Arsenyevich) 1932-1986 .... **CLC 75**
   See also CA 127

Tartt, Donna 1964(?)- .... **CLC 76**
   See also AAYA 56; CA 142; CANR 135; LNFS 2; MTFW 2005

Tasso, Torquato 1544-1595 .... **LC 5, 94**
   See also EFS 2; EW 2; RGWL 2, 3; WLIT 7

Tate, (John Orley) Allen 1899-1979 .. **CLC 2, 4, 6, 9, 11, 14, 24; PC 50**
   See also AMW; CA 5-8R; 85-88; CANR 32, 108; CN 1, 2; CP 1, 2; DLB 4, 45, 63; DLBD 17; EWL 3; MAL 5; MTCW 1, 2; MTFW 2005; RGAL 4; RHW

Tate, Ellalice
   See Hibbert, Eleanor Alice Burford

Tate, James (Vincent) 1943- ..... **CLC 2, 6, 25**
   See also CA 21-24R; CANR 29, 57, 114; CP 1, 2, 3, 4, 5, 6, 7; DLB 5, 169; EWL 3; PFS 10, 15; RGAL 4; WP

Tate, Nahum 1652(?)-1715 .... **LC 109**
   See also DLB 80; RGEL 2

Tauler, Johannes c. 1300-1361 ...... **CMLC 37**
   See also DLB 179; LMFS 1

Tavel, Ronald 1936-2009 .... **CLC 6**
   See also CA 21-24R; 284; CAD; CANR 33; CD 5, 6

Taviani, Paolo 1931- .... **CLC 70**
   See also CA 153

Taylor, Bayard 1825-1878 .... **NCLC 89**
   See also DLB 3, 189, 250, 254; RGAL 4

Taylor, C(ecil) P(hilip) 1929-1981 .... **CLC 27**
   See also CA 25-28R; 105; CANR 47; CBD

Taylor, Edward 1642(?)-1729 ..... **LC 11, 163; PC 63**
   See also AMW; DA; DAB; DAC; DAM MST, POET; DLB 24; EXPP; PFS 31; RGAL 4; TUS

Taylor, Eleanor Ross 1920- .... **CLC 5**
   See also CA 81-84; CANR 70

Taylor, Elizabeth 1912-1975 .... **CLC 2, 4, 29; SSC 100**
   See also CA 13-16R; CANR 9, 70; CN 1, 2; DLB 139; MTCW 1; RGEL 2; SATA 13

Taylor, Frederick Winslow 1856-1915 .... **TCLC 76**
   See also CA 188

Taylor, Henry 1942- .... **CLC 44**
   See also CA 33-36R; CAAS 7; CANR 31, 178; CP 6, 7; DLB 5; PFS 10

Taylor, Henry Splawn
   See Taylor, Henry

Taylor, Kamala
   See Markandaya, Kamala

Taylor, Mildred D. 1943- .... **CLC 21**
   See also AAYA 10, 47; BW 1; BYA 3, 8; CA 85-88; CANR 25, 115, 136; CLR 9, 59, 90, 144; CSW; DLB 52; JRDA; LAIT 3; MAICYA 1, 2; MTFW 2005; SAAS 5; SATA 135; WYA; YAW

Taylor, Peter (Hillsman) 1917-1994 .. **CLC 1, 4, 18, 37, 44, 50, 71; SSC 10, 84**
   See also AMWS 5; BPFB 3; CA 13-16R; 147; CANR 9, 50; CN 1, 2, 3, 4, 5; CSW; DLB 218, 278; DLBY 1981, 1994; EWL 3; EXPS; INT CANR-9; MAL 5; MTCW 1, 2; MTFW 2005; RGSF 2; SSFS 9; TUS

Taylor, Robert Lewis 1912-1998 .... **CLC 14**
   See also CA 1-4R; 170; CANR 3, 64; CN 1, 2; SATA 10; TCWW 1, 2

Tchekhov, Anton
   See Chekhov, Anton

Tchicaya, Gerald Felix 1931-1988 .. **CLC 101**
   See also CA 129; 125; CANR 81; EWL 3

Tchicaya U Tam'si
   See Tchicaya, Gerald Felix

Teasdale, Sara 1884-1933 .... **PC 31; TCLC 4**
   See also CA 104; 163; DLB 45; GLL 1; PFS 14; RGAL 4; SATA 32; TUS

Tecumseh 1768-1813 .... **NNAL**
   See also DAM MULT

Tegner, Esaias 1782-1846 .... **NCLC 2**

Teilhard de Chardin, (Marie Joseph) Pierre 1881-1955 .... **TCLC 9**
   See also CA 105; 210; GFL 1789 to the Present

Temple, Ann
   See Mortimer, Penelope (Ruth)

Tennant, Emma 1937- .... **CLC 13, 52**
   See also BRWS 9; CA 65-68; CAAS 9; CANR 10, 38, 59, 88, 177; CN 3, 4, 5, 6, 7; DLB 14; EWL 3; SFW 4

Tenneshaw, S.M.
   See Silverberg, Robert

Tenney, Tabitha Gilman 1762-1837 .... **NCLC 122**
   See also DLB 37, 200

Tennyson, Alfred 1809-1892 ... **NCLC 30, 65, 115, 202; PC 6, 101; WLC 6**
   See also AAYA 50; BRW 4; BRWR 3; CD-BLB 1832-1890; DA; DA3; DAB; DAC; DAM MST, POET; DLB 32; EXPP; PAB; PFS 1, 2, 4, 11, 15, 19; RGEL 2; TEA; WLIT 4; WP

Teran, Lisa St. Aubin de
   See St. Aubin de Teran, Lisa

Terence c. 184B.C.-c. 159B.C. ...... **CMLC 14; DC 7**
   See also AW 1; CDWLB 1; DLB 211; RGWL 2, 3; TWA; WLIT 8

Teresa de Jesus, St. 1515-1582 .... **LC 18, 149**

Teresa of Avila, St.
   See Teresa de Jesus, St.

Terkel, Louis
   See Terkel, Studs

Terkel, Studs 1912-2008 .... **CLC 38**
   See also AAYA 32; AITN 1; CA 57-60; 278; CANR 18, 45, 67, 132, 195; DA3; MTCW 1, 2; MTFW 2005; TUS

Terkel, Studs Louis
   See Terkel, Studs

Terry, C. V.
   See Slaughter, Frank G(ill)

Terry, Megan 1932- .... **CLC 19; DC 13**
   See also CA 77-80; CABS 3; CAD; CANR 43; CD 5, 6; CWD; DFS 18; DLB 7, 249; GLL 2

Tertullian c. 155-c. 245 .... **CMLC 29**

Tertz, Abram
   See Sinyavsky, Andrei (Donatevich)

Tesich, Steve 1943(?)-1996 .... **CLC 40, 69**
   See also CA 105; 152; CAD; DLBY 1983

Tesla, Nikola 1856-1943 .... **TCLC 88**
   See also CA 157

Teternikov, Fyodor Kuzmich 1863-1927 .... **TCLC 9**
   See also CA 104; DLB 295; EWL 3

Tevis, Walter 1928-1984 .... **CLC 42**
   See also CA 113; SFW 4

Tey, Josephine
   See Mackintosh, Elizabeth

Thackeray, William Makepeace 1811-1863 ...... **NCLC 5, 14, 22, 43, 169, 213; WLC 6**
   See also BRW 5; BRWC 2; CDBLB 1832-1890; DA; DA3; DAB; DAC; DAM MST, NOV; DLB 21, 55, 159, 163; NFS 13; RGEL 2; SATA 23; TEA; WLIT 3

Thakura, Ravindranatha
   See Tagore, Rabindranath

Thames, C. H.
   See Marlowe, Stephen

Tharoor, Shashi 1956- .... **CLC 70**
   See also CA 141; CANR 91, 201; CN 6, 7

Thelwall, John 1764-1834 .... **NCLC 162**
   See also DLB 93, 158

Thelwell, Michael Miles 1939- .... **CLC 22**
   See also BW 2; CA 101

Theo, Ion
   See Theodorescu, Ion N.

Theobald, Lewis, Jr.
   See Lovecraft, H. P.

Theocritus c. 310B.C.- .... **CMLC 45**
   See also AW 1; DLB 176; RGWL 2, 3

Theodorescu, Ion N. 1880-1967 .... **CLC 80**
   See also CA 167; 116; CDWLB 4; DLB 220; EWL 3

Theriault, Yves 1915-1983 .... **CLC 79**
   See also CA 102; CANR 150; CCA 1; DAC; DAM MST; DLB 88; EWL 3

Therion, Master
   See Crowley, Edward Alexander

Theroux, Alexander 1939- .... **CLC 2, 25**
   See also CA 85-88; CANR 20, 63, 190; CN 4, 5, 6, 7

Theroux, Alexander Louis
See Theroux, Alexander

Theroux, Paul 1941- .... **CLC 5, 8, 11, 15, 28, 46, 159**
See also AAYA 28; AMWS 8; BEST 89:4; BPFB 3; CA 33-36R; CANR 20, 45, 74, 133, 179; CDALBS; CN 1, 2, 3, 4, 5, 6, 7; CP 1; CPW 1; DA3; DAM POP; DLB 2, 218; EWL 3; HGG; MAL 5; MTCW 1, 2; MTFW 2005; RGAL 4; SATA 44, 109; TUS

Theroux, Paul Edward
See Theroux, Paul

Thesen, Sharon 1946- .... **CLC 56**
See also CA 163; CANR 125; CP 5, 6, 7; CWP

Thespis fl. 6th cent. B.C.- .... **CMLC 51**
See also LMFS 1

Thevenin, Denis
See Duhamel, Georges

Thibault, Jacques Anatole Francois
See France, Anatole

Thiele, Colin 1920-2006 .... **CLC 17**
See also CA 29-32R; CANR 12, 28, 53, 105; CLR 27; CP 1, 2; DLB 289; MAICYA 1, 2; SAAS 2; SATA 14, 72, 125; YAW

Thiong'o, Ngugi Wa
See Ngugi wa Thiong'o

Thistlethwaite, Bel
See Wetherald, Agnes Ethelwyn

Thomas, Audrey (Callahan) 1935- .... **CLC 7, 13, 37, 107, 289; SSC 20**
See also AITN 2; CA 21-24R, 237; CAAE 237; CAAS 19; CANR 36, 58; CN 2, 3, 4, 5, 6, 7; DLB 60; MTCW 1; RGSF 2

Thomas, Augustus 1857-1934 .... **TCLC 97**
See also MAL 5

Thomas, D.M. 1935- ..... **CLC 13, 22, 31, 132**
See also BPFB 3; BRWS 4; CA 61-64; CAAS 11; CANR 17, 45, 75; CDBLB 1960 to Present; CN 4, 5, 6, 7; CP 1, 2, 3, 4, 5, 6, 7; DA3; DLB 40, 207, 299; HGG; INT CANR-17; MTCW 1, 2; MTFW 2005; RGHL; SFW 4

Thomas, Dylan 1914-1953 . **PC 2, 52; SSC 3, 44; TCLC 1, 8, 45, 105; WLC 6**
See also AAYA 45; BRWR 3; BRWS 1; CA 104; 120; CANR 65; CDBLB 1945-1960; DA; DA3; DAB; DAC; DAM DRAM, MST, POET; DLB 13, 20, 139; EWL 3; EXPP; LAIT 3; MTCW 1, 2; MTFW 2005; PAB; PFS 1, 3, 8; RGEL 2; RGSF 2; SATA 60; TEA; WLIT 4; WP

Thomas, Dylan Marlais
See Thomas, Dylan

Thomas, (Philip) Edward 1878-1917 . **PC 53; TCLC 10**
See also BRW 6; BRWS 3; CA 106; 153; DAM POET; DLB 19, 98, 156, 216; EWL 3; PAB; RGEL 2

Thomas, J. F.
See Fleming, Thomas

Thomas, Joyce Carol 1938- .... **CLC 35**
See also AAYA 12, 54; BW 2, 3; CA 113; 116; CANR 48, 114, 135; CLR 19; DLB 33; INT CA-116; JRDA; MAICYA 1, 2; MTCW 1, 2; MTFW 2005; SAAS 7; SATA 40, 78, 123, 137; SATA-Essay 137; WYA; YAW

Thomas, Lewis 1913-1993 .... **CLC 35**
See also ANW; CA 85-88; 143; CANR 38, 60; DLB 275; MTCW 1, 2

Thomas, M. Carey 1857-1935 .... **TCLC 89**
See also FW

Thomas, Paul
See Mann, Thomas

Thomas, Piri 1928- .... **CLC 17; HLCS 2**
See also CA 73-76; HW 1; LLW

Thomas, R(onald) S(tuart)
1913-2000 .... **CLC 6, 13, 48; PC 99**
See also BRWS 12; CA 89-92; 189; CAAS 4; CANR 30; CDBLB 1960 to Present; CP 1, 2, 3, 4, 5, 6, 7; DAB; DAM POET; DLB 27; EWL 3; MTCW 1; RGEL 2

Thomas, Ross (Elmore) 1926-1995 .. **CLC 39**
See also CA 33-36R; 150; CANR 22, 63; CMW 4

Thompson, Francis (Joseph)
1859-1907 .... **TCLC 4**
See also BRW 5; CA 104; 189; CDBLB 1890-1914; DLB 19; RGEL 2; TEA

Thompson, Francis Clegg
See Mencken, H. L.

Thompson, Hunter S. 1937(?)-2005 .. **CLC 9, 17, 40, 104, 229**
See also AAYA 45; BEST 89:1; BPFB 3; CA 17-20R; 236; CANR 23, 46, 74, 77, 111, 133; CPW; CSW; DA3; DAM POP; DLB 185; MTCW 1, 2; MTFW 2005; TUS

Thompson, Hunter Stockton
See Thompson, Hunter S.

Thompson, James Myers
See Thompson, Jim

Thompson, Jim 1906-1977 .... **CLC 69**
See also BPFB 3; CA 140; CMW 4; CPW; DLB 226; MSW

Thompson, Judith (Clare Francesca)
1954- .... **CLC 39**
See also CA 143; CD 5, 6; CWD; DFS 22; DLB 334

Thomson, James 1700-1748 .... **LC 16, 29, 40**
See also BRWS 3; DAM POET; DLB 95; RGEL 2

Thomson, James 1834-1882 .... **NCLC 18**
See also DAM POET; DLB 35; RGEL 2

Thoreau, Henry David 1817-1862 .. **NCLC 7, 21, 61, 138, 207; PC 30; WLC 6**
See also AAYA 42; AMW; ANW; BYA 3; CDALB 1640-1865; DA; DA3; DAB; DAC; DAM MST; DLB 1, 183, 223, 270, 298; LAIT 2; LMFS 1; NCFS 3; RGAL 4; TUS

Thorndike, E. L.
See Thorndike, Edward L(ee)

Thorndike, Edward L(ee)
1874-1949 .... **TCLC 107**
See also CA 121

Thornton, Hall
See Silverberg, Robert

Thorpe, Adam 1956- .... **CLC 176**
See also CA 129; CANR 92, 160; DLB 231

Thorpe, Thomas Bangs
1815-1878 .... **NCLC 183**
See also DLB 3, 11, 248; RGAL 4

Thubron, Colin 1939- .... **CLC 163**
See also CA 25-28R; CANR 12, 29, 59, 95, 171; CN 5, 6, 7; DLB 204, 231

Thubron, Colin Gerald Dryden
See Thubron, Colin

Thucydides c. 455B.C.-c.
399B.C. .... **CMLC 17, 117**
See also AW 1; DLB 176; RGWL 2, 3; WLIT 8

Thumboo, Edwin Nadason 1933- .... **PC 30**
See also CA 194; CP 1

Thurber, James 1894-1961 .... **CLC 5, 11, 25, 125; SSC 1, 47, 137**
See also AAYA 56; AMWS 1; BPFB 3; BYA 5; CA 73-76; CANR 17, 39; CDALB 1929-1941; CWRI 5; DA; DA3; DAB; DAC; DAM DRAM, MST, NOV; DLB 4, 11, 22, 102; EWL 3; EXPS; FANT; LAIT 3; MAICYA 1, 2; MAL 5; MTCW 1, 2; MTFW 2005; RGAL 4; RGSF 2; SATA 13; SSFS 1, 10, 19; SUFW; TUS

Thurber, James Grover
See Thurber, James

Thurman, Wallace (Henry)
1902-1934 .. **BLC 1:3; HR 1:3; TCLC 6**
See also BW 1, 3; CA 104; 124; CANR 81; DAM MULT; DLB 51

Tibullus c. 54B.C.-c. 18B.C. .... **CMLC 36**
See also AW 2; DLB 211; RGWL 2, 3; WLIT 8

Ticheburn, Cheviot
See Ainsworth, William Harrison

Tieck, (Johann) Ludwig
1773-1853 ..... **NCLC 5, 46; SSC 31, 100**
See also CDWLB 2; DLB 90; EW 5; IDTP; RGSF 2; RGWL 2, 3; SUFW

Tiger, Derry
See Ellison, Harlan

Tilghman, Christopher 1946- .... **CLC 65**
See also CA 159; CANR 135, 151; CSW; DLB 244

Tillich, Paul (Johannes)
1886-1965 .... **CLC 131**
See also CA 5-8R; 25-28R; CANR 33; MTCW 1, 2

Tillinghast, Richard (Williford)
1940- .... **CLC 29**
See also CA 29-32R; CAAS 23; CANR 26, 51, 96; CP 2, 3, 4, 5, 6, 7; CSW

Tillman, Lynne (?)- .... **CLC 231**
See also CA 173; CANR 144, 172

Timrod, Henry 1828-1867 .... **NCLC 25**
See also DLB 3, 248; RGAL 4

Tindall, Gillian (Elizabeth) 1938- ...... **CLC 7**
See also CA 21-24R; CANR 11, 65, 107; CN 1, 2, 3, 4, 5, 6, 7

Ting Ling
See Chiang, Pin-chin

Tiptree, James, Jr.
See Sheldon, Alice Hastings Bradley

Tirone Smith, Mary-Ann 1944- .... **CLC 39**
See also CA 118; 136; CANR 113; SATA 143

Tirso de Molina 1580(?)-1648 .... **DC 13; HLCS 2; LC 73**
See also RGWL 2, 3

Titmarsh, Michael Angelo
See Thackeray, William Makepeace

Tocqueville, Alexis (Charles Henri Maurice Clerel Comte) de 1805-1859 .. **NCLC 7, 63**
See also EW 6; GFL 1789 to the Present; TWA

Toe, Tucker
See Westlake, Donald E.

Toer, Pramoedya Ananta
1925-2006 .... **CLC 186**
See also CA 197; 251; CANR 170; DLB 348; RGWL 3

Toffler, Alvin 1928- .... **CLC 168**
See also CA 13-16R; CANR 15, 46, 67, 183; CPW; DAM POP; MTCW 1, 2

Toibin, Colm 1955- .... **CLC 162, 285**
See also CA 142; CANR 81, 149; CN 7; DLB 271

Tolkien, J. R. R. 1892-1973 ... **CLC 1, 2, 3, 8, 12, 38; TCLC 137; WLC 6**
See also AAYA 10; AITN 1; BPFB 3; BRWC 2; BRWS 2; CA 17-18; 45-48; CANR 36, 134; CAP 2; CDBLB 1914-1945; CLR 56; CN 1; CPW 1; CWRI 5; DA; DA3; DAB; DAC; DAM MST, NOV, POP; DLB 15, 160, 255; EFS 2; EWL 3; FANT; JRDA; LAIT 1; LATS 1:2; LMFS 2; MAICYA 1, 2; MTCW 1, 2; MTFW 2005; NFS 8, 26; RGEL 2; SATA 2, 32, 100; SATA-Obit 24; SFW 4; SUFW; TEA; WCH; WYA; YAW

Tolkien, John Ronald Reuel
See Tolkien, J. R. R.

von Horvath, Odon 1901-1938 .... **TCLC 45**
See also CA 118; 184, 194; DLB 85, 124;
RGWL 2, 3
von Horvath, Oedoen
See von Horvath, Odon
von Kleist, Heinrich
See Kleist, Heinrich von
Vonnegut, Kurt, Jr.
See Vonnegut, Kurt
Vonnegut, Kurt 1922-2007 .... **CLC 1, 2, 3, 4,
5, 8, 12, 22, 40, 60, 111, 212, 254; SSC
8; WLC 6**
See also AAYA 6, 44; AITN 1; AMWS 2;
BEST 90:4; BPFB 3; BYA 3, 14; CA
1-4R; 259; CANR 1, 25, 49, 75, 92;
CDALB 1968-1988; CN 1, 2, 3, 4, 5, 6,
7; CPW 1; DA; DA3; DAB; DAC; DAM
MST, NOV, POP; DLB 2, 8, 152; DLBD
3; DLBY 1980; EWL 3; EXPN; EXPS;
LAIT 4; LMFS 2; MAL 5; MTCW 1, 2;
MTFW 2005; NFS 3, 28; RGAL 4;
SCFW; SFW 4; SSFS 5; TUS; YAW
Von Rachen, Kurt
See Hubbard, L. Ron
von Sternberg, Josef
See Sternberg, Josef von
Vorster, Gordon 1924- .... **CLC 34**
See also CA 133
Vosce, Trudie
See Ozick, Cynthia
Voznesensky, Andrei 1933- ..... **CLC 1, 15, 57**
See also CA 89-92; CANR 37; CWW 2;
DAM POET; EWL 3; MTCW 1
Voznesensky, Andrei Andreievich
See Voznesensky, Andrei
Voznesensky, Andrey
See Voznesensky, Andrei
Wace, Robert c. 1100-c. 1175 .... **CMLC 55**
See also DLB 146
Waddington, Miriam 1917-2004 .... **CLC 28**
See also CA 21-24R; 225; CANR 12, 30;
CCA 1; CP 1, 2, 3, 4, 5, 6, 7; DLB 68
Wade, Alan
See Vance, Jack
Wagman, Fredrica 1937- .... **CLC 7**
See also CA 97-100; CANR 166; INT CA-
97-100
Wagner, Linda W.
See Wagner-Martin, Linda (C.)
Wagner, Linda Welshimer
See Wagner-Martin, Linda (C.)
Wagner, Richard 1813-1883 ..... **NCLC 9, 119**
See also DLB 129; EW 6
Wagner-Martin, Linda (C.) 1936- .... **CLC 50**
See also CA 159; CANR 135
Wagoner, David (Russell) 1926- .... **CLC 3, 5,
15; PC 33**
See also AMWS 9; CA 1-4R; CAAS 3;
CANR 2, 71; CN 1, 2, 3, 4, 5, 6, 7; CP 1,
2, 3, 4, 5, 6, 7; DLB 5, 256; SATA 14;
TCWW 1, 2
Wah, Fred(erick James) 1939- .... **CLC 44**
See also CA 107; 141; CP 1, 6, 7; DLB 60
Wahloo, Per 1926-1975 .... **CLC 7**
See also BPFB 3; CA 61-64; CANR 73;
CMW 4; MSW
Wahloo, Peter
See Wahloo, Per
Wain, John (Barrington) 1925-1994 . **CLC 2,
11, 15, 46**
See also CA 5-8R; 145; CAAS 4; CANR
23, 54; CDBLB 1960 to Present; CN 1, 2,
3, 4, 5; CP 1, 2, 3, 4, 5; DLB 15, 27, 139,
155; EWL 3; MTCW 1, 2; MTFW 2005
Wajda, Andrzej 1926- .... **CLC 16, 219**
See also CA 102
Wakefield, Dan 1932- .... **CLC 7**
See also CA 21-24R; 211; CAAE 211;
CAAS 7; CN 4, 5, 6, 7

Wakefield, Herbert Russell
1888-1965 .... **TCLC 120**
See also CA 5-8R; CANR 77; HGG; SUFW
Wakoski, Diane 1937- ...... **CLC 2, 4, 7, 9, 11,
40; PC 15**
See also CA 13-16R, 216; CAAE 216;
CAAS 1; CANR 9, 60, 106; CP 1, 2, 3, 4,
5, 6, 7; CWP; DAM POET; DLB 5; INT
CANR-9; MAL 5; MTCW 2; MTFW
2005
Wakoski-Sherbell, Diane
See Wakoski, Diane
Walcott, Derek 1930- . **BLC 1:3, 2:3; CLC 2,
4, 9, 14, 25, 42, 67, 76, 160, 282; DC 7;
PC 46**
See also BW 2; CA 89-92; CANR 26, 47,
75, 80, 130; CBD; CD 5, 6; CDWLB 3;
CP 1, 2, 3, 4, 5, 6, 7; DA3; DAB; DAC;
DAM MST, MULT, POET; DLB 117,
332; DLBY 1981; DNFS 1; EFS 1; EWL
3; LMFS 2; MTCW 1, 2; MTFW 2005;
PFS 6; RGEL 2; TWA; WWE 1
Walcott, Derek Alton
See Walcott, Derek
Waldman, Anne (Lesley) 1945- .... **CLC 7**
See also BG 1:3; CA 37-40R; CAAS 17;
CANR 34, 69, 116; CP 1, 2, 3, 4, 5, 6, 7;
CWP; DLB 16
Waldo, E. Hunter
See Sturgeon, Theodore (Hamilton)
Waldo, Edward Hamilton
See Sturgeon, Theodore (Hamilton)
Walker, Alice 1944- .... **BLC 1:3, 2:3; CLC 5,
6, 9, 19, 27, 46, 58, 103, 167; PC 30;
SSC 5; WLCS**
See also AAYA 3, 33; AFAW 1, 2; AMWS
3; BEST 89:4; BPFB 3; BW 2, 3; CA 37-
40R; CANR 9, 27, 49, 66, 82, 131, 191;
CDALB 1968-1988; CN 4, 5, 6, 7; CPW;
CSW; DA; DA3; DAB; DAC; DAM MST,
MULT, NOV, POET, POP; DLB 6, 33,
143; EWL 3; EXPN; EXPS; FL 1:6; FW;
INT CANR-27; LAIT 3; MAL 5; MBL;
MTCW 1, 2; MTFW 2005; NFS 5; PFS
30; RGAL 4; RGSF 2; SATA 31; SSFS 2,
11; TUS; YAW
Walker, Alice Malsenior
See Walker, Alice
Walker, David Harry 1911-1992 ...... **CLC 14**
See also CA 1-4R; 137; CANR 1; CN 1, 2;
CWRI 5; SATA 8; SATA-Obit 71
Walker, Edward Joseph 1934-2004 .. **CLC 13**
See also CA 21-24R; 226; CANR 12, 28,
53; CP 1, 2, 3, 4, 5, 6, 7; DLB 40
Walker, George F(rederick) 1947- .. **CLC 44,
61**
See also CA 103; CANR 21, 43, 59; CD 5,
6; DAB; DAC; DAM MST; DLB 60
Walker, Joseph A. 1935-2003 .... **CLC 19**
See also BW 1, 3; CA 89-92; CAD; CANR
26, 143; CD 5, 6; DAM DRAM, MST;
DFS 12; DLB 38
Walker, Margaret 1915-1998 .... **BLC 1:3;
CLC 1, 6; PC 20; TCLC 129**
See also AFAW 1, 2; BW 2, 3; CA 73-76;
172; CANR 26, 54, 76, 136; CN 1, 2, 3,
4, 5, 6; CP 1, 2, 3, 4, 5, 6; CSW; DAM
MULT; DLB 76, 152; EXPP; FW; MAL
5; MTCW 1, 2; MTFW 2005; PFS 31;
RGAL 4; RHW
Walker, Ted
See Walker, Edward Joseph
Wallace, David Foster 1962-2008 .... **CLC 50,
114, 271, 281; SSC 68**
See also AAYA 50; AMWS 10; CA 132;
277; CANR 59, 133, 190; CN 7; DA3;
DLB 350; MTCW 2; MTFW 2005
Wallace, Dexter
See Masters, Edgar Lee

Wallace, (Richard Horatio) Edgar
1875-1932 .... **TCLC 57**
See also CA 115; 218; CMW 4; DLB 70;
MSW; RGEL 2
Wallace, Irving 1916-1990 .... **CLC 7, 13**
See also AITN 1; BPFB 3; CA 1-4R; 132;
CAAS 1; CANR 1, 27; CPW; DAM NOV,
POP; INT CANR-27; MTCW 1, 2
Wallant, Edward Lewis 1926-1962 ... **CLC 5,
10**
See also CA 1-4R; CANR 22; DLB 2, 28,
143, 299; EWL 3; MAL 5; MTCW 1, 2;
RGAL 4; RGHL
Wallas, Graham 1858-1932 .... **TCLC 91**
Waller, Edmund 1606-1687 .... **LC 86; PC 72**
See also BRW 2; DAM POET; DLB 126;
PAB; RGEL 2
Walley, Byron
See Card, Orson Scott
Walpole, Horace 1717-1797 ..... **LC 2, 49, 152**
See also BRW 3; DLB 39, 104, 213; GL 3;
HGG; LMFS 1; RGEL 2; SUFW 1; TEA
Walpole, Hugh 1884-1941 .... **TCLC 5**
See also CA 104; 165; DLB 34; HGG;
MTCW 2; RGEL 2; RHW
Walpole, Hugh Seymour
See Walpole, Hugh
Walrond, Eric (Derwent) 1898-1966 . **HR 1:3**
See also BW 1; CA 125; DLB 51
Walser, Martin 1927- .... **CLC 27, 183**
See also CA 57-60; CANR 8, 46, 145;
CWW 2; DLB 75, 124; EWL 3
Walser, Robert 1878-1956 ..... **SSC 20; TCLC
18**
See also CA 118; 165; CANR 100, 194;
DLB 66; EWL 3
Walsh, Gillian Paton
See Paton Walsh, Jill
Walsh, Jill Paton
See Paton Walsh, Jill
Walter, Villiam Christian
See Andersen, Hans Christian
Walter of Chatillon c. 1135-c.
1202 .... **CMLC 111**
Walters, Anna L(ee) 1946- .... **NNAL**
See also CA 73-76
Walther von der Vogelweide c.
1170-1228 .... **CMLC 56**
Walton, Izaak 1593-1683 .... **LC 72**
See also BRW 2; CDBLB Before 1660;
DLB 151, 213; RGEL 2
Walzer, Michael 1935- .... **CLC 238**
See also CA 37-40R; CANR 15, 48, 127,
190
Walzer, Michael Laban
See Walzer, Michael
Wambaugh, Joseph, Jr. 1937- ...... **CLC 3, 18**
See also AITN 1; BEST 89:3; BPFB 3; CA
33-36R; CANR 42, 65, 115, 167; CMW
4; CPW 1; DA3; DAM NOV, POP; DLB
6; DLBY 1983; MSW; MTCW 1, 2
Wambaugh, Joseph Aloysius
See Wambaugh, Joseph, Jr.
Wang Wei 699(?)-761(?) . **CMLC 100; PC 18**
See also TWA
Warburton, William 1698-1779 .... **LC 97**
See also DLB 104
Ward, Arthur Henry Sarsfield
1883-1959 .... **TCLC 28**
See also AAYA 80; CA 108; 173; CMW 4;
DLB 70; HGG; MSW; SUFW
Ward, Douglas Turner 1930- .... **CLC 19**
See also BW 1; CA 81-84; CAD; CANR
27; CD 5, 6; DLB 7, 38
Ward, E. D.
See Lucas, E(dward) V(errall)
Ward, Mrs. Humphry 1851-1920
See Ward, Mary Augusta
See also RGEL 2

Weldon, Fay 1931- . **CLC 6, 9, 11, 19, 36, 59, 122**
See also BRWS 4; CA 21-24R; CANR 16, 46, 63, 97, 137; CDBLB 1960 to Present; CN 3, 4, 5, 6, 7; CPW; DAM POP; DLB 14, 194, 319; EWL 3; FW; HGG; INT CANR-16; MTCW 1, 2; MTFW 2005; RGEL 2; RGSF 2

Wellek, Rene 1903-1995 .... **CLC 28**
See also CA 5-8R; 150; CAAS 7; CANR 8; DLB 63; EWL 3; INT CANR-8

Weller, Michael 1942- .... **CLC 10, 53**
See also CA 85-88; CAD; CD 5, 6

Weller, Paul 1958- .... **CLC 26**

Wellershoff, Dieter 1925- .... **CLC 46**
See also CA 89-92; CANR 16, 37

Welles, (George) Orson 1915-1985 .. **CLC 20, 80**
See also AAYA 40; CA 93-96; 117

Wellman, John McDowell 1945- ...... **CLC 65**
See also CA 166; CAD; CD 5, 6; RGAL 4

Wellman, Mac
See Wellman, John McDowell; Wellman, John McDowell

Wellman, Manly Wade 1903-1986 ... **CLC 49**
See also CA 1-4R; 118; CANR 6, 16, 44; FANT; SATA 6; SATA-Obit 47; SFW 4; SUFW

Wells, Carolyn 1869(?)-1942 .... **TCLC 35**
See also CA 113; 185; CMW 4; DLB 11

Wells, H. G. 1866-1946 . **SSC 6, 70; TCLC 6, 12, 19, 133; WLC 6**
See also AAYA 18; BPFB 3; BRW 6; CA 110; 121; CDBLB 1914-1945; CLR 64, 133; DA; DA3; DAB; DAC; DAM MST, NOV; DLB 34, 70, 156, 178; EWL 3; EXPS; HGG; LAIT 3; LMFS 2; MTCW 1, 2; MTFW 2005; NFS 17, 20; RGEL 2; RGSF 2; SATA 20; SCFW 1, 2; SFW 4; SSFS 3; SUFW; TEA; WCH; WLIT 4; YAW

Wells, Herbert George
See Wells, H. G.

Wells, Rosemary 1943- .... **CLC 12**
See also AAYA 13; BYA 7, 8; CA 85-88; CANR 48, 120, 179; CLR 16, 69; CWRI 5; MAICYA 1, 2; SAAS 1; SATA 18, 69, 114, 156, 207; YAW

Wells-Barnett, Ida B(ell) 1862-1931 .... **TCLC 125**
See also CA 182; DLB 23, 221

Welsh, Irvine 1958- .... **CLC 144, 276**
See also CA 173; CANR 146, 196; CN 7; DLB 271

Welty, Eudora 1909-2001 .... **CLC 1, 2, 5, 14, 22, 33, 105, 220; SSC 1, 27, 51, 111; WLC 6**
See also AAYA 48; AMW; AMWR 1; BPFB 3; CA 9-12R; 199; CABS 1; CANR 32, 65, 128; CDALB 1941-1968; CN 1, 2, 3, 4, 5, 6, 7; CSW; DA; DA3; DAB; DAC; DAM MST, NOV; DFS 26; DLB 2, 102, 143; DLBD 12; DLBY 1987, 2001; EWL 3; EXPS; HGG; LAIT 3; MAL 5; MBL; MTCW 1, 2; MTFW 2005; NFS 13, 15; RGAL 4; RGSF 2; RHW; SSFS 2, 10, 26; TUS

Welty, Eudora Alice
See Welty, Eudora

Wen I-to 1899-1946 .... **TCLC 28**
See also EWL 3

Wentworth, Robert
See Hamilton, Edmond

Werewere Liking 1950- .... **BLC 2:2**
See also EWL 3

Werfel, Franz (Viktor) 1890-1945 .... **PC 101; TCLC 8**
See also CA 104; 161; DLB 81, 124; EWL 3; RGWL 2, 3

Wergeland, Henrik Arnold 1808-1845 .... **NCLC 5**
See also DLB 354

Werner, Friedrich Ludwig Zacharias 1768-1823 .... **NCLC 189**
See also DLB 94

Werner, Zacharias
See Werner, Friedrich Ludwig Zacharias

Wersba, Barbara 1932- .... **CLC 30**
See also AAYA 2, 30; BYA 6, 12, 13; CA 29-32R, 182; CAAE 182; CANR 16, 38; CLR 3, 78; DLB 52; JRDA; MAICYA 1, 2; SAAS 2; SATA 1, 58; SATA-Essay 103; WYA; YAW

Wertmueller, Lina 1928- .... **CLC 16**
See also CA 97-100; CANR 39, 78

Wescott, Glenway 1901-1987 .. **CLC 13; SSC 35**
See also CA 13-16R; 121; CANR 23, 70; CN 1, 2, 3, 4; DLB 4, 9, 102; MAL 5; RGAL 4

Wesker, Arnold 1932- .... **CLC 3, 5, 42**
See also CA 1-4R; CAAS 7; CANR 1, 33; CBD; CD 5, 6; CDBLB 1960 to Present; DAB; DAM DRAM; DLB 13, 310, 319; EWL 3; MTCW 1; RGEL 2; TEA

Wesley, Charles 1707-1788 .... **LC 128**
See also DLB 95; RGEL 2

Wesley, John 1703-1791 .... **LC 88**
See also DLB 104

Wesley, Richard (Errol) 1945- .... **CLC 7**
See also BW 1; CA 57-60; CAD; CANR 27; CD 5, 6; DLB 38

Wessel, Johan Herman 1742-1785 .... **LC 7**
See also DLB 300

West, Anthony (Panther) 1914-1987 .... **CLC 50**
See also CA 45-48; 124; CANR 3, 19; CN 1, 2, 3, 4; DLB 15

West, C. P.
See Wodehouse, P. G.

West, Cornel 1953- .... **BLCS; CLC 134**
See also CA 144; CANR 91, 159; DLB 246

West, Cornel Ronald
See West, Cornel

West, Delno C(loyde), Jr. 1936- .... **CLC 70**
See also CA 57-60

West, Dorothy 1907-1998 ...... **HR 1:3; TCLC 108**
See also AMWS 18; BW 2; CA 143; 169; DLB 76

West, Edwin
See Westlake, Donald E.

West, (Mary) Jessamyn 1902-1984 ... **CLC 7, 17**
See also CA 9-12R; 112; CANR 27; CN 1, 2, 3; DLB 6; DLBY 1984; MTCW 1, 2; RGAL 4; RHW; SATA-Obit 37; TCWW 2; TUS; YAW

West, Morris L(anglo) 1916-1999 ..... **CLC 6, 33**
See also BPFB 3; CA 5-8R; 187; CANR 24, 49, 64; CN 1, 2, 3, 4, 5, 6; CPW; DLB 289; MTCW 1, 2; MTFW 2005

West, Nathanael 1903-1940 ...... **SSC 16, 116; TCLC 1, 14, 44, 235**
See also AAYA 77; AMW; AMWR 2; BPFB 3; CA 104; 125; CDALB 1929-1941; DA3; DLB 4, 9, 28; EWL 3; MAL 5; MTCW 1, 2; MTFW 2005; NFS 16; RGAL 4; TUS

West, Owen
See Koontz, Dean

West, Paul 1930- .... **CLC 7, 14, 96, 226**
See also CA 13-16R; CAAS 7; CANR 22, 53, 76, 89, 136; CN 1, 2, 3, 4, 5, 6, 7; DLB 14; INT CANR-22; MTCW 2; MTFW 2005

West, Rebecca 1892-1983 ... **CLC 7, 9, 31, 50**
See also BPFB 3; BRWS 3; CA 5-8R; 109; CANR 19; CN 1, 2, 3; DLB 36; DLBY 1983; EWL 3; FW; MTCW 1, 2; MTFW 2005; NCFS 4; RGEL 2; TEA

Westall, Robert (Atkinson) 1929-1993 .... **CLC 17**
See also AAYA 12; BYA 2, 6, 7, 8, 9, 15; CA 69-72; 141; CANR 18, 68; CLR 13; FANT; JRDA; MAICYA 1, 2; MAICYAS 1; SAAS 2; SATA 23, 69; SATA-Obit 75; WYA; YAW

Westermarck, Edward 1862-1939 . **TCLC 87**

Westlake, Donald E. 1933-2008 ... **CLC 7, 33**
See also BPFB 3; CA 17-20R; 280; CAAS 13; CANR 16, 44, 65, 94, 137, 192; CMW 4; CPW; DAM POP; INT CANR-16; MSW; MTCW 2; MTFW 2005

Westlake, Donald E. Edmund
See Westlake, Donald E.

Westlake, Donald Edwin
See Westlake, Donald E.

Westlake, Donald Edwin Edmund
See Westlake, Donald E.

Westmacott, Mary
See Christie, Agatha

Weston, Allen
See Norton, Andre

Wetcheek, J. L.
See Feuchtwanger, Lion

Wetering, Janwillem van de
See van de Wetering, Janwillem

Wetherald, Agnes Ethelwyn 1857-1940 .... **TCLC 81**
See also CA 202; DLB 99

Wetherell, Elizabeth
See Warner, Susan (Bogert)

Whale, James 1889-1957 .... **TCLC 63**
See also AAYA 75

Whalen, Philip (Glenn) 1923-2002 .... **CLC 6, 29**
See also BG 1:3; CA 9-12R; 209; CANR 5, 39; CP 1, 2, 3, 4, 5, 6, 7; DLB 16; WP

Wharton, Edith 1862-1937 ... **SSC 6, 84, 120; TCLC 3, 9, 27, 53, 129, 149; WLC 6**
See also AAYA 25; AMW; AMWC 2; AMWR 1; BPFB 3; CA 104; 132; CDALB 1865-1917; CLR 136; DA; DA3; DAB; DAC; DAM MST, NOV; DLB 4, 9, 12, 78, 189; DLBD 13; EWL 3; EXPS; FL 1:6; GL 3; HGG; LAIT 2, 3; LATS 1:1; MAL 5; MBL; MTCW 1, 2; MTFW 2005; NFS 5, 11, 15, 20; RGAL 4; RGSF 2; RHW; SSFS 6, 7; SUFW; TUS

Wharton, Edith Newbold Jones
See Wharton, Edith

Wharton, James
See Mencken, H. L.

Wharton, William 1925-2008 ..... **CLC 18, 37**
See also CA 93-96; 278; CN 4, 5, 6, 7; DLBY 1980; INT CA-93-96

Wheatley, Phillis 1753(?)-1784 .... **BLC 1:3; LC 3, 50; PC 3; WLC 6**
See also AFAW 1, 2; CDALB 1640-1865; DA; DA3; DAC; DAM MST, MULT, POET; DLB 31, 50; EXPP; FL 1:1; PFS 13, 29; RGAL 4

Wheatley Peters, Phillis
See Wheatley, Phillis

Wheelock, John Hall 1886-1978 .... **CLC 14**
See also CA 13-16R; 77-80; CANR 14; CP 1, 2; DLB 45; MAL 5

Whim-Wham
See Curnow, (Thomas) Allen (Monro)

Whisp, Kennilworthy
See Rowling, J. K.

Whitaker, Rod 1931-2005 .... **CLC 29**
See also CA 29-32R; 246; CANR 45, 153; CMW 4

Whitaker, Rodney
See Whitaker, Rod

Whitaker, Rodney William
See Whitaker, Rod

White, Babington
See Braddon, Mary Elizabeth

White, E. B. 1899-1985 .... **CLC 10, 34, 39**
See also AAYA 62; AITN 2; AMWS 1; CA 13-16R; 116; CANR 16, 37; CDALBS; CLR 1, 21, 107; CPW; DA3; DAM POP; DLB 11, 22; EWL 3; FANT; MAICYA 1, 2; MAL 5; MTCW 1, 2; MTFW 2005; NCFS 5; RGAL 4; SATA 2, 29, 100; SATA-Obit 44; TUS

White, Edmund 1940- .... **CLC 27, 110**
See also AAYA 7; CA 45-48; CANR 3, 19, 36, 62, 107, 133, 172; CN 5, 6, 7; DA3; DAM POP; DLB 227; MTCW 1, 2; MTFW 2005

White, Edmund Valentine III
See White, Edmund

White, Elwyn Brooks
See White, E. B.

White, Hayden V. 1928- .... **CLC 148**
See also CA 128; CANR 135; DLB 246

White, Patrick 1912-1990 . **CLC 3, 4, 5, 7, 9, 18, 65, 69; SSC 39; TCLC 176**
See also BRWS 1; CA 81-84; 132; CANR 43; CN 1, 2, 3, 4; DLB 260, 332; EWL 3; MTCW 1; RGEL 2; RGSF 2; RHW; TWA; WWE 1

White, Patrick Victor Martindale
See White, Patrick

White, Phyllis Dorothy James
See James, P.D.

White, T(erence) H(anbury) 1906-1964 .... **CLC 30**
See also AAYA 22; BPFB 3; BYA 4, 5; CA 73-76; CANR 37; CLR 139; DLB 160; FANT; JRDA; LAIT 1; MAICYA 1, 2; NFS 30; RGEL 2; SATA 12; SUFW 1; YAW

White, Terence de Vere 1912-1994 ... **CLC 49**
See also CA 49-52; 145; CANR 3

White, Walter
See White, Walter F(rancis)

White, Walter F(rancis) 1893-1955 ..... **BLC 1:3; HR 1:3; TCLC 15**
See also BW 1; CA 115; 124; DAM MULT; DLB 51

White, William Hale 1831-1913 ..... **TCLC 25**
See also CA 121; 189; DLB 18; RGEL 2

Whitehead, Alfred North 1861-1947 .... **TCLC 97**
See also CA 117; 165; DLB 100, 262

Whitehead, Colson 1969- ...... **BLC 2:3; CLC 232**
See also CA 202; CANR 162

Whitehead, E(dward) A(nthony) 1933- .... **CLC 5**
See also CA 65-68; CANR 58, 118; CBD; CD 5, 6; DLB 310

Whitehead, Ted
See Whitehead, E(dward) A(nthony)

Whiteman, Roberta J. Hill 1947- ...... **NNAL**
See also CA 146

Whitemore, Hugh (John) 1936- .... **CLC 37**
See also CA 132; CANR 77; CBD; CD 5, 6; INT CA-132

Whitman, Sarah Helen (Power) 1803-1878 .... **NCLC 19**
See also DLB 1, 243

Whitman, Walt 1819-1892 .. **NCLC 4, 31, 81, 205; PC 3, 91; WLC 6**
See also AAYA 42; AMW; AMWR 1; CDALB 1640-1865; DA; DA3; DAB; DAC; DAM MST, POET; DLB 3, 64, 224, 250; EXPP; LAIT 2; LMFS 1; PAB; PFS 2, 3, 13, 22, 31; RGAL 4; SATA 20; TUS; WP; WYAS 1

Whitman, Walter
See Whitman, Walt

Whitney, Isabella fl. 1565-fl. 1575 ..... **LC 130**
See also DLB 136

Whitney, Phyllis A. 1903-2008 .... **CLC 42**
See also AAYA 36; AITN 2; BEST 90:3; CA 1-4R; 269; CANR 3, 25, 38, 60; CLR 59; CMW 4; CPW; DA3; DAM POP; JRDA; MAICYA 1, 2; MTCW 2; RHW; SATA 1, 30; SATA-Obit 189; YAW

Whitney, Phyllis Ayame
See Whitney, Phyllis A.

Whitney, Phyllis Ayame
See Whitney, Phyllis A.

Whittemore, (Edward) Reed, Jr. 1919- .... **CLC 4**
See also CA 9-12R, 219; CAAE 219; CAAS 8; CANR 4, 119; CP 1, 2, 3, 4, 5, 6, 7; DLB 5; MAL 5

Whittier, John Greenleaf 1807-1892 .... **NCLC 8, 59; PC 93**
See also AMWS 1; DLB 1, 243; RGAL 4

Whittlebot, Hernia
See Coward, Noel

Wicker, Thomas Grey
See Wicker, Tom

Wicker, Tom 1926- .... **CLC 7**
See also CA 65-68; CANR 21, 46, 141, 179

Wicomb, Zoe 1948- .... **BLC 2:3**
See also CA 127; CANR 106, 167; DLB 225

Wideman, John Edgar 1941- .. **BLC 1:3, 2:3; CLC 5, 34, 36, 67, 122; SSC 62**
See also AFAW 1, 2; AMWS 10; BPFB 4; BW 2, 3; CA 85-88; CANR 14, 42, 67, 109, 140, 187; CN 4, 5, 6, 7; DAM MULT; DLB 33, 143; MAL 5; MTCW 2; MTFW 2005; RGAL 4; RGSF 2; SSFS 6, 12, 24; TCLE 1:2

Wiebe, Rudy 1934- . **CLC 6, 11, 14, 138, 263**
See also CA 37-40R; CANR 42, 67, 123, 202; CN 1, 2, 3, 4, 5, 6, 7; DAC; DAM MST; DLB 60; RHW; SATA 156

Wiebe, Rudy Henry
See Wiebe, Rudy

Wieland, Christoph Martin 1733-1813 .... **NCLC 17, 177**
See also DLB 97; EW 4; LMFS 1; RGWL 2, 3

Wiene, Robert 1881-1938 .... **TCLC 56**

Wieners, John 1934- .... **CLC 7**
See also BG 1:3; CA 13-16R; CP 1, 2, 3, 4, 5, 6, 7; DLB 16; WP

Wiesel, Elie 1928- ...... **CLC 3, 5, 11, 37, 165; WLCS**
See also AAYA 7, 54; AITN 1; CA 5-8R; CAAS 4; CANR 8, 40, 65, 125; CDALBS; CWW 2; DA; DA3; DAB; DAC; DAM MST, NOV; DLB 83, 299; DLBY 1987; EWL 3; INT CANR-8; LAIT 4; MTCW 1, 2; MTFW 2005; NCFS 4; NFS 4; RGHL; RGWL 3; SATA 56; YAW

Wiesel, Eliezer
See Wiesel, Elie

Wiggins, Marianne 1947- .... **CLC 57**
See also AAYA 70; BEST 89:3; CA 130; CANR 60, 139, 180; CN 7; DLB 335

Wigglesworth, Michael 1631-1705 .... **LC 106**
See also DLB 24; RGAL 4

Wiggs, Susan CLC 70
See also CA 201; CANR 173

Wight, James Alfred 1916-1995 .... **CLC 12**
See also AAYA 1, 54; BPFB 2; CA 77-80; 148; CANR 40; CLR 80; CPW; DAM POP; LAIT 3; MAICYA 2; MAICYAS 1; MTCW 2; SATA 86, 135; SATA-Brief 44; TEA; YAW

Wilbur, Richard 1921- .. **CLC 3, 6, 9, 14, 53, 110; PC 51**
See also AAYA 72; AMWS 3; CA 1-4R; CABS 2; CANR 2, 29, 76, 93, 139; CDALBS; CP 1, 2, 3, 4, 5, 6, 7; DA; DAB; DAC; DAM MST, POET; DLB 5, 169; EWL 3; EXPP; INT CANR-29; MAL 5; MTCW 1, 2; MTFW 2005; PAB; PFS 11, 12, 16, 29; RGAL 4; SATA 9, 108; WP

Wilbur, Richard Purdy
See Wilbur, Richard

Wild, Peter 1940- .... **CLC 14**
See also CA 37-40R; CP 1, 2, 3, 4, 5, 6, 7; DLB 5

Wilde, Oscar 1854(?)-1900 ... **DC 17; SSC 11, 77; TCLC 1, 8, 23, 41, 175; WLC 6**
See also AAYA 49; BRW 5; BRWC 1, 2; BRWR 2; BYA 15; CA 104; 119; CANR 112; CDBLB 1890-1914; CLR 114; DA; DA3; DAB; DAC; DAM DRAM, MST, NOV; DFS 4, 8, 9, 21; DLB 10, 19, 34, 57, 141, 156, 190, 344; EXPS; FANT; GL 3; LATS 1:1; NFS 20; RGEL 2; RGSF 2; SATA 24; SSFS 7; SUFW; TEA; WCH; WLIT 4

Wilde, Oscar Fingal O'Flahertie Willis
See Wilde, Oscar

Wilder, Billy
See Wilder, Samuel

Wilder, Samuel 1906-2002 .... **CLC 20**
See also AAYA 66; CA 89-92; 205; DLB 26

Wilder, Stephen
See Marlowe, Stephen

Wilder, Thornton 1897-1975 ..... **CLC 1, 5, 6, 10, 15, 35, 82; DC 1, 24; WLC 6**
See also AAYA 29; AITN 2; AMW; CA 13-16R; 61-64; CAD; CANR 40, 132; CDALBS; CN 1, 2; DA; DA3; DAB; DAC; DAM DRAM, MST, NOV; DFS 1, 4, 16; DLB 4, 7, 9, 228; DLBY 1997; EWL 3; LAIT 3; MAL 5; MTCW 1, 2; MTFW 2005; NFS 24; RGAL 4; RHW; WYAS 1

Wilder, Thornton Niven
See Wilder, Thornton

Wilding, Michael 1942- ...... **CLC 73; SSC 50**
See also CA 104; CANR 24, 49, 106; CN 4, 5, 6, 7; DLB 325; RGSF 2

Wiley, Richard 1944- .... **CLC 44**
See also CA 121; 129; CANR 71

Wilhelm, Kate
See Wilhelm, Katie

Wilhelm, Katie 1928- .... **CLC 7**
See also AAYA 20; BYA 16; CA 37-40R; CAAS 5; CANR 17, 36, 60, 94; DLB 8; INT CANR-17; MTCW 1; SCFW 2; SFW 4

Wilhelm, Katie Gertrude
See Wilhelm, Katie

Wilkins, Mary
See Freeman, Mary E(leanor) Wilkins

Willard, Nancy 1936- .... **CLC 7, 37**
See also BYA 5; CA 89-92; CANR 10, 39, 68, 107, 152, 186; CLR 5; CP 2, 3, 4, 5; CWP; CWRI 5; DLB 5, 52; FANT; MAICYA 1, 2; MTCW 1; SATA 37, 71, 127, 191; SATA-Brief 30; SUFW 2; TCLE 1:2

William of Malmesbury c. 1090B.C.-c. 1140B.C. .... **CMLC 57**

William of Moerbeke c. 1215-c. 1286 .... **CMLC 91**

William of Ockham 1290-1349 ..... **CMLC 32**

Williams, Ben Ames 1889-1953 ..... **TCLC 89**
See also CA 183; DLB 102

Williams, Charles
See Collier, James Lincoln

PC Cumulative Nationality Index

Valéry, (Ambroise) Paul (Toussaint Jules) **9**
Verlaine, Paul (Marie) **2, 32**
Vigny, Alfred (Victor) de **26**
Villon, François **13**

GERMAN

Benn, Gottfried **35**
Bukowski, Charles **18**
Enzensberger, Hans Magnus **28**
Goethe, Johann Wolfgang von **5**
Heine, Heinrich **25**
Hölderlin, (Johann Christian) Friedrich **4**
Mueller, Lisel **33**
Rilke, Rainer Maria **2**
Sachs, Nelly **78**
Stramm, August **50**

GREEK

Cavafy, C(onstantine) P(eter) **36**
Elytis, Odysseus **21**
Homer **23**
Pindar **19**
Sappho **5**
Seferis, George **66**
Sikelianos, Angelos **29**

HUNGARIAN

Illyés, Gyula **16**
Szirtes, George **51**

INDIAN

Das, Kamala **43**
Kabir **56**
Kalidasa **22**
Mirabai **48**
Tagore, Rabindranath **8**

IRISH

Boland, Eavan **58**
Day Lewis, C(ecil) **11**
Goldsmith, Oliver **77**
Heaney, Seamus (Justin) **18, 100**
Joyce, James (Augustine Aloysius) **22**
Kavanagh, Patrick (Joseph) **33, 105**
Kinsella, Thomas **69**
MacNeice, Louis **61**
Mahon, Derek **60**
McGuckian, Medbh **27**
Montague, John **106**
Ní Chuilleanáin, Eiléan **34**
Swift, Jonathan **9**
Yeats, William Butler **20, 51**

ISRAELI

Amichai, Yehuda **38**

ITALIAN

Ariosto, Ludovico **42**
Carducci, Giosue **46**
Dante **21**
Gozzano, Guido **10**
Leopardi, Giacomo **37**
Martial **10**
Michelangelo **103**
Montale, Eugenio **13**
Pasolini, Pier Paolo **17**

Pavese, Cesare **13**
Petrarch **8**
Quasimodo, Salvatore **47**
Stampa, Gaspara **43**
Ungaretti, Giuseppe **57**
Zanzotto, Andrea **65**

JAMAICAN

Goodison, Lorna **36**

JAPANESE

Hagiwara, Sakutaro **18**
Ishikawa, Takuboku **10**
Matsuo Basho **3**
Nishiwaki, Junzaburō **15**
Yosano Akiko **11**

LEBANESE

Gibran, Kahlil **9**

MARTINICAN

Césaire, Aimé (Fernand) **25**

MEXICAN

Juana Inés de la Cruz **24**
Paz, Octavio **1, 48**
Urista, Alberto H. **34**

NEW ZEALAND

Curnow, (Thomas) Allen (Monro) **48**

NICARAGUAN

Alegria, Claribel **26**
Cardenal, Ernesto **22**
Darío, Rubén **15**

NIGERIAN

Okigbo, Christopher (Ifenayichukwu) **7**

PALESTINIAN

Darwish, Mahmoud **86**

PERSIAN

Khayyam, Omar **8**
Rumi, Jalâl al-Din **45**

POLISH

Herbert, Zbigniew **50**
Mickiewicz, Adam **38**
Milosz, Czeslaw **8**
Szymborska, Wisława **44**
Zagajewski, Adam **27**

PORTUGUESE

Camões, Luís de **31**
Pessoa, Fernando (António Nogueira) **20**

PUERTO RICAN

Cruz, Victor Hernández **37**

ROMAN

Horace **46**
Martial **10**
Ovid **2**
Vergil **12**

ROMANIAN

Cassian, Nina **17**
Celan, Paul **10**
Tzara, Tristan **27**

RUSSIAN

Akhmadulina, Bella **43**
Akhmatova, Anna **2, 55**
Bely, Andrey **11**
Blok, Alexander (Alexandrovich) **21**
Brodsky, Joseph **9**
Lermontov, Mikhail Yuryevich **18**
Mandelstam, Osip (Emilievich) **14**
Pasternak, Boris (Leonidovich) **6**
Pushkin, Alexander (Sergeyevich) **10**
Shvarts, Elena **50**
Tsvetaeva (Efron), Marina (Ivanovna) **14**
Yevtushenko, Yevgeny (Alexandrovich) **40**

SALVADORAN

Alegria, Claribel **26**
Dalton, Roque **36**

SCOTTISH

Burns, Robert **6**
Dunbar, William **67**
Henryson, Robert **65**
Macpherson, James **97**
Muir, Edwin **49**
Scott, Walter **13**
Spark, Muriel **72**
Stevenson, Robert Louis **84**

SENEGALESE

Senghor, Léopold Sédar **25**

SINGAPORAN

Thumboo, Edwin Nadason **30**

SOUTH AFRICAN

Brutus, Dennis **24**

SPANISH

Castro, Rosalia de **41**
Cernuda, Luis **62**
Fuertes, Gloria **27**
García Lorca, Federico **3**
Guillén, Jorge **35**
Jiménez (Mantecón), Juan Ramón **7**

ST. LUCIAN

Walcott, Derek **46**

SWEDISH

Ekeloef, (Bengt) Gunnar **23**

SWISS

Jaccottet, Philippe **98**

SYRIAN

Gibran, Kahlil **9**

WELSH

Abse, Dannie **41**
Dafydd ap Gwilym **56**
Thomas, Dylan (Marlais) **2, 52**
Thomas, R. S. **99**

Nationality Index

PC-106 Title Index

ISBN-13: 978-1-4144-4761-2
ISBN-10: 1-4144-4761-2

224—

224—